S0-BAY-091

Principles of Financial and Managerial Accounting

Second Edition

Carl S. Warren, PhD, CPA, CMA, CIA
Professor of Accounting
University of Georgia, Athens

Philip E. Fess, PhD, CPA
Professor Emeritus of Accountancy
University of Illinois, Champaign-Urbana

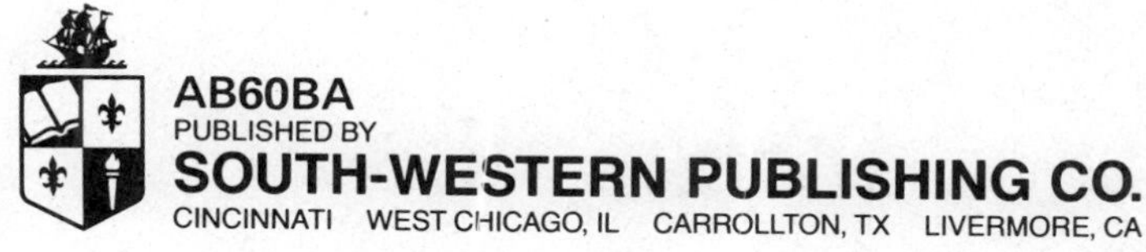
AB60BA
PUBLISHED BY
SOUTH-WESTERN PUBLISHING CO.
CINCINNATI WEST CHICAGO, IL CARROLLTON, TX LIVERMORE, CA

Copyright © 1989
by South-Western Publishing Co.
Cincinnati, Ohio

All Rights Reserved

The text of this publication, or any part thereof, may not be reproduced or transmitted in any form or by any means, electronic or mechanical, including photocopying, recording, storage in an information retrieval system, or otherwise, without the prior written permission of the publisher.

ISBN: 0-538-80171-9

Library of Congress Catalog Card Number: 88-61712

2 3 4 5 6 7 8 9 Ki 1 0 9

Printed in the United States of America

Preface

The second edition of PRINCIPLES OF FINANCIAL AND MANAGERIAL ACCOUNTING is a student-oriented text. It presents the fundamental accounting concepts and principles in a logical, concise, and clear manner. The text provides a solid educational foundation that allows instructors to focus on clarifying issues and increasing the student's understanding of accounting and its uses.

Fundamental accounting concepts and principles are presented in the text in a business setting that allows students to understand accounting as it is applied in serving not only the business world but all of society. Such an approach meets the needs of students planning careers in accounting as well as in business administration, in liberal arts areas, in law, or in other disciplines.

IMPORTANT FEATURES OF THE SECOND EDITION

The basic foundation of PRINCIPLES OF FINANCIAL AND MANAGERIAL ACCOUNTING has been retained in the second edition. However, many new features have been added and the coverage of some topics has been modified, based on extensive feedback from current users and on independent reviews by scholars and educators. The most significant new features and the quality features introduced in the first edition are described in the following paragraphs.

Financial Accounting Cycle

The accounting cycle for a merchandising enterprise is presented in the first four chapters. In Chapter 1, the unique presentation integrates the accounting equation with the accounts and journal entries.

Form of Business Organization

The corporate form of business organization is used in the illustrations and discussions of accounting concepts and principles beginning in Chapter 1. The concepts and principles applicable to the sole proprietorship and partnership are presented in Chapter 10.

Accounting for Merchandise Inventory

The discussion of accounting for merchandise inventory has been revised to facilitate student understanding.

- The accounts *Purchases Returns and Allowances* and *Transportation In* are used in the discussion of accounting for merchandise enterprises.
- An alternate method of handling merchandise inventory at the end of an accounting period has been added as Appendix B. This method, sometimes referred to as the adjusting method, can be used instead of the method presented in the merchandising chapters. The Solutions Manual includes solutions for both approaches.
- The discussion of the periodic and perpetual methods of accounting for merchandise inventories has been revised and expanded. A comparison of the journal entries under each method has been added. Also, a discussion of the use of the perpetual inventory system in computerized environments is included.

Statement of Cash Flows

The requirements of the Financial Accounting Standards Board pronouncement on cash flows have been incorporated into Chapter 14. The indirect method of reporting cash flows from operating activities is described and illustrated in the chapter. The direct method of reporting cash flows from operations is described and illustrated in Appendix E. Appendix F provides a work sheet approach to preparing the statement of cash flows.

Nature of Managerial Accounting

Chapter 15 eases the transition from financial accounting to managerial accounting by contrasting the nature of managerial accounting with financial accounting. Included in this discussion is a description of the management process, including the management functions of planning, organizing and directing, controlling, and decision making. The role of managerial accounting has been integrated into this discussion as an essential element of the management process. Students are also introduced to the basic cost concepts and classifications, such as product costs, period costs, differential costs, variable costs, and fixed costs.

Average Cost Method

A discussion and illustration of the average cost method has been added to the process cost chapter of the text. In this way, students will gain a better understanding of the importance of cost methods in inventory costing.

Cost Behavior and Cost Estimation

A new chapter (Chapter 18) on cost behavior and cost estimation has been added. The chapter begins with a description of the distinction between cost behavior and cost estimation, and concludes with descriptions and illustrations of the basic cost estimation methods, such as the high-low method, the scattergraph method, and the least squares method. The learning effect and current cost trends are also described. By discussing cost estimation methods at this point, students are better able to understand subsequent topics, such as cost-volume-profit analysis.

Contribution Margin Analysis

Chapter 20, Profit Reporting for Management Analysis, has been revised by deleting the discussion of gross profit analysis and adding discussion and illustration of contribution margin analysis in the context of uses of variable costing.

Product Life Cycle

The use of alternative price strategies during a product's life cycle has been added to Chapter 25. In addition, a discussion of the effect of elasticity of demand and competitive market conditions on pricing strategies has also been added.

Tax Law Changes

Tax law changes have been integrated throughout the text. For example, Chapter 26 describes and illustrates the effect of the Modified Accelerated Cost Recovery Systems (MACRS) on capital investment decisions. In addition, a brief coverage of income taxes has been condensed and is presented in Appendix D. This appendix, which incorporates the 1986 and 1987 changes in the tax law, provides students with an understanding of the basic nature of the federal income tax system and its effects on personal and business income.

Financial Statement Analysis and Annual Reports

Chapter 28 retains its managerial emphasis from the first edition, but has been revised to include a section on corporate annual reports and price-level changes.

Managerial Accounting for Service Enterprises and Activities

Appendix H describes and illustrates the managerial accounting concepts and procedures that are especially relevant for service enterprises. These concepts include job order cost accounting, budgeting, responsibility accounting, standard costs, and setting fees.

Trends in Managerial Accounting

Appendix I describes trends in manufacturing and in managerial accounting. Some of the trends described in this appendix include automation, controlling product quality, materials requirements planning, just-in-time inventory systems, and information technology. A selected bibliography has also been included to provide students additional readings on these current developments and trends.

Present Value and Future Value Tables

More detailed present value tables, as well as future value tables, are included in an appendix.

Chapter Objectives

The chapter objectives have been revised and expanded to enable students and instructors to integrate the chapter materials with the overall learning objectives more successfully.

Illustrations

Many additional charts, graphs, and diagrams have been added throughout the text to enable students to visualize important concepts and principles more efficiently. These charts, graphs, and diagrams are highlighted with color to enhance the learning process.

Real-World Examples

Real-world business examples have been integrated throughout the text to provide students with a flavor for the real-world impact of accounting. These examples add concrete meaning to concepts and principles which might otherwise appear abstract. Many of these examples were taken directly from the latest annual reports of companies such as Pepsico and General Motors. In addition, the American Institute of Certified Public Accountants' publication, *Accounting Trends & Techniques,* is cited where appropriate to indicate the frequency with which alternative accounting presentations and methods are used in the real world.

Enrichment Material

Excerpts from well-known business periodicals, such as the *Journal of Accountancy, Management Accounting,* the *Wall Street Journal,* and *Forbes,* have been added to each chapter. Each excerpt was adapted and designed to stir the students' interest and enrich their learning experience by providing real-world information relevant to the topics that are discussed in the chapter.

Chapter Reviews

A chapter review has been added at the end of each chapter. The chapter reviews are designed to increase and enhance student retention of important chapter concepts and principles. Each chapter review includes key points, key terms, self-examination questions, and an illustrative problem and solution.

- The **key points** summarize the major concepts presented in a chapter. By studying the key points, students can quickly review the major concepts and principles of each chapter.
- Each **key term** listed in the chapter review is followed by the page number indicating where the key term was first presented in color and discussed in the chapter. Students may also refer to Appendix A, where all the key terms in the text are listed alphabetically and defined.
- Five **self-examination questions** are provided for each chapter. After studying the chapter, students can answer these questions and compare their answers with the correct ones that appear at the end of the chapter. An explanation of both the correct

and incorrect answers for each question is provided in order to increase students' understanding and enhance the learning process further.

- The **illustrative problem** with suggested solution focuses on the concepts and principles discussed in the chapter. Students can use these problems as a means of building confidence in their ability to apply a chapter's concepts and principles to a problem situation.

End-of-Chapter Materials

The end-of-chapter exercises and problems have been carefully written and revised to be both practical and comprehensive. The variety and volume of the assignment materials presented at the end of each chapter provide a wide choice of subject matter and range of difficulty. In addition, selected problems may be solved using general ledger and spreadsheet software that is available from South-Western Publishing Co. As in the first edition, each chapter contains a mini-case for stimulating student interest. Each case, which presents situations with which students can easily identify, emphasizes important chapter concepts and principles.

Real-World Focus Questions

A discussion question that requires students to interpret and respond to a real-world business situation is contained in each chapter. In some chapters, a real-world exercise is also included. These questions and exercises, which are labeled "Real World Focus," are based on actual business data.

Comprehensive Problem

A comprehensive problem has been added at the end of Chapter 4 to integrate and summarize the concepts and principles of the first four chapters.

Alternate Problems

The alternate problems appear at the end of each chapter in order to facilitate student and instructor usage.

Check Figures

Check figures are presented at the end of the textbook for student use in solving end-of-chapter problems. Agreement with the check figures is an indication that a significant portion of the solution is basically correct.

SUPPLEMENTARY MATERIALS

PRINCIPLES OF FINANCIAL AND MANAGERIAL ACCOUNTING is part of a well-integrated educational package that includes materials designed for the instructor's use and for the students' use. These materials are carefully prepared and reviewed to maintain consistency and high quality throughout.

Available to Instructors

Solutions Manuals. These manuals contain solutions to all end-of-chapter materials, including the discussion questions, exercises, problems, mini-cases, and comprehensive problem. The first volume is for use with Chapters 1–14, and the second volume is for use with Chapters 15–28.

Spreadsheet Applications, prepared by Gaylord N. Smith of Albion College. These template diskettes are used with Lotus™ 1-2-3™[1] for solving selected end-of-

[1]Lotus™ 1-2-3™ are trademarks of the Lotus Development Corporation. Any reference to Lotus or 1-2-3 refers to this footnote.

chapter exercises and problems that are identified with the symbol at the right. These diskettes, which also provide a tutorial and "what if" analysis, may be ordered upon adoption from South-Western Publishing Co.

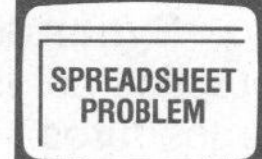

Instructor's Manual. This manual contains a summary of the chapter objectives, terminology, and concepts. In a section organized according to chapter objectives, a basis for developing class lectures and assigning homework is provided. In addition, exercise and problem descriptions, estimated time requirements for the problems, and suggestions for use of the appendixes and other supplementary items are included.

Transparencies of solutions to all exercises and problems and **Teaching Transparencies** are packaged in two binders—one for Chapters 1–14 and the other for Chapters 15–28. The Teaching Transparencies are designed to aid the instructor's focus on key concepts and principles discussed in the text.

Test Bank. A collection of examination problems, multiple-choice questions, and true or false questions for each chapter, accompanied by solutions, is available in both printed and microcomputer (MicroSWAT II) versions. The Test Bank is designed to save time in preparing and grading periodic and final examinations. Individual items may also be selected for use as short quizzes. The number of questions is sufficient to provide variety from year to year and from class section to class section.

Achievement Tests. Two sets of preprinted objective tests are available. Each test covers a group of chapters and may be machine graded. Comprehensive tests are also included.

The Administrator. A software management package is available to adopters. This package is specifically designed for use in maintaining a grade book, creating an interactive testing and/or study guide file, and generating tests.

Available to Students

Solutions: Financial Applications Software, prepared by Warren W. Allen and Dale H. Klooster of Educational Technical Systems. This software, which may be ordered with the textbook, is a general ledger program tailored specifically to the financial accounting portion of the text. It may be used with the IBM PC, IBM PCjr, the IBM Personal System/2,[2] and the Tandy® 1000[3] microcomputers to solve selected end-of-chapter problems and the comprehensive problem, which are identified with the symbol at the right. This software may also be used to solve the financial accounting practice set.

SOLUTIONS SOFTWARE

Working Papers. Appropriate printed forms on which to work end-of-chapter problems and mini-cases are available in two bound volumes. The first volume is for use with Chapters 1–14, and the second volume is for use with Chapters 15–28.

Study Guide. The Study Guide is designed to assist in comprehending the concepts and principles presented in the text. This publication includes an outline for each chapter as well as brief objective questions and problems. Solutions to these questions and problems are presented at the back of the Study Guide. The **Microcomputer Study Guide** is the microcomputer version of the manual Study Guide and may be used with the IBM PC, the IBM PCjr, the IBM Personal System/2, and the Tandy 1000.

Campus Collections Inc. II, prepared by Herman R. Andress of Santa Fe Community College. This short practice set requires the recording, analysis, interpretation, and reporting of accounting data for a corporation. It is available in either a manual or computerized version.

---

[2]IBM is a registered trademark of International Business Machines Corporation. Any reference to the IBM Personal Computer, the IBM PCjr, or the IBM Personal System/2 refers to this footnote.

[3]Tandy® 1000 is a registered trademark of the Radio Shack Division of Tandy Corporation. Any reference to the Tandy 1000 microcomputer refers to this footnote.

Synertech Inc., prepared by Dieter H. Weiss of Ferris State College. This short practice set is a budgeting set that emphasizes decision making rather than forms and procedures. The set is available in either a manual version or a computerized version based on Lotus 1-2-3.

ORGANIZATION OF THE SECOND EDITION

PRINCIPLES OF FINANCIAL AND MANAGERIAL ACCOUNTING has been organized to facilitate the learning of accounting and the overall educational process. Concepts and principles are introduced in a logical, step-by-step way and are reinforced by applications from the business world.

Each chapter builds on the terminology, concepts, and principles introduced in previous chapters. The chapter objectives provide students with a basis for beginning their study of each chapter. In turn, each chapter is organized around the chapter objectives in an educationally sound approach. The chapter reviews provide students with a means for review and a basis for assessing their knowledge of each chapter. The end-of-chapter discussion questions, exercises, problems, and mini-cases provide a vehicle for the instructor to assess the students' knowledge of each chapter's concepts and principles. Periodic giving of examinations provides instructors with a means for assessing students' cumulative knowledge.

The organization of the second edition of PRINCIPLES OF FINANCIAL AND MANAGERIAL ACCOUNTING is briefly summarized in the following paragraphs.

Introduction: Evolution of Accounting

The introduction presents a summary of the beginnings of accounting in 1494 and its development to the present. Emphasis is given to the present-day profession of accountancy and its future. This overview provides students of all backgrounds an excellent perspective on the importance and influence of accounting on all phases of society.

Part 1 — Fundamentals of Financial Accounting

- Chapter 1 presents the rules of debit and credit, the use of accounts, the preparation of a trial balance, and the preparation of financial statements, including the statement of cash flows, for a corporate form of organization.
- Chapter 2 reinforces the principles and concepts introduced in Chapter 1 by discussing basic financial principles and concepts in the context of merchandising enterprises.
- Chapters 3 and 4 complete the accounting cycle by discussing the matching concept, the adjusting process, and periodic reporting.

Part 2 — Financial Accounting Systems

- Chapters 5–9 begin with a brief discussion of the basic concepts of accounting systems design. Financial accounting principles for cash, receivables and temporary investments, inventories, plant and intangible assets, and payroll and other current liabilities are then discussed in depth in balance sheet order.

Part 3 — Accounting for Equity Rights

- Chapters 10 and 11 discuss alternative forms of business organization — sole proprietorships and partnerships — and complex business transactions affecting stockholders' equity.
- Chapter 12 discusses long-term liabilities and investments in bonds. Present value concepts are integrated throughout this chapter.
- Chapter 13 discusses principles and concepts involving long-term investments in stocks, consolidations, and accounting for international operations. Accounting for international operations is increasing in importance as more and more businesses of all sizes engage in foreign transactions.

Part 4—Reporting Changes in Cash Flows

- Chapter 14 emphasizes the principles and conceptual logic of the statement of cash flows. Appendixes are provided for those instructors who wish to use a work sheet for preparing the statement of cash flows and to emphasize the direct method of reporting cash flows from operations.

Part 5—Managerial Accounting Concepts and Systems

- Chapter 15 provides students with an overview of the nature of the management process and the essential role of managerial accounting in this process. It also provides an overview of the manufacturing process and managerial accounting terminology. After completing Chapter 15, students will have been exposed to the majority of the terminology they will need in completing the remainder of the chapters on managerial accounting. This allows instructors flexibility in the order in which they assign subsequent chapters.
- Chapters 16 and 17 provide illustrations of the application of managerial accounting concepts to a manufacturing environment. Chapter 16 describes and illustrates job order cost accounting systems, and Chapter 17 describes and illustrates process cost accounting systems.

Part 6—Planning and Control

- This part emphasizes managerial accounting concepts and principles for planning and control. Chapter 18 describes and illustrates cost behavior and cost estimation.
- Chapter 19 describes and illustrates cost-volume-profit analysis.
- Chapter 20 describes and illustrates profit reporting for management analysis, including absorption costing and variable costing. The importance of the contribution margin in managerial decision making is emphasized.
- Chapter 21 describes and illustrates budgeting, including an integrated example of the preparation of the master budget.
- Chapter 22 concludes this part by describing and illustrating standard cost systems.

Part 7—Accounting for Decentralized Operations

- Chapter 23 describes responsibility accounting for decentralized operations. The chapter concludes with a description and illustration of responsibility accounting for cost and profit centers.
- Chapter 24 describes and illustrates responsibility accounting for investment centers and includes a discussion of transfer pricing.

Part 8—Analyses for Decision Making

- Chapter 25 describes and illustrates the use of differential analysis in decision making. Also included in Chapter 25 is a discussion of pricing, including short-term special pricing situations and the setting of long-term prices. Integrated into this discussion is the economic approach to pricing and the impact of a product's life cycle on setting prices.
- Chapter 26 describes and illustrates capital investment analysis, including the discounted internal rate of return method. Chapter 26 also includes a detailed illustration of the impact of MACRS depreciation on capital investment decisions.
- Chapter 27 describes and illustrates quantitative techniques for controlling inventory and making decisions under uncertainty.

Part 9—Financial Analysis for Management Use

- Chapter 28 describes and illustrates the usefulness of financial statement analysis to management. Chapter 28 also includes a description of the essential elements and content of corporate annual reports.

Appendixes

- Appendix A contains a glossary of the key terms.
- Appendix B presents an alternative method of recording merchandise inventory at the end of an accounting period. This method is sometimes referred to as the adjusting method. Solutions to problems using this method are presented in the Solutions Manual.
- Appendix C discusses and illustrates special journals and subsidiary ledgers.
- Appendix D discusses income taxes for individuals and business enterprises. Question and exercise materials are included with the appendix.
- Appendix E discusses and illustrates the direct method of reporting cash flows from operating activities for the statement of cash flows. Exercise and problem materials are included with the appendix.
- Appendix F presents a work sheet approach to the preparation of the statement of cash flows. The Solutions Manual includes solutions to problems using the work sheet.
- Appendix G presents complete present value and future value tables.
- Appendix H describes the use of managerial concepts and principles by service enterprises.
- Appendix I describes the trends in managerial accounting, including just-in-time manufacturing systems, automation, and quality control.
- Appendix J contains selected financial statements for real companies.

ACKNOWLEDGMENTS

Throughout the textbook, relevant professional statements of the Financial Accounting Standards Board, the National Association of Accountants, and other authoritative publications are discussed, quoted, paraphrased, or footnoted. We are indebted to the American Accounting Association, the American Institute of Certified Public Accountants, the Financial Accounting Standards Board, and the National Association of Accountants for material from their publications.

We thank the following faculty who provided helpful suggestions for this revision: Chris Bjornson, University of Illinois; Ken Macur, University of Wisconsin; William K. Carter, University of Virginia; William R. Pasewark, University of Georgia; Emmanuel Amobi, Northern Arizona University; Stephen Del Vecchio, Southeast Missouri State University; Wilbur L. Garland, Coastal Carolina College; James M. Emig, Villanova University; John T. Martinelli, Sr., California State University at Long Beach; and Keith A. Russell, Southeast Missouri State University.

Carl S. Warren
Philip E. Fess

About the Authors

Professor Carl S. Warren is the Arthur Andersen & Co. Alumni Professor of Accounting at the J. M. Tull School of Accounting at the University of Georgia, Athens. Professor Warren received his PhD from Michigan State University in 1973 and has taught accounting at the University of Iowa, Michigan State University, the University of Chicago, and the University of Georgia. He has received teaching awards from three different student organizations at the University of Georgia.

Professor Warren is a CMA and a CPA. He was awarded a Certificate of Distinguished Performance for his scores on the CMA examination and a Certificate of Honorable Mention for his scores on the CPA examination. He is a member of the National Association of Accountants, the American Institute of CPAs, the Georgia Society of CPAs, the American Accounting Association, the Georgia Association of Accounting Educators, and the Financial Executives Institute. Professor Warren has served on numerous professional committees and editorial boards, including a term as editor of the American Accounting Association publication *Auditing: A Journal of Practice and Theory.* He has written five textbooks and numerous articles in such journals as the *Journal of Accountancy,* the *Accounting Review,* the *Journal of Accounting Research,* the *CPA Journal, Corporate Accounting, Cost and Management,* and *Managerial Planning.* Professor Warren is also the Consulting Editor for South-Western Publishing Co.'s accounting series.

Professor Warren resides in Athens, Georgia, with his wife, Sharon, and two children, Stephanie (age 15) and Jeffrey (age 13). Professor Warren's hobbies include coaching Little League Baseball, golf, tennis, and fishing.

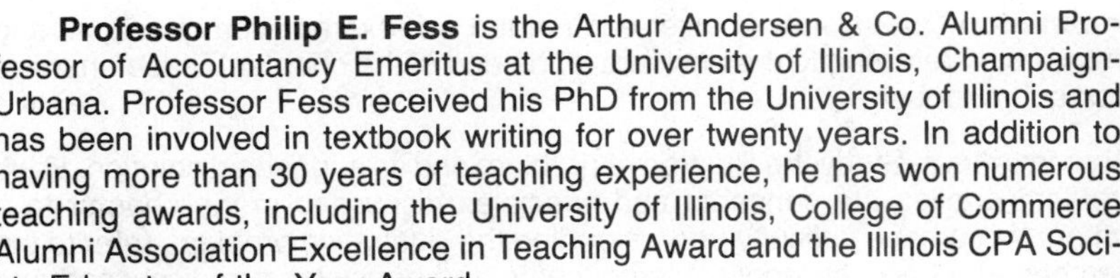

Professor Philip E. Fess is the Arthur Andersen & Co. Alumni Professor of Accountancy Emeritus at the University of Illinois, Champaign-Urbana. Professor Fess received his PhD from the University of Illinois and has been involved in textbook writing for over twenty years. In addition to having more than 30 years of teaching experience, he has won numerous teaching awards, including the University of Illinois, College of Commerce Alumni Association Excellence in Teaching Award and the Illinois CPA Society Educator of the Year Award.

Professor Fess is a CPA and a member of the American Institute of CPAs and the Illinois Society of CPAs. He is also a member of the National Association of Accountants and the American Accounting Association. He has served many professional associations in a variety of ways, including a term as a member of the Auditing Standards Board, editorial advisor to the *Journal of Accountancy,* and chairperson of the American Accounting Association Committee on CPA Examinations. Professor Fess has written more than 100 books and articles, which have appeared in such journals as the *Journal of Accountancy,* the *Accounting Review,* the *CPA Journal,* and *Management Accounting.* He has also served as an expert witness before the U.S. Tax Court and is a member of the Cost Advisory Panel for the Secretary of the Air Force.

Professor Fess and his wife, Suzanne, have three daughters: Linda, who is completing a PhD in accounting at Arizona State University; Ginny, who is a CPA and is employed by Solar Turbine Co.; and Martha, who has a degree in finance from the University of Illinois. Professor Fess' hobby is tennis, and he has represented the United States in international tennis competition.

Note to Students

This text was written with the objective of preparing you for your future professional career. Accounting is a stimulating, rewarding field of study. To be effective, professionals in all areas of business, such as finance, production, marketing, personnel, and general management, must have a good understanding of accounting. In addition, men and women whose careers are in nonbusiness areas can use a knowledge of accounting to perform more effectively in society.

As you begin your study of accounting, you may find the following suggestions helpful:

- Read each chapter objective before you begin studying a chapter.
- Take a few minutes and scan the chapter to get a flavor of the material before you begin a detailed reading of the chapter.
- As you read each chapter, you may wish to underline points that you feel are especially important. Also, you should give special attention to key terms which are identified in color when they first appear in the chapter.
- After reading the text of the chapter, carefully study the Chapter Review, giving special attention to the following items:

Key Points. You should thoroughly understand each of the key points presented in the chapter. If you have difficulty understanding any of the key points, review the section of the chapter where the key point is discussed and illustrated. The key points are organized as major chapter headings that appear sequentially throughout the chapter.

Key Terms. You should be able to define each key term. If you cannot, refer to the page of the chapter where the key term is first presented and discussed. You may also refer to Appendix A, where all of the key terms are listed in alphabetical order and defined.

Self-Examination Questions. Answer each of the self-examination questions and check your answers by referring to the answers at the end of the chapter. These answers explain the correct response.

Illustrative Problem. Study the illustrative problem and its suggested solution. Each illustrative problem applies the concepts and principles discussed in the chapter to a problem situation. If you have difficulty understanding the illustrative problem, refer to the section of the chapter where the applicable concepts and principles are discussed and illustrated.

- Work all assigned homework. In many cases, the homework is related to specific chapter illustrations, and you may find it helpful to review the relevant chapter sections before you begin a homework assignment.
- Take notes during class lectures and discussions and give attention to the topics covered by your instructor.
- In reviewing for examinations, keep in mind those topics that your instructor has emphasized, and review your class notes and the text.
- If you feel you need additional aid, you may find the Study Guide that accompanies this textbook helpful. The Study Guide can be ordered from South-Western Publishing Co. by your college or university bookstore.

Contents in Brief

Contents

APPENDIXES

TEXT OBJECTIVES

•

•

Describe the evolution of accounting.

•

Describe the basic structure of the accounting profession.

•

Describe and illustrate the basic financial accounting concepts and principles.

•

Describe and illustrate accounting systems for service and merchandising enterprises.

•

Describe and illustrate accounting concepts and principles for sole proprietorships, partnerships, and corporations.

•

Describe the basic nature and structure of managerial accounting.

•

Describe and illustrate the accounting systems for manufacturing operations.

•

Describe and illustrate managerial accounting concepts for planning and controlling operations and decision making.

•

Describe and illustrate financial analyses for management use.

•

Introduction: Evolution of Accounting

Accounting has evolved, as have medicine, law, and most other fields of human activity, in response to the social and economic needs of society. As business and society have become more complex over the years, accounting has developed new concepts and techniques to meet the ever increasing needs for financial information. Without such information, many complex economic developments and social programs might never have been undertaken. This introduction is devoted to a brief résumé of the evolution of accounting.

PRIMITIVE ACCOUNTING

People in all civilizations have maintained various types of records of business activities. The oldest known are clay tablet records of the payment of wages in Babylonia around 3600 B.C. There are numerous evidences of record keeping and systems of accounting control in ancient Egypt and in the Greek city-states. The earliest known English records were compiled at the direction of William the Conqueror in the eleventh century to ascertain the financial resources of the kingdom.

For the most part, early accounting dealt only with limited aspects of the financial operations of private or governmental enterprises. There was no systematic accounting for all transactions of a particular unit, only for specific types or portions of transactions. Complete accounting for an enterprise developed somewhat later in response to the needs of the commercial republics of Italy.

DOUBLE-ENTRY SYSTEM

The evolution of the system of record keeping which came to be called "double entry" was strongly influenced by Venetian merchants. The first known description of the system was published in Italy in 1494. The author, a Franciscan monk by the name of Luca Pacioli, was a mathematician who taught in various universities in Perugia, Naples, Pisa, and Florence. Evidence of the position that Pacioli occupied among the intellectuals of his day was his close friendship with Leonardo da Vinci, with whom he collaborated on a mathematics book. Pacioli did the text and da Vinci the illustrations.

Goethe, the German poet, novelist, scientist, and universal genius, wrote about double entry as follows: "It is one of the most beautiful inventions of the human spirit, and every good businessman should use it in his economic undertakings."[1] Double entry provides for recording both aspects of a transaction in such a manner as to establish an equilibrium. For example, if an individual borrows $1,000 from a bank, the amount of the loan is recorded both as cash of $1,000 and as an obligation to repay $1,000. Either of the $1,000 amounts is balanced by the other $1,000 amount. As the basic principles are developed further in the early chapters of this book, it will become evident that "double entry" provides for the recording of all business transactions in a systematic manner. It also provides for a set of integrated financial statements reporting in monetary terms the amount of (1) the profit (net income) for a single venture or for a specified period, and (2) the properties (assets) owned by the enterprise and the ownership rights (equities) to the properties.

When the resources of a number of people were pooled to finance a single venture, such as a voyage of a merchant ship, the double-entry system provided records and reports of the income of the venture and the equity of the various participants. As single ventures were replaced by more permanent business organizations, the double-entry system was easily adapted to meet their needs. In spite of the tremendous development of business operations since 1494, and the ever increasing complexities of business and governmental organizations, the basic elements of the double-entry system have continued virtually unchanged.

INDUSTRIAL REVOLUTION

The Industrial Revolution, which occurred in England from the mid-eighteenth to the mid-nineteenth century, brought many social and economic changes, notably a change from the handicraft method of producing marketable goods to the factory system. The use of machinery in turning out many identical products gave rise to the need to determine the cost of a large volume of machine-made products instead of the cost of a relatively small number of individually handcrafted products. The specialized field of cost accounting emerged to meet this need for the analysis of various costs and for recording techniques.

In the early days of manufacturing operations, when business enterprises were relatively small and often isolated geographically, competition was frequently not very keen. Cost accounting was primitive and focused primarily on providing management with records and reports on past operations. Most business decisions were made on the basis of this historical financial information combined with intuition or hunches about the potential success of proposed courses of action.

As manufacturing enterprises became larger and more complex and as competition among manufacturers increased, the "scientific management concept" evolved. This concept emphasized a systematic approach to the solution of management problems. Paralleling this trend was the development of more sophisticated cost accounting concepts to supply

[1]Goethe, Johann Wolfgang von, *Samtliche Werke,* edited by Edward von der Hellen (Stuttgart and Berlin: J. G. Cotta, 1902–07), Vol. XVII, p. 37.

management with analytical techniques for measuring the efficiency of current operations and in planning for future operations. This trend was accelerated in the twentieth century by the advent of the electronic computer with its capacity for manipulating large masses of data and its ability to determine the potential effect of alternative courses of action.

CORPORATE ORGANIZATION

The expanded business operations initiated by the Industrial Revolution required increasingly large amounts of money to build factories and purchase machinery. This need for large amounts of capital resulted in the development of the corporate form of organization, which was first legally established in England in 1845. The Industrial Revolution spread rapidly to the United States, which became one of the world's leading industrial nations shortly after the Civil War. The accumulation of large amounts of capital was essential for establishment of new businesses in industries such as manufacturing, transportation, mining, electric power, and communications. In the United States, as in England, the corporation was the form of organization that facilitated the accumulation of the substantial amounts of capital needed.

Almost all large American business enterprises, and many small ones, are organized as corporations largely because ownership is evidenced by readily transferable shares of stock. The shareholders of a corporation control the management of corporate affairs only indirectly. They elect a board of directors, which establishes general policies and selects officers who actively manage the corporation. The development of a class of owners far removed from active participation in the management of the business created an additional dimension for accounting. Accounting information was needed not only by management in directing the affairs of the corporation but also by the shareholders, who required periodic financial statements in order to appraise management's performance.

As corporations became larger, an increasing number of individuals and institutions looked to accountants to provide economic information about these enterprises. Prospective shareholders and creditors sought information about a corporation's financial status and its prospects for the future. Governmental agencies required financial information for purposes of taxation and regulation. Employees, union representatives, and customers demanded information upon which to judge the stability and profitability of corporate enterprises. Thus accounting began to expand its function of meeting the needs of a relatively few owners to a public role of meeting the needs of a variety of interested parties.

PUBLIC ACCOUNTING

The development of the corporation also created a new social need — the need for an independent audit to provide some assurance that management's financial representations were reliable. This audit function, often referred to as the "attest function," was chiefly responsible for the creation and growth of the public accounting profession. Unlike private accountants, public accountants are independent of the enterprises for which they perform services.

Recognizing the need for accounting services of professional caliber, all of the states provide for the licensing of certified public accountants (*CPAs*). In

1944, fifty years after the enactment of the first CPA law, there were approximately 25,000 CPAs in the United States. During the next four decades the number increased tenfold, and currently the number exceeds 250,000.

Auditing is still a major service offered by CPAs, but presently they also devote much of their time to assisting their clients with problems related to planning, controlling, and decision making. Such services, known as management advisory services or management consulting, have increased in volume over the years until today they comprise a significant part of the practice of most public accounting firms.

INCOME TAX

Enactment of the federal income tax law in 1913 resulted in a tremendous stimulus to accounting activity. All business enterprises organized as corporations or partnerships, as well as many individuals, were required to maintain sufficient records to enable them to file accurate tax returns. Since that time the income tax laws and regulations have become increasingly complex. As a consequence businesses have depended upon both private anc public accountants for advice on legal methods of tax minimization, for preparing tax returns, and for representing them in tax disputes with governmental agencies.

It should also be noted that accounting has influenced the development of income tax law to a great degree. Had not accounting progressed to a point where periodic net income could be determined, the enactment and enforcement of any tax law undoubtedly would have been extremely difficult, if not impossible.

GOVERNMENT INFLUENCE

Over the years government at various levels has intervened to an increasing extent in economic and social matters affecting ever greater numbers of people. Accounting has played an important role by providing the financial information needed to achieve the desired goals.

As the number and size of corporate enterprises grew and an ever increasing number of shares of stock were traded in the market place, laws regulating the activities of stock exchanges, stockbrokers, and investment companies were enacted for the protection of investors. These regulations involve accounting requirements. To protect the public from excessive charges by railroads and other monopolies, commissions were established to limit their rates to levels yielding net income considered to be a "fair return" on invested capital. This rate-making process required extensive accounting information. Regulated banks and savings and loan associations also had to meet record-keeping and reporting requirements and permit periodic examination of their records by governmental agencies. As labor unions became larger and more powerful, regulatory laws were enacted requiring them to submit periodic financial reports. With the enactment of social security and medicare legislation came record-keeping and reporting requirements for almost all businesses and many individuals.

As the federal government exercised increasing control over economic activities, accounting information became more essential as a basis for formulating legislation. One of the areas in which the government has influenced economic and social behavior has been through the income tax. For example, contributions to charitable organizations have been encouraged by permitting their deduction in determining taxable income. Controls over wages and prices have also been enacted at various times in attempts to control the economy by reducing the rate of inflation. An enormous volume of accounting data must be reported, summarized, and studied before proceeding with the evaluation of various governmental proposals such as the foregoing.

CURRENT ACCOUNTING PRACTICE

Accounting as a profession has experienced rapid development during the past 25 years. During the period 1960–1984, the profession of accountancy grew to approximately double its size in 1960. This expansion of career opportunities in accounting and of professionally trained accountants is expected to continue.

The following table indicates the projected growth of the profession of accountancy relative to the projected growth of the legal and medical professions:

Profession	*Projected Rate of Increase 1982–1995*
Accountancy	40.2%
Legal	34.3
Medical	34.0

Source: U. S. Department of Labor, Bureau of Labor Statistics, *Occupational Projections and Training Data: 1984 Edition* (Washington: U. S. Government Printing Office, May, 1984).

Profession of Accountancy

Accountancy is a profession whose members may be viewed as engaged in either (1) private accounting or (2) public accounting. Accountants employed by a particular business firm or not-for-profit organization, perhaps as chief accountant, controller, or financial vice-president, are said to be engaged in **private accounting.** Accountants who render accounting services on a fee basis, and staff accountants employed by them, are said to be engaged in **public accounting.**

Both private and public accounting have long been recognized as excellent training for top managerial responsibilities. Many executive positions in government and in industry are held by men and women with education and experience in accounting.

Private Accounting. The scope of activities and responsibilities of private accountants varies widely. They are frequently referred to as administrative or managerial accountants, or, if they are employed by a manufacturing concern, as industrial accountants. Various governmental units and other not-for-profit organizations also employ accountants.

The Institute of Certified Management Accounting, which is an affiliate of the National Association of Accountants, grants the certificate in management accounting (CMA) as evidence of professional competence in that field. Requirements for the CMA designation include the baccalaureate degree or equivalent, two years of experience in management accounting, and successful completion of examinations occupying two and one-half days. Participation in a program of continuing professional education is also required

GROWTH TRENDS IN THE ACCOUNTING PROFESSION

The accounting profession has been growing at a much faster rate than the population of the United States, according to occupational surveys issued by the Bureau of the Census, which count all employed accountants and auditors regardless of the nature of their employer. These figures, which are summarized in the following chart, include accountants in public practice, in industry, and in government, but exclude bookkeepers and other semiprofessionals.

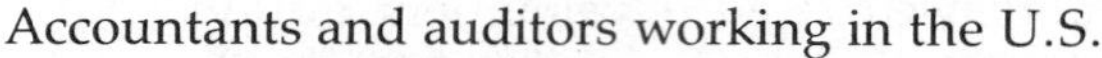

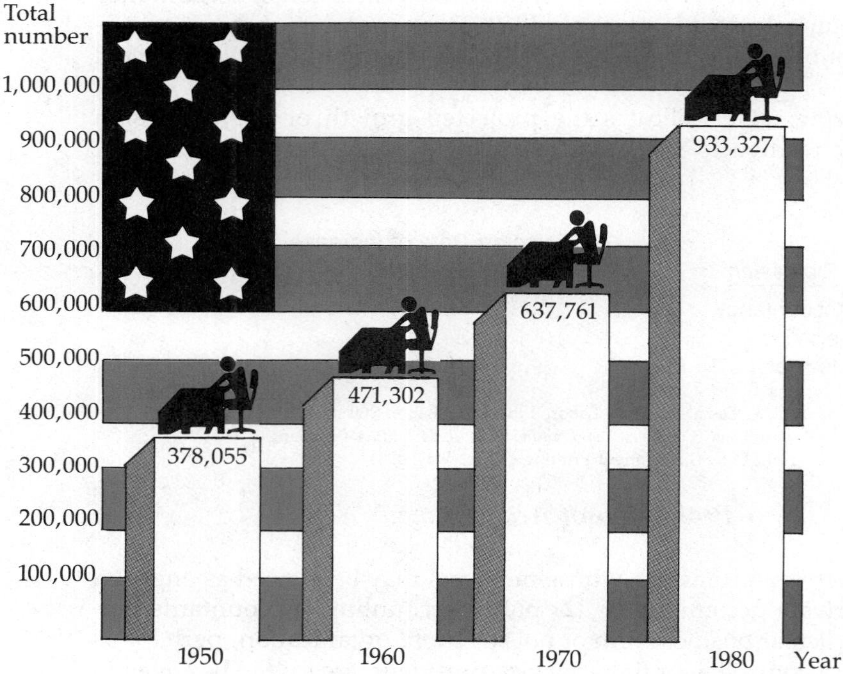

Source: "Growth Trends in the Accounting Profession," *Journal of Accountancy* (May, 1985), pp. 139–144.

for renewal of the certificate. The Institute of Internal Auditors administers a similar program for internal auditors—accountants who review the accounting and operating procedures prescribed by their firms. Accountants qualifying under this program are entitled to use the designation Certified Internal Auditor (CIA).

Public Accounting. In public accounting, an accountant may practice as an individual or as a member of a public accounting firm. Public accountants who have met a state's education, experience, and examination requirements may become **certified public accountants,** commonly called **CPAs**.

Qualifications of CPAs. The qualifications required for the CPA certificate differ among the various states. A specified level of education is required, often the completion of a collegiate course of study in accounting. All states require that a candidate pass an examination prepared by the **American Institute of Certified Public Accountants (AICPA).** The examination is administered twice a year, in May and November. Many states permit candidates to take the examination upon graduation from college or during the term in which they will complete the educational requirements. The examination, which occupies one afternoon and two all-day sessions, is divided into four parts: Accounting Theory, Accounting Practice, Auditing, and Business Law. Some states also require an examination in an additional subject, such as Rules of Professional Conduct. Most states do not permit successful candidates to practice as independent CPAs until they have had from one to three years' experience in public accounting or in employment considered equivalent.

In recent years a majority of the states have enacted laws requiring public practitioners to participate in a program of continuing professional education or forfeit their right to continue in public practice. According to the statutes of one of the states, the continuing education must be a "formal program of learning which contributes directly to the professional competence of an individual after he or she has been licensed to practice public accounting." The states differ as to some of the details of the requirement, such as the number of hours of formal education required for renewal of the permit to practice. The rules adopted by a number of State Boards of Accountancy require forty hours per year (a fifty-minute class period counts as one hour).

Details regarding the requirements for practice as a CPA in any particular state can be obtained from the respective State Board of Accountancy.

Professional Ethics for CPAs. CPAs have a duty not only to their clients but to their colleagues and the public to perform services competently and with integrity. However, many clients and much of the public do not have the capability of evaluating a CPA's performance. Therefore, standards of conduct have been established to guide CPAs in the conduct of their practices. These standards, called **codes of professional conduct** or **codes of professional ethics,** have been established by professional organizations of CPAs, such as the AICPA and state societies of CPAs, and by regulatory agencies, such as State Boards of Accountancy and the Securities and Exchange Commission.

The purpose of codes of professional conduct is to instill confidence in the quality of services rendered by the profession of public accounting. Such codes establish minimum standards of acceptable conduct, which often extend beyond behavior which is otherwise acceptable under the law. For example, under the current AICPA code of professional conduct, CPAs are prohibited from practicing under a firm name that is misleading.[2]

A CPA who violates the code of ethics is subject to disciplinary proceedings. The AICPA and state societies of CPAs have authority to revoke a CPA's membership in their organizations. If the violation also involves a regulatory agency, such as a State Board of Accountancy or the Securities and Exchange Commission, the CPA's ability to practice within the agency's jurisdiction may be revoked or otherwise limited. The combination of professional organization and regulatory agency sanctions guards against unethical behavior by the public accounting profession.

To meet the public's expectations of the role and responsibilities of the CPA, codes of professional conduct change as society changes. However, ethical conduct is more than simply conforming to written standards of professional behavior. In a true sense, ethical conduct requires a personal commitment to honorable behavior. This thought was best expressed by Marcus Aurelius, who said, "A man should *be* upright; not be *kept* upright."

---

[2]*The Code of Professional Conduct,* American Institute of Certified Public Accountants (New York, 1988).

ACCOUNTING'S FUTURE

Accounting is capable of supplying financial information that is essential for the efficient operation and for the evaluation of performance of any economic unit in society. Changes in the environment in which such organizations operate will inevitably be accompanied by alterations in accounting concepts and techniques. Although long-range predictions as to environmental changes are risky and of doubtful value, there are three areas that promise to receive increased attention in the immediate future—computerized accounting systems, international accounting, and socio-economic accounting.

Computerized Accounting Systems

Since the electronic computer was first used to process business data in the middle of the twentieth century, it has played an ever increasing role in the design of accounting systems and the processing of economic data. It has generally enabled interested users of accounting information to receive relevant economic data on a more timely basis at a lower cost.

The integration of the electronic computer into accounting systems has created both opportunities and challenges for accountants. The computer provides opportunities for accountants to analyze efficiently a greater quantity of economic data for reporting to users. As the use of computers in business continues to accelerate, there will be an increasing demand for accountants to aid in the analysis, design, and implementation of these systems. This responsibility, in turn, will create ever greater challenges for accountants to obtain a complete understanding of business operations and the principles of designing systems that will gather all accurate, relevant data on a timely basis.

International Accounting

The rapid growth of multinational firms in recent years has had a significant impact on accounting because of the different environments existing in the various countries in which such firms operate. Currently, a major problem is the need to develop more uniform accounting standards among countries. Working toward this end are such international organizations as the International Accounting Standards Committee and the International Federation of Accountants.

Socioeconomic Accounting

The term socioeconomic accounting refers to the measurement and communication of information about the impact of various organizations on society. Three major areas of social measurement can be identified. First, at the societal level the interest is on the total impact of all institutions on matters that affect the quality of life. The second area is concerned with the programs undertaken by the government and socially oriented not-for-profit organizations to accomplish specific social objectives. The third area, sometimes referred to as corporate social responsibility, focuses on the public interest in corporate social performance in such areas as reduction of water and air pollution, conservation of natural resources, improvement in quality of product and customer service, and employment practices regarding minority groups and females. The concept of social measurement is relatively simple as a theory, but much additional study and research will be needed before measurement can be expressed in terms of monetary costs and benefits.

Part One

Fundamentals of Financial Accounting

1
Concepts and Principles of Accounting

CHAPTER OBJECTIVES

Describe accounting and the users of accounting information.

Describe financial accounting and managerial accounting.

Describe the development of financial accounting concepts and principles.

Identify and illustrate the application of the following basic financial accounting concepts and principles:

Business entity
Cost principle
Business transactions
Unit of measurement
Matching concept
Adequate disclosure
Consistency
Materiality
Going concern

Identify the accounting equation and its basic elements.

Describe and illustrate how all business transactions can be recorded.

Identify and describe the financial statements of a corporation.

Income statement
Balance sheet
Retained earnings statement
Statement of cash flows

Accounting plays an important role in our economic and social system. Sound decisions made by individuals, businesses, governments, and other entities are essential for the efficient distribution and use of the nation's scarce resources. To make such decisions, these groups must have reliable information provided by the accounting system. The objective of accounting, therefore, is to record, summarize, report, and interpret economic data for use by many groups within our economic and social system.

ACCOUNTING AND THE USERS OF ACCOUNTING INFORMATION

Accounting[1] is often called the "language of business." This language can be viewed as an information system that provides essential information about the financial activities of an entity to various individuals or groups for their use in making informed judgments and decisions. As such, accounting information is composed principally of financial data about business transactions, expressed in terms of money.

Accounting provides the techniques for gathering economic data and the language for communicating these data to different individuals and institutions. Investors in a business enterprise need information about its financial status and its future prospects. Bankers and suppliers appraise the financial soundness of a business organization and assess the risks involved before making loans or granting credit. Government agencies are concerned with the financial activities of business organizations for purposes of taxation and regulation. Employees and their union representatives are also vitally interested in the stability and the profitability of the organization that hires them.

The individuals who depend upon and make the most use of accounting are those charged with the responsibility for directing the operations of enterprises. They are often referred to collectively as "management." Management relies upon many types of accounting data in conducting day-to-day operations, in evaluating current operations, and in planning future operations.

The process of using accounting to provide information to users is illustrated in the following diagram:

Accounting as a Provider of Information to Users

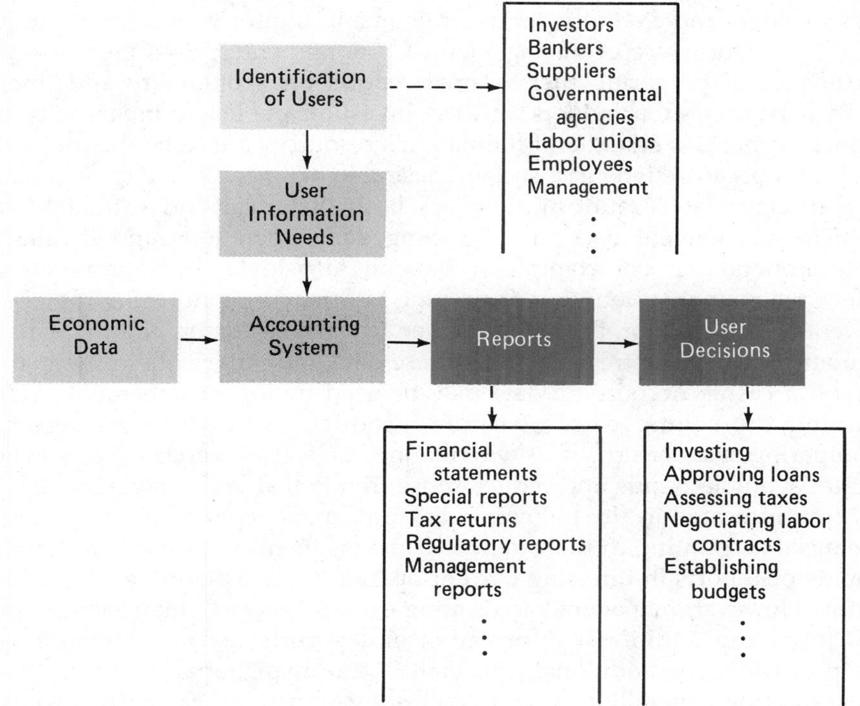

[1] A glossary of terms appears in Appendix A. The terms included in the glossary are printed in color the first time they appear in the text.

First, user groups are identified and their information needs determined. These needs determine which economic data are gathered and processed by the accounting system. Finally, the accounting system generates reports that communicate essential information to users. For example, investors need information on the financial condition and results of operations of an enterprise to assess the profitability and riskiness of their investments in the enterprise. The accounting system satisfies these needs by recording essential information and periodically summarizing this information in financial reports. Although the information for one category of users may differ markedly from that needed by other users, accounting can provide each user group with economic information to assist them in making decisions regarding future actions.

FINANCIAL AND MANAGERIAL ACCOUNTING

As a result of rapid technological advances and accelerated economic growth, a number of specialized fields in accounting have evolved. The two most important accounting fields are financial accounting and managerial accounting.

Financial accounting is concerned with the measuring and recording of transactions for a business enterprise or other economic unit and the periodic preparation of various reports from such records. The reports, which may be for general purposes or for a special purpose, provide useful information for managers, owners, creditors, governmental agencies, and the general public. Of particular importance to financial accountants are the principles of accounting, termed **generally accepted accounting principles (GAAP).** These principles were developed because of the demand by "Outsiders," such as stockholders and creditors, for accurate financial information for use in judging the performance of management. Corporate enterprises must use these principles in preparing their annual reports on profitability and financial status for their stockholders and the investing public. Comparability of financial reports is essential if the nation's resources are to be divided among business organizations in a socially desirable manner.

Managerial accounting employs both historical and estimated data, which management uses in conducting daily operations and in planning future operations. For example, in directing day-to-day operations, management relies upon accounting to provide information concerning the amount owed to each creditor, the amount owed by each customer, and the date each amount is due. The treasurer uses these data and other data in the management of cash. Accounting data may be used by top management in determining the selling price of a new product. Production managers, by comparing past performances with planned objectives, can take steps to accelerate favorable trends and reduce those trends that are unfavorable.

As indicated in the following diagram, managerial accounting overlaps financial accounting to the extent that management uses the financial statements or reports in directing current operations and planning future operations. However, managerial accounting extends beyond financial accounting by providing additional information and reports for management's use. In providing this additional information, the managerial accountant is *not* governed by generally accepted accounting principles. Since these data are used only by management, the accountant provides the data in the format that is most useful for management. The principle of "usefulness," then, is dominant in guiding the accountant in preparing management reports.

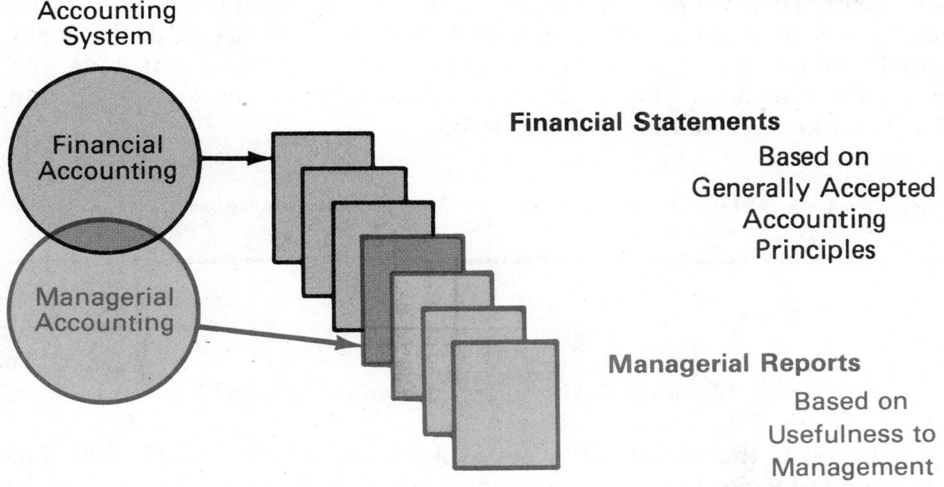

The first fourteen chapters of this text focus on financial accounting and the concepts and principles underlying the preparation and use of financial statements. Managerial accounting and the principles and concepts underlying the preparation of managerial accounting reports are discussed in Chapters 15–28.

DEVELOPMENT OF FINANCIAL ACCOUNTING CONCEPTS AND PRINCIPLES

The word "principle" as used in the context of generally accepted accounting principles does not have the same authoritativeness as universal principles or natural laws relating to the study of astronomy, physics, or other physical sciences. Accounting principles have been developed by individuals to help make accounting data more useful in an ever-changing society. They represent guides for the achievement of the desired results, based on reason, observation, and experimentation. The selection of the best method from among many alternatives has come about gradually, and in some areas a clear consensus is still lacking. These principles are continually reexamined and revised to keep pace with the increasing complexity of business operations. General acceptance among the members of the accounting profession is the criterion for determining an accounting principle.

Responsibility for the development of accounting principles has rested primarily on practicing accountants and accounting educators, working both independently and under the sponsorship of various accounting organizations. These principles are also influenced by business practices and customs, ideas and beliefs of the users of the financial statements, governmental agencies, stock exchanges, and other business groups.

The Importance of Accounting Standards

No amount of policing by the public accounting profession or regulatory agencies to prevent abuses in financial reporting can satisfy the public need for comparable information from all companies. Only financial accounting and reporting standards can satisfy that need. The challenge to the FASB is to strike a reasonable balance between the prevention of abuses and the portrayal of economic reality. As standard setters, we must try to avoid the concern about potential abuses leading to standards that make significantly different situations look the same — in other words, forcing square pegs into round holes.

Source: Donald J. Kirk, FASB chairman (From a speech before the National Association of Accountants Second Annual International-European Conference, Paris, April 19, 1985).

Financial Accounting Standards Board

In 1973, the **Financial Accounting Standards Board (FASB)** was appointed by the Financial Accounting Foundation (FAF). The FAF is an independent, nonprofit organization that was created in 1972 to oversee the standard-setting process, to appoint members of standard-setting boards and advisory councils, and to raise funds for the operation of the standard-setting process.

The FASB, which is presently the dominant body in the development of generally accepted accounting principles, is composed of seven members, four of whom must be CPAs drawn from public practice. These seven members serve full time, receive a salary, and must resign from the firm or institution with which they have been affiliated. The FASB is assisted by an advisory council of approximately forty members, whose major responsibilities include the recommendation of priorities and agenda and the review of FASB plans, activities, and statements proposed for issuance. The FASB employs a full-time research staff and administrative staff as well as task forces to study specific matters from time to time.

As problems in financial reporting are identified, the FASB conducts extensive research to identify the principal issues involved and the possible solutions. Generally, after issuing discussion memoranda and preliminary proposals and evaluating comments from interested parties, the Board issues *Statements of Financial Accounting Standards,* which become part of generally accepted accounting principles. To explain, clarify, or elaborate on existing pronouncements, the Board also issues *Interpretations,* which have the same authority as the standards.

Presently, the Board is in the process of developing a broad conceptual framework for financial accounting. This project, which is expected to take many years to complete, is an attempt to develop a "constitution" that can be used to evaluate current standards and can serve as the basis for future standards. The results of the completed portion of this project have been published as six *Statements of Financial Accounting Concepts,* which are briefly described as follows:

- **Objectives of Financial Reporting by Business Enterprises (No. 1)**
  Sets forth three broad objectives of financial reporting:
  1. To provide financial information that is useful in making rational investment, credit, and similar decisions;
  2. To provide financial information to enable users to predict cash flows to the business and subsequently to themselves;
  3. To provide financial information about business resources, claims to these resources, and changes in these resources and claims.
- **Qualitative Characteristics of Accounting Information (No. 2)**
  Identifies the essential qualities of the accounting information included in financial reports as follows: usefulness, understandability, relevance, reliability, verifiability, timeliness, neutrality, completeness, and comparability.
- **Elements of Financial Statements of Business Enterprises (No. 3)**
  Replaced by Statement No. 6.
- **Objectives of Financial Reporting by Nonbusiness Organizations (No. 4)**
  Sets forth the objectives that guide the preparation of the financial statements for nonbusiness organizations.
- **Recognition and Measurement in Financial Statements of Business Enterprises (No. 5)**
  Identifies the financial statements that should be prepared to meet the objectives of financial reporting for business enterprises.
- **Elements of Financial Statements (No. 6)**
  Replaces Statement No. 3 and defines the interrelated elements of financial statements that are directly related to measuring the performance and status of businesses and nonprofit organizations.

Governmental Accounting Standards Board

The **Governmental Accounting Standards Board (GASB)** was formed in 1984 as an arm of the Financial Accounting Foundation. The GASB has a full-time chairperson and four part-time members who have responsibility for establishing the accounting standards to be followed by state and municipal governments. The GASB employs a full-time research staff and administrative staff. An advisory council of approximately 20 members assists the GASB and also has fund-raising responsibilities.

Accounting Organizations

Among the oldest and most influential organizations of accountants are the **American Institute of Certified Public Accountants (AICPA)** and the **American Accounting Association (AAA)**. Each organization publishes a monthly or quarterly periodical and, from time to time, issues other publications in the form of research studies, technical opinions, and monographs. There are also other national accounting organizations as well as many state societies and local chapters of the national and state organizations. These groups provide forums for the interchange of ideas and discussion of accounting principles.

Government Organizations

Of the various governmental agencies with an interest in the development of accounting principles, the **Securities and Exchange Commission (SEC)** has been the most influential. Established by an act of Congress in 1934, the SEC issues regulations that must be observed in the preparation of financial statements and other reports filed with the Commission.

The **Internal Revenue Service (IRS)** issues regulations that govern the determination of income for purposes of federal income taxation. Because these regulations sometimes conflict with financial accounting principles, many enterprises maintain two sets of accounts to satisfy both reporting requirements. To avoid this increased record keeping, there have been times when firms have adopted practices that are acceptable for tax purposes as generally accepted accounting principles. A discussion of the nature of the income tax is presented in more detail in Appendix D.

Other regulatory agencies exercise a dominant influence on the accounting principles of the industries under their jurisdiction. In rare situations, Congress may also enact legislation that dictates accounting principles. These situations usually involve controversial issues on which no clear consensus has been reached within the profession.

Other Influential Organizations

The **Financial Executives Institute (FEI)** has influenced the development of accounting principles by encouraging and sponsoring accounting research. The FEI also comments on proposed pronouncements of the FASB, the SEC, and other organizations.

The **National Association of Accountants (NAA)** is one of the largest organizations of accountants. It is primarily concerned with management's use of accounting information in directing business operations. Since management is responsible for the preparation of the basic financial statements, however, the NAA communicates its recommendations on generally accepted accounting principles to appropriate organizations.

Other organizations representing users of accounting reports are increasingly making their views known. Prominent in this group are the **Financial Analysts Federation** (investors and investment advisors) and the **Securities Industry Associates** (investment bankers).

FINANCIAL ACCOUNTING CONCEPTS AND PRINCIPLES

The remainder of this chapter is devoted to the underlying assumptions, concepts, and principles of the greatest importance and widest applicability. Attention will also be directed toward applications of financial accounting concepts and principles to specific situations.

Business Entity Concept

The **business entity concept** is based on the applicability of accounting to individual economic units in society. These individual economic units include all business enterprises organized for profit; numerous governmental units, such as states, cities, and school districts; other not-for-profit units, such as charities, churches, hospitals, and social clubs; and individual persons and family units. The basic economic data for a unit must first be recorded, followed by analysis and summarization, and finally by periodic reporting. Thus, accounting applies to each separate economic unit.

Profit-Making Businesses

This textbook is concerned primarily with the accounting principles and techniques applicable to profit-making businesses. Such businesses are customarily organized as sole proprietorships, partnerships, or corporations. A **sole proprietorship** is owned by one individual. A **partnership** is owned by two or more individuals in accordance with a contractual arrangement. A **corporation**, organized in accordance with state or federal statutes, is a separate legal entity in which ownership is divided into shares of stock. Although the sole proprietorship is the most common business form, the corporation is the dominant form in terms of dollars of business activity, as indicated in the following charts:

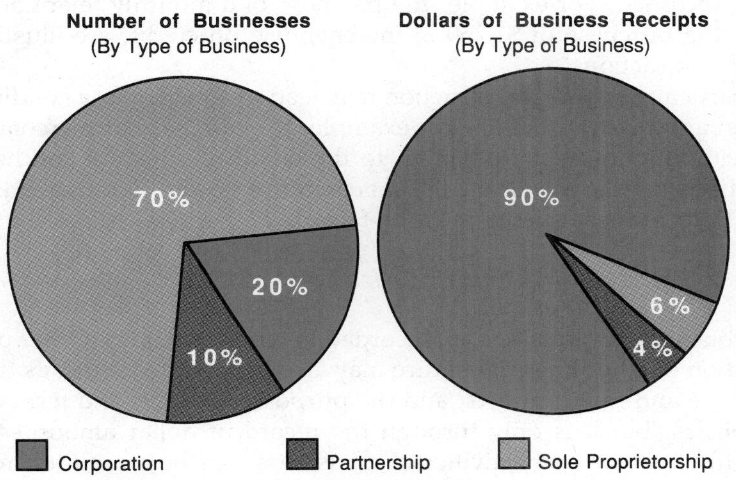

SOURCE: U.S. Bureau of the Census, *Statistical Abstract of the United States: 1987* (107th edition; Washington: U.S. Government Printing Office, 1986).

The Cost Principle

The records of properties and services purchased by a business are maintained in accordance with the **cost principle**, which requires that the monetary record be in terms of *cost*. For example, if a building is purchased at a cost of $150,000, that is the amount used in the buyer's accounting record. The seller may have been asking $170,000 for the building up to the time of the sale; the buyer may have initially offered $130,000 for it; the building may have been assessed at $125,000 for property tax purposes and insured for $135,000; and the buyer may have received an offer of $175,000 for the building the day after it was acquired. These latter amounts have no effect on the accounting records because they do not originate from an exchange. The exchange price, or cost, of $150,000 determines the monetary amount used in the records for the building.

Continuing the illustration, the $175,000 offer received by the buyer is an indication that the building was a bargain purchase at $150,000. To use

$175,000 in the accounting records, however, would give recognition to an illusory or unrealized profit. If, after purchasing the building, the buyer should accept the offer and sell the building for $175,000, a profit of $25,000 would be realized, and the new owner would use $175,000 as the cost of the building.

The determination of costs incurred and revenues earned is fundamental to accounting. In exchanges between buyer and seller, both attempt to get the best price. Only the amount agreed upon is objective enough for accounting purposes. If the monetary amounts at which the accounting records for properties are maintained were constantly revised upward and downward on the basis of mere offers, appraisals, and opinions, accounting reports would soon become unstable and unreliable.

Business Transactions

A **business transaction** is the occurrence of an event or of a condition that must be recorded. For example, the payment of a monthly telephone bill of $68 and the purchase of $1,750 of merchandise on credit, are illustrative of business transactions.

A particular business transaction may lead to an event or a condition that results in another transaction. For example, the purchase of merchandise on credit will be followed by payment to the creditor, which is another transaction. Each time a portion of the merchandise is sold, another transaction occurs. Each of these events must be recorded.

Unit of Measurement

All business transactions are recorded in terms of money. Other pertinent information of a nonfinancial nature may also be recorded, such as the terms of purchase and sale contracts, and the purpose, amount, and term of insurance policies. But it is only through the record of dollar amounts that the diverse transactions and activities of a business may be measured, reported, and periodically compared. Money is both the common factor of all business transactions and the only feasible unit of measurement that can be used to achieve uniform financial data.

As a unit of measurement, the dollar differs from such quantitative standards as the kilogram, liter, or meter, which have not changed for centuries. The instability of the purchasing power of the dollar is well known, and the disruptive effect of the declining value of the dollar is acknowledged by accountants. In the past, however, this declining value generally was not given recognition in the financial statements.

The use of a monetary unit that is assumed to be stable insures **objectivity**. In spite of the inflationary trend in the United States, historical-dollar financial statements are considered to be better than statements based on movements of the general price level. Many accountants recommend that businesses use supplemental statements to indicate the effect of changing prices.

ASSETS, LIABILITIES, AND OWNER'S EQUITY

The properties owned by a business enterprise are referred to as **assets** and the rights or claims to the properties are referred to as **equities**. If the assets owned by a business amount to $100,000, the equities in the assets must also amount to $100,000. The relationship between the two may be stated in the form of an equation, as follows:

Assets = Equities

Equities may be subdivided into two principal types: the rights of creditors and the rights of owners. The rights of creditors represent *debts* of the business and are called **liabilities**. The rights of the owner or owners are called **owner's equity**. Expansion of the equation to give recognition to the two basic types of equities yields the following, which is known as the **accounting equation**:

Assets = Liabilities + Owner's Equity

It is customary to place "Liabilities" before "Owner's Equity" in the accounting equation because creditors have preferential rights to the assets. The residual claim of the owner or owners is sometimes given greater emphasis by transposing liabilities to the other side of the equation, yielding:

Assets − Liabilities = Owner's Equity

TRANSACTIONS AND THE ACCOUNTING EQUATION

All business transactions, from the simplest to the most complex, can be stated in terms of the resulting change in the three basic elements of the accounting equation. In all cases, the recording of the effects of transactions on the elements of the accounting equation must be such that the equality of the equation is maintained. For example, if a business organizes as a corporation by selling shares of ownership interests, generally referred to as **capital stock**, for $50,000, the asset cash will increase by **$50,000** and the owner's equity will increase by **$50,000**. The effect of this transaction on the accounting equation is as follows:

Assets	=	Liabilities +	Owner's Equity
Cash			Capital Stock
+$50,000			+$50,000

The transactions completed by an enterprise during a specific period may number into the thousands and may cause increases and decreases in many different asset, liability, and owner's equity items. To provide timely reports on the effects of these transactions, accountants must record them in a systematic manner. Although the effects of transactions can be recorded in terms of the accounting equation, as illustrated, such a format is not practical as a design for actual accounting systems. On a day-to-day basis, separate records are maintained for each major asset, liability, and owner's equity item of a business entity. For example, a single record must be used only for recording increases and decreases in cash.

The type of record traditionally used for the purpose of recording individual transactions is called an **account**. A group of related accounts that comprise a complete unit, such as all of the accounts of a specific business enterprise, is called a **ledger**. These individual accounts are summarized at periodic intervals, and the information thus obtained is presented in financial statements.

NATURE OF AN ACCOUNT

The simplest form of an account has three parts: (1) a title, which is the name of the item recorded in the account; (2) a space for recording increases in the amount of the item, in terms of money; and (3) a space for recording decreases in the amount of the item, also in monetary terms. This form of an account, illustrated below, is known as a **T account** because of its similarity to the letter T.

Title	
Left side	Right side
debit	*credit*

T-Account

The left side of the account is called the **debit** side and the right side is called the **credit** side.[2] Amounts entered on the left side of an account, regardless of the account title, are called **debits** to the account, and the account is said to be **debited**. Amounts entered on the right side of an account are called **credits**, and the account is said to be **credited**.

In the following illustration, receipts of cash during a period of time have been listed vertically on the debit side of the cash account. The cash payments for the same period have been listed in similar fashion on the credit side of the account. A memorandum total of the cash receipts for the period to date, **$109,500** in the illustration, may be inserted below the last debit at any time the information is desired. This figure should be identified in such a way that it is not mistaken for an additional debit. The total of the cash payments, $68,500 in the illustration, may be inserted on the credit side in a similar manner. Subtraction of the smaller sum from the larger, $109,500 − $68,500, yields the amount of cash on hand, $41,000, which is called the **balance of the account.** This amount is inserted on the debit side of the account, next to the total of the debits, thus identifying the balance of the account as a debit balance. If financial statements were to be prepared at this time, the amount of cash reported thereon would be $41,000.

Cash		
	50,000	8,500
	30,500	14,000
	29,000	7,000
41,000	*109,500*	29,000
		10,000
		68,500

RECORDING TRANSACTIONS IN ACCOUNTS

To illustrate the manner of recording transactions, assume that Ingram Corporation is to be organized on January 1, 1989. Each transaction or group

---

[2]Often abbreviated as *Dr.* for "debit" and *Cr.* for "credit," derived from the Latin *debere* and *credere*.

of similar transactions that occurs during January, the first month of operations, is described. The recording of the transaction in the accounts is then illustrated.

Transaction (a)

Ingram Corporation sells $60,000 of capital stock.

As illustrated previously, assets can be reported on the left side of the accounting equation. Consistent with this presentation, transactions increasing assets are entered on the left side of asset accounts as debits, and decreases are entered on the right side as credits. This pattern was followed in recording the debits and credits in the cash account illustrated on page 20. Since liabilities and owner's equity can be reported on the right side of the accounting equation, the procedure for entering increases and decreases is reversed. Therefore, increases in liabilities and owner's equity are entered on the right side of those accounts as credits and decreases are entered on the left side as debits. Thus, the effect of Ingram Corporation's first transaction on the accounts in the ledger can be described as a $60,000 debit (increase) to Cash and a $60,000 credit (increase) to Capital Stock. The equation is maintained by the equality of the debit and credit.

Transaction information is initially entered in a record called a **journal**. The process of recording a transaction in the journal is called **journalizing**, and the form of presentation is called a **journal entry.** In the journal, the transaction information is recorded by listing the title of the account and the amount to be debited, followed by a similar listing, below and to the right of the debit, of the title of the account and the amount to be credited. For transaction (a), the journal entry is as follows:

(a)	Cash	60,000	
	Capital Stock		60,000

The data in the journal entry are transferred to the appropriate accounts by a process known as **posting**. The posting process for transaction (a) is illustrated as follows:

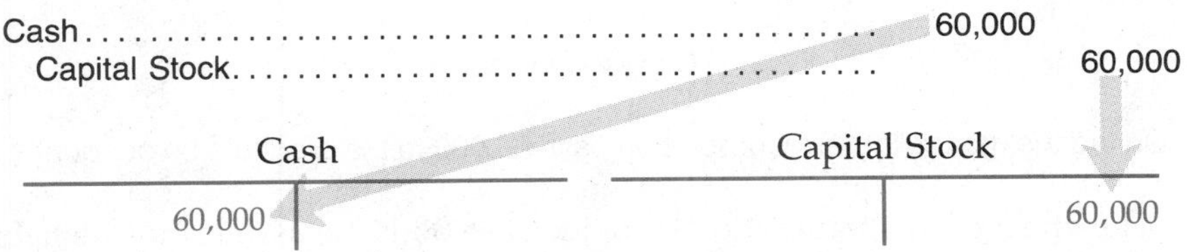

After recording the transaction through the use of a journal entry and posting it to the accounts, the accounting equation and the accounts would appear as follows:

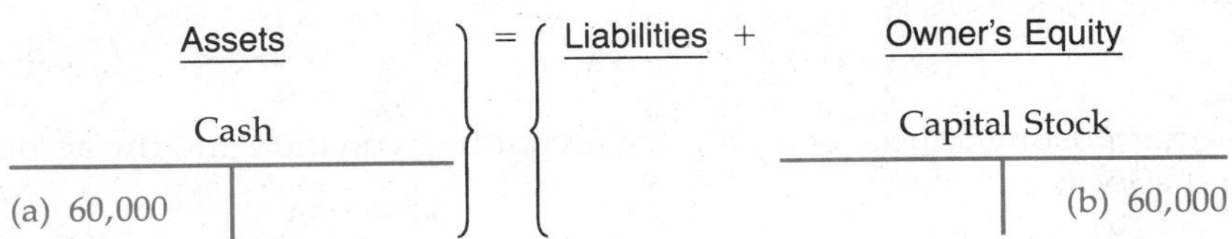

Note that the amount of cash, which is reported on the left side of the accounting equation under Assets, is posted to the left (debit) side of Cash. The owner's equity in the enterprise, which is reported on the right side of the accounting equation, is posted to the right (credit) side of Capital Stock.

Transaction (b)

During the month, Ingram Corporation purchases $12,000 of supplies from various suppliers, agreeing to pay in the near future.

Consumable goods purchased, such as supplies, and advance payments of expenses, such as insurance, are considered to be **prepaid expenses,** or assets. These assets may be acquired by the payment of cash, or they may be acquired on credit, as in this case, in which the buyer agrees to make the payment in the near future. The type of credit transaction is called a purchase on *account,* and the liability created is termed an **account payable.** Liabilities of various types are commonly described as **payables.**

The effect of this transaction on the accounts in the ledger can be described as a $12,000 debit (increase) to Supplies and a $12,000 credit (increase) to Accounts Payable. Transaction (b) is recorded in the journal by the following entry:

(b)	Supplies	12,000	
	Accounts Payable		12,000

After posting journal entry (b), the accounting equation and the accounts would appear as follows:

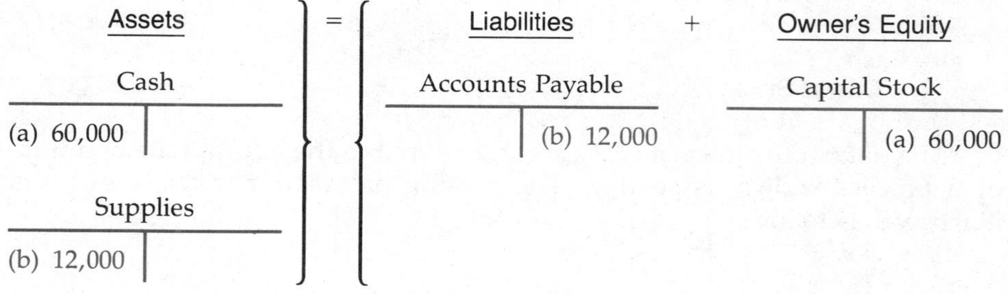

Transaction (c)

During the month, Ingram Corporation pays $8,000 to the creditors on account.

The effect of this transaction is to decrease both the assets and the liabilities of the enterprise. The effect on the accounts in the ledger can be described as an $8,000 credit (decrease) to Cash and an $8,000 debit (decrease) to Accounts Payable. Transaction (c) is recorded in the journal by the following entry:

(c)	Accounts Payable	8,000	
	Cash		8,000

After posting journal entry (c), the accounting equation and the accounts would appear as follows:

Assets		=	Liabilities		+	Owner's Equity	
Cash			Accounts Payable			Capital Stock	
(a) 60,000	(c) 8,000		(c) 8,000	(b) 12,000			(a) 60,000
Supplies							
(b) 12,000							

Before continuing with the illustration, the general rules for recording transactions in the asset, liability, and owner's equity accounts are summarized. As illustrated in the recording of transactions (a), (b), and (c), the left side of asset accounts is used for recording increases and the right side is used for recording decreases.

It was also illustrated that the right side of liability and owner's equity accounts is used to record increases. It naturally follows that the left side of such accounts is used to record decreases. The left side of all accounts, whether asset, liability, or owner's equity, is the debit side and the right side is the credit side. Consequently, a debit may be either an increase or a decrease, depending on the nature of the account affected. A credit may likewise be either an increase or a decrease, depending on the nature of the account. The rules of debit and credit for asset, liability, and owner's equity accounts may therefore be stated as follows:

Rules of Debit and Credit—Asset, Liability, and Owner's Equity Accounts

Debit may signify:	*Credit* may signify:
Increase in asset accounts	Decrease in asset accounts
Decrease in liability accounts	Increase in liability accounts
Decrease in owner's equity accounts	Increase in owner's equity accounts

The general rules of debit and credit for asset, liability, and owner's equity accounts may also be stated in relationship to the accounting equation, as in the following diagram:

General Rules of Debit and Credit—The Accounting Equation

ASSETS		=	LIABILITIES		+	OWNER'S EQUITY	
Asset Accounts			Liability Accounts			Owner's Equity Accounts	
Debit for increases	Credit for decreases		Debit for decreases	Credit for increases		Debit for decreases	Credit for increases

Every business transaction affects a minimum of two accounts. Regardless of the complexity of a transaction or the number of accounts affected, the sum of the debits is always equal to the sum of the credits. This equality of debit and credit for each transaction is inherent in the equation A = L + OE. It is also because of this duality that the system is known as **double-entry accounting.**

The manner of recording additional types of transactions is described in the remainder of the illustration for Ingram Corporation.

Transaction (d)

During the first month of operations, Ingram Corporation earned fees of $62,000, receiving the amount in cash.

The principal objective of a business enterprise is to increase owner's equity through earnings. For Ingram Corporation, this objective means that the cash and other assets acquired through the rendering of services must be greater than the cost of the supplies used, the wages of employees, the rent, and all the other expenses of operating the business.

In general, the amount charged to customers for goods or services sold to them is called **revenue**. Other terms may be used for certain kinds of revenue, such as *sales* for the sale of merchandise, *fares earned* for an enterprise that provides transportation services, *rent earned* for the use of real estate or other property, and *fees earned* for charges by a professional, such as an accountant or physician, to clients.

The rules of debit and credit for revenue accounts are based upon the relationship of revenue transactions to owner's equity. Revenues increase the owner's equity in the business enterprise. Just as increases in owner's equity are recorded as credits, increases in revenues during an accounting period are recorded as credits.

The effect of transaction (d) on the accounts in the ledger can be described as a $62,000 debit (increase) to Cash and a $62,000 credit (increase) to Fees Earned. Transaction (d) is recorded in the journal by the following entry:

		Debit	Credit
(d)	Cash	62,000	
	Fees Earned		62,000

After posting journal entry (d), the accounting equation and the accounts would appear as follows:

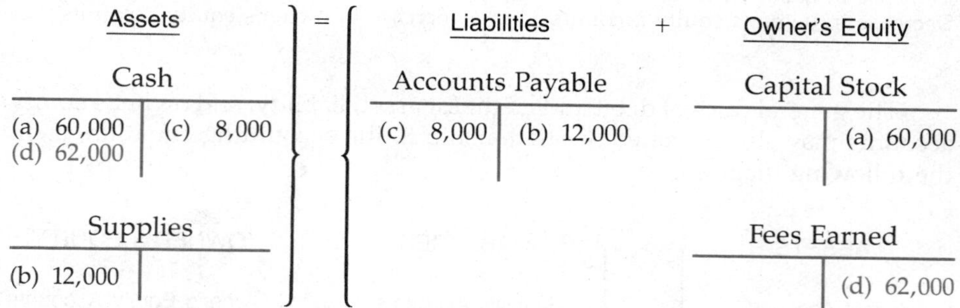

Instead of requiring the payment of cash at the time goods or services are sold, a business may make sales *on account,* allowing the customer to pay later. In such cases the firm acquires an **account receivable,** which is a claim against the customer. An account receivable is as much an asset as cash, and the revenue is realized in exactly the same manner as if cash had been immediately received. At a later date, when the money is collected, there is only an exchange of one asset for another, with cash increasing and accounts receivable decreasing.

Transaction (e)

Various business expenses incurred and paid during the month were as follows: wages, $25,000; rent, $10,000; utilities, $6,000; miscellaneous, $2,500.

In a broad sense, the amount of assets consumed or services used in the process of earning revenue is called **expense**. Expenses would include supplies used, wages of employees, and other assets and services used in operating the business.

The rules of debit and credit for expense accounts are based upon the relationship of expense transactions to owner's equity. Expenses decrease the owner's equity in the business enterprise. Just as decreases in owner's equity are recorded as debits, increases in expenses during an accounting period are recorded as debits.

The effect of transaction (e) on the accounts in the ledger can be described as a $25,000 debit (increase) to Wages Expense, a $10,000 debit (increase) to Rent Expense, a $6,000 debit (increase) to Utilities Expense, a $2,500 debit (increase) to Miscellaneous Expense, and a $43,500 credit (decrease) to Cash. Transaction (e) is recorded in the journal by the following entry:

		Debit	Credit
(e)	Wages Expense	25,000	
	Rent Expense	10,000	
	Utilities Expense	6,000	
	Miscellaneous Expense	2,500	
	Cash		43,500

Entry (e) is called a **compound journal entry** because it is composed of two or more debits or two or more credits. In all compound entries, the total debits must equal the total credits. After posting journal entry (e), the accounting equation and the accounts would appear as follows:

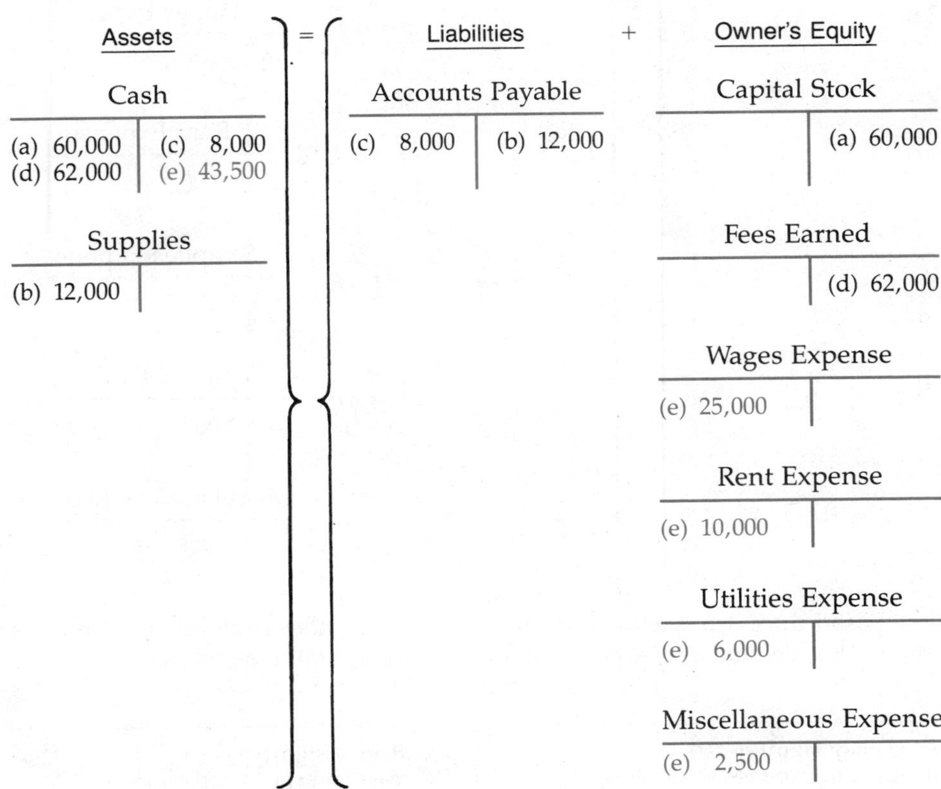

Transaction (f)

At the end of the month, it is determined that the cost of the supplies on hand is $4,500. The remainder of the supplies purchased in transaction (b), $7,500 ($12,000 – $4,500), were used in the operations of the business.

The effect of transaction (f) on the accounts in the ledger can be described as a $7,500 debit (increase) to Supplies Expense and a $7,500 credit (decrease) to Supplies. Transaction (f) is recorded in the journal by the following entry:

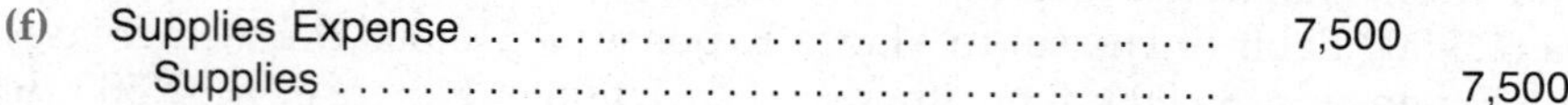

		Debit	Credit
(f)	Supplies Expense	7,500	
	Supplies		7,500

After posting journal entry (f), the accounting equation and the accounts would appear as follows:

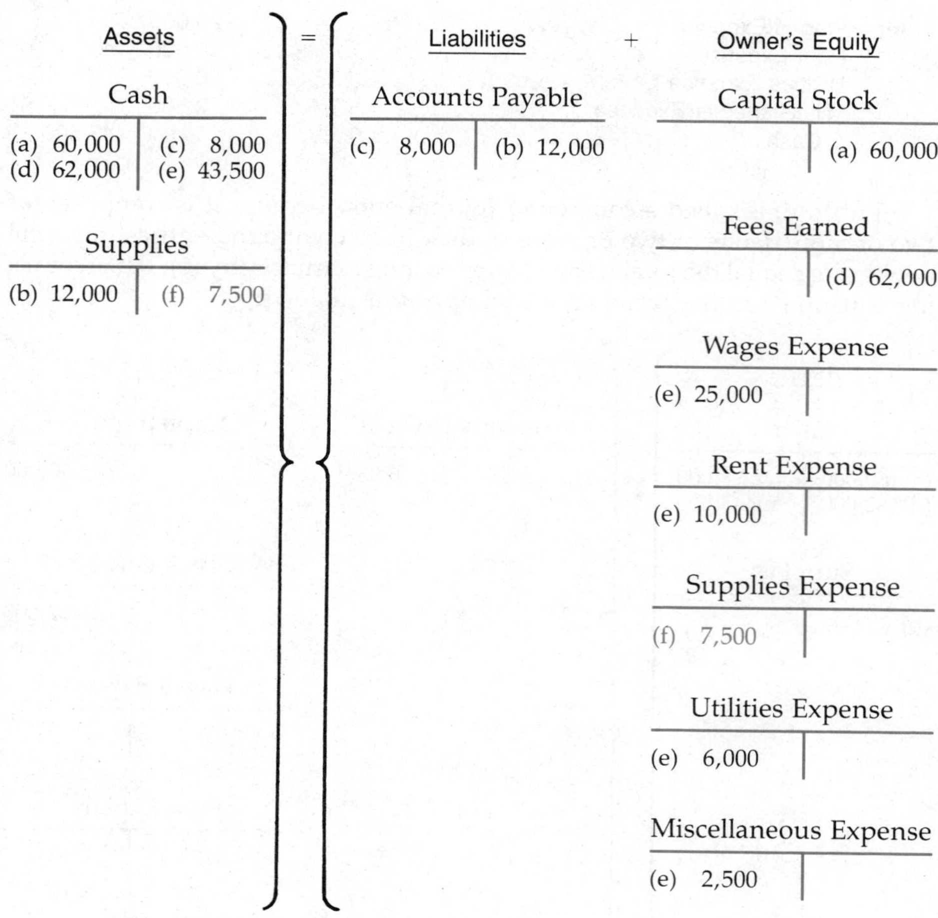

Based upon transactions (d), (e), and (f), the rules of debit and credit as applied to revenue and expense accounts may be stated as follows:

Rules of Debit and Credit–Revenue and Expense Accounts

Debit **may signify:**	*Credit* **may signify:**
Increase in expense accounts	Decrease in expense accounts
Decrease in revenue accounts	Increase in revenue accounts

In summary, the general rules of debit and credit for asset, liability, owner's equity, revenue, and expense accounts may be stated in relationship to the accounting equation, as shown in the following diagram:

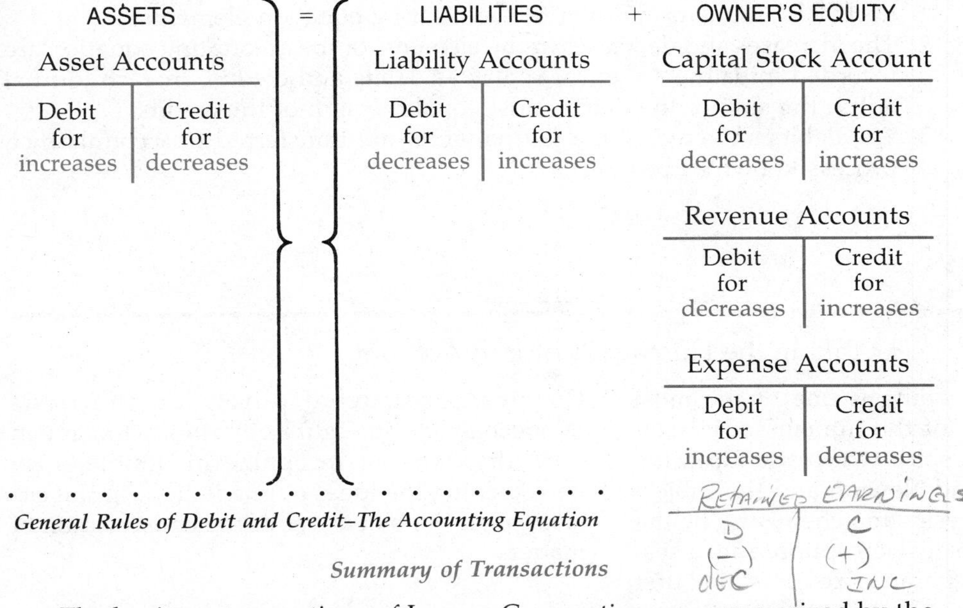

General Rules of Debit and Credit–The Accounting Equation

Summary of Transactions

The business transactions of Ingram Corporation are summarized by the accounting equation and accounts as follows. The transactions are identified by letter, and the balance of each account at the end of the month is shown.

Summary of Transactions

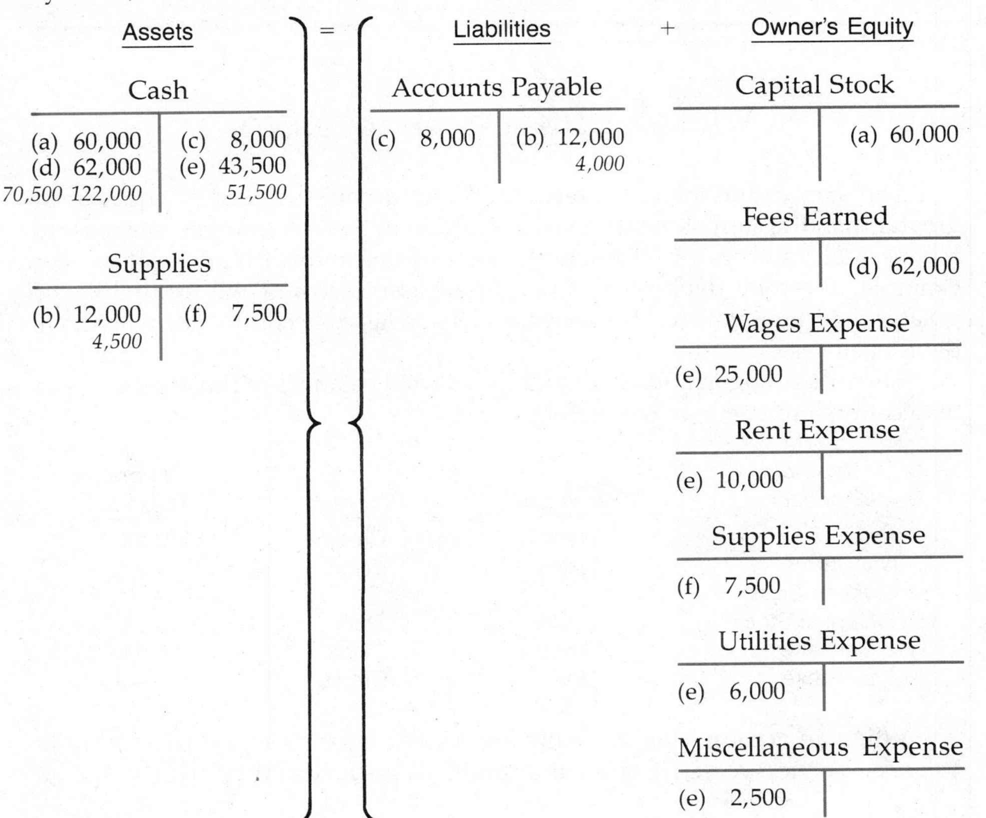

The following observations, which apply to all types of businesses, should be noted:

1. The effect of every transaction can be stated in terms of increases and/or decreases in one or more of the accounting equation elements.
2. The increases and decreases in the elements of the accounting equation are recorded initially in a journal entry as debits and credits. In each journal entry, the sum of the debits must equal the sum of the credits.
3. The debits and credits in a journal entry are transferred to accounts by a process known as posting.

Taking the Human Spirit into Account

Double-entry bookkeeping is one of the most beautiful discoveries of the human spirit. . . . It came from the same spirit which produced the systems of Galileo and Newton and the subject matter of modern physics and chemistry. By the same means, it organizes perceptions into a system, and one can characterize it as the first Cosmos constructed purely on the basis of mechanistic thought. . . . Without too much difficulty, we can recognize in double-entry bookkeeping the ideas of gravitation, of the circulation of the blood and of the conservation of matter.

Source: From the novel, *Wilhelm Meister's Lehrjahre* (Apprenticeship), written in 1795–6 by the German poet Johann Wolfgang von Goethe, translated by the German political economist Werner Sombart (1863–1941)

NORMAL BALANCES OF ACCOUNTS

The sum of the increases recorded in an account is usually equal to or greater than the sum of the decreases recorded in the account. For this reason, the normal balances of all accounts are positive rather than negative. For example, the total debits (increases) in an asset account will ordinarily be greater than the total credits (decreases). Thus, asset accounts normally have debit balances.

The rules of debit and credit and the normal balances of the various types of accounts are summarized as follows:

Normal Account Balances

Type of Account	Increase	Decrease	Normal Balance
Asset	Debit	Credit	Debit
Liability	Credit	Debit	Credit
Owner's Equity			
Capital Stock	Credit	Debit	Credit
Revenue	Credit	Debit	Credit
Expense	Debit	Credit	Debit

When an account that normally has a debit balance actually has a credit balance, or vice versa, it is an indication of an accounting error or of an unusual situation. For example, a credit balance in the supplies account could result only from an accounting error. On the other hand, a debit balance in an accounts payable account could result from an overpayment.

TRIAL BALANCE

Because of the way in which business transactions are recorded in the accounts by following the rules of debit and credit, the total of the accounts with debit balances must always equal the total of the accounts with credit balances. A listing of the account balances which verifies this equality is known as a **trial balance.** The trial balance for Ingram Corporation as of January 31, 1989, is as follows:

Ingram Corporation
Trial Balance
January 31, 1989

Cash	70,500	
Supplies	4,500	
Accounts Payable		4,000
Capital Stock		60,000
Fees Earned		62,000
Wages Expense	25,000	
Rent Expense	10,000	
Supplies Expense	7,500	
Utilities Expense	6,000	
Miscellaneous Expense	2,500	
	126,000	126,000

If the two totals of the trial balance are not equal, an error has occurred. Chapter 2 discusses the types of errors that could occur and how errors may be discovered.

FINANCIAL STATEMENTS

The principal financial statements of a corporation are the income statement, the retained earnings statement, the balance sheet, and the statement of cash flows. The nature of the data presented in each statement, in general terms, is as follows:

Income statement
A summary of the revenue and the expenses of a business entity for a specific period of time, such as a month or a year.

Retained earnings statement
A summary of the changes in the earnings retained in the business entity for a specific period of time, such as a month or a year.

Balance sheet

A list of the assets, liabilities, and owner's equity of a business entity on a specific date, usually at the close of the last day of a month or a year.

Statement of cash flows

A summary of the cash receipts and cash payments of a business entity for a specific period of time, such as a month or year.

The basic features of these four statements are described and illustrated in the following paragraphs. The data for the statements were taken from the summary of transactions and the trial balance of Ingram Corporation previously presented.

All financial statements should be identified by the name of the business, the title of the statement, and the date or period of time. The data presented in the balance sheet are for a specific date. The data presented in the income statement, the retained earnings statement, and the statement of cash flows are for a period of time.

Income Statement

The excess of the revenue over the expenses incurred in earning the revenue is called **net income** or **net profit.** If the expenses of the enterprise exceed the revenue, the excess is a **net loss.** It is ordinarily impossible to determine the exact amount of expense incurred in connection with each revenue transaction. Therefore, it is satisfactory to determine the net income or the net loss for a stated period of time, such as a month or a year, rather than for each revenue transaction or group of transactions.

The revenue earned and the expenses incurred during the month by Ingram Corporation were recorded in the revenue and expense accounts. The balances of these accounts provide the basis for matching the revenues earned during the month and the expenses incurred in earning these revenues to determine the amount of net income or net loss. The details of this matching for Ingram Corporation, together with the net income in the amount of $11,000, are reported in the following income statement:

Income Statement

Ingram Corporation
Income Statement
For Month Ended January 31, 1989

Fees earned		$62,000
Operating expenses:		
Wages expense	$25,000	
Rent expense	10,000	
Supplies expense	7,500	
Utilities expense	6,000	
Miscellaneous expense	2,500	
Total operating expenses		51,000
Net income		$11,000

The order in which the operating expenses are presented in the income statement varies among businesses. One of the arrangements commonly followed is to list them in the order of size, beginning with the larger items. Miscellaneous expense is usually shown as the last item, regardless of the amount.

Retained Earnings Statement

It is customary for corporations to distinguish between (1) the investment of the owners, who are called **stockholders,** and (2) the **retained earnings,** or net income retained in the business. Because changes in the amounts invested by stockholders occur infrequently, the primary focus for analyzing changes in the owner's equity of a corporation is the retained earnings statement. If there have been significant changes in capital stock during a period, such data should be reported in a separate additional statement. The details of minor changes in capital stock need not be reported.

The retained earnings statement for Ingram Corporation for the month of January is as follows:

Retained Earnings Statement

Ingram Corporation
Retained Earnings Statement
For Month Ended January 31, 1989

Net income for the month	$11,000
Retained earnings, January 31, 1989	$11,000

Since January was Ingram Corporation's first month of operations, the January 31, 1989 retained earnings equals the month's net income of $11,000. Changes in Ingram Corporation's retained earnings in future months may result from (1) additional net income (or net loss) and (2) the distribution of earnings, called **dividends,** to stockholders. To illustrate, assume that Ingram Corporation earned net income of $35,000 and paid dividends of $15,000 during February. The retained earnings statement for Ingram Corporation for February would appear as follows:

Ingram Corporation
Retained Earnings Statement
For Month Ended February 28, 1989

Retained earnings, February 1, 1989		$11,000
Net income for the month	$35,000	
Less dividends	15,000	
Increase in retained earnings		20,000
Retained earnings, February 28, 1989		$31,000

In the retained earnings statement for Ingram Corporation, the distribution of dividends decreases retained earnings. Since decreases in owner's equity accounts are recorded as debits, the distribution of dividends could be recorded initially as a debit to the retained earnings account. Alternatively, the distribution of dividends could be recorded initially as a debit to the dividends account. Throughout this text, this latter alternative will be used for recording dividends, because the balance of the dividends account is a convenient summary of the total dividends declared during the period. Thus, the distribution of $15,000 of dividends in February by Ingram Corporation is recorded as a debit (increase) to Dividends and a credit (decrease) to Cash, as shown in the following journal entry:

Dividends	15,000	
Cash		15,000

Balance Sheet

The balance sheet for Ingram Corporation is as follows:

Balance Sheet

Ingram Corporation
Balance Sheet
January 31, 1989

Assets		
Cash		$70,500
Supplies		4,500
Total assets		$75,000
Liabilities		
Accounts payable		$ 4,000
Stockholders' Equity		
Capital stock	$60,000	
Retained earnings	11,000	
Total stockholders' equity		71,000
Total liabilities and stockholders' equity		$75,000

It is customary to begin the asset section with cash. This item is followed by receivables, supplies, and other assets that will be converted into cash or used up in the near future. It is also customary on corporation balance sheets to refer to the owner's equity as **stockholders' equity.** For Ingram Corporation, the January 31, 1989 stockholders' equity consists of $60,000 of capital stock and retained earnings of $11,000. The retained earnings amount of $11,000 is taken from the retained earnings statement.

The form of balance sheet illustrated for Ingram Corporation, with liability and owner's equity sections presented below the asset section, is called the **report form.** Another arrangement in common use lists the assets on the left and the liabilities and owner's equity on the right. Because of its similarity to the T account, it is referred to as the **account form of balance sheet.**

The statement of cash flows for Ingram Corporation is as follows:

Ingram Corporation Statement of Cash Flows For Month Ended January 31, 1989		
Cash flows from operating activities:		
Cash received from customers	$62,000	
Deduct cash payments for expenses and payments to creditors	51,500	
Net cash flow from operating activities		$10,500
Cash flows from financing activities:		
Cash received from sale of capital stock		60,000
Net cash flow and January 31, 1989 cash balance		$70,500

Statement of Cash Flows

It is customary to report cash flows in three sections: (1) operating activities, (2) financing activities, and (3) investing activities. Data for the preparation of these three sections of the statement of cash flows for Ingram Corporation can be obtained from an examination of the transactions in the cash account.[3]

The cash flows from operating activities section includes cash transactions that enter into the determination of net income. For Ingram Corporation, the cash received from customers' fees was $62,000. The cash payments totaled $51,500, which consisted of $8,000 paid to creditors for supplies purchased and $43,500 paid for wages, rent, utilities, and miscellaneous expense. The net cash flow from operating activities is $10,500 ($62,000 − $51,500).

The net cash flow from operating activities will normally differ from the amount of net income for the period. For Ingram Corporation, the net cash flow from operating activities ($10,500) differs from the net income ($11,000) by $500. This difference arises because $8,000 was paid for supplies during January, but only $7,500 of supplies were used. Thus, while the income statement reports supplies expense of $7,500, the statement of cash flows includes in cash payments the $8,000 paid for supplies.

The cash flows from financing activities section reports the cash transactions related to the issuance of capital stock and debt securities and the payment of dividends. For Ingram Corporation, the cash flows from financing activities were $60,000 from the sale of capital stock.

The cash flows from investing activities section reports the cash transactions for the acquisition and sale of relatively fixed or permanent-type assets. Ingram Corporation had no cash flows related to investing activities.

Since January was Ingram Corporation's first month of operations, the increase in cash flows for January is the January 31, 1989 cash balance. In future statements, the cash balance at the beginning of the period is added to

[3]In practice, it is more efficient to accumulate the data needed to prepare the statement of cash flows by analysis of the accounts giving rise to cash receipts and cash payments. The discussion of this method and additional complexities is reserved until Chapter 14, after various necessary concepts and principles have been explained and illustrated.

the increase (or decrease) in cash for the period to indicate the cash balance at the end of the period. To illustrate, assume that Ingram Corporation's net cash flows for February increased by $12,500. The increase resulted from the following cash transactions:

Cash received from customers	$75,000
Cash received from sale of capital stock	20,000
Cash payments for expenses and payments to creditors	67,500
Cash paid for dividends	15,000

The statement of cash flows for Ingram Corporation for February would appear as follows:

Ingram Corporation
Statement of Cash Flows
For Month Ended February 28,1989

Cash flows from operating activities:		
Cash received from customers	$75,000	
Deduct cash payments for expenses and payments to creditors	67,500	
Net cash flow from operating activities		$ 7,500
Cash flows from financing activities:		
Cash received from sale of capital stock	$20,000	
Less cash paid for dividends	15,000	
Net cash flow from financing activities		5,000
Increase in cash		$12,500
Cash balance, February 1, 1989		70,500
Cash balance, February 28, 1989		$83,000

The statement of cash flows for Ingram Corporation reported cash received from sale of capital stock of $20,000. When the $15,000 of dividends paid to stockholders was deducted, the net cash flow from financing activities was $5,000.

Preparation of Financial Statements

In preparing the financial statements of a business enterprise, the income statement is usually prepared first because the net income for the period is needed in order to prepare the retained earnings statement. The retained earnings statement is prepared next because the ending balance of retained earnings for the period is needed for the preparation of the balance sheet. Then the balance sheet and the statement of cash flows are prepared.

ADDITIONAL CONCEPTS AND PRINCIPLES

The remainder of this chapter is devoted to some additional financial accounting concepts and principles. These concepts and principles require an understanding of the process of recording transactions and preparing financial statements, as discussed previously.

Matching Concept

The determination of the periodic net income (or net loss) is a two-step process. First, revenues are recognized during the period. Second, the costs of assets consumed in generating the revenues must be matched against the revenues in order to determine the net income or the net loss.

Revenues are recognized and recorded in the accounts according to various criteria. Generally, revenues for the rendering of services are recognized after the service has been rendered to the customer. Revenues for the sale of merchandise are generally recognized after the ownership of the goods has passed to the buyer. Depending upon the terms of shipment, ownership may pass upon shipment of the merchandise or when the goods are delivered to their final destination. Shipping terms are discussed in Chapter 2.

The costs of assets consumed in generating revenue during a period must be recognized as expenses. In this way, the expenses are properly matched against the revenues generated. Some assets are treated as expenses at the time of purchase because they will expire by the end of the period. For example, when monthly rent is paid at the beginning of the month, the asset purchased (the right to use property for a month) will be wholly expired at the end of the month. For this reason, the rental payment is usually debited directly to an expense account. The allocation **(matching)** to proper periods of the costs of assets consumed is an important consideration, which will be further discussed in later chapters.

Adequate Disclosure

Financial statements and their accompanying footnotes or other explanatory materials should contain all of the pertinent data believed essential to the reader's understanding of the enterprise's financial status. Criteria for standards of disclosure often must be based on value judgments rather than on objective facts.

The use of headings and subheadings and the merging of items in significant categories in the financial statements illustrated in the preceding paragraphs are examples of the application of the concept of adequate disclosure. Additional examples will be presented in many of the remaining chapters after more complex accounting matters have been presented.

Consistency

A number of accepted alternative principles affecting the determination of income statement and balance sheet amounts will be presented in later chapters. Recognizing that different methods may be used under varying circumstances, some guide or standard is needed to assure that the periodic financial statements of an enterprise can be compared. It is common practice to compare an enterprise's current income statement and balance sheet with the statements of the preceding year.

The amount and the direction of change in net income and financial position from period to period is very important to readers and may greatly influence their decisions. Therefore, interested persons should be able to assume that successive financial statements of an enterprise are based consistently on the same generally accepted accounting principles. If the principles are not applied consistently, the trends indicated could be the result of changes in the principles used rather than the result of changes in business conditions or managerial effectiveness.

The concept of **consistency** does not completely prohibit changes in the accounting principles used. Changes are permissible when it is believed that the use of a different principle will more fairly state net income and financial position. In such cases, the reason for the change and its effect on income should be disclosed in the financial statements of the period in which the change in principle is made.

Materiality

In following generally accepted accounting principles, the accountant must consider the relative importance of any event, accounting procedure, or change in procedure that affects items on the financial statements. Absolute accuracy in accounting and full disclosure in reporting are not ends in themselves, and there is no need to exceed the limits of practicality. The determination of what is significant and what is not requires the exercise of judgment. Precise criteria cannot be formulated.

To determine **materiality**, the size of an item and its nature must be considered in relationship to the size and the nature of other items. The erroneous identification of a $10,000 expense on an income statement exhibiting total expenses of $10,000,000 would probably be immaterial. In this situation, the size of the error would not necessitate a correction. If the total expenses were $20,000, however, the error would certainly be material and the income statement should be corrected.

Custom and practicality also influence criteria of materiality. Corporate financial statements seldom report the cents amounts or even the hundreds of dollars. A common practice is to round to the nearest thousand. For large corporations, there is an increasing tendency to report financial data in terms of millions, carrying figures to one decimal. For example, an amount stated in millions as $907.4 may be read as nine hundred seven million, four hundred thousand.[4]

Going Concern

Generally, a business is not organized with the expectation of operating for only a certain period of time. In most cases, it is not possible to determine in advance the length of life of an enterprise, and so an assumption must be made. The nature of the assumption will affect the manner of recording some of the business transactions, which in turn will affect the data reported in the financial statements.

It is customary to assume that a business entity has a reasonable expectation of continuing in business at a profit for an indefinite period of time. This **going concern concept** provides much of the justification for recording the purchase of a building at the price paid and subsequently recognizing a portion of this purchase price as the cost of using the building. The current value of the building is not reported in the basic financial statements because there is no immediate expectation of selling it. If the firm continues to use the

---

[4]Examples are presented in Appendix J.

building, the fluctuation in market value causes no gain or loss, nor does it increase or decrease the usefulness of the building. Thus, if the going concern assumption is a valid concept, the investment in the building will serve the purpose for which it was made.

When there is conclusive evidence that a business entity has a limited life, the accounting procedures should be appropriate to the expected terminal date of the entity. Changes in the application of normal accounting procedures may be needed for business organizations in receivership or bankruptcy, for example. In such cases, the financial statements should clearly disclose the limited life of the enterprise and should be prepared from the "quitting concern" or liquidation point of view, rather than from a "going concern" point of view.

Chapter Review

KEY POINTS

1. Accounting and the Users of Accounting Information.
The objective of accounting is to record, summarize, report, and interpret economic data for use by many groups within our economic and social system. In this sense, accounting is often called the "language of business." This language can be viewed as an information system that provides essential information about the financial activities of an entity to various individuals or groups for their use in making informed judgments and decisions.

Accounting provides for the gathering of economic data and the communication of these data to different individuals and institutions. Examples of users of accounting information include investors, bankers, suppliers, government agencies, employees, and managers of the entity.

2. Financial and Managerial Accounting.
Financial accounting is concerned with the measuring and recording of transactions for a business enterprise and the periodic preparation of various reports from such records. Corporate enterprises must use generally accepted accounting principles in preparing their annual financial statements. Managerial accounting uses both historical and estimated data to assist management in conducting daily operations and in planning future operations. The principle of "usefulness" is dominant in guiding the accountant in preparing management reports.

3. Development of Financial Accounting Concepts and Principles.
As the American economy developed and as business organizations grew in size and complexity, there came an awareness of the need for a framework of concepts and generally accepted accounting principles to serve as guidelines for the preparation of the basic financial statements. These principles represent the best possible guides, based on reason, observation, and experimentation, to help make accounting data more useful in an ever-changing society.

Currently, the Financial Accounting Standards Board establishes accounting standards for business enterprises. The Governmental Accounting Standards Board has responsibility for establishing accounting standards to be followed by state and municipal governments.

Among the other organizations which have had an effect on the development of accounting principles are the American Institute of Certified Public Accountants, the American Accounting Association, the Securities and Exchange Commission, the Internal Revenue Service, the Financial Executives Institute, and the National Association of Accountants.

4. Financial Accounting Concepts and Principles.
Four of the most important accounting concepts relate to the business entity, the cost of properties and services, business transactions, and the unit of measurement.

The business entity concept is based on the applicability of accounting to individual economic units in society. Profit-making businesses are customarily organized as sole proprietorships, partnerships, or corporations.

The cost principle requires that properties and services purchased by a business be recorded in terms of cost.

A business transaction is the occurrence of an event or a condition that must be recorded. Business transactions may be either simple or complex and may lead to an event or a condition that results in yet another transaction.

All business transactions are recorded in terms of money. The use of the monetary unit in accounting for and reporting the activities of an enterprise assumes stability of the measurement unit.

5. Assets, Liabilities, and Owner's Equity.
The properties owned by a business and the rights or claims to properties may be stated in the form of an equation as follows: Assets = Equities. The expansion of the equation to give recognition to two basic types of equities yields the following, which is known as the accounting equation: Assets = Liabilities + Owner's Equity.

6. Transactions and the Accounting Equation.
All transactions, from the simplest to the most complex, can be stated in terms of the resulting change in the three basic elements of the accounting equation. That is, the effect of every transaction can be stated in terms of increases and/or decreases in one or more of the accounting equation elements such that the equality of the two sides of the accounting equation is always maintained.

7. Nature of an Account and Recording Transactions in Accounts.
The record traditionally kept for each item that appears on the financial statements is the account. A group of related accounts that comprise a complete unit, such as all the accounts of a specific business enterprise, is called the ledger.

Increases and decreases in an account are recorded as debits (entries on the left side of the account) and credits (entries on the right side of the account). Periodically, the debits and the credits in an account are summed and the difference between the two sums is determined. This difference is called the balance of the account.

The effects of transactions are initially entered in a record called a journal. Periodically, transactions that have been journalized are transferred to the accounts by a process known as posting.

8. Normal Balances of Accounts.
The sum of the increases recorded in an account is usually equal to or greater than the sum of the decreases recorded in the account. For this reason, the normal balance of an account is indicated by the side of the account (debit or credit) that receives the increases.

The rules of debit and credit and normal account balances are summarized in the following table:

	Increase	*Decrease*	*Normal Balance*
Asset	Debit	Credit	Debit
Liability	Credit	Debit	Credit
Owner's Equity			
Capital Stock	Credit	Debit	Credit
Retained Earnings	Credit	Debit	Credit
Dividends	Debit	Credit	Debit
Revenue	Credit	Debit	Credit
Expense	Debit	Credit	Debit

9. Trial Balance.
The equality of the debits and credits in a ledger is verified periodically by the preparation of a trial balance. The trial balance does not provide complete proof of accuracy of the ledger, but only indicates that the debits and credits are equal.

10. Financial Statements.
After the effects of individual transactions have been determined and recorded, reports (financial statements) summarizing these effects are prepared and communicated to users. The principal accounting statements of a corporation are the income statement, the retained earnings statement, the balance sheet, and the statement of cash flows.

11. Additional Concepts and Principles.
Matching concept: The determination of periodic net income is a two-step process involving (1) the recognition of revenue during the period and (2) the allocation of asset costs to the period. Thus, revenues and expired costs must be matched to determine net income or net loss for the period.

Adequate disclosure: Financial statements and their accompanying footnotes or other explanatory materials should contain all of the pertinent data believed essential to the reader's understanding of the enterprise's financial status.

Consistency: A number of acceptable alternative principles affecting the determination of income statement and balance sheet amounts exist. The concept of consistency implies that the financial statements should be prepared by applying the same principles year after year. If changes in principles do occur, their effect on the financial statements should be disclosed.

Materiality: In following generally accepted accounting principles, the accountant must consider the relative importance of any event, accounting procedure, or change in procedure that affects items on the financial statements. The concept of materiality implies that accountants need not strictly adhere to generally accepted accounting principles if the amounts involved are not significant.

Going concern: In most cases, it is not possible to determine in advance the length of life of an enterprise, and so an assumption must be made. It is customary to assume that a business entity has a reasonable expectation of continuing in business at a profit for an indefinite period of time.

KEY TERMS

accounting 11
financial accounting 12
generally accepted accounting principles (GAAP) 12
managerial accounting 12
Financial Accounting Standards Board (FASB) 14
Governmental Accounting Standards Board (GASB) 15
business entity concept 16
sole proprietorship 17
partnership 17
corporation 17
cost principle 17
business transaction 18
assets 18
equities 18
liabilities 19
owner's equity 19
accounting equation 19
capital stock 19
account 19
ledger 20
T account 20
debit 20
credit 20
journal 21
posting 21
account payable 22
prepaid expenses 22
double-entry accounting 23
revenue 24
account receivable 24
expense 25
trial balance 29
income statement 29
retained earnings statement 29
balance sheet 30
statement of cash flows 30
net income 30
net loss 30
stockholders 31
retained earnings 31
dividends 31
stockholders' equity 32
report form of balance sheet 32
account form of balance sheet 32
matching 35
consistency 36
materiality 36
going concern concept 36

SELF-EXAMINATION QUESTIONS

(Answers at End of Chapter)

1. A profit-making business that is a separate legal entity and in which ownership is divided into shares of stock is known as a:
   A. sole proprietorship
   B. single proprietorship
   C. partnership
   D. corporation
2. The properties owned by a business enterprise are called:
   A. assets
   B. liabilities
   C. capital stock
   D. owner's equity
3. A debit may signify:
   A. an increase in an asset account
   B. a decrease in an asset account
   C. an increase in a liability account
   D. an increase in an owner's equity account

4. The type of account with a normal credit balance is:
   A. an asset
   B. a dividend
   C. a revenue
   D. an expense

5. A list of assets, liabilities, and owner's equity of a business entity as of a specific date is:
   A. a balance sheet
   B. an income statement
   C. a statement of cash flows
   D. a retained earnings statement

ILLUSTRATIVE PROBLEM

Acme Cleaners Inc. is a corporation that was organized recently. Currently, a building and equipment are being rented pending completion of construction of new facilities. The actual work of dry cleaning is done by another company at wholesale rates. The assets, liabilities, and owner's equity of the business on May 1 of the current year are as follows: Cash, $5,400; Accounts Receivable, $3,700; Supplies, $410; Land, $9,500; Accounts Payable, $2,380; Capital Stock, $10,000; Retained Earnings, $6,630. Business transactions during May are summarized as follows:

(a) Paid rent for the month, $850.
(b) Charged customers for dry cleaning sales on account, $5,646.
(c) Paid creditors on account, $1,680.
(d) Purchased supplies on account, $254.
(e) Received cash from cash customers for dry cleaning sales, $2,894.
(f) Received cash from customers on account, $2,750.
(g) Paid dividends of $760.
(h) Received monthly invoice for dry cleaning expense for May (to be paid on June 10), $3,416.
(i) Paid the following: wages expense, $675; truck expense, $310; utilities expense, $260; miscellaneous expense, $89.
(j) Received cash from sale of capital stock, $2,000.
(k) Determined the cost of supplies used during the month, $328.

Instructions:

1. Prepare a ledger of T accounts for Acme Cleaners Inc., using the following account titles: Cash, Accounts Receivable, Supplies, Land, Accounts Payable, Capital Stock, Retained Earnings, Dividends, Dry Cleaning Sales, Dry Cleaning Expense, Rent Expense, Wages Expense, Supplies Expense, Truck Expense, Utilities Expense, Miscellaneous Expense. Record the normal balances in the T accounts by writing "Bal." and entering the appropriate amount on the debit or credit side of the account.
2. Prepare journal entries for transactions (a) through (k).
3. Post the journal to the ledger, and determine the balances after all posting is complete.
4. Prepare a trial balance as of May 31, 19--.
5. Prepare an income statement and retained earnings statement, for May.
6. Prepare a balance sheet as of May 31, 19--.
7. Prepare a statement of cash flows for May.

SOLUTION

		Dr.	Cr.
(2) (a)	Rent Expense	850	
	Cash		850
(b)	Accounts Receivable	5,646	
	Dry Cleaning Sales		5,646
(c)	Accounts Payable	1,680	
	Cash		1,680
(d)	Supplies	254	
	Accounts Payable		254
(e)	Cash	2,894	
	Dry Cleaning Sales		2,894
(f)	Cash	2,750	
	Accounts Receivable		2,750
(g)	Dividends	760	
	Cash		760
(h)	Dry Cleaning Expense	3,416	
	Accounts Payable		3,416
(i)	Wages Expense	675	
	Truck Expense	310	
	Utilities Expense	260	
	Miscellaneous Expense	89	
	Cash		1,334
(j)	Cash	2,000	
	Capital Stock		2,000
(k)	Supplies Expense	328	
	Supplies		328

(1) and (3)

Cash

Bal.	5,400	(a)	850
(e)	2,894	(c)	1,680
(f)	2,750	(g)	760
(j)	2,000	(i)	1,334
8,420	*13,044*		*4,624*

Supplies

Bal.	410	(k)	328
(d)	254		
336	*664*		

Land

Bal.	9,500		

Accounts Receivable

Bal.	3,700	(f)	2,750
(b)	5,646		
6,596	*9,346*		

Accounts Payable

(c)	1,680	Bal.	2,380
		(d)	254
		(h)	3,416
		4,370	*6,050*

Capital Stock

	Bal.	10,000
	(j)	2,000
		12,000

Retained Earnings

	Bal.	6,630

Dividends

(g)	760	

Dry Cleaning Sales

	(b)	5,646
	(e)	2,894
		8,540

Dry Cleaning Expense

(h)	3,416	

Rent Expense

(a)	850	

Wages Expense

(i)	675	

Supplies Expense

(k)	328	

Truck Expense

(i)	310	

Utilities Expense

(i)	260	

Miscellaneous Expense

(i)	89	

(4)

ACME CLEANERS INC.
Trial Balance
May 31, 19--

Cash	8,420	
Accounts Receivable	6,596	
Supplies	336	
Land	9,500	
Accounts Payable		4,370
Capital Stock		12,000
Retained Earnings		6,630
Dividends	760	
Dry Cleaning Sales		8,540
Dry Cleaning Expense	3,416	
Rent Expense	850	
Wages Expense	675	
Supplies Expense	328	
Truck Expense	310	
Utilities Expense	260	
Miscellaneous Expense	89	
	31,540	31,540

(5)

ACME CLEANERS INC.
Income Statement
For Month Ended May 31, 19--

Dry cleaning sales		$8,540
Operating expenses:		
Dry cleaning expense	$3,416	
Rent expense	850	
Wages expense	675	
Supplies expense	328	
Truck expense	310	
Utilities expense	260	
Miscellaneous expense	89	
Total operating expenses		5,928
Net income		$2,612

ACME CLEANERS INC.
Retained Earnings Statement
For Month Ended May 31, 19--

Retained earnings, May 1, 19--		$6,630
Net income for the month	$2,612	
Less dividends	760	
Increase in retained earnings		1,852
Retained earnings, May 31, 19--		$8,482

(6)

ACME CLEANERS INC.
Balance Sheet
May 31, 19--

Assets		
Cash		$ 8,420
Accounts receivable		6,596
Supplies		336
Land		9,500
Total assets		$24,852
Liabilities		
Accounts payable		$ 4,370
Stockholders' Equity		
Capital stock	$12,000	
Retained earnings	8,482	
Total stockholders' equity		20,482
Total liabilities and stockholders' equity		$24,852

(7)

ACME CLEANERS INC.
Statement of Cash Flows
For Month Ended May 31, 19--

Cash flows from operating activities:		
Cash received from customers	$5,644*	
Deduct cash payments for expenses and payments to creditors	3,864**	
Net cash flow from operating activities		$1,780
Cash flows from financing activities:		
Cash received from sale of capital stock	$2,000	
Less cash paid for dividends	760	
Net cash flow from financing activities		1,240
Increase in cash		$3,020
Cash balance, May 1, 19--		5,400
Cash balance, May 31, 19--		$8,420

*$2,894 (e) + $2,750 (f) = $5,644
**$850 (a) + $1,680 (c) + $1,334 (i) = $3,864

Discussion Questions

1–1. What is the objective of accounting?

1–2. Name some of the categories of individuals and institutions who use accounting information.

1–3. Distinguish between financial accounting and managerial accounting.

1–4. Accounting principles are broad guides to accounting practice. (a) How do these principles differ from the principles relating to the physical sciences? (b) Of what significance is acceptability in the development of accounting principles? (c) Why must accounting principles be continually reexamined and revised?

1–5. What role does the Financial Accounting Foundation play in the development of accounting principles?

1–6. What body is currently dominant in the development of (a) generally accepted accounting principles for business enterprises and (b) principles for state and municipal governments?

1–7. (a) Name the three principal forms of profit-making business organizations. (b) Which of these forms is identified with the greatest number of businesses?

1–8. What is meant by the cost principle?

1–9. (a) Land with an assessed value of $90,000 for property tax purposes is acquired by a business enterprise for $195,000. At what amount should the land be recorded by the buyer?
(b) Five years later the plot of land in (a) has an assessed value of $145,000 and the business enterprise receives an offer of $300,000 for it. Should the monetary amount assigned to the land in the business records now be increased and, if so, by what amount?
(c) Assuming that the land acquired in (a) was sold for $325,000, (1) how much would the owner's equity increase, and (2) at what amount would the buyer record the land?

1–10. Conventional financial statements do not give recognition to the instability of the purchasing power of the dollar. How can the effect of the fluctuating dollar on business operations be presented to the users of the financial statements?

1–11. (a) If the assets owned by a business enterprise total $500,000, what is the amount of the equities of the enterprise? (b) What are the two principal types of equities?

1–12. (a) An enterprise has assets of $290,000 and liabilities of $175,000. What is the amount of its owner's equity?
(b) An enterprise has assets of $410,000 and owner's equity of $150,000. What is the total amount of its liabilities?
(c) A corporation has assets of $970,000, liabilities of $615,000, and capital stock of $200,000. What is the amount of its retained earnings?
(d) An enterprise has liabilities of $400,000 and owner's equity of $200,000. What is the total amount of its assets?

1–13. Describe how the following business transactions affect the three elements of the accounting equation.
(a) Issued capital stock for cash.
(b) Purchased supplies on account.
(c) Received cash for services performed.
(d) Paid for utilities used in the business.

1–14. (a) A vacant lot acquired for $80,000, on which there is a balance owed of $25,000, is sold for $110,000 in cash. What is the effect of the sale on the total amount of the seller's (1) assets, (2) liabilities, and (3) owner's equity?
(b) After receiving the $110,000 cash in (a), the seller pays the $25,000 owed. What is the effect of the payment on the total amount of the seller's (1) assets, (2) liabilities, and (3) owner's equity?

1–15. Differentiate between an account and a ledger.

1–16. What is the name of the accounting record in which transaction data are initially entered?

1–17. Define posting.

1–18. Do the terms *debit* and *credit* signify increase or decrease, or may they signify either? Explain.

1–19. Indicate whether each of the following is recorded by a debit or by a credit: (a) decrease in an asset account, (b) decrease in a liability account, (c) increase in an owner's equity account.

1–20. What is the effect (increase or decrease) of debits to expense accounts (a) in terms of owner's equity, (b) in terms of expense?

1–21. (a) Describe the form known as a trial balance. (b) What proof is provided by a trial balance?

1–22. During the month, a business corporation received $725,000 in cash and paid out $675,000 in cash. Do the data indicate that the corporation earned $50,000 during the month? Explain.

1–23. Operations of an enterprise for a particular month are summarized as follows:
Service sales: on account, $42,000; for cash, $82,000
Expenses incurred: on account, $56,000; for cash, $51,000
What was the amount of the enterprise's (a) revenue, (b) expenses, and (c) net income?

1–24. A business enterprise had revenues of $65,000 and operating expenses of $72,750. Did the enterprise (a) incur a net loss or (b) realize a net income?

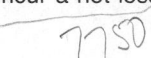

1–25. Indicate whether each of the following types of transactions will (a) increase owner's equity or (b) decrease owner's equity:
(1) issuance of capital stock
(2) dividends
(3) revenues
(4) expenses

1–26. Give the title of a corporation's four major financial statements illustrated in this chapter, and briefly describe the nature of the information provided by each.

1–27. What particular item of financial or operating data of a service enterprise, organized as a corporation, appears on (a) both the income statement and the retained earnings statement, and (b) both the balance sheet and the retained earnings statement?

1–28. Video Center had an owner's equity balance at the beginning of the period of $110,000. At the end of the period, the company had total assets of $198,000 and total liabilities of $93,000. (a) What was the net income or net loss for the period, assuming no additional changes in owner's equity? (b) What was the net income or net loss for the period, assuming a dividend of $35,000 had been paid during the period?

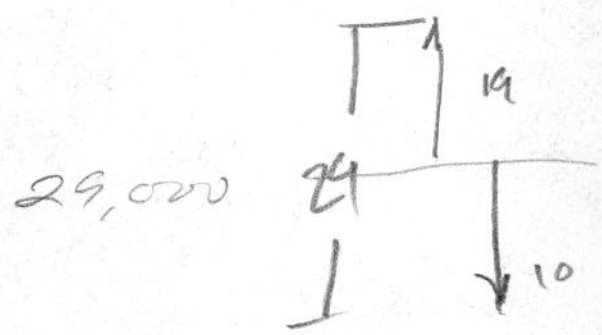

1–29. If total assets have increased by $19,000 during a specific period of time and owner's equity has decreased by $10,000 during the same period, what was the amount and direction (increase or decrease) of the period's change in total liabilities?

1–30. For accounting purposes, what is the nature of the assumption as to the length of life of an enterprise?

1–31. Real World Focus. Based upon the annual report of The Procter & Gamble Company, presented in Appendix J, what are (a) the total assets at June 30, 1987, (b) the total liabilities and shareholders' equity at June 30, 1987, (c) the net sales for the year ended June 30, 1987, (d) the net earnings for the year ended June 30, 1987, (e) the ratio of the net earnings to the net sales for the year ended June 30, 1987?

Exercises

1–32. Balance sheet items. From the following list of selected accounts taken from the records of J. A. Buck Corporation as of a specific date, identify those that would appear on the balance sheet:

(1) Capital Stock
(2) Fees Earned
(3) Land
(4) Salaries Expense
(5) Accounts Payable
(6) Retained Earnings
(7) Cash
(8) Utilities Expense
(9) Supplies
(10) Salaries Payable

1–33. Transactions of corporation. The following selected transactions were completed by Owen Delivery Company during May:

(1) Sold capital stock, $25,000.
(2) Purchased supplies of gas and oil for cash, $925.
(3) Paid advertising expense, $700.

(4) Received cash from cash customers, $1,500.
(5) Billed customers for delivery services on account, $1,100.
(6) Paid rent for May, $900.
(7) Paid creditors on account, $470.
(8) Received cash from customers on account, $910.
(9) Paid cash dividends, $1,000.
(10) Determined by taking an inventory that $650 of supplies of gas and oil had been used during the month.

Indicate the effect of each transaction on the accounting equation by listing the numbers identifying the transactions, (1) through (10), in a vertical column, and inserting at the right of each number the appropriate letter from the following list:

(a) Increase in one asset, decrease in another asset.
(b) Increase in an asset, increase in a liability.
(c) Increase in an asset, increase in owner's equity.
(d) Decrease in an asset, decrease in a liability.
(e) Decrease in an asset, decrease in owner's equity.

1–34. Transactions of corporation. Sims Corporation, engaged in a service business, completed the following selected transactions during the period:

(1) Purchased supplies on account.
(2) Issued additional capital stock, receiving cash.
(3) Charged customers for services sold on account.
(4) Paid utilities expense.
(5) Returned defective supplies purchased on account for which payment has not yet been made.
(6) Received cash as a refund from the erroneous overpayment of an expense.
(7) Paid a creditor on account.
(8) Received cash from customers on account.
(9) Determined the amount of supplies used during the month.
(10) Paid cash dividends to stockholders.

Using a tabular form with four column headings entitled Transaction, Assets, Liabilities, and Owner's Equity, respectively, indicate the effect of each transaction. Use + for increase and − for decrease.

1–35. Missing amounts from balance sheet and income statement data. One item is omitted in each of the following summaries of balance sheet and income statement data for four different corporations, A, B, C, and D.

	A	B	C	D
Beginning of the year:				
Assets	$200,000	$60,000	$97,000	(d)
Liabilities	90,000	20,000	76,000	$22,100
End of the year:				
Assets	240,000	95,000	94,000	68,000
Liabilities	110,000	20,000	77,000	37,000
During the year:				
Additional issuance of capital stock	(a)	7,000	5,000	30,000
Dividends	20,000	12,000	(c)	21,000
Revenue	90,000	(b)	82,100	99,000
Expenses	75,000	40,000	83,600	88,000

Determine the amounts of the missing items, identifying them by letter. (*Suggestion:* First determine the amount of increase or decrease in owner's equity during the year.)

1–36. Journal entries for corporation. Cey Company has the following accounts in its ledger: Cash; Accounts Receivable; Supplies; Office Equipment; Accounts Payable; Capital Stock; Retained Earnings; Dividends; Fees Earned; Rent Expense; Advertising Expense; Utilities Expense; Miscellaneous Expense.

Record the following transactions in a journal:

(a) Paid advertising expense, $500.
(b) Paid rent for the month, $900.
(c) Paid cash for supplies, $95.
(d) Purchased office equipment on account, $4,100.
(e) Received cash from customers on account, $5,600.
(f) Paid cash for repairs to office equipment, $60.
(g) Paid creditor on account, $2,150.
(h) Paid cash dividends, $1,200.
(i) Paid telephone bill for the month, $160.
(j) Fees earned and billed to customers for the month, $8,550.
(k) Paid electricity bill for the month, $415.

1–37. Identify transactions for corporation. Eight transactions are recorded in the following T accounts:

Cash	
(1) 15,000	(2) 7,500
(7) 10,600	(3) 950
	(4) 225
	(5) 5,000
	(8) 3,000

Equipment	
(2) 20,000	

Dividends	
(8) 3,000	

Accounts Receivable	
(6) 27,500	(7) 10,600

Accounts Payable	
(5) 5,000	(2) 12,500

Service Revenue	
	(6) 27,500

Supplies	
(4) 225	

Capital Stock	
	(1) 15,000

Operating Expenses	
(3) 950	

Indicate for each debit and each credit: (a) whether an asset, liability, owner's equity, dividend, revenue, or expense account was affected and (b) whether the account was increased (+) or decreased (−). Answers should be presented in the following form (transaction (1) is given as an example):

	Account Debited		Account Credited	
Transaction	Type	Effect	Type	Effect
(1)	asset	+	owner's equity	+

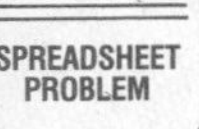

1–38. Trial balance for corporation. The accounts in the ledger of Corley Realty as of June 30 of the current year are listed in alphabetical order as follows. All accounts have normal balances. The balance of the cash account has been intentionally omitted.

Accounts Payable	$ 18,910
Accounts Receivable	23,750
Capital Stock	100,000
Cash	?
Fees Earned	270,000
Land	120,000
Miscellaneous Expense	9,900

Notes Payable	$ 25,000
Prepaid Insurance	3,850
Retained Earnings	22,000
Salary Expense	210,000
Supplies	3,900
Supplies Expense	6,100
Utilities Expense	21,500

Prepare a trial balance, listing the accounts in their proper order and inserting the missing figure for cash.

1–39. Income statement, retained earnings statement, and balance sheet for corporation. The trial balance for Dawson Corporation as of December 31, the end of the current year is as follows.

Dawson Corporation
Trial Balance
December 31, 19--

Cash	49,910	
Accounts Receivable	103,300	
Prepaid Insurance	20,400	
Supplies	14,500	
Land	100,000	
Accounts Payable		19,610
Notes Payable		50,000
Capital Stock		100,000
Retained Earnings		52,000
Dividends	20,000	
Fees Earned		587,500
Salary Expense	267,500	
Rent Expense	98,750	
Utilities Expense	57,500	
Supplies Expense	36,500	
Insurance Expense	21,000	
Miscellaneous Expense	19,750	
	809,110	809,110

Prepare an income statement for the current year ended December 31, 19--, a retained earnings statement for the current year ended December 31, 19--, and a balance sheet as of December 31, 19--. The amount of retained earnings in the trial balance represents the balance on January 1, the beginning of the current year.

1–40. Trial balance and financial statements for corporation. The accounts (all normal balances) in the ledger of A. D. Cowan Inc. as of June 30, the *end* of the current year, are in alphabetical order as follows.

Accounts Payable	$ 9,610
Accounts Receivable	13,300
Buildings	210,000
Capital Stock	300,000
Cash	59,910
Dividends	20,000
Equipment	162,280
Fees Earned	287,500
Land	120,000
Miscellaneous Expense	2,500
Note Payable	25,000
Prepaid Insurance	2,400

Retained Earnings	$175,000
Salary Expense	187,500
Supplies	4,500
Supplies Expense	3,120
Utilities Expense	11,600

(a) Prepare a trial balance, listing the accounts in the following order: assets, liabilities, owner's equity, revenues, and expenses.
(b) Prepare an income statement for the current year ended June 30, 19--.
(c) Prepare a retained earnings statement for the current year ended June 30, 19--. The amount of retained earnings in the trial balance represents the balance on July 1, the *beginning* of the current year.
(d) Prepare a balance sheet as of June 30, 19--.
(e) Prepare a statement of cash flows for the year. The cash balance on July 1, the beginning of the current year, was $9,910. During the year, cash receipts from customers were $275,000, and cash payments for expenses and to creditors was $230,000. Cash received from the sale of capital stock was $25,000 and cash dividends paid were $20,000.

Problems

1–41. Journal entries and trial balance. On July 1 of the current year, D. D. Robb established a corporation under the name of Robb Realty Inc. Robb Realty Inc. completed the following transactions during the month:

(a) Issued capital stock for $50,000.
(b) Paid rent on office and equipment for the month, $15,000.
(c) Purchased supplies (stationery, stamps, pencils, ink, etc.) on account, $3,900.
(d) Paid creditor on account, $2,900.
(e) Earned sales commissions, receiving cash, $41,500.
(f) Paid dividends, $5,000.
(g) Paid automobile expenses (including rental charge) for month, $2,900, and miscellaneous expenses, $1,950.
(h) Paid office salaries, $8,000.
(i) Determined that the cost of supplies used was $650.

Instructions: (1) Prepare a ledger of T accounts for the following accounts: Cash, Supplies, Accounts Payable, Capital Stock, Dividends, Sales Commissions, Rent Expense, Office Salaries Expense, Automobile Expense, Supplies Expense, Miscellaneous Expense.
(2) Prepare journal entries for transactions (a) through (i).
(3) Post the journal to the ledger, and determine the account balances after all posting is complete.
(4) Prepare a trial balance as of July 31, 19--.
(5) Determine the following:
 (a) Amount of total revenue recorded in the ledger.
 (b) Amount of total expenses recorded in the ledger.
 (c) Amount of net income for July.

1–42. Financial statements. Following are the amounts of Fulton Corporation's assets and liabilities at July 31, the end of the current year, and its revenue and expenses for the year ended on that date, listed in alphabetical order. Fulton Corporation had capital stock of $100,000 and retained earnings of $97,890 on August 1, the beginning of the current year. During the current year, the corporation paid cash dividends of $40,000 and received cash from the sale of capital stock of $50,000. Cash received from customers was $790,000 and cash paid for expenses and to creditors was $765,000.

Accounts payable	$ 61,250
Accounts receivable	120,500
Advertising expense	30,000
Cash	64,515
Insurance expense	24,000
Land	200,000
Miscellaneous expense	8,125
Notes payable	25,000
Prepaid insurance	6,000
Rent expense	160,500
Salaries payable	9,000
Salary expense	410,500
Sales	845,500
Supplies	5,500
Supplies expense	19,750
Taxes expense	33,500
Utilities expense	65,750

Instructions: (1) Prepare an income statement for the current year ended July 31.
(2) Prepare a retained earnings statement for the current year ended July 31.
(3) Prepare a balance sheet as of July 31 of the current year.
(4) Prepare a statement of cash flows for the current year ended July 31. The cash balance on August 1, the beginning of the current year was $29,515

1–43. Transactions; financial statements. Berry Dry Cleaners Inc. is a corporation operated by R. C. Berry. Currently, a building, delivery truck, and equipment are being rented, pending completion of construction of new facilities. The actual work of dry cleaning is done by another company at wholesale rates. The assets, liabilities, and owner's equity of the business on May 1 of the current year are as follows: Cash, $7,750; Accounts Receivable, $15,600; Supplies, $800; Land, $25,000; Accounts Payable, $9,700; Capital Stock, $25,000; Retained Earnings, $14,450. Business transactions during May are summarized as follows:

(a) Received cash from cash customers for dry cleaning sales, $9,150.
(b) Paid rent for the month, $900.
(c) Purchased supplies on account, $220.
(d) Paid creditors on account, $8,000.
(e) Charged customers for dry cleaning sales on account, $3,520.
(f) Received monthly invoice for dry cleaning expense for May (to be paid on June 10), $6,800.
(g) Paid dividends, $1,750.
(h) Received cash from sale of capital stock, $5,000.
(i) Paid the following: wages expense, $1,400; truck expense, $580; utilities expense, $460; miscellaneous expense, $130.
(j) Received cash from customers on account, $8,100.
(k) Determined the cost of supplies used during the month, $270.

Instructions: (1) Prepare a ledger of T accounts for Berry Dry Cleaners Inc., using the following account titles: Cash, Accounts Receivable, Supplies, Land, Accounts Payable, Capital Stock, Retained Earnings, Dividends, Dry Cleaning Sales, Dry Cleaning Expense, Wages Expense, Rent Expense, Truck Expense, Utilities Expense, Supplies Expense, Miscellaneous Expense.
(2) Record the normal balances in the T accounts by writing "Bal." and entering the appropriate amount on the debit or credit side of the account.
(3) Prepare journal entries for transactions (a) through (k).
(4) Post the journal to the ledger, and determine the account balances after all posting is complete.

(5) Prepare a trial balance as of May 31, 19--.
(6) Prepare an income statement and retained earnings statement for May.
(7) Prepare a balance sheet as of May 31, 19--.
(8) Prepare a statement of cash flows for May.

1–44. Journal entries and trial balance. The following business transactions were completed by Dunway Theatre Corporation during May of the current year:

(a) Deposited in a bank account $65,000 cash received for capital stock.
(b) Purchased the Waddell Drive-In Theatre for $225,000, divided as follows: land, $125,000; buildings, $75,000; equipment, $25,000. Paid $50,000 in cash and gave a note payable for the remainder.
(c) Entered into a contract for the operation of the refreshment stand concession at a rental of 25% of the concessionaire's sales, with a guaranteed minimum of $1,000 a month, payable in advance. Received cash of $1,000 as the advance payment for the month of May.
(d) Paid for advertising leaflets for May, $225.
(e) Paid premiums for property and casualty insurance policies, $3,700.
(f) Purchased supplies, $650, and equipment, $3,150, on account.
(g) Paid for May billboard and newspaper advertising, $1,500.
(h) Paid miscellaneous expense, $220.
(i) Cash received from admissions for the week, $5,125.
(j) Paid semimonthly wages, $1,670.
(k) Cash received from admissions for the week, $4,900.
(l) Paid miscellaneous expenses, $210.
(m) Returned a portion of the supplies purchased in transaction (f) to the supplier, receiving full credit for the cost, $160.
(n) Paid cash to creditors on account, $2,350.
(o) Cash received from admissions for the week, $3,910.
(p) Purchased supplies for cash, $300.
(q) Recorded invoice of $5,800 for rental of film for May. Payment is due on June 6.
(r) Paid electricity and water bills, $625.
(s) Paid semimonthly wages, $1,720.
(t) Cash received from admissions for remainder of the month, $3,100.
(u) Recorded additional amount owed by the concessionaire for the month of May; sales for the month totaled $5,280. Rental charges in excess of the advance payment of $1,000 are not due and payable until June 10.

Instructions: (1) Prepare a ledger of T accounts for Dunway Theatre Corporation, using the following account titles: Cash, Accounts Receivable, Prepaid Insurance, Supplies, Land, Buildings, Equipment, Accounts Payable, Note Payable, Capital Stock, Admissions Income, Concession Income, Wages Expense, Film Rental Expense, Advertising Expense, Electricity and Water Expense, Miscellaneous Expense.
(2) Prepare journal entries for transactions (a) through (u).
(3) Post the journal to the ledger, and determine the balances after all posting is complete.
(4) Prepare a trial balance as of May 31, 19--.
(5) Determine the following:
  (a) Amount of total revenue recorded in the ledger.
  (b) Amount of total expenses recorded in the ledger.
  (c) Amount of the net income for May, assuming that additional unrecorded expenses (including supplies used, insurance expired, etc.) totaled $2,450.
  (d) The understatement or overstatement of net income for May that would have resulted from the failure to record the invoice for film rental until it was paid in June. (see transaction q).
  (e) The understatement or overstatement of liabilities as of May 31 that would have resulted from the failure to record the invoice for film rental in May (see transaction q).

1–45. Journal entries and trial balance. Hill Realty Inc. acts as an agent in buying, selling, renting, and managing real estate. The account balances at the end of March of the current year are as follows:

Cash	36,150	
Accounts Receivable	28,750	
Prepaid Insurance	1,100	
Office Supplies	715	
Land	—0—	
Accounts Payable		6,175
Notes Payable		—0—
Capital Stock		30,000
Retained Earnings		10,840
Dividends	2,000	
Fees Earned		125,500
Salary and Commission Expense	92,100	
Rent Expense	4,500	
Advertising Expense	3,900	
Automobile Expense	2,750	
Miscellaneous Expense	550	
	172,515	172,515

The following business transactions were completed by Hill Realty Inc. during April of the current year:

(a) Paid rent on office for month, $1,500.
(b) Purchased office supplies on account, $375.
(c) Paid insurance premiums, $1,650.
(d) Received cash from clients on account, $18,200.
(e) Paid salaries and commissions, $16,650.
(f) Purchased land for a future building site for $55,000, paying $11,000 in cash and giving a note payable for the remainder.
(g) Recorded revenue earned and billed to clients during first half of month, $19,100.
(h) Paid creditors on account, $4,150.
(i) Returned a portion of the office supplies purchased in (b), receiving full credit for their cost, $75.
(j) Received cash from clients on account, $16,700.
(k) Paid advertising expense, $1,550.
(l) Discovered an error in computing a commission; received cash from the salesperson for the overpayment, $350.
(m) Paid automobile expense (including rental charges for an automobile), $715.
(n) Paid miscellaneous expenses, $215.
(o) Recorded revenue earned and billed to clients during second half of month, $16,300.
(p) Paid salaries and commissions, $19,850.
(q) Paid dividends, $2,000.

Instructions: (1) Prepare a ledger of T accounts, using the account titles in the trial balance as of March 31. Record the balances in the accounts by writing "Bal." and entering the appropriate amount on the debit or credit side of the account.
(2) Prepare journal entries for transactions (a) through (q) completed during April.
(3) Post the journal to the ledger, and determine the balances after all posting is complete.
(4) Prepare a trial balance of the ledger as of April 30.

1–46. Transactions; income statement, retained earnings statement, and balance sheet. On June 1 of the current year, Rapid Delivery Inc. was organized as a corporation. The summarized transactions of the business for its first two months of operations, ending on July 31, are as follows:

(a) Received cash from stockholders for capital stock		$60,000
(b) Purchased a portion of a delivery service that had been operating as a sole proprietorship in accordance with the following details:		
Assets acquired by the corporation:		
Accounts receivable	$14,000	
Truck supplies	4,550	
Office supplies	750	$19,300
Liabilities assumed by the corporation:		
Accounts payable		9,300
Payment to be made as follows:		
Cash	$ 2,500	
Three non-interest-bearing notes payable of $2,500 each, due at two-month intervals	7,500	$10,000
(c) Purchased truck supplies on account		$ 1,150
(d) Purchased office supplies for cash		250
(e) Paid creditors on account		5,000
(f) Received cash from customers on account		9,500
(g) Paid insurance premiums in advance		1,800
(h) Paid advertising expense		1,100
(i) Charged delivery service sales to customers on account		39,250
(j) Paid rent expense on office and trucks		4,100
(k) Paid utilities expense		925
(l) Paid first of the three notes payable		2,500
(m) Paid miscellaneous expenses		1,475
(n) Paid taxes expense		275
(o) Paid wages expense		17,100
(p) Truck supplies used		2,720
(q) Office supplies used		325
(r) Insurance premiums that expired and became an expense		300
(s) Purchased land as future building site, paying $15,000 cash and giving a note payable due in 5 years for the balance of $25,000		40,000
(t) Paid cash dividends to stockholders		1,000

Instructions: (1) Prepare a ledger of T accounts, using the following account titles: Cash, Accounts Receivable, Truck Supplies, Office Supplies, Prepaid Insurance, Land, Notes Payable, Accounts Payable, Capital Stock, Dividends, Delivery Service Sales, Wages Expense, Rent Expense, Truck Supplies Expense, Advertising Expense, Utilities Expense, Office Supplies Expense, Taxes Expense, Insurance Expense, Miscellaneous Expense.

(2) Prepare journal entries for transactions (a) through (t) completed during June and July.

(3) Post the journal to the ledger, and determine the balances after all posting is complete.

(4) Prepare a trial balance of the ledger as of July 31.

(5) Prepare the following: (a) income statement for two months, (b) retained earnings statement for two months, and (c) balance sheet as of July 31.

1–42A. Financial statements. Following are the amounts of Baker Corporation's assets and liabilities at October 31, the end of the current year, and its revenue and expenses for the year ended on that date, listed in alphabetical order. Baker Corporation had capital stock of $50,000 and retained earnings of $16,765 on November 1, the beginning of the current year. During the current year, the corporation paid cash dividends of $15,000 and received cash from the sale of capital stock of $20,000. Cash received from customers was $189,500 and cash paid for expenses and to creditors was $185,500.

Accounts payable	$ 5,600
Accounts receivable	19,750
Advertising expense	5,000
Cash	16,500
Insurance expense	1,900
Land	80,000
Miscellaneous expense	1,250
Notes payable	5,000
Prepaid insurance	950
Rent expense	42,000
Salaries payable	2,250
Salary expense	90,500
Sales	205,500
Supplies	865
Supplies expense	6,125
Taxes expense	5,775
Utilities expense	19,500

Instructions: (1) Prepare an income statement for the current year ended October 31.
(2) Prepare a retained earnings statement for the current year ended October 31.
(3) Prepare a balance sheet as of October 31 of the current year.
(4) Prepare a statement of cash flows for the current year ended October 31. The cash balance on November 1, the beginning of the current year was $7,500.

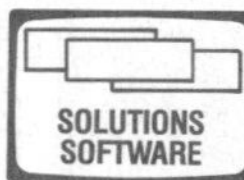

1–43A. Transactions; financial statements. Berry Dry Cleaners Inc. is a corporation operated by R. C. Berry. Currently, a building and equipment are being rented, pending expansion to new facilities. The actual work of dry cleaning is done by another company at wholesale rates. The assets, liabilities, and owner's equity of the business on June 1 of the current year are as follows: Cash, $9,400; Accounts Receivable, $3,900; Supplies, $410; Land, $15,000; Accounts Payable, $2,880; Capital Stock, $20,000; Retained Earnings, $5,830. Business transactions during June are summarized as follows:

(a) Paid rent for the month, $1,050.
(b) Charged customers for dry cleaning sales on account, $6,250.
(c) Paid creditors on account, $1,680.
(d) Purchased supplies on account, $310.
(e) Received cash from cash customers for dry cleaning sales, $3,200.
(f) Received cash from customers on account, $3,750.
(g) Paid dividends, $2,000.
(h) Received monthly invoice for dry cleaning expense for June (to be paid on July 10), $3,200.
(i) Paid the following: wages expense, $1,200; truck expense, $675; utilities expense, $460; miscellaneous expense, $190.
(j) Received cash from sale of capital stock, $2,500.
(k) Determined the cost of supplies used during the month, $420.

Instructions: (1) Prepare a ledger of T accounts for Berry Dry Cleaners Inc., using the following account titles: Cash, Accounts Receivable, Supplies, Land, Accounts Payable, Capital Stock, Retained Earnings, Dividends, Dry Cleaning Sales, Dry Cleaning Expense, Wages Expense, Rent Expense, Truck Expense, Utilities Expense, Supplies Expense, Miscellaneous Expense.

(2) Record the normal balances in the T accounts by writing "Bal." and entering the appropriate amount on the debit or credit side of the account.

(3) Prepare journal entries for transactions (a) through (k).

(4) Post the journal to the ledger, and determine the balances after all posting is complete.

(5) Prepare a trial balance as of June 30, 19--.

(6) Prepare an income statement and retained earnings statement for June.

(7) Prepare a balance sheet as of June 30, 19--.

(8) Prepare a statement of cash flows for June.

1–44A. Journal entries and trial balance. The following business transactions were completed by Carr Theatre Corporation during July of the current year:

(a) Received and deposited in a bank account $50,000 cash for capital stock.
(b) Purchased the Lincoln Drive-In Theatre for $120,000, divided as follows: land, $60,000; buildings, $40,000; equipment, $20,000. Paid $35,000 in cash and gave a note payable for the remainder.
(c) Entered into a contract for the operation of the refreshment stand concession at a rental of 20% of the concessionaire's sales, with a guaranteed minimum of $600 a month, payable in advance. Received cash of $600 as the advance payment for the month of July.
(d) Purchased supplies, $390, and equipment, $4,200, on account.
(e) Paid premiums for property and casualty insurance policies, $2,250.
(f) Paid for July billboard and newspaper advertising, $750.
(g) Cash received from admissions for the week, $2,730.
(h) Paid miscellaneous expense, $265.
(i) Paid semimonthly wages, $1,360.
(j) Cash received from admissions for the week, $2,980.
(k) Paid miscellaneous expenses, $310.
(l) Returned a portion of the supplies purchased in transaction (d) to the supplier, receiving full credit for the cost, $60.
(m) Paid cash to creditors on account, $2,250.
(n) Cash received from admissions for the week, $2,420.
(o) Purchased supplies for cash, $210.
(p) Paid for advertising leaflets for special promotion during last week in July, $375.
(q) Recorded invoice of $4,400 for rental of film for July. Payment is due on August 7.
(r) Paid electricity and water bills, $890.
(s) Paid semimonthly wages, $1,450.
(t) Cash received from admissions for remainder of the month, $3,600.
(u) Recorded additional amount owed by the concessionaire for the month of July; sales for the month totaled $4,500. Rental charges in excess of the advance payment of $600 are not due and payable until August 5.

Instructions: (1) Prepare a ledger of T accounts for Carr Theatre Corporation, using the following account titles: Cash, Accounts Receivable, Prepaid Insurance, Supplies, Land, Buildings, Equipment, Accounts Payable, Note Payable, Capital Stock, Admissions Income, Concession Income, Wages Expense, Film Rental Expense, Advertising Expense, Electricity and Water Expense, Miscellaneous Expense.

(2) Prepare journal entries for transactions (a) through (u).

(3) Post the journal to the ledger, and determine the balances after all posting is complete.
(4) Prepare a trial balance as of July 31, 19--.
(5) Determine the following:
   (a) Amount of total revenue recorded in the ledger.
   (b) Amount of total expenses recorded in the ledger.
   (c) Amount of net income for July, assuming that additional unrecorded expenses (including supplies used, insurance expired, etc.) totaled $610.
   (d) The understatement or overstatement of net income for July that would have resulted from the failure to record the invoice for film rental until it was paid in August (see transaction q).
   (e) The understatement or overstatement of liabilities as of July 31 that would have resulted from the failure to record the invoice for film rental in July (see transaction q).

Mini-Case 1

Ann Wolf, a junior in college, has been seeking ways to earn extra spending money. As an active sports enthusiast, Ann plays tennis regularly at the Royal Golf and Tennis Club, where her family has a membership. The president of the club recently approached Ann with the proposal that she manage the club's tennis courts on weekends. Ann's primary duty would be to supervise the operation of the club's two indoor and six outdoor courts, including court reservations. In return for her services, the club would pay Ann $80 per weekend, plus Ann could keep whatever she earned from lessons and the fees from the use of the ball machine. The club and Ann agreed to a one-month trial, after which both would consider an arrangement for the remaining two years of Ann's college career. On this basis, Ann organized Tennis Services Unlimited. During September, Ann managed the tennis courts and entered into the following transactions:

(a) Opened a business account by depositing $500.
(b) Paid $100 for tennis supplies (practice tennis balls, etc.)
(c) Paid $125 for the rental of video tape equipment to be used in offering lessons during September.
(d) Arranged for the rental of a ball machine during September for $50. Paid $25 in advance, with the remaining $25 due October 1.
(e) Received $450 for lessons given during September.
(f) Received $90 in fees from the use of the ball machine during September.

(g) Paid $120 for salaries of part-time employees who answered the telephone and took reservations while Ann was giving lessons.
(h) Paid $75 for miscellaneous expenses.
(i) Received $320 from the club for managing the tennis courts during September.
(j) Supplies on hand at the end of the month totaled $55.
(k) Ann withdrew $400 for personal use on September 30.

As a friend and accounting student, Ann has asked you to aid her in assessing the venture.

Instructions:

(1) To assist Ann with her record keeping, prepare a ledger of T accounts that would be appropriate. Note: Small business enterprises such as Tennis Services Unlimited are often organized as sole proprietorships. The accounting for sole proprietorships is similar to that for a corporation, except that the owner's equity accounts differ. Specifically, instead of the account Capital Stock, a capital account entitled Ann Wolf, Capital is used to record investments in the business. In addition, instead of a dividends account, withdrawals from the business enterprise are debited to Ann Wolf, Drawing.
(2) Prepare journal entries for transactions (a) through (k).
(3) Post the journal to the ledger, and determine the balances after all posting is complete.
(4) Prepare a trial balance as of September 30, 19--.
(5) Prepare an income statement for September.
(6) (a) Assume that Ann Wolf could earn $4.50 per hour working 16 hours per weekend for a fast food restaurant. Evaluate which of the two alternatives, the fast food restaurant or Tennis Services Unlimited, would provide Ann with the most income per month.
    (b) Discuss any other factors that you believe Ann should consider before discussing a long-term arrangement with Royal Golf and Tennis Club.

Answers to Self-Examination Questions

1. D A corporation, organized in accordance with state or federal statutes, is a separate legal entity in which ownership is divided into shares of stock (answer D). A sole proprietorship, sometimes referred to as a single proprietorship (answers A and B), is a business enterprise owned by one individual. A partnership (answer C) is a business enterprise owned by two or more individuals.

2. A The properties owned by a business enterprise are referred to as assets (answer A). The debts of the business are called liabilities (answer B), and the equity of the owners is represented by capital stock or owner's equity (answers C and D).
3. A A debit may signify an increase in asset accounts (answer A) or a decrease in liability and owner's equity accounts. A credit may signify a decrease in asset accounts (answer B) or an increase in liability and owner's equity accounts (answers C and D).
4. C Liability, capital stock, and revenue (answer C) accounts have normal credit balances. Asset (answer A), dividend (answer B), and expense (answer D) accounts have normal debit balances.
5. A The balance sheet is a listing of the assets, liabilities, and owner's equity of a business entity at a specific date (answer A). The income statement (answer B) is a summary of the revenue and expenses of a business entity for a specific period of time. The statement of cash flows (answer C) summarizes the changes in the cash of a business entity. The retained earnings statement (answer D) summarizes the changes in retained earnings for a corporation during a specific period of time.

2
Accounting for Merchandise Transactions

CHAPTER OBJECTIVES

Describe and illustrate the accounting for purchases of merchandise.

Describe and illustrate the accounting for sales of merchandise.

Describe the major classifications of accounts.

Describe and illustrate the chart of accounts of a merchandising enterprise.

Describe and illustrate the use of the standard account form.

Describe the procedures for discovering errors in accounts.

The recording of business transactions for a service enterprise was described and illustrated in Chapter 1. This chapter describes the recording of transactions for an enterprise that sells merchandise, and describes the classification of accounts, the standard account form, and the general journal. In Chapters 3 and 4, a merchandising enterprise's summarizing and reporting procedures at year end, including the preparation of financial statements, are discussed.

PURCHASING AND SELLING PROCEDURES

Merchandising enterprises acquire merchandise for resale to customers. These purchases and the sales of merchandise are the transactions that differ from those of enterprises that render services. Although these transactions result in differences in accounting for merchandising enterprises and service enterprises, the flow of accounting data, as described in Chapter 1, is the same. This flow, from the time a transaction occurs to its recording in the ledger, may be diagrammed as follows:

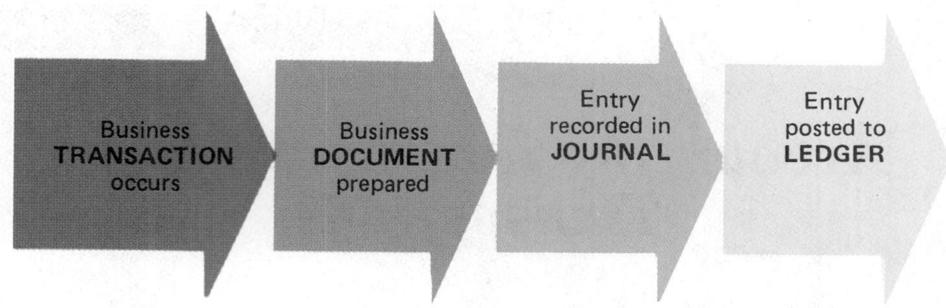

The initial record of each transaction, or a group of similar transactions, is evidenced by a business document such as a sales ticket, a check stub, or a cash register tape. On the basis of the evidence provided by the business documents, the transactions are entered in chronological order in a journal. The amounts of the debits and the credits in the journal are then transferred or posted to the accounts in the ledger.

The common procedures for recording purchasing and selling transactions are discussed in the following paragraphs. These procedures may vary from business to business, however. For example, purchases and sales may be made for cash or on credit (on account), and many different arrangements may be made for making payments on account. In addition, policies for the return of merchandise and for the payment of transportation costs may be different.

ACCOUNTING FOR PURCHASES

Purchases of merchandise are usually identified in the ledger as *Purchases*. A more exact account title, such as "Purchases of Merchandise," could be used, but the briefer title is customarily used. Thus, a merchandising enterprise can accumulate in the purchases account the cost of all merchandise purchased for resale during the accounting period.

When purchases are made for cash, the transaction may be recorded in the journal as follows:

Purchases	510	
Cash		510

Most purchases of merchandise are made on account and may be recorded as follows:

Purchases	925	
Accounts Payable		925

Purchases Discounts

The arrangements agreed upon by the buyer and the seller as to when payments for merchandise are to be made are called the **credit terms.** If payment is required immediately upon delivery, the terms are said to be "cash" or "net cash." Otherwise, the buyer is allowed a certain amount of time, known as the **credit period,** in which to pay.

It is usual for the credit period to begin with the date of the sale as shown by the date of the **invoice** or **bill**. If payment is due within a stated number of days after the date of the invoice, for example 30 days, the terms are said to be "net 30 days," which may be written as "n/30."[1] If payment is due by the end of the month in which the sale was made, it may be expressed as "n/eom."

As a means of encouraging payment before the end of the credit period, the seller may offer a discount for the early payment of cash. Thus the expression "2/10, n/30" means that, although the credit period is 30 days, the buyer may deduct 2% of the amount of the invoice if payment is made within 10 days of the invoice date. This deduction is known as a **cash discount.** The essentials of credit terms of 2/10, n/30 are summarized in the following diagram:

Credit Terms

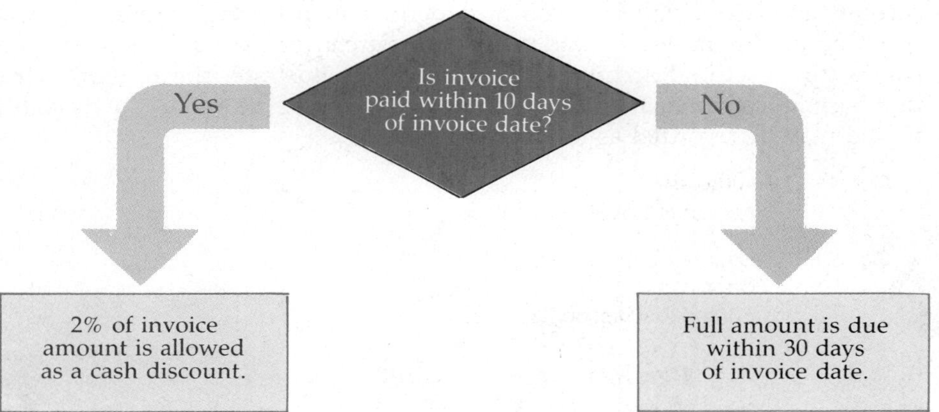

From the buyer's standpoint, it is important to take advantage of all available discounts, even though it may be necessary to borrow the money to make the payment. To illustrate, assume that the following invoice for $1,500 is received by Midtown Electric Corporation:

Invoice

Wallace Electronics Supply
3800 MISSION STREET
SAN FRANCISCO, CA 94110-1732

FOR CUSTOMER'S USE ONLY
Calculations Checked: W.M.L. | Price Approved
Material Received: 10-13 1989 A.S. Rec. Cl. (Date / Signature / Title)
Audited: L.R.A. | Final Approval

Customer's Order No. & Date: 412 Oct. 9, 1989
Refer to Invoice No. 106-8
Invoice Date Oct. 11, 1989
Vendor's Nos.

SOLD TO Midtown Electric Corporation
1200 San Vicente Blvd.
Los Angeles, CA 90019-2350

Date Shipped Oct. 11, 1989 From San Francisco
Prepaid or Collect? Prepaid
How Shipped and Route Western Trucking Co.
F.O.B. Los Angeles
Terms 2/10, n/30
Made in U. S. A.

QUANTITY	DESCRIPTION	UNIT PRICE	AMOUNT
20	392E Transformers	75.00	1,500.00

[1]The word "net" in this context does not have the usual meaning of a remainder after all relevant deductions have been subtracted, as in "net income," for example.

The invoice, with terms of 2/10, n/30, is to be paid within the discount period with money borrowed for the remaining 20 days of the credit period. If an annual interest rate of 12% is assumed, the net savings to the buyer is $20.20, determined as follows:

Discount of 2% on $1,500	$30.00
Interest for 20 days, at rate of 12% on $1,470 ($1,500 − $30)	9.80[2]
Savings effected by borrowing	$20.20

Discounts taken by the buyer for early payment of an invoice are called **purchases discounts**. They are recorded by crediting the purchases discounts account and are usually viewed as a deduction from the amount initially recorded as Purchases. In this sense, the purchases discounts account is a contra (or offsetting) account to Purchases. To illustrate, the receipt of the purchase invoice presented above and its payment at the end of the discount period may be recorded as follows:

Oct. 11	Purchases	1,500	
	Accounts Payable		1,500
Oct. 21	Accounts Payable	1,500	
	Cash		1,470
	Purchases Discounts		30

Purchases Returns and Allowances

When merchandise is returned **(purchases return)** or a price adjustment **(purchases allowance)** is requested, the buyer usually communicates with the seller in writing. The details may be stated in a letter, or the buyer (debtor) may use a **debit memorandum** form. This form, illustrated at the top of page 65, is a convenient medium for informing the seller (creditor) of the amount the buyer proposes to debit to the accounts payable account. It also states the reasons for the return or request for a price reduction.

The debtor may use a copy of the debit memorandum as the basis for an entry or may wait for confirmation from the creditor, which is usually in the form of a **credit memorandum.** In either event, Accounts Payable must be debited and Purchases Returns and Allowances must be credited.[3] The purchases returns and allowances account can be viewed as a deduction from the amount initially recorded as Purchases. In this sense, like Purchases Discounts, the purchases returns and allowances account is a contra (or offsetting) account to Purchases. To illustrate, the entry by Martin and Thomas Inc. to record the return of the merchandise identified in the debit memo on page 65 would be as follows:

July 7	Accounts Payable	62.50	
	Purchases Returns and Allowances		62.50

[2]Following the usual commercial practice of using 360 days as a year, the interest of $9.80 is computed as follows:

$$\$1,470 \times \frac{12}{100} \times \frac{20}{360} = \$9.80$$

[3]Many businesses credit the purchases returns and allowances account for merchandise returned and allowances granted. However, some businesses prefer to credit the purchases account. If this alternative is used, the balance of the purchases account will be a net amount—the total purchases less the total returns and allowances for the period.

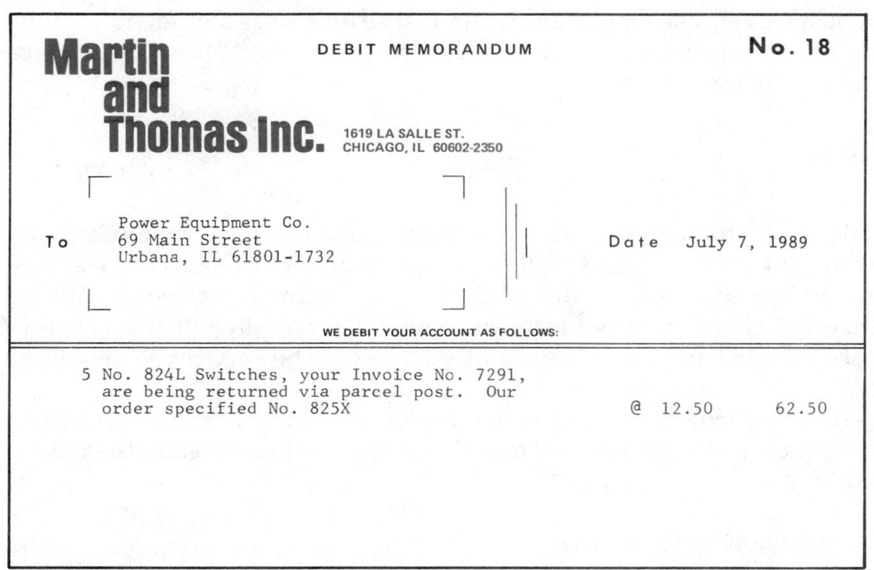

Martin and Thomas Inc. 1619 LA SALLE ST. CHICAGO, IL 60602-2350

DEBIT MEMORANDUM

No. 18

To Power Equipment Co.
69 Main Street
Urbana, IL 61801-1732

Date July 7, 1989

WE DEBIT YOUR ACCOUNT AS FOLLOWS:

5 No. 824L Switches, your Invoice No. 7291, are being returned via parcel post. Our order specified No. 825X @ 12.50 62.50

Debit Memorandum

When a buyer returns merchandise or has been granted an allowance prior to the payment of the invoice, the amount of the debit memorandum is deducted from the invoice amount before the purchases discount is computed. For example, assume that the details related to the amount payable to Power Equipment Co., for which the debit memo illustrated above was issued, are as follows:

Invoice No. 7291 dated July 1 (terms 2/10, n/30)	$2,045.00
Debit Memo No. 18 dated July 7	62.50
Balance of account	$1,982.50
Discount (2% of $1,982.50)	39.65
Cash payment, July 11	$1,942.85

The cash payment could be recorded by Martin and Thomas Inc. as follows:

July 11	Accounts Payable	1,982.50	
	Cash		1,942.85
	Purchases Discounts		39.65

ACCOUNTING FOR SALES

Merchandise sales are usually identified in the ledger as *Sales*, or *Sales of Merchandise*. Sales are recorded in the accounting records based upon the **realization principle.** Under this principle, sales are generally recorded when the title to the merchandise passes to the buyer. The passing of title usually occurs when the merchandise has been delivered to the buyer or when the merchandise has been placed in the custody of a shipping agent, such as a freight company. Usually at that time, rather than when a sales order is received, the buyer incurs a specific obligation to pay for the merchandise.

A business may sell merchandise for cash. These sales are generally "rung up" on a cash register and totaled at the end of the day. Such sales may be recorded as follows:

Jan. 7	Cash	1,872.50	
	Sales		1,872.50

Sales to customers who use bank credit cards (such as MasterCard and VISA) are generally treated as cash sales. The credit card invoices representing these sales are deposited by the seller directly into the bank, along with the currency and checks received from customers. Periodically, the bank charges a service fee for handling these credit card sales. The service fee should be debited to an expense account.

A business may also sell merchandise on account. Such sales result in a debit to Accounts Receivable and a credit to Sales, as illustrated in the following entry:

Jan. 12	Accounts Receivable	510	
	Sales		510

Sales made by the use of nonbank credit cards (such as American Express) generally must be reported periodically to the card company before cash is received. Therefore, such sales create a receivable with the card company. Before the card company remits cash, it normally deducts a service fee. To illustrate, assume that nonbank credit card sales of $1,000 are made and reported to the card company on January 20. On January 27, the company deducts a service fee of $50 and remits $950. The transactions may be recorded as follows:

Jan. 20	Accounts Receivable	1,000	
	Sales		1,000
Jan. 27	Cash	950	
	Credit Card Collection Expense	50	
	Accounts Receivable		1,000

CREDIT CARDS AND CASH DISCOUNTS

The extensive use of credit cards by the American consumer has led some analysts to predict that the "cashless society" is on the horizon. In an effort to reduce operating costs, however, many businesses have encouraged consumers to use cash rather than credit cards. For example, some oil companies are now offering incentives for their customers to use cash, described as follows in an article that appeared in the *Harvard Business Review:*

... Exxon, Amoco, Sohio, and Mobil have been trying out various ways of offering discounts for cash in lieu of credit card sales. Mobil has lowered its wholesale price while adding a 3% processing fee for credit card sales to induce station managers to favor cash sales. As a result, ... Mobil stations [are] offering consumers gasoline at 4 cents a gallon less if they pay cash....

The idea received a boost in the summer of 1981 when Congress passed the Cash Discount Act, permitting businesses to give discounts exceeding 5% to consumers paying cash. Previously, a rebate of more than 5% was considered a finance charge levied against credit card users and was therefore illegal.

The retailer incurs two costs in each credit card transaction: the [collection] fee to convert the charge to cash and the interest expense arising from the time lag between the sale and collection of funds. If, for example, his cost of [funds] is 20%, if an average six days elapse between the sale and the collection of the proceeds, and if the [collector's] fee is 5%, then $10,000 in credit sales are equivalent to $9,472 in cash sales. The retailer could offer a cash discount of 5.3% and still be as well off as with a credit card sale.

Although many retailers might like to reject credit cards altogether because of their expense, up to now they have been ill-advised to take this step unless most of their competitors followed suit. Otherwise, they could suffer a . . . disadvantage.

The retailer should consider four elements before adopting a discount-for-cash policy:

The reasons why his customers use credit cards. If it's just because they like the convenience of not carrying cash or consider it an advantage to buy now and pay later, they are candidates for a cash discount strategy. If, however, customers need the credit in order to make a purchase, a small cash reduction for cash payment probably would not deter their use of credit cards.

The proportion of his volume made up by cash sales. If the proportion is high, a discount-for-cash policy would give many customers who would have paid cash anyway a "free" deduction. Obviously, the effect on the retailer's earnings would not be healthy.

The cost of implementing the new policy. Computerized cash registers permit programming of a discount. Without electronic cash-handling technology, calculating the rebates could result in slower checkouts and clerical errors.

His customers' attitudes toward such an incentive—if he can ascertain them. If his competitors have a cash discount policy, the retailer could match this and wait for customer reaction. This "competitive parity" assumes, however, that rivals have determined an optimal discount policy that is applicable to others . . ."

Source: Michael Levy and Charles A. Ingene, "Retailers: Head off Credit Cards with Cash Discounts?" *Harvard Business Review* (May–June, 1983), pp. 18–22.

Sales Discounts

The seller refers to the discounts taken by the buyer for early payment of an invoice as **sales discounts.** They are recorded by debiting the sales discounts account and are considered to be a reduction in the amount initially recorded as Sales. In this sense, the balance of the sales discounts account is viewed as a contra (or offsetting) account to Sales. To illustrate, if cash is received within the discount period from a previously recorded credit sale of $500, 2/10, n/30, the transaction may be recorded as follows:

June 10	Cash	490	
	Sales Discounts	10	
	Accounts Receivable		500

Sales Returns and Allowances

Merchandise sold may be returned by the buyer **(sales return)** or, because of defects or for other reasons, the buyer may be allowed a reduction from the original price at which the goods were sold **(sales allowance).** If the return or allowance is for a sale on account, the seller usually gives the buyer a **credit memorandum.** This memorandum shows the amount for which the buyer is to be credited and the reason therefor. A typical credit memorandum is illustrated as follows:

CREDIT MEMORANDUM No. 32

Baker Manufacturing Company
1277 SIXTH AVENUE
LOS ANGELES, CA 90019-2350

Date October 13, 1989

CREDIT TO
Berry Company
7608 Melton Avenue
Los Angeles, CA 90025-3942

WE CREDIT YOUR ACCOUNT AS FOLLOWS:

1 Model 393 F Transformer returned 225.00

Credit Memorandum

The effect of a sales return or allowance is a reduction in sales revenue and a reduction in cash or accounts receivable. If the sales account is debited, however, the balance of the account at the end of the period will represent net sales, and the volume of returns and allowances will not be disclosed. Because of the loss in revenue resulting from allowances, and the various expenses (transportation, unpacking, repairing, reselling, etc.) related to returns, it is advisable that management know the amount of such transactions. Such a policy will allow management to determine the causes of returns and allowances, should they become excessive, and to take corrective action. It is therefore preferable to debit an account entitled Sales Returns and Allowances. If the original sale is on account, the remainder of the transaction is recorded as a credit to Accounts Receivable. Because sales returns and allowances are viewed as reductions of the amount initially recorded as Sales, the sales returns and allowances account is a contra (or offsetting) account to Sales. To illustrate, the following entry would be made by Baker Manufacturing Company to record the credit memo presented above:

Oct. 13	Sales Returns and Allowances	225	
	Accounts Receivable		225

If a cash refund is made because of merchandise returned or for an allowance, Sales Returns and Allowances is debited and Cash is credited.

TRANSPORTATION COSTS

The terms of the agreement between buyer and seller include provisions concerning (1) when the ownership (title) of the merchandise passes to the buyer and (2) which party is to bear the cost of delivering the merchandise to the buyer. If the ownership passes to the buyer when the seller delivers the merchandise to the shipper, the buyer is to absorb the transportation costs, and the terms are said to be **FOB (free on board) shipping point.** If ownership passes to the buyer when the merchandise is received by the buyer, the seller is to assume the costs of transportation, and the terms are said to be **FOB (free on board) destination**. The relationship of the shipping terms to the passage of ownership and who is to bear the costs of transportation is summarized in the following table:

Shipping Terms

	FOB shipping point	*FOB destination*
Ownership (title) passes to buyer when merchandise is	delivered to shipper	delivered to buyer
Transportation costs are borne by	buyer	seller

When merchandise is purchased on terms of FOB shipping point, the transportation costs paid by the buyer should be debited to Transportation In or Freight In and credited to Cash. The balance of the transportation in or freight in account should be added to net purchases in determining the total cost of merchandise purchased.[4]

In some cases, the seller may prepay the transportation costs and add them to the invoice, as an accommodation or courtesy to the buyer, even though the agreement states that the buyer bear such costs (terms FOB shipping point). If the seller prepays the transportation charges, the buyer will debit Transportation In for the transportation costs. To illustrate, assume that on June 10, Durban Co. purchases merchandise from Bell Corp. on account, $900, terms FOB shipping point, 2/10, n/30, with prepaid transportation costs of $50 added to the invoice. The entry by Durban Co. would be as follows:

June 10	Purchases..	900	
	Transportation In...................................	50	
	Accounts Payable................................		950

When the terms provide for a discount for early payment, the discount is based on the amount of the sale rather than on the invoice total. To illustrate, if Durban Co. pays the amount due on the purchase of June 10 within 10 days, the amount of the discount and the amount of the payment may be determined as follows:

Invoice from Bell Corp., including prepaid transportation of $50		$950
Amount subject to discount..............................	$900	
Rate of discount	2%	
Amount of purchases discount............................		18
Amount of payment		$932

[4]Some businesses prefer to debit the purchases account for transportation charges paid on merchandise purchased FOB shipping point. If this alternative is used, the balance of the purchases account will include the transportation costs borne by the buyer. The total cost of merchandise purchased will be the same as when a separate transportation in or freight in account is used.

Durban Co. may record the payment as follows:

June 20	Accounts Payable	950	
	Cash		932
	Purchases Discounts		18

When the seller prepays the transportation costs and the terms are FOB shipping point, as in the illustration above, the seller adds these costs to the invoice that is sent to the buyer. Therefore, the seller records the payment of the transportation costs by debiting Accounts Receivable. In the illustration above, for example, Bell Corp. would record the following entry on June 10, in addition to the entry to record the sale to Durban Co.:

June 10	Accounts Receivable	50	
	Cash		50

When the agreement states that the seller is to bear the delivery costs (FOB destination), the amounts paid by the seller for delivery are debited to Transportation Out, Delivery Expense, or a similarly titled account. The total of such costs incurred during a period is reported on the seller's income statement as a selling expense.

SALES TAXES

Almost all states and many other taxing units levy a tax on sales of merchandise. The liability for the sales tax is ordinarily incurred at the time the sale is made, regardless of the terms of the sale.

Sales Tax for Seller

At the time of a cash sale, the seller collects the sales tax. When a sale is made on account, the buyer is charged for the tax. The seller credits the sales account for only the amount of the sale, and credits the tax to Sales Tax Payable. For example, a sale of $100 on account, subject to a tax of 4%, may be recorded by the following entry:

Aug. 12	Accounts Receivable	104	
	Sales		100
	Sales Tax Payable		4

Periodically, the appropriate amount of the sales tax is paid to the taxing unit, and Sales Tax Payable is debited.

Sales Tax for Buyer

The buyer debits the purchases account for the full amount of the merchandise acquired, including the sales tax. For example, a purchase of $100 on account, subject to a tax of 4%, may be recorded by the following entry:

Aug. 12	Purchases	104	
	Accounts Payable		104

CLASSIFICATION OF ACCOUNTS

Before the recording of a series of transactions for a merchandising enterprise is illustrated, the classifications and accounts characteristically used are described in the following paragraphs. Accounts in the ledger are customarily classified according to a common characteristic: assets, liabilities, owner's equity, revenue, and expenses. In addition, there may be subgroupings within these major categories.

Assets

Any physical object or right that has a money value is an asset. Assets are customarily divided into groups for presentation on the balance sheet. The two groups used most often — current assets and plant assets — are discussed in the following paragraphs. Additional groups, such as investments and intangible assets, are discussed in later chapters.

Current assets. Cash and other assets that a business may reasonably expect to be sold, used up, or realized in cash through the normal operations of the business, usually within a year, are called **current assets.** Current assets are generally listed on the balance sheet in the order of liquidity. Cash is therefore listed first, followed by marketable securities, accounts receivable, notes receivable, merchandise inventory, supplies, and other prepaid expenses in the order in which they will be converted to cash or consumed.

Cash is any medium of exchange that a bank will accept at face value. It includes bank deposits, currency, checks, bank drafts, and money orders. **Notes receivable** are claims against debtors evidenced by a written promise to pay a certain sum in money at a definite time to the order of a specified person or to bearer. **Accounts receivable** are also claims against debtors, but are less formal than notes. **Merchandise inventory** is unsold merchandise that is held for resale to customers. **Prepaid expenses** include supplies on hand and advance payments of expenses such as insurance and property taxes.

Plant assets. Tangible assets used in the business that are of a permanent or relatively fixed nature are called **plant assets** or **fixed assets.** Plant assets include equipment, machinery, buildings, and land. With the exception of land, these assets gradually lose their usefulness with the passage of time. They are said to **depreciate.** The concept of depreciation is discussed in more detail in Chapter 3.

Liabilities

Liabilities are debts owed to outsiders (creditors) and are frequently described on the balance sheet by titles that include the word "payable." The two categories occurring most frequently are (1) current liabilities and (2) long-term liabilities.

Current liabilities. Liabilities that will be due within a short time (usually one year or less) and that are to be paid out of current assets are called **current liabilities.** The most common liabilities in this group are **notes payable** and **accounts payable,** which are exactly like their receivable counterparts except that the debtor-creditor relationship is reversed. Other current liability accounts commonly found in the ledger are Salaries Payable, Interest Payable, and Taxes Payable.

Long-term liabilities. Liabilities that will not be due for a comparatively long time (usually more than one year) are called **long-term liabilities** or **fixed liabilities.** As they come within the one-year range and are to be paid, these liabilities become current. If the obligation is to be renewed rather than paid at maturity, however, it would continue to be classified as long-term. When a long-term debt is to be paid over a number of years, the installments due within one year from a balance sheet date are classified as a current liability. When a note is accompanied by security in the form of a mortgage, the obligation may be referred to as *mortgage note payable* or *mortgage payable.*

Owner's Equity

Owner's equity is the residual claim of the owner or owners against the assets of the business after the total liabilities are deducted. Other commonly used terms for owner's equity are **stockholders' equity,** *shareholders' equity, shareholders' investment,* and **net worth** (or *capital* in referring to a sole proprietorship or partnership).

Revenue

Revenue is the gross increase in owner's equity attributable to business activities. It results from the sale of merchandise, the performance of services for a customer or a client, the rental of property, the lending of money, and other business and professional activities entered into for the purpose of earning income. Revenue from sales of merchandise is often identified merely as sales.

Expense

Costs that have been consumed in the process of producing revenue are **expired costs** or **expenses.** The number of expense categories and individual expense accounts maintained in the ledger varies with the nature and the size of an enterprise. A large business with authority and responsibility spread among many employees may use an elaborate classification and hundreds of accounts as an aid in controlling expenses.

For merchandise enterprises, the cost of merchandise purchased for resale is identified as purchases. The merchandise purchased is an asset until it is sold. At the time of sale, the cost of the merchandise purchased becomes an expense and is identified as **cost of merchandise sold.** The recording of the cost of merchandise sold and its presentation on the income statement is discussed and illustrated in Chapters 3 and 4.

CHART OF ACCOUNTS — MERCHANDISING ENTERPRISE

The number of accounts maintained by a specific enterprise is affected by the nature of its operations, its volume of business, and the extent to which details are needed for taxing authorities, managerial decisions, credit purposes, etc. For example, one enterprise may have separate accounts for executive salaries, office salaries, and sales salaries, while another may find it satisfactory to record all types of salaries in a single salary expense account.

Insofar as possible, the order of the accounts in the ledger should agree with the order of the items in the balance sheet and the income statement.

The accounts are numbered to permit indexing and also for use as posting references.

Although accounts in the ledger may be numbered consecutively as in the pages of a book, a flexible system of indexing is preferable. In the following listing of accounts, called a **chart of accounts,** for Taylor Inc., each account number has two digits. The first digit indicates the major division of the ledger in which the account is placed. Accounts beginning with 1 represent assets; 2, liabilities; 3, owner's equity; 4, revenue; and 5, expenses. The second digit indicates the position of the account within its division. A numbering system of this type has the advantage of permitting the later insertion of new accounts in their proper sequence without disturbing the other account numbers. For a large enterprise with a number of departments or branches, it is not unusual for each account number to have four or more digits.

Charts of Accounts for Taylor Inc.

Balance Sheet Accounts

1. Assets

11 Cash
12 Accounts Receivable
13 Merchandise Inventory
14 Store Supplies
15 Prepaid Rent
18 Store Equipment
19 Accumulated Depreciation

2. Liabilities

21 Accounts Payable
22 Salaries Payable

3. Owner's Equity

31 Capital Stock
32 Retained Earnings
33 Dividends
34 Income Summary

Income Statement Accounts

4. Revenue

41 Sales
42 Sales Returns and Allowances
43 Sales Discounts

5. Expenses

51 Purchases
52 Purchases Discounts
53 Transportation In
54 Advertising Expense
55 Salary Expense
56 Rent Expense
57 Depreciation Expense
58 Utilities Expense
59 Miscellaneous Expense

LEDGER ACCOUNTS

Accounts in the simple T form were used for illustrative purposes in Chapter 1. A more formal form is the **standard account form,** which includes balance columns. The primary advantage of the standard account form is that the account balance is readily available, as shown in the following illustration:

Standard Account Form

ACCOUNT Cash — ACCOUNT NO. 11

DATE		ITEM	POST. REF.	DEBIT	CREDIT	BALANCE DEBIT	BALANCE CREDIT
1989 May	1	Balance	✓			5 245 00	
	1		17	1 822 25		7 067 25	
	1		17		350 00	6 717 25	
	1		17		995 50	5 721 75	
	3		17	960 40		6 682 15	
	3		17		192 00	6 490 15	
	3		17		1 882 25	4 607 90	

The basic features of a journal entry and posting were illustrated in Chapter 1 when the use of accounts and debit and credit were introduced. The **general journal** is the formalized device used for recording journal entries in chronological order, illustrated as follows:

General Journal

JOURNAL PAGE 17

DATE		DESCRIPTION	POST. REF.	DEBIT	CREDIT
1989 May	1	Cash		1822 25	
		Sales			1822 25
		Cash sales for the day.			
	1	Advertising Expense		350 00	
		Cash			350 00
		Advertisements in Lima News.			
	1	Store Supplies		175 00	
		Accounts Payable			175 00
		On account from Crom Co.			

Note that brief explanations have been written below each journal entry. Many accountants prefer to omit explanations when the nature of the entry is obvious.

The posting of a debit or credit general journal entry to a standard ledger account is performed in the following manner:

1. Record the date and the amount of the entry in the account.
2. Insert the number of the journal page in the Posting Reference column of the account.
3. Insert the ledger account number in the Posting Reference column of the journal.

These procedures are illustrated as follows by the posting of a debit to the cash account. The posting of a credit uses the same sequence of procedures.

JOURNAL PAGE 17

	DATE		DESCRIPTION	POST. REF.	DEBIT	CREDIT	
1	1989 May	1	Cash	11	1 8 2 2 25		1
2			Sales			1 8 2 2 25	2
3			Cash sales for the day.				3
4							4

① ② ① ③

ACCOUNT Cash ACCOUNT NO. 11

DATE		ITEM	POST. REF.	DEBIT	CREDIT	BALANCE DEBIT	BALANCE CREDIT
1989 May	1	Balance	✓			5 2 4 5 00	
	1		17	1 8 2 2 25		7 0 6 7 25	

Diagram of the Posting of a Debit

ILLUSTRATION OF JOURNALIZING, POSTING, AND TRIAL BALANCE

To illustrate the procedures discussed in the preceding sections, assume that Taylor Inc. is organized as a corporation on June 1, 1989, to sell merchandise. The transactions for Taylor Inc.'s first month of operations are described below, followed by the appropriate journal entry. To reduce repetition, some of the transactions are stated as a summary. For example, sales for cash are ordinarily recorded on a daily basis, but in this illustration, summary totals are given only at the middle and end of the month.

June 1. Taylor Inc. was organized by issuing shares of capital stock for $80,000 in cash.

JOURNAL PAGE 1

	DATE		DESCRIPTION	POST. REF.	DEBIT	CREDIT	
1	1986 June	1	Cash	11	80 0 0 0 00		1
2			Capital Stock	31		80 0 0 0 00	2

June 2. Paid $3,600 on a lease rental contract, the payment representing two months' rent of store space in a local shopping mall. The asset acquired in exchange for the cash payment is the use of the property for two months. Thus, an asset entitled Prepaid Rent is debited for $3,600.

3							3
4		2	Prepaid Rent	15	3 6 0 0 00		4
5			Cash	11		3 6 0 0 00	5

June 3. Purchased store equipment on account from Roswell Equipment Suppliers for $15,000, terms n/60. The terms of the purchase indicate that the full amount of the liability is due at the end of 60 days.

3	Store Equipment	18	15 000 00	
	Accounts Payable	21		15 000 00

June 5. Purchased $30,000 of merchandise on account from Owen Clothing, terms 2/10, n/30. The terms of the purchase indicate that a 2% discount is available if the amount is paid within 10 days, but that the full amount is due, in any case, at the end of 30 days.

5	Purchases	51	30 000 00	
	Accounts Payable	21		30 000 00

June 8. Paid $600 for a newspaper advertisement.

8	Advertising Expense	54	600 00	
	Cash	11		600 00

June 10. Purchased $3,000 of store supplies, paying one half in cash and agreeing to pay the remainder in 30 days.

10	Store Supplies	14	3 000 00	
	Cash	11		1 500 00
	Accounts Payable	21		1 500 00

June 14. Paid salesperson $600 for two weeks' salary.

14	Salary Expense	55	600 00	
	Cash	11		600 00

June 15. Received $8,000 from cash sales for the first half of June.

Date	Description	Post. Ref.	Debit	Credit
15	Cash	11	8 0 0 0 00	
	Sales	41		8 0 0 0 00

June 15. Paid Owen Clothing for purchases of June 5 on account, less discount of $600 ($30,000 × 2%).

Date	Description	Post. Ref.	Debit	Credit
15	Accounts Payable	21	30 0 0 0 00	
	Cash	11		29 4 0 0 00
	Purchases Discounts	52		6 0 0 00

June 15. Sales on account totaled $12,500 for the first half of June. All sales are made with terms 1/10, n/30.

Date	Description	Post. Ref.	Debit	Credit
15	Accounts Receivable	12	12 5 0 0 00	
	Sales	41		12 5 0 0 00

June 19. Received merchandise returned on account, $4,000.

Date	Description	Post. Ref.	Debit	Credit
19	Sales Returns and Allowances	42	4 0 0 0 00	
	Accounts Receivable	12		4 0 0 0 00

June 22. Purchased merchandise from Norcross Clothiers, $15,000, terms FOB shipping point, 2/15, n/30, with prepaid transportation charges of $750 added to the invoice. The prepaid transportation charges of $750 must be added to the accounts payable, since the merchandise was shipped FOB shipping point. The transportation charges are not eligible for the 2% discount.

Date	Description	Post. Ref.	Debit	Credit
22	Purchases	51	15 0 0 0 00	
	Transportation In	53	7 5 0 00	
	Accounts Payable	21		15 7 5 0 00

June 25. Received $6,930 cash from customers on account, after discounts of $70 had been deducted.

39						39
40	25	Cash	11	6 930 00		40
41		Sales Discounts	43	70 00		41
42		Accounts Receivable	12		7 000 00	42

June 28. Paid $1,400 for electricity and telephone charges for the month.

43						43
44	28	Utilities Expense	58	1 400 00		44
45		Cash	11		1 400 00	45

June 30. Paid $380 for postage and other miscellaneous expenses for the month.

JOURNAL — PAGE 2

	DATE		DESCRIPTION	POST. REF.	DEBIT	CREDIT	
1	1989 June	30	Miscellaneous Expense	59	380 00		1
2			Cash	11		380 00	2

June 30. Paid salesperson $600 for two weeks' salary.

3						3
4	30	Salary Expense	55	600 00		4
5		Cash	11		600 00	5

June 30. Received $11,000 from cash sales for the second half of June.

6						6
7	30	Cash	11	11 000 00		7
8		Sales	41		11 000 00	8

June 30. Sales on account totaled $14,000 for the second half of June. All sales are made with terms 1/10, n/30.

9						9
10	30	Accounts Receivable	12	14 000 00		10
11		Sales	41		14 000 00	11

After all entries for the month have been posted, the ledger will appear as shown below and on pages 80–81. In practice, each account would appear on a separate page in the ledger. Tracing each entry from the journal to the accounts in the ledger will give a clear understanding of the posting process.

The accounts are numbered in accordance with the chart shown on page 73. However, some of the accounts listed in the chart are not shown in the illustrative ledger. The additional accounts will be used later when the work of the accounting period is completed.

ACCOUNT Cash ACCOUNT NO. 11

DATE		ITEM	POST. REF.	DEBIT	CREDIT	BALANCE DEBIT	BALANCE CREDIT
1989 June	1		1	80 000 00		80 000 00	
	2		1		3 600 00	76 400 00	
	8		1		600 00	75 800 00	
	10		1		1 500 00	74 300 00	
	14		1		600 00	73 700 00	
	15		1	8 000 00		81 700 00	
	15		1		29 400 00	52 300 00	
	25		1	6 930 00		59 230 00	
	28		1		1 400 00	57 830 00	
	30		2		380 00	57 450 00	
	30		2		600 00	56 850 00	
	30		2	11 000 00		67 850 00	

ACCOUNT Accounts Receivable ACCOUNT NO. 12

DATE		ITEM	POST. REF.	DEBIT	CREDIT	BALANCE DEBIT	BALANCE CREDIT
1989 June	15		1	12 500 00		12 500 00	
	19		1		4 000 00	8 500 00	
	25		1		7 000 00	1 500 00	
	30		2	14 000 00		15 500 00	

ACCOUNT Store Supplies ACCOUNT NO. 14

DATE		ITEM	POST. REF.	DEBIT	CREDIT	BALANCE DEBIT	BALANCE CREDIT
1989 June	10		1	3 000 00		3 000 00	

ACCOUNT Prepaid Rent ACCOUNT NO. 15

DATE		ITEM	POST. REF.	DEBIT	CREDIT	BALANCE DEBIT	BALANCE CREDIT
1989 June	2		1	3 600 00		3 600 00	

ACCOUNT Store Equipment — ACCOUNT NO. 18

DATE		ITEM	POST. REF.	DEBIT	CREDIT	BALANCE DEBIT	BALANCE CREDIT
1989 June	3		1	15 000 00		15 000 00	

ACCOUNT Accounts Payable — ACCOUNT NO. 21

DATE		ITEM	POST. REF.	DEBIT	CREDIT	BALANCE DEBIT	BALANCE CREDIT
1989 June	3		1		15 000 00		15 000 00
	5		1		30 000 00		45 000 00
	10		1		1 500 00		46 500 00
	15		1	30 000 00			16 500 00
	22		1		15 750 00		32 250 00

ACCOUNT Capital Stock — ACCOUNT NO. 31

DATE		ITEM	POST. REF.	DEBIT	CREDIT	BALANCE DEBIT	BALANCE CREDIT
1989 June	1		1		80 000 00		80 000 00

ACCOUNT Sales — ACCOUNT NO. 41

DATE		ITEM	POST. REF.	DEBIT	CREDIT	BALANCE DEBIT	BALANCE CREDIT
1989 June	15		1		8 000 00		8 000 00
	15		1		12 500 00		20 500 00
	30		2		11 000 00		31 500 00
	30		2		14 000 00		45 500 00

ACCOUNT Sales Returns and Allowances — ACCOUNT NO. 42

DATE		ITEM	POST. REF.	DEBIT	CREDIT	BALANCE DEBIT	BALANCE CREDIT
1989 June	19		1	4 000 00		4 000 00	

ACCOUNT Sales Discounts — ACCOUNT NO. 43

DATE		ITEM	POST. REF.	DEBIT	CREDIT	BALANCE DEBIT	BALANCE CREDIT
1989 June	25		1	70 00		70 00	

ACCOUNT Purchases — ACCOUNT NO. 51

DATE		ITEM	POST. REF.	DEBIT	CREDIT	BALANCE DEBIT	BALANCE CREDIT
1989 June	5		1	30,000 00		30,000 00	
	22		1	15,000 00		45,000 00	

ACCOUNT Purchases Discounts — ACCOUNT NO. 52

DATE		ITEM	POST. REF.	DEBIT	CREDIT	BALANCE DEBIT	BALANCE CREDIT
1989 June	15		1		600 00		600 00

ACCOUNT Transportation In — ACCOUNT NO. 53

DATE		ITEM	POST. REF.	DEBIT	CREDIT	BALANCE DEBIT	BALANCE CREDIT
1989 June	22		1	750 00		750 00	

ACCOUNT Advertising Expense — ACCOUNT NO. 54

DATE		ITEM	POST. REF.	DEBIT	CREDIT	BALANCE DEBIT	BALANCE CREDIT
1989 June	8		1	600 00		600 00	

ACCOUNT Salary Expense — ACCOUNT NO. 55

DATE		ITEM	POST. REF.	DEBIT	CREDIT	BALANCE DEBIT	BALANCE CREDIT
1989 June	14		1	600 00		600 00	
	30		2	600 00		1,200 00	

ACCOUNT Utilities Expense — ACCOUNT NO. 58

DATE		ITEM	POST. REF.	DEBIT	CREDIT	BALANCE DEBIT	BALANCE CREDIT
1989 June	28		1	1,400 00		1,400 00	

ACCOUNT Miscellaneous Expense — ACCOUNT NO. 59

DATE		ITEM	POST. REF.	DEBIT	CREDIT	BALANCE DEBIT	BALANCE CREDIT
1989 June	30		2	380 00		380 00	

As discussed in Chapter 1, the equality of debits and credits in the ledger should be verified at the end of each accounting period, if not more often, through preparing a **trial balance,** which is illustrated as follows:

Taylor Inc. Trial Balance June 30, 1989		
Cash	67,850.00	
Accounts Receivable	15,500.00	
Store Supplies	3,000.00	
Prepaid Rent	3,600.00	
Store Equipment	15,000.00	
Accounts Payable		32,250.00
Capital Stock		80,000.00
Sales		45,500.00
Sales Returns and Allowances	4,000.00	
Sales Discounts	70.00	
Purchases	45,000.00	
Purchases Discount		600.00
Transportation In	700.00	
Advertising Expense	600.00	
Salary Expense	1,200.00	
Utilities Expense	1,400.00	
Miscellaneous Expense	380.00	
	158,350.00	158,350.00

DISCOVERY OF ERRORS

The existence of errors in the accounts may be determined in various ways: (1) by audit procedures, (2) by chance discovery, or (3) by preparing a trial balance. If the debit and the credit totals of the trial balance are not in agreement, the exact amount of the difference between the totals should be determined before proceeding to search for the error.

The trial balance does not provide complete proof of the accuracy of the ledger. It indicates only that the *debits* and the *credits* are *equal*. This proof is of value, however, because errors frequently affect the equality of debits and credits. If the two totals of a trial balance are not equal, it is probably due to one or more of the following types of errors:

1. Error in preparing the trial balance, such as:
   a. One of the columns of the trial balance was incorrectly added.
   b. The amount of an account balance was incorrectly recorded on the trial balance.
   c. A debit balance was recorded on the trial balance as a credit, or vice versa, or a balance was omitted entirely.
2. Error in determining the account balances, such as:
   a. A balance was incorrectly computed.
   b. A balance was entered in the wrong balance column.

3. Error in recording a transaction in the ledger, such as:
   a. An erroneous amount was posted to the account.
   b. A debit entry was posted as a credit, or vice versa.
   c. A debit or a credit posting was omitted.

Among the types of errors that will not cause an inequality in the trial balance totals are the following:

1. Failure to record a transaction or to post a transaction.
2. Recording the same erroneous amount for both the debit and the credit parts of a transaction.
3. Recording the same transaction more than once.
4. Posting a part of a transaction correctly as a debit or credit but to the wrong account.

The amount of the difference between the two totals of a trial balance sometimes gives a clue as to the nature of the error or where it occurred. For example, a difference of 10, 100, or 1,000 between two totals is frequently the result of an error in addition. A difference between totals can also be due to the omission of a debit or a credit posting or, if the difference is divisible evenly by 2, to the posting of a debit as a credit, or vice versa. For example, if the debit and the credit totals of a trial balance are $20,640 and $20,236 respectively, the difference of $404 may indicate that a credit posting of that amount was omitted or that a credit of $202 was erroneously posted as a debit.

Two other common types of errors are known as **transpositions** and **slides.** A transposition is the erroneous rearrangement of digits, such as writing $542 as $452 or $524. In a slide, the entire number is erroneously moved one or more spaces to the right or the left, such as writing $542.00 as $54.20 or $5,420.00. If an error of either type has occurred and there are no other errors, the discrepancy between the two trial balance totals will be evenly divisible by 9.

A preliminary examination along the lines suggested by the preceding paragraphs will frequently disclose the error. If it does not, the general procedure is to retrace the various steps in the accounting process, beginning with the last step and working back to the original entries in the journal. While there are no rigid rules for discovering errors, the errors that have caused the trial balance totals to be unequal will ordinarily be discovered before all of the procedures outlined in the following suggested plan have been completed:

1. Verify the accuracy of the trial balance totals by re-adding the columns.
2. Compare the listings in the trial balance with the balances shown in the ledger, making certain that no accounts have been omitted.
3. Recompute the balance of each account in the ledger.
4. Trace the postings in the ledger back to the journal, placing a small check mark by the item in the ledger and also in the journal. If the error is not found, examine each account to see if there is an entry without a check mark. Do the same with the entries in the journal.
5. Verify the equality of the debits and the credits in the journal.

It is readily apparent that care should be exercised both in recording transactions in the journal and in posting to the accounts. The desirability of accuracy in determining account balances and reporting them on the trial balance is equally obvious.

Chapter Review

KEY POINTS

1. Purchasing and Selling Procedures.
Merchandising enterprises acquire merchandise for resale to customers. It is the selling of merchandise, instead of a service, that makes the activities of merchandising enterprises differ from the activities of service enterprises.

2. Accounting for Purchases.
Purchases of merchandise, which may be made for cash or on account, are usually identified in the ledger as Purchases. For purchases of merchandise on account, the credit terms may allow cash discounts for early payment. Such discounts are recorded by the buyer as purchases discounts and are usually viewed as a deduction from the amount initially recorded as Purchases. Likewise, when merchandise is returned or a price adjustment is granted, the buyer records the adjustment as a purchases return and allowance.

3. Accounting for Sales.
Merchandise sales, which may be for cash or on account, are usually identified in the ledger as Sales. Sales are generally recorded based on the realization principle, i.e., when title to the merchandise passes to the buyer. The seller refers to the discounts taken by the buyer for early payment of an invoice as sales discounts, which are viewed as a reduction in the amount initially recorded as Sales. Merchandise returned or an allowance for reduction in the original price at which the goods were sold is treated as a sales return or allowance. Like sales discounts, sales returns and allowances are treated as a reduction in the initial amount recorded as Sales.

4. Transportation Costs.
The terms of a sale between a buyer and seller will include provisions concerning when ownership of the merchandise passes to the buyer and which party is to bear the cost of delivering merchandise to the buyer. If the ownership passes to the buyer when the seller delivers the merchandise to the shipper, the buyer is to absorb the transportation costs, and the terms are said to be FOB shipping point. If the ownership passes to the buyer when the merchandise is received by the buyer, the seller is to assume the cost of transportation, and the terms are said to be FOB destination.

5. Sales Taxes.
The liability for the sales tax is ordinarily incurred at the time the sale is made and is recorded by the seller as a credit to the sales tax payable account. The offsetting debit will be to Accounts Receivable if the merchandise is purchased on account, or to Cash if the cash is collected at the time of the sale. From the buyer's perspective, the cost of the purchases will include the original list price of the merchandise plus the sales tax.

6. Classification of Accounts.
Accounts in the ledger are customarily listed in the order in which they appear in the financial statements and are classified according to common characteristics. Balance sheet accounts are classified as asset, liability, or owner's equity accounts. Income statement accounts are classified as revenues or expenses. There may also be subgroupings within the major categories.

7. Chart of Accounts.
Accounts in the ledger are numbered so as to permit easy indexing and for use in posting. A listing of the accounts used by a specific enterprise in its ledger is referred to as a chart of accounts.

8. Ledger Accounts.
T accounts are used primarily for illustrative purposes, but are seldom used in practice. A standard account form with four columns, including debit balance and credit balance columns, is widely used in practice.

9. General Journal and Posting.
The general journal is the formalized device used for recording journal entries in chronological order. Periodically, transaction data are transferred from the journal to the accounts in the ledger through a process known as posting.

10. Discovery of Errors.
The existence of errors in the accounts may be determined in various ways: (1) by audit procedures, (2) by chance discovery, or (3) by preparing a trial balance. The trial balance does not provide complete proof of accuracy of the ledger, but only indicates that the debits and credits are equal.

KEY TERMS

invoice 62
cash discount 63
purchases discounts 64
purchases returns and allowances 64
debit memorandum 64
credit memorandum 64
realization principle 65
sales discounts 67
sales returns and allowances 67
FOB shipping point 69
FOB destination 69
current assets 71
plant assets 71
current liabilities 71
long-term liabilities 72
stockholders' equity 72
net worth 72
revenue 72
expenses 72
chart of accounts 73
transpositions 83
slides 83

SELF-EXAMINATION QUESTIONS

(Answers at End of Chapter)

1. Credit terms of 1/10, n/30 mean that:
   A. the credit period is 30 days
   B. 1% of the amount of the invoice can be deducted if payment is made within 10 days
   C. the 1% referred to in B is a cash discount
   D. all of the above

2. If merchandise purchased on account is returned, the buyer may inform the seller of the details by issuing:
   A. a debit memorandum
   B. a credit memorandum
   C. an invoice
   D. a bill

3. If merchandise is sold on account to a customer for $1,000, terms FOB shipping point, 1/10, n/30, and the seller prepays $50 in transportation costs, the amount of the discount for early payment would be:
   A. $0
   B. $5.00
   C. $10.00
   D. $10.50

4. Merchandise is sold on account to a customer for $1,000, terms FOB destination, 1/10, n/30. If the seller pays $50 in transportation costs and the customer returns $100 of the merchandise prior to payment, what is the amount of the discount for early payment?
   A. $0
   B. $9.00
   C. $10.00
   D. $10.50

5. If merchandise is purchased FOB shipping point:
   A. ownership (title) passes to the buyer when the merchandise is delivered to the shipper
   B. ownership (title) passes to the buyer when the merchandise is delivered to the buyer
   C. transportation costs are borne by the seller
   D. none of the above

ILLUSTRATIVE PROBLEM

MacBride Discount Stores Inc. entered into the following selected transactions during August of the current year:

Aug. 1. Purchased merchandise on account, terms 2/10, n/30, FOB shipping point, $28,500.
1. Paid rent for August, $4,500.
2. Paid transportation charges on purchase of August 1, $1,180.
5. Purchased office supplies for cash, $600.
7. Sold merchandise on account, terms 1/10, n/30, FOB destination, $12,400.
8. Paid transportation charges on sale of August 7, $550.
11. Paid for merchandise purchased on August 1, less discount.
12. Received merchandise returned from sale of August 7, $3,200.
14. Purchased merchandise on account, terms 4/15, n/30, FOB destination, $18,300.
15. Paid transportation charges on purchase of August 14, $750.
16. Returned merchandise purchased on August 14, $5,200.
17. Received cash on account from sale of August 7, less return and discount.
18. Sold merchandise on account, terms 1/10, n/30, FOB shipping point, $8,800. Prepaid transportation costs as an accommodation to the customer, $250.
26. Sold merchandise on bank credit cards, $3,700.

Aug. 29. Paid for merchandise purchased on August 14, less prepaid transportation charges, return, and discount.
31. Received cash on account from sale of August 18, $9,050.

Instructions:

Record the August transactions in a journal.

SOLUTION

Aug. 1	Purchases	28,500	
	Accounts Payable		28,500
1	Rent Expense	4,500	
	Cash		4,500
2	Transportation In	1,180	
	Cash		1,180
5	Office Supplies	600	
	Cash		600
7	Accounts Receivable	12,400	
	Sales		12,400
8	Transportation Out	550	
	Cash		550
11	Accounts Payable	28,500	
	Purchases Discounts		570
	Cash		27,930
12	Sales Returns and Allowances	3,200	
	Accounts Receivable		3,200
14	Purchases	18,300	
	Accounts Payable		18,300
15	Accounts Payable	750	
	Cash		750
16	Accounts Payable	5,200	
	Purchases Returns and Allowances		5,200
17	Cash	9,108	
	Sales Discounts	92	
	Accounts Receivable		9,200
18	Accounts Receivable	8,800	
	Sales		8,800
18	Accounts Receivable	250	
	Cash		250
26	Cash	3,700	
	Sales		3,700
29	Accounts Payable	12,350	
	Purchases Discounts		524
	Cash		11,826
31	Cash	9,050	
	Accounts Receivable		9,050

Discussion Questions

2–1. Rearrange the following in proper sequence: (a) entry recorded in journal, (b) business document prepared, (c) entry posted to ledger, (d) business transaction occurs.

2–2. What distinguishes a merchandising enterprise from a service enterprise?

2–3. The credit period during which the buyer of merchandise is allowed to pay usually begins with what date?

2–4. Nash Inc. ordered $3,000 of merchandise on account on October 2, terms 2/10, n/30. Although the supplier shipped the merchandise on October 3, the merchandise was not received by Nash Inc. until October 6. The invoice received with the merchandise by Nash Inc. was dated October 3. What is the last date Nash Inc. could pay the invoice and still receive the discount?

2–5. What is the meaning of (a) 2/10, n/30; (b) n/60; (c) n/eom?

2–6. What is the term applied to discounts for early payment by (a) the buyer; (b) the seller?

2–7. Thomas Company purchased merchandise on account from a supplier for $4,000, terms 1/10, n/30. Thomas Company returned $500 of the merchandise and received full credit. (a) If Thomas Company pays the invoice within the discount period, what is the amount of cash required for the payment? (b) What accounts are credited to record the return and the cash discount?

2–8. The debits and credits from four related transactions are presented in the following T accounts. (a) Describe each transaction. (b) What is the rate of the discount and on what amount was it computed?

Cash

		(2)	250
		(4)	6,664

Transportation In

(2)	250		

Accounts Payable

(3)	400	(1)	7,200
(4)	6,800		

Purchases Discounts

		(4)	136

Purchases

(1)	7,200		

Purchases Returns and Allowances

		(3)	400

2–9. How does the accounting for sales to customers using bank credit cards, such as MasterCard and VISA, differ from accounting for sales to customers using nonbank credit cards, such as American Express?

2–10. After the amount due on a sale of $2,000, terms 2/10, n/eom, is received from a customer within the discount period, the seller consents to the return of the entire shipment. (a) What is the amount of the refund owed to the customer? (b) What accounts should be debited and credited by the seller to record the return and the refund?

2–11. Who bears the transportation costs when the terms of sale are (a) FOB shipping point, (b) FOB destination?

2–12. Merchandise is sold on account to a customer for $8,000, terms FOB shipping point, 2/10, n/30, the seller paying the transportation costs of $300. Determine the following: (a) amount of the sale, (b) amount debited to Accounts Receivable, (c) amount of the discount for early payment, (d) amount of the remittance due within the discount period.

2–13. A retailer is considering the purchase of 10 units of a specific commodity from either of two suppliers. Their offers are as follows:
A: $200 a unit, total of $2,000, 2/10, n/30, plus transportation costs of $250.
B: $220 a unit, total of $2,200, 1/10, n/30, no charge for transportation.
Which of the two offers, A or B, yields the lower price?

2–14. A sale of merchandise on account for $400 is subject to a 6% sales tax. (a) Should the sales tax be recorded at the time of sale or when payment is received? (b) What is the amount of the sale? (c) What is the amount debited to Accounts Receivable? (d) What is the title of the account to which the $24 is credited?

2–15. Describe the nature of the assets that compose the following categories: (a) current assets, (b) plant assets.

2–16. As of the time a balance sheet is being prepared, a business enterprise owes a mortgage note payable of $80,000, the terms of which provide for monthly payments of $2,000. How should the liability be classified on the balance sheet?

2–17. Identify each of the following as (a) a current asset or (b) a plant asset: (1) land, (2) cash, (3) building, (4) accounts receivable, (5) supplies.

2–18. Describe in general terms the sequence of accounts in the ledger.

2–19. When a trial balance is prepared, an account balance of $36,750 is listed as $3,675, and an account balance of $54,000 is listed as $45,000. Identify the transposition and the slide.

2–20. When a purchase of supplies of $750 for cash was recorded, both the debit and the credit were journalized and posted as $570. (a) Would this error cause the trial balance to be out of balance? (b) Would the answer be the same if the $750 entry had been journalized correctly, the debit to Supplies had been posted correctly, but the credit to Cash had been posted as $570?

2–21. Indicate which of the following errors, each considered individually, would cause the trial balance totals to be unequal:
(a) A fee of $3,500 earned and due from a client was not debited to Accounts Receivable or credited to a revenue account, because the cash had not been received.
(b) A payment of $45,000 for equipment purchased was posted as a debit of $54,000 to Equipment and a credit of $45,000 to Cash.
(c) A payment of $625 to a creditor was posted as a credit of $625 to Accounts Payable and a credit of $625 to Cash.
(d) A receipt of $550 from an account receivable was journalized and posted as a debit of $550 to Cash and a credit of $550 to Sales.

2–22. Real World Focus. The current asset and current liability data adapted from a recent Hershey Food Corporation balance sheet are as follows:

Current Assets (in thousands):	
Cash and short-term investments	$110,636
Accounts receivable	76,617
Inventories	192,678
Other current assets	32,359
Total current assets	$412,290

Current Liabilities (in thousands):	
Accounts payable	$ 87,799
Payroll and other compensation costs	37,275
Advertising and promotional expenses	19,828
Income taxes	9,253
Short-term debt and current portion of long-term debt	9,623
Other	31,544
Total current liabilities	$195,322

(a) Based upon the preceding data, determine (1) the difference between the total current assets and the total current liabilities, and (2) the ratio of the total current assets to the total current liabilities. (b) Based upon the solution in (a), is it likely that Hershey Food Corporation will be able to pay its current liabilities as they become due?

Exercises

2–23. Purchase-related transactions. Sutton Co. purchases $4,000 of merchandise from a supplier on account, terms FOB shipping point, 1/10, n/30. The supplier adds transportation charges of $150 to the invoice. Sutton Co. returns some of the merchandise, receiving a credit memorandum for $500, and then pays the amount due within the discount period. Present Sutton Co.'s entries to record (a) the purchase, (b) the merchandise return, and (c) the payment.

2–24. Determination of amounts to be paid on invoices. Determine the amount to be paid in full settlement of each of the following invoices, assuming that credit for returns and allowances was received prior to payment and that all invoices were paid within the discount period.

	Purchase Invoice			Returns and
	Merchandise	Transportation	Terms	Allowances
(a)	$5,000	—	FOB destination, n/30	$1,000
(b)	4,000	—	FOB destination, 2/10, n/30	—
(c)	7,500	—	FOB shipping point, 1/10, n/30	500
(d)	3,200	$ 80	FOB shipping point, 1/10, n/30	100
(e)	6,000	240	FOB shipping point, 2/10, n/30	800

2–25. Sales-related transactions, including the use of credit cards. Present entries for the following transactions of Hodges Inc.:

(a) Sold merchandise for cash, $5,200.
(b) Sold merchandise on account, $6,800.
(c) Sold merchandise to customers who used MasterCard and VISA, $2,600.
(d) Sold merchandise to customers who used American Express, $1,300.
(e) Paid an invoice from First National Bank for $130, representing a service fee for processing of MasterCard and VISA sales.
(f) Received $1,235 from American Express Company after a $65 collection fee had been deducted.

2–26. Sales-related transactions. Present entries for the following related transactions.

Feb. 4. Sold merchandise to a customer for $12,000, terms FOB shipping point, 2/10, n/30.
4. Paid the transportation charges of $310, debiting the amount to Accounts Receivable.
8. Issued a credit memorandum for $1,500 to the customer for merchandise returned.
14. Received a check for the amount due from the sale.

2–27. Sales-related transactions. Lowe Corp. sells merchandise to Howard Co. on account for $6,800, FOB shipping point, 1/10, n/30. Lowe Corp. pays the transportation charges of $400 as an accommodation and adds it to the invoice. Lowe Corp. issues a credit memorandum for $800 for merchandise returned and subsequently receives the amount due within the discount period. Present Lowe Corp.'s entries to record (a) the sale and the transportation costs, (b) the credit memorandum, and (c) the receipt of the check for the amount due.

2–28. Purchase-related transactions. Based upon the data presented in 2–27, present Howard Co.'s entries to record (a) the purchase, including the transportation charges, (b) the return of the merchandise for credit, and (c) the payment of the invoice within the discount period.

2–29. Purchase-related transactions. Present entries for the following related transactions of Thompson Inc.:

(a) Purchased $3,000 of merchandise from Delano Co. on account, terms 2/10, n/30.
(b) Paid the amount owed on the invoice within the discount period.
(c) Discovered that some of the merchandise was defective and returned items with an invoice price of $1,000, receiving credit.
(d) Purchased an additional $800 of fabrics from Delano Co. on account, terms 2/10, n/30.
(e) Received a check for the balance owed from the return in (c), after deducting for the purchase in (d).

2–30. Sales tax-related transactions. Present entries to record the following related transactions of Sanders Co.:

(a) Purchased merchandise on account, $3,200, terms 2/10, n/30. The merchandise was subject to a sales tax of 6%.
(b) Sold $2,000 of merchandise on account, subject to a sales tax of 6%.
(c) Paid the amount owed in (a) within the discount period.
(d) Paid $1,200 to the state revenue department for sales taxes collected.

2–31. Chart of accounts. Alexis Services Co. is a newly organized enterprise. The list of accounts to be opened in the general ledger is as follows:

Retained Earnings	Accounts Receivable
Miscellaneous Expense	Equipment
Sales	Salary Expense
Accumulated Depreciation	Cash
Capital Stock	Accounts Payable
Supplies	Supplies Expense
Prepaid Rent	Salaries Payable
Rent Expense	Depreciation Expense

List the accounts in the order in which they should appear in the ledger of Alexis Services Co. and assign account numbers. Each account number is to have two digits: the first digit is to indicate the major classification ("1" for assets, etc.), and the second digit is to identify the specific account within each major classification ("11" for Cash, etc.).

2–32. Effect of errors on trial balance. The following errors occurred in posting from a journal:

(1) A debit of $2,500 to Equipment was posted twice.
(2) A debit of $200 to Cash was posted as $20.
(3) A debit of $810 to Supplies was posted as $180.
(4) A credit of $225 to Accounts Receivable was not posted.
(5) A debit of $1,000 to Cash was posted to Sales.
(6) A credit of $420 to Accounts Payable was posted as a debit.
(7) An entry debiting Rent Expense and crediting Cash for $750 was not posted.

Considering each case individually (i.e., assuming that no other errors had occurred), indicate: (a) by "yes" or "no" whether the trial balance would be out of balance; (b) if answer to (a) is "yes", the amount by which the trial balance totals would differ; and (c) the column of the trial balance that would have the larger total. Answers should be presented in the following form (error (1) is given as an example):

Error	(a) Out of Balance	(b) Difference	(c) Larger Total
(1)	yes	$2,500	debit

Problems

2–33. Purchase-related and sales-related transactions. The following selected transactions were completed during June between Hogan Company and Sneed Inc.:

June 3. Hogan Company sold merchandise on account to Sneed Inc., $12,500, terms FOB shipping point, 2/10, n/30. Hogan Company prepaid transportation costs of $600 which were added to the invoice.
8. Hogan Company sold merchandise on account to Sneed Inc., $16,000, terms FOB destination, 1/15, n/eom.
8. Hogan Company paid transportation costs of $800 for delivery of merchandise sold to Sneed Inc. on June 8.
11. Sneed Inc. returned merchandise purchased on account on June 8 from Hogan Company, $4,000.
13. Sneed Inc. paid Hogan Company for purchases of June 3, less discount.
23. Sneed Inc. paid Hogan Company for purchases of June 8, less discount and less return of June 11.
24. Hogan Company sold merchandise on account to Sneed Inc., $8,000, terms FOB destination, n/eom.
27. Sneed Inc. paid transportation charges of $300 on June 24 purchase from Hogan Company. Hogan Company was not notified of this transaction until June 30.
30. Sneed Inc. paid Hogan Company on account for purchases of June 24, less transportation charges paid.

Instructions: Journalize the June transactions for (1) Hogan Company and (2) Sneed Inc.

2–34. Purchase-related and sales-related transactions. The following were selected from among the transactions completed by Kline Company during May of the current year:

May 3. Purchased merchandise on account from Floyd Inc., $4,000, terms FOB shipping point, 2/10, n/30, with prepaid transportation costs of $120 added to the invoice.

May 5. Purchased merchandise on account from Kramer Co., $8,500, terms FOB destination, 1/10, n/30.
6. Sold merchandise on account to C.F. Howell Co., $2,800, terms 2/10, n/30.
8. Purchased office supplies for cash, $650.
10. Returned merchandise purchased on May 5 from Kramer Co., $1,300.
13. Paid Floyd Inc. on account for purchases of May 3, less discount.
14. Purchased merchandise for cash, $10,500.
15. Paid Kramer Co. on account for purchases of May 5, less return of May 10 and discount.
16. Received cash on account from sale of May 6 to C.F. Howell Co., less discount.
19. Sold merchandise on nonbank credit cards and reported accounts to the card company, $2,450.
22. Sold merchandise on account to Comer Co., $3,480, terms 2/10, n/30.
24. Sold merchandise for cash, $4,350.
25. Received merchandise returned by Comer Co. from sale of May 22, $1,480.
31. Received cash from card company for nonbank credit card sales of May 19, less $140 service fee.

Instructions: Journalize the transactions.

2–35. Purchase-related and sales-related transactions; ledger accounts. The account balances at July 1 of the current year of Haynes Company are as follows:

11 Cash	$ 15,540
12 Accounts Receivable	31,800
13 Merchandise Inventory	82,600
14 Prepaid Insurance	2,500
15 Store Supplies	1,700
21 Accounts Payable	28,300
31 Capital Stock	75,000
32 Retained Earnings	30,840
33 Dividends	—
41 Sales	—
42 Sales Returns and Allowances	—
43 Sales Discounts	—
51 Purchases	—
52 Purchases Returns and Allowances	—
53 Purchases Discounts	—
54 Transportation In	—
55 Sales Salaries Expense	—
56 Advertising Expense	—
57 Store Supplies Expense	—
58 Miscellaneous Selling Expense	—
59 Office Salaries Expense	—
60 Rent Expense	—
61 Insurance Expense	—
62 Miscellaneous General Expense	—

The following transactions were completed during July of the current year:

July 1. Paid rent for month, $2,500.
3. Purchased merchandise on account, $11,200.
5. Purchased merchandise on account, FOB shipping point, $18,600.
8. Sold merchandise on account, $12,300.
9. Paid transportation charges on the purchase of July 5, $450.

July 10. Received $14,750 cash from customers on account, after discounts of $250 were deducted.
11. Paid creditors $16,700 on account, after discounts of $280 had been deducted.
14. Sold merchandise for cash, $9,500.
15. Received merchandise returned on account, $800.
16. Paid sales salaries of $3,400 and office salaries of $1,100.
17. Paid creditors $12,750 on account, after discounts of $200 had been deducted.
18. Received $9,500 cash from customers on account, after discounts of $120 had been deducted.
21. Purchased merchandise on account, $15,200.
22. Paid advertising expense, $3,000.
23. Sold merchandise for cash, $8,100.
24. Returned merchandise purchased on account, $6,800.
25. Sold merchandise for cash, $4,600.
28. Sold merchandise on account, $27,300.
28. Refunded $350 cash on sales made for cash.
29. Paid sales salaries of $2,800 and office salaries of $1,100.
30. Paid creditors $10,900 on account, no discount.
31. Received $12,500 cash from customers on account, no discount.

Instructions: (1) Open a ledger of standard accounts for the accounts listed. Record the balances in the appropriate balance column as of July 1, write "Balance" in the item section, and place a check mark (√) in the posting reference column.
(2) Record the transactions for July in a journal.
(3) Post to the ledger, extending the month-end balances to the appropriate balance columns after all posting is completed.
(4) Prepare a trial balance of the ledger as of July 31.

2–36. Journal entries and trial balance for service corporation. T. A. Thomas Inc. was recently organized to offer management consulting services. The account balances at the end of July of the current year are as follows:

Account	Debit	Credit
11 Cash	46,240	
12 Accounts Receivable	23,600	
13 Prepaid Insurance	240	
14 Office Supplies	830	
16 Land	0	
21 Accounts Payable		4,250
22 Notes Payable		0
31 Capital Stock		20,000
32 Retained Earnings		19,606
33 Dividends	2,000	
41 Fees Earned		305,600
51 Salary and Commission Expense	244,480	
52 Rent Expense	12,000	
53 Advertising Expense	10,300	
54 Automobile Expense	8,450	
59 Miscellaneous Expense	1,316	
	349,456	349,456

The following business transactions were completed during August of the current year.

Aug. 2. Paid rent on office for month, $1,000.
3. Purchased office supplies on account, $250.
5. Received cash from clients on account, $16,280.

Aug. 7. Paid insurance premiums, $1,400.
12. Paid salaries and commissions, $12,870.
14. Purchased land for a future building site for $20,500, paying $5,500 in cash and giving a note payable for the remainder.
15. Recorded revenue earned and billed to clients during first half of month, $14,160.
18. Paid creditors on account, $2,420.
20. Returned a portion of the supplies purchased on August 3, receiving full credit for their cost, $80.
23. Received cash from clients on account, $10,190.
24. Paid advertising expense, $820.
27. Discovered an error in computing a salary; received cash from the employee for the overpayment, $350.
28. Paid automobile expenses (including rental charges), $630.
30. Paid miscellaneous expenses, $216.
31. Recorded revenue earned and billed to clients during second half of month, $16,300.
31. Paid salaries and commissions, $19,840.
31. Paid dividend, $2,000.

Instructions: (1) Open a ledger of standard accounts for the accounts listed. Record the balances in the appropriate balance columns as of August 1, write "Balance" in the item section, and place a check mark (√) in the posting reference column.
(2) Record the transactions for August in a journal.
(3) Post to the ledger, extending the month-end balances to the appropriate balance columns after all posting is completed.
(4) Prepare a trial balance of the ledger as of August 31.

(If the working papers correlating with the textbook are not used, omit Problem 2–37.)

2–37. Errors in trial balance. The following records of Hutton TV Repair are presented in the working papers:

Journal containing entries for the period March 1–31.
Ledger to which the March entries have been posted.
Preliminary trial balance as of March 31, which does not balance.

Locate the errors, supply the information requested, and prepare a corrected trial balance, proceeding in accordance with the following detailed instructions. The balances recorded in the accounts as of March 1 and the entries in the journal are correctly stated. If it is necessary to correct any posted amounts in the ledger, a line should be drawn through the erroneous figure and the correct amount inserted above. Corrections or notations may be inserted on the preliminary trial balance in any manner desired. It is not necessary to complete all of the instructions if equal trial balance totals can be obtained earlier. However, the requirements of instructions (6) and (7) should be completed in any event.

Instructions: (1) Verify the totals of the preliminary trial balance, inserting the correct amounts in the schedule provided in the working papers.
(2) Compute the difference between the trial balance totals.
(3) Compare the listings in the trial balance with the balances appearing in the ledger and list the errors found in the space provided in the working papers.
(4) Verify the accuracy of the balance of each account in the ledger and list the errors found in the space provided in the working papers.
(5) Trace the postings in the ledger back to the journal, using small check marks to identify items traced. Correct any amounts in the ledger that may be necessitated by errors in posting, and list the errors in the space provided in the working papers.
(6) Journalize as of March 31 the payment of $160 for gas and electricity. The bill had been paid on March 31 but was inadvertently omitted from the journal. Post to the ledger. (Revise any amounts necessitated by posting this entry.)
(7) Prepare a new trial balance.

2–38. Corrected trial balance. Martino Photography Inc. prepared the following trial balance as of October 31 of the current year:

Cash	4,735	
Accounts Receivable	9,925	
Supplies	1,277	
Prepaid Insurance	330	
Equipment	12,500	
Notes Payable		5,000
Accounts Payable		3,025
Capital Stock		7,500
Retained Earnings		4,990
Dividends	6,750	
Sales		80,750
Wages Expense	48,150	
Rent Expense	750	
Advertising Expense	5,250	
Gas, Electricity, and Water Expense	3,150	
	92,817	101,265

The debit and credit totals are not equal as a result of the following errors:

(a) The balance of cash was understated by $1,000.
(b) A cash payment of $450 was posted as a credit to Cash of $540.
(c) A debit of $175 to Accounts Receivable was not posted.
(d) A return of $252 of defective supplies was erroneously posted as a $225 credit to Supplies.
(e) An insurance policy acquired at a cost of $310 was posted as a credit to Prepaid Insurance.
(f) The balance of Notes Payable was understated by $2,500.
(g) A credit of $75 in Accounts Payable was overlooked when the balance of the account was determined.
(h) A debit of $750 for a dividend was posted as a credit to Retained Earnings.
(i) The balance of $7,500 in Rent Expense was entered as $750 in the trial balance.
(j) Miscellaneous Expense, with a balance of $915, was omitted from the trial balance.

Instructions: Prepare a corrected trial balance as of October 31 of the current year.

ALTERNATE PROBLEMS

2–33A. Purchase-related and sales-related transactions. The following selected transactions were completed during October between Early Company and Flynn Inc.:

Oct. 4. Early Company sold merchandise on account to Flynn Inc., $10,000, terms FOB destination, 1/15, n/eom.
4. Early Company paid transportation costs of $600 for delivery of merchandise sold to Flynn Inc. on October 4.
10. Early Company sold merchandise on account to Flynn Inc., $15,000, terms FOB destination, n/eom.
12. Flynn Inc. returned merchandise purchased on account on October 4 from Early Company, $2,000.
14. Flynn Inc. paid transportation charges of $1,200 on October 10 purchase from Early Company.

Oct. 18. Early Company sold merchandise on account to Flynn Inc., $18,000, terms FOB shipping point, 2/10, n/30. Early Company prepaid transportation costs of $1,500 which were added to the invoice.
19. Flynn Inc. paid Early Company on account for purchases of October 4, less discount and less return of October 12.
28. Flynn Inc. paid Early Company on account for purchases of October 18, less discount.
31. Flynn Inc. paid Early Company on account for purchases of October 10, less transportation charges paid.

Instructions: Journalize the October transactions for (1) Early Company and (2) Flynn Inc.

2–34A. Purchase-related and sales-related transactions. The following were selected from among the transactions completed by Brooks Co. during November of the current year:

Nov. 3. Purchased office supplies for cash, $720.
5. Purchased merchandise on account from Butler Co., $12,500, terms FOB destination, 1/10, n/30.
6. Sold merchandise for cash, $2,950.
7. Purchased merchandise on account from Mattox Co., $6,400, terms FOB shipping point, 2/10, n/30, with prepaid transportation costs of $190 added to the invoice.
7. Returned merchandise purchased on November 5 from Butler Co., $2,500.
11. Sold merchandise on account to Bowles Co., $1,800, terms 1/10, n/30.
15. Paid Butler Co. on account for purchases of November 5, less return of November 7 and discount.
16. Sold merchandise on nonbank credit cards and reported accounts to the card company, $3,850.
17. Paid Mattox Co. on account for purchases of November 7, less discount.
19. Purchased merchandise for cash, $3,500.
21. Received cash on account from sale of November 11 to Bowles Co., less discount.
24. Sold merchandise on account to Clemons Inc., $4,200, terms 1/10, n/30.
28. Received cash from card company for nonbank credit card sales of November 16, less $190 service fee.
30. Received merchandise returned by Clemons Inc. from sale of November 24, $2,700.

Instructions: Journalize the transactions.

If the working papers correlating with the textbook are not used, omit Problem 2–37A.

2–37A. Errors in trial balance. The following records of Hutton TV Repair are presented in the working papers:

Journal containing entries for the period March 1–31.
Ledger to which the March entries have been posted.
Preliminary trial balance as of March 31, which does not balance.

Locate the errors, supply the information requested, and prepare a corrected trial balance, proceeding in accordance with the following detailed instructions. The balances recorded in the accounts as of March 1 and the entries in the journal are correctly stated. If it is necessary to correct any posted amounts in the ledger, a line should be drawn through the erroneous figure and the correct amount inserted above. Corrections or notations may be inserted on the preliminary trial balance in any manner desired. It is not necessary to complete all of the instructions if equal trial balance totals can be obtained earlier. However, the requirements of instructions (6) and (7) should be completed in any event.

Instructions: (1) Verify the totals of the preliminary trial balance, inserting the correct amounts in the schedule provided in the working papers.

(2) Compute the difference between the trial balance totals.

(3) Compare the listings in the trial balance with the balances appearing in the ledger and list the errors found in the space provided in the working papers.

(4) Verify the accuracy of the balance of each account in the ledger and list the errors found in the space provided in the working papers.

(5) Trace the postings in the ledger back to the journal, using small check marks to identify items traced. Correct any amounts in the ledger that may be necessitated by errors in posting and list the errors in the space provided in the working papers.

(6) Journalize as of March 31 the payment of $125 for advertising expense. The bill had been paid on March 31 but was inadvertently omitted from the journal. Post to the ledger. (Revise any amounts necessitated by posting this entry.)

(7) Prepare a new trial balance.

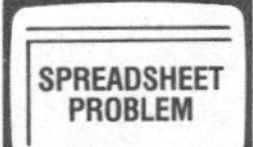

2–38A. Corrected trial balance. Collins Carpet Company has the following trial balance as of August 31 of the current year:

Account	Debit	Credit
Cash	4,400	
Accounts Receivable	6,400	
Supplies	1,010	
Prepaid Insurance	150	
Equipment	15,500	
Notes Payable		15,000
Accounts Payable		4,620
Capital Stock		10,000
Retained Earnings		5,300
Dividends	7,000	
Sales		49,980
Wages Expense	28,500	
Rent Expense	6,400	
Advertising Expense	320	
Gas, Electricity, and Water Expense	3,150	
	72,830	84,900

The debit and credit totals are not equal as a result of the following errors:

(a) The balance of cash was overstated by $500.
(b) A cash receipt of $240 was posted as a debit to Cash of $420.
(c) A debit of $1,000 for a dividend was posted as a credit to Retained Earnings.
(d) The balance of $3,200 in Advertising Expense was entered as $320 in the trial balance.
(e) A debit of $725 to Accounts Receivable was not posted.
(f) A return of $125 of defective supplies was erroneously posted as a $215 credit to Supplies.
(g) The balance of Notes Payable was overstated by $5,000.
(h) An insurance policy acquired at a cost of $200 was posted as a credit to Prepaid Insurance.
(i) Miscellaneous Expense, with a balance of $945, was omitted from the trial balance.
(j) A debit of $710 in Accounts Payable was overlooked when determining the balance of the account.

Instructions: Prepare a corrected trial balance as of August 31 of the current year.

Mini-Case 2

GIBBONS
DISCOUNT INC.

For the past twenty years, your father has managed and operated Gibbons Discount Inc., a regional chain of retail stores. You have recently accepted a position with Gibbons Discount Inc. as a special assistant to the president. As a first assignment, you are to review the purchasing and disbursing policies of the enterprise.

For your analysis, the controller has gathered the following data covering the past three years:

	19X3	19X2	19X1
Purchases..........	$20,400,000	$18,200,000	$16,300,000
Purchases returns and allowances ...	204,000	136,500	81,500
Transportation in	591,600	564,200	489,000

After reviewing these data, you ask the controller why no purchases discounts are shown for the three-year period. The controller responded as follows:

> Your father won't let us take purchases discounts. It doesn't make sense to me. The industry standard is 2/10, n/30. Your father always has believed in paying the bills on the final due date and not a day before. I've tried to convince him that we should take the discounts, but he won't budge.

The controller also indicated that the company has recently entered into a store expansion program that will likely create a cash shortage. Because of this situation, the company has negotiated a $500,000 line of credit with its bank at an interest rate of 11%.

Instructions:

(1) Prepare an analysis indicating the net savings that the company could have earned from taking all discounts for the past three years. Assume that discounts are available on all purchases. In addition, assume that the company had sufficient cash to pay all invoices without borrowing and that the average rates at which the excess cash could have been invested in each of the past three years were as follows:

19X3...............................	11%
19X2...............................	12%
19X1...............................	14%

(Hint: You should take into consideration the interest income the company would have forgone by paying the invoices within the discount period.)

(continued)

(2) Assume that you are able to convince your father to use the new line of credit to pay all invoices within the discount period during 19X4. The net purchases for 19X4 are projected to increase 15% over the net purchases for 19X3. Compute the expected net savings for 19X4 by taking all the available purchases discounts.

(3) Based upon the purchase data for 19X3, 19X2, and 19X1, what other questions might you raise concerning the company's purchasing and disbursing policies?

Answers to Self-Examination Questions

1. D Credit terms of 1/10, n/30 mean that the credit period is 30 days (answer A), the cash discount is 1% (answer C), and the cash discount can be deducted from the invoice amount if payment is made within 10 days of the invoice date (answer B).
2. A A debit memorandum (answer A), issued by the buyer, indicates the amount the buyer proposes to debit to the accounts payable account. A credit memorandum (answer B), issued by the seller, indicates the amount the seller proposes to credit to the accounts receivable account. An invoice (answer C) or a bill (answer D), issued by the seller, indicates the amount and terms of the sale.
3. C The amount of discount for early payment is $10 (answer C), or 1% of $1,000. Although the $50 of transportation costs paid by the seller are debited to the customer's account, the customer is not entitled to a discount on that amount.
4. B The customer is entitled to a discount of $9 (answer B) for early payment. This amount is 1% of $900, which is the sales price of $1,000 less the return of $100. The $50 of transportation costs is an expense of the seller.
5. A Ownership (title) to merchandise shipped FOB shipping point passes to the buyer when the merchandise is delivered to the shipper (answer A). When merchandise is shipped FOB destination, title passes to the buyer when the merchandise is delivered to the buyer (answer B). If merchandise is shipped FOB destination, the transportation costs are borne by the seller (answer C).

3
The Matching Concept and the Adjusting Process

CHAPTER OBJECTIVES

Describe what is meant by a fiscal year and a natural business year.

Discuss the matching concept as it relates to the cash basis and the accrual basis of accounting.

Describe and illustrate the need for adjusting the accounting records to comply with the matching concept.

Describe the nature of the adjusting process.

Describe and illustrate the preparation of adjusting entries related to:
plant assets
prepaid expenses
unearned revenues
accrued assets
accrued liabilities

Describe and illustrate the effect on the financial statements of the failure to record adjusting entries.

As was demonstrated in the preceding chapters, transactions are recorded during an accounting period as they occur. At the end of the period, the ledger accounts must be brought up-to-date (adjusted) to assure that revenues and expenses are properly matched (matching concept), so that the financial statements will fairly present the results of operations for the period and the financial condition at the end of the period. In addition to further discussing the matching concept, which was discussed briefly in Chapter 1, this chapter discusses and illustrates the use of the adjusting process to achieve the proper matching of revenues and expenses. In Chapter 4, the preparation of the financial statements will be addressed.

FISCAL YEAR

The maximum length of an accounting period is usually one year, which includes a complete cycle of the seasons and of business activities. Income and property taxes are also based on yearly periods and thus require that annual determinations be made.

The annual accounting period adopted by an enterprise is known as its **fiscal year.** Fiscal years ordinarily begin with the first day of the particular month selected and end on the last day of the twelfth month hence. The period most commonly adopted is the calendar year, although other periods are not unusual, particularly for incorporated businesses.

The 1986 edition of *Accounting Trends & Techniques,* published by the American Institute of Certified Public Accountants, reported the following results of a survey of 600 industrial and merchandising companies concerning the month of their fiscal year end:

Percentage of companies with fiscal years ending in the month of:

January	4%
February	3
March	2
April	1
May	2
June	7
July	3
August	3
September	7
October	4
November	2
December	62

A period ending when a business's activities have reached the lowest point in its annual operating cycle is termed the **natural business year.**

The long-term financial history of a business enterprise may be shown by a succession of balance sheets, prepared every year. The history of operations for the intervening periods is presented in a series of income statements. If the life of a business enterprise is represented by a line moving from left to right, a series of balance sheets and income statements may be diagrammed as follows:

THE LIFE OF A BUSINESS

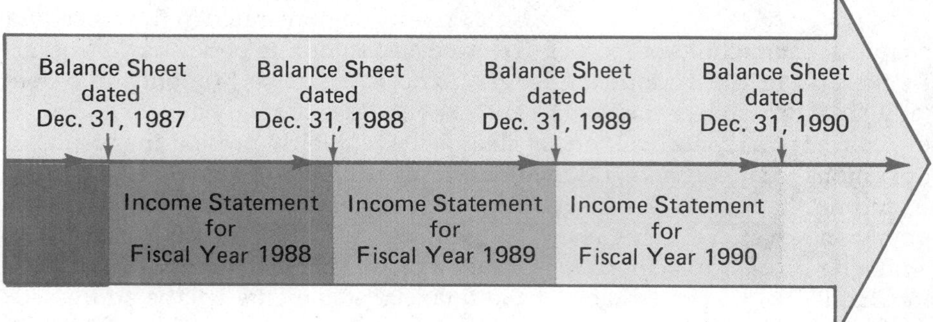

MATCHING CONCEPT

Revenues and expenses may be reported on the income statement by (1) the **cash basis** or (2) the **accrual basis** of accounting. When the cash basis is used, revenues are recognized in the period in which cash is received, and expenses are recognized in the period in which cash is paid. For example, sales would be recorded only when cash is received from customers, and salaries expense would be recorded only when cash is paid to employees. The net income (or net loss) is the difference between the cash receipts (revenues) and the cash disbursements (expenses). Small service enterprises and practicing professionals that have few receivables and payables may use the cash basis. For most businesses, however, the cash basis does not measure revenues and expenses accurately enough to be considered an acceptable method.

Generally accepted accounting principles require the use of the accrual basis of accounting. Therefore, most enterprises use this basis, under which revenues are recognized in the period earned and expenses are recognized in the period incurred in the process of generating revenues, as discussed in Chapter 1. For example, sales would be recognized when the merchandise is sold to customers and not when the cash is received from those customers. Supplies expense would be recognized when the supplies are used and not when the supplies are purchased.

The accrual basis of accounting requires the use of an adjusting process at the end of the accounting period in order to match revenues and expenses for the period properly. The common characteristics of the adjusting process are discussed in the remainder of the chapter.

NATURE OF THE ADJUSTING PROCESS

The entries required at the end of an accounting period to bring the accounts up to date and to assure the proper matching of revenues and expenses are called **adjusting entries.** In a broad sense, they may be called corrections to the ledger. But bringing the ledger up to date at the end of a period is part of the accounting procedure; it is not caused by errors. The term "adjusting entries" is therefore more appropriate than the term "correcting entries."

The following ledger accounts require adjustment: plant assets, prepaid expenses, unearned revenues, accrued assets, and accrued liabilities. The entries that adjust these accounts affect both the balance sheet and the income statement. To illustrate, assume that the effect of the credit portion of a particular adjusting entry is to increase a liability account (balance sheet). It follows that the effect of the debit portion of the entry will be either (1) to increase an expense account (income statement) or (2) to decrease a revenue account (income statement). In no case will an adjustment affect only an asset and a liability (both balance sheet) or only an expense and a revenue (both income statement).

PLANT ASSETS

As time passes, many plant assets, such as buildings, lose their capacity to provide useful services. This decrease in usefulness is a business expense called **depreciation.** The factors involved in computing depreciation are discussed in a later chapter.

The adjusting entry to record depreciation must recognize the expense as well as the decrease in the plant assets. However, for reasons to be described in a later chapter, it is not practical to reduce plant asset accounts by the amount estimated as depreciation. In addition, it is common practice to show on the balance sheet both the original cost of plant assets and the amount of depreciation accumulated since their acquisition. Accordingly, the costs of plant assets are recorded as debits to the appropriate asset accounts, and the decreases in usefulness are recorded as credits to the related **accumulated depreciation accounts.** The latter are called **contra accounts** because they are offset against the plant asset accounts. The unexpired or remaining cost of a plant asset is the debit balance in the plant asset account minus the credit balance in the related accumulated depreciation account.

Typical titles for plant asset accounts and their related contra asset accounts are as follows:

Plant Asset	Contra Asset
Land	*None—land does not usually depreciate*
Buildings	Accumulated Depreciation—Buildings
Equipment	Accumulated Depreciation—Equipment

The ledger could show more detail by having a separate account for each of a number of buildings. Equipment may also be subdivided according to function, such as Delivery Equipment, Store Equipment, and Office Equipment, with a related accumulated depreciation account for each plant asset account.

To illustrate an adjusting entry to record depreciation, assume that a building was purchased on January 2, 1989. If the estimated amount of depreciation for 1989 is $2,250, the adjusting entry to record the $2,250 decrease in the asset and the corresponding increase in the expense is as follows:

Adjusting Entry

Dec. 31	Depreciation Expense—Buildings	2,250	
	Accumulated Depreciation—Buildings..........		2,250

After the entry has been posted, the accounts affected appear as follows:

Adjustment for Depreciation

ACCOUNT BUILDINGS — ACCOUNT NO. 131

Date		Item	Debit	Credit	Balance Debit	Balance Credit
1989 Jan.	2		90,000.00		90,000.00	

ACCOUNT DEPRECIATION EXPENSE—BUILDINGS — ACCOUNT NO. 522

Date		Item	Debit	Credit	Balance Debit	Balance Credit
1989 Dec.	31	Adjusting	2,250.00		2,250.00	

ACCOUNT ACCUMULATED DEPRECIATION—BUILDINGS — ACCOUNT NO. 132

Date		Item	Debit	Credit	Balance Debit	Balance Credit
1989 Dec.	31	Adjusting		2,250.00		2,250.00

The difference between the balance of a plant asset account and its related accumulated depreciation account represents the undepreciated original cost of the asset and is called the **book value** of the asset. This book value, which would generally differ from the asset's current market value, may be presented on the balance sheet in the following manner:

Plant assets:		
Buildings	$90,000	
Less accumulated depreciation	2,250	$87,750

PREPAID EXPENSES

Prepaid expenses are the costs of goods and services that have been purchased but not used at the end of the accounting period. The portion of the asset that has been used during the period has become an expense. Since the remainder will not become an expense until some time in the near future, it will be listed as a current asset on the balance sheet. Prepaid expenses include such items as prepaid insurance, prepaid rent, prepaid advertising, prepaid interest, and various kinds of supplies.

At the time an expense is prepaid, it may be debited either to an asset account or to an expense account. The two alternative systems are explained and illustrated in the paragraphs that follow. In any particular situation, either alternative may be elected. The only difference between the systems is in the procedure used. Their effect on the financial statements is the same.

Prepaid Expenses Recorded Initially as Assets

Insurance premiums or other services or supplies that are used may be debited to asset accounts when purchased, even though all or a part of them is expected to be consumed during the accounting period. The amount actually used is then determined at the end of the period and the accounts adjusted accordingly.

To illustrate, assume that the prepaid insurance account has a balance of $2,034 at the end of the year. This amount represents the total of premiums on policies purchased during the year. Assume further that $906 of insurance premiums has expired during the year. The adjusting entry to record the $906 decrease of the asset and the corresponding increase in expense is as follows:

Adjusting Entry

Dec. 31	Insurance Expense	906	
	Prepaid Insurance		906

After this entry has been posted, the two accounts affected appear as follows:

Adjustment for Prepaid Expense Recorded as Asset

ACCOUNT INSURANCE EXPENSE ACCOUNT NO. 716

Date		Item	Debit	Credit	Balance	
					Debit	Credit
1989 Dec.	31	Adjusting	906		906	

ACCOUNT PREPAID INSURANCE ACCOUNT NO. 118

Date		Item	Debit	Credit	Balance	
					Debit	Credit
1989						
Jan.	1		1,250		1,250	
Mar.	18		225		1,475	
Aug.	26		379		1,854	
Nov.	11		180		2,034	
Dec.	31	Adjusting		906	1,128	

After the $906 of expired insurance is transferred to the expense account, the balance of $1,128 in Prepaid Insurance represents the cost of premiums on various policies that apply to future periods. The $906 expense appears on the income statement for the period and the $1,128 asset appears on the balance sheet as of the end of the period as a current asset.

Prepaid Expenses Recorded Initially as Expenses

Instead of being debited to an asset account, prepaid expenses may be debited to an expense account at the time of the expenditure, even though all or a part of the prepayment is expected to be unused at the end of the accounting period. The amount actually unused is then determined at the end of the period and the accounts are adjusted accordingly.

To illustrate this alternative system, assume that the insurance expense account has a balance of $2,034 at the end of the year. This amount represents the total premiums on policies purchased during the year. Assume further that $1,128 of the insurance premiums applies to future periods. The adjusting entry to record the $1,128 decrease of the expense and the corresponding increase in the asset is as follows:

Adjusting Entry

Dec. 31	Prepaid Insurance	1,128	
	Insurance Expense		1,128

After this entry has been posted, the two accounts affected appear as follows:

Adjustment for Prepaid Expense Recorded as Expense

ACCOUNT PREPAID INSURANCE ACCOUNT NO. 118

Date		Item	Debit	Credit	Balance	
					Debit	Credit
1989						
Dec.	31	Adjusting	1,128		1,128	

ACCOUNT INSURANCE EXPENSE ACCOUNT NO. 716

Date		Item	Debit	Credit	Balance	
					Debit	Credit
1989						
Jan.	1		1,250		1,250	
Mar.	18		225		1,475	
Aug.	26		379		1,854	
Nov.	11		180		2,034	
Dec.	31	Adjusting		1,128	906	

After the $1,128 of unexpired insurance is transferred to the asset account, the balance of $906 in Insurance Expense represents the cost of premiums on various policies that has expired during the year. The $1,128 asset appears on the balance sheet at the end of the period and the $906 expense appears on the income statement for the period.

Comparison of the Two Systems

The basic features of the two systems of recording prepaid expenses, including the adjusting entries at the end of the accounting period, can be summarized as follows, using the data in the preceding illustration:

Prepaid Expense **Recorded Initially as Asset**			Prepaid Expense **Recorded Initially as Expense**		
Initial entries (to record initial expenditures):			Initial entries (to record initial expenditures):		
Prepaid Insurance..........	1,250		Insurance Expense..........	1,250	
Cash		1,250	Cash		1,250
Prepaid Insurance..........	180		Insurance Expense..........	180	
Cash		180	Cash		180
Adjusting entry (to transfer amount **used** to appropriate **expense** account):			Adjusting entry (to transfer amount **unused** to the appropriate **asset** account):		
Insurance Expense..........	906		Prepaid Insurance..........	1,128	
Prepaid Insurance.........		906	Insurance Expense........		1,128

NOTE: Both methods will result in the same account balances.

Systems of Recording Prepaid Expenses

Either of the two systems of recording prepaid expenses may be used for all of the prepaid expenses of an enterprise, or one system may be used for some kinds of prepaid expenses and the other system for other kinds. Initial debits to the asset account seem to be logical for prepayments of insurance, which are usually for periods of from one to three years. On the other hand, interest charges on notes payable are usually for short periods. Some charges may be recorded when a note is issued; other charges may be recorded when a note is paid; and few, if any, of the debits for interest may require adjustment at the end of the period. It therefore seems logical to record all interest charges initially by debiting the expense account rather than the asset account.[1]

As was noted earlier, the amounts reported as expenses in the income statement and as assets on the balance sheet will not be affected by the system used. To avoid confusion, the system adopted by an enterprise for each kind of prepaid expense should be followed consistently from year to year.

UNEARNED REVENUES

READ ↓

Revenue received during a particular period may be only partly earned by the end of the period. Items of revenue that are received in advance represent

[1]Notes payable and related interest charges are discussed in more detail in Chapter 9.

a liability that may be termed **unearned revenue**. The portion of the liability that is discharged during the period through delivery of goods or services has been earned; the remainder will be earned in the future. For example, magazine publishers usually receive advance payment for subscriptions covering periods ranging from a few months to a number of years. At the end of an accounting period, that portion of the receipts which is related to future periods has not been earned and should, therefore, appear in the balance sheet as a liability.

Other examples of unearned revenue are rent received in advance on property owned, premiums received in advance by an insurance company, tuition received in advance by a school, an annual retainer fee received in advance by an attorney, and amounts received in advance by an advertising firm for advertising services to be rendered in the future.

By accepting advance payment for a good or service, a business commits itself to furnish the good or the service at some future time. At the end of the accounting period, if some portion of the good or the service has been furnished, part of the revenue has been earned. The earned portion appears in the income statement. The unearned portion represents a liability of the business to furnish the good or the service in a future period and is reported in the balance sheet as a liability. As in the case of prepaid expenses, two systems of accounting are explained and illustrated.

Unearned Revenues Recorded Initially as Liabilities

When revenue is received in advance, it may be credited to a liability account. To illustrate, assume that on October 1 a business rents a portion of its building for a period of one year, receiving $7,200 in payment for the entire term of the lease. Assume also that the transaction was originally recorded by a debit to Cash and a credit to the liability account Unearned Rent. On December 31, the end of the fiscal year, one fourth of the amount has been earned and three fourths of the amount remains a liability. The entry to record the revenue and reduce the liability appears as follows:

Adjusting Entry

Dec. 31	Unearned Rent	1,800	
	Rent Income		1,800

After this entry has been posted, the unearned rent account and the rent income account appear as follows:

Adjustment for Unearned Revenue Recorded as Liability

ACCOUNT UNEARNED RENT — ACCOUNT NO. 218

Date		Item	Debit	Credit	Balance Debit	Balance Credit
1989						
Oct.	1			7,200		7,200
Dec.	31	Adjusting	1,800			5,400

ACCOUNT RENT INCOME — ACCOUNT NO. 812

Date		Item	Debit	Credit	Balance Debit	Balance Credit
1989						
Dec.	31	Adjusting		1,800		1,800

After the amount earned, $1,800, is transferred to Rent Income, the balance of $5,400 remaining in Unearned Rent is a liability to render a service in the future. It appears as a current liability in the balance sheet because the service is to be rendered within the next accounting period. Rent Income is reported in the income statement.

Unearned Revenues Recorded Initially as Revenues

Instead of being credited to a liability account, unearned revenue may be credited to a revenue account as the cash is received. To illustrate this alternative, assume the same facts as in the preceding illustration, except that the transaction was originally recorded on October 1 by a debit to Cash and a credit to Rent Income. On December 31, the end of the fiscal year, three fourths of the balance in Rent Income is still unearned and the remaining one fourth has been earned. The entry to record the transfer to the liability account appears as follows:

Adjusting Entry

Dec. 31	Rent Income	5,400	
	Unearned Rent		5,400

After this entry has been posted, the unearned rent account and the rent income account appear as follows:

Adjustment for Unearned Revenue Recorded as Revenue

ACCOUNT UNEARNED RENT — ACCOUNT NO. 218

Date		Item	Debit	Credit	Balance Debit	Balance Credit
1989						
Dec.	31	Adjusting		5,400		5,400

ACCOUNT RENT INCOME — ACCOUNT NO. 812

Date		Item	Debit	Credit	Balance Debit	Balance Credit
1989						
Oct.	1			7,200		7,200
Dec.	31	Adjusting	5,400			1,800

The unearned rent of $5,400 is listed in the current liability section of the balance sheet, and the rent income of $1,800 is reported in the income statement.

Comparison of the Two Systems

The basic features of the two systems of recording unearned revenue, including the adjusting entries at the end of the accounting period, can be summarized as follows, using the data in the preceding illustration:

Unearned Revenue Recorded Initially as Liability			Unearned Revenue Recorded Initially as Revenue		
Initial entry (to record initial receipt):			Initial entry (to record initial receipt):		
Cash	7,200		Cash	7,200	
Unearned Rent		7,200	Rent Income		7,200
Adjusting entry (to transfer amount earned to appropriate revenue account):			Adjusting entry (to transfer amount unearned to appropriate liability account):		
Unearned Rent	1,800		Rent Income	5,400	
Rent Income		1,800	Unearned Rent		5,400

NOTE: Both methods will result in the same account balances.

Systems of Recording Unearned Revenue

Either of the systems may be used for all revenues received in advance, or the first system may be used for advance receipts of some kinds of revenue and the second system for other kinds. The results obtained are the same under both systems, but to avoid confusion the system used should be followed consistently from year to year.

ACCRUED ASSETS (ACCRUED REVENUES)

All assets belonging to the business at the end of an accounting period and all revenues earned during the period should be recorded in the ledger. But during a fiscal period it is common to record some types of revenue only as the cash is received; consequently, at the end of the period there may be items of revenue that have not been recorded. The amounts of any such accrued but unrecorded revenues at the end of the fiscal period are both an asset and a revenue. The amount of the accrued revenue must be recorded by debiting an asset account and crediting a revenue account. Because of the dual nature of such accruals, they are called **accrued assets** or **accrued revenues.**

To illustrate the adjusting entry for an accrued asset, assume that on December 31, the end of the fiscal year, the fees earned account has a credit balance of $50,500. Assume further that on the same date unbilled services have been performed for a client for $8,050. The entry to record this increase in the amount due from clients and the additional revenue earned is as follows:

Adjusting Entry

Dec. 31	Fees Receivable	8,050	
	Fees Earned		8,050

After this entry has been posted, the fees receivable account and the fees earned account appear as follows:

Adjustment for Accrued Asset

ACCOUNT FEES RECEIVABLE — ACCOUNT NO. 114

Date		Item	Debit	Credit	Balance Debit	Balance Credit
1989 Dec.	31	Adjusting	8,050		8,050	

ACCOUNT FEES EARNED — ACCOUNT NO. 401

Date		Item	Debit	Credit	Balance Debit	Balance Credit
1989						
Dec.	12			4,750		50,500
	31	Adjusting		8,050		58,550

The accrued fees of $8,050 recorded in Fees Receivable will appear in the balance sheet of December 31 as a current asset. The credit balance of $58,550 in Fees Earned will appear in the income statement for the year ended December 31.

The treatment of accrued fees illustrates the method of handling accrued assets in general. If there are other accrued assets at the end of a fiscal period, separate accounts may be set up. Each of these accounts will be similar to the fees receivable account. When such items are numerous, a single account entitled Accrued Receivables or Accrued Assets may be used. All accrued assets may then be recorded as debits to this account.

ACCRUED LIABILITIES (ACCRUED EXPENSES)

Some expenses accrue from day to day but are usually recorded only when they are paid. Examples are salaries paid to employees and interest paid on notes payable. The amounts of such accrued but unpaid items at the end of the fiscal period are both an expense and a liability. It is for this reason that such accruals are called **accrued liabilities** or **accrued expenses.**

To illustrate the adjusting entry for an accrued liability, assume that on December 31, the end of the fiscal year, the salary expense account has a debit balance of $72,800. During the year, salaries have been paid each Friday for the five-day week then ended. For this particular fiscal year, December 31 falls on Wednesday. The records of the business show that the salary accrued for these last three days of the year amounts to $940. The entry to record the additional expense and the liability is as follows:

Adjusting Entry

Dec. 31	Salaries Expense	940	
	Salaries Payable..............................		940

Adjustment for Accrued Liability

After the adjusting entry has been posted to the two accounts, they appear as follows:

ACCOUNT SALARIES PAYABLE — ACCOUNT NO. 214

Date		Item	Debit	Credit	Balance Debit	Balance Credit
1989						
Dec.	31	Adjusting		940		940

ACCOUNT SALARIES EXPENSE — ACCOUNT NO. 611

Date		Item	Debit	Credit	Balance Debit	Balance Credit
1989						
Dec.	26		1,425		72,800	
	31	Adjusting	940		73,740	

The accrued salaries of $940 recorded in Salaries Payable will appear in the balance sheet of December 31 as a current liability. The balance of $73,740 now recorded in Salaries Expense will appear in the income statement for the year ended December 31.

The discussion of the treatment of accrued salary expense illustrates the method of handling accrued liabilities in general. If, in addition to accrued salaries, there are other accrued liabilities at the end of a fiscal period, separate liability accounts may be set up for each type. When there are many accrued liability items, however, a single account entitled Accrued Payables or Accrued Liabilities may be used. All accrued liabilities may then be recorded as credits to this account instead of to separate accounts.

What Happened to the Accrued Liabilities?

The accounting systems and procedures for recording accruals and the related adjusting entries for one company are not always applicable to another company. This was never better illustrated than in a court case involving the Yale Express and Republic Carloading companies.

Yale Express was a New York-based short-haul trucker specializing in carrying less than truckload freight to points along the east coast within 500 miles of New York. Yale Express kept its books on a semi-cash basis and recorded all adjusting entries for accrued liabilities based upon a cutoff period ending twenty days into the following period. Any bills for unpaid expenses related to the prior accounting period received during this twenty-day period would be recorded through the use of adjusting entries. Over the years, this procedure had proven adequate for preparing the financial statements of Yale Express, since few bills relating to a prior period were received beyond the twenty-day cutoff point.

Republic Carloading was basically a sales organization that held an ICC certificate authorizing it to serve as a freight forwarder in all fifty states. As a freight forwarder, Republic moved little freight itself, but contracted for others to actually move the freight. Republic kept its books on a full accrual basis and recorded adjusting entries for accrued liabilities at the end of its fiscal year for anticipated expenses and transportation bills that often arrived months into the new accounting period. These accrued liabilities were recorded as debits to various expense accounts and credits to Accounts Payable and other liability accounts.

When Yale Express acquired Republic in a merger, the administrative vice-president of Yale Express decided to use Yale Express' semi-cash, twenty-day cutoff procedure for accrued liabilities for Republic. Later it was discovered that millions of dollars of accrued liabilities had not been recorded by Republic. These accrued liabilities, along with other miscellaneous errors, misstated the financial statements of the combined companies, such that an original profit of $1.14 million was restated to a loss of $1.88 million. As a result of the misstated financial statements, several lawsuits were filed by the stockholders and creditors against the management and auditor for Yale Express.

Source: Richard J. Whalen, "The Big Skid at Yale Express," *Fortune* (November, 1965).

EFFECT OF OMITTING ADJUSTING ENTRIES

Adjusting entries are required at the end of the accounting period to match revenues and expenses properly. Since each adjusting entry affects both an income statement account and a balance sheet account, the failure to record them, or an error in recording them, will result in an incorrect income statement, retained earnings statement, and balance sheet. To illustrate, assume that a business acquired $75,000 of equipment on January 3. If the estimated amount of depreciation for the year is $3,000, the equipment, accumulated depreciation, and depreciation expense accounts would appear as follows, after the adjusting entry on December 31 for depreciation:

Equipment

	Debit		Credit
Jan. 3	75,000		

Accumulated Depreciation

	Debit		Credit
		Dec. 31	3,000

Depreciation Expense

	Debit		Credit
Dec. 31	3,000		

As was noted earlier in the chapter, the $3,000 increase in the accumulated depreciation account represents a reduction in the $75,000 cost recorded in the plant asset account. The resulting book value of the asset is reported on the balance sheet as follows:

Plant assets:		
Equipment.	$75,000	
Less accumulated depreciation	3,000	$72,000

If the $3,000 adjustment for depreciation is omitted, the net income reported on the income statement will be overstated by $3,000 because the depreciation expense will be understated by $3,000. The ending balance for retained earnings reported on the retained earnings statement will be overstated by $3,000 because the net income reported on the retained earnings statement will be overstated by that amount. On the balance sheet, both the book value of the asset and the retained earnings will be overstated by $3,000. The effect on the financial statements of omitting this adjustment for depreciation can be summarized as follows:

Income statement	
Expenses will be understated.	$3,000
Net income will be overstated.	3,000
Retained earnings statement	
Net income will be overstated.	$3,000
Ending retained earnings will be overstated	3,000
Balance Sheet	
Assets will be overstated.	$3,000
Retained earnings will be overstated.	3,000

The two items that are overstated on the balance sheet (assets and retained earnings) will also be overstated on future balance sheets until the equipment is disposed of or a correction is made. When the equipment is disposed of, the incorrect amounts will be removed from the asset accounts.[2]

[2]The accounting for the disposal of plant assets is discussed in Chapter 8.

Note that the failure to record any adjusting entry will result in an error on all three financial statements. As another illustration, assume that a business enterprise was organized on May 1, and salaries of $5,000 and $5,200 were paid on May 14 and May 28 respectively. If salaries accrued were $1,100 on May 31, the salaries expense and salaries payable accounts would appear as follows, after the adjustment on May 31:

Salaries Payable				Salaries Expense			
		May 31	1,100	May 14	5,000		
				28	5,200		
				31	1,100		

If the $1,100 adjustment for accrued salaries is omitted, the net income reported on the income statement will be overstated by $1,100 because the salaries expense is understated by $1,100. The ending balance of retained earnings reported on the retained earnings statement will be overstated by $1,100 because of the overstatement of net income. On the balance sheet, the liability for salaries payable will be understated by $1,100, and the retained earnings will be overstated by $1,100. The effect on the financial statements of omitting the adjustment for accrued salaries can be summarized as follows:

Income statement	
Expenses will be understated	$1,100
Net income will be overstated	1,100
Retained earnings statement	
Net income will be overstated	$1,100
Ending retained earnings will be overstated	1,100
Balance sheet	
Liabilities will be understated	$1,100
Retained earnings will be overstated	1,100

Unless a correction is made, the salaries expense for the following period will be overstated by the amount of the omitted adjusting entry. This overstatement results because the accrued salaries will be included in the first salary payment of the succeeding period and will be recorded as salaries expense of that period. In the illustration, for example, the first salary payment in June will be made on June 11 and will include the accrued salaries of $1,100. Assuming that the salaries paid on June 11 total $5,250 (the $1,100 accrued on May 31 and $4,150 for the period from June 1–11), the entire $5,250 will be debited to Salaries Expense. The result is an $1,100 overstatement of salaries expense and an $1,100 understatement of net income for June.

Chapter Review

KEY POINTS

1. Fiscal Year

The annual accounting period adopted by an enterprise is known as the fiscal year. The period most commonly adopted is the calendar year, although other periods corresponding to the enterprise's natural business year may be used, particularly for incorporated enterprises.

2. Matching Concept.
Revenues and expenses may be reported on the income statement by (1) the cash basis or (2) the accrual basis of accounting. When the cash basis is used, revenues are reported in the period in which cash is received, and expenses are reported in the period in which cash is paid. Most enterprises, however, use the accrual basis of accounting. Under the accrual method, revenues are reported in the period in which they are earned, and expenses are reported in the period in which they are incurred in the process of generating revenues. The accrual basis of accounting requires the use of an adjusting process at the end of the accounting period to match properly the revenues and expenses within the period.

3. Nature of the Adjusting Process.
At the end of the accounting period, some of the account balances are not necessarily correct. For example, the balances of prepaid expense accounts are normally overstated because the day-to-day consumption or expiration of these assets has not been recorded. Likewise, some revenue or expense items related to the period may not be recorded, since these items are customarily recorded only when cash has been received or paid. The entries required at the end of the accounting period to bring the accounts up to date and to insure the proper matching of revenues and expenses under the accrual method are called adjusting entries. Adjusting entries are required for plant assets, prepaid expenses, unearned revenues, accrued assets, and accrued liabilities.

4. Plant Assets.
The decrease in usefulness of plant assets is called depreciation. The adjusting entry to record depreciation must recognize the expense as well as the decrease in plant assets. The adjusting entry debits a depreciation expense account and credits the related accumulated depreciation account. The latter account is called a contra account because it is offset against the related plant asset account. The difference between the balance of the asset account and the balance of the related accumulated depreciation account is referred to as the book value of the asset.

5. Prepaid Expenses.
Prepaid expenses are the costs of goods and services that have been purchased but not used. The portion of the asset that has been used during the period has become an expense; the remainder will not become an expense until some time in the future. At the time an expense is prepaid, it may be debited to either an asset account or an expense account. Either alternative may be elected, since the effect on the financial statements, after adjusting entries, is the same.

6. Unearned Revenues.
Items of revenue that are received in advance represent a liability that may be termed unearned revenue. The portion of the liability that is discharged during the period, through the delivery of goods or services, has been earned; the remainder will be earned in the future. When revenue is received in advance, it may be credited to either a liability account or a revenue account. Either alternative may be used, since the effect on the financial statements, after adjusting entries, is the same.

7. Accrued Assets (Accrued Revenues).
All assets belonging to the business at the end of an accounting period and all revenues earned during the period should be recorded in the ledger. But during a fiscal period it is common to record some types of revenue only as cash is received; consequently, at the end of the period there may be items of revenue that have not been recorded. In such cases, the amount of the accrued revenue must be recorded by an adjusting entry which debits an asset account and credits a revenue account.

8. Accrued Liabilities (Accrued Expenses).
Some expenses accrue from day to day but are usually recorded only when paid. The amounts of such accrued but unpaid items at the end of the fiscal period are both an expense and a liability. It is for this reason that accruals are called accrued liabilities or accrued expenses. At the end of the accounting period, the amount of the accrued liability must be recorded by an adjusting entry that debits an expense account and credits a liability account.

9. Effect of Omitting Adjusting Entries.
Since each adjusting entry affects both an income statement account and a balance sheet account, the failure to record them will result in an incorrect income statement, retained earnings statement, and balance sheet.

KEY TERMS

fiscal year 102
natural business year 102
cash basis 103
accrual basis 103
adjusting entries 103
depreciation 103
accumulated depreciation account 104
contra account 104
book value 105
prepaid expenses 105
unearned revenues 108
accrued assets 110
accrued revenues 110
accrued liabilities 111
accrued expenses 111

SELF-EXAMINATION QUESTIONS

(Answers at End of Chapter)

1. If the effect of the debit portion of a specific adjusting entry is to increase an asset account, the effect of the credit portion of the entry would be to:
   A. decrease an asset account
   B. increase a liability account
   C. decrease a liability account
   D. decrease an expense account

2. If the estimated amount of depreciation on equipment for a period is $2,000, the adjusting entry to record depreciation would be:
   A. debit Depreciation Expense, $2,000; credit Equipment, $2,000
   B. debit Equipment, $2,000; credit Depreciation Expense, $2,000
   C. debit Depreciation Expense, $2,000; credit Accumulated Depreciation, $2,000
   D. debit Accumulated Depreciation, $2,000; credit Depreciation Expense, $2,000

3. Purchases of office supplies during the year were $2,910, and inventory at the end of the year was $595. If office supplies are initially recorded as an expense, the adjusting entry at the end of the year would be:

A. Dr. Office Supplies, $595; Cr. Office Supplies Expense, $595
B. Dr. Office Supplies, $2,315; Cr. Office Supplies Expense, $2,315
C. Dr. Office Supplies Expense, $595; Cr. Office Supplies, $595
D. Dr. Office Supplies Expense, $2,315; Cr. Office Supplies, $2,315

4. Prepaid expenses are listed on the balance sheet under:
   A. current assets
   B. plant assets
   C. current liabilities
   D. long-term liabilities

5. The balance in Unearned Rent at the end of a period represents:
   A. an asset
   B. a liability
   C. a revenue
   D. an expense

ILLUSTRATIVE PROBLEM

From a review of the ledger (before adjustment) and other records of Epstein Company, the following data were obtained for the current fiscal year ending May 31:

(a) As insurance premiums are paid, they have been debited to Prepaid Insurance, which has a balance of $4,120 at May 31. An analysis of the insurance policies and premiums indicates that $2,940 of the insurance has expired during the year.
(b) Rent Income has a balance at May 31 of $20,320, composed of the following:
   (1) the beginning balance at June 1 of $7,420, representing rent prepaid for six months;
   (2) a credit of $12,900, representing advance payment of rent for twelve months beginning December 1.
(c) Sales salaries are uniformly $16,800 for a six-day workweek ending on Saturday. The last payday of the year was Saturday, May 27.
(d) Unbilled service fees total $13,600 at May 31.
(e) Depreciation on equipment used during the year totals $35,000.

Instructions:

Journalize the adjusting entries as of May 31 of the current fiscal year, identifying each entry by letter.

SOLUTION

(a) Insurance Expense	2,940	
Prepaid Insurance		2,940
(b) Rent Income	6,450	
Unearned Rent		6,450
(c) Sales Salaries Expense	8,400	
Sales Salaries Payable		8,400
(d) Service Fees Receivable	13,600	
Service Fee Revenue		13,600
(e) Depreciation Expense—Equipment	35,000	
Accumulated Depreciation—Equipment		35,000

Discussion Questions

3–1. What term is applied to the annual accounting period adopted by a business enterprise?

3–2. Why are adjusting entries needed at the end of an accounting period?

3–3. If the effect of the debit portion of an adjusting entry is to increase the balance of an asset account, which of the following statements describes the effect of the credit portion of the entry: (a) increases the balance of a liability account, (b) increases the balance of a revenue account?

3–4. Does every adjusting entry have an effect on the determination of the amount of net income for a period? Explain.

3–5. (a) Explain the purpose of the two accounts, Depreciation Expense and Accumulated Depreciation. (b) What is the normal balance of each account? (c) In what financial statements, if any, will each account appear?

3–6. What term is applied to the difference between the balance in a plant asset account and its related accumulated depreciation account?

3–7. A purchase of supplies can be debited to one of two types of accounts. Name the two types of accounts that can be debited.

3–8. From time to time during the fiscal year, an enterprise makes an advance payment of premiums on three-year and one-year property insurance policies. Which of the following types of accounts will be affected by the related adjusting entry at the end of the fiscal year: (1) asset, (2) liability, (3) revenue, (4) expense?

3–9. (a) Will a business enterprise that occasionally places advertisements in the local newspaper, for which it makes advance payments, always have prepaid advertising at the end of each fiscal year? Explain.
(b) Will a business enterprise almost always have prepaid property and casualty insurance at the end of each fiscal year? Explain.
(c) Would it be logical to record prepayments of the type referred to in (a) as expenses and prepayments of the type referred to in (b) as assets? Discuss.

3–10. Where are prepaid expenses reported on the balance sheet?

3–11. On January 2, an enterprise receives $24,000 from a tenant as rent for the current calendar year. The fiscal year of the enterprise is from July 1 to June 30. (a) Which of the following types of accounts will be affected by the adjusting entry as of June 30: (1) asset, (2) liability, (3) revenue, (4) expense? (b) How much of the $24,000 rent should be reported as revenue for the current fiscal year ending June 30?

3–12. On June 30, the end of its fiscal year, an enterprise owed salaries of $3,100 for an incomplete payroll period. Which of the following types of accounts will be affected by the related adjusting entry: (1) asset, (2) liability, (3) revenue, (4) expense?

3–13. Where would (a) accrued expenses and (b) accrued revenues, both due within a year, appear on the balance sheet?

3–14. Classify the following items as (a) prepaid expense, (b) unearned revenue, (c) accrued expense, or (d) accrued revenue.
(1) Receipts from sales of meal tickets by a restaurant.
(2) Property taxes paid in advance.
(3) A two-year premium paid on a fire insurance policy.
(4) Life insurance premiums received by an insurance company.
(5) Utilities owed but not yet paid.
(6) Fees earned but not yet received.

(7) Supplies on hand.
(8) Tuition collected in advance by a university.
(9) Storage fees earned but not yet received.
(10) Taxes owed but payable in the following period.
(11) Salary owed but not yet due.
(12) Fees received but not yet earned.

3–15. Each of the following debits and credits represents one half of an adjusting entry. Name the title of the account that would be used for the remaining half of the entry.
(a) Fees Earned is debited.
(b) Office Supplies Expense is debited.
(c) Unearned Subscriptions is credited.
(d) Salary Expense is debited.
(e) Property Tax Payable is credited.
(f) Prepaid Insurance is credited.
(g) Unearned Rent is debited.

3–16. At the end of July, the first month of the fiscal year, the usual adjusting entry transferring supplies used to an expense account is inadvertently omitted. Which items will be incorrectly stated, because of the error, on (a) the income statement for July and (b) the balance sheet as of July 31? Also indicate whether the items in error will be overstated or understated.

3–17. Accrued salaries of $7,500 owed to employees for December 29, 30, and 31 are not taken into consideration in preparing the financial statements for the fiscal year ended December 31. Which items will be erroneously stated, because of the error, on (a) the income statement for the year and (b) the balance sheet as of December 31? Also indicate whether the items in error will be overstated or understated.

3–18. Assume that the error in 3–17 was not corrected and that the $7,500 of accrued salaries was included in the first salary payment in January. Which items will be erroneously stated, because of failure to correct the initial error, on (a) the income statement for the month of January and (b) the balance sheet as of January 31?

3–19. If the adjusting entry for depreciation for the current year is omitted, which items will be affected on (a) the income statement for the current year, (b) the retained earnings statement for the current year, and (c) the balance sheet at the end of the current year?

3–20. Real World Focus. The fiscal years for several well-known companies were as follows:

Company	Fiscal Year Ending
K Mart	January 30
J. C. Penney	January 26
Zayre Corp.	January 26
Toys “R” Us, Inc.	February 3
Federated Department Stores	February 2
The Limited, Inc.	February 2

What general characteristic of these companies explains why they do not have fiscal years ending December 31?

3–21. Real World Focus. The balance sheet for Tandy Corporation as of June 30, 1986, includes accrued expenses as current liabilities. Notes to the balance sheet indicate that the following items are a major portion of the accrued expenses:

Accrued payroll and bonuses	$66,452,000
Accrued sales and payroll taxes	12,843,000
Accrued insurance	14,654,000
Accrued interest expense	18,419,000

The net income for Tandy Corporation for the year ended June 30, 1986, was $197,659,000. (a) If the accrued expenses had *not* been recorded at June 30, 1986, how much would net income have been misstated for the fiscal year ended June 30, 1986? (b) What is the percentage of the misstatement in (a) to the actual net income of $197,659,000?

Exercises

3–22. Adjusting entries for depreciation; effect of error. On December 31, a business enterprise estimates depreciation on equipment used during the first year of operations to be $2,910. (a) Journalize the adjusting entry required as of December 31. (b) If the adjusting entry in (a) were omitted, which items would be erroneously stated on (1) the income statement for the year, and (2) the balance sheet as of December 31?

3–23. Adjusting entries for prepaid insurance. The balance in the prepaid insurance account, before adjustment at the end of the year, is $4,525. Journalize the adjusting entry required under each of the following alternatives: (a) the amount of insurance expired during the year is $3,225; (b) the amount of unexpired insurance applicable to future periods is $1,300.

3–24. Adjusting entries for office supplies. The office supplies purchased during the year total $5,450, and the inventory at the end of the year is $1,530.

(a) Set up T accounts for Office Supplies and Office Supplies Expense, and record the following directly in the accounts, employing the system of initially recording supplies as an asset (identify each entry by number): (1) purchases for the period; (2) adjusting entry at the end of the period.

(b) Set up T accounts for Office Supplies and Office Supplies Expense, and record the following directly in the accounts, employing the system of initially recording supplies as an expense (identify each entry by number): (1) purchases for the period; (2) adjusting entry at the end of the period.

3–25. Adjusting entries for advertising revenues. The advertising revenues received during the year total $280,000, and the unearned advertising revenue at the end of the year is $40,000.

(a) Set up T accounts for Unearned Advertising Revenue and Advertising Revenue and record the following directly in the accounts, employing the system of initially recording advertising fees as a liability (identify each entry by number): (1) revenues received during the period; (2) adjusting entry at the end of the period.

(b) Set up T accounts for Unearned Advertising Revenue and Advertising Revenue and record the following directly in the accounts, employing the system of initially recording advertising fees as a revenue (identify each entry by number): (1) revenues received during the period; (2) adjusting entry at the end of the period.

3–26. Adjusting entries for unearned revenues; effect of errors. In its first year of operations, Southern Publishing Co. received $250,000 from advertising contracts and $425,000 from magazine subscriptions, crediting the two amounts to Advertising Revenue and Circulation Revenue respectively. At the end of the year, the unearned advertising revenue amounts to $32,000 and the unearned circulation revenue amounts to $197,000. (a) If no adjustments are made at the end of the year, will revenue for the year be overstated or understated, and by what amount? (b) Present the adjusting entries that should be made at the end of the year.

3–27. Adjusting entry for accrued assets. During the current fiscal year, a business enterprise billed customers $191,750 for fees earned. At the end of the fiscal year, unbilled services totaling $20,100 had been performed for customers. Present the adjusting entry that should be made at the end of the fiscal year.

3–28. Adjusting entries for prepaid and accrued taxes. A business enterprise was organized on July 1 of the current year. On July 2, the enterprise paid $3,600 to the city for taxes (license fees) for the next 12 months, and debited the prepaid taxes account. The same enterprise is also required to pay in January an annual tax (on property) for the previous calendar year. The estimated amount of the property tax for the current year is $3,950. (a) Journalize the two adjusting entries required to bring the accounts affected by the two taxes up to date as of December 31, the end of the current year. (b) What is the amount of tax expense for the current year?

3–29. Adjusting entries for accrued salaries. A business enterprise pays weekly salaries of $11,300 on Friday for a five-day week ending on that day. Journalize the necessary adjusting entry at the end of the fiscal period, assuming that the fiscal period ends (a) on Monday, (b) on Wednesday.

3–30. Adjusting entry for accrued interest. A business enterprise issued a note payable for $100,000. If interest of $1,500 has accrued as of the end of the accounting period, journalize the necessary adjusting entry at the end of the period.

Problems

3–31. Adjusting entries. Beacon Bowl Inc. prepared the following trial balance at June 30, the end of the current fiscal year:

Beacon Bowl Inc.
Trial Balance
June 30, 19--

Cash	11,500	
Prepaid Insurance	2,400	
Supplies	1,950	
Land	40,000	
Building	122,000	
Accumulated Depreciation—Building		31,700
Equipment	72,400	
Accumulated Depreciation—Equipment		15,300
Accounts Payable		6,100
Capital Stock		100,000
Retained Earnings		60,500
Dividends	15,000	
Bowling Revenue		161,200
Salaries and Wages Expense	60,200	
Advertising Expense	19,000	
Utilities Expense	18,200	
Repairs Expense	8,100	
Miscellaneous Expense	4,050	
	374,800	374,800

The data needed to determine year-end adjustments are as follows:

(a) Insurance expired during the year	$1,050
(b) Inventory of supplies at June 30	450
(c) Depreciation of building for the year	1,620
(d) Depreciation of equipment for the year	5,160
(e) Accrued salaries and wages at June 30	1,950

Instructions: Prepare journal entries to adjust the accounts at June 30, identifying each entry by letter.

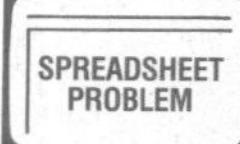

3–32. Adjusting entries. As of April 30, the end of the current fiscal year, the accountant for Benedict Company prepared a trial balance, journalized and posted the adjusting entries, and prepared an adjusted trial balance. The two trial balances as of April 30, one before adjustments and the other after adjustments, are as follows:

Benedict Company
Trial Balance
April 30, 19--

	Unadjusted		Adjusted	
Cash	7,325		7,325	
Supplies	6,920		1,610	
Prepaid Rent	16,900		1,300	
Prepaid Insurance	1,275		350	
Equipment	69,750		69,750	
Accumulated Depreciation—Equipment		33,480		36,270
Automobiles	54,800		54,800	
Accumulated Depreciation—Automobiles		18,250		21,900
Accounts Payable		4,310		4,530
Salaries Payable		—		3,480
Taxes Payable		—		1,200
Capital Stock		25,000		25,000
Retained Earnings		12,375		12,375
Service Fees Earned		181,200		181,200
Salary Expense	112,300		115,780	
Rent Expense	—		15,600	
Supplies Expense	—		5,310	
Depreciation Expense—Equipment	—		2,790	
Depreciation Expense—Automobiles	—		3,650	
Utilities Expense	2,720		2,940	
Taxes Expense	915		2,115	
Insurance Expense	—		925	
Miscellaneous Expense	1,710		1,710	
	274,615	274,615	285,955	285,955

Instructions: Present the eight journal entries that were required to adjust the accounts at April 30. None of the accounts was affected by more than one adjusting entry.

3–33. Adjusting entries. The following information was obtained from a review of the ledger (before adjustments) and other records of Hass Company at December 31, the end of the current year:

(a) As advance premiums have been paid on insurance policies during the year, they have been debited to Prepaid Insurance, which has a balance of $3,258 at December 31. Details of premium expirations are as follows:

Policy No.	Premium Cost per Month	Period in Effect During Year
SB106	$50	Jan. 1–June 30
84162	20	Feb. 1–Dec. 31
C84DE	45	Jan. 1–Oct. 31
01CF2	32	Mar. 1–Dec. 31
Z149C	15	Aug. 1–Dec. 31

(b) Management Fees Earned has a credit balance of $156,900 at December 31. The unbilled fees at December 31 total $9,500.

(c) As office supplies have been purchased during the year, they have been debited to Office Supplies Expense, which has a balance of $1,280 at December 31. The inventory of supplies at that date totals $390.

(d) On December 31, Rent Expense has a debit balance of $19,500, which includes rent of $1,500 for January of the following year, paid on December 31 of the preceding year.

(e) Sales commissions are uniformly 2% of net sales and are paid on the tenth of the month following the sales. Net sales for the month ended December 31 were $108,600. Only commissions paid have been recorded during the year.

(f) Prepaid Advertising has a debit balance of $13,000 at December 31, which represents the advance payment on April 1 of a yearly contract for a uniform amount of space in 52 consecutive issues of a weekly publication. As of December 31, advertisements had appeared in 39 issues.

(g) Unearned Rent has a credit balance of $18,900, composed of the following: (1) January 1 balance of $4,500, representing rent prepaid for four months, January through April, and (2) a credit of $14,400, representing advance payment of rent for twelve months at $1,200 a month, beginning with May.

Instructions: (1) Determine the amount of each adjustment, identifying all principal figures used in the computations.

(2) Journalize the adjusting entries as of December 31 of the current fiscal year, identifying each entry by letter.

3–34. Year-end adjusting entries; general ledger accounts. The following accounts appear in the ledger of Frost Inc. at January 31, the end of the current fiscal year. None of the year-end adjustments have been recorded.

113	Fees Receivable	—	411	Fees Earned	$99,600
114	Supplies	$1,080	511	Salary Expense	66,720
115	Prepaid Insurance	5,960	513	Advertising Expense	16,540
116	Prepaid Advertising	—	514	Insurance Expense	—
213	Salaries Payable	—	515	Supplies Expense	—
215	Unearned Rent	—	611	Rent Income	14,560

The following information relating to adjustments at January 31 is obtained from physical inventories, supplementary records, and other sources:

(a) Unbilled fees at January 31, $12,400.

(b) Inventory of supplies at January 31, $320.

(c) The insurance record indicates that $3,360 of insurance has expired during the year.

(d) Of a prepayment of $2,500 for advertising space on a billboard, 80% of the time has expired, and the remainder will expire in the following year. The payment of the $2,500 was recorded in Advertising Expense.

(e) Salaries accrued at January 31, $1,850.

(f) Rent collected in advance that will not be earned until the following year, $1,120.

Instructions: (1) Open the accounts listed and record the balances in the appropriate balance columns, as of January 31.

(2) Journalize the adjusting entries and post to the appropriate accounts after each entry, extending the balances. Identify the postings by writing "Adjusting" in the item column.

3–35. Adjusting entries from ledger account balances. Selected accounts from the ledger of Jesse Moody Inc. at the end of the fiscal year are as follows. The account balances are shown before and after adjustment.

	Unadjusted Balance	Adjusted Balance
Fees Receivable	—	$ 3,900
Supplies	$ 2,550	810
Prepaid Insurance	6,720	2,940
Wages Payable	—	3,560
Utilities Payable	—	570
Unearned Rent	—	720
Fees Earned	109,200	113,100
Wages Expense	72,600	76,160
Utilities Expense	5,940	6,510
Insurance Expense	—	3,780
Supplies Expense	—	1,740
Rent Income	9,360	8,640

Instructions: Journalize the adjusting entries that were posted to the ledger at the end of the fiscal year.

3–36. Two methods of recording advertising expense and rent income. The following transactions relate to advertising and rent. Accounts are adjusted at December 31, the end of the fiscal year.

Advertising

June 1. Payment of $6,600 (allocable at $550 a month for 12 months beginning June 1).

Rent

Mar. 1. Receipt of $14,400 (allocable at $1,200 a month for 12 months beginning March 1).

Sept. 1. Receipt of $15,300 (allocable at $1,275 a month for 12 months beginning September 1).

Instructions: (1) Open accounts for Prepaid Advertising, Advertising Expense, Unearned Rent, and Rent Income. Using the system of initially recording prepaid expense as an asset and unearned revenue as a liability, record the following directly in the accounts: (a) transactions of March 1, June 1, and September 1 and (b) adjusting entries at December 31. Identify each entry in the item section of the accounts as transaction or adjusting, and extend the balance after each entry.

(2) Open a duplicate set of accounts and follow the remaining instructions in Instruction (1), except to employ the system of initially recording prepaid expense as an expense and unearned revenue as revenue.

(3) Determine the amounts that would appear in the balance sheet at December 31 as asset and liability respectively, and in the income statement for the year as expense and revenue respectively, according to the system employed in Instruction (1) and the system employed in Instruction (2). Present your answers in the following form:

System	Asset	Expense	Liability	Revenue
Instruction (1)	$	$	$	$
Instruction (2)				

3–31A. Adjusting entries. Professional Lawn Service Inc. prepares financial statements at the end of each month. The trial balance at September 30 and the adjustment data needed at September 30 are as follows:

Professional Lawn Service Inc.
Trial Balance
September 30, 19--

Cash	7,990	
Prepaid Insurance	1,200	
Supplies	1,120	
Land	30,000	
Building	79,500	
Accumulated Depreciation—Building		31,725
Equipment	74,750	
Accumulated Depreciation—Equipment		35,200
Accounts Payable		3,170
Capital Stock		50,000
Retained Earnings		36,255
Service Revenue		80,600
Salaries and Wages Expense	31,150	
Advertising Expense	4,500	
Utilities Expense	4,380	
Repairs Expense	1,320	
Miscellaneous Expense	1,040	
	236,950	236,950

Adjustment data at September 30:

(a) Insurance unexpired at September 30	$ 300
(b) Inventory of supplies on September 30	270
(c) Depreciation of building for September	1,620
(d) Depreciation of equipment for September	5,150
(e) Accrued salaries and wages on September 30	1,820

Instructions: Journalize the adjusting entries at September 30, identifying each entry by letter.

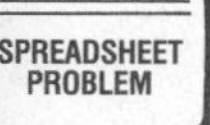

3–32A. Adjusting entries. As of December 31, the end of the current fiscal year, the accountant for Bonner Company prepared a trial balance, journalized and posted the adjusting entries, and prepared an adjusted trial balance. The two trial balances as of December 31, one before adjustments and the other after adjustments, are as follows:

Bonner Company
Trial Balance
December 31, 19--

	Unadjusted		Adjusted	
Cash	13,650		13,650	
Supplies	10,380		3,960	
Prepaid Rent	9,750		750	
Prepaid Insurance	2,400		800	
Land	42,500		42,500	
Buildings	116,000		116,000	
Accumulated Depreciation—Buildings		77,600		82,400
Trucks	103,000		103,000	
Accumulated Depreciation—Trucks		32,800		50,900
Accounts Payable		7,120		7,520

Salaries Payable	—			1,450
Taxes Payable	—			920
Capital Stock		100,000		100,000
Retained Earnings		16,790		16,790
Service Fees Earned		140,680		140,680
Salary Expense	71,200		72,650	
Depreciation Expense—Trucks	—		18,100	
Rent Expense	—		9,000	
Supplies Expense	—		6,420	
Utilities Expense	4,550		4,950	
Depreciation Expense—Buildings	—		4,800	
Taxes Expense	600		1,520	
Insurance Expense	—		1,600	
Miscellaneous Expense	960		960	
	374,990	374,990	400,660	400,660

Instructions: Present the eight journal entries that were required to adjust the accounts at December 31. None of the accounts was affected by more than one adjusting entry.

3–33A. Adjusting entries. The following information was obtained from a review of the ledger (before adjustments) and other records of Koo Company at December 31, the end of the current fiscal year:

(a) As advance premiums have been paid on insurance policies during the year, they have been debited to Prepaid Insurance, which has a balance of $1,236 at December 31. Details of premium expirations are as follows:

Policy No.	Premium Cost per Month	Period in Effect During Year
B115	$25	Jan. 1–June 30
210A	27	July 1–Dec. 31
917Y	12	Jan. 1–Dec. 31
881C	30	Jan. 1–Apr. 30
419X	29	May 1–Dec. 31

(b) Prepaid Advertising has a debit balance of $7,800 at December 31, which represents the advance payment on March 1 of a yearly contract for a uniform amount of space in 52 consecutive issues of a weekly publication. As of December 31, advertisements had appeared in 44 issues.

(c) Unearned Rent has a credit balance of $14,700, composed of the following: (1) January 1 balance of $2,700, representing rent prepaid for three months, January through March, and (2) a credit of $12,000, representing advance payment of rent for twelve months at $1,000 a month, beginning with April.

(d) Management Fees Earned has a credit balance of $130,750 at December 31. The unbilled fees at December 31 total $7,150.

(e) As office supplies have been purchased during the year, they have been debited to Office Supplies Expense, which has a balance of $930 at December 31. The inventory of supplies at that date totals $345.

(f) On December 31, Rent Expense has a debit balance of $19,500, which includes rent of $1,500 for January of the following year, paid on December 31 of this year.

(g) Sales commissions are uniformly 2% of net sales and are paid the tenth of the month following the sales. Net sales for December were $70,000. Only commissions paid have been recorded during the year.

Instructions: (1) Determine the amount of each adjustment, identifying all principal figures used in the computations.
(2) Journalize the adjusting entries as of December 31 of the current fiscal year, identifying each entry by letter.

3–34A. Year-end adjusting entries; general ledger accounts. The following accounts appear in the ledger of Jackson Company at April 30, the end of the current fiscal year. None of the year-end adjustments have been recorded.

113	Fees Receivable	—	411	Fees Earned	$152,000
114	Supplies	$1,560	511	Salary Expense	92,600
115	Prepaid Insurance	3,840	513	Advertising Expense	20,400
116	Prepaid Advertising	—	514	Insurance Expense	—
213	Salaries Payable	—	515	Supplies Expense	—
215	Unearned Rent	—	611	Rent Income	15,600

The following information relating to adjustments at April 30 is obtained from physical inventories, supplementary records, and other sources:

(a) Salaries accrued at April 30, $2,380.
(b) Unbilled fees at April 30, $6,800.
(c) Rent collected in advance that will not be earned until the following year, $1,200.
(d) The insurance record indicates that $1,300 of insurance relates to future years.
(e) Inventory of supplies at April 30, $540.
(f) Of a prepayment of $6,000 for advertising space on a billboard, 60% of the time has expired, and the remainder will expire in the following year. The payment of the $6,000 was recorded in Advertising Expense.

Instructions: (1) Open the accounts listed and record the balances in the appropriate balance columns, as of April 30.
(2) Journalize the adjusting entries and post to the appropriate accounts after each entry, extending the balances. Identify the postings by writing "Adjusting" in the item column.

3–35A. Adjusting entries from ledger account balances. Selected accounts from the ledger of Groves Company at the end of the fiscal year are as follows. The account balances are shown before and after adjustment.

	Unadjusted Balance	Adjusted Balance
Fees Receivable	—	$ 9,000
Supplies	$ 1,860	780
Prepaid Insurance	4,720	2,120
Wages Payable	—	2,472
Advertising Payable	—	3,000
Unearned Rent	—	400
Fees Earned	149,600	158,600
Wages Expense	63,280	65,752
Insurance Expense	—	2,600
Advertising Expense	16,200	19,200
Supplies Expense	—	1,080
Rent Income	5,200	4,800

Instructions: Journalize the adjusting entries that were posted to the ledger at the end of the fiscal year.

Mini-Case 3

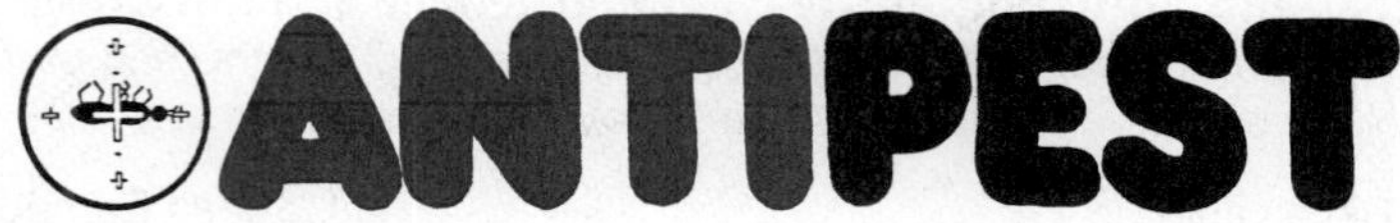

Assume that you recently accepted a position with the American National Bank as an assistant loan officer. As one of your first duties, you have been assigned the responsibility of evaluating a loan request for $75,000 from Antipest, a small local corporation. In support of the loan application, Donna Polk, principal stockholder, submitted the following "Statement of Accounts" (trial balance) for the first year of operations ended December 31, 1989:

Antipest
Statement of Accounts
December 31, 1989

Cash	4,120	
Billings Due from Others	7,740	
Supplies (chemicals, etc.)	14,950	
Trucks	32,750	
Equipment	16,150	
Amounts Owed to Others		4,700
Capital Stock		47,500
Service Revenue		97,650
Wages Expense	60,100	
Utilities Expense	6,900	
Rent Expense	4,800	
Insurance Expense	1,400	
Other Expenses	940	
	149,850	149,850

Instructions:

(1) Explain to Donna Polk why a set of financial statements (income statement, retained earnings statement, and a balance sheet) would be useful to you in evaluating the loan request.
(2) In discussing the "Statement of Accounts" with Donna Polk, you discovered that the accounts had not been adjusted at December 31. Through analysis of the "Statement of Accounts," indicate possible adjusting entries that might be necessary before an accurate set of financial statements could be prepared.
(3) Assuming that an accurate set of financial statements will be submitted by Donna Polk in a few days, what other considerations or information would you require before making a decision on the loan request?

Answers to Self-Examination Questions

1. D Every adjusting entry affects both a balance sheet account and an income statement account. Therefore, if the debit portion of an adjusting entry increases an asset (balance sheet) account, the credit portion of the entry must affect an income statement account, as would be the case for a decrease in an expense account (answer D).
2. C Since increases in expense accounts (such as depreciation expense) are recorded by debits and it is customary to record the decreases in usefulness of plant assets as credits to accumulated depreciation accounts, answer C is the correct entry.
3. A Under the system of initially recording office supplies as an expense, the office supplies expense account would have a balance of $2,910 before adjustment, representing the cost of office supplies purchased during the year.The accounts are therefore adjusted by debiting Office Supplies and crediting Office Supplies Expense for $595 (answer A). The adjustment transfers $595, representing the unconsumed supplies on hand at the end of the year, to the asset account.
4. A Prepaid expenses are listed on the balance sheet among the current assets (answer A), because they are expected to become an expense in the current accounting period.
5. B Unearned revenues are revenues received in advance that will be earned in the future. They represent a liability (answer B) of the business to furnish the service in a future period.

4
Periodic Reporting

CHAPTER OBJECTIVES

Describe and illustrate the use of the work sheet for summarizing the accounting data needed to prepare the financial statements.

Describe alternative formats and terminology for the income statement, retained earnings statement, and balance sheet.

Illustrate the preparation of an income statement, retained earnings statement, and balance sheet from the work sheet.

Describe and illustrate the preparation of adjusting entries and closing entries.

Describe and illustrate the preparation of reversing entries.

At the end of each accounting period, the operating data for the period must be summarized, adjusted, and reported in the financial statements for the use of managers, owners, creditors, various governmental agencies, and other interested persons. The ledger, which contains the basic data for the reports, must then be prepared to receive entries for transactions that will occur in the following period.

The sequence of the end-of-period procedures, which are discussed and illustrated in this chapter, may be outlined as follows:

1. Prepare a trial balance of the ledger on a work sheet form.
2. Review the accounts and gather the data required for the adjustments.
3. Insert the adjustments and complete the work sheet.
4. Prepare financial statements from the data in the work sheet.
5. Journalize the adjusting entries and post to the ledger.
6. Journalize the closing entries and post to the ledger.
7. Prepare a post-closing trial balance of the ledger.
8. Journalize the reversing entries required to facilitate the recording of transactions in the following period and post to the ledger.

The most significant output of the end-of-period procedures is the financial statements. To assist the accountant in accumulating data for the statements, a **work sheet** is often used. The work sheet provides a convenient means of accumulating essential data, verifying arithmetical accuracy, and arranging data in a logical form.

The work sheet for Midtown Electric Corporation is presented on pages 132–133. It has an account title column and eight money columns arranged in four pairs of debit and credit columns. The main headings for the four sets of money columns are:

1. Trial Balance
2. Adjustments
3. Income Statement
4. Balance Sheet

Trial Balance on the Work Sheet

The trial balance data for Midtown Electric Corporation appear on the work sheet on page 132. All of the accounts, with their balances, are listed in the order in which they appear in the ledger.

Adjustments on the Work Sheet

Both the debit and the credit parts of an adjustment should be inserted on the appropriate lines before going on to another adjustment. Cross-referencing the related debit and credit of each adjustment by letters is useful to anyone who may have occasion to review the work sheet. It is also helpful later when the adjusting entries are recorded in the journal. The sequence of adjustments is not important, except that there is a time and accuracy advantage in following the order in which the adjustment data are assembled.

The data needed for adjusting the accounts of Midtown Electric Corporation are summarized as follows:

Office supplies as of December 31, 1989		$ 480
Insurance expired during 1989		1,910
Depreciation during 1989 on:		
Store equipment		3,100
Office equipment		2,490
Salaries accrued on December 31, 1989:		
Sales salaries	$780	
Office salaries	360	1,140

Explanations of the adjusting entries in the work sheet above are given in the paragraphs that follow.

(a) **Office Supplies.** The $1,090 balance of the office supplies account in the trial balance is the combined cost of office supplies on hand at the beginning of the year and the cost of office supplies purchased during the year. The physical inventory at the end of the year indicates office supplies on hand totaling $480. The excess of $1,090 over the inventory of $480 is $610, which is the cost of the office supplies used during the period. The accounts are adjusted by debiting Office Supplies Expense and crediting Office Supplies for $610.

Midtown Electric
Work
For Year Ended

ACCOUNT TITLE	TRIAL BALANCE	
	DEBIT	CREDIT
Cash	62,950	
Notes Receivable	40,000	
Accounts Receivable	60,880	
Merchandise Inventory	59,700	
Office Supplies	1,090	
Prepaid Insurance	4,560	
Store Equipment	27,100	
Accumulated Depreciation—Store Equipment		12,600
Office Equipment	15,570	
Accumulated Depreciation—Office Equipment		7,230
Accounts Payable		22,420
Salaries Payable		
Mortgage Note Payable		25,000
Capital Stock		100,000
Retained Earnings		41,200
Dividends	18,000	
Sales		720,185
Sales Returns and Allowances	6,140	
Sales Discounts	5,790	
Purchases	521,980	
Purchases Returns and Allowances		9,100
Purchases Discounts		2,525
Transportation In	17,400	
Sales Salaries Expense	59,250	
Advertising Expense	10,860	
Depreciation Expense—Store Equipment		
Miscellaneous Selling Expense	630	
Office Salaries Expense	20,660	
Rent Expense	8,100	
Depreciation Expense—Office Equipment		
Insurance Expense		
Office Supplies Expense		
Miscellaneous General Expense	760	
Interest Income		3,600
Interest Expense	2,440	
	943,860	943,860
Net Income		

Work Sheet

(b) Prepaid Insurance. The adjustment for insurance expired is similar to the adjustment for supplies consumed. The balance in Prepaid Insurance is the amount prepaid at the beginning of the year plus the additional premium costs incurred during the year. Analysis of the various insurance policies reveals that a total of $1,910 in premiums has expired. Insurance Expense is debited and Prepaid Insurance is credited for $1,910.

(c), (d) Depreciation of Plant Assets. The expired cost of a plant asset is debited to a depreciation expense account and credited to an accumulated depreciation account. A separate account for the current period's expense and for the accumulation of prior periods is maintained for each plant asset account. Thus, the adjustment for depreciation of the store equipment is recorded by a debit to Depreciation Expense—

Corporation
Sheet
December 31, 1989

ADJUSTMENTS		INCOME STATEMENT		BALANCE SHEET	
DEBIT	CREDIT	DEBIT	CREDIT	DEBIT	CREDIT
				62,950	
				40,000	
				60,880	
		59,700	62,150	62,150	
	(a) 610			480	
	(b) 1,910			2,650	
				27,100	
	(c) 3,100				15,700
				15,570	
	(d) 2,490				9,720
					22,420
	(e) 1,140				1,140
					25,000
					100,000
					41,200
				18,000	
			720,185		
		6,140			
		5,790			
		521,980			
			9,100		
			2,525		
		17,400			
(e) 780		60,030			
		10,860			
(c) 3,100		3,100			
		630			
(e) 360		21,020			
		8,100			
(d) 2,490		2,490			
(b) 1,910		1,910			
(a) 610		610			
		760			
			3,600		
		2,440			
9,250	9,250	722,960	797,560	289,780	215,180
		74,600			74,600
		797,560	797,560	289,780	289,780

Store Equipment and a credit to Accumulated Depreciation—Store Equipment for $3,100 [entry (c)]. The adjustment for depreciation of the office equipment is recorded in a similar manner [entry (d)].

(e) Salaries Payable. The liability for salaries earned by employees but not yet paid is recorded by a credit of $1,140 to Salaries Payable and debits of $780 and $360 to Sales Salaries Expense and Office Salaries Expense respectively.

Completing the Work Sheet

The data in the trial balance columns are combined with the adjustments data and extended to one of the remaining four columns. The amounts of assets, liabilities, and stockholders' equity (including dividends) are extended to the Balance Sheet columns. The revenues and expenses are extended to the Income Statement columns. This procedure must be applied to the balance of each account listed.

In the illustrative work sheet, the first account listed is Cash and the balance appearing in the Trial Balance Debit column is $62,950. Since there are no adjustments to Cash, the trial balance amount should be extended to the appropriate column. Cash is an asset, it is listed on the balance sheet, and it has a debit balance. Accordingly, the $62,950 amount is extended to the Debit column of the Balance Sheet section. The balances of Notes Receivable and Accounts Receivable are extended in similar fashion. Office Supplies has an initial debit balance of $1,090 and a credit adjustment (decrease) of $610. The amount to be extended to the Balance Sheet Debit column is the remaining debit balance of $480. The same procedure is continued until all account balances, including any adjustments, have been extended to the appropriate columns. The balances of the retained earnings and dividends accounts are extended to the Balance Sheet section, because this work sheet does not provide for separate Retained Earnings Statement columns.

An exception to the usual practice of extending account balances should be noted for Merchandise Inventory. The amount reported as merchandise inventory in the trial balance represents the unsold merchandise held for sale at the beginning of the year. It is reported as a part of the cost of merchandise sold on the income statement. It is therefore extended from the Trial Balance Debit column to the Income Statement Debit column. Similarly, the merchandise on hand at the end of the year ($62,150 for Midtown Electric Corporation) is reported on the income statement as a deduction in determining the cost of merchandise sold. It is therefore entered on the work sheet as a credit in the Income Statement Credit column. This inventory at the end of the year is also reported on the balance sheet as an asset and is therefore entered on the work sheet in the Balance Sheet Debit column. It should be noted that the amount for the ending inventory is placed on the same line as that used for the beginning merchandise inventory.

After all of the balances have been extended, each of the four columns is totaled. The net income or the net loss for the period is the amount of the difference between the totals of the two income statement columns. If the credit column total is greater than the debit column total, the excess is the net income. For the work sheet presented on pages 132–133, the computation of net income is as follows:

Total of Income Statement Credit Column	$797,560
Total of Income Statement Debit column	722,960
Net income	$ 74,600

Revenue and expense accounts, which are in reality subdivisions of stockholders' equity, are temporary in nature. They are used during the accounting period to facilitate the accumulation of detailed operating data. After they have served their purpose, the net balance will be transferred to the retained earnings account in the ledger. This transfer is accomplished on the work sheet by entries in the Income Statement Debit column and the Balance Sheet Credit column, as illustrated on page 133. If there had been a net loss instead of a net income, the amount would have been entered in the Income Statement Credit column and the Balance Sheet Debit column.

After the net income or net loss is entered in the appropriate columns on the work sheet, each of the four statement columns is totaled to verify the arithmetic accuracy of the amount of net income or net loss transferred from the income statement to the balance sheet. The totals of the two income statement columns must be equal, as must the totals of the two balance sheet columns. The work sheet may be expanded by the addition of a pair of columns solely for retained earnings statement data. However, because of the very few items involved, this variation is not illustrated. If there are a great many adjustments, it may be advisable to insert a section entitled Adjusted Trial Balance between the adjustments section and the income statement section. The arithmetic of combining the data may then be verified before extending balances to the statement sections.

PREPARATION OF FINANCIAL STATEMENTS

The income statement, the retained earnings statement, and the balance sheet are prepared from the account titles and the data in the statement sections of the work sheet.[1] Many variations are possible in the general format, the terminology used, and the extent to which details are presented in these statements. The forms most frequently used are described and illustrated in the sections that follow.[2]

Income Statement

There are two widely used forms for the income statement: **multiple-step** and **single-step.** Both forms are used with approximately the same frequency among large corporations. The 1987 edition of *Accounting Trends & Techniques* reported that 54% of the 600 industrial and merchandising companies surveyed use the multiple-step form, while 46% use the single-step form.

Multiple-Step Form. The multiple-step income statement is so called because of its many sections, subsections, and intermediate balances. In practice, there is considerable variation in the amount of detail presented in these sections. For example, instead of reporting separately gross sales and the related returns, allowances, and discounts, the statement may begin with net sales. Similarly, the supporting data for the determination of the cost of merchandise sold may be omitted from the statement. A multiple-step income statement for Midtown Electric Corporation is presented on page 136.

The various sections of a conventional multiple-step income statement for Midtown Electric Corporation are discussed briefly in the paragraphs that follow.

Revenue from sales. The total of all charges to customers for merchandise sold, both for cash and on account, is reported in this section. Sales returns and allowances and sales discounts are deducted from the gross amount to yield net sales.

Cost of merchandise sold. The **cost of merchandise sold** to customers is reported in this section. It is made up of that portion of the beginning inventory and purchases that have been sold. The cost of merchandise sold, some-

[1]The preparation of the cash flow statement is discussed in Chapter 14.
[2]Examples of some of the forms described are presented in Appendix H.

Midtown Electric Corporation
Income Statement
For Year Ended December 31, 1989

Revenue from sales:				
Sales			$720,185	
Less: Sales returns and allowances		$ 6,140		
Sales discounts		5,790	11,930	
Net sales				$708,255
Cost of merchandise sold:				
Merchandise inventory, January 1, 1989			$ 59,700	
Purchases		$521,980		
Less: Purchases returns and allowances	$9,100			
Purchases discounts	2,525	11,625		
Net purchases		$510,355		
Add transportation in		17,400		
Cost of merchandise purchased			527,755	
Merchandise available for sale			$587,455	
Less merchandise inventory, December 31, 1989			62,150	
Cost of merchandise sold				525,305
Gross profit				$182,950
Operating expenses:				
Selling expenses:				
Sales salaries expense		$ 60,030		
Advertising expense		10,860		
Depreciation expense—store equipment		3,100		
Miscellaneous selling expense		630		
Total selling expenses			$ 74,620	
General expenses:				
Office salaries expense		$ 21,020		
Rent expense		8,100		
Depreciation expense—office equipment		2,490		
Insurance expense		1,910		
Office supplies expense		610		
Miscellaneous general expense		760		
Total general expenses			34,890	
Total operating expenses				109,510
Income from operations				$ 73,440
Other income:				
Interest income			$ 3,600	
Other expense:				
Interest expense			2,440	1,160
Net income[3]				$ 74,600

Multiple-Step Form of Income Statement

[3] This amount is further reduced by corporation income tax. The discussion of income taxes levied on corporate entities is reserved for later chapters.

times referred to as **cost of goods sold** or **cost of sales,** is often the largest deduction from sales. The manner in which this important figure is determined for a merchandising enterprise depends upon whether the accounting for merchandise is by the perpetual or the periodic system.

Under the **perpetual inventory system,** both the sales amount and the cost of merchandise sold amount are recorded when each item of merchandise is sold. In this manner, the accounting records continuously (perpetually) disclose the inventory on hand. The perpetual system is discussed in later chapters.

Many merchandising enterprises use the **periodic inventory system.** In this system, the revenues from sales are recorded when sales are made, but no attempt is made on the sales date to record the cost of the merchandise sold. It is only by a detailed listing of the merchandise on hand (called a **physical inventory**) at the end of the accounting period that a determination is made of (1) the cost of the merchandise sold during the period and (2) the cost of the inventory on hand at the end of the period. The periodic method is assumed for the illustrations in this chapter.

For merchandising enterprises that use the periodic system, the details of the cost of merchandise sold during a period is reported in a separate section in the income statement, as illustrated in Midtown Electric Corporation's income statement. In this illustration, note that the purchases returns and allowances and the purchases discounts are deducted from the purchases to yield the **net purchases,** and the transportation costs are added to the net purchases to yield the **cost of merchandise purchased.** This cost of merchandise purchased is added to the beginning inventory to yield the **merchandise available for sale.** The ending inventory is then subtracted from the merchandise available for sale to yield the cost of merchandise sold.

Gross profit. The excess of the net revenue from sales over the cost of merchandise sold is called **gross profit, gross profit on sales,** or **gross margin.** It is called *gross* because operating expenses must be deducted from it.

Operating expenses. The operating expenses of a business may be grouped under any desired number of headings and subheadings. In a retail business of the kind that has been used for illustrative purposes, it is usually satisfactory to subdivide operating expenses into two categories, selling and general.

Expenses that are incurred directly and entirely in connection with the sale of merchandise are classified as **selling expenses.** They include such expenses as salaries of the sales force, store supplies used, depreciation of store equipment, and advertising.

Expenses incurred in the general operations of the business are classified as **general expenses** or **administrative expenses.** Examples of these expenses are office salaries, depreciation of office equipment, and office supplies used. Expenses that are partly connected with selling and partly connected with the general operations of the business may be divided between the two categories. In a small business, however, such expenses as rent, insurance, and taxes are commonly reported as general expenses.

Expenses of relatively small amounts that cannot be identified with the principal accounts are usually accumulated in accounts entitled Miscellaneous Selling Expense and Miscellaneous General Expense.

Income from operations. The excess of gross profit over total operating expenses is called **income from operations,** or **operating income.** The amount of the income from operations and its relationship to capital investment and to net sales are important factors in judging the efficiency of management and the degree of profitability of an enterprise. If operating expenses are greater than the gross profit, the excess is called **loss from operations.**

Other income. Revenue from sources other than the principal activity of a business is classified as **other income,** or **nonoperating income.** In a merchandising business, this category often includes income from interest, rent, dividends, and gains resulting from the sale of plant assets.

Other expense. Expenses that cannot be associated definitely with operations are identified as **other expense,** or **nonoperating expense.** Interest expense that results from financing activities and losses incurred in the disposal of plant assets are examples of items that are reported in this section.

The two categories of nonoperating items are offset against each other on the income statement. If the total of other income exceeds the total of other expense, the difference is added to income from operations. If the reverse is true, the difference is subtracted from income from operations.

Net income. The final figure on the income statement is labeled **net income** (or **net loss**). It is the net increase (or net decrease) in stockholders' equity as a result of profit-making activities. (As noted previously, the reporting of corporation income tax is discussed later.)

Single-Step Form. The single-step form of income statement derives its name from the fact that the total of all expenses is deducted from the total of all revenues. Such a statement is illustrated as follows for Midtown Electric Corporation. The illustration has been condensed to focus attention on its principal features. Such condensation is not an essential characteristic of the form.

Single-Step Form of Income Statement

Midtown Electric Corporation
Income Statement
For Year Ended December 31, 1989

Revenues:		
Net sales		$708,255
Interest income		3,600
Total revenues		$711,855
Expenses:		
Cost of merchandise sold	$525,305	
Selling expenses	74,620	
General expenses	34,890	
Interest expense	2,440	
Total expenses		637,255
Net income		$ 74,600

The single-step form has the advantage of being simple and it emphasizes total revenues and total expenses as the factors that determine net income. An objection to the single-step form is that such relationships as gross profit to sales and income from operations to sales are not as readily determinable as they are when the multiple-step form is used.

Retained Earnings Statement

The **retained earnings statement** summarizes the changes which have occurred in the retained earnings account during the fiscal period. It serves as a connecting link between the income statement and the balance sheet. The retained earnings statement for Midtown Electric Corporation is illustrated as follows:

Retained Earnings Statement

Midtown Electric Corporation
Retained Earnings Statement
For Year Ended December 31, 1989

Retained earnings, January 1, 1989		$41,200
Net income for the year	$74,600	
Less dividends	18,000	
Increase in retained earnings		56,600
Retained earnings, December 31, 1989		$97,800

It is not unusual to add the analysis of retained earnings at the bottom of the income statement to form a **combined income and retained earnings statement.** This combined form was used by 10% of the 600 industrial and merchandising companies surveyed in the 1987 edition of *Accounting Trends & Techniques.* The income statement portion of the combined statement may be shown either in multiple-step form or in a single-step form, as in the following illustration:

Combined Income and Retained Earnings Statement

Midtown Electric Corporation
Income and Retained Earnings Statement
For Year Ended December 31, 1989

Revenues:		
Net sales		$708,255
Interest income		3,600
Total revenues		$711,855
Expenses:		
Cost of merchandise sold	$525,305	
Selling expenses	74,620	
General expenses	34,890	
Interest expense	2,440	
Total expenses		637,255
Net income		$ 74,600
Retained earnings, January 1, 1989		41,200
		$115,800
Less dividends		18,000
Retained earnings, December 31, 1989		$ 97,800

The combined statement form emphasizes net income as the connecting link between the income statement and the retained earnings portion of stockholders' equity and thus helps the reader's understanding. A criticism of the combined statement is that the net income figure is buried in the body of the statement.

Balance Sheet

The traditional arrangement of assets on the left-hand side of the balance sheet, with the liabilities and stockholders' equity on the right-hand side, is referred to as the **account form.**[4] If the entire statement is presented on a single page, it is customary to present the three sections in a downward sequence, with the total of the assets section equaling the combined totals of the other two sections. The latter form, called the **report form,** is illustrated in the following balance sheet for Midtown Electric Corporation:

Report Form of Balance Sheet

Midtown Electric Corporation
Balance Sheet
December 31, 1989

Assets			
Current assets:			
Cash		$ 62,950	
Notes receivable		40,000	
Accounts receivable		60,880	
Merchandise inventory		62,150	
Office supplies		480	
Prepaid insurance		2,650	
Total current assets			$229,110
Plant assets:			
Store equipment	$27,100		
Less accumulated depreciation	15,700	$ 11,400	
Office equipment	$15,570		
Less accumulated depreciation	9,720	5,850	
Total plant assets			17,250
Total assets			$246,360
Liabilities			
Current liabilities:			
Accounts payable		$ 22,420	
Mortgage note payable (current portion)		5,000	
Salaries payable		1,140	
Total current liabilities			$ 28,560
Long-term liabilities:			
Mortgage note payable (final payment, 1999)			20,000
Total liabilities			$ 48,560
Stockholders' Equity			
Capital stock		$100,000	
Retained earnings		97,800	
Total stockholders' equity			197,800
Total liabilities and stockholders' equity			$246,360

[4]An account form of balance sheet is illustrated on pages 502 and 503.

ADJUSTING ENTRIES

The analyses required to make the adjustments were completed during the process of preparing the work sheet. It is therefore unnecessary to refer again to the basic data when recording the adjusting entries in the journal. The adjusting entries for Midtown Electric Corporation are as follows:

Adjusting Entries

JOURNAL — PAGE 28

DATE		DESCRIPTION	POST. REF.	DEBIT	CREDIT
		Adjusting Entries			
1989 Dec.	31	Office Supplies Expense	717	610 00	
		Office Supplies	116		610 00
	31	Insurance Expense	716	1910 00	
		Prepaid Insurance	117		1910 00
	31	Depreciation Expense—Store Equip.	613	3100 00	
		Accumulated Depr.—Store Equip.	122		3100 00
	31	Depreciation Expense—Office Equip.	715	2490 00	
		Accumulated Depr.—Office Equip.	124		2490 00
	31	Sales Salaries Expense	611	780 00	
		Office Salaries Expense	711	360 00	
		Salaries Payable	213		1140 00

CLOSING ENTRIES

As was discussed in Chapter 1, the revenue, expense, and dividends accounts are used in classifying and summarizing changes in stockholders' equity during the accounting period. At the end of the period, the net effect of the balances in these accounts must be recorded in the retained earnings account. The balances must also be removed from the revenue, expense, and dividends accounts, so that they will be ready for use in accumulating data for the following accounting period. Both of these goals are accomplished by a series of entries called **closing entries.**

The account titled **Income Summary** is used for summarizing the data in the revenue and expense accounts. Thus, Income Summary is used only at the end of the accounting period during the closing process.

Four entries are required to close the revenue, expense, and dividend accounts of a corporation at the end of the period. They may be described as follows:

1. The first entry closes all income statement accounts with *credit* balances by transferring the total of the credit balances to the *credit* side of Income Summary. Note that the credit to Income Summary is the total of the Income Statement Credit column in the work sheet.
2. The second entry closes all income statement accounts with *debit* balances by transferring the total of the debit balances to the *debit* side of Income Summary. The debit to Income Summary is the subtotal of the Income Statement Debit column in the work sheet.
3. The third entry closes Income Summary by transferring its balance, the net income or the net loss for the year, to Retained Earnings. The amount of the debit (or credit) to Income Summary is the amount of net income (or net loss) reported on the work sheet.
4. The fourth entry closes Dividends by transferring its balance to Retained Earnings.

The closing entries are recorded in the journal immediately following the adjusting entries. The closing entries for Midtown Electric Corporation are shown on page 143.[5]

The income summary account, as it will appear after the closing entries have been posted, is as follows:

Income Summary Account

ACCOUNT Income Summary ACCOUNT NO. 313

DATE		ITEM	POST. REF.	DEBIT	CREDIT	BALANCE DEBIT	BALANCE CREDIT
1989 Dec.	31	Revenue, etc.	29		797 560 00		797 560 00
	31	Expenses, etc.	29	722 960 00			74 600 00
	31	Net Income	29	74 600 00		—	—

After the closing entries have been recorded and posted, the revenue, expense, and dividend accounts have zero balances. The only accounts with balances are the asset, contra asset, liability, and stockholders' equity accounts. The balances of these accounts in the ledger will correspond exactly with the amounts appearing on the balance sheet on page 140.

POST-CLOSING TRIAL BALANCE

After the adjusting and closing entries have been recorded, it is advisable to take another trial balance to verify the debit-credit equality of the ledger at the beginning of the following year. This post-closing trial balance may consist of two calculator tape listings, one for the debit balances and the other for the credit balances, or its details may be shown in a more formal fashion, as was illustrated in Chapter 1 on page 29.

[5]An alternative method of recording merchandise inventory is presented in Appendix B. This alternative method is sometimes referred to as the adjusting method. Under this method, the entries for beginning and ending merchandise inventory are classified as adjusting entries rather than closing entries.

JOURNAL PAGE 29

	DATE		DESCRIPTION	POST. REF.	DEBIT	CREDIT	
1			Closing Entries				1
2	1989 Dec.	31	Merchandise Inventory	114	62 150 00		2
3			Sales	411	720 185 00		3
4			Purchases Returns and Allowances	512	9 100 00		4
5			Purchases Discounts	518	2 525 00		5
6			Interest Income	812	3 600 00		6
7			Income Summary	313		797 560 00	7
8							8
9		31	Income Summary	313	722 960 00		9
10			Merchandise Inventory	114		59 700 00	10
11			Sales Returns and Allowances	412		6 140 00	11
12			Sales Discounts	413		5 790 00	12
13			Purchases	511		521 980 00	13
14			Transportation In	514		17 400 00	14
15			Sales Salaries Expense	611		60 030 00	15
16			Advertising Expense	612		10 860 00	16
17			Depreciation Exp.—Store Equip.	613		3 100 00	17
18			Miscellaneous Selling Expense	619		630 00	18
19			Office Salaries Expense	711		21 020 00	19
20			Rent Expense	712		8 100 00	20
21			Depreciation Exp.—Office Equip.	715		2 490 00	21
22			Insurance Expense	716		1 910 00	22
23			Office Supplies Expense	717		610 00	23
24			Miscellaneous General Expense	719		760 00	24
25			Interest Expense	911		2 440 00	25
26							26
27		31	Income Summary	313	74 600 00		27
28			Retained Earnings	311		74 600 00	28
29							29
30		31	Retained Earnings	311	18 000 00		30
31			Dividends	312		18 000 00	31
32							32
33							33
34							34
35							35

Closing Entries

FLOW OF DATA THROUGH ACCOUNTING SYSTEM

An understanding of the principal accounting procedures of a fiscal period, which were presented in this and preceding chapters, is essential as a foundation for further study of accounting principles. The flow of data through the accounting system begins with the analysis and the journalizing of transactions and ends with the post-closing trial balance, with the financial statements being the most significant outputs. The flowchart on page 144 shows the following phases of this flow, by number:

1. Transactions are analyzed and recorded in a journal.
2. Transactions are posted to the ledger.
3. Trial balance is prepared, data needed to adjust the accounts are assembled, and the work sheet is completed.
4. Financial statements are prepared.
5. Adjusting and closing entries are journalized.
6. Adjusting and closing entries are posted to the ledger.
7. Post-closing trial balance is prepared.

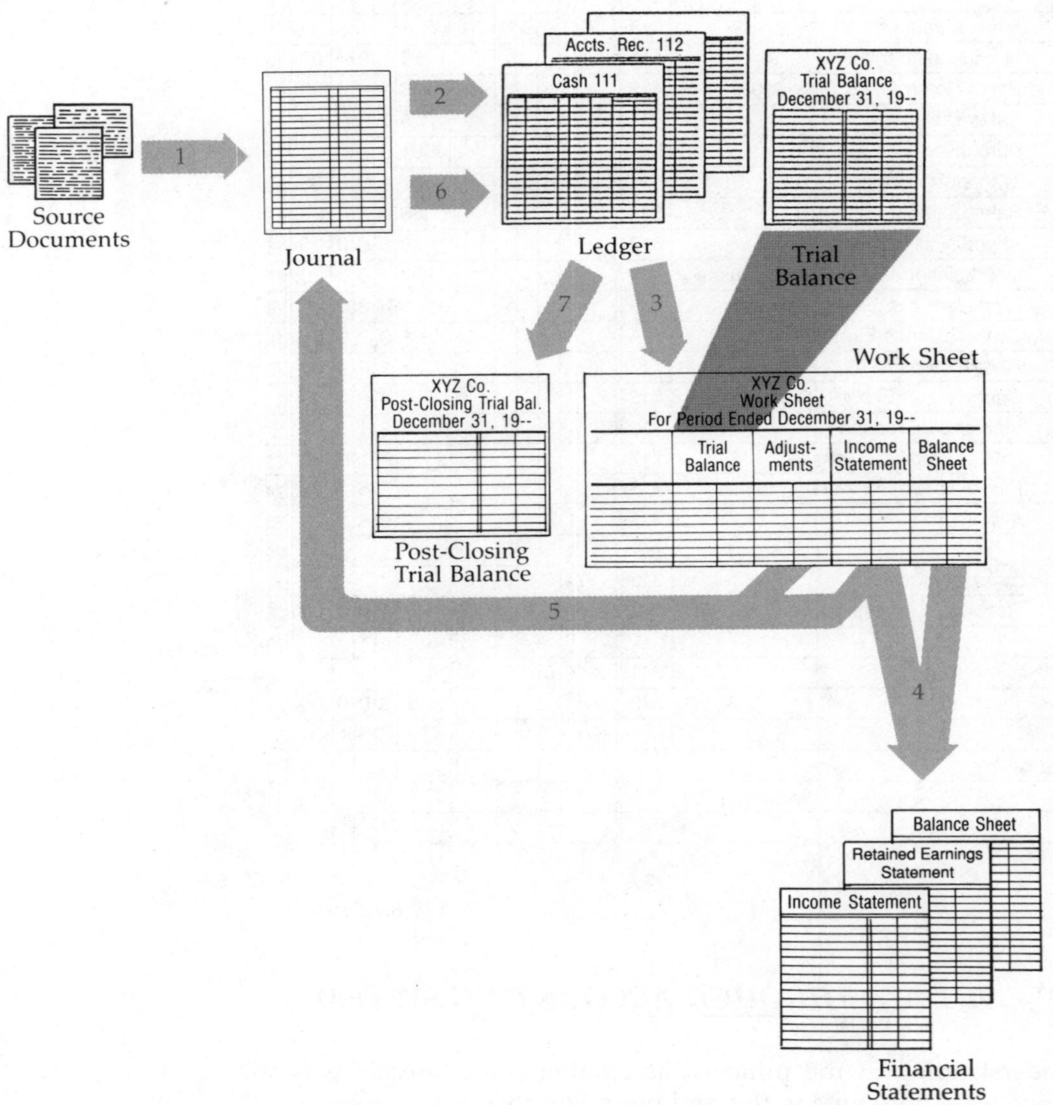

Flow of Data Through Accounting System

REVERSING ENTRIES

At the beginning of a new fiscal period, after the post-closing trial balance for the preceding period has been prepared, **reversing entries** may be recorded. These entries, which are optional, are the exact reverse of the related adjusting entries made at the end of the preceding period. Some of these adjusting entries have an important effect on otherwise routine transactions that occur in the following period. The purpose of reversing entries is to make the recording of these routine transactions more efficient.

A typical example of an adjusting entry that affects a transaction in the following period is the adjusting entry for accrued salaries owed to employees at the end of the year. The wage or salary expense of an enterprise and the accompanying liability to employees actually accumulates or accrues day by day, or even hour by hour, during any part of the fiscal year. Nevertheless, the practice of recording the expense only at the time of payment is more efficient. When salaries are paid weekly, an entry debiting Salary Expense and crediting Cash will be recorded 52 or 53 times during the year. If there has been an adjusting entry for accrued salaries at the end of the year, however, the first payment of salaries in the following year will include such year-end accrual. In the absence of some special provision, it will be necessary to debit Salaries Payable for the amount owed for the earlier year and Salary Expense for the portion of the payroll that represents expense for the later year.

To illustrate, assume the following facts for an enterprise that pays salaries weekly and ends its fiscal year on December 31:

1. Salaries are paid on Friday for the five-day week ending on Friday.
2. The balance in Salary Expense as of Friday, December 27, is $62,500.
3. Salaries accrued for Monday and Tuesday, December 30 and 31, total $500.
4. Salaries paid on Friday, January 3, of the following year total $1,250.

The foregoing data may be diagrammed as follows:

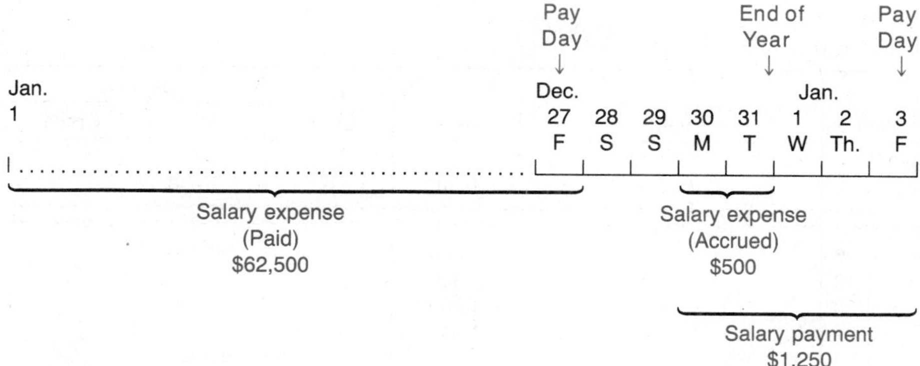

The adjusting entry to record the accrued salary expense and salaries payable for Monday and Tuesday, December 30 and 31, is as follows:

Dec. 31	Salary Expense	500	
	Salaries Payable		500

After the adjusting entry has been posted, Salary Expense will have a debit balance of $63,000 ($62,500 + $500) and Salaries Payable will have a credit balance of $500. After the closing process is completed, Salary Expense is in balance and ready for entries of the following year, but Salaries Payable continues to have a credit balance of $500. As matters now stand, it would be necessary to record the $1,250 payroll on January 3 as a debit of $500 to Salaries Payable and a debit of $750 to Salary Expense. This situation means that the employee who records payroll entries must not only record this particular payroll in a different manner from all other weekly payrolls for the year, but must also refer to the adjusting entries in the journal or the ledger to determine the amount of the $1,250 payment to be debited to each of the two accounts.

The need to refer to earlier entries and to divide the debit between two accounts can be avoided by recording a reversing entry as of the first day of the following fiscal period. Continuing with the illustration, the reversing entry for the accrued salaries is as follows:

Jan. 1	Salaries Payable	500	
	Salary Expense		500

The amounts and the accounts in the reversing entry are the same as in the adjusting entry; the debits and credits are merely reversed. The effect of the reversing entry is to transfer the $500 liability from Salaries Payable to the credit side of Salary Expense. The real nature of the $500 balance is unchanged; it remains a liability. When the payroll is paid on January 3, Salary Expense will be debited and Cash will be credited for $1,250, the entire amount of the weekly salaries. After the entry is posted, Salary Expense will have a debit balance of $750, which is the amount of expense incurred for January 1–3. The sequence of entries, including adjusting, closing, and reversing entries, may be traced in the following accounts:

Adjustment and Reversal for Accrued Salaries

ACCOUNT SALARY EXPENSE ACCOUNT NO. 611

Date		Item	Debit	Credit	Balance Debit	Balance Credit
1989						
Jan.	5		1,240		1,240	
Dec.	6		1,300		58,440	
	13		1,450		59,890	
	20		1,260		61,150	
	27		1,350		62,500	
	31	Adjusting	500		63,000	
	31	Closing		63,000	—	—
1990						
Jan.	1	Reversing		500		500
	3		1,250		750	

ACCOUNT SALARIES PAYABLE ACCOUNT NO. 213

Date		Item	Debit	Credit	Balance Debit	Balance Credit
1989 Dec.	31	Adjusting		500		500
1990 Jan.	1	Reversing	500		—	—

Reversing entries can be used with the adjustments for all accrued liabilities and accrued assets. They are also appropriate with the adjustments for prepaid expenses recorded initially as expenses and unearned revenues recorded initially as revenues.

The only reversing entry that would be made by Midtown Electric Corporation is the reversing entry for accrued salaries. This entry is journalized as follows:

Reversing Entry

JOURNAL PAGE 29

	DATE		DESCRIPTION	POST. REF.	DEBIT	CREDIT	
33			Reversing Entry				33
34	1989 Jan.	1	Salaries Payable	213	1 1 4 0 00		34
35			Sales Salaries Expense	611		7 8 0 00	35
36			Office Salaries Expense	711		3 6 0 00	36
37							37
38							38

After the reversing entry is posted, Salaries Payable is in balance and the liabilities for sales and office salaries appear as credits in the respective expense accounts. The entire amount of the first payroll in January will be debited to the salary expense accounts, and the balances of the accounts will then automatically represent the expense of the new period.

Reversing Entries: Once or Twice?

The use of reversing entries is an optional procedure designed to simplify the recording of transactions that follow, reduce the time required to record such transactions, avoid errors, and promote efficiency in general. In one case, however, a reversing entry created rather than prevented an error from occurring.

The error occurred when two companies merged and combined their accounting systems. The accounting systems for the two companies were incompatible—and so, unfortunately, were the chief accounting personnel of the two companies, who were jockeying for position and scarcely speaking to each other. Competent enough to perform routine functions for the separate companies, they were unable to cope with the change brought about by the merger. Furthermore, the basic data which the accounting systems provided were suspect; one company's computerized accounting system was badly programmed and almost nightmarishly erratic.

Amid the confusion of closing and opening the books while the two accounting departments were being combined, an accrued liability was reversed twice instead of once. The net effect was that earnings were overstated by $790,000 and accounts payable were understated by the same amount.

Source: Richard J. Whalen, "The Big Skid at Yale Express," *Fortune* (November, 1965).

Chapter Review

KEY POINTS

1. Work Sheet for Financial Statements.
To assist the accountant in accumulating data for the financial statements, a work sheet is often used. The work sheet can also assist the accountant in preparing adjusting and closing entries.

2. Preparation of Financial Statements.
The basic financial statements for an enterprise are the income statement, retained earnings statement, and balance sheet.

There are two widely used forms for the income statement: multiple-step and single-step. The multiple-step income statement is so called because of its many sections, subsections, and intermediate balances. The single-step income statement derives its name from the fact that the total of all expenses is deducted from the total of all revenues.

The retained earnings statement summarizes the changes that have occurred in the retained earnings account during a fiscal period. It is not unusual to add the analysis of retained earnings at the bottom of the income statement to form a combined income and retained earnings statement.

The balance sheet may be prepared using the account form or the report form. The account form lists assets on the left-hand side of the statement, with liabilities and stockholders' equity on the right-hand side. The report form lists assets, liabilities, and stockholders' equity in a downward sequence.

3. Adjusting and Closing Entries.
The adjusting entries are prepared from the work sheet adjustments columns. The closing entries are recorded in the journal immediately following the adjusting entries. The revenue and expense accounts are cleared of their balances, reducing them to zero. The final effect of closing out such balances is a net increase or decrease in the retained earnings account. The final closing entry reduces the dividends account to a zero balance by transferring it to the retained earnings account.

4. Post-Closing Trial Balance.
After the adjusting and closing entries have been recorded, it is advisable to take another trial balance to verify the debit-credit equality of the ledger as of the beginning of the following year.

5. Reversing Entries.
Some of the adjusting entries recorded at the end of the fiscal year have an important effect on otherwise routine transactions that occur in the following year. To simplify the recording of transactions in the following year, to reduce the time required to record such transactions, to avoid errors, and to promote efficiency, reversing entries may be prepared. As the term implies, a reversing entry is the exact reverse of the adjusting entry to which it relates. The amounts are the same; the debits and credits are merely reversed.

KEY TERMS

work sheet 131
multiple-step income statement 135
single-step income statement 135
cost of merchandise sold 135
perpetual inventory system 137
periodic inventory system 137
physical inventory 137
gross profit 137
selling expenses 137
general expenses 137
income from operations 137
other income 138
other expense 138
net income 138
net loss 138
retained earnings statement 139
account form of balance sheet 140
report form of balance sheet 140
closing entries 141
Income Summary 141
reversing entry 145

SELF-EXAMINATION QUESTIONS

(Answers at End of Chapter)

1. The income statement in which the total of all expenses is deducted from the total of all revenues is termed:
   A. multiple-step form
   B. single-step form
   C. account form
   D. report form
2. On a multiple-step income statement, the excess of net sales over the cost of merchandise sold is called:
   A. operating income
   B. income from operations
   C. gross profit
   D. net income
3. Which of the following expenses would normally be classified as "other expense" on a multiple-step income statement?
   A. Depreciation expense—office equipment
   B. Sales salaries expense
   C. Insurance expense
   D. Interest expense
4. Which of the following accounts would be closed to the income summary account at the end of a period?
   A. Sales
   B. Salary Expense
   C. Both Sales and Salary Expense
   D. Neither Sales nor Salary Expense
5. The post-closing trial balance would include which of the following accounts?
   A. Cash
   B. Sales
   C. Salary Expense
   D. All of the above

ILLUSTRATIVE PROBLEM

A partially completed work sheet for Hadley Inc., including all adjustments, is presented on page 151.

Instructions:

1. Complete the work sheet for Hadley Inc. The merchandise inventory at October 31, 1989, as determined by a physical count, was $156,000.
2. Prepare a multiple-step income statement.
3. Prepare a retained earnings statement.
4. Prepare a report form of balance sheet, assuming that the current portion of the mortgage note payable is $7,500.
5. Journalize the adjusting entries.
6. Journalize the closing entries.
7. Journalize any reversing entries as of November 1, 1989.

Hadley Inc.

Work Sheet

For Year Ended October 31, 1989

	ACCOUNT TITLE	TRIAL BALANCE		ADJUSTMENTS	
		DEBIT	CREDIT	DEBIT	CREDIT
1	Cash	26400 00			
2	Accounts Receivable	62200 00			
3	Merchandise Inventory	141300 00			
4	Prepaid Insurance	6800 00			(a) 4300 00
5	Store Supplies	1250 00			(b) 660 00
6	Office Supplies	800 00			(c) 480 00
7	Store Equipment	65000 00			
8	Accumulated Depreciation—Store Equipment		20100 00		(d) 5850 00
9	Office Equipment	19600 00			
10	Accumulated Depreciation—Office Equipment		8100 00		(e) 2160 00
11	Accounts Payable		36400 00		
12	Salaries Payable				(f) 2700 00
13	Mortgage Note Payable (final payment, 1998)		75000 00		
14	Capital Stock		50000 00		
15	Retained Earnings		63420 00		
16	Dividends	8000 00			
17	Sales		540000 00		
18	Sales Returns and Allowances	4300 00			
19	Sales Discounts	2500 00			
20	Purchases	360000 00			
21	Purchases Returns and Allowances		9000 00		
22	Purchases Discounts		4680 00		
23	Transportation In	1800 00			
24	Sales Salaries Expense	43200 00		(f) 1800 00	
25	Advertising Expense	15000 00			
26	Depreciation Expense—Store Equipment			(d) 5850 00	
27	Store Supplies Expense			(b) 660 00	
28	Miscellaneous Selling Expense	970 00			
29	Office Salaries Expense	30000 00		(f) 900 00	
30	Rent Expense	8500 00			
31	Insurance Expense			(a) 4300 00	
32	Depreciation Expense—Office Equipment			(e) 2160 00	
33	Office Supplies Expense			(c) 480 00	
34	Miscellaneous General Expense	830 00			
35	Interest Expense	8250 00			
36		806700 00	806700 00	16150 00	16150 00
37	Net Income				
38					

SOLUTION

(1)

Hadley

Work

For Year Ended

ACCOUNT TITLE	TRIAL BALANCE DEBIT	TRIAL BALANCE CREDIT	ADJUSTMENTS DEBIT	ADJUSTMENTS CREDIT
Cash	26,400.00			
Accounts Receivable	62,200.00			
Merchandise Inventory	141,300.00			
Prepaid Insurance	6,800.00			(a) 4,300.00
Store Supplies	1,250.00			(b) 660.00
Office Supplies	800.00			(c) 480.00
Store Equipment	65,000.00			
Accumulated Depreciation—Store Equipment		20,100.00		(d) 5,850.00
Office Equipment	19,600.00			
Accumulated Depreciation—Office Equipment		8,100.00		(e) 2,160.00
Accounts Payable		36,400.00		
Salaries Payable				(f) 2,700.00
Mortgage Note Payable (final payment, 1998)		75,000.00		
Capital Stock		50,000.00		
Retained Earnings		63,420.00		
Dividends	8,000.00			
Sales		540,000.00		
Sales Returns and Allowances	4,300.00			
Sales Discounts	2,500.00			
Purchases	360,000.00			
Purchases Returns and Allowances		9,000.00		
Purchases Discounts		4,680.00		
Transportation In	1,800.00			
Sales Salaries Expense	43,200.00		(f) 1,800.00	
Advertising Expense	15,000.00			
Depreciation Expense—Store Equipment			(d) 5,850.00	
Store Supplies Expense			(b) 660.00	
Miscellaneous Selling Expense	970.00			
Office Salaries Expense	30,000.00		(f) 900.00	
Rent Expense	8,500.00			
Insurance Expense			(a) 4,300.00	
Depreciation Expense—Office Equipment			(e) 2,160.00	
Office Supplies Expense			(c) 480.00	
Miscellaneous General Expense	830.00			
Interest Expense	8,250.00			
	806,700.00	806,700.00	16,150.00	16,150.00
Net Income				

Inc.

Sheet

October 31, 1989

INCOME STATEMENT		BALANCE SHEET		
DEBIT	CREDIT	DEBIT	CREDIT	
		26400 00		1
		62200 00		2
141300 00	156000 00	156000 00		3
		2500 00		4
		590 00		5
		320 00		6
		65000 00		7
			25950 00	8
		19600 00		9
			10260 00	10
			36400 00	11
			2700 00	12
			75000 00	13
			50000 00	14
			63420 00	15
		8000 00		16
	540000 00			17
4300 00				18
2500 00				19
360000 00				20
	9000 00			21
	4680 00			22
1800 00				23
45000 00				24
15000 00				25
5850 00				26
660 00				27
970 00				28
30900 00				29
8500 00				30
4300 00				31
2160 00				32
480 00				33
830 00				34
8250 00				35
632800 00	709680 00	340610 00	263730 00	36
76880 00			76880 00	37
709680 00	709680 00	340610 00	340610 00	38
				39
				40

(2)

Hadley Inc.
Income Statement
For Year Ended October 31, 1989

Revenue from sales:				
Sales			$540,000	
Less: Sales returns and allowances		$ 4,300		
Sales discounts		2,500	6,800	
Net sales				$533,200
Cost of merchandise sold:				
Merchandise inventory, November 1, 1988			$141,300	
Purchases		$360,000		
Less: Purchases returns and allowances	$9,000			
Purchases discounts	4,680	13,680		
Net purchases		$346,320		
Add transportation in		1,800		
Cost of merchandise purchased			348,120	
Merchandise available for sale			$489,420	
Less merchandise inventory, October 31, 1989			156,000	
Cost of merchandise sold				333,420
Gross profit				$199,780
Operating expenses:				
Selling expenses:				
Sales salaries expense		$ 45,000		
Advertising expense		15,000		
Depreciation expense—store equipment		5,850		
Store supplies expense		660		
Miscellaneous selling expense		970		
Total selling expenses			$ 67,480	
General expenses:				
Office salaries expense		$ 30,900		
Rent expense		8,500		
Insurance expense		4,300		
Depreciation expense—office equipment		2,160		
Office supplies expense		480		
Miscellaneous general expense		830		
Total general expenses			47,170	
Total operating expenses				114,650
Income from operations				$ 85,130
Other expense:				
Interest expense				8,250
Net income				$ 76,880

(3)

Hadley Inc.
Retained Earnings Statement
For Year Ended October 31, 1989

Retained earnings, November 1, 1988		$ 63,420
Net income for the year	$76,880	
Less dividends	8,000	
Increase in retained earnings		68,880
Retained earnings, October 31, 1989		$132,300

(4)

Hadley Inc.
Balance Sheet
October 31, 1989

Assets			
Current assets:			
Cash		$ 26,400	
Accounts receivable		62,200	
Merchandise inventory		156,000	
Prepaid insurance		2,500	
Store supplies		590	
Office supplies		320	
Total current assets			$248,010
Plant assets:			
Store equipment	$65,000		
Less accumulated depreciation	25,950	$ 39,050	
Office equipment	$19,600		
Less accumulated depreciation	10,260	9,340	
Total plant assets			48,390
Total assets			$296,400
Liabilities			
Current liabilities:			
Accounts payable		$ 36,400	
Mortgage note payable (current portion)		7,500	
Salaries payable		2,700	
Total current liabilities			$ 46,600
Long-term liabilities:			
Mortgage note payable (final payment, 1998)			67,500
Total liabilities			$114,100
Stockholders' Equity			
Capital stock		$ 50,000	
Retained earnings		132,300	
Total stockholders' equity			182,300
Total liabilities and stockholders' equity			$296,400

(5)

JOURNAL PAGE 27

DATE		DESCRIPTION	POST. REF.	DEBIT	CREDIT
		Adjusting Entries			
1989 Oct.	31	Insurance Expense		4300 00	
		Prepaid Insurance			4300 00
	31	Store Supplies Expense		660 00	
		Store Supplies			660 00
	31	Office Supplies Expense		480 00	
		Office Supplies			480 00
	31	Depr. Expense — Store Equipment		5850 00	
		Accumulated Depr. — Store Equip.			5850 00
	31	Depr. Expense — Office Equipment		2160 00	
		Accumulated Depr. — Office Equip.			2160 00
	31	Sales Salaries Expense		1800 00	
		Office Salaries Expense		900 00	
		Salaries Payable			2700 00

(6)

DATE		DESCRIPTION	POST. REF.	DEBIT	CREDIT
		Closing Entries			
	31	Merchandise Inventory		156000 00	
		Sales		540000 00	
		Purchases Returns and Allowances		9000 00	
		Purchases Discounts		4680 00	
		Income Summary			709680 00
	31	Income Summary		632800 00	
		Merchandise Inventory			141300 00
		Sales Returns and Allowances			4300 00
		Sales Discounts			2500 00
		Purchases			360000 00
		Transportation In			1800 00
		Sales Salaries Expense			45000 00
		Advertising Expense			15000 00
		Depr. Expense — Store Equipment			5850 00
		Store Supplies Expense			660 00
		Miscellaneous Selling Expense			970 00
		Office Salaries Expense			30900 00

Date		Description	Post. Ref.	Debit	Credit
		Rent Expense			8500 00
		Insurance Expense			4300 00
		Depr. Expense—Office Equipment			2160 00
		Office Supplies Expense			480 00
		Miscellaneous General Expense			830 00
		Interest Expense			8250 00
		Income Summary		76880 00	
		Retained Earnings			76880 00
		Retained Earnings		8000 00	
		Dividends			8000 00

(7)

JOURNAL PAGE 28

DATE		DESCRIPTION	POST. REF.	DEBIT	CREDIT
		Reversing Entry			
1989 Nov.	1	Salaries Payable		2700 00	
		Sales Salaries Expense			1800 00
		Office Salaries Expense			900 00

Discussion Questions

4–1. Is the work sheet a substitute for the financial statements? Discuss.

4–2. What is the name of the account in which unsold merchandise at the end of a period is recorded?

4–3. In the Balance Sheet columns of the work sheet for Fox Company for the current year, the Debit column total is $22,150 greater than the Credit column total. Would the income statement report a net income or a net loss? Explain.

4–4. Differentiate between the multiple-step and the single-step forms of the income statement.

4–5. What is the primary characteristic of the multiple-step income statement?

4–6. Is there uniformity in the amount of detail presented in a multiple-step income statement? Explain.

4–7. In which type of system for accounting for merchandise held for sale is there no attempt to record the cost of merchandise sold until the end of the period, when a physical inventory is taken?

4–8. The account Merchandise Inventory is listed at $150,000 on the trial balance (before adjustments) as of October 31, the end of the first month in the fiscal year. Which one of the following phrases describes the item correctly?
(a) Inventory of merchandise at October 1, beginning of the month.
(b) Purchases of merchandise during October.
(c) Merchandise available for sale during October.
(d) Inventory of merchandise at October 31, end of the month.
(e) Cost of merchandise sold during October.

4–9. In the following questions, identify the items designated by "X":
(a) Purchases − (X + X) = Net purchases
(b) Net purchases + X = Cost of merchandise purchased
(c) X + Cost of merchandise purchased = Merchandise available for sale
(d) Merchandise available for sale − X = Cost of merchandise sold

4–10. For the fiscal year, net sales were $780,000 and the cost of merchandise purchased was $520,000. Merchandise inventory at the beginning of the year was $60,000, and at the end of the year it was $70,000. Determine the following amounts:
(a) Merchandise available for sale.
(b) Cost of merchandise sold.
(c) Gross profit.
(d) Merchandise inventory listed on the balance sheet as of the end of the year.

4–11. Into what two categories are operating expenses of a merchandising enterprise usually separated?

4–12. The following expenses were incurred by a merchandising enterprise during the year. In which expense section of the income statement should each be reported: (a) selling, (b) general, or (c) other?
(1) Interest expense on notes payable.
(2) Salaries of salespersons.
(3) Insurance expense on office equipment.
(4) Advertising expense.
(5) Office supplies used.
(6) Depreciation expense on store equipment.
(7) Rent expense.
(8) Salary of general manager.

4–13. What major advantages and disadvantages does the single-step form of income statement have in comparison to the multiple-step statement?

4–14. (a) What two financial statements are frequently combined and presented as a single statement? (b) What is the major criticism directed at the combined statement?

4–15. Differentiate between the account form and the report form of balance sheet.

4–16. Why are closing entries required at the end of an accounting period?

4–17. What type of accounts are closed by transferring their balances to Income Summary (a) as a debit, (b) as a credit?

4–18. To what account is the income summary account closed for a corporation?

4–19. To what account in the ledger of a corporation is the account Dividends periodically closed?

4–20. From the following list, identify the accounts that should be closed to Income Summary at the end of the fiscal year: (a) Accounts Receivable, (b) Salaries Expense, (c) Capital Stock, (d) Salaries Payable, (e) Depreciation Expense—Equipment, (f) Utilities Expense, (g) Equipment, (h) Supplies, (i) Retained Earnings, (j) Sales, (k) Land, (l) Accumulated Depreciation—Equipment.

4–21. (a) What is the effect of closing the revenue, expense, and dividends accounts of a corporation at the end of a fiscal year? (b) After the closing entries have been posted, what type of accounts remain with balances?

4–22. Which of the following accounts in the ledger of a corporation will ordinarily appear in the post-closing trial balance? (a) Accounts Payable, (b) Accumulated Depreciation, (c) Capital Stock, (d) Supplies, (e) Depreciation Expense, (f) Sales, (g) Equipment, (h) Retained Earnings, (i) Dividends, (j) Cash, (k) Wages Expense, (l) Wages Payable.

4–23. Before adjustment at October 31, the end of the fiscal year, the salary expense account has a debit balance of $370,000. The amount of salary accrued (owed but not paid) on the same date is $7,800. Indicate the necessary (a) adjusting entry, and (b) reversing entry.

4–24. As of November 1, the first day of the fiscal year, Salary Expense has a credit balance of $4,800. On November 4, the first payday of the year, salaries of $13,100 are paid. (a) What is the salary expense for November 1–4? (b) What entry should be made to record the payment on November 4?

4–25. Real World Focus. A recent trend in retailing is the establishment of warehouse clubs. These clubs offer name-brand merchandise at prices ranging from 20 to 40 percent below discount store prices to their members who pay a nominal yearly fee. The Price Club is one of the leaders in this growing area of retailing. The following graph compares the gross profit as a percent of sales of The Price Club with that of K Mart Corp.:

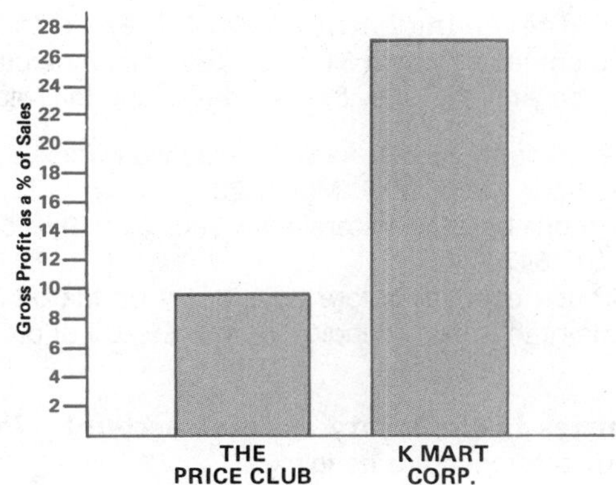

How can the Price Club remain profitable with a gross profit percentage less than one half that of K Mart Corp.?

Exercises

4–26. Closing entries for corporation. After all revenue and expense accounts have been closed at the end of the fiscal year, Income Summary has a debit of $919,750 and a credit of $889,250. As of the same date, Retained Earnings has a credit balance of $310,600, and Dividends has a balance of $25,000. (a) Journalize the entries required to complete the closing of the accounts. (b) State the amount of Retained Earnings at the end of the period.

4–27. Identification of items missing from income statement. For (a) through (i), identify the items designated by "X".

(a) Sales − (X + X) = Net sales
(b) Purchases − (X + X) = Net purchases
(c) Net purchases + X = Cost of merchandise purchased
(d) Merchandise inventory (beginning) + cost of merchandise purchased = X
(e) Merchandise available for sale − X = Cost of merchandise sold
(f) Net sales − cost of merchandise sold = X
(g) X + X = Operating expenses
(h) Gross profit − operating expenses = X
(i) Income from operations + X − X = Net income

4–28. Determination of amounts for items omitted from income statement. Three items are omitted in each of the following tabulations of income statement data. Determine the amounts of the missing items, identifying them by letter.

Sales	$ (a)	$560,000	$880,000	$750,000
Sales returns and allowances	8,000	20,000	(g)	18,000
Sales discounts	2,000	10,000	5,000	(j)
Net sales	100,000	(d)	860,000	(k)
Beginning inventory	(b)	120,000	215,000	(l)
Cost of merchandise purchased	60,000	(e)	500,000	580,000
Ending inventory	30,000	100,000	(h)	120,000
Cost of merchandise sold	50,000	340,000	(i)	540,000
Gross profit	(c)	(f)	385,000	180,000

4–29. Adjusting and reversing entries. On the basis of the following data, journalize (a) the adjusting entries at March 31, 1989, the end of the current fiscal year, and (b) the reversing entry on April 1, 1989, the first day of the following year.

(1) Sales salaries are uniformly $9,000 for a five-day workweek, ending on Friday. The last payday of the year was Friday, March 28.
(2) Store supplies account balance before adjusting, $1,250; store supplies physical inventory, March 31, $470.
(3) The prepaid insurance account before adjustment on March 31 has a balance of $8,270. An analysis of the policies indicates that $5,230 of premiums have expired during the year.

4–30. Identify entries in the salary expense account. Portions of the salary expense account of an enterprise are as follows:

ACCOUNT Salary Expense — ACCOUNT NO. 54

Date		Item	Dr.	Cr.	Balance Dr.	Balance Cr.
19--						
Jan.	2			1,250		1,250
	6		6,000		4,750	
Dec.	27	(1)	7,500		245,500	
	31	(2)	3,000		248,500	
	31	(3)		248,500	—	—
19--						
Jan.	2	(4)		3,000		3,000
	5	(5)	7,500		4,500	

(a) Indicate the nature of the entry (payment, adjusting, closing, reversing) for each numbered item. (b) Present the complete journal entry for each numbered item.

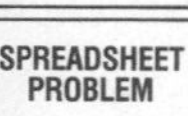

4–31. Cost of merchandise sold section of income statement. On the basis of the following data, prepare the cost of merchandise sold section of the income statement for the fiscal year ended March 31, 1989, for Tysan Inc.

Merchandise Inventory, March 31, 1989	$150,000
Merchandise Inventory, April 1, 1988	120,000
Purchases	600,000
Purchases Returns and Allowances	5,500
Purchases Discounts	3,200
Transportation In	2,800

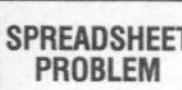

4–32. Multiple-step income statement and closing entries. Selected account titles and related amounts appearing in the income statement and balance sheet columns of the work sheet of North Company for the year ended December 31 are listed in alphabetical order as follows:

Building	$260,000	Purchases Discounts	$ 10,000
Capital Stock	100,000	Purchases Returns and Allowances	15,000
Cash	57,800	Retained Earnings	300,000
Dividends	15,000	Salaries Payable	3,720
General Expenses	87,200	Sales	1,200,000
Interest Expense	7,500	Sales Discounts	9,500
Merchandise Inventory (1/1)	200,000	Sales Returns and Allowances	28,000
Merchandise Inventory (12/31)	230,000	Selling Expenses	125,000
Office Supplies	8,500	Store Supplies	7,200
Purchases	850,000	Transportation In	6,300

All selling expenses have been recorded in the account entitled "Selling Expenses," and all general expenses have been recorded in the account entitled "General Expenses."

(a) Prepare a multiple-step income statement for the year.
(b) Determine the amount of retained earnings to be reported in the balance sheet at the end of the year.
(c) Journalize the closing entries.

4–33. Single-step income statement. Summary operating data for Ronald Childers Inc. during the current year ended August 31, 1989, are as follows: cost of merchandise sold, $850,000; general expenses, $150,000; interest expense, $30,000; rent income, $50,000; net sales, $1,400,000; and selling expenses, $200,000. Prepare a single-step income statement.

4–34. Combined income and retained earnings statement. From the data presented in Exercise 4–33 and assuming that the balance of Retained Earnings was $610,000 on September 1, 1988, and that $40,000 of dividends were paid during the year, prepare a combined income and retained earnings statement for Ronald Childers Inc. (Use the single-step form for the income statement portion.)

Problems

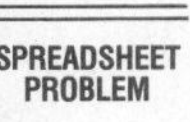

4–35. Preparation of work sheet. The accounts in the ledger of Bemis Company, with the unadjusted balances on August 31, the end of the current fiscal year, are as follows:

Cash	$ 17,760	Sales	$790,500
Accounts Receivable	53,340	Purchases	513,700
Merchandise Inventory	121,400	Sales Salaries Expense	82,800
Prepaid Insurance	2,480	Advertising Expense	23,300
Store Supplies	2,120	Depreciation Expense—Store Equipment	—
Store Equipment	166,200	Store Supplies Expense	—
Accumulated Depreciation—Store Equipment	84,600	Miscellaneous Selling Expense	1,600
Accounts Payable	32,000	Office Salaries Expense	52,200
Salaries Payable	—	Rent Expense	25,000
Capital Stock	100,000	Heating and Lighting Expense	17,400
Retained Earnings	99,550	Taxes Expense	7,850
Dividends	16,000	Insurance Expense	—
		Miscellaneous General Expense	3,500

The data needed for year-end adjustments on August 31 are as follows:

Insurance expired during the year		$1,560
Store supplies inventory on August 31		520
Depreciation for the current year		9,300
Accrued salaries on August 31:		
Sales salaries	$1,500	
Office salaries	1,200	2,700

Instructions: (1) Prepare a work sheet for the fiscal year ended August 31. The merchandise inventory on August 31 is $100,000.
(2) Compute the percent of net income to sales.

4–36. Preparation of multiple-step income statement and report form of balance sheet. The following selected accounts and their normal balances appear in the income statement and balance sheet columns of the work sheet of Thaxton Inc. for the fiscal year ended November 30, 1989:

Cash	$ 95,000
Notes Receivable	60,000
Accounts Receivable	92,000
Merchandise Inventory, Dec. 1, 1988	90,000
Merchandise Inventory, Nov. 30, 1989	100,000
Office Supplies	1,600
Prepaid Insurance	6,800
Office Equipment	24,000
Accumulated Depreciation—Office Equipment	10,800
Store Equipment	40,500
Accumulated Depreciation—Store Equipment	18,900
Accounts Payable	32,000
Salaries Payable	1,700
Mortgage Note Payable (final payment, 1998)	35,000
Capital Stock	150,000
Retained Earnings	144,010
Dividends	25,000
Sales	1,000,000
Sales Returns and Allowances	9,000
Sales Discounts	8,500
Purchases	790,000
Purchases Returns and Allowances	16,200
Purchases Discounts	3,800
Transportation In	10,300
Sales Salaries Expense	88,000
Advertising Expense	16,300
Depreciation Expense—Store Equipment	4,600
Miscellaneous Selling Expense	1,000
Office Salaries Expense	30,900

Rent Expense	$12,150
Depreciation Expense—Office Equipment	3,700
Insurance Expense	2,750
Office Supplies Expense	900
Miscellaneous General Expense	1,150
Interest Income	5,400
Interest Expense	3,660

Instructions: (1) Prepare a multiple-step income statement.
(2) Prepare a retained earnings statement.
(3) Prepare a report form of balance sheet, assuming that the current portion of the mortgage note payable is $3,500.

4–37. Preparation of single-step income statement and combined income and retained earnings statement. Selected accounts and related amounts for Thaxton Inc. for the fiscal year ended November 30, 1989, are presented in Problem 4–36.

Instructions: (1) Prepare a single-step income statement.
(2) Prepare a combined income and retained earnings statement, using the single-step form for the income statement portion.

SPREADSHEET PROBLEM

4–38. Combined income and retained earnings statement; balance sheet. The following data are derived from the records of Tift Co. at December 31, 1989, the end of the current fiscal year:

Accounts payable	$ 50,700
Accounts receivable	161,100
Accumulated depreciation—office equipment	40,800
Accumulated depreciation—store equipment	75,200
Capital stock	150,000
Cash	105,600
Cost of merchandise sold	726,600
Dividends	40,000
Dividends payable	10,000
General expenses	207,300
Interest expense	18,250
Merchandise inventory, December 31, 1989	175,000
Mortgage note payable (due in 1995)	150,000
Office equipment	72,200
Prepaid insurance	10,700
Rent income	15,500
Retained earnings	156,100
Salaries payable	9,750
Sales	1,267,000
Selling expenses	233,500
Store equipment	174,800

Instructions: (1) Prepare a combined income and retained earnings statement, using the single-step form for the income statement portion.
(2) Prepare a balance sheet in report form.

If the working papers correlating with this textbook are not used, omit Problem 4–39.

SPREADSHEET PROBLEM

4–39. Completion of work sheet and preparation of financial statements. A partially completed work sheet for Feldman Inc. is presented in the working papers. All adjustments have been entered on the work sheet. The ending inventory is $260,000.

Instructions: (1) Complete the work sheet for Feldman Inc.
(2) Prepare a multiple-step income statement.
(3) Prepare a retained earnings statement.
(4) Prepare a report form of balance sheet, assuming that the current portion of the mortgage note payable is $10,000.

4–40. Preparation of work sheet, financial statements, and adjusting, closing, and reversing entries. The accounts and their balances in the ledger of Fischer Company on December 31 of the current year are as follows:

Cash	$ 53,160
Accounts Receivable	125,000
Merchandise Inventory	180,000
Prepaid Insurance	9,540
Store Supplies	2,500
Office Supplies	1,700
Store Equipment	134,000
Accumulated Depreciation—Store Equipment	40,300
Office Equipment	40,000
Accumulated Depreciation—Office Equipment	17,200
Accounts Payable	62,540
Salaries Payable	—
Note Payable (final payment, 1994)	105,000
Capital Stock	150,000
Retained Earnings	70,510
Dividends	40,000
Sales	1,080,000
Sales Returns and Allowances	12,500
Sales Discounts	6,500
Purchases	720,000
Purchases Returns and Allowances	8,200
Purchases Discounts	6,800
Transportation In	5,000
Sales Salaries Expense	86,400
Advertising Expense	30,000
Depreciation Expense—Store Equipment	—
Store Supplies Expense	—
Miscellaneous Selling Expense	2,000
Office Salaries Expense	60,000
Rent Expense	18,000
Insurance Expense	—
Depreciation Expense—Office Equipment	—
Office Supplies Expense	—
Miscellaneous General Expense	1,650
Interest Expense	12,600

The data for year-end adjustments on December 31 are as follows:

Insurance expired during the year		$ 6,200
Inventory of supplies on December 31:		
Store supplies		800
Office supplies		400
Depreciation for the year:		
Store equipment		13,400
Office equipment		5,200
Salaries payable on December 31:		
Sales salaries	$2,750	
Office salaries	1,150	3,900

Instructions: (1) Prepare a work sheet for the fiscal year ended December 31, listing all accounts in the order given. The merchandise inventory on December 31 is $220,000.
(2) Prepare a multiple-step income statement.
(3) Prepare a retained earnings statement.
(4) Prepare a report form of balance sheet, assuming that the current portion of the note payable is $15,000.
(5) Journalize the adjusting entries.
(6) Journalize the closing entries.
(7) Journalize the reversing entries as of January 1.

4–41. Work sheet and statements for service corporation. Beacon Bowl Inc. prepared the following trial balance at June 30, 19--, the end of the current fiscal year:

Beacon Bowl Inc.
Trial Balance
June 30, 19--

Cash	11,500	
Prepaid Insurance	2,400	
Supplies	1,950	
Land	40,000	
Building	122,000	
Accumulated Depreciation—Building		31,700
Equipment	72,400	
Accumulated Depreciation—Equipment		15,300
Accounts Payable		6,100
Capital Stock		100,000
Retained Earnings		60,500
Dividends	15,000	
Bowling Revenue		161,200
Salaries and Wages Expense	60,200	
Advertising Expense	19,000	
Utilities Expense	18,200	
Repairs Expense	8,100	
Miscellaneous Expense	4,050	
	374,800	374,800

The data needed to determine year-end adjustments are as follows:

(a) Insurance expired during the year	$1,050
(b) Inventory of supplies at June 30	450
(c) Depreciation of building for the year	1,620
(d) Depreciation of equipment for the year	5,160
(e) Accrued salaries and wages at June 30	1,950

Instructions: (1) Record the trial balance on a work sheet and complete the work sheet.
(2) Prepare an income statement for the year ended June 30.
(3) Prepare a retained earnings statement for the year ended June 30.
(4) Prepare a report form of balance sheet as of June 30.
(5) Compute the percent of net income to revenue for the year.
(6) Compute the percent of net income for the year ended June 30 to total stockholders' equity as of the beginning of the fiscal year. The capital stock account remained unchanged during the year.

4–42. Adjusting entries from work sheet. A portion of the work sheet of Monfort Co. for the current year ended October 31 is as follows:

Account Title	Income Statement		Balance Sheet	
	Debit	Credit	Debit	Credit
Cash			57,900	
Accounts Receivable			122,500	
Merchandise Inventory	354,000	335,000	335,000	
Prepaid Rent			3,000	
Prepaid Insurance			2,340	
Supplies			1,380	
Store Equipment			152,300	
Accumulated Depr.—Store Equipment				51,000
Office Equipment			44,520	
Accumulated Depr.—Office Equipment				35,000
Accounts Payable				115,600
Sales Salaries Payable				4,500
Mortgage Note Payable				250,000
Capital Stock				150,000
Retained Earnings				90,850
Dividends			43,200	
Sales		1,020,000		
Sales Returns and Allowances	12,000			
Sales Discounts	8,500			
Purchases	617,720			
Purchases Returns and Allowances		14,650		
Purchases Discounts		10,140		
Transportation In	7,230			
Sales Salaries Expense	124,000			
Depreciation Expense—Store Equipment	16,460			
Supplies Expense	960			
Miscellaneous Selling Expense	3,800			
Office Salaries Expense	70,000			
Rent Expense	36,000			
Heating and Lighting Expense	21,750			
Insurance Expense	4,100			
Depreciation Expense—Office Equipment	5,180			
Miscellaneous General Expense	2,900			
Interest Expense	30,000			
	1,314,600	1,379,790	762,140	696,950

Instructions: (1) From the partial work sheet, determine the six entries that appeared in the adjustments columns and present them in journal form. The balance in Prepaid Rent before adjustment was $39,000, representing 13 months' rent at $3,000 per month.
(2) Determine the following:
(a) Amount of net income for the year.
(b) Balance of the retained earnings account at the end of the year.

ALTERNATE PROBLEMS

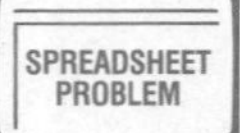

4–35A. Preparation of work sheet. The accounts in the ledger of Argo Company, with the unadjusted balances on April 30, the end of the current fiscal year, are as follows:

Cash	$ 26,250	Purchases	$360,000
Accounts Receivable	57,600	Sales Salaries Expense	46,500
Merchandise Inventory	87,150	Advertising Expense	15,800
Prepaid Insurance	7,600	Depreciation Expense—	
Store Supplies	4,950	Store Equipment	—
Store Equipment	53,700	Store Supplies Expense	—
Accumulated Depreciation—		Miscellaneous Selling Expense	2,750
Store Equipment	15,180	Office Salaries Expense	30,000
Accounts Payable	26,800	Rent Expense	24,000
Salaries Payable	—	Heating and Lighting Expense	9,660
Capital Stock	75,000	Taxes Expense	5,100
Retained Earnings	69,020	Insurance Expense	—
Dividends	15,000	Miscellaneous General Expense	2,140
Sales	562,200		

The data needed for year-end adjustments on April 30 are as follows:

Insurance expired during the year		$ 3,800
Store supplies inventory on April 30		1,250
Depreciation for the current year		11,500
Accrued salaries on April 30:		
Sales salaries	$1,600	
Office salaries	750	2,350

Instructions: (1) Prepare a work sheet for the fiscal year ended April 30. The merchandise inventory on April 30 is $90,000.
(2) Compute the percent of net income to sales.

4–36A. Preparation of multiple-step income statement and report form of balance sheet. The following selected accounts and their normal balances appear in the income statement and balance sheet columns of the work sheet of Daisy Inc. for the fiscal year ended January 31, 1989:

Cash	$ 41,000
Notes Receivable	120,000
Accounts Receivable	210,000
Merchandise Inventory, Feb. 1, 1988	125,000
Merchandise Inventory, Jan. 31, 1989	100,000
Office Supplies	5,600
Prepaid Insurance	3,400
Office Equipment	35,000
Accumulated Depreciation—Office Equipment	12,800
Store Equipment	72,000
Accumulated Depreciation—Store Equipment	24,200
Accounts Payable	45,600
Salaries Payable	2,400
Mortgage Note Payable (final payment, 1998)	56,000
Capital Stock	100,000
Retained Earnings	291,000
Dividends	15,000
Sales	1,400,000
Sales Returns and Allowances	12,100
Sales Discounts	11,900
Purchases	1,100,000

Purchases Returns and Allowances	$ 24,600
Purchases Discounts	15,400
Transportation In	15,000
Sales Salaries Expense	123,200
Advertising Expense	22,800
Depreciation Expense—Store Equipment	6,400
Miscellaneous Selling Expense	1,600
Office Salaries Expense	31,150
Rent Expense	16,350
Depreciation Expense—Office Equipment	12,700
Insurance Expense	3,900
Office Supplies Expense	1,300
Miscellaneous General Expense	1,600
Interest Income	21,000
Interest Expense	6,000

Instructions: (1) Prepare a multiple-step income statement.
(2) Prepare a retained earnings statement.
(3) Prepare a report form balance sheet, assuming that the current portion of the mortgage note payable is $6,000.

4–37A. Preparation of single-step income statement and combined income and retained earnings statement. Selected accounts and related amounts for Daisy Inc. for the fiscal year ended January 31, 1989, are presented in Problem 4–36A.

Instructions: (1) Prepare a single-step income statement.
(2) Prepare a combined income and retained earnings statement, using the single-step form for the income statement portion.

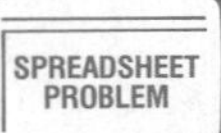

4–38A. Combined income and retained earnings statement; balance sheet. The following data are derived from the records of Jenner Co. at April 30, 1989, the end of the current fiscal year:

Accounts payable	$ 68,700
Accounts receivable	132,100
Accumulated depreciation—office equipment	30,750
Accumulated depreciation—store equipment	91,050
Capital stock	100,000
Cash	45,300
Cost of merchandise sold	860,400
Dividends	20,000
Dividends payable	5,000
General expenses	108,720
Interest expense	18,000
Merchandise inventory, April 30, 1989	280,200
Mortgage note payable (due in 1998)	150,000
Office equipment	110,800
Prepaid insurance	5,250
Rent income	19,260
Retained earnings	281,500
Salaries payable	4,640
Sales	1,240,700
Selling expenses	170,580
Store equipment	240,250

Instructions: (1) Prepare a combined income and retained earnings statement, using the single-step form for the income statement portion.
(2) Prepare a balance sheet in report form.

SOLUTIONS SOFTWARE

4–42A. Adjusting entries from work sheet. A portion of the work sheet of Shriver Inc. for the current year ended November 30 is as follows:

Account Title	Income Statement Debit	Income Statement Credit	Balance Sheet Debit	Balance Sheet Credit
Cash			62,650	
Accounts Receivable			210,800	
Merchandise Inventory	260,500	241,650	241,650	
Prepaid Rent			8,400	
Prepaid Insurance			17,200	
Supplies			3,360	
Store Equipment			87,750	
Accumulated Depr.—Store Equipment				33,490
Office Equipment			45,600	
Accumulated Depr.—Office Equipment				15,750
Accounts Payable				93,750
Sales Salaries Payable				4,500
Mortgage Note Payable				180,000
Capital Stock				100,000
Retained Earnings				117,160
Dividends			15,000	
Sales		1,240,700		
Sales Returns and Allowances	31,400			
Sales Discounts	12,900			
Purchases	770,650			
Purchases Returns and Allowances		18,050		
Purchases Discounts		8,600		
Transportation In	12,100			
Sales Salaries Expense	120,750			
Depreciation Expense—Store Equipment	11,800			
Supplies Expense	2,040			
Miscellaneous Selling Expense	1,600			
Office Salaries Expense	50,300			
Rent Expense	33,600			
Heating and Lighting Expense	13,420			
Insurance Expense	11,500			
Depreciation Expense—Office Equipment	5,180			
Miscellaneous General Expense	1,900			
Interest Expense	21,600			
	1,361,240	1,509,000	692,410	544,650

Instructions: (1) From the partial work sheet, determine the six entries that appeared in the adjustments columns and present them in journal form. The balance in Prepaid Rent before adjustment was $42,000, representing 15 months' rent at $2,800 per month.

(2) Determine the following:

(a) Amount of net income for the year.

(b) Balance of the retained earnings account at the end of the year.

Mini-Case 4

Your brother operates Video Connection Inc., a video tape distributorship that is in its third year of operation. Recently, Jane Crawley, the firm's accountant, resigned to enter nursing school. Before leaving, she completed the work sheet for the year ended May 31, 1989, and recorded the necessary adjusting entries. From this work sheet, your brother prepared the following financial statements:

Video Connection Inc.
Income Statement
For Year Ended May 31, 1989

Sales		$308,200
Less cost of merchandise sold:		
Purchases	$231,600	
Net increase in merchandise inventory	17,500	214,100
Gross profit		$ 94,100
Operating expenses:		
Salaries expense	$ 29,600	
Heat and lighting expense	5,750	
Insurance expense	4,050	
Depreciation expense—building	2,880	
Depreciation expense—office equipment	1,260	
Depreciation expense—store equipment	2,160	
Supplies expense	2,440	
Miscellaneous expense	1,620	
Transportation in	7,100	56,860
		$ 37,240
Selling expenses:		
Advertising expense	$ 6,940	
Transportation out	14,160	21,100
Income from operations		$ 16,140
Other income:		
Purchases discounts	$ 2,480	
Purchases returns and allowances	3,820	
Interest income	500	6,800
		$ 22,940
Other expenses:		
Sales returns	$ 1,200	
Dividends	15,000	
Interest expense	6,000	22,200
Net income		$ 740

Video Connection Inc.
Retained Earnings Statement
For Year Ended May 31, 1989

Retained earnings, June 1, 1988	$30,760
Net income for the year	740
Retained earnings, May 31, 1989	$31,500

Video Connection Inc.
Balance Sheet
May 31, 1989

Assets	
Cash	$ 15,100
Merchandise inventory	62,300
Supplies	1,820
Prepaid insurance	1,680
Accounts receivable	25,600
Store equipment	12,800
Office equipment	6,300
Building	58,900
Land	30,000
Notes receivable	5,000
Total assets	$219,500
Liabilities and Stockholders' Equity	
Accumulated depreciation—store equipment	$ 4,320
Accumulated depreciation—office equipment	2,520
Accumulated depreciation—building	5,760
Accounts payable	13,800
Salaries payable	1,600
Mortgage note payable—First National Bank (due in 1996)	60,000
Capital stock	100,000
Retained earnings	31,500
Total liabilities and stockholders' equity	$219,500

As part of the existing loan agreement with First National Bank, Video Connection Inc. must submit financial statements annually to the bank. In reviewing your brother's statements and supporting records before he submits the statements to the bank, you discover the following information:

Merchandise inventory:	
June 1, 1988	$44,800
May 31, 1989	62,300
Salaries expense:	
Sales salaries	$20,200
Office salaries	9,400
Supplies expense:	
Store supplies	$ 1,600
Office supplies	840
Miscellaneous expense:	
Selling	$ 1,020
General	600

Instructions:

(1) Revise your brother's statements as necessary to conform to proper form for a multiple-step income statement, a retained earnings statement, and a report form of balance sheet.

(2) Prepare a projected single-step income statement based upon the following data:

Your brother is considering a proposal to increase net income by offering sales discounts of 2/15, n/30, and by shipping all merchandise FOB shipping point. Currently, no sales discounts are allowed and merchandise is shipped FOB destination. It is estimated that these credit terms will increase net sales by 10%. The ratio of cost of merchandise sold to net sales is 70% and is not expected to change under the proposed plan. All selling and general expenses are expected to remain unchanged, except for store supplies, miscellaneous selling, office supplies, and miscellaneous general expenses, which are expected to increase proportionately with increased net sales. The other income and other expense items will remain unchanged. The shipment of all merchandise FOB shipping point will eliminate all transportation out expenses.

(3) (a) Based upon the projected income statement in (2), would you recommend the implementation of the proposed changes?

(b) Describe any possible concerns you may have related to the proposed changes described in (2).

Answers to Self-Examination Questions

1. B The single-step form of income statement (answer B) is so named because the total of all expenses is deducted from the total of all revenues. The multiple-step form (answer A) includes numerous sections and subsections with several intermediate balances before arriving at net income. The account form (answer C) and the report form (answer D) are two common forms of the balance sheet.
2. C Gross profit (answer C) is the excess of net sales over the cost of merchandise sold. Operating income (answer A) or income from operations (answer B) is the excess of gross profit over operating expenses. Net income (answer D) is the final figure on the income statement after all revenues and expenses have been reported.
3. D Expenses such as interest expense (answer D) that cannot be associated definitely with operations are identified as other expense or nonoperating expense. Depreciation expense—office equipment (answer A) is a general expense. Sales salaries expense (answer B) is a selling expense. Insurance expense (answer C) is a mixed expense with elements of both selling expense and general expense. For small businesses, however, insurance expense is usually reported as a general expense.
4. C Since all revenue and expense accounts are closed at the end of the period, both Sales (revenue) and Salary Expense (expense) would be closed to Income Summary (answer C).

5. A Since the post-closing trial balance includes only balance sheet accounts (all of the revenue and expense accounts have been previously closed), Cash (answer A) would appear on the post-closing trial balance. Both Sales (answer B) and Salary Expense (answer C) are income statement accounts that are closed prior to the preparation of the post-closing trial balance.

Comprehensive Problem

The account balances for Lyons Inc. are as follows. All balances are stated as of May 1, 1989, unless otherwise indicated.

101	Cash	39,160
102	Accounts Receivable	50,220
103	Merchandise Inventory, June 1, 1988	123,900
104	Prepaid Insurance	3,750
105	Store Supplies	2,550
111	Store Equipment	44,300
112	Accumulated Depreciation	12,600
201	Accounts Payable	38,500
202	Salaries Payable	—
301	Capital Stock	50,000
302	Retained Earnings, June 1, 1988	113,270
303	Dividends	4,500
305	Income Summary	—
401	Sales	741,600
402	Sales Returns and Allowances	13,600
403	Sales Discounts	5,200
501	Purchases	540,000
502	Purchases Returns and Allowances	21,600
503	Purchases Discounts	5,760
504	Transportation In	5,400
601	Sales Salaries Expense	74,400
602	Advertising Expense	18,000
603	Depreciation Expense	—
604	Store Supplies Expense	—
605	Miscellaneous Selling Expense	2,800
611	Office Salaries Expense	29,400
612	Rent Expense	24,500
613	Insurance Expense	—
614	Miscellaneous General Expense	1,650

During May, the last month of Lyons Inc.'s fiscal year, the following transactions were completed:

May 1. Paid rent for May, $2,500.
2. Purchased merchandise on account, terms 2/10, n/30, FOB shipping point, $22,000.
3. Paid transportation charges on purchase of May 2, $860.
4. Purchased merchandise on account, terms 1/10, n/30, FOB destination, $16,200.
5. Sold merchandise on account, terms 2/10, n/30, FOB shipping point, $8,500.
8. Received $14,900 cash from customers on account, no discount.
10. Sold merchandise for cash, $18,300.
11. Paid $12,800 to creditors on account, after discounts of $200 had been deducted.
12. Paid for merchandise purchased on May 2, less discount.

May 13. Received merchandise returned on sale of May 5, $1,000.
14. Paid advertising expense for last half of May, $2,000.
15. Received cash from sale of May 5, less return and discount.
18. Paid sales salaries of $1,500 and office salaries of $500.
18. Received $28,500 cash from customers on account, after discounts of $400 had been deducted.
19. Purchased merchandise for cash, $6,400.
19. Paid $13,150 to creditors on account, after discounts of $250 had been deducted.
20. Sold merchandise on account, terms 1/10, n/30, FOB shipping point, $16,000.
21. As an accommodation to the customer, paid shipping charges on sale of May 20, $600.
21. Purchased merchandise on account, terms 1/10, n/30, FOB destination, $15,000.
22. Paid for merchandise purchased on May 4.
24. Returned damaged merchandise purchased on May 21, receiving credit from the seller, $3,000.
25. Refunded cash on sales made for cash, $400.
27. Paid sales salaries of $1,200 and office salaries of $400.
28. Sold merchandise on account, terms 2/10, n/30, FOB shipping point, $24,700.
29. Purchased store supplies for cash, $350.
30. Received cash from sale of May 20, less discount, plus transportation paid on May 21.
31. Paid for purchase of May 21, less return and discount.
31. Sold merchandise on account, terms 2/10, n/30, FOB shipping point, $17,400.
31. Purchased merchandise on account, terms 1/10, n/30, FOB destination, $19,700.

Instructions: (1) Record the balances of each of the accounts as of May 1 in the appropriate balance column of a standard account form. Write "Balance" in the item section, and place a check mark (√) in the posting reference column.

(2) Record the transactions for May in a general journal.

(3) Post to the ledger, extending the month-end balances to the appropriate balance columns after all posting is completed.

(4) Prepare a trial balance as of May 31 on a work sheet, listing all the accounts in the order given in the ledger. Complete the work sheet for the fiscal year ended May 31, using the following adjustment and other data:

(a) Insurance expired during the year		$2,250
(b) Store supplies inventory on May 31		750
(c) Depreciation for the current year		8,860
(d) Accrued salaries on May 31:		
Sales salaries	$400	
Office salaries	140	540

The physical count of merchandise on hand on May 31 totaled $134,150.

(5) Prepare a multiple-step income statement, a retained earnings statement, and a report form of balance sheet.

(6) Journalize and post the adjusting entries.

(7) Journalize and post the closing entries. Indicate closed accounts by inserting a line in both balance columns opposite the closing entry. Insert the new balance in the retained earnings account.

(8) Prepare a post-closing trial balance.

(9) Journalize and post any reversing entries as of June 1, 1989.

Part Two

Financial Accounting Systems

5
Accounting Systems and Cash

CHAPTER OBJECTIVES

Describe the principles of properly designed accounting systems.

Describe the three phases of accounting system installation and revision.

Describe and illustrate the principles of internal control.

Describe and illustrate the use of a bank account for controlling cash, including the preparation of a bank reconciliation.

Describe internal controls for cash receipts, including the handling of mail receipts, the use of a cash short and over account, and the use of cash change funds.

Describe and illustrate the use of the voucher system for controlling cash payments.

Describe and illustrate the use of a discounts lost account and a petty cash account for controlling cash payments.

Describe recent trends in the use of electronic funds transfer to process cash transactions.

The way in which management is given the information for use in conducting the affairs of the business and in reporting to owners, creditors, and other interested parties is called the **accounting system.** In a general sense, an accounting system includes the entire network of communications used by a business organization to provide needed information.

In this chapter, the qualities of a properly designed accounting system and the principles of internal control for directing operations are discussed. The chapter also presents the application of these internal control principles to the design of an effective system for controlling cash and accounting for cash transactions.

The entire amount of data needed by an enterprise is called its **data base.** Depending upon the enterprise, the variety and amount of data included in the data base, and the uses made of the data, various accounting systems—manual and computerized—may be used.

In preceding chapters, manual accounting systems were illustrated because they are the easiest systems to understand. If the data base is relatively small, the manual system illustrated may serve a business reasonably well. As an enterprise becomes larger and more complex, the manual system can be modified in order to make the system more efficient and to better meet the needs of the enterprise. For example, as the number of sales on account increases, including in the ledger with all of the other accounts an account for each customer may result in a ledger that is unwieldy. In such a case, the individual customers' accounts could be placed in a separate ledger called a **subsidiary ledger.** This subsidiary ledger would be represented in the principal ledger (now called the **general ledger**) by a summarizing account called a **controlling account.** The balance in the accounts receivable controlling account in the general ledger would agree with the total of the balances of all of the customers' accounts in the subsidiary ledger.[1]

The concept of the subsidiary ledger can be extended to any group of individual accounts with a common characteristic, when it is desirable to reduce the number of accounts in the principal ledger. For example, a subsidiary ledger for creditors' accounts payable could be used, with Accounts Payable serving as the controlling account in the general ledger.

When the data base for an enterprise becomes too large and complex for the manual system to handle efficiently, the manual accounting system may be replaced by a computerized system. Regardless of whether the accounting system for a particular enterprise uses manual or computerized procedures to process its transactions, however, there are basic principles of accounting systems that are applicable in all cases. These principles are discussed in the following paragraphs.

Cost-Effectiveness Balance

An accounting system must be tailored to meet the specific needs of each business. Since costs must be incurred in meeting these needs, one of the major considerations in developing an accounting system is cost effectiveness. For example, although the reports produced by an accounting system are a valuable end product of the system, the value of the reports produced should be at least equal to the cost of producing them. No matter how detailed or informational a report may be, it should not be produced if it costs more than the benefits received by those who use it.

[1]Another means by which the manual system can be modified in order to reduce costs and more efficiently process accounting data is to use special journals, in which selected kinds of transactions are recorded. The basic features of special journals and a more detailed discussion of subsidiary ledgers are presented in Appendix C.

Flexibility to Meet Future Needs

A characteristic of the modern business environment is change. Each business must adapt to the constantly changing environment in which it operates. Whether the changes are the result of new government regulations, changes in accounting principles, organizational changes necessary to meet practices of competing businesses, changes in data processing technology, or other factors, the accounting system must be flexible enough to meet the changing demands made of it. For example, when granting credit to customers became a common practice, it was necessary for many businesses to maintain accounts receivable, accounts payable, and related statistical and other useful information. Regulatory agencies, such as the Securities and Exchange Commission, often require a continually changing variety of reports that require changes in the accounting system.

Adequate Internal Controls

An accounting system must provide the information needed by management in reporting to owners, creditors, and other interested parties. In addition, the system should aid management in directing operations. The detailed policies and procedures used by management to direct operations so that enterprise goals can be achieved are called **internal controls**. The broad principles of internal control are discussed later in the chapter.

Effective Reporting

Users of the information provided by the accounting system rely on various reports for relevant information presented in an understandable manner. When these reports are prepared, the requirements and knowledge of the user should be recognized. For example, management may need detailed reports for controlling operations on a weekly or even daily basis, and regulatory agencies often require uniform data and establish certain deadlines for the submission of certain reports.

Adaptation to Organizational Structure

Only by effectively using and adapting to the human resources of a business can the accounting system meet information needs at the lowest cost. Since no two businesses are structured alike, the accounting system must be tailored to the organizational structure of each business. The lines of authority and responsibility will affect the information requirements of each business. In addition, an effective system needs the approval and support of all levels of management.

ACCOUNTING SYSTEM INSTALLATION AND REVISION

Before designing and installing an accounting system for an enterprise, the designer must have a complete knowledge of the business' operations. However, the designer should recognize that some areas of the system, such as the types and design of the forms needed and the number and titles of the accounts required, may be affected by factors that are not known when a business is first organized. As new information about a business is obtained and as a business "outgrows" its accounting system when it expands to new operational areas, the system will need to be revised.

Many large businesses continually review their accounting system and may constantly be involved in changing some part of it. The job of installing or changing an accounting system, either in its entirety or only in part, is made up of three phases: (1) analysis, (2) design, and (3) implementation.

Systems Analysis

The goal of **systems analysis** is to determine information needs, the sources of such information, and the deficiencies in procedures and data processing methods presently used. The analysis usually begins with a review of the organizational structure and the job descriptions of the personnel affected. This review is followed by a study of the forms, records, procedures, processing methods, and reports used by the enterprise. The source of such information is usually the firm's *Systems Manual.*

In addition to looking at the shortcomings of the present system, the analyst should determine management's plans for changes in operations (volume, products, territories, etc.) in the foreseeable future.

Systems Design

Accounting systems are changed as a result of the kind of analysis previously described. The design of the new system may involve only minor changes from the existing system, such as revision of a particular form and the related procedures and processing methods, or it may be a complete revision of the entire system. Systems designers must have a general knowledge of the qualities of different kinds of data processing equipment, and the ability to evaluate alternatives. Although successful systems design depends to a large extent upon the creativity, imagination, and general capabilities of the designer, observance of the broad principles previously discussed is necessary.

Systems Implementation

The final phase of the creation or revision of an accounting system is to carry out, or implement, the proposals. New or revised forms, records, procedures, and equipment must be installed, and any that are no longer useful must be withdrawn. All personnel responsible for operating the system must be carefully trained and closely supervised until satisfactory efficiency is achieved.

For a large organization, a major revision such as a change from an obsolete to a modern computer processing system is usually done gradually over an extended period rather than all at once. With such a procedure, there is less likelihood that the flow of useful data will be seriously slowed down during the critical phase of implementation. Weaknesses and conflicting or unnecessary elements in the design may also become apparent during the implementation phase. They are more easily seen and corrected when changes in a system are adopted gradually, and possible chaos is thereby avoided.

Accounting Systems, Profit Measurement, and Management

A Greek restaurant owner in Canada had his own system of accounting. He kept his accounts payable in a cigar box on the left-hand side of his cash register, his daily cash returns on the cash register, and his receipts for paid bills in another cigar box on the right.

When his youngest son graduated as an accountant, he was appalled by his father's primitive methods. "I don't know how you can run a business that way," he said. "How do you know what your profits are?"

"Well, son," the father replied, "when I got off the boat from Greece, I had nothing but the pants I was wearing. Today, your brother is a doctor. You are an accountant. Your sister is a speech therapist. Your mother and I have a nice car, and city house, a country home. We have a good business, and everything is paid for. . ."

"So, you add all that together, subtract the pants, and there's your profit!"

Source: Anonymous.

INTERNAL CONTROLS

Internal controls are established by an enterprise to provide reasonable assurance that the enterprise's goals will be achieved. Internal controls consist of three elements: (1) the control environment, (2) the control procedures, and (3) the accounting system. The control environment refers to the employees' overall attitude toward internal controls. The proper control environment exists when all employees are aware of the importance of internal controls. The control procedures are the policies and methods established within the control environment. The accounting system provides the information needed by management in planning and directing operations toward achieving the enterprise's goals.

Details of a system of internal control will vary according to the size and type of business enterprise. In a small business where it is possible for the owner-manager to personally supervise the employees and to direct the affairs of the business, few controls are necessary. As the number of employees and the complexities of an enterprise increase, it becomes more difficult for management to maintain control over all phases of operations. As a firm grows, management needs to delegate authority and to place more reliance on the internal controls to achieve the enterprise's goals.

Several broad principles of internal control are discussed in the following paragraphs. Many of these principles should be considered by all businesses, large and small.

Competent Personnel and Rotation of Duties

The successful operation of an accounting system requires people who are able to perform the duties to which they are assigned. Hence, it is necessary that all accounting employees be adequately trained and supervised to perform their jobs. It is also advisable to rotate clerical personnel periodically from job to job. In addition to broadening their understanding of the system, the knowledge that others may in the future perform their jobs tends to discourage deviations from prescribed procedures. Rotation of duties is also very helpful in disclosing any irregularities that may have occurred.

Assignment of Responsibility

If employees are to work efficiently, their responsibilities must be clearly defined. There should be no overlapping or undefined areas of responsibility. For example, if a certain cash register is to be used by two or more salesclerks, each one should be assigned a separate cash drawer and register key. Thus, daily proof of the handling of cash can be obtained for each clerk.

Separation of Responsibility for Related Operations

To decrease the possibility of inefficiency, errors, and fraud, responsibility for a sequence of related operations should be divided among two or more persons. For example, no one individual should be authorized to order merchandise, verify the receipt of the goods, and pay the supplier. To do so would invite abuses such as the following:

1. Placing orders with a supplier on the basis of friendship rather than on price, quality, and other objective factors.
2. Indifferent and routine verification of the quantity and the quality of goods received.
3. Conversion of goods to the personal use of the employee.
4. Carelessness in verifying the validity and the accuracy of invoices.
5. Payment of false invoices.

When the responsibility for purchasing, receiving, and paying are divided among three persons or departments, the possibilities of such abuses are minimized.

The "checks and balances" provided by distributing responsibility among various departments requires no duplication of effort. The business documents prepared as a result of the work of each department must "fit" with those prepared by the other departments.

Separation of Operations and Accounting

Responsibility for maintaining the accounting records should be separated from the responsibility for engaging in business transactions and for the custody of the firm's assets. By so doing, the accounting records serve as an independent check on the business operations. For example, the employees entrusted with handling cash receipts from credit customers should not have access to the journal or ledger. Separation of the two functions reduces the possibilities of errors and embezzlement.

Proofs and Security Measures

Proofs and security measures should be used to safeguard business assets and assure reliable accounting data. This principle applies to many different techniques and procedures, such as the use of a bank account and other safekeeping measures for cash and other valuable documents. Cash registers are widely used in making the initial record of cash sales. The conditioning of the public to observe the amount recorded as the sale or to accept a printed receipt from the salesclerk increases the machine's effectiveness as a part of internal control.

The use of fidelity insurance is also an aid to internal control. It insures against losses caused by fraud on the part of employees who are entrusted with company assets.

Independent Review

To determine whether the other internal control principles are being effectively applied, the system should be periodically reviewed and evaluated by internal auditors. These auditors must be independent of the employees responsible for operations. An example of the use of internal auditors for review of internal controls is described in the annual report of Rose's Stores Inc., as follows:

> To meet its responsibilities with respect to financial information, management maintains and enforces internal accounting policies, procedures, and controls which are designed to provide reasonable assurance that assets are safeguarded and that transactions are properly recorded and executed in accordance with management's authorization. The concept of reasonable assurance is based on the recognition that the cost of controls should not exceed the expected benefits. Management maintains an internal audit function and an internal control function which are responsible for evaluating the adequacy and application of financial and operating controls and for testing compliance with Company policies and procedures.

Internal auditors should report any weaknesses and recommend changes to correct them. For example, a review of cash disbursements may disclose that invoices were not paid within the discount period, even though enough cash was available.

CONTROL OVER CASH

Because of the ease with which money can be transferred, cash is the asset most likely to be diverted and used improperly by employees. In addition, many transactions either directly or indirectly affect the receipt or payment of cash. It is therefore necessary that cash be effectively safeguarded by special controls.

The Bank Account as a Tool for Controlling Cash

One of the major devices for maintaining control over cash is the bank account. To get the most benefit from a bank account, all cash received must be deposited in the bank and all payments must be made by checks drawn on the bank or from special cash funds. When such a system is strictly followed, there is a double record of cash, one maintained by the business and the other by the bank.

In some cases, a bank may require a business to maintain a minimum cash balance in a bank account. This requirement for a minimum balance, called a **compensating balance,** may be imposed by the bank as a part of a loan agreement. Compensating balance requirements should be disclosed in notes to the financial statements, as indicated in the following note taken from the 1986 financial statements of Research Incorporated:

> The Company has a $3,000,000 unsecured bank line of credit.... The Company generally maintains a compensating balance of 5% of the amount of the line.

The forms used by a business in connection with a bank account are a signature card, deposit ticket, check, and a record of checks drawn.

Signature Card. At the time an account is opened, an identifying number is assigned to the account, and a **signature card** must be signed by each person authorized to sign checks drawn on the account. The card is used by the bank to determine the authenticity of the signature on checks presented to it for payment.

Deposit Ticket. The details of a deposit are listed by the depositor on a printed form supplied by the bank. **Deposit tickets** may be prepared in duplicate, in which case the copy is stamped or initialed by the bank's teller and given to the depositor as a receipt. The receipt of a deposit may be indicated by means other than a duplicate deposit ticket, but all methods give the depositor written proof of the date and the total amount of the deposit.

Check. A **check** is a written instrument signed by the depositor, ordering the bank to pay a certain sum of money to the order of a designated person. There are three parties to a check: the **drawer,** the one who signs the check; the **drawee,** the bank on which the check is drawn; and the **payee,** the one to whose order the check is drawn. When checks are issued to pay bills, they are recorded as credits to Cash on the day issued, even though they are not presented to the drawer's bank until some later time. When checks are received from customers, they are recorded as debits to Cash, on the assumption that the customer has enough money on deposit.

Check forms may be obtained in many styles. The name and the address of the depositor are often printed on each check, and the checks are usually numbered in sequence to facilitate the depositor's internal control. Most banks use automatic sorting and posting equipment and, therefore, provide check forms on which the bank's identification number and the depositor's account number are printed along the lower margin in machine-readable magnetic ink. When the check is presented for payment, the amount for which it is drawn is inserted next to the account number, also in magnetic ink.

Record of Checks Drawn. A memorandum record of the basic details of a check should be prepared at the time the check is written. The record may be a stub from which the check is detached or it may be a small booklet designed to be kept with the check forms. Each type of record also provides spaces for recording deposits and the current bank balance.

Business firms may prepare a copy of each check drawn and then use it as a basis for recording the transaction. Checks issued to a creditor on account are usually accompanied by a notification of the specific invoice that is being paid. The purpose of such notification, sometimes called a **remittance advice,** is to make sure that proper credit is recorded in the accounts of the creditor. Mistakes are less likely to happen and the possible need for exchanges of correspondence is reduced. The invoice number or other descriptive data may be inserted in spaces provided on the face or on the back of the check or on an attachment to the check, as in the following illustration:

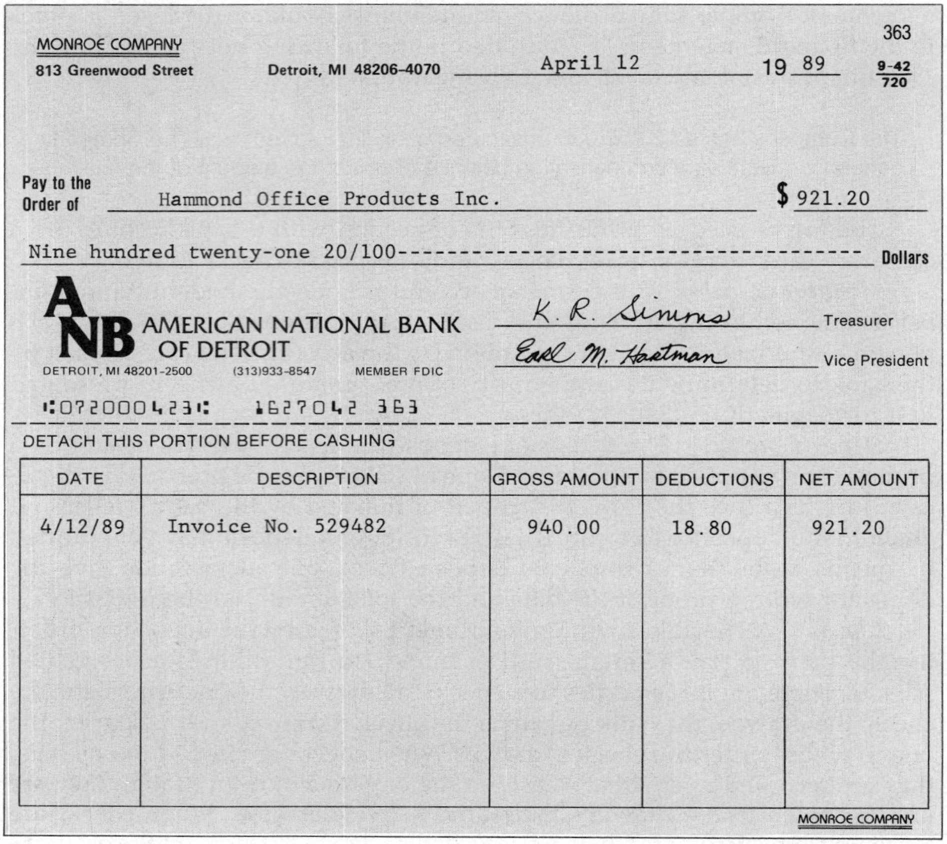

MONROE COMPANY 363
813 Greenwood Street Detroit, MI 48206-4070 April 12 19 89 9-42/720

Pay to the Order of Hammond Office Products Inc. $ 921.20

Nine hundred twenty-one 20/100------------------------------------- Dollars

ANB AMERICAN NATIONAL BANK OF DETROIT
DETROIT, MI 48201-2500 (313)933-8547 MEMBER FDIC

K. R. Simons Treasurer
Earl M. Hartman Vice President

⑆072000423⑆ 1627042 363

DETACH THIS PORTION BEFORE CASHING

DATE	DESCRIPTION	GROSS AMOUNT	DEDUCTIONS	NET AMOUNT
4/12/89	Invoice No. 529482	940.00	18.80	921.20

MONROE COMPANY

Check and Remittance Advice

Before depositing the check at the bank, the payee removes the part of the check containing the remittance information. The removed part may then be used by the payee as written proof of the details of the cash receipt.

Bank Statement

Although there are some differences in procedure, banks usually maintain an original and a copy of all checking account transactions. When this is done, the original becomes the statement of account that is mailed to the depositor, usually once each month. Like any account with a customer or a creditor, the bank statement shows the beginning balance, checks and other debits (deductions by the bank), deposits and other credits (additions by the bank), and the balance at the end of the period. The depositor's checks received by the bank during the period may accompany the bank statement, arranged in the order of payment. The paid or canceled checks are perforated or stamped "Paid," together with the date of payment.

Debit or credit memorandums describing other entries in the depositor's account may also be enclosed with the statement. For example, the bank may have debited the depositor's account for service charges or for deposited checks returned because of insufficient funds. It may have credited the account for receipts from notes receivable left for collection, for loans to the depositor, or for interest.[2] A typical bank statement is illustrated as follows:

Bank Statement

ANB
MEMBER FDIC
AMERICAN NATIONAL BANK
OF DETROIT
DETROIT, MI 48201-2500 (313)933-8547

PAGE 1
ACCOUNT NUMBER 1627042

FROM 6/30/89 TO 7/31/89

	BALANCE	4,218.60
22	DEPOSITS	13,749.75
52	WITHDRAWALS	15,013.57
2	OTHER DEBITS AND CREDITS	405.00CR
	NEW BALANCE	3,359.78

MONROE COMPANY
813 GREENWOOD STREET
DETROIT, MI 48206-4070

CHECKS AND OTHER DEBITS			DEPOSITS	DATE	BALANCE
819.40	122.54		585.75	07/01	3,862.41
369.50	732.26	20.15	421.53	07/02	3,162.03
600.00	190.70	52.50	781.30	07/03	3,100.13
25.93	160.00		662.50	07/05	3,576.70
36.80	181.02		503.18	07/07	3,862.06
32.26	535.09		932.00	07/29	3,389.40
21.10	126.20		705.21	07/30	3,947.31
		SC 3.00	MS 408.00	07/30	4,352.31
26.12	1,615.13		648.72	07/31	3,359.78

EC--ERROR CORRECTION
MS--MISCELLANEOUS
NSF--NOT SUFFICIENT FUNDS

OD--OVERDRAFT
PS--PAYMENT STOPPED
SC--SERVICE CHARGE

*** *** ***

THE RECONCILEMENT OF THIS STATEMENT WITH YOUR RECORDS IS ESSENTIAL.
ANY ERROR OR EXCEPTION SHOULD BE REPORTED IMMEDIATELY.

Bank Reconciliation

When all cash receipts are deposited in the bank and all payments are made by check, the cash account is often called Cash in Bank. This account in the depositor's ledger is the reciprocal of the account with the depositor in the bank's ledger. Cash in Bank in the depositor's ledger is an asset with a debit balance, and the account with the depositor in the bank's ledger is a liability with a credit balance.

It might seem that the two balances should be equal, but they are not likely to be equal on any specific date because of either or both of the following: (1) delay by either party in recording transactions, and (2) errors by either party in recording transactions. Ordinarily, there is a time lag of one day or

---

[2]Although interest-bearing checking accounts are common for individuals, Federal Reserve Regulation Q prohibits the paying of interest on corporate checking accounts.

more between the date a check is written and the date that it is presented to the bank for payment. If the depositor mails deposits to the bank or uses the night depository, a time lag between the date of the deposit and the date that it is recorded by the bank is also probable. Conversely, the bank may debit or credit the depositor's account for transactions about which the depositor will not be informed until later. Examples are service or collection fees charged by the bank and the proceeds of notes receivable sent to the bank for collection.

To determine the reasons for any difference and to correct any errors that may have been made by the bank or the depositor, the depositor's own records should be reconciled with the bank statement. The **bank reconciliation** is divided into two major sections: one section begins with the balance according to the bank statement and ends with the adjusted balance; the other section begins with the balance according to the depositor's records and also ends with the adjusted balance. The two amounts designated as the adjusted balance must be equal. The form and the content of the bank reconciliation are outlined as follows:

Format for Bank Reconciliation

Bank balance according to bank statement		$XXX
Add: Additions by depositor not on bank statement	$XX	
Bank errors	XX	XX
		$XXX
Deduct: Deductions by depositor not on bank statement	$XX	
Bank errors	XX	XX
Adjusted balance		$XXX
Bank balance according to depositor's records		$XXX
Add: Additions by bank not recorded by depositor	$XX	
Depositor errors	XX	XX
		$XXX
Deduct: Deductions by bank not recorded by depositor	$XX	
Depositor errors	XX	XX
Adjusted balance		$XXX

The following procedures are used in finding the reconciling items and determining the adjusted balance of Cash in Bank:

1. Individual deposits listed on the bank statement are compared with unrecorded deposits appearing in the preceding reconciliation and with deposit receipts or other records of deposits. Deposits not recorded by the bank are added to the balance according to the bank statement.
2. Paid checks are compared with outstanding checks appearing on the preceding reconciliation and with the record of checks written. Checks issued that have not been paid by the bank are outstanding and are deducted from the balance according to the bank statement.
3. Bank credit memorandums, representing additions made by the bank, are traced to the records of cash receipts. Credit memorandums that have not been recorded are added to the balance according to the depositor's records.
4. Bank debit memorandums, representing deductions made by the bank, are traced to the records of cash payments. Debit memorandums that have not been recorded are deducted from the balance according to the depositor's records.

5. Errors discovered during the process of making the foregoing comparisons are listed separately on the reconciliation. For example, if the amount for which a check was written had been recorded erroneously by the depositor, the amount of the error should be added to or deducted from the balance according to the depositor's records. Similarly, errors by the bank should be added to or deducted from the balance according to the bank statement.

Illustration of Bank Reconciliation. The bank statement for Monroe Company, reproduced on page 185, indicates a balance of $3,359.78 as of July 31. The balance in Cash in Bank in Monroe Company's ledger as of the same date is $2,234.99. Use of the procedures outlined above reveals the following reconciling items:

Deposit of July 31 not recorded on bank statement..............	$ 816.20
Checks outstanding: No. 812, $1,061.00; No. 878, $435.39; No. 883, $48.60..	1,544.99
Note from Wilson Co. plus interest of $8 collected by bank (credit memorandum), not recorded by Monroe Company........	408.00
Bank service charges (debit memorandum) not recorded by Monroe Company	3.00
Check No. 879 for $732.26 to Taylor Co. on account, recorded by Monroe Company as $723.26.............................	9.00

The bank reconciliation based on the bank statement and the reconciling items is as follows:

Monroe Company
Bank Reconciliation
July 31, 1989

Balance per bank statement		$3,359.78
Add deposit of July 31, not recorded by bank		816.20
		$4,175.98
Deduct outstanding checks:		
No. 812	$1,061.00	
No. 878	435.39	
No. 883	48.60	1,544.99
Adjusted balance		$2,630.99
Balance per depositor's records....................		$2,234.99
Add note and interest collected by bank		408.00
		$2,642.99
Deduct: Bank service charges	$ 3.00	
Error in recording Check No. 879	9.00	12.00
Adjusted balance		$2,630.99

Entries Based on Bank Reconciliation. Bank memorandums not recorded by the depositor and depositor's errors shown by the bank reconciliation require that entries be made in the accounts. The entries for Monroe Company, based on the bank reconciliation above, are as follows:

July 31	Cash in Bank	408	
	Notes Receivable		400
	Interest Income		8
	Note collected by bank.		
31	Miscellaneous General Expense	3	
	Accounts Payable—Taylor Co.	9	
	Cash in Bank		12
	Bank service charges and error in recording Check No. 879.		

The data needed for these entries are provided by the section of the bank reconciliation that begins with the balance per depositor's records. No entries are necessary on the depositor's books as a result of the information included in the section that begins with the balance per bank statement.

After the foregoing entries are posted, the cash in bank account will have a debit balance of $2,630.99, which agrees with the adjusted balance shown on the bank reconciliation. This is the amount of cash available for use as of July 31 and the amount that would be reported on the balance sheet on that date.

Importance of Bank Reconciliation. The bank reconciliation is an important part of the system of internal control because it is a means of comparing recorded cash, as shown by the accounting records, with the amount of cash reported by the bank. It thus provides for finding and correcting errors and irregularities. Greater internal control is achieved when the bank reconciliation is prepared by an employee who does not take part in or record cash transactions with the bank. Without a proper separation of these duties, cash is more likely to be embezzled. For example, an employee who takes part in all of these duties could prepare an unauthorized check, omit it from the accounts, and cash it. Then to account for the canceled check when returned by the bank, the employee could understate the amount of the outstanding checks on future bank reconciliations by the amount of the embezzlement.

Check-Churning Frenzy

In today's high-tech economy, a cash manager's responsibility is to maximize cash inflows. One means of accomplishing this goal is to transfer bank balances by wire to New York and other money centers every night. The amounts are then invested in commercial paper and government securities. As the money is needed, it is wired back to the banks. Thus, corporate deposits in these banks may be turned over every day. This activity in the wire transfers of cash was described in a *Wall Street Journal* article, as follows:

... The nation's cash managers and bankers transact more than $600 billion a day in wire transfers alone. The great majority of this is on Fedwire—the wire service operated by the Federal Reserve System. This daily dollar volume is triple the federal budget deficit for [1985] and annually amounts to more than $170 trillion, which makes our annual gross national product of close to $4 trillion look [small]....

The technological and management sophistication required to churn money on this massive scale has led many in the banking industry to boast that we have the most advanced payments system in the world. This is true. But this sophistication is largely a direct result of efforts to abuse existing clearing rules, which are the most backward and wasteful of any developed country, and to avoid Regulation Q's nonsensical prohibition against paying interest on deposits of corporations, including banks and other depository institutions. Congressional deregulation has phased out Regulation Q as it relates to consumers but it still applies to corporations....

Another important reason for the heavy use of Fedwire is that it grants interest-free loans, or float. In an effort to attract business, the Fed (which competes directly against banks in both check clearing and wire transfers) gives immediate and irrevocable credit and availability of funds to recipients of wires but does not require senders to pay until the end of the day. Such a policy causes the Fed to extend unsecured, and to a large extent uncontrollable, intraday loans to some wire users. Recent estimates are that such loans, called "daylight overdrafts" or float, often exceed $100 billion by day's end. . . .

. . . Float is the principal reason for the existence of cash management. A cash manager's job is to make payments to others clear as slowly as possible and to clear payments received from others as quickly as possible. The clearing of payments to others is slowed through techniques such as remote disbursement. This involves issuing corporate checks on, say, First National Remote Bank. Almost everyone has received a check from a local company written on a bank in Butte, Mont., or Bangor, Maine. The clearing of checks from other banks is expedited through the use of a sophisticated and expensive network of jets, helicopters and couriers (First National Remote Bank is always located far from an airport, and ideally has a parking lot too small for a helicopter). . . .

Source: J. W. Henry Watson, "End the Check-Churning Frenzy," *Wall Street Journal,* May 24, 1985.

INTERNAL CONTROL OF CASH RECEIPTS

Department stores and other retail businesses ordinarily receive cash from two main sources: (1) over the counter from cash customers and (2) by mail from charge customers making payments on account. At the end of the business day, each salesclerk counts the cash in the assigned cash drawer and records the amount on a memorandum form. An employee from the cashier's department removes the cash register tapes on which total receipts were recorded for each cash drawer, counts the cash, and compares the total with the memorandum and the tape, noting any differences. The cash is then taken to the cashier's office and the tapes and memorandum forms are forwarded to the accounting department, where they become the basis for journal entries.

The employees who open incoming mail compare the amount of cash received with the amount shown on the accompanying remittance advice to be certain that the two amounts agree. If there is no separate remittance advice, an employee prepares one on a form designed for such use. All cash received, usually in the form of checks and money orders, is sent to the cashier's department, where it is combined with the receipts from cash sales and a deposit ticket is prepared. The remittance advices are delivered to the accounting department, where they become the basis for journal entries.

The duplicate deposit tickets or other bank receipt forms obtained by the cashier are sent to the controller or other financial officer, who compares the total amount with that reported by the accounting department as the total debit to Cash in Bank for the period.

Cash Short and Over

The amount of cash actually received during a day often does not agree with the record of cash receipts. Whenever there is a difference between the record and the actual cash and no error can be found in the record, it must be assumed that the mistake occurred in making change. The cash shortage or overage is recorded in an account entitled Cash Short and Over. For example, if the actual cash received from cash sales is less than the amount indicated by the cash register tally, the entry would include a debit to Cash Short and Over. An example for one day's receipts follows:

Cash in Bank	4,577.60	
Cash Short and Over	3.16	
Sales		4,580.76

If there is a debit balance in the cash short and over account at the end of the fiscal period, it is an expense and may be included in "Miscellaneous general expense" on the income statement. If there is a credit balance, it is revenue and may be listed in the "Other income" section. If the balance becomes larger than may be accounted for by minor errors in making change, the management should take corrective measures.

Cash Change Funds

Retail stores and other businesses that receive cash directly from customers must maintain a fund of currency and coins in order to make change. The fund may be established by drawing a check for the required amount, debiting the account Cash on Hand and crediting Cash in Bank. No additional charges or credits to the cash on hand account are necessary unless the amount of the fund is to be increased or decreased. At the end of each business day, the total amount of cash received during the day is deposited and the original amount of the change fund is retained. The desired composition of the fund is maintained by exchanging bills or coins for those of other denominations at the bank.

INTERNAL CONTROL OF CASH PAYMENTS

It is common practice for business enterprises to require that every payment of cash be evidenced by a check signed by a designated official. As an additional control, some firms require two signatures on all checks or only on checks which are larger than a certain amount. It is also common to use a check protector, which produces amounts on the check that are not easily removed or changed.

When the owner of a business has personal knowledge of all goods and services purchased, the owner may sign checks, with the assurance that the creditors have followed the terms of their contracts and that the exact amount of the obligation is being paid. Disbursing officials are seldom able to have such a complete knowledge of affairs, however. In enterprises of even moderate size, the responsibility for issuing purchase orders, inspecting goods received, and verifying contractual and arithmetical details of invoices is divided among the employees of several departments. It is desirable, therefore, to coordinate these related activities and to link them with the final issuance of checks to creditors. One of the best systems used for this purpose is the voucher system.

The Voucher System

A **voucher system** is made up of records, methods, and procedures used in proving and recording liabilities and in paying and recording cash payments. A voucher system uses (1) vouchers, (2) a file for unpaid vouchers, and (3) a file for paid vouchers. As in all areas of accounting systems and internal controls, many differences in detail are possible. The discussion that follows refers to a medium-size merchandising enterprise with separate departments for purchasing, receiving, accounting, and disbursing.

Vouchers. The term **voucher** is widely used in accounting. In a general sense, it means any document that serves as proof of authority to pay cash, such as an invoice approved for payment, or as evidence that cash has been paid, such as a canceled check. The term has a narrower meaning when applied to the voucher system: a voucher is a special form on which is recorded relevant data about a liability and the details of its payment.

An important characteristic of the voucher system is the requirement that a voucher be prepared for each expenditure. In fact, a check may not be issued except in payment of a properly authorized voucher. Vouchers may be paid immediately after they are prepared or at a later date, depending upon the circumstances and the credit terms.

A voucher form is illustrated below. The face of the voucher provides space for the name and address of the creditor, the date and number of the voucher, and basic details of the invoice or other supporting document, such as the vendor's invoice number and the amount and terms of the invoice. One half of the back of the voucher is devoted to the account distribution and the other half to summaries of the voucher and the details of payment. Spaces are also provided for the signature or initials of certain employees.

VOUCHER — JANSEN AUTO SUPPLY INC.

Date July 1, 1989 Voucher No. 451

Payee Allied Manufacturing Company
683 Fairmont Road
Chicago, IL 60630-3168

DATE	DETAILS	AMOUNT
June 28, 1989	Invoice No. 4693-C FOB Chicago, 2/10, n/30	450.00

Attach Supporting Documents

ACCOUNT DISTRIBUTION

DEBIT	AMOUNT
PURCHASES	450 00
SUPPLIES	
ADVERTISING EXPENSE	
DELIVERY EXPENSE	
MISC. SELLING EXPENSE	
MISC. GENERAL EXPENSE	
CREDIT ACCOUNTS PAYABLE	450 00

DISTRIBUTION APPROVED *L. Donnelly*

VOUCHER NO. 451

DATE 7/1/89 DUE 7/8/89

PAYEE
Allied Manufacturing Company
683 Fairmont Road
Chicago, IL 60630-3168

VOUCHER SUMMARY

AMOUNT	450 00
ADJUSTMENT	
DISCOUNT	9 00
NET	441 00
APPROVED *H. C. Lesher*	CONTROLLER
RECORDED *WB*	

PAYMENT SUMMARY

DATE	7/8/89
AMOUNT	441.00
CHECK NO.	863
APPROVED	*A. T. Wood*
RECORDED	*L. K. R.* *A.S.*

Voucher

Vouchers are customarily prepared by the accounting department on the basis of an invoice or a memorandum that serves as proof of an expenditure. This is usually done only after the following comparisons and verifications have been completed and noted on the invoice:

1. Comparison of the invoice with a copy of the purchase order to verify quantities, prices, and terms.
2. Comparison of the invoice with the receiving report to verify receipt of the items billed.
3. Verification of the arithmetical accuracy of the invoice.

After all data except details of payment have been inserted, the invoice or other supporting evidence is attached to the face of the voucher, which is then folded with the account distribution and summaries on the outside. The voucher is then given to the designated official or officials for final approval.

Unpaid Voucher File. After approval by the designated official, each voucher is recorded as a credit to Accounts Payable and a debit to the appropriate account or accounts. For example, the entry to record the voucher prepared by Jansen Auto Supply Inc., illustrated above, is as follows:

Purchases	450	
Accounts Payable		450

After the voucher is recorded, it is filed in an unpaid voucher file, where it remains until it is paid. The amount due on each voucher represents the credit balance of an account payable.

All voucher systems include some way to assure payment within the discount period or on the last day of the credit period. A simple but effective method is to file each voucher in the unpaid voucher file according to the earliest date that consideration should be given to its payment. The file may be made up of a group of folders, numbered from 1 to 31, the numbers representing days of a month. Such a system brings to the attention of the disbursing official the vouchers that are to be paid on each day. It also provides management with a convenient means of forecasting the amount of cash needed to meet maturing obligations.

When a voucher is to be paid, it is removed from the unpaid voucher file and a check is issued in payment. The date, the number, and the amount of the check are listed on the back of the voucher for use in recording the payment. Paid vouchers and the supporting documents are often run through a canceling machine to prevent accidental or intentional reuse.

An exception to the general rule that vouchers be prepared for all expenditures may be made for bank charges shown by debit memorandums or notations on the bank statement. For example, such items as bank service charges, safe-deposit box rentals, and returned NSF (Not Sufficient Funds) checks from customers may be charged to the depositor's account without either a formal voucher or a check. For large expenditures, such as the repayment of a bank loan, a supporting voucher may be prepared, if desired, even though a check is not written. The paid note may then be attached to the voucher as evidence of the obligation. All bank debit memorandums are the equivalent of checks as evidence of payment.

Paid Voucher File. The payment of a voucher is recorded in the same manner as payment of an account payable. For example, the entry to record the check issued in payment of the Jansen Auto Supply Inc. voucher would be as follows:

Accounts Payable	450	
Cash in Bank		441
Purchases Discounts		9

After payment, vouchers are usually filed in numerical order in a paid voucher file. They are then readily available for examination by employees or independent auditors needing information about a certain expenditure. Eventually the paid vouchers are destroyed according to the firm's policies concerning the retention of records.

Voucher System and Management. The voucher system not only provides effective accounting controls but also aids management in discharging other responsibilities. For example, the voucher system gives greater assurance that all payments are in liquidation of valid liabilities. In addition, current information is always available for use in determining future cash requirements, which in turn enables management to make the best use of cash resources. Invoices on which cash discounts are allowed can be paid within the discount period and other invoices can be paid on the final day of the credit period, thus reducing costs and maintaining a favorable credit standing. Seasonal borrowing for working capital purposes can also be planned more accurately, with a consequent saving in interest costs.

Purchases Discounts

In earlier chapters, purchases of merchandise were recorded at the invoice price, and cash discounts taken were credited to the purchases discounts account at the time of payment. There are two opposing views on how discounts taken should be reported in the income statement.

The most widely accepted view, which has been followed in this textbook, is that purchases discounts should be reported as a deduction from purchases. For example, the cost of merchandise with an invoice price of $1,000, subject to terms of 2/10, n/30, is recorded initially at $1,000. If payment is made within the discount period, the discount of $20 reduces the cost to $980. If the invoice is not paid within the discount period, the cost of the merchandise remains $1,000. This treatment of purchases discounts may be attacked on the grounds that the date of payment should not affect the cost of a commodity. The additional payment required beyond the discount period adds nothing to the value of the commodities purchased.

The second view reports discounts taken as "other income." In terms of the preceding example, the cost of the merchandise is considered to be $1,000, regardless of the time of payment. If payment is made within the discount period, revenue of $20 is considered to be realized. The objection to this procedure lies in the recognition of revenue from the act of purchasing and paying for a commodity. Theoretically, an enterprise might make no sales of merchandise during an accounting period and yet might report as revenue the amount of cash discounts taken.

A major disadvantage of recording purchases at the invoice price and recognizing purchases discounts at the time of payment is that this method does not measure the cost of failing to take discounts. Well-managed enterprises maintain enough cash to pay within the discount period all invoices subject to a discount, and view the failure to take a discount as an inefficiency. To measure the cost of this inefficiency, purchases invoices may be recorded at the net amount, assuming that all discounts will be taken. Any discounts *not* taken are then recorded in an expense account called Discounts Lost. This method measures the cost of failure to take cash discounts and gives management an opportunity to take remedial action. Again assuming the same data, the invoice for $1,000 would be recorded as a debit to Purchases of $980 and a credit to Accounts Payable for the same amount. If the invoice is not paid until after the discount period has passed, the entry would be as follows:

Accounts Payable	980	
Discounts Lost	20	
Cash in Bank		1,000

When this method is used with the voucher system, all vouchers are prepared and recorded at the net amount. Any discount lost is noted on the related voucher and recorded in the journal when the voucher is paid.

Another advantage of this treatment of purchases discounts is that all merchandise purchased is recorded initially at the net price, and hence no later adjustments to cost are necessary. An objection, however, is that the amount reported as accounts payable in the balance sheet may be less than the amount needed to discharge the liability.

Petty Cash

In most businesses there is a frequent need for the payment of relatively small amounts, such as for postage due, for transportation charges, or for the purchase of urgently needed supplies at a nearby retail store. Payment by check in such cases would result in delay, annoyance, and excessive expense of maintaining the records. Yet because these small payments may occur frequently and therefore amount to a considerable total sum, it is desirable to retain close control over such payments. This may be done by maintaining a special cash fund called **petty cash.**

In establishing a petty cash fund, the first step is to estimate the amount of cash needed for disbursements of relatively small amounts during a certain period, such as a week or a month. If the voucher system is used, a voucher is then prepared for this amount and it is recorded as a debit to Petty Cash and a credit to Accounts Payable. The check drawn to pay the voucher is recorded as a debit to Accounts Payable and a credit to Cash in Bank.

The money obtained from cashing the check is placed in the custody of a specific employee who is authorized to disburse the fund according to restrictions as to maximum amount and purpose. Each time a disbursement is made from the fund, the employee records the essential details on a receipt form, obtains the signature of the payee as proof of the payment, and initials the completed form.

When the amount of money in the petty cash fund is reduced to the predetermined minimum amount, the fund is replenished. If the voucher system is used, the accounts debited on the replenishing voucher are those indicated by a summary of expenditures. The voucher is then recorded as a debit to the various expense and asset accounts and a credit to Accounts Payable. The check in payment of the voucher is recorded in the usual manner.

To illustrate the entries that would be made in accounting for petty cash, assume that a voucher system is used and that a petty cash fund of $100 is established on August 1. At the end of August, the petty cash receipts indicate expenditures for the following items: office supplies, $28; postage (office supplies), $22; store supplies, $35; and daily newspaper (miscellaneous general expense), $3.70. To record the establishment and replenishment of the petty cash fund, the entries would be as follows:

Aug.	1	Petty Cash	100.00	
		Accounts Payable		100.00
	1	Accounts Payable	100.00	
		Cash in Bank		100.00
	31	Office Supplies	50.00	
		Store Supplies	35.00	
		Miscellaneous General Expense	3.70	
		Accounts Payable		88.70
	31	Accounts Payable	88.70	
		Cash in Bank		88.70

Replenishing the petty cash fund restores it to its original amount. It should be noted that the only entry in the petty cash account will be the initial debit, unless at some later time the standard amount of the fund is increased or decreased.

Because disbursements are not recorded in the accounts until the fund is replenished, petty cash funds and other special funds that operate in a like manner should always be replenished at the end of an accounting period. The amount of money actually in the fund will then agree with the balance in the related fund account, and the expenses and the assets for which payment has been made will be recorded in the proper period.

Other Cash Funds

Cash funds may also be established to meet other special needs of a business. For example, money may be advanced for travel expenses as needed. Then periodically, after expense reports have been received, the expenses are recorded and the fund is replenished. A similar procedure may be used to provide a working fund for a sales office located in another city. The amount of the fund may be deposited in a local bank and the sales representative may be authorized to draw checks for payment of rent, salaries, and other operating expenses. Each month, the representative sends the invoices, bank statement, paid checks, bank reconciliation, and other business documents to the home office. The data are audited, the expenditures are recorded, and a reimbursing check is returned for deposit in the local bank.

CASH TRANSACTIONS AND ELECTRONIC FUNDS TRANSFER

Currently most cash transactions are in the form of currency or check. The broad principles discussed in earlier sections provide the basis for developing an effective system to control such cash transactions. However, the development of **electronic funds transfer (EFT)** may eventually change the form in which many cash transactions are executed and could affect the processing and controlling of cash transactions.

EFT can be defined as a payment system that uses computerized electronic impulses rather than paper (money, checks, etc.) to effect a cash transaction. For example, a business may pay its employees by means of EFT. Under such a system, employees who want their payroll checks deposited directly in a checking account sign an authorization form. For each pay period, the business' computer produces a magnetic tape with computer-sensitive notations for relevant payroll data. The magnetic tape is delivered to the bank, or the data are transmitted over telephone lines. The bank then debits the business' account for the entire payroll and credits the checking account of each employee. Similar cash payments might be made for other preauthorized payments. The federal government currently processes several million social security checks through EFT.

EFT is also beginning to play a role in retail sales. Through a point-of-sale (POS) system, a customer pays for goods at the time of purchase by presenting a plastic card. The card is used to activate a terminal in the store and thereby effect an immediate transfer from the customer's checking account to the retailer's account at the bank.

Studies have indicated that EFT systems may reduce the cost of processing certain cash transactions and contribute to better control over cash receipts and cash payments. Offsetting these potential advantages are problems of protecting the privacy of information stored in computers, and difficulties in documenting purchase and sale transactions. In any event, developments with EFT systems are likely to be followed very closely by most businesses over the next few years.

Chapter Review

KEY POINTS

1. Principles of Accounting Systems.
Although accounting systems will vary from business to business, the following broad principles will apply to all systems: cost-effectiveness balance; flexibility to meet future needs; adequate internal controls; effective reporting; and adaptation to organizational structure.

2. Accounting System Installation and Revision.
Accounting system installation and revision involves three phases: (1) analysis of information needs, (2) design of the new system, and (3) implementation of proposals.

3. Internal Controls.
Internal controls are the detailed policies and procedures used by management to achieve goals. Although the details of the system of internal control will vary according to size and type of business, the following broad principles of internal control apply to most businesses: competent personnel and rotation of duties, assignment of responsibility, separation of responsibility for related operations, separation of operations and accounting, proofs and security measures, and independent review.

4. Control Over Cash.
It is necessary to safeguard cash effectively because of the ease with which it can be transferred. One of the major devices for maintaining control over cash is the bank account. To obtain the most benefit from a bank account, all cash received must be deposited in the bank and all payments must be made by checks drawn on the bank or from special cash funds.

Periodically, the bank mails to the depositor a statement of account. This statement of account should be reconciled with the depositor's records by preparing a bank reconciliation. The bank reconciliation is divided into two major sections: one section begins with the balance according to the bank statement and ends with an adjusted balance; the other section begins with the balance according to the depositor's records and also ends with an adjusted balance. After all reconciling items have been considered, the two amounts designated as the adjusted balance must be equal.

After a bank reconciliation has been prepared, the items which appear in the section of the bank reconciliation beginning with the balance according to the depositor's records must be entered into the accounting records through the use of journal entries.

5. Internal Control of Cash Receipts.
The bank reconciliation is an important part of the system of internal control over cash. Other controls of cash receipts include the separation of responsibilities for recording cash transactions from the handling of cash, the use of a cash short and over account for differences between recorded receipts and actual receipts, and the use of cash change funds.

6. Internal Control of Cash Payments.
One of the best systems for establishing control of cash payments is the use of a voucher system. A voucher system is made up of records, methods, and procedures used in proving and recording liabilities and in making and recording cash payments. A voucher system uses (1) vouchers, (2) a file for unpaid vouchers, and (3) a file for paid vouchers.

Because of the importance of taking advantage of all purchases discounts, a business may use a separate account, called Discounts Lost, to account for any discounts not taken during the discount period. When this method is used with the voucher system, all vouchers are prepared and recorded at the net amount, assuming that the discount will be taken.

A special cash fund, called petty cash, may be used by a business to make small payments that occur frequently, for which payment by check would cause delay, annoyance, and excessive expense of maintaining records. The amount of money maintained in a petty cash fund is placed in the custody of a specific employee, who authorizes disbursement of the fund according to specific restrictions as to maximum amount and purpose. When the amount of money in the petty cash fund is reduced to a predetermined minimum amount, the fund is replenished. Other cash funds may be established by businesses for purposes such as travel expenses, selling expenses, and other operating expenses.

7. Cash Transactions and Electronic Funds Transfer.
Electronic funds transfer is a payment system that uses computerized electronic impulses rather than paper (money, checks, etc.) to effect cash transactions. EFT is beginning to play an important role in retail sales.

KEY TERMS

accounting system 176
data base 177
subsidiary ledger 177
general ledger 177
controlling account 177
internal controls 178
bank reconciliation 185
voucher system 190
voucher 191
petty cash 194
electronic funds transfer (EFT) 195

SELF-EXAMINATION QUESTIONS

(Answers at End of Chapter)

1. The detailed procedures used by management to direct operations so that enterprise goals can be achieved are termed:
   A. internal controls
   B. systems analysis
   C. systems design
   D. systems implementation
2. In preparing a bank reconciliation, the amount of checks outstanding would be:
   A. added to the bank balance according to the bank statement
   B. deducted from the bank balance according to the bank statement
   C. added to the bank balance according to the depositor's records
   D. deducted from the bank balance according to the depositor's records
3. Journal entries based on the bank reconciliation are required for:
   A. additions to the bank balance according to the depositor's records
   B. deductions from the bank balance according to the depositor's records
   C. both A and B
   D. neither A nor B
4. A voucher system is used, all vouchers for purchases are recorded at the net amount, and a purchase is made for $500 under terms 1/10, n/30.
   A. Purchases would be debited for $495 to record the purchase.
   B. Discounts Lost would be debited for $5 if the voucher is not paid within the discount period.
   C. If the voucher is not paid until after the discount period has expired, the discount lost would be reported as an expense on the income statement.
   D. All of the above
5. A petty cash fund is:
   A. used to pay relatively small amounts
   B. established by estimating the amount of cash needed for disbursements of relatively small amounts during a specified period
   C. reimbursed when the amount of money in the fund is reduced to a predetermined minimum amount
   D. all of the above

ILLUSTRATIVE PROBLEM

The bank statement for Dunlap Company for April 30 indicates a balance of $10,443.11. The Dunlap Company employs the voucher system in controlling expenditures and disbursements. All cash receipts are deposited each evening in a night depository, after banking hours. The accounting records indicate the following summary data for April:

balance as of April 1	$ 5,143.50
Total cash receipts for April	28,971.60
Total amount of checks issued in April	26,060.85

Comparison of the bank statement and the accompanying canceled checks and memorandums with the records revealed the following reconciling items:

(a) The bank had collected for Dunlap Company $912 on a note left for collection. The face of the note was $900.
(b) A deposit of $1,852.21, representing receipts of April 30, had been made too late to appear on the bank statement.
(c) Checks outstanding totaled $3,265.27.
(d) A check drawn for $79 had been erroneously charged by the bank as $97.
(e) A check for $10 returned with the statement had been recorded in the records as $100. The check was for the payment of an obligation to Davis Equipment Company for the purchase of office supplies on account.
(f) Bank service charges for April amounted to $8.20.

Instructions:

1. Prepare a bank reconciliation for April.
2. Journalize the entries that should be made by Dunlap Company.

SOLUTION

(1)

Dunlap Company
Bank Reconciliation
April 30, 19--

Balance per bank statement		$10,443.11
Add: Deposit of April 30 not recorded by bank	$1,852.21	
Bank error in charging check for $97 instead of $79	18.00	1,870.21
		$12,313.32
Deduct: Outstanding checks		3,265.27
Adjusted balance		$ 9,048.05
Balance per depositor's records		$ 8,054.25*
Add: Proceeds of note collected by bank including $12 interest	$ 912.00	
Error in recording check	90.00	1,002.00
		$ 9,056.25
Deduct: Bank service charges		8.20
Adjusted balance		$ 9,048.05

*$5,143.50 + $28,971.60 − $26,060.85

(2)

Cash in Bank	1,002.00	
Notes Receivable		900.00
Interest Income		12.00
Accounts Payable		90.00
Miscellaneous General Expense	8.20	
Cash in Bank		8.20

Discussion Questions

5–1. Why is the accounting system of an enterprise an information system?

5–2. What are internal controls?

5–3. What is the objective of systems analysis?

5–4. What is included in an enterprise's systems manual?

5–5. How does a policy of rotating clerical employees from job to job aid in strengthening internal control?

5–6. Why should the responsibility for a sequence of related operations be divided among different persons?

5–7. The ticket seller at a movie theater doubles as ticket taker for a few minutes each day while the ticket taker is on a "break." Which principle of internal control is violated in this situation?

5–8. Why should the responsibility for maintaining the accounting records be separated from the responsibility for operations?

5–9. How can the use of fidelity insurance aid internal control?

5–10. How does a periodic review by internal auditors strengthen the system of internal control?

5–11. Why is cash the asset that often warrants the most attention in the design of an effective internal control system?

5–12. (a) What is meant by the term *compensating balance* as applied to the checking account of a firm? (b) How is the compensating balance reported in the financial statements?

5–13. What name is often given to the notification attached to a check that indicates the specific invoice that is being paid?

5–14. When checks are received, they are recorded as debits to Cash, the assumption being that the drawer has sufficient funds on deposit. What entry should be made if a check received from a customer and deposited is returned by the bank for lack of sufficient funds (NSF)?

5–15. Do items reported on the bank statement as debits represent (a) deductions made by the bank from the depositor's balance, or (b) additions made by the bank to the depositor's balance?

5–16. What is the purpose of preparing a bank reconciliation?

5–17. Identify each of the following reconciling items as: (a) an addition to the balance per bank statement, (b) a deduction from the balance per bank statement, (c) an addition to the balance per depositor's records, or (d) a deduction from the balance per depositor's records. (None of the transactions reported by bank debit and credit memorandums have been recorded by the depositor.)

(1) Outstanding checks, $4,210.50.
(2) Note collected by bank, $5,150.
(3) Deposit in transit, $3,305.75.
(4) Check for $2,000 charged by bank as $200.
(5) Check drawn by depositor for $520 but recorded as $250.
(6) Check of a customer returned by bank to depositor because of insufficient funds, $92.55.
(7) Bank service charges, $22.50.

5–18. Which of the reconciling items listed in Question 5–17 necessitate an entry in the depositor's accounts?

5–19. The procedures employed by Garcia's for over-the-counter receipts are as follows: At the close of each day's business, the salesclerks count the cash in their respective cash drawers, after which they determine the amount recorded on the cash register tapes and prepare the memorandum cash form, noting any discrepancies. An employee from the cashier's office counts the cash, compares the total with the memorandum, and takes the cash to the cashier's office. (a) Indicate the weak link in internal control. (b) How can the weakness be corrected?

5–20. The mailroom employees of C. L. Dunn Co. send all remittances and remittance advices to the cashier. The cashier deposits the cash in the bank and forwards the remittance advices and duplicate deposit slips to the accounting department. (a) Indicate the weak link in internal control in the handling of cash receipts. (b) How can the weakness be corrected?

5–21. The combined cash count of all cash registers at the close of business is $4.35 less than the cash sales indicated by the cash register tapes. (a) In what account is the cash shortage recorded? (b) Are cash shortages debited or credited to this account?

5–22. The bookkeeper pays all obligations by prenumbered checks. What are the strengths and weaknesses in the internal control over cash disbursements in this situation?

5–23. What is meant by the term *voucher* as applied to the voucher system?

5–24. Before a voucher for the purchase of merchandise is approved for payment, three documents should be compared to verify the accuracy of the liability. Name these three documents.

5–25. Ann Jacobs, controller of D. D. West and Company, approves all vouchers before they are submitted to the treasurer for payment. What procedure can Jacobs add to the system to assure that the documents accompanying the vouchers and supporting the expenditures are not "reused" to support future vouchers improperly?

5–26. In what order are vouchers ordinarily filed (a) in the unpaid voucher file, and (b) in the paid voucher file? Give reasons for answers.

5–27. What are the two possibilities for reporting purchases discounts on the income statement?

5–28. Merchandise with an invoice price of $5,000 is purchased subject to terms of 2/10, n/30. Determine the cost of the merchandise according to each of the following systems:

(a) Discounts taken are treated as deductions from the invoice price.
   (1) The invoice is paid within the discount period.
   (2) The invoice is paid after the discount period has expired.
(b) Discounts taken are treated as other income.
   (1) The invoice is paid within the discount period.
   (2) The invoice is paid after the discount period has expired.
(c) Discounts allowable are treated as deductions from the invoice price, regardless of when payment is made.
   (1) The invoice is paid within the discount period.
   (2) The invoice is paid after the discount period has expired.

5–29. What account or accounts are debited when recording the voucher (a) establishing a petty cash fund and (b) replenishing a petty cash fund?

5–30. The petty cash account has a debit balance of $250. At the end of the accounting period, there is $33 in the petty cash fund along with petty cash receipts totaling $217. Should the fund be replenished as of the last day of the period? Discuss.

5–31. What is meant by electronic funds transfer?

5–32. Real World Focus. Between September 3 and September 22, seventeen prenumbered checks totaling $1,129,232.39 were forged and cashed on the accounts of Perini Corporation, a construction company based in the Boston suburb of Framingham. Perini Corporation kept its supply of blank prenumbered checks in an unlocked storeroom with items such as styrofoam coffee cups. Every clerk and secretary had access to this storeroom. It was later discovered that someone had apparently stolen two boxes of prenumbered checks. The numbers of the missing checks matched the numbers of the out-of-sequence checks cashed by the banks. What fundamental principle of control over cash was violated in this case?

Exercises

5–33. Bank reconciliation. The following data are accumulated for use in reconciling the bank account of Lambert and Mann Inc. for June:

(a) Balance per bank statement at June 30, $8,791.22.
(b) Balance per depositor's records at June 30, $7,548.02.
(c) Checks outstanding, $1,955.25.
(d) Deposit in transit, not recorded by bank, $787.50.
(e) A check for $122 in payment of a voucher was erroneously recorded as $212.
(f) Bank debit memorandum for service charges, $14.55.

Prepare a bank reconciliation.

5–34. Entries for bank reconciliation. Using the data presented in Exercise 5–33, prepare the entry or entries that should be made by the depositor.

5–35. Entries for note collected by bank. Accompanying a bank statement for DeMaris and Son is a credit memorandum for $5,150, representing the principal ($5,000) and interest ($150) on a note that had been collected by the bank. The depositor had been notified by the bank at the time of the collection, but had made no entries. Present the entry that should be made by the depositor.

5–36. Entry for cash sales. The actual cash received from cash sales for Susan Clark Company was $3,745.75, and the amount indicated by the cash register tally was $3,750.25. Prepare the entry to record the cash receipts and cash sales.

5–37. Entries for vouchers and checks; purchases at gross amount. Present entries for the following selected transactions. All invoices are recorded at invoice price.

July 1. Recorded Voucher No. 792 for $2,000, payable to Corley Co., for merchandise purchased, terms 2/10, n/30.
2. Recorded Voucher No. 793 for $300, payable to B. M. Systems, for merchandise purchased, terms 1/10, n/30.
11. Issued Check No. 779 in payment of Voucher No. 793.
13. Recorded Voucher No. 812 for $2,500, payable to Glos Inc., for merchandise purchased, terms 2/10, n/30.
23. Issued Check No. 799 in payment of Voucher No. 812.
30. Recorded Voucher No. 840 for $212.10 to replenish the petty cash fund for the following disbursements: store supplies, $72.50; office supplies, $51.25; miscellaneous general expense, $46.10; miscellaneous selling expense, $42.25.
30. Issued Check No. 815 in payment of Voucher No. 840.
30. Issued Check No. 816 in payment of Voucher No. 792.

5–38. Entries for purchases at net amount. Record the following related transactions, assuming that invoices for commodities purchased are recorded at their net price after deducting the allowable discount:

June 10. Voucher No. 801 is prepared for merchandise purchased from Klein Co., $3,000, terms 2/10, n/30.
15. Voucher No. 811 is prepared for merchandise purchased from Zimmer Co., $1,500, terms 1/10, n/30.
25. Check No. 798 is issued in payment of Voucher No. 811.
July 10. Check No. 808 is issued in payment of Voucher No. 801.

5–39. Petty cash fund entries. Prepare the entries to record the following:

(a) Voucher No. 19 is prepared to establish a petty cash fund of $200.
(b) Check No. 15 is issued in payment of Voucher No. 19.
(c) The amount of cash in the petty cash fund is now $19.90. Voucher No. 80 is prepared to replenish the fund, based on the following summary of petty cash receipts: office supplies, $62.20; miscellaneous selling expense, $59.15; miscellaneous general expense, $57.50. (Since the amount of the petty cash receipts in the fund plus the balance in the fund do not equal $200, record the discrepancy in the cash short and over account.)
(d) Check No. 73 is issued by the disbursing officer in payment of Voucher No. 80. The check is cashed and the money is placed in the fund.

5–40. Cash change fund entries. Record the following transactions:

(a) Voucher No. 440 is prepared to establish a change fund of $250.
(b) Check No. 419 is issued in payment of Voucher No. 440.
(c) Cash sales for the day, according to the cash register tapes, were $1,900.05, and cash on hand is $2,152.15. A bank deposit ticket was prepared for $1,902.15.

5–41. Procedures for internal control of cash payments. D. Hogan Corp. is a medium-size merchandising enterprise. When its current income statement was reviewed, it was noted that the amount of purchases discounts was disproportionately small in comparison with earlier periods. Further investigation revealed that in spite of a sufficient bank balance, a significant amount of available cash discounts had been lost because of failure to make timely payments. In addition, it was discovered that several purchases invoices had been paid twice.

Outline procedures for the payment of vendor's invoices so that the possibilities of losing available cash discounts and of paying an invoice a second time will be minimized.

Problems

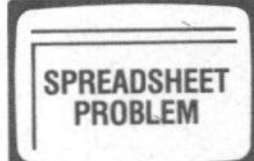

5–42. Bank reconciliation and entries. The cash in bank account for J. C. Peters Co. at June 30 of the current year indicated a balance of $18,500.30. The bank statement indicated a balance of $29,106.30 on June 30. Comparison of the bank statement and the accompanying canceled checks and memorandums with the records revealed the following reconciling items:

(a) Checks outstanding totaled $13,441.50.
(b) A deposit of $6,917.75, representing receipts of June 30, had been made too late to appear on the bank statement.
(c) The bank had collected for J. C. Peters Co. $4,240 on a note left for collection. The face of the note was $4,000.
(d) A check for $92.50 returned with the statement had been recorded erro-neously as $9.25. The check was for the payment of an obligation to Allen Supply Company for the purchase of office equipment on account.
(e) A check drawn for $505 had been erroneously charged by the bank as $550.
(f) Bank service charges for June amounted to $29.50.

Instructions: (1) Prepare a bank reconciliation.
(2) Record the necessary entries. The accounts have not been closed.

5–43. Bank reconciliation and entries. The cash in bank account for Baker Co. at July 1 of the current year indicated a balance of $11,221.70. Cash deposited and checks written during July totaled $20,650.75 and $21,770.25, respectively. The bank statement indicated a balance of $18,243.30 on July 31. Comparison of the bank statement, the canceled checks, and the accompanying memorandums with the records revealed the following reconciling items:

(a) Checks outstanding totaled $9,103.84.
(b) A deposit of $3,248.21, representing receipts of July 31, had been made too late to appear on the bank statement.
(c) The bank had collected for Baker Co. $2,650 on a note left for collection. The face of the note was $2,500.
(d) A check drawn for $360 had been erroneously charged by the bank as $630.
(e) A check for $84.20 returned with the statement had been recorded by Baker Co. as $8.42. The check was for the payment of an obligation to Barker Equipment Company for the purchase of office equipment on account.
(f) Bank service charges for July amounted to $18.75.

Instructions: (1) Prepare a bank reconciliation as of July 31.
(2) Journalize the necessary entries. The accounts have not been closed.

5–44. Bank reconciliation and related entries. Quartz Company employs the voucher system in controlling expenditures and disbursements. All cash receipts are deposited each Wednesday and Friday in a night depository after banking hours. The data required to reconcile the bank statement as of April 30 have been abstracted from various documents and records and are reproduced as follows:

CASH IN BANK ACCOUNT BALANCE AS OF APRIL 1................ $8,217.40

CASH RECEIPTS FOR MONTH OF APRIL......................... 7,829.58

DUPLICATE DEPOSIT TICKETS:

Date and amount of each deposit in April:

Date	Amount	Date	Amount	Date	Amount
April 1	$798.63	April 10	$971.71	April 22	$972.34
3	894.04	15	957.85	24	867.71
8	910.50	17	946.74	29	510.06

CHECKS WRITTEN:

Number and amount of each check issued in April:

Check No.	Amount	Check No.	Amount	Check No.	Amount
725	$327.50	732	$490.90	739	$172.75
726	515.15	733	VOID	740	249.75
727	401.90	734	640.13	741	113.95
728	771.30	735	376.77	742	907.95
729	506.88	736	299.37	743	359.60
730	117.25	737	537.01	744	601.50
731	298.66	738	380.95	745	486.39

Total amount of checks issued in April.......................... $8,555.66

APRIL BANK STATEMENT:

Balance as of April 1	$ 8,347.20
Deposits and other credits	10,602.77
Checks and other debits	(8,182.21)
Balance as of April 30	$10,767.76

Date and amount of each deposit in April:

Date	Amount	Date	Amount	Date	Amount
April 1	$690.25	April 9	$910.50	April 18	$946.74
2	798.63	11	971.71	23	972.34
4	894.04	16	975.85	25	867.71

CHECKS ACCOMPANYING APRIL BANK STATEMENT:

Number and amount of each check, rearranged in numerical sequence:

Check No.	Amount	Check No.	Amount	Check No.	Amount
716	$112.15	729	$506.88	736	$299.37
723	301.40	730	117.25	737	537.01
724	60.55	731	298.66	738	380.95
725	327.50	732	490.90	740	249.75
726	515.15	734	640.13	741	113.95
727	401.90	735	376.77	742	907.95
728	771.30			745	486.39

BANK MEMORANDUMS ACCOMPANYING APRIL BANK STATEMENT:

Date, description, and amount of each memorandum:

Date	Description	Amount
April 4	Bank credit memo for note collected:	
	Principal	$2,500.00
	Interest	75.00
24	Bank debit memo for check returned because of insufficient funds	266.80
30	Bank debit memo for service charges	19.50

BANK RECONCILIATION FOR PRECEDING MONTH:

Quartz Company
Bank Reconciliation
March 31, 19--

Balance per bank statement		$8,347.20
Add deposit for March 31, not recorded by bank		690.25
		$9,037.45
Deduct outstanding checks:		
No. 716	$112.15	
721	345.95	
723	301.40	
724	60.55	820.05
Adjusted balance		$8,217.40
Balance per depositor's records		$8,230.50
Deduct service charges		13.10
Adjusted balance		$8,217.40

Instructions: (1) Prepare a bank reconciliation as of April 30. If errors in recording deposits or checks are discovered, assume that the errors were made by the company. Assume that all deposits are from cash sales. All checks are in payment of vouchers.
(2) Journalize the necessary entries. The accounts have not been closed.
(3) What is the amount of cash in bank that should appear on the balance sheet as of April 30?

5–45. Entries for voucher system. The following selected transactions were completed by a company that uses a voucher system, with all invoices recorded at their net price.

July 2. Recorded Voucher No. 240 for $1,100, payable to Davis Supply Co., for office supplies purchased on terms n/30.
5. Recorded Voucher No. 242 for $5,000, payable to A. Adair Co., for merchandise purchased on terms 1/10, n/30.
7. Recorded Voucher No. 248 for $1,400, payable to Kennedy Inc., for merchandise purchased on terms 1/10, n/30.
17. Issued Check No. 364 in payment of Voucher No. 248.
22. Recorded Voucher No. 260 for $239.84 to replenish the petty cash fund for the following disbursements: store supplies, $92.88; office supplies, $69.95; miscellaneous general expense, $42.45; miscellaneous selling expense, $34.56.
23. Issued Check No. 370 in payment of Voucher No. 260.
31. Issued Check No. 377 in payment of Voucher No. 242.
31. Issued Check No. 389 in payment of Voucher No. 240.

Instructions: Record the transactions.

5–46. Transactions for petty cash, advances to salespersons fund; cash short and over. Martin Company has just adopted the policy of depositing all cash receipts in the bank and of making all payments by check in conjunction with the voucher system. The following transactions were selected from those completed in June of the current year:

June 1. Recorded Voucher No. 1 to establish a petty cash fund of $200 and a change fund of $500.
1. Issued Check No. 909 in payment of Voucher No. 1.
4. Recorded Voucher No. 5 to establish an advances to salespersons fund of $1,000.
4. Issued Check No. 912 in payment of Voucher No. 5.

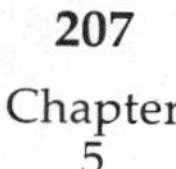

10. The cash sales for the day, according to the cash register tapes, totaled $3,107.90. The combined count of all cash on hand (including the change fund) totaled $3,610.50.
25. Recorded Voucher No. 35 to reimburse the petty cash fund for the following disbursements, each evidenced by a petty cash receipt:
    June 5. Store supplies, $15.50.
    6. Express charges on merchandise purchased, $14.50.
    8. Office supplies, $12.75
    9. Office supplies, $9.20.
    12. Postage stamps, $22 (Office Supplies).
    12. Repair to calculator, $27.50 (Miscellaneous General Expense).
    16. Repair to typewriter, $20.50 (Miscellaneous General Expense).
    18. Postage due on special delivery letter, $1.05 (Miscellaneous General Expense).
    20. Express charges on merchandise purchased, $19.50.
    24. Telegram charges, $7.75 (Miscellaneous Selling Expense).
25. Issued Check No. 942 in payment of Voucher No. 35.
28. The cash sales for the day, according to the cash register tapes, totaled $2,605.50. The count of all cash on hand (including the change fund) totaled $3,101.60.
30. Recorded Voucher No. 40 to replenish the advances to salespersons fund for the following expenditures for travel: Ann Brennon, $197.50; John Kottes, $297.40; Jane Palmer, $311.15.
30. Issued Check No. 948 in payment of Voucher No. 40.

Instructions: Record the transactions.

ALTERNATE PROBLEMS

5–42A. Bank reconciliation and entries. The cash in bank account for L. L. Holmes Co. at May 31 of the current year indicated a balance of $12,643.35. The bank statement indicated a balance of $17,762.90 on May 31. Comparison of the bank statement and the accompanying canceled checks and memorandums with the records revealed the following reconciling items:

(a) Checks outstanding totaled $6,172.25.
(b) A deposit of $3,770.10, representing receipts of May 31, had been made too late to appear on the bank statement.
(c) The bank had collected for L. L. Holmes Co. $2,575 on an interest-bearing note left for collection. The face of the note was $2,500.
(d) A check for $47 returned with the statement had been recorded erroneously as $74. The check was for the payment of an obligation to Durham Bros. for the purchase of office supplies on account.
(e) A check drawn for $150 had been erroneously charged by the bank as $15.
(f) Bank service charges for May amounted to $19.60.

Instructions: (1) Prepare a bank reconciliation.
(2) Record the necessary entries. The accounts have not been closed.

5–43A. Bank reconciliation and entries. The cash in bank account for Parr Co. at April 1 of the current year indicated a balance of $9,992.50. Cash deposited and checks written during April totaled $20,500.40 and $18,850.47, respectively. The bank statement indicated a balance of $14,519.55 on April 30. Comparison of the bank statement, the canceled checks, and the accompanying memorandums with the records revealed the following reconciling items:

(a) Checks outstanding totaled $4,291.37.
(b) A deposit of $2,592.80, representing receipts of April 30, had been made too late to appear on the bank statement.
(c) A check for $100 had been erroneously charged by the bank as $10.
(d) A check for $57.45 returned with the statement had been recorded by Parr Co. as $75.45. The check was for the payment of an obligation to Brandon Office Supply Co. for the purchase of office supplies on account.
(e) The bank had collected for Parr Co. $1,080 on a note left for collection. The face of the note was $1,000.
(f) Bank service charges for April amounted to $9.45.

Instructions: (1) Prepare a bank reconciliation as of April 30.
(2) Journalize the necessary entries. The accounts have not been closed.

5–44A. Bank reconciliation and related entries. Venice Company employs the voucher system in controlling expenditures and disbursements. All cash receipts are deposited each Wednesday and Friday in a night depository after banking hours. The data required to reconcile the bank statement as of July 31 have been abstracted from various documents and records and are reproduced as follows.

CASH IN BANK ACCOUNT BALANCE AS OF JULY 1 .... $10,905.50

CASH RECEIPTS FOR MONTH OF JULY.......................... $ 7,005.10

DUPLICATE DEPOSIT TICKETS:

Date and amount of each deposit in July:

Date	Amount	Date	Amount	Date	Amount
July 2	$850.40	July 11	$616.70	July 23	$881.45
4	709.90	16	797.60	25	601.50
9	919.24	18	701.26	30	927.05

CHECKS WRITTEN:

Number and amount of each check issued in July:

Check No.	Amount	Check No.	Amount	Check No.	Amount
414	$152.50	421	$399.50	428	$717.70
415	710.10	422	VOID	429	349.90
416	289.90	423	VOID	430	882.20
417	595.50	424	918.01	431	982.16
418	335.40	425	558.63	432	62.40
419	220.10	426	530.03	433	675.48
420	238.87	427	338.73	434	97.90

Total amount of checks issued in July $9,055.01

JULY BANK STATEMENT:

Balance as of July 1	$11,017.02
Deposits and other credits	14,508.85
Checks and other debits	(9,559.03)
Balance as of July 31	$15,966.84

Date and amount of each deposit in July:

Date	Amount	Date	Amount	Date	Amount
July 1	$780.80	July 11	$919.24	July 21	$701.26
3	850.40	13	616.70	24	881.45
6	709.90	17	797.60	28	601.50

CHECKS ACCOMPANYING JULY BANK STATEMENT:

Number and amount of each check, rearranged in numerical sequence:

Check No.	Amount	Check No.	Amount	Check No.	Amount
400	$390.40	418	$335.40	426	$530.03
412	110.25	419	220.10	427	338.73
413	219.17	420	238.87	429	359.90
414	152.50	421	399.50	430	882.20
415	710.10	424	918.01	431	982.16
416	289.90	425	558.63	432	62.40
417	595.50			433	675.48

BANK MEMORANDUMS ACCOMPANYING JULY BANK STATEMENT:

Date, description, and amount of each memorandum:

Date	Description	Amount
July 3	Bank credit memo for note collected:	
	Principal	$7,500.00
	Interest	150.00
16	Bank debit memo for check returned because of insufficient funds	575.50
31	Bank debit memo for service charges	14.30

BANK RECONCILIATION FOR PRECEDING MONTH:

Venice Company
Bank Reconciliation
June 30, 19--

Balance per bank statement		$11,017.02
Add deposit of June 30, not recorded by bank		780.80
		$11,797.82
Deduct outstanding checks:		
No. 400	$390.40	
406	172.50	
412	110.25	
413	219.17	892.32
Adjusted balance		$10,905.50
Balance per depositor's records		$10,917.75
Deduct service charges		12.25
Adjusted balance		$10,905.50

Instructions: (1) Prepare a bank reconciliation as of July 31. If errors in recording deposits or checks are discovered, assume that the errors were made by the company. Assume that all deposits are from cash sales. All checks are in payment of vouchers.
(2) Journalize the necessary entries. The accounts have not been closed.
(3) What is the amount of cash in bank that should appear on the balance sheet as of July 31?

Mini-Case 5

The records of Perez Company indicate an April 30 cash in bank balance of $30,777.35, which includes undeposited receipts for April 29 and 30. The cash balance on the bank statement as of April 30 is $27,196.30. This balance includes a note of $1,500 plus $60 interest collected by the bank but not recorded in the journal. Checks outstanding on April 30 were as follows: No. 110, $713.40; No. 177, $300.00; No. 201, $522.40; No. 882, $825.15; No. 885, $327.70; and No. 886, $466.10.

On April 10, the Perez Company cashier resigned, effective at the end of the month. Before leaving on April 30, the cashier prepared the following bank reconciliation:

Balance per books, April 30		$30,777.35
Add outstanding checks:		
882	$825.15	
885	327.70	
886	466.10	1,418.95
		$32,196.30
Less undeposited receipts		5,000.00
Balance per bank, April 30		$27,196.30
Deduct unrecorded note with interest		1,560.00
True cash, April 30		$25,636.30

Calculator Tape of Outstanding Checks

```
       0.  *

  825.15  +
  327.70  +
  466.10  +
1,418.95  *
```

Subsequently, the owner of Perez Company discovered that the cashier had stolen all undeposited receipts on hand on April 30 in excess of $5,000. The owner, a close family friend, has asked your help in determining the amount that the former cashier has stolen.

Instructions:

(1) Determine the amount the cashier stole from Perez Company. Show your computations in good form.
(2) How did the cashier attempt to conceal the theft?

(3) (a) Identify two major weaknesses in Perez Company's internal accounting controls, which allowed the cashier to steal the undeposited cash receipts.
(b) Recommend improvements in Perez Company's internal accounting controls, so that similar types of thefts of undeposited cash receipts could be prevented.

(AICPA adapted)

Answers to Self-Examination Questions

1. A The policies and procedures established by an enterprise to provide reasonable assurance that the enterprise's goals will be achieved are called internal controls (answer A). The three phases of installing or changing an accounting system are: analysis (answer B), design (answer C), and implementation (answer D). System analysis is the determination of the information needs, the sources of such information, and the deficiencies in procedures and data processing methods presently used. Systems design refers to the creation of a new system or a change in the present system, based on the analysis. The carrying out of the proposals for the design of a system is referred to as systems implementation.

2. B On any specific date, the cash in bank account in a depositor's ledger may not agree with the reciprocal account in the bank's ledger because of delays and/or errors by either party in recording transactions. The purpose of a bank reconciliation, therefore, is to determine the reasons for any discrepancies between the two account balances. All errors should then be corrected by the depositor or the bank as appropriate. In arriving at the adjusted (correct) balance according to the bank statement, outstanding checks must be deducted (answer B) to adjust for checks that have been written by the depositor but that have not yet been presented to the bank for payment.

3. C All reconciling items that are added to and deducted from the "balance per depositor's records" on the bank reconciliation (answer C) require that journal entries be made by the depositor to correct errors made in recording transactions or to bring the cash account up to date for delays in recording transactions.

4. D A major advantage of recording purchases at the net amount (answer A) is that the cost of failing to take discounts is recorded in the accounts (answer B) and then reported as an expense on the income statement (answer C).

5. D To avoid the delay, annoyance, and expense that is associated with paying all obligations by check, relatively small amounts (answer A) are paid from a petty cash fund. The fund is established by estimating the amount of cash needed to pay these small amounts during a specified period (answer B) and it is then reimbursed when the amount of money in the fund is reduced to a predetermined minimum amount (answer C).

6 Receivables and Temporary Investments

CHAPTER OBJECTIVES

Describe the common classifications of receivables.

Describe the basic principles of internal control over receivables.

Describe and illustrate the accounting for notes receivable, including the determination of interest and proceeds from discounting notes.

Describe and illustrate the allowance method of accounting for uncollectible receivables, including the estimation of uncollectibles based on sales and an analysis of receivables.

Describe and illustrate the direct write-off method of accounting for uncollectible receivables.

Describe and illustrate the accounting for receivables from installment sales.

Describe and illustrate the accounting for temporary investments.

Describe and illustrate the presentation of temporary investments and receivables in the balance sheet.

For many businesses, the revenue from sales on a credit basis is the largest factor influencing the amount of net income. As credit is granted, businesses must account for the resulting receivables, which may represent a substantial portion of the total current assets. As the receivables are collected, the cash realized is accounted for in the manner discussed in Chapter 5. If the amount of cash on hand exceeds immediate cash requirements, the excess cash might be invested in securities until needed. These securities are accounted for as temporary investments.

CLASSIFICATION OF RECEIVABLES

The term **receivables** includes all money claims against people, organizations, or other debtors. Receivables are acquired by a business enterprise in various kinds of transactions, the most common being the sale of merchandise or services on a credit basis.

Credit may be granted on open account or on the basis of a formal instrument of credit, such as a promissory note. Promissory notes are usually used for credit periods of more than sixty days, as in sales of equipment on the installment plan, and for transactions of relatively large dollar amounts. Promissory notes may also be used in settlement of an open account and in borrowing or lending money.

A **promissory note,** frequently referred to simply as a **note,** is a written promise to pay a sum of money on demand or at a definite time. As in the case of a check, it must be payable to the order of a certain person or firm, or to bearer. It must also be signed by the person or firm that makes the promise. The one to whose order the note is payable is called the **payee,** and the one making the promise is called the **maker.** The enterprise owning a note refers to it as a **note receivable** and records it as an asset at its face amount.

A note that provides for the payment of interest for the period between the issuance date and the due date is called an **interest-bearing note.** If a note makes no provision for interest, it is said to be **non-interest-bearing.**

The amount that is due at the maturity or due date is called the **maturity value.** The maturity value of a non-interest-bearing note is the face amount. The maturity value of an interest-bearing note is the sum of the face amount and the interest.

From the point of view of the creditor, a claim evidenced by a note has some advantages over a claim in the form of an account receivable. By signing a note, the debtor acknowledges the debt and agrees to pay it according to the terms given. The note is therefore a stronger legal claim if there is court action. It is also more liquid than an open account because the holder can usually transfer it more readily to a bank or other financial agency in exchange for cash.

Accounts and notes receivable originating from sales transactions are sometimes called **trade receivables.** In the absence of other descriptive words or phrases, accounts and notes receivable may be assumed to have originated from sales in the usual course of the business.

Other receivables include interest receivable, loans to officers or employees, and loans to affiliated companies. To facilitate their classification and presentation on the balance sheet, a general ledger account should be maintained for each type of receivable, with proper subsidiary ledgers.

All receivables that are expected to be realized in cash within a year are presented in the current assets section of the balance sheet. Those that are not currently collectible, such as long-term loans, should be listed under the caption "Investments" below the current assets section.

CONTROL OVER RECEIVABLES

As is the case for all assets, the broad principles of internal control discussed in Chapter 5 can be used to establish procedures to safeguard receivables. These controls would include the separation of the business operations and the accounting for receivables, so that the accounting records can serve as an independent check on operations. Thus the employee who handles the accounting for notes and accounts receivable should not be involved with credit approvals or collections of receivables. Separation of these functions reduces the possibility of errors and embezzlement. The controls would also include the separation of responsibility for related functions, so that the work of one employee can serve as a check on the work of another employee.

For most businesses, the principal receivables are notes receivable and accounts receivable. Generally, notes receivable are recorded in a single general ledger account. If there are numerous notes, the general ledger account can be supported by a notes receivable register. The register would contain details of each note, such as the name of the maker, place of payment, amount, term, interest rate, and due date. Frequent reference to the due date section directs attention to those notes that are due for payment. In this way, the maker of the note can be notified when the note is due, and the risk that the maker will overlook the due date can be minimized.

Adequate control over accounts receivable begins with the approval of the sale by a responsible company official or the credit department, after the customer's credit rating has been reviewed. Likewise, adjustments of accounts receivable, such as for sales returns and allowances and sales discounts, should be authorized or reviewed by a responsible party. Effective collection procedures should also be established to ensure timely collection of accounts receivable and to minimize losses from uncollectible accounts.

Effective Control of Accounts Receivable

Companies should make every effort to speed up the process of changing receivables into cash, as well as establish controls that help assure the quality of the receivables. These aspects of effective receivables control were addressed in the following paragraph from an article in *CFO*:

[A] common mistake . . . is having customers send payments to the company. "Checks sit on someone's desk for a few days, then they are sent through the mail, then they are processed at the bank, and then they sit for a while until they clear," says Andrea Bierce, manager for Peat, Marwick, Mitchell & Co.'s financial management division in New York City. Instead, she says, have customers send payments directly to a bank lockbox. "I've seen companies free up $100,000 to $1 million this way," says Bierce. Anthony Timiraos, manager of the accounting and business advisory service department in Laventhol & Horwath's Boston office, tells clients strapped for financial manpower to split up the cash management responsibilities. "Sometimes the salespeople make a sale to someone just to make their department look good," he observes. "They don't always check with the credit manager to approve the sale." Next thing you know, says Timiraos, goods are going out to customers who can't pay their bills. Instead, he says, "Small companies need to split up cash management responsibilities among different departments." Managers should work out collection goals for the sales and marketing department, for instance, to help them determine the validity of sales. . . .

Source: Leslie Schultz, "Which Ever Way the Cash Flows," *CFO* (March, 1986), p. 20.

DETERMINING INTEREST

Interest rates are usually stated in terms of a period of a year, regardless of the actual period of time involved. Thus the interest on $2,000 for a year at 12% would be $240 (12% of $2,000); the interest on $2,000 for one fourth of a year at 12% would be $60 (¼ of $240).

Notes covering a period of time longer than a year ordinarily provide that the interest be paid semiannually, quarterly, or at some other stated interval. The time involved in commercial credit transactions is usually less than a year, and the interest provided for by a note is payable at the time the note is paid.

In computing interest for a period of less than a year, agencies of the federal government use the actual number of days in the year. For example, 90 days is considered to be 90/365 of a year. The usual commercial practice is to use 360 as the denominator of the fraction; thus 90 days is considered to be 90/360 of a year.

The basic formula for computing interest is as follows:

$$\text{Principal} \times \text{Rate} \times \text{Time} = \text{Interest}$$

To illustrate the use of the formula, assume that a note for $1,500 is payable in 20 days with interest at 12%. The interest would be $10, computed as follows:

$$\$1{,}500 \times \frac{12}{100} \times \frac{20}{360} = \$10 \quad \text{interest}$$

One of the commonly used shortcut methods of computing interest is called the 60-day, 6% method. The 6% annual rate is converted to the effective rate of 1% for a 60-day period (60/360 of 6%). Accordingly, the interest on any amount for 60 days at 6% is determined by moving the decimal point in the principal two places to the left. For example, the interest on $1,500 at 6% for 60 days is $15. The amount obtained by moving the decimal point must be adjusted (1) for interest rates greater or less than 6% and (2) for periods of time greater or less than 60 days. For example, the interest on $1,500 at 6% for 90 days is $22.50 (90/60 of $15). The interest on $1,500 at 12% for 60 days is $30 (12/6 of $15).

Comprehensive interest tables are available and are commonly used by financial institutions and other enterprises that require frequent interest calculations. Nevertheless, students of business should know the mechanics of interest computations well enough to use them with complete accuracy and to recognize major errors in interest amounts that come to their attention.

When the term of a note is stated in months instead of in days, each month may be considered as being 1/12 of a year, or, alternatively, the actual number of days in the term may be counted. For example, the interest on a 3-month note dated June 1 could be computed on the basis of 3/12 of a year or on the basis of 92/360 of a year. It is the usual commercial practice to use the first method, while banks usually charge interest for the exact number of days. For the sake of simplicity, the usual commercial practice will be assumed in all cases.

The Bobtailed Year

The practice of using the 360-day year for determining interest has a surprisingly significant effect on the economy as a whole. Both the background of the practice and its effect are described in the following excerpts from an article in the *Wall Street Journal*:

In 46 B.C., Julius Caesar proclaimed that a year would be pegged at 365 days, with an extra day added every fourth year. What was good enough for Caesar has been good enough for the rest of us ever since except for the nation's bankers.

A lot of bankers are using a 360-day year to

compute the interest they charge to borrowers on commercial and corporate loans. This means, in effect, that they are collecting a smidgin more interest on these loans than their stated "annual" interest rates would indicate. . . .

Though only small amounts of money are involved in the difference between 365- and 360-day charges on any one loan, the nickels and dimes add up to an impressive pile. . . . [In fact, the overcharges that result from the use of the bobtailed year have been estimated to be at least $145 million a year.]

According to the bankers, use of the bobtailed year began before the widespread use of adding machines; clerks who had to do the computations with pencil and paper found it a lot easier to multiply and divide by 360 rather than 365 or 366. Since nobody seemed to care much, the 360-day base continued in use through the age of calculators and now is imbedded in the banks' computer programs. "Converting our computers to a 365-day year would be a massive job," says one officer of a major bank.

Source: James F. Carberry, "365 Days May Have Been Good Enough For Caesar, But Lenders Find That 360 Provide More Profit," *The Wall Street Journal,* March 30, 1973.

DETERMINING DUE DATE

The period of time between the issuance date and the maturity date of a short-term note may be stated in either days or months. When the term of a note is stated in days, the due date is the specified number of days after its issuance. To illustrate, the due date of a 90-day note dated March 16 may be determined as follows:

Determination of Due Date of Note

Term of the note		90
March (days)	31	
Date of note	16	15
Number of days remaining		75
April (days)		30
		45
May (days)		31
Due date, June		14

When the term of a note is stated as a certain number of months after the issuance date, the due date is determined by counting the number of months from the issuance date. Thus, a 3-month note dated June 5 would be due on September 5. In those cases in which there is no date in the month of maturity that corresponds to the issuance date, the due date becomes the last day of the month. For example, a 2-month note dated July 31 would be due on September 30.

NOTES RECEIVABLE AND INTEREST INCOME

The typical retail enterprise makes most of its sales for cash or on account. If the account of a customer becomes delinquent, the creditor may insist that the account be converted into a note. In this way, the debtor is given more time, and if the creditor needs more funds, the note may be endorsed and transferred to a bank or other financial agency. Notes may also be received by retail firms that sell merchandise on long-term credit. For example, a dealer in household appliances may require a down payment at the time of sale and accept a note or a series of notes for the remainder. Such arrangements usually provide for monthly payments. Wholesale firms and manufacturers are likely to receive notes more often than retailers, although here, too, much depends upon the kind of product and the length of the credit period.

When a note is received from a customer to apply on account, the facts are recorded by debiting the notes receivable account and crediting the accounts receivable controlling account and the account of the customer from whom the note is received. If the note is interest-bearing, interest must also be recorded as appropriate.

To illustrate, assume that the account of W. A. Bunn Co., which has a debit balance of $6,000, is past due. A 30-day, 12% note for that amount, dated December 21, 1989, is accepted in settlement of the account. The entry to record the transaction is as follows:

Dec. 21	Notes Receivable	6,000	
	Accounts Receivable—W. A. Bunn Co.		6,000
	Received a 30-day, 12% note dated December 21, 1989.		

On December 31, 1989, the end of the fiscal year, an adjusting entry would be recorded for the accrual of the interest from December 21 to December 31. The entry to record the accrued revenue of $20 ($6,000 × 12/100 × 10/360) is as follows:

Adjusting Entry

Dec. 31	Interest Receivable....................................	20	
	Interest Income		20

Interest receivable is reported on the balance sheet at December 31, 1989, as a current asset. The interest income account is closed at December 31 and the amount is reported in the Other Income section of the income statement for the year ended December 31, 1989.

When the amount due on the note is collected in 1990, part of the interest received will effect a reduction of the interest that was receivable at December 31, 1989, and the remainder will represent revenue for 1990. To avoid the possibility of failing to recognize this division and to avoid the inconvenience of analyzing the receipt of interest in 1990, a reversing entry is made after the accounts are closed. The effect of the entry, which is illustrated as follows, is to transfer the debit balance in the interest receivable account to the debit side of the interest income account.

Reversing Entry

Jan. 1	Interest Income	20	
	Interest Receivable		20

At the time the note matures and payment is received, the entire amount of the interest received is credited to Interest Income, as illustrated by the following entry:

Jan. 20	Cash	6,060	
	Notes Receivable		6,000
	Interest Income		60

After the foregoing entries are posted, the interest income account will appear as follows:

ACCOUNT INTEREST INCOME ACCOUNT NO. 811

Date		Item	Debit	Credit	Balance	
					Debit	Credit
1989						
Dec.	12			120		946
	31	Adjusting		20		966
	31	Closing	966		—	—
1990						
Jan.	1	Reversing	20		20	
	20			60		40

The adjusting and reversing process divided the $60 of interest received on January 20, 1990, into two parts for accounting purposes: (1) **$20** representing the interest income for 1989 (recorded by the adjusting entry) and (2) **$40** representing the interest income for 1990 (the balance in the interest income account at January 20, 1990).

Discounting Notes Receivable

Although it is not a common transaction, a company in need of cash may transfer its notes receivable to a bank by endorsement. The **discount** (interest) charged by the bank is computed on the maturity value of the note for the period of time the bank must hold the note, namely the time that will pass between the date of the transfer and the due date of the note. The amount of the **proceeds** paid to the endorser is the excess of the maturity value over the discount.

To illustrate, assume that a 90-day, 12% note receivable for $1,800, dated November 8, is discounted at the payee's bank on December 3 at the rate of 14%. The data used in determining the effect of the transaction are as follows:

Face value of note dated Nov. 8		$1,800.00
Interest on note—90 days at 12%		54.00
Maturity value of note due Feb. 6		$1,854.00
Discount period—Dec. 3 to Feb. 6	65 days	
Discount on maturity value—65 days at 14%		46.87
Proceeds		$1,807.13

The same information is presented graphically in the following flow diagram. In reading the data, follow the direction of the arrows.

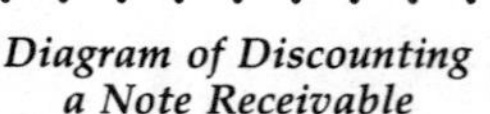
Diagram of Discounting a Note Receivable

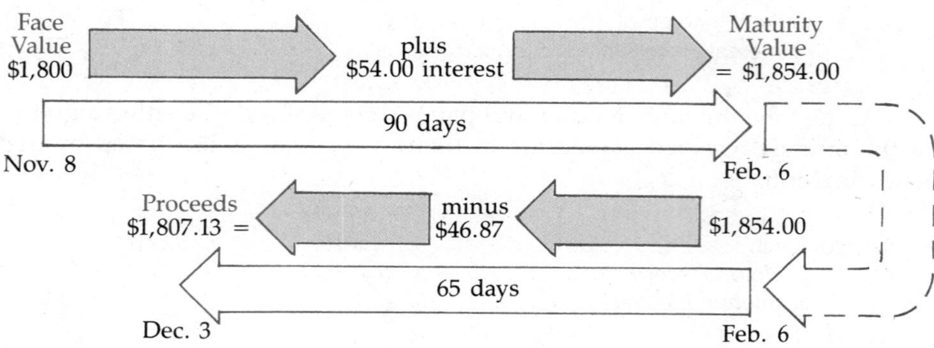

The excess of the proceeds from discounting the note, $1,807.13, over its face value, $1,800, is recorded as interest income. The entry for the transaction is as follows:

Dec. 3	Cash	1,807.13	
	Notes Receivable		1,800.00
	Interest Income		7.13

It should be observed that the proceeds from discounting a note receivable may be less than the face value. When this situation occurs, the excess of the face value over the proceeds is recorded as interest expense. The amount and direction of the difference between the interest rate and the discount rate will affect the result, as will the relationship between the full term of the note and the length of the discount period.

Without a statement limiting responsibility, the endorser of a note is committed to paying the note if the maker should default. Such potential obligations that will become actual liabilities only if certain events occur in the future are called **contingent liabilities.** Thus, the endorser of a note that has been discounted has a contingent liability that is in effect until the due date. If the maker pays the promised amount at maturity, the contingent liability is removed without any action on the part of the endorser. If, on the other hand, the maker defaults and the endorser is notified according to legal requirements, the liability becomes an actual one.

Significant contingent liabilities should be disclosed on the balance sheet or in an accompanying note. Disclosure requirements for contingent liabilities are discussed and illustrated in Chapter 9.

Dishonored Notes Receivable

If the maker of a note fails to pay the debt on the due date, the note is said to be **dishonored.** A dishonored note receivable is no longer negotiable, and for that reason the holder usually transfers the claim, including any interest due, to the accounts receivable account. For example, if the $6,000, 30-day, 12% note received and recorded on December 21 (page 217) had been dishonored at maturity, the entry to charge the note, including the interest, back to the customer's account would have been as follows:

Jan. 20	Accounts Receivable—W. A. Bunn Co.	6,060	
	Notes Receivable		6,000
	Interest Income		60
	Dishonored note and interest.		

If there had been some assurance that the maker would pay the note within a relatively short time, action would have been delayed until the matter was resolved. However, for future guidance in extending credit, it may be desirable that the customer's account in the subsidiary ledger disclose the dishonor of the note.

When a discounted note receivable is dishonored, the holder usually notifies the endorser of such fact and asks for payment. If the request for payment and notification of dishonor are timely, the endorser is legally obligated to pay the amount due on the note. The entire amount paid to the holder by the endorser, including the interest, should be debited to the account receivable of the maker. To illustrate, assume that the $1,800, 90-day, 12% note discounted on December 3 (page 218) is dishonored at maturity by the maker, Pryor & Co. The entry to record the payment by the endorser would be as follows:

Feb. 6	Accounts Receivable — Pryor & Co.	1,854	
	Cash		1,854

In some cases, the holder of a dishonored note gives the endorser a notarized statement of the facts of the dishonor. The fee for this statement, known as a **protest fee,** is charged to the endorser, who in turn charges it to the maker of the note. If there had been a protest fee of $6 in connection with the dishonor and the payment previously recorded, the debit to the maker's account and the credit to Cash would have been $1,860.

UNCOLLECTIBLE RECEIVABLES

Bad Debt expense

When merchandise or services are sold without the immediate receipt of cash, a part of the claims against customers usually proves to be uncollectible. This situation is common, regardless of the care used in granting credit and the effectiveness of the collection procedures used. The operating expense incurred because of the failure to collect receivables is called an expense or a loss from **uncollectible accounts, doubtful accounts,** or **bad debts.**[1]

There is no single general rule for determining when an account or a note becomes uncollectible. The fact that a debtor fails to pay an account according to a sales contract or dishonors a note on the due date does not necessarily mean that the account will be uncollectible. Bankruptcy of the debtor is one of the most positive indications of partial or complete worthlessness of a receivable. Other evidence includes closing of the debtor's business, disappearance of the debtor, failure of repeated attempts to collect, and the barring of collection by the statute of limitations.

There are two methods of accounting for receivables that are believed to be uncollectible. The **allowance method,** which is sometimes called the **reserve method,** provides in advance for uncollectible receivables. The other procedure, called the **direct write-off method** or **direct charge-off method,** recognizes the expense only when certain accounts are judged to be worthless.

ALLOWANCE METHOD OF ACCOUNTING FOR UNCOLLECTIBLES

Most large business enterprises provide currently for the amount of their trade receivables estimated to become uncollectible in the future. The advance provision for future uncollectibility is made by an adjusting entry at the end of the fiscal period. As with all periodic adjustments, the entry serves two purposes. In this instance, it provides for (1) the reduction of the value of the receivables to the amount of cash expected to be realized from them in the

---

[1]If both notes and accounts are involved, both may be included in the title, as in "uncollectible notes and accounts expense," or the general term "uncollectible receivables expense" may be substituted. Because of its wide usage and simplicity, "uncollectible accounts expense" will be used in this text.

future, and (2) the allocation to the current period of the expected expense resulting from such reduction.

Assumed data for a new business firm, Richards Company, will be used to explain and illustrate the allowance method. The enterprise began business in August and chose to use the calendar year as its fiscal year. The accounts receivable account, illustrated as follows, has a balance of $105,000 at the end of the period.

ACCOUNT ACCOUNTS RECEIVABLE — ACCOUNT NO. 114

Date		Item	Debit	Credit	Balance Debit	Balance Credit
19--						
Aug.	31		20,000		20,000	
Sept.	30		25,000		45,000	
	30			15,000	30,000	
Oct.	31		40,000		70,000	
	31			25,000	45,000	
Nov.	30		38,000		83,000	
	30			23,000	60,000	
Dec.	31		75,000		135,000	
	31			30,000	105,000	

Among the individual customers accounts making up the $105,000 balance in Accounts Receivable are a number of balances which are a varying number of days past due. No specific accounts are believed to be wholly uncollectible at this time, but it seems likely that some will be collected only in part and that others are likely to become entirely worthless. Based on a careful study, it is estimated that a total of $3,000 will eventually prove to be uncollectible. The amount expected to be realized from the accounts receivable is, therefore, $102,000 ($105,000 − $3,000), and the $3,000 reduction in value is the uncollectible accounts expense for the period.

The $3,000 reduction in accounts receivable cannot yet be identified with specific customers accounts in the subsidiary ledger and should therefore not be credited to the controlling account in the general ledger. The customary practice is to use a contra asset account entitled Allowance for Doubtful Accounts. The adjusting entry to record the expense and the reduction in the asset is as follows:

Adjusting Entry

Dec. 31	Uncollectible Accounts Expense	3,000	
	Allowance for Doubtful Accounts...............		3,000

The two accounts to which the entry is posted are illustrated as follows:

ACCOUNT UNCOLLECTIBLE ACCOUNTS EXPENSE — ACCOUNT NO. 717

Date		Item	Debit	Credit	Balance Debit	Balance Credit
19--						
Dec.	31	Adjusting	3,000		3,000	

ACCOUNT ALLOWANCE FOR DOUBTFUL ACCOUNTS — ACCOUNT NO. 115

Date		Item	Debit	Credit	Balance	
					Debit	Credit
19-- Dec.	31	Adjusting		3,000		3,000

The debit balance of $105,000 in Accounts Receivable is the amount of the total claims against customers on open account, and the credit balance of $3,000 in Allowance for Doubtful Accounts is the amount to be deducted from Accounts Receivable to determine the **expected realizable value.** The $3,000 reduction in the asset was transferred to Uncollectible Accounts Expense, which will in turn be closed to Income Summary.

Uncollectible accounts expense is generally reported on the income statement as a general expense, because the credit-granting and collection duties are the responsibilities of departments within the general administrative framework. The accounts receivable may be listed on the balance sheet at the net amount of $102,000, with a notation in parentheses showing the amount of the allowance, or the details may be presented as shown on the following partial balance sheet. When the allowance account includes provision for doubtful notes as well as accounts, it should be deducted from the total of Notes Receivable and Accounts Receivable.

Accounts Receivable on the Balance Sheet

look →

Richards Company
Balance Sheet
December 31, 19--

Assets

Current assets:		
Cash		$ 21,600
Accounts receivable	$105,000	
Less allowance for doubtful accounts	3,000	102,000

Write-Offs to the Allowance Account

When an account is believed to be uncollectible, it is written off against the allowance account as in the following entry:

Jan. 21	Allowance for Doubtful Accounts	110	
	Accounts Receivable—John Parker		110
	To write off the uncollectible account.		

During the year, as more accounts or portions of accounts are determined to be uncollectible, they are written off against Allowance for Doubtful Accounts in the same manner. Instructions for write-offs should originate with the credit manager or other designated official. The authorizations, which should always be written, serve as objective evidence in support of the accounting entry.

Naturally enough, the total amount written off against the allowance account during the period will rarely be equal to the amount in the account at the beginning of the period. The allowance account will have a credit balance at the end of the period if the write-offs during the period amount to less than the beginning balance. It will have a debit balance if the write-offs exceed the beginning balance. After the year-end adjusting entry is recorded, the allowance account will have a credit balance.

An account receivable that has been written off against the allowance account may later be collected. In such cases, the account should be reinstated by an entry that is the exact reverse of the write-off entry. For example, assume that the account of $110 written off in the preceding journal entry is later collected. The entry to reinstate the account would be as follows:

June 10	Accounts Receivable—John Parker	110	
	Allowance for Doubtful Accounts................		110
	To reinstate account written off earlier in the year.		

The cash received in payment would be recorded as a receipt on account. Although it is possible to combine the reinstatement and the receipt of cash into a single debit and credit, the entries in the customer's account, with a proper notation, provide useful credit information.

Estimating Uncollectibles

The estimate of uncollectibles at the end of the fiscal period is based on past experience and forecasts of future business activity. When the trend of general sales volume is upward and there is relatively full employment, the amount of the expense should usually be less than when the trend is in the opposite direction. The estimate is customarily based on either (1) the amount of sales for the entire fiscal period or (2) the amount and the age of the receivable accounts at the end of the fiscal period.

Estimate Based on Sales. Accounts receivable are acquired as a result of sales on account. The amount of such sales during the year may therefore be used to determine the probable amount of the accounts that will be uncollectible. The amount of this estimate is added to whatever balance exists in Allowance for Doubtful Accounts. To illustrate, assume that the allowance account has a credit balance of $700 before adjustment. If it is known from past experience that about 1% of charge sales will be uncollectible and the charge sales for a certain year amount to $300,000, the adjusting entry for uncollectible accounts at the end of the year would be as follows:

Adjusting Entry

Dec. 31	Uncollectible Accounts Expense..................	3,000	
	Allowance for Doubtful Accounts................		3,000

After the adjusting entry is posted, the balance in the allowance account is $3,700. If there had been a debit balance of $200 in the allowance account before the year-end adjustment, the amount of the adjustment would still have been $3,000. The balance in the allowance account, after the adjusting entry is posted, would be $2,800 ($3,000 − $200).

Instead of charge sales, total sales (including those made for cash) may be used in developing the percentage. Total sales is obtainable from the ledger without the analysis that may be needed to determine charge sales. If the ratio of sales on account to cash sales does not change very much from year to year, the results obtained will be equally satisfactory. If in the above example the balance of the sales account at the end of the year is assumed to be $400,000, the application of 3/4 of 1% to that amount would also yield an estimate of $3,000.

If it becomes apparent over a period of time that the amount of write-offs is always greater or less than the amount provided by the adjusting entry, the percentage applied to sales data should be changed accordingly. A newly established business enterprise, having no record of credit experience, may obtain data on the probable amount of the expense from trade association journals and other publications containing information on credit and collections.

The estimate-based-on-sales method of determining the uncollectible accounts expense is widely used. It is simple and it provides the best basis for charging uncollectible accounts expense to the period in which the related sales were made.

Estimate Based on Analysis of Receivables. The process of analyzing the receivable accounts in terms of the length of time past due is sometimes called **aging the receivables.** The base point for determining age is the due date of the account. The number and breadth of the time intervals used will vary according to the credit terms granted to customers. A portion of a typical analysis is as follows:

Analysis of Accounts Receivable

		NOT	DAYS PAST DUE					
CUSTOMER	BALANCE	DUE	1–30	31–60	61–90	91–180	181–365	over 365
Ashby & Co. . . .	$ 150			$ 150				
B. T. Barr	610					$ 350	$260	
Brock Co.	470	$ 470						
J. Zimmer Co..	160							160
Total	$86,300	$75,000	$4,000	$3,100	$1,900	$1,200	$800	$300

The analysis is completed by adding the columns to determine the total amount of receivables in each age group. A sliding scale of percentages, based on experience, is next applied to obtain the estimated amount of uncollectibles in each group. The manner in which the data may be presented is illustrated as follows:

Estimate of Uncollectible Accounts

Age Interval	*Balance*	*Estimated Uncollectible Accounts*	
		Percent	*Amount*
Not due.	$75,000	2%	$1,500
1–30 days past due	4,000	5	200
31–60 days past due	3,100	10	310
61–90 days past due	1,900	20	380
91–180 days past due	1,200	30	360
181–365 days past due	800	50	400
Over 365 days past due	300	80	240
Total.	$86,300		$3,390

The estimate of uncollectible accounts, $3,390 in the example above, is the amount to be deducted from accounts receivable to yield their expected realizable value. It is thus the amount of the desired balance of the allowance account after adjustment. The excess of this figure over the balance of the allowance account before adjustment is the amount of the current provision to be made for uncollectible accounts expense.

To continue the illustration, assume that the allowance account has a credit balance of $510 before adjustment. The amount to be added to this balance is therefore $2,880 ($3,390 − $510), and the adjusting entry is as follows:

Adjusting Entry

Dec. 31	Uncollectible Accounts Expense	2,880	
	Allowance for Doubtful Accounts................		2,880

After the adjusting entry is posted, the credit balance in the allowance account will be $3,390, which is the desired amount. If there had been a debit balance of $300 in the allowance account before the year-end adjustment, the amount of the adjustment would have been $3,690 ($3,390 desired balance + $300 negative balance).

Estimations of uncollectible accounts expense based on an analysis of receivables are less common than estimations based on sales volume. Estimations based on receivables analyses are sometimes preferred because they give more accurate estimates of the current realizable values of the receivables.

DIRECT WRITE-OFF METHOD OF ACCOUNTING FOR UNCOLLECTIBLES

The use of the allowance method, as previously illustrated, results in the uncollectible accounts expense being reported in the period in which the sales are made. This matching of expenses with related revenue is the preferred method of accounting for uncollectible receivables. However, there are situations in which it is impossible to estimate, with reasonable accuracy, the uncollectibles at the end of the period. Also if an enterprise sells most of its goods or services on a cash basis, the amount of its expense from uncollectible accounts is usually small in relation to its revenue. The amount of its receivables at any time is also likely to represent a relatively small part of its total current assets. In such cases, it is satisfactory to delay recognition of uncollectibility until the period in which certain amounts are believed to be worthless and are actually written off as an expense. Accordingly, an allowance account or an adjusting entry is not needed at the end of the period. The entry to write off an account when it is believed to be uncollectible is as follows:

May 10	Uncollectible Accounts Expense	42	
	Accounts Receivable — D. L. Ross		42
	To write off uncollectible account.		

If an account that has been written off is collected later, the account should be reinstated. If the recovery is in the same fiscal year as the write-off, the earlier entry should be reversed to reinstate the account. To illustrate, assume that the account written off in the May 10 entry is collected in November of the same fiscal year. The entry to reinstate the account would be as follows:

Nov. 21	Accounts Receivable—D. L. Ross	42	
	Uncollectible Accounts Expense		42
	To reinstate account written off earlier in the year.		

The receipt of cash in payment of the reinstated amount would be recorded in the usual manner.

When an account that has been written off is collected in a later fiscal year, it may be reinstated by an entry like that just illustrated. An alternative is to credit some other appropriately titled account, such as Recovery of Uncollectible Accounts Written Off. The credit balance in such an account at the end of the year may then be reported on the income statement as a deduction from Uncollectible Accounts Expense, or the net expense only may be reported. Such amounts are likely to be small compared to net income.

RECEIVABLES FROM INSTALLMENT SALES

In some businesses, especially in the retail field, it is common to make sales on the installment plan. In the typical installment sale, the buyer makes a down payment and agrees to pay the remainder in specified amounts at stated intervals over a period of time. The seller may retain technical title to the goods or may take other means to make repossession easier in the event that the purchaser defaults on the payments. Despite such provisions, installment sales should ordinarily be treated in the same manner as any other sale on account, in which case the revenue is considered to be realized at the point of sale.[2]

In some exceptional cases, the circumstances are such that the collection of receivables is not reasonably assured. In these cases, another method of determining revenue may be used.[3] The alternative is to consider each receipt of cash to be revenue and to be composed of partial amounts of (1) the cost of merchandise sold and (2) gross profit on the sale.

As a basis for illustration, assume that in the first year of operations, a dealer in household appliances had total installment sales of $300,000, and the cost of the merchandise sold amounted to $180,000. Assume also that collections of the installment accounts receivable were spread over three years as follows: 1st year, $140,000; 2d year, $100,000; 3d year, $60,000. According to the **point of sale method,** under which revenue is realized at the time title passes to the buyer, all of the revenue would be recognized in the first year. The gross profit realized in that year would be determined as follows:

Point of Sale Method

Installment sales	$300,000
Cost of the merchandise sold	180,000
Gross profit	$120,000

The alternative to the point of sale method, the **installment method,** allocates gross profit according to the amount of receivables collected in each

[2]*Opinions of the Accounting Principles Board, No. 10,* "Omnibus Opinion—1966" (New York: American Institute of Certified Public Accountants, 1966), par. 12.
[3]*Ibid.*

year, based on the percent of gross profit to sales. The rate of gross profit to sales is determined as follows:

$$\frac{\text{Gross Profit}}{\text{Installment Sales}} = \frac{\$120{,}000}{\$300{,}000} = 40\%$$

The amounts reported as gross profit for each of the three years, based on collections of installment accounts receivable, are as follows:

Installment Method

1st year collections:	\$140,000 × 40%	\$ 56,000
2d year collections:	\$100,000 × 40%	40,000
3d year collections:	\$ 60,000 × 40%	24,000
Total	\$300,000	\$120,000

TEMPORARY INVESTMENTS

A business may have a large amount of cash on hand that is not needed immediately, but this cash may be needed later in operating the business, possibly within the coming year. Rather than allow this excess cash to lie idle until it is actually needed, the business may put all or a part of it into income-yielding investments, such as certificates of deposit and money market funds. In many cases, the idle cash is invested in securities that can be quickly sold when cash is needed. Such securities are known as **temporary investments** or **marketable securities.** Although they may be retained as an investment for a number of years, they continue to be classified as temporary, provided that: (1) the securities are readily marketable and thus can be sold for cash at any time, and (2) management intends to sell them at such time as the enterprise needs more cash for normal operations.

Temporary investments in securities include stocks and bonds. **Stocks** are equity securities issued by corporations, and **bonds** are debt securities issued by corporations and various government agencies. Stocks and bonds held as temporary investments are classified on the balance sheet as current assets. They may be listed after "Cash," or they may be combined with cash and described as "Cash and marketable securities."

A temporary investment in a portfolio of debt securities is usually carried at cost. However, the **carrying amount** (also called **basis**) of a temporary investment in a portfolio of equity securities is the lower of its total cost or market value, determined at the date of the balance sheet.[4] Note that in the following illustration, the carrying amount is based on the comparison between the *total* cost and the *total* market value of the portfolio, rather than the lower of cost or market price of *each item*.

Temporary Investment Portfolio	*Cost*	*Market*	*Unrealized Gain (Loss)*
Equity security A	\$150,000	\$100,000	\$(50,000)
Equity security B	200,000	200,000	—
Equity security C	180,000	210,000	30,000
Equity security D	160,000	150,000	(10,000)
Total	\$690,000	\$660,000	\$(30,000)

[4]*Statement of Financial Accounting Standards, No. 12,* "Accounting for Certain Marketable Securities" (Stamford: Financial Accounting Standards Board, 1975), par. 8.

The marketable equity securities would be reported in the current assets section of the balance sheet at a cost of $690,000 less an allowance for decline to market value of $30,000 to yield a carrying amount of $660,000. The unrealized loss of $30,000 is included in the determination of net income and reported as a separate item on the income statement. If the market value of the portfolio later rises, the unrealized loss is reversed and included in net income, but only to the extent that it does not exceed the original cost. In such cases, the increase is reported separately in the Other Income section of the income statement, and the amount reported on the balance sheet is likewise adjusted.[5]

Some accountants believe that marketable equity securities should be valued at their current market prices, regardless of whether these prices are above or below cost. They argue for current market prices because (1) the securities are readily marketable, (2) the current market prices can be objectively and simply determined, and (3) current market prices are more useful as an indication of the amount of cash that can be made available for normal operations. Although the merits of the valuation of marketable equity securities at current market prices continues to be debated within the profession, the lower of cost or market price method is the current generally accepted method of valuation. To date, only certain industries, such as securities brokers and mutual fund dealers, are permitted to report their marketable equity securities at current market prices.

TEMPORARY INVESTMENTS AND RECEIVABLES IN THE BALANCE SHEET

Temporary investments and all receivables that are expected to be realized in cash within a year are presented in the current assets section of the balance sheet. It is customary to list the assets in the order of their liquidity, that is, in the order in which they can be converted to cash in normal operations. An illustration of the presentation of receivables and temporary investments is shown in the following partial balance sheet for Pilar Enterprises Inc.:

Temporary Investments and Receivables in Balance Sheet

Pilar Enterprises Inc.
Balance Sheet
December 31, 19--

Assets		
Current assets:		
Cash		$119,500
Marketable equity securities	$690,000	
Less allowance for decline to market	30,000	660,000
Notes receivable		250,000
Accounts receivable	$445,000	
Less allowance for doubtful accounts	15,000	430,000
Interest receivable		14,500

[5] *Ibid.*, par. 11.

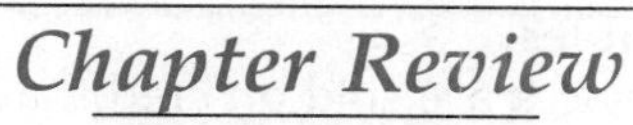

Chapter Review

KEY POINTS

1. Classification of Receivables.
The term receivables includes all money claims against people, organizations, or other debtors. A promissory note is a written promise to pay a sum of money on demand or at a definite time. Accounts and notes receivable originating from sales transactions are called trade receivables.

2. Control Over Receivables.
The internal controls that apply to receivables include the separation of responsibility for related functions, so that the work of one employee can serve as a check on the work of another employee. For most businesses, the principal receivables are notes receivable and accounts receivable. If there are numerous notes receivable, a general ledger account for notes receivable should be supported by a notes receivable register.

3. Determining Interest.
Interest rates are usually stated in terms of a period of a year, regardless of the actual period of time involved. Notes covering a period of time longer than a year ordinarily provide that the interest be paid semiannually, quarterly, or at some other stated interval. The basic formula for computing interest is as follows: Principal × Rate × Time = Interest

4. Determining Due Date.
The period of time between the issuance date and the maturity date of a short-term note may be stated in either days or months. When the term of a note is stated in days, the due date is the specified number of days after its issuance. When the term of a note is stated as a number of months after the issuance date, the due date is determined by counting the number of months from the issuance date.

5. Notes Receivable and Interest Income.
Notes may be received by retail firms that sell merchandise on long-term credit. Such notes usually provide for monthly payments. In addition, if an account receivable becomes delinquent, the account may be converted to a note. Instead of retaining the note receivable until maturity, a note receivable may be transferred to a bank by endorsement. This transfer to a bank is called discounting the note receivable. The discount (interest) charged by the bank is computed on the maturity value of the note for the period of time the bank must hold the note until the due date. The amount of the proceeds paid to the endorser is the excess of the maturity value over the discount. Without a statement limiting responsibility, the endorser of a note is committed to paying the note if the maker should default. Such potential obligations that will become actual liabilities only if certain events occur in the future are called contingent liabilities.

If the maker of a note fails to pay the debt on the due date, the note is said to be dishonored. A dishonored note receivable is no longer negotiable, and the amount of the claim against the maker is transferred to an accounts receivable account.

6. Uncollectible Receivables.
When merchandise or services are sold on credit, a part of the claims against customers may prove to be uncollectible. The operating expense incurred because of the failure to collect receivables is called uncollectible accounts expense. There are two methods of accounting for receivables that are believed to be uncollectible: the allowance method and the direct write-off method.

7. Allowance Method of Accounting for Uncollectibles.
Most large business enterprises provide currently for the amount of their trade receivables estimated to become uncollectible. The estimate of the amount of uncollectibles may be based on either (1) the amount of sales for the entire fiscal period, or (2) the amount and the age of the receivable accounts at the end of the fiscal period. An adjusting entry made at the end of the fiscal period provides for (1) the reduction of the value of the receivables to the amount of cash expected to be realized from them in the future and (2) the allocation to the current period of the expected expense resulting from such reduction. The adjusting entry debits Uncollectible Accounts Expense and credits Allowance for Doubtful Accounts. When an account is believed to be uncollectible, it is written off against the allowance account.

The allowance account, which will normally have a credit balance after the adjusting entry has been posted, is a contra asset account. The uncollectible accounts expense is generally reported on the income statement as a general expense.

8. Direct Write-Off Method of Accounting for Uncollectibles.
If it is impossible to estimate uncollectibles with reasonable accuracy or if most sales are made on a cash basis, it is satisfactory to delay recognition of the uncollectibility of accounts receivable until the period in which certain accounts are believed to be worthless and are actually written off as an expense. Accordingly, under this method neither an allowance account nor an adjusting entry is needed at the end of the period. The entry in this case to write off an account debits Uncollectible Accounts Expense and credits Accounts Receivable.

9. Receivables from Installment Sales.
Revenue from sales made on the installment plan should ordinarily be accounted for by the point of sale method, under which revenue is realized at the time title passes to the buyer. When the collection of the receivables is not reasonably assured, the installment method may be used. Under this method, the gross profit from installment sales is recognized according to the amount of receivables collected in each year, based on the percent of gross profit to sales.

10. Temporary Investments.
A business may put all or part of any excess cash on hand into income-yielding investments that are readily marketable and are known as temporary investments or marketable securities. These investments may include stocks and bonds. Stocks are equity securities issued by corporations, and bonds are debt securities issued by corporations and various governmental agencies. A temporary investment of debt securities is usually carried in the records at cost. However, a temporary investment in equity securities must be carried at the lower of its total cost or market value at the balance sheet date.

11. Temporary Investments and Receivables in the Balance Sheet. Temporary investments and all receivables that are expected to be realized in cash within a year are presented in the current assets section of the balance sheet. It is customary to list the assets in the order of their liquidity, that is, in the order in which they can be converted to cash in normal operations.

KEY TERMS

promissory note 213
note receivable 213
maturity value 213
discount 218
proceeds 218
contingent liabilities 219
dishonored 219
allowance method 220
direct write-off method 220
aging the receivables 224
point of sale method 226
installment method 226
temporary investments 227
marketable securities 227
carrying amount 227

SELF-EXAMINATION QUESTIONS

(Answers at End of Chapter)

1. What is the maturity value of a 90-day, 12% note for $10,000?
   A. $8,800
   B. $10,000
   C. $10,300
   D. $11,200

2. On June 16, an enterprise discounts a 60-day, 10% note receivable for $15,000, dated June 1, at the rate of 12%. The proceeds are:
   A. $15,000.00
   B. $15,021.25
   C. $15,250.00
   D. $15,478.75

3. At the end of the fiscal year, before the accounts are adjusted, Accounts Receivable has a balance of $200,000 and Allowance for Doubtful Accounts has a credit balance of $2,500. If the estimate of uncollectible accounts determined by aging the receivables is $8,500, the current provision to be made for uncollectible accounts expense would be:
   A. $2,500
   B. $6,000
   C. $8,500
   D. $200,000

4. At the end of the fiscal year, Accounts Receivable has a balance of $100,000 and Allowance for Doubtful Accounts has a balance of $7,000. The expected realizable value of the accounts receivable is:
   A. $7,000
   B. $93,000
   C. $100,000
   D. $107,000

5. Under what caption would a temporary investment in stock be reported in the balance sheet?
   A. Current assets
   B. Plant assets
   C. Investments
   D. None of the above

ILLUSTRATIVE PROBLEM

Selected transactions completed by Rodriguez Company are as follows. Rodriguez Company uses the allowance method of accounting for uncollectible accounts receivable.

Jan. 28. Sold merchandise on account to Lakeland Inc., $10,000.
Mar. 1. Accepted a 60-day, 12% note for $10,000 from Lakeland Inc. on account.
Apr. 11. Wrote off a $4,500 account from Exdel Inc. as uncollectible.
16. Loaned $7,500 cash to Thomas Glazer, receiving a 90-day, 14% note.
30. Received the interest due from Lakeland Inc. and a new 90-day, 14% note as a renewal of the loan. (Record both the debit and credit to the notes receivable account.)
May 1. Discounted the note from Thomas Glazer at the First National Bank at 10%.
June 13. Reinstated the account of Exdel Inc., written off on April 11, and received $4,500 in full payment.
July 15. Received notice from First National Bank that Thomas Glazer dishonored his note. Paid the bank the maturity value of the note plus a $20 protest fee.
29. Received from Lakeland Inc. the amount due on its note of April 30.
Aug. 14. Received from Thomas Glazer the amount owed on the dishonored note, plus interest for 30 days at 15%, computed on the maturity value of the note and the protest fee.
Dec. 31. It is estimated that 2% of the credit sales of $958,600 for the year ended December 31 will be uncollectible.

Instructions:

Present entries to record the transactions.

SOLUTION

Date	Account	Debit	Credit
Jan. 28	Accounts Receivable—Lakeland Inc.	10,000.00	
	Sales		10,000.00
Mar. 1	Notes Receivable—Lakeland Inc.	10,000.00	
	Accounts Receivable—Lakeland Inc		10,000.00
Apr. 11	Allowance for Doubtful Accounts	4,500.00	
	Accounts Receivable—Exdel Inc.		4,500.00
16	Notes Receivable—Thomas Glazer	7,500.00	
	Cash		7,500.00
30	Notes Receivable—Lakeland Inc.	10,000.00	
	Cash	200.00	
	Notes Receivable—Lakeland Inc.		10,000.00
	Interest Income		200.00

		Debit	Credit
May 1	Cash	7,600.78	
	Notes Receivable—Thomas Glazer		7,500.00
	Interest Income		100.78
	Face value $7,500.00		
	Interest on note (90 days at 14%) 262.50		
	Maturity value $7,762.50		
	Discount on maturity value (75 days at 10%) 161.72		
	Proceeds $7,600.78		
June 13	Accounts Receivable—Exdel Inc.	4,500.00	
	Allowance for Doubtful Accounts		4,500.00
13	Cash	4,500.00	
	Accounts Receivable—Exdel Inc.		4,500.00
July 15	Accounts Receivable—Thomas Glazer	7,782.50	
	Cash		7,782.50
29	Cash	10,350.00	
	Notes Receivable—Lakeland Inc.		10,000.00
	Interest Income		350.00
Aug. 14	Cash	7,879.78	
	Accounts Receivable—Thomas Glazer		7,782.50
	Interest Income ($7,782.50 × 15% × 30/360)		97.28
Dec. 31	Uncollectible Accounts Expense	19,172.00	
	Allowance for Doubtful Accounts		19,172.00

Discussion Questions

6–1. Johnson Corporation issued a promissory note to Madrid Company. (a) Who is the payee? (b) What is the title of the account employed by Madrid Company in recording the note?

6–2. What are the advantages, to the creditor, of a note receivable in comparison to an account receivable?

6–3. In what section of the balance sheet should a note receivable be listed if its term is (a) 90 days, (b) 5 years?

6–4. The clerk who maintains the accounts receivable records is also responsible for handling cash receipts. Which principle of internal control is violated in this situation?

6–5. If a note provides for payment of principal of $1,000 and interest at the rate of 10%, will the interest amount to $100? Explain.

6–6. The following questions refer to a 60-day, 12% note for $20,000, dated April 1: (a) What is the face value of the note? (b) What is the amount of interest payable at maturity? (c) What is the maturity value of the note? (d) What is the due date of the note?

6–7. At the end of the fiscal year, an enterprise holds a 90-day note receivable accepted from a customer fifteen days earlier. (a) Which of the following types of accounts will be affected by the related adjusting entry at the end of the year: (1) asset, (2) liability, (3) revenue, (4) expense? (b) If the note is held until maturity, what fraction of the total interest should be allocated to the year in which the note is collected?

6–8. The payee of a 90-day, 10% note for $4,000, dated May 1, endorses it to a bank on May 31. The bank discounts the note at 12%, paying the endorser $4,018. Identify or determine the following as they relate to the note: (a) face value, (b) maturity value, (c) due date, (d) number of days in the discount period, (e) proceeds, (f) interest income or expense recorded by endorser, (g) amount payable to the bank if the maker should default.

6–9. During the year, notes receivable of $250,000 were discounted at a bank by an enterprise. By the end of the year, $220,000 of these notes have matured. What is the amount of the endorser's contingent liability for notes receivable discounted at the end of the year?

6–10. The maker of a $5,000, 12%, 30-day note receivable failed to pay the note on the due date. What entry should be made in the accounts of the payee to record the dishonored note receivable?

6–11. A discounted note receivable is dishonored by the maker and the endorser pays the bank the face of the note, $10,000, the interest, $150, and a protest fee of $8. What entry should be made in the accounts of the endorser to record the payment?

6–12. The series of six transactions recorded in the following T accounts were related to a sale to a customer on account and receipt of the amount owed. Briefly describe each transaction.

Cash

Debit	Credit
(4) 4,854	(5) 4,956
(6) 4,980	

Notes Receivable

Debit	Credit
(3) 4,900	(4) 4,900

Accounts Receivable

Debit	Credit
(1) 5,000	(2) 100
(5) 4,956	(3) 4,900
	(6) 4,956

Sales

Debit	Credit
(2) 100	(1) 5,000

Interest Income

Debit	Credit
	(6) 24

Interest Expense

Debit	Credit
(4) 46	

6–13. Which of the two methods of accounting for uncollectible accounts provides for the recognition of the expense at the earlier date?

6–14. What kind of an account (asset, liability, etc.) is Allowance for Doubtful Accounts, and is its normal balance a debit or a credit?

6–15. Give the adjusting entry to increase Allowance for Doubtful Accounts by $9,450.

6–16. After the accounts are adjusted and closed at the end of the fiscal year, Accounts Receivable has a balance of $260,500 and Allowance for Doubtful Accounts has a balance of $9,900.

(a) What is the expected realizable value of the accounts receivable?

(b) If an account receivable of $1,500 is written off against the allowance account, what will be the expected realizable value of the accounts receivable after the write-off, assuming that no other changes in either account have occurred in the meantime?

6–17. A firm has consistently adjusted its allowance account at the end of the fiscal year by adding a fixed percent of the period's net sales on account. After five years, the balance in Allowance for Doubtful Accounts has become disproportionately large in relationship to the balance in Accounts Receivable. Give two possible explanations.

6–18. The $250 balance of an account owed by a customer is considered to be uncollectible and is to be written off. Give the entry to record the write-off in the general ledger, (a) assuming that the allowance method is used and (b) assuming that the direct write-off method is used.

6–19. Which of the two methods of estimating uncollectibles, when advance provision for uncollectible receivables is made, provides for the most accurate estimate of the current realizable value of the receivables?

6–20. Is revenue from sales of merchandise on account more commonly recognized at the time of sale or at the time of cash receipt?

6–21. During the current year, merchandise costing $150,000 was sold on the installment plan for $250,000. The down payments and the installment payments received during the current year totaled $125,000. What is the amount of gross profit considered to be realized in the current year, applying (a) the point of sale method and (b) the installment method of revenue recognition?

6–22. Under what caption should securities held as a temporary investment be reported on the balance sheet?

6–23. A corporation has two equity securities which it holds as a temporary investment. If they have a total cost of $210,000 and a fair market value of $200,000, at what amount should these securities be reported in the current assets section of the corporation's balance sheet?

6–24. Real World Focus. Receivables and related allowances for doubtful accounts for fiscal years ending in 1984 and 1983 for six corporations are as follows:

	1984		1983	
	Receivables	Allowance for Doubtful Accounts	Receivables	Allowance for Doubtful Accounts
Chrysler Corp. . . .	$ 346,000,000	$13,800,000	$ 316,700,000	$ 25,500,000
PepsiCo, Inc.	672,047,000	31,966,000	681,067,000	33,738,000
General Electric. .	5,602,000,000	93,000,000	5,351,000,000	102,000,000
W. R. Grace & Co.	678,200,000	25,700,000	670,900,000	28,000,000
Fuqua Industries .	181,071,000	8,096,000	155,653,000	7,383,000
Gannett Co., Inc..	262,918,000	7,748,000	220,386,000	7,051,000

For 1984 and 1983, compute for each company (a) the realizable value of the receivables and (b) the percent of the allowance for doubtful accounts to the total receivables, rounding to the nearest tenth of a percent. (c) What might explain the general decrease from 1983 to 1984 in the percentages computed in (b)?

Exercises

6–25. Determination of due date and interest on notes. Determine the due date and the amount of interest due at maturity on the following notes:

Date of Note	Face Amount	Term of Note	Interest Rate
(a) March 1	$12,000	60 days	10%
(b) April 10	3,000	60 days	12%
(c) May 16	6,000	75 days	14%
(d) June 5	4,000	90 days	15%
(e) July 22	7,200	120 days	10%

6–26. Entries for notes receivable. Leigh Company issues a 90-day, 12% note for $5,000, dated July 20, to Lakes Corporation on account.

(a) Determine the due date of the note.
(b) Determine the maturity value of the note.
(c) Present entries to record the following:
 (1) Receipt of the note by the payee.
 (2) Receipt by payee of payment of the note at maturity.

6–27. Entries for note receivable and related year-end adjustments. The following selected transactions were completed by Bering Co. during the current year:

May 1. Received from Adams Co., on account, an $8,000, 90-day, 12% note dated May 1.
 31. Recorded an adjusting entry for accrued interest on the note of May 1.
 31. Closed the interest income account. The only entry in this account originated from the May 31 adjustment.
June 1. Recorded a reversing entry for accrued interest.
July 30. Received $8,240 from Adams Co. for the note due today.

(a) Present entries to record the transactions.
(b) What is the balance in interest income after the entry of July 30?
(c) How many days' interest on $8,000 at 12% does the amount reported in (b) represent?

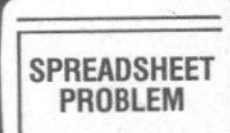

6–28. Discounting note receivable. Lincoln Co. holds a 60-day, 12% note for $7,500, dated April 20, that was received from a customer on account. On May 10, the note is discounted at the Franklin National Bank at the rate of 15%.

(a) Determine the maturity value of the note.
(b) Determine the number of days in the discount period.
(c) Determine the amount of the discount.
(d) Determine the amount of the proceeds.
(e) Present the entry to record the discounting of the note on May 10.

6–29. Entries for receipt and discounting of note receivable and dishonored note. Record the following transactions in the accounts of D. Shuman and Son.

April 6. Received a $9,000, 60-day, 14% note dated April 6 from B. C. Andrews on account.
 26. Discounted the note at Paxton National Bank at 15%.
June 5. The note is dishonored; paid the bank the amount due on the note plus a protest fee of $10.
 25. Received the amount due on the dishonored note plus interest for 20 days at 14% on the total amount charged to B. C. Andrews on June 5.

6–30. Entries for receipt and dishonor of notes receivable. Record the following transactions in the accounts of Jane Thomas and Daughter.

May 1. Received a $40,000, 90-day, 14% note dated May 1 from A. B. James Corp. on account.
 10. Received a $12,000, 60-day, 15% note dated May 10 from Clark and Dodds on account.
July 9. The note dated May 10 from Clark and Dodds is dishonored and the customer's account is charged for the note, including interest.
 30. The note dated May 1 from A. B. James Corp. is dishonored and the customer's account is charged for the note, including interest.

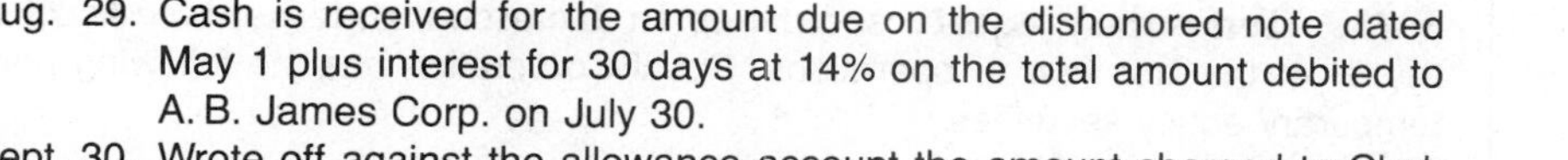

Aug. 29. Cash is received for the amount due on the dishonored note dated May 1 plus interest for 30 days at 14% on the total amount debited to A. B. James Corp. on July 30.

Sept. 30. Wrote off against the allowance account the amount charged to Clark and Dodds on July 9 for the dishonored note dated May 10.

6–31. Provision for doubtful accounts. At the end of the current year, the accounts receivable account has a debit balance of $95,000, and net sales for the year total $900,000. Determine the amount of the adjusting entry to record the provision for doubtful accounts under each of the following assumptions:

(a) The allowance account before adjustment has a credit balance of $500.
  (1) Uncollectible accounts expense is estimated at 1% of net sales.
  (2) Analysis of the individual customers accounts indicates doubtful accounts of $9,950.
(b) The allowance account before adjustment has a debit balance of $250.
  (1) Uncollectible accounts expense is estimated at 3/4 of 1% of net sales.
  (2) Analysis of the individual customers accounts indicates doubtful accounts of $5,900.

6–32. Entries for uncollectible receivables using allowance method. Present entries to record the following transactions in the accounts of Baker Corporation, which uses the allowance method of accounting for uncollectible receivables.

Feb. 10. Sold merchandise on account to J. A. Jacobs, $2,500.

June 30. Received $1,250 from J. A. Jacobs and wrote off the remainder owed on the sale of February 10 as uncollectible.

Dec. 15. Reinstated the account of J. A. Jacobs that had been written off on June 30 and received $1,250 cash in full payment.

6–33. Entries for uncollectible accounts, using direct write-off method. Present entries to record the following transactions in the accounts of Dexter and Parker, which uses the direct write-off method of accounting for uncollectible receivables.

Jan. 5. Sold merchandise on account to P. P. Rossi, $1,000.

May 12. Received $600 from P. P. Rossi and wrote off the remainder owed on the sale of January 5 as uncollectible.

Nov. 30. Reinstated the account of P. P. Rossi that had been written off on May 12 and received $400 cash in full payment.

6–34. Gross profit by point of sale and installment methods. Sexton Company makes all sales on the installment plan. Data related to merchandise sold during the current fiscal year are as follows:

Sales	$900,000
Cash received on the $900,000 of installment contracts	340,000
Merchandise inventory, beginning of year	102,500
Merchandise inventory, end of year	107,500
Purchases	635,000

Determine the amount of gross profit that would be recognized for the current fiscal year according to (a) the point of sale method and (b) the installment method.

6–35. Temporary equity securities in financial statements. As of December 31 of the first year of operations, Royal Corporation has the following portfolio of temporary equity securities:

	Cost	Market
Security A	$22,100	$19,750
Security B	18,000	16,200
Security C	17,750	19,500
Security D	85,800	81,000

Describe how the portfolio of temporary equity securities would affect the year-end balance sheet and income statement of Royal Corporation.

Problems

6–36. Sales, notes receivable, discounting notes receivable transactions. The following were selected from among the transactions completed by Alex Gomez and Co. during the current year:

Jan. 20. Loaned $5,000 cash to Ann Santos, receiving a 90-day, 12% note.
Mar. 1. Sold merchandise on account to J. A. Block Co., $10,000.
20. Sold merchandise on account to C. D. Connors Co., $7,100.
30. Received from C. D. Conners Co. the amount of the invoice of March 20, less 2% discount.
31. Accepted a 30-day, 15% note for $10,000 from J. A. Block Co. on account.
Apr. 20. Received the interest due from Ann Santos and a new 90-day, 14% note as a renewal of the loan of January 20. (Record both the debit and the credit to the notes receivable account.)
30. Received from J. A. Block Co. the amount due on the note of March 31.
July 12. Sold merchandise on account to Swartz and Sons, $20,000.
19. Received from Ann Santos the amount due on her note of April 20.
Aug. 11. Accepted a 60-day, 12% note for $20,000 from Swartz and Sons on account.
Sept. 10. Discounted the note from Swartz and Sons at the American National Bank at 14%.
Oct. 10. Received notice from the American National Bank that Swartz and Sons had dishonored its note. Paid the bank the maturity value of the note.
Nov. 9. Received from Swartz and Sons the amount owed on the dishonored note, plus interest for 30 days at 12% computed on the maturity value of the note.

Instructions: Present the entries to record the transactions.

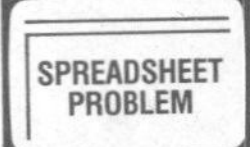

6–37. Details of notes receivable, including discounting. During the last three months of the current fiscal year, Atkins Co. received the following notes. Notes (1), (2), (3), and (4) were discounted on the dates and at the rates indicated.

	Date	Face Amount	Term	Interest Rate	Date Discounted	Discount Rate
(1)	Oct. 1	$7,200	60 days	14%	Oct. 21	12%
(2)	Oct. 11	9,500	30 days	12%	Oct. 26	14%
(3)	Oct. 28	3,100	90 days	14%	Dec. 27	15%
(4)	Nov. 8	8,000	60 days	12%	Nov. 23	16%
(5)	Dec. 11	9,000	60 days	11%	—	—
(6)	Dec. 21	8,700	30 days	12%	—	—

Instructions: (1) Determine for each note (a) the due date and (b) the amount of interest due at maturity, identifying each note by number.
(2) Determine for each of the first four notes (a) the maturity value, (b) the discount period, (c) the discount, (d) the proceeds, and (e) the interest income or interest expense, identifying each note by number.
(3) Present the entries to record the discounting of notes (2) and (4) at a bank.
(4) Assuming that notes (5) and (6) are held until maturity, determine for each the amount of interest earned (a) in the current fiscal year and (b) in the following fiscal year.

6–38. Notes receivable entries and year-end entries; general ledger accounts. A. C. Cohen Co. closes its accounts annually as of December 31, the end of the fiscal year. The following data relate to notes receivable and interest from November 1, 1989, through March 11, 1990. (All notes are dated as of the day they are received.)

Nov. 1. Received a $6,750, 12%, 60-day note on account.
11. Received a $30,000, 15%, 120-day note on account.
Dec. 16. Received a $12,000, 13%, 60-day note on account.
21. Received an $18,000, 12%, 30-day note on account.
31. Received $6,885 on note of November 1.
31. Recorded an adjusting entry for the interest accrued on the notes dated November 11, December 16, and December 21. There are no other notes receivable on this date.
31. Closed the interest income account.
Jan. 1. Recorded a reversing entry for the accrued interest.
20. Received $18,180 on note of December 21.
26. Received a $7,000, 12%, 30-day note on account.
Feb. 14. Received $12,260 on note of December 16.
25. Received $7,070 on note of January 26.
Mar. 11. Received $31,500 on note of November 11.

Instructions: (1) Open accounts for Interest Receivable (Account No. 116) and Interest Income (Account No. 611), and record a credit balance of $4,450 in the latter account as of November 1, 1989.
(2) Present entries to record the transactions and other data, posting to the two accounts after each entry affecting them.
(3) If the reversing entry had not been recorded as of January 1, indicate how each interest receipt in January, February, and March should be allocated. Submit the data in the following form:

Note (Face Amount)	Total Interest Received	Cr. Interest Receivable	Cr. Interest Income
$18,000	$	$	$
12,000			
7,000			
30,000			
Total	$	$	$

(4) Do the March 11 balances of Interest Receivable and Interest Income obtained by use of the reversing entry technique correspond to the balances that would have been obtained by analyzing each receipt?

6–39. Entries related to uncollectible accounts. The following transactions, adjusting entries, and closing entries were completed during the current fiscal year ended December 31.

Feb. 8. Received 60% of the $5,000 balance owed by Flowers Co., a bankrupt business, and wrote off the remainder as uncollectible.

May 29. Reinstated the account of James Gray, which had been written off in the preceding year as uncollectible. Recorded the receipt of $990 cash in full payment of Gray's account.

Aug. 16. Wrote off the $5,300 balance owed by Shaw Corp., which has no assets.

Oct. 1. Reinstated the account of W. Ricardo Inc. which had been written off in the preceding year as uncollectible. Recorded the receipt of $2,950 cash in full payment of W. Ricardo Inc.'s account.

Dec. 30. Wrote off the following accounts as uncollectible (compound entry): Mertz and Dodds, $4,920; Nance Inc., $3,975; Powell Distributors, $9,700; J. J. Stevens, $4,200.

31. Based on an analysis of the $610,000 of accounts receivable, it was estimated that $31,250 will be uncollectible. Recorded the adjusting entry.

31. Recorded the entry to close the appropriate account to Income Summary.

Instructions: (1) Open the following selected accounts, recording the credit balance indicated as of January 1 of the current fiscal year:

115	Allowance for Doubtful Accounts	$29,500
313	Income Summary	—
718	Uncollectible Accounts Expense	—

(2) Record the transactions and the adjusting and closing entries previously described. After each entry, post to the three selected accounts affected and extend the new balances.
(3) Determine the expected realizable value of the accounts receivable as of December 31.
(4) Assuming that, instead of basing the provision for uncollectible accounts on an analysis of receivables, the adjusting entry on December 31 had been based on an estimated loss of 1/2 of 1% of the net sales of $5,700,000 for the year, determine the following:
(a) Uncollectible accounts expense for the year.
(b) Balance in the allowance account after the adjustment of December 31.
(c) Expected realizable value of the accounts receivable as of December 31.

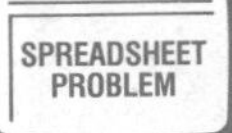

6–40. Comparison of two methods of accounting for receivables. AID Corporation has just completed its fourth year of operations. The direct write-off method of recording uncollectible accounts expense has been employed during the entire period. Because of substantial increases in sales volume and amount of uncollectible accounts, the firm is considering the possibility of changing to the allowance method. Information is requested as to the effect that an annual provision of 1% of sales would have had on the amount of uncollectible accounts expense reported for each of the past four years. It is also considered desirable to know what the balance of Allowance for Doubtful Accounts would have been at the end of each year. The following data have been obtained from the accounts:

Year	Sales	Uncollectible Accounts Written Off	Year of Origin of Accounts Receivable Written off as Uncollectible: 1st	2d	3d	4th
1st	$450,000	$2,500	$2,500			
2d	600,000	2,950	1,500	$1,450		
3d	850,000	4,700	700	2,400	$1,600	
4th	950,000	6,450		1,900	2,950	$1,600

Instructions: (1) Assemble the desired data, using the following columnar captions:

	Uncollectible Accounts Expense			
Year	Expense Actually Reported	Expense Based on Estimate	Increase in Amount of Expense	Balance of Allowance Account, End of Year

(2) Experience during the first four years of operation indicated that the receivables were either collected within two years or had to be written off as uncollectible. Does the estimate of 1% of sales appear to be reasonably close to the actual experience with uncollectible accounts originating during the first two years?

6–41. Installment sales. R. C. Nunn Inc. makes all sales on the installment basis and recognizes revenue at the point of sale. Condensed income statements and the amounts collected from customers for each of the first three years of operations are as follows:

	First Year	Second Year	Third Year
Sales	$300,000	$340,000	$440,000
Cost of merchandise sold	195,000	224,400	281,600
Gross profit	$105,000	$115,600	$158,400
Operating expenses	62,500	68,500	98,400
Net income	$ 42,500	$ 47,100	$ 60,000
Collected from sales of first year	$ 75,000	$125,000	$100,000
Collected from sales of second year		110,000	180,000
Collected from sales of third year			115,000

Instructions: Determine the amount of net income that would have been reported in each year if the installment method of recognizing revenue had been employed, ignoring the possible effects of uncollectible accounts on the computation. Present figures in good order.

6–42. Installment sale and repossession. Fuller Video employs the installment method of recognizing gross profit for sales made on the installment plan. Details of a particular installment sale, amounts collected from the buyer, and the repossession of the item sold are as follows.

First year:
Sold for $900 a color television set having a cost of $720; received a down payment of $150.

Second year:
Received 12 monthly payments of $30 each.

Third year:
The buyer defaulted on the monthly payments, the set was repossessed, and the remaining 13 installments were canceled. The set was estimated to be worth $350.

Instructions: (1) Determine the gross profit to be recognized in the first year.

(2) Determine the gross profit to be recognized in the second year.

(3) Determine the gain or loss to be recognized from the repossession of the set. (*Suggestion:* First determine the amount of the unrecovered cost in the canceled installments. The gain or loss on repossession will then be the difference between this unrecovered cost and the value of the repossessed set.)

6–43. Financial statements for corporation. The following data for N. B. Neter Company were selected from the ledger, after adjustment at December 31, the end of the current fiscal year.

Accounts payable	$ 25,750
Accounts receivable	51,500
Accumulated depreciation—building	175,000
Accumulated depreciation—office equipment	49,750
Allowance for decline to market of marketable securities	1,100
Allowance for doubtful accounts	1,500
Building	325,000
Capital stock	250,000
Cash	35,500
Cost of merchandise sold	510,000
Dividends	60,000
General expenses	73,500
Interest and dividend income	6,100
Land	75,000
Marketable equity securities	60,000
Notes receivable	40,000
Office equipment	79,750
Office supplies	7,500
Prepaid insurance	5,000
Retained earnings	205,900
Salaries payable	3,250
Sales	795,000
Sales discounts	6,500
Selling expenses	110,500
Unrealized loss from decline to market of marketable securities	1,100

Instructions: (1) Prepare an income statement in multiple-step form. The merchandise inventory at December 31 is $72,500.
(2) Prepare a retained earnings statement.
(3) Prepare a balance sheet in report form.

ALTERNATE PROBLEMS

6–36A. Sales, notes receivable, discounting notes receivable transactions. The following were selected from among the transactions completed by D. L. Parton Co. during the current year:

Jan. 20. Sold merchandise on account to Grant Co., $10,000.
30. Accepted a 60-day, 12% note for $10,000 from Grant Co. on account.
Mar. 31. Received from Grant Co. the amount due on the note of January 30.
May 1. Sold merchandise on account to W. A. Lewis Co. for $2,000.
5. Loaned $6,000 cash to Frank Nelson, receiving a 30-day, 14% note.
11. Received from W. A. Lewis Co. the amount due on the invoice of May 1, less 1% discount.
June 4. Received the interest due from Frank Nelson and a new 60-day, 14% note as a renewal of the loan of May 5. (Record both the debit and the credit to the notes receivable account.)
Aug. 3. Received from Frank Nelson the amount due on his note of June 4.
16. Sold merchandise on account to J. A. Rohr, $8,000.
Sept. 10. Accepted a 60-day, 12% note for $8,000 from J. A. Rohr on account.
Oct. 10. Discounted the note from J. A. Rohr at the Collier National Bank at 10%.
Nov. 9. Received notice from Collier National Bank that J. A. Rohr had dishonored its note. Paid the bank the maturity value of the note.
Dec. 9. Received from J. A. Rohr the amount owed on the dishonored note, plus interest for 30 days at 10% computed on the maturity value of the note.

Instructions: Present the entries to record the transactions.

SPREADSHEET PROBLEM

6–37A. Details of notes receivable, including discounting. During the last six months of the current year, Amos Co. received the following notes. Notes (1), (2), (3), and (4) were discounted on the dates and at the rates indicated.

Date	Face Amount	Term	Interest Rate	Date Discounted	Discount Rate
(1) June 5	$13,500	60 days	12%	June 25	10%
(2) July 30	8,000	60 days	12%	Aug. 9	15%
(3) Aug. 19	15,000	90 days	10%	Sept. 18	12%
(4) Sept. 1	10,800	60 days	11%	Oct. 11	12%
(5) Dec. 11	9,000	30 days	14%	—	—
(6) Dec. 16	12,000	60 days	13%	—	—

Instructions: (1) Determine for each note (a) the due date and (b) the amount of interest due at maturity, identifying each note by number.

(2) Determine for each of the first four notes (a) the maturity value, (b) the discount period, (c) the discount, (d) the proceeds, and (e) the interest income or interest expense, identifying each note by number.

(3) Present the entries to record the discounting of notes (2) and (3) at a bank.

(4) Assuming that notes (5) and (6) are held until maturity, determine for each the amount of interest earned (a) in the current fiscal year and (b) in the following fiscal year.

6–38A. Notes receivable entries and year-end entries; general ledger accounts. Tracy Co. closes its accounts annually as of December 31, the end of the fiscal year. The following data relate to notes receivable and interest from November 1, 1989, through March 16, 1990. (All notes are dated as of the day they are received.)

Nov. 1. Received a $20,000, 12%, 60-day note on account.
21. Received a $9,000, 14%, 90-day note on account.
Dec. 16. Received a $12,000, 15%, 90-day note on account.
21. Received a $3,600, 13%, 30-day note on account.
31. Received $20,400 on note of November 1.
31. Recorded an adjusting entry for the interest accrued on the notes dated November 21, December 16, and December 21. There are no other notes receivable on this date.
31. Closed the interest income account.
Jan. 1. Recorded a reversing entry for the accrued interest.
20. Received $3,639 on note of December 21.
21. Received a $7,000, 12%, 30-day note on account.
Feb. 19. Received $9,315 on note of November 21.
20. Received $7,070 on note of January 21.
Mar. 16. Received $12,450 on note of December 16.

Instructions: (1) Open accounts for Interest Receivable (Account No. 116) and Interest Income (Account No. 611), and record a credit balance of $2,050 in the latter account as of November 1, 1989.

(2) Present entries to record the transactions and other data, posting to the two accounts after each entry affecting them.

(3) If the reversing entry had not been recorded as of January 1, indicate how each interest receipt in January, February, and March should be allocated. Submit the data in the following form:

Note (Face Amount)	Total Interest Received	Cr. Interest Receivable	Cr. Interest Income
$ 9,000	$	$	$
12,000			
3,600			
7,000			
Total	$	$	$

(continued)

(4) Do the March 16 balances of Interest Receivable and Interest Income obtained by the use of the reversing entry technique correspond to the balances that would have been obtained by analyzing each receipt?

6–39A. Entries related to uncollectible accounts. The following transactions, adjusting entries, and closing entries were completed during the current fiscal year ended December 31:

Feb. 22. Reinstated the account of Bob Lowe, which had been written off in the preceding year as uncollectible. Recorded the receipt of $610 cash in full payment of Lowe's account.
May 3. Wrote off the $3,925 balance owed by Licci Co., which has no assets.
Aug. 7. Received 30% of the $5,000 balance owed by C. O'Rourke Corp., a bankrupt business, and wrote off the remainder as uncollectible.
Oct. 19. Reinstated the account of John Nowak, which had been written off two years earlier as uncollectible. Recorded the receipt of $925 cash in full payment.
Dec. 20. Wrote off the following accounts as uncollectible (compound entry): Cain Bros., $480; Gerber and Hertz, $1,900; Jenson Furniture, $2,775; Charles Menke, $840.
31. Based on an analysis of the $234,250 of accounts receivable, it was estimated that $15,000 will be uncollectible. Recorded the adjusting entry.
31. Recorded the entry to close the appropriate account to Income Summary.

Instructions: (1) Open the following selected accounts, recording the credit balance indicated as of January 1 of the current fiscal year:

115	Allowance for Doubtful Accounts	$13,050
313	Income Summary	—
718	Uncollectible Accounts Expense	—

(2) Record the transactions and the adjusting and closing entries described. After each entry, post to the three selected accounts affected and extend the new balances.
(3) Determine the expected realizable value of the accounts receivable as of December 31.
(4) Assuming that, instead of basing the provision for uncollectible accounts on an analysis of receivables, the adjusting entry on December 31 had been based on an estimated loss of 1/2 of 1% of the net sales of $2,700,000 for the year, determine the following:
(a) Uncollectible accounts expense for the year.
(b) Balance in the allowance account after the adjustment of December 31.
(c) Expected realizable value of the accounts receivable as of December 31.

6–41A. Installment sales. Watson Co. makes all sales on the installment basis and recognizes revenue at the point of sale. Condensed income statements and the amounts collected from customers for each of the first three years of operations are as follows:

	First Year	Second Year	Third Year
Sales	$398,750	$340,000	$382,000
Cost of merchandise sold	271,150	227,800	248,300
Gross profit	$127,600	$112,200	$133,700
Operating expenses	60,000	51,500	62,250
Net income	$ 67,600	$ 60,700	$ 71,450
Collected from sales of first year	$121,250	$157,500	$120,000
Collected from sales of second year		95,000	145,000
Collected from sales of third year			99,000

Instructions: Determine the amount of net income that would have been reported in each year if the installment method of recognizing revenue had been employed, ignoring the possible effects of uncollectible accounts on the computation. Present figures in good order.

Mini-Case 6

For several years, Cannons' sales have been on a "cash only" basis. On January 1, 1986, however, Cannons began offering credit on terms of n/30. The amount of the adjusting entry to record the estimated uncollectible receivables at the end of each year has been 1/2 of 1% of credit sales, which is the rate reported as the average for the industry. Credit sales and the year-end credit balances in Allowance for Doubtful Accounts for the past four years are as follows:

Year	Credit Sales	Allowance for Doubtful Accounts
1986	$3,900,000	$ 6,000
1987	3,600,000	8,000
1988	4,000,000	11,500
1989	3,750,000	14,000

Jane Cannon, president of Cannons, is concerned that the method used to account for and write off uncollectible receivables is unsatisfactory. She has asked for your advice in the analysis of past operations in this area and for recommendations for change.

Instructions:

(1) Determine the amount of (a) the addition to Allowance for Doubtful Accounts and (b) the accounts written off for each of the four years.

(2) Advise Jane Cannon as to whether the estimate of 1/2 of 1% of credit sales appears reasonable.

(3) Assume that after discussing item (2) with Jane Cannon, she asked you what action might be taken to determine what the balance of Allowance for Doubtful Accounts should be at December 31, 1989, and possible changes, if any, you might recommend in accounting for uncollectible receivables. How would you respond?

Answers to Self-Examination Questions

1. C Maturity value is the amount that is due at the maturity or due date. The maturity value of $10,300 (answer C) is determined as follows:

Face amount of note	$10,000
Plus interest ($10,000 × 12/100 × 90/360)	300
Maturity value of note	$10,300

2. B The proceeds of $15,021.25 (answer B) are determined as follows:

Face value of note dated June 1	$15,000.00
Interest on note (60 days at 10%)	250.00
Maturity value of note due July 31	$15,250.00
Discount on maturity value (45 days, from June 16 to July 31 at 12%)	228.75
Proceeds	$15,021.25

3. B The estimate of uncollectible accounts, $8,500 (answer C), is the amount of the desired balance of Allowance for Doubtful Accounts *after adjustment.* The amount of the current provision to be made for uncollectible accounts expense is thus $6,000 (answer B), which is the amount that must be added to the Allowance for Doubtful Accounts credit balance of $2,500 (answer A), so that the account will have the desired balance of $8,500.
4. B The amount expected to be realized from accounts receivable is the balance of Accounts Receivable, $100,000, less the balance of Allowance for Doubtful Accounts, $7,000, or $93,000 (answer B).
5. A Securities held as temporary investments are classified on the balance sheet as current assets (answer A).

7
Inventories

CHAPTER OBJECTIVES

Describe and illustrate the effect of inventory on the financial statements of the current period and the following period.

Identify and describe the two principal inventory systems.

Identify and illustrate the procedures for determining the actual quantity in inventory.

Describe and illustrate the most common methods of determining the cost of inventory, including the comparison of the effect of the methods on operating results.

Describe and illustrate the valuation of inventory at the lower of cost or market.

Describe and illustrate the perpetual inventory system.

Identify and illustrate the proper presentation of inventory in the financial statements.

Describe and illustrate methods of estimating the cost of inventory.

Describe and illustrate inventories of manufacturing enterprises.

Describe and illustrate accounting for long-term construction contracts.

The term **inventories** is used to designate (1) merchandise held for sale in the normal course of business, and (2) materials in the process of production or held for such use. This chapter discusses the determination of the inventory of merchandise purchased for resale, commonly called **merchandise inventory.** Inventories of raw materials and partially processed materials of a manufacturing enterprise are also discussed.

IMPORTANCE OF INVENTORIES

Merchandise, being continually purchased and sold, is one of the most active elements in the operation of wholesale and retail businesses. The sale of merchandise provides the principal source of revenue for such enterprises. When the net income is determined, the cost of merchandise sold is normally the largest deduction from sales. In fact, it is usually larger than all other deductions combined. In addition, a substantial part of a merchandising firm's resources is invested in inventory. It is frequently the largest of the current assets of such a firm.

The Effect of Inventory on the Current Period's Statement

Inventory determination plays an important role in matching expired costs with revenues of the period. As was explained and illustrated in Chapter 4, the total cost of merchandise available for sale during a period of time must be divided into two parts at the end of the period. The cost of the merchandise determined to be in the inventory will appear on the balance sheet as a current asset. The other element, which is the cost of the merchandise sold, will be reported on the income statement as a deduction from net sales to yield gross profit. An error in the determination of the inventory amount at the end of the period will cause an equal misstatement of gross profit and net income, and the amount reported for both assets and owner's equity in the balance sheet will be incorrect by the same amount. The effects of understatements and overstatements of merchandise inventory at the end of the period are demonstrated in the following three sets of condensed income statements and balance sheets. The first set of statements is based on a correct ending inventory of $20,000; the second set, on an *incorrect ending inventory of $12,000;* and the third set, on an *incorrect ending inventory of $27,000.* In all three cases, net sales are $200,000, merchandise available for sale is $140,000, and expenses are $55,000.

1. Inventory at end of period correctly stated at $20,000.

Income Statement for the Year		Balance Sheet at End of Year	
Net sales	$200,000	Merchandise inventory	$ 20,000
Cost of merchandise sold	120,000	Other assets	80,000
Gross profit	$ 80,000	Total	$100,000
Expenses	55,000		
Net income	$ 25,000	Liabilities	$ 30,000
		Owner's equity	70,000
		Total	$100,000

2. Inventory at end of period incorrectly stated at $12,000; (understated by $8,000).

Income Statement for the Year		Balance Sheet at End of Year	
Net sales	$200,000	Merchandise inventory	$ 12,000
Cost of merchandise sold	128,000	Other assets	80,000
Gross profit	$ 72,000	Total	$ 92,000
Expenses	55,000		
Net income	$ 17,000	Liabilities	$ 30,000
		Owner's equity	62,000
		Total	$ 92,000

3. Inventory at end of period incorrectly stated at $27,000; (overstated by $7,000).

Income Statement for the Year		Balance Sheet at End of Year	
Net sales	$200,000	Merchandise inventory	$ 27,000
Cost of merchandise sold	113,000	Other assets	80,000
Gross profit	$ 87,000	Total	$107,000
Expenses	55,000		
Net income	$ 32,000	Liabilities	$ 30,000
		Owner's equity	77,000
		Total	$107,000

Note that in the illustration the total cost of merchandise available for sale was constant at $140,000. It was the way in which the cost was allocated that varied. The variations in allocating the $140,000 of merchandise cost are summarized as follows:

	Merchandise Available		
	Total	*Inventory*	*Sold*
1. Inventory correctly stated.............	$140,000	$20,000	$120,000
2. Inventory understated by $8,000	140,000	12,000	128,000
3. Inventory overstated by $7,000	140,000	27,000	113,000

The effect of the errors on net income, assets, and owner's equity may also be summarized. Comparison of the financial statements in *2* and *3* with the financial statements in *1* yields the following:

	Net Income	*Assets*	*Owner's Equity*
2. Ending inventory understated $8,000	Understated $8,000	Understated $8,000	Understated $8,000
3. Ending inventory overstated $7,000	Overstated $7,000	Overstated $7,000	Overstated $7,000

The Effect of Inventory on the Following Period's Statements

The inventory at the end of one period becomes the inventory for the beginning of the following period. Thus, if the inventory is incorrectly stated at the end of the period, the net income of that period will be misstated and so will the net income for the following period. The amount of the two misstatements will be equal and in opposite directions. Therefore, the effect on net income of an incorrectly stated inventory, if not corrected, is limited to the period of the error and the following period. At the end of this following period, assuming no additional errors, both assets and owner's equity will be correctly stated. To illustrate, assume that the ending inventory for period *1* was understated by $10,000, and no other errors are made. The gross profit (and net income) would be understated for period *1* and overstated for period *2* by $10,000, indicated as follows:

	Period 1				*Period 2*			
	No Error		*Error*		*Error*		*No Error*	
Net sales		$90,000		$90,000		$85,000		$85,000
Cost of merchandise sold:								
Beginning inventory...........	$25,000		$25,000		$20,000		$30,000	
Purchases	70,000		70,000		65,000		65,000	
Merchandise available for sale.	$95,000		$95,000		$85,000		$95,000	
Less ending inventory.........	30,000		20,000		28,000		28,000	
Cost of merchandise sold ...		65,000		75,000		57,000		67,000
Gross profit		$25,000		$15,000		$28,000		$18,000
				Understated $10,000		Overstated $10,000		

In the illustration, the $10,000 understatement of inventory at the end of period *1* resulted in an overstatement of the cost of merchandise sold and thus an understatement of gross profit by $10,000. On the balance sheet, merchandise inventory and owner's equity would both be understated by $10,000. Because the ending inventory of period *1* becomes the beginning inventory for period *2,* the cost of merchandise sold was understated and gross profit was overstated by $10,000 for period *2.* Both merchandise inventory and owner's equity will be correct at the end of period *2.*

INVENTORY SYSTEMS

As discussed in Chapter 4, there are two principal systems of inventory accounting— periodic and perpetual. When the **periodic inventory system** is used, only the revenue from sales is recorded each time a sale is made. No entry is made at the time of the sale to record the cost of the merchandise that has been sold. Consequently, a **physical inventory** must be taken in order to determine the cost of the inventory at the end of an accounting period. Ordinarily, it is practical to take a complete physical inventory only at the end of the fiscal year. In the earlier chapters dealing with purchases and sales of merchandise, the use of the periodic system was assumed.

In contrast to the periodic system, the **perpetual inventory system** uses accounting records that continuously disclose the amount of the inventory. A separate account for each type of merchandise is maintained in a subsidiary ledger. Increases in inventory items are recorded as debits to the proper accounts, and decreases are recorded as credits. The balances of the accounts are called the **book inventories** of the items on hand. Regardless of the care with which the perpetual inventory records are maintained, their accuracy must be tested by taking a physical inventory of each type of commodity at least once a year. The records are then compared with the actual quantities on hand and any differences are corrected.

The periodic inventory system is often used by retail enterprises that sell many kinds of low unit cost merchandise, such as groceries, hardware, and drugs. The expense of maintaining perpetual inventory records may be prohibitive in such cases. In recent years, however, the use of computerized systems in such businesses has reduced this expense considerably. Firms selling a relatively small number of high unit cost items, such as office equipment, automobiles, or fur garments, are more likely to use the perpetual system.

Although much of the discussion that follows applies to both systems, the use of the periodic inventory system will be assumed. Later in the chapter, principles and procedures related only to the perpetual inventory system will be presented.

DETERMINING ACTUAL QUANTITIES IN THE INVENTORY

The first stage in the process of "taking" an inventory is to determine the quantity of each kind of merchandise owned by the enterprise. When the periodic system is used, the counting, weighing, and measuring should be done at the end of the accounting period. To accomplish this, the inventory crew may work during the night, or business operations may be stopped until the count is finished.

The details of the specific procedures for determining quantities and assembling the data differ among companies. A common practice is to use teams made up of two persons. One person counts, weighs, or otherwise determines quantity, and the other lists the description and the quantity on inventory sheets. The quantity indicated for high-cost items is verified by a third person at some time during the inventory-taking period. It is also advisable for the third person to verify other items selected at random from the inventory sheets.

All of the merchandise owned by the business on the inventory date, and only such merchandise, should be included in the inventory. It may be necessary to examine purchase and sales invoices of the last few days of the accounting period and the first few days of the following period to determine who has legal title to merchandise in transit on the inventory date. When goods are purchased or sold **FOB shipping point,** title usually passes to the buyer when the goods are shipped. When the terms are **FOB destination,** title usually does not pass to the buyer until the goods are delivered. To illustrate, assume that merchandise purchased FOB shipping point is shipped by the seller on the last day of the buyer's fiscal period. The merchandise does not arrive until the following period and hence is not available for "counting" by the inventory crew. However, such merchandise should be included in the buyer's inventory because title has passed. It is also evident that a debit to Purchases and a credit to Accounts Payable should be recorded by the buyer as of the end of the period, rather than recording it as a transaction of the following period.

Another example, although less common, will further show the importance of closely examining transactions involving shipments of merchandise. Manufacturers sometimes ship merchandise on a consignment basis to retailers who act as the manufacturer's agent when selling the merchandise. The manufacturer retains title until the goods are sold. Obviously, such unsold merchandise is a part of the manufacturer's (consignor's) inventory, even though the manufacturer does not have physical possession. It is just as obvious that the consigned merchandise should not be included in the retailer's (consignee's) inventory.

DETERMINING THE COST OF INVENTORY

The cost of merchandise inventory is made up of the purchase price and all expenditures incurred in acquiring such merchandise, including transportation, customs duties, and insurance against losses in transit. The purchase price can be readily determined, as may some of the other costs. Those that are difficult to associate with specific inventory items may be prorated on some equitable basis. Minor costs that are difficult to allocate may be left out entirely from inventory cost and treated as operating expenses of the period.

If purchases discounts are treated as a deduction from purchases on the income statement, they should also be deducted from the purchase price of items in the inventory. If it is not possible to determine the exact amount of discount applicable to each inventory item, a pro rata amount of the total discount for the period may be deducted instead. For example, if net purchases and purchases discounts for the period amount to $200,000 and $3,000 respectively, the discounts represent 1½% of net purchases. If the inventory cost, before considering the cash discounts is $30,000, the amount may be reduced by 1½%, or $450, to yield an inventory cost of $29,550.

One of the most significant problems in determining inventory cost comes about when identical units of a certain commodity have been acquired at different unit cost prices during the period. In such cases, it is necessary to determine the unit prices of the items still on hand. To illustrate this problem and its relationship to the determination of net income and inventory cost, assume that three identical units of Commodity X were available for sale to customers during the fiscal year. One of these units was in the inventory at the beginning of the year, and the other two were purchased on March 4 and May 9 respectively. The costs per unit are as follows:

Commodity X		*Units*	*Cost*
Jan. 1	Inventory	1	$ 9
Mar. 4	Purchase	1	13
May 9	Purchase	1	14
Total		3	$36
Average cost per unit			$12

During the year, two units of Commodity X were sold, leaving one unit in the inventory at the end of the year. In the illustration and in actual practice, it may be possible to identify units with specific expenditures if both the variety of merchandise carried in stock and the volume of sales are relatively small. Ordinarily, however, **specific identification** procedures are too costly and too time consuming to justify their use. It is customary, therefore, to use an arbitrary assumption as to the *flow of costs* of merchandise through the enterprise. The three most common assumptions of determining the cost of the merchandise sold are as follows:

1. Cost flow is in the order in which the expenditures were made—first-in, first-out.
2. Cost flow is in the reverse order in which the expenditures were made—last-in, first-out.
3. Cost flow is an average of the expenditures.

Details of the cost of the two units of Commodity X assumed to be sold and the cost of the one unit remaining, determined in accordance with each of these assumptions, are as follows:

	Commodity X Costs				
	Units Available		*Units Sold*		*Unit Remaining*
1. In order of expenditures (first-in, first-out)	$36	−	($ 9 + $13)	=	$14
2. In reverse order of expenditures (last-in, first-out)	36	−	(14 + 13)	=	9
3. In accordance with average expenditures	36	−	(12 + 12)	=	12

The three most widely used inventory costing methods (which correspond to the three assumptions of cost flows illustrated) are:

1. **First-in, first-out (fifo)**
2. **Last-in, first-out (lifo)**
3. **Average**

Know

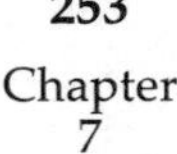

The extent of the use of these three methods is indicated by the following chart:

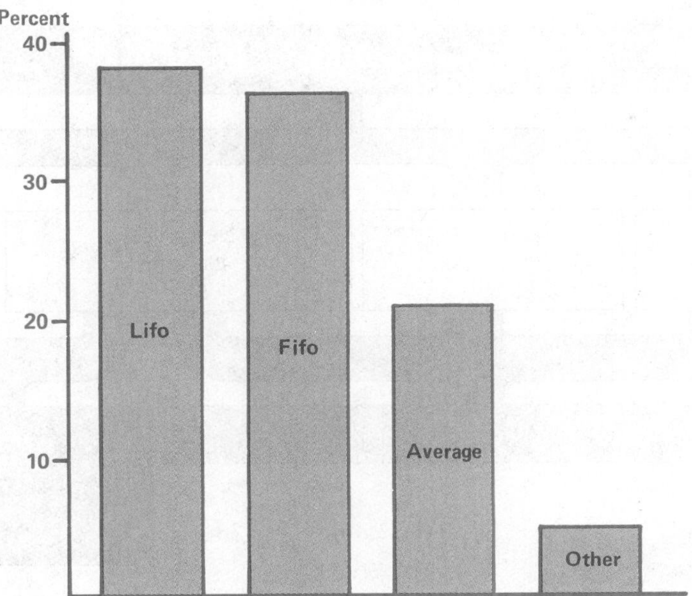

Source: Accounting Trends & Techniques, 41st ed. (New York: American Institute of Certified Public Accountants, 1987).

First-In, First-Out Method

The **first-in, first-out (fifo) method** of costing inventory is based on the assumption that costs should be charged against revenue in the order in which they were incurred. Hence the inventory remaining is assumed to be made up of the most recent costs. The illustration of the application of this method is based on the following data for a particular commodity:

Jan. 1	Inventory	200 units at $ 9	$ 1,800
Mar. 10	Purchase	300 units at 10	3,000
Sept. 21	Purchase	400 units at 11	4,400
Nov. 18	Purchase	100 units at 12	1,200
	Available for sale during year	1,000	$10,400

The physical count on December 31 shows that 300 units of the particular commodity are on hand. In accordance with the assumption that the inventory is composed of the most recent costs, the cost of the 300 units is determined as follows:

Most recent costs, Nov. 18	100 units at $12	$1,200
Next most recent costs, Sept. 21	200 units at 11	2,200
Inventory, Dec. 31	300	$3,400

Deduction of the inventory of $3,400 from the $10,400 of merchandise available for sale yields $7,000 as the cost of merchandise sold, which represents the earliest costs incurred for this commodity. The relationship of the inventory at December 31 and the cost of merchandise sold during the year is illustrated in the following diagram:

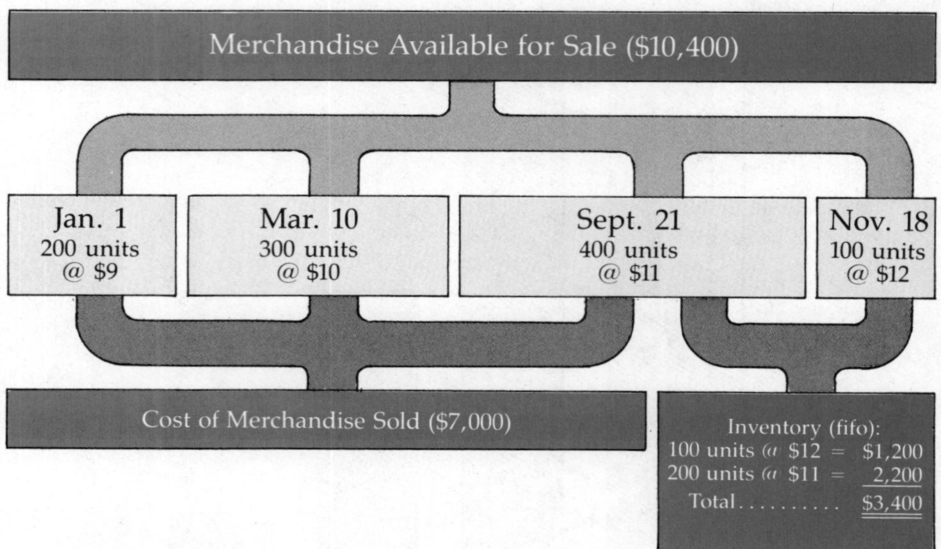

In most businesses, there is a tendency to dispose of goods in the order of their acquisition. This would be particularly true of perishable merchandise and goods in which style or model changes are frequent. Thus, the fifo method is generally in harmony with the physical movement of merchandise in an enterprise. To the extent that this is the case, the fifo method approximates the results that would be obtained by the specific identification of costs.

Last-In, First-Out Method

The **last-in, first-out (lifo) method** is based on the assumption that the most recent costs incurred should be charged against revenue. Hence the inventory remaining is assumed to be composed of the earliest costs. Based on the illustrative data presented in the preceding section, the cost of the 300 units of inventory is determined in the following manner:

Earliest costs, Jan. 1	200 units at $ 9............	$1,800
Next earliest costs, Mar. 10	100 units at 10............	1,000
Inventory, Dec. 31..............	300	$2,800

Deduction of the inventory of $2,800 from the $10,400 of merchandise available for sale yields $7,600 as the cost of merchandise sold, which represents the most recent costs incurred for this particular commodity. The relationship of the inventory at December 31 and the cost of merchandise sold during the year is illustrated in the following diagram:

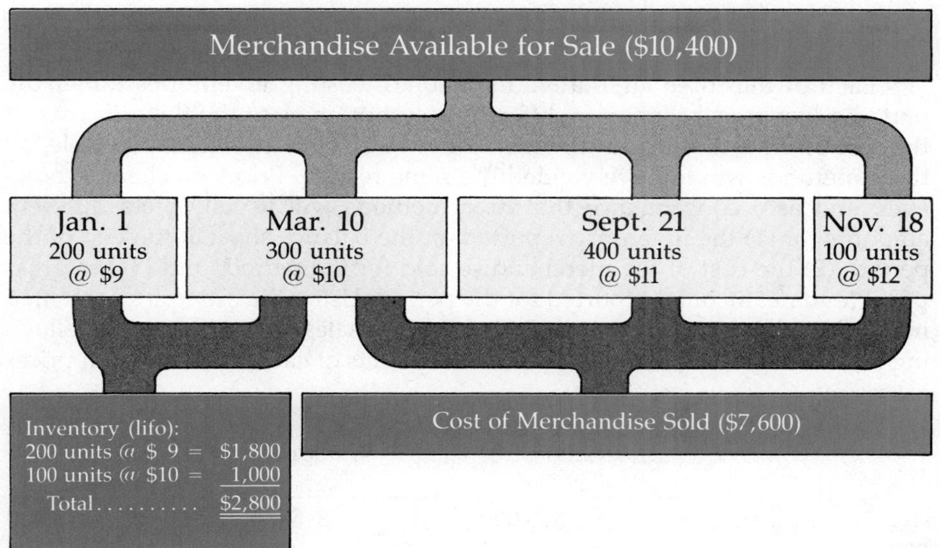

The use of the lifo method was originally confined to the relatively rare situations in which the units sold were taken from the most recently acquired stock. Its use has greatly increased during the past few decades, and it is now often used even when it does not represent the physical flow of goods.

Average Cost Method

The **average cost method,** sometimes called the **weighted average method,** is based on the assumption that costs should be charged against revenue according to the weighted average unit costs of the goods sold. The same weighted average unit costs are used in determining the cost of the merchandise remaining in the inventory. The weighted average unit cost is determined by dividing the total cost of the identical units of each commodity available for sale during the period by the related number of units of that commodity. Assuming the same cost data as in the preceding illustrations, the average cost of the 1,000 units and the cost of the 300 units in inventory are determined as follows:

Average unit cost	$10,400 ÷ 1,000 = $10.40	
Inventory, Dec. 31..........	300 units at $10.40	$3,120

Deduction of the inventory of $3,120 from the $10,400 of merchandise available for sale yields $7,280 as the cost of merchandise sold, which represents the average of the costs incurred for this commodity.

For businesses in which various purchases of identical units of a commodity are mingled, the average method has some relationship to the physical flow of goods.

Stop here

Comparison of Inventory Costing Methods

Each of the three alternative methods of costing inventories under the periodic system is based on a different assumption as to the flow of costs. If the cost of units and prices at which they were sold had remained stable, all three methods would have yielded the same results. Prices do change, however, and as a consequence the three methods will usually yield different amounts for (1) the inventory reported on the balance sheet at the end of the period, (2) the cost of the merchandise sold for the period, and (3) the gross profit (and net income) reported for the period. Using the examples presented in the preceding sections and assuming that net sales were $15,000, the following partial income statements indicate the effects of each method when prices are rising:

	First-In, First-Out		Average Cost		Last-In, First-Out	
Net sales		$15,000		$15,000		$15,000
Cost of merchandise sold:						
Beginning inventory	$ 1,800		$ 1,800		$ 1,800	
Purchases	8,600		8,600		8,600	
Merchandise available for sale	$10,400		$10,400		$10,400	
Less ending inventory	3,400		3,120		2,800	
Cost of merchandise sold		7,000		7,280		7,600
Gross profit		$ 8,000		$ 7,720		$ 7,400

As shown in the income statements, the fifo method yielded the lowest amount for the cost of merchandise sold and the highest amount for gross profit (and net income). It also yielded the highest amount for the ending inventory. On the other hand, the lifo method yielded the highest amount for the cost of merchandise sold, the lowest amount for gross profit (and net income), and the lowest amount for ending inventory. The average cost method yielded results that were between those of fifo and lifo.

Use of the First-In, First-Out Method. During a period of inflation or rising prices, the use of the fifo method will result in the effects shown in the illustration because the costs of the units sold are assumed to be in the order in which they were incurred, and the earlier unit costs were lower than the more recent unit costs. Much of the benefit of the larger amount of gross profit is lost, however, as the inventory is continually replenished at ever higher prices. During the 1970s, when the rate of inflation increased to double-digit percentages, the larger gross profits that resulted were frequently referred to as *inventory profits* or *illusory profits*.

In a period of deflation or declining prices, the effect described above is reversed, and the fifo method yields the lowest amount of gross profit. The major criticism of the fifo method is this tendency to maximize the effect of inflationary and deflationary trends on amounts reported as gross profit. However, the dollar amount reported as merchandise inventory on the balance sheet will usually be about the same as its current replacement cost.

Use of the Last-In, First-Out Method. During a period of rising prices, the use of the last-in, first-out method will result in a lower amount of inventory at the end of the period, a higher amount of cost of merchandise sold, and a lower amount of gross profit than the other two methods. The reason for these effects is that the cost of the most recently acquired units most nearly approximates the cost of their replacement, and the more recent unit costs were higher than the earlier unit costs. Thus, it can be argued that the use of the lifo method more nearly matches current costs with current revenues. This latter point was one reason that Chrysler Corporation changed from the fifo method to the lifo method in 1984, as stated in the following footnote that accompanied Chrysler's financial statements for 1984:

> Effective January 1, 1984, Chrysler changed its method of accounting from first-in, first-out (fifo) to last-in, first-out (lifo) for substantially all of its domestic productive inventories. The change to lifo was made to more accurately match current costs with current revenues. Had the inventory, at December 31, 1984, been valued on the fifo basis, it would have been $29.7 million higher than reported.

During periods of rising prices, the use of lifo offers a savings in income taxes. The income tax savings results because lifo reports the lowest amount of net income of the three methods. During the accelerated inflationary trend of the 1970s, many business enterprises changed from fifo to lifo to take advantage of this tax savings.

In a period of deflation or falling price levels, the effect described above is reversed and the lifo method yields the highest amount of gross profit. The major justification for lifo is this tendency to minimize the effect of price trends on reported gross profit and, therefore, to exert a stabilizing influence on the economy. A criticism of the use of lifo is that the dollar amount reported for merchandise inventory on the balance sheet may be quite far removed from the current replacement cost. In such situations, however, it is customary to indicate in a note accompanying the published financial statements the approximate difference between the lifo inventory amount and the inventory amount if fifo had been used. The following note accompanying the 1986 statements of The Walgreen Co. is illustrative:

> Inventories are valued on a last-in, first-out (LIFO) cost basis. At August 31, 1986 and 1985, inventories would have been greater by $162,698,000 and $149,134,000 respectively, if they had been valued on a lower of first-in, first-out (FIFO) cost or market basis.

Inflation and Adoption of Lifo

The effects of using lifo and some of the reasons that the method is adopted (or not adopted) by businesses were discussed in an article in *Management Accounting*. Some excerpts from that article follow.

. . . The primary advantage of lifo is that in today's inflationary environment lifo defers (not avoids) income taxes by reducing income. The improved cash flow, then, can be profitably invested or used to reduce borrowings. . . .

In addition to deferring income taxes, though, lifo has a great deal of theoretical justification. By matching current costs against current sales, lifo produces a truer picture of income; that is, the quality of income produced by the use of lifo is higher because it more nearly approximates disposable income....

Even though the primary advantage of lifo—reduced tax payments—is a function of lower income, the negative earnings impact ironically continues to cloud corporate managers' decisions about the adoption of lifo. Managers fear that lower reported earnings will [have unfavorable effects on the stock price, executive compensation contracts, and credit ratings. However,] there is little evidence to suggest that stock price is adversely affected by lifo adoption. Furthermore, [lifo should have no effect on executive compensation contracts or credit ratings.]

The Internal Revenue Code...and Treasury Regulations...[mandate] that taxpayers who avail themselves of the federal income tax benefits of the lifo method also must use lifo "...for credit purposes or for purposes of reports to shareholders, partners, or other proprietors, or to beneficiaries...." Thus, the lifo conformity requirement is the culprit behind the negative earnings impact issue. However, regulations adopted in January, 1981, although not going to the extent of allowing the use of lifo in tax returns and a non-lifo method elsewhere, did relax the conformity requirement significantly, such that it is now possible to present non-lifo information very favorably in lifo-based reports....

...[The] non-lifo data may be presented in the notes to the financial statements as in the 1981 Merck & Co. Inc. Annual Report: "...Lifo had the effect of reducing 1981 net income by $21,108,000 ($.28 per share)...with a positive increase to cash flow of $19,500,000...as a result of decreased U.S. taxes."

...Another concern about lifo commonly expressed by corporate managers is misstatement of the inventories on the lifo balance sheet. Particularly over a period of rapidly rising inventory quantities and prices, the use of lifo can lead to a valuation of inventories that is significantly less than current replacement cost. However, this misstatement can be mitigated by presenting inventories valued on a non-lifo basis and deducting the lifo valuation [allowance to reduce the balance sheet inventory to the lifo amount, as follows:]

Inventory	XXX
Less reduction to lifo cost	XXX
Total	XXX

Source: Clayton T. Rumble, "So You Still Have Not Adopted Lifo," *Management Accounting* (October, 1983), pp. 59–67.

Use of the Average Cost Method. The average cost method of inventory costing is, in a sense, a compromise between fifo and lifo. The effect of price trends is averaged, both in the determination of gross profit and in the determination of inventory cost. For any given series of acquisitions, the average cost will be the same, regardless of the direction of price trends. For example, a complete reversal of the sequence of unit costs presented in the illustration on page 253 would not affect the reported gross profit or the inventory cost. The time required to assemble the data is likely to be greater for the average cost method than for the other two methods. The additional expense incurred could be large if there are many purchases of a wide variety of merchandise items.

Selection of an Inventory Costing Method. The foregoing comparisons show the importance attached to the selection of the inventory costing method. It is not unusual for manufacturing enterprises to apply one method to a particular class of inventory, such as merchandise ready for sale, and a different method to another class, such as raw materials purchased. The method(s) used may be changed for a valid reason. The effect of any change in method and the reason for the change should be fully disclosed in the financial statements for the fiscal period in which the change occurred.

VALUATION OF INVENTORY AT OTHER THAN COST

As discussed in the preceding section, cost is the primary basis for the valuation of inventories. Under certain circumstances, however, inventory is valued at other than cost. Two such circumstances arise when (1) the cost of replacing items in inventory is below recorded cost, and (2) the inventory is not salable at normal sales prices because of imperfections, shop wear, style changes, or other causes.

Valuation at Lower of Cost or Market

If the market price of an item in inventory is lower than its cost, the **lower of cost or market** method is used to value inventory. It should be noted that regardless of the method used (cost, or lower of cost or market), it is first necessary to determine the cost of the inventory. "Market," as used in the phrase lower of cost or market, is interpreted to mean the cost to replace the merchandise on the inventory date, based on quantities typically purchased from the usual source of supply. In the discussion that follows, the salability of the merchandise at normal sales prices will be assumed. Articles that have to be sold at a price below their cost would be valued at their net realizable value, as described on page 260.

If the replacement price of an item in the inventory is lower than its cost, the use of the lower of cost or market method provides two advantages: (1) the gross profit (and net income) are reduced for the period in which the decline occurred and (2) an approximately normal gross profit is realized during the period in which the item is sold. To illustrate, assume that merchandise with a unit cost of $70 has sold at $100 during the period, yielding a gross profit of $30 a unit, or 30% of sales. Assume also that at the end of the year, there is a single unit of the commodity in the inventory and that its replacement price has declined to $63. Under such circumstances it would be reasonable to expect that the selling price would also decline, if indeed it had not already done so. Assuming a reduction in selling price to $90, the gross profit based on replacement cost of $63 would be $27, which is also 30% of the selling price. Accordingly, valuation of the unit in the inventory at $63 reduces gross profit of the past period by $7 and permits a normal gross profit of $27 to be realized on its sale in the following period. If the unit had been valued at its original cost of $70, the gross profit determined for the past year would have been $7 greater, and the gross profit attributable to the sale of the item in the following period would have been $7 less.

It would be possible to apply the lower of cost or market basis (1) to each item in the inventory, (2) to major classes or categories, or (3) to the inventory as a whole. The first procedure is the one usually followed in practice. To illustrate the application of the lower of cost or market to individual items, assume that there are 400 identical units of Commodity A in the inventory, each acquired at a unit cost of $10.25. If at the inventory date the commodity would cost $10.50 to replace, the cost price of $10.25 would be multiplied by 400 to determine the inventory value. On the other hand, if the commodity could be replaced at $9.50 a unit, the replacement price of $9.50 would be used for valuation purposes. The following tabulation illustrates one of the forms that may be followed in assembling inventory data.

Description	Quantity	Unit Cost Price	Unit Market Price	Total Cost	Total Lower of C or M
Commodity A	400	$10.25	$ 9.50	$ 4,100	$ 3,800
Commodity B	120	22.50	24.10	2,700	2,700
Commodity C	600	8.00	7.75	4,800	4,650
Commodity D	280	14.00	14.00	3,920	3,920
Total				$15,520	$15,070

Determination of Inventory at Lower of Cost or Market

Although it is not essential to accumulate the data for total cost, as in the illustration, it permits the measurement of the reduction in inventory value as a result of a decline in market prices. When the amount of the market decline is known ($15,520−$15,070, or $450), it may be reported as a separate item on the income statement. Otherwise, the market decline will be included in the amount reported as the cost of merchandise sold and will reduce gross profit by a corresponding amount. In any event, the amount reported as net income will not be affected. It will be the same, regardless of whether the amount of the market decline is determined and separately stated.

Valuation at Net Realizable Value

Obsolete, spoiled, or damaged merchandise and other merchandise that can be sold only at prices below cost should be valued at **net realizable value.** For this purpose, net realizable value is the estimated selling price less any direct cost of disposition, such as sales commissions. To illustrate, assume that damaged merchandise that had a cost of $1,000 can be sold for only $800, and direct selling expenses are estimated at $150. This inventory would be valued at $650 ($800−$150), which is its net realizable value.

ACCOUNTING FOR AND REPORTING INVENTORY UNDER A PERPETUAL SYSTEM

The use of a perpetual inventory system for merchandise provides the most effective means of control over this important asset. Although it is possible to maintain a perpetual inventory in memorandum records only or to limit the data to quantities, a complete set of records integrated with the general ledger is preferable. With the widespread use of computers, integrated perpetual inventory systems are being used by more and more companies.

Under the periodic inventory system, as described in earlier chapters, the merchandise inventory account at the beginning of an accounting period reflects the merchandise on hand on that date. Purchases of merchandise are recorded in the purchases account, and sales of merchandise are recorded in the sales account. The cost of the merchandise sold is not determined for each sale. Instead, at the end of an accounting period, when a physical inventory is taken, the beginning inventory is removed from the merchandise inventory account and is replaced by the ending inventory. This ending balance of merchandise inventory is reported on the balance sheet. The cost of merchandise sold is then determined, and this amount is reported on the income statement.

Under the perpetual inventory system, all merchandise increases and decreases are recorded in a manner somewhat similar to the recording of increases and decreases in cash. The merchandise inventory account at the beginning of an accounting period reflects the merchandise on hand on that date. Sales are recorded in the sales account and, on the date of each sale, the cost of the merchandise sold is recorded by debiting Cost of Merchandise Sold and crediting Merchandise Inventory. Thus, in the perpetual system, the merchandise inventory account continuously (perpetually) discloses the balance of merchandise on hand. At the end of the period, the balance in the merchandise inventory account is reported on the balance sheet, and the balance in the cost of merchandise sold account is reported on the income statement.

The accounting for and reporting of merchandise inventory transactions under the periodic and perpetual systems are compared and illustrated as follows:

Comparison of Periodic and Perpetual Systems

Inventory, Purchases, and Sales Data

January	1	Merchandise inventory (beginning)	$52,500
	1–31	Purchases (on account)	26,200
	1–31	Sales (on account)—selling price	49,750
		Sales—cost price	28,000
	31	Merchandise inventory (ending)	50,700

Periodic			Perpetual		
January 1 Merchandise Inventory					
Merchandise inventory account reflects inventory on hand, $52,500.			Merchandise inventory account reflects inventory on hand, $52,500.		
Entries to Record Purchases, January 1–31					
Purchases	26,200		Merchandise Inventory	26,200	
Accounts Payable		26,200	Accounts Payable		26,200
Entries to Record Sales, January 1–31					
Accounts Receivable	49,750		Accounts Receivable	49,750	
Sales		49,750	Sales		49,750
			Cost of Merchandise Sold	28,000	
			Merchandise Inventory		28,000
January 31 Merchandise Inventory					
Merchandise inventory account will reflect the inventory on hand at January 31, $50,700, after the accounts are closed.			Merchandise inventory account perpetually discloses the inventory on hand, which at January 31 is $50,700.		

Periodic			Perpetual	
Reporting Cost of Merchandise Sold in January on Income Statement				
Cost of merchandise sold:			Cost of merchandise sold........	$28,000
Jan. 1 inventory	$52,500			
January purchases....	26,200			
Merchandise available for sale...........	$78,700			
Less Jan. 31 inventory .	50,700			
Cost of merchandise sold..............		$28,000		
Reporting Merchandise Inventory, January 31, on Balance Sheet				
Merchandise inventory		$50,700	Merchandise inventory	$50,700

INVENTORY COSTING METHODS UNDER A PERPETUAL SYSTEM

Unlike cash, merchandise is a mixed mass of goods. Details of the cost of each type of merchandise purchased and sold, together with such related transactions as returns and allowances, could be maintained in a subsidiary **inventory ledger,** with a separate account for each type. Whether this ledger is computerized or maintained manually, it is customary to use one of the three costing methods—first-in, first out; last-in, first-out; or average.

In the following paragraphs, the fifo and lifo methods in a perpetual system are discussed and illustrated. The average cost method is briefly discussed also, but an illustration is reserved for advanced texts.

The basis for the fifo and lifo illustrations is the following data for merchandise identified as Commodity 127B:

			Units	*Cost*
Jan.	1	Inventory..............................	10	$20
	4	Sale...................................	7	
	10	Purchase	8	21
	22	Sale...................................	4	
	28	Sale...................................	2	
	30	Purchase	10	22

First-In, First-Out Method

To illustrate the first-in, first-out method of cost flow in a perpetual inventory system, the inventory ledger account for Commodity 127B is shown at the top of page 263. The number of units on hand after each transaction, together with total costs and unit costs, appears in the inventory section of the account.

Note that after the 7 units of the commodity were sold on January 4, there was a remaining inventory of 3 units at $20 each. The 8 units purchased on January 10 were acquired at a unit cost of $21, instead of $20, and hence could not be combined with the 3 units. The inventory after the January 10 purchase is therefore reported on two lines, 3 units at $20 each and 8 units at $21 each. Next, it should be noted that the $81 cost of the 4 units sold on

January 22 is composed of the remaining 3 units at $20 each and 1 unit at $21. At this point, 7 units remain in inventory at a cost of $21 per unit. The remainder of the illustration is explained in a similar manner.

Commodity 127B

	Purchases			Cost of Merchandise Sold			Inventory		
Date	Quantity	Unit Cost	Total Cost	Quantity	Unit Cost	Total Cost	Quantity	Unit Cost	Total Cost
Jan. 1							10	20	200
4				7	20	140	3	20	60
10	8	21	168				3 8	20 21	60 168
22				3 1	20 21	60 21	7	21	147
28				2	21	42	5	21	105
30	10	22	220				5 10	21 22	105 220

Perpetual Inventory Account (FIFO)

Last-In, First-Out Method

When the last-in, first-out method is used in a perpetual inventory system, the cost of the units sold is the cost of the most recent purchases. To illustrate, the ledger account for Commodity 127B, prepared on a lifo basis, is as follows:

Commodity 127B

	Purchases			Cost of Merchandise Sold			Inventory		
Date	Quantity	Unit Cost	Total Cost	Quantity	Unit Cost	Total Cost	Quantity	Unit Cost	Total Cost
Jan. 1							10	20	200
4				7	20	140	3	20	60
10	8	21	168				3 8	20 21	60 168
22				4	21	84	3 4	20 21	60 84
28				2	21	42	3 2	20 21	60 42
30	10	22	220				3 2 10	20 21 22	60 42 220

Perpetual Inventory Account (LIFO)

A comparison of the ledger accounts for the fifo perpetual system and the lifo perpetual system indicates that the accounts are the same through the January 10 purchase. Using the lifo perpetual system, however, the cost of the 4 units sold on January 22 is the cost of the units from the January 10 purchase ($21 per unit). The cost of the 7 units in inventory after the sale on January 22 is the cost of the 3 units remaining from the beginning inventory and the cost of the 4 units remaining from the January 10 purchase. The remainder of the lifo illustration is explained in a similar manner.

Average Cost Method

When the average cost method is used in a perpetual inventory system, an average unit cost for each type of commodity is computed each time a purchase is made, rather than at the end of the period. This unit cost is then used to determine the cost of each sale, until another purchase is made and a new average is computed. This averaging technique is called a **moving average.**

INTERNAL CONTROL AND PERPETUAL INVENTORY SYSTEMS

The control feature is the most important advantage of the perpetual system. The inventory of each type of merchandise is always readily available in the subsidiary ledger. A physical count of any type of merchandise can be made at any time and compared with the balance of the subsidiary account to determine the existence and seriousness of any shortages. When a shortage is discovered, an entry is made debiting Inventory Shortages and crediting Merchandise Inventory for the cost. If the balance of the inventory shortages account at the end of a fiscal period is relatively small, it may be included in miscellaneous general expense on the income statement. Otherwise it may be separately reported in the general expense section.

In addition to the usefulness of the perpetual inventory system in the preparation of interim statements, the subsidiary ledger can be an aid in maintaining inventory quantities at an optimum level. Frequent comparisons of balances with predetermined maximum and minimum levels facilitate both (1) the timely reordering of merchandise to avoid the loss of sales and (2) the avoidance of excess inventory.

AUTOMATED PERPETUAL INVENTORY RECORDS

A perpetual inventory system may be maintained using manually kept records. However, such a system is often too costly and too time consuming for enterprises with a large number of inventory items and/or with many purchase and sales transactions. In such cases, because of the mass of data to be processed, the frequently recurring and routine nature of the processing, and the importance of speed and accuracy, the record keeping is often computerized. A computerized inventory system operates with little human intervention.

One use of computers in maintaining perpetual inventory records for retail stores is described in the following outline:

1. The quantity of inventory for each commodity, along with its color, unit size or other descriptive data, and any other information desired, is stored in the computer.
2. Each time a commodity is purchased, or is returned by a customer, the data are recorded and processed by the computer, so that the inventory records are updated.
3. Each time a commodity is sold, a salesclerk passes an electronic wand over the price tag attached to the merchandise. The electronic wand "reads" the magnetic code on the price tag. The information provided in the magnetic code is used by the computer to update the inventory records.
4. Data from a physical inventory count are periodically entered into the computer. These data are compared with the current balances and a listing of the overages and shortages is printed. The appropriate commodity balances are adjusted to the quantities determined by the physical count.

By entering additional data, the system described can be extended to aid in maintaining inventory quantities at optimum levels. For example, data on the most economical quantity to be purchased in a single order and the minimum quantity to be maintained for each commodity can be entered into the computer. The equipment is then programmed to compare these data with data on actual inventory and to start the purchasing activity by preparing purchase orders.

The system can also be extended to aid in processing the related accounting transactions. For example, as cash sales are entered on an electronic cash register, the sales data can be accumulated and used for the appropriate accounting entries. These entries would include a debit to Cash and a credit to Sales as well as a debit to Cost of Merchandise Sold and a credit to Merchandise Inventory.

Computer Finds a Role In Buying and Selling

A growing number of companies are buying and selling merchandise by computer. The effect of the computer on some of these companies is described in the following excerpts from an article in the *Wall Street Journal:*

. . . Philip Cavavetta buys merchandise for his Boston-area drugstores from two wholesalers. One of them, McKesson, is getting more of his business these days. Why? "Their computer system is so good," he says.

Not long ago, salesmen from McKesson, as those from other wholesalers, would drop by Mr. Cavavetta's Econo Drug Marts to take orders for cough syrup, aspirin, penicillin and Valium. When the store ran short between salesmen's visits, clerks would read new orders over the phone to tape recorders at McKesson's warehouse.

Today, a clerk in Mr. Cavavetta's stores walks the aisles once a week with a McKesson-supplied computer in his palm. If the store is low on, say, bottles of cough syrup, the clerk waves a scanner over a McKesson-provided label stuck to the shelf. The computer takes note, and, when the clerk is finished, transmits the order to McKesson.

At first glance, it appears that McKesson has simply automated a costly, labor-intensive chore. But far more has happened: McKesson's computers not only dispatch the orders to a warehouse but also print price stickers that add in the precise profit margin that Mr. Cavavetta has selected and tell him monthly how profitable each of his departments is. . . .

Not surprisingly, some competitors matched McKesson's computer systems. In what once was a fragmented market, the top four distributors have increased their combined market share substantially to 60%, largely by squeezing out or acquiring small distributors who couldn't keep pace. Big distributors now compete for new accounts by offering increasingly sophisticated computer services. The Foxmeyer unit of National Intergroup Inc., for instance, is about to offer pharmacists personal-computer software that will draw pictures telling them how to rearrange shelves to maximize profits. . . .

In San Francisco, Levi Strauss & Co. soon will begin telling retailers, among other things, how their sales of popular Levi products compare with those of other stores in the same area. "We hope to give small retailers something to help them manage their business," says R. W. Eaton, Levi's vice president for corporate information systems. . . .

GM and Ford Motor Co. have indicated that in the future they will do business only with suppliers who can receive and send messages electronically. The auto companies say they need to cut inventories by arranging for parts to arrive just before they are needed on the assembly line, a cost-saving trick borrowed from the Japanese that requires quick, frequent communication with suppliers. Toward that end, Ford is electronically sending more than 700 suppliers of its Wixom, Mich., assembly plant daily updates on the parts the plants need. Previously, the information was available only once a week.

The auto industry hasn't enough experience to show how significantly inventories can be reduced, but others do. Levi Strauss, for one, says conversing electronically with denim suppliers has helped the company reduce inventories of uncut fabric to three days' worth or less; in the past, the company had enough fabric on hand to make a month's worth of blue jeans. Denim mills tell Levi not only how many rolls of denim are arriving on the next truck but also what shade of fabric is placed where on that truck. "This translated last year into the largest drop in days of inventory we've ever had in our history," says Thomas Tusher, Levi's executive vice president.

Source: David Wessel, "Computer Finds a Role in Buying and Selling, Reshaping Businesses," *Wall Street Journal,* March 17, 1987.

PRESENTATION OF MERCHANDISE INVENTORY ON THE BALANCE SHEET

Merchandise inventory is usually presented on the balance sheet immediately following receivables. Both the method of determining the cost of the inventory (fifo, lifo, or average) and the method of valuing the inventory (cost, or lower of cost or market) should be shown. Both are important to the reader. The details may be disclosed by a parenthetical notation or a footnote. The use of a parenthetical notation is illustrated by the following partial balance sheet:

Merchandise Inventory on Balance Sheet

Afro-Arts Company
Balance Sheet
December 31, 1989

Assets		
Current assets:		
Cash		$ 19,400
Accounts receivable	$80,000	
Less allowance for doubtful accounts	3,000	77,000
Merchandise inventory—at lower of cost (first-in, first-out method) or market		216,300

It is not unusual for large enterprises with diversified activities to use different costing methods for different segments of their inventories. The following note taken from the 1986 financial statements of General Motors Corporation is illustrative:

> Inventories are stated generally at cost, which is not in excess of market. The cost of substantially all domestic inventories other than the inventories of GM Hughes Electronics Corporation (GMHE) is determined by the last-in, first-out (lifo) method. . . . The cost of inventories outside the United States and of the inventories of GMHE is determined generally by fifo or average cost methods.

ESTIMATING INVENTORY COST

In practice, an inventory amount may be needed in order to prepare an income statement when it is impractical or impossible to take a physical inventory or to maintain perpetual inventory records. For example, taking a physical inventory each month may be too costly, even though monthly income statements are desired. Taking a physical inventory may be impossible when a catastrophe, such as a fire, has destroyed the inventory. In such cases, the inventory cost might be estimated for use in preparing the income statement. Two commonly used methods of estimating inventory cost are (1) the retail method and (2) the gross profit method.

Retail Method of Inventory Costing

The **retail inventory method** of inventory costing is widely used by retail businesses, particularly department stores. It is based on the relationship of the cost of merchandise available for sale to the retail price of the same merchandise. The retail prices of all merchandise acquired are accumulated in supplementary records, and the inventory at retail is determined by deducting sales for the period from the retail price of the goods that were available for sale during the period. The inventory at retail is then converted to cost on the basis of the ratio of cost to selling (retail) price for the merchandise available for sale. Determination of inventory by the retail method is illustrated as follows:

Determination of Inventory By Retail Method

	Cost	*Retail*
Merchandise inventory, January 1	$19,400	$ 36,000
Purchases in January (net)	42,600	64,000
Merchandise available for sale	$62,000	$100,000
Ratio of cost to retail price: $\frac{\$62,000}{\$100,000} = 62\%$		
Sales for January (net)		70,000
Merchandise inventory, January 31, at retail		$ 30,000
Merchandise inventory, January 31, at estimated cost ($30,000 × 62%)		$ 18,600

There is an inherent assumption in the retail method of inventory costing that the composition or "mix" of the commodities in the ending inventory, in terms of percent of cost to selling price, is comparable to the entire stock of merchandise available for sale. In the illustration, for example, it is unlikely that the retail price of every item was composed of exactly 62% cost and

38% gross profit. It is assumed, however, that the weighted average of the cost percentages of the merchandise in the inventory ($30,000) is the same as in the merchandise available for sale ($100,000). When the inventory is made up of different classes of merchandise with very different gross profit rates, the cost percentages and the inventory should be developed separately for each class.

One of the major advantages of the retail method is that it provides inventory figures for use in preparing interim statements. Department stores and similar merchandisers usually determine gross profit and operating income each month but take a physical inventory only once a year. In addition to facilitating frequent income determinations, a comparison of the computed ending inventory with the physical ending inventory, both at retail prices, will help identify inventory shortages resulting from shoplifting and other causes. The appropriate corrective measures can then be taken.

The retail method can also be used in conjunction with the periodic system when a physical inventory is taken at the end of the year. In such a case, the items counted are recorded on the inventory sheets at their selling prices instead of their cost prices. The physical inventory at selling price is then converted to cost by applying the ratio of cost to selling (retail) price for the merchandise available for sale. To illustrate, assume that the data presented in the example above are for an entire fiscal year rather than for the first month of the year only. If the physical inventory taken on December 31 totaled $29,000, priced at retail, it would be this amount rather than the $30,000 that would be converted to cost. Accordingly, the inventory at cost would be $17,980 ($29,000 × 62%) instead of $18,600 ($30,000 × 62%). The $17,980 is generally accepted for use on the year-end financial statements and for income tax purposes.

Know

Gross Profit Method of Estimating Inventories

The **gross profit method** uses an estimate of the gross profit realized during the period to estimate the inventory at the end of the period. By using the rate of gross profit, the dollar amount of sales for a period can be divided into its two components: (1) gross profit and (2) cost of merchandise sold. The latter may then be deducted from the cost of merchandise available for sale to yield the estimated inventory of merchandise on hand.

always a % of sales

To illustrate this method, assume that the inventory on January 1 is $57,000, that net purchases during the month are $180,000, that net sales during the month are $250,000, and finally that gross profit is *estimated* to be 30% of net sales. The inventory on January 31 may be estimated as follows:

Estimate of Inventory By Gross Profit Method

Merchandise inventory, January 1		$ 57,000
Purchases in January (net)		180,000
Merchandise available for sale		$237,000
Sales in January (net)	$250,000	
Less estimated gross profit ($250,000 × 30%)	75,000	
Estimated cost of merchandise sold		175,000
Estimated merchandise inventory, January 31		$ 62,000

The estimate of the rate of gross profit is ordinarily based on the actual rate for the preceding year, adjusted for any changes made in the cost and sales prices during the current period. Inventories estimated in this manner are useful in preparing interim statements. The method may also be used in establishing an estimate of the cost of merchandise destroyed by fire or other disaster.

INVENTORIES OF MANUFACTURING ENTERPRISES

In the preceding discussion, the principles and procedures for inventory were presented in the context of a merchandising enterprise. These same principles and procedures, with some modification, also apply to inventories of a manufacturing enterprise. Although attention is directed to these basic principles and procedures in the following paragraphs, it should be noted that they are discussed in more detail in managerial accounting texts.

Manufacturing businesses maintain three inventory accounts instead of a single merchandise inventory account. Separate accounts are maintained for (1) goods in the state in which they are to be sold, (2) goods in the process of manufacture, and (3) goods in the state in which they were acquired. These inventories are called respectively **finished goods, work in process,** and **materials.** The balances in the inventory accounts may be presented in the balance sheet in the following manner:

Inventories:		
Finished goods	$300,000	
Work in process	55,000	
Materials	123,000	$478,000

The finished goods inventory and work in process inventory are composed of three separate categories of manufacturing costs: direct materials, direct labor, and factory overhead. **Direct materials** represent the delivered cost of the materials that enter directly into the finished product. **Direct labor** represents the wages of the factory workers who change the materials into a finished product. **Factory overhead** includes all of the remaining costs of operating the factory, such as wages for factory supervision, supplies used in the factory but not entering directly into the finished product, and taxes, insurance, depreciation, and maintenance related to factory plant and equipment.

LONG-TERM CONSTRUCTION CONTRACTS

Enterprises engaged in large construction projects may devote several years to the completion of a particular contract or project. In such cases, the costs incurred in construction may be accumulated in a work in process account, called Construction in Progress, until the project is completed. After the project is completed and accepted by the customer, the full revenue and the related net income are recognized. To illustrate, assume that a contractor engages in a project that will require three years to complete, for a contract price of $50,000,000. If the total costs accumulated during construction total $44,000,000, the revenue of $50,000,000 and the net income of $6,000,000 would be reported in the third year.

Whenever the total cost of a long-term contract and the extent of the project's progress can be reasonably estimated, it is preferable to consider the revenue as being realized over the entire life of the contract.[1] The amount of revenue to be recognized in any particular period is then determined on the basis of the estimated percentage of the contract that has been completed during the period. The estimated percentage of completion can be developed by comparing the incurred costs with the most recent estimates of total costs or by estimates by engineers, architects, or other qualified personnel of the progress of the work performed. To continue with the illustration, assume that by the end of the first fiscal year the contract is estimated to be one-fourth completed and the costs incurred during the year were $11,200,000. According to the **percentage-of-completion method,** the revenue to be recognized and the income for the year would be determined as follows:

Revenue ($50,000,000 × 25%)	$12,500,000
Costs incurred..........................	11,200,000
Income (Year 1)	$ 1,300,000

The costs actually incurred during the year (rather than one fourth of the original cost estimate of $44,000,000, or $11,000,000) are deducted from the revenue recognized.

The 1987 edition of *Accounting Trends & Techniques* indicated that 89% of the surveyed companies with long-term contracts used the percentage-of-completion method. Although the use of this method involves some subjectivity, and hence possible error, in the determination of the amount of reported revenue, the financial statements may be more informative and more useful than they would be if none of the revenue was recognized until completion of the contract.

The method used to recognize revenue on a long-term contract should be noted in the financial statements, as indicated in the following excerpt taken from a note to the financial statements of Martin Marietta Corporation:

> Revenue Recognition. Sales under long-term contracts generally are recognized under the percentage-of-completion method, and include a proportion of the earnings expected to be realized on the contract.... Other sales are recorded upon shipment of products or performance of services.

Chapter Review

KEY POINTS

1. Importance of Inventories.

Inventory determination plays an important role in matching expired costs with revenues of the period. An error in the determination of the inventory amount at the end of the period will cause an equal misstatement of gross

[1] *Accounting Research and Terminology Bulletins—Final Edition,* "No. 45, Long-term Construction-type Contracts" (New York: American Institute of Certified Public Accountants, 1961), par. 15.

profit and net income. The amount reported for both assets and owner's equity in the balance sheet will also be incorrect by the same amount. In addition, because the inventory at the end of one period becomes the inventory for the beginning of the following period, an error in inventory at the end of the period will cause the net income of the following period to be misstated. The effect of the two misstatements in income will be equal and in opposite directions. Therefore, the effect on net income of an incorrectly stated inventory is limited to the period of the error and the following period. At the end of this following period, assuming no additional errors, both assets and owner's equity will be correctly stated.

2. Inventory Systems.
There are two principal systems of inventory accounting—periodic and perpetual. In the periodic system, only the revenue from sales is recorded at the time a sale is made. No entry is made until the end of the period to record the cost of merchandise sold. In the perpetual inventory system, sales and cost of merchandise sold are recorded at the time each sale is made. In this way, the accounting records continuously disclose the amount of inventory on hand. In a perpetual inventory system, a subsidiary ledger is maintained with a separate account for each type of merchandise.

3. Determining Actual Quantities in the Inventory.
All the merchandise owned by a business on the inventory date, and only such merchandise, should be included in the inventory. The first step in "taking" an inventory is to count the merchandise on hand. To this count is added merchandise in transit that is owned. Therefore, it is normally necessary to examine purchases and sales invoices of the last few days of the accounting period and the first few days of the following period to determine who has legal title to merchandise in transit on the inventory date.

4. Determining the Cost of Inventory.
The cost of merchandise inventory is made up of the purchase price and all expenditures incurred in acquiring such merchandise, including transportation, customs duties, and insurance against losses in transit.

5. Inventory Costing Methods Under a Periodic System.
In determining the cost of merchandise sold and the inventory cost at the end of the period, it is customary to use an assumption as to the flow of costs of merchandise through an enterprise. The three most common assumptions of determining the cost of merchandise sold are as follows: first-in, first-out (fifo), last-in, first-out (lifo), and average cost. The fifo method of costing inventory is based on the assumption that costs should be charged against revenue in the order in which they were incurred. The lifo method is based on the assumption that the most recent costs incurred should be charged against revenues. The average cost method, sometimes called the weighted average method, is based on the assumption that costs should be charged against revenue according to the weighted average unit costs of the goods sold.

If the cost of units and the prices at which they are sold remain stable, all three inventory costing methods will yield the same results. However, during a period of rising prices, the use of the fifo method will result in a higher amount of gross profit than the other two methods. In a period of declining prices, the use of the lifo method will result in a higher amount of gross profit than the other two methods. The average cost method of inventory costing is often viewed as a compromise between the fifo and lifo methods.

6. Valuation of Inventory at Other than Cost.
If the market price of an item of inventory is lower than its cost, the lower of cost or market method is used to value inventory. Market, as used in the phrase *lower of cost or market,* is interpreted to mean the cost to replace the merchandise on the inventory date. It is possible to apply the lower of cost or market basis to each item in the inventory, to major classes or categories, or to the inventory as a whole.

Merchandise that can be sold only at prices below cost should be valued at net realizable value, which is the estimated selling price less any direct cost of disposition.

7. Accounting for and Reporting Inventory Under a Perpetual System.
The use of a perpetual inventory system for merchandise provides the most effective means of control over this important asset. Under this system, sales are recorded in the sales account and, on the date of each sale, the cost of the merchandise sold is recorded by debiting Cost of Merchandise Sold and crediting Merchandise Inventory.

8. Inventory Costing Methods Under a Perpetual System.
In a perpetual system, the details of merchandise increases and decreases are maintained in a subsidiary ledger, called an inventory ledger, with a separate account for each type of merchandise. As in a periodic system, it is customary to use one of the three costing methods — fifo, lifo, or average.

9. Internal Control and Perpetual Inventory Systems.
In a perpetual system, the existence of shortages can be determined by taking a physical count of the merchandise and comparing the count with the balance of the subsidiary ledger. The timely reordering of merchandise and the avoidance of excess inventory can be accomplished by comparing the balance of the subsidiary ledger with predetermined maximum and minimum levels of inventory.

10. Automated Perpetual Inventory Records.
The basic inventory records in a perpetual inventory system may be maintained by using a computer. The system can be extended to aid in maintaining inventory quantities at optimum levels and in processing the inventory-related accounting transactions.

11. Presentation of Merchandise Inventory on the Balance Sheet.
Merchandise inventory is usually presented in the current assets section of the balance sheet immediately following receivables. Both the method of determining the cost of the inventory (lifo, fifo, or average) and the method of valuing the inventory (cost, or lower of cost or market) should be shown.

12. Estimating Inventory Cost.
When it is impractical or impossible to take a physical inventory or to maintain perpetual inventory records, two commonly used methods of estimating inventory may be used: (1) the retail method, and (2) the gross profit method. The retail method of inventory estimation is based on the relationship of the cost of merchandise available for sale to the retail price of the same merchandise. The inventory at retail is determined by deducting sales for the period from the retail price of the goods that were available for sale during the period. The inventory at retail is then converted to cost on the basis of the ratio of cost to selling (retail) price for the merchandise available for sale.

The gross profit method of estimating inventory is based upon the historical relationship of the gross profit to the dollar amount of sales. The rate of gross profit is multiplied by the current period sales in order to estimate the gross profit for the period. To determine the estimate of the cost of merchandise sold, the estimated gross profit is then subtracted from the sales of the period. The estimated cost of merchandise sold can then be subtracted from the merchandise available for sale for the period to determine an estimate of the ending inventory.

13. Inventories of Manufacturing Enterprises.
Manufacturing enterprises maintain three separate inventory accounts for (1) goods in the state in which they are to be sold (finished goods), (2) goods in the process of manufacture (work in process), and (3) goods in the state in which they were acquired (materials). The finished goods inventory and work in process inventory are composed of three separate manufacturing costs: direct materials, direct labor, and factory overhead.

14. Long-Term Construction Contracts.
Enterprises engaged in large, long-term construction projects may determine revenue and income by the percentage-of-completion method. Under this method, the revenue to be recognized each year of the life of the contract is based on the estimated percentage of the contract that has been completed during each year.

KEY TERMS

merchandise inventory 247
periodic inventory system 250
physical inventory 250
perpetual inventory system 250
first-in, first-out (fifo) method 253
last-in, first-out (lifo) method 254
average cost method 255
lower of cost or market 259
net realizable value 260
retail inventory method 267
gross profit method 268
finished goods 269
work in process 269
materials 269
direct materials 269
direct labor 269
factory overhead 269
percentage-of-completion method 270

SELF-EXAMINATION QUESTIONS

(Answers at End of Chapter)

1. If the merchandise inventory at the end of the year is overstated by $7,500, the error will cause an:
   A. overstatement of cost of merchandise sold for the year by $7,500
   B. understatement of gross profit for the year by $7,500
   C. overstatement of net income for the year by $7,500
   D. understatement of net income for the year by $7,500

2. The inventory system employing accounting records that continuously disclose the amount of inventory is called:
   A. periodic
   B. perpetual
   C. physical
   D. retail

3. The inventory costing method that is based on the assumption that costs should be charged against revenue in the order in which they were incurred is:
   A. fifo C. average cost
   B. lifo D. perpetual inventory

4. The following units of a particular commodity were available for sale during the period:

Beginning inventory	40 units at $20
First purchase	50 units at $21
Second purchase	50 units at $22
Third purchase	50 units at $23

   What is the unit cost of the 35 units on hand at the end of the period as determined under the periodic system by the fifo costing method?
   A. $20 C. $22
   B. $21 D. $23

5. If merchandise inventory is being valued at cost and the price level is steadily rising, the method of costing that will yield the highest net income is:
   A. lifo C. average
   B. fifo D. periodic

ILLUSTRATIVE PROBLEM

Stewart Inc.'s beginning inventory and purchases during the fiscal year ended March 31, 1989, were as follows:

		Units	Unit Cost	Total Cost
April 1, 1989	Inventory	1,000	$50.00	$ 50,000
April 10, 1989	Purchase	1,200	52.50	63,000
May 30, 1989	Purchase	800	55.00	44,000
August 26, 1989	Purchase	2,000	56.00	112,000
October 15, 1989	Purchase	1,500	57.00	85,500
December 31, 1989	Purchase	700	58.00	40,600
January 18, 1990	Purchase	1,350	60.00	81,000
March 21, 1990	Purchase	450	62.00	27,900
Total		9,000		$504,000

Stewart Inc. uses the periodic inventory system, and there are 3,200 units of inventory on hand on March 31, 1990.

Instructions:

1. Determine the cost of inventory on March 31, 1990, under each of the following inventory costing methods:
   a. First-in, first-out
   b. Last-in, first-out
   c. Average cost

2. Assume that during the fiscal year ended March 31, 1990, sales of $536,000 were made at an estimated gross profit rate of 40%. Estimate the ending inventory at March 31, 1990, using the gross profit method.

SOLUTION

(1)

(a) First-in, first-out method:

450 units @ $62	$ 27,900
1,350 units @ $60	81,000
700 units @ $58	40,600
700 units @ $57	39,900
3,200 units	$189,400

(b) Last-in, first-out method:

1,000 units @ $50.00	$ 50,000
1,200 units @ $52.50	63,000
800 units @ $55.00	44,000
200 units @ $56.00	11,200
3,200 units	$168,200

(c) Average cost method:

Average cost per unit	$504,000 ÷ 9,000 units = $56	
Inventory, March 31	3,200 units at $56	$179,200

(2)

Merchandise inventory, April 1, 1989		$ 50,000
Purchases (net), April 1, 1989–March 31, 1990		454,000
Merchandise available for sale		$504,000
Sales (net), April 1, 1989–March 31, 1990	$536,000	
Less estimated gross profit ($536,000 × 40%)	214,400	
Estimated cost of merchandise sold		321,600
Estimated merchandise inventory, March 31, 1990		$182,400

Discussion Questions

7–1. The merchandise inventory at the end of the year was inadvertently overstated by $5,000. (a) Did the error cause an overstatement or an understatement of the gross profit for the year? (b) Which items on the balance sheet at the end of the year were overstated or understated as a result of the error?

7–2. The $5,000 inventory error in Question 7–1 was not discovered, and the inventory at the end of the following year was correctly stated. (a) Will the earlier error cause an overstatement or an understatement of the gross profit for the following year? (b) Which items on the balance sheet at the end of the following year will be overstated or understated as a result of the error in the earlier year?

7–3. (a) Differentiate between the periodic system and the perpetual system of inventory determination. (b) Which system is more costly to maintain?

7–4. If the perpetual inventory system is used, is it necessary to take a physical inventory? Discuss.

7–5. What is the meaning of the following terms: (a) physical inventory; (b) book inventory?

7–6. In which of the following types of businesses would a perpetual inventory system ordinarily be used: (a) retail hardware store, (b) retail yacht dealer, (c) grocery store, (d) retail sports car dealer, (e) retail drugstore?

7–7. When does title to merchandise pass from the seller to the buyer if the terms of shipment are (a) FOB shipping point; (b) FOB destination?

7–8. Which of the three methods of inventory costing—fifo, lifo, or average cost—is based on the assumption that costs should be charged against revenue in the reverse order in which they were incurred?

7–9. Do the terms *fifo* and *lifo* refer to techniques employed in determining quantities of the various classes of merchandise on hand? Explain.

7–10. Does the term *last-in* in the lifo method mean that the items in the inventory are assumed to be the most recent (last) acquisitions? Explain.

7–11. Under which method of cost flow are (a) the earliest costs assigned to inventory; (b) the most recent costs assigned to inventory; (c) average costs assigned to inventory?

7–12. The following units of a particular commodity were available for sale during the year:

Beginning inventory	10 units at $50
First purchase	15 units at $54
Second purchase	20 units at $65

The firm uses the periodic system, and there are 9 units of the commodity on hand at the end of the year. What is their unit cost according to (a) fifo, (b) lifo, (c) average cost?

7–13. If merchandise inventory is being valued at cost and the price level is steadily rising, which of the three methods of costing—fifo, lifo, or average cost—will yield (a) the highest inventory cost, (b) the lowest inventory cost, (c) the highest gross profit, (d) the lowest gross profit?

7–14. Which of the three methods of inventory costing—fifo, lifo, or average cost—will in general yield an inventory cost most nearly approximating current replacement cost?

7–15. In the phrase *lower of cost or market,* what is meant by "market"?

7–16. The cost of a particular inventory item is $125, the current replacement cost is $115, and the selling price is $180. At what amount should the item be included in the inventory according to the lower of cost or market basis?

7–17. Because of imperfections, an item of merchandise cannot be sold at its normal selling price. How should this item be valued for financial statement purposes?

7–18. An enterprise using a perpetual inventory system sells merchandise to a customer on account for $475; the cost of the merchandise was $300.
(a) What entries would be made on the general ledger accounts as a result of the transaction?
(b) What is the amount and direction of the net change in the amount of assets and owner's equity resulting from the transaction?

7–19. What are the three most important advantages of the perpetual inventory system over the periodic system?

7–20. An enterprise using the retail method of inventory costing determines that merchandise inventory at retail is $100,000. If the ratio of cost to retail price is 70%, what is the amount of inventory to be reported on the financial statements?

7–21. What uses can be made of the estimate of the cost of inventory determined by the gross profit method?

7–22. Name the three inventory accounts for a manufacturing business and describe what each balance represents at the end of an accounting period.

7–23. Name and describe the three categories of manufacturing costs included in the cost of finished goods and the cost of work in process.

7–24. What are the advantages and disadvantages of using the percentage-of-completion method for reporting income on long-term construction projects?

7–25. Real World Focus. The following footnote was taken from the 1986 financial statements of Teledyne Inc.:

> Inventories stated on the last-in, first-out basis were $187.1 million and $199.4 million less than their first-in, first-out values at December 31, 1986 and 1985, respectively. These first-in, first-out values do not differ materially from current cost.

Additional data are as follows:

Operating income for 1986	$238,300,000
Total lifo inventories, December 31, 1986	211,000,000

Based on the preceding data, determine (a) what the total inventories at December 31, 1986 would have been, using the fifo method, and (b) what the operating income for 1986 would have been if fifo had been used instead of lifo.

Exercises

7–26. Periodic inventory by three methods. The beginning inventory and the purchases of an item during the year were as follows:

Jan. 1	Inventory	15 units at $60
Feb. 12	Purchase	10 units at $62
June 24	Purchase	20 units at $65
Oct. 8	Purchase	15 units at $70

There are 20 units of the commodity in the physical inventory at December 31. The periodic system is used. Determine the inventory cost and the cost of merchandise sold by three methods, presenting your answers in the following form:

	Cost	
Inventory Method	Merchandise Inventory	Merchandise Sold
(1) First-in, first-out	$	$
(2) Last-in, first-out		
(3) Average cost		

7–27. Lower of cost or market inventory. On the basis of the following data, determine the value of the inventory at the lower of cost or market. Assemble the data in the form illustrated on page 260.

Commodity	Inventory Quantity	Unit Cost	Unit Market Price
12A	8	$340	$350
78G	17	110	105
33P	12	275	260
90R	35	60	65
45T	20	95	100

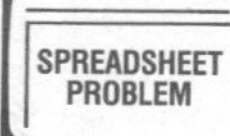

7–28. Perpetual inventory using fifo. Beginning inventory, purchases, and sales data for Commodity A12 are as follows:

Jan. 1.	Inventory	20 units at $45
4.	Sold	10 units
9.	Purchased	15 units at $47
15.	Sold	18 units
22.	Sold	3 units
30.	Purchased	10 units at $48

The enterprise maintains a perpetual inventory system, costing by the first-in, first-out method. Determine the cost of the merchandise sold in each sale and the inventory balance after each sale, presenting the data in the form illustrated on page 263.

7–29. Perpetual inventory using lifo. Beginning inventory, purchases, and sales data for Commodity C33 for June are as follows:

Inventory:	
June 1	30 units at $30
Sales:	
June 8	15 units
17	10 units
27	10 units
Purchases:	
June 5	20 units at $31
20	15 units at $32

Assuming that the perpetual inventory system is used, costing by the lifo method, determine the cost of the inventory balance at June 30, presenting data in the form illustrated on page 263.

7–30. Perpetual inventory entries. The perpetual inventory system is used, and the merchandise inventory account (controlling) had a balance of $394,250 on January 1, the beginning of the current year. The account was debited for $776,750 for purchases made during the year.

(a) Journalize the entries required to record sales for the year (all sales are made on account): sales price, $1,150,000; cost, $782,500.
(b) If a physical count of inventory on December 31 revealed a cost of $381,200, prepare the entry to record the inventory shortage.

7–31. Retail inventory method. On the basis of the following data, estimate the cost of the merchandise inventory at October 31 by the retail method:

		Cost	Retail
October 1	Merchandise inventory	$244,500	$370,500
October 1–31	Purchases (net)	164,700	249,500
October 1–31	Sales (net)		259,000

7–32. Gross profit inventory method. The merchandise inventory of Joop Company was destroyed by fire on June 10. The following data were obtained from the accounting records:

Jan. 1	Merchandise inventory........................	$172,250
Jan. 1–June 10	Purchases (net).............................	212,250
	Sales (net).................................	380,000
	Estimated gross profit rate..................	40%

384,500

SALES

Estimate the cost of the merchandise destroyed.

7–33. Percentage-of-completion method. During the current year, Evans Construction Company obtained a contract to build an apartment building. The total contract price was $6,000,000, and the estimated construction costs were $4,950,000. During the current year, the project was estimated to be 40% completed, and the costs incurred totaled $2,290,000. Under the percentage-of-completion method of revenue recognition, what amount of (a) revenue, (b) cost, and (c) income should be recognized from the contract for the current year?

Problems

7–34. Periodic inventory by three methods. B & M Television employs the periodic inventory system. Details regarding the inventory of television sets at July 1, 1989, purchases invoices during the year, and the inventory count at June 30, 1990, are summarized as follows:

		Purchases Invoices			
Model	Inventory, July 1	1st	2d	3d	Inventory Count, June 30
C10	6 at $238	4 at $250	8 at $260	10 at $266	12
D05	6 at 77	5 at 82	8 at 89	8 at 99	10
L10	2 at 108	2 at 110	3 at 128	3 at 130	3
O18	8 at 88	4 at 79	3 at 85	6 at 92	8
K72	2 at 250	2 at 260	4 at 271	4 at 275	4
S91	5 at 160	4 at 170	4 at 175	7 at 180	8
V17	—	4 at 150	4 at 200	2 at 205	5

Instructions: (1) Determine the cost of the inventory on June 30, 1990, by the first-in, first-out method. Present data in columnar form, using the following headings:

Model	Quantity	Unit Cost	Total Cost

If the inventory of a particular model is composed of an entire lot plus a portion of another lot acquired at a different unit cost, use a separate line for each lot.

(2) Determine the cost of the inventory on June 30, 1990, by the last-in, first-out method, following the procedures indicated in (1).

(3) Determine the cost of the inventory on June 30, 1990, by the average cost method, using the columnar headings indicated in (1).

7–35. Fifo and lifo perpetual inventory. The beginning inventory of soybeans at the Urbana Co-Op and data on purchases and sales for a three-month period are as follows:

Date		Transaction	Number of Bushels	Per Unit	Total
July	1.	Inventory	25,000	$6.10	$152,500
	10.	Purchase	75,000	6.15	461,250
	15.	Sale	35,000	7.00	245,000
	25.	Sale	30,000	7.00	210,000
Aug.	8.	Sale	10,000	7.10	71,000
	12.	Purchase	50,000	6.20	310,000
	17.	Sale	35,000	7.20	252,000
	28.	Sale	20,000	7.15	143,000
Sept.	5.	Purchase	60,000	6.10	366,000
	17.	Sale	40,000	7.00	280,000
	20.	Purchase	30,000	6.00	180,000
	30.	Sale	45,000	7.00	315,000

Instructions: (1) Record the inventory, purchases, and cost of merchandise sold data in a perpetual inventory record similar to the one illustrated on page 263, using the first-in, first-out method.

(2) Determine the total sales and the total cost of soybeans sold for the period and indicate their effect on the general ledger, using two journal entries. Assume that all sales were on account.

(3) Determine the gross profit from sales of soybeans for the period.

(4) Record the inventory, purchases, and cost of merchandise sold data in a perpetual inventory record similar to the one illustrated on page 263, using the last-in, first-out method.

If the working papers correlating with the textbook are not used, omit Problem 7–36.

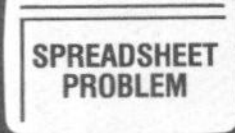

7–36. Lower of cost or market inventory. Data on the physical inventory of Dent Corporation as of April 30, the end of the current fiscal year, are presented in the working papers. The quantity of each commodity on hand has been determined and recorded on the inventory sheet. Unit market prices have also been determined as of April 30 and recorded on the sheet. The inventory is to be determined at cost and also at the lower of cost or market, using the first-in, first-out method. Quantity and cost data from the last purchases invoice of the year and the next-to-the-last purchases invoice are summarized as follows:

	Last Purchases Invoice		Next-to-the-Last Purchases Invoice	
Description	Quantity Purchased	Unit Cost	Quantity Purchased	Unit Cost
A71	20	$ 60	30	$ 59
C22	25	210	20	205
D82	10	145	25	142
E34	150	25	100	24
F17	10	560	10	570
J19	100	15	100	14
K41	10	380	5	385
P21	500	6	500	6
R72	80	17	50	18
T15	5	250	4	260
V55	700	9	500	9
AC2	100	45	50	46
BB7	5	420	5	425
BD1	100	20	75	19
CC1	60	16	40	17
EB2	50	29	25	28
FF7	75	26	60	25
GE4	5	710	5	715

Instructions: Record the appropriate unit costs on the inventory sheet and complete the pricing of the inventory. When there are two different unit costs applicable to a commodity, proceed as follows:

(1) Draw a line through the quantity and insert the quantity and unit cost of the last purchase.

(2) On the following line, insert the quantity and unit cost of the next-to-the-last purchase. The first item on the inventory sheet has been completed as an example.

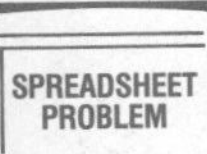

7–37. Retail method; gross profit method. Selected data on merchandise inventory, purchases, and sales for Payton Co. and Reese Co. are as follows:

Payton Co.

	Cost	Retail
Merchandise inventory, July 1	$259,800	$370,000
Transactions during July:		
Purchases	366,840	521,000
Purchases discounts	2,940	
Sales		600,000
Sales returns and allowances		5,000

Reese Co.

Merchandise inventory, April 1	$317,500
Transactions during April and May:	
Purchases	410,250
Purchases discounts	5,250
Sales	625,000
Sales returns and allowances	5,000
Estimated gross profit rate	40%

Instructions: (1) Determine the estimated cost of the merchandise inventory of Payton Co. on July 31 by the retail method, presenting details of the computations.

(2) Estimate the cost of the merchandise inventory of Reese Co. on May 31 by the gross profit method, presenting details of the computations.

7–38. Corrections to inventory; revised income statement. The following preliminary income statement of Jordan Enterprises Inc. was prepared after the accounts were adjusted and closed at the end of the fiscal year. The company uses the periodic inventory system.

Jordan Enterprises Inc.
Income Statement
For Year Ended December 31, 19--

Sales (net)		$985,750
Cost of merchandise sold:		
Merchandise inventory, January 1, 19--	$230,000	
Purchases (net)	695,000	
Merchandise available for sale	$925,000	
Less merchandise inventory, December 31, 19--	245,000	
Cost of merchandise sold		680,000
Gross profit		$305,750
Operating expenses		202,250
Net income		$103,500

The following errors in the ledger and on the inventory sheets for the physical inventory on December 31 were discovered by the independent CPA retained to conduct the annual audit:

(a) A number of errors were discovered in pricing inventory items, in extending amounts, and in footing inventory sheets. The net effect of the errors, exclusive of those described below, was to overstate by $5,000 the amount of ending inventory on the income statement.
(b) A purchases invoice for merchandise of $1,500, dated December 30, had been received and correctly recorded, but the merchandise was not received until January 3 and had not been included in the December 31 inventory. Title had passed to Jordan Enterprises Inc. on December 30.
(c) A purchases invoice for merchandise of $3,000, dated December 31, was not received until January 4 and had not been recorded by December 31. However, the merchandise, to which title had passed, had arrived and had been included in the December 31 inventory.
(d) A sales order for $10,000, dated December 31, had been recorded as a sale on that date, but title did not pass to the buyer until shipment was made on January 3. The merchandise, which had cost $6,500, was excluded from the December 31 inventory.
(e) A sales invoice for $1,250, dated December 30, had not been recorded. The merchandise was shipped on December 30, FOB shipping point, and its cost, $775, was excluded from the December 31 inventory.
(f) An item of office equipment, received on December 27, was erroneously included in the December 31 merchandise inventory at its cost of $8,500. The invoice had been recorded correctly.

Instructions: (1) Determine the correct inventory for December 31, beginning your analysis with the $245,000 inventory shown on the preliminary income statement. Assemble the corrections in two groupings, "Additions" and "Deductions," allowing six lines for each group. Identify each correction by the appropriate letter.
(2) Prepare a revised income statement.

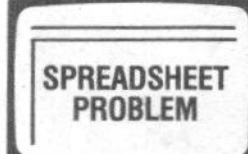

7–39. Percentage-of-completion method. Newell Company began construction on three contracts during 1989. The contract prices and construction activities for each of the years 1989, 1990, and 1991 were as follows:

		1989		1990		1991	
Contract	Contract Price	Costs Incurred	Percent Completed	Costs Incurred	Percent Completed	Costs Incurred	Percent Completed
1	$6,000,000	$2,175,000	40%	$3,250,000	60%	—	—
2	4,000,000	600,000	20	1,375,000	40	$1,500,000	40%
3	3,500,000	455,000	15	985,000	30	1,575,000	50

Instructions: Determine the amount of revenue and income to be recognized from the contracts for each of the years 1989, 1990, and 1991. Revenue is to be recognized by the percentage-of-completion method. Present computations in good order.

ALTERNATE PROBLEMS

7–34A. Periodic inventory by three methods. Allen Stereo employs the periodic inventory system. Details regarding the inventory of television sets at January 1, purchases invoices during the year, and the inventory count at December 31 are summarized as follows:

Model	Inventory, January 1	Purchases Invoices 1st	2d	3d	Inventory Count, December 31
B91	4 at $150	6 at $150	8 at $155	7 at $155	5
F10	3 at 210	3 at 215	5 at 213	4 at 225	3
H21	2 at 520	2 at 530	2 at 530	2 at 536	3
J39	6 at 520	8 at 531	4 at 549	6 at 542	8
P80	9 at 213	7 at 215	6 at 222	6 at 225	8
T15	6 at 305	3 at 310	3 at 316	4 at 321	5
V11	—	4 at 220	4 at 230	—	2

Instructions: (1) Determine the cost of the inventory on December 31 by the first-in, first-out method. Present data in columnar form, using the following headings:

Model	Quantity	Unit Cost	Total Cost

If the inventory of a particular model is composed of an entire lot plus a portion of another lot acquired at a different unit cost, use a separate line for each lot.

(2) Determine the cost of the inventory on December 31 by the last-in, first-out method, following the procedures indicated in (1).

(3) Determine the cost of the inventory on December 31 by the average cost method, using the columnar headings indicated in (1).

7–35A. Fifo and lifo perpetual inventory. The beginning inventory of Commodity 12A and data on purchases and sales for a three-month period are as follows:

Date		Transaction	Number of Units	Per Unit	Total
April	1.	Inventory	9	$220	$1,980
	5.	Purchase	25	225	5,625
	12.	Sale	10	300	3,000
	22.	Sale	6	300	1,800
May	4.	Purchase	10	230	2,300
	6.	Sale	8	310	2,480
	21.	Sale	5	310	1,550
	28.	Purchase	15	235	3,525
June	5.	Sale	9	315	2,835
	13.	Sale	10	315	3,150
	19.	Purchase	10	240	2,400
	26.	Sale	8	320	2,560

Instructions: (1) Record the inventory, purchases, and cost of merchandise sold data in a perpetual inventory record similar to the one illustrated on page 263, using the first-in, first-out method.

(2) Determine the total sales and the total cost of Commodity 12A sold for the period and indicate their effect on the general ledger, using two journal entries. Assume that all sales were on account.

(3) Determine the gross profit from sales of Commodity 12A for the period.

(4) Record the inventory, purchases, and cost of merchandise sold data in a perpetual inventory record similar to the one illustrated on page 263, using the last-in, first-out method.

If the working papers correlating with the textbook are not used, omit Problem 7–36A.

7–36A. Lower of cost or market inventory. Data on the physical inventory of W. A. Anderson Co. as of December 31, the end of the current fiscal year, are presented in the working papers. The quantity of each commodity on hand has been determined and recorded on the inventory sheet. Unit market prices have also been determined as of

December 31 and recorded on the sheet. The inventory is to be determined at cost and also at the lower of cost or market, using the first-in, first-out method. Quantity and cost data from the last purchases invoice of the year and the next-to-the-last purchases invoice are summarized as follows:

	Last Purchases Invoice		Next-to-the-Last Purchases Invoice	
Description	Quantity Purchased	Unit Cost	Quantity Purchased	Unit Cost
A71	20	$ 60	40	$ 59
C22	25	190	15	190
D82	15	145	15	142
E34	150	25	100	27
F17	6	550	15	540
J19	75	16	100	17
K41	8	400	5	410
P21	500	6	500	7
P72	70	17	50	16
T15	5	250	4	260
V55	1,000	10	500	10
AC2	100	45	100	46
BB7	5	410	5	400
BD1	100	20	100	19
CC1	50	15	40	16
EB2	40	29	50	28
FF7	55	28	50	28
GE4	6	690	5	700

Instructions: Record the appropriate unit costs on the inventory sheet and complete the pricing of the inventory. When there are two different unit costs applicable to a commodity, proceed as follows:

(1) Draw a line through the quantity and insert the quantity and unit cost of the last purchase.

(2) On the following line, insert the quantity and unit cost of the next-to-the-last purchase. The first item on the inventory sheet has been completed as an example.

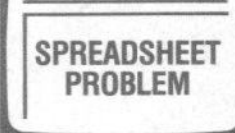

7–37A. Retail method; gross profit method. Selected data on merchandise inventory, purchases, and sales for Boyd Co. and Carson Supply Co. are as follows:

Boyd Co.

	Cost	Retail
Merchandise inventory, January 1	$377,100	$579,100
Transactions during January:		
Purchases	186,600	298,400
Purchases discounts	2,100	
Sales		340,500
Sales returns and allowances		5,500

Carson Supply Co.

Merchandise inventory, July 1	$517,900
Transactions during July and August:	
Purchases	425,500
Purchases discounts	3,600
Sales	570,250
Sales returns and allowances	5,250
Estimated gross profit rate	35%

Instructions: (1) Determine the estimated cost of the merchandise inventory of Boyd Co. on January 31 by the retail method, presenting details of the computations.

(2) Estimate the cost of the merchandise inventory of Carson Supply Co. on August 31 by the gross profit method, presenting details of the computations.

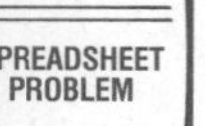

7–39A. Percentage-of-completion method. Sheppard Company began construction on three contracts during 1989. The contract prices and construction activities for 1989, 1990, and 1991 were as follows:

		1989		1990		1991	
Contract	Contract Price	Costs Incurred	Percent Completed	Costs Incurred	Percent Completed	Costs Incurred	Percent Completed
1	$ 5,000,000	$1,810,000	40%	$1,575,000	35%	$1,090,000	25%
2	10,000,000	2,550,000	30	2,625,000	30	2,695,000	30
3	8,000,000	3,710,000	50	3,815,000	50	—	—

Instructions: Determine the amount of revenue and the income to be recognized for each of the years, 1989, 1990, and 1991. Revenue is to be recognized by the percentage-of-completion method. Present computations in good order.

Mini-Case 7

Drew Company began operations in 1989 by selling a single product. Data on purchases and sales for the year were as follows:

Purchases

Date	Units Purchased	Unit Cost	Total Cost
April 5	5,000	$13.20	$ 66,000
May 2	5,000	14.00	70,000
June 4	5,000	14.20	71,000
July 10	5,000	15.00	75,000
August 7	3,000	15.25	45,750
October 5	2,000	15.50	31,000
November 1	1,000	15.75	15,750
December 10	1,000	17.00	17,000
	27,000		$391,500

Sales

April	2,000 units	September	3,500 units
May	2,000	October	2,250
June.	3,500	November	2,250
July	4,000	December	1,000
August.	3,500		

Total sales . . $454,000

On January 2, 1990, the president of the company, Ann Drew, asked for your advice on costing the 3,000-unit physical inventory that was taken on December 31, 1989. Also, since the firm plans to expand its product line, she asked for your advice on the use of a perpetual inventory system in the future.

Instructions:

(1) Determine the cost of the December 31, 1989 inventory under the periodic system, using the (a) first-in, first-out method, (b) last-in, first-out method, and (c) average cost method.
(2) Determine the gross profit for the year under each of the three methods in (1).
(3) (a) In your opinion, which of the three inventory costing methods best reflects the results of operations for 1989? Why?
    (b) In your opinion, which of the three inventory costing methods best reflects the replacement cost of the inventory on the balance sheet as of December 31, 1989? Why?
    (c) Which inventory costing method would you choose to use for income tax purposes? Why?
(4) Discuss the advantages and disadvantages of using a perpetual inventory system. From the data presented in this case, is there any indication of the adequacy of inventory levels during the year?

Answers to Self-Examination Questions

1. C The overstatement of inventory by $7,500 at the end of a period will cause the cost of merchandise sold for the period to be understated by $7,500, the gross profit for the period to be overstated by $7,500, and the net income for the period to be overstated by $7,500 (answer C).
2. B The perpetual system (answer B) continuously discloses the amount of inventory. The periodic inventory system (answer A) relies upon a detailed listing of the merchandise on hand, called a physical inventory (answer C), to determine the cost of inventory at the end of a period. The retail inventory method (answer D) is employed in connection with the periodic system and is based on the relationship of the cost of merchandise available for sale to the retail price of the same merchandise.
3. A The fifo method (answer A) is based on the assumption that costs are charged against revenue in the order in which they were incurred. The lifo method (answer B) charges the most recent costs incurred against revenue, and the average cost method (answer C) charges a weighted average of unit costs of commodities sold against revenue. The perpetual inventory system (answer D) is a system that continuously discloses the amount of inventory.
4. D The fifo method of costing is based on the assumption that costs should be charged against revenue in the order in which they were incurred (first-in, first-out). Thus the most recent costs are assigned to inventory. The 35 units would be assigned a unit cost of $23 (answer D).
5. B When the price level is steadily rising, the earlier unit costs are lower than recent unit costs. Under the fifo method (answer B), these earlier costs are matched against revenue to yield the highest possible net income. The periodic inventory system (answer D) is a system and not a method of costing.

8
Plant Assets and Intangible Assets

CHAPTER OBJECTIVES

Describe the characteristics of plant assets and illustrate the accounting for the acquisition of plant assets.

Describe the nature of depreciation and illustrate the accounting for depreciation.

Describe and illustrate the accounting for plant asset disposals.

Describe and illustrate the accounting for the leasing of plant assets.

Describe and illustrate the accounting for depletion.

Describe and illustrate the accounting for intangible assets.

Describe and illustrate the reporting of depreciation expense, plant assets, and intangible assets in the financial statements.

Long-lived is a general term that may be applied to assets of a relatively fixed or permanent nature owned by a business enterprise. Such assets that are tangible in nature, used in the operations of the business, and not held for sale in the ordinary course of the business are classified on the balance sheet as **plant assets** or **fixed assets.** Other descriptive titles frequently used are **property, plant, and equipment,** used either alone or in various combinations. The properties most frequently included in plant assets may be described in more specific terms as equipment, furniture, tools, machinery, buildings, and land. Although there is no standard criterion as to the minimum length of life necessary for classification as plant assets, such assets must be capable of repeated use and are ordinarily expected to last more than a year. However, the asset need not actually be used continuously or even often. Items of standby equipment held for use in the event of a breakdown of regular equipment or for use only during peak periods of activity are included in plant assets.

Assets acquired for resale in the normal course of business cannot be characterized as plant assets, regardless of their durability or the length of time they are held. For example, undeveloped land or other real estate acquired as a speculation should be listed on the balance sheet in the asset section entitled "Investments."

INITIAL COSTS OF PLANT ASSETS

The initial cost of a plant asset includes all expenditures *necessary* to get it in place and ready for use. Sales tax, transportation charges, insurance on the asset while in transit, special foundations, and installation costs should be added to the purchase price of the related plant asset. Similarly, when a secondhand asset is purchased, the initial costs of getting it ready for use, such as expenditures for new parts, repairs, and painting, are debited to the asset account. On the other hand, costs associated with the acquisition of a plant asset should be excluded from the asset account if they are not necessary for getting the asset ready for use and therefore do not increase the asset's usefulness. Expenditures resulting from carelessness or errors in installing the asset, from vandalism, or from other unusual occurrences do not increase the usefulness of the asset and should be allocated to the period as an expense.

The cost of constructing a building includes the fees paid to architects and engineers for plans and supervision, insurance incurred during construction, and all other needed expenditures related to the project. Generally, interest incurred during the construction period on money borrowed to finance construction should also be treated as part of the cost of the building.[1]

The cost of land includes not only the negotiated price but also broker's commissions, title fees, surveying fees, and other expenditures connected with securing title. If delinquent real estate taxes are assumed by the buyer, they also are chargeable to the land account. If unwanted buildings are located on land acquired for a plant site, the cost of their razing or removal, less any salvage recovered, is properly chargeable to the land account. The cost of leveling or otherwise permanently changing the contour is also an additional cost of the land.

Other expenditures related to the land may be charged to Land, Buildings, or Land Improvements, depending upon the circumstances. If the property owner bears the initial cost of paving the public street bordering the land, either by direct payment or by special tax assessment, the paving may be considered to be as permanent as the land. On the other hand, the cost of constructing walkways to and around the building may be added to the building account if the walkways are expected to last as long as the building. Expenditures for improvements that are neither as permanent as the land nor directly associated with the building may be set apart in a land improvements account and depreciated according to their different life spans. Some of the more usual items of this nature are trees and shrubs, fences, outdoor lighting systems, and paved parking areas.

NATURE OF DEPRECIATION

As time passes, all plant assets with the exception of land lose their capacity to yield services.[2] Accordingly, the cost of such assets should be

---

[1]*Statement of Financial Accounting Standards, No. 34,* "Capitalization of Interest Cost" (Stamford: Financial Accounting Standards Board, 1979), par. 6.

[2]Land is here assumed to be used only as a site. Consideration will be given later in the chapter to land acquired for its mineral deposits or other natural resources.

transferred to the related expense accounts in an orderly manner during their expected useful life. This periodic cost expiration is called **depreciation.**

Factors contributing to a decline in usefulness may be divided into two categories: *physical* depreciation, which includes wear from use and deterioration from the action of the elements, and *functional* depreciation, which includes inadequacy and obsolescence. A plant asset becomes inadequate if its capacity is not sufficient to meet the demands of increased production. A plant asset is obsolete if the commodity that it produces is no longer in demand or if a newer machine can produce a commodity of better quality or at a great reduction in cost. The continued growth of technological progress during this century has made obsolescence an increasingly important part of depreciation. Although the several factors comprising depreciation can be defined, it is not feasible to identify them when recording depreciation expense.

The meaning of the term "depreciation" as used in accounting is often misunderstood because the same term is also commonly used in business to mean a decline in the market value of an asset. The amount of unexpired cost of plant assets reported in the balance sheet is not likely to agree with the amount that could be realized from their sale. Plant assets are held for use in the enterprise rather than for sale. It is assumed that the enterprise will continue forever as a **going concern.** Consequently, the decision to dispose of a plant asset is based mainly on its usefulness to the enterprise and not on its market value.

Another common misunderstanding is that depreciation accounting automatically provides the cash needed to replace plant assets as they wear out. The cash account is neither increased nor decreased by the periodic entries that transfer the cost of plant assets to depreciation expense accounts. The misconception probably occurs because depreciation expense, unlike most expenses, does not require an equivalent outlay of cash in the period in which the expense is recorded.

DETERMINING DEPRECIATION

If a plant asset is expected to have no value at the time that it is retired from service, its entire initial cost should be spread over the expected useful life of the asset as depreciation expense. Also, if a plant asset's value at the time of retirement is expected to be very small in comparison with the cost of the asset, this value may be ignored and the entire cost spread over the asset's expected useful life. If a plant asset is expected to have a significant value at the time that it is retired from service, the difference between its initial cost and this value is the cost (depreciable cost) that should be spread over the useful life of the asset as depreciation expense. The plant asset's estimated value at the time that it is to be retired from service is called its **residual value, scrap value, salvage value,** or **trade-in value**.

In determining the amount of depreciable cost that is to be recognized as periodic depreciation expense, three factors need to be considered: the plant asset's (a) initial cost, (b) residual value, and (c) useful life. The relationship between these three factors and the periodic depreciation expense is presented in the following diagram:

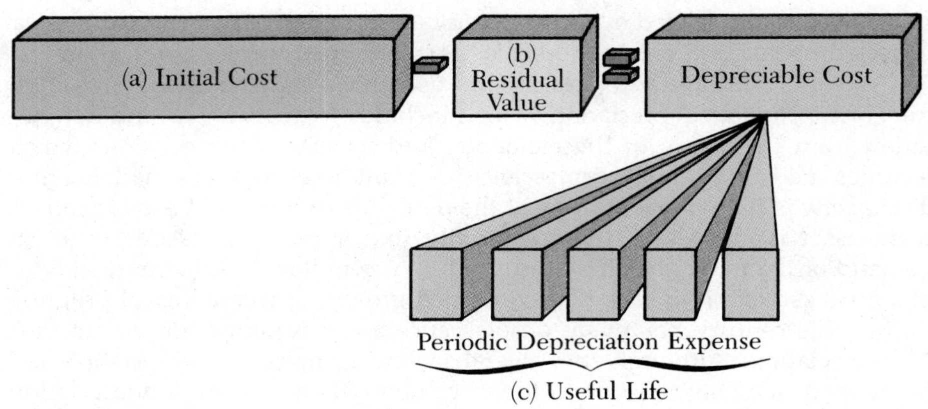

Factors that Determine Depreciation Expense

Neither the period of usefulness of a plant asset nor its residual value at the end of that period can be accurately determined until the asset is retired. However, in determining the amount of the periodic depreciation, these two related factors must be estimated at the time the asset is placed in service.

There are no hard-and-fast rules for estimating either factor, and both factors may be greatly affected by management policies. For example, the estimates of a company that provides its sales representatives with a new automobile every year will differ from those of a firm that keeps its cars for three years. Such variables as climate, frequency of use, maintenance, and minimum standards of efficiency will also affect the estimates.

Life estimates for depreciable assets are available in various trade association and other publications. For federal income tax purposes, the Internal Revenue Service has also established guidelines for life estimates. These guidelines may be useful in determining depreciation for financial reporting purposes.

In addition to the many factors that may influence the life estimate of an asset, there is a wide range in the degree of exactness used in the computation. A calendar month is ordinarily the smallest unit of time used. When this period of time is used, all assets placed in service or retired from service during the first half of a month are treated as if the event had occurred on the first day of that month. Similarly, all plant asset additions and reductions during the second half of a month are considered to have occurred on the first day of the next month. In the absence of any statement to the contrary, this practice will be assumed throughout this chapter.

It is not necessary that an enterprise use a single method of computing depreciation for all classes of its depreciable assets. The methods used in the accounts and financial statements may also differ from the methods used in determining income taxes and property taxes. The four methods used most often are straight-line, units-of-production, declining-balance, and sum-of-the-years-digits. The extent of the use of these methods in financial statements is presented in the following chart:

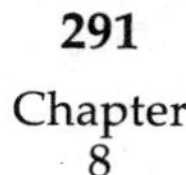

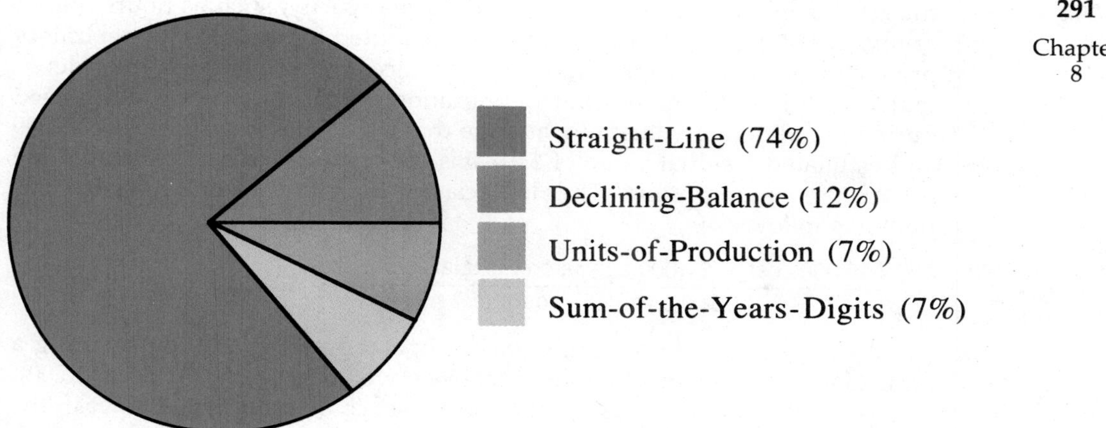

Source: Accounting Trends & Techniques, 41st ed. (New York: American Institute of Certified Public Accountants, 1987).

Use of Depreciation Methods

Straight-Line Method

The **straight-line method** of determining depreciation provides for equal periodic charges to expense over the estimated life of the asset. To illustrate this method, assume that the cost of a depreciable asset is $16,000, its estimated residual value is $1,000, and its estimated life is 5 years. The annual depreciation is computed as follows:

$$\frac{\$16{,}000 \text{ cost} - \$1{,}000 \text{ estimated residual value}}{5 \text{ years estimated life}} = \$3{,}000 \text{ annual depreciation}$$

Straight-Line Method of Depreciation

The annual depreciation of $3,000 would be prorated for the first and the last partial years of use. Assuming a fiscal year ending on December 31 and first use of the asset on October 15, the depreciation for that fiscal year would be $750 (3 months). If usage had begun on October 16, the depreciation for the year would be $500 (2 months).

The annual straight-line depreciation may be converted to a percentage rate, determined on the basis of cost and the estimated life of the asset without regard to residual value. The conversion to an annual percentage rate is accomplished by dividing 100 by the number of years of life. Thus a life of 50 years is equivalent to a 2% depreciation rate, 20 years is equivalent to a 5% rate, 8 years is equivalent to a 12½% rate, and so on.

The straight-line method is widely used because of its simplicity. In addition, it provides a reasonable allocation of costs to periodic revenue when usage is relatively the same from period to period.

Units-of-Production Method

The **units-of-production method** yields a depreciation charge that varies with the amount of asset usage. To apply this method, the length of life of the asset is expressed in terms of productive capacity, such as hours, miles, or number of units. Depreciation is first computed for the appropriate unit of production, and the depreciation for each accounting period is then determined by multiplying the unit depreciation by the number of units used during the period. To illustrate, assume that a machine with a cost of $16,000 and estimated residual value of $1,000 is expected to have an estimated life of 10,000 operating hours. The depreciation for a unit of one hour is computed as follows:

Units-of-Production Method of Depreciation

$$\frac{\$16{,}000 \text{ cost} - \$1{,}000 \text{ estimated residual value}}{10{,}000 \text{ estimated hours}} = \$1.50 \text{ hourly depreciation}$$

Assuming that the machine was in operation for 2,200 hours during a particular year, the depreciation for that year would be $3,300 ($1.50 × 2,200).

When the amount of usage of a plant asset changes from year to year, the units-of-production method is more logical than the straight-line method. It may yield fairer allocations of cost against periodic revenue.

Declining-Balance Method

The **declining-balance method** yields a declining periodic depreciation charge over the estimated life of the asset. The most common technique is to double the straight-line depreciation rate, computed as explained previously, and apply the resulting rate to the cost of the asset less its accumulated depreciation. For example, the declining-balance rate for an asset with an estimated life of five years would be double the straight-line rate of 20%, or 40%. This rate is then applied to the cost of the asset for the first year of its use and thereafter to the declining book value (cost minus accumulated depreciation). The method is illustrated in the following table:

Declining-Balance Method of Depreciation

Year	Cost	Accumulated Depreciation at Beginning of Year	Book Value at Beginning of Year	Rate	Depreciation for Year	Book Value at End of Year
1	$16,000	—	$16,000.00	40%	$6,400.00	$9,600.00
2	16,000	$ 6,400.00	9,600.00	40%	3,840.00	5,760.00
3	16,000	10,240.00	5,760.00	40%	2,304.00	3,456.00
4	16,000	12,544.00	3,456.00	40%	1,382.40	2,073.60
5	16,000	13,926.40	2,073.60	40%	829.44	1,244.16

Note that estimated residual value is not considered in determining the depreciation rate. It is also ignored in computing periodic depreciation, except that the asset should not be depreciated below the estimated residual value. In the above example, it was assumed that the estimated residual value at the end of the fifth year approximates the book value of $1,244.16. If the residual value had been estimated at $1,500, the depreciation for the fifth year would have been $573.60 ($2,073.60 − $1,500) instead of $829.44.

There was an implicit assumption in the above illustration that the first use of the asset coincided with the beginning of the fiscal year. This would usually not occur in actual practice, however, and would require a slight change in the computation for the first partial year of use. If the asset in the example had been placed in service at the end of the third month of the fiscal year, only the pro rata portion of the first full year's depreciation, $4,800 (9/12 × 40% × $16,000), would be allocated to the first fiscal year. The method of computing the depreciation for the following years would not be affected. Thus, the depreciation for the second fiscal year would be $4,480 [40% × ($16,000 − $4,800)].

Sum-of-the-Years-Digits Method

Know

The **sum-of-the-years-digits method** yields results like those obtained by use of the declining-balance method. The periodic charge for depreciation declines steadily over the estimated life of the asset because a successively smaller fraction is applied each year to the original cost of the asset less the estimated residual value. The denominator of the fraction, which remains the same, is the sum of the digits representing the years of life. The numerator of the fraction, which changes each year, is the number of years of life remaining at the beginning of the year for which depreciation is being computed. For an asset with an estimated life of 5 years, the denominator is 5 + 4 + 3 + 2 + 1, or 15.[3] For the first year, the numerator is 5, for the second year 4, and so on. The method is illustrated by the following depreciation schedule for an asset with an assumed cost of $16,000, residual value of $1,000, and life of 5 years:

Sum-of-the-Years-Digits Method of Depreciation

Year	*Cost Less Residual Value*	*Rate*	*Depreciation for Year*	*Accumulated Depreciation at End of Year*	*Book Value at End of Year*
1	$15,000	5/15	$5,000	$ 5,000	$11,000
2	15,000	4/15	4,000	9,000	7,000
3	15,000	3/15	3,000	12,000	4,000
4	15,000	2/15	2,000	14,000	2,000
5	15,000	1/15	1,000	15,000	1,000

When the first use of the asset does not coincide with the beginning of a fiscal year, it is necessary to allocate each full year's depreciation between the two fiscal years benefited. Assuming that the asset in the example was placed in service after three months of the fiscal year had elapsed, the depreciation for that fiscal year would be $3,750 (9/12 × 5/15 × $15,000). The depreciation for the second year would be $4,250, computed as follows:

3/12 × 5/15 × $15,000....................	$1,250
9/12 × 4/15 × $15,000....................	3,000
Total, second fiscal year	$4,250

Comparison of Depreciation Methods

The straight-line method provides for uniform periodic charges to depreciation expense over the life of the asset. The units-of-production method provides for periodic charges to depreciation expense that may vary considerably, depending upon the amount of usage of the asset.

Both the declining-balance and the sum-of-the-years-digits methods provide for a higher depreciation charge in the first year of use of the asset and a gradually declining periodic charge thereafter. For this reason they are

[3]The denominator can also be determined from the following formula, where S = sum of the digits and N = number of years of estimated life: $S = N[(N + 1) \div 2]$.

frequently referred to as **accelerated depreciation methods.** These methods are most appropriate for situations in which the decline in productivity or earning power of the asset is proportionately greater in the early years of its use than in later years. Further justification for their use is based on the tendency of repairs to increase with the age of an asset. The reduced amounts of depreciation in later years are therefore offset to some extent by increased maintenance expenses.

The periodic depreciation charges for the straight-line method and the accelerated methods are compared in the following chart. This chart is based on an asset cost of $16,000, an estimated life of 5 years, and an estimated residual value of $1,000.

Comparison of Depreciation Methods

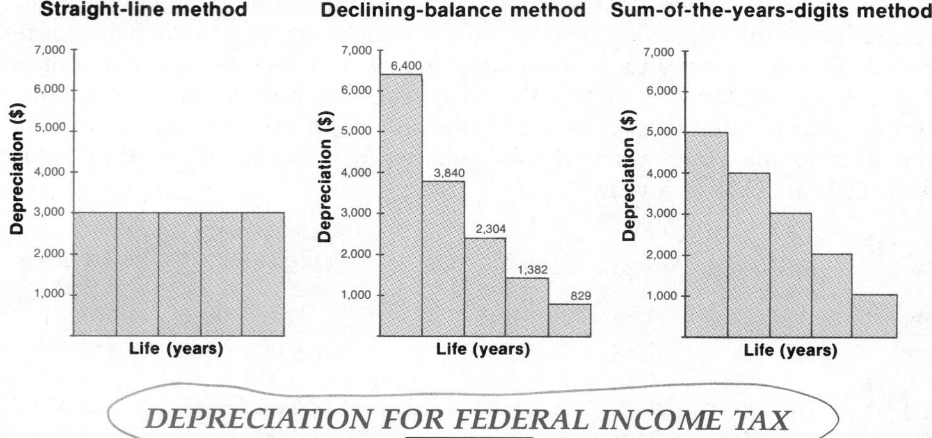

DEPRECIATION FOR FEDERAL INCOME TAX

Each of the four depreciation methods described in the preceding paragraphs can be used to determine the amount of depreciation for federal income tax purposes for plant assets acquired prior to 1981. The accelerated depreciation methods are widely used. Acceleration of the "write-off" of the asset reduces the income tax liability in the earlier years and thus increases the amount of cash available in those years to pay for the asset or for other purposes.

For plant assets acquired after 1980 and before 1987, either the straight-line method or the Accelerated Cost Recovery System (ACRS) could be used for federal income tax purposes. ACRS provided for depreciation deductions that approximated the depreciation calculated by the 150-percent declining-balance method. For most business property, ACRS also provided for three classes of useful life. Each class of useful life was often much shorter than the actual useful life of the asset in that class.

Under the Tax Reform Act of 1986, Modified ACRS (MACRS) provides for eight classes of useful life for plant assets acquired after 1986. The two most common classes, other than real estate, are the 5-year class and the 7-year class.[4] The 5-year class includes automobiles and light-duty trucks, and the 7-year class includes most machinery and equipment. The depreciation deduction for these two classes approximates the use of the 200-percent declining-balance method.

[4]Real estate is classified into 27 1/2-year and 31 1/2-year classes and is depreciated by the straight-line method.

The Internal Revenue Service has prescribed methods that result in annual percentages to be used in determining depreciation for each class. In using these rates, salvage value is ignored, and all plant assets are assumed to be placed in service in the middle of the year and taken out of service in the middle of the year. Thus, for the 5-year-class assets, for example, depreciation is spread over six years, as shown in the following schedule of MACRS depreciation rates:

MACRS Depreciation Rate Schedule

Year	*5-Year-Class Depreciation Rates*
1	20.0%
2	32.0
3	19.2
4	11.5
5	11.5
6	5.8
	100.0%

REVISION OF PERIODIC DEPRECIATION

Earlier in this chapter, it was noted that two of the factors that must be considered in computing the periodic depreciation of a plant asset—its residual value at the time it is retired from service and its useful life—must be estimated at the time the asset is placed in service. Minor errors resulting from the use of these estimates are normal and tend to be recurring.[5] When such errors occur, the revised estimates are used to determine the amount of the remaining undepreciated asset cost to be charged as an expense in future periods.

To illustrate, assume that a plant asset purchased for $130,000 and originally estimated to have a useful life of 30 years and a residual value of $10,000 has been depreciated for 10 years by the straight-line method. At the end of ten years, its book value (undepreciated cost) would be $90,000, determined as follows:

Asset cost	$130,000
Less accumulated depreciation ($4,000 per year × 10 years)	40,000
Book value (undepreciated cost), end of tenth year	$ 90,000

If during the eleventh year it is estimated that the remaining useful life is 25 years (instead of 20) and that the residual value is $5,000 (instead of $10,000), the depreciation expense for each of the remaining 25 years would be $3,400, determined as follows:

Book value (undepreciated cost), end of tenth year	$90,000
Less revised estimated residual value	5,000
Revised remaining depreciation	$85,000
Revised annual depreciation expense ($85,000 ÷ 25)	$ 3,400

Note that the correction of minor errors in the estimates used in the determination of depreciation does not affect the amounts of depreciation expense recorded in earlier years. The use of estimates, and the resulting likelihood of minor errors in such estimates, is inherent in the accounting

[5]The correction of material or large errors made in computing depreciation is discussed in Chapter 11.

process. Therefore when such errors do occur, the amounts recorded for depreciation expense in the past are not corrected; only future depreciation expense amounts are affected.

RECORDING DEPRECIATION

Depreciation may be recorded by an entry at the end of each month, or the adjustment may be delayed until the end of the year. As illustrated on page 104, the part of the entry that records the decrease in the plant asset is credited to a contra asset account entitled Accumulated Depreciation or Allowance for Depreciation. The use of a contra asset account permits the original cost to remain unchanged in the plant asset account. This facilitates the computation of periodic depreciation, the listing of both cost and accumulated depreciation on the balance sheet, and the reporting required for property tax and income tax purposes.

An exception to the general procedure of recording depreciation monthly or annually is often made when a plant asset is sold, traded in, or scrapped. As discussed and illustrated later in the chapter, the disposal is recorded by removing from the accounts both the cost of the asset and its related accumulated depreciation as of the date of the disposal. Hence, it is advisable to record the additional depreciation on the item for the current period before recording the transaction disposing of the asset. A further advantage of recording the depreciation at the time of the disposal of the asset is that no additional attention need be given the transaction when the amount of the periodic depreciation adjustment for the other plant assets is later determined.

CAPITAL AND REVENUE EXPENDITURES

In addition to the initial cost of acquiring a plant asset, costs for additions made to the asset and other costs related to its efficiency or capacity may be incurred during its service life. Expenditures for additions to a plant asset or expenditures that add to the utility of the asset for more than one accounting period are called **capital expenditures.** Such expenditures are debited to the asset account or to a related accumulated depreciation account. Expenditures that benefit only the current period and that are made in order to maintain normal operating efficiency are called **revenue expenditures.** Such expenditures are debited to expense accounts. Although it may be difficult to distinguish between capital and revenue expenditures, care should be exercised so that revenues and expenses will be matched properly. Capital expenditures will affect the depreciation expense of more than one period, while revenue expenditures will affect the expenses of only the current period.

Capital Expenditures

Expenditures for an addition to a plant asset are capital expenditures and should be debited to the plant asset account. For example, the cost of installing an air conditioning unit in an automobile or of adding a wing to a building should be debited to the respective asset account.

Expenditures that increase operating efficiency or capacity for the remaining useful life of an asset should be treated as capital expenditures. For example, if the power unit attached to a machine is replaced by one of greater capacity, the cost should be added to the plant asset account. Also, the cost and the accumulated depreciation related to the old motor should be removed from the accounts. The cost of the new power unit would be depreciated over its estimated useful life.

Expenditures that increase the useful life of an asset beyond the original estimate are also capital expenditures. They should be debited to the appropriate accumulated depreciation account, however, rather than to the asset account. In such circumstances, the expenditures may be said to restore or "make good" a portion of the depreciation accumulated in prior years. To illustrate, assume that a machine with an estimated life of ten years is substantially rebuilt at the end of its seventh year of use, and that the extraordinary repairs are expected to extend the life of the machine an additional three years beyond the original estimate. In this case, the expenditure would be debited to the accumulated depreciation account. In addition, the periodic depreciation for future periods would be redetermined on the basis of the new book value of the asset and the new estimate of the remaining useful life.

Revenue Expenditures

Expenditures for ordinary maintenance and repairs of a recurring nature should be classified as revenue expenditures and debited to expense accounts. For example, the cost of replacing spark plugs in an automobile or the cost of repainting a building should be debited to proper expense accounts.

Small expenditures are usually treated as repair expense, even though they may have the characteristics of capital expenditures. The saving in time and clerical expenses justifies the sacrifice of the small degree of accuracy. Some businesses establish a minimum amount required to classify an item as a capital expenditure.

Summary of Capital and Revenue Expenditures

The initial cost of acquiring a plant asset is debited to a plant asset account. Subsequent to the initial expenditures, the accounting for expenditures related to the plant asset is summarized in the following diagram:

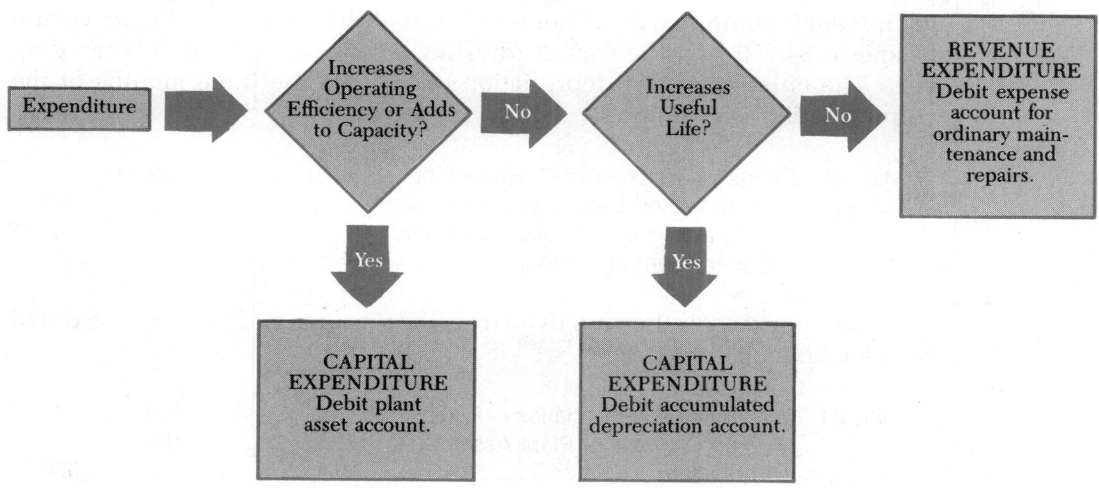

DISPOSAL OF PLANT ASSETS

Plant assets that are no longer useful may be discarded, sold, or applied toward the purchase of other plant assets. The details of the entry to record a disposal will vary, but in all cases it is necessary to remove the book value of the asset from the accounts. This is done by debiting the proper accumulated depreciation account for the total depreciation to the date of disposal and crediting the asset account for the cost of the asset.

A plant asset should not be removed from the accounts only because it has been depreciated for the full period of its estimated life. If the asset is still useful to the enterprise, the cost and accumulated depreciation should remain in the ledger. Otherwise the accounts would contain no evidence of the continued existence of such plant assets and the control function of the ledger would be impaired. In addition, the cost and the accumulated depreciation data on such assets are often needed in reporting for property tax and income tax purposes.

Discarding Plant Assets

When plant assets are no longer useful to the business and have no market value, they are discarded. If the asset has been fully depreciated, no loss is realized. To illustrate, assume that an item of equipment acquired at a cost of $6,000 became fully depreciated at December 31, the end of the preceding fiscal year, and is now to be discarded as worthless. The entry to record the disposal is as follows:

Mar. 24	Accumulated Depreciation — Equipment	6,000	
	Equipment		6,000
	To write off equipment discarded.		

If the accumulated depreciation applicable to the $6,000 of discarded equipment had been less than $6,000, there would have been a loss on its disposal. Furthermore, it would have been necessary to record depreciation for the three months of use in the current period before recording the disposal. To illustrate these differences, assume that annual depreciation on the equipment is computed at 10% of cost and that the accumulated depreciation balance is $4,750 after the annual adjusting entry at the end of the preceding year. The entry to record depreciation of $150 for the three months of the current period is as follows:

Mar. 24	Depreciation Expense — Equipment	150	
	Accumulated Depreciation — Equipment		150
	To record current depreciation on equipment discarded.		

The equipment is then removed from the accounts and the loss is recorded by the following entry:

Mar. 24	Accumulated Depreciation — Equipment	4,900	
	Loss on Disposal of Plant Assets	1,100	
	Equipment		6,000
	To write off equipment discarded.		

Ordinary losses and gains on the disposal of plant assets are nonoperating items and may be reported in the Other Expense and Other Income sections, respectively, of the income statement.

Sale of Plant Assets

The entry to record the sale of a plant asset is like the entries illustrated in the preceding section, except that the cash or other asset received must also be recorded. If the selling price is more than the book value of the asset, the transaction results in a gain; if the selling price is less than the book value, there is a loss. To illustrate some possibilities, assume that equipment acquired at a cost of $10,000 and depreciated at the annual rate of 10% of cost is sold for cash on October 12 of the eighth year of its use. The accumulated depreciation in the account as of the preceding December 31 is $7,000. The entry to record the depreciation for the nine months of the current year is as follows:

Oct. 12	Depreciation Expense—Equipment	750	
	Accumulated Depreciation—Equipment		750
	To record current depreciation on equipment sold.		

After the current depreciation is recorded, the book value of the asset is $2,250. The entries to record the sale under three different assumptions as to selling price are as follows:

	Sold at book value, for $2,250. No gain or loss.		
Oct. 12	Cash	2,250	
	Accumulated Depreciation—Equipment	7,750	
	Equipment		10,000
	Sold below book value, for $1,000. Loss of $1,250.		
Oct. 12	Cash	1,000	
	Accumulated Depreciation—Equipment	7,750	
	Loss on Disposal of Plant Assets	1,250	
	Equipment		10,000
	Sold above book value, for $3,000. Gain of $750.		
Oct. 12	Cash	3,000	
	Accumulated Depreciation—Equipment	7,750	
	Equipment		10,000
	Gain on Disposal of Plant Assets		750

Exchange of Plant Assets

Old equipment is often traded in for new equipment having a similar use. The trade-in allowance is deducted from the price of the new equipment, and the balance owed **(boot)** is paid according to the credit terms. The trade-in allowance given by the seller is often greater or less than the book value of the old equipment traded in. In the past, it was acceptable for financial reporting purposes to recognize the difference between the trade-in allowance and the book value as a gain or a loss. For example, a trade-in allowance of $1,500 on equipment with a book value of $1,000 would have yielded a recognized gain of $500. Such treatment is no longer acceptable for financial reporting purposes on the theory that revenue occurs from the production and sale of items produced by plant assets and not from the exchange of similar plant assets. However, if the trade-in allowance is less than the book value of the old equipment, the loss is recognized immediately.

Nonrecognition of Gain. The acceptable method of accounting for an exchange in which the trade-in allowance exceeds the book value of the old plant asset requires that the cost of the new asset be determined by adding the amount of boot given to the book value of the old asset. To illustrate, assume an exchange based on the following data:

Equipment traded in (old):	
Cost of old equipment	$4,000
Accumulated depreciation at date of exchange	3,200
Book value at June 19, date of exchange	$ 800

Similar equipment acquired (new):	
Price of new equipment	$5,000
Trade-in allowance on old equipment	1,100
Boot given (cash)	$3,900

The cost basis of the new equipment is **$4,700,** which is determined by adding the boot given **($3,900)** to the book value of the old equipment **($800).** The compound entry to record the exchange and the payment of cash is as follows:

June 19	Accumulated Depreciation—Equipment	3,200	
	Equipment	4,700	
	Equipment		4,000
	Cash		3,900

It should be noted that the nonrecognition of the $300 gain ($1,100 trade-in allowance minus $800 book value) at the time of the exchange is really a postponement. The periodic depreciation expense is based on a cost of $4,700 rather than on the quoted price of $5,000. The unrecognized gain of $300 at the time of the exchange will be matched by a reduction of $300 in the total amount of depreciation taken during the life of the equipment.

Recognition of Loss. To illustrate the accounting for a loss on the exchange of one plant asset for another which is similar in use, assume an exchange based on the following data:

Equipment traded in (old):	
Cost of old equipment	$ 7,000
Accumulated depreciation at date of exchange	4,600
Book value at September 7, date of exchange	$ 2,400

Similar equipment acquired (new):	
Price of new equipment	$10,000
Trade-in allowance on old equipment	2,000
Boot given (cash)	$ 8,000

The amount of the loss to be recognized on the exchange is the excess of the book value of the equipment traded in **($2,400)** over the trade-in allowance **($2,000)**, or **$400**. The entry to record the exchange is as follows:

Sept. 7	Accumulated Depreciation—Equipment	4,600	
	Equipment	10,000	
	Loss on Disposal of Plant Assets	400	
	Equipment		7,000
	Cash		8,000

Federal Income Tax Requirements. The Internal Revenue Code (IRC) requires that neither gains nor losses be recognized for income tax purposes if (1) the asset acquired by the taxpayer is similar in use to the asset given in exchange and (2) any boot involved is given (rather than received) by the taxpayer. Thus, the treatment of a nonrecognized gain corresponds to the acceptable method prescribed for financial reporting purposes, the boot given being added to the book value of the old equipment. In the first illustration, the cost basis for federal income tax purposes corresponds to the amount recorded as the cost of the new equipment, namely $4,700.

The cost basis of the new equipment in the second illustration, for federal income tax purposes, is determined in a like manner. The boot given ($8,000) is added to the book value of the old equipment ($2,400), yielding a cost basis of $10,400. The unrecognized loss of $400 at the time of the exchange will be matched by an increase of $400 in the total amount of depreciation allowed for income tax purposes during the life of the asset.

AT&T-Line Depreciation

When plant assets are being disposed of, the effects of improperly determining depreciation can be clearly seen. One such example is the nation's 1,400 local telephone companies, which are reporting some $26 billion in old equipment on their balance sheets. This amount should have been depreciated in past years, and now the equipment is obsolete and must be replaced. The problems caused by this underdepreciation are addressed in the following excerpts from an article in *Forbes*:

That $26 billion represents over 10% of the operating companies' $195.8 billion physical plant—telephone poles, miles of copper wire and giant switching stations, all built in the days when telecommunications was dominated by a monopoly jointly overseen by the Bell system and the government. Indeed, the 22 Bell operating companies account for over $20 billion of the total shortfall.

In the monopoly days, Bell executives sat down with state and federal regulators, estimated how long a new piece of equipment would last, and stretched the depreciation accordingly—sometimes for longer than 40 years. Independent companies followed the pattern. That cozy arrangement suited everybody's purposes: The companies could count on a steady revenue stream, shareholders got a stable return, and consumers benefited from low telephone rates.

Result: As Cornell's Alfred E. Kahn... puts it: "Depreciation lives were set under a monopoly that was in a position to control the rate of innovation." No matter how long the costs were stretched out, they were certain to be recovered. And if the geniuses at Bell Labs came up with something new—improved fiber optics, say—it was unlikely that billions of dollars' worth of copper wire would be pulled out until it was fully depreciated.

No more. With deregulation, anybody with the wherewithal can put in a state-of-the-art telephone system vastly more efficient and cheaper than old-fashioned copper wires and mechanical switching. Some of the telephone companies' biggest customers are doing just that....

All in all, says a study by the U.S. Telephone Association, local operating companies could lose $8.4 billion in annual revenues by 1995 because big customers are bypassing them....

So the local companies are spending big—an estimated $18 billion this year on capital construction—in a rush to install digital switching and fiber optics before their big customers desert them for good. Trouble is, they still have that $26 billion in old plant on their books that won't be depreciated for years....

...What will happen? Unless somebody comes up with a better solution, which isn't likely, the telephone companies are going to have to write off some of that $26 billion, probably a lot of it. Alfred Kahn compares their plight to that of a utility with an abandoned nuclear plant. "You just have to eat some of that deficiency," he says. "You have to write down the assets to something more closely approximating what you can hope to get back in the future, write down your equity on the other side of the balance sheet, and take your loss."

Source: Howard Gold, "The $26 Billion Solution," *Forbes* (July 29, 1985), pp. 40–41.

SUBSIDIARY LEDGERS FOR PLANT ASSETS

When depreciation is to be computed individually on a large number of assets making up a functional group, it is advisable to maintain a subsidiary ledger. To illustrate, assume that an enterprise owns about 200 items of office equipment with a total cost of about $100,000. Unless the business is newly organized, the equipment would have been acquired over a number of years. The individual cost, estimated residual value, and estimated useful life would be different in each case, and the makeup of the group will continually change because of acquisitions and disposals.

There are many variations in the form of subsidiary records for depreciable assets. Multicolumn analysis sheets may be used, or a separate ledger account may be maintained for each asset. The form should be designed to provide spaces for recording the acquisition and the disposal of the asset, the depreciation charged each period, the accumulated depreciation to date, and any other pertinent data desired. Following is an example of a subsidiary ledger account for a plant asset:

An Account in the Office Equipment Ledger

Plant Asset Record

Account No.: 123-215 General Ledger Account: Office Equipment

Item: SF 490 COPIER

Serial No.: AT 47-3926

From Whom Purchased: Hamilton Office Machines Co. Inc.

Estimated Useful Life: 10 Years Estimated Residual Value: $500 Depreciation per Year: $240

	Asset			Accumulated Depreciation			Book
Date	Debit	Credit	Balance	Debit	Credit	Balance	Value
04/08/89	2,900		2,900				2,900
12/31/89					180	180	2,720
12/31/90					240	420	2,480

The number assigned to the account illustrated is made up of the number of the office equipment account in the general ledger (123) followed by the number assigned to the specific item of office equipment purchased (215). An identification tag or plaque with the corresponding account number is attached to the asset. Depreciation for the year in which the asset was acquired, computed for nine months on a straight-line basis, is $180; for the following year it is $240. These amounts, together with the corresponding amounts from all other accounts in the subsidiary ledger, provide the figures for the respective year-end adjusting entries debiting the depreciation expense account and crediting the accumulated depreciation account.

The sum of the asset balances and the sum of the accumulated depreciation balances in all of the accounts should be compared periodically with the balances of their respective controlling accounts in the general ledger. When a certain asset is disposed of, the asset section of the subsidiary account is credited and the accumulated depreciation section is debited. This reduces the balances of both sections to zero. The account is then removed from the ledger and filed for possible future reference.

Subsidiary ledgers for plant assets are useful to the accounting department in (1) determining the periodic depreciation expense, (2) recording the disposal of individual items, (3) preparing tax returns, and (4) preparing insurance claims in the event of insured losses. The forms may also be expanded to provide spaces for accumulating data on the operating efficiency of the asset. Such information as number of breakdowns, length of time out of service, and cost of repairs is useful in comparing similar equipment produced by different manufacturers. When new equipment is to be purchased, the data are useful to management in deciding upon size, model, and other specifications and the best source of supply.

Regardless of whether subsidiary equipment ledgers are maintained, plant assets should be inspected periodically in order to determine their state of repair and whether or not they are still in use.

COMPOSITE-RATE DEPRECIATION METHOD

In the preceding illustrations, depreciation has been computed on each individual plant asset and, unless otherwise stated, this procedure will be assumed in the problem materials at the end of the chapter. Another procedure, called the **composite-rate depreciation method**, is to determine depreciation for entire groups of assets by use of a single rate. The basis for grouping may be similarity in life estimates or other common traits, or it may be broadened to include all assets within a functional class, such as office equipment or factory equipment.

When depreciation is computed on the basis of a composite group of assets of differing life spans, a rate based on averages must be developed. This may be done by (1) computing the annual depreciation for each asset, (2) determining the total annual depreciation, and (3) dividing the sum thus determined by the total cost of the assets. The procedure is illustrated as follows:

Composite-Rate Method of Depreciation

Asset No.	*Cost*	*Estimated Residual Value*	*Estimated Life*	*Annual Depreciation*
101	$ 20,000	$4,000	10 years	$ 1,600
102	15,600	1,500	15 years	940
~~				
147	41,000	1,000	8 years	5,000
Total	$473,400			$49,707

$$\frac{\$49{,}707 \text{ annual depreciation}}{\$473{,}400 \text{ cost}} = 10.5\% \text{ composite rate}$$

Although new assets of differing life spans and residual values will be added to the group and old assets will be retired, the "mix" is assumed to remain relatively unchanged. Accordingly, a depreciation rate based on averages (10.5% in the illustration) also remains unchanged for an indefinite time in the future.

When a composite rate is used, it may be applied against total asset cost on a monthly basis, or some reasonable assumption may be made regarding the timing of increases and decreases in the group. A common practice is to assume that all additions and retirements have occurred uniformly throughout the year. The composite rate is then applied to the average of the beginning and the ending balances of the account. Another acceptable averaging technique is to assume that all additions and retirements during the first half of the year occurred as of the first day of the year, and that all additions and retirements during the second half of the year occurred on the first day of the following year.

When assets within the composite group are retired, no gain or loss should be recognized. Instead, the asset account is credited for the cost of the asset and the accumulated depreciation account is debited for the excess of cost over the amount realized from the disposal. Any deficiency in the amount of depreciation recorded on the shorter-lived assets is presumed to be balanced by excessive depreciation on the longer-lived assets.

Regardless of whether depreciation is computed for each individual unit or for composite groups, the periodic depreciation charge is based on estimates. The effect of obsolescence and inadequacy on the life of plant assets is particularly difficult to forecast. Any system that provides for the allocation of depreciation in a systematic and rational manner fulfills the requirements of good accounting.

DEPRECIATION OF PLANT ASSETS OF LOW UNIT COST

Subsidiary ledgers are not usually maintained for classes of plant assets that are made up of individual items of low unit cost. Hand tools and other portable equipment of small size and value are typical examples. Because of hard usage, breakage, and pilferage, such assets may be relatively short-lived and may require constant replacement. In such cases, the usual depreciation methods are not practical. One common method of determining cost expiration is to take a periodic inventory of the items on hand, estimate their fair value based on original cost, and transfer the remaining amount from the asset account to an appropriately titled account, such as Tools Expense. Other categories to which the same method is often applied are dies, molds, patterns, and spare parts.

ACQUISITION OF PLANT ASSETS THROUGH LEASING

Instead of owning a plant asset, a business may acquire the use of a plant asset through a lease. A **lease** is a contractual agreement that conveys the right to use an asset for a stated period of time. The two parties to a lease contract are the **lessor** and the **lessee.** The lessor is the party who legally owns the asset and who conveys the rights to use the asset to the lessee. Typical lease transactions include the leasing of automobiles, computers, airplanes, and communication satellites.

In agreeing to a lease, the lessee incurs an obligation to make periodic rent payments for the lease term. In accounting for lease obligations, all leases are classified by the lessee as either capital leases or operating leases. **Capital leases** are defined as leases which include one or more of the following provisions: (1) the lease transfers ownership of the leased asset to the lessee at the end of the lease term; (2) the lease contains an option for a bargain purchase of the leased asset by the lessee; (3) the lease term extends over most of the economic life of the leased asset; or (4) the lease requires rental payments which approximate the fair market value of the leased asset.[6] Leases which do not meet the preceding criteria for a capital lease are classified as **operating leases.**

A capital lease is accounted for as if the lessee has, in fact, purchased the asset. Accordingly, when a lease is executed, the lessee would debit an asset account for the fair market value of the leased asset and would credit a long-term lease liability account. The complex accounting procedures applicable to capital leases are discussed in detail in more advanced accounting texts.

In accounting for operating leases, rent expense is recognized as the leased asset is used. Neither future lease obligations nor the future rights to use the leased asset are recognized in the accounts. However, the lessee must disclose future lease commitments in footnotes to the financial statements.[7] An example of the disclosure of future lease commitments taken from the 1986 annual report of The Pillsbury Company is as follows:

omit

Minimum future obligations on leases with an initial term greater than one year for the fiscal years ending May 31:	*Capital leases*	*Operating leases*
	(In millions)	
1987	$ 15.7	$ 69.1
1988	14.2	62.5
1989	13.1	59.4
1990	12.2	54.9
1991	11.6	49.3
Later	71.8	488.9
Total minimum obligations	138.6	784.1

DEPLETION

Know

The periodic allocation of the cost of metal ores and other minerals removed from the earth is called **depletion.** The amount of the periodic cost allocation is based on the relationship of the cost to the estimated size of the mineral deposit and on the quantity extracted during the particular period. To illustrate, assume that the cost of certain mineral rights is $400,000 and that the deposit is estimated at 1,000,000 tons of ore of uniform grade. The depletion rate would be $400,000 ÷ 1,000,000, or $.40 a ton. If 90,000 tons are mined during the year, the depletion, amounting to $36,000, would be recorded by the following entry:

Read

[6] *Statement of Financial Accounting Standards, No. 13,* "Accounting for Leases" (Stamford: Financial Accounting Standards Board, 1976), par. 7.

[7] *Ibid.,* par. 16.

Adjusting Entry

Dec. 31	Depletion Expense	36,000	
	Accumulated Depletion		36,000

The accumulated depletion account is a contra asset account and is presented in the balance sheet as a deduction from the cost of the mineral deposit.

In determining income subject to the federal income tax, the IRC permits, with certain limitations, a depletion deduction equal to a specified percent of gross income from the extractive operations. Thus, for income tax purposes, it is possible for total depletion deductions to be more than the cost of the property. A detailed examination of the tax law and regulations regarding "percentage depletion" is beyond the scope of this discussion, however.

INTANGIBLE ASSETS

Long-lived assets that are useful in the operations of an enterprise, not held for sale, and without physical qualities are usually classified as **intangible assets.** The basic principles of accounting for intangible assets are like those described earlier for plant assets. The major concerns are the determination of the initial costs and the recognition of periodic cost expiration, called **amortization**, due to the passage of time or a decline in usefulness. Intangible assets often include patents, copyrights, and goodwill.

Patents

Manufacturers may acquire exclusive rights to produce and sell goods with one or more unique features. Such rights are evidenced by **patents,** which are issued to inventors by the federal government. They continue in effect for 17 years. An enterprise may purchase patent rights from others or it may obtain patents on new products developed in its own research laboratories.

The initial cost of a purchased patent should be debited to an asset account and then written off, or amortized, over the years of its expected usefulness. This period of time may be less than the remaining legal life of the patent, and the expectations are also subject to change in the future. The straight-line method of amortization should be used unless it can be shown that another method is more appropriate.[8]

A separate contra asset account is normally not credited for the write-off or amortization of patents. In most situations, the credit is recorded directly in the patents account. This practice is common for all intangible assets. To illustrate, assume that at the beginning of its fiscal year an enterprise acquires for $100,000 a patent granted six years earlier. Although the patent will not expire for another eleven years, it is expected to be of value for only five years. The entry to amortize the patent at the end of the fiscal year is as follows:

Adjusting Entry

Dec. 31	Amortization Expense—Patents	20,000	
	Patents		20,000

[8]*Opinions of the Accounting Principles Board, No. 17,* "Intangible Assets" (New York: American Institute of Certified Public Accountants, 1970), par. 30.

Continuing the illustration, assume that after two years of use it appears that the patent will have no value at the end of an additional two years. The cost to be amortized in the third year would be the balance of the asset account, $60,000, divided by the remaining two years, or $30,000.

An enterprise that develops patentable products in its own research laboratories often incurs substantial costs for the experimental work involved. In theory, some accountants believe that such costs, normally referred to as **research and development costs,** should be treated as an asset in the same manner as patent rights purchased from others. However, business enterprises are generally required to treat expenditures for research and development as current operating expenses.[9] The reason for this requirement is that there is a high degree of uncertainty about their future benefits, and therefore expensing these costs as incurred seems most appropriate. In addition, from a practical standpoint, a reasonably fair cost figure for each patent is difficult to establish because a number of research projects may be in process at the same time or work on some projects may extend over a number of years. As a result, a specific relationship between research and development costs and future revenue seldom can be established.

Whether patent rights are purchased from others or result from the effort of its own research laboratories, an enterprise often incurs substantial legal fees related to the patents. For example, legal fees may be incurred in establishing the legal validity of the patents. Such fees should be debited to an asset account and then amortized over the years of the usefulness of the patents.

Copyrights

The exclusive right to publish and sell a literary, artistic, or musical composition is obtained by a **copyright.** Copyrights are issued by the federal government and extend for 50 years beyond the author's death. The costs assigned to a copyright include all costs of creating the work plus the cost of obtaining the copyright. A copyright that is purchased from another should be recorded at the price paid for it. Because of the uncertainty regarding the useful life of a copyright, it is usually amortized over a relatively short period of time.

Goodwill

In the sense that it is used in business, **goodwill** is an intangible asset that attaches to a business as a result of such favorable factors as location, product superiority, reputation, and managerial skill. Its existence is evidenced by the ability of the business to earn a rate of return on the investment that is in excess of the normal rate for other firms in the same line of business.

Accountants are in general agreement that goodwill should be recognized in the accounts only if it can be objectively determined by an event or transaction, such as the purchase or sale of a business. Accountants also agree that the value of goodwill eventually disappears and that the recorded costs should be amortized over the years during which the goodwill is expected to be of value. This period should not, however, exceed 40 years.[10]

[9] *Statement of Financial Accounting Standards, No. 2,* "Accounting for Research and Development Costs" (Stamford: Financial Accounting Standards Board, 1974), par. 12.

[10] *Opinions of the Accounting Principles Board, No. 17,* "Intangible Assets," *op. cit.,* par. 29.

REPORTING DEPRECIATION EXPENSE, PLANT ASSETS, AND INTANGIBLE ASSETS IN THE FINANCIAL STATEMENTS

The amount of depreciation expense of a period should be set forth separately in the income statement or disclosed in some other manner. A general description of the method or methods used in computing depreciation should also accompany the financial statements.[11]

The balance of each major class of depreciable assets should be disclosed in the balance sheet or in notes thereto, together with the related accumulated depreciation, either by major class or in total.[12] When there are too many classes of plant assets to permit such a detailed listing in the balance sheet, a single figure may be presented, supported by a separate schedule.

Intangible assets are usually presented in the balance sheet in a separate section immediately following plant assets. The balance of each major class of intangible assets should be disclosed at an amount net of amortization taken to date.

An illustration of the presentation of plant assets and intangible assets is shown in the following partial balance sheet:

Plant Assets and Intangible Assets in the Balance Sheet

Clinton Door Inc.
Balance Sheet
December 31, 19--

Assets

	Cost	Accumulated Depreciation	Book Value	
Total current assets				$462,500
Plant assets:				
Land	$ 30,000	—	$ 30,000	
Buildings..................	110,000	$ 26,000	84,000	
Factory equipment........	650,000	192,000	458,000	
Office equipment	120,000	13,000	107,000	
Total plant assets	$910,000	$231,000		679,000
Intangible assets:				
Patents			$ 75,000	
Goodwill			50,000	
Total intangible assets....				125,000

REPLACEMENT COST OF PLANT ASSETS

In preceding illustrations, plant assets were recorded at the cost actually incurred in acquiring them (historical cost), and depreciation was based on this cost. This principle is generally accepted for financial reporting purposes. The basic financial statements, therefore, do not indicate the effect

[11]*Opinions of the Accounting Principles Board, No. 22,* "Disclosure of Accounting Policies" (New York: American Institute of Certified Public Accountants, 1972), par. 13.

[12]*Opinions of the Accounting Principles Board, No. 12,* "Omnibus Opinion—1967" (New York: American Institute of Certified Public Accountants, 1967), par. 5.

of changes in price levels on plant assets and depreciation. In periods of inflation, which have been common in the past, many accountants have questioned the usefulness of financial statements that ignore the effects of inflation on operations.

To indicate the nature of the problem, assume that plant assets acquired by an enterprise ten years ago for $1,000,000 are now to replaced with similar assets which, at present price levels, will cost $2,000,000. Assume further that during the ten-year period the plant assets had been fully depreciated and that the net income of the enterprise had amounted to $5,000,000. Although the initial outlay of $1,000,000 for the plant assets was recovered through depreciation charges, the amount represents only one half of the cost of replacing the assets. Instead of considering the current value of the new assets to have doubled compared to a decade earlier, the dollars recovered can be said to have declined to one half of their earlier value. From either point of view, the firm has suffered a loss in purchasing power, which is the same as a loss of capital. In addition, $1,000,000 of the net income reported during the period might be said to be illusory, since it must be used to replace the assets.

The use of historical cost in accounting for plant assets insures objectivity. Therefore, in spite of inflationary trends, historical-cost financial statements are considered to be better than statements based on movements in the price level. Many accountants, however, recommend that businesses provide supplemental information that indicates the replacement cost, or current cost, of plant assets and the depreciation based on such cost. This supplemental information would match current costs for depreciation against current revenues and would therefore give a net income figure that would be useful in evaluating operating results. For example, a net income figure that has been determined after considering plant asset depreciation based on replacement cost would be especially useful in evaluating the amount of net income that should be made available for dividends.

There are many obstacles to the use of replacement costs for accounting for plant assets. For many businesses, such as a steel company with its many buildings and special machinery and equipment, it would be difficult to determine replacement costs with reasonable accuracy. In addition, if replacement costs were used, the process of estimating costs would have to be repeated each year, which would further increase the subjectivity of the accounting method. For reasons such as these, the use of replacement costs in accounting for plant assets has been generally restricted to experimental situations involving supplementary data.

Chapter Review

KEY POINTS

1. Initial Costs of Plant Assets.

The initial cost of a plant asset includes all expenditures necessary to get it in place and ready for use. Such expenditures include sales taxes, transportation charges, insurance on the asset while in transit, special foundations, installation costs, broker's commissions, and title fees.

2. Nature of Depreciation.
As time passes, all plant assets with the exception of land lose their capacity to yield services. This expiration of the cost of plant assets is called depreciation.

3. Determining Depreciation.
In determining the amount of depreciation, three factors need to be considered: (1) the plant asset's initial cost, (2) the residual value of the asset, and (3) the useful life of the asset. The difference between a plant asset's initial cost and its residual value is the cost that is to be spread over the useful life of the asset.

The four methods of depreciation used most often are summarized as follows:

Straight-line	Provides for equal periodic charges to expense over the estimated useful life of the asset.
Units-of-production..........	Yields a depreciation charge that varies with the amount of asset usage. Length of useful life of asset expressed in terms of productive capacity.
Declining-balance...........	Yields a declining periodic depreciation charge over the estimated useful life of the asset. Rate of depreciation usually twice the straight-line rate. Computed without regard to residual value. Resulting rate applied to cost of asset less accumulated depreciation.
Sum-of-the-year-digits.......	Yields a steadily declining periodic depreciation charge over the estimated useful life of the asset. Successively smaller fraction applied each year to the original cost of the asset less the estimated residual value.

All four depreciation methods will yield identical amounts of total depreciation over the life of the asset. However, each method will yield periodic charges which may vary significantly. Because the declining-balance and the sum-of-the-years-digits methods provide a higher depreciation charge in the early years of the life of the asset and a gradually declining charge thereafter, they are referred to as accelerated depreciation methods.

4. Depreciation for Federal Income Tax.
Each of the four depreciation methods described in this chapter can be used to determine the amount of depreciation for federal income tax purposes for plant assets acquired prior to 1981. For plant assets acquired after 1980, and before 1987, either the straight-line method or the Accelerated Cost Recovery System (ACRS) may be used. Under the Tax Reform Act of 1986, Modified ACRS (MACRS) must be used for plant assets acquired after 1986.

5. Revision of Periodic Depreciation.
Minor errors resulting from incorrect estimates of a plant asset's useful life and residual value are corrected by revising estimates used to determine the amount of remaining undepreciated asset cost to be charged to expense in future periods.

6. Recording Depreciation.
Depreciation is recorded periodically by debiting Depreciation Expense and crediting a contra asset account entitled Accumulated Depreciation. The use of a contra asset account permits the original cost to remain unchanged in the plant asset account.

7. Capital and Revenue Expenditures.
In addition to the initial cost of acquiring a plant asset, costs for additions made to the asset and other costs related to its efficiency or capacity may be incurred during its service life. Costs for additions or costs that add to the utility of the asset for more than one period are chargeable to an asset account or to a related accumulated depreciation account and are called capital expenditures. Expenditures that benefit only the current period and that are made in order to maintain normal operating efficiency are chargeable to expense accounts and are called revenue expenditures.

8. Disposal of Plant Assets.
Plant assets that are no longer useful may be discarded, sold, or traded in on other plant assets. When disposal of a plant asset occurs, the cost of the plant asset and the accumulated depreciation must be removed from the accounts and any related gain or loss recognized.

9. Subsidiary Ledgers for Plant Assets.
When depreciation is to be computed individually on a large number of assets making up a functional group, it is advisable to maintain a subsidiary ledger. Subsidiary ledgers for plant assets are useful in determining the periodic depreciation expense, recording the disposal of individual items, preparing tax returns, and preparing insurance claims in the event of insured losses.

10. Composite-Rate Depreciation Method.
Depreciation determined for an entire group of assets by use of a single rate is referred to as composite-rate depreciation. When this method is used to compute depreciation on a group of assets of differing life spans, a rate based on averages must be developed.

11. Depreciation of Plant Assets of Low Unit Cost.
For classes of plant assets that are made up of individual items of low unit cost, depreciation is often determined by periodically taking an inventory of items on hand, estimating their fair value based on original cost, and transferring the remaining amount from the asset account to an expense account.

12. Acquisition of Plant Assets Through Leasing.
Instead of owning a plant asset, a business may acquire the use of a plant asset through a lease. A lease agreement conveys the right to use an asset for a stated period of time. A capital lease is accounted for as if the lessee has, in fact, purchased the asset. An operating lease recognizes lease payments as rent expense for the lessee and as rent income for the lessor.

13. Depletion.
The periodic allocation of the cost of metal ores and other minerals removed from the earth is called depletion. The amount of the periodic cost allocation is based on the relationship of the cost to the estimated size of the mineral deposit, and on the quantity extracted during the particular period. An accumulated depletion account is maintained as a contra account to the original cost of the mineral deposit.

14. Intangible Assets.
Long-lived assets that are useful in the operations of an enterprise, not held for sale, and without physical qualities are usually classified as intangible assets. The initial cost of an intangible asset is normally amortized over its useful life. Intangible assets include patents, copyrights, and goodwill.

15. Reporting Depreciation Expense, Plant Assets, and Intangible Assets in the Financial Statements.
The amount of depreciation expense and the method or methods used in computing depreciation should be disclosed in the financial statements. In addition, each major class of depreciable assets should be disclosed, along with the related accumulated depreciation. Intangible assets are usually presented in the balance sheet in a separate section immediately following plant assets. Each major class of intangible assets should be disclosed at an amount net of amortization taken to date.

16. Replacement Cost of Plant Assets.
Plant assets are recorded at cost, and depreciation is based on this cost for financial reporting purposes. However, many accountants recommend that businesses provide supplemental information that indicates the replacement cost, or current cost, of plant assets and the depreciation based on such costs. Such supplemental information would be especially useful in evaluating operating results in periods of inflation.

KEY TERMS

plant assets 287
depreciation 289
residual value 289
straight-line method 291
units-of-production method 291
declining-balance method 292
sum-of-the-years-digits method 293
accelerated depreciation method 294
capital expenditures 296
revenue expenditures 296
boot 299
composite-rate depreciation method 303
capital leases 305
operating leases 305
depletion 305
intangible assets 306
amortization 306
goodwill 307

SELF-EXAMINATION QUESTIONS

(Answers at End of Chapter)

1. Which of the following expenditures incurred in connection with the acquisition of machinery is a proper charge to the asset account?
   A. Transportation charges
   B. Installation costs
   C. Both A and B
   D. Neither A nor B

2. What is the amount of depreciation, using the sum-of-the-years-digits method, for the first year of use for equipment costing $9,500, with an estimated residual value of $500 and an estimated life of 3 years?
   A. $4,500.00
   B. $3,166.67
   C. $3,000.00
   D. None of the above

3. An example of an accelerated depreciation method is:
   A. straight-line
   B. sum-of-the-years-digits
   C. units-of-production
   D. none of the above

4. A plant asset priced at $100,000 is acquired by trading in a similar asset that has a book value of $25,000. Assuming that the trade-in allowance is

$30,000 and that $70,000 cash is paid for the new asset, what is the cost basis for the new asset for financial reporting purposes?
A. $100,000
B. $70,000
C. $30,000
D. None of the above

5. Which of the following is an example of an intangible asset?
A. Patents
B. Goodwill
C. Copyrights
D. All of the above

ILLUSTRATIVE PROBLEM

Florence Company acquired new equipment at a cost of $75,000 at the beginning of the fiscal year. The equipment has an estimated life of five years and an estimated residual value of $6,000. The president, John C. Florence, has requested information regarding the alternative depreciation methods.

Instructions:

1. Determine the annual depreciation for each of the five years of estimated useful life of the equipment, the accumulated depreciation at the end of each year, and the book value of the equipment at the end of each year by (a) the straight-line method, (b) the declining-balance method (at twice the straight-line rate), and (c) the sum-of-the-years-digits method.
2. Assume that the equipment was depreciated under the declining-balance method. In the first week of the fifth year, the equipment was traded in for similar equipment priced at $90,000. The trade-in allowance on the old equipment was $8,000, and cash was paid for the balance.
   a. Prepare the journal entry to record the exchange.
   b. What is the cost basis of the new equipment for computing the amount of depreciation allowable for income tax purposes?

SOLUTION

(1)

	Year	Depreciation Expense	Accumulated Depreciation, End of Year	Book Value, End of Year
(a)	1	$13,800	$13,800	$61,200
	2	13,800	27,600	47,400
	3	13,800	41,400	33,600
	4	13,800	55,200	19,800
	5	13,800	69,000	6,000
(b)	1	$30,000	$30,000	$45,000
	2	18,000	48,000	27,000
	3	10,800	58,800	16,200
	4	6,480	65,280	9,720
	5	3,720*	69,000	6,000
(c)	1	$23,000	$23,000	$52,000
	2	18,400	41,400	33,600
	3	13,800	55,200	19,800
	4	9,200	64,400	10,600
	5	4,600	69,000	6,000

*The asset is not depreciated below the estimated residual value of $6,000.

(2)(a)	Accumulated Depreciation—Equipment	65,280	
	Equipment	90,000	
	Loss on Disposal of Plant Assets	1,720	
	Equipment		75,000
	Cash		82,000

(b)	Book value of old equipment	$ 9,720
	Boot given (cash)	82,000
	Cost basis of new equipment for income tax purposes	$91,720

or

Price of new equipment	$90,000
Plus unrecognized loss on old equipment	1,720
Cost basis of new equipment for income tax purposes	$91,720

Discussion Questions

8–1. Which of the following qualities are characteristic of plant assets? (a) tangible, (b) intangible, (c) capable of repeated use in the operations of the business, (d) long-lived, (e) held for sale in the normal course of business, (f) used continuously in the operations of the business.

8–2. Shay Office Equipment Co. has a fleet of automobiles and trucks for use by salespersons and for delivery of office supplies and equipment. Martin Auto Sales Inc. has automobiles and trucks for sale. Under what caption would the automobiles and trucks be reported on the balance sheet of (a) Shay Office Equipment Co., (b) Martin Auto Sales Inc.?

8–3. Roarke and Simons Co. acquired an adjacent vacant lot as a speculation. The lot will hopefully be sold in the future at a gain. Where should such real estate be listed in the balance sheet?

8–4. Which of the following expenditures incurred in connection with the acquisition of a lathe should be charged to the asset account? (a) sales tax on purchase price, (b) freight charges, (c) insurance while in transit, (d) cost of special foundation (e) new parts to replace those damaged in unloading, (f) fee paid to factory representative for installation.

8–5. Which of the following expenditures incurred in connection with the purchase of a secondhand printing press should be debited to the asset account? (a) freight charges, (b) installation costs, (c) repair of vandalism damages that occurred during installation, (d) replacement of worn-out parts.

8–6. To increase its parking area, Market Place Shopping Center acquired adjoining land for $80,000 and a building located on the land for $40,000. The net cost of razing the building and leveling the land was $10,000, after amounts received from the sale of salvaged building materials were deducted. What accounts should be debited for (a) the cost of the land ($80,000), (b) the cost of the building ($40,000), (c) the net cost of preparing the land ($10,000)?

8–7. Are the amounts at which plant assets are reported in the balance sheet their approximate market values as of the balance sheet date? Discuss.

8–8. (a) Does the recognition of depreciation in the accounts provide a special cash fund for the replacement of plant assets? Explain. (b) Describe the nature of depreciation as the term is used in accounting.

8–9. Name the three factors that need to be considered in determining the amount of periodic depreciation.

8–10. Is it necessary for an enterprise to use the same method of computing depreciation (a) for all classes of its depreciable assets, (b) in the financial statements and in the determination of income taxes?

8–11. Of the four common depreciation methods, which is most widely used?

8–12. Convert each of the following estimates of useful life to a straight-line depreciation rate, stated as a percent, assuming that the residual value of the plant asset is to be ignored: (a) 4 years, (b) 5 years, (c) 10 years, (d) 20 years, (e) 25 years, (f) 40 years, (g) 50 years.

8–13. A plant asset with a cost of $85,000 has an estimated residual value of $5,000 and an estimated useful life of 4 years. What is the amount of the annual depreciation, computed by the straight-line method?

8–14. A plant asset with a cost of $95,000 has an estimated residual value of $5,000 and an estimated productive capacity of 900,000 units. What is the amount of annual depreciation, computed by the units-of-production method, for a year in which production is (a) 90,000 units, (b) 60,000 units?

8–15. The declining-balance method, at double the straight-line rate, is to be used for an asset with a cost of $100,000, estimated residual value of $10,000, and estimated useful life of 10 years. What is the depreciation for the first fiscal year, assuming that the asset was placed in service at the beginning of the year?

8–16. An asset with a cost of $26,000, an estimated residual value of $1,000, and an estimated useful life of 4 years is to be depreciated by the sum-of-the-years-digits method. (a) What is the denominator of the depreciation fraction? (b) What is the amount of depreciation for the first full year of use? (c) What is the amount of depreciation for the second full year of use?

8–17. (a) Name the two accelerated depreciation methods described in this chapter. (b) Why are the accelerated depreciation methods used frequently for income tax purposes?

8–18. A plant asset with a cost of $205,000 has an estimated residual value of $5,000, an estimated useful life of 40 years, and is depreciated by the straight-line method. (a) What is the amount of the annual depreciation? (b) What is the book value at the end of the twentieth year of use? (c) If at the start of the twenty-first year it is estimated that the remaining life is 25 years and that the residual value is $5,000, what is the depreciation expense for each of the remaining 25 years?

8–19. (a) Differentiate between capital expenditures and revenue expenditures. (b) Why are some items that have the characteristics of capital expenditures treated as revenue expenditures?

8–20. Immediately after a used truck is acquired, a new motor is installed and the tires are replaced at a total cost of $3,500. Is this a capital expenditure or a revenue expenditure?

8–21. For a number of subsidiary plant ledger accounts of an enterprise, the balance in accumulated depreciation is exactly equal to the cost of the asset. (a) Is it permissible to record additional depreciation on the assets if they are still useful to the enterprise? Explain. (b) When should an entry be made to remove the cost and accumulated depreciation from the accounts?

8–22. In what sections of the income statement are gains and losses from the disposal of plant assets presented?

8–23. A plant asset priced at $120,000 is acquired by trading in a similar asset and paying cash for the remainder. (a) Assuming that the trade-in allowance is $50,000, what is the amount of boot given? (b) Assuming that the book value of the asset traded in is $40,000, what is the cost basis of the new asset for financial reporting purposes? (c) What is the cost basis of the new asset for the computation of depreciation for federal income tax purposes?

8–24. Assume the same facts as in Question 8–23, except that the book value of the asset traded in is $60,000. (a) What is the cost basis of the new asset for financial reporting purposes? (b) What is the cost basis of the new asset for the computation of depreciation for federal income tax purposes?

8–25. The cost of a composite group of equipment is $700,000 and the annual depreciation, computed on the individual items, totals $77,000 (a) What is the composite straight-line depreciation rate? (b) What would the rate be if the total depreciation amounted to $56,000 instead of $77,000?

8–26. Differentiate between a capital lease and an operating lease.

8–27. What is the term applied to the periodic charge for (a) ore removed from a mine, (b) the write-off of the cost of an intangible asset?

8–28. (a) Over what period of time should the cost of a patent acquired by purchase be amortized? (b) In general, what is the required treatment for research and development costs?

8–29. Is the use of replacement cost generally accepted for accounting for plant assets and depreciation?

8–30. Real World Focus. The financial statements of La-Z-Boy Chair Company contain the following footnote:

> The Company has several long-term leases covering manufacturing facilities. The lease agreements require the Company to insure and maintain the facilities and provide for annual payments, which include interest. These leases give the Company the option to purchase the facilities for nominal amounts, or in some instances to renew the leases for extended periods at nominal annual rentals.

Would these leases be classified as operating or capital leases? Discuss.

Exercises

8–31. Depreciation by three methods. A plant asset acquired on January 2 at a cost of $220,000 has an estimated useful life of 10 years. Assuming that it will have no residual value, determine the depreciation for each of the first two years (a) by the straight-line method, (b) by the declining-balance method, using twice the straight-line rate, and (c) by the sum-of-the-years-digits method.

8–32. Depreciation by units-of-production method. A diesel-powered generator with a cost of $160,000 and estimated salvage value of $10,000 is expected to have a useful operating life of 50,000 hours. During June, the generator was operated 360 hours. Determine the depreciation for the month.

SPREADSHEET PROBLEM

8–33. Depreciation by units-of-production method. Balances in Trucks and in Accumulated Depreciation—Trucks at the end of the year, prior to adjustment, are $109,600 and $53,500, respectively. Details of the subsidiary ledger are as follows:

Truck No.	Cost	Estimated Residual Value	Estimated Useful Life in Miles	Accumulated Depreciation at Beginning of Year	Miles Operated During Year
1	$45,000	$5,000	200,000	$22,500	25,000
2	17,600	2,600	100,000	7,700	20,000
3	28,000	4,000	150,000	23,300	4,500
4	19,000	1,000	200,000	—	12,000

(a) Determine the depreciation rates per mile and the amount to be credited to the accumulated depreciation section of each of the subsidiary accounts for the current year. (b) Present the journal entry to record depreciation for the year.

8–34. Depreciation by three methods. An item of equipment acquired at the beginning of the fiscal year at a cost of $45,200 has an estimated residual value of $2,000 and an estimated useful life of 8 years. Determine the following: (a) the amount of annual depreciation by the straight-line method, (b) the amount of depreciation for the second year computed by the declining-balance method (at twice the straight-line rate), (c) the amount of depreciation for the second year computed by the sum-of-the-years-digits method.

8–35. Depreciation by accelerated depreciation methods. A piece of machinery acquired at a cost of $33,000 has an estimated residual value of $3,000 and an estimated useful life of 5 years. It was placed in service on April 1 of the current fiscal year, which ends on December 31. Determine the depreciation for the current fiscal year and for the following fiscal year by (a) the declining-balance method, at twice the straight-line rate, and (b) the sum-of-the-years-digits method.

8–36. Revision of depreciation. An item of equipment acquired on January 3, 1985, at a cost of $32,500 has an estimated residual value of $2,500 and an estimated useful life of 10 years. Depreciation has been recorded for the first four years ended December 31, 1988, by the straight-line method. Determine the amount of depreciation for the current year ended December 31, 1989, if the revised estimated residual value is $2,100 and the revised estimated remaining useful life (including the current year) is 8 years.

8–37. Entries for sale of plant asset. A piece of equipment acquired on January 2, 1987, at a cost of $55,000 has an estimated useful life of five years, an estimated residual value of $5,000, and is depreciated by the straight-line method. (a) What was the book value of the equipment at December 31, 1990, the end of the fiscal year? (b) Assuming that the equipment was sold on July 1, 1991, for $7,500, prepare journal entries to record (1) depreciation for the six months of the current year ending December 31, 1991, and (2) the sale of the equipment.

8–38. Disposal of plant asset. A piece of equipment acquired on January 3, 1986, at a cost of $22,500 has an estimated useful life of 4 years and an estimated residual value of $2,500. (a) What was the annual amount of depreciation for the years 1986, 1987, and 1988, assuming the use of the straight-line method of depreciation? (b) What was the book value of the equipment on January 1, 1989? (c) Assuming that the equipment was sold on January 2, 1989, for $6,000, prepare the journal entry to record the sale. (d) Assuming that the equipment had been sold for $9,000 on January 2, 1989, instead of $6,000, prepare the journal entry to record the sale.

8–39. Major repair to plant asset. A number of major structural repairs completed at the beginning of the current fiscal year at a cost of $90,000 are expected to extend the life of a building 10 years beyond the original estimate. The original cost of the building was $800,000, and it has been depreciated by the straight-line method for 25 years. Residual value is expected to be negligible and has been ignored. The balance of the related accumulated depreciation account after the depreciation adjustment at the end of the preceding year is $400,000. (a) What has the amount of annual depreciation been in past years? (b) To what account should the cost of repairs ($90,000) be debited? (c) What is the book value of the building after the repairs have been recorded? (d) What is the amount of depreciation for the current year, using the straight-line method (assume that the repairs were completed at the very beginning of the year)?

8–40. Entries for loss on trade of plant asset. On July 1, Ross Co. acquired a new computer with a list price of $125,000. Ross received a trade-in allowance of $15,000 on an old computer of a similar type, paid cash of $30,000, and gave a series of five notes payable for the remainder. The following information about the old computer is obtained from the account in the office equipment ledger: cost, $82,500; accumulated depreciation on December 31, the end of the preceding fiscal year, $50,000; annual depreciation, $15,000. Present entries to record: (a) the current depreciation on the old computer to the date of trade-in; (b) the transaction on July 1 for financial reporting purposes.

8–41. Depreciation on asset acquired by exchange. On the first day of the fiscal year, a delivery truck with a list price of $30,000 was acquired in an exchange for an old delivery truck and $26,000 cash. The old truck has a book value of $2,500 at the date of the exchange. The new truck is to be depreciated over 5 years by the straight-line method. The estimated residual value is $2,000. Determine the following: (a) annual depreciation for financial reporting purposes, (b) annual depreciation for income tax purposes, (c) annual depreciation for financial reporting purposes, assuming that the book value of the old delivery truck was $5,000, (d) annual depreciation for income tax purposes, assuming the same book value as indicated in (c).

8–42. Composite depreciation rate. A composite depreciation rate of 15% is applied annually to a plant asset account. Details of the account for the fiscal year ended December 31 are as follows:

Delivery Equipment

Jan. 1	Balance	297,750	May 1	16,500
Mar. 2		27,250	Sept. 7	11,750
Apr. 29		14,000	Dec. 15	15,500
Aug. 22		20,500		
Nov. 14		17,500		

Determine the depreciation for the year according to each of the following assumptions: (a) that all additions and retirements have occurred uniformly throughout the year, (b) that additions and retirements during the first half of the year occurred on the first day of that year and those during the second half occurred on the first day of the succeeding year.

8–43. Amortization and depletion entries. On July 1 of the current fiscal year ended December 31, Huff Co. acquired a patent for $75,000 and mineral rights for $200,000. The patent, which expires in 9 years, is expected to have value for 6 years. The mineral deposit is estimated at 500,000 tons of ore of uniform grade. Present entries to record the following for the current year: (a) amortization of the patent, (b) depletion, assuming that 50,000 tons were mined during the year.

8–44. Amortization and depletion entries. For each of the following unrelated transactions, (a) determine the amount of the amortization or depletion expense for the current year, and (b) present the adjusting entries required to record each expense.

(1) Timber rights on a tract of land were purchased for $50,000. The stand of timber is estimated at 500,000 board feet. During the current year, 75,000 board feet of timber were cut.
(2) Goodwill in the amount of $160,000 was purchased on January 4, the first month of the fiscal year. It is decided to amortize over the maximum period allowable.
(3) Governmental and legal costs of $24,800 were incurred at midyear in obtaining a patent with an estimated economic life of 8 years. Amortization is to be for one-half year.

Problems

SPREADSHEET PROBLEM

8–45. Allocation of expenditures and receipts to plant asset accounts. The following expenditures and receipts are related to land, land improvements, and buildings acquired for use in a business enterprise. The receipts are identified by an asterisk.

(a) Cost of real estate acquired as a plant site: Land	$125,000
Building	45,000
(b) Delinquent real estate taxes on property assumed by purchaser	8,750
(c) Cost of razing and removing the building	5,800
(d) Fee paid to attorney for title search	900
(e) Cost of land fill and grading	9,700
(f) Architect's and engineer's fees for plans and supervision	60,000
(g) Premium on 1-year insurance policy during construction	5,500
(h) Paid to building contractor for new building	750,000
(i) Cost of repairing windstorm damage during construction	1,500
(j) Cost of paving parking lot to be used by customers	12,500
(k) Cost of trees and shrubbery planted	15,000
(l) Special assessment paid to city for extension of water main to the property	2,500
(m) Cost of repairing vandalism damage during construction	500
(n) Interest incurred on building loan during construction	39,000
(o) Cost of floodlights installed on parking lot	13,500
(p) Proceeds from sale of salvage materials from old building	1,100*
(q) Money borrowed to pay building contractor	600,000*
(r) Proceeds from insurance company for windstorm damage	1,000*
(s) Refund of premium on insurance policy (g) canceled after 11 months	350*

Instructions: Assign each expenditure and receipt (indicate receipts by an asterisk) to Land (permanently capitalized), Land Improvements (limited life), Building, or Other Accounts. Identify each item by letter and list the amounts in columnar form, as follows:

Item	Land	Land Improvements	Building	Other Accounts
	$	$	$	$

8–46. Depreciation by four methods. North Company purchased equipment on January 1, 1988, for $75,000. The equipment was expected to have a useful life of 4 years, or 14,000 operating hours, and a residual value of $5,000. The equipment was used for 3,200 hours during 1988 and for 4,000, 3,800, and 3,000 hours for 1989, 1990, and 1991 respectively. The equipment was sold for $5,000 on January 4, 1992.

Instructions: Determine the amount of depreciation expense for 1988, 1989, 1990, and 1991 by (a) the straight-line method, (b) the declining-balance method, using twice the straight-line rate, (c) the sum-of-the-years-digits method, and (d) the units-of-production method.

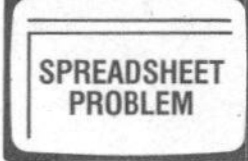

8–47. Depreciation by three methods; trade of plant asset. An item of new equipment, acquired at a cost of $125,000 at the beginning of a fiscal year, has an estimated useful life of 5 years and an estimated residual value of $5,000. The manager requested information regarding the effect of alternative methods on the amount of depreciation expense each year. Upon the basis of the data presented to the manager, the declining-balance method was elected.

In the first week of the fifth year, the equipment was traded in for similar equipment priced at $170,000. The trade-in allowance on the old equipment was $20,000, cash of $25,000 was paid, and a note payable was issued for the balance.

Instructions: (1) Determine the annual depreciation expense for each of the estimated 5 years of use, the accumulated depreciation at the end of each year, and the book value of the equipment at the end of each year by (a) the straight-line method, (b) the sum-of-the-years-digits method, and (c) the declining-balance method (at twice the straight-line rate). The following columnar headings are suggested for each schedule:

Year	Depreciation Expense	Accumulated Depreciation, End of Year	Book Value, End of Year

(2) For financial reporting purposes, determine the cost basis of the new equipment acquired in the exchange.
(3) Present the entries to record the exchange.
(4) What is the cost basis of the new equipment for purposes of computing the amount of depreciation allowable for income tax purposes?
(5) Present the entries to record the exchange, assuming that the trade-in allowance was $10,000 instead of $20,000.
(6) What is the cost basis of the new equipment for purposes of computing the amount of depreciation allowable for income tax purposes, assuming the data presented in Instruction (5)?

If the working papers correlating with the textbook are not used, omit Problem 8–48.

8–48. Plant asset transactions and subsidiary plant asset ledger. Victor Press Inc. maintains a subsidiary equipment ledger for the printing equipment and accumulated depreciation accounts in the general ledger. A small portion of the subsidiary ledger, the two controlling accounts, and a journal are presented in the working papers. The company computes depreciation on each individual item of equipment. Transaction and adjusting entries affecting the printing equipment are described as follows:

1989

Sept. 1. Purchased a power binder (Model 4C, Serial No. 7765) from Ryan Manufacturing Co. on account for $60,000. The estimated useful life of the asset is 10 years, it is expected to have no residual value, and the straight-line method of depreciation is to be used. (This is the only transaction of the year that directly affected the printing equipment account.)

Dec. 31. Recorded depreciation for the year in subsidiary accounts 125-30 to 125-32, and inserted the balances. (An assistant recorded the depreciation and the new balances in accounts 125-1 to 125-29.)

31. Journalized and posted the annual adjusting entry for depreciation on printing equipment. The depreciation for the year, recorded in subsidiary accounts 125-1 to 125-29, totaled $68,200, to which was added the depreciation entered in accounts 125-30 to 125-32.

1990
Mar. 31 Purchased a Model 32 rotary press from Jackson Press Inc., priced at $50,000, giving the Model G3 flatbed press (Account No. 125-31) in exchange plus $7,500 cash and a series of four $5,000 notes payable, maturing at 6-month intervals. The estimated useful life of the new press is 10 years, and it is expected to have a residual value of $2,000. (Recorded depreciation to date in 1990 on item traded in.)

Instructions: (1) Journalize the transaction of September 1. Post to Printing Equipment in the general ledger and to Account No. 125-32 in the subsidiary ledger.

(2) Journalize the adjusting entry required on December 31 and post to Accumulated Depreciation—Printing Equipment in the general ledger. Also post the appropriate amounts to Account Nos. 125-30 to 125-32.

(3) Journalize the entries required by the purchase of printing equipment on March 31. Post to Printing Equipment and to Accumulated Depreciation—Printing Equipment in the general ledger and to Account Nos. 125-31 and 125-33 in the subsidiary ledger.

(4) If the rotary press purchased on March 31 had been depreciated by the declining-balance method at twice the straight-line rate, determine the depreciation on this press for the fiscal years ending (a) December 31, 1990, and (b) December 31, 1991.

8–49. Transactions for plant assets, including trade. The following transactions, adjusting entries, and closing entries were completed by Urbana Furniture Co. during a 3-year period. All are related to the use of delivery equipment. The declining-balance method (twice the straight-line rate) of depreciation is used.

1989
Jan. 2. Purchased a used delivery truck for $10,800, paying cash.
5. Paid $1,200 for major repairs to the truck.
Sept. 17. Paid garage $225 for miscellaneous repairs to the truck.
Dec. 31. Recorded depreciation on the truck for the fiscal year. The estimated useful life of the truck is 4 years, with a residual value of $1,800.
31. Closed the appropriate accounts to the income summary account.

1990
June 30. Traded in the used truck for a new truck priced at $25,000, receiving a trade-in allowance of $5,000 and paying the balance in cash. (Record depreciation to date in 1990.)
Nov. 4. Paid garage $195 for miscellaneous repairs to the truck.
Dec. 31. Recorded depreciation on the truck. It has an estimated residual value of $4,500 and an estimated useful life of 5 years.
31. Closed the appropriate accounts to the income summary account.

1991
Oct. 1. Purchased a new truck for $24,400, paying cash.
2. Sold the truck purchased in 1990 for $15,000. (Record depreciation to date in 1991.)
Dec. 31. Recorded depreciation on the remaining truck. It has an estimated residual value of $1,500 and an estimated useful life of 8 years.
31. Closed the appropriate accounts to the income summary account.

Instructions: (1) Open the following accounts in the ledger:

122 Delivery Equipment
123 Accumulated Depreciation—Delivery Equipment
616 Depreciation Expense—Delivery Equipment
617 Truck Repair Expense
812 Gain on Disposal of Plant Assets

(2) Record the transactions and the adjusting and closing entries. Post to the accounts and extend the balances after each posting.

8–50. Correcting entries. The following recording errors occurred and were discovered during the current year:

(a) The $750 cost of repairing factory equipment damaged in the process of installation was charged to Factory Equipment.

(b) The sale of an electronic typewriter for $475 was recorded by a $475 credit to Office Equipment. The original cost of the machine was $1,450, and the related balance in Accumulated Depreciation at the beginning of the current year was $925. Depreciation of $100 accrued during the current year, prior to the sale, had not been recorded.

(c) Property taxes of $5,000 were paid on real estate acquired during the year and were debited to Property Tax Expense. Of this amount, $4,000 was for taxes that were delinquent at the time the property was acquired.

(d) Office equipment with a book value of $11,200 was traded in for similar equipment with a list price of $60,000. The trade-in allowance on the old equipment was $15,000, and a note payable was given for the balance. A gain on disposal of plant assets of $3,800 was recorded.

(e) The $1,100 cost of a major motor overhaul expected to prolong the life of a truck two years beyond the original estimate was debited to Delivery Expense. The truck was acquired new four years earlier.

(f) A $450 charge for incoming transportation on an item of factory equipment was debited to Transportation In.

(g) The cost of a razed building, $30,000, was debited to Loss on Disposal of Plant Assets and credited to Building. The building and the land on which it was located had been acquired at a total cost of $110,000 ($80,000 debited to Land, $30,000 debited to Building) as a parking area for the adjacent plant.

(h) The fee of $7,500 paid to the wrecking contractor to raze the building in (g) was debited to Miscellaneous Expense.

(i) The $7,750 cost of repainting several interior rooms of a building was debited to Building. The building had been owned and occupied for 20 years.

Instructions: Journalize the entries to correct the errors during the current year. Identify each entry by letter.

8–51. Income statement and balance sheet for corporation. The trial balance of Shaul Corporation at the end of the current fiscal year, before adjustments, is as follows:

Account	Debit	Credit
Cash	29,600	
Accounts Receivable	60,700	
Allowance for Doubtful Accounts		500
Merchandise Inventory	178,700	
Prepaid Expense	11,250	
Land	50,000	
Buildings	225,000	
Accumulated Depreciation—Buildings		86,000
Office Equipment	31,100	
Accumulated Depreciation—Office Equipment		11,600
Store Equipment	51,500	
Accumulated Depreciation—Store Equipment		21,400
Delivery Equipment	57,850	
Accumulated Depreciation—Delivery Equipment		21,750
Patents	18,000	
Accounts Payable		40,200
Notes Payable (short-term)		20,000
Capital Stock		250,000
Retained Earnings		179,750
Dividends	70,000	
Sales (net)		996,950
Purchases (net)	702,350	
Operating Expenses (controlling account)	140,500	
Interest Expense	1,600	
	1,628,150	1,628,150

Data needed for year-end adjustments:

(a) Estimated uncollectible accounts at December 31, $6,100.
(b) Insurance and other prepaid operating expenses expired during the year, $7,250.
(c) Depreciation is computed at composite rates on the average of the beginning and the ending balances of the plant asset accounts. The beginning balances and rates are as follows:

Office Equipment, $27,900; 10%	Delivery Equipment, $57,150; 20%
Store Equipment, $48,500; 8%	Buildings, $225,000; 2%

(d) Amortization of patents computed for the year, $3,000.
(e) Accrued liabilities at the end of the year, $3,000, of which $300 is for interest on the notes and $2,700 is for wages and other operating expenses.

Instructions: (1) Prepare a multiple-step income statement for the current year. The merchandise inventory at December 31 is $171,000.
(2) Prepare a balance sheet in report form, presenting the plant assets in the manner illustrated in this chapter.

ALTERNATE PROBLEMS

SPREADSHEET PROBLEM

8–45A. Allocation of expenditures and receipts to plant asset accounts. The following expenditures and receipts are related to land, land improvements, and buildings acquired for use in a business enterprise. The receipts are identified by an asterisk.

(a)	Cost of real estate acquired as a plant site: Land	$ 225,000
	Building	65,000
(b)	Finder's fee paid to real estate agency	15,000
(c)	Fee paid to attorney for title search	900
(d)	Delinquent real estate taxes on property, assumed by purchaser	18,500
(e)	Cost of razing and removing the building	11,250
(f)	Proceeds from sale of salvage materials from old building	1,500*
(g)	Cost of land fill and grading	13,500
(h)	Architect's and engineer's fees for plans and supervision	105,000
(i)	Premium on 1-year insurance policy during construction	9,000
(j)	Cost of paving parking lot to be used by customers	17,500
(k)	Cost of trees and shrubbery planted	10,000
(l)	Special assessment paid to city for extension of water main to the property	4,500
(m)	Cost of repairing windstorm damage during construction	3,500
(n)	Cost of repairing vandalism damage during construction	800
(o)	Proceeds from insurance company for windstorm and vandalism damage	3,300*
(p)	Interest incurred on building loan during construction	85,000
(q)	Money borrowed to pay building contractor	1,000,000*
(r)	Paid to building contractor for new building	1,250,000
(s)	Refund of premium on insurance policy (i) canceled after 10 months	750*

Instructions: Assign each expenditure and receipt (indicate receipts by an asterisk) to Land (permanently capitalized), Land Improvements (limited life), Building, or Other Accounts. Identify each item by letter and list the amounts in columnar form, as follows:

Item	Land	Land Improvements	Building	Other Accounts
	$	$	$	$

8–46A. Depreciation by four methods. Colby Company purchased equipment on July 1, 1988, for $72,000. The equipment was expected to have a useful life of 3 years, or 6,900 operating hours, and a residual value of $3,000. The equipment was used for 700 hours during 1988 and for 2,800, 2,400 and 1,000 hours for 1989, 1990, and 1991 respectively. The equipment was sold for $3,000 on July 3, 1991.

Instructions: Determine the amount of depreciation expense for 1988, 1989, 1990, and 1991 by (a) the straight-line method, (b) the declining-balance method, using twice the straight-line rate, (c) the sum-of-the-years-digits method, and (d) the units-of-production method.

8–47A. Determination of depreciation by three methods; trade of plant asset. An item of new equipment, acquired at a cost of $80,000 at the beginning of a fiscal year, has an estimated useful life of 4 years and an estimated residual value of $5,000. The manager requested information regarding the effect of alternative methods on the amount of depreciation expense each year. Upon the basis of the data presented to the manager, the declining-balance method was elected.

In the first week of the fourth year, the equipment was traded in for similar equipment priced at $200,000. The trade-in allowance on the old equipment was $15,000, cash of $15,000 was paid, and a note payable was issued for the balance.

Instructions: (1) Determine the annual depreciation expense for each of the estimated 4 years of use, the accumulated depreciation at the end of each year, and the book value of the equipment at the end of each year by (a) the straight-line method, (b) the declining-balance method (at twice the straight-line rate), and (c) the sum-of-the-years-digits method. The following columnar headings are suggested for each schedule:

Year	Depreciation Expense	Accumulated Depreciation, End of Year	Book Value, End of Year

(2) For financial reporting purposes, determine the cost basis of the new equipment acquired in the exchange.
(3) Present the entries to record the exchange.
(4) What is the cost basis of the new equipment for purposes of computing the amount of depreciation allowable for income tax purposes?
(5) Present the entries to record the exchange, assuming that the trade-in allowance was $5,000 instead of $15,000.
(6) What is the cost basis of the new equipment for purposes of computing the amount of depreciation allowable for income tax purposes, assuming the data presented in Instruction (5)?

If the working papers correlating with the textbook are not used, omit Problem 8–48A.

8–48A. Plant asset transactions and subsidiary plant asset ledger. Hamilton Press Co. maintains a subsidiary equipment ledger for the printing equipment and accumulated depreciation accounts in the general ledger. A small portion of the subsidiary ledger, the two controlling accounts, and a journal are presented in the working papers. The company computes depreciation on each individual item of equipment. Transactions and adjusting entries affecting the printing equipment are described as follows:

1989

June 30. Purchased a power binder (Model 14, Serial No. D7351) from Evans Manufacturing Co. on account for $108,000. The estimated useful life of the asset is 12 years, it is expected to have no residual value, and the straight-line method of depreciation is to be used. (This is the only transaction of the year that directly affected the printing equipment account.)

Dec. 31. Recorded depreciation for the year in subsidiary accounts 125-30 to 125-32, and inserted the new balances. (An assistant recorded the depreciation and the new balances in accounts 125-1 to 125-29.)

31. Journalized and posted the annual adjusting entry for depreciation on printing equipment. The depreciation for the year, recorded in subsidiary accounts 125-1 to 125-29, totaled $61,200, to which was added the depreciation entered in accounts 125-30 to 125-32.

1990

Sept. 30. Purchased a Model F5 rotary press from Wei Press Inc., priced at $60,000, giving the Model G3 flatbed press (Account No. 125-31) in exchange plus $20,000 cash and a series of ten $2,500 notes payable, maturing at 6-month intervals. The estimated useful life of the new press is 10 years, and it is expected to have a residual value of $6,250. (Recorded depreciation to date in 1990 on item traded in.)

Instructions: (1) Journalize the transaction of June 30. Post to Printing Equipment in the general ledger and to Account No. 125-32 in the subsidiary ledger.

(2) Journalize the adjusting entry on December 31 and post to Accumulated Depreciation — Printing Equipment in the general ledger. Also post the appropriate amounts to Account Nos. 125-30 to 125-32.

(3) Journalize the entries required by the purchase of printing equipment on September 30. Post to Printing Equipment and to Accumulated Depreciation — Printing Equipment in the general ledger and to Account Nos. 125-31 and 125-33 in the subsidiary ledger.

(4) If the rotary press purchased on September 30 had been depreciated by the declining-balance method at twice the straight-line rate, determine the depreciation on this press for the fiscal years ending (a) December 31, 1990, and (b) December 31, 1991.

8–49A. Transactions for plant assets, including trade. The following transactions, adjusting entries, and closing entries were completed by Reliable Furniture Co. during 3 fiscal years ending on June 30. All are related to the use of delivery equipment. The declining-balance method (twice the straight-line rate) of depreciation is used.

1988–1989 Fiscal Year

July 3. Purchased a used delivery truck for $15,000, paying cash.
6. Paid $1,000 to replace the automatic transmission and install new brakes on the truck. (Debit Delivery Equipment.)

Dec. 7. Paid garage $215 for changing the oil, replacing the oil filter, and tuning the engine on the delivery truck.

June 30. Recorded depreciation on the truck for the fiscal year. The estimated useful life of the truck is 8 years, with a residual value of $3,000.
30. Closed the appropriate accounts to the income summary account.

1989–1990 Fiscal Year

Aug. 29. Paid garage $240 to tune the engine and make other minor repairs on the truck.

Oct. 31. Traded in the used truck for a new truck priced at $28,000, receiving a trade-in allowance of $12,000 and paying the balance in cash. (Record depreciation to date in 1989.)

June 30. Recorded depreciation on the truck. It has an estimated trade-in value of $2,750 and an estimated life of 10 years.
30. Closed the appropriate accounts to the income summary account.

1990–1991 Fiscal Year

Apr. 1. Purchased a new truck for $30,000, paying cash.
2. Sold the truck purchased October 31, 1988, for $20,500. (Record depreciation for the year.)

June 30. Recorded depreciation on the remaining truck. It has an estimated residual value of $4,500 and an estimated useful life of 8 years.
30. Closed the appropriate accounts to the income summary account.

Instructions: (1) Open the following accounts in the ledger:

122 Delivery Equipment
123 Accumulated Depreciation — Delivery Equipment
616 Depreciation Expense — Delivery Equipment

617 Truck Repair Expense
812 Gain on Disposal of Plant Assets

(2) Record the transactions and the adjusting and closing entries. Post to the accounts and extend the balances after each posting.

Mini-Case 8

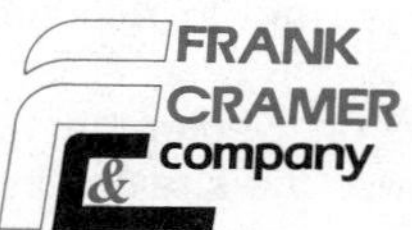

Frank Cramer, president of Frank Cramer and Company, is considering the purchase of machinery for $120,000. The machinery has a useful life of 5 years and no residual value. In the past, all plant assets have been leased. Cramer is considering depreciating the machinery by either the straight-line method or the sum-of-the-years-digits method, and has asked for your advice as to which method to use.

Instructions:

(1) Compute depreciation for each of the five years of useful life by (a) the straight-line method and (b) the sum-of-the-years-digits method.

(2) Assuming that income before depreciation and income tax is estimated to be uniformly $100,000 per year, that the depreciation method selected will be used for both financial reporting and income tax purposes, and that the income tax rate is 30%, compute the net income for each of the five years of useful life if (a) the straight-line method is used and (b) the sum-of-the-years-digits method is used.

(3) What factors would you present for Cramer's consideration in the selection of a depreciation method?

Answers to Self-Examination Questions

1. C All expenditures necessary to get a plant asset (such as machinery) in place and ready for use are proper charges to the asset account. In the case of machinery acquired, the transportation costs (answer A) and the installation costs (answer B) are both (answer C) proper charges to the machinery account.

2. A The periodic charge for depreciation under the sum-of-the-years-digits method is determined by multiplying a fraction by the original cost of the asset after the estimated residual value has been subtracted. The denominator of the fraction, which remains constant, is the sum of the digits representing the years of life, or 6 (3 + 2 + 1), in the question. The numerator of the fraction, which changes each year, is the number of years of life remaining at the beginning of the year for which depreciation is being computed, or 3 for the first year, 2 for the second year, and 1 for the third year in the question. The $4,500 (answer A) of depreciation for the first year is determined as follows:

$$\frac{\text{Years of Life Remaining at Beginning of Year}}{\text{Sum of Digits for Years of Life}} \times \left[\text{Cost} - \begin{array}{c}\text{Estimated} \\ \text{Residual Value}\end{array}\right]$$

$$\frac{3}{3 + 2 + 1} \times (\$9{,}500 - \$500)$$

$$= \frac{1}{2} \times \$9{,}000 = \$4{,}500$$

3. B Depreciation methods that provide for a higher depreciation charge in the first year of the use of an asset and a gradually declining periodic charge thereafter are referred to as accelerated depreciation methods. Examples of such methods are the sum-of-the-years-digits (answer B) and the declining-balance methods.

4. D The acceptable method of accounting for an exchange of similar assets in which the trade-in allowance ($30,000) exceeds the book value of the old asset ($25,000) requires that the cost of the new asset be determined by adding the amount of boot given ($70,000) to the book value of the old asset ($25,000), which totals $95,000.

5. D Long-lived assets that are useful in operations, not held for sale, and without physical qualities are referred to as intangible assets. Patents, goodwill, and copyrights are examples of intangible assets (answer D).

9
Payroll, Notes Payable, and Other Current Liabilities

CHAPTER OBJECTIVES

Describe and illustrate accounting for payrolls, including liabilities arising from employee earnings, deductions from earnings, and employer's payroll taxes.

Describe and illustrate accounting systems for payroll and payroll taxes.

Describe the principles of internal control for payroll systems.

Describe and illustrate accounting for employee fringe benefits, including vacation pay, pensions, and stock options.

Describe and illustrate accounting for short-term notes payable.

Describe and illustrate accounting for product warranties.

Describe and illustrate accounting for contingent liabilities.

Payables are the opposite of receivables. They are debts owed by an enterprise to its creditors. Money claims against a firm may originate in many ways, such as purchases of merchandise or services on account, loans from banks, and purchases of equipment and marketable securities on a credit basis. At any particular moment, a business may also owe its employees for wages or salaries accrued, banks or other creditors for interest accrued on notes, and governmental agencies for taxes.

In addition to known liabilities of a definite or reasonably approximate amount, there may be potential obligations that will materialize only if certain events take place in the future. Such uncertain liabilities are termed **contingent liabilities.**

Some types of current liabilities, such as accounts payable, have been discussed in earlier chapters. Additional types of current liabilities, including liabilities arising from payrolls, pensions, and notes payable, are discussed in this chapter. Contingent liabilities are also discussed. Long-term liabilities are presented in Chapter 12.

PAYROLL

The term **payroll** is often used to refer to the total amount paid to employees for a certain period. Payroll expenditures are usually significant for several reasons. First, employees are sensitive to payroll errors or irregularities, and maintaining good employee morale requires that the payroll be paid on a timely, accurate basis. Second, payroll expenditures are subject to various federal and state regulations. Finally, the amount of these payroll expenditures and related payroll taxes has a significant effect on the net income of most business enterprises. Although the degree of importance of such expenses varies widely, it is not unusual for a business to expend nearly a third of its sales revenue for payroll and payroll-related expenses. These expenses and their related liabilities are discussed in the following sections.

LIABILITY FOR PAYROLL

The term **salary** is usually applied to payment for managerial, administrative, or similar services. The rate of salary is ordinarily expressed in terms of a month or a year. Remuneration for manual labor, both skilled and unskilled, is commonly called **wages** and is stated on an hourly, weekly, or piecework basis. In practice, the terms salary and wages are often used interchangeably.

The basic salary or wage of an employee may be supplemented by commissions, bonuses, profit sharing, or cost-of-living adjustments. The form in which remuneration is paid generally has no effect on the manner in which it is treated by either the employer or the employee. Although payment is usually in terms of cash, it may take such forms as securities, notes, lodging, or other property or services.

Salary and wage rates are determined, in general, by agreement between the employer and the employees. Enterprises engaged in interstate commerce must also follow the requirements of the Fair Labor Standards Act. Employers covered by this legislation, which is commonly called the Federal Wage and Hour Law, are required to pay a minimum rate of 1½ times the regular rate for all hours worked in excess of 40 hours per week. Exemptions from the requirements are provided for executive, administrative, and certain supervisory positions. Premium rates for overtime or for working at night or other less desirable times are fairly common, even when not required by law, and the premium rates may be as much as twice the base rate.

Determination of Employee Earnings

To illustrate the computation of the earnings of an employee, it is assumed that Thomas C. Johnson is employed at the rate of $20 per hour for the first 40 hours in the weekly pay period and at $30 ($20 + $10) per hour for any additional hours. His time card shows that he worked 43 hours during the week ended December 27. His earnings for that week are computed as follows:

Earnings at base rate (40 × $20)	$800.00
Earnings at overtime rate (3 × $30)	90.00
Total earnings	$890.00

The foregoing computations can be stated in generalized arithmetic formulas or algorithms. If the hours worked during the week are less than or equal to (≤) 40, the formula may be expressed by the following equation, where E represents total earnings, H represents hours worked, and R represents hourly rate:

$$E = H \times R$$

This equation cannot be used to determine the earnings of an employee who has worked more than (>) 40 hours during the week, because the overtime rate differs from the basic rate. The expansion of the equation to include the additional factor of overtime yields the following:

$$E = 40\ R + 1.5\ R(H - 40)$$

The two equations can be expressed as shown in the following algorithm:

If	Then
$H \leq 40$	$E = H \times R$
$H > 40$	$E = 40R + 1.5R(H - 40)$

After the value of H and R are known for each employee at the end of a payroll period, the earnings of each employee can be computed accurately and speedily. Application of the standardized procedure of the algorithm to computers makes it possible to process a payroll routinely, regardless of its size.

Determination of Profit-Sharing Bonuses

Many enterprises pay their employees an annual bonus in addition to their regular salary or wage. The amount of the bonus is often based on the productivity of the employees, as measured by the net income of the enterprise. Such profit-sharing bonuses are treated in the same manner as wages and salaries.

The method used in determining the amount of a profit-sharing bonus is usually stated in the agreement between the employer and the employees. When the amount of the bonus is measured by a certain percentage of income, there are four basic formulas for the computation. The percentage may be applied (1) to income before deducting the bonus and income taxes, (2) to income after deducting the bonus but before deducting income taxes, (3) to income before deducting the bonus but after deducting income taxes, or (4) to net income after deducting both the bonus and income taxes.

Determination of a 10% bonus according to each of the four methods is illustrated as follows, based on the assumption that the employer's income before deducting the bonus and income taxes amounts to $150,000, and that income taxes are levied at the rate of 40% of income. Bonus and income taxes are abbreviated as B and T respectively.

(1) Bonus based on income before deducting bonus and taxes.

$$B = .10\ (\$150{,}000)$$
$$\text{Bonus} = \$15{,}000$$

(2) Bonus based on income after deducting bonus but before deducting taxes.

$$B = .10\ (\$150{,}000 - B)$$
Simplifying: $$B = \$15{,}000 - .10B$$
Transposing: $$1.10B = \$15{,}000$$
$$\text{Bonus} = \$13{,}636.36$$

(3) Bonus based on income before deducting bonus but after deducting taxes.

B equation: $$B = .10\ (\$150{,}000 - T)$$
T equation: $$T = .40\ (\$150{,}000 - B)$$

Substituting for T in the B equation and solving for B:

$$B = .10\ [\$150{,}000 - .40\ (\$150{,}000 - B)]$$
Simplifying: $$B = .10\ (\$150{,}000 - \$60{,}000 + .40B)$$
Simplifying: $$B = \$15{,}000 - \$6{,}000 + .04B$$
Transposing: $$.96B = \$9{,}000$$
$$\text{Bonus} = \$9{,}375$$

(4) Bonus based on net income after deducting bonus and taxes.

B equation: $$B = .10\ (\$150{,}000 - B - T)$$
T equation: $$T = .40\ (\$150{,}000 - B)$$

Substituting for T in the B equation and solving for B:

$$B = .10\ [\$150{,}000 - B - .40\ (\$150{,}000 - B)]$$
Simplifying: $$B = .10\ (\$150{,}000 - B - \$60{,}000 + .40B)$$
Simplifying: $$B = \$15{,}000 - .10B - \$6{,}000 + .04B$$
Transposing: $$1.06B = \$9{,}000$$
$$\text{Bonus} = \$8{,}490.57$$

With the amount of the bonus possibilities ranging from the high of $15,000 to the low of $8,490.57, the importance of strictly following the agreement is evident. If the bonus is to be shared by all of the employees, the agreement must also provide for the manner by which the bonus is divided among them. A common method is to express the bonus as a percentage of total earnings for the year. For example, if the bonus were computed to be $15,000 and employee earnings before the bonus had been $100,000, the bonus for each of the employees could be stated as 15% of their earnings.

Managers' Rewards for Corporate Performance

The role of bonuses in compensation plans is becoming increasingly important in many companies. Examples of how and why companies are using bonuses, particularly for their executives, were given in articles in *The Wall Street Journal,* excerpts from which are as follows:

David Margolis works for a [very] generous company.... [In 1985,] Mr. Margolis, the president, chairman and chief executive officer of Colt Industries Inc., received a bonus of $555,000, more than double the average bonus for chief executives of similar-sized companies. And that bonus was $115,680 more than his base salary. Total compensation: close to $1 million.

... On top of his regular salary of $363,931, [Paul Fireman, Chairman of Reebok International Ltd.] received a bonus of $12.7 million... [for 1986.]

That sum reflects an agreement under which Mr. Fireman is entitled to an annual bonus equal to 5% of the amount by which the company's annual pre-tax earnings exceeds $20 million. Pre-tax earnings for the *maker of athletic shoes soared to $261.2 million in 1986 from $78.1 million in 1985. . . .*

. . . After years of regularly receiving hefty increases in salary and bonus — regardless of their company's success or failure — more top executives are now finding their compensation linked directly to corporate performance. . . .

"There's been so much scrutiny that boards have been taking a closer look" at compensation, says Pete Smith, national director of Wyatt Co.'s compensation consulting business. As a result, companies are relying less on salary and more on bonuses and other performance-linked compensation to reward executives. They are also tightening the criteria for earning those rewards. . . . [For example,] more compensation is being pegged to three-year or five-year gains in . . . performance. . . .

Some companies also want to extend bonuses, which are usually limited to senior executives, to lower-level managers. Specialists believe that bonuses work successfully as incentives only if they amount to 15% or more of total compensation. But most lower-level managers are unwilling to risk that large a proportion of their income. . . .

The solution — adding bonuses to existing salaries — means a big increase in costs. But some executives say those costs are worth it to retain first-class management. Says David Jones, chairman and chief executive of Humana Corp.: "You don't pay executives with cornflakes. There's always costs of employing executives. If the costs are reasonable, you pay them. You have to pay what the marketplace demands."

Source: Amanda Bennett, "More Managers Find Salary, Bonus Are Tied Directly to Performance," *The Wall Street Journal,* February 28, 1986 and Christopher J. Chipello, "Reebok's Chairman Got Bonuses Totaling $12.7 Million in '86," *The Wall Street Journal,* April 14, 1987.

DEDUCTIONS FROM EMPLOYEE EARNINGS

The total earnings of an employee for a payroll period, including bonuses and overtime pay, are often called the **gross pay.** From this amount is subtracted one or more **deductions** to arrive at the **net pay,** which is the amount the employer must pay the employee. The deductions for federal taxes are of the widest applicability and usually the largest in amount. Deductions may also be needed for state or local income taxes and for contributions to state unemployment compensation programs. Other deductions may be made for contributions to pension plans and for items authorized by individual employees.

FICA Tax

Most employers are required by the Federal Insurance Contributions Act (FICA) to withhold a portion of the earnings of each of their employees. The amount of **FICA tax** withheld is the employees' contribution to the combined federal programs for old-age and disability benefits, insurance benefits to survivors, and health insurance for the aged (medicare). With very few exceptions, employers are required to withhold from each employee a tax at a specified rate on earnings up to a specified amount paid in the calendar year. Although both the schedule of future tax rates and the maximum amount subject to tax are revised often by Congress, such changes have no effect on the basic outline of the payroll system.[1] For purposes of illustration, a rate of 7.5% on maximum annual earnings of $45,000, or a maximum annual tax of $3,375, will be assumed.

[1]Current tax rates and the amount of earnings subject to tax may be located in Internal Revenue Service publications and in standard tax reporting services.

Federal Income Tax

Except for certain types of employment, all employers must withhold a portion of the earnings of their employees for payment of the employees' liability for federal income tax. The amount that must be withheld from each employee differs according to the amount of gross pay, marital status, and the estimated deductions and exemptions claimed when filing the annual income tax return.

Other Deductions

Deductions from gross earnings for payment of taxes are compulsory. Neither the employer nor the employee has any choice in the matter. In addition, however, there may be other deductions authorized by individual employees or by the union representing them. For example, an employee may authorize deductions for the purchase of United States savings bonds, for contributions to a United Fund or other charitable organization, for payment of premiums on various types of employee insurance, or for the purchase of a retirement annuity. The union contract may also require the deduction of union dues or other deductions for group benefits.

COMPUTATION OF EMPLOYEE NET PAY

Gross earnings for a payroll period less the payroll deductions yields the amount to be paid to the employee, which is often called the **net pay** or **take-home pay.** The amount to be paid Thomas C. Johnson for the week ended December 27 is $640.80, based on the following summary:

Gross earnings for the week		$890.00
Deductions:		
FICA tax	$ 37.50	
Federal income tax	186.70	
U.S. savings bonds	20.00	
United Fund	5.00	
Total deductions		249.20
Net pay		$640.80

As has been indicated, there is a ceiling on the annual earnings subject to the FICA tax, and consequently the amount of the annual tax is also limited. Therefore, when the amount of FICA tax to withhold from an employee is determined for a payroll period, it is necessary to refer to one of the following cumulative amounts:

1. Employee gross earnings for the year up to, but not including, the current payroll period, or
2. Employee tax withheld for the year up to, but not including, the current payroll period.

To continue with the illustration, reference to Johnson's earnings record shows cumulative earnings of $44,500 prior to the current week's earnings of $890. The amount of the current week's earnings subject to FICA tax is therefore the maximum of \$500 (\$45,000 − \$44,500), and the FICA tax to be withheld is \$37.50 (7.5% of \$500). Alternatively, the determination could be based on the amount of FICA tax withheld from Johnson prior to the current payroll period. This amount, according to the employee record, is \$3,337.50, and the amount to be withheld is the maximum of \$37.50 (\$3,375 − \$3,337.50).

There is no ceiling on the amount of earnings subject to withholding for income taxes and hence no need to consider the cumulative earnings. The amount of federal income tax withheld would be determined by reference to official withholding tax tables issued by the Internal Revenue Service. For purposes of this illustration, the amount of federal income tax withheld was assumed to be \$186.70. The deductions for the purchase of bonds and for the charitable contribution were in accordance with Johnson's authorizations.

As in the determination of gross earnings when overtime rates are a factor, the computation of some deductions can be generalized in the form of algorithms. The algorithm for the determination of the FICA tax deduction, based on the maximum deduction approach, is as follows, where E represents current period's earnings, F represents current period's FICA deduction, and f represents cumulative FICA deductions prior to the current period:

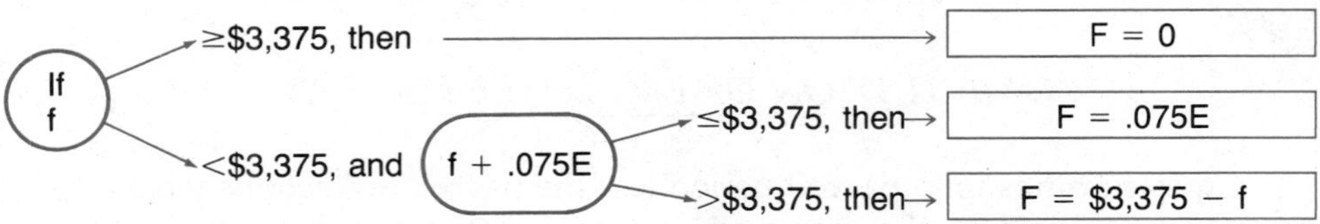

An alternative generalization of the method of determining FICA deductions, based on the maximum taxable earnings approach, is illustrated by the following decision diagram. The additional symbol "e" represents cumulative earnings prior to the current period.

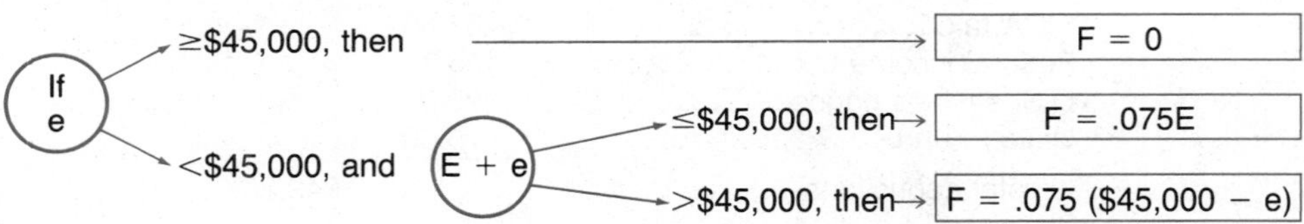

The elements of the decision diagram are examples of standardized instructions that can be applied to computations involving many variables. They are used in many situations as an aid to routine processing of repetitive data, regardless of whether the processing is performed manually or with a computer.

LIABILITY FOR EMPLOYER'S PAYROLL TAXES

Thus far the discussion of taxes has been limited to those levied against employees and withheld by employers. Most employers are subject to federal and state taxes based on the amount of remuneration earned by their employees. Such taxes are an operating expense of the business and may amount to a relatively large sum.

FICA Tax

Employers are required to contribute to the Federal Insurance Contributions Act program for each employee. The tax rate and the maximum amount of employee remuneration entering into an employer's tax base are the same as those applicable to employees, which for purposes of illustration are assumed to be 7.5% and $45,000 respectively.

Your Social Security Taxes

In its 1936 publication, *Security in Your Old Age,* the Social Security Board set forth the following explanation of how the social security tax would affect a worker's paycheck:

> *The taxes called for in this law will be paid both by your employer and by you. For the next 3 years you will pay maybe 15 cents a week, maybe 25 cents a week, maybe 30 cents or more, according to what you earn. That is to say, during the next 3 years, beginning January 1, 1937, you will pay 1 cent for every dollar you earn, and at the same time your employer will pay 1 cent for every dollar you earn, up to $3,000 a year. Twenty-six million other workers and their employers will be paying at the same time.*
>
> *After the first 3 years—that is to say, beginning in 1940—you will pay, and your employer will pay, 1½ cents for each dollar you earn, up to $3,000 a year. This will be the tax for 3 years, and then beginning in 1943, you will pay 2 cents, and so will your employer, for every dollar you earn for the next three years. After that, you and your employer will each pay half a cent more for 3 years, and finally, beginning in 1949, twelve years from now, you and your employer will each pay 3 cents on each dollar you earn, up to $3,000 a year. That is the most you will ever pay.*

The rate on January 1, 1988, is estimated to be 7.51 cents per dollar earned (7.51%) up to the first $45,000 of earnings.

Source: Arthur Lodge, "That Is the Most You Will Ever Pay," *Journal of Accountancy* (October, 1985), p. 44.

Federal Unemployment Compensation Tax

Unemployment insurance provides temporary relief to those who become unemployed as a result of economic forces beyond their control. Types of employment subject to the unemployment insurance program are similar to those covered by the FICA tax. The tax of .8% is levied on employers only, rather than on both employers and employees. It is applicable only to the first $7,000 of the remuneration of each covered employee during a calendar year. As with the FICA tax, the rate and the maximum amount subject to federal unemployment compensation tax are revised often by Congress. The funds collected by the federal government are not paid out as benefits to the unemployed, but are allocated among the states for use in administering state programs.

State Unemployment Compensation Tax

The amounts paid as benefits to unemployed persons are obtained, for the most part, by taxes levied upon employers only. A very few states also require employee contributions. The rates of tax and the tax base vary, and in most states, employers who provide steady employment for their employees are awarded reduced rates. The employment experience and the status of each employer's tax account are reviewed annually, and the merit ratings and tax rates are revised accordingly.[2]

ACCOUNTING SYSTEMS FOR PAYROLL AND PAYROLL TAXES

Accounting systems for payroll and payroll taxes are concerned with the records and reports associated with the employer-employee relationship. It is important that the accounting system provide safeguards to insure that payments are in accord with management's general plans and its specific authorizations.

All employees of a firm expect and are entitled to receive their remuneration at regular intervals following the close of each payroll period. Regardless of the number of employees and the difficulties in computing the amounts to be paid, the payroll system must be designed to process the necessary data quickly and assure payment of the correct amount to each employee. The system must also provide adequate safeguards against payments to fictitious persons and other misappropriations of funds.

Various federal, state, and local laws require that employers accumulate certain specified data in their payroll records, not only for each payroll period but also for each employee. Periodic reports of such data must be submitted to the appropriate governmental agencies and remittances made for amounts withheld from employees and for taxes levied on the employer. The records must be retained for specified periods of time and be available for inspection by those responsible for enforcement of the laws. In addition, payroll data may be useful in negotiations with labor unions, in settling employee grievances, and in determining rights to vacations, sick leaves, and retirement pensions.

Although complex organizational structures may necessitate the use of detailed subsystems, the major parts common to most payroll systems are the

Payroll Register

PAYROLL FOR WEEK ENDING

NAME	TOTAL HOURS	EARNINGS REGULAR	EARNINGS OVERTIME	EARNINGS TOTAL	TAXABLE EARNINGS UNEMPLOYMENT COMP.	TAXABLE EARNINGS FICA
ARKIN, JOAN E.	40	500.00		500.00	500.00	500.00
DAWSON, LOREN A.	44	392.00	58.80	450.80		450.80
GREEN, MINDY M.		840.00		840.00		
JOHNSON, THOMAS C.	43	800.00	90.00	890.00		500.00
WYATT, WILLIAM R.	40	480.00		480.00		480.00
ZACHS, ANNA H.		600.00		600.00	150.00	600.00
TOTAL		13,328.70	574.00	13,902.70	2,710.00	11,354.70

[2]As of January 1, 1989, the maximum state rate recognized by the federal unemployment system was 5.4% of the first $7,000 of each employee's earnings during a calendar year.

payroll register, employee's earnings record, and payroll checks. Each of these major payroll components is illustrated and discussed in the following sections. Although the illustrations are relatively simple, many modifications might be introduced in actual practice.

Payroll Register

The multicolumn form used in assembling and summarizing the data needed at the end of each payroll period is called the **payroll register.** Its design varies according to the number and classes of employees and the extent to which computers are used. A form suitable for a small number of employees is illustrated at the bottom of pages 336 and 337.

The nature of most of the data appearing in the illustrative payroll register is evident from the columnar headings. The number of hours worked and the earnings and deduction data are inserted in the appropriate columns. The sum of the deductions applicable to an employee is then deducted from the total earnings to yield the amount to be paid. Recording the check numbers in the payroll register as the checks are written eliminates the need to maintain other detailed records of the payments.

The two columns under the general heading of Taxable Earnings are used in accumulating data needed to compute the employer's payroll taxes. The last two columns of the payroll register are used to accumulate the total wages or salaries to be charged to the expense accounts. This process is usually termed **payroll distribution.** If there is an extensive account classification of labor expense, the charges may be analyzed on a separate payroll distribution sheet.

The format of the illustrative payroll register aids the determination of arithmetic accuracy before checks are issued to employees and before the summary amounts are formally recorded. Specifically, all columnar totals except those in the Taxable Earnings columns should be cross-verified. The miscellaneous deductions must also be summarized by account classification.

DECEMBER 27, 19--

DEDUCTIONS					PAID		ACCOUNTS DEBITED	
FICA TAX	FEDERAL INCOME TAX	U.S. SAVINGS BONDS	MISCELLANEOUS	TOTAL	NET AMOUNT	CHECK NO.	SALES SALARIES EXPENSE	OFFICE SALARIES EXPENSE
37.50	74.10	20.00	UF 10.00	141.60	358.40	6857	500.00	
33.81	62.60		AR 50.00	146.41	304.39	6858		450.80
	186.30	25.00	UF 10.00	221.30	618.70	6859	840.00	
37.50	186.70	20.00	UF 5.00	249.20	640.80	6860	890.00	
36.00	69.20	10.00		115.20	364.80	6880	480.00	
45.00	71.36	5.00	UF 2.00	123.36	476.64	6881		600.00
851.60	3,332.18	680.00	UF 470.00 AR 50.00	5,383.78	8,518.92		11,122.16	2,780.54

MISCELLANEOUS DEDUCTIONS: AR—ACCOUNTS RECEIVABLE UF—UNITED FUND

The following tabulation illustrates the method of cross-verification:

Earnings:		
Regular	$13,328.70	
Overtime	574.00	
Total		$13,902.70
Deductions:		
FICA tax	$ 851.60	
Federal income tax	3,332.18	
U.S. savings bonds	680.00	
United Fund	470.00	
Accounts receivable	50.00	
Total		5,383.78
Paid—net amount		$ 8,518.92
Accounts debited:		
Sales Salaries Expense		$11,122.16
Office Salaries Expense		2,780.54
Total (as above)		$13,902.70

Recording Employees' Earnings. The payroll register may be used as a supporting record for a journal entry that records the payroll data. The entry based on the payroll register illustrated is as follows:

Dec. 27	Sales Salaries Expense	11,122.16	
	Office Salaries Expense	2,780.54	
	FICA Tax Payable		851.60
	Employees Federal Income Tax Payable		3,332.18
	Bond Deductions Payable		680.00
	United Fund Deductions Payable		470.00
	Accounts Receivable—Loren A. Dawson		50.00
	Salaries Payable		8,518.92
	Payroll for week ended December 27.		

The total expense incurred for the services of employees is recorded by the debits to the salary expense accounts. Amounts withheld from employees' earnings have no effect on the debits to these accounts. Five of the credits in the entry represent increases in specific liability accounts and one represents a decrease in the accounts receivable account.

Recording and Paying Payroll Taxes. Each time the payroll register is prepared, the amounts of all employees' current earnings entering the tax base are listed in the respective taxable earnings columns. As explained earlier, the cumulative amounts of each employee's earnings just prior to the current period are available in the employee's earnings record.

According to the payroll register illustrated for the week ended December 27, the amount of remuneration subject to FICA tax was $11,354.70, and the amount subject to state and federal unemployment compensation taxes was $2,710. Multiplication by the applicable tax rates yields the following amounts:

FICA tax	$ 851.60
State unemployment compensation tax (5.4% × $2,710)	146.34
Federal unemployment compensation tax (.8% × $2,710)	21.68
Total payroll taxes expense	$1,019.62

The journal entry to record the payroll tax expense for the week and the liability for the taxes accrued is as follows:

Dec. 27	Payroll Taxes Expense	1,019.62	
	FICA Tax Payable........................		851.60
	State Unemployment Tax Payable		146.34
	Federal Unemployment Tax Payable		21.68
	Payroll taxes for week ended December 27.		

Payment of the liability for each of the taxes is recorded in the same manner as the payment of other liabilities. Employers are required to compute and report all payroll taxes on the calendar-year basis, regardless of the fiscal year they may use for financial reporting and income tax purposes. Details of the federal income tax and FICA tax withheld from employees are combined with the employer's FICA tax on a single return accompanied by the amount of tax due. Payments are required on a weekly, semimonthly, monthly, or quarterly basis, depending on the amount of the combined taxes. Unemployment compensation tax returns and payments are required by the federal government on an annual basis. Earlier payments are required when the tax exceeds a certain minimum. Unemployment compensation tax returns and payments are required by most states on a basis similar to that required by the federal government.

All payroll taxes levied against employers become liabilities at the time the related remuneration is *paid* to employees, rather than at the time the liability to the employees is incurred. Observance of this requirement may cause a problem of expense allocation between fiscal periods. To illustrate, assume that an enterprise using the calendar year as its fiscal year pays its employees on Friday for a weekly payroll period ending the preceding Wednesday, the two-day lag between Wednesday and Friday being needed to process the payroll. Regardless of the day of the week on which the year ends, there will be some accrued wages. If it ends on a Thursday, the accrual will cover a full week plus an extra day. Logically, the unpaid wages and the related payroll taxes should both be charged to the period that benefited from the services performed by the employees. On the other hand, there is legally no liability for the payroll taxes until the wages are paid in January, when a new cycle of earnings subject to tax is begun. The distortion of net income that would result from failure to accrue the payroll taxes might well be insignificant. The practice adopted should be followed consistently.

Employee's Earnings Record

The necessity of having the cumulative amount of each employee's earnings readily available at the end of each payroll period was discussed earlier. Without such information or the related data on the cumulative amount of FICA tax previously withheld, there would be no means of determining the appropriate amount to withhold from current earnings. It is essential, therefore, that detailed records be maintained for each employee.

A portion of the **employee's earnings record** is illustrated on pages 340 and 341. The relationship between this record and the payroll register can be seen by tracing the amounts entered on Johnson's earnings record for December 27 back to its source, which is the fourth line of the payroll register illustrated on pages 336 and 337.

THOMAS C. JOHNSON 4990 COLUMBUS AVENUE STATESVILLE, IA 52732-6142						PHONE: 555-3148
MARRIED		NUMBER OF WITHHOLDING ALLOWANCES: 4			PAY RATE: $800.00 PER WEEK	
OCCUPATION: SALESPERSON					EQUIVALENT HOURLY RATE: $20	
				EARNINGS		
LINE NO.	PERIOD ENDED	TOTAL HOURS	REGULAR EARNINGS	OVERTIME	TOTAL EARNINGS	CUMULATIVE TOTAL
39	SEPT. 27	41	800.00	30.00	830.00	34,690.00
THIRD QUARTER			10,400.00	270.00	10,670.00	
40	OCT. 4	40	800.00		800.00	35,490.00
46	NOV. 15	41	800.00	30.00	830.00	40,320.00
47	NOV. 22	40	800.00		800.00	41,120.00
48	NOV. 29	42	800.00	60.00	860.00	41,980.00
49	DEC. 6	40	800.00		800.00	42,780.00
50	DEC. 13	40	800.00		800.00	43,580.00
51	DEC. 20	44	800.00	120.00	920.00	44,500.00
52	DEC. 27	43	800.00	90.00	890.00	45,390.00
FOURTH QUARTER			10,400.00	300.00	10,700.00	
YEARLY TOTAL			41,600.00	3,790.00	45,390.00	

Employee's Earnings Record

In addition to spaces for recording data for each payroll period and the cumulative total of earnings, there are spaces for quarterly totals and the yearly total. These totals are used in various reports for tax, insurance, and other purposes. Copies of one such annual report, known as Form W-2 Wage and Tax Statement, must be given to each employee as well as to the Social Security Administration.

The source of the amounts inserted in the following statement was the employee's earnings record.

1 Control number		OMB No. 1545-0008	
2 Employer's name, address, and ZIP code Langford Supply Co. 560 Hudson Avenue Cedar Rapids, IA 52731-6148		3 Employer's identification number 61-843652	4 Employer's state I.D. number
		5 Statutory employee ☐ Deceased ☐ Pension plan ☐ Legal rep. ☐	942 emp. ☐ Subtotal ☐ Deferred compensation ☐ Void ☐
		6 Allocated tips	7 Advance EIC payment
8 Employee's social security number 381-48-9120	9 Federal income tax withheld $8,942.06	10 Wages, tips, other compensation $45,390.00	11 Social security tax withheld $3,375.00
12 Employee's name, address, and ZIP code Thomas C. Johnson 4990 Columbus Avenue Statesville, IA 52732-6142		13 Social security wages $45,000.00	14 Social security tips
		16	16a Fringe benefits incl. in Box 10
		17 State income tax / 18 State wages, tips, etc.	19 Name of state
		20 Local income tax / 21 Local wages, tips, etc.	22 Name of locality
Form W-2 Wage and Tax Statement 19-- This information is being furnished to the Internal Revenue Service.		Copy B To be filed with employee's FEDERAL tax return	Dept. of the Treasury—IRS

Wage and Tax Statement

SOC. SEC. NO.: 381-48-9120							EMPLOYEE NO.: 814
DATE EMPLOYED: FEBRUARY 15, 1974							
DATE OF BIRTH: OCTOBER 4, 1952							
DATE EMPLOYMENT TERMINATED:							
DEDUCTIONS					PAID		
FICA TAX	FEDERAL INCOME TAX	U.S. SAVINGS BONDS	MISC.	TOTAL	NET AMOUNT	CHECK NO.	LINE NO.
62.25	174.11	20.00		256.36	573.64	6175	39
800.25	2,238.30	260.00	AR 40.00	3,338.55	7,331.45		
60.00	167.82	20.00	UF 5.00	252.82	547.18	6225	40
62.25	174.11	20.00		256.36	573.64	6530	46
60.00	167.82	20.00		247.82	552.18	6582	47
64.50	180.41	20.00		264.91	595.09	6640	48
60.00	167.82	20.00	UF 5.00	252.82	547.18	6688	49
60.00	167.82	20.00		247.82	552.18	6743	50
69.00	192.99	20.00		281.99	638.01	6801	51
37.50	186.70	20.00	UF 5.00	249.20	640.80	6860	52
773.25	2,244.60	260.00	UF 15.00	3,292.85	7,407.15		
3,375.00	8,942.06	1,040.00	AR 40.00 UF 60.00	13,457.06	31,932.94		

Payroll Checks

One of the principal outputs of most payroll systems is a series of **payroll checks** at the end of each pay period. The data needed for this purpose are provided by the payroll register, each line of which applies to an individual employee. It is possible to prepare the checks solely by reference to the Net Amount column of the register. However, the customary practice is to provide each employee with a statement of the details of the computation. The statement may be entirely separate from the check or it may be in the form of a detachable stub attached to the check.

When employees are paid by checks drawn on the regular bank account and the voucher system is used, it is necessary to prepare a voucher for the net amount to be paid the employees. The voucher is then recorded as a debit to Salaries Payable and a credit to Accounts Payable, and payment is recorded in the usual manner. If the voucher system is not used, the payment would be recorded by a debit to Salaries Payable and a credit to Cash.

It should be understood that the journal entry derived from the payroll register, such as the entry illustrated on page 337, would precede the entries just described. It should also be noted that the entire amount paid may be recorded as a single item, regardless of the number of employees. There is no need to record each check separately because all of the details are available in the payroll register for future reference.

Most employers with a large number of employees use a special bank account and payroll checks designed specifically for the purpose. After the data for the payroll period have been recorded and summarized in the payroll register, a single check for the total amount to be paid is drawn on the firm's regular bank account and deposited in a special account. The individual payroll checks are then drawn against the special payroll account, and the numbers of the payroll checks are inserted in the payroll register.

The use of special payroll checks relieves the treasurer or other executives of the task of signing a large number of regular checks each payday. The responsibility for signing payroll checks may be given to the paymaster, or mechanical means of signing the checks may be used. Another advantage of this system is that reconciling the regular bank statement is simplified. The paid payroll checks are returned by the bank separately from regular checks and are accompanied by a statement of the special bank account. Any balance shown on the bank's statement will correspond to the sum of the payroll checks outstanding because the amount of each deposit is exactly the same as the total amount of checks drawn. The recording procedures are the same as when checks on the regular bank account are used.

Currency is sometimes used as the medium of payment when the payroll is paid each week or when the business location or the time of payment is such that banking or check-cashing facilities are not readily available to employees. In such cases, a single check, payable to Payroll, is drawn for the entire amount to be paid. The check is then cashed at the bank and the money is inserted in individual pay envelopes. Each employee should be required to sign a receipt which serves as evidence of payment. The procedures for recording the payment correspond to those outlined for payroll checks.

PAYROLL SYSTEM DIAGRAM

The flow of data within segments of an accounting system may be shown by diagrams such as the one illustrated on page 343. It depicts the interrelationships of the principal parts of the payroll system described in this chapter. The requirement of constant updating of the employee's earnings record is indicated by the dotted line.

Attention thus far has been directed to the end product or *output* of a payroll system, namely the payroll register, the checks payable to individual employees, the earnings records for each employee, and reports for tax and other purposes. The basic data entering the payroll systems are sometimes called the *input* of the system. Input data that remain relatively unchanged and do not need to be reintroduced into the system for each payroll period are characterized as *constants.* Those data that differ from period to period are termed *variables.*

Constants include such data for each employee as name and social security number, marital status, number of income tax withholding allowances claimed, rate of pay, functional category (office, sales, etc.), and department where employed. The FICA tax rate, maximum earnings subject to tax, and various tax tables are also constants which apply to all employees. The variable data for each employee include the number of hours or days worked during each payroll period, days of sick leave with pay, vacation credits, and cumulative amounts of earnings and taxes withheld. If salespersons are employed on a commission basis, the amount of their sales would also vary from period to period. The forms used in initially recording both the constant and the variable data vary widely according to the complexities of the payroll system and the processing methods used.

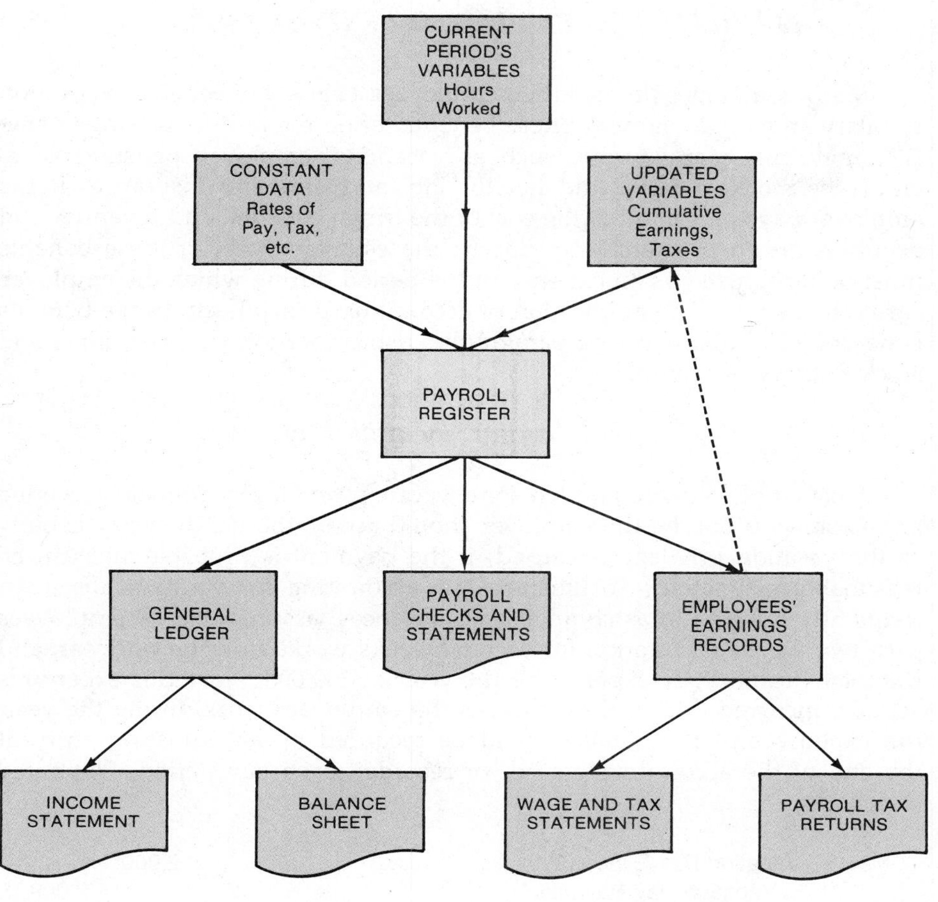

Flow Diagram of a Payroll System

INTERNAL CONTROLS FOR PAYROLL SYSTEMS

The large amount of data and the computations necessary to process the payroll are evident. As the number of employees and the mass of data increase, the number of individuals needed to manage and process payroll data likewise increases. Such characteristics, together with the relative magnitude of labor costs, indicate the need for controls that will assure the reliability of the data and minimize the opportunity for misuse of funds.

The cash disbursement controls discussed in Chapter 5 are applicable to payrolls. Thus, the use of the voucher system and the requirement that all payments be supported by vouchers are desirable. The addition or deletion of names on the payroll should be supported by written authorizations from the personnel department. It is also essential that employees' attendance records be controlled in such a manner as to prevent errors and abuses. Perhaps the most basic and widely used records are "In and Out" cards, whereby employees indicate, often by "punching" a time clock, their time of arrival and departure. Employee identification cards or badges may also be used in this connection to assure that all salaries and wages are paid to the proper individuals.

LIABILITY FOR EMPLOYEES' FRINGE BENEFITS

Many companies provide their employees a variety of benefits in addition to salary and wages earned. These benefits, often referred to as **fringe benefits,** may take many forms, such as vacations, employee pension plans, employee stock options, and health, life, and disability insurance. If the employer pays part or all of the cost of the fringe benefits, and revenues and expenses are to be matched properly, the estimated cost of these benefits must be recognized as an expense of the period during which the employee earns the benefit. The application of accounting principles to fringe benefits is described in the following paragraphs, using vacation pay, pensions, and stock options as examples.

Liability for Vacation Pay

Most employees are granted some vacation privileges. To match revenue and expense properly, the employer should accrue the vacation pay liability as the vacation privilege is earned, if the payment is probable and can be reasonably estimated.[3] To illustrate the accounting for vacation absences, frequently referred to as compensated absences, assume that all employees earn two weeks of vacation for each 50 weeks worked during the year, and the total vacation pay expense for the year is $100,000. Since this expense is actually incurred during the 50 weeks the employees work during the year, the expense and the liability could be recorded by an adjusting entry at the end of the accounting period, or recorded each pay period, illustrated as follows:

May 5	Vacation Pay Expense	2,000	
	Vacation Pay Payable............................		2,000
	Vacation pay for week ended May 5		
	(1/50 of annual vacation pay of $100,000)		

Depending upon when it is to be paid, the vacation liability will be classified in the balance sheet as either a current liability or a long-term liability. When the payroll in which the employees are paid for their vacations is prepared, Vacation Pay Payable would be debited, and Salaries Payable and the appropriate accounts for recording taxes and withholdings would be credited.

Liability for Pensions

In recent years, retirement pension plans have increased rapidly in number, variety, and complexity. Although the details of the plans vary from employer to employer, pension benefits are usually based on factors such as employee age, years of service, and salary level. In 1974, Congress enacted the Employee Retirement Income Security Act (ERISA), which established guidelines for safeguarding employee benefits.

Pension plans may be classified as contributory or noncontributory, funded or unfunded, and qualified or unqualified. A **contributory plan** requires

[3] *Statement of Financial Accounting Standards, No. 43,* "Accounting for Compensated Absences" (Stamford: Financial Accounting Standards Board, 1980), par. 6.

the employer to withhold a portion of each employee's earnings as a contribution to the plan. The employer then makes a contribution according to the provisions of the plan. A **noncontributory plan** requires the employer to bear the entire cost. A **funded plan** requires the employer to set aside funds to meet future pension benefits by making payments to an independent funding agency. The funding agency is responsible for managing the assets of the pension fund and for disbursing the pension benefits to employees. For many pension plans, insurance companies serve as the funding agency. An **unfunded plan** is managed entirely by the employer instead of by an independent agency. A **qualified plan** is designed to comply with federal income tax requirements which allow the employer to deduct pension contributions for tax purposes and which exempt pension fund income from tax. Most pension plans are qualified.

The accounting for pension plans can be complex due to the uncertainties of projecting future pension obligations. Future pension obligations depend upon such factors as employee life expectancies, expected employee compensation levels, and investment income on pension contributions. Pension funding requirements are estimated by individuals known as actuaries, who use sophisticated mathematical and statistical models.

The employer's cost of an employee's pension plan in a given year, referred to as the **net periodic pension cost,** is debited to an operating expense account, Pension Expense.[4] The credit is to Cash if the pension cost is fully funded. If the pension cost is partially funded, any unfunded amount is credited to Unfunded Accrued Pension Cost. To illustrate, assume that the pension plan of Flossmoor Industries requires an annual pension cost of $25,000, and Flossmoor Industries pays $15,000 to the fund trustee, Equity Insurance Company. The entry to record the transaction is as follows:

Pension Expense	25,000	
Cash		15,000
Unfunded Accrued Pension Cost......................		10,000

Depending upon when the pension liability (unfunded accrued pension cost) is to be paid, the $10,000 will be classified on the balance sheet as either a long-term or a current liability.

An entity's financial statements should fully disclose the nature of its pension plans and pension obligations. The financial statement disclosures should include the net periodic pension cost for the year and a description of the pension plan, including such items as the employee groups covered, the entity's accounting and funding policies, and any pension changes affecting comparability among years.

When an employer first adopts or changes a pension plan, the employer must consider whether to grant employees credit for prior years service. If a company does grant credit to employees for prior service, a prior service cost obligation must be recognized. The funding of prior service cost is normally provided for over a number of years, thus creating a long-term prior service pension cost liability. The complex nature of accounting for prior service costs is left for more advanced accounting study.

---

[4]*Statement of Financial Accounting Standards, No. 87,* "Employers' Accounting for Pensions" (Stamford: Financial Accounting Standards Board, 1985), par. 6.

Employee Stock Options

Stock options are rights given by a corporation to its employees to purchase shares of the corporation's stock at a stated price. Employee stock options generally involve an element of salary expense when the employees have the right to purchase the corporation's stock at a price below market value. In such a case, the expense is the difference between the market price of the stock and the amount the employees are required to pay for it. The amount of the expense is debited to an appropriate expense account and credited to an owner's equity account. The details of accounting for employee stock options are discussed in more advanced accounting texts.

NOTES PAYABLE AND INTEREST EXPENSE

Notes may be issued to creditors in temporary satisfaction of an account payable created earlier, or they may be issued at the time merchandise or other assets are purchased. To illustrate the former, assume that an enterprise issues to Murray Co. a 90-day, 12% note for $1,000, dated December 1, 1989, in settlement of a $1,000 overdue account. The entry to record the transaction is as follows:

Dec. 1	Accounts Payable—Murray Co.	1,000	
	Notes Payable		1,000
	Issued a 90-day, 12% note on account.		

On December 31, 1989, the end of the fiscal year, an adjusting entry would be recorded for the accrual of the interest from December 1 to December 31. The entry to record the accrued expense of $10 ($1,000 × 12/100 × 30/360) is as follows:

Adjusting Entry

Dec. 31	Interest Expense	10	
	Interest Payable		10

Interest payable is reported on the balance sheet at December 31, 1989, as a current liability. The interest expense account is closed at December 31, and the amount is reported in the Other Expense section of the income statement for the year ended December 31, 1989.

When the amount due on the note is paid in 1990, part of the interest paid will effect a reduction of the interest that was payable at December 31, 1989, and the remainder will represent expense for 1990. To avoid the possibility of failing to recognize this division and to avoid the inconvenience of analyzing the payment of interest in 1990, a reversing entry is made after the accounts are closed. The effect of the entry, illustrated as follows, is to transfer the credit balance in the interest payable account to the credit side of the interest expense account.

Reversing Entry

Jan. 1	Interest Payable	10	
	Interest Expense		10

At the time the note matures and payment is made, the entire amount of the interest payment is debited to Interest Expense, as illustrated by the following entry:

Mar. 1	Notes Payable	1,000	
	Interest Expense	30	
	Cash		1,030

After the foregoing entries are posted, the interest expense account will appear as follows:

ACCOUNT INTEREST EXPENSE — ACCOUNT NO. 911

Date		Item	Debit	Credit	Balance Debit	Balance Credit
1989						
Nov.	10		250		890	
Dec.	31	Adjusting	10		900	
	31	Closing		900	—	—
1990						
Jan.	1	Reversing		10		10
Mar.	1		30		20	

The adjusting and reversing process divided the $30 of interest paid on March 1, 1990, into two parts for accounting purposes: (1) $10 representing the interest expense for 1989 (recorded by the adjusting entry) and (2) $20 representing the interest expense for 1990 (the balance in the interest expense account at March 1, 1990).

Notes may also be issued when money is borrowed from banks. Although there are many variations in interest and repayment terms, the most direct procedure is for the borrower to issue an interest-bearing note for the amount of the loan. For example, assume that on September 19 a firm borrows $4,000 from the First National Bank, with the loan evidenced by the firm's 90-day, 15% note. The effect of this transaction is as follows:

Sept. 19	Cash	4,000	
	Notes Payable		4,000

On the due date of the note, ninety days later, the borrower owes $4,000, the face amount of the note, and interest of $150. The accounts are affected by the payment as follows:

Dec. 18	Notes Payable	4,000	
	Interest Expense	150	
	Cash		4,150

A variant of the bank loan transaction just illustrated is to issue a non-interest-bearing note for the amount that is to be paid at maturity. Although the note issued is non-interest-bearing, interest is deducted from the maturity value of the note and the borrower receives the remainder. The deduction of interest from a future value is termed **discounting.** The rate used in computing the interest may be termed the **discount rate,** the deduction may be called the **discount,** and the net amount available to the borrower is called the **proceeds.**

To illustrate the discounting of a note payable, assume that on August 10 an enterprise issued to a bank a $4,000, 90-day, non-interest-bearing note and that the bank discount rate is 15%. The amount of the discount is $150, and the proceeds are $3,850. The entry to record the transaction is as follows:

Aug. 10	Cash	3,850	
	Interest Expense	150	
	Notes Payable		4,000

The note payable is recorded at its face value, which is also its maturity value, and the interest expense is recorded at the time the note is issued. When the note is paid, the following entry is recorded:

Nov. 8	Notes Payable	4,000	
	Cash		4,000

PRODUCT WARRANTY LIABILITY

At the time of sale, a company may grant a warranty on a product. If revenues and expenses are to be matched properly, a liability to cover the warranty must be recorded in the period of the sale.[5] Later, when the product is repaired or replaced, the liability will be reduced. To illustrate, assume that during June a company sells $60,000 of a product, on which there is a 36-month warranty for repairing defects in the product. If past experience indicates that the average cost to repair defects is 5% of the sales price, the entry to record the product warranty liability would be as follows:

June 30	Product Warranty Expense	3,000	
	Product Warranty Payable.....................		3,000
	Product warranty for June, 5% × $60,000.		

When the defective product is repaired, the repair costs would be recorded by debiting Product Warranty Payable and crediting Cash, Supplies, or other appropriate account.

CONTINGENT LIABILITIES

As discussed previously, contingent liabilities are potential obligations that will materialize only if certain events occur in the future. They arise from

[5] *Statement of Financial Accounting Standards, No. 5,* "Accounting for Contingencies" (Stamford: Financial Accounting Standards Board, 1975), pars. 8, 24.

discounting notes receivable, litigation, possible tax assessments, or other causes. If the liability is probable and the amount of the liability can be reasonably estimated, it should be recorded in the accounts. If the amount cannot be reasonably estimated, the details of the contingency should be disclosed. Following is an example of a note disclosing a contingent liability in the 1986 financial statements of Florida Steel Corporation:

> The Company is defending various claims and legal actions which are common to its operations. This includes a suit in the Commonwealth of Puerto Rico against the Company and others for alleged violations of Puerto Rican antidumping statutes asking damages in excess of $5,000,000. While it is not feasible to predict or determine the ultimate outcome of these matters, none of them, in the opinion of management, will have a material effect on the Company's financial position or results of operations.

Chapter Review

KEY POINTS

1. Payroll and Liability for Payroll.
The term payroll is used to refer to the total amount paid to employees for a certain period. Payroll includes amounts paid for salaries to managerial or administrative employees as well as wages paid for manual labor.

Many enterprises pay their employees an annual bonus in addition to their regular salary or wage. The amount of the bonus may be measured by a certain percentage of income, which may be computed in a variety of ways.

2. Deductions from Employee Earnings and Computation of Employee Net Pay.
The total earnings of an employee for a payroll period, including bonuses and overtime pay, are often called the gross pay. From this amount is subtracted one or more deductions to arrive at the net pay. Deductions normally include FICA tax, federal income tax, and state and local income taxes, and may include union dues, charitable contributions, or employee insurance.

3. Liability for Employer's Payroll Taxes.
Most employers are subject to federal and state taxes based on the amount of remuneration earned by their employees. Such taxes include FICA tax, federal unemployment compensation tax, and state unemployment compensation tax.

4. Accounting Systems for Payroll and Payroll Taxes.
Although payroll systems will vary, the major parts common to most payroll systems include the payroll register, payroll checks, and employee's earnings

record. Based upon the data in the payroll register, a journal entry is usually prepared to record the payroll for a period. This entry recognizes employer and employee payroll taxes as well as the liability for the net pay to the employees. The payment of the payroll liabilities is recorded in the usual manner. The payment of the payroll is usually accomplished through the use of payroll checks.

The employee's earnings record is updated after each payroll period and is used for preparing reports for tax, insurance, and other purposes.

5. Internal Controls for Payroll Systems.
Cash disbursement controls are applicable to payrolls. Thus, the use of the voucher system and the requirement that all payments be supported by vouchers is desirable. Additional controls, such as the maintenance of employees' attendance records, are also desirable.

6. Liability for Employees' Fringe Benefits.
Most companies provide their employees a variety of benefits in addition to salary and wages earned. These benefits are referred to as fringe benefits and may take the form of vacations, employee pension plans, stock options, health insurance, etc. The estimated cost of these benefits should be recognized as an expense of the period during which the employee earns the benefit.

7. Notes Payable and Interest Expense.
Notes may be issued to creditors in temporary satisfaction of an account payable created earlier, or they may be issued at the time merchandise or other assets are purchased. At the end of the fiscal period, an adjusting entry is normally prepared for the accrual of interest. The interest payable is reported on the balance sheet as a current liability. The adjusting entry for accrued interest at the end of the period is normally reversed to simplify the accounting process in the following period.

Notes may also be issued to borrow money from banks. The notes may be interest-bearing or non-interest-bearing. In the case of non-interest-bearing notes, the interest (discount) is deducted from the face of the note and the borrower receives the balance (proceeds).

8. Product Warranty Liability.
At the time of sale, a company may grant a warranty on a product. A liability to cover the warranty should be recorded during the period of the sale.

9. Contingent Liabilities.
Contingent liabilities are potential obligations that will materialize only if certain events occur in the future. If the liability is probable and the amount of the liability can be reasonably estimated, it should be recorded in the accounts. If the amount cannot be reasonably estimated, the details of the contingency should be disclosed in the financial statements.

KEY TERMS

contingent liabilities 328
payroll 329
gross pay 332
net pay 332
FICA tax 332
payroll register 337
employee's earnings record 339
stock options 346
discount rate 348
discount 348
proceeds 348

SELF-EXAMINATION QUESTIONS

(Answers at End of Chapter)

1. An employee's rate of pay is $20 per hour, with time and a half for all hours worked in excess of 40 during a week. The following data are available:

Hours worked during current week	45
Year's cumulative earnings prior to current week	$44,400
FICA rate, on maximum of $45,000 of annual earnings	7.5%
Federal income tax withheld	$ 212

Based on these data, the amount of the employee's net pay for the current week is:
A. $600 C. $800
B. $693 D. $950

2. Which of the following taxes are employers usually required to withhold from employees?
A. Federal income tax
B. Federal unemployment compensation tax
C. State unemployment compensation tax
D. All of the above

3. With limitations on the maximum earnings subject to the tax, employers incur operating costs for which of the following payroll taxes?
A. FICA tax
B. Federal unemployment compensation tax
C. State unemployment compensation tax
D. All of the above

4. The unpaid balance of a mortgage note payable is $50,000 at the end of the current fiscal year. If the terms of the note provide for monthly principal payments of $1,000, how should the liability for the principal be presented on the balance sheet?
A. $50,000 current liability
B. $50,000 long-term liability
C. $12,000 current liability; $38,000 long-term liability
D. $12,000 long-term liability; $38,000 current liability

5. An enterprise issued a $5,000, 60-day, non-interest-bearing note to the bank, and the bank discounts the note at 12%. The proceeds are:
A. $4,400 C. $5,000
B. $4,900 D. $5,100

ILLUSTRATIVE PROBLEM

Selected transactions of Grainger Company, completed during the fiscal year ended December 31, are as follows:

Mar. 1. Purchased merchandise on account from Perry Inc., $15,000.
Apr. 10. Issued a 60-day, 12% note for $15,000 to Perry Inc., on account.
June 9. Paid Perry Inc. the amount owed on the note of April 10.
Aug. 1. Issued a 90-day, non-interest-bearing note for $30,000 to Atlantic Coast National Bank. The bank discounted the note at 15%.
Oct. 30. Paid Atlantic Coast National Bank the amount due on the note of August 1.

Dec. 15. Prepared the journal entry to record the biweekly payroll. A summary of the payroll record follows:

Deductions:	
FICA tax	$ 4,820
Federal income tax withheld	13,280
State income tax withheld	3,840
Savings bond deductions	630
Medical insurance deductions	960
Salary distribution:	
Sales	$50,800
Officers	25,800
Office	6,400
Net amount	$59,470

30. Issued a check in payment of employees' federal income tax of $68,550 and FICA tax of $24,650 due.
31. Issued a check for $8,600 to the pension fund trustee to fully fund the pension cost for December.
31. Prepared a journal entry to record the employees' accrued vacation pay, $32,200.
31. Prepared a journal entry to record the estimated accrued product warranty liability, $41,360.

Instructions:

Prepare entries to record the preceding transactions.

SOLUTION

Date	Account	Debit	Credit
Mar. 1	Purchases	15,000	
	Accounts Payable—Perry Inc.		15,000
Apr. 10	Accounts Payable—Perry Inc.	15,000	
	Notes Payable		15,000
June 9	Notes Payable	15,000	
	Interest Expense	300	
	Cash		15,300
Aug. 1	Cash	28,875	
	Interest Expense	1,125	
	Notes Payable		30,000
Oct. 30	Notes Payable	30,000	
	Cash		30,000
Dec. 15	Sales Salaries Expense	50,800	
	Officers Salaries Expense	25,800	
	Office Salaries Expense	6,400	
	FICA Tax Payable		4,820
	Employees Federal Income Tax Payable		13,280
	Employees State Income Tax Payable		3,840
	Bond Deductions Payable		630
	Medical Insurance Payable		960
	Salaries Payable		59,470

30	Employees Federal Income Tax Payable . . .	68,550	
	FICA Tax Payable	24,650	
	Cash		93,200
31	Pension Expense	8,600	
	Cash		8,600
31	Vacation Pay Expense	32,200	
	Vacation Pay Payable		32,200
31	Product Warranty Expense	41,360	
	Product Warranty Payable		41,360

Discussion Questions

9–1. If an employee is granted a profit-sharing bonus, is the amount of the bonus (a) part of the employee's earnings and (b) deductible as an expense of the enterprise in determining the federal income tax?

9–2. The general manager of a business enterprise is entitled to an annual profit-sharing bonus of 8%. For the current year, income before bonus and income taxes is $202,500, and income taxes are estimated at 40% of income before income taxes. Determine the amount of the bonus, assuming that the bonus is based on net income after deducting both bonus and income taxes.

9–3. What is (a) gross pay? (b) net or take-home pay?

9–4. (a) Identify the federal taxes that most employers are required to withhold from employees. (b) Give the titles of the accounts to which the amounts withheld are credited.

9–5. For each of the following payroll-related taxes, indicate whether there is a ceiling on the annual earnings subject to the tax: (a) FICA tax, (b) federal income tax, (c) federal unemployment compensation tax.

9–6. Identify the payroll taxes levied against employers.

9–7. Do payroll taxes levied against employers become liabilities at the time the liabilities for wages are incurred or at the time the wages are paid?

9–8. Prior to the last weekly payroll period of the calendar year, the cumulative earnings of employees A and B are $44,800 and $45,500, respectively. Their earnings for the last completed payroll period of the year are $900 each, which will be paid in January. If the amount of earnings subject to FICA tax is $45,000 and the tax rate is 7.5%, (a) what will be the employer's FICA tax on the earnings of employees A and B in the last payroll period; (b) what is the employer's total FICA tax expense for employees A and B for the calendar year just ended?

9–9. Indicate the principal functions served by the employee's earnings record.

9–10. Explain how a payroll system that is properly designed and operated tends to give assurance (a) that wages paid are based upon hours actually worked, and (b) that payroll checks are not issued to fictitious employees.

9–11. An employer pays the employees in currency and the pay envelopes are prepared by an employee rather than by the bank. (a) Why would it be advisable to obtain from the bank the exact amount of money needed for a payroll? (b) How could the exact number of each bill and coin denomination needed be determined efficiently in advance?

9–12. A company uses a weekly payroll period and a special bank account for payroll. (a) When should deposits be made in the account? (b) How is the amount of the deposit determined? (c) Is it necessary to have in the general ledger an account entitled "Cash—Special Payroll Account"? Explain. (d) The bank statement for the payroll bank account for the month ended November 30 indicates a bank balance of $11,705.50. Assuming that the bank has made no errors, what does this amount represent?

9–13. To match revenues and expenses properly, should the expense for employee vacation pay be recorded in the period during which the vacation privilege is earned or during the period in which the vacation is taken? Discuss.

9–14. Differentiate between a contributory and a noncontributory pension plan.

9–15. Identify several factors which influence the future pension obligation of an enterprise.

9–16. How does prior service cost arise in a new or revised pension plan?

9–17. What are employee stock options?

9–18. The unpaid balance of a mortgage note payable is $500,000 at the end of the current fiscal year. The terms of the note provide for quarterly principal payments of $20,000. How should the liability for the principal be presented on the balance sheet as of this date?

9–19. A business enterprise issued a 90-day, 12% note for $10,000 to a creditor on account. Give the entries to record (a) the issuance of the note and (b) the payment of the note at maturity, including interest of $300.

9–20. In borrowing money from a bank, an enterprise issued a $50,000, 60-day, non-interest-bearing note, which the bank discounted at 15%. Are the proceeds $50,000? Explain.

9–21. When should the liability associated with a product warranty be recorded? Discuss.

9–22. A business firm is contesting a suit for damages of a substantial amount, brought by a customer for an alleged faulty product. Is this a contingent liability for the defendant? If so, should it be disclosed in financial statements issued during the period of litigation? Discuss.

9–23. Real World Focus. The 1986 annual report for Whirlpool Corporation reports in the liability section of the December 31, 1986 balance sheet the following data with respect to product warranties:

Current Liabilities:	
Product warranty	19,200,000
Other Liabilities:	
Product warranty	11,900,000

(a) What entry would have been made to record the accrued product warranty costs at December 31, 1986, assuming that no entry had been made in prior years? (b) How would costs of repairing a defective product be recorded?

Exercises

9–24. Algorithm. Develop an algorithm, in the form illustrated in this chapter, to compute the amount of each employee's weekly earnings subject to state unemployment compensation tax. Assume that the tax is 4.2% on the first $7,000 of each employee's earnings during the year and that the following symbols are to be used:

e—Cumulative earnings subject to state unemployment compensation tax prior to current week
E—Current week's earnings
S—Amount of current week's earnings subject to state unemployment compensation tax

SPREADSHEET PROBLEM

9–25. Profit-sharing bonus. The general manager of a business enterprise is entitled to an annual profit-sharing bonus of 5%. For the current year, income before bonus and income taxes is $400,000, and income taxes are estimated at 40% of income before income taxes. Determine the amount of the bonus, assuming that (a) the bonus is based on income before deductions for bonus and income taxes and (b) the bonus is based on income after deduction for both bonus and income taxes.

9–26. Summary payroll data. In the following summary of data for a payroll period, some amounts have been intentionally omitted:

Earnings:		Deductions:	
(1) At regular rate.	—	(4) FICA tax.	$ 4,315.20
(2) At overtime rate . . .	$ 4,144.00	(5) Income tax withheld.	9,281.60
(3) Total earnings.	—	(6) Medical insurance. .	710.00
		(7) Union dues.	—
		(8) Total deductions . . .	15,766.40
		(9) Net amount paid. . .	59,116.80

Accounts debited:	
(10) Factory Wages. . .	$53,984.40
(11) Sales Salaries . . .	—
(12) Office Salaries . . .	4,872.00

(a) Determine the amounts omitted in lines (1), (3), (7), and (11). (b) Present the entry to record the payroll. (c) Present the entry to record the voucher for the payroll. (d) Present the entry to record the payment of the voucher. (e) From the data given in this exercise and your answer to (a), would you conclude that this payroll was paid sometime during the first few weeks of the calendar year? Explain.

9–27. Payroll tax entries. According to a summary of the payroll of McMann Distributing Co., the amount of earnings for the four weekly payrolls paid in December of the current year was $360,000, of which $25,000 was not subject to FICA tax and $345,000 was not subject to state and federal unemployment taxes. (a) Determine the employer's payroll taxes expense for the month, using the following rates: FICA, 7.5%; state unemployment, 4.8%; federal unemployment, .8%. (b) Present the entry to record the accrual of payroll taxes for the month of December.

9–28. Accrued vacation pay and product warranty. A business enterprise provides its employees with varying amounts of vacation per year, depending on the length of employment. It also warrants its products for one year. The estimated total amount of the current year's vacation pay is $180,000, and the estimated product warranty is 2% of sales. If sales were $650,000 for January, prepare the adjusting entries required at January 31, the end of the first month of the current year, to record (a) the accrued vacation pay and (b) the accrued product warranty.

9–29. Pension plan entries. Jefferson Corporation maintains a funded pension plan for its employees. The plan requires quarterly installments to be paid to the funding agent, Curtin Insurance Company, by the fifteenth of the month following the end of each quarter. If for the quarter ended December 31, the pension cost is $45,000, prepare entries to record (a) the accrued pension liability on December 31 and (b) the payment to the funding agent on January 15.

9–30. Entries for discounting notes. Newhart Co. issues a 90-day, non-interest-bearing note for $100,000 to Roberts Bank and Trust Co., and the bank discounts the note at 15%. (a) Present the maker's entries to record (1) the issuance of the note and (2) the payment of the note at maturity. (b) Present the payee's entries to record (1) the receipt of the note and (2) the receipt of payment of the note at maturity.

9–31. Determination of interest on notes issued. In negotiating a 120-day loan, an enterprise has the option of either (1) issuing a $200,000, non-interest-bearing note that will be discounted at the rate of 12%, or (2) issuing a $200,000 note that bears interest at the rate of 12% and that will be accepted at face value.

(a) Determine the amount of the interest expense for each option.
(b) Determine the amount of the proceeds for each option.
(c) Indicate the option that is more favorable to the borrower.

9–32. Plant asset purchases with note. On September 1, Oliver Company purchased land for $150,000 and a building for $500,000, paying $130,000 cash and issuing a 12% note for the balance, secured by a mortgage on the property. The terms of the note provide for 26 semiannual payments of $20,000 on the principal plus the interest accrued from the date of the preceding payment. Present the entry to record (a) the transaction on September 1, (b) the adjustment for accrued interest on December 31, (c) the reversal of the adjustment on January 1, (d) the payment of the first installment on February 28, and (e) the payment of the second installment the following August 31.

Problems

9–33. Profit-sharing bonuses. The president of Wagner Company is entitled to an annual profit-sharing bonus of 4%. For the current year, income before bonus and income taxes is $720,000, and income taxes are estimated at 40% of income before income taxes.

Instructions: (1) Determine the amount of the bonus, assuming that:
(a) The bonus is based on income before deductions for bonus and income taxes.
(b) The bonus is based on income after deduction for bonus but before deduction for income taxes.
(c) The bonus is based on income after deduction for income taxes but before deduction for bonus.
(d) The bonus is based on income after deduction for both bonus and income taxes.
(2) (a) Which bonus plan would the president prefer? (b) Would this plan always be the president's choice, regardless of Wagner Company's income level?

9–34. Entries for payroll and payroll taxes. The following information relative to the payroll for the week ended December 30 was obtained from the records of E. Thurmond Inc.:

Salaries:		Deductions:	
Sales salaries	$148,700	Income tax withheld	$33,850
Warehouse salaries	21,280	U.S. savings bonds	4,400
Office salaries	12,020	Group insurance	2,800
	$182,000	FICA tax withheld totals the same amount as the employer's tax.	

Tax rates assumed:
FICA, 7.5%
State unemployment (employer only), 3.8%
Federal unemployment, .8%

Instructions: (1) Assuming that the payroll for the last week of the year is to be paid on December 31, present the following entries:

(a) December 30, to record the payroll. Of the total payroll for the last week of the year, $112,800 is subject to FICA tax and $15,000 is subject to unemployment compensation taxes.

(b) December 30, to record the employer's payroll taxes on the payroll to be paid on December 31.

(2) Assuming that the payroll for the last week of the year is to be paid on January 4 of the following year, present the following entries:

(a) December 30, to record the payroll.

(b) January 4, to record the employer's payroll taxes on the payroll to be paid on January 4.

If the working papers correlating with the textbook are not used, omit Problem 9–35.

9–35. Payroll register. The payroll register for H. A. Howe Company for the week ending December 7 of the current fiscal year is presented in the working papers.

Instructions: (1) Journalize the entry to record the payroll for the week.

(2) Assuming the use of a voucher system and payment by regular check, present the entries to record the payroll voucher and the issuance of the checks to employees.

(3) Journalize the entry to record the employer's payroll taxes for the week. Assume the following tax rates: FICA, 7.5%; state unemployment, 3.8%; federal unemployment, .8%.

(4) Present the entries to record the following selected transactions:

Dec. 15. Prepared a voucher, payable to First National Bank, for employees income taxes, $3,750.60, and FICA taxes, $2,369.15, on salaries paid in November.

15. Issued a check to First National Bank in payment of the voucher.

9–36. Payroll entries. The following accounts, with the balances indicated, appear in the ledger of Monico Company on December 1 of the current year:

212	Salaries Payable	—
213	FICA Tax Payable	$ 14,910
214	Employees Federal Income Tax Payable	44,800
215	Employees State Income Tax Payable	13,260
216	State Unemployment Tax Payable	1,710
217	Federal Unemployment Tax Payable	360
218	Bond Deductions Payable	715
219	Medical Insurance Payable	3,875
611	Sales Salaries Expense	631,300
711	Officers Salaries Expense	311,800
712	Office Salaries Expense	85,500
719	Payroll Taxes Expense	92,430

The following transactions relating to payroll, payroll deductions, and payroll taxes occurred during December:

Dec. 2. Prepared Voucher No. 638 for $715, payable to Marine National Bank, to purchase United States savings bonds for employees.

2. Issued Check No. 621 in payment of Voucher No. 638.

14. Prepared a journal entry to record the biweekly payroll. A summary of the payroll record follows:

Deductions:

FICA tax	$ 3,250
Federal income tax withheld	7,790
State income tax withheld	1,920
Savings bond deductions	315
Medical insurance deductions	480

Salary distributions:

Sales	$30,600
Officers	15,200
Office	3,800
Net amount	$35,845

Dec. 14. Prepared Voucher No. 646, payable to Payroll Bank Account, for the net amount of the biweekly payroll.

14. Issued Check No. 627 in payment of Voucher No. 646.

15. Prepared Voucher No. 647 for $59,710, payable to Marine National Bank for $44,800 of employees' federal income tax and $14,910 of FICA tax due on December 15.

15. Issued Check No. 633 in payment of Voucher No. 647.

18. Prepared Voucher No. 650 for $3,875, payable to Wilson Insurance Company, for the semiannual premium on the group medical insurance policy.

19. Issued Check No. 639 in payment of Voucher No. 650.

28. Prepared a journal entry to record the biweekly payroll. A summary of the payroll record follows:

Deductions:

FICA tax	$ 3,010
Federal income tax withheld	7,565
State income tax withheld	1,845
Savings bond deductions	315

Salary distribution:

Sales	$28,500
Officers	15,200
Office	3,800
Net amount	$34,765

Dec. 28. Prepared Voucher No. 684, payable to Payroll Bank Account, for the net amount of the biweekly payroll.

28. Issued Check No. 671 in payment of Voucher No. 684.

30. Prepared Voucher No. 690 for $630, payable to Marine National Bank, to purchase United States savings bonds for employees.

30. Issued Check No. 680 in payment of Voucher No. 690.

30. Prepared Voucher No. 691 for $13,260, payable to Marine National Bank, for employees' state income tax due on December 31.

30. Issued Check No. 681 in payment of Voucher No. 691.

31. Prepared a journal entry to record the employer's payroll taxes on earnings paid in December. FICA tax totals $6,260, and taxable earnings subject to unemployment compensation tax are $8,500. Assume the following tax rates: state unemployment, 3.8%; federal unemployment, .8%.

Instructions: (1) Record the transactions in a journal.

(2) Journalize the adjusting entry on December 31 to record salaries for the incomplete payroll period. Salaries accrued are as follows: sales salaries, $2,950; officers salaries, $1,640; office salaries, $410. The payroll taxes are immaterial and are not accrued.

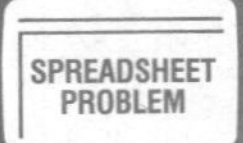

9–37. Wage and Tax Statement data and employer FICA tax. Griffin Company began business on January 2 of last year. Salaries were paid to employees on the last day of each month, and both FICA tax and federal income tax were withheld in the required amounts. An employee who is hired in the middle of the month receives half the monthly salary for that month. All required payroll tax reports were filed and the correct amount of payroll taxes was remitted by the company for the calendar year. Before the Wage and Tax Statements (Form W-2) could be prepared for distributing to employees and filing with the Social Security Administration, the employees' earnings records were inadvertently destroyed.

None of the employees resigned or were discharged during the year, and there were no changes in salary rates. The FICA tax was withheld at the rate of 7.5% on the first $45,000 of salary. Data on dates of employment, salary rates, and employees' income taxes withheld, which are summarized as follows, were obtained from personnel records and payroll records.

Employee	Date First Employed	Monthly Salary	Monthly Income Tax Withheld
Allen	June 2	$2,500	$ 417.50
Cox	Jan. 2	4,200	854.50
Gower	Mar. 1	3,800	748.15
Nunn	Jan. 2	4,000	810.10
Quinn	Nov. 15	3,600	652.30
Ruiz	Apr. 15	2,800	461.10
Wu	Jan. 16	5,200	1,261.40

Instructions: (1) Determine the amounts to be reported on each employee's Wage and Tax Statement (Form W-2) for the year, arranging the data in the following form:

Employee	Gross Earnings	Federal Income Tax Withheld	Earnings Subject to FICA Tax	FICA Tax Withheld

(2) Determine the following employer payroll taxes for the year: (a) FICA; (b) state unemployment compensation at 3.8% on the first $7,000 of each employee's earnings; (c) federal unemployment compensation at .8% of the first $7,000 of each employee's earnings; (d) total.

(3) In a manner similar to the illustrations in this chapter, develop four algorithms to describe the computations required to determine the four amounts in (1), using the following symbols:

n = Numbered of payroll periods
g = Monthly gross earnings
f = Monthly federal income tax withheld
G = Total gross earnings
F = Total federal income tax withheld
T = Total earnings subject to FICA tax
S = Total FICA tax withheld

9–38. Purchases and notes payable transactions. The following items were selected from among the transactions completed by Flowers Co. during the current year:

Mar. 2. Purchased merchandise on account from Hines and York, $5,400.
8. Purchased merchandise on account from Malone Co., $10,000.
12. Paid Hines and York for the invoice of March 2, less 2% discount.
Apr. 1. Issued a 60-day, 12% note for $10,000 to Malone Co., on account.
May 10. Issued a 120-day, non-interest-bearing note for $45,000 to Garden City Bank. The bank discounted the note at the rate of 14%.
31. Paid Malone Co. the amount owed on the note of April 1.
Aug. 5. Borrowed $7,500 from First Financial Corporation, issuing a 60-day, 14% note for that amount.
Sept. 7. Paid Garden City Bank the amount due on the note of May 10.
Oct. 4. Paid First Financial Corporation the interest due on the note of August 5 and renewed the loan by issuing a new 30-day, 16% note for $7,500. (Record both the debit and the credit to the notes payable account.)

Nov. 3. Paid First Financial Corporation the amount due on the note of October 4.

15. Purchased store equipment from Sims Equipment Co. for $50,000, paying $8,000 and issuing a series of seven 12% notes for $6,000 each, coming due at 30-day intervals.

Dec. 15. Paid the amount due Sims Equipment Co. on the first note in the series issued on November 15.

Instructions: (1) Record the transactions.

(2) Determine the total amount of interest accrued as of December 31 on the six notes owed to Sims Equipment Co.

(3) Record the adjusting journal entry for the accrued interest at December 31 and the reversing entry on January 1.

(4) Assume that a single note for $42,000 had been issued on November 15 instead of the series of seven notes, and that its terms required principal payments of $6,000 each 30 days, with interest at 12% on the principal balance before applying the $6,000 payment. Determine the amount that would have been due and payable on December 15.

ALTERNATE PROBLEMS

9–33A. Profit-sharing bonuses. The president of Wilson Products is entitled to an annual profit-sharing bonus of 5%. For the current year, income before bonus and income taxes is $309,000, and income taxes are estimated at 40% of income before income taxes.

Instructions: (1) Determine the amount of the bonus, assuming that:

(a) The bonus is based on income before deductions for bonus and income taxes.

(b) The bonus is based on income after deduction for bonus but before deduction for income taxes.

(c) The bonus is based on income after deduction for income taxes but before deduction for bonus.

(d) The bonus is based on income after deduction for both bonus and income taxes.

(2) (a) Which bonus plan would the president prefer? (b) Would this plan always be the president's choice, regardless of Wilson Products' income level?

9–34A. Entries for payroll and payroll taxes. The following information relative to the payroll for the week ended December 30 was obtained from the records of C. H. Beal Inc.:

Salaries:		Deductions:	
Sales salaries	$ 86,500	Income tax withheld	$18,050
Warehouse salaries	18,980	Group insurance	1,350
Office salaries	9,520	U.S. savings bonds	1,200
	$115,000	FICA tax withheld totals the same amount as the employer's tax.	

Tax rates assumed:
FICA, 7.5%
State unemployment (employer only), 4.2%
Federal unemployment, .8%

Instructions: (1) Assuming that the payroll for the last week of the year is to be paid on December 31, present the following entries:
(a) December 30, to record the payroll. Of the total payroll for the last week of the year, $109,000 is subject to FICA tax and $9,000 is subject to unemployment compensation taxes.
(b) December 30, to record the employer's payroll taxes on the payroll to be paid on December 31.
(2) Assuming that the payroll for the last week of the year is to be paid on January 5 of the following fiscal year, present the following entries:
(a) December 31, to record the payroll.
(b) January 5, to record the employer's payroll taxes on the payroll to be paid on January 5.

If the working papers correlating with the textbook are not used, omit Problem 9–35A.

9–35A. Payroll register. The payroll register for Ann Murphy Co. for the week ending December 7 of the current fiscal year is presented in the working papers.

Instructions: (1) Journalize the entry to record the payroll for the week.
(2) Assuming the use of a voucher system and payment by regular check, present the entries to record the payroll voucher and the issuance of the checks to employees.
(3) Journalize the entry to record the employer's payroll taxes for the week. Assume the following tax rates: FICA, 7.5%; state unemployment, 3.1%; federal unemployment, .8%.
(4) Present the entries to record the following selected transactions:

Dec. 16. Prepared a voucher, payable to Palmer National Bank, for employees income taxes, $3,192.50, and FICA taxes, $2,172.25, on salaries paid in November.
16. Issued a check to Palmer National Bank in payment of the above voucher.

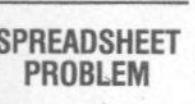

9–37A. Wage and Tax Statement data and employer FICA tax. Stoner Company began business on January 2 of last year. Salaries were paid to employees on the last day of each month, and both FICA tax and federal income tax were withheld in the required amounts. An employee who is hired in the middle of the month receives half the monthly salary for that month. All required payroll tax reports were filed and the correct amount of payroll taxes was remitted by the company for the calendar year. Before the Wage and Tax Statements (Form W-2) could be prepared for distributing to employees and filing with the Social Security Administration, the employees' earnings records were inadvertently destroyed.

None of the employees resigned or were discharged during the year, and there were no changes in salary rates. The FICA tax was withheld at the rate of 7.5% on the first $45,000 of salary. Data on dates of employment, salary rates, and employees' income taxes withheld, which are summarized as follows, were obtained from personnel records and payroll records.

Employee	Date First Employed	Monthly Salary	Monthly Income Tax Withheld
Alvarez	Jan. 16	$2,800	$ 471.20
Cruz	Nov. 1	2,500	394.25
Funk	Jan. 2	4,200	895.60
Little	July 16	3,400	636.50
Powell	Jan. 2	5,400	1,374.10
Soong	May 1	3,600	652.30
Wilson	Feb. 16	4,000	864.10

Instructions: (1) Determine the amounts to be reported on each employee's Wage and Tax Statement (Form W-2) for the year, arranging the data in the following form:

Employee	Gross Earnings	Federal Income Tax Withheld	Earnings Subject to FICA Tax	FICA Tax Withheld

(2) Determine the following employer payroll taxes for the year: (a) FICA; (b) state unemployment compensation at 4.2% on the first $7,000 of each employee's earnings; (c) federal unemployment compensation at .8% on the first $7,000 of each employee's earnings; (d) total.

(3) In a manner similar to the illustrations in this chapter, develop four algorithms to describe the computations required to determine the four amounts in (1), using the following symbols:

n = Number of payroll periods
g = Monthly gross earnings
f = Monthly federal income tax withheld
G = Total gross earnings
F = Total federal income tax withheld
T = Total earnings subject to FICA tax
S = Total FICA tax withheld

9–38A. Purchases and notes payable transactions. The following items were selected from among the transactions completed by Douglas Co. during the current year:

Jan. 15. Purchased merchandise on account from Davis Co., $7,800.
Mar. 1. Purchased merchandise on account from Evans Co., $9,600.
6. Issued a 30-day, 12% note for $7,800 to Davis Co., on account.
10. Paid Evans Co. for the invoice of March 1, less 1% discount.
Apr. 5. Paid Davis Co. the amount owed on the note of March 6.
July 15. Borrowed $8,000 from Royal National Bank, issuing a 90-day, 13% note for that amount.
25. Issued a 120-day, non-interest-bearing note for $20,000 to Barnett State Bank. The bank discounted the note at the rate of 15%.
Oct. 13. Paid Royal National Bank the interest due on the note of July 15 and renewed the loan by issuing a new 30-day, 15% note for $8,000. (Record both the debit and credit to the notes payable account.)
Nov. 12. Paid Royal National Bank the amount due on the note of October 13.
22. Paid Barnett State Bank the amount due on the note of July 25.
Dec. 1. Purchased office equipment from Bunn Equipment Co. for $57,500, paying $7,500 and issuing a series of ten 12% notes for $5,000 each, coming due at 30-day intervals.
31. Paid the amount due Bunn Equipment Co. on the first note in the series issued on December 1.

Instructions: (1) Record the transactions.

(2) Determine the total amount of interest accrued as of December 31 on the nine notes owed to Bunn Equipment Co.

(3) Record the adjusting entry for the accrued interest at December 31 and the reversing entry on January 1.

(4) Assume that a single note for $50,000 had been issued on December 1 instead of the series of ten notes, and that its terms required principal payments of $5,000 each 30 days, with interest at 12% on the principal balance before applying the $5,000 payment. Determine the amount that would have been due and payable on December 31.

Mini-Case 9

In 1988, your father retired as president of the family-owned business, MG Inc., and a new president was recruited by an executive search firm. The new president's contract called for an annual base salary of $50,000 plus a bonus of 12% of income after deducting the bonus but before deducting income taxes.

In 1989, the first full year under the new president, MG Inc. reported income of $910,000 before deducting the bonus and income taxes. After being fired on January 3, 1990, the new president demanded immediate payment of a $109,200 bonus for 1989.

Your father was concerned about the accounting practices used during 1989, and he has asked you to help him in reviewing the accounting records before the bonus is paid. Upon investigation, you have discovered the following facts:

(a) The payroll for December 27–31, 1989, was not accrued at the end of the year. The salaries for the five-day period and the applicable payroll taxes are as follows:

Sales salaries	$5,500
Warehouse salaries	3,500
Office salaries	3,000
FICA tax	7.5%
State unemployment tax (employer only)	3.2%
Federal unemployment tax	.8%

The payroll was paid on January 9, 1990, for the period December 27, 1989, through January 7, 1990.

(b) The semiannual pension cost of $25,000 was not accrued for the last half of 1989. The pension cost was paid to Equity Insurance Company on January 12, 1990, and was recorded by a debit to Pension Expense and a credit to Cash for $25,000.

(c) The estimated product warranty liability of $10,000 for products sold during the year ended December 31, 1989, was not recorded.

(d) On July 1, 1989, MG Inc. purchased a one-year insurance policy for $9,640, debiting the cost to Prepaid Insurance. No adjusting entry was made for insurance expired at December 31, 1989.

(e) The vacation pay liability of $12,000 for December, 1989, was not recorded.

Instructions:

(1) Based on reported 1989 income of $910,000 before deducting the bonus and income taxes, was the president's calculation of the $109,200 bonus correct? Explain.

(2) What accounting errors were made in 1989 which would affect the amount of the president's bonus?
(3) Based on the employment contract and your answer to (2), what is the correct amount of the president's bonus for 1989?
(4) How much did the president's demand for a $109,200 bonus exceed the correct amount of the bonus under the employment contract?
(5) Late in 1990, MG Inc. paid the president the amount of the bonus computed in (3), after which the president sued MG Inc. for breach of contract. The suit requested compensatory and punitive damages of $500,000. Should the lawsuit be reported on the 1990 financial statements?
(6) Describe the major advantage and disadvantage of using profit-sharing bonuses in employment contracts.

Answers to Self-Examination Questions

1. B The amount of net pay of $693 (answer B) is determined as follows:

Gross pay:		
40 hours at $20	$800	
5 hours at $30	150	$950
Deductions:		
Federal income tax withheld	$212	
FICA ($600 × .075)	45	257
Net pay		$693

2. A Employers are usually required to withhold a portion of the earnings of their employees for payment of federal income taxes (answer A). Generally, federal (answer B) and state (answer C) unemployment compensation taxes are levied against the employer only and thus are not deducted from employee earnings.
3. D The employer incurs operating costs for FICA tax (answer A), federal unemployment compensation tax (answer B), and state unemployment compensation tax (answer C). These costs add significantly to the total labor costs for most businesses.
4. C Liabilities due within a year should be presented as current liabilities, and those with a more distant future due date should be presented as long-term liabilities on the balance sheet. Therefore, the 12 monthly payments of $1,000 each, for a total of $12,000, represent a current liability, and the remaining $38,000 is a long-term liability(answer C).
5. B The net amount available to a borrower from discounting a note payable is termed the proceeds. The proceeds of $4,900 (answer B) is determined as follows:

Face amount of note	$5,000
Less discount ($5,000 × 12/100 × 60/360)	100
Proceeds	$4,900

Part Three

Accounting for Equity Rights

10
Forms of Business Organization

CHAPTER OBJECTIVES

Identify basic sole proprietorship characteristics which have accounting implications.

Describe and illustrate the accounting for sole proprietorships.

Identify basic partnership characteristics which have accounting implications.

Describe and illustrate the accounting for partnerships.

Identify basic corporation characteristics which have accounting implications.

Describe and illustrate the accounting for stockholders' equity.

Describe and illustrate the computation of equity per share of stock.

Describe and illustrate the accounting for organization costs.

In preceding chapters, the corporate enterprise was used in illustrations. The transactions affecting the stockholders' equity of these enterprises focused on basic accounting concepts and principles. In this chapter, consideration will be given to the two other types of business organizations — sole proprietorships and partnerships. In addition, the accounting for more complex transactions affecting stockholders' equity will be discussed.

CHARACTERISTICS OF SOLE PROPRIETORSHIPS

A sole proprietorship is a business enterprise owned by one individual. Approximately 74% of all business enterprises in the United States are sole proprietorships. However, sole proprietorships account for only 7% of all business revenues. These statistics indicate that sole proprietorships, although numerous, consist mostly of small enterprises.

A business may be started and operated relatively easily as a sole proprietorship. There are few legal restrictions to establishing a sole proprietorship, and the individual owner can usually make all business decisions without being accountable to others. This ability to be one's own boss is a major reason why many individuals organize their business enterprises as sole proprietorships.

A sole proprietorship is a separate entity for accounting purposes, and when the owner dies or retires, the sole proprietorship ceases to exist. For federal income tax purposes, however, the sole proprietorship is not treated as a separate taxable entity. The income (or loss) is allocated to the owner and is included on the owner's personal tax return.

A primary disadvantage of a sole proprietorship may be the difficulty in raising funds. Investment in the business is limited to the amounts that the owner can provide from personal resources, plus any additional amounts that can be raised through borrowing. The owner is also personally liable for any debts of the business. Thus, if the business becomes insolvent, creditors have rights to the personal assets of the owner, regardless of the amount of the owner's investment in the enterprise.

ACCOUNTING FOR SOLE PROPRIETORSHIPS

Since the sole proprietorship is a separate business entity for accounting purposes, the transactions of the sole proprietorship must be kept separate from the personal financial affairs of the owner. Only in this way can the financial condition and the results of operations of the sole proprietorship be accurately measured and reported.

The day-to-day accounting entries for a sole proprietorship are much the same as for a corporation. The primary differences in accounting for a sole proprietorship include the use of an owner's **capital account,** rather than a capital stock account, to record investments in the enterprise. In addition, this capital account, rather than a retained earnings account, is used to record changes in owner's equity from net income or net loss. Finally, instead of a dividends account, distributions to the owner are recorded in the owner's **drawing account.** At the end of the period, the drawing account is closed to the owner's capital account, and a statement of owner's equity is prepared. The statement of owner's equity thus summarizes changes in owner's equity that have occurred during a specific period of time.

CHARACTERISTICS OF PARTNERSHIPS

The Uniform Partnership Act, which has been adopted by more than ninety percent of the states, defines a partnership as "an association of two or more persons to carry on as co-owners a business for profit." The partnership form of business organization is widely used for comparatively small businesses that wish to take advantage of the combined capital, managerial talent, and experience of two or more persons. In many cases, the alternative to securing the amount of investment needed or the various skills needed to operate a business is to adopt the corporate form of organization. The typical corporate form of organization is sometimes not permitted, however, because of restrictions in state laws. In addition, a group of physicians, attorneys, or certified public accountants who wish to band together to practice a profession often organize as a partnership. Medical and legal partnerships made up of 20 or more partners are not unusual, and the number of partners in some CPA firms exceeds 1,000.

Partnerships have several characteristics that have accounting implications. These characteristics are described in the following paragraphs.

A partnership has a **limited life.** Dissolution of a partnership occurs whenever a partner ceases to be a member of the firm for any reason, including withdrawal, bankruptcy, incapacity, or death. Similarly, admission of a new partner dissolves the old partnership. In case of dissolution, a new partnership must be formed if the operations of the business are to be continued without interruption. This situation frequently occurs with professional partnerships. Their composition may change often as new partners are admitted and others are retired.

Most partnerships are *general partnerships,* in which the partners have **unlimited liability.** Each partner is individually liable to creditors for debts incurred by the partnership. Thus, if a partnership becomes insolvent, the partners must contribute sufficient personal assets to settle the debts of the partnership. In some states, a *limited partnership* may be formed, in which the liability of some partners may be limited to the amount of their capital investment. However, a limited partnership must have at least one general partner who has unlimited liability. In this chapter, the discussion is focused on the general partnership.

Partners have **co-ownership of partnership property.** The property invested in a partnership by a partner becomes the property of all the partners jointly. Upon dissolution of the partnership and distribution of its assets, the partners' claims against the assets are measured by the amount of the balances in their capital accounts.

Another characteristic of a partnership is **mutual agency.** This feature means that each partner is an agent of the partnership, with the authority to enter into contracts for the partnership. Thus, the acts of each partner bind the partnership and become the responsibility of all partners.

A significant right of partners is **participation in income** of the partnership. Net income and net loss are distributed among the partners according to their agreement. In the absence of any agreement, all partners share equally. If the agreement specifies profit distribution but is silent as to losses, the losses are shared in the same manner as profits.

A partnership, like a sole proprietorship, is a **nontaxable entity** and is therefore not required to pay federal income taxes. However, revenue and expense and other financial details of partnership operations must be reported annually on official Internal Revenue Service forms known as *information returns*. The individual partners must report their distributive share of partnership income on their personal tax returns.

A partnership is created by a voluntary contract containing all the elements essential to any other enforceable contract. It is not necessary that this contract be in writing, nor even that its terms be specifically expressed. However, good business practice dictates that the contract should be in writing and should clearly express the intentions of the partners. The contract, known as the **articles of partnership** or **partnership agreement,** should contain provisions regarding such matters as the amount of investment to be made, limitations on withdrawals of funds, the manner in which net income and net loss are to be divided, and the admission and withdrawal of partners.

Most of the day-to-day accounting for a partnership is the same as the accounting for a sole proprietorship and a corporation. It is in the areas of the formation, income distribution, dissolution, and liquidation that transactions peculiar to partnerships arise.

Recording Investments

A separate entry is made for the investment of each partner in a partnership. The various assets contributed by a partner are debited to the proper asset accounts. If liabilities are assumed by the partnership, the appropriate liability accounts are credited. The partner's capital account is credited for the net amount.

To illustrate the entry to record an initial investment, assume that Robert A. Stevens and Earl S. Foster, who are sole owners of competing hardware stores, agree to combine their businesses in a partnership. Each is to contribute certain amounts of cash and other business assets. It is also agreed that the partnership is to assume the liabilities of the separate businesses. The entry to record the assets contributed and the liabilities transferred by Robert A. Stevens is as follows:

Apr.	1	Cash	7,200	
		Accounts Receivable	16,300	
		Merchandise Inventory	28,700	
		Store Equipment	5,400	
		Office Equipment	1,500	
		Allowance for Doubtful Accounts		1,500
		Accounts Payable		2,600
		Robert A. Stevens, Capital		55,000

The monetary amounts at which the noncash assets are stated are those agreed upon by the partners. In arriving at an appropriate amount for such assets, consideration should be given to their market values at the time the partnership is formed. The values agreed upon represent the acquisition cost to the accounting entity created by the formation of the partnership. These amounts may differ from the balances appearing in the accounts of the separate businesses before the partnership was organized.

Division of Net Income or Net Loss

As in the case of a sole proprietorship, the net income of a partnership may be said to include a return for the services of the owners, for the capital invested, and for economic or pure profit. Partners are not legally employees of the partnership, nor are their capital contributions a loan. If each of two partners is to contribute equal services and amounts of capital, an equal sharing in partnership net income would be equitable. But if one partner is to contribute a larger portion of capital than the other, provision for unequal capital contributions should be given recognition in the agreement for dividing net income. Or, if the services of one partner are much more valuable to the partnership than those of the other, provision for unequal service contributions should be given recognition in their agreement.

To illustrate the division of net income and the accounting for this division, assume that Stone and Mills (1) are allowed monthly salaries of $2,500 and $2,000 respectively; (2) are allowed interest at 12% on capital balances at January 1 of the current fiscal year, which amounted to $80,000 and $60,000 respectively; and (3) divide the remainder of net income equally. A report of the division of net income may be presented as a separate statement accompanying the balance sheet and the income statement, or it may be added at the bottom of the income statement. If the latter procedure is adopted, the lower part of the income statement would appear as follows:

Net income			$75,000
	J. L. Stone	*C. R. Mills*	*Total*
Division of net income:			
Salary allowance	$30,000	$24,000	$54,000
Interest allowance	9,600	7,200	16,800
Remaining income	2,100	2,100	4,200
Net income	$41,700	$33,300	$75,000

The division of net income is recorded as a closing entry, regardless of whether the partners actually withdraw any amounts from the partnership. The entry for the division of net income is as follows:

Dec. 31	Income Summary	75,000	
	J. L. Stone, Capital		41,700
	C. R. Mills, Capital		33,300

If Stone and Mills had withdrawn any amounts, the withdrawals would have accumulated as debits in the drawing accounts during the year. At the end of the year, the debit balances in their drawing accounts would be transferred to their respective capital accounts.

In the above illustration, the net income exceeded the sum of the allowances for salary and interest. If the net income is less than the total of the special allowances, the "remaining balance" will be a negative figure that must be divided among the partners as though it were a net loss. The effect of this situation may be illustrated by assuming the same salary and interest allowances as in the preceding illustration, but changing the amount of net income to $50,000. The salary and interest allowances to Stone total $39,600 and the comparable figure for Mills is $31,200. The sum of these amounts, $70,800, exceeds the net income of $50,000 by $20,800. It is therefore necessary to deduct $10,400 (½ of $20,800) from each partner's share to arrive at the net income, as follows:

Net income			$50,000
	J. L. Stone	*C. R. Mills*	*Total*
Division of net income:			
Salary allowance	$30,000	$24,000	$54,000
Interest allowance	9,600	7,200	16,800
Total	$39,600	$31,200	$70,800
Excess of allowances over income	10,400	10,400	20,800
Net income	$29,200	$20,800	$50,000

In closing Income Summary at the end of the year, $29,200 would be credited to J. L. Stone, Capital, and $20,800 would be credited to C. R. Mills, Capital.

Executive Compensation—A Partnership Vs. A Corporation

In a report prepared for a Congressional subcommittee, Deloitte, Haskins & Sells (a public accounting partnership) described their firm's view of partner compensation and the division of the firm's income. Excerpts from that report are as follows:

...As a general rule, compensation in major mid-sized corporations (to which we might be compared based on revenue size, number of personnel, etc.) consists of current cash, deferred payments, payments made on behalf of an individual for retirement benefits, and perquisites. In addition, options to purchase stock at potentially favorable prices may also be an attractive compensation component. Unlike a corporation, partners...must provide from their own earnings for their own retirement benefits, as well as paying for self-employment taxes, group insurance, and other benefit programs. As a partnership, of course, our partners...do not have stock options available....

Each year the majority of the firm's earnings are distributed to the partners. Some small percentage is usually retained for working capital needs. No amounts are guaranteed, like a "pre-set" annual salary. If earnings decline, partners'...individual earnings also decline. Partners...are also required to invest capital in the firm. As such, part of their earnings represent a return on their investment.... With regard to their firm activities, partners have a much broader exposure to personal liability than do most corporate officers.

The factors mentioned above must be considered in making meaningful comparisons of partners' compensation with other business executives. To simply compare amounts would be misleading.

Our partnership is a private organization and many of the partners feel strongly that their compensation should not be disclosed. Nonetheless, firm management has concluded that the public may be better served if we disclose selective compensation data. We hope this disclosure demonstrates to the public that our earnings enable us to retain competent professionals, that we do not earn excessive amounts, and that we have no special agreements that would compromise our integrity or our independence.

The average earnings of all of our partners for fiscal year 1985 was approximately $143,000. As to our five most highly compensated partners, their individual earnings ranged from $385,000 to $725,000, and their average was $500,000....

Source: Deloitte, Haskins & Sells, *A Report for Congress and the Public* (September, 1985).

Partnership Dissolution

One of the basic characteristics of the partnership form of organization is its limited life. Any change in the personnel of the ownership results in the dissolution of the partnership. Thus, admission of a new partner dissolves the old firm. Similarly, death, bankruptcy, or withdrawal of a partner causes dissolution.

Dissolution of the partnership is not necessarily followed by the winding up of the affairs of the business. For example, a partnership composed of two partners may admit an additional partner. Or if one of three partners in a business withdraws, the remaining two partners may continue to operate the business.

Admission of a Partner

An additional person may be admitted to a partnership enterprise only with the consent of all the current partners. It does not follow, however, that a partner's interest, or part of that interest, cannot be disposed of without the consent of the remaining partners. Under common law, if a partner's interest was assigned to an outside party, the partnership was automatically dissolved. Under the Uniform Partnership Act, a partner's interest can be disposed of without the consent of the remaining partners. The person who buys the interest acquires the selling partner's rights to share in net income and in assets upon liquidation. The buyer does not automatically become a partner, however, and has no voice in partnership affairs unless admitted to the firm.

An additional person may be admitted to a partnership through either of two procedures:

1. Purchase of an interest from one or more of the current partners.
2. Contribution of assets to the partnership.

When the first procedure is followed, the capital interest of the incoming partner is obtained from current partners, and *neither the total assets nor the total owner's equity of the business is affected.* When the second procedure is followed, *both the total assets and the total owner's equity of the business are increased.*

Admission by Purchase of an Interest. When an additional person is admitted to a firm by purchasing an interest from one or more of the partners, the purchase price is paid directly to the selling partners. Payment is for partnership equity owned by the partners as individuals, and hence the cash or other consideration paid is not recorded in the accounts of the partnership. The only entry needed is the transfer of the proper amounts of owner's equity from the capital accounts of the selling partners to the capital account established for the incoming partner.

As an example, assume that partners Tom Andrews and George Bell have capital balances of $50,000 each. On June 1, each sells one fifth of his respective equity to Joe Canter for $10,000 in cash. The exchange of cash is not a partnership transaction and thus is not recorded by the partnership. The only entry required in the partnership accounts is as follows:

June 1	Tom Andrews, Capital	10,000	
	George Bell, Capital	10,000	
	Joe Canter, Capital		20,000

The effect of the transaction on the partnership accounts is presented in the following diagram:

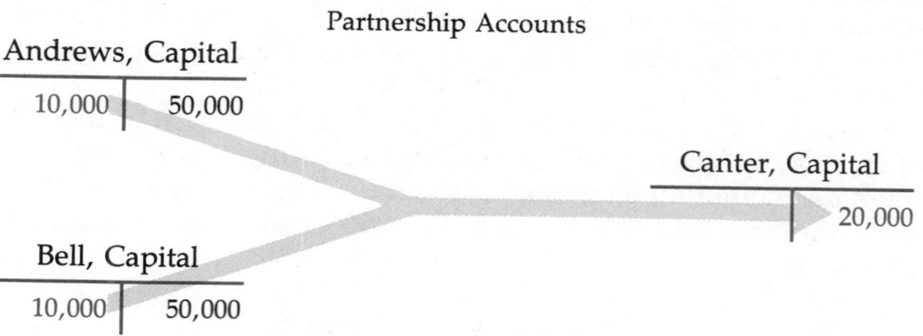

The foregoing entry is not affected by the amount paid by Canter for the one-fifth interest. If the firm had been earning a high rate of return on the investment and Canter had been very eager to obtain the one-fifth interest, he might have paid considerably more than $20,000. Had other circumstances prevailed, he might have acquired the one-fifth interest for considerably less than $20,000. In either event, the entry to transfer the capital interests would be as illustrated.

After the admission of Canter, the total owner's equity of the firm is $100,000, of which Canter has a one-fifth interest, or $20,000. It does not necessarily follow that he will be entitled to a similar share of the partnership net income. Division of net income or net loss will be in accordance with the new partnership agreement.

Admission by Contribution of Assets. Instead of buying an interest from the current partners, the incoming partner may contribute assets to the partnership. In this case, both the assets and the owner's equity of the firm are increased. To illustrate, assume that Donald Lewis and Gerald Morton are partners with capital accounts of $35,000 and $25,000 respectively. On June 1, Sharon Nelson invests $20,000 cash in the business, for which she is to receive an ownership equity of $20,000. The entry to record this transaction is as follows:

June 1	Cash	20,000	
	Sharon Nelson, Capital		20,000

The major difference between the circumstances of the admission of Nelson and the admission of Canter in the preceding example may be observed by comparing the following diagram with the one at the bottom of page 372.

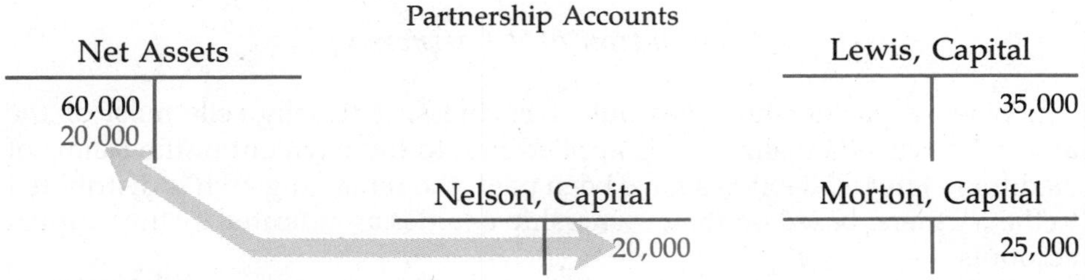

Partnership Accounts

Net Assets	
60,000	
20,000	

Nelson, Capital	
	20,000

Lewis, Capital	
	35,000

Morton, Capital	
	25,000

With the admission of Nelson, the total owners' equity of the new partnership becomes $80,000, of which Nelson has a one-fourth interest, or $20,000. The extent of her participation in partnership net income will be governed by the articles of partnership.

Withdrawal of a Partner

When a partner retires or for some other reason wishes to withdraw from the firm, one or more of the remaining partners may purchase the withdrawing partner's interest and the business may be continued without apparent interruption. In such cases, settlement for the purchase and sale is made between the partners as individuals, in a manner similar to the admission of a new partner by purchase of an interest, and thus is not recorded by the partnership. The only entry required by the partnership is a debit to the capital account of the partner withdrawing and a credit to the capital account of the partner or partners acquiring the interest.

If the settlement with the withdrawing partner is made by the partnership, the effect is to reduce the assets and the owner's equity of the firm. To determine the ownership equity of the withdrawing partner, the asset accounts should be adjusted to current market prices. The net amount of the adjustments should be divided among the capital accounts of the partners according to the income-sharing ratio. In the event that the cash or the other available assets are insufficient to make complete payment at the time of withdrawal, a liability account should be credited for the balance owed to the withdrawing partner.

Death of a Partner

The death of a partner dissolves the partnership. In the absence of any contrary agreement, the accounts should be closed as of the date of death, and the net income for the fractional part of the year should be transferred to the capital accounts. It is not unusual, however, for the partnership agreement to stipulate that the accounts remain open to the end of the fiscal year or until the affairs are wound up, if that should occur earlier. The net income of the entire period is then divided, as provided by the agreement, between the respective periods occurring before and after dissolution.

The balance in the capital account of the deceased partner is then transferred to a liability account with the deceased's estate. The surviving partner or partners may continue the business or the affairs may be wound up. If the former course is followed, the procedures for settling with the estate will conform to those outlined earlier for the withdrawal of a partner from the business.

Liquidation of a Partnership

When a partnership goes out of business, it usually sells most of the assets. As cash is realized, it is applied first to the payment of the claims of creditors. After all liabilities have been paid, the remaining cash is distributed to the partners, based on their ownership equities as indicated by their capital accounts.

If the assets are sold piecemeal, the liquidation process may extend over a considerable period of time. This situation creates no special problem, however, if the distribution of cash to the partners is delayed until all of the assets have been sold.

As a basis for illustration, assume that Farley, Greene, and Hill decide to liquidate their partnership. Their income-sharing ratio is 5:3:2 (5/10, 3/10, 2/10). On April 9, after discontinuing the ordinary business operations and closing the accounts, the following summary of the general ledger is prepared:

Cash	$11,000	
Noncash Assets	64,000	
Liabilities		$ 9,000
Jane Farley, Capital		22,000
Brad Greene, Capital		22,000
Alice Hill, Capital		22,000
Total	$75,000	$75,000

For the sake of brevity, it will be assumed that all noncash assets are disposed of in a single transaction and that all liabilities are paid at one time.

In addition, Noncash Assets and Liabilities will be used as account titles in place of the various asset, contra asset, and liability accounts that in actual practice would be affected by the transactions.

Between April 10 and April 30 of the current year, Farley, Greene, and Hill sell all noncash assets for $72,000, realizing a gain of $8,000 ($72,000 − $64,000). The gain is divided among the capital accounts in the income-sharing ratio of 5:3:2. The liabilities are paid, and *the remaining cash is distributed to the partners according to the balances in their capital accounts.* A statement of partnership liquidation, which summarizes the liquidation process, follows:

Farley, Greene, and Hill
Statement of Partnership Liquidation
For Period April 10–30, 19--

						Capital					
	Cash	+	Noncash Assets	=	Liabilities	+	Farley (50%)	+	Greene (30%)	+	Hill (20%)
Balances before realization . . .	$11,000		$64,000		$9,000		$22,000		$22,000		$22,000
Sale of noncash assets and division of gain	+72,000		−64,000		—		+ 4,000		+ 2,400		+ 1,600
Balances after realization	$83,000		0		$9,000		$26,000		$24,400		$23,600
Payment of liabilities.	− 9,000		—		−9,000		—		—		—
Balances after payment of liabilities	$74,000		0		0		$26,000		$24,400		$23,600
Distribution of cash to partners.	−74,000		—		—		−26,000		−24,400		−23,600
Final balances.	0		0		0		0		0		0

As shown in the foregoing illustration, the distribution of the cash among the partners is determined by reference to the balances of their respective capital accounts after the gain on realization has been allocated. Under no circumstances should the income-sharing ratio be used as a basis for distributing the cash.

If the sale of assets were to result in a loss, the loss would be divided among the partners' capital accounts in the income-sharing ratio. The cash would then be applied first to the payment of the claims of creditors and the remainder would be distributed to the partners according to the balances in their respective capital accounts.

CHARACTERISTICS OF A CORPORATION

start here

In the Dartmouth College case in 1819, Chief Justice Marshall stated: "A corporation is an artificial being, invisible, intangible, and existing only in contemplation of the law." The concept underlying this definition has become the foundation for the prevailing legal doctrine that a corporation is an artificial person, created by law and having a distinct existence separate and apart from the natural persons who are responsible for its creation and operation. Almost all large business enterprises in the United States are organized as corporations.

As a legal entity, the corporation has certain characteristics that make it different from other types of business organizations. The most important characteristics with accounting implications are described briefly in the following paragraphs.

A corporation has a **separate legal existence.** It may acquire, own, and dispose of property in its corporate name. It may also incur liabilities and enter into other types of contracts according to the provisions of its **charter** (also called **articles of incorporation**).

The ownership of a corporation, of which there may be several categories or classes, is divided into **transferable units** known as **shares of stock.** Each share of stock of a certain class has the same rights and privileges as every other share of the same class. The **stockholders** (also called **shareholders**) may buy and sell shares without interfering with the activities of the corporation. The millions of transactions that occur daily on stock exchanges are independent transactions between buyers and sellers. Thus, in contrast to the partnership, the existence of the corporation is not affected by changes in ownership.

The stockholders of a corporation have **limited liability.** A corporation is responsible for its own acts and obligations, and therefore its creditors usually may not look beyond the assets of the corporation for satisfaction of their claims. Thus, the financial loss that a stockholder may suffer is limited to the amount invested. The phenomenal growth of the corporate form of business would not have been possible without this limited liability feature.

The stockholders, who are, in fact, the owners of the corporation, exercise control over the management of corporate affairs indirectly by electing a **board of directors.** It is the responsibility of the board of directors to meet from time to time to determine the corporate policies and to select the officers who manage the corporation. The following chart shows the **organizational structure** of a corporation:

Organizational Structure of a Corporate Enterprise

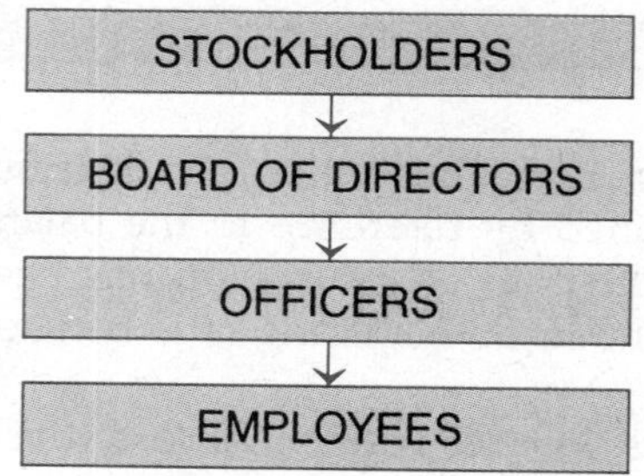

As a separate entity, a corporation is subject to **additional taxes.** It must pay a charter fee to the state at the time of its organization and annual taxes thereafter. If the corporation does business in states other than the one in which it is incorporated, it may also be required to pay annual taxes to such states. The earnings of a corporation may also be subject to a state income tax.

The earnings of a corporation are subject to the federal income tax. When the remaining earnings are distributed to stockholders as dividends, they are again taxed as income to the individuals receiving them. Under certain conditions specified in the Internal Revenue Code, a corporation with a few stockholders may elect to be treated in a manner similar to a partnership for income tax purposes. A corporation electing this optional treatment does not pay federal income taxes. Instead, its stockholders include their distributive shares of corporate income in their own taxable income, regardless of whether the income is distributed to them.

Being a creature of the state and being owned by stockholders who have limited liability, a corporation has less freedom of action than a sole proprietorship and a partnership. There may be **government regulations** in such matters as ownership of real estate, retention of earnings, and purchase of its own stock.

STOCKHOLDERS' EQUITY

The owners' equity in a corporation is commonly called **stockholders' equity, shareholders' equity, shareholders' investment,** or **capital.** The two main sources of stockholders' equity are (1) investments contributed by the stockholders, called **paid-in capital** or **contributed capital,** and (2) net income retained in the business, called **retained earnings.** As shown in the following illustration, the stockholders' equity section of corporation balance sheets is divided into subsections based on these two sources.

Stockholders' Equity		
Paid-in capital:		
Common stock	$330,000	
Retained earnings	80,000	
Total stockholders' equity		$410,000

The paid-in capital contributed by the stockholders is recorded in accounts maintained for each class of stock. If there is only one class of stock, the account is entitled Common Stock or Capital Stock.

The retained earnings amount results from transferring the balance in the income summary account (the net income) to a retained earnings account at the end of a fiscal year. The dividends account, to which distributions of earnings to stockholders have been debited, is also closed to Retained Earnings. If the occurrence of net losses results in a debit balance in Retained Earnings, it is termed a **deficit.** In the stockholders' equity section of the balance sheet, a deficit is deducted from paid-in capital to determine total stockholders' equity.

There are a number of acceptable variants of the term "retained earnings," among which are *earnings retained for use in the business, earnings reinvested in the business, earnings employed in the business,* and *accumulated earnings.* For many years, the term applied to retained earnings was *earned surplus.* However, the use of this term in published financial statements has generally been discontinued.[1] Because of its connotation as an excess, or something left over, "surplus" was sometimes erroneously interpreted by readers of financial statements to mean "cash available for dividends."

CHARACTERISTICS OF STOCK

The general term applied to the shares of ownership of a corporation is **capital stock.** The number of shares that a corporation is *authorized* to issue is set forth in its charter. The term *issued* is applied to the shares issued to the stockholders. A corporation may, under circumstances discussed later in the chapter, reacquire some of the stock that it has issued. The stock remaining in the hands of the stockholders is then referred to as the **stock outstanding.**

[1] *Accounting Research and Terminology Bulletins—Final Edition.* "Accounting Terminology Bulletins, No. 1, Review and Résumé" (New York: American Institute of Certified Public Accountants, 1961), par. 65–69.

The shares of capital stock are often assigned an arbitrary monetary figure, known as **par.** The par amount is printed on the **stock certificate,** which is the evidence of ownership issued to the stockholder. Stock may also be issued without par, in which case it is called **no-par** stock. Many states provide that the board of directors must assign a **stated value** to no-par stock, which makes it similar to par stock.

Because of the limited liability feature, the creditors of a corporation have no claim against the personal assets of stockholders. However, the law requires that some specific minimum contribution by the stockholders be retained by the corporation for the protection of its creditors. This amount, called **legal capital,** varies among the states but usually includes the par or stated value of the shares of capital stock issued.

End to Paper Stock Certificates

The stock certificate as it is known today may someday succumb to the computer era. A strong advocate of computerized buying and selling of securities is John Shad, former Chairman of the Securities and Exchange Commission. Some of the efforts of Mr. Shad, as well as the concerns of those who oppose such computerization, are described in the following excerpts from an article in *The Wall Street Journal:*

...[In speeches, personal letters, and meetings,] Mr. Shad has been jawboning issuers and dealers,... [urging] them to adopt computerized "book entry" clearing systems.... Mr. Shad acknowledges that his goal—complete elimination of the paper certificate—won't come any time soon. His ideal is to limit each security issue to a single, "global" certificate that would rest, forever immobilized, in a central depository. All sales and purchases of the issue would be tracked by computer....

"Billion-dollar benefits," Mr. Shad says, "will be realized by gradually turning off the flow of new paper into the system." The SEC says computerized clearing would cost brokers six to 10 times less than physically transferring certificates from sellers to buyers....

Mr. Shad promises book-entry systems will improve the market's speed, simplicity, and safety. Certificates, he says, waste time and energy. "They are inspected, counted, and sorted over and over again, repackaged and sent by couriers and insured mail to investors and depositories, and stored in vaults and safety deposit boxes. Millions of dollars of securities are counterfeited, lost, stolen, and accidentally mutilated and destroyed annually."

Issuers agree. "It's a real pain in the neck to print certificates," says Weyland F. Blood, vice president and treasurer of Ford Motor Credit Co....

Many issuers worry that investors might balk at buying book-entry securities, making it more difficult to sell the issue. "All other things being equal, Citicorp favors the book-entry notion," says Robert M. Butcher, vice president. But he would want to find out if the lack of a certificate would hurt the distribution of a book-entry issue. "If the answer is no, fine. If it's yes, forget it. If it's maybe, forget it."

Some investors do face obstacles in buying book-entry issues. Some states require government pension funds and insurance companies to keep their certificates on hand.... At the SEC's urging, most of the states that require certificates are considering changing their regulations....

Other investors, suspicious of computer glitches, take comfort in holding paper. Chrysler Corp. would gladly issue book-entry securities, says Frederick W. Zuckerman, treasurer, but would hesitate before buying them. When Chrysler holds certificates, he explains, he can make a "surprise visit" to the bank that holds them. "In a world where not everybody is always honest and always careful, that gives me a sense of comfort."

...Unlike the French government, which has mandated the conversion of all securities to electronic book entry, the SEC has relied on persuasion.... Most market participants agree that although a book-entry system is painfully slow in coming, it's inevitable....

Source: Ann Monroe and Bruce Ingersoll, "SEC Chief Seeks End to Paper Securities," *The Wall Street Journal* (April 28, 1986), p. 6.

Classes of Stock

The major basic rights that accompany ownership of a share of stock are (1) the right to vote in matters concerning the corporation, (2) the right to share in distributions of earnings, (3) the **preemptive right,** which is the right to maintain the same fractional interest in the corporation by purchasing a proportionate number of shares of any additional issuances of stock[2], and (4) the right to share in assets upon liquidation.

If a corporation issues only **common stock,** each share generally has equal rights. In order to appeal to a broader investment market, a corporation may provide for one or more classes of stock with various preferential rights. The preference usually relates to the right to share in distributions of earnings. Such stock is generally called **preferred stock.**

The board of directors has the sole authority to distribute earnings to the stockholders. When such action is taken, the directors are said to *declare a dividend.* A corporation cannot guarantee that its operations will be profitable and hence it cannot guarantee dividends to its stockholders. Furthermore, the directors have wide discretionary powers in determining the extent to which earnings should be retained by the corporation to provide for expansion, to offset possible future losses, or to provide for other contingencies.

A corporation with both preferred stock and common stock may declare dividends on the common only after it meets the requirements of the stated dividend on the preferred (which may be stated in monetary terms or as a percent of par). To illustrate, assume that a corporation has 1,000 shares of $10 preferred stock (that is, the preferred has a prior claim to an annual $10 per share dividend) and 4,000 shares of common stock outstanding. Assume also that in the first three years of operations, net income was $30,000, $55,000, and $100,000 respectively. The directors authorize the retention of a portion of each year's earnings and the distribution of the remainder. Details of the dividend distribution are presented in the following tabulation:

	First Year	Second Year	Third Year
Net income	$30,000	$55,000	$100,000
Amount retained	10,000	20,000	40,000
Amount distributed	$20,000	$35,000	$ 60,000
Preferred dividend (1,000 shares)	10,000	10,000	10,000
Common dividend (4,000 shares)	$10,000	$25,000	$ 50,000
Dividends per share:			
Preferred	$10.00	$10.00	$10.00
Common	$ 2.50	$ 6.25	$12.50

Participating and Nonparticipating Preferred Stock

In the foregoing illustration, the holders of preferred stock received an annual dividend of $10 per share, in contrast to the common stockholders, whose annual per share dividends were $2.50, $6.25, and $12.50 respectively. It is apparent from the example that holders of preferred stock have relatively

[2]In recent years the stockholders of a significant number of corporations have, by formal action, given up their preemptive rights.

greater assurance than common stockholders of receiving dividends regularly. On the other hand, holders of common stock have the possibility of receiving larger dividends than preferred stockholders. The preferred stockholders' preferential right to dividends is usually limited to a certain amount, which was assumed to be the case in the preceding example. Such stock is said to be **nonparticipating.**

Preferred stock which provides for the possibility of dividends in excess of a certain amount is said to be **participating.** Preferred shares may participate with common shares to varying degrees, and the agreement with the shareholders must be examined to determine the extent of this participation. To illustrate, assume that the contract covering the preferred stock of the corporation in the preceding illustration provides that if the total dividends to be distributed exceed the regular preferred dividend and a comparable dividend on common, the preferred shall share in the excess ratably on a share-for-share basis with the common. According to such terms, the $60,000 dividend distribution in the third year would be allocated as follows:

	Preferred Dividend	*Common Dividend*	*Total Dividends*
Regular dividend to preferred (1,000 × $10)	$10,000	—	$10,000
Comparable dividend to common (4,000 × $10)	—	$40,000	40,000
Remainder to 5,000 shares ratably ($2 per share)	2,000	8,000	10,000
Total	$12,000	$48,000	$60,000
Dividends per share	$12	$12	

Cumulative and Noncumulative Preferred Stock

As was indicated in the preceding section, most preferred stock is nonparticipating. Provision is usually made, however, to assure the continuation of the preferential dividend right if at any time the directors *pass* (do not declare) the usual dividend. The preferential dividend right is assured by providing that dividends may not be paid on the common stock if any preferred dividends have been passed (are in *arrears*). Such preferred stock is said to be **cumulative.** To illustrate, assume that a corporation has outstanding 5,000 shares of cumulative preferred 9% stock of $100 par (that is, the preferred stockholders have a prior claim to an annual 9% dividend, or $9 per share). In addition, assume that dividends have been passed for the preceding two years. In the current year, no dividend may be declared on the common stock unless the directors first declare preferred dividends of $90,000 for the past two years and $45,000 for the current year. Preferred stock not having this cumulative right is called **noncumulative.**

Other Preferential Rights

Thus far the discussion of preferential rights of preferred stock has related to dividend distributions. Preferred stock may also be given a preference in its claim to assets upon liquidation of the corporation. If the assets remaining after payment of creditors are not sufficient to return the capital contributions of both classes of stock, payment would first be made to the preferred stockholders and any balance remaining would go to the common stockholders. Another difference between preferred and common stock is that the former may have no voting rights. A corporation may also have more than one class of preferred stock, with differences as to the amount of dividends, priority of claims upon liquidation, and voting rights. In any particular case, the rights of a class of stock may be determined by reference to the charter, the stock certificate, or some other abstract of the agreement.

ISSUING STOCK

The entries to record investments of stockholders in a corporation are like those for investments by owners of other types of business organizations, in that cash and other assets received are debited and any liabilities assumed are credited. The credit to stockholders' equity differs, however, in that there are accounts for each class of stock. To illustrate, assume that a corporation, with an authorization of 10,000 shares of preferred stock of $100 par and 100,000 shares of common stock of $20 par, issues one half of each authorization at par for cash. The entry to record the stockholders' investment and the receipt of the cash is as follows:

Cash	1,500,000	
Preferred Stock		500,000
Common Stock		1,000,000

The capital stock accounts (Preferred Stock, Common Stock) are controlling accounts. It is necessary to maintain records of each stockholder's name, address, and number of shares held in order to issue dividend checks, proxy forms, and financial reports. Individual stockholders accounts are kept in a subsidiary ledger known as the **stockholders ledger.**

Par stock is often issued by a corporation at a price other than par. When it is issued for more than par, the excess of the contract price over par is termed a **premium** on stock. When it is issued at a price that is below par, the difference is called a **discount** on stock. Thus, if stock with a par of $50 is issued at $60, the amount of the premium is $10. If the same stock is issued at $45, the amount of the discount is $5.

Theoretically, there is no reason for a newly organized corporation to issue stock at a price other than par. The par designation is merely a part of the plan of dividing owners' equity into a number of units of ownership. Hence, a group of persons investing their funds in a new corporation might all be expected to pay par for the shares. The fortunes of an enterprise do not remain the same, however, even when it is still in the process of organizing. The changing prospects for its future success may affect the price per share at which the incorporators can secure other investors.

A need for additional paid-in capital may arise long after a corporation has become established. Losses during prior fiscal periods may have depleted operating funds or the operations may have been successful enough to warrant a substantial expansion of plant and equipment. If the funds are to be obtained by the issuance of additional stock, it is apparent that the current price at which the original stock is selling in the market will affect the price that can be obtained for the new shares.

Generally speaking, the price at which stock can be sold by a corporation is influenced by (1) the financial condition, the earnings record, and the dividend record of the corporation, (2) its potential earning power, (3) the availability of money for investment purposes, and (4) general business and economic conditions and prospects.

Premium on Stock

When capital stock is issued at a premium, cash or other assets are debited for the amount received. The stock account is then credited for the par amount, and a premium account, sometimes called Paid-In Capital in Excess of Par, is credited for the amount of the premium. For example, if Caldwell Company issues 2,000 shares of $50 par preferred stock for cash at $55, the entry to record the transaction would be as follows:

Cash	110,000	
Preferred Stock		100,000
Premium on Preferred Stock		10,000

The premium of $10,000 is a part of the investment of the stockholders and is therefore a part of paid-in capital. It is distinguished from the capital stock account because usually it is not a part of legal capital and in many states may be used as a basis for dividends to stockholders. However, if the premium is returned to stockholders as a dividend at a later date, it should be emphasized that the dividend is a return of paid-in capital rather than a distribution of earnings.

Discount on Stock

Some states do not permit the issuance of stock at a discount. In others, it may be done only under certain conditions. When stock is issued at less than its par, it is considered to be fully paid as between the corporation and the stockholder. In some states, however, the stockholders are contingently liable to creditors for the amount of the discount. If the corporation is liquidated and there are not enough assets to pay creditors in full, the stockholders may be assessed for an additional contribution up to the amount of the discount on their stock.

When capital stock is issued at a discount, cash or other assets are debited for the amount received, and a discount account is debited for the amount of the discount. The capital stock account is then credited for the par amount. For example, if Caldwell Company issues 20,000 shares of $25 par common stock for cash at $23, the entry to record the transaction would be as follows:

Cash	460,000	
Discount on Common Stock	40,000	
Common Stock		500,000

The discount of $40,000 is a contra paid-in capital account and must be offset against Common Stock to arrive at the amount actually invested by the holders of common stock. The discount is not an asset, nor should it be amortized against revenue as though it were an expense.

Premiums and Discounts on the Balance Sheet

The manner in which premiums and discounts may be presented in the stockholders' equity section of the balance sheet is illustrated as follows, based on the two illustrative entries for Caldwell Company:

Stockholders' Equity			
Paid-in capital:			
Preferred 10% stock, cumulative, $50 par (2,000 shares authorized and issued)	$100,000		
Premium on preferred stock	10,000	$110,000	
Common stock, $25 par (50,000 shares authorized, 20,000 shares issued)	$500,000		
Less discount on common stock	40,000	460,000	
Total paid-in capital		$570,000	
Retained earnings		175,000	
Total stockholders' equity			$745,000

The following stockholders' equity section illustrates the reporting of a deficit and some differences in terminology from that in the foregoing example:

Shareholders' Equity			
Paid-in capital:			
Preferred $3 stock, cumulative, $25 par (10,000 shares authorized and issued)	$ 250,000		
Excess of issuance price over par	20,000	$ 270,000	
Common stock, $10 par (200,000 shares authorized, 100,000 shares issued)	$1,000,000		
Less excess of par over issuance price	100,000	900,000	
Total paid in by stockholders		$1,170,000	
Less deficit		75,000	
Total shareholders' equity			$1,095,000

Issuing Stock for Assets Other Than Cash

When capital stock is issued in exchange for assets other than cash, such as land, buildings, and equipment, the assets acquired should be recorded at their fair market price or at the fair market price of the stock issued, whichever is more objectively determinable. The determination of the values to be assigned to the assets is the responsibility of the board of directors.

As a basis for illustration, assume that a corporation acquired land for which the fair market price is not determinable. In exchange, the corporation issued 10,000 shares of its $10 par common stock with a current market price of $12 per share. The transaction could be recorded as follows:

Dec. 5	Land	120,000	
	Common Stock		100,000
	Premium on Common Stock		20,000

No-Par Stock

In the early days of rapid industrial expansion and increasing use of the corporate form of business organization, it was customary to assign a par of $100 to shares of stock. It is not surprising that unsophisticated investors, mistakenly considering "par value" to be the equivalent of "value," were often induced to invest in mining and other highly speculative enterprises by the simple means of being offered $100 par stock at "bargain" prices. Another misleading practice was the use of par in assigning highly inflated values to assets acquired in exchange for stock. For example, stock with a total par of $1,000,000 might be issued in exchange for patents, mineral rights, or other properties with a conservatively estimated value of $50,000. The assets would be recorded at the full par of $1,000,000, whereas in reality the stock had been issued at a discount of $950,000. Balance sheets that were "window-dressed" in this manner were obviously deceptive.

To combat such abuses and also to eliminate the troublesome discount liability of stockholders, stock without par was conceived. The issuance of stock without par was first permitted by New York in 1912. Its use is now authorized in nearly all of the states.

Over the years, questionable practices in the issuance of securities have been virtually eliminated. Today federal and state laws and rules imposed by organized stock exchanges and governmental agencies such as the Securities and Exchange Commission combine to protect the investor from misrepresentations that were common in earlier days.

In most states, both preferred and common stock may be issued without a par designation. However, preferred stock is usually assigned a par. When no-par stock is issued, the entire proceeds may be credited to the capital stock account, even though the issuance price varies from time to time. For example, if at the time of organization a corporation issues no-par common stock at $40 a share and at a later date issues additional shares at $36, the entries would be as follows:

1. *Original issuance of 10,000 shares of no-par common at $40:*

Cash	400,000	
Common Stock		400,000

2. *Subsequent issuance of 1,000 shares of no-par common at $36:*

Cash	36,000	
Common Stock		36,000

The laws of some states require that the entire proceeds from the issuance of no-par stock be regarded as legal capital. The preceding entries conform to this principle, which also conforms to the original concept of no-par stock. In other states, no-par stock may be assigned a stated value per share, and the excess of the proceeds over the stated value may be credited to Paid-In Capital in Excess of Stated Value. Assuming that in the previous example the stated value is $25 and the board of directors wishes to credit the common stock for stated value, the transactions would be recorded as follows:

1. *Original issuance of 10,000 shares of no-par common, stated value $25, at $40:*

Cash	400,000	
Common Stock		250,000
Paid-In Capital in Excess of Stated Value		150,000

2. *Subsequent issuance of 1,000 shares of no-par common, stated value $25, at $36:*

Cash	36,000	
Common Stock		25,000
Paid-In Capital in Excess of Stated Value		11,000

It is readily apparent that the accounting for no-par stock with a stated value may follow the same pattern as the accounting for par stock.

TREASURY STOCK

Although there are some legal restrictions on the practice, a corporation may purchase shares of its own outstanding stock from stockholders. It may also accept shares of its own stock in payment of a debt owed by a stockholder, which in essence is much the same as acquisition by purchase. A corporation may buy its own stock in order to provide shares for resale to employees, to provide shares for reissuance to employees as a bonus, or to support the market price of the stock. In March, 1986, for example, General Motors announced that it would buy back as much as $1.95 billion of its common stock. General Motors officials stated that two primary uses of the treasury stock would be for incentive compensation plans and employee savings plans.

The term **treasury stock** may be applied only to the issuing corporation's stock that (1) has been issued as fully paid, (2) has later been reacquired by the corporation, and (3) has not been canceled or reissued. In the past, corporations would occasionally list treasury stock on the balance sheet as an asset. The justification for such treatment was that the stock could be reissued and was thus like an investment in the stock of another corporation. The same argument, though indefensible, might well be extended to authorized but unissued stock.

Today, it is generally agreed among accountants that treasury stock should not be reported as an asset. A corporation cannot own a part of itself. Treasury stock has no voting rights, it does not have the preemptive right to participate in additional issuances of stock, nor does it generally participate in cash dividends. When a corporation purchases its own stock, it is returning capital to the stockholders from whom the purchase was made.

There are several methods of accounting for the purchase and the resale of treasury stock. A commonly used method is the **cost basis.** When the stock is purchased by the corporation, the account Treasury Stock is debited for the price paid for it. The par and the price at which the stock was originally issued are ignored. When the stock is resold, Treasury Stock is credited at the price paid for it, and the difference between the price paid and the selling price is debited or credited to an account entitled Paid-In Capital from Sale of Treasury Stock.

As a basis for illustrating the cost method, assume that the paid-in capital of a corporation is composed of common stock issued at a premium, detailed as follows:

Common stock, $25 par (20,000 shares authorized and issued)	$500,000
Premium on common stock	150,000

The assumed transactions involving treasury stock and the required entries are as follows:

1. Purchased 1,000 shares of treasury stock at $45.		
Treasury Stock	45,000	
Cash		45,000
2. Sold 200 shares of treasury stock at $55.		
Cash	11,000	
Treasury Stock		9,000
Paid-In Capital from Sale of Treasury Stock		2,000
3. Sold 200 shares of treasury stock at $40.		
Cash	8,000	
Paid-In Capital from Sale of Treasury Stock	1,000	
Treasury Stock		9,000

Paid-In Capital from Sale of Treasury Stock is reported in the paid-in capital section of the balance sheet. Treasury Stock is deducted from the total of the paid-in capital and retained earnings. After the foregoing transactions are completed, the stockholders' equity section of the balance sheet would appear as follows:

Stockholders' Equity

Paid-in capital:			
Common stock, $25 par (20,000 shares authorized and issued)	$500,000		
Premium on common stock	150,000	$650,000	
From sale of treasury stock		1,000	
Total paid-in capital		$651,000	
Retained earnings		130,000	
Total		$781,000	
Deduct treasury stock (600 shares at cost)		27,000	
Total stockholders' equity			$754,000

The stockholders' equity section of the balance sheet indicates that 20,000 shares of stock were issued, of which 600 are held as treasury stock. The number of shares outstanding is therefore 19,400. If cash dividends are declared at this time, the declaration would apply to only 19,400 shares of stock. Similarly, 19,400 shares could be voted at a stockholders' meeting.

If sales of treasury stock result in a net decrease in paid-in capital, the decrease may be reported on the balance sheet as a reduction of paid-in capital or it may be debited to the retained earnings account.

EQUITY PER SHARE

The amount appearing on the balance sheet as total stockholders' equity can be stated in terms of the **equity per share.** Another term sometimes used in referring to the equity allocable to a single share of stock is **book value per share.** The latter term is not only less accurate but its use of "value" may also be interpreted by nonaccountants to mean "market value" or "actual worth."

When there is only one class of stock, the equity per share is determined by dividing total stockholders' equity by the number of shares outstanding.

For a corporation with both preferred and common stock, it is necessary first to allocate the total equity between the two classes. In making the allocation, consideration must be given to the liquidation rights of the preferred stock, including any participating and cumulative dividend features. After the total is allocated to the two classes, the equity per share of each class may then be determined by dividing the respective amounts by the related number of shares outstanding.

To illustrate, assume that as of the end of the current fiscal year, a corporation has both preferred and common shares outstanding, that there are no preferred dividends in arrears, and that the preferred stock is entitled to receive $105 per share upon liquidation. The amounts of the stockholders' equity accounts of the corporation and the computation of the equity per share are as follows:

Stockholders' Equity

Preferred $9 stock, cumulative, $100 par (1,000 shares outstanding)	$100,000
Premium on preferred stock	2,000
Common stock, $10 par (50,000 shares outstanding)	500,000
Premium on common stock	50,000
Retained earnings	253,000
Total equity	$905,000

Allocation of Total Equity to Preferred and Common Stock

Total equity	$905,000
Allocated to preferred stock:	
Liquidation price	105,000
Allocated to common stock	$800,000

Equity Per Share

Preferred stock: $105,000 ÷ 1,000 shares = $105 per share
Common stock: $800,000 ÷ 50,000 shares = $ 16 per share

If it is assumed that the preferred stock is entitled to dividends in arrears in the event of liquidation, and that there is an arrearage of two years, the computations for the foregoing illustration would be as follows:

Allocation of Total Equity to Preferred and Common Stock

Total equity		$905,000
Allocated to preferred stock:		
Liquidation price	$105,000	
Dividends in arrears	18,000	123,000
Allocated to common stock		$782,000

Equity Per Share

Preferred stock: $123,000 ÷ 1,000 shares = $123.00 per share
Common stock: $782,000 ÷ 50,000 shares = $ 15.64 per share

Equity per share, particularly of common stock, is often stated in corporation reports to stockholders and quoted in the financial press. It is one of the many factors affecting the **market price,** that is, the price at which a share is bought and sold at a particular moment. However, it should be noted that earning capacity, dividend rates, and prospects for the future usually affect the market price of listed stocks to a much greater extent than does equity per share. So-called "glamour" stocks may at times sell at more than ten times the amount of the equity per share. On the other hand, stock in corporations that have suffered severe declines in earnings or whose future prospects appear to be unfavorable may sell at prices which are much less than the equity per share.

ORGANIZATION COSTS

Expenditures incurred in organizing a corporation, such as legal fees, taxes and fees paid to the state, and promotional costs, are charged to an intangible asset account entitled Organization Costs. Although such costs have no realizable value upon liquidation, they are as essential as plant and equipment, for without the expenditures the corporation could not have been created. If the life of a corporation is limited to a definite period of time, the organization costs should be amortized over the period by annual charges to an expense account. However, at the time of incorporation the length of life of most corporations is indeterminate.

There are two possible extreme viewpoints on the proper accounting for organization costs and other intangibles of indeterminate life. One extreme would consider the cost of intangibles as a permanent asset until there was convincing evidence of loss in value. The other extreme would consider the cost of intangibles as an expense in the period in which the cost is incurred. The practical solution to the problem is expressed in the following quotation:

> *. . . . Allocating the cost of goodwill or other intangible assets with an indeterminate life over time is necessary because the value almost inevitably becomes zero at some future date. Since the date at which the value becomes zero is indeterminate, the end of the useful life must necessarily be set arbitrarily at some point or within some range of time for accounting purposes.*[3]

The Internal Revenue Code permits the amortization of organization costs equally over a period of not less than sixty months beginning with the month the corporation commences business. Since the amount of such costs is generally small in relation to total assets and the effect on net income is ordinarily not significant, amortization of organization costs over sixty months is generally accepted in accounting practice.

---

[3]*Opinions of the Accounting Principles Board, No. 17,* "Intangible Assets" (New York: American Institute of Certified Public Accountants, 1970), par. 23.

Chapter Review

KEY POINTS

1. Characteristics of Sole Proprietorships.
A sole proprietorship, which is a business owned by one individual, is a separate entity for accounting purposes. There are few legal restrictions to establishing a sole proprietorship, and the individual owner can usually make all business decisions without being accountable to others. A primary disadvantage of a sole proprietorship may be the difficulty in raising funds.

2. Accounting for Sole Proprietorships.
The primary differences in accounting for a sole proprietorship as compared with a corporation include the use of an owner's capital account (rather than a capital stock account) to record investments in the enterprise. This capital account is also used to record changes in owner's equity from net income or net loss. Instead of a dividends account, distributions to the owner are recorded in the owner's drawing account.

3. Characteristics of Partnerships.
Partnership characteristics that have accounting implications are: limited life, unlimited liability, co-ownership of property, mutual agency, and participation in income. In addition, a partnership is a nontaxable entity and is therefore not required to pay federal income taxes. Individual partners must report their distributive share of partnership income on their personal returns.

4. Accounting for Partnerships.
Most of the day-to-day accounting for partnerships is the same as the accounting for any other form of business organization. It is in the areas of formation, income distribution, dissolution, and liquidation that transactions peculiar to partnerships arise.

To record the investment of each partner in a partnership, the various assets contributed by a partner are debited to the proper asset accounts, the liabilities assumed are credited to the appropriate liability accounts, and the partner's capital account is credited for the net amount. The monetary amounts at which noncash assets are stated are those agreed upon by the partners.

The net income of a partnership can be divided among the partners in any manner agreed to by the partners. The net income is often divided on the basis of services rendered by individual partners and/or on the basis of the investments of the individual partners. In the absence of any agreement, net income is divided equally among the partners.

Any change in the personnel of ownership results in the dissolution of the partnership. However, dissolution of the partnership is not necessarily followed by a winding up of the affairs of the business. A partnership may be dissolved by admission of a new partner, or the withdrawal, bankruptcy, or death of a partner.

When a partnership goes out of business, it usually sells the noncash assets, pays the creditors, and distributes the remaining cash or other assets to the partners according to the balances of the partners' capital accounts. Any gain or loss on the realization of the assets should be allocated to the partners' capital accounts in the income-sharing ratio. The distribution of assets to the partners is equal to the credit balances in their respective capital accounts after all gains and losses on realization have been divided.

5. Characteristics of a Corporation.
The most important corporation characteristics with accounting implications are the following: separate legal existence, transferable units of stock, limited liability, and organizational structure. In addition, a corporation as a separate entity is subject to federal income taxes.

6. Stockholders' Equity.
The stockholders' equity section of a corporation balance sheet is divided into two subsections: paid-in capital and retained earnings.

7. Characteristics of Stock.
The stock of a corporation may be classified according to its par, right to vote, preference as to dividends, and preference as to liquidation rights. Various types of stock include par common stock, no-par common stock, participating preferred stock, nonparticipating preferred stock, cumulative preferred stock, and noncumulative preferred stock.

8. Issuing Stock.
When a corporation issues stock at par, each class of stock is credited for its par amount. When a corporation issues stock at more than par, a premium is recognized in the records, and when stock is issued at less than par, a discount is recognized. Balances in the premium and discount accounts appear with their related class of stock in the stockholders' equity section of the balance sheet.

When capital stock is issued and exchanged for assets other than cash, the assets acquired should be recorded at their fair market price or at the fair market price of the stock issued, whichever is more objectively determinable.

When no-par stock is issued, the entire proceeds may be credited to the capital stock account, even though the issue price varies from time to time. In some cases, no-par stock may be assigned a stated value per share, and the excess of the proceeds over the stated value may be credited to a separate paid-in capital account.

9. Treasury Stock.
A corporation may purchase shares of its own outstanding stock from stockholders. Any treasury stock held at the end of an accounting period is deducted from the total of the paid-in capital and retained earnings of the corporation. Any difference between the price paid for and the selling price of the treasury stock is usually recorded in a paid-in capital account for treasury stock transactions.

10. Equity per Share.
The amount appearing on the balance sheet as total stockholders' equity can be stated in terms of the equity per share. For a corporation with both preferred and common stock outstanding, it is necessary to allocate the total equity between the two classes of stock. The equity allocated to each class is divided by the number of shares outstanding of the respective class to determine the equity per share.

11. Organization Costs.
Expenditures incurred in organizing a corporation are charged to an intangible asset account entitled Organization Costs. The generally accepted accounting

practice is to amortize organization costs over a period of sixty months, which conforms with federal income tax regulations.

KEY TERMS

articles of partnership 368
stockholders 376
stockholders' equity 377
paid-in capital 377
retained earnings 377
deficit 377
capital stock 377
stock outstanding 377
par 378
stated value 378
preemptive right 379
common stock 379
preferred stock 379
participating preferred stock 380
cumulative preferred stock 380
premium on stock 381
discount on stock 381
treasury stock 385
equity per share 386

SELF-EXAMINATION QUESTIONS

(Answers at End of Chapter)

1. X and Y invest $100,000 and $50,000 respectively in a partnership and agree to a division of net income that provides for an allowance of interest at 10% on original investments, salary allowances of $12,000 and $24,000, with the remainder divided equally. What would be X's share of a periodic net income of $45,000?
   A. $22,500
   B. $22,000
   C. $19,000
   D. $10,000

2. If a corporation has outstanding 1,000 shares of $9 cumulative preferred stock of $100 par and dividends have been passed for the preceding three years, what is the amount of preferred dividends that must be declared in the current year before a dividend can be declared on common stock?
   A. $9,000
   B. $27,000
   C. $36,000
   D. None of the above

3. The stockholders' equity section of the balance sheet may include:
   A. Discount on Common Stock
   B. Common Stock
   C. Premium on Preferred Stock
   D. all of the above

4. If a corporation reacquires its own stock, the stock is listed on the balance sheet in the:
   A. current assets section
   B. long-term liabilities section
   C. stockholders' equity section
   D. none of the above

5. A corporation's balance sheet includes 10,000 outstanding shares of $8 cumulative preferred stock of $100 par; 100,000 outstanding shares of $20 par common stock; premium on common stock of $100,000; and retained earnings of $540,000. If preferred dividends are three years in arrears and the preferred stock is entitled to dividends in arrears plus $110 per share in the event of liquidation, what is the equity per common share?
   A. $20.00
   B. $23.00
   C. $25.40
   D. None of the above

ILLUSTRATIVE PROBLEM

The stockholders' equity and related accounts of Rockton Manufacturing Corporation as of January 1, the beginning of the fiscal year, are as follows:

Preferred 8% Stock, $50 par (100,000 shares authorized, 23,000 shares issued)	$1,150,000
Premium on Preferred Stock	80,000
Common Stock, $25 par (500,000 shares authorized, 100,000 shares issued)	2,500,000
Premium on Common Stock	600,000
Retained Earnings	3,150,000

During the fiscal year, Rockton Manufacturing Corporation completed the following transactions affecting stockholders' equity:

(a) Purchased 5,000 shares of treasury common for $130,000.
(b) Sold 3,000 shares of treasury common for $81,000.
(c) Issued 40,000 shares of common stock at $27, receiving cash.
(d) Sold 1,000 shares of treasury common for $24,000.

Instructions:

1. Prepare the journal entries to record the transactions listed, identifying each transaction by the appropriate letter.
2. Prepare the stockholders' equity section for the balance sheet at December 31, the end of the fiscal year. The beginning retained earnings balance must be increased by the net income for the year, $710,000, and reduced by the dividends declared and paid, $280,000.

SOLUTION

(1)

	Debit	Credit
(a) Treasury Stock	130,000	
Cash		130,000
(b) Cash	81,000	
Treasury Stock		78,000
Paid-In Capital from Sale of Treasury Stock		3,000
(c) Cash	1,080,000	
Common Stock		1,000,000
Premium on Common Stock		80,000
(d) Cash	24,000	
Paid-In Capital from Sale of Treasury Stock	2,000	
Treasury Stock		26,000

(2)

Stockholders' Equity

Paid-in capital:			
Preferred 8% stock, $50 par (100,000 shares authorized, 23,000 shares issued)	$1,150,000		
Premium on preferred stock .	80,000	$1,230,000	
Common stock, $25 par (500,000 shares authorized, 140,000 shares issued)	$3,500,000		
Premium on common stock ..	680,000	4,180,000	
From sale of treasury stock ..		1,000	
Total paid-in capital		$5,411,000	
Retained earnings		3,580,000	
Total		$8,991,000	
Deduct treasury common stock (1,000 shares at cost)		26,000	
Total stockholders' equity			$8,965,000

Discussion Questions

10–1. What form of business organization is used most frequently in the United States?

10–2. What is the primary disadvantage of organizing a business enterprise as a sole proprietorship?

10–3. What are the primary differences in accounting for a sole proprietorship and accounting for a corporation?

10–4. At the end of the accounting period for a sole proprietorship, the owner's drawing account is closed to what account?

10–5. Must a partnership (a) file a federal income tax return or (b) pay federal income taxes? Explain.

10–6. The partnership agreement between Weiss and Young provides for the sharing of partnership net income in the ratio of 2:1. Since the agreement is silent concerning the sharing of net losses, in what ratio will they be shared?

10–7. In the absence of an agreement, how will the net income be distributed between Joe Morris and Ann Peters, partners in the firm of Morris and Peters Consultants?

10–8. Martha Shaul and Barbara Towne are contemplating the formation of a partnership in which Shaul is to devote full time and Towne is to devote one-half time. In the absence of any agreement, will the partners share in net income or net loss in the ratio of 2:1? Explain.

10–9. Sue Ness and Frank Owens are partners who share in net income equally and have capital balances of $80,000 and $62,500 respectively. Ness, with the consent of Owens, sells one fourth of her interest to Joe Atles. What entry is required by the partnership if the sale price is (a) $20,000? (b) $30,000?

10–10. In the liquidation process, (a) how are losses and gains on realization divided among the partners, and (b) how is cash distributed among the partners?

10–11. Vance and Wallace are partners, sharing gains and losses equally. At the time they decide to terminate their partnership, their capital balances are $55,000 and $30,000 respectively. After all noncash assets are sold and all liabilities are paid, there is a cash balance of $70,000. (a) What is the amount of gain or loss on realization? (b) How should the gain or loss be divided between Vance and Wallace? (c) How should the cash be divided between Vance and Wallace?

10–12. Why is it said that the earnings of a corporation are subject to "double taxation"? Discuss.

10–13. What are the two principal sources of stockholders' equity?

10–14. The retained earnings account of a corporation at the beginning of the year had a credit balance of $60,000. The only other entry in the account during the year was a debit of $75,000 transferred from the income summary account at the end of the year. (a) What is the term applied to the $75,000 debit? (b) What is the balance in Retained Earnings at the end of the year? (c) What is the term applied to the balance determined in (b)?

10–15. The charter of a corporation provides for the issuance of a maximum of 50,000 shares of common stock. The corporation issued 40,000 shares of common stock, and two years later it reacquired 5,000 shares. After the reacquisition, what is the number of shares of stock (a) authorized, (b) issued, and (c) outstanding?

10–16. (a) Differentiate between common stock and preferred stock. (b) Describe briefly (1) participating preferred stock and (2) cumulative preferred stock.

10–17. Assume that a corporation has had outstanding 100,000 shares of $5 cumulative preferred stock of $50 par and dividends were passed for the preceding three years. What amount of total dividends must be paid to the preferred stockholders before the common stockholders are entitled to any dividends in the current year?

10–18. When a corporation issues stock at a premium, does the premium constitute income? Explain.

10–19. In which section of the corporation balance sheet would Discount on Preferred Stock appear?

10–20. The stockholders' equity section of a corporation balance sheet is composed of the following items:

Preferred $10 stock	$400,000			
Premium on preferred stock	40,000	$440,000		
Common stock...........	$800,000			
Discount on common stock	70,000	730,000	$1,170,000	
Retained earnings........			330,000	$1,500,000

Determine the following amounts: (a) paid-in capital attributable to preferred stock, (b) paid-in capital attributable to common stock, (c) earnings retained for use in the business, and (d) total stockholders' equity.

10–21. Land is acquired by a corporation for 10,000 shares of its $20 par common stock, which is currently selling for $35 per share on a national stock exchange. (a) At what value should the land be recorded? (b) What accounts and amounts should be credited to record the transaction?

10–22. (a) In what respect does treasury stock differ from unissued stock? (b) For what reasons might a company purchase treasury stock? (c) How should treasury stock be presented on the balance sheet?

10–23. A corporation reacquires 1,000 shares of its own $20 par common stock for $30,000, recording it at cost. (a) What effect does this transaction have on revenue or expense of the period? (b) What effect does it have on stockholders' equity?

10–24. The treasury stock in Question 10–23 is resold for $35,000. (a) What is the effect on the corporation's revenue of the period? (b) What is the effect on stockholders' equity?

10–25. A corporation that had issued 80,000 shares of $10 par common stock subsequently reacquired 10,000 shares, which it now holds as treasury stock. If the board of directors declares a cash dividend of $1 per share, what will be the total amount of the dividend?

10–26. At the end of the current period, a corporation has 10,000 shares of preferred stock and 100,000 shares of common stock outstanding. Assuming that there are no preferred dividends in arrears, that the preferred stock is entitled to receive $55 per share upon liquidation, and that total stockholders' equity is $2,750,000, determine the following amounts: (a) equity per share of preferred stock, and (b) equity per share of common stock.

10–27. Common stock has a par of $10 per share, the current equity per share is $37.25, and the market price per share is $45. Suggest reasons for the comparatively high market price in relation to par and to equity per share.

10–28. (a) What type of expenditure is charged to the organization costs account? (b) Give examples of such expenditures. (c) In what section of the balance sheet is the balance of Organization Costs listed?

10–29. Identify each of the following accounts as asset, liability, stockholders' equity, revenue, or expense, and indicate the normal balance of each:

(1) Preferred Stock
(2) Paid-In Capital from Sale of Treasury Stock
(3) Treasury Stock
(4) Organization Costs
(5) Discount on Common Stock
(6) Common Stock
(7) Premium on Preferred Stock
(8) Retained Earnings

10–30. Real World Focus. The following excerpt was taken from the January 31, 1986 balance sheet of Deb Shops Inc.

Shareholders' Equity	
Series A Preferred Stock, par value $1.00 a share:	
Authorized—5,000,000 shares	
Issued and outstanding—460 shares	$ 460
Common Stock, par value $.01 a share:	
Authorized—25,000,000 shares	
Issued and outstanding—7,579,321 shares	75,793
Additional paid-in capital	1,282,634
Retained earnings	38,287,626
	$39,646,513
Less: 26,631 common treasury shares at cost	519,927
Total	$39,126,586

Notes to the financial statements indicate that the holders of the Series A Preferred Stock are entitled to a $1,000 per share liquidation preference and a $120 per share annual dividend, which is cumulative. (a) If no dividends are in arrears on January 31, 1986, what is the total liquidation value of the Series A Preferred Stock? (b) What is the equity per share of the outstanding common stock as of January 31, 1986?

Exercises

SPREADSHEET PROBLEM

10–31. Division of partnership income. John Martin and Larry North formed a partnership, investing $100,000 and $50,000 respectively. Determine their participation in the year's net income of $60,000 under each of the following assumptions: (a) no agreement concerning division of net income; (b) divided in the ratio of original capital investment; (c) interest at the rate of 12% allowed on original investments and the remainder divided in the ratio of 2:3; (d) salary allowances of $15,000 and $30,000 respectively, and the balance divided equally; (e) allowance of interest at the rate of 12% on original investments, salary allowances of $15,000 and $30,000 respectively, and the remainder divided equally.

10–32. Admission of new partners. The capital accounts of Alan Evans and Mary Farr have balances of $60,000 and $100,000 respectively. Don Reese and Gloria Swain are to be admitted to the partnership. Reese purchases one fourth of Evans' interest for $22,500 and one fifth of Farr's interest for $30,000. Swain contributes $60,000 cash to the partnership, for which she is to receive an ownership equity of $60,000. (a) Present the entries to record the admission of (1) Reese and (2) Swain. (b) What are the capital balances of each partner after the admission of Reese and Swain?

10–33. Distribution of cash on partnership liquidation. John Gann and Juan Herr, with capital balances of $51,000 and $36,000 respectively, decided to liquidate their partnership. After selling the noncash assets and paying the liabilities, there is $67,000 of cash remaining. If the partners share income and losses equally, how should the cash be distributed?

10–34. Dividends per share. A. P. Nelson Company has stock outstanding as follows: 10,000 shares of $8 cumulative, nonparticipating preferred stock of $100 par, and 100,000 shares of $20 par common. During its first five years of operations, the following amounts were distributed as dividends: first year, none; second year, $120,000; third year, $180,000; fourth year, $230,000; fifth year, $200,000. Determine the dividends per share on each class of stock for each of the five years.

10–35. Dividends per share. CDP Inc. has outstanding stock composed of 1,000 shares of 10%, $100 par, participating preferred stock and 10,000 shares of no-par common stock. The preferred stock is entitled to participate equally with the common, on a share-for-share basis, in any dividend distributions which exceed the regular preferred dividend and a $2 per share common dividend. The directors declare dividends of $41,000 for the current year. Determine the amount of the dividend per share on (a) the preferred stock and (b) the common stock.

10–36. Entries for stock issuance. On February 20, Adams Company issued for cash 5,000 shares of no-par common stock (with a stated value of $20) at $22, and on August 7 it issued for cash 2,000 shares of $50 par preferred stock at $52. (a) Give the entries for February 20 and August 7, assuming that the common stock is to be credited with the stated value. (b) What is the total amount invested by all stockholders as of August 7?

10–37. Corporate organization; stockholders' equity section. Sanderson Products Inc. was organized on January 9 of the current year, with an authorization of 10,000 shares of $11 cumulative preferred stock, $100 par, and 100,000 shares of $10 par common stock.

The following selected transactions were completed during the first year of operations:

Jan. 9. Issued 20,000 shares of common stock at par for cash.
9. Issued 950 shares of common stock to an attorney in payment of legal fees for organizing the corporation.

Feb. 4. Issued 20,000 shares of common stock in exchange for land, buildings, and equipment with fair market prices of $40,000, $120,000, and $45,000 respectively.
Oct. 15. Issued 2,000 shares of preferred stock at $96 for cash.

(a) Record the transactions. (b) Prepare the stockholders' equity section of the balance sheet as of December 31, the end of the current year. The net income for the year amounted to $37,500.

10–38. Treasury stock transactions. On January 11 of the current year, Lang Company reacquired 1,000 shares of its common stock at $22 per share. On July 2, 500 of the reacquired shares were sold at $25 per share. The remaining 500 shares were sold at $20 per share on December 19. (a) Record the transactions of January 11, July 2, and December 19. (b) What is the balance in Paid-In Capital from Sale of Treasury Stock on December 31 of the current year? (c) Where will the balance in Paid-In Capital from Sale of Treasury Stock be reported on the balance sheet?

SPREADSHEET PROBLEM

10–39. Equity per share. The stockholders' equity accounts of Diaz Company at the end of the current fiscal year are as follows: Preferred $5 Stock, $50 par, $1,000,000; Common Stock, $25 par, $5,000,000; Premium on Common Stock, $200,000; Premium on Preferred Stock, $40,000; Retained Earnings, $860,000. (a) Determine the equity per share of each class of stock, assuming that the preferred stock is entitled to receive $60 upon liquidation. (b) Determine the equity per share of each class of stock, assuming that the preferred stock is to receive $60 per share plus the dividends in arrears in the event of liquidation, and that only the dividends for the current year are in arrears.

10–40. Treasury stock and equity per share. The following items were listed in the stockholders' equity section of the balance sheet of June 30: Common stock, $10 par (50,000 shares outstanding), $500,000; Premium on common stock, $150,000; Retained earnings, $190,000. On July 1, the corporation purchased 2,000 shares of its stock for $24,000. (a) Determine the equity per share of stock on June 30. (b) Present the entry to record the purchase of the stock on July 1. (c) Determine the equity per share on July 1.

10–41. Equity per share; liquidation amounts. The following items were listed in the stockholders' equity section of the balance sheet on July 31: Preferred stock, $50 par, $500,000; Common stock, $20 par, $1,500,000; Premium on common stock, $150,000; Deficit, $250,000. On August 1, the board of directors voted to dissolve the corporation immediately. A short time later, after all noncash assets were sold and liabilities were paid, cash of $1,525,000 remained for distribution to stockholders. (a) Assuming that preferred stock is entitled to preference in liquidation of $55 per share, determine the equity per share on July 31 of (1) preferred stock and (2) common stock. (b) Determine the amount of the $1,525,000 that will be distributed for each share of (1) preferred stock and (2) common stock. (c) Explain the reason for the difference between the common stock equity per share on July 31 and the amount of the cash distribution per common share.

Problems

10–42. Division of partnership income. Martha Cole and Ann Dunn have decided to form a partnership. They have agreed that Cole is to invest $60,000 and that Dunn is to invest $90,000. Cole is to devote full time to the business and Dunn is to devote one-half time. The following plans for the division of income are being considered:

(a) Equal division.
(b) In the ratio of original investments.

(c) In the ratio of time devoted to the business.
(d) Interest of 10% on original investments and the remainder in the ratio of 3:2.
(e) Interest of 10% on original investments, salary allowances of $30,000 to Cole and $15,000 to Dunn, and the remainder equally.
(f) Plan (e), except that Cole is also to be allowed a bonus equal to 20% of the amount by which net income exceeds the salary allowances.

Instructions: For each plan, determine the division of the net income under each of the following assumptions: (1) net income of $75,000; and (2) net income of $45,000. Present the data in tabular form, using the following columnar headings:

	$75,000		$45,000	
Plan	Cole	Dunn	Cole	Dunn

10–43. Statement of partnership liquidation. After closing the accounts on August 1, prior to liquidating the partnership, the capital account balances of Gertz, Hart, and Imes are $21,000, $26,000, and $13,000 respectively. Cash, noncash assets, and liabilities total $11,000, $79,000, and $30,000 respectively. Between August 1 and August 30, the noncash assets are sold for $49,000, the liabilities are paid, and the remaining cash is distributed to the partners. The partners share net income and loss in the ratio of 3:2:1.

Instructions: Prepare a statement of partnership liquidation for the period August 1–30.

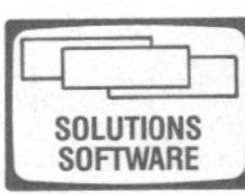

10–44. Corporation organization; stockholders' equity section. Lincolnshire West Corp. was organized by Dunn, Howe, and Radner. The charter authorized 50,000 shares of common stock with a par of $10. The following transactions affecting stockholders' equity were completed during the first year of operations:

(a) Issued 5,000 shares of stock at par to Dunn for cash.
(b) Issued 500 shares of stock at par to Howe for promotional services rendered in connection with the organization of the corporation, and issued 4,500 shares of stock at par to Howe for cash.
(c) Purchased land and a building from Radner. The building is encumbered by a 13%, 16-year mortgage of $95,500, and there is accrued interest of $4,000 on the mortgage note at the time of the purchase. It is agreed that the land is to be priced at $40,000 and the building at $125,000, and that Radner's equity will be exchanged for stock at par. The corporation agreed to assume responsibility for paying the mortgage note and the accrued interest.
(d) Issued 10,000 shares of stock at $12 to various investors for cash.
(e) Purchased equipment for $75,000. The seller accepted a 6-month, 11% note for $25,000 and 5,000 shares of stock in exchange for the equipment.

Instructions: (1) Prepare entries to record the transactions.
(2) Prepare the stockholders' equity section of the balance sheet as of the end of the first year of operations. The retained earnings balance is the net income for the year, $77,500, less dividends declared and paid during the year, $1 per share.

10–45. Dividends on preferred and common stock. The annual dividends declared by Cullum Company during a six-year period are presented in the following table:

	Total	Preferred Dividends		Common Dividends	
Year	Dividends	Total	Per Share	Total	Per Share
1984	$ 62,000				
1985	128,000				
1986	12,000				
1987	5,000				
1988	6,000				
1989	45,000				

During the entire period, the outstanding stock of the company was composed of 2,000 shares of cumulative, participating, $5 preferred stock, $50 par, and 20,000 shares of common stock, $10 par. The preferred stock contract provides that the preferred stock shall participate in distributions of additional dividends after allowance of a $2 dividend per share on the common stock, the additional dividends to be prorated among common and preferred shares on the basis of the total par of the stock outstanding.

Instructions: (1) Determine the total dividends and the per-share dividends declared on each class of stock for each of the six years, using the headings presented above. There were no dividends in arrears on January 1, 1984.

(2) Determine the average annual dividend per share for each class of stock for the six-year period.

(3) Assuming that the preferred stock was sold at par and common stock was sold at $28 at the beginning of the six-year period, determine the percentage return on initial shareholders' investment, based on the average annual dividend per share (a) for preferred stock and (b) for common stock.

10–46. Equity per share. Selected data from the balance sheets of six corporations, identified by letter, are as follows:

A.	Common stock, no par, 50,000 shares outstanding	$ 750,000
	Deficit	90,000
B.	Preferred $2 stock, $25 par	$ 750,000
	Common stock, $10 par	2,000,000
	Premium on common stock	50,000
	Retained earnings	450,000
	Preferred stock has prior claim to assets on liquidation to the extent of par.	
C.	Preferred $12 stock, $100 par	$ 500,000
	Premium on preferred stock	30,000
	Common stock, $5 par	1,000,000
	Discount on common stock	55,000
	Deficit	95,000
	Preferred stock has prior claim to assets on liquidation to the extent of par.	
D.	Preferred 10% stock, $100 par	$ 750,000
	Premium on preferred stock	100,000
	Common stock, $20 par	2,500,000
	Deficit	75,000
	Preferred stock has prior claim to assets on liquidation to the extent of 110% of par.	
E.	Preferred 11% stock, $100 par	$ 800,000
	Common stock, $5 par	2,000,000
	Premium on common stock	300,000
	Retained earnings	104,000
	Dividends on preferred stock are in arrears for 2 years, including the dividend passed during the current year. Preferred stock is entitled to par plus unpaid cumulative dividends upon liquidation to the extent of retained earnings.	
F.	Preferred $2 stock, $25 par	$ 500,000
	Premium on preferred stock	10,000
	Common stock, $10 par	1,500,000
	Deficit	55,000
	Dividends on preferred stock are in arrears for 3 years, including the dividend passed during the current year. Preferred stock is entitled to par plus unpaid cumulative dividends upon liquidation, regardless of the availability of retained earnings.	

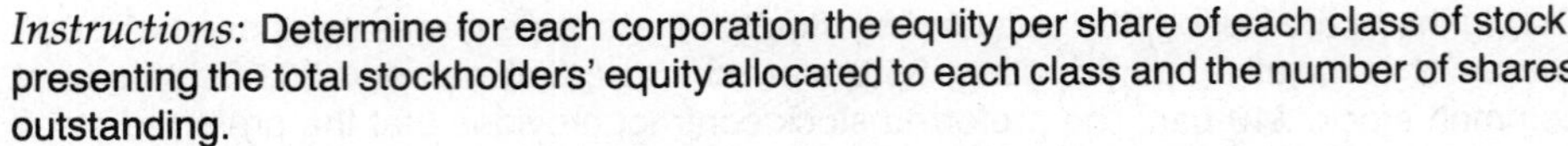

Instructions: Determine for each corporation the equity per share of each class of stock, presenting the total stockholders' equity allocated to each class and the number of shares outstanding.

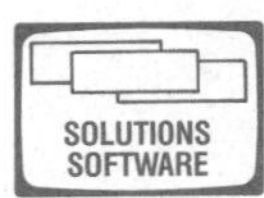

10–47. Corporate expansion; stockholders' equity section. The following accounts and their balances appear in the ledger of Fred Sims and Co. on June 30 of the current year:

Preferred $9 Stock, $100 par (10,000 shares authorized, 8,000 shares issued)	$ 800,000
Premium on Preferred Stock	16,000
Common Stock, $20 par (100,000 shares authorized, 75,000 shares issued)	1,500,000
Premium on Common Stock	210,000
Retained Earnings	305,000

At the annual stockholders' meeting on July 9, the board of directors presented a plan for modernizing and expanding plant operations at a cost of approximately $500,000. The plan provided (a) that the corporation borrow $200,000, (b) that 1,000 shares of the unissued preferred stock be issued through an underwriter, and (c) that a building, valued at $155,000, and the land on which it is located, valued at $40,000, be acquired in accordance with preliminary negotiations by the issuance of 8,000 shares of common stock. The plan was approved by the stockholders and accomplished by the following transactions:

July 24. Issued 8,000 shares of common stock in exchange for land and building in accordance with the plan.
30. Issued 1,000 shares of preferred stock, receiving $105 per share in cash from the underwriter.
31. Borrowed $200,000 from Palmer National Bank, giving a 14% mortgage note.

Instructions: Assuming for the purpose of the problem that no other transactions occurred during July:

(1) Prepare the entries to record the foregoing transactions.
(2) Prepare the stockholders' equity section of the balance sheet as of July 31.

ALTERNATE PROBLEMS

10–42A. Division of partnership income. Chin and Dyke have decided to form a partnership. They have agreed that Chin is to invest $100,000 and that Dyke is to invest $50,000. Chin is to devote one-half time to the business and Dyke is to devote full time. The following plans for the division of income are being considered:

(a) Equal division.
(b) In the ratio of original investments.
(c) In the ratio of time devoted to the business.
(d) Interest of 12% on original investments and the remainder equally.
(e) Interest of 12% on original investments, salaries of $15,000 to Chin and $30,000 to Dyke, and the remainder equally.
(f) Plan (e), except that Dyke is also to be allowed a bonus equal to 20% of the amount by which net income exceeds the salary allowances.

Instructions: For each plan, determine the division of the net income under each of the following assumptions: (1) net income of $45,000; (2) net income of $120,000. Present the data in tabular form, using the following columnar headings:

Plan	$45,000 Chin	$45,000 Dyke	$120,000 Chin	$120,000 Dyke

10–45A. Dividends on preferred and common stock. The annual dividends declared by A. W. Twig Company during a six-year period are presented in the following table:

Year	Total Dividends	Preferred Dividends Total	Preferred Dividends Per Share	Common Dividends Total	Common Dividends Per Share
1984	$ 4,000				
1985	11,000				
1986	30,000				
1987	84,000				
1988	72,000				
1989	21,000				

During the entire period, the outstanding stock of the company was composed of 1,000 shares of cumulative, participating, 10% preferred stock, $100 par, and 10,000 shares of common stock, $50 par. The preferred stock contract provides that the preferred stock shall participate in distributions of additional dividends after allowance of a $5 dividend per share on the common stock, the additional dividends to be prorated among common and preferred shares on the basis of the total par of the stock outstanding.

Instructions: (1) Determine the total dividends and the per share dividends declared on each class of stock for each of the six years, using the headings presented above. There were no dividends in arrears on January 1, 1984.

(2) Determine the average annual dividend per share for each class of stock for the six-year period.

(3) Assuming that the preferred stock was sold at par and common stock was sold at $40 at the beginning of the six-year period, determine the percentage return on initial shareholders' investment, based on the average annual dividend per share (a) for preferred stock and (b) for common stock.

10–46A. Equity per share. Selected data from the balance sheets of six corporations, identified by letter, are as follows:

A.	Common stock, $10 par	$ 500,000
	Premium on common stock	100,000
	Deficit	75,000
B.	Preferred $10 stock, $25 par	$ 500,000
	Common stock, $20 par	1,500,000
	Premium on common stock	130,000
	Retained earnings	410,000
	Preferred stock has prior claim to assets on liquidation to the extent of par.	
C.	Preferred $9 stock, $100 par	$1,000,000
	Premium on preferred stock	50,000
	Common stock, no par, 25,000 shares outstanding	1,250,000
	Deficit	200,000
	Preferred stock has prior claim to assets on liquidation to the extent of par.	
D.	Preferred 11% stock, $50 par	$2,000,000
	Premium on preferred stock	275,000
	Common stock, $25 par	3,750,000
	Retained earnings	450,000
	Preferred stock has prior claim to assets on liquidation to the extent of 110% of par.	

E. Preferred 9% stock, $100 par $1,200,000
Common stock, $50 par 4,000,000
Premium on common stock 340,000
Retained earnings 108,000

Dividends on preferred stock are in arrears for 2 years, including the dividend passed during the current year. Preferred stock is entitled to par plus unpaid cumulative dividends upon liquidation to the extent of retained earnings.

F. Preferred $2 stock, $25 par .... $ 500,000
Discount on preferred stock 40,000
Common stock, $10 par 2,000,000
Deficit 130,000

Dividends on preferred stock are in arrears for 3 years, including the dividend passed during the current year. Preferred stock is entitled to par plus unpaid cumulative dividends upon liquidation, regardless of the availability of retained earnings.

Instructions: Determine for each corporation the equity per share of each class of stock, presenting the total stockholders' equity allocated to each class and the number of shares outstanding.

Mini-Case 10

Miami Valley Cooperative Electric Corporation needs $2,000,000 to finance a major plant expansion. To raise the $2,000,000, the chairman of the board of directors suggested that the cooperative first offer common stock for sale at a price equal to the January 1, 1989 equity per share of common stock. The chairman indicated that by setting the price in this way, the value of the current common stockholders' interest in the cooperative would be preserved. Any additional funds that might be needed after this offer expired could be obtained from the issuance of preferred stock.

Since no preferred stock is authorized, the board is considering characteristics of the stock, such as the dividend rate and the cumulative and participating features. So as not to jeopardize common stockholder dividends, the board of directors tentatively approved a dividend rate of 4% for the preferred stock. The board agreed to delay any final action on other aspects of the financing plan until the legal counsel can be contacted to determine the procedures necessary to seek authorization of the preferred stock.

As of January 1, 1989, the stockholders' equity is as follows:

Paid-in capital:		
Common stock, $50 par (100,000 shares authorized, 60,000 shares issued)	$3,000,000	
Premium on common stock	450,000	
Total paid-in capital		$3,450,000
Retained earnings		1,350,000
Total stockholders' equity		$4,800,000

Instructions:

(1) Determine the equity per share of common stock on January 1, 1989.
(2) During the board meeting, the chairman asked for your opinion of the suggestion for determining the selling price of the common stock. How would you respond?
(3) What characteristics might you suggest the board consider in designing the preferred stock? Comment on the low preferred stock dividend rate tentatively approved by the board.

Answers to Self-Examination Questions

1. C X's share of the $45,000 of net income is $19,000 (answer C), determined as follows:

	X	Y	Total
Interest allowance	$10,000	$ 5,000	$15,000
Salary allowance	12,000	24,000	36,000
Total	$22,000	$29,000	$51,000
Excess of allowances over income	3,000	3,000	6,000
Net income distribution	$19,000	$26,000	$45,000

2. C If a corporation has cumulative preferred stock outstanding, dividends that have been passed for prior years plus the dividend for the current year must be paid before dividends may be declared on common stock. In this case, dividends of $27,000 ($9,000 × 3) have been passed for the preceding three years and the current year's dividends are $9,000, making a total of $36,000 (answer C) that must be paid to preferred stockholders before dividends can be declared on common stock.

3. D The stockholders' equity section of corporate balance sheets is divided into two principal subsections: (1) investments contributed by the stockholders and (2) net income retained in the business. Included as part of the investments by stockholders is the excess of par over issued price of stock, such as discount on common stock (answer A); the par of common stock (answer B); and the excess of issued price of stock over par, such as premium on preferred stock (answer C).

4. C Reacquired stock, known as treasury stock, should be listed in the stockholders' equity section (answer C) of the balance sheet. The price paid for the treasury stock is deducted from the total of all of the stockholders' equity accounts.

5. B The total stockholders' equity is determined as follows:

Preferred stock	$1,000,000
Common stock	2,000,000
Premium on common stock	100,000
Retained earnings	540,000
Total equity	$3,640,000

The amount allocated to common stock is determined as follows:

Total equity		$3,640,000
Allocated to preferred stock:		
Liquidation price	$1,100,000	
Dividends in arrears	240,000	1,340,000
Allocated to common stock		$2,300,000

The equity per common share is determined as follows:

$2,300,000 ÷ 100,000 shares = $23 per share

11
Stockholders' Equity Earnings, and Dividends

CHAPTER OBJECTIVES

Identify and illustrate alternative terminology used in preparing the stockholders' equity section of the balance sheet.

Describe and illustrate the accounting for corporate income taxes.

Describe and illustrate the accounting for unusual items in the financial statements.

Describe and illustrate the computation of earnings per share.

Describe and illustrate the accounting for appropriations of retained earnings and the preparation of a retained earnings statement.

Describe and illustrate the accounting for dividends, including cash dividends, stock dividends, and liquidating dividends.

Describe and illustrate the accounting for stock splits.

As has been indicated, the stockholders' equity section of the balance sheet is divided into two major subdivisions, *paid-in capital* (or contributed capital) and *retained earnings*. Although in practice there is wide variation in the amount of detail presented and the descriptive captions used, sources of significant amounts of stockholders' equity should be properly disclosed.

The emphasis on disclosure and clarity of expression by the accounting profession has been relatively recent. In earlier days, it was not unusual to present for stockholders' equity only the amount of the par of the preferred and common stock outstanding and a balancing amount described simply as "Surplus." Readers of the balance sheet could only assume that par represented the amount paid in by stockholders and that surplus represented retained earnings. Although it was possible for a "surplus" of $1,000,000, for example, to be composed solely of retained earnings, it could represent paid-in capital from premiums on stock issued or even an excess of $1,200,000 of such premiums over an accumulated deficit of $200,000 of retained earnings.

As illustrated in Chapter 10, the main credits to paid-in capital accounts result from the issuance of stock. If par stock is issued at a price above or below par, the difference is recorded in a separate premium or discount account. It is also common to use two accounts in recording the issuance of no-par stock, one for the stated value and the other for the excess over stated value. Another account for paid-in capital discussed in the preceding chapter was Paid-In Capital from Sale of Treasury Stock.

Paid-in capital may also originate from donated real estate and redemptions of a corporation's own stock. Civic organizations sometimes give land or land and buildings to a corporate enterprise as an inducement to locate in the community. In such cases, the assets are recorded in the corporate accounts at fair market value, with a credit to Donated Capital. Preferred stock contracts may give to the issuing corporation the right to redeem the stock at varying redemption prices at varying future dates. If the redemption price paid to the stockholder is greater than the original issuance price, the excess is considered to be a distribution of retained earnings. On the other hand, if the amount paid is less than the amount originally received by the corporation, the difference is a retention of capital and should be credited to Paid-In Capital from Preferred Stock Redemption or a similarly titled account.

As with other sections of the balance sheet, there are many variations in terminology and arrangement of the paid-in capital section. Some of these variations are illustrated by the following three examples. The details of each class of stock, including related stock premium or discount, are commonly listed first, followed by the other paid-in capital accounts. Instead of describing the source of each amount in excess of par or stated value, a common practice is to combine all such accounts into a single amount. It is then listed below the capital stock accounts and described as "Additional paid-in capital," "Capital in excess of par (or stated value) of shares," or by a similarly descriptive phrase.

Stockholders' Equity

Paid-in capital:			
Common stock, $20 par (50,000 shares authorized, 45,000 shares issued)	$900,000		
Premium on common stock	132,000	$1,032,000	
From stock redemption		60,000	
From sale of treasury stock		25,000	
Total paid-in capital			$1,117,000

Shareholders' Equity

Paid-in capital:			
Common stock, $20 par (50,000 shares authorized, 45,000 shares issued)		$ 900,000	
Excess of issuance price over par	$132,000		
From redemption of common stock	60,000		
From transactions in own stock	25,000	217,000	
Total paid-in capital			$1,117,000

Shareholders' Investment		
Contributed capital:		
Common stock, $20 par (50,000 shares authorized, 45,000 shares issued)	$ 900,000	
Additional paid-in capital	217,000	
Total contributed capital		$1,117,000

Significant changes in paid-in capital during the period should also be disclosed. The details of these changes may be presented either in a separate paid-in capital statement or in notes to other financial statements.

CORPORATE EARNINGS AND INCOME TAXES

The determination of the net income or net loss of a corporation is comparable, in most respects, to that of other forms of business organization. Unlike sole proprietorships and partnerships, however, corporations are distinct legal entities. In general, they are subject to the federal income tax and, in many cases, to income taxes levied by states or other political subdivisions. Although the discussion that follows is limited to the income tax levied by the federal government, the basic concepts apply also to state and local income taxes.

For several years, most corporations have been required to estimate the amount of their federal income tax expense for the year and to make advance payments, usually in four installments. To illustrate, assume that a calendar-year corporation estimates its income tax expense for the year to be $84,000. The required entry for each of the four payments of $21,000 (1/4 of $84,000) would be as follows:

	Debit	Credit
Income Tax	21,000	
Cash		21,000

At year end, the actual taxable income and the actual tax are determined. If an additional amount is owed, this liability must be recorded. Continuing with the illustration, assume that the corporation's actual tax, based on actual taxable income, is $86,000 instead of $84,000. The following entry would be required in order to include the income tax expense in the fiscal year in which the related income was earned:

		Debit	Credit
Dec. 31	Income Tax	2,000	
	Income Tax Payable		2,000

If the amount of the advance payments exceeds the tax liability based on actual income, the amount of the overpayment would be debited to a receivable account and credited to Income Tax.

Income tax returns and related records and documents are subject to review by the taxing authority, usually for a period of three years after the return is filed. Consequently, the determination made by the taxpayer is provisional rather than final. In recognition of the possibility of an assessment for a tax deficiency, the liability for income taxes is sometimes described in the current liability section of the balance sheet as "Estimated income tax payable."

Because of its substantial size in relationship to net income, income tax is often reported on the income statement as a special deduction, as follows:

Palmer Corporation Income Statement For Year Ended December 31, 19--	
Sales	$980,000
Income before income tax	$200,000
Income tax	82,500
Net Income	$117,500

ALLOCATION OF INCOME TAX BETWEEN PERIODS

The **taxable income** of a corporation, determined according to the tax laws, is often different from the amount of income (before income tax) determined from the accounts and reported in the income statement. This difference may need to be allocated between periods, depending upon whether it is a permanent difference or a temporary difference.[1]

Permanent Differences

The tax laws provide for special treatment of certain revenue and expense items. This special treatment results in permanent differences between the amount of income tax actually owed and the amount that would be owed if the tax were based on income before income tax. These items may be described as follows:

1. An expense for a specified purpose is not deductible in determining taxable income, or revenue from a specified source is excludable from taxable income. Example: Interest income on tax-exempt municipal bonds.
2. A deduction is allowed in determining taxable income, but there is no actual expenditure and hence no expense. Example: The excess of the allowable deduction for percentage depletion of natural resources over depletion expense based on cost.

Permanent differences cause no problem for financial reporting. The amount of income tax determined in accordance with the tax laws is the amount reported on the income statement.

---

[1] *Statement of Financial Accounting Standards, No. 96,* "Accounting for Income Taxes" (Stamford: Financial Accounting Standards Board, 1987), par. 14.

Temporary Differences

The treatment of certain items results in differences between income before income tax and taxable income, because the items are recognized in one period for income statement purposes and in another period for tax purposes. These temporary differences, sometimes referred to as timing differences, reverse or turn around in later years. The cases in which such differences occur are described as follows:

1. The method used in determining the amount of a specified revenue or expense for income tax purposes differs from the method used in determining net income for reporting purposes. Example: The installment method of determining revenue is used in determining taxable income and the point of sale method is used for reporting purposes.
2. The manner prescribed for the treatment of a specified revenue or expense in determining taxable income is contrary to generally accepted accounting principles and hence not acceptable in determining net income for reporting purposes. Example: Revenue received in advance for magazine subscriptions must be included in taxable income in the year received, which is contrary to the basic accounting principle that such revenue be allocated to the years benefited.

Temporary differences require special treatment in the accounts. To illustrate the effect of temporary differences and their related effect on the amount of income tax reported in corporate financial statements, assume that a corporation that sells its product on the installment basis recognizes the revenue at the time of sale and maintains its accounts accordingly. At the end of the first year of operations, the income before income tax according to the ledger is $300,000. Realizing the advantage of reducing current income tax, the corporation elects the installment method of determining revenue and cost of merchandise sold, which yields taxable income of only $100,000. Assuming an income tax rate of 40%, the income tax on $300,000 of income would amount to $120,000. The income tax actually due for the year would only be $40,000 (40% of $100,000). The $80,000 difference between the two amounts is due to the timing difference in recognizing revenue. It represents a deferment of $80,000 of income tax to future years. As the installment accounts receivable are collected in later years, the additional $200,000 of income will be included in the taxable income, and the $80,000 deferment will become a tax liability of those years.[2] The situation may be summarized as follows:

Income before income tax according to ledger	$300,000	
Income tax based on $300,000 at 40%		$120,000
Taxable income according to tax return	$100,000	
Income tax based on $100,000 at 40%		40,000
Income tax deferred to future years		$ 80,000

The income tax to be reported on the income statement should be the total tax ($120,000 in the illustration) expected to result from the net income of the

[2]If the tax rates change, companies are required to recompute their tax liabilities and to recognize the effect of the change in net income. This topic is discussed in more detail in advanced texts.

year. In this manner, the revenue reported on the income statement will be matched with the expenses (including income tax) related to that revenue, regardless of when the tax will become an actual liability to be paid. Applying the concept of the allocation of income tax between periods to the illustrative data yields the following results, stated in terms of a journal entry:

Income Tax	120,000	
Income Tax Payable		40,000
Deferred Income Tax Payable		80,000

Continuing with the illustration, the $80,000 in Deferred Income Tax Payable will be transferred to Income Tax Payable as the remaining $200,000 of income becomes taxable in later years. If, for example, $120,000 of untaxed income of the first year of the corporation's operations becomes taxable in the second year, the effect would be as follows, stated as a journal entry:

Deferred Income Tax Payable	48,000	
Income Tax Payable		48,000

In the illustration, the amount in Deferred Income Tax Payable at the end of a year will be reported as a liability. The amount due within one year will be classified as a current liability, and the remainder will be classified as a long-term liability or reported in a Deferred Credits section following the Long-Term Liabilities section.

If installment sales are made in later years, there will be more differences between taxable income and reported income, and an accompanying deferment of tax liability. During periods of growth, the amount of deferred income taxes for an enterprise may increase rapidly and can become a significant amount. The amounts of deferred income taxes listed as long-term liabilities on the 1986 annual reports of nine major companies were as follows:

Procter & Gamble Company	$1,121,000,000
PPG Industries, Inc.	367,700,000
Xerox	342,000,000
The New York Times Company	120,795,000
Sherwin-Williams Company	78,863,000
Teledyne, Inc.	78,800,000
Kidde, Inc.	51,383,000
Hartmarx Corporation	21,443,000
Graphic Industries, Inc.	5,430,993

Are Deferred Taxes Really a Liability?

For those companies that show a significant amount of deferred taxes on their balance sheets, the question that may arise is whether such amounts are really liabilities. For example, the reporting of a liability for "deferred income taxes, $267.7 million," on Anheuser-Busch's 1980 balance sheet was discussed in *Forbes*. In this article, excerpts from which follow, it was noted that Anheuser-Busch's deferred tax liability was equal to 19% of the total liabilities and 26% of the stockholders' equity.

... Says Harvey D. Moskowitz, national director of accounting and auditing for Seidman & Seidman, "The deferred taxes on the balance sheet bear no relationship to what is actually going to be owed. So the current method of income tax accounting makes it impossible for the investor to evaluate a company's liquidity, solvency or cash flow."

Here's the explanation for this curious state of affairs: Anheuser-Busch had pretax income of $271.5 million, so, using standard corporate tax rates (less credits), it owed $99.7 million to Uncle Sam. That's what it set aside as "provision for income taxes" on its income statement. But it's not what the company actually paid. Like most businesses Anheuser keeps two sets of books, one for tax purposes, one for stock owners. It uses accelerated depreciation for taxes but straight line for reporting to investors.... So, out-of-pocket, it really had to pay only $31.9 million in taxes in 1980—the line marked "current" on the income statement. The other $67.8 million, called "deferred," represents cash that's squirreled away in liabilities on the balance sheet, under the assumption that the company will pay those taxes eventually—when accelerated depreciation runs out, for example.

That assumption is probably wrong, though. As long as the company keeps growing—in real terms or because of inflation—it will keep adding new assets and new interest costs to replace the ones that are running out. That means those deferred taxes, instead of getting paid, will simply roll over. And over and over and over. It could almost make you dizzy.

Source: Jane Carmichael, "Rollover," *Forbes* (January 18, 1982), pp. 75, 78.

REPORTING UNUSUAL ITEMS IN THE FINANCIAL STATEMENTS

In recent years, professional accounting organizations have devoted much time to the development of guidelines for reporting unusual items relating to the determination of net income. These items may be divided into four relatively well-defined categories, as follows:

1. Adjustments or corrections of net income of prior fiscal periods.
2. Segregation of the results of discontinued operations from the results of continuing operations.
3. Recognition of extraordinary items of gain or loss.
4. Change from one generally accepted accounting principle to another.

Before examining the guidelines that are presently in effect, a brief summary of earlier viewpoints is in order. For several years, there were two conflicting theories about the proper function of the income statement: (1) to report the *current operating performance* and (2) to be *all-inclusive.* According to the first theory, only the effects of the ordinary, normal, and recurring operations were to be reported in the income statement. It was considered better to report nonrecurring items of significant amount in the retained earnings statement. By so doing, it was argued that readers of the income statement would not draw incorrect conclusions about the "normal operating performance" of an enterprise.

On the other hand, the all-inclusive point of view was exactly the opposite of the current operating performance viewpoint. It required that all revenue and expense items recorded in the current period be reported in the income statement, with significant amounts of a nonrecurring nature properly identified. If nonrecurring items were "buried" in the retained earnings statement, they were likely to be overlooked and the total amount of the periodic net income reported over the entire life of an enterprise could not be determined from its income statements. The all-inclusive viewpoint has prevailed, and most professional accountants agree that it is preferable. The generally accepted guidelines on the subject are discussed briefly in the subsections that follow.

Prior Period Adjustments

Minor accounting errors often result from the use of estimates that are inherent in the accounting process. For example, relatively small errors in amounts provided for income taxes of one or more periods are not unusual. Similarly, annual provisions for the uncollectibility of receivables seldom agree with the amounts of the accounts actually written off. Such minor errors are normal and tend to be recurring. The effect of these errors should be included in determining amounts for the current period.

Material errors may result from mathematical mistakes and from mistakes in the application of accounting principles or oversight or misuse of facts that existed at the time transactions were recorded. The treatment of material errors depends on when they are discovered. The procedure recommended for correcting errors that are discovered in the same period in which they occurred and that have been posted to the ledger is summarized as follows: (1) set forth the entire entry in which the error occurred by the use of memorandum T accounts or a journal entry; (2) set forth the entry that should have been made, using a second set of T accounts or a journal entry; and (3) formulate the debits and credits needed to bring the erroneous entry into agreement with the correct entry. This procedure is entirely a matter of technique, and no question of principle is involved. After the correction has been made, the account balances are the same as they would have been in the absence of error, and the information given in the income statement and the balance sheet is unaffected.

The effect of material errors that are not discovered within the same fiscal period in which they occurred should not be included in the determination of net income for the current period.[3] Corrections of this type of error, usually called **prior period adjustments,** should be reported as an adjustment of the retained earnings balance at the beginning of the period in which the correction is made. Prior period adjustments would include, for example, the correction of a material error in computing depreciation expense for a prior period. In addition, a change from an unacceptable accounting principle to an acceptable accounting principle is considered to be a correction of a material error and should be treated as a prior period adjustment. An example of such a situation would be the correction resulting from changing from the cash basis to the accrual basis of accounting for a business enterprise that buys and sells merchandise. The manner in which a prior period adjustment is presented in the retained earnings statement is illustrated as follows:

---

[3]*Statement of Financial Accounting Standards, No. 16,* "Prior Period Adjustments" (Stamford: Financial Accounting Standards Board, 1977), par. 11.

Palmer Company Retained Earnings Statement For Year Ended December 31, 1989		
Retained earnings, January 1, 1989		$310,500
Less prior period adjustment:		
Correction of error in depreciation expense in 1988, net of applicable income tax of $13,000		29,200
Corrected retained earnings, January 1, 1989		$281,300
Net income for year	$77,350	
Less dividends	40,000	
Increase in retained earnings		37,350
Retained earnings, December 31, 1989		$318,650

Note that the amount reported as a prior period adjustment is reported net of the related income tax. In addition, if financial statements are presented only for the current period, the effect of the adjustment on the net income of the preceding period should also be disclosed. If financial statements for prior periods are presented, as is preferable, the statements should be adjusted and the amount of each adjustment should be disclosed.

Adjustments applicable to prior periods that meet the criteria for a prior period adjustment are rare in modern financial accounting. Annual audits by independent public accountants, combined with the internal control features of accounting systems, lessen the chances of errors justifying such treatment.

Discontinued Operations

A gain or loss resulting from the disposal of a segment of a business should be identified on the income statement as a gain or loss from **discontinued operations.** The term *discontinued* refers to "the operations of a segment of a business . . . that has been sold, abandoned, spun off, or otherwise disposed of or . . . is the subject of a formal plan for disposal."[4] The term "segment of a business" refers to a part of an enterprise whose activities represent a major line of business, such as a division or department or a certain class of customer.[5] For example, if an enterprise owning newspapers, television stations, and radio stations were to sell its radio stations, the results of the sale would be reported as a gain or loss on discontinued operations.

When an enterprise discontinues a segment of its operations and identifies the gain or loss therefrom, the results of "continuing operations" should also be identified in the income statement. The net income or loss from continuing operations is presented first, beginning with sales and followed by the enterprise's customary analysis of its costs and expenses. In addition to the data on discontinued operations presented in the body of the statement, such details as the identity of the segment disposed of, the disposal date, a descrip-

[4]*Opinions of the Accounting Principles Board, No. 30,* "Reporting the Results of Operations" (New York: American Institute of Certified Public Accountants, 1973), par. 8.
[5]*Ibid.,* par. 13.

tion of the assets and liabilities involved, and the manner of disposal should be disclosed in a note to the financial statements.[6]

Extraordinary Items

Extraordinary gains and losses result from "events and transactions that are distinguished by their unusual nature *and* by the infrequency of their occurrence."[7] Such gains and losses, other than those from the disposal of a segment of a business, should be identified in the income statement as **extraordinary items.** To be so classified, an event or transaction must meet both of the following criteria:

1. Unusual nature—*the underlying event or transaction should possess a high degree of abnormality and be of a type clearly unrelated to, or only incidentally related to, the ordinary and typical activities of the entity, taking into account the environment in which the entity operates.*
2. Infrequency of occurrence—*the underlying event or transaction should be of a type that would not reasonably be expected to recur in the foreseeable future, taking into account the environment in which the entity operates.*[8]

Transactions that meet both of the criteria are rare. For example, the 1987 edition of *Accounting Trends & Techniques* indicated that only 104 of the 600 industrial and merchandising companies surveyed reported extraordinary items on their income statements. Usually, extraordinary items result from major casualties, such as floods, earthquakes, and other rare catastrophes not expected to recur. In addition, gains or losses that result when land or buildings are condemned for public use are considered extraordinary.

Gains and losses on the disposal of plant assets do not qualify as extraordinary items because (1) they are not unusual and (2) they recur from time to time in the ordinary course of business activities. Similarly, gains and losses incurred on the sale of investments are usual and recurring for most enterprises. However, if a company had owned only one investment during its entire existence, a gain or loss on its sale might qualify as an extraordinary item, provided there was no intention of acquiring other investments in the foreseeable future.

Changes in Accounting Principles

A change in accounting principle "results from adoption of a generally accepted accounting principle different from the one used previously for reporting purposes."[9] The concept of consistency and its relationship to changes in accounting methods were discussed in Chapter 1. A change from one generally accepted accounting principle or method to another generally accepted principle or method should be disclosed in the financial statements of the period in which the change is made. In addition to describing the nature of the change, the justification for the change should be stated and the effect of the change on net income should be disclosed.

[6] *Ibid.*, par. 18.
[7] *Ibid.*, par. 20.
[8] *Ibid.*
[9] *Opinions of the Accounting Principles Board, No. 20,* "Accounting Changes" (New York: American Institute of Certified Public Accountants, 1971), par. 7.

The generally accepted procedures for disclosing the effect on net income of a change in principle are as follows: (1) report the cumulative effect of the change on net income of prior periods as a special item on the income statement, and (2) report the effect of the change on net income of the current period. If the financial statements for prior periods are presented in conjunction with the current statements, the effect of the change in accounting principle should also be applied retroactively to the published statements of the prior periods and reported either on their face or in accompanying notes.

The amount of the cumulative effect on net income of prior periods should be reported in a special section of the income statement located immediately prior to the net income. If an extraordinary item or items are reported on the statement, the amount related to the change in principle should follow the extraordinary items.

The procedures should be modified for a change from the lifo assumption for inventory costing to another method or for a change in the method of accounting for long-term construction contracts. For these changes in principle, the cumulative effect on prior years' income is not reported as a special item on the income statement. Instead, the newly adopted principle should be applied retroactively to the income statements of the prior periods and the effect on income disclosed, either on the face of the statements or in accompanying notes. Financial statements of subsequent periods need not repeat the disclosures.[10]

Allocation of Income Tax to Unusual Items

The amount reported as a prior period adjustment, a gain or loss from a discontinued operation, an extraordinary item, or the cumulative effect of a change in accounting principle should be net of the related income tax. The amount of income tax allocable to each of these items may be disclosed on the face of the appropriate financial statement or by an accompanying note.

Presentation of Unusual Items in the Income Statement

The manner in which gains or losses from discontinued operations, extraordinary items, and the cumulative effect of a change in accounting principle may be presented in the income statement is illustrated for CAP Corporation on page 416. Many variations in terminology and format are possible.

EARNINGS PER COMMON SHARE

The absolute amounts of net income are often useful in evaluating a company's profitability. However, these absolute amounts are difficult to use in comparing companies of different sizes. For example, a net income of $750,000 may be very satisfactory for a small computer manufacturer, but it may be very unsatisfactory for a very large computer manufacturer. Likewise, the absolute amount of net income is difficult to use in evaluating a company's profitability when the amount of stockholders' equity changes significantly. In such cases, the profitability of a company may be expressed as earnings per

[10] *Ibid.*, pars. 27 and 28.

CAP Corporation
Income Statement
For the Year Ended August 31, 19--

Net sales	$9,600,950

Income from continuing operations before income tax	$1,310,000
Income tax	620,000
Income from continuing operations	$ 690,000
Loss on discontinued operations (Note A)	100,000
Income before extraordinary item and cumulative effect of a change in accounting principle	$ 590,000
Extraordinary item:	
Gain on condemnation of land, net of applicable income tax of $65,000	150,000
Cumulative effect on prior years of changing to a different depreciation method (Note B)	92,000
Net income	$ 832,000

Note A. On July 1 of the current year, the entire electrical products division of the corporation was sold at a loss of $100,000, net of applicable income tax of $50,000. The net sales of the division for the current year were $2,900,000. The assets sold were composed of inventories, equipment, and plant totaling $2,100,000, and the liabilities assumed by the purchaser amounted to $600,000.

Note B. Depreciation of property, plant, and equipment has been computed by the straight-line method at all manufacturing facilities in 19--. Prior to 19--, depreciation of equipment for one of the divisions had been computed on the double-declining balance method. In 19--, the straight-line method was adopted for this division in order to achieve uniformity and to more appropriately match the remaining depreciation charges with the estimated economic utility of such assets. Pursuant to APB Opinion 20, this change in depreciation has been applied retroactively to prior years. The effect of the change was to increase income before extraordinary items for 19-- by approximately $30,000. The adjustment of $92,000 (after reduction for income tax of $68,000) to apply retroactively the new method is also included in income for 19--.

share. The term **earnings per share** refers to the net income per share of common stock outstanding during a given period. For public corporations, data on earnings per share of common stock must be reported on the income statement.[11] Earnings per share is often the item of greatest interest contained in corporate financial statements. these data are also often reported by the financial press and by various statistical services.

If a company has only common stock outstanding, the earnings per share of common stock is determined by dividing net income by the number of common shares outstanding. If preferred stock is outstanding, the net income must be reduced by the amount of any preferred divided requirements before dividing by the number of common shares outstanding.

[11]Nonpublic corporations are exempt from this requirement, according to *Statement of Financial Accounting Standards, No. 21*, "Suspension of the Reporting of Earnings per Share and Segment Information by Nonpublic Enterprises" (Stamford: Financial Accounting Standards Board, 1978).

The effect of nonrecurring additions to or deductions from income of a period should be considered in computing earnings per share. Otherwise, a single per share amount based on net income would be misleading. To illustrate this point, assume that CAP Corporation, whose partial income statement for the current year was presented above, reported net income of $700,000 for the preceding year, with no extraordinary or other special items. Assume also that the corporation's capital stock was composed of 200,000 common shares outstanding during the entire two-year period. If the earnings per share of $3.50 ($700,000 ÷ 200,000) for the preceding year were compared with the earnings per share of $4.16 ($832,000 ÷ 200,000) for the current year, it would appear that operations had greatly improved. However, the current year's per share amount that is comparable to $3.50 is in reality $3.45 ($690,000 ÷ 200,000), which indicates a slight downward trend in normal operations.

Data on earnings per share should be presented in conjunction with the income statement. If there are nonrecurring items on the statement, the per share amounts should be presented for (1) income from continuing operations, (2) income before extraordinary items and the cumulative effect of a change in accounting principle, (3) the cumulative effect of a change in accounting principle, and (4) net income.[12] Presentation of per share amounts is optional for the gain or loss on discontinued operations and for extraordinary items. The per share data may be shown in parentheses or added at the bottom of the statement, as in the following illustration for CAP Corporation:

CAP Corporation
Income Statement
For the Year Ended August 31, 19--

Income from continuing operations	$690,000
...	
Net income	$832,000
Earnings per common share:	
Income from continuing operations	$3.45
Loss on discontinued operations	.50
Income before extraordinary item and cumulative effect of a change in accounting principle	$2.95
Extraordinary item	.75
Cumulative effect on prior years of changing to a different depreciation method	.46
Net income	$4.16

In computing the earnings per share of common stock, all factors that affect the number of common shares outstanding must be considered. If there

[12] *Opinions of the Accounting Principles Board, No. 15,* "Earnings per Share" (New York: American Institute of Certified Public Accountants, 1969) as amended by *Opinions of the Accounting Principles Board, No. 20,* and *Opinions of the Accounting Principles Board, No. 30.*

is an issue of preferred stock or bonds (debt) with the privilege of converting to common stock, two different amounts of per share earnings should ordinarily be reported. One amount is computed without regard to the conversion privilege and is referred to as "Earnings per common share—assuming no dilution" or "Primary earnings per share." The other computation is based on the assumption that the convertible preferred stock or bonds are converted to common stock, and the amount is referred to as "Earnings per common share—assuming full dilution" or "Fully diluted earnings per share."[13]

The details of the computation of earnings per share should be disclosed in notes to the financial statements, as indicated by the following note adapted from the 1986 statements of Colgate-Palmolive Company:

> Earnings per common share is determined by dividing net earnings (after deducting dividends on preferred shares) by the weighted average number of shares outstanding. The dilution that could result from the exercise of stock options and conversion of second preferred stock is not material.

The complexities of the computation of earnings per share and other complexities of capital structure are discussed in more advanced accounting texts.

Start here
go to end

APPROPRIATION OF RETAINED EARNINGS

The amount of a corporation's retained earnings available for distribution to its shareholders may be limited by action of the board of directors. The amount restricted, which is called an **appropriation** or a **reserve,** remains a part of retained earnings and should be so classified in the financial statements. An appropriation can be effected by transferring the desired amount from Retained Earnings to a special account designating its purpose, such as Appropriation for Plant Expansion.

Appropriations may be initiated by the directors, or they may be required by law or contract. Some states require that a corporation retain earnings equal to the amount paid for treasury stock. For example, if a corporation with accumulated earnings of $200,000 purchases shares of its own issued stock for $50,000, the corporation would not be permitted to pay more than $150,000 in dividends. The restriction is equal to the $50,000 paid for the treasury stock and assures that legal capital will not be impaired by a declaration of dividends. The entry to record the appropriation would be:

Apr. 24	Retained Earnings	50,000	
	Appropriation for Treasury Stock		50,000

When a part or all of an appropriation is no longer needed, the amount should be transferred back to the retained earnings account. Thus, if the corporation in the above illustration sells the treasury stock, the appropriation would be eliminated by the following entry:

[13] *Opinions of the Accounting Principles Board, No. 15,* "Earnings per Share" (New York: American Institute of Certified Public Accountants, 1969) par. 16.

Nov. 10	Appropriation for Treasury Stock	50,000	
	Retained Earnings		50,000

When a corporation borrows a large amount through the issuance of bonds (debt), the agreement may provide for restrictions on dividends until the debt is paid. The contract may stipulate that retained earnings equal to the amount borrowed be restricted during the entire period of the loan, or it may require that the restriction be built up by annual appropriations. For example, assume that a corporation borrows $700,000 on ten-year bonds. If equal annual appropriations were to be made over the life of the bonds, there would be a series of ten entries, each in the amount of $70,000, debiting Retained Earnings and crediting an appropriation account entitled Appropriation for Bonded Indebtedness. Even if the bond agreement did not require the restriction on retained earnings, the directors might decide to establish the appropriation. In that case, it would be a *discretionary* rather than a *contractual* appropriation. The entries would be the same in either case.

It must be clearly understood that the appropriation account is not directly related to any certain group of asset accounts. Its existence does not imply that there is an equivalent amount of cash or other assets set aside in a special fund. The appropriation serves the purpose of restricting dividends, but it does not assure that the cash that might otherwise be distributed as dividends will not be invested in additional inventories or other assets, or used to reduce liabilities.

Appropriations of retained earnings may be accompanied by a segregation of cash or marketable securities, in which case the appropriation is said to be **funded.** Accumulation of such funds is discussed in Chapter 12.

There are other purposes for which the directors may consider appropriations desirable. A company may earmark earnings for specific contingencies, such as inventory price declines or an adverse decision on a pending lawsuit. Some companies with properties in many locations may assume their own risk of losses from fire, windstorm, and other casualties rather than obtain protection from insurance companies. In such cases, the appropriation account would be entitled Appropriation for Self-Insurance. Such an appropriation is likely to be permanent, although its amount may vary as the total value of properties and the extent of casualty protection change. If a loss occurs, it should be debited to a special loss account rather than to the appropriation account. It is definitely a loss of the particular period and should be reported in the income statement.

The details of retained earnings may be presented in the balance sheet in the following manner. The item designated "Unappropriated" is the balance of the retained earnings account.

Retained earnings:		
Appropriated:		
For plant expansion	$ 250,000	
Unappropriated	1,800,000	
Total retained earnings		$2,050,000

Restrictions on retained earnings do not need to be formalized in the ledger. However, following legal requirements and contractual restrictions is necessary, and the nature and the amount of all restrictions should always be disclosed in the balance sheet. For example, the appropriations data appearing in the foregoing illustration could be presented in a note accompanying the balance sheet. Such an alternative might also be used as a means of simplifying or condensing the balance sheet, even though appropriation accounts are maintained in the ledger. The alternative balance sheet presentation, including the note, might appear as follows:

Retained earnings (see note)	$2,050,000

Note: Retained earnings in the amount of $250,000 are appropriated for expansion of plant facilities; the remaining $1,800,000 is unrestricted.

When there are accounts for appropriations, it is customary to divide the retained earnings statement into two major sections: (1) appropriated and (2) unappropriated. The first section is composed of an analysis of all appropriation accounts, beginning with the opening balance, followed by the additions or the deductions during the period, and ending with the closing balance. The second section is composed of an analysis of the retained earnings account, beginning with the opening balance, followed by the period's net income, dividends, and transfers to and from the appropriation accounts, and ending with the closing balance. The final figure on the statement is the total retained earnings as of the last day of the period. This form of the statement is illustrated for Shaw Corporation as follows:

Shaw Corporation
Retained Earnings Statement
For Year Ended December 31, 19--

Appropriated:			
Appropriation for plant expansion, January 1, 19--		$ 180,000	
Additional appropriation (see below)		100,000	
Retained earnings appropriated, December 31, 19--			$ 280,000
Unappropriated:			
Balance, January 1, 19--	$1,414,500		
Net income for the year	580,000	$1,994,500	
Cash dividends declared	$ 125,000		
Transfer to appropriation for plant expansion (see above)	100,000	225,000	
Retained earnings unappropriated, December 31, 19--			1,769,500
Total retained earnings, December 31, 19--			$2,049,500

Retained Earnings Statement

There are many possible variations in the form of the retained earnings statement. It may also be added to the income statement to form a combined statement of income and retained earnings, as illustrated in Chapter 4.

NATURE OF DIVIDENDS

A **dividend** is a distribution by a corporation to its shareholders. On common shares, the dividend is usually stated in terms of dollars and cents rather than as a percentage of par. On preferred shares, the dividend may be stated either in monetary terms or as a percentage of par. For example, the annual dividend rate on a particular $100 par preferred stock may be stated as either $10 or 10%.

A dividend usually represents a distribution from retained earnings, and may be paid in cash, in stock of the company, or in other property. A dividend may also represent a distribution from paid-in capital. The types of dividends are discussed in the following paragraphs.

Cash Dividends

A cash distribution of earnings by a corporation to its shareholders is called a **cash dividend.** Cash dividends are the most usual form of dividend. Usually there are three prerequisites to paying a cash dividend:

1. Sufficient unappropriated retained earnings,
2. Sufficient cash, and
3. Formal action by the board of directors.

A large amount of accumulated earnings does not always mean that a corporation is able to pay dividends. There must also be enough cash in excess of routine requirements. The amount of retained earnings, which represents net income retained in the business, is not directly related to cash. The cash provided by the net income may have been used to purchase assets, to reduce liabilities, or for other purposes. The directors are not required by law to declare dividends, even when both retained earnings and cash appear to be sufficient. When a dividend has been declared, however, it becomes a liability of the corporation.

Corporations with a wide distribution of stock usually try to maintain a stable dividend record. They may retain a large part of earnings in good years in order to be able to continue dividend payments in lean years. Dividends may be paid once a year or on a semiannual or quarterly basis. The tendency is to pay quarterly dividends on both common and preferred stock. In particularly good years, the directors may declare an "extra" dividend on common stock. It may be paid at one of the usual dividend dates or at some other date. The designation "extra" indicates that the board of directors does not anticipate an increase in the amount of the "regular" dividend.

Notice of a dividend declaration is usually reported in financial publications and newspapers. The notice identifies three different dates related to a declaration:

1. The date of declaration,
2. The date of record, and
3. The date of payment.

The first is the date the directors take formal action declaring the dividend, the second is the date as of which ownership of shares is to be determined, and the third is the date payment is to be made. For example, a notice read: "On June 26, the board of directors of Campbell Soup Co. declared a quarterly cash dividend of $.33 per common share to stockholders of record as of the close of business on July 8, payable on July 31."

The liability for a dividend is recorded on the declaration date, when the formal action is taken by the directors. No entry is required on the date of record, which merely fixes the date for determining the identity of the stockholders entitled to receive the dividend. The period of time between the record date and the payment date is provided to permit completion of postings to the stockholders ledger and preparation of the dividend checks. The liability of the corporation is paid by the mailing of the checks.

To illustrate the entries required in the declaration and the payment of cash dividends, assume that on December 1 the board of directors of Hiber Corporation declares the regular quarterly dividend of $2.50 on the 5,000 shares of $100 par, 10% preferred stock outstanding (total dividend of $12,500), and a quarterly dividend of 30¢ on the 100,000 shares of $10 par common stock outstanding (total dividend of $30,000). Both dividends are to stockholders of record on December 10, and checks are to be issued to stockholders on January 2. The entry to record the declaration of the dividends is as follows:

Dec. 1	Cash Dividends	42,500	
	Cash Dividends Payable		42,500

The balance in Cash Dividends would be transferred to Retained Earnings as a part of the closing process and Cash Dividends Payable would be listed on the balance sheet as a current liability. Payment of the liability on January 2 would be recorded in the usual manner as a debit to Cash Dividends Payable and a credit to Cash for $42,500.

Dividends on cumulative preferred stock do not become a liability of the corporation until formal action is taken by the board of directors. However, dividends in arrears at a balance sheet date should be disclosed by a footnote, a parenthetical notation, or a segregation of retained earnings similar to the following:

Retained earnings:		
Required to meet dividends in arrears on preferred stock	$30,000	
Remainder, unrestricted	16,000	
Total retained earnings		$46,000

Stock Dividends

A pro rata distribution of shares of stock of a company to the stockholders, accompanied by a transfer of retained earnings to paid-in capital accounts, is called a **stock dividend**. Such distributions are usually in common stock and are issued to holders of common stock. It is possible to issue common stock to preferred stockholders or vice versa, but such stock dividends are too unusual to warrant their consideration here.

Stock dividends are quite unlike cash dividends, in that there is no distribution of cash or other corporate assets to the stockholders. They are ordinarily issued by corporations that "plow back" (retain) earnings for use in acquiring new facilities or for expanding their operations.

The effect of a stock dividend on the capital structure of the issuing corporation is to transfer accumulated earnings to paid-in capital. The statutes of most states require that an amount equivalent to the par or stated value of a stock dividend be transferred from the retained earnings account to the common stock account. Compliance with this minimum requirement is considered by accountants to be satisfactory for a nonpublic corporation, whose stockholders are presumed to have enough knowledge of the corporation's affairs to recognize the true import of the dividend. However, many investors in the stock of public corporations are often less knowledgeable. An analysis of this latter situation, and the widely accepted viewpoint of professional accountants, has been expressed as follows:

> *. . . many recipients of stock dividends look upon them as distributions of corporate earnings and usually in an amount equivalent to the fair value of the additional shares received. Furthermore, it is to be presumed that such views of recipients are materially strengthened in those instances, which are by far the most numerous, where the issuances are so small in comparison with the shares previously outstanding that they do not have any apparent effect upon the share market price and, consequently, the market value of the shares previously held remains substantially unchanged. The committee therefore believes that where these circumstances exist the corporation should in the public interest account for the transaction by transferring from [retained earnings] to the category of permanent capitalization . . . an amount equal to the fair value of the additional shares issued. Unless this is done, the amount of earnings which the shareholder may believe to have been distributed to him will be left, except to the extent otherwise dictated by legal requirements, in [retained earnings] subject to possible further similar stock issuances or cash distributions.*[14]

To illustrate the issuance of a stock dividend according to the procedure recommended above, assume the following balances in the stockholders' equity accounts of Montag Corporation as of December 15:

Common Stock, $20 par (2,000,000 shares issued)	$40,000,000
Premium on Common Stock	9,000,000
Retained Earnings	26,600,000

On December 15, the board of directors declares a 5% stock dividend (100,000 shares, $20 par), to be issued on January 10. Assuming that the average of the high and low market prices on the declaration date is $31 a share, the entry to record the declaration would be as follows:

Dec. 15	Stock Dividends	3,100,000	
	Stock Dividends Distributable		2,000,000
	Premium on Common Stock		1,100,000

The $3,100,000 debit to Stock Dividends would be transferred to Retained Earnings as a part of the closing process. The issuance of the stock certificates would be recorded on January 10 as follows:

Jan. 10	Stock Dividends Distributable	2,000,000	
	Common Stock		2,000,000

The effect of the stock dividend is to transfer $3,100,000 from the retained earnings account to paid-in capital accounts and to increase by 100,000 the number of shares outstanding. There is no change in the assets, liabilities, or total stockholders' equity of the corporation. If financial statements are pre-

---

[14] *Accounting Research and Terminology Bulletins—Final Edition,* "No. 43, Restatement and Revision of Accounting Research Bulletins" (New York: American Institute of Certified Public Accountants, 1961), Ch. 7, Sec. B, par. 10.

pared between the date of declaration and the date of issuance, the stock dividends distributable account should be listed in the paid-in capital section of the balance sheet.

The issuance of the additional shares does not affect the total amount of a stockholder's equity and proportionate interest in the corporation. The effect of the stock dividend on the accounts of a corporation and on the equity of a stockholder owning 1,000 shares is demonstrated by the following tabulation:

The Corporation	*Before Stock Dividend*	*After Stock Dividend*
Common stock	$40,000,000	$42,000,000
Premium on common stock	9,000,000	10,100,000
Retained earnings	26,600,000	23,500,000
Total stockholders' equity	$75,600,000	$75,600,000
Number of shares outstanding	2,000,000	2,100,000
Equity per share	$37.80	$36.00
A Stockholder		
Number of shares owned	1,000	1,050
Total equity	$37,800	$37,800
Portion of corporation owned	.05%	.05%

Liquidating Dividends

The term **liquidating dividend** is applied to a distribution to stockholders from paid-in capital. Such dividends are unusual, but in many states they may be declared from the excess of paid-in capital over par or stated value. Liquidating dividends are usually paid when a corporation permanently reduces its operations or winds up its affairs completely. Since dividends are normally paid from retained earnings, dividends that reduce paid-in capital should be identified as liquidating dividends when paid.

STOCK SPLITS

Corporations sometimes reduce the par or stated value of their common stock and issue a proportionate number of additional shares. Such a procedure is called a **stock split** or **stock split-up.** The primary purpose of a stock split is to bring about a reduction in the market price per share and thus to encourage more investors to enter the market for the company's shares. This purpose was expressed by the Chairman and Chief Executive Officer of Nord Resources Corporation in a letter to shareholders on January 28, 1987, in these terms: "This stock split will be a significant step in improving the market liquidity of the Corporation's shares and further enhance the Corporation's ability to compete in the financial marketplace."

To illustrate a stock split, assume that the board of directors of Riley Corporation, which has 10,000 shares of $100 par stock outstanding, reduces the par to $20 and increases the number of shares to 50,000. The amount of stock outstanding is $1,000,000 both before and after the stock split. Only the number of shares and the par per share are changed. Since there are no changes in the balances of any of the corporation's accounts, no entry to record the stock split is required.

Each shareholder in a corporation whose stock is split owns the same total par amount of stock before and after the stock split. For example, a Riley Corporation stockholder who owned 100 shares of $100 par stock before the split (total par of $10,000) would own 500 shares of $20 par stock after the split (total par of $10,000).

DIVIDENDS AND STOCK SPLITS FOR TREASURY STOCK

Cash or property dividends are not paid on treasury stock. To do so would place the corporation in the position of earning income through dealing with itself. Accordingly, the total amount of a cash (or property) dividend should be based on the number of shares outstanding at the record date.

When a corporation holding treasury stock declares a stock dividend, the number of shares to be issued may be based on either (1) the number of shares outstanding or (2) the number of shares issued. In practice, the number of shares held as treasury stock represents a small percent of the number of shares issued. Also, the rate of dividend is usually small, so that the difference between the end results of both methods is usually not significant.

There is no legal, theoretical, or practical reason for excluding treasury stock when computing the number of shares to be issued in a stock split. The reduction in par or stated value would apply to all shares of the class, including the unissued, issued, and treasury shares.

Chapter Review

KEY POINTS

1. Paid-In Capital.
Although paid-in capital usually results from the issuance of stock, it may also originate from donated assets and redemptions of a corporation's own stock. Many variations in terminology and arrangement of the paid-in capital section of the balance sheet exist. Significant changes in paid-in capital during a period should be disclosed.

2. Corporate Earnings and Income Taxes.
Unlike sole proprietorships and partnerships, corporations are subject to federal income tax and, in many cases, to income taxes levied by states or other political subdivisions. Most corporations are required to estimate the amount of their federal income tax expense for the year and make advance payment, usually in four installments. At the end of the year, the actual taxable income and the actual tax are determined. If an additional amount is owed, a liability is recorded. If an overpayment occurs, the amount would be debited to a receivable account and credited to Income Tax.

3. Allocation of Income Tax Between Periods.
The taxable income of a corporation, determined according to the tax laws, is often different from the amount of income (before income tax) determined from the accounts and reported in the income statement. This difference may

need to be allocated between periods, depending upon whether it is a permanent difference or a temporary difference.

The tax laws provide for special treatment of certain revenue and expense items. This special treatment results in permanent differences between the amount of income tax actually owed and the amount that would be owed if the tax laws were based on income before income tax. Permanent differences cause no problems for financial reporting. The amount of income tax determined in accordance with the tax laws is the amount reported on the income statement.

The treatment of certain items results in differences between income before income tax and taxable income, because the items are recognized in one period for income statement purposes and in another period for tax purposes. These temporary differences turn around in later years. Temporary differences require special treatment in the accounts. The income tax to be reported on the income statement should be the total tax expected to result from the net income reported for that period. The difference between the amount of income tax based on reported net income and the amount based on taxable income is debited or credited to a deferred income tax account. The deferred income tax account will normally have a credit balance and is reported on the balance sheet as a current liability or a long-term liability, depending on when the items to which it relates will reverse their effects on taxable income.

4. Reporting Unusual Items in the Financial Statements.
General guidelines have been developed for reporting unusual items related to the determination of net income. Material errors related to a prior period are reported as an adjustment to the retained earnings balance at the beginning of the period in which the correction is made. Any financial statements presented for the prior period should be restated, and the current period financial statements should clearly set forth the adjustment necessary to the retained earnings account.

A gain or loss resulting from the disposal of a segment of a business should be identified on the income statement as a gain or loss from discontinued operations. In addition, the results of continuing operations should be identified in the income statement. Details of the discontinued operations should also be disclosed in a note to the financial statements.

Extraordinary gains and losses result from events and transactions that are distinguished by their unusual nature and the infrequency of their occurrence. Such gains and losses, other than those from the disposal of a segment of a business, should be identified in the income statement as extraordinary items.

A change in accounting principle results from the adoption of a generally accepted accounting principle different from the one used previously for reporting purposes. The effect of the change in principle on net income in the current period, as well as the cumulative effect on income of prior periods, should be disclosed. Details describing the change in accounting principle are also normally disclosed in an accompanying note to the financial statements.

The amount reported as a prior period adjustment, a gain or loss from discontinued operations, an extraordinary item, or the cumulative effect of a change in accounting principle should be net of the related income tax. The amount of income tax allocable to each of these items should bé disclosed on the face of the appropriate financial statement or by an accompanying note.

5. Earnings per Common Share.
Data on earnings per share of common stock are reported on the income statements of public corporations. If preferred stock is outstanding, the net income must be reduced by the amount of any preferred dividend requirements before dividing by the number of common shares outstanding. If there are nonrecurring items on the income statement, the per share amount should be presented for (1) income from continuing operations, (2) income before extraordinary items and the cumulative effect of a change in accounting principle, (3) the cumulative effect of a change in accounting principle, and (4) net income. Presentation of per share amounts is optional for a gain or loss on discontinued operations and for extraordinary items.

6. Appropriation of Retained Earnings.
The amount of a corporation's retained earnings available for distribution to its shareholders may be limited by action of the board of directors or by law or contract. The amount restricted, called an appropriation or a reserve, remains a part of retained earnings. An appropriation of retained earnings is not directly related to any certain group of assets, and its existence does not imply that there is an equivalent amount of cash or other assets set aside in a special fund. However, appropriations may be accompanied by a segregation of cash or marketable securities, in which case the appropriation is said to be funded. Appropriations of retained earnings should be clearly set forth in the retained earnings statement and should be properly identified on the face of the balance sheet or in an accompanying note.

It is customary to divide the retained earnings statement into two major sections: (1) appropriated and (2) unappropriated. Each of these sections should identify the beginning balance and any additions or deductions during the period.

7. Nature of Dividends.
A dividend is a distribution by a corporation to its shareholders. Dividends may be paid in cash, in stock of the company, or in other property. Three dates are important in the distribution of dividends. (1) The date of declaration is the date on which the directors take formal action to declare the dividend and on which the dividend is recorded in the accounting records. (2) The date of record is the date on which ownership of shares is to be determined for purposes of distribution of the dividend. (3) The date of payment is the date on which the dividend is to be distributed or paid.

Dividends on cumulative preferred stock do not become a liability of the corporation until formal action is taken by the board of directors. However, dividends in arrears at a balance sheet date should be disclosed by a footnote, a parenthetical notation, or a segregation of retained earnings.

A stock dividend is a pro rata distribution of shares of stock to stockholders. The effect of a stock dividend on the capital structure of the issuing corporation is to transfer accumulated earnings to paid-in capital. There is no change in the assets, liabilities, or total stockholders' equity of the corporation.

A dividend distribution to stockholders from paid-in capital is known as a liquidating dividend. Such dividends are usually paid when a corporation permanently reduces its operations or winds up its affairs completely. Because of the unusual nature of liquidating dividends, they should be clearly identified in the financial statements.

8. Stock Splits.
When a corporation reduces the par or stated value of its common stock and issues a proportionate number of additional shares, a stock split or stock split-up has occurred. Because only the number of shares and the par amount per share of stock is changed during a stock split, there are no changes in the balances of any corporation accounts, and no entry is required. Each shareholder owns the same total par amount of stock before and after a stock split. The primary purpose of a stock split is to reduce the market price per share and encourage more investors to enter the market for the company's shares.

9. Dividends and Stock Splits for Treasury Stock.
Cash or property dividends are not paid on treasury stock. To do so would place the corporation in a position of earning income through dealing with itself. However, when a stock dividend or a stock split occurs, treasury shares may or may not participate, depending upon action of the board of directors.

KEY TERMS

taxable income 408
prior period adjustments 412
discontinued operations 413
extraordinary items 414
earnings per share 416
appropriation of
  retained earnings 418
funded 419
dividend 420
cash dividend 421
stock dividend 422
liquidating dividend 424
stock split 424

SELF-EXAMINATION QUESTIONS

(Answers at End of Chapter)

1. Paid-in capital for a corporation may originate from which of the following sources?
   A. Real estate donated to the corporation
   B. Redemption of the corporation's own stock
   C. Sale of the corporation's treasury stock
   D. All of the above

2. During its first year of operations, a corporation elected to use the straight-line method of depreciation for financial reporting purposes and the sum-of-the-years-digits method in determining taxable income. If the income tax is 40% and the amount of depreciation expense is $60,000 under the straight-line method and $100,000 under the sum-of-the-years-digits method, what is the amount of income tax deferred to future years?
   A. $16,000 C. $40,000
   B. $24,000 D. None of the above

3. An item treated as a prior period adjustment should be reported in the financial statements as:
   A. an extraordinary item
   B. an other expense item
   C. an adjustment of the beginning balance of retained earnings
   D. none of the above

4. A material gain resulting from the condemnation of land for public use would be reported on the income statement as:
   A. an extraordinary item
   B. an other income item
   C. an item of revenue from sales
   D. none of the above

5. An appropriation for plant expansion would be reported on the balance sheet in:
   A. the plant assets section
   B. the long-term liabilities section
   C. the stockholders' equity section
   D. none of the above

ILLUSTRATIVE PROBLEM

During its current fiscal year ended December 31, Block Inc. completed the following selected transactions:

Jan. 9. Purchased 1,500 shares of own common stock at $16, recording the stock at cost. (Prior to the purchase there were 70,000 shares of $10 par common stock outstanding.)

Mar. 16. Discovered that a receipt of $500 cash on account from I. Jonson had been posted in error to the account of I. Johnson. The transaction was recorded correctly in the journal.

May 18. Declared a semiannual dividend of $1 on the 10,000 shares of preferred stock and a 20¢ dividend on the common stock to stockholders of record on May 28, payable on June 10.

June 10. Paid the cash dividends.

Aug. 23. Sold 1,000 shares of treasury stock at $18, receiving cash.

Nov. 12. Declared semiannual dividends of $1 on the preferred stock and 20¢ on the common stock. In addition, a 5% common stock dividend was declared on the common stock outstanding, to be capitalized at the fair market value of the common stock, which is estimated at $16.

Dec. 4. Paid the cash dividends and issued the certificates for the common stock dividend.

31. Recorded $75,000 additional federal income tax allocable to net income for the year. Of this amount, $65,600 is a current liability and $9,400 is deferred.

31. The board of directors authorized the appropriation necessitated by the holding of treasury stock.

Instructions:

Prepare the journal entries to record the transactions for Block Inc.

SOLUTION

Jan. 9	Treasury Stock	24,000	
	Cash		24,000
Mar. 16	No entry. Error can be corrected by revising the postings in the subsidiary accounts receivable ledger.		

May 18	Cash Dividends	23,700	
	Cash Dividends Payable		23,700
June 10	Cash Dividends Payable	23,700	
	Cash		23,700
Aug. 23	Cash	18,000	
	Treasury Stock		16,000
	Paid-In Capital from Sale of Treasury Stock		2,000
Nov. 12	Cash Dividends	23,900	
	Stock Dividends	55,600	
	Cash Dividends Payable		23,900
	Stock Dividends Distributable		34,750
	Premium on Common Stock		20,850
Dec. 4	Cash Dividends Payable	23,900	
	Stock Dividends Distributable	34,750	
	Cash		23,900
	Common Stock		34,750
31	Income Tax	75,000	
	Income Tax Payable		65,600
	Deferred Income Tax Payable		9,400
31	Retained Earnings	8,000	
	Appropriation for Treasury Stock		8,000

Discussion Questions

11–1. What are the titles of the two principal subdivisions of the stockholders' equity section of a corporate balance sheet?

11–2. If a corporation is given land as an inducement to locate in a particular community, (a) how should the amount of the debit to the land account be determined, and (b) what is the title of the account that should be credited for the same amount?

11–3. A corporation has paid $300,000 of federal income tax during the year on the basis of its estimated income. What entry should be recorded as of the end of the year if it determines that (a) it owes an additional $10,000? (b) it overpaid its tax by $20,000?

11–4. The income before income tax reported on the income statement for the year is $600,000. Because of timing differences between accounting and tax methods, the taxable income for the same year is $450,000. Assuming an income tax rate of 40%, state (a) the amount of income tax to be deducted from the $600,000 on the income statement, (b) the amount of the actual income tax that should be paid for the year, and (c) the amount of the deferred income tax liability.

11–5. How would the amount of deferred income tax payable be reported in the balance sheet (a) if it is payable within one year, and (b) if it is payable beyond one year?

11–6. Indicate how prior period adjustments would be reported on the financial statements presented only for the current period.

11–7. Indicate where the following should be reported in the financial statements, assuming that financial statements are presented only for the current year:
(a) Loss on disposal of equipment considered to be obsolete.
(b) Uninsured loss on building due to hurricane damage. The firm was organized in 1905, and had not previously incurred hurricane damage.

11–8. Classify each of the following revenue and expense items as either (a) normally recurring or (b) extraordinary. Assume that the amount of each item is material.

(1) Uninsured flood loss. (Flood insurance is unavailable because of periodic flooding in the area.)
(2) Uncollectible accounts expense.
(3) Interest income on notes receivable.
(4) Gain on sale of land condemned for public use.
(5) Loss on sale of plant assets.
(6) Salaries of corporate officers.

11–9. During the current year, ten acres of land which cost $75,000 were condemned for construction of an interstate highway. Assuming that an award of $125,000 in cash was received and that the applicable income tax on this transaction is 25%, how would this information be presented in the income statement?

11–10. A corporation reports earnings per share of $5.75 for the most recent year and $4.75 for the preceding year. The $5.75 includes $1.50 per share gain from a sale of the only investment owned since the business was organized in 1939. (a) Should the composition of the $5.75 be disclosed in the financial reports? (b) What is the earnings per share amount for the most recent year that is comparable to the $4.75 earnings per share of the preceding year? (c) On the basis of the limited information presented, would you conclude that operations had improved or declined?

11–11. Appropriations of retained earnings may be (a) required by law, (b) required by contract, or (c) made at the discretion of the board of directors. Give an illustration of each type of appropriation.

11–12. A credit balance in Retained Earnings does not represent cash. Explain.

11–13. The board of directors votes to appropriate $100,000 of retained earnings for bonded indebtedness. What is the effect of this action on (a) cash, (b) total retained earnings, and (c) retained earnings available for dividends?

11–14. What are the three prerequisites of the declaration and the payment of a cash dividend?

11–15. The dates in connection with the declaration of a cash dividend are June 15, July 1, and July 15. Identify each date.

11–16. A corporation with both cumulative preferred stock and common stock outstanding has a substantial credit balance in its retained earnings account at the beginning of the current fiscal year. Although net income for the current year is sufficient to pay the preferred dividend of $25,000 each quarter and a common dividend of $40,000 each quarter, the board of directors declares dividends only on the preferred stock. Suggest possible reasons for passing the dividends on the common stock.

11–17. State the effect of the following actions on a corporation's assets, liabilities, and stockholders' equity: (a) declaration of a cash dividend; (b) payment of the cash dividend declared in (a); (c) declaration of a stock dividend; (d) issuance of stock certificates for the stock dividend declared in (c); (e) authorization and issuance of stock certificates in a stock split.

11–18. An owner of 100 shares of Randall Company common stock receives a stock dividend of 5 shares. (a) What is the effect of the stock dividend on the equity per share of the stock? (b) How does the total equity of 105 shares compare with the total equity of 100 shares before the stock dividend?

11–19. What term is used to identify a distribution to stockholders from paid-in capital?

11–20. A corporation with 5,000 shares of no-par common stock issued, of which 200 shares are held as treasury stock, declares a cash dividend of $1 a share. What is the total amount of the dividend?

11–21. If a corporation with 10,000 shares of common stock outstanding has a 4-for-1 stock split (3 additional shares each share issued), what will be the number of shares outstanding after the split?

11–22. If the common stock in Question 11–21 had a market price of $200 per share before the stock split, what would be an approximate market price per share after the split?

11–23. Real World Focus. The 1986 annual report of The Sherwin-Williams Company disclosed the discontinuance of its drug stores segment. The summarized 1986 operating results (in thousands of dollars) for the discontinued operations are as follows:

Net sales	$700,258
Operating profit	10,072
Income (loss) before income tax benefit	8,448
Income tax benefit	1,543
Income from discontinued operations—net of tax	$ 9,991

Indicate how the income (loss) from discontinued operations should be reported by Sherwin-Williams Company on its income statement for the year ended December 31, 1986.

Exercises

11–24. Income tax entries. Present entries to record the following selected transactions of CPD Inc.:

Apr. 15. Paid the first installment of the estimated income tax for the current fiscal year ending December 31, $175,000. No entry had been made to record the liability.

June 15. Paid the second installment of $175,000.

Dec. 31. Recorded the additional income tax liability for the year just ended and the deferred income tax liability, based on the two transactions above and the following data:

Income tax rate	40%
Income before income tax	$1,900,000
Taxable income according to tax return	1,775,000
Third installment paid on September 15	175,000
Fourth installment paid on December 15	175,000

11–25. Retained earnings statement with prior period adjustment. Howard Trier and Company reported the following results of transactions affecting retained earnings for the current year ended December 31, 1989:

Net income	$97,500
Dividends	50,000
Prior period adjustment for understatement of merchandise inventory on December 31, 1988, net of applicable income tax of $8,000	11,000

Assuming that the retained earnings balance reported on the retained earnings statement as of December 31, 1988, was $212,500, prepare a retained earnings statement for the year ended December 31, 1989.

11–26. Income statement. On the basis of the following data for the current fiscal year ended September 30, prepare an income statement for Stein Company, including an analysis of earnings per share in the form illustrated in this chapter. There were 50,000 shares of $25 par common stock outstanding throughout the year.

Cost of merchandise sold	$609,600
Cumulative effect on prior years of changing to a different depreciation method	68,500
Gain on condemnation of land (extraordinary item)	57,750
General expenses	46,250
Income tax applicable to change in depreciation method	20,500
Income tax applicable to gain on condemnation of land	16,750
Income tax reduction applicable to loss from discontinued operations	22,500
Income tax applicable to ordinary income	108,000
Loss on discontinued operations	74,500
Sales	979,600
Selling expenses	74,750

11–27. Entries for treasury stock. A corporation purchased for cash 5,000 shares of its own $10 par common stock at $15 a share. In the following year, it sold 2,000 of the treasury shares at $18 a share for cash. (a) Present the entries (1) to record the purchase (treasury stock is recorded at cost) and (2) to provide for the appropriation of retained earnings. (b) Present the entries (1) to record the sale of the stock and (2) to reduce the appropriation.

11–28. Entries for cash dividends. The dates in connection with a cash dividend of $25,000 on a corporation's common stock are January 9, January 28, and February 14. Present the entries required on each date.

11–29. Stock dividends; equity per share. The following account balances appear on the balance sheet of Haris Company: Common stock (10,000 shares authorized), $50 par, $400,000; Premium on common stock, $52,250; and Retained earnings, $219,750. The board of directors declared a 5% stock dividend when the market price of the stock was $65 a share. (a) Present entries to record (1) the declaration of the dividend, capitalizing an amount equal to market value, and (2) the issuance of the stock certificates. (b) Determine the equity per share (1) before the stock dividend and (2) after the stock dividend. (c) Linda Celise owned 100 shares of the common stock before the stock dividend was declared. Determine the total equity of her holdings (1) before the stock dividend and (2) after the stock dividend.

11–30. Stock split. The board of directors of Magno Corporation authorized the reduction of par of its common shares from $100 to $25, increasing the number of outstanding shares to 400,000. The market price of the stock immediately before the stock split was $180 a share. (a) Determine the number of outstanding shares prior to the stock split. (b) Present the entry to record the stock split. (c) At approximately what price would a share of stock be expected to sell immediately after the stock split?

11–31. Retained earnings statement. Rittenhouse Corporation reports the following results of transactions affecting net income and retained earnings for its first fiscal year of operations ended on December 31:

Appropriation for plant expansion	$ 25,000
Cash dividends declared	50,000
Income before income tax	147,500
Income tax	49,500

Prepare a retained earnings statement for the fiscal year ended December 31.

Problems

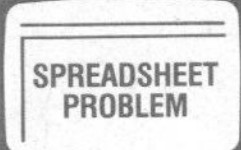

11–32. Income tax allocation. Differences between the accounting methods applied to accounts and financial reports and those used in determining taxable income yielded the following amounts for the first four years of a corporation's operations:

	First Year	Second Year	Third Year	Fourth Year
Income before income tax.	$290,000	$370,000	$460,000	$440,000
Taxable income.	240,000	340,000	470,000	480,000

The income tax rate for each of the four years was 35% of taxable income, and each year's taxes were promptly paid.

Instructions: (1) Determine for each year the amounts described in the following columnar captions, presenting the information in the form indicated:

			Deferred Income Tax Payable	
Year	Income Tax Deducted on Income Statement	Income Tax Payments for the Year	Year's Addition (Deduction)	Year-End Balance

(2) Total the first three amount columns.

11–33. Entries for selected corporate transactions. Selected transactions completed by Golan Corporation during the current fiscal year are as follows:

Jan. 4. Split the common stock 5 for 1 and reduced the par from $50 to $10 per share. After the split, there were 80,000 common shares outstanding.

25. Declared semiannual dividends of $5 on 10,000 shares of preferred stock and 50¢ on the 80,000 shares of $10 par common stock to stockholders of record on February 14, payable on February 22.

Feb. 22. Paid the cash dividends.

Mar. 6. Purchased 5,000 shares of the corporation's own common stock at $16, recording the stock at cost.

Apr. 29. Discovered that a receipt of $1,725 cash on account from C. W. Smith Co. had been posted in error to the account of John Smid Inc. The transaction was recorded correctly in the journal.

July 10. Sold 1,000 shares of treasury stock at $22, receiving cash.

23. Declared semiannual dividends of $5 on the preferred stock and 50¢ on the common stock. In addition, a 2% common stock dividend was declared on the common stock outstanding, to be capitalized at the fair market value of the common stock, which is estimated at $20.

Aug. 25. Paid the cash dividends and issued the certificates for the common stock dividend.

Nov. 8. Discovered that an invoice of $825 for utilities expense for the month of October was debited to Office Supplies.

Dec. 31. Recorded $112,500 additional federal income tax allocable to net income for the year. Of this amount, $83,000 is a current liability and $29,500 is deferred.

31. The board of directors authorized the appropriation necessitated by the holding of treasury stock.

Instructions: Record the transactions.

11–34. Retained earnings statement. The retained earnings accounts of Tardy Corporation for the current fiscal year ended December 31 are as follows:

ACCOUNT APPROPRIATION FOR PLANT EXPANSION ACCOUNT NO. 3201

Date		Item	Debit	Credit	Balance Debit	Balance Credit
19--						
Jan.	1	Balance				200,000
Dec.	31	Retained earnings		50,000		250,000

ACCOUNT APPROPRIATION FOR TREASURY STOCK ACCOUNT NO. 3202

Date		Item	Debit	Credit	Balance Debit	Balance Credit
19--						
Jan.	1	Balance				300,000
Dec.	31	Retained earnings	30,000			270,000

ACCOUNT RETAINED EARNINGS ACCOUNT NO. 3301

Date		Item	Debit	Credit	Balance Debit	Balance Credit
19--						
Jan.	1	Balance				515,000
Dec.	31	Income summary		190,000		705,000
	31	Appropriation for plant expansion	50,000			655,000
	31	Appropriation for treasury stock		30,000		685,000
	31	Cash dividends	50,000			635,000
	31	Stock dividends	100,000			535,000

ACCOUNT CASH DIVIDENDS ACCOUNT NO. 3302

Date		Item	Debit	Credit	Balance Debit	Balance Credit
19--						
Mar.	2		25,000		25,000	
Sept.	7		25,000		50,000	
Dec.	31	Retained earnings		50,000	—	—

ACCOUNT STOCK DIVIDENDS ACCOUNT NO. 3303

Date		Item	Debit	Credit	Balance Debit	Balance Credit
19--						
Sept.	7		100,000		100,000	
Dec.	31	Retained earnings		100,000	—	—

Instructions: Prepare a retained earnings statement for the fiscal year ended December 31.

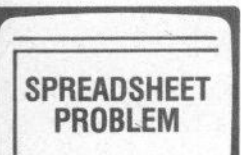

11–35. Income statement. The following data were selected from the records of A. Jones Inc. for the current fiscal year ended December 31:

Advertising expense	$ 24,000
Delivery expense	9,900
Depreciation expense—office equipment	4,250
Depreciation expense—store equipment	11,000
Gain on condemnation of land	50,000

Income tax:	
Applicable to continuing operations	$ 55,000
Applicable to loss from disposal of a segment of a business (reduction)	5,000
Applicable to gain on condemnation of land	15,000
Insurance expense	9,100
Interest income	13,700
Loss from disposal of a segment of the business	25,000
Merchandise inventory (January 1)	97,750
Merchandise inventory (December 31)	105,000
Miscellaneous general expense	2,800
Miscellaneous selling expense	3,500
Office salaries expense	46,000
Office supplies expense	1,750
Purchases	602,250
Rent expense	30,000
Sales	987,500
Sales commissions expense	44,900
Sales salaries expense	56,400
Store supplies expense	2,600

Instructions: Prepare a multiple-step income statement, concluding with a section for earnings per share in the form illustrated in this chapter. There were 50,000 shares of common stock (no preferred) outstanding throughout the year. Assume that the condemnation of land is an extraordinary item.

11–36. Entries for selected corporate transactions. The stockholders' equity accounts of Wright Enterprises Inc., with balances on January 1 of the current fiscal year, are as follows:

Common Stock, stated value $10 (100,000 shares authorized, 80,000 shares issued)	$800,000
Paid-In Capital in Excess of Stated Value	70,000
Appropriation for Plant Expansion	100,000
Appropriation for Treasury Stock	37,500
Retained Earnings	422,750
Treasury Stock (3,000 shares, at cost)	37,500

The following selected transactions occurred during the year:

Jan. 29. Paid cash dividends of $1 per share on the common stock. The dividend had been properly recorded when declared on December 28 of the preceding fiscal year.
Feb. 25. Sold all of the treasury stock for $45,000.
May 5. Issued 10,000 shares of common stock for $130,000 cash.
June 11. Received land with an estimated fair market value of $50,000 from the Naples City Council as a donation.
July 30. Declared a 5% stock dividend on common stock, to be capitalized at the market price of the stock, which is $15 a share.
Aug. 27. Issued the certificates for the dividend declared on July 30.
Oct. 8. Purchased 2,500 shares of treasury stock for $25,000.
Dec. 20. Declared a $1 per share dividend on common stock.
20. The board of directors authorized the increase of the appropriation for plant expansion by $25,000.
20. Decreased the appropriation for treasury stock to $25,000.
31. Closed the credit balance of the income summary account, $132,500.
31. Closed the two dividends accounts to Retained Earnings.

Instructions: (1) Open T accounts for the stockholders' equity accounts listed and enter the balances as of January 1. Also open T accounts for the following: Paid-In Capital from

Sale of Treasury Stock; Donated Capital; Stock Dividends Distributable; Stock Dividends; Cash Dividends.

(2) Prepare entries to record the transactions and post to the eleven selected accounts.

(3) Prepare the stockholders' equity section of the balance sheet as of December 31 of the current fiscal year.

11–37. Stockholders' equity transactions and statements. The stockholders' equity section of the balance sheet of KGM Industries as of January 1 is as follows:

Stockholders' Equity			
Paid-in capital:			
Common stock, $20 par (100,000 shares authorized, 40,000 shares issued)	$800,000		
Premium on common stock	150,000		
Total paid-in capital		$ 950,000	
Retained earnings:			
Appropriated for bonded indebtedness	$275,000		
Unappropriated	530,000		
Total retained earnings		805,000	
Total		$1,755,000	
Deduct treasury stock (5,000 shares at cost) ..		125,000	
Total stockholders' equity			$1,630,000

The following selected transactions occurred during the fiscal year:

Feb. 2. Issued 10,000 shares of stock in exchange for land and buildings with an estimated fair market value of $75,000 and $300,000 respectively. The property was encumbered by a mortgage of $125,000, and the company agreed to assume the responsibility for paying the mortgage note.

May 30. Sold all of the treasury stock for $150,000.

June 25. Declared a cash dividend of $2 per share to stockholders of record on July 15, payable on July 30.

July 30. Paid the cash dividend declared on June 25.

Sept. 2. Received additional land valued at $50,000. The land was donated for a plant site by the Bonita Industrial Development Council.

Dec. 1. Issued 1,000 shares of stock to officers as a salary bonus. Market price of the stock is $30 a share. (Debit Officers Salaries Expense.)

Dec. 10. Declared a 4% stock dividend on the stock outstanding to stockholders of record on December 30 to be issued on January 20. The stock dividend is to be capitalized at the market price of $30 a share.

31. Increased the appropriation for bonded indebtedness by $25,000.

31. Closed the income summary account. After closing all revenue and expense accounts, Income Summary has a credit balance of $195,000.

31. Closed the two dividends accounts to Retained Earnings.

Instructions: (1) Open T accounts for the accounts appearing in the stockholders' equity section of the balance sheet and enter the balances as of January 1. Also open T accounts for the following: Paid-In Capital from Sale of Treasury Stock; Donated Capital; Cash Dividends; Stock Dividends; Stock Dividends Distributable.

(2) Prepare entries to record the transactions and post to the ten selected accounts.

(3) Prepare the stockholders' equity section of the balance sheet as of December 31, the end of the fiscal year.

(4) Prepare a retained earnings statement for the fiscal year ended December 31.

11–38. Correcting entries and financial statements. C. L. Eddy Company is in need of additional cash to expand operations. To raise the needed funds, the company is applying to the Collier County Bank for a loan. For this purpose, the bank requests that the financial statements be audited. To assist the auditor, C. L. Eddy Company's accountant prepared the following financial statements related to the current year:

C. L. Eddy Company
Balance Sheet
December 31, 19--

Current assets:		
Cash	$ 56,250	
Accounts receivable	64,500	
Merchandise inventory	85,750	
Supplies	7,250	$213,750
Plant assets:		
Land	$ 90,000	
Buildings	325,000	
Equipment	132,500	
Patents	45,000	592,500
Total assets		$806,250
Current liabilities:		
Accounts payable	$ 46,500	
Salaries payable	3,500	$ 50,000
Deferred charges:		
Accumulated depreciation—buildings	$ 72,500	
Accumulated depreciation—equipment	37,500	
Allowance for doubtful accounts	3,700	113,700
Stockholders' equity:		
Common stock (100,000 shares authorized, $10 par)	$350,000	
Premium on common stock	45,000	
Retained earnings	165,000	
Net income	82,550	642,550
Total liabilities and stockholders' equity		$806,250

C. L. Eddy Company
Income Statement
For Year Ended December 31, 19--

Revenues:		
Net sales	$722,500	
Gain on expropriation of land	42,000	
Total revenues		$764,500
Expenses:		
Cost of merchandise sold	$440,500	
Salary expense	60,250	
Depreciation expense—buildings	36,900	
Loss on discontinued operations	35,550	
Utilities expense	20,750	
Insurance expense	10,400	
Depreciation expense—equipment	8,500	
Amortization expense—patents	5,000	
Uncollectible accounts expense	3,750	
Miscellaneous general expense	3,350	
Income tax	32,000	
Dividends expense	25,000	
Total expenses		681,950
Net income		$ 82,550

In the course of the audit, the auditor examined the common stock and retained earnings accounts, which appeared as follows:

ACCOUNT COMMON STOCK ($10 Par) ACCOUNT NO. 3200

Date		Item	Debit	Credit	Balance Debit	Balance Credit
19--						
Jan.	1	Balance—30,000 shares				300,000
	2	Issued 3,000 shares for patents		50,000		350,000

ACCOUNT RETAINED EARNINGS ACCOUNT NO. 3300

Date		Item	Debit	Credit	Balance Debit	Balance Credit
19--						
Jan.	1	Balance				97,500
Feb.	1	Donation of land		50,000		147,500
	10	Error correction	7,500			140,000
Dec.	28	Appropriation for land acquisition		25,000		165,000

A closer examination of the transactions in these and other accounts revealed the following details:

(a) The patent acquired on January 2 by an issuance of 3,000 shares of common stock had a fair market value of $50,000 and an estimated useful life of 10 years.

(b) On February 1, the company received a donation of land. The land account was debited for $50,000, the fair market value of the land at that date.

(c) A computational error was made in the calculation of a prior year's dividend. The corrected amount of the dividend was paid on February 10 and debited to the retained earnings account.

(d) In anticipation of further land acquisition, the board of directors on December 28 authorized a $25,000 appropriation of retained earnings that resulted in a debit to Land and a credit to Retained Earnings.

(e) After three years of using the straight-line method of depreciation for the buildings, the company changed to the sum-of-the-years-digits method. The following entry recorded this change:

Depreciation Expense—Buildings	26,900	
Accumulated Depreciation—Buildings		26,900

(f) A $1 cash dividend declared on December 28 and payable on February 9 of the next fiscal year was not recorded. The $25,000 of dividends expense represents the mid-year cash dividend paid on July 30 of the current year.

(g) The income tax of $32,000 is the estimated tax paid during the year. The tax based on the corrected net income was determined to be $33,950, allocated as follows:

(1) Income from continuing operations	$44,500
(2) Loss from discontinued operations	14,100
(3) Gain on expropriation of land	12,300
(4) Cumulative effect of change in depreciation method	8,750

The tax owed of $1,950 at December 31 had not been recorded.

Instructions: (1) Prepare the necessary correcting entries for the items discovered by the independent auditor. Assume that the accounts have not been closed for the current fiscal year.

(2) Prepare a multiple-step income statement for the current fiscal year, including the appropriate earnings per share disclosure. Operating expenses need not be divided into selling and general expense categories.

(continued)

(3) Prepare the retained earnings statement for the current fiscal year.
(4) Prepare a balance sheet as of the end of the current fiscal year.

ALTERNATE PROBLEMS

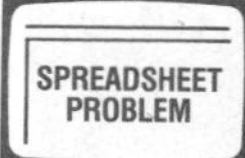

11–32A. Income tax allocation. Differences between the accounting methods applied to accounts and financial reports and those used in determining taxable income yielded the following amounts for the first four years of a corporation's operations:

	First Year	Second Year	Third Year	Fourth Year
Income before income tax.	$210,000	$300,000	$450,000	$488,000
Taxable income.	150,000	260,000	430,000	518,000

The income tax rate for each of the four years was 35% of taxable income, and each year's taxes were promptly paid.

Instructions: (1) Determine for each year the amounts described in the following columnar captions, presenting the information in the form indicated:

Year	Income Tax Deducted on Income Statement	Income Tax Payments for the Year	Deferred Income Tax Payable: Year's Addition (Deduction)	Deferred Income Tax Payable: Year-End Balance

(2) Total the first three amount columns.

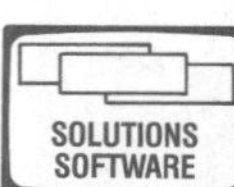

11–33A. Entries for selected corporate transactions. Selected transactions completed by Odell Company during the current fiscal year are as follows:

Jan. 2. Split the common stock 4 for 1 and reduced the par from $100 to $25 per share. After the split, there were 40,000 common shares outstanding.
Feb. 3. Purchased 1,000 shares of the corporation's own common stock at $62, recording the stock at cost.
Mar. 2. Discovered that a receipt of $600 cash on account from A. Baker had been posted in error to the account of C. Barker. The transaction was recorded correctly in the journal.
May 1. Declared semiannual dividends of $5 on 5,000 shares of preferred stock and $1 on the common stock to stockholders of record on May 20, payable on July 15.
July 15. Paid the cash dividends.
Aug. 22. Sold 500 shares of treasury stock at $70, receiving cash.
Nov. 30. Declared semiannual dividends of $5 on the preferred stock and $1.25 on the common stock. In addition, a 5% common stock dividend was declared on the common stock outstanding, to be capitalized at the fair market value of the common stock, which is estimated at $72.
Dec. 30. Paid the cash dividends and issued the certificates for the common stock dividend.
30. Recorded $76,500 additional federal income tax allocable to net income for the year. Of this amount, $51,500 is a current liability and $25,000 is deferred.
30. The board of directors authorized the appropriation necessitated by the holding of treasury stock.

Instructions: Record the transactions.

11–34A. Retained earnings statement. The retained earnings accounts of Pena Corporation for the current fiscal year ended December 31 are as follows:

ACCOUNT APPROPRIATION FOR PLANT EXPANSION ACCOUNT NO. 3201

Date		Item	Debit	Credit	Balance Debit	Balance Credit
19--						
Jan.	1	Balance				300,000
Dec.	31	Retained earnings		50,000		350,000

ACCOUNT APPROPRIATION FOR TREASURY STOCK ACCOUNT NO. 3202

Date		Item	Debit	Credit	Balance Debit	Balance Credit
19--						
Jan.	1	Balance				225,000
Dec.	31	Retained earnings	125,000			100,000

ACCOUNT RETAINED EARNINGS ACCOUNT NO. 3301

Date		Item	Debit	Credit	Balance Debit	Balance Credit
19--						
Jan.	1	Balance				515,000
Dec.	31	Income summary		175,000		690,000
	31	Appropriation for plant expansion	50,000			640,000
	31	Appropriation for treasury stock		125,000		765,000
	31	Cash dividends	150,000			615,000
	31	Stock dividends	125,000			490,000

ACCOUNT CASH DIVIDENDS ACCOUNT NO. 3302

Date		Item	Debit	Credit	Balance Debit	Balance Credit
19--						
Oct.	11		150,000		150,000	
Dec.	31	Retained earnings		150,000	—	—

ACCOUNT STOCK DIVIDENDS ACCOUNT NO. 3303

Date		Item	Debit	Credit	Balance Debit	Balance Credit
19--						
Oct.	11		125,000		125,000	
Dec.	31	Retained earnings		125,000	—	—

Instructions: Prepare a retained earnings statement for the fiscal year ended December 31.

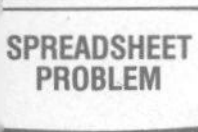

11–35A. Income statement. The following data were selected from the records of A. P. Davis Co. for the current fiscal year ended December 31:

Merchandise inventory (January 1)	$130,000
Merchandise inventory (December 31)	135,500
Office salaries expense	42,750
Depreciation expense—store equipment	9,000
Sales	997,500
Sales salaries expense	42,500
Sales commissions expense	53,500
Advertising expense	27,250
Purchases	605,500
Rent expense	21,000
Delivery expense	19,750
Store supplies expense	7,500
Office supplies expense	1,700
Insurance expense	9,000
Depreciation expense—office equipment	5,200
Miscellaneous selling expense	8,600
Miscellaneous general expense	4,550
Interest expense	25,200
Loss from disposal of a segment of the business	40,200
Gain on condemnation of land	20,000
Income tax:	
Applicable to continuing operations	35,000
Applicable to loss from disposal of a segment of the business (reduction)	8,200
Applicable to gain on condemnation of land	4,000

Instructions: Prepare a multiple-step income statement, concluding with a section for earnings per share in the form illustrated in this chapter. There were 25,000 shares of common stock (no preferred) outstanding throughout the year. Assume that the gain on condemnation of land is an extraordinary item.

11–36A. Entries for selected corporate transactions. The stockholders' equity accounts of Anderson Enterprises Inc., with balances on January 1 of the current fiscal year, are as follows:

Common Stock, stated value $25 (100,000 shares authorized, 50,000 shares issued)	$1,250,000
Paid-In Capital in Excess of Stated Value	450,000
Appropriation for Plant Expansion	250,000
Appropriation for Treasury Stock	120,000
Retained Earnings	575,000
Treasury Stock (4,000 shares, at cost)	120,000

The following selected transactions occurred during the year:

Jan. 15. Received land with an estimated fair market value of $65,000 from the city as a donation.

Jan. 30. Paid cash dividends of $1 per share on the common stock. The dividend had been properly recorded when declared on December 20 of the preceding fiscal year for $46,000.

Feb. 25. Sold all of the treasury stock for $150,000.

Apr. 1. Issued 5,000 shares of common stock for $190,000.

July 1. Declared a 4% stock dividend on common stock, to be capitalized at the market price of the stock, which is $40 a share.

Aug. 11. Issued the certificates for the dividend declared on July 1.

Nov. 20. Purchased 2,000 shares of treasury stock for $72,000.

Dec. 21. The board of directors authorized an increase of the appropriation for plant expansion by $50,000.

21. Declared a $1.10 per share dividend on common stock.

21. Decreased the appropriation for treasury stock to $72,000.

Dec. 31. Closed the credit balance of the income summary account, $196,700.
31. Closed the two dividends accounts to Retained Earnings.

Instructions: (1) Open T accounts for the stockholders' equity accounts listed and enter the balances as of January 1. Also open T accounts for the following: Paid-in Capital from Sale of Treasury Stock; Donated Capital; Stock Dividends Distributable; Stock Dividends; Cash Dividends.

(2) Prepare entries to record the transactions and post to the eleven selected accounts.

(3) Prepare the stockholders' equity section of the balance sheet as of December 31 of the current fiscal year.

Mini-Case 11

Kahn Co. has paid quarterly cash dividends since 1980. These dividends have steadily increased from $.20 per share to the latest dividend declaration of $.50 per share. The board of directors would like to continue this trend and are hesitant to suspend or decrease the amount of quarterly dividends. Unfortunately, sales of Kahn Co. dropped sharply in the fourth quarter of 1989 due to worsening economic conditions and increased competition. As a result, the board is uncertain as to whether it should declare a dividend for the last quarter of 1989.

On November 1, 1989, Kahn Co. borrowed $500,000 from Citizens National Bank to use in modernizing its retail stores and to expand its product line in reaction to its competition. The terms of the 10-year, 12% loan require Kahn Co. to:

(a) Pay monthly the total interest due,
(b) Pay $50,000 of the principal each November 1, beginning in 1990,
(c) Maintain a current ratio (current assets ÷ current liabilities) of 2:1,
(d) Appropriate $500,000 of retained earnings until the loan is fully paid, and
(e) Maintain a minimum balance of $25,000 (called a compensating balance) in its Citizens National Bank account.

On December 31, 1989, 25% of the $500,000 loan had been disbursed in modernization of the retail stores and in expansion of the product line, and the remainder is temporarily invested in U.S. Treasury notes. Kahn Co.'s balance sheet as of December 31, 1989, as follows:

Kahn Co.
Balance Sheet
December 31, 1989

Assets			
Current assets:			
Cash		$ 40,000	
Marketable securities, at cost (market price, $379,500)		375,000	
Accounts receivable	$ 91,500		
Less allowance for doubtful accounts	6,500	85,000	
Merchandise inventory		120,500	
Prepaid expenses		4,500	
Total current assets			$ 625,000
Plant assets:			
Land		$150,000	
Buildings	$950,000		
Less accumulated depreciation	215,000	735,000	
Equipment	$460,000		
Less accumulated depreciation	110,000	350,000	
Total plant assets			1,235,000
Total assets			$1,860,000
Liabilities			
Current liabilities:			
Accounts payable	$ 71,800		
Notes payable (Citizens National Bank)	50,000		
Salaries payable	3,200		
Total current liabilities		$125,000	
Long-term liabilities:			
Notes payable (Citizens National Bank)		450,000	
Total liabilities			$ 575,000
Stockholders' Equity			
Paid-in capital:			
Common stock, $20 par (50,000 shares authorized, 25,000 shares issued)	$500,000		
Premium on common stock	40,000		
Total paid-in capital		$540,000	
Retained earnings:			
Appropriated for provision of Citizens National Bank loan	$500,000		
Unappropriated	245,000		
Total retained earnings		745,000	
Total stockholders' equity			1,285,000
Total liabilities and stockholders' equity			$1,860,000

The board of directors is scheduled to meet January 10, 1990, to discuss the results of operations for 1989 and to consider the declaration of dividends for the fourth quarter of 1989. The chairman of the board has asked for your advice on the declaration of dividends.

Instructions:

(1) What factors should the board consider in deciding whether to declare a cash dividend?
(2) The board is considering the declaration of a stock dividend instead of a cash dividend. Discuss the issuance of a stock dividend from the point of view of (a) a stockholder and (b) the board of directors.

Answers to Self-Examination Questions

1. D Paid-in capital is one of the two major subdivisions of the stockholders' equity of a corporation. It may result from many sources, including the receipt of donated real estate, (answer A), the redemption of a corporation's own stock (answer B), and the sale of a corporation's treasury stock (answer C).

2. A The amount of income tax deferred to future years is $16,000 (answer A), determined as follows:

Depreciation expense, sum-of-the-years-digits method	$100,000
Depreciation expense, straight-line method	60,000
Excess expense in determination of taxable income	$ 40,000
Income tax rate	× 40%
Income tax deferred to future years	$ 16,000

3. C The correction of a material error related to a prior period should be excluded from the determination of net income of the current period and reported as an adjustment of the balance of retained earnings at the beginning of the current period (answer C).

4. A Events and transactions that are distinguished by their unusual nature and by the infrequency of their occurrence, such as a gain on condemnation of land for public use, are reported in the income statement as extraordinary items (answer A).

5. C An appropriation for plant expansion is a portion of total retained earnings and would be reported in the stockholders' equity section of the balance sheet (answer C).

12
Long-Term Liabilities and Investments in Bonds

CHAPTER OBJECTIVES

Describe and illustrate the impact of borrowing on a long-term basis as a means of financing corporations.

Describe the characteristics of bonds.

Describe and illustrate the concept of present value and how it relates to bonds.

Describe and illustrate the accounting for bonds payable.

Describe and illustrate the accounting for bond sinking funds.

Describe and illustrate the accounting for long-term investments in bonds.

The acquisition of cash and other assets by a corporation through the issuance of its stock has been discussed in earlier chapters. Expansion of corporate enterprises through the retention of earnings, in some instances accompanied by the issuance of stock dividends, has also been explored. In addition to these two methods of obtaining relatively permanent funds, corporations may also borrow money on a long-term basis by issuing notes or **bonds,** which are a form of interest-bearing note. Long-term notes may be issued to relatively few lending agencies or to a single investor such as an insurance company. Bonds are usually sold to underwriters (dealers and brokers in securities), who in turn sell them to investors. Although the discussion that follows will be limited to bonds, the accounting principles involved apply equally to long-term notes.

When funds are borrowed through the issuance of bonds, there is a definite commitment to pay interest and to repay the principal at a stated future date. Bondholders are creditors of the issuing corporation and their claims for interest and for repayment of principal rank ahead of the claims of stockholders.

Many factors influence the incorporators or the board of directors in deciding upon the best means of obtaining funds. The subject will be limited here to a brief illustration of the effect of different financing methods on the income of a corporation and the common stockholders. To illustrate, assume that three different plans for financing a $4,000,000 corporation are under consideration by its organizers, and that in each case the securities will be issued at their par or face amount. The incorporators estimate that the enterprise will earn $800,000 annually, before deducting interest on the bonds and income tax estimated at 40% of income. The following tabulation indicates the amount of earnings that would be available to common stockholders under each of the three plans:

	Plan 1	*Plan 2*	*Plan 3*
12% bonds	—	—	$2,000,000
Preferred 9% stock, $50 par	—	$2,000,000	1,000,000
Common stock, $10 par	$4,000,000	2,000,000	1,000,000
Total	$4,000,000	$4,000,000	$4,000,000
Earnings before interest and income tax	$ 800,000	$ 800,000	$ 800,000
Deduct interest on bonds	—	—	240,000
Income before income tax	$ 800,000	$ 800,000	$ 560,000
Deduct income tax	320,000	320,000	224,000
Net income	$ 480,000	$ 480,000	$ 336,000
Dividends on preferred stock	—	180,000	90,000
Available for dividends on common stock	$ 480,000	$ 300,000	$ 246,000
Shares of common stock outstanding	400,000	200,000	100,000
Earnings per share on common stock	$1.20	$1.50	$2.46

If Plan 1 is adopted and the entire financing is from the issuance of common stock, the earnings per share on the common stock would be $1.20 per share. Under Plan 2, the effect of using 9% preferred stock for half of the capitalization would result in $1.50 earnings per common share. The issuance of 12% bonds in Plan 3, with the remaining capitalization split between preferred and common stock, would yield a return of $2.46 per share on common stock.

Under the assumed conditions, Plan 3 would obviously be the most attractive for common stockholders. If the anticipated earnings should increase beyond $800,000, the spread between the earnings per share to common stockholders under Plan 1 and Plan 3 would become even greater. But if successively smaller amounts of earnings are assumed, the attractiveness of Plan 2 and Plan 3 decreases. The effect of lower earnings is illustrated by the following tabulation, in which earnings, before interest and income tax are deducted, are assumed to be $440,000 instead of $800,000:

	Plan 1	*Plan 2*	*Plan 3*
12% bonds	—	—	$2,000,000
Preferred 9% stock, $50 par	—	$2,000,000	1,000,000
Common stock, $10 par	$4,000,000	2,000,000	1,000,000
Total	$4,000,000	$4,000,000	$4,000,000

	Plan 1	Plan 2	Plan 3
Earnings before interest and income tax ..	$ 440,000	$ 440,000	$ 440,000
Deduct interest on bonds...............	—	—	240,000
Income before income tax............	$ 440,000	$ 440,000	$ 200,000
Deduct income tax.....................	176,000	176,000	80,000
Net income	$ 264,000	$ 264,000	$ 120,000
Dividends on preferred stock............	—	180,000	90,000
Available for dividends on common stock .	$ 264,000	$ 84,000	$ 30,000
Shares of common stock outstanding.....	400,000	200,000	100,000
Earnings per share on common stock	$.66	$.42	$.30

The preceding analysis focused attention on the effect of the different plans on earnings per share of common stock. There are other factors that must be considered when different methods of financing are evaluated. The issuance of bonds represents a fixed annual interest charge that, in contrast to dividends, is not subject to corporate control. Provision must also be made for the eventual repayment of the principal amount of the bonds, in contrast to the absence of any such obligation to stockholders. On the other hand, a decision to finance entirely by an issuance of common stock would require substantial investment by a single stockholder or small group of stockholders who desire to control the corporation.

How Refinancing Works

Some of the same factors that influence a corporation's decision on financing will also be considered when a company refinances, or changes the structure of its debt and stockholders' equity. In refinancing, however, both management and the stockholders are concerned about the effect of *changes* in the debt and equity relationship. These concerns are described in the following excerpt from an article in *USA TODAY:*

When a major company like Allegis Corp. announces that it is "recapitalizing" [refinancing], many shareholders may be baffled.... Recapitalization plans aren't as complicated as they seem, however. Here are some basic questions and answers:

What is capital?

Simply put, it's a company's money. It can come from two sources: stockholders and lenders.

The stockholders' share is called equity. It represents cash the company has raised by selling stock, and profits the company has built up.

The other part of capital is money borrowed from banks or raised by selling bonds.

How companies balance equity and debt is up to them. At IBM Corp., only 11% of total capital is debt. Sears, Roebuck and Co. has 46% debt. The level of debt a company keeps depends on the risk its managers are willing to assume.

What does risk have to do with it?

It's no different for a company than for an individual. The more debt you have, the greater the risk. Reason: Any profit you earn first must go to meet interest payments. If earnings aren't sufficient to cover the interest owed, you'll have to deplete your savings—or sell something—to raise the needed cash.

What happens in a recapitalization?

A company decides to borrow heavily to raise cash for a large, one-time cash... payment to shareholders.... [In addition,]... shareholders also receive new shares to replace their old shares in the company.... [In] the process, the company generally wipes out its equity. It's replaced with debt.

How can the company afford the debt load?

The company is forced to operate more efficiently than ever. It will have to slash expenses to keep earnings up in the face of higher interest expenses. Owens-Corning Fiberglas Corp., for example, pared its research costs significantly after its recapitalization last year....

Is there any advantage in being so heavily in debt?

Debt does have a good side. By borrowing, you gain "leverage"—the ability to control more assets by using someone else's money. That can magnify the return to shareholders, if business is good and the firm operates efficiently....

Source; Neil Budde, "How Company Recapitalization Plans Work," *USA TODAY,* (June 8, 1987).

CHARACTERISTICS OF BONDS

When a corporation issues bonds, it executes a contract with the bondholders known as a **bond indenture** or **trust indenture.** The entire issue is divided into a number of individual bonds, which may be of varying denominations. Usually the principal of each bond, also called the **face value,** is $1,000 or a multiple thereof. The interest on bonds may be payable at annual, semiannual, or quarterly intervals. Most bonds provide for payment on a semiannual basis.

Registered bonds may be transferred from one owner to another only by endorsement on the bond certificate, and the issuing corporation must maintain a record of the name and the address of each bondholder. Interest payments are made by check to the owner of record. Title to **bearer bonds,** which are also called **coupon bonds,** is transferred merely by delivery, and the issuing corporation does not know the identity of the bondholders. Interest coupons for the entire term, in the form of checks or drafts payable to bearer, are attached to the bond certificate. At each interest date, the holder detaches the appropriate coupon and presents it to a bank for payment.

When all bonds of an issue mature at the same time, they are called **term bonds.** If the maturities are spread over several dates, they are called **serial bonds.** For example, one tenth of an issue of $1,000,000, or $100,000, may mature eleven years from the issuance date, another $100,000 may mature twelve years from the issuance date, and so on until the final $100,000 matures at the end of the twentieth year.

Bonds that may be exchanged for other securities under certain conditions are called **convertible bonds.** Bonds issued by a corporation that reserves the right to redeem them before maturity are referred to as **callable bonds.**

A **secured bond** is one that gives the bondholder a claim on specific assets in case the issuing corporation fails to meet its obligations on the bonds. The properties mortgaged or pledged may be specific buildings and equipment, the entire plant, or stocks and bonds of other companies owned by the debtor corporation. Unsecured bonds issued on the basis of the general credit of the corporation are called **debenture bonds.**

PRESENT VALUE CONCEPTS

omit

The concept of present value plays an important role in many accounting analyses and business decisions. For example, accounting analyses based on the present value concept are useful for evaluating proposals for long-term investments in plant and equipment. Such analyses are discussed in managerial accounting textbooks. In this chapter, the concept of present value will be discussed in the context of the role that it plays in determining the selling price of bonds.

The concept of **the time value of money** is that an amount of cash to be received at some date in the future is not the equivalent of the same amount of cash held at an earlier date. In other words, a sum of cash to be received in the future is not as valuable as the same sum on hand today, because cash on hand today can be invested to earn income. For example, $100 on hand today would be more valuable than $100 to be received a year from today. In this case, if the $100 cash on hand today can be invested to earn 10% per year, the $100 will accumulate to $110 ($100 plus $10 earnings) by one year from today. The $100 on hand today can be referred to as the **present value** amount that is equivalent to $110 to be received a year from today.

PRESENT VALUE CONCEPTS FOR BONDS PAYABLE

When a corporation issues bonds, it usually incurs two distinct obligations: (1) to pay the face amount of the bonds at a specified maturity date, and (2) to pay periodic interest at a specified percentage of the face amount. The price that a buyer is willing to pay for these future benefits is the sum of (1) the *present value* of the face amount of the bonds at the maturity date and (2) the *present value* of the periodic interest payments.

Present Value of $1

The present value of the face amount of bonds at the maturity date is the value today of the promise to pay the face amount at some future date. To illustrate, assume that $1,000 is to be paid in one year and that the rate of earnings is 12%. The present value amount is $892.86 ($1,000 ÷ 1.12). If the $1,000 is to be paid one year later (two years in all), with the earnings compounded at the end of the first year, the present value amount would be $797.20 ($892.86 ÷ 1.12).

Instead of determining the present value of a future cash sum by a series of divisions in the manner just illustrated, it is customary to use a table of present values to find the present value of $1 for the appropriate number of periods, and to multiply that present value factor by the amount of the future cash sum. A partial table of the present value of $1 appears as follows:[1]

Periods	5%	5½%	6%	6½%	7%	10%	11%	12%	13%	14%
1	0.9524	0.9479	0.9434	0.9390	0.9346	0.9091	0.9009	0.8929	0.8850	0.8772
2	0.9070	0.8985	0.8900	0.8817	0.8734	0.8264	0.8116	0.7972	0.7831	0.7695
3	0.8638	0.8516	0.8396	0.8278	0.8163	0.7513	0.7312	0.7118	0.6931	0.6750
4	0.8227	0.8072	0.7921	0.7773	0.7629	0.6830	0.6587	0.6355	0.6133	0.5921
5	0.7835	0.7651	0.7473	0.7299	0.7130	0.6209	0.5935	0.5674	0.5428	0.5194
6	0.7462	0.7252	0.7050	0.6853	0.6663	0.5645	0.5346	0.5066	0.4803	0.4556
7	0.7107	0.6874	0.6651	0.6435	0.6228	0.5132	0.4817	0.4523	0.4251	0.3996
8	0.6768	0.6516	0.6274	0.6042	0.5820	0.4665	0.4339	0.4039	0.3762	0.3506
9	0.6446	0.6176	0.5919	0.5674	0.5439	0.4241	0.3909	0.3606	0.3329	0.3075
10	0.6139	0.5854	0.5584	0.5327	0.5083	0.3855	0.3522	0.3220	0.2946	0.2697
11	0.5847	0.5549	0.5268	0.5002	0.4751	0.3505	0.3173	0.2875	0.2607	0.2366
12	0.5568	0.5260	0.4970	0.4697	0.4440	0.3186	0.2858	0.2567	0.2307	0.2076
13	0.5303	0.4986	0.4688	0.4410	0.4150	0.2897	0.2575	0.2292	0.2042	0.1821
14	0.5051	0.4726	0.4423	0.4141	0.3878	0.2633	0.2320	0.2046	0.1807	0.1597
15	0.4810	0.4479	0.4173	0.3888	0.3624	0.2394	0.2090	0.1827	0.1599	0.1401
16	0.4581	0.4246	0.3936	0.3651	0.3387	0.2176	0.1883	0.1631	0.1415	0.1229
17	0.4363	0.4024	0.3714	0.3428	0.3166	0.1978	0.1696	0.1456	0.1252	0.1078
18	0.4155	0.3815	0.3503	0.3219	0.2959	0.1799	0.1528	0.1300	0.1108	0.0946
19	0.3957	0.3616	0.3305	0.3022	0.2765	0.1635	0.1377	0.1161	0.0981	0.0829
20	0.3769	0.3427	0.3118	0.2838	0.2584	0.1486	0.1240	0.1037	0.0868	0.0728

Present Value of $1 at Compound Interest

[1]The tables illustrated are limited to 20 periods for a small number of interest rates, and the amounts are carried to only four decimal places. Books of tables are available with as many as 360 periods, 45 interest rates (including many fractional rates), and amounts carried to eight decimal places. More complete interest tables can be found in Appendix G.

For the previous example, the table indicates that the present value of $1 to be received two years hence, with earnings at the rate of 12% a year, is .7972. Multiplying $1,000 by .7972 yields $797.20, which is the same amount that was determined previously by two successive divisions. In using the table, it should be noted that the "periods" column represents the number of compounding periods, while the "percentage" columns represent the compound interest rate per period. For example, 12% for two years compounded annually, as in the preceding illustration, is 12% for two periods; 12% for two years compounded semiannually would be 6% (12% per year ÷ 2 semiannual periods) for four periods (2 years × 2 semiannual periods); and 12% for three years compounded semiannually would be 6% (12% ÷ 2) for six periods (3 years × 2 semiannual periods).

Present Value of Annuity of $1

The present value of the periodic interest payments on bonds is the value today of the promise to pay a fixed amount of interest at the end of each of a number of periods. Such a series of fixed payments at fixed intervals is called an **annuity**.

The following partial table of the present value of an annuity of $1 at compound interest indicates the value now (present value) of $1 to be received at the end of *each* period at various compound rates of interest. For example, the present value of $1,000 to be received at the end of each of the next 5 periods at 10% compound interest per period is $3,790.80 (3.7908 × $1,000).

Periods	5%	5½%	6%	6½%	7%	10%	11%	12%	13%	14%
1	0.9524	0.9479	0.9434	0.9390	0.9346	0.9091	0.9009	0.8929	0.8850	0.8772
2	1.8594	1.8463	1.8334	1.8206	1.8080	1.7355	1.7125	1.6901	1.6681	1.6467
3	2.7232	2.6979	2.6730	2.6485	2.6243	2.4869	2.4437	2.4018	2.3612	2.3216
4	3.5460	3.5052	3.4651	3.4258	3.3872	3.1699	3.1024	3.0373	2.9745	2.9137
5	4.3295	4.2703	4.2124	4.1557	4.1002	3.7908	3.6959	3.6048	3.5172	3.4331
6	5.0757	4.9955	4.9173	4.8410	4.7665	4.3553	4.2305	4.1114	3.9976	3.8887
7	5.7864	5.6830	5.5824	5.4845	5.3893	4.8684	4.7122	4.5638	4.4226	4.2883
8	6.4632	6.3346	6.2098	6.0888	5.9713	5.3349	5.1461	4.9676	4.7988	4.6389
9	7.1078	6.9522	6.8017	6.6561	6.5152	5.7590	5.5370	5.3283	5.1317	4.9464
10	7.7217	7.5376	7.3601	7.1888	7.0236	6.1446	5.8892	5.6502	5.4262	5.2161
11	8.3064	8.0925	7.8869	7.6890	7.4987	6.4951	6.2065	5.9377	5.6869	5.4527
12	8.8633	8.6185	8.3838	8.1587	7.9427	6.8137	6.4924	6.1944	5.9176	5.6603
13	9.3936	9.1171	8.8527	8.5997	8.3577	7.1034	6.7499	6.4235	6.1218	5.8424
14	9.8986	9.5896	9.2950	9.0138	8.7455	7.3667	6.9819	6.6282	6.3025	6.0021
15	10.3797	10.0376	9.7123	9.4027	9.1079	7.6061	7.1909	6.8109	6.4624	6.1422
16	10.8378	10.4622	10.1059	9.7678	9.4467	7.8237	7.3792	6.9740	6.6039	6.2651
17	11.2741	10.8646	10.4773	10.1106	9.7632	8.0216	7.5488	7.1196	6.7291	6.3729
18	11.6896	11.2461	10.8276	10.4325	10.0591	8.2014	7.7016	7.2497	6.8399	6.4674
19	12.0853	11.6077	11.1581	10.7347	10.3356	8.3649	7.8393	7.3658	6.9380	6.5504
20	12.4622	11.9504	11.4699	11.0185	10.5940	8.5136	7.9633	7.4694	7.0248	6.6231

Present Value of Annuity of $1 at Compound Interest

ACCOUNTING FOR BONDS PAYABLE

The interest rate specified in the bond indenture is called the **contract** or **coupon rate,** which may differ from the rate prevailing in the market at the time the bonds are issued. If the **market** or **effective rate** is higher than the contract rate, the bonds will sell at a **discount,** or less than their face amount. This discount results because buyers are unwilling to pay the face amount for bonds whose contract rate is lower than the prevailing market rate. The discount, therefore, represents the amount necessary to make up for the difference in the market and the contract interest rates. Conversely, if the market rate is lower than the contract rate, the bonds will sell at a **premium,** or more than their face amount. In this case, buyers are willing to pay more than the face amount for bonds whose contract rate is higher than the market rate.

Bonds Issued at Face Amount

To illustrate an issuance of bonds, assume that on January 1 a corporation issues for cash $100,000 of 12%, five-year bonds, with interest of $6,000 payable semiannually. The market rate of interest at the time the bonds are issued is 12%. Since the contract rate and the market rate of interest are the same, the bonds will sell at their face amount. This amount, calculated as follows, is the sum of (1) the present value of the face amount of $100,000 to be repaid in 5 years and (2) the present value of 10 semiannual interest payments of $6,000 each.[2]

Present value of face amount of $100,000 due in 5 years, at 12% compounded semiannually: $100,000 × .5584 (present value of $1 for 10 periods at 6%)	$ 55,840
Present value of 10 semiannual interest payments of $6,000, at 12% compounded semiannually: $6,000 × 7.3601 (present value of annuity of $1 for 10 periods at 6%)	44,160
Total present value of bonds	$100,000

The basic data for computing the two present values totaling $100,000 were obtained from the two present value tables presented on pages 510 and 511. The first of the two amounts, **$55,840,** is the present value of the $100,000 that is to be repaid in 5 years. The $55,840 is determined by locating the present value of $1 for 10 periods (5 years of semiannual payments) at 6% semiannually (12% annual rate) in the present value of $1 table and multiplying by $100,000. If the bond indenture provided that no interest would be paid during the entire 5-year period, the bonds would be worth only $55,840 at the time of their issuance. To express the concept of present value from a different viewpoint, if $55,840 were invested today, with interest at 12% compounded semiannually, the sum accumulated at the end of 10 semiannual periods would be $100,000.

The second of the two amounts, **$44,160,** is the present value of the series of ten $6,000 payments. The $44,160 is determined by locating the present value of an annuity of $1 for 10 periods (5 years of semiannual payments) at 6% semiannually (12% annual rate) in the present value of an annuity of $1 table and multiplying by $6,000. The present value of $44,160 can also be viewed as the amount of a current deposit earning 12% that would yield ten semiannual withdrawals of $6,000, with the original deposit being reduced to zero by the tenth withdrawal.

The entry to record the issuance of the $100,000 bonds at their face amount is as follows:

[2]Because the present value tables are rounded to four decimal places, minor rounding errors may appear in the illustrations.

Jan. 1	Cash	100,000	
	Bonds Payable		100,000

At six-month intervals following the issuance of the 12% bonds, the interest payment of $6,000 is recorded in the usual manner by a debit to Interest Expense and a credit to Cash. At the maturity date, the payment of the principal sum of $100,000 would be recorded by a debit to Bonds Payable and a credit to Cash.

Bonds Issued at a Discount

If the market rate of interest is 13% and the contract rate is 12%, the bonds will sell at a discount. The present value of the five-year, $100,000 bonds with a market rate of 13% may be calculated as follows:

Present value of $100,000 due in 5 years, at 13% compounded semiannually:	
$100,000 × .5327 (present value of $1 for 10 periods at 6 1/2%)	$53,270
Present value of 10 semiannual interest payments of $6,000 at 13% compounded semiannually: $6,000 × 7.1888 (present value of an annuity of $1 for 10 periods at 6 1/2%)	43,133
Total present value of bonds	$96,403

The two present values that make up the total are both somewhat less than the comparable amounts in the first illustration, where the contract rate and the market rate were exactly the same. The reason for the lesser present value is that the value now of a future amount becomes less and less as the interest rate rises. In other words, the sum that would have to be invested today to equal a fixed future amount becomes less and less as the interest rate earned on the investment rises.

In the following entry to record the issuance of the 12% bonds, the bond liability is recorded at the face amount, and the discount is recorded in a separate contra account:

Jan. 1	Cash	96,403	
	Discount on Bonds Payable	3,597	
	Bonds Payable		100,000

The $3,597 discount may be viewed as the amount that is needed to compensate the investor for accepting a contract rate of interest that is below the prevailing market rate. From another view, the $3,597 represents the additional amount that must be returned by the issuer at maturity; that is, the issuer received $96,403 at the sale date but must return $100,000 at the maturity date. The $3,597 discount must therefore be amortized as additional interest expense over the five-year life of the bonds. There are two widely used methods of allocating bond discount to the various periods: (1) **straight-line** and (2) **interest**. Although the interest method is the recommended method, the straight-line method is acceptable if the results obtained by its use do not materially differ from the results that would be obtained by the use of the interest method.[3]

[3]*Opinions of the Accounting Principles Board, No. 21*, "Interest on Receivables and Payables" (New York: American Institute of Certified Public Accountants, 1971), par. 14.

Amortization of Discount by the Straight-Line Method. The straight-line method is the simpler of the two methods and provides for amortization in equal periodic amounts. Application of this method to the illustration would yield amortization of 1/10 of $3,597, or $359.70, each half year. The amount of the interest expense on the bonds would remain constant for each half year at $6,000 plus $359.70, or $6,359.70. The entry to record the first interest payment and the amortization of the related amount of discount is as follows:

July 1	Interest Expense	6,359.70	
	Discount on Bonds Payable		359.70
	Cash		6,000.00

use only st. line

As an alternative to recording the amortization each time the interest is paid, it may be recorded only at the end of the year. When this procedure is used, each interest payment is recorded as a debit to Interest Expense and a credit to Cash. In terms of the illustration, the entry to amortize the discount at the end of the first year would be as follows:

Dec. 31	Interest Expense	719.40	
	Discount on Bonds Payable		719.40

The amount of the discount amortized, $719.40, is made up of the two semiannual amortization amounts of $359.70.

omit

Amortization of Discount by the Interest Method. In contrast to the straight-line method, which provides for a constant *amount* of interest expense, the interest method provides for a constant *rate* of interest on the **carrying amount** (also called **book value**) of the bonds at the beginning of each period. The interest rate used in the computation is the market rate as of the date the bonds were issued, and the carrying amount of the bonds is their face amount minus the unamortized discount. The difference between the interest expense computed in this manner and the amount of the periodic interest payment is the amount of discount to be amortized for the period. Application of this method to the illustration yields the following data:

Amortization of Discount on Bonds Payable

Interest Payment	A Interest Paid (6% of Face Amount)	B Interest Expense (6½% of Bond Carrying Amount)	C Discount Amortization (B–A)	D Unamortized Discount (D–C)	E Bond Carrying Amount ($100,000–D)
				$3,597	$ 96,403
1	$6,000	$6,266(6½% of $96,403)	$266	3,331	96,669
2	6,000	6,284(6½% of $96,669)	284	3,047	96,953
3	6,000	6,302(6½% of $96,953)	302	2,745	97,255
4	6,000	6,322(6½% of $97,255)	322	2,423	97,577
5	6,000	6,343(6½% of $97,577)	343	2,080	97,920
6	6,000	6,365(6½% of $97,920)	365	1,715	98,285
7	6,000	6,389(6½% of $98,285)	389	1,326	98,674
8	6,000	6,415(6½% of $98,674)	415	911	99,089
9	6,000	6,441(6½% of $99,089)	441	470	99,530
10	6,000	6,470(6½% of $99,530)	470	—	100,000

The following important details should be observed:

1. The interest paid (column A) remains constant at 6% of $100,000, the face amount of the bonds.
2. The interest expense (column B) is computed at 6 1/2% of the bond carrying amount at the beginning of each period, yielding a gradually increasing amount.
3. The excess of the interest expense over the interest payment of $6,000 is the amount of discount to be amortized (column C).
4. The unamortized discount (column D) decreases from the initial balance, $3,597, to a zero balance at the maturity date of the bonds.
5. The carrying amount (column E) increases from $96,403, the amount received for the bonds, to $100,000 at maturity.

The entry to record the first interest payment and the amortization of the related amount of discount is as follows:

July 1	Interest Expense	6,266	
	Discount on Bonds Payable		266
	Cash		6,000

If the amortization is recorded only at the end of the year, the amount of the discount amortized on December 31 would be $550, which is the sum of the first two semiannual amortization amounts ($266 and $284) from the preceding table.

Bonds Issued at a Premium

If the market rate of interest is 11% and the contract rate is 12%, the bonds will sell at a premium. The present value of the five-year, $100,000 bonds, with a market rate of 11%, may be calculated as follows:

Present value of $100,000 due in 5 years, at 11% compounded semiannually: $100,000 × .5854 (present value of $1 for 10 periods at 5 1/2%)	$ 58,540
Present value of 10 semiannual interest payments of $6,000, at 11% compounded semiannually: $6,000 × 7.5376 (present value of an annuity of $1 for 10 periods at 5 1/2%)	45,226
Total present value of bonds	$103,766

The entry to record the issuance of the bonds is as follows:

Jan. 1	Cash	103,766	
	Bonds Payable		100,000
	Premium on Bonds Payable		3,766

Procedures for amortization of the premium and determination of the periodic interest expense are basically the same as those used for bonds issued at a discount.

Amortization of Premium by the Straight-Line Method. Application of the straight-line method to the illustration would yield amortization of 1/10 of $3,766, or $376.60 each half year. Just as bond discount can be viewed as additional interest expense, bond premium can be viewed as a reduction in the amount of interest expense. The entry to record the first interest payment and the amortization of the related amount of premium is as follows:

July 1	Interest Expense	5,623.40	
	Premium on Bonds Payable	376.60	
	Cash..		6,000.00

If the amortization of the premium is recorded only at the end of the year, each interest payment would be recorded by debiting Interest Expense and crediting Cash. The amortization of the premium at the end of the year, in the illustration, would then be recorded as follows:

Dec. 31	Premium on Bonds Payable....................	753.20	
	Interest Expense............................		753.20

The amount of the premium amortized, $753.20, is the sum of the two semiannual amounts of $376.60.

Amortization of Premium by the Interest Method. Application of the interest method of amortization yields the following data:

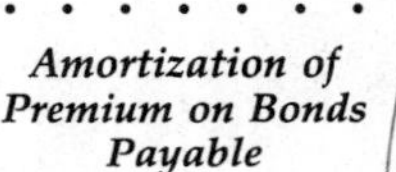

Amortization of Premium on Bonds Payable

Interest Payment	A Interest Paid (6% of Face Amount)	B Interest Expense (5½% of Bond Carrying Amount)	C Premium Amortization (A–B)	D Unamortized Premium (D–C)	E Bond Carrying Amount ($100,000 + D)
				$3,766	$103,766
1	$6,000	$5,707(5½% of $103,766)	$293	3,473	103,473
2	6,000	$5,691(5½% of $103,473)	309	3,164	103,164
3	6,000	$5,674(5½% of $103,164)	326	2,838	102,838
4	6,000	$5,657(5½% of $102,838)	343	2,495	102,495
5	6,000	$5,638(5½% of $102,495)	362	2,133	102,133
6	6,000	$5,618(5½% of $102,133)	382	1,751	101,751
7	6,000	$5,597(5½% of $101,751)	403	1,348	101,348
8	6,000	$5,575(5½% of $101,348)	425	923	100,923
9	6,000	$5,551(5½% of $100,923)	449	474	100,474
10	6,000	$5,526(5½% of $100,474)	474	—	100,000

The following important details should be observed:

1. The interest paid (column A) remains constant at 6% of $100,000, the face amount of the bonds.
2. The interest expense (column B) is computed at 5 1/2% of the bond carrying amount at the beginning of each period, yielding a gradually decreasing amount.
3. The excess of the periodic interest payment of $6,000 over the interest expense is the amount of premium to be amortized (column C).
4. The unamortized premium (column D) decreases from the initial balance, $3,766, to a zero balance at the maturity date of the bonds.
5. The carrying amount (column E) decreases from $103,766, the amount received for the bonds, to $100,000 at maturity.

The entry to record the first payment and the amortization of the related amount of premium is as follows:

July 1	Interest Expense	5,707	
	Premium on Bonds Payable	293	
	Cash		6,000

If the amortization is recorded only at the end of the year, the amount of the premium amortized on December 31 would be $602, which is the sum of the first two semiannual amounts ($293 and $309) from the preceding table.

BOND SINKING FUND

The bond indenture may provide that funds for the payment of bonds at maturity be accumulated over the life of the issue. The amounts set aside are kept separate from other assets in a special fund called a **sinking fund.** Cash deposited in the fund is usually invested in income-producing securities. The periodic deposits plus the earnings on the investments should approximately equal the face amount of the bonds at maturity. In determining the amount of these periodic deposits, the concept of future value can be used.

Future Value Concepts

Future value is the amount that will accumulate at some future date as a result of an investment or a series of investments. For example, if $1,000 is invested to earn 10% per year, the future value at the end of a year will be $1,100 ($1,000 plus $100 earnings). If the $1,100 is left to accumulate additional compounded earnings for three years, the future value at the end of the second year will be $1,210 ($1,100 plus $110 earnings), and at the end of the third year, $1,331 ($1,210 plus $121 earnings).

The future value of an investment can also be determined by using a table of future values to find the future value of $1 for the appropriate number of periods, and then multiplying the amount of the investment by this future value factor. A partial table of the future value of $1 appears as follows:

Periods	5%	5½%	6%	6½%	7%	10%	11%	12%	13%	14%
1	1.0500	1.0550	1.0600	1.0650	1.0700	1.1000	1.1100	1.1200	1.1300	1.1400
2	1.1025	1.1130	1.1236	1.1342	1.1449	1.2100	1.2321	1.2544	1.2769	1.2996
3	1.1576	1.1742	1.1910	1.2080	1.2250	1.3310	1.3676	1.4049	1.4429	1.4815
4	1.2155	1.2388	1.2625	1.2865	1.3108	1.4641	1.5181	1.5735	1.6305	1.6890
5	1.2763	1.3070	1.3382	1.3701	1.4026	1.6105	1.6851	1.7623	1.8424	1.9254
6	1.3401	1.3788	1.4185	1.4591	1.5007	1.7716	1.8704	1.9738	2.0820	2.1950
7	1.4071	1.4547	1.5036	1.5540	1.6058	1.9487	2.0762	2.2107	2.3526	2.5023
8	1.4775	1.5347	1.5939	1.6550	1.7182	2.1436	2.3045	2.4760	2.6584	2.8526
9	1.5513	1.6191	1.6895	1.7626	1.8385	2.3580	2.5580	2.7731	3.0040	3.2520
10	1.6289	1.7081	1.7909	1.8771	1.9672	2.5937	2.8394	3.1059	3.3946	3.7072
11	1.7103	1.8021	1.8983	1.9992	2.1049	2.8531	3.1518	3.4786	3.8359	4.2262
12	1.7959	1.9012	2.0122	2.1291	2.2522	3.1384	3.4985	3.8960	4.3345	4.8179
13	1.8857	2.0058	2.1329	2.2675	2.4099	3.4523	3.8833	4.3635	4.8980	5.4924
14	1.9799	2.1161	2.2609	2.4149	2.5785	3.7975	4.3104	4.8871	5.5348	6.2614
15	2.0789	2.2325	2.3966	2.5718	2.7590	4.1773	4.7846	5.4736	6.2543	7.1379
16	2.1829	2.3553	2.5404	2.7390	2.9522	4.5950	5.3109	6.1304	7.0673	8.1373
17	2.2920	2.4848	2.6928	2.9171	3.1588	5.0545	5.8951	6.8660	7.9861	9.2765
18	2.4066	2.6215	2.8543	3.1067	3.3799	5.5599	6.5436	7.6900	9.0243	10.5752
19	2.5270	2.7657	3.0256	3.3086	3.6165	6.1159	7.2633	8.6128	10.1974	12.0557
20	2.6533	2.9178	3.2071	3.5237	3.8697	6.7275	8.0623	9.6463	11.5231	13.7435

Future Value of $1 at Compound Interest

For the previous example, the table indicates that the future value of $1 three years (periods) hence, with earnings at the rate of 10% a year, is 1.331. Multiplying $1,000 by 1.331 yields $1,331, which is the same amount as determined previously.

Future value may also arise from a series of equal investments made at fixed intervals (an annuity).[4] For example, if $1,000 is invested at the end of each year to earn 10% per year compounded annually, the future value of the annuity at the end of the third year would be $3,310, determined as follows:

Year	*Beginning Balance*	*Earnings During Year (10% × Beginning Balance)*	*Annual Deposit (End of Year)*	*Accumulation at End of Year*
1	—	—	$1,000	$1,000
2	$1,000	$100	1,000	2,100
3	2,100	210	1,000	3,310

The future value of a series of investments can also be determined by using a table of future values to find the future value of an annuity of $1 for the appropriate number of periods, and then multiplying the amount of the investment by the future value factor. A partial table of the future value of an annuity of $1 appears as follows:

Periods	5%	5½%	6%	6½%	7%	10%	11%	12%	13%	14%
1	1.0000	1.0000	1.0000	1.0000	1.0000	1.0000	1.0000	1.0000	1.0000	1.0000
2	2.0500	2.0550	2.0600	2.0650	2.0700	2.1000	2.1100	2.1200	2.1300	2.1400
3	3.1525	3.1680	3.1836	3.1992	3.2149	3.3100	3.3421	3.3744	3.4069	3.4396
4	4.3101	4.3423	4.3746	4.4072	4.4399	4.6410	4.7097	4.7793	4.8498	4.9211
5	5.5256	5.5811	5.6371	5.6936	5.7507	6.1051	6.2278	6.3529	6.4803	6.6101
6	6.8019	6.8881	6.9753	7.0637	7.1533	7.7156	7.9129	8.1152	8.3227	8.5355
7	8.1420	8.2669	8.3938	8.5229	8.6540	9.4872	9.7833	10.0890	10.4047	10.7305
8	9.5491	9.7216	9.8975	10.0769	10.2598	11.4359	11.8594	12.2997	12.7573	13.2328
9	11.0266	11.2563	11.4913	11.7319	11.9780	13.5795	14.1640	14.7757	15.4157	16.0854
10	12.5779	12.8754	13.1808	13.4944	13.8165	15.9374	16.7220	17.5487	18.4198	19.3373
11	14.2068	14.5835	14.9716	15.3716	15.7836	18.5312	19.5614	20.6546	21.8143	23.0445
12	15.9171	16.3856	16.8699	17.3707	17.8885	21.3843	22.7132	24.1331	25.6502	27.2708
13	17.7130	18.2868	18.8821	19.4998	20.1406	24.5227	26.2116	28.0291	29.9847	32.0887
14	19.5986	20.2926	21.0151	21.7673	22.5505	27.9750	30.0949	32.3926	34.8827	37.5811
15	21.5786	22.4087	23.2760	24.1822	25.1290	31.7725	34.4054	37.2797	40.4175	43.8424
16	23.6575	24.6411	25.6725	26.7540	27.8881	35.9497	39.1900	42.7533	46.6717	50.9804
17	25.8404	26.9964	28.2129	29.4930	30.8402	40.5447	44.5008	48.8837	53.7391	59.1176
18	28.1324	29.4812	30.9057	32.4104	33.9990	45.5992	50.3959	55.7497	61.7251	68.3941
19	30.5390	32.1027	33.7600	35.5167	37.3790	51.1591	56.9395	63.4397	70.7494	78.9692
20	33.0660	34.8683	36.7856	38.8253	40.9955	57.2750	64.2028	72.0524	80.9468	91.0249

Future Value of Annuity of $1 at Compound Interest (Investments at end of period)

For the previous example, the table indicates that the future value of an annuity of $1 three years (periods) hence, with earnings at the rate of 10% a year, is 3.310. Multiplying $1,000 by 3.310 yields $3,310, which is the same amount as determined previously.

To illustrate the concept of the future value of an annuity for the periodic deposits in a bond sinking fund, assume that a corporation issues $100,000 of 10-year bonds, dated January 1. A bond sinking fund for the payment of the bonds at maturity is established, with deposits to be made at the end of each

---

[4]As discussed in a preceding section, a series of fixed payments or investments at fixed intervals is called an annuity.

year. If the deposits are expected to earn 14% per year, the annual deposit would be $5,171, determined as follows:

$$\text{Annual Deposit} = \frac{\text{Maturity Value of Bonds}}{\text{Future Value of Annuity of \$1 for 10 Periods at 14\%}}$$

$$\text{Annual Deposit} = \frac{\$100{,}000}{19.3373}$$

$$\text{Annual Deposit} = \$5{,}171 \text{ (rounded)}$$

Accounting for Bond Sinking Fund

When cash is transferred to the sinking fund, an account called Sinking Fund Cash is debited and Cash is credited. The purchase of investments is recorded by a debit to Sinking Fund Investments and a credit to Sinking Fund Cash. As income (interest or dividends) is received, the cash is debited to Sinking Fund Cash and Sinking Fund Income is credited.

The accounting for a bond sinking fund is illustrated by using the preceding example, in which a corporation issues $100,000 of 10-year bonds dated January 1. As indicated in the preceding section, annual deposits of $5,171, invested in securities that will yield approximately 14% per year, are sufficient to provide a fund of approximately $100,000 at the end of 10 years. A few of the typical transactions and the related entries affecting the sinking fund during the 10-year period are illustrated as follows:

Deposit of cash in the fund

The first deposit in the sinking fund is recorded. A similar entry would be recorded as deposits are made at the end of each of the 9 remaining years.

		Debit	Credit
Entry:	Sinking Fund Cash	5,171	
	Cash		5,171

Purchase of investments

The purchases of securities after the first deposit was made are recorded in a summary entry. The time of purchase and the amount invested at any one time vary, depending upon market conditions and the unit price of securities purchased.

		Debit	Credit
Entry:	Sinking Fund Investments	5,000	
	Sinking Fund Cash		5,000

Receipt of income from investments

The receipt of income for the year on the securities purchased is recorded in a summary entry. Interest and dividends are received at different times during the year, and the amount earned per year normally increases as the fund increases.

		Debit	Credit
Entry:	Sinking Fund Cash	700	
	Sinking Fund Income		700

Sale of investments

The sale of all securities at the end of the tenth year is recorded. Investments may be sold from time to time and the proceeds reinvested. Prior to maturity, all investments are converted into cash.

Entry:	Sinking Fund Cash	85,100	
	Sinking Fund Investments		82,480
	Gain on Sale of Investments		2,620

Payment of bonds

The payment of the bonds and the transfer of the remaining sinking fund cash to the cash account is recorded. The cash available in the fund at the end of the tenth year is assumed to be composed of the following:

Proceeds from sale of investments	$ 85,100
Income earned during tenth year	11,520
Last annual deposit	5,171
Total	$101,791

Entry:	Bonds Payable	100,000	
	Cash	1,791	
	Sinking Fund Cash		101,791

In the illustration, the amount of the fund exceeded the amount of the liability by $1,791. This excess was transferred to the regular cash account. If the fund had been less than the amount of the liability, $99,500 for example, the regular cash account would have been drawn upon for the $500 deficiency.

Sinking fund income represents earnings of the corporation and is reported in the income statement as "Other income." The cash and the securities making up the sinking fund are classified in the balance sheet as "Investments," which usually appears immediately below the current assets section.

APPROPRIATION FOR BONDED INDEBTEDNESS

The restriction of dividends during the life of a bond issue is another means of increasing the assurance that the obligation will be paid at maturity. Assuming that the corporation in the preceding example is required by the bond indenture to appropriate $10,000 of retained earnings each year for the 10-year life of the bonds, the following entry would be made annually:

Dec. 31	Retained Earnings	10,000	
	Appropriation for Bonded Indebtedness		10,000

As was indicated in Chapter 11, an appropriation has no direct relationship to a sinking fund. Each is independent of the other. When there is both a fund and an appropriation for the same purpose, the appropriation may be said to be **funded.**

BOND REDEMPTION

Callable bonds are redeemable by the issuing corporation within the period of time and at the price stated in the bond indenture. Usually the call price is above the face value. If the market rate of interest declines after the issuance of the bonds, the corporation may sell new bonds at a lower interest rate and use the funds to redeem the original issue. The reduction of future interest expense is always an incentive for bond redemption. A corporation may also redeem all or a portion of its bonds before maturity by purchasing them on the open market.

When a corporation redeems bonds at a price below their carrying amount, the corporation realizes a gain. If the price is in excess of the carrying amount, a loss is incurred. To illustrate redemption, assume that on June 30 a corporation has a bond issue of $100,000 outstanding, on which there is an unamortized premium of $4,000. The corporation has the option of calling the bonds for $105,000, which it exercises on this date. The entry to record the redemption is:

June 30	Bonds Payable	100,000	
	Premium on Bonds Payable	4,000	
	Loss on Redemption of Bonds	1,000	
	Cash		105,000

If the bonds were not callable, the corporation might purchase a portion on the open market. Assuming that the corporation purchases one fourth ($25,000) of the bonds for $24,000 on June 30, the entry to record the redemption would be as follows:

June 30	Bonds Payable	25,000	
	Premium on Bonds Payable	1,000	
	Cash		24,000
	Gain on Redemption of Bonds		2,000

Note that only the portion of the premium relating to the bonds redeemed is written off. The excess of the carrying amount of the bonds purchased, $26,000, over the cash paid, $24,000, is recognized as a gain.

BALANCE SHEET PRESENTATION OF BONDS PAYABLE

Bonds payable are usually reported on the balance sheet as long-term liabilities. If there are two or more bond issues, separate accounts should be maintained and the details of each should be reported on the balance sheet or in a supporting schedule or note. When the balance sheet date is within one year of the bond maturity date, the bonds should be transferred to the current liability classification if they are to be paid out of current assets. If they are to be paid with funds that have been set aside or if they are to be replaced with another bond issue, they should remain in the noncurrent category and their anticipated liquidation disclosed in an explanatory note.

The balance in a discount account should be reported in the balance sheet as a deduction from the related bonds payable. Conversely, the balance in a premium account should be reported as an addition to the related bonds payable. Either in the financial statements or in accompanying notes, the description of the bonds (terms, security, due date, etc.) should also include the effective interest rate and the maturities and sinking fund requirements for each of the next five years.[5]

INVESTMENTS IN BONDS

The issuance of bonds and related transactions were discussed in the preceding paragraphs from the standpoint of the issuing corporation. Whenever a corporation records a transaction between itself and the owners of its bonds, there is a reciprocal entry in the accounts of the investor.

In the following discussion, attention will be given to the principles underlying the accounting for investments in **debt securities** (bonds and notes) that are identified as long-term investments. **Long-term investments** are investments that are not intended as a ready source of cash in the normal operations of the business. These long-term investments are listed in the balance sheet under the caption "Investments," which usually follows the current assets. By contrast, temporary investments or marketable securities, which were discussed in Chapter 6, are available to meet the needs for additional cash for normal operations and are classified as current assets.

A business may make long-term investments simply because it has cash that is not needed in its normal operations. As discussed previously, cash and securities in bond sinking funds are considered long-term investments, since they are accumulated for the purpose of paying the bond liability. A corporation may also purchase bonds as a means of establishing or maintaining business relations with the issuing company.

Investments in corporate bonds may be purchased directly from the issuing corporation or from other investors. The services of a broker are usually employed in buying and selling bonds listed on the organized exchanges. The record of transactions on bond exchanges is reported daily in the financial pages of newspapers. This record usually includes data on the bond interest rate, maturity date, volume of sales, and the high, low, and closing prices for each corporation's bonds traded during the day. Prices for bonds are quoted as a percentage of the face amount. Thus, the price of a $1,000 bond quoted at 104 1/2 would be $1,045.

ACCOUNTING FOR INVESTMENTS IN BONDS

A long-term investment in debt securities is customarily carried at cost. The cost of bonds purchased includes the amount paid to the seller plus other costs related to the purchase, such as the broker's commission. When bonds are purchased between interest dates, the buyer pays the seller the interest accrued from the last interest payment date to the date of purchase. The amount of the interest paid should be debited to Interest Income, since it is an

[5] *Statement of Financial Accounting Standards, No. 47,* "Disclosure of Long-Term Obligations" (Stamford: Financial Accounting Standards Board, 1981), par. 10.

offset against the amount that will be received at the next interest date. To illustrate, assume that a $1,000 bond is purchased at 102 plus a brokerage fee of $5.30 and accrued interest of $10.20. The transaction is recorded by the following entry. Note that the cost of the bond is recorded in a single account, i.e., the face amount of the bond and the premium paid are not recorded in separate accounts.

Apr. 2	Investment in Lewis Co. Bonds	1,025.30	
	Interest Income	10.20	
	Cash		1,035.50

As discussed previously, the price investors pay for bonds may be much greater or less than the face amount or the original issuance price. When bonds held as long-term investments are purchased at a price other than the face amount, the discount or premium should be amortized over the remaining life of the bonds. The amortization of discount increases the amount of the investment account and interest income. The amortization of premium decreases the amount of the investment account and interest income. The procedures for determining the amount of amortization each period correspond to those described and illustrated on pages 454 to 457.

Interest received on bond investments is recorded by a debit to Cash and a credit to Interest Income. At the end of a fiscal year, the interest accrued should be recorded by a debit to Interest Receivable and a credit to Interest Income. The adjusting entry should be reversed after the accounts are closed, so that all receipts of bond interest during the following year may be recorded without referring to the adjustment data.

As a basis for illustrating the transactions associated with long-term investments in bonds, assume that $50,000 of 8% bonds of Nowell Corporation, due in 8 3/4 years, are purchased on July 1 to yield approximately 11%. The purchase price is $41,706 plus interest of $1,000 accrued from April 1, the date of the last semiannual interest payment. Entries in the accounts of the purchaser at the time of purchase and for the remainder of the fiscal year, ending December 31, are as follows:

July 1 Payment for investment in bonds and accrued interest

Cost of $50,000 of Nowell Corp. bonds	$41,706
Interest accrued on $50,000 at 8%, April 1–July 1 (3 months)	1,000
Total	$42,706

Entry:	Investment in Nowell Corp. Bonds	41,706	
	Interest Income	1,000	
	Cash		42,706

October 1 Receipt of semiannual interest

Interest on $50,000 at 8%, April 1–October 1 (6 months), $2,000

Entry:	Cash	2,000	
	Interest Income		2,000

December 31 Adjusting entries

Interest accrued on $50,000 at 8%, October 1–December 31 (3 months), $1,000

Entry: Interest Receivable	1,000	
Interest Income		1,000

Discount to be amortized by interest method, July 1–December 31 (6 months):

Interest income (5 1/2% of bond carrying amount of $41,706)................................	$2,294
Less interest received (4% of face amount of $50,000) ...	2,000
Amount to be amortized............................	$ 294

Entry: Investment in Nowell Corp. Bonds...............	294	
Interest Income		294

The entries in the interest income account in the above illustration may be summarized as follows:

July 1	Paid accrued interest—3 months........................	$(1,000)
Oct. 1	Received interest payment—6 months	2,000
Dec. 31	Recorded accrued interest—3 months..................	1,000
31	Recorded amortization of discount—6 months	294
	Interest earned—6 months	$ 2,294

SALE OF INVESTMENTS IN BONDS

When bonds held as long-term investments are sold, the seller will receive the sales price (less commissions and other selling costs) plus the interest accrued since the last payment date. Before recording the proceeds, the seller should record the appropriate amount of the amortization of discount or premium for the current period, up to the date of sale. Then, in recording the proceeds, any gain or loss incurred on the sale can be recognized. To illustrate the recording of a sale of bonds held as a long-term investment, assume that the Nowell Corporation bonds of the preceding example are sold for $47,350 plus accrued interest on June 30, seven years after their purchase. The carrying amount of the bonds (cost plus amortized discount) as of January 1 of the year of sale is $47,080. The entries to record the amortization of discount for the current year and the sale of the bonds are as follows:

June 30 Amortization of discount for current year

Discount to be amortized by the interest method, January 1–June 30, $589

Entry: Investment in Nowell Corp. Bonds...............	589	
Interest Income		589

June 30 Receipt of interest and sale of bonds

Interest accrued on $50,000 at 8%, April 1–June 30 (3 months), $1,000

Carrying amount of bonds on January 1 of current year	$47,080
Discount amortized in current year	589
Carrying amount of bonds on June 30	$47,669
Proceeds of sale	47,350
Loss on sale	$ 319

Entry: Cash	48,350	
Loss on Sale of Investments	319	
Interest Income		1,000
Investment in Nowell Corp. Bonds		47,669

Chapter Review

KEY POINTS

1. Financing Corporations.
Business enterprises may raise funds for long-term financing in various ways. They may sell capital stock or issue notes or bonds, which are a form of interest-bearing note. When funds are borrowed through the issuance of bonds, there is a definite commitment to pay periodic interest and to repay the principal at a stated future date. There are many factors that must be considered when different methods of financing are evaluated. One such factor is the impact on the corporation's earnings per share of common stock.

2. Characteristics of Bonds.
When a corporation issues bonds, it executes a contract, known as a bond indenture or trust indenture, with bondholders. The principal amount of each bond is called its face value and is usually in a multiple of $1,000. Different types of bonds that may be issued by a corporation include registered bonds, bearer bonds, coupon bonds, term bonds, serial bonds, convertible bonds, callable bonds, secured bonds, and debenture bonds.

3. Present Value Concepts.
The concept of present value plays an important role in many accounting analyses and business decisions. The concept of the time value of money is that an amount of cash to be received at some date in the future is not the equivalent of the same amount of cash held at an earlier date. In other words, a sum of cash to be received in the future is not as valuable as the same sum on hand today, because cash on hand today can be invested to earn income.

4. Present Value Concepts for Bonds Payable.
When a corporation issues bonds, it incurs two distinct obligations: (1) to pay the face amount of the bonds at a specified maturity date, and (2) to pay periodic interest at a specified percentage of the face amount. A price that a buyer is willing to pay for these future benefits is the sum of (1) the present

value of the face amount of the bonds at the maturity date and (2) the present value of the periodic interest payments. The present value of $1 table is used to compute the present value of the face amount of the bonds at the maturity date. The present value of an annuity of $1 table is used to compute the present value of the periodic interest payments on the bonds.

5. Accounting for Bonds Payable.
The interest rate specified in the bond indenture is called the contract or coupon rate, which may differ from the rate prevailing in the market at the time the bonds are issued. If the market or effective rate is higher than the contract rate, the bonds will sell at a discount, or less than their face amount. The discount results because buyers are unwilling to pay the face amount for bonds whose contract rate is lower than the prevailing market rate. If the market rate is lower than the contract rate, the bonds will sell at a premium, or more than their face amount. In this case, buyers are willing to pay more than the face amount for bonds whose contract rate is higher than the market rate.

When bonds are issued at a discount, Discount on Bonds Payable is debited for the amount of the discount. When bonds are issued at a premium, Premium on Bonds Payable is credited for the amount of the premium. The amount of the discount or premium must be allocated to interest expense over the life of the bonds by using either the straight-line method or the interest method. The straight-line method provides for a constant amount of interest expense. The interest method provides for a constant rate of interest. A discount is amortized by crediting Discount on Bonds Payable. A premium is amortized by debiting Premium on Bonds Payable. The amortization of a discount increases interest expense, and the amortization of a premium decreases interest expense. The amortization entry may be recorded at either the date of periodic interest payments or the end of the accounting period.

6. Bond Sinking Fund.
The bond indenture may provide that funds for the payment of bonds at maturity be accumulated over the life of the issue. The amounts set aside are accounted for separately from other assets in a special fund called a sinking fund. Cash deposited in this fund is usually invested in income-producing securities. The periodic deposits plus the earnings on the investments should approximately equal the face amount of the bonds at maturity. The concept of future value may be used to determine the amount of the periodic deposits.

7. Appropriation for Bonded Indebtedness.
The bond indenture may require a board of directors to restrict dividends during the life of a bond issue through the use of an appropriation of retained earnings. This action may also be taken voluntarily. When there is both a bond sinking fund and an appropriation of retained earnings for the purpose of redeeming bonds at maturity, the appropriation is said to be funded.

8. Bond Redemption.
Callable bonds are redeemable by the issuing corporation at the price stated in the bond indenture. If the bonds are not callable, they may be purchased on the open market. When a corporation redeems bonds, any gain or loss on the redemption is recognized in the accounts.

9. Balance Sheet Presentation of Bonds Payable.
Bonds payable are usually reported on the balance sheet as long-term liabilities. When the balance sheet date is within one year of the bond maturity date, the bonds should be transferred to the current liability classification if they are to be paid out of current assets. If they are to be paid with funds that have been set aside or if they are to be replaced with another bond issue, they should remain in the noncurrent category and their anticipated liquidation disclosed in an explanatory note. The balance in a discount account should be reported in the balance sheet as a deduction from the related bonds payable, and the balance in a premium account should be reported as an addition to the related bonds payable.

10. Investments in Bonds.
A corporation may purchase bonds of another corporation as a long-term investment that is not intended as a ready source of cash in the normal operations of the business. These long-term investments are listed in the balance sheet under the caption "Investments," following the current assets section.

11. Accounting for Investments in Bonds.
A long-term investment in debt securities is customarily carried at cost. The cost of the bonds purchased includes the amount paid to the seller plus other costs related to the purchase, such as the broker's commission. When bonds are purchased between interest dates, the buyer pays the seller the interest accrued from the last interest payment date to the date of the purchase. The amount of the interest paid should be debited to Interest Income, since it is an offset against the amount that will be received at the next interest date. When bonds held as long-term investments are purchased at a price other than the face amount, the discount or premium should be amortized over the remaining life of the bonds. The procedures for determining the amount of amortization are similar to those for bonds payable. The amortization of a discount increases the amount of the investment account and interest income. The amortization of a premium decreases the amount of the investment account and interest income.

12. Sale of Investments in Bonds.
When bonds held as long-term investments are sold, the seller will receive the sales price (less commissions and other selling costs) plus the interest accrued since the last payment date. Before recording the proceeds, the seller should record the appropriate amount of the amortization of discount or premium for the current period, up to the date of sale. Then, in recording the proceeds, any gain or loss incurred on the sale can be recognized.

KEY TERMS

bonds 446
bond indenture 449
present value 450
annuity 451
contract rate of interest 451
effective rate of interest 451
bond discount 451
bond premium 452
carrying amount 454
sinking fund 457
future value 457
debt securities 462
long-term investments 462

SELF-EXAMINATION QUESTIONS

(Answers at End of Chapter)

1. If a corporation plans to issue $1,000,000 of 12% bonds at a time when the market rate for similar bonds is 10%, the bonds can be expected to sell:
   A. at their face amount
   B. at a premium
   C. at a discount
   D. at a price below their face amount
2. If the bonds payable account has a balance of $500,000 and the discount on bonds payable account has a balance of $40,000, what is the carrying amount of the bonds?
   A. $460,000
   B. $500,000
   C. $540,000
   D. none of the above
3. The cash and the securities comprising the sinking fund established for the payment of bonds at maturity are classified on the balance sheet as:
   A. current assets
   B. investments
   C. long-term liabilities
   D. none of the above
4. If a firm purchases $100,000 of bonds of X Company at 101 plus accrued interest of $2,000 and pays broker's commissions of $50, the amount debited to Investment in X Company Bonds would be:
   A. $100,000
   B. $101,050
   C. $103,000
   D. none of the above
5. The balance in the discount on bonds payable account would usually be reported in the balance sheet in the:
   A. current assets section
   B. current liabilities section
   C. long-term liabilities section
   D. none of the above

ILLUSTRATIVE PROBLEM

Dent Inc.'s fiscal year ends December 31. Selected transactions for the period 1989 through 1996 involving bonds payable issued by Dent Inc. are as follows:

1989

Nov. 30. Issued $4,000,000 of 25-year, 9% callable bonds dated November 30, 1989, for cash of $3,840,000. Interest is payable semiannually on November 30 and May 31.

Dec. 31. Recorded the adjusting entry for interest payable.

31. Recorded amortization of $533 discount on the bonds.

31. Closed the interest expense account.

1990

Jan. 1. Reversed the adjusting entry for interest payable.

May 31. Paid the semiannual interest on the bonds.

Nov. 30. Paid the semiannual interest on the bonds.

Dec. 31. Recorded the adjusting entry for interest payable.

31. Recorded amortization of $6,400 discount on the bonds.

31. Closed the interest expense account.

1996

Nov. 30. Recorded the redemption of the bonds, which were called at 102. The balance in the bond discount account is $115,200 after the payment of interest and amortization of discount have been recorded. (Record the redemption only.)

Instructions:

1. Prepare journal entries to record the preceding transactions.
2. Determine the amount of interest expense for 1989 and 1990.
3. Estimate the effective annual interest rate by dividing the interest expense for 1989 by the bond carrying amount at the time of issuance and multiplying by 12.
4. Determine the carrying amount of the bonds as of December 31, 1990.

SOLUTION

(1)

Date	Account	Debit	Credit
1989			
Nov. 30	Cash	3,840,000	
	Discount on Bonds Payable	160,000	
	Bonds Payable		4,000,000
Dec. 31	Interest Expense	30,000	
	Interest Payable		30,000
31	Interest Expense	533	
	Discount on Bonds Payable		533
31	Income Summary	30,533	
	Interest Expense		30,533
1990			
Jan. 1	Interest Payable	30,000	
	Interest Expense		30,000
May 31	Interest Expense	180,000	
	Cash		180,000
Nov. 30	Interest Expense	180,000	
	Cash		180,000
Dec. 31	Interest Expense	30,000	
	Interest Payable		30,000
31	Interest Expense	6,400	
	Discount on Bonds Payable		6,400
31	Income Summary	366,400	
	Interest Expense		366,400
1996			
Nov. 30	Bonds Payable	4,000,000	
	Loss on Redemption of Bonds Payable	195,200	
	Discount on Bonds Payable		115,200
	Cash		4,080,000

(2) (a) 1989—$ 30,533
(b) 1990—$366,400

(3) $30,533 ÷ $3,840,000 = .8% rate for one month of a year
.8% × 12 = 9.6% annual rate

(4) Initial carrying amount of bonds.	$3,840,000
Discount amortized on December 31, 1989	533
Discount amortized on December 31, 1990	6,400
Carrying amount of bonds, December 31, 1990	$3,846,933

Discussion Questions

12–1. When underwriters are used by the corporation issuing bonds, what function do the underwriters perform?

12–2. How are interest payments made to holders of (a) bearer or coupon bonds and (b) registered bonds?

12–3. Explain the meaning of each of the following terms as they relate to a bond issue: (a) secured, (b) convertible, (c) callable, and (d) debenture.

12–4. Describe the two distinct obligations incurred by a corporation when issuing bonds.

12–5. What is the present value of $1,000 due in 2 years, if the market rate of interest is 11%?

12–6. What is the present value of $1,000 to be received in each of the next 2 years, if the market rate of interest is 11%?

12–7. A corporation issues $5,000,000 of 12% coupon bonds to yield interest at the rate of 11%. (a) Was the amount of cash received from the sale of the bonds greater or less than $5,000,000? (b) Identify the following terms related to the bond issue: (1) face amount, (2) market or effective rate of interest, (3) contract or coupon rate of interest, and (4) maturity amount.

12–8. If bonds issued by a corporation are sold at a premium, is the market rate of interest greater or less than the coupon rate?

12–9. If the bonds payable account has a balance of $1,000,000 and the premium on bonds payable account has a balance of $37,420, what is the carrying amount of the bonds?

12–10. The following data are related to a $500,000, 12% bond issue for a selected semiannual interest period:

Bond carrying amount at beginning of period	$531,000
Interest paid at end of period	30,000
Interest expense allocable to the period	28,450

(a) Were the bonds issued at a discount or at a premium? (b) What is the balance of the discount or premium account at the beginning of the period? (c) How much amortization of discount or premium is allocable to the period?

12–11. A corporation issues 10%, 20-year debenture bonds, with a face amount of $5,000,000, for 102 1/2 at the beginning of the current year. Assuming that the premium is to be amortized on a straight-line basis, what is the total amount of interest expense for the current year?

12–12. Indicate the title of (a) the account to be debited and (b) the account to be credited in the entry made at year-end for amortization of (1) discount on bonds payable and (2) premium on bonds payable.

12–13. When the premium on bonds payable is amortized by the interest method, does the interest expense increase or decrease over the amortization period?

12–14. What is the purpose of a bond sinking fund?

12–15. What would be the value at the end of the second year for a $1,000 investment if the earnings rate is 12% compounded annually?

12–16. What would be the value at the end of the sixth year for a $5,000 investment if the earnings rate is 10% compounded annually? Use the table of the future value of $1 presented in this chapter to determine the value.

12–17. What would be the value at the end of the second year from a series of investments of $10,000 each to be made at the end of each of the first two years, with earnings of 12% compounded annually?

12–18. If Cowan Company invests $10,000 at the end of each of the next 5 years in a sinking fund, what is the value of the fund at the end of 5 years if the fund investments yield 12% per year, compounded annually? Use the table of the future value of an annuity of $1 presented in this chapter to determine the value.

12–19. What amount must be invested at the end of each of the next 5 years, in a sinking fund that earns 12% compounded annually, to accumulate to $10,000 at the end of the fifth year? Use the table of the future value of an annuity of $1 presented in this chapter to determine the amount.

12–20. If the amount accumulated in a sinking fund account exceeds the amount of liability at the redemption date, to what account is the excess transferred?

12–21. How are cash and securities comprising a sinking fund classified on the balance sheet?

12–22. Bonds Payable has a balance of $300,000 and Premium on Bonds Payable has a balance of $11,400. If the issuing corporation redeems the bonds at 102, what is the amount of gain or loss on redemption?

12–23. Indicate how the following accounts should be reported in the balance sheet: (a) Premium on Bonds Payable, and (b) Discount on Bonds Payable.

12–24. Under what caption are "Long-term investments in bonds" listed on the balance sheet?

12–25. The quoted price of Turpin Corp. bonds on May 1 is 105. On the same day the interest accrued is 4% of the face amount. (a) Does the quoted price include accrued interest? (b) If $20,000 face amount of Turpin Corp. bonds is purchased on May 1 at the quoted price, what is the cost of the bonds, exclusive of commission?

12–26. An investor sells $20,000 of bonds of ICC Corp. carried at $20,450, for $20,900 plus accrued interest of $200. The broker remits the balance due after deducting a commission of $80. Present the entry to record this transaction.

12–27. Real World Focus. General Electric Company 8 1/2% debenture bonds due in 2004 were reported in *The Wall Street Journal* as selling for 101 3/8 on February 6, 1987. (a) Were the bonds selling at a premium or at a discount on February 6, 1987? (b) Was the market rate of interest for similar quality bonds higher or lower than 8 1/2% on February 6, 1987?

Exercises

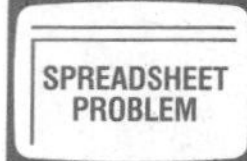

12–28. Effect of financing on earnings per share. Two companies are financed as follows:

	Sims Inc.	Tone Co.
Bonds payable, 10% (issued at face value)	$2,000,000	$1,000,000
Preferred 9% stock (nonparticipating).............	2,000,000	1,000,000
Common stock, $10 par	2,000,000	4,000,000

Income tax is estimated at 40% of income. Determine for each company the earnings per share of common stock, assuming that the income before bond interest and income tax for each company is (a) $500,000, (b) $1,000,000, and (c) $1,600,000.

12–29. Entries for issuance and calling of bonds. F. C. Classic Company issued $5,000,000 of 20-year, 12% callable bonds on March 1, 1989, with interest payable on March 1 and September 1. The fiscal year of the company is the calendar year. Present the entries to record the following selected transactions:

1989
Mar. 1. Issued the bonds for cash at their face amount.
Sept. 1. Paid the interest on the bonds.
Dec. 31. Recorded accrued interest for four months.
31. Closed the interest expense account.

1990
Jan. 1. Reversed the adjusting entry for accrued interest.
Mar. 1. Paid the interest on the bonds.

1994
Sept. 1. Called the bond issue at 102, the rate provided in the bond indenture. (Omit entry for payment of interest.)

12–30. Entries for bond issuance; amortization of discount by straight-line method. On the first day of its fiscal year, Grant Corporation issued $10,000,000 of 10-year, 10% bonds, interest payable semiannually, at an effective interest rate of 12%, receiving cash of $8,852,950.

(a) Present the entries to record the following:
 (1) Sale of the bonds.
 (2) First semiannual interest payment. (Amortization of discount is to be recorded annually.)
 (3) Second semiannual interest payment.
 (4) Amortization of discount at the end of the first year, using the straight-line method.
(b) Determine the amount of the bond interest expense for the first year.

12–31. Computation of bond proceeds, entries for bond issuance, and amortization of premium by straight-line method. On March 1, 1989, Allen Corporation issued $5,000,000 of 10-year, 12% bonds at an effective interest rate of 11%. Interest is payable semiannually on March 1 and September 1. Present the entries to record the following:

(a) Sale of bonds on March 1, 1989. (Use the tables of present values appearing in the chapter to determine the bond proceeds.)
(b) First interest payment on September 1, 1989, including amortization of bond premium for 6 months, using the straight-line method.

SPREADSHEET PROBLEM

12–32. Computation of bond proceeds, amortization of premium by interest method, and interest expense. On the first day of its fiscal year, Harris Co. issued $10,000,000 of 10-year, 12% bonds at an effective interest rate of 10%, with interest payable semiannually. Compute the following, presenting figures used in your computations and rounding to the nearest dollar:

(a) The amount of cash proceeds from the sale of the bonds. (Use the tables of present values appearing in the chapter.)
(b) The amount of premium to be amortized for the first semiannual interest payment period, using the interest method.
(c) The amount of premium to be amortized for the second semiannual interest payment period, using the interest method.
(d) The amount of the bond interest expense for the first year.

12–33. Determination of sinking fund deposit and entry. C. C. Cutler Co. issued $10,000,000 of 20-year bonds on January 1 of the current year. The bond indenture requires that equal deposits be made in a bond sinking fund at the end of each of the 20 years. The fund is expected to be invested in securities that will yield 12% per year compounded annually.

(a) Determine the amount of each of the 20 deposits to be made in the bond sinking fund.
(b) Prepare the entry to record the first deposit made in the sinking fund.

12–34. Entries for bond sinking fund and appropriation of retained earnings. Yaxley Corporation issued $20,000,000 of 20-year bonds on the first day of the fiscal year. The bond indenture provides that a sinking fund be accumulated by 20 annual deposits of $550,000, beginning at the end of the first year.

Present the entries to record the following selected transactions related to the bond issue:

(a) The required amount is deposited in the sinking fund.
(b) Investments in securities from the first sinking fund deposit total $539,100.
(c) Appropriated $1,000,000 of retained earnings for bonded indebtedness.
(d) The sinking fund earned $36,500 during the year following the first deposit (summarizing entry).
(e) The bonds are paid at maturity, and excess cash of $97,750 in the fund is transferred to the cash account.
(f) Transferred the appropriation for bonded indebtedness balance of $20,000,000 back to retained earnings.

12–35. Computation of amortization of bond discount by both straight-line and interest methods. On July 1 of the current fiscal year, Rockford Company purchased $500,000 of 10-year, 10% bonds as a long-term investment directly from the issuing company for $442,650. The effective rate of interest is 12%, and the interest is payable semiannually. Compute the amount of discount to be amortized for the first semiannual interest payment period, using (a) the straight-line method and (b) the interest method.

12–36. Entries for purchase and sale of investment in bonds. Present entries to record the following selected transactions of Hackman Corporation:

(a) Purchased for cash $200,000 of Dirch Co. 11% bonds at 102 plus accrued interest of $5,500.
(b) Received first semiannual interest.
(c) Amortized $360 on the bond investment at the end of the first year.
(d) Sold the bonds at 99 plus accrued interest of $2,775. The bonds were carried at $201,500 at the time of the sale.

12–37. Entries for bonds payable transactions. The following transactions were completed by Harlow Co., whose fiscal year is the calendar year:

1989

Oct. 1. Issued $10,000,000 of 10-year, 12% callable bonds dated October 1, 1989, for cash of $11,246,320. Interest is payable semiannually on October 1 and April 1.

Dec. 31. Recorded the adjusting entry for interest payable.

31. Recorded bond premium amortization of $18,842, which was determined using the interest method.

31. Closed the interest expense account.

1990

Jan. 1. Reversed the adjusting entry for interest payable.

Apr. 1. Paid the semiannual interest on the bonds.

Oct. 1. Paid the semiannual interest on the bonds.

Dec. 31. Recorded the adjusting entry for interest payable.

31. Recorded bond premium amortization of $79,184, which was determined by using the interest method.

31. Closed the interest expense account.

1996

Oct. 1. Recorded the redemption of the bonds, which were called at 102. The balance in the bond premium account is $507,764 after the payment of interest and amortization of premium have been recorded. (Record the redemption only.)

Instructions: (1) Prepare entries to record the foregoing transactions.

(2) Indicate the amount of the interest expense in (a) 1989 and (b) 1990.

(3) Determine the effective interest rate by dividing the interest expense for 1989 by the bond carrying amount at the time of issuance and converting the result to an annual rate.

(4) Determine the carrying amount of the bonds as of December 31, 1990.

12–38. Entries for bonds payable transactions. On July 1, 1989, Betz Corporation issued $12,000,000 of 10-year, 10% bonds at an effective interest rate of 11%. Interest on the bonds is payable semiannually on December 31 and June 30. The fiscal year of the company is the calendar year.

Instructions: (1) Present the entry to record the amount of the cash proceeds from the sale of the bonds. Use the tables of present values appearing in this chapter to compute the cash proceeds, rounding to the nearest dollar.

(2) Present the entries to record the following selected transactions for 1989 and 1990:

(a) The entry for the payment of interest and the amortization of the bond discount on December 31, 1989, using the interest method.

(b) The semiannual interest payment on June 30, 1990, including the amortization of the bond discount, using the interest method.

(3) Present the entries for Instruction (2), using the straight-line method of discount amortization.

(4) What is the total interest expense for 1989 for (a) the interest method of discount amortization and (b) the straight-line method of discount amortization? (c) Will the annual interest expense using the interest method of discount amortization always be less than the annual interest expense using the straight-line method of discount amortization?

12–39. Entries for bond and sinking fund transactions, including appropriation of retained earnings. During 1989 and 1990, Watts Company completed the following transactions relating to its $4,500,000 issue of 30-year, 11% bonds dated September 1, 1989. Interest is payable on September 1 and March 1. The corporation's fiscal year is the calendar year.

1989
Sept. 1. Sold the bond issue for $4,197,600.
Dec. 31. Recorded the adjusting entry for interest payable.
Dec. 31. Recorded bond discount amortization of $3,360, which was determined by using the straight-line method.
31. Deposited $20,000 cash in a bond sinking fund.
31. Appropriated $50,000 of retained earnings for bonded indebtedness.
31. Closed the interest expense account.

1990
Jan. 1. Reversed the adjustment for interest payable.
15. Purchased various securities with sinking fund cash, cost $17,400.
Mar. 1. Paid the semiannual interest on the bonds.
Sept. 1. Paid the semiannual interest on the bonds.
Dec. 15. Recorded the receipt of $1,900 of income on sinking fund securities, depositing the cash in the sinking fund.
Dec. 31. Recorded the adjusting entry for interest payable.
31. Recorded bond discount amortization of $10,080, which was determined by using the straight-line method.
31. Deposited $60,000 cash in the sinking fund.
31. Appropriated $150,000 of retained earnings for bonded indebtedness.
31. Closed the interest expense account.

Instructions: (1) Prepare entries to record the foregoing transactions.
(2) Prepare a columnar table, using the following headings, and list the information for each of the two years.

			Account Balances at End of Year				
					Sinking Fund		
Year	Bond Interest Expense for Year	Sinking Fund Income for Year	Bonds Payable	Discount on Bonds	Cash	Investments	Appropriation For Bonded Indebtedness

12–40. Entries for bond and sinking fund transactions. The following transactions relate to the issuance of $900,000 of 10-year, 8% bonds dated January 1, 1980, and the accumulations in a sinking fund to redeem the bonds at maturity. Interest on the bonds is payable on June 30 and December 31.

1980
Jan. 2. Sold the bond issue at 100.
June 30. Paid semiannual interest on bonds.
Dec. 31. Paid semiannual interest on bonds and deposited $52,000 in a bond sinking fund.

1981
Jan. 13. Purchased $50,100 of investments with bond sinking fund cash.
June 30. Paid semiannual interest on bonds.
Nov. 11. Received $3,890 income on investments.
Dec. 31. Paid semiannual interest on bonds.

(Assume that all intervening transactions have been properly recorded.)

1990
Jan. 2. Sold all investments in the bond sinking fund for $880,500. The sinking fund investments had a book carrying value of $899,200.

Jan. 9. Paid the bonds at maturity from the sinking fund cash and the regular cash account. The cash available in the sinking fund at this date was $891,900.

Instructions: Prepare journal entries to record the foregoing transactions.

12–41. Entries for bond investments. The following transactions relate to certain securities acquired by Crawford Company, whose fiscal year ends on December 31:

1989

Nov. 1. Purchased $400,000 of Watson Company 20-year, 9% coupon bonds dated September 1, 1989, directly from the issuing company for $388,100 plus $6,000 accrued interest.

Dec. 31. Recorded the adjustment for interest receivable on the Watson Company bonds.

31. Recorded bond discount amortization of $100 on the Watson Company bonds. The amortization amount was determined by using the straight-line method.

(Assume that all intervening transactions and adjustments have been properly recorded, and that the number of bonds owned has not changed from December 31, 1989, to December 31, 1993.)

1994

Jan. 1. Reversed the adjustment of December 31, 1993, for interest receivable on the Watson Company bonds.

Mar. 1. Deposited the coupons for semiannual interest on the Watson Company bonds.

June 1. Sold one half of the Watson Company bonds at 98 plus accrued interest. The broker deducted $1,240 for commission, etc., remitting the balance. Before the sale was recorded, $125 of discount on one half of the bonds was amortized, increasing the carrying amount of those bonds to $195,425.

Sept. 1. Deposited coupons for semiannual interest on the Watson Company bonds.

Dec. 31. Recorded the adjustment for interest receivable on the Watson Company bonds.

31. Recorded bond discount amortization of $300 on the Watson Company bonds.

Instructions: (1) Prepare entries to record the foregoing transactions.
(2) Determine the amount of interest earned on the bonds in 1989.
(3) Determine the amount of interest earned on the bonds in 1994.

12–42. Work sheet and financial statements for corporation. The accounts in the ledger of Roberts Industries Inc., with the balances on December 31, 1989, the end of the current fiscal year, are as follows:

Cash	$ 56,200
Marketable Securities	30,000
Accounts Receivable	127,660
Allowance for Doubtful Accounts	1,200
Merchandise Inventory	130,000
Prepaid Insurance	9,120
Store Supplies	4,120
Bond Sinking Fund	70,100
Store Equipment	377,600
Accumulated Depreciation—Store Equipment	84,000
Office Equipment	136,000
Accumulated Depreciation—Office Equipment	51,080
Accounts Payable	55,900

Interest Payable	—
12% Bonds Payable	$ 160,000
Premium on Bonds Payable	9,800
Common Stock, $20 par	200,000
Retained Earnings	232,672
Sales	1,638,200
Purchases	1,239,960
Purchases Discounts	14,480
Sales Salaries and Commissions Expense	88,000
Advertising Expense	25,200
Depreciation Expense—Store Equipment	—
Store Supplies Expense	—
Miscellaneous Selling Expense	7,500
Office and Officers Salaries Expense	74,000
Rent Expense	48,000
Depreciation Expense—Office Equipment	—
Uncollectible Accounts Expense	—
Insurance Expense	—
Miscellaneous General Expense	6,380
Interest Expense	16,000
Sinking Fund Income	7,708
Interest Income	800
Income Tax	10,000

The data needed for year-end adjustments on December 31, 1989, are as follows:

Insurance expired during the year	$ 6,140
Store supplies inventory on December 31	1,520
Depreciation (straight-line method) for the current year on:	
Store equipment	30,800
Office equipment	18,720
Uncollectible accounts expense is estimated at 1% of sales.	
Bonds payable are due on November 1, 1994. Interest on bonds is payable on May 1 and November 1. Premium to be amortized on bonds payable, using the straight-line method	1,680

Instructions: (1) Prepare a work sheet for the fiscal year ended December 31. The merchandise inventory on December 31, 1989, using the first-in, first-out method, is $142,000.

(2) Prepare a multiple-step income statement.

(3) Prepare a report form balance sheet. (The market price of marketable securities is $31,600).

ALTERNATE PROBLEMS

12–37A. Entries for bonds payable transactions. The following transactions were completed by Valdez Industries Inc., whose fiscal year is the calendar year:

1989

Mar. 31. Issued $8,000,000 of 10-year, 10% callable bonds dated March 31, 1989, receiving cash of $7,521,760. Interest is payable semiannually on March 31 and September 30.

Sept. 30. Paid the semiannual interest on the bonds.

Dec. 31. Recorded the adjusting entry for interest payable.

31. Recorded bond discount amortization of $20,922, which was determined by using the interest method.

31. Closed the interest expense account.

1990
Jan. 1. Reversed the adjusting entry for interest payable.
Mar. 31. Paid the semiannual interest on the bonds.
Sept. 30. Paid the semiannual interest on the bonds.
Dec. 31. Recorded the adjusting entry for interest payable.
31. Recorded bond discount amortization of $30,512, which was determined by using the interest method.
31. Closed the interest expense account.

1997
Mar. 31. Recorded the redemption of the bonds, which were called at 102 1/2. The balance in the bond discount account is $140,738 after the payment of interest and amortization of discount have been recorded. (Record the redemption only.)

Instructions: (1) Prepare entries to record the foregoing transactions.
(2) Indicate the amount of the interest expense in (a) 1989 and (b) 1990.
(3) Determine the effective interest rate by dividing the interest expense for 1989 by the bond carrying amount at the time of issuance and converting the result to an annual rate.
(4) Determine the carrying amount of the bonds as of December 31, 1990.

12–38A. Entries for bonds payable transactions. On July 1, 1989, Pender Corporation issued $20,000,000 of 10-year, 12% bonds at an effective interest rate of 11%. Interest on the bonds is payable semiannually on December 31 and June 30. The fiscal year of the company is the calendar year.

Instructions: (1) Present the entry to record the amount of the cash proceeds from the sale of the bonds. Use the tables of present values appearing in this chapter to compute the cash proceeds, rounding to the nearest dollar.
(2) Present the entries to record the following:
(a) The first semiannual interest payment on December 31, 1989, including the amortization of the bond premium, using the interest method.
(b) The interest payment on June 30, 1990, including the amortization of the bond premium, using the interest method.
(3) Present the entries for Instruction (2), using the straight-line method of amortization.
(4) Determine the total interest expense for 1989 under (a) the interest method of premium amortization and (b) the straight-line method of premium amortization. (c) Will the annual interest expense using the interest method of premium amortization always be greater than the annual interest expense using the straight-line method of premium amortization?

12–39A. Entries for bond and sinking fund transactions, including appropriation of retained earnings. During 1989 and 1990, Carr Company completed the following transactions relating to its $5,000,000 issue of 20-year, 12% bonds dated February 1, 1989. Interest is payable on February 1 and August 1. The corporation's fiscal year is the calendar year.

1989
Feb. 1. Sold the bond issue for $5,402,000 cash.
Aug. 1. Paid the semiannual interest on the bonds.
Dec. 31. Recorded the adjusting entry for interest payable.
31. Recorded bond premium amortization of $18,425, which was determined by using the straight-line method.
31. Deposited $264,000 cash in a bond sinking fund.
31. Appropriated $440,000 of retained earnings for bonded indebtedness.
31. Closed the interest expense account.

1990
Jan. 1. Reversed the adjustment for interest payable.
9. Purchased various securities with sinking fund cash, cost $256,500.

Feb. 1. Paid the semiannual interest on the bonds.
Aug. 1. Paid the semiannual interest on the bonds.
Dec. 20. Recorded the receipt of $22,150 of income on sinking fund securities, depositing the cash in the sinking fund.
31. Recorded the adjusting entry for interest payable.
31. Recorded bond premium amortization of $20,100, which was determined by using the straight-line method.
31. Deposited $288,000 cash in the sinking fund.
31. Appropriated $480,000 of retained earnings for bonded indebtedness.
31. Closed the interest expense account.

Instructions: (1) Prepare entries to record the foregoing transactions.
(2) Prepare a columnar table, using the following headings, and list the information for each of the two years.

			Account Balances at End of Year				
					Sinking Fund		
Year	Bond Interest Expense for Year	Sinking Fund Income for Year	Bonds Payable	Premium on Bonds	Cash	Investments	Appropriation for Bonded Indebtedness

12–41A. Entries for bond investments. The following transactions relate to certain securities acquired as a long-term investment by Power Company, whose fiscal year ends on December 31:

1989
May 1. Purchased $100,000 of Bowen Company 15-year, 12% coupon bonds dated April 1, 1989, directly from the issuing company for $101,790 plus accrued interest of $1,000.
Oct. 1. Deposited the coupons for semiannual interest on the Bowen Company bonds.
Dec. 31. Recorded the adjustment for interest receivable on the Bowen Company bonds.
31. Recorded bond premium amortization of $80 on the Bowen Company bonds. The amortization amount was determined by using the straight-line method.

(Assume that all intervening transactions and adjustments have been properly recorded, and that the number of bonds owned has not changed from December 31, 1989, to December 31, 1994.)

1995
Jan. 1. Reversed the adjustment of December 31, 1994, for interest receivable on the Bowen Company bonds.
Apr. 1. Deposited coupons for semiannual interest on the Bowen Company bonds.
July 1. Sold one half of the Bowen Company bonds at 103 plus accrued interest. The broker deducted $540 for commission, etc., remitting the balance. Before the sale was recorded, $30 of premium on one half of the bonds was amortized, reducing the carrying amount of those bonds to $50,525.
Oct. 1. Deposited coupons for semiannual interest on the Bowen Company bonds.
Dec. 31. Recorded the adjustment for interest receivable on the Bowen Company bonds.
31. Recorded bond premium amortization of $60 on the Bowen Company bonds.

Instructions: (1) Prepare entries to record the foregoing transactions.
(2) Determine the amount of interest earned on the bonds in 1989.
(3) Determine the amount of interest earned on the bonds in 1995.

Mini-Case 12

You hold a 10% common stock interest in the family-owned business, a soft drink bottling distributorship. Your father, who is the manager, has proposed an expansion of plant facilities at an expected cost of $1,500,000. Two alternative plans have been suggested as methods of financing the expansion. Each plan is briefly described as follows:

Plan 1. Issue an additional 20,000 shares of $20 par common stock at $25 per share, and $1,000,000 of 20-year, 12% bonds at face amount.

Plan 2. Issue $1,500,000 of 20-year, 12% bonds at face amount.

The balance sheet as of the end of the previous fiscal year is as follows:

C-U Bottling Co.
Balance Sheet
December 31, 19--

Assets	
Current assets	$1,200,000
Plant assets	5,800,000
Total assets	$7,000,000
Liabilities and Stockholders' Equity	
Current liabilities	$1,800,000
Common stock, $20	600,000
Premium on common stock	150,000
Retained earnings	4,450,000
Total liabilities and stockholders' equity	$7,000,000

Net income has remained relatively constant over the past several years. The expansion program is expected to increase yearly income before bond interest and income tax from $700,000 to $960,000.

Your father has asked you, as the company treasurer, to prepare an analysis of each financing plan.

Instructions:

(1) Prepare a tabulation indicating the expected earnings per share on the common stock under each plan. Assume an income tax rate of 40%.
(2) List factors other than earnings per share that should be considered in evaluating the two plans.
(3) Which plan offers the greater benefit to the present stockholders? Give reasons for your opinion.

Answers to Self-Examination Questions

1. B Since the contract rate on the bonds is higher than the prevailing market rate, a rational investor would be willing to pay more than the face amount, or a premium (answer B), for the bonds. If the contract rate and the market rate were equal, the bonds could be expected to sell at their face amount (answer A). Likewise, if the market rate is higher than the contract rate, the bonds would sell at a price below their face amount (answer D) or at a discount (answer C).
2. A The bond carrying amount, sometimes called the book value, is the face amount plus unamortized premium or less unamortized discount. For this question, the carrying amount is $500,000 less $40,000, or $460,000 (answer A).
3. B Although the sinking fund may consist of cash as well as securities, the fund is listed on the balance sheet as an investment (answer B) because it is to be used to pay the long-term liability at maturity.
4. B The amount debited to the investment account is the cost of the bonds, which includes the amount paid to the seller for the bonds (101% × $100,000) plus broker's commissions ($50), or $101,050 (answer B). The $2,000 of accrued interest that is paid to the seller should be debited to Interest Income, since it is an offset against the amount that will be received as interest at the next interest date.
5. C The balance of Discount on Bonds Payable is usually reported as a deduction from Bonds Payable in the long-term liabilities section (answer C) of the balance sheet. Likewise, a balance in a premium on bonds payable account would usually be reported as an addition to Bonds Payable in the long-term liabilities section of the balance sheet.

13
Investments in Stocks; Consolidated Statements; International Operations

CHAPTER OBJECTIVES

Describe and illustrate the accounting for long-term investments in stocks.

Describe alternative methods of combining businesses.

Describe and illustrate the accounting for parent-subsidiary affiliations and the preparation of consolidated financial statements.

Illustrate a corporate balance sheet for a parent company and its subsidiaries.

Describe and illustrate the accounting for international operations.

In the preceding chapter, the principles of accounting for long-term investments in bonds were discussed. In this chapter, the principles of accounting for long-term investments in stocks will be presented. Accounting for the combining of the operations of two corporations and the expansion of operations into international markets will also be discussed.

INVESTMENTS IN STOCKS

A business may make long-term investments in **equity securities** (preferred and common shares), simply because it has cash that it does not need for normal operations. A corporation may also purchase stocks as a means of establishing or maintaining business relations with the issuing company. In some cases, a corporation may acquire all or a large part of the voting stock of another corporation in order to control its activities. Similarly, a corporation may organize a new corporation for the purpose of marketing a new product or for some other business reason, receiving stock in exchange for the assets transferred to the new corporation.

Investments in stocks may be purchased directly from the issuing corporation or from other investors. Both preferred and common stocks may be *listed* on an organized stock exchange, or they may be *unlisted*, in which case they are said to be bought or sold *over the counter.* The services of a broker are usually used in buying and selling both listed and unlisted securities.

The record of transactions on the stock exchanges is reported daily by the financial press. This record usually includes, for each stock traded, the high and low price for the past year, the current annual dividend, the volume of sales for the day, and the high, low, and closing price for the day. Prices for stocks are quoted in terms of fractional dollars, with 1/8 of a dollar being the usual minimum fraction, although some low-priced stocks are sold in lower fractions of a dollar, such as 1/16 or 1/32. Thus, a price of 40 3/8 per share means $40.375; a price of 40 1/2 means $40.50.

In the following discussion, attention will be given to the principles underlying the accounting for investments in stocks that are not intended as a ready source of cash in the normal operations of the business. Such investments are identified as long-term investments and are reported in the balance sheet under the caption "Investments." The principles underlying the accounting for investments in stocks that are classified as temporary investments or marketable securities were discussed in Chapter 6.

More Americans Than Ever Before Own Stock

About 47 million Americans own stock, more than ever before, but many are participants through stock mutual funds, according to a New York Stock Exchange survey.

The survey said the 47 million investors tallied as of mid-1985 were an 11 percent increase over the 42 million found in the exchange's last survey in mid-1983.

That means that one in five Americans is now a stock investor, as opposed to one of every six two years ago.

Women account for 57 percent of the new investors, the survey said; typically, she is married, employed in a technical or professional job, has an annual household income of $35,000 and a portfolio of $2,200.

Source: "More Americans Than Ever Before Own Stock," *Champaign-Urbana News Gazette,* December 5, 1985. © Associated Press.

ACCOUNTING FOR LONG-TERM INVESTMENTS IN STOCK

There are two methods of accounting for long-term investments in stock: (1) the **cost method** and (2) the **equity method.** The method used depends upon whether the investor owns enough of the voting stock of the investee (company whose stock is owned by the investor) to have a significant influence over its operating and financing policies. If the investor does not have a significant influence, the cost method (with the lower of cost or market rule) must be used. If the investor can exercise a significant influence in a long-term investment situation, the equity method must be used. Evidence of such influence includes, but is not limited to, representation on the board of directors, material intercompany transactions, and interchange of managerial personnel. Guidelines to be applied in making the election are as follows:

In order to achieve a reasonable degree of uniformity in application, the Board concludes that an investment (direct or indirect) of 20% or more of the voting stock of an investee should lead to a presumption that in the absence of evidence to the contrary an investor has the ability to exercise significant influence over an investee. Conversely, an investment of less than 20% of the voting stock of an investee should lead to a presumption that an investor does not have the ability to exercise significant influence unless such ability can be demonstrated.[1]

Cost Method

The cost of stocks purchased includes not only the amount paid to the seller but also other costs related to the purchase, such as the broker's commission and postage charges for delivery. When stocks are purchased between dividend dates, there is no separate charge for the pro rata amount of the dividend. Dividends do not accrue from day to day, since they become an obligation of the issuing corporation only when they are declared by the board of directors. The prices of stocks may be affected by the anticipated dividend as the usual declaration date approaches, but this anticipated dividend is only one of many factors that influence stock prices.

The total cost of stocks purchased should be debited to an investment account. When the cost method is used, cash dividends on capital stock held as an investment may be recorded as an increase in the appropriate income and asset accounts. To illustrate, assume that Ingle Corporation purchases 100 shares of Howe Corporation common stock at 55 plus a brokerage fee of $42. At the end of the year, Howe Corporation declares a $2 per share cash dividend. Entries in the accounts of Ingle Corporation, the investor, are as follows:

Record purchase of Howe Corp. common stock for $5,542 cash

		Debit	Credit
Entry:	Investment in Howe Corp. Stock..................	5,542	
	Cash		5,542

Record share of cash dividends paid by Howe Corp.

		Debit	Credit
Entry:	Cash	200	
	Dividend Income		200

In the illustration, the dividend was recorded when it became taxable to Ingle Corporation, which occurred when the cash was received. An alternative would be to record the cash dividend when it is declared by the investee corporation. If this alternative had been used, Ingle Corporation would have debited Dividends Receivable and credited Dividend Income when the dividend was declared. When the dividend was paid, Ingle Corporation would have debited Cash and credited the receivable.

A dividend in the form of additional shares of stock is usually not income, and therefore no entry is needed beyond a notation as to the additional number of shares acquired. The receipt of a stock dividend does, however, affect the carrying amount of each share of stock. Thus, if a 5-share common stock dividend is received on 100 shares of common stock with a current carrying amount of $4,200 ($42 per share), the unit carrying amount of the 105 shares becomes $4,200 ÷ 105, or $40 per share.

---

[1]*Opinions of the Accounting Principles Board, No. 18,* "The Equity Method of Accounting for Investments in Common Stock" (New York: American Institute of Certified Public Accountants, 1971), par. 17.

Long-term investments in stocks of a company over which the investor does not exercise significant influence are subject to the lower of cost or market rule. In applying the rule, the carrying amount of a long-term investment in a portfolio of equity securities is the lower of the *total* cost or *total* market price of the portfolio at the date of the balance sheet. Any market value changes that are recognized are not included in net income, but are reported as a separate item in the stockholders' equity section of the balance sheet.[2] If the decline in market value below cost of an individual security as of the balance sheet date is other than temporary, the cost basis of the individual security is written down and the amount of the write-down is accounted for as a realized loss. After the write-down, the carrying amount of the individual security cannot be changed for subsequent recoveries in market value.[3]

Equity Method

When the equity method of accounting is used, a stock purchase is recorded at cost as under the cost method. The features that distinguish the equity method from the cost method relate to the net income and cash dividends of the investee and are summarized as follows:

1. The investor records its share of the periodic net income of the investee as an increase in the investment account and as revenue of the period. Conversely, the investor's share of the investee's periodic loss is recorded as a decrease in the investment and a loss of the period.
2. The investor records its share of cash or property dividends on the stock as a decrease in the investment account and an increase in the appropriate asset accounts.

To illustrate the foregoing, assume that as of the beginning of the fiscal years of Otto Corporation and Parker Corporation, Otto acquires 40% of the common (voting) stock of Parker for $350,000 in cash, that Parker reports net income of $105,000 for the year, and that Parker declared and paid $45,000 in cash dividends during the year. Entries in the accounts of the investor to record these transactions are as follows:

Record purchase of 40% of Parker Corp. common stock for $350,000 cash

Entry:	Investment in Parker Corp. Stock	350,000	
	Cash		350,000

Record 40% of Parker Corp. net income of $105,000

Entry:	Investment in Parker Corp. Stock	42,000	
	Income of Parker Corp.		42,000

Record 40% of cash dividends of $45,000 paid by Parker Corp.

Entry:	Cash	18,000	
	Investment in Parker Corp. Stock		18,000

---

[2] *Statement of Financial Accounting Standards, No. 12*, "Accounting for Certain Marketable Securities" (Stamford: Financial Accounting Standards Board, 1975), par. 11.

[3] *Ibid.*, par. 21.

The combined effect of recording 40% of Parker Corporation's income and the dividends received was to increase Cash by $18,000, Investment in Parker Corp. Stock by $24,000, and Income of Parker Corp. by $42,000.

SALE OF LONG-TERM INVESTMENTS IN STOCKS

When shares of stock held as a long-term investment are sold, the investment account is credited for the carrying amount of the shares sold and the cash or appropriate receivable account is debited for the proceeds (sales price less commission and other selling costs). Any difference between the proceeds and the carrying amount is recorded as a gain or loss on the sale. To illustrate, assume that an investment in Drey Corporation stock has a carrying amount of $15,700. If the proceeds from the sale of the stock are $17,500, the entry to record the transaction is as follows:

Cash	17,500	
Investment in Drey Corp. Stock		15,700
Gain on Sale of Investments		1,800

BUSINESS COMBINATIONS

The history of business organization in the United States has been characterized by continuous growth in the size of business entities and the combining of separate enterprises to form even larger operating units. Over the past several years, the combining of businesses has increased dramatically both in numbers and dollars. In 1986, for example, more than 3,300 combinations took place, involving the exchange of cash, debt obligations, or capital stock of approximately $175 billion.[4] These combinations were influenced by such objectives as efficiencies of large-scale production, broadening of markets and sales volume, reduction of competition, diversification of product lines, and savings in income taxes.

The combining of businesses is often announced to the public, especially if the businesses are well known. For example, the advertisement at the top of page 487 appeared in *The Wall Street Journal* (February 9, 1987), announcing the acquisition of *Esquire Magazine* by the Hearst Corporation.

The combining of businesses that are engaged either in similar types of activity or in totally different kinds of pursuits may be effected (1) through a joining of two or more corporations to form a single unit by merger or by consolidation, or (2) through common control of two or more corporations by means of stock ownership that results in a parent-subsidiary affiliation. These methods of combining separate corporations into larger operating units are complex. Therefore, the discussion that follows is intended to be introductory, with major emphasis on the financial statements of business combinations.

Mergers and Consolidations

When one corporation acquires the properties of another corporation and the latter then dissolves, the joining of the two enterprises is called a **merger.** Usually, all of the assets of the acquired company, as well as its liabilities, are

[4]"Corporate Mergers Climbed 12% for 1986, Grimm Says," *The Wall Street Journal,* February 12, 1987.

Esquire Magazine Group, Inc.

has sold

Esquire Magazine

to

The Hearst Corporation

The undersigned acted as financial advisor to
Esquire Magazine Group, Inc.

The First Boston Corporation

February 9, 1987

taken over by the acquiring company, which continues its operations as a single unit. Payment may be in the form of cash, obligations, or capital stock of the acquiring corporation, or there may be a combination of several kinds of consideration. In any event, the consideration received by the dissolving corporation is distributed to its stockholders in final liquidation.

When two or more corporations transfer their assets and liabilities to a corporation which has been created for purposes of the takeover, the combination is called a **consolidation.** The new corporation usually issues its own securities in exchange for the properties acquired, and the original corporations are dissolved.

There are many legal, financial, managerial, and accounting problems associated with mergers and consolidations. Perhaps the most important matter is the determination of the class and amount of securities to be issued to the owners of the dissolving corporations. In resolving this problem, several factors are considered, including the relative value of the net assets contributed, the relative earning capacities, and the market price of the securities of the respective companies. Bargaining between the parties to the combination may also affect the final outcome.

Parent and Subsidiary Corporations

A common means of achieving a business combination is by one corporation owning a controlling share of the outstanding voting stock of one or more other corporations. When this method is used, none of the participants dissolves. All continue as separate legal entities. The corporation owning all or a majority of the voting stock of another corporation is known as the **parent company.** The corporation that is controlled is known as the **subsidiary company.** Two or more corporations closely related through stock ownership are sometimes called **affiliated** or **associated** companies.

The relationship of a parent and a subsidiary may be established by "purchase" or by a "pooling of interests." When a corporation acquires a controlling share of the voting common stock of another corporation in exchange for cash, other assets, issuance of notes or other debt obligations, or by a combination of these items, the transaction is treated as a purchase. It is accounted for by the **purchase method.** When this method of effecting a parent-subsidiary affiliation is used, the stockholders of the acquired company transfer their stock to the parent corporation.

Alternatively, when two corporations become affiliated by means of an exchange of voting common stock of one corporation (the parent) for substantially all (at least 90%) of the voting common stock of the other corporation (the subsidiary), the transaction is termed a pooling of interests. It is accounted for by the **pooling of interests method.** When this method of effecting a parent-subsidiary affiliation is used, the former stockholders of the subsidiary become stockholders of the parent company.

The accounting implications of the two affiliation methods are very different. The method first described is a "sale-purchase" transaction in contrast to the second method, in which there is a "joining of ownership interests" in the two companies.

The Accounting Principles Board established very strict criteria that must be met before the pooling of interests method can be used.[5] As a result, most business combinations are accounted for as a purchase. The 1987 edition of *Accounting Trends & Techniques* reported that, of the applicable companies surveyed, 92% of the business combinations were accounted for by the purchase method and 8% were accounted for by the pooling of interests method.

ACCOUNTING FOR PARENT-SUBSIDIARY AFFILIATIONS

Although the corporations that make up a parent-subsidiary affiliation may operate as a single economic unit, they continue to maintain separate accounting records and prepare their own periodic financial statements. The parent corporation uses the equity method of accounting for its investment in the stock of a subsidiary.

After the parent-subsidiary relationship has been established, the investment account of the parent is periodically increased by its share of the subsidiary's net income and decreased by its share of dividends received from the subsidiary. At the end of each fiscal year, the parent reports the investment account balance on its own balance sheet as a long-term investment, and its current share of the subsidiary's net income on its own income statement as a separate item.

In addition to the interrelationship through stock ownership, there are usually other intercorporate transactions which have an effect on the financial

[5] *Opinions of the Accounting Principles Board, No. 16,* "Business Combinations" (New York: American Institute of Certified Public Accountants, 1970).

statements of both the parent and the subsidiary. For example, either may own bonds or other evidences of indebtedness issued by the other and either may purchase or sell goods or services to the other.

Because of the central managerial control factor and the intertwining of relationships, it is usually desirable to present the results of operations and the financial position of a parent company and its subsidiaries as if the group were a single company with one or more branches or divisions. Such statements are likely to be more meaningful to stockholders of the parent company than separate statements for each corporation. Thus, with few exceptions, the financial statements of all subsidiaries should be combined with those of the parent.[6] The financial statements resulting from the combining of parent and subsidiary statements are generally called **consolidated statements.** Specifically, such statements may be identified by the addition of "and subsidiary(ies)" to the name of the parent corporation or by modification of the title of the respective statement, as in *consolidated balance sheet* or *consolidated income statement*.

BASIC PRINCIPLES OF CONSOLIDATION OF FINANCIAL STATEMENTS

When the data on the financial statements of the parent corporation and its subsidiaries are combined to form the consolidated statements, special attention should be given to the ties of relationship between the separate corporations. These ties are represented by the intercompany items appearing in their respective ledgers and statements. Examples of such intercompany items include notes receivable and notes payable, accounts receivable and accounts payable, interest receivable and interest payable, sales and purchases (or cost of merchandise sold), and interest expense and interest income. The intercompany items, which are called **reciprocals**, must be eliminated from the statements that are to be consolidated. For example, a note representing a loan by a parent corporation to its subsidiary would appear as a note receivable in the parent's balance sheet and a note payable in the subsidiary's balance sheet. When the two balance sheets are combined, the note receivable and the note payable would be eliminated because the consolidated balance sheet is prepared as if the parent and subsidiary were one operating unit. After the proper eliminations are made, the remaining items on the financial statements of the subsidiary are combined with the like items on the financial statements of the parent.

The intercompany accounts of a parent and its subsidiaries may not be entirely reciprocal in amount. Differences may be caused by the manner in which the parent-subsidiary relationship was created, by the extent of the parent's ownership of the subsidiary, or by the nature of their subsequent intercompany transactions. Such factors must be considered when the financial statements of affiliated corporations are consolidated.

To direct attention to the basic concepts of consolidation, most of the data appearing in financial statements will be omitted from many of the illustra-

[6] *Statement of Financial Accounting Standards, No. 94,* "Consolidation of All Majority-Owned Subsidiaries" (Stamford: Financial Accounting Standards Board, 1987). Examples of consolidated statements are presented in Appendix J.

tions in the following paragraphs. The term "net assets" will be used as a substitute for the specific assets and liabilities that appear in the balance sheet. Explanations will also be simplified by using the term "book equity" in referring to the monetary amount of the stockholders' equity of the subsidiary acquired by the parent. The illustrative companies will be identified as Parent and Subsidiary.

Purchase Method

When a parent-subsidiary affiliation is effected as a purchase, the parent corporation is deemed to have purchased all or a major part of the subsidiary corporation's net assets. Accordingly, the principles of accounting for a sale-purchase transaction are applied to the consolidation of the parent and the subsidiary.

Consolidated Balance Sheet at Date of Acquisition. At the date of acquisition, the assets of the subsidiary should be reported on the consolidated balance sheet at their cost to the parent, as measured by the amount of the consideration given in acquiring the stock. The reciprocal of the investment account in the parent's ledger at the date of acquisition is the composite of all of the stockholders' equity accounts in the subsidiary's ledger. Any difference between the cost to the parent and the amounts reported on the subsidiary's balance sheet must be given recognition on the consolidated balance sheet.

Income from an investment in assets does not accrue to an investor until after the assets have been purchased. Therefore, subsidiary company earnings accumulated prior to the date of the parent-subsidiary purchase affiliation must be excluded from the consolidated balance sheet and the income statement. Only those earnings of the subsidiary realized subsequent to the affiliation are includable in the consolidated statements.

Wholly Owned Subsidiary Acquired at a Cost Equal to Book Equity. Assume that Parent creates Subsidiary, transferring to it $120,000 of assets and $20,000 of liabilities, and taking in exchange 10,000 shares of $10 par common stock of Subsidiary. The effect of the transaction on Parent's ledger is to replace the various assets and liabilities (net assets of $100,000) with a single account: Investment in Subsidiary, $100,000. The effect on the balance sheet of Parent, together with the balance sheet of Subsidiary prepared immediately after the transaction, is as follows:

	Assets	Stockholders' Equity
Parent:		
Investment in Subsidiary, 10,000 shares	$100,000	
Subsidiary:		
Net assets	$100,000	
Common stock, 10,000 shares, $10 par		$100,000

When the balance sheets of the two corporations are consolidated, the reciprocal accounts Investment in Subsidiary and Common Stock are offset against each other, or *eliminated*. The individual assets (Cash, Equipment, etc.) and the individual liabilities (Accounts Payable, etc.) making up the $100,000 of net assets on the balance sheet of Subsidiary are then added to the corresponding items on the balance sheet of Parent. The consolidated balance sheet is completed by listing Parent's paid-in capital accounts and retained earnings.

Wholly Owned Subsidiary Acquired at a Cost Above Book Equity. Instead of creating a new subsidiary, a corporation may acquire an already established corporation by purchasing its stock. In such cases, the subsidiary stock's total cost to the parent usually differs from the book equity of such stock. To illustrate, assume that Parent acquires for $180,000 all of the outstanding stock of Subsidiary, a going concern, from Subsidiary's stockholders. Assume further that the stockholders' equity of Subsidiary is made up of common stock of $100,000 (10,000 shares, $10 par) and $50,000 of retained earnings. Parent records the investment at its cost of $180,000, regardless of the amount of the book equity of Subsidiary. It should also be noted that the $180,000 paid to Subsidiary's stockholders has no effect on the assets, liabilities, or stockholders' equity of Subsidiary. The situation immediately after the transaction may be presented as follows:

	Assets	*Stockholders' Equity*
Parent:		
Investment in Subsidiary, 10,000 shares	$180,000	
Subsidiary:		
Net assets	$150,000	
Common stock, 10,000 shares, $10 par		$100,000
Retained earnings		50,000

It is readily apparent that the reciprocal items on the separate balance sheets differ by $30,000. If the reciprocals were eliminated, as in the preceding illustration, and were replaced solely by Subsidiary's net assets of $150,000, the consolidated balance sheet would be out of balance.

The treatment of the $30,000 difference depends upon the reason that Parent paid more than book equity for Subsidiary's stock. When the amount paid above book equity is due to an excess of fair market value over book value of Subsidiary's assets, the values of the appropriate assets should be revised upward by $30,000. For example, if land that Subsidiary had acquired several years previously at a cost of $50,000 (book value) has a current fair market value of $80,000, the book amount should be increased from $50,000 to $80,000 when the asset is reported on the consolidated balance sheet. When Parent has paid more for Subsidiary's stock because Subsidiary has prospects for high future earnings, the $30,000 should be reported on the consolidated balance sheet under a description such as "Goodwill" or "Excess of cost of business acquired over related net assets."

When the amount paid above book equity is due to both an excess of fair market value over book value of assets and high future earnings prospects, the excess of cost over book equity should be allocated accordingly.[7] To illustrate, assume that the $30,000 difference in the illustration is due to a $20,000 excess of fair value over book value of Subsidiary's land and Subsidiary prospects for high future earnings. The book amount of the land, which had cost $50,000, would be increased to $70,000, and goodwill of $10,000 would be reported on the consolidated balance sheet.

[7] *Opinions of the Accounting Principles Board, No. 16, op. cit.,* par. 87.

Wholly Owned Subsidiary Acquired at a Cost Below Book Equity. All of the stock of a corporation may be acquired from its stockholders at a cost that is less than book equity. To illustrate, assume that the stock in Subsidiary is acquired for $130,000 and that the composition of the stockholders' equity of Subsidiary is the same as in the preceding illustration. Parent records the investment at its cost of $130,000. The situation immediately after the transaction is as follows:

	Assets	Stockholders' Equity
Parent:		
Investment in Subsidiary, 10,000 shares	$130,000	
Subsidiary:		
Net assets	$150,000	
Common stock, 10,000 shares, $10 par......		$100,000
Retained earnings..........................		50,000

Elimination of the reciprocal accounts and reporting the $150,000 of net assets of Subsidiary on the consolidated balance sheet creates an imbalance of $20,000. The possible reasons for the apparent "bargain" purchase and the treatment of the imbalance are generally the reverse of those given in explaining acquisition at a price higher than book equity. The complexities that might arise in some instances are discussed in advanced texts.

Partially Owned Subsidiary Acquired at a Cost Above or Below Book Equity. When one corporation seeks to gain control over another by purchase of its stock, it is not necessary and often not possible to acquire all of the stock. To illustrate this situation, assume that Parent acquires, at a total cost of $190,000, 80% of the stock of Subsidiary, whose book equity is composed of common stock of $100,000 (10,000 shares, $10 par) and $80,000 of retained earnings. The relevant data immediately after the acquisition of the stock are as follows:

	Assets	Stockholders' Equity
Parent:		
Investment in Subsidiary, 8,000 shares	$190,000	
Subsidiary:		
Net assets	$180,000	
Common stock, 10,000 shares, $10 par......		$100,000
Retained earnings..........................		80,000

The explanation of the $10,000 imbalance in the reciprocal items in this illustration is more complex than in the preceding illustrations. Two factors are involved: (1) the amount paid for the stock is greater than 80% of Subsidiary's book equity and (2) only 80% of Subsidiary's stock was purchased. Since Parent acquired 8,000 shares or 80% of the outstanding shares of Subsidiary, only 80% of the stockholders' equity accounts of Subsidiary can be eliminated. The remaining 20% of the stock is owned by outsiders, who are called collectively the **minority interest.** The eliminations from the partially reciprocal accounts and the amounts to be reported on the consolidated balance sheet, including the minority interest, are determined as follows:

Parent:		
Investment in Subsidiary		$190,000
Eliminate 80% of Subsidiary stock	$ 80,000	
Eliminate 80% of Subsidiary retained earnings	64,000	144,000
Excess of cost over book equity of Subsidiary interest		$ 46,000
Subsidiary:		
Common stock	$100,000	
Eliminate 80% of Subsidiary stock	80,000	
Remainder		$ 20,000
Retained earnings	$ 80,000	
Eliminate 80% of Subsidiary retained earnings	64,000	
Remainder		16,000
Minority interest		$ 36,000

The excess cost of $46,000 is reported on the consolidated balance sheet as goodwill or the valuation placed on other assets is increased by $46,000, according to the principles explained earlier. The minority interest of $36,000, which is the amount of Subsidiary's book equity allocable to outsiders, is reported on the consolidated balance sheet, usually preceding the stockholders' equity accounts of Parent. The 1987 edition of *Accounting Trends & Techniques* indicates that minority interest is reported in the long-term liabilities section by most of the companies surveyed.

Consolidated Balance Sheet Subsequent to Acquisition. Subsequent to acquisition of a subsidiary, the parent company uses the equity method to account for its investment in the subsidiary. Thus, the parent company's investment account is increased periodically for its share of the subsidiary's earnings and decreased for the related dividends received. Correspondingly, the retained earnings account of the subsidiary will be increased periodically by the amount of its net income and reduced by dividend distributions. Because of these periodic changes in the balances of the reciprocal accounts, the eliminations required in preparing a consolidated balance sheet will change each year.

To illustrate consolidation of balance sheets subsequent to acquisition, assume that Subsidiary in the preceding illustration earned net income of $50,000 and paid dividends of $20,000 during the year subsequent to Parent's acquisition of 80% of its stock. The net effect of the year's transactions on Subsidiary were as follows:

	Net Assets	*Common Stock*	*Retained Earnings*
Subsidiary:			
Date of acquisition	$180,000	$100,000	$ 80,000
Add net income	50,000		50,000
Deduct dividends	(20,000)		(20,000)
Date subsequent to acquisition	$210,000	$100,000	$110,000

Parent's entries to record its 80% share of subsidiary's net income and dividends are as follows:

Parent:		
Investment in Subsidiary	40,000	
Income of Subsidiary		40,000
Cash	16,000	
Investment in Subsidiary		16,000

The net effect of the foregoing entries on Parent's investment account is to increase the balance by $24,000, as follows:

Parent:		
Investment in subsidiary, 8,000 shares:		
Date of acquisition		$190,000
Add 80% of Subsidiary's net income	$40,000	
Deduct 80% of Subsidiary's dividends	(16,000)	24,000
One year subsequent to acquisition		$214,000

Continuing the illustration, the eliminations from the partially reciprocal accounts and the amounts to be reported on the consolidated balance sheet are determined as follows:

Parent:		
Investment in Subsidiary		$214,000
Eliminate 80% of Subsidiary stock	$ 80,000	
Eliminate 80% of Subsidiary retained earnings	88,000	168,000
Excess of cost over book equity of Subsidiary interest		$ 46,000
Subsidiary:		
Common stock	$100,000	
Eliminate 80% of Subsidiary stock	80,000	
Remainder		$ 20,000
Retained earnings	$110,000	
Eliminate 80% of Subsidiary retained earnings	88,000	
Remainder		22,000
Minority interest		$ 42,000

A comparison of the data with the analysis as of the date of acquisition shows the following:

1. Minority interest increased $6,000 (from $36,000 to $42,000), which is equivalent to 20% of the $30,000 net increase ($50,000 of net income less $20,000 of dividends) in Subsidiary's retained earnings.
2. Excess of cost over book equity of the subsidiary interest remained unchanged at $46,000.

To avoid additional complexities, it was assumed that the $46,000 excess at the date of acquisition was not due to goodwill or to assets subject to depreciation or amortization.[8]

Work Sheet for Consolidated Balance Sheet. The preceding discussion focused on the basic concepts associated with the process of preparing consolidated balance sheets. If the consolidation process becomes quite complex or if the amount of data to be processed is substantial, all of the relevant data for the consolidated statements may be assembled on work sheets. Although a work sheet is not essential, it is used in the following illustration to show an alternate method of accumulating all relevant data for the consolidated balance sheet. Whether or not a work sheet is used, the basic concepts and the consolidated balance sheet would not be affected.

To illustrate the use of the work sheet, assume that (as was the case in the illustration in the preceding section) Parent had purchased 80% of Subsidiary stock for $190,000. For the year since the acquisition, Parent had debited the investment account for its share of Subsidiary earnings and had credited the investment account for its share of dividends declared by Subsidiary. Balance sheet data for Parent and Subsidiary as of December 31 of the year subsequent to acquisition appear as follows. Although these data include amounts for land, other assets, and liabilities, the net assets and stockholders' equity for Subsidiary are the same as in the preceding illustration.

	Parent	*Subsidiary*
Investment in Subsidiary	$214,000	
Land	100,000	$ 60,000
Other assets	400,000	200,000
	$714,000	$260,000
Liabilities	$164,000	$ 50,000
Common stock:		
Parent	300,000	
Subsidiary		100,000
Retained earnings:		
Parent	250,000	
Subsidiary		110,000
	$714,000	$260,000

The account balances at December 31 and the eliminations from the reciprocal accounts would be entered on the work sheet. The amounts would be determined for the consolidated balance sheet items as follows (the right margin notations are added as an aid to understanding):

[8] Any portion of the excess of cost over book equity assigned to goodwill must be amortized according to *Opinions of the Accounting Principles Board, No. 17,* "Intangible Assets." Similarly, any excess of cost over book equity assigned to plant assets of limited life must be gradually reduced by depreciation. The application of such amortization and depreciation techniques to consolidated statements goes beyond the scope of the discussion here.

Parent and Subsidiary
Work Sheet for Consolidated Balance Sheet
December 31, 19--

	Parent	Subsidiary	Eliminations Debit	Eliminations Credit	Consolidated Balance Sheet	
Investment in Subsidiary . .	214,000			168,000	46,000	Excess of cost over book equity
Land	100,000	60,000			160,000	
Other Assets	400,000	200,000			600,000	
	714,000	260,000			806,000	
Liabilities	164,000	50,000			214,000	
Common Stock:						
Parent	300,000				300,000	
Subsidiary		100,000	80,000		20,000	minority interest
Retained Earnings:						
Parent	250,000				250,000	
Subsidiary		110,000	88,000		22,000	minority interest
	714,000	260,000	168,000	168,000	806,000	

It should be noted that the work sheet is only an aid for accumulating the data for the consolidated balance sheet. It is not the consolidated balance sheet. Also, if there are other intercompany items that must be eliminated from the statements that are to be consolidated, those eliminations would be entered in the eliminations columns of the work sheet. For example, a loan by a parent to its subsidiary on a note would require an elimination of the amount of the note from both notes receivable and notes payable in the work sheet.

When 80% of Subsidiary common stock and Subsidiary retained earnings is eliminated against the Investment in Subsidiary, as indicated in the eliminations columns of the work sheet, (1) the $46,000 excess of cost over book equity of the subsidiary interest can be identified and (2) the minority interest of $42,000 (consisting of $20,000 related to subsidiary common stock and $22,000 related to subsidiary retained earnings) can be identified. The $46,000 excess of cost over book equity is reported on the consolidated balance sheet according to the principles explained earlier.

In the following balance sheet, it is assumed that the $46,000 is due to an excess of fair value over book value of Subsidiary's land. Thus, the amount for land as reported on the consolidated balance sheet would be $206,000, consisting of the parent's amount of $100,000 plus the subsidiary's amount of $106,000 (the $60,000 book amount plus the $46,000 excess of cost over book equity attributable to the land). The minority interest of $42,000 is also reported on the consolidated balance sheet as explained earlier.

Parent and Subsidiary Consolidated Balance Sheet December 31, 19--	
Assets	
Land	$206,000
Other assets	600,000
Total assets	$806,000
Liabilities and Stockholders' Equity	
Liabilities	$134,000
Minority interest in subsidiary	42,000
Common stock	300,000
Retained earnings	250,000
Total liabilities and stockholders' equity	$806,000

Pooling of Interests Method

When a parent-subsidiary affiliation is effected as a pooling of interests, the ownership of the two companies is joined together in the parent corporation. The parent deems its investment in the subsidiary to be equal to the carrying amount of the subsidiary's net assets. Any difference that may exist between such carrying amount and the fair value of the subsidiary's assets does not affect the amount recorded by the parent as the investment.

Consolidated Balance Sheet at Date of Affiliation. Since the parent's investment in the subsidiary is equal to the carrying amount of the subsidiary's net assets, no change is needed in the amounts at which the subsidiary's assets should be included in the consolidated balance sheet prepared at the date of affiliation. The subsidiary's assets are reported as they appear in the subsidiary's separate balance sheet.

The credit to the parent company's stockholders' equity accounts for the stock issued in exchange for the subsidiary company's stock corresponds to the amount debited to the investment account. In addition to the common stock account, the paid-in capital accounts may be affected, as well as the retained earnings account. According to the concept of continuity of ownership interests, subsidiary earnings accumulated prior to the affiliation should be combined with those of the parent on the consolidated balance sheet. It is as though there had been a single economic unit from the time the enterprises had begun.

To illustrate the procedure for consolidating the balance sheets of two corporations by the pooling of interests method, their respective financial positions immediately prior to the exchange of stock are assumed to be as follows:

	Assets	*Stockholders' Equity*
Parent:		
Net assets	$230,000	
Common stock, 4,000 shares, $25 par		$100,000
Retained earnings		130,000

	Assets	Stockholders' Equity
Subsidiary:		
Net assets	$150,000	
Common stock, 10,000 shares, $10 par		$100,000
Retained earnings		50,000

Since poolings must involve substantially all (90% or more) of the stock of the subsidiary, the illustration will assume an exchange of 100% of the stock. It is also assumed that the fair market value of the net assets of both companies is greater than the amounts reported above and that there appears to be an element of goodwill in both cases. Based on recent price quotations, it is agreed that for the purpose of the exchange, Parent's common stock is to be valued at $45 a share and Subsidiary's at $18 a share.[9] According to the agreement, the exchange of stock is brought about as follows:

Parent issues 4,000 shares valued at $45 per share	$180,000
in exchange for	
Subsidiary's 10,000 shares valued at $18 per share	$180,000

The excess of the $180,000 value of Parent's stock issued over the $150,000 of net assets of Subsidiary may be ignored and the investment recorded as follows:

Parent:		
Investment in Subsidiary	150,000	
Common Stock		100,000
Retained Earnings		50,000

After the foregoing entry has been recorded, the basic balance sheet data of the two companies are as follows:

	Assets	Stockholders' Equity
Parent:		
Investment in Subsidiary, 10,000 shares	$150,000	
Other net assets	230,000	
Common stock, 8,000 shares, $25 par		$200,000
Retained earnings		180,000
Subsidiary:		
Net assets	$150,000	
Common stock, 10,000 shares, $10 par		$100,000
Retained earnings		50,000

To consolidate the balance sheets of the two companies, Parent's investment account and Subsidiary's common stock and retained earnings accounts are eliminated. The net assets of the two companies, $230,000 and $150,000, are combined without any changes in valuation, making a total of

[9] In practice, it may be necessary to pay cash for fractional shares or for subsidiary shares held by dissenting stockholders.

$380,000. The consolidated stockholders' equity is composed of common stock of $200,000 and retained earnings of $180,000, for a total of $380,000.

Consolidated Balance Sheet Subsequent to Affiliation. The equity method is used by the parent corporation in recording changes in its investment account subsequent to acquisition. Thus, the account is increased by the parent's share of the subsidiary's earnings and decreased by its share of dividends. Continuing the illustration of the preceding section, assume that Subsidiary's net income and dividends paid during the year subsequent to affiliation with Parent are $20,000 and $5,000 respectively. After Parent has recorded Subsidiary's net income and dividends, the Parent's investment in Subsidiary increases by $15,000, and the Subsidiary's net assets and retained earnings increase by $15,000, yielding the following account balances:

	Assets	*Stockholders' Equity*
Parent:		
Investment in Subsidiary, 10,000 shares	$165,000	
Subsidiary:		
Net assets	$165,000	
Common stock, 10,000 shares, $10 par.......		$100,000
Retained earnings..........................		65,000

When the balance sheets of the affiliated corporations are consolidated, the reciprocal accounts are eliminated and the $165,000 of net assets of Subsidiary are combined with those of Parent.

Work Sheet for Consolidated Balance Sheet. To illustrate the use of the work sheet to assemble the relevant data for the consolidated balance sheet for an affiliation effected as a pooling of interests, assume that (as was the case in the illustration in the preceding section) Parent had exchanged 4,000 shares of its common stock for all of the 10,000 shares of Subsidiary common stock. For the year since the acquisition, Parent had debited the investment account for its share (100%) of Subsidiary earnings and had credited the investment account for its share (100%) of dividends declared by Subsidiary. Balance sheet data for Parent and Subsidiary as of December 31 of the year subsequent to acquisition appear as follows. As in the purchase illustration, amounts for land, other assets, and liabilities have been added, but the amounts for net assets and stockholders' equity for Subsidiary are the same as in the preceding illustration.

	Parent	*Subsidiary*
Investment in Subsidiary	$165,000	
Land..	80,000	$ 40,000
Other assets..................................	325,000	175,000
	$570,000	$215,000
Liabilities....................................	$140,000	$ 50,000
Common stock:		
Parent	200,000	
Subsidiary..................................		100,000
Retained earnings:		
Parent	230,000	
Subsidiary..................................		65,000
	$570,000	$215,000

The account balances at December 31 and the eliminations from the reciprocal accounts would be entered on the work sheet and the amounts determined for the consolidated balance sheet items as follows:

Parent and Subsidiary
Work Sheet for Consolidated Balance Sheet
December 31, 19--

	Parent	Subsidiary	Eliminations		Consolidated Balance Sheet
			Debit	Credit	
Investment in Subsidiary	165,000			165,000	
Land	80,000	40,000			120,000
Other Assets	325,000	175,000			500,000
	570,000	215,000			620,000
Liabilities	140,000	50,000			190,000
Common Stock:					
Parent	200,000				200,000
Subsidiary		100,000	100,000		
Retained Earnings:					
Parent	230,000				230,000
Subsidiary		65,000	65,000		
	570,000	215,000	165,000	165,000	620,000

After 100% of Subsidiary common stock and Subsidiary retained earnings is eliminated against Investment in Subsidiary, as indicated in the eliminations columns of the work sheet, the amounts for the two companies are combined, without any changes in valuation, and are then reported on the consolidated balance sheet.

As previously discussed, the work sheet is only an aid for accumulating the data for the consolidated balance sheet. These data are the basis for the consolidated balance sheet, which is prepared in the normal manner.

Consolidated Income Statement and Other Statements

Consolidation of income statements and other statements of affiliated companies usually presents fewer difficulties than those encountered in balance sheet consolidations. The difference is largely because of the inherent nature of the statements. The balance sheet reports cumulative effects of all transactions from the very beginning of an enterprise to a current date, whereas the income statement, the retained earnings statement, and the statement of cash flows (or statement of changes in financial position) report selected transactions only and are for a limited period of time, usually a year.

The principles used in the consolidation of the income statements of a parent and its subsidiaries are the same, regardless of whether the affiliation is deemed to be a purchase or a pooling of interests. When the income statements are consolidated, all amounts resulting from intercompany transactions, such as management fees or interest on loans charged by one affiliate to another, must be eliminated. Any intercompany profit included in inventories must also be eliminated. The remaining amounts of sales, cost of merchandise sold, operating expenses, and other revenues and expenses reported on the income statements of the affiliated corporations are then combined. The eliminations required in consolidating the retained earnings statement and other statements are based largely on data assembled in consolidating the balance sheet and income statement.

CORPORATION FINANCIAL STATEMENTS

Examples of retained earnings statements and sections of income statements affected by the corporate form of organization have been presented in preceding chapters. A complete balance sheet of a corporation, containing items discussed in this and preceding chapters, is illustrated on pages 502 and 503.

ACCOUNTING FOR INTERNATIONAL OPERATIONS

In an effort to expand operations, many U.S. companies conduct business in foreign countries. If the operations of these multinational companies involve currencies other than the dollar, special accounting problems may arise (1) in accounting for transactions with the foreign companies and (2) in the preparation of consolidated statements for domestic and foreign companies that are affiliated. The basic principles used in such situations are presented in the following paragraphs. Details and complexities are reserved for advanced texts.

Accounting for Transactions with Foreign Companies

If transactions with foreign companies are executed in dollars, no special accounting problems arise. Such transactions would be recorded as illustrated in the text. For example, the sale of merchandise to a Japanese company that is billed in and paid in dollars would be recorded by the U.S. company in the normal manner, using dollar amounts. However, if transactions involve receivables or payables that are to be received or paid in a foreign currency, the U.S. company may incur an exchange gain or loss.

Realized Currency Exchange Gains and Losses. When a U.S. company executes a transaction with a company in a foreign country using a currency other than the dollar, one currency needs to be converted into another to settle the transaction. For example, a U.S. company purchasing merchandise from a British company that requires payment in British pounds must exchange dollars ($) for pounds (£) to settle the transaction. This exchange of one currency into another involves the use of an exchange rate. The **exchange rate** is the rate at which one unit of currency (the dollar, for example) can be converted into another currency (the British pound, for example). To continue with the illustration, if the U.S. company had purchased merchandise for £1,000 from a British company on June 1, when the exchange rate was $1.40 per British pound, $1,400 would need to be exchanged for £1,000 to make the purchase.[10] Since the U.S. company maintains its accounts in dollars, the transaction would be recorded as follows:

[10]Foreign exchange rates are quoted in major financial reporting services. Because the exchange rates are quite volatile, those used in this chapter are assumed rates which do not necessarily reflect current rates.

June 1	Purchases	1,400	
	Cash		1,400
	Payment of Invoice No. 1725 from W. A. Sterling Co., £1,000; exchange rate, $1.40 per British pound.		

Special accounting problems arise when the exchange rate fluctuates between the date of the original transaction (such as a purchase on account) and the settlement of that transaction in cash in the foreign currency (such

Balance Sheet of a Corporation

Connor Corporation
Consolidated
December

Assets				
Current assets:				
Cash			$ 255,000	
Marketable securities, at cost (market price, $160,000)			152,500	
Accounts and notes receivable		$ 722,000		
Less allowance for doubtful receivables		37,000	685,000	
Inventories, at lower of cost (first-in, first-out) or market			917,500	
Prepaid expenses			70,000	
Total current assets				$2,080,000
Investments:				
Bond sinking fund			$ 422,500	
Investment in bonds of Dalton Company			240,000	
Total investments				662,500
	Cost	Accumulated Depreciation	Book Value	
Plant assets (depreciated by the straight-line method):				
Land	$ 250,000	—	$ 250,000	
Buildings	920,000	$ 379,955	540,045	
Machinery and equipment	2,764,400	766,200	1,998,200	
Total plant assets	$3,934,400	$1,146,155		2,788,245
Intangible assets:				
Goodwill			$ 300,000	
Organization costs			50,000	
Total intangible assets				350,000
Total assets				$5,880,745

as the payment of an account payable). In practice, such fluctuations are frequent. To illustrate, assume that on July 10, when the exchange rate was \$.004 per yen (Y), a purchase for Y100,000 was made from a Japanese company. Since the U.S. company maintains its accounts in dollars, the entry would be recorded at \$400 (Y100,000 × \$.004), as follows:

July 10	Purchases	400	
	Accounts Payable—M. Suzuki and Son		400
	Invoice No. 818, Y100,000, exchange rate, \$.004 per yen.		

and Subsidiaries
Balance Sheet
31, 19--

Liabilities				
Current liabilities:				
Accounts payable			\$ 508,810	
Income tax payable			120,500	
Dividends payable			94,000	
Accrued liabilities			81,400	
Total current liabilities				\$ 804,710
Long-term liabilities:				
Debenture 8% bonds payable, due December 31, 19--		\$1,000,000		
Less unamortized discount		60,000	\$ 940,000	
Minority interest in subsidiaries			115,000	
Total long-term liabilities				1,055,000
Deferred credits:				
Deferred income tax payable				95,500
Total liabilities				\$1,955,210
Stockholders' Equity				
Paid-in capital:				
Common stock, \$20 par (250,000 shares authorized, 100,000 shares issued)		\$2,000,000		
Premium on common stock		320,000		
Total paid-in capital			\$2,320,000	
Retained earnings:				
Appropriated:				
For bonded indebtedness	\$250,000			
For plant expansion	750,000	\$1,000,000		
Unappropriated		605,535		
Total retained earnings			1,605,535	
Total stockholders' equity				3,925,535
Total liabilities and stockholders' equity				\$5,880,745

If on the date of payment, August 9, the exchange rate had increased to \$.005 per yen, the Y100,000 account payable must be settled by exchanging \$500 (Y100,000 × \$.005) for Y100,000. In such a case, the U.S. company incurs an exchange loss of \$100, because \$500 was needed to settle a \$400 debt (account payable). The cash payment would be recorded as follows:

Aug. 9	Accounts Payable—M. Suzuki and Son	400	
	Exchange Loss	100	
	Cash		500
	Cash paid on Invoice No. 818, for Y100,000, or \$400, when exchange rate was \$.005 per yen.		

All transactions with foreign companies can be analyzed in the manner described above. For example, assume that on May 1, when the exchange rate was \$.25 per Swiss franc (F), a sale on account for \$1,000 to a Swiss company was billed in Swiss francs. The transaction would be recorded as follows:

May 1	Accounts Receivable—D. W. Robinson Co.	1,000	
	Sales		1,000
	Invoice No. 9772, F4,000; exchange rate, \$.25 per Swiss franc.		

If the exchange rate had increased to \$.30 per Swiss franc on May 31, the date of receipt of cash, the U.S. company would realize an exchange gain of \$200. The gain was realized because the F4,000, which had a value of \$1,000 on the date of sale, had increased in value to \$1,200 (F4,000 × \$.30) on May 31 when payment was received. The receipt of the cash would be recorded as follows:

May 31	Cash	1,200	
	Accounts Receivable—D. W. Robinson Co.		1,000
	Exchange Gain		200
	Cash received on Invoice No. 9772, for F4,000, or \$1,000, when exchange rate was \$.30 per Swiss franc.		

Unrealized Currency Exchange Gains and Losses. In the previous illustrations, the transactions were completed by either the receipt or the payment of cash. Therefore, any exchange gain or loss was realized and, in an accounting sense, was "recognized" at the date of the cash receipt or cash payment. However, if financial statements are prepared between the date of the original transaction (sale or purchase on account, for example) and the date of the cash receipt or cash payment, and the exchange rate has changed since the original transaction, an unrealized gain or loss must be recognized in the statements. To illustrate, assume that a sale on account for \$1,000 had been made to a German company on December 20, when the exchange rate was \$.50 per deutsche mark (DM), and that the transaction had been recorded as follows:

Dec. 20	Accounts Receivable—T. A. Mueller Inc.	1,000	
	Sales		1,000
	Invoice No. 1793, DM2,000; exchange rate, $.50 per deutsche mark.		

If the exchange rate had decreased to $.45 per deutsche mark on December 31, the date of the balance sheet, the $1,000 account receivable would have a value of only $900 (DM2,000 × $.45). This "unrealized" loss would be recorded as follows:

Dec. 31	Exchange Loss	100	
	Accounts Receivable—T. A. Mueller Inc.		100
	Invoice No. 1793, DM2,000 × $.05 decrease in exchange rate.		

Assuming that DM2,000 are received on January 19 in the following year, when the exchange rate is $.42, the additional decline in the exchange rate from $.45 to $.42 per deutsche mark must be recognized. The cash receipt would be recorded as follows:

Jan. 19	Cash	840	
	Exchange Loss ($.03 × DM2,000)	60	
	Accounts Receivable—T. A. Mueller Inc.		900
	Cash received on Invoice No. 1793, for DM2,000, or $900, when exchange rate was $.42 per deutsche mark.		

If the exchange rate had increased between December 31 and January 19, an exchange gain would be recorded on January 19. For example, if the exchange rate had increased from $.45 to $.47 per deutsche mark during this period, Exchange Gain would be credited for $40 ($.02 × DM2,000).

A balance in the exchange loss account at the end of the fiscal period should be reported in the Other Expense section of the income statement. A balance in the exchange gain account should be reported in the Other Income section.

Consolidated Financial Statements with Foreign Subsidiaries

Before the financial statements of domestic and foreign companies are consolidated, the amounts shown on the statements for the foreign companies must be converted to U.S. dollars. Asset and liability amounts are normally converted to U.S. dollars by using the exchange rates as of the balance sheet date. Revenues and expenses are normally converted by using the exchange rates that were in effect when those transactions were executed. (For practical purposes, a weighted average rate for the period is generally used.) The adjustments (gains or losses) resulting from the conversion are reported as a separate item in the stockholders' equity section of the balance sheets of the foreign companies.[11]

After the foreign company statements have been converted to U.S. dollars, the financial statements of U.S. and foreign subsidiaries are consolidated in the normal manner as described previously in this chapter.

Chapter Review

KEY POINTS

1. Investments in Stocks.
A business may make long-term investments in equity securities (preferred and common shares) with cash that it does not need for normal operations. A corporation may also purchase stocks as a means of establishing or maintaining business relations with the issuing company. In other cases, a corporation may acquire all or a large part of the voting stock of another corporation in order to control its activities.

2. Accounting for Long-Term Investments in Stock.
There are two methods of accounting for long-term investments in stock: (1) the cost method and (2) the equity method. The method used depends upon whether the investor owns enough of the voting stock of the investee (company whose stock is owned by the investor) to have a significant influence over its operating and financing policies. If the investor does not have a significant influence, the cost method (with the lower of cost or market rule) must be used. If the investor can exercise significant influence in a long-term investment situation, the equity method must be used.

The cost of stocks purchased includes not only the amount paid to the seller but also other costs related to the purchase, such as the broker's commission and postage charges for delivery. When the cost method is used, cash dividends on capital stock held as an investment may be recorded as an increase in the appropriate income and asset accounts. Under the cost method, the lower of cost or market rule must be applied to the total cost or total market price of the stock as of the date of the balance sheet. Any market value changes that are recognized are not included in net income, but are reported as a separate item in the stockholders' equity section of the balance sheet. If the decline in market value below cost for an individual security as of the balance sheet date is other than temporary, the cost basis of the individual security is written down and the amount of the write-down is accounted for as a realized loss. After the write-down, the carrying amount of the individual security cannot be changed for subsequent recoveries in market value.

When the equity method of accounting is used, a stock purchase is recorded at cost. The investor records its share of periodic net income of the investee as an increase in the investment account and as revenue of the period. Conversely, the investor's share of the investee's periodic loss is

[11] *Statement of Financial Accounting Standards, No. 52,* "Foreign Currency Translation" (Stamford: Financial Accounting Standards Board, 1981).

recorded as a decrease in the investment and a loss of the period. In addition, the investor records its share of cash or property dividends on the stock as a decrease in the investment account and as an increase in the appropriate asset accounts.

3. Sale of Long-Term Investments in Stocks.

When shares of stock held as a long-term investment are sold, the investment account is credited for the carrying amount of the shares sold and the cash or appropriate receivable account is debited for the proceeds (sales price less commission and other selling costs). Any difference between the proceeds and the carrying amount is recorded as a gain or loss on the sale.

4. Business Combinations.

Combinations of businesses may be effected (1) through a joining of two or more corporations to form a single unit by either merger or consolidation, or (2) through common control of two or more corporations by means of stock ownership that results in a parent-subsidiary affiliation. When a corporation acquires the properties of another corporation and the latter then dissolves, the joining of the two enterprises is called a merger. When two or more corporations transfer their assets and liabilities to a corporation which has been created for purposes of the takeover, the combination is called a consolidation. When a business combination is effected by one corporation acquiring a controlling share of the outstanding voting stock of one or more other corporations, the corporation owning the majority of the voting stock is known as the parent company. The corporation that is controlled is known as the subsidiary company. When a corporation acquires a controlling share of the voting stock of another corporation in exchange for cash, other assets, issuance of notes or other debt obligations, or by a combination of these items, the transaction is accounted for by the purchase method. When two corporations are combined by exchanging the voting common stock of one corporation (the parent) for substantially all (at least 90%) of the voting common stock of the other corporation (the subsidiary), the transaction is accounted for by the pooling of interests method.

5. Accounting for Parent-Subsidiary Affiliations.

Although the corporations that make up a parent-subsidiary affiliation may operate as a single economic unit, they usually continue to maintain separate accounting records and prepare their own periodic financial statements. The parent corporation uses the equity method of accounting for its investment in the stock of the subsidiary. The financial statements resulting from combining the parent and subsidiary statements are generally called consolidated statements.

6. Basic Principles of Consolidation of Financial Statements.

When the data on the financial statements of the parent corporation and its subsidiaries are combined to form the consolidated statements, special attention should be given to the intercompany items appearing on the separate corporation financial statements. These intercompany items must be eliminated in preparing financial statements for the consolidated entity.

When a parent-subsidiary affiliation is effected as a purchase, the parent corporation is deemed to have purchased all or a major part of the subsidiary corporation's net assets. Accordingly, the assets of the subsidiary should be reported on the consolidated balance sheet at their cost to the parent. The reciprocal of the investment account in the parent's ledger at the date of acquisition is the composite of all the stockholders' equity accounts in the subsidiary's ledger. In some cases, a parent corporation may pay an amount above the book equity of a subsidiary because the subsidiary has prospects for high future earnings. The amount of this excess should be identified on the consolidated balance sheet as goodwill. When a parent corporation purchases less than 100% of the subsidiary's stock, the remaining stockholders' equity is identified as minority interest. The minority interest is reported on the consolidated balance sheet, usually preceding the stockholders' equity accounts of the parent.

When a parent-subsidiary affiliation is effected as a pooling of interests, the ownership of the two companies is joined together in the parent corporation. The parent deems its investment in the subsidiary to be equal to the carrying amount of the subsidiary's net assets. Any difference that may exist between such carrying amount and the fair value of the subsidiary's assets does not affect the amount recorded by the parent as the investment. Consequently, no change is needed in the amounts at which the subsidiary's assets should be included in the consolidated balance sheet.

The principles used in the consolidation of income statements of a parent and its subsidiary are the same, regardless of whether the affiliation is deemed to be a purchase or a pooling of interests. When the income statements are consolidated, all amounts resulting from intercompany transactions, such as management fees or interest on loans charged by one affiliate to another, must be eliminated. Any intercompany profit included in inventories must also be eliminated.

7. Accounting for International Operations.
When U.S. companies conduct business in foreign countries, special accounting problems may arise (1) in accounting for transactions with foreign companies and (2) in the preparation of consolidated statements for domestic and foreign companies that are affiliated. When a U.S. company executes a transaction with a company in a foreign country using a currency other than the dollar, an exchange rate should be used to convert one currency into another to settle the transaction. Because of this conversion process, gains and losses on foreign transactions may arise. If a foreign transaction has not been completed by the end of the year, an unrealized currency exchange gain or loss may need to be recognized, depending upon fluctuations in the exchange rates.

Before the financial statements of domestic and foreign companies are consolidated, the statements of the foreign companies must be converted to U.S. dollars. Asset and liability amounts are normally converted to U.S. dollars by using the exchange rates as of the balance sheet date. Revenues and expenses are normally converted by using the exchange rates that were in effect when those transactions were executed.

KEY TERMS

equity securities 482
cost method 483
equity method 483
merger 486
consolidation 487
parent company 488
subsidiary company 488
purchase method 488
pooling of interests method 488
consolidated statements 489
minority interest 492
exchange rate 501

SELF-EXAMINATION QUESTIONS

(Answers at End of Chapter)

1. Which of the following are characteristic of a parent-subsidiary relationship known as a pooling of interests?
   A. Parent acquires substantially all of the voting stock of subsidiary in exchange for cash
   B. Parent acquires substantially all of the voting stock of subsidiary in exchange for its bonds payable
   C. Parent acquires substantially all of the voting stock of subsidiary in exchange for its voting common stock
   D. All of the above

2. P Co. purchased the entire outstanding stock of S Co. for $1,000,000 in cash. If at the date of acquisition, S Co.'s stockholders' equity consisted of $750,000 of common stock and $150,000 of retained earnings, what is the amount of the difference between cost and book equity of the subsidiary interest?
   A. Excess of cost over book equity of subsidiary interest, $250,000
   B. Excess of cost over book equity of subsidiary interest, $100,000
   C. Excess of book equity over cost of subsidiary interest, $250,000
   D. None of the above

3. If in Question 2, P Co. had purchased 90% of the outstanding stock of S Co. for $1,000,000, what is the amount of the difference between cost and book equity of subsidiary interest?
   A. Excess of cost over book equity of subsidiary interest, $100,000
   B. Excess of cost over book equity of subsidiary interest, $190,000
   C. Excess of cost over book equity of subsidiary interest, $250,000
   D. None of the above

4. Based on the data in Question 3, what is the amount of the minority interest at the date of acquisition?
   A. $15,000
   B. $75,000
   C. $100,000
   D. None of the above

5. On July 9, 1989, a sale on account for $10,000 to a Mexican company was billed for 250,000 pesos. The exchange rate was $.04 per peso on July 9 and $.05 per peso on August 8, 1989, when the cash was received on account. Which of the following statements identifies the exchange gain or loss for the fiscal year ended December 31, 1989?
   A. Realized exchange loss, $2,500
   B. Realized exchange gain, $2,500
   C. Unrealized exchange loss, $2,500
   D. Unrealized exchange gain, $2,500

ILLUSTRATIVE PROBLEM

All of Stereophonic Inc.'s outstanding shares of stock were acquired on October 1, 1989, by Piedmont Inc. After lengthy negotiations with Stereophonic Inc.'s major shareholder, it was agreed that (1) the current management of Stereophonic Inc. would be retained for a minimum of five years, (2) Stereophonic Inc. would be operated as an independent subsidiary, and (3) Piedmont Inc. would issue 1,200 of its own $100 par common stock in exchange for all of Stereophonic Inc.'s stock.

The balance sheets of the two corporations on September 30, 1989, were as follows:

	Piedmont Inc.	Stereophonic Inc.
Assets		
Cash	$ 124,200	$ 18,120
Accounts receivable	238,150	36,810
Inventory	405,750	61,300
Land	120,000	50,000
Plant and equipment (net)	612,300	120,450
	$1,500,400	$286,680
Liabilities and Stockholders' Equity		
Accounts payable	$ 136,400	$ 41,500
Common stock	900,000	120,000
Retained earnings	464,000	125,180
	$1,500,400	$286,680

Instructions:

1. Prepare the entry that should be made by Piedmont Inc. to record the combination as a pooling of interests.
2. Assuming the business combination is to be recorded as a pooling of interests, prepare a consolidated balance sheet for Piedmont Inc. and Stereophonic Inc. as of October 1, 1989.
3. Assume that Piedmont Inc. paid $106,000 in cash and issued 1,500 shares of Piedmont Inc. common stock with a fair market value of $212,000 for all the common stock of Stereophonic Inc. Prepare the entry for Piedmont Inc. to record the combination as a purchase.
4. Assuming that the business combination is to be recorded as a purchase and that the book values of the net assets of Stereophonic Inc. are approximately equal to their fair market values, prepare a consolidated balance sheet for Piedmont Inc. and Stereophonic Inc. as of October 1, 1989.

SOLUTION

(1)

Investment in Stereophonic Inc.	245,180	
Common Stock		120,000
Retained Earnings		125,180

(2) Piedmont Inc. and Subsidiary Stereophonic Inc.
Consolidated Balance Sheet
October 1, 1989

Assets		
Current assets:		
Cash	$ 142,320	
Accounts receivable	274,960	
Inventory	467,050	
Total current assets		$ 884,330
Plant assets:		
Land	$ 170,000	
Plant and equipment (net)	732,750	
Total plant assets		902,750
Total assets		$1,787,080
Liabilities		
Accounts payable		$ 177,900
Stockholders' Equity		
Common stock	$1,020,000	
Retained earnings	589,180	
Total stockholders' equity		1,609,180
Total liabilities and stockholders' equity		$1,787,080

(3)

Investment in Stereophonic Inc.	318,000	
Cash		106,000
Common Stock		150,000
Premium on Common Stock		62,000

(4) Piedmont Inc. and Subsidiary Stereophonic Inc.
Consolidated Balance Sheet
October 1, 1989

Assets		
Current assets:		
Cash*	$ 36,320	
Accounts receivable	274,960	
Inventory	467,050	
Total current assets		$ 778,330
Plant assets:		
Land	$ 170,000	
Plant and equipment (net)	732,750	
Total plant assets		902,750
Intangible assets:		
Goodwill**		72,820
Total assets		$1,753,900

Liabilities		
Accounts payable		$ 177,900
Stockholders' Equity		
Common stock,	$1,050,000	
Premium on common stock	62,000	
Retained earnings	464,000	
Total stockholders' equity		1,576,000
Total liabilities and stockholders' equity		$1,753,900

*$124,200 + $18,120 − $106,000 = $36,320
**$318,000 − $245,180 = $72,820

Discussion Questions

13–1. (a) What are two methods of accounting for long-term investments in stock? (b) Under what caption are long-term investments in stocks reported on the balance sheet?

13–2. When stocks are purchased between dividend dates, does the purchaser pay the seller the dividend accrued since the last dividend payment date? Explain.

13–3. A stockholder owning 200 shares of Tone Co. common stock, acquired at a total cost of $5,880, receives a common stock dividend of 10 shares. What is the carrying amount per share after the stock dividend?

13–4. What terms are applied to the following: (a) a corporation that is controlled by another corporation through ownership of a controlling interest in its stock; (b) a corporation that owns a controlling interest in the voting stock of another corporation; (c) a group of corporations related through stock ownership?

13–5. What are the two methods by which the relationship of parent-subsidiary may be established?

13–6. P Company purchases for $5,000,000 the entire common stock of S Corporation. What type of accounts on S's balance sheet are reciprocal to the investment account on P's balance sheet?

13–7. Are the eliminations of the reciprocal accounts in consolidating the balance sheets of P and S in Question 13–6 recorded in the respective ledgers of the two companies? Explain.

13–8. Powers Company purchased from stockholders the entire outstanding stock of Sanders Inc. for a total of $4,500,000 in cash. At the date of acquisition, Sanders Inc. had $2,500,000 of liabilities and total stockholders' equity of $4,000,000. (a) As of the acquisition date, what was the total amount of the assets of Sanders Inc.? (b) As of the acquisition date, what was the amount of the net assets of Sanders Inc.? (c) What is the amount of difference between the investment account and the book equity of the subsidiary interest acquired by Powers Company?

13–9. What is the possible explanation of the difference determined in Question 13–8(c) and how will it affect the reporting of the difference on the consolidated balance sheet?

13–10. If, in Question 13–8, Powers Company had paid only $3,700,000 for the stock of Sanders Inc., what would the solution to part (c) have been?

13–11. Parent Corporation owns 90% of the outstanding common stock of Subsidiary Corporation, which has no preferred stock. (a) What is the term applied to the remaining 10% interest? (b) If the total stockholders' equity of Subsidiary Corporation is $700,000, what is the amount of Subsidiary's book equity allocable to outsiders? (c) Where is the amount determined in (b) reported on the consolidated balance sheet?

13–12. P Corporation owns 85% of the outstanding common stock of S Co., which has no preferred stock. Net income of S Co. was $300,000 for the year, and cash dividends declared and paid during the year amounted to $200,000. What entries should be made by P Corporation to record its share of S Co.'s (a) net income and (b) dividends? (c) What is the amount of the net increase in the equity of the minority interest?

13–13. (a) What purpose is served by the work sheet for a consolidated balance sheet? (b) Is the work sheet a substitute for the consolidated balance sheet?

13–14. At the end of the fiscal year, the amount of notes receivable and notes payable reported on the respective balance sheets of a parent and its wholly owned subsidiary are as follows:

	Parent	Subsidiary
Notes Receivable	$ 400,000	$50,000
Notes Payable	175,000	45,000

If $25,000 of Subsidiary's notes receivable are owed by Parent, determine the amount of notes receivable and notes payable to be reported on the consolidated balance sheet.

13–15. Sales and purchases of merchandise by a parent corporation and its wholly owned subsidiary during the year were as follows:

	Parent	Subsidiary
Sales	$6,000,000	$910,000
Purchases.	3,600,000	595,000

If $500,000 of the sales of Parent were made to Subsidiary, determine the amount of sales and purchases to be reported on the consolidated income statement.

13–16. The relationships of parent and subsidiary were established by the following transactions. Identify each affiliation as a "purchase" or a "pooling of interests."

(a) Company P receives 100% of the voting common stock of Company S in exchange for cash and long-term bonds payable.
(b) Company P receives 95% of the voting common stock of Company S in exchange for voting common stock of Company P.
(c) Company P receives 95% of the voting common stock of Company S in exchange for cash.
(d) Company P receives 70% of the voting common stock of Company S in exchange for voting common stock of Company P.

13–17. Which of the following procedures for consolidating the balance sheet of a parent and wholly owned subsidiary are characteristic of acquisition of control by purchase and which are characteristic of a pooling of interests? (a) Retained earnings of subsidiary at date of acquisition are eliminated. (b) Retained earnings of subsidiary at date of acquisition are combined with retained earnings of parent. (c) Assets are not revalued. (d) Goodwill may not be recognized.

13–18. On July 31, Penn Corp. issued 10,000 shares of its $20 par common stock, with a total market value of $330,000, to the stockholders of Sands Inc. in exchange for all of

Sands' common stock. Penn Corp. records its investment at $300,000. The net assets and stockholders' equities of the two companies just prior to the affiliation are summarized as follows:

	Penn Corp.	Sands Inc.
Net assets	$910,000	$300,000
Common stock	$700,000	$200,000
Retained earnings	210,000	100,000
	$910,000	$300,000

(a) At what amounts would the following be reported on the consolidated balance sheet as of July 31, applying the pooling of interests method: (1) Net assets, (2) Retained earnings?

(b) Assume that, instead of issuing shares of stock, Penn Corp. had given $330,000 in cash and long-term notes. At what amounts would the following be reported on the consolidated balance sheet as of July 31: (1) Net assets, (2) Retained earnings?

13–19. Can a U.S. company incur an exchange gain or loss because of fluctuations in the exchange rate if its transactions with foreign countries, involving receivables or payables, are executed in (a) dollars, (b) the foreign currency?

13–20. A U.S. company purchased merchandise for 10,000 francs on account from a French company. If the exchange rate was $.22 per franc on the date of purchase and $.20 per franc on the date of payment of the account, what was the amount of exchange gain or loss realized by the U.S. company?

13–21. What two conditions give rise to unrealized currency exchange gains and losses from sales and purchases on account that are to be settled in the foreign currency?

13–22. Real World Focus. The income statement of Xerox Corporation for the year ended December 31, 1986, reports "Equity in income from continuing operations of Xerox Financial Services Inc., $278,000,000." Xerox Financial Services Inc. is Xerox Corporation's domestic financial services subsidiary. Xerox Financial Services Inc. also paid Xerox Corporation $108,000,000 in dividends during 1986. (a) Prepare the entry that Xerox Corporation would have made to record its equity interest in Xerox Financial Services Inc.'s income for 1986. (b) Prepare the entry that Xerox Corporation would have made to record the receipt of the dividends in 1986 from Xerox Financial Services Inc.

Exercises

13–23. Entries for investment in stock, receipt of dividends, and sale of shares. On March 2, Linn Corporation acquired 500 shares of the 50,000 outstanding shares of Wills Co. common stock at 53 1/4 plus commission and postage charges of $150. On July 15, a cash dividend of $3 per share and a 5% stock dividend were received. On November 25, 200 shares were sold at 55 1/2 less commission and postage charges of $45. Present entries to record (a) the purchase of the stock, (b) the receipt of the dividends, and (c) the sale of the 200 shares.

13–24. Entries using equity method for stock investment. At a total cost of $2,200,000, Dunn Corporation acquired 100,000 shares of Mini-Systems Co. common stock as a long-term investment. Dunn Corporation uses the equity method of accounting for this investment. Mini-Systems Co. has 250,000 shares of common stock outstanding, including the shares acquired by Dunn Corporation. Present the entries by Dunn Corporation to record the following information:

(a) Mini-Systems Co. reports net income of $600,000 for the current period.
(b) A cash dividend of $.50 per common share is paid by Mini-Systems Co. during the current period.

13–25. Determination and reporting of items related to consolidated statements. On the last day of the fiscal year, Pullen Inc. purchased 85% of the common stock of Starr Company for $600,000, at which time Starr Company reported the following on its balance sheet: assets, $980,000; liabilities, $300,000; common stock, $10 par, $500,000; retained earnings, $180,000. In negotiating the stock sale, it was determined that the book carrying amounts of Starr's recorded assets and equities approximated their current market values.

(a) Indicate for each of the following the section, the title of the item, and the amount to be reported on the consolidated balance sheet as of the date of acquisition:
    (1) Difference between cost and book equity of subsidiary interest.
    (2) Minority interest.
(b) During the following year, Pullen Inc. realized net income of $810,000, exclusive of the income of the subsidiary, and Starr Company realized net income of $150,000. In preparing a consolidated income statement, indicate in what amounts the following would be reported:
    (1) Minority interest's share of net income.
    (2) Consolidated net income.

13–26. Consolidated balance sheet from affiliation effected as a purchase. On December 31 of the current year, P Corporation purchased 90% of the stock of S Company. The data reported on their separate balance sheets immediately after the acquisition are as follows:

	P Corporation	S Company
Assets		
Cash	$ 32,200	$ 21,250
Accounts receivable (net)	50,800	35,000
Inventories	141,000	61,750
Investment in S Company	370,000	—
Equipment (net)	400,000	291,500
	$994,000	$409,500
Liabilities and Stockholders' Equity		
Accounts payable	$ 99,000	$ 49,500
Common stock, $10 par	750,000	250,000
Retained earnings	145,000	110,000
	$994,000	$409,500

The fair value of S Company's assets corresponds to their book carrying amounts, except for equipment, which is valued at $325,000 for consolidation purposes. Prepare a consolidated balance sheet as of December 31, in report form, omitting captions for current assets, plant assets, etc. (A work sheet need not be used.)

13–27. Consolidated balance sheet from affiliation effected as a pooling. As of July 31 of the current year, Pike Corporation exchanged 5,000 shares of its $10 par common stock for the 1,000 shares of Seed Company $50 par common stock held by Seed stockholders. The separate balance sheets of the two enterprises, immediately after the exchange of shares, are as follows:

	Pike Corporation	Seed Company
Assets		
Cash	$ 22,500	$ 15,500
Accounts receivable (net)	27,250	20,000
Inventories	75,750	32,750
Investment in Seed Company	87,500	—
Equipment (net)	329,000	44,250
	$542,000	$112,500
Liabilities and Stockholders' Equity		
Accounts payable	$ 77,000	$ 25,000
Common stock	300,000	50,000
Retained earnings	165,000	37,500
	$542,000	$112,500

Prepare a consolidated balance sheet as of July 31, in report form, omitting captions for current assets, plant assets, etc. (A work sheet need not be used.)

13–28. Consolidated income statement. For the current year ended June 30, the results of operations of Packer Corporation and its wholly owned subsidiary, Sullen Enterprises, are as follows:

	Packer Corporation		Sullen Enterprises	
Sales		$990,000		$410,000
Cost of merchandise sold	$655,000		$245,000	
Selling expenses	155,000		60,000	
General expenses	85,000		40,000	
Interest expense (income)	(12,000)	883,000	12,000	357,000
Net income		$107,000		$ 53,000

During the year, Packer sold merchandise to Sullen for $75,000. The merchandise was sold by Sullen to nonaffiliated companies for $100,000. Packer's interest income was realized from a long-term loan to Sullen.

(a) Prepare a consolidated income statement for the current year for Packer and its subsidiary. Use the single-step form and disregard income taxes. (A work sheet need not be used.)

(b) Assuming that none of the merchandise sold by Packer to Sullen had been sold during the year to nonaffiliated companies, and that Packer's cost of the merchandise had been $51,000, determine the amounts that would have been reported for the following items on the consolidated income statement: (1) sales, (2) cost of merchandise sold, (3) net income.

13–29. Determination of consolidated balance sheet amounts for affiliation effected as a pooling and as a purchase. Summarized data from the balance sheets of Page Company and Swartz Inc., as of June 30 of the current year, are as follows:

	Page Company	Swartz Inc.
Net assets	$900,000	$120,000
Common stock:		
50,000 shares, $10 par	500,000	
2,500 shares, $20 par		50,000
Retained earnings	400,000	70,000

(a) On July 1 of the current year, the two companies combine. Page Company issues 5,000 shares of its $10 par common stock, valued at $130,000, to Swartz's stockholders in exchange for the 2,500 shares of Swartz's $20 par common stock, also valued at $130,000. Assuming that the affiliation is effected as a pooling of interests, what are the amounts that would be reported for net assets, common stock, and retained earnings as of July 1 of the current year?

(b) Assume that Page Company had paid cash of $130,000 for all of Swartz Inc.'s common stock on July 1 of the current year and that the book value of the net assets of Swartz Inc. is deemed to reflect fair value. (1) What are the amounts that would be reported for net assets, common stock, and retained earnings as of July 1 of the current year, using the purchase method? (2) How much goodwill will be reported on the combined balance sheet?

13–30. Entries for sales made in foreign currency. Omar Company makes sales on account to several Mexican companies which it bills in pesos. Record the entries for the following selected transactions completed during the current year:

Feb. 2. Sold merchandise on account, 100,000 pesos; exchange rate, $.04 per peso.
Mar. 4. Received cash from sale of February 2, 100,000 pesos; exchange rate, $.05 per peso.
May 30. Sold merchandise on account, 120,000 pesos; exchange rate, $.05 per peso.
June 30. Received cash from sale of May 30, 120,000 pesos; exchange rate, $.04 per peso.

13–31. Entries for purchases made in foreign currency. Schoenfeld Company purchases merchandise from a German company that requires payment in deutsche marks. Record the entries for the following selected transactions completed during the current year:

June 10. Purchased merchandise on account, net 30, 5,000 deutsche marks; exchange rate, $.51 per deutsche mark.
July 10. Paid invoice of June 10; exchange rate, $.52 per deutsche mark.
Sept. 1. Purchased merchandise on account, net 30, 4,000 deutsche marks; exchange rate, $.52 per deutsche mark.
Oct. 1. Paid invoice of September 1; exchange rate, $.50 per deutsche mark.

Problems

13–32. Entries for investments in stock. The following transactions relate to certain securities acquired by Griffin Company, whose fiscal year ends on December 31:

1989
Mar. 8. Purchased 1,000 shares of the 10,000 outstanding common shares of Howard Corporation at 35 plus commission and other costs of $175.
May 15. Received the regular cash dividend of 80¢ a share on Howard Corporation stock.
Nov. 15. Received the regular cash dividend of 80¢ a share plus an extra dividend of 10¢ a share on Howard Corporation stock.

(Assume that all intervening transactions have been recorded properly, and that the number of shares of stock owned has not changed from December 31, 1989, to December 31, 1993.)

1994
May 20. Received the regular cash dividend of 80¢ a share and a 5% stock dividend on the Howard Corporation stock.
July 20. Sold 500 shares of Howard Corporation stock at 40. The broker deducted commission and other costs of $125, remitting the balance.
Nov. 18. Received a cash dividend at the new rate of 84¢ a share on the Howard Corporation stock.

Instructions: Record the entries for the foregoing transactions.

13–33. Work sheet and consolidated balance sheet from affiliation effected as a purchase. On May 1 of the current year, Park Company purchased 90% of the stock of Summa Company. On the same date, Park Company loaned Summa Company $50,000 on a 90-day note. The data reported on their separate balance sheets immediately after the acquisition and loan are as follows:

	Park Company	Summa Company
Assets		
Cash	$ 50,750	$ 25,750
Accounts receivable (net)	48,500	32,000
Notes receivable	50,000	—
Inventories	164,750	52,250
Investment in Summa Company	290,000	—
Equipment (net)	340,000	215,000
	$944,000	$325,000
Liabilities and Stockholders' Equity		
Accounts payable	$175,000	$ 29,500
Notes payable	—	50,000
Common stock, $20 par	500,000	—
Common stock, $10 par	—	200,000
Retained earnings	269,000	45,500
	$944,000	$325,000

The fair value of Summa Company's assets corresponds to the book carrying amounts, except for equipment, which is valued at $265,000 for consolidation purposes.

Instructions: (1) Prepare a work sheet for a consolidated balance sheet as of May 1 of the current year.

(2) Prepare in report form a consolidated balance sheet as of May 1, omitting captions for current assets, plant assets, etc.

13–34. Work sheet and consolidated balance sheet; year-end minority interest; increase in investment account during year. On June 30, Pole Company purchased 80% of the outstanding stock of Selma Company for $360,000. Balance sheet data for the two corporations immediately after the transaction are as follows:

	Pole Company	Selma Company
Assets		
Cash and marketable securities	$ 86,700	$ 31,050
Accounts receivable	120,500	59,160
Allowance for doubtful accounts	(9,500)	(1,320)
Inventories	475,000	115,440
Investment in Selma Company	360,000	—
Land	100,000	21,000
Building and equipment	990,000	297,000
Accumulated depreciation	(200,000)	(66,000)
	$1,922,700	$456,330

	Pole Company	Selma Company
Liabilities and Stockholders' Equity		
Accounts payable	$ 152,500	$ 42,990
Income tax payable	41,500	5,940
Bonds payable (due in 2005)	500,000	—
Common stock, $20 par	900,000	—
Common stock, $10 par	—	300,000
Retained earnings	328,700	107,400
	$1,922,700	$456,330

Instructions: (1) Prepare a work sheet for a consolidated balance sheet as of the date of acquisition.

(2) Prepare in report form a detailed consolidated balance sheet as of the date of acquisition. The fair value of Selma Company's assets are deemed to correspond to the book carrying amounts, except for land, which is to be increased by $30,000 for consolidation purposes.

(3) Assuming that Selma Company earns net income of $60,000 and pays cash dividends of $40,000 during the ensuing fiscal year and that Pole Company records its share of the earnings and dividends, determine the following as of the end of the year:

(a) The net amount added to Pole Company's investment account as a result of Selma Company's earnings and dividends.

(b) The amount of the minority interest.

13–35. Consolidated balance sheet from affiliation effected as a purchase. Several years ago, Price Corporation purchased 9,000 shares of the 10,000 outstanding shares of stock of Sax Company. Since the date of acquisition, Price Corporation has debited the investment account for its share of the subsidiary's earnings and has credited the account for its share of dividends declared. Balance sheet data for the two corporations as of December 31 of the current year are as follows:

	Price Corp.	Sax Co.
Assets		
Cash	$ 57,750	$ 21,050
Notes receivable	40,000	15,000
Accounts receivable (net)	140,750	49,650
Interest receivable	3,000	600
Dividends receivable	4,500	—
Inventories	199,500	65,000
Prepaid expenses	5,100	1,700
Investment in Sax Co.	180,180	—
Land	75,000	45,000
Buildings and equipment	411,000	240,000
Accumulated depreciation	(200,000)	(95,400)
	$916,780	$342,600
Liabilities and Stockholders' Equity		
Notes payable	$ 45,000	$ 50,000
Accounts payable	99,500	65,500
Income tax payable	35,000	13,900
Dividends payable	15,000	5,000
Interest payable	2,450	3,000
Common stock, $20 par	600,000	—
Common stock, $10 par	—	100,000
Premium on common stock	—	25,000
Retained earnings	119,830	80,200
	$916,780	$342,600

Price Corporation holds $35,000 of short-term notes of Sax Company, on which there is accrued interest of $3,000. Sax Company owes Price Corporation $15,000 for a management advisory fee for the year. It has been recorded by both corporations in their respective accounts payable and accounts receivable accounts.

Instructions: Prepare in report form a detailed consolidated balance sheet as of December 31 of the current year. (A work sheet is not required.) The excess of book equity in Sax Company over the balance of the Price Corporation's investment account is attributable to overvaluation of Sax Company's land.

13–36. Consolidated balance sheet from both pooling and purchase methods. On July 1 of the current year, after several months of negotiations, Peck Company issued 15,000 shares of its own $10 par common stock for all of Scott Inc.'s outstanding shares of stock. The fair market value of the Peck Company shares issued is $22.50 per share, or a total of $337,500. Scott Inc. is to be operated as a separate subsidiary. The balance sheets of the two firms on June 30 of the current year are as follows:

	Peck Company	Scott Inc.
Assets		
Cash	$ 202,500	$ 23,500
Accounts receivable (net)	245,000	41,900
Inventory	428,250	61,450
Land	120,000	50,000
Plant and equipment (net)	504,250	123,150
	$1,500,000	$300,000
Liabilities and Stockholders' Equity		
Accounts payable	$ 145,000	$ 52,500
Common stock ($10 par)	1,000,000	150,000
Retained earnings	355,000	97,500
	$1,500,000	$300,000

Instructions: (1) (a) What entry would be made by Peck Company to record the combination as a pooling of interests? (b) Prepare a consolidated balance sheet for Peck Company and Scott Inc. as of July 1 of the current year, assuming that the business combination has been recorded as a pooling of interests. (A work sheet is not required.)

(2) (a) Assume that Peck Company paid $150,000 in cash and issued 12,500 shares of Peck common stock with a fair market value of $187,500 for all the common stock of Scott Inc. What entry would Peck Company make to record the combination as a purchase? (b) Prepare a consolidated balance sheet as of July 1 of the current year, assuming that the business combination has been recorded as a purchase, and that the book values of the net assets of Scott Inc. are deemed to represent fair value. (A work sheet is not required.)

(3) Assume the same situation as in (2), except that the fair value of the land of Scott Inc. was $60,000. Prepare a consolidated balance sheet as of July 1 of the current year. (A work sheet is not required.)

SPREADSHEET PROBLEM

13–37. Eliminations for and preparation of consolidated balance sheet and income statement. On January 1 of the current year, Polk Corporation exchanged 25,000 shares of its $10 par common stock for 10,000 shares (the entire issue) of Swain Company's $25 par common stock. Later in the year, Swain purchased from Polk Corporation $100,000 of its $200,000 issue of bonds payable, at face amount. All of the items for "interest" appearing on the balance sheets and income statements of both corporations are related to the bonds.

During the year, Polk Corporation sold merchandise with a cost of $175,000 to Swain Company for $250,000, all of which was sold by Swain Company before the end of the year.

Polk Corporation has correctly recorded the income and dividends reported for the year by Swain Company. Data for the income statements for both companies for the current year are as follows:

	Polk Corporation	Swain Company
Revenues:		
Sales	$1,900,000	$625,000
Income of subsidiary	125,000	—
Interest income	—	3,125
	$2,025,000	$628,125
Expenses:		
Cost of merchandise sold	$1,219,600	$315,750
Selling expenses	185,000	62,275
General expenses	135,000	37,000
Interest expense	12,500	—
Income tax	155,100	88,100
	$1,707,200	$503,125
Net income	$ 317,800	$125,000

Data for the balance sheets of both companies as of the end of the current year are as follows:

	Polk Corporation	Swain Company
Assets		
Cash	$ 86,200	$ 37,150
Accounts receivable (net)	138,400	62,800
Dividends receivable	12,500	—
Interest receivable	—	3,125
Inventories	549,550	199,000
Investment in Swain Co. (10,000 shares)	505,800	—
Investment in Polk Corp. bonds (at face amount)	—	100,000
Plant and equipment	837,850	312,000
Accumulated depreciation	(230,300)	(164,075)
	$1,900,000	$550,000
Liabilities and Stockholders' Equity		
Accounts payable	$ 154,400	$ 26,100
Income tax payable	20,000	5,600
Dividends payable	20,000	12,500
Interest payable	6,250	—
Bonds payable, 12 1/2% (due in 2004)	200,000	—
Common stock, $10 par	1,000,000	—
Common stock, $25 par	—	250,000
Premium on common stock	40,000	80,000
Retained earnings	459,350	175,800
	$1,900,000	$550,000

Instructions: (1) Determine the amounts to be eliminated from the following items in preparing the consolidated balance sheet as of December 31 of the current year: (a) dividends receivable and dividends payable; (b) interest receivable and interest payable; (c) investment in Swain Co. and stockholders' equity; (d) investment in Polk Corp. bonds and bonds payable.

(2) Prepare a detailed consolidated balance sheet as of December 31 in report form.

(3) Determine the amounts to be eliminated from the following items in preparing the consolidated income statement for the current year ended December 31: (a) sales and cost of merchandise sold; (b) interest income and interest expense; (c) income of subsidiary and net income.

(4) Prepare a single-step consolidated income statement, inserting the earnings per share in parentheses on the same line with net income.

(5) Determine the amount of the reduction in consolidated inventories, net income, and retained earnings if Swain Company's inventory had included $75,000 of the merchandise purchased from Polk Corporation.

13–38. Foreign currency transactions. Waddell Company sells merchandise to and purchases merchandise from various Canadian and Mexican companies. These transactions are settled in the foreign currency. The following selected transactions were completed during the current fiscal year:

Jan. 10. Purchased merchandise on account from Javier Company, net 30, $10,000 Canadian; exchange rate, $.88 per Canadian dollar.
Feb. 9. Issued check for amount owed to Javier Company; exchange rate, $.90 per Canadian dollar.
Mar. 30. Sold merchandise on account to Valdez Company, net 30, 500,000 pesos; exchange rate, $.045 per Mexican peso.
Apr. 29. Received cash from Valdez Company; exchange rate, $.046 per Mexican peso.
June 1. Purchased merchandise on account from Blume Company, net 30, $30,000 Canadian; exchange rate, $.88 per Canadian dollar.
July 1. Issued check for amount owed to Blume Company; exchange rate, $.87 per Canadian dollar.
Oct. 5. Sold merchandise on account to Osuna Company, net 30, 300,000 pesos; exchange rate, $.044 per Mexican peso.
Nov. 4. Received cash from Osuna Company; exchange rate, $.043 per Mexican peso.
Dec. 15. Sold merchandise on account to Gresky Company, net 30, $50,000 Canadian; exchange rate, $.85 per Canadian dollar.
21. Purchased merchandise on account from Ortega Company, net 30, 250,000 pesos; exchange rate, $.047 per Mexican peso.
31. Recorded unrealized currency exchange gain and/or loss on transactions of December 15 and 21. Exchange rates on December 31: $.84 per Canadian dollar; $.046 per Mexican peso.

Instructions: (1) Present the entries to record the transactions and adjustments for the year.

(2) Present the entries to record the payment of the December 21st purchase on January 20, when the exchange rate was $.048 per Mexican peso, and the receipt of cash from the December 15th sale, on January 21, when the exchange rate was $.83 per Canadian dollar.

ALTERNATE PROBLEMS

SPREADSHEET PROBLEM

13–33A. Work sheet and consolidated balance sheet from affiliation effected as a purchase. On June 30 of the current year, Putman Company purchased

85% of the stock of Searcy Company. On the same date, Putman Company loaned Searcy Company $50,000 on a 60-day note. The data reported on their separate balance sheets immediately after the acquisition and loan are as follows:

	Putman Company	Searcy Company
Assets		
Cash	$ 56,500	$ 55,000
Accounts receivable (net)	95,250	70,000
Notes receivable	75,000	—
Inventories	179,250	98,000
Investment in Searcy Company	520,000	—
Equipment (net)	425,000	430,000
	$1,351,000	$653,000
Liabilities and Stockholders' Equity		
Accounts payable	$ 210,000	$ 45,000
Notes payable	—	50,000
Common stock, $20 par	800,000	—
Common stock, $10 par	—	400,000
Retained earnings	341,000	158,000
	$1,351,000	$653,000

The fair value of Searcy Company's assets correspond to the book carrying amounts, except for equipment, which is valued at $450,000 for consolidation purposes.

Instructions: (1) Prepare a work sheet for a consolidated balance sheet as of June 30 of the current year.

(2) Prepare in report form a consolidated balance sheet as of June 30, omitting captions for current assets, plant assets, etc.

13–34A. Work sheet and consolidated balance sheet; year-end minority interest; increase in investment account during year. On July 31, Perry Company purchased 80% of the outstanding stock of Sims Company for $600,000. Balance sheet data for the two corporations immediately after the transaction are as follows:

	Perry Company	Sims Company
Assets		
Cash and marketable securities	$ 263,200	$ 35,400
Accounts receivable	369,225	66,225
Allowance for doubtful accounts	(30,150)	(12,075)
Inventories	735,375	183,150
Investment in Sims Company	600,000	—
Land	210,000	112,500
Building and equipment	1,093,950	741,900
Accumulated depreciation	(348,600)	(392,850)
	$2,893,000	$734,250

	Perry Company	Sims Company
Liabilities and Stockholders' Equity		
Accounts payable	$ 308,575	$106,725
Income tax payable	63,000	9,075
Bonds payable (due in 2007)	600,000	—
Common stock, $20 par	1,125,000	—
Common stock, $5 par	—	450,000
Retained earnings	796,425	168,450
	$2,893,000	$734,250

Instructions: (1) Prepare a work sheet for a consolidated balance sheet as of the date of acquisition.

(2) Prepare in report form a detailed consolidated balance sheet as of the date of acquisition. The fair value of Sims Company's assets are deemed to correspond to the book carrying amounts, except for land, which is to be increased by $70,000.

(3) Assuming that Sims Company earns net income of $135,000 and pays cash dividends of $60,000 during the following fiscal year and that Perry Company records its share of the earnings and dividends, determine the following as of the end of the year:

(a) The net amount added to Perry Company's investment account as a result of Sims Company's earnings and dividends.

(b) The amount of the minority interest.

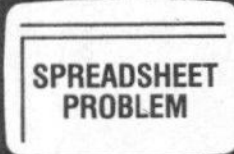

13–37A. Eliminations for and preparation of consolidated balance sheet and income statement. On January 2 of the current year, Pella Corporation exchanged 15,000 shares of its $20 par common stock for 12,000 shares (the entire issue) of Stein Company's $25 par common stock. Stein purchased from Pella Corporation $150,000 of its $250,000 issue of bonds payable, at face amount. All of the items for "interest" appearing on the balance sheets and income statements of both corporations are related to the bonds.

During the year, Pella Corporation sold merchandise with a cost of $184,000 to Stein Company for $230,000, all of which was sold by Stein Company before the end of the year.

Pella Corporation has correctly recorded the income and dividends reported for the year by Stein Company. Data for the income statements for both companies for the current year are as follows:

	Pella Corporation	Stein Company
Revenues:		
Sales	$1,600,000	$500,000
Income of subsidiary	110,000	—
Interest income	—	15,000
	$1,710,000	$515,000
Expenses:		
Cost of merchandise sold	$ 950,000	$280,000
Selling expenses	165,000	52,000
General expenses	125,000	37,000
Interest expense	25,000	—
Income tax	195,000	36,000
	$1,460,000	$405,000
Net income	$ 250,000	$110,000

Data for the balance sheets of both companies as of the end of the current year are as follows:

	Pella Corporation	Stein Company
Assets		
Cash	$ 62,500	$ 25,800
Accounts receivable (net)	165,000	51,800
Dividends receivable	50,000	—
Interest receivable	—	7,500
Inventories	275,000	126,300
Investment in Stein Co. (12,000 shares)	641,550	—
Investment in Pella Corp. bonds (at face amount)	—	150,000
Plant and equipment	1,150,000	471,950
Accumulated depreciation	(650,000)	(108,350)
	$1,694,050	$725,000

	Pella Corporation	Stein Company
Liabilities and Stockholders' Equity		
Accounts payable	$ 75,200	$ 27,750
Income tax payable	20,510	5,700
Dividends payable	30,000	50,000
Interest payable	12,500	—
Bonds payable, 10% (due in 2003)	250,000	—
Common stock, $20 par	1,000,000	—
Common stock, $25 par	—	300,000
Premium on common stock	100,000	50,000
Retained earnings	205,840	291,550
	$1,694,050	$725,000

Instructions: (1) Determine the amounts to be eliminated from the following items in preparing the consolidated balance sheet as of December 31 of the current year: (a) dividends receivable and dividends payable; (b) interest receivable and interest payable; (c) investment in Stein Co. and stockholders' equity; (d) investment in Pella Corp. bonds and bonds payable.

(2) Prepare a detailed consolidated balance sheet as of December 31 in report form.

(3) Determine the amounts to be eliminated from the following items in preparing the consolidated income statement for the current year ended December 31: (a) sales and cost of merchandise sold; (b) interest income and interest expense; (c) income of subsidiary and net income.

(4) Prepare a single-step consolidated income statement, inserting the earnings per share in parentheses on the same line with net income.

(5) Determine the amount of the reduction in consolidated inventories, net income, and retained earnings if Stein Company's inventory had included $50,000 of the merchandise purchased from Pella Corporation.

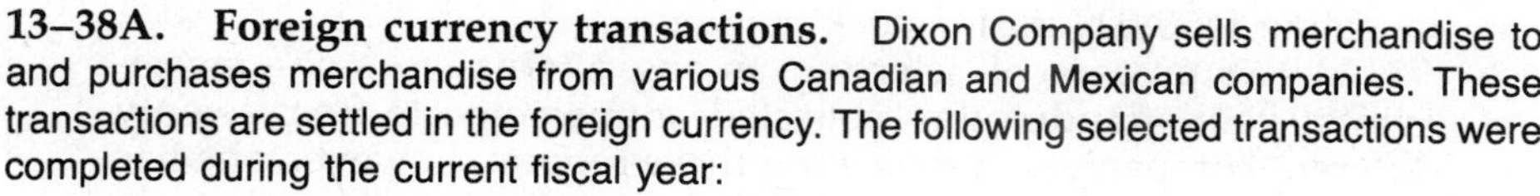

13–38A. Foreign currency transactions. Dixon Company sells merchandise to and purchases merchandise from various Canadian and Mexican companies. These transactions are settled in the foreign currency. The following selected transactions were completed during the current fiscal year:

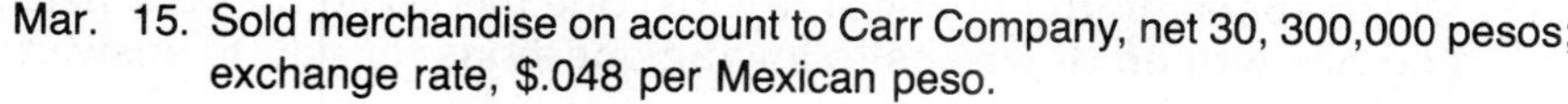

Mar. 15. Sold merchandise on account to Carr Company, net 30, 300,000 pesos; exchange rate, $.048 per Mexican peso.

Apr. 14. Received cash from Carr Company; exchange rate, $.047 per Mexican peso.
May 5. Purchased merchandise on account from Lofgren Company, net 30, $5,000 Canadian; exchange rate, $.82 per Canadian dollar.
June 4. Issued check for amount owed to Lofgren Company; exchange rate, $.81 per Canadian dollar.
Aug. 31. Sold merchandise on account to Sanchez Company, net 30, 300,000 pesos; exchange rate, $.044 per Mexican peso.
Sept. 30. Received cash from Sanchez Company; exchange rate, $.046 per Mexican peso.
Oct. 10. Purchased merchandise on account from Chevalier Company, net 30, $20,000 Canadian; exchange rate, $.83 per Canadian dollar.
Nov. 9. Issued check for amount owed to Chevalier Company; exchange rate, $.84 per Canadian dollar.
Dec. 15. Sold merchandise on account to Adams Company, net 30, $50,000 Canadian; exchange rate, $.85 per Canadian dollar.
16. Purchased merchandise on account from Santos Company, net 30, 250,000 pesos; exchange rate, $.047 per Mexican peso.
31. Recorded unrealized currency exchange gain and/or loss on transactions of December 15 and 16. Exchange rates on December 31: $.86 per Canadian dollar; $.048 per Mexican peso.

Instructions: (1) Present entries to record the transactions and adjustments for the year.
(2) Present entries to record the payment of the December 16th purchase, on January 15, when the exchange rate was $.046 per Mexican peso, and the receipt of cash from the December 15th sale, on January 17, when the exchange rate was $.87 per Canadian dollar.

Mini-Case 13

Stella Wilkinson

Your grandmother recently retired, sold her home in Kansas City, and moved to a retirement community in Palm Springs. With some of the proceeds from the sale of her home, she is considering investing $150,000 in the stock market.

In the process of selecting among alternative stock investments, your grandmother collected annual reports from twenty different companies. In reviewing these reports, however, she has become confused and has questions concerning several items which appear in the financial reports. She has asked for your help and has written down the following questions for you to answer:

(a) "In reviewing the annual reports, I noticed many references to 'consolidated financial statements.' What are consolidated financial statements?"
(b) " 'Excess of cost of business acquired over related net assets' appears on the consolidated balance sheets in several annual reports. What does this mean? Is it an asset (it appears with other assets)?"
(c) "What is minority interest?"
(d) "A footnote to one of the consolidated statements indicated interest and the amount of a loan from one company to another had been eliminated. Is this good accounting? A loan is a loan. How can a company just eliminate a loan that hasn't been paid off?"
(e) "How can financial statements for an American company (in dollars) be combined with a British subsidiary (in pounds)?"

Instructions:

(1) Briefly respond to each of your grandmother's questions.
(2) While discussing the items in (1) with your grandmother, she asked for your advice on whether she should limit her investment to one stock. What would you advise?

Answers to Self-Examination Questions

1. C When parent acquires substantially all of the voting stock of subsidiary in exchange for its voting common stock (answer C), the affiliation is termed a "pooling of interests." When parent acquires substantially all of the voting stock of subsidiary in exchange for cash (answer A), other assets, issuances of debt obligations (answer B), or a combination of the foregoing, it is termed a "purchase."

2. B The excess of cost over book equity of interest in S Co. is $100,000 (answer B), determined as follows:

Investment in S Co. (cost)	$1,000,000
Eliminate 100% of S Co. stock	(750,000)
Eliminate 100% of S Co. retained earnings	(150,000)
Excess of cost over book equity of subsidiary interest	$ 100,000

3. B The excess of cost over book equity of interest in S Co. is $190,000 (answer B), determined as follows:

Investment in S Co. (cost)	$1,000,000
Eliminate 90% of S Co. stock	(675,000)
Eliminate 90% of S Co. retained earnings	(135,000)
Excess of cost over book equity of subsidiary interest	$ 190,000

4. D The 10% of the stock owned by outsiders is referred to as the minority interest. It amounts to $90,000, determined as follows:

10% of common stock	$75,000
10% of retained earnings	15,000
Total minority interest	$90,000

5. B The 250,000 pesos ($10,000 ÷ $.04) representing the billed price, which had a value of $10,000 on July 9, 1989, had increased in value to $12,500 (250,000 pesos × $.05) on August 8, 1989, when payment was received. The gain, which was realized because the transaction was completed by the receipt of cash, was $2,500 (answer B).

Part Four

Reporting Changes in Cash Flows

14
Statement of Cash Flows

CHAPTER OBJECTIVES

Describe the nature and purpose of the statement of cash flows.

Describe and illustrate the following types of cash flow activities:
- Cash flows from operating activities
- Cash flows from financing activities
- Cash flows from investing activities

Describe and illustrate the preparation of the statement of cash flows.

The four basic financial statements are the balance sheet, the income statement, the retained earnings statement (statement of owner's equity), and the statement of cash flows. The preparation and use of the first three statements were thoroughly discussed in preceding chapters. This chapter is devoted to an in-depth discussion of the nature and purpose of the statement of cash flows. Such a statement is useful to managers in evaluating past and planning future financing and investing activities. It is also useful to creditors and investors in their analysis of a firm's financial condition and profitability.

NATURE OF THE STATEMENT OF CASH FLOWS

In 1987, the Financial Accounting Standards Board (FASB) issued Statement of Financial Accounting Standards No. 95, which requires the inclusion of a statement of cash flows as part of the basic set of financial statements. The statement of cash flows replaces the statement of changes in financial position (frequently called the funds statement).

The statement of changes in financial position reported a firm's significant financing and investing activities for a period. These activities were generally described in terms of the inflow and outflow of "funds," with funds defined either as "cash" or "working capital" (current assets − current liabilities). After considerable research and experimentation, the FASB decided that a statement of cash flows would better meet the objectives of financial reporting, expressed as follows:

Financial reporting should provide information to help present and potential investors and creditors and other users in assessing the amounts, timing, and uncertainty of prospective cash receipts from dividends or interest and the proceeds from the sale, redemption, or maturity of securities or loans. The prospects for those cash receipts are affected by an enterprise's ability to generate enough cash to meet its obligations when due and its other cash operating needs, to reinvest in operations, and to pay cash dividends.... [1]

The **statement of cash flows** reports a firm's major sources of cash receipts and major uses of cash payments for a period.[2] Such a statement provides useful information about a firm's activities in generating cash from operations, meeting its financial obligations, paying dividends, and maintaining and expanding operating capacity. Such information, when used in conjunction with the other financial statements, assists investors, creditors, and others in assessing the entity's profitability and solvency (the ability to meet currently maturing debt). For example, the receipt of cash from issuing bonds indicates that the firm is not only committed to the payment of periodic interest expense (which affects profitability and solvency), but also to the redemption of the bonds at maturity (which affects solvency). Thus, the statement of cash flows is useful in analyzing both past and future profitability and solvency of the firm.

Focus on Cash Flow

In the past, investors have relied almost exclusively on a company's earnings information in judging the company's performance. But this information may be misleading. Therefore, as described in the following excerpt from an article in *The Wall Street Journal,* more and more investors are focusing on cash flows.

Follow the money.

That's a guiding principle for the increasing number of stock analysts and investors who study corporate cash flows. While none of them advocates using cash-flow analysis by itself, they say it can be an important tool in piercing the camouflage that sometimes makes reported earnings misleading.

As the term suggests, cash flow is basically a measure of the money flowing into—or out of—a business. If large companies were run, like lemonade stands, on a cash basis, earnings and cash flow would be identical.

Every major corporation, however, keeps its books on an accrual basis. When it builds a new plant or receives a large multiyear contract, it generally staggers the expense or income over a period of years. That can give a truer picture of corporate profitability, but sometimes it obscures important developments.

Take a company that spent $140 million on new machinery last year. If it depreciates the equipment over a seven-year period, it will be subtracting $20 million from reported profits each year.

But if the machines will stay up-to-date and useful for 25 years, the company's reported earnings may understate its true strength....

...Sometimes the reverse is true. If a company has been neglecting capital spending, its earnings may look good. But on a cash-flow basis, it will look no better, and perhaps worse, than its competitors.

Thus, focusing on cash flow makes the investor confront an important question: whether...assets being depreciated really do wear out as rapidly as they are being depreciated....

...Joseph Battipaglia, an analyst with Gruntal & Co. in New York, says that cash-flow trends gave alert investors an early warning of the auto industry's problems in the 1970's. By the end of the decade, he notes, poor earnings made those problems apparent to everyone. But by then, he says, "everyone was going through the same door at the same time."

Source: John R. Dorfman, "Stock Analysts Increase Focus on Cash Flow," *The Wall Street Journal* (February 17, 1987), Section 2, page 1.

[1] *Statement of Financial Accounting Concepts, No. 1,* "Objectives of Financial Reporting by Business Enterprises" (Stamford: Financial Accounting Standards Board, 1978), par. 37.

[2] Cash is the most useful concept for the statement of cash flows. However, cash in excess of immediate needs may be invested in income-producing, short-term, highly liquid investments, called cash equivalents, such as Treasury bills and money market funds. In such cases, the statement of cash flows may report changes during the period in cash and cash equivalents.

FORM OF THE STATEMENT OF CASH FLOWS

The statement of cash flows classifies cash receipts and cash payments by three types of activities:

1. **Cash flows from operating activities,** which include cash transactions that enter into the determination of net income.
2. **Cash flows from financing activities,** which include receipts from the issuance of equity and debt securities; and payments for dividends, repurchase of equity securities, and redemption of debt securities.
3. **Cash flows from investing activities,** which include receipts from the sale of investments and plant assets and other noncurrent assets; and payments for the acquisition of investments and plant assets and other noncurrent assets.

By grouping cash flows by operating, financing, and investing activities, significant relationships within and among the activities can be evaluated. For example, cash receipts from borrowings can easily be related to repayments of borrowings when both are reported as financing activities. Also, the impact of each of the three activities (operating, financing, and investing) on cash flows can be evaluated. Such relationships assist investors and creditors in evaluating the effects of cash flows on profitability and solvency.

The common transactions giving rise to cash flows that would be reported in one of the three sections of the statement of cash flows are presented in the diagram below and are discussed in the following paragraphs. The focus in this chapter is on presenting the basic concept of cash flows and on providing an understanding of the preparation, interpretation, and use of the statement of cash flows.

Cash Flows

OPERATING ACTIVITIES
(receipts from revenues and payments for expenses)

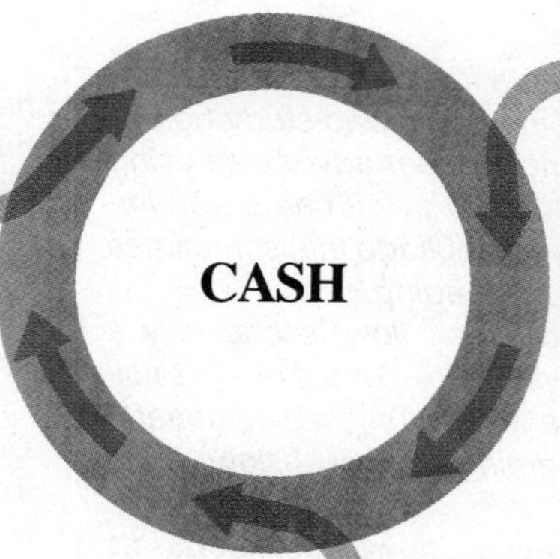

FINANCING ACTIVITIES
(receipts from issuance of equity and debt securities; payments for treasury stock and dividends and for redemption of debt securities)

INVESTING ACTIVITIES
(receipts from sale of noncurrent assets and payments to acquire noncurrent assets)

Operating Activities

The most frequent and often the most important cash flows relate to operating activities entered into for the purpose of earning net income. There are two alternatives to reporting cash flows from such operating activities in the statement of cash flows: (1) the direct method and (2) the indirect method. The **direct method** reports the major classes of operating cash receipts (cash collected from customers and cash received from interest and dividends, for example) and of operating cash payments (cash paid to suppliers for merchandise and services, to employees for wages, and to creditors for interest, for example). The difference between these operating cash receipts and cash payments would be reported as the net cash flow from operating activities. The principal advantage of the direct method is that it presents the major categories of cash receipts and cash payments. Its principal disadvantage is that the necessary data are often costly to accumulate.

When the **indirect method** is used, the effects of all deferrals of past cash receipts and payments and all accruals of expected future cash receipts and payments are removed from the net income reported on the income statement. This removal is accomplished by adjusting the amount reported as net income upward or downward to determine the net amount of cash flows from operating activities. One of the major advantages of the indirect method is that it focuses on the differences between net income and cash flows from operating activities. In addition, the data needed for the indirect method are generally more readily available and less costly to obtain than the data needed for the direct method.

Because of its more frequent usage, the indirect method will be used in this chapter.[3] Regardless of which method is used, the same amount of net cash flow from operating activities will be reported in the statement of cash flows.

Financing Activities

Cash inflows from financing activities include proceeds from the issuance of equity securities, such as preferred and common stocks. Cash inflows also arise from the issuance of bonds, mortgage notes payable, and notes and other long-term and short-term borrowings. Cash outflows from financing activities include the payment of cash dividends, the acquisition of treasury stock, and the repayment of amounts borrowed.

In reporting cash flows from financing activities on the statement of cash flows, the cash inflows are usually reported first, followed by the cash outflows. If the inflows exceed the outflows, the net cash flow can be described as "Net cash flow provided by financing activities." If the cash outflows exceed the cash inflows, the difference can be described as "Net cash flow used for financing activities."

Investing Activities

Cash inflows from investing activities generally arise from the sale of investments, plant assets, and intangible assets. Cash outflows generally include payments to acquire investments, plant assets, and intangible assets.

In reporting cash flows from investing activities on the statement of cash flows, the cash inflows are usually reported first, followed by the cash outflows. If the inflows exceed the outflows, the net cash flow can be described

---

[3]A brief discussion of the direct method of reporting cash flows from operating activities is presented in Appendix E.

as "Net cash flow provided by investing activities." If the cash outflows exceed the cash inflows, the difference can be described as "Net cash flow used for investing activities."

Noncash Financing and Investing Activities

In addition to the financing and investing activities described in the preceding sections, financing and investing may be affected by transactions that do not involve cash. If such transactions have occurred during the period, their effect, if significant, should be reported in a separate schedule to accompany the statement of cash flows. This broadened concept recognizes that some financing and investing transactions do not involve cash receipts and payments but have a significant effect on future cash flows. For example, the issuance of common stock in liquidation of long-term debt has no effect on cash. However, the transaction will eliminate the future cash payments to retire the bonds and future cash payments for interest. Therefore, it should be reported.

A complete discussion of the kinds of noncash transactions that usually have a significant effect on financing and investing activities is beyond the scope of discussion here. The following transactions are illustrative of the many possibilities: issuance of bonds or capital stock in exchange for plant assets, issuance of common stock in exchange for convertible preferred stock, and issuance of long-term investments in exchange for machinery and equipment.

ASSEMBLING DATA FOR THE STATEMENT OF CASH FLOWS

To collect the data for the statement of cash flows, all the cash receipts and disbursements for a period could be analyzed and then reported by activity (operating, financing, or investing) on the statement. However, this direct method of analyzing and reporting cash flows is expensive and time consuming. An indirect method is the more efficient procedure of examining the noncash balance sheet accounts and determining the type of cash flow activity that leads to changes in these accounts during the period. In performing this analysis, supplementary explanatory data can be obtained from the income statement and other records as needed. Such a procedure is not only efficient but also logical, because all transactions eventually affect balance sheet accounts. For example, although revenues and expenses are not shown directly on the balance sheet, the retained earnings account on the balance sheet is affected as revenues and expenses are closed at the end of a period.

Although there is no order in which the noncash balance sheet accounts must be analyzed, time can be saved and greater accuracy can be achieved by selecting the accounts in the reverse order in which they appear on the balance sheet. Therefore, the retained earnings account provides the starting point for determining the cash flows from operating activities that normally appear first on the statement of cash flows.

To illustrate this approach to assembling the data for the statement of cash flows, the following comparative balance sheet for T. R. Morgan Corporation for the year ended December 31, 1990, will be used. Selected ledger

Comparative Balance Sheet

T. R. Morgan Corporation
Comparative Balance Sheet
December 31, 1990 and 1989

	1990	1989	Increase Decrease*
Assets			
Cash	$ 49,000	$ 26,000	$ 23,000
Trade receivables (net)	74,000	65,000	9,000
Inventories	172,000	180,000	8,000*
Prepaid expenses	4,000	3,000	1,000
Investments (long-term)	—	45,000	45,000*
Land	90,000	40,000	50,000
Building	200,000	200,000	—
Accumulated depreciation—building	(36,000)	(30,000)	(6,000)
Equipment	290,000	142,000	148,000
Accumulated depreciation—equipment	(43,000)	(40,000)	(3,000)
Total assets	$800,000	$631,000	$169,000
Liabilities			
Accounts payable (merchandise creditors)	$ 50,000	$ 32,000	$ 18,000
Income tax payable	2,500	4,000	1,500*
Dividends payable	15,000	8,000	7,000
Bonds payable	120,000	245,000	125,000*
Total liabilities	$187,500	$289,000	$101,500*
Stockholders' Equity			
Preferred stock	$150,000	—	$150,000
Premium on preferred stock	10,000	—	10,000
Common stock	280,000	$230,000	50,000
Retained earnings	172,500	112,000	60,500
Total stockholders' equity	$612,500	$342,000	$270,500
Total liabilities and stockholders' equity	$800,000	$631,000	$169,000

accounts will be presented as needed, along with supplementary data taken from the income statement.[4]

Retained Earnings

According to the comparative balance sheet for T. R. Morgan Corporation, there was an increase of $60,500 in retained earnings during the year. The retained earnings account, as shown below, indicates the nature of the entries made during the year that resulted in this increase.

[4]When the volume of data is substantial, experienced accountants may first assemble all relevant facts in working papers designed for the purpose. Specialized working papers are not essential, however. Because of their complexity, they tend to obscure the basic concepts of cash flow analysis for anyone who is not already familiar with the subject. For this reason, special working papers will not be used in the following discussion. Instead, the emphasis will be on the basic analyses. The use of a work sheet as an aid in assembling data for the statement of cash flows is presented in Appendix F.

ACCOUNT RETAINED EARNINGS — ACCOUNT NO.

Date		Item	Debit	Credit	Balance Debit	Balance Credit
1990						
Jan.	1	Balance				112,000
Dec.	31	Net income		90,500		
	31	Cash dividends	30,000			172,500

The retained earnings account indicates net income of $90,500 and cash dividends declared of $30,000. The determination of the amount of cash flows from operating activities and the cash flows for the payment of dividends is discussed in the following paragraphs. It should be noted that there may be entries in the retained earnings account that do not affect cash, such as a transfer of retained earnings to paid-in capital accounts in the issuance of a stock dividend. Similarly, transfers between the retained earnings account and appropriations accounts have no effect on cash. Such transactions would not be reported on the statement of cash flows.

Cash Flows from Operating Activities. The amount of net income, $90,500, which is reported on the income statement, was determined by the accrual method of accounting. It is therefore necessary to recognize the relationship of the accrual method to the movement of cash. Usually, a part of some of the costs and expenses reported on the income statement, as well as a part of the revenue earned, is not accompanied by cash outflow or inflow.

There is often a period of time between the accrual of a revenue and the receipt of the related cash. Perhaps the most common example is the sale of merchandise or a service on account, for which payment is received at a later point in time. Hence, the amount reported on the income statement as revenue from sales is not likely to correspond with the amount of the related cash inflow for the same period.

Timing differences between the incurrence of an expense and the related cash outflow must also be considered in determining the amount of cash flows from operating activities. For example, the amount reported on the income statement as insurance expense is the amount of insurance premiums expired rather than the amount of premiums paid during the period. Similarly, supplies paid for in one year may be used and thus converted to an expense in a later year. Conversely, a portion of some of the expenses incurred near the end of one period, such as wages and taxes, may not require a cash outlay until the following period.

Some revenues and expenses related to noncurrent accounts do not provide or use cash. For example, depreciation expense is a proper expense for the purpose of determining net income, but it does not require an outlay of cash.

To determine the amount of cash flows from operating activities, the accrual basis net income, as reported on the income statement, must be converted to the cash basis. For purposes of illustration, the types of accounts that must be analyzed to convert net income from the accrual basis to the cash basis can be placed in two categories, described as follows:

1. Expenses affecting noncurrent accounts but not cash. For example, depreciation of plant assets and amortization of intangible assets are deducted from revenue but have no effect on cash. Similarly, the amortization of

premium on bonds payable, which decreases interest expense and therefore increases operating income, does not affect cash.

2. Revenues and expenses affecting current asset and current liability accounts in amounts that differ from cash flows. For example, a sale of $10,000 on account, on which $8,000 has subsequently been collected, increases revenue by $10,000 but increases cash by only $8,000. In this case, to convert the revenue reported on the income statement ($10,000) to the cash basis, the increase in accounts receivable of $2,000 ($10,000 sale less $8,000 collection) can be deducted from the $10,000 of revenue to yield a cash flow of $8,000.

Generally accepted accounting principles require that cash flows be classified according to the nature of the underlying transaction.[5] This requirement means that cash flows from operating activities should not include transactions which are financing activities or investing activities. For example, the gain or loss from the sale of noncurrent assets would be reported as part of the total cash flows from investing activities arising from the sale of noncurrent assets. To illustrate, assume that land costing $50,000 was sold for $90,000 (a gain of $40,000). The sale should be reported in the investing activities section as "Cash receipts from the sale of land, $90,000." Since the $40,000 gain on the sale of the land is reported in the income statement, the $40,000 must be deducted from net income in converting the reported net income to cash flows from operations. Otherwise, the $40,000 gain would be reported twice on the statement of cash flows. Similarly, losses resulting from such transactions would be added to net income in determining the net cash flow from operating activities. Also, gains or losses arising from the retirement of debt would need to be deducted from or added to net income as reported on the income statement to determine the net cash flow from operating activities.

The conversion of the net income reported on the income statement to cash flows from operating activities can be summarized as follows:

Net income, per income statement		$XX
Add: Depreciation of plant assets	$XX	
Amortization of bond discount and intangible assets	XX	
Decreases in current assets (receivables, inventories, prepaid expenses)	XX	
Increases in current liabilities (accounts and notes payable, accrued liabilities)	XX	
Losses on disposal of assets and retirement of debt	XX	XX
Deduct: Amortization of bond premium	$XX	
Increases in current assets (receivables, inventories, prepaid expenses)	XX	
Decreases in current liabilities (accounts and notes payable, accrued liabilities)	XX	
Gains on disposal of assets and retirement of debt	XX	XX
Net cash flow from operating activities		$XX

Note that two current accounts—cash and dividends payable—are not included in this conversion schedule. Cash is omitted because it is the focus

[5] *Statement of Financial Accounting Standards, No. 95,* "Statement of Cash Flows" (Stamford: Financial Accounting Standards Board, 1987), par. 14.

of the analysis. Dividends payable is omitted because dividends are a distribution of earnings and do not affect net income. The treatment of dividends as they affect the statement of cash flows will be discussed later in the chapter. In the following paragraphs, the manner in which the net income reported by T. R. Morgan Corporation is converted to "Cash flows from operating activities" is discussed.

Depreciation. The comparative balance sheet for T. R. Morgan Corporation indicates that Accumulated Depreciation—Equipment increased by $3,000, and Accumulated Depreciation—Building increased by $6,000. Reference to these two accounts, shown as follows, indicates that depreciation for the year was $12,000 for the equipment and $6,000 for the building, or a total of $18,000.

ACCOUNT ACCUMULATED DEPRECIATION—EQUIPMENT ACCOUNT NO.

Date		Item	Debit	Credit	Balance Debit	Balance Credit
1990						
Jan.	1	Balance				40,000
May	9	Discarded, no salvage	9,000			
Dec.	31	Depreciation for year		12,000		43,000

ACCOUNT ACCUMULATED DEPRECIATION—BUILDING ACCOUNT NO.

Date		Item	Debit	Credit	Balance Debit	Balance Credit
1990						
Jan.	1	Balance				30,000
Dec.	31	Depreciation for year		6,000		36,000

Since the $18,000 of depreciation expense reduces net income but did not require an outlay of cash, $18,000 is added to net income in the process of determining the cash flows from operating activities, as follows:

Cash flows from operating activities:		
Net income	$90,500	
Add: Depreciation	18,000	$108,500

Current assets and current liabilities. In the process of determining cash flows from operating activities, decreases in the noncash current assets and increases in the current liabilities must be added to the amount reported as net income. Conversely, increases in the noncash current assets and decreases in the current liabilities must be deducted from the amount reported as net income. The relevant current asset and current liability accounts of T. R. Morgan Corporation are as follows:

Accounts	December 31 1990	December 31 1989	Increase Decrease*
Trade receivables (net)	$ 74,000	$ 65,000	$ 9,000
Inventories	172,000	180,000	8,000*
Prepaid expenses	4,000	3,000	1,000
Accounts payable (merchandise creditors)	50,000	32,000	18,000
Income tax payable	2,500	4,000	1,500*

The additions to ***trade receivables*** for sales on account during the year were $9,000 more than the deductions for amounts collected from customers on account. The amount reported on the income statement as sales therefore included $9,000 that did not yield cash inflow during the year. Accordingly, $9,000 must be deducted from net income.

The $8,000 decrease in ***inventories*** indicates that the merchandise sold exceeded the cost of the merchandise purchased by $8,000. The amount reported on the income statement as a deduction from the revenue therefore included $8,000 that did not require cash outflow during the year. Accordingly, $8,000 must be added to net income.

The outlay of cash for ***prepaid expenses*** exceeded by $1,000 the amount deducted as an expense during the year. Hence, $1,000 must be deducted from net income.

The effect of the increase in ***accounts payable***, which is the amount owed creditors for goods and services, was to include in expired costs and expenses the sum of $18,000 for which there had been no cash outlay during the year. Income was thereby reduced by $18,000, though there was no cash outlay. Hence, $18,000 must be added to net income.

The outlay of cash for ***income taxes*** exceeded by $1,500 the amount of income tax deducted as an expense during the period. Accordingly, $1,500 must be deducted from net income.

The foregoing adjustments to income, including the adjustment for depreciation, may be summarized as follows:

Cash flows from operating activities:			
Net income		$ 90,500	
Add: Depreciation	$18,000		
Decrease in inventories	8,000		
Increase in accounts payable	18,000	44,000	
		$134,500	
Deduct: Increase in trade receivables	$ 9,000		
Increase in prepaid expenses	1,000		
Decrease in income tax payable	1,500	11,500	$123,000

Gain on sale of investments. Reference to the ledger or income statement would indicate that the sale of investments resulted in a gain of $30,000. As discussed in preceding paragraphs, to avoid the double reporting of this $30,000 in the statement of cash flows, it must be deducted from the net income reported on the income statement as follows:[6]

Cash flows from operating activities:		
Net income	$90,500	
Deduct: Gain on sale of investments	30,000	$60,500

Reporting cash flows from operating activities. All the adjustments that are necessary to convert the net income to cash flows from operating activities for T. R. Morgan Corporation are presented in a format suitable for the statement of cash flows, as follows:

[6]The reporting of the cash flows from the sale of investments, which is an investing activity, is discussed in a later paragraph.

Cash flows from operating activities:

Net income, per income statement		$ 90,500	
Add: Depreciation	$18,000		
Decrease in inventories	8,000		
Increase in accounts payable	18,000	44,000	
		$134,500	
Deduct: Increase in trade receivables	$ 9,000		
Increase in prepaid expenses	1,000		
Decrease in income tax payable	1,500		
Gain on sale of investments	30,000	41,500	
Net cash flow from operating activities			$93,000

Cash Flows for Payment of Dividends. According to the retained earnings account of T. R. Morgan Corporation (page 536), cash dividends of $30,000 were declared during the year. However, according to the dividends payable account, shown as follows, dividend payments during the year totaled $23,000, revealing a timing difference between the declaration and the payment.

ACCOUNT DIVIDENDS PAYABLE ACCOUNT NO.

Date		Item	Debit	Credit	Balance Debit	Balance Credit
1990						
Jan.	1	Balance				8,000
	10	Cash paid	8,000		—	—
June	20	Dividend declared		15,000		15,000
July	10	Cash paid	15,000		—	—
Dec.	20	Dividend declared		15,000		15,000

The $23,000 of cash dividend payments would be reported in the financing activities section and may be noted on the statement of cash flows as follows:

Cash flows from financing activities:
Cash paid for dividends $23,000

Common Stock

The increase of $50,000 in the common stock account, shown as follows, is the result of stock being issued in exchange for land valued at $50,000.

ACCOUNT COMMON STOCK ACCOUNT NO.

Date		Item	Debit	Credit	Balance Debit	Balance Credit
1990						
Jan.	1	Balance				230,000
Dec.	28	Issued at par in exchange for land		50,000		280,000

Although cash was not involved, the transaction represents a significant financing and investing transaction that should be reported in a separate schedule to the statement of cash flows, as discussed previously. In this schedule, the transaction may be noted as follows:

Noncash financing and investing activities:
Issuance of common stock at par for land $50,000

Preferred Stock

The increase of $150,000 in the preferred stock account and the increase of $10,000 in the premium on preferred stock account, shown as follows, is the result of an issuance of preferred stock for $160,000.

ACCOUNT PREFERRED STOCK, $50 PAR — ACCOUNT NO.

Date		Item	Debit	Credit	Balance	
					Debit	Credit
1990						
Nov.	1	3,000 shares issued for cash		150,000		150,000

ACCOUNT PREMIUM ON PREFERRED STOCK — ACCOUNT NO.

Date		Item	Debit	Credit	Balance	
					Debit	Credit
1990						
Nov.	1	3,000 shares issued for cash		10,000		10,000

This cash flow would be reported in the financing activities section and may be noted on the statement of cash flows as follows:

Cash flows from financing activities:
Cash received from sale of preferred stock $160,000

Bonds Payable

The next item listed on the balance sheet, bonds payable, decreased $125,000 during the year. Examination of the bonds payable account, which appears as follows, indicates that $125,000 of the bonds payable were retired by payment of the face amount.

ACCOUNT BONDS PAYABLE — ACCOUNT NO.

Date		Item	Debit	Credit	Balance	
					Debit	Credit
1990						
Jan.	1	Balance				245,000
June	30	Retired by payment of cash at face amount	125,000			120,000

This cash flow would be reported in the financing activities section and may be noted as follows:

Cash flows from financing activities:
Cash paid to retire bonds payable $125,000

Equipment

The comparative balance sheet indicates that the cost of equipment increased $148,000. The following equipment account and the accumulated depreciation account reveal that the net change of $148,000 was the result of two separate transactions — the discarding of equipment that had cost $9,000 and the purchase of equipment for $157,000. The equipment discarded had been fully depreciated, as indicated by the debit of $9,000 in the accumulated depreciation account, and no salvage was realized from its disposal. Hence, the transaction had no effect on cash and is not reported on the statement of cash flows.

ACCOUNT EQUIPMENT ACCOUNT NO.

Date		Item	Debit	Credit	Balance Debit	Balance Credit
1990						
Jan.	1	Balance			142,000	
May	9	Discarded, no salvage		9,000		
Dec.	7	Purchased for cash	157,000		290,000	

ACCOUNT ACCUMULATED DEPRECIATION — EQUIPMENT ACCOUNT NO.

Date		Item	Debit	Credit	Balance Debit	Balance Credit
1990						
Jan.	1	Balance				40,000
May	9	Discarded, no salvage	9,000			
Dec.	31	Depreciation for year		12,000		43,000

The effect on cash flows from the purchase of equipment for $157,000 would be reported in the investing activities section and may be noted as follows:

Cash flows from investing activities:
Cash paid for purchase of equipment $157,000

The credit in the accumulated depreciation account had the effect of reducing the book value of equipment by $12,000 but caused no change in cash. The depreciation was treated previously as an addition to net income in determining cash flows from operating activities.

Building

According to the comparative balance sheet, there was no change in the $200,000 balance in the building account between the beginning and end of the year. Reference to the ledger confirms the absence of entries in the building account during the year, and hence the account is not shown here. The credit in the related accumulated depreciation account reduced the book value of the building, but, as indicated previously, cash was not affected. The depreciation was treated previously as an addition to net income in determining cash flows from operating activities.

Land

The comparative balance sheet indicates that land increased by $50,000. The notation in the land account, which follows, indicates that the land was acquired by issuance of common stock at par.

ACCOUNT LAND ACCOUNT NO.

Date		Item	Debit	Credit	Balance	
					Debit	Credit
1990						
Jan.	1	Balance			40,000	
Dec.	28	Acquired by issuance of common stock at par	50,000		90,000	

Although cash was not involved in this transaction, as indicated previously, the acquisition represents a significant financing and investing activity. Therefore, the transaction would be reported in a separate schedule as follows:

Noncash financing and investing activities:
Issuance of common stock at par for land $50,000

Investments

The comparative balance sheet indicates that investments decreased by $45,000. The notation in the following investments account indicates that the investments were sold for $75,000 in cash.

ACCOUNT INVESTMENTS ACCOUNT NO.

Date		Item	Debit	Credit	Balance	
					Debit	Credit
1990						
Jan.	1	Balance			45,000	
June	8	Sold for $75,000 cash		45,000	—	—

The $75,000 received from the sale of the investments must be reported as a cash flow from investing activities. Accordingly, the notation in the statement of cash flows is as follows:

Cash flows from investing activities:
Cash received from sale of investments (includes $30,000 gain reported in net income).. $75,000

Note that the $30,000 gain on the sale is included in the net income reported on the income statement. As indicated previously, this gain was deducted from the net income in determining the cash flows from operating activities.

ILLUSTRATION OF THE STATEMENT OF CASH FLOWS

As mentioned previously, the statement of cash flows is divided into three sections—cash flows from operating activities, cash flows from financing activities, and cash flows from investing activities. Although different formats are possible, the cash flows from operating activities section is generally presented first, followed by the sections for cash flows from financing activities and investing activities. The total of the net cash flows from the three sections is the increase or decrease in cash for the period. The change in cash should be added to the cash balance at the beginning of the year in order to reconcile the beginning and ending cash balances. If there were noncash financing and investing activities during the period, a separate schedule reporting such transactions would accompany the statement of cash flows.

An analysis of the statement of cash flows for T. R. Morgan Corporation, presented below, indicates that the cash position increased by $23,000 during the year. The most significant increase in net cash flows was from operating activities ($93,000). The investing activities used $82,000 of cash flows during the year.

Statement of Cash Flows

example

T. R. Morgan Corporation
Statement of Cash Flows
For Year Ended December 31, 1990

Cash flows from operating activities:			
Net income, per income statement		$ 90,500	
Add: Depreciation	$ 18,000		
Decrease in inventories	8,000		
Increase in accounts payable	18,000	44,000	
		$134,500	
Deduct: Increase in trade receivables	$ 9,000		
Increase in prepaid expenses	1,000		
Decrease in income tax payable	1,500		
Gain on sale of investments	30,000	41,500	
Net cash flow from operating activities			$93,000
Cash flows from financing activities:			
Cash received from sale of preferred stock		$160,000	
Less: Cash paid for dividends	$ 23,000		
Cash paid to retire bonds payable	125,000	148,000	
Net cash flow provided by financing activities			12,000
Cash flows from investing activities:			
Cash received from sale of investments		$ 75,000	
Less: Cash paid for purchase of equipment		157,000	
Net cash flow used for investing activities			(82,000)
Increase in cash			$23,000
Cash at the beginning of the year			26,000
Cash at the end of the year			$49,000

Schedule of Noncash Financing and Investing Activities

Issuance of common stock at par for land	$50,000

CASH FLOW PER SHARE

The term "cash flow per share" is sometimes encountered in the financial press. In many cases, the reference is to cash flows from operations per share. Such reporting of cash flow per share might mislead readers into thinking that cash flow is equivalent to or perhaps superior to earnings per share in appraising the relative success of operations. For example, users might interpret the cash flow from operations per share as being the amount available for dividends, when most of the cash generated by operations may be required for repaying loans or for reinvesting in the business. The financial statements, including the statement of cash flows, should therefore not report a cash flow per share amount.

Chapter Review

KEY POINTS

1. Nature of the Statement of Cash Flows.
The statement of cash flows reports a firm's major sources of cash receipts and major uses of cash payments for a period. The statement of cash flows provides useful information about a firm's activities in generating cash from operations, meeting its financial obligations, paying dividends, and maintaining and expanding operating capacity. When used in conjunction with the other financial statements, the statement of cash flows is useful in analyzing both past and future profitability and solvency of a firm.

2. Form of the Statement of Cash Flows.
The statement of cash flows reports cash receipts and cash payments by three types of activities: (1) operating activities, (2) financing activities, and (3) investing activities. Operating activities include cash transactions that enter into the determination of net income. Financing activities include receipts from the issuance of equity and debt securities and payments for dividends, repurchase of equity securities, and redemption of debt securities. Investing activities include receipts from the sale of noncurrent assets, such as investments and plant assets, and payments for the acquisition of noncurrent assets. If financing and investing transactions that do not involve cash have occurred during the period, their effect should be reported in a separate schedule to the statement of cash flows.

3. Assembling Data for the Statement of Cash Flows.
The common and most efficient procedure for determining the data for the statement of cash flows is to examine the noncash balance sheet accounts and determine the type of cash flow activity related to changes in these accounts.

4. Illustration of the Statement of Cash Flows.
The statement of cash flows is divided into three sections, with the cash flows from operating activities generally placed first, followed by the cash flows from financing activities and the cash flows from investing activities. A separate schedule is used to report noncash financing and investing activities.

5. Cash Flow per Share.
Sometimes the financial press refers to cash flows from operations per share. Such reporting of cash flow per share data might mislead readers into thinking that cash flow is equivalent to or perhaps superior to earnings per share in appraising the relative success of operations. The financial statements, including the statement of cash flows, should therefore not report a cash flow per share amount.

KEY TERMS

statement of cash flows 531
cash flows from operating activities 532
cash flows from financing activities 532
cash flows from investing activities 532
direct method 533
indirect method 533

SELF-EXAMINATION QUESTIONS

(Answers at End of Chapter)

1. A full set of financial statements for a corporation would include:
   A. a balance sheet
   B. an income statement
   C. a statement of cash flows
   D. all of the above

2. An example of a cash flow from an operating activity is:
   A. receipt of cash from the sale of capital stock
   B. receipt of cash from the sale of bonds
   C. payment of cash for dividends
   D. none of the above

3. An example of a cash flow from a financing activity is:
   A. receipt of cash from the sale of capital stock
   B. receipt of cash from the sale of bonds
   C. payment of cash for dividends
   D. all of the above

4. An example of a cash flow from an investing activity is:
   A. receipt of cash from the sale of equipment
   B. receipt of cash from the sale of capital stock
   C. payment of cash for dividends
   D. payment of cash to repurchase equity securities

5. The net income reported on the income statement for the year was $55,000 and depreciation on plant assets for the year was $22,000. The balances of the current asset and current liability accounts at the beginning and end of the year are as follows:

	End	Beginning
Cash	$ 65,000	$ 70,000
Trade receivables	100,000	90,000
Inventories	145,000	150,000
Prepaid expenses	7,500	8,000
Accounts payable (merchandise creditors)	51,000	58,000

The total amount reported for cash flows from operating activities in the statement of cash flows would be:

A. $33,000
B. $55,000
C. $77,000
D. none of the above

ILLUSTRATIVE PROBLEM

The comparative balance sheet of Jones Inc. for December 31, 1990 and 1989, is as follows:

Assets	1990	1989
Cash	$ 65,100	$ 42,500
Trade receivables (net)	91,350	61,150
Inventories	104,500	109,500
Prepaid expenses	3,600	2,700
Land	30,000	50,000
Buildings	345,000	245,000
Accumulated depreciation—buildings	(120,600)	(110,400)
Machinery and equipment	255,000	255,000
Accumulated depreciation—machinery and equipment	(92,000)	(65,000)
Patents	35,000	40,000
	$716,950	$630,450
Liabilities and Stockholders' Equity		
Accounts payable (merchandise creditors)	$ 61,150	$ 75,000
Dividends payable	15,000	10,000
Salaries payable	6,650	7,550
Mortgage note payable, due 1995	60,000	—
Bonds payable	—	75,000
Common stock, $20 par	300,000	250,000
Premium on common stock	100,000	75,000
Retained earnings	174,150	137,900
	$716,950	$630,450

An examination of the income statement and the accounting records revealed the following additional information applicable to 1990:

(a) Net income, $96,250.
(b) Depreciation expense reported on the income statement: buildings, $10,200; machinery and equipment, $27,000.
(c) Land costing $20,000 was sold for $20,000.
(d) Patent amortization reported on the income statement, $5,000
(e) A mortgage note was issued for $60,000.

(f) A building costing $100,000 was constructed.
(g) 2,500 shares of common stock were issued at 30 in exchange for the bonds payable.
(h) Cash dividends declared, $60,000.

Instructions:
Prepare a statement of cash flows.

SOLUTION

Jones Inc.
Statement of Cash Flows
For Year Ended December 31, 1990

Cash flows from operating activities:			
Net income, per income statement		$ 96,250	
Add: Depreciation	$ 37,200		
Amortization of patents	5,000		
Decrease in inventories	5,000	47,200	
		$143,450	
Deduct: Increase in trade receivables (net)	$ 30,200		
Increase in prepaid expenses	900		
Decrease in accounts payable	13,850		
Decrease in salaries payable	900	45,850	
Net cash flow from operating activities			$97,600
Cash flows from financing activities:			
Cash received from issuance of mortgage note payable		$ 60,000	
Less: Cash paid for dividends		55,000	
Net cash flow provided by financing activities			5,000
Cash flows from investing activities:			
Cash received from sale of land		$ 20,000	
Less: Cash paid for construction of building		100,000	
Net cash flow used for investing activities			(80,000)
Increase in cash			$22,600
Cash at the beginning of the year			42,500
Cash at the end of the year			$65,100

Schedule of Noncash Financing and Investing Activities

Issuance of common stock to retire bonds payable	$75,000

Discussion Questions

14–1. Name the four principal financial statements comprising a full set of statements.

14–2. Which of the four principal financial statements is most useful in evaluating past and planning future financing and investing activities?

14–3. What financial statement was replaced by the statement of cash flows?

14–4. For the statement of changes in financial position, the working capital basis was often employed. What is working capital?

14–5. What are the three types of activities reported on the statement of cash flows?

14–6. State the effect of each of the following transactions, considered individually, on cash flows (cash receipt or payment, and amount):
(a) Sold a new issue of $100,000 of bonds at 102.
(b) Sold equipment with a book value of $37,500 for $40,000.
(c) Sold 5,000 shares of $50 par common stock at $45 per share.
(d) Retired $500,000 of bonds on which there was $2,500 of unamortized bond discount for $501,000.

14–7. Identify each of the following as to type of cash flow activity (operating, financing, or investing):
(a) sale of investments
(b) issuance of common stock
(c) purchase of buildings
(d) net income
(e) issuance of bonds
(f) payment of cash dividends
(g) purchase of treasury stock
(h) redemption of bonds
(i) sale of equipment
(j) issuance of preferred stock
(k) purchase of patents

14–8. Name the two alternatives to reporting cash flows from operating activities in the statement of cash flows.

14–9. What is the principal disadvantage of the direct method of reporting cash flows from operating activities?

14–10. What are the major advantages of the indirect method of reporting cash flows from operating activities?

14–11. On the statement of cash flows, if the cash inflows from financing activities exceed the cash outflows, how is the difference described?

14–12. On the statement of cash flows, if the cash outflows from financing activities exceed the cash inflows, how is the difference described?

14–13. On the statement of cash flows, if the cash inflows from investing activities exceed the cash outflows, how is the difference described?

14–14. On the statement of cash flows, if the cash outflows from investing activities exceed the cash inflows, how is the difference described?

14–15. A corporation issued $250,000 of common stock in exchange for $250,000 of plant assets. Where would this transaction be reported on the statement of cash flows?

14–16. A corporation acquired as a long-term investment all of the capital stock of AJC Co., valued at $5,000,000, by issuance of $5,000,000 of its own common stock. Where should the transaction be reported on the statement of cash flows?

14–17. (a) What is the effect on cash flows of the declaration and issuance of a stock dividend?
(b) Is the stock dividend reported on the statement of cash flows?

14–18. On its income statement for the current year, a company reported a net loss of $50,000 from operations. On its statement of cash flows, it reported $25,000 of cash flows from operating activities. Explain the seeming contradiction between the loss and the cash flows.

14–19. What is the effect on cash flows of an appropriation of retained earnings for bonded indebtedness?

14–20. A retail enterprise, employing the accrual method of accounting, owed merchandise creditors (accounts payable) $295,000 at the beginning of the year and $320,000 at the end of the year. What adjustment for the $25,000 increase must be made to net income in determining the amount of cash flows from operating activities? Explain.

14–21. If revenue from sales amounted to $940,000 for the year and trade receivables totaled $120,000 and $135,000 at the beginning and end of the year respectively, what was the amount of cash received from customers during the year?

14–22. If salaries payable was $95,000 and $85,000 at the beginning and end of the year respectively, should $10,000 be added to or deducted from income to determine the amount of cash flows from operating activities? Explain.

14–23. The board of directors declared cash dividends totaling $120,000 during the current year. The comparative balance sheet indicates dividends payable of $25,000 at the beginning of the year and $30,000 at the end of the year. What was the amount of cash payments to stockholders during the year?

14–24. A long-term investment in bonds with a cost of $70,000 was sold for $75,000 cash. (a) What was the gain or loss on the sale? (b) What was the effect of the transaction on cash flows? (c) How should the transaction be reported in the statement of cash flows?

14–25. A corporation issued $5,000,000 of 20-year bonds for cash at 105. How would the transaction be reported on the statement of cash flows?

14–26. Fully depreciated equipment costing $75,000 was discarded. What was the effect of the transaction on cash flows if (a) $5,000 cash is received, (b) there is no salvage value?

14–27. Real World Focus. Tandy Corporation converted approximately $100 million of 6½% debenture bonds into shares of common stock. How would this transaction be reported on the statement of cash flows?

Exercises

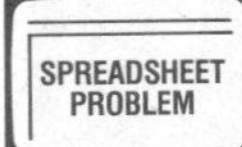

14–28. Cash flows from operating activities section. The net income reported on the income statement for the current year was $87,100. Depreciation recorded on equipment and a building amounted to $32,250 for the year. Balances of the current asset and current liability accounts at the beginning and end of the year are as follows:

	End of Year	Beginning of Year
Cash	$ 61,125	$58,725
Trade receivables (net)	87,500	80,000
Inventories	110,000	95,000
Prepaid expenses	6,900	7,650
Accounts payable (merchandise creditors)	77,200	72,700
Salaries payable	3,750	6,250

Prepare the cash flows from operating activities section of the statement of cash flows.

14–29. Cash flows from operating activities section. The net income reported on an income statement for the current year was $92,125. Depreciation recorded on store equipment for the year amounted to $43,500. Balances of the current asset and current liability accounts at the beginning and end of the year are as follows:

	End of Year	Beginning of Year
Cash	$ 69,750	$61,250
Trade receivable (net)	80,500	85,000
Merchandise inventory	110,000	97,000
Prepaid expenses	7,900	7,400
Accounts payable (merchandise creditors)	69,700	72,700
Wages payable	7,500	6,250

Prepare the cash flows from operating activities section of a statement of cash flows.

14–30. Reporting changes in equipment on statement of cash flows. An analysis of the general ledger accounts indicated that office equipment, which had cost $60,000 and on which accumulated depreciation totaled $52,500 on the date of sale, was sold for $7,000 during the year. Using this information, indicate the items to be reported on the statement of cash flows.

14–31. Reporting changes in equipment on statement of cash flows. An analysis of the general ledger accounts indicated that delivery equipment, which had cost $35,000 and on which accumulated depreciation totaled $29,750 on the date of sale, was sold for $7,000 during the year. Using this information, indicate the items to be reported on the statement of cash flows.

14–32. Reporting land transactions on statement of cash flows. On the basis of the details of the following plant asset account, indicate the items to be reported on the statement of cash flows.

ACCOUNT LAND ACCOUNT NO.

Date		Item	Debit	Credit	Balance Debit	Balance Credit
19--						
Jan.	1	Balance			650,000	
Aug.	29	Purchased for cash	200,000			
Nov.	20	Sold for $75,000		40,000	810,000	

14–33. Reporting stockholders' equity items on statement of cash flows. On the basis of the following stockholders' equity accounts, indicate the items, exclusive of net income, to be reported on the statement of cash flows. There were no unpaid dividends at either the beginning or end of the year.

ACCOUNT COMMON STOCK, $10 PAR ACCOUNT NO.

Date		Item	Debit	Credit	Balance Debit	Balance Credit
19--						
Jan.	1	Balance, 50,000 shares				500,000
	20	5,000 shares issued for cash		50,000		
June	25	2,750-share stock dividend		27,500		577,500

ACCOUNT PREMIUM ON COMMON STOCK ACCOUNT NO.

Date		Item	Debit	Credit	Balance Debit	Balance Credit
19--						
Jan.	1	Balance				50,000
	20	5,000 shares issued for cash		10,000		
June	25	Stock dividend		5,000		65,000

(continued)

ACCOUNT RETAINED EARNINGS ACCOUNT NO.

Date		Item	Debit	Credit	Balance Debit	Balance Credit
19--						
Jan.	1	Balance				225,000
June	25	Stock dividend	32,500			
Dec.	15	Cash dividend	55,000			
	31	Net income		97,500		235,000

14–34. Reporting land acquisition for cash and mortgage note on statement of cash flows. On the basis of the details of the following plant asset account, indicate the items to be reported on the statement of cash flows.

ACCOUNT LAND ACCOUNT NO.

Date		Item	Debit	Credit	Balance Debit	Balance Credit
19--						
Jan.	1	Balance			750,000	
Mar.	2	Purchased for cash	100,000			
Oct.	29	Purchased with long-term mortgage note	300,000		1,150,000	

Problems

14–35. Statement of cash flows. The comparative balance sheet of R. N. Corley Inc. for December 31 of the current year and the preceding year is as follows:

	December 31 Current Year	Preceding Year
Cash	$ 72,000	$ 50,500
Trade receivables (net)	88,000	80,000
Inventories	105,900	91,400
Investments	—	50,000
Land	50,000	—
Equipment	375,000	275,000
Accumulated depreciation	(149,000)	(114,000)
	$541,900	$432,900
Accounts payable (merchandise creditors)	$ 57,000	$ 55,000
Dividends payable	15,000	10,000
Common stock, $40 par	320,000	250,000
Premium on common stock	17,000	12,000
Retained earnings	132,900	105,900
	$541,900	$432,900

The following additional information was taken from Corley's records:

(a) The investments were sold for $60,000 cash.
(b) Equipment and land were acquired for cash.
(c) There were no disposals of equipment during the year.
(d) The common stock was issued for cash.

(e) There was a $64,500 credit to Retained Earnings for net income.
(f) There was a $37,500 debit to Retained Earnings for cash dividends declared.

Instructions: Prepare a statement of cash flows.

14–36. Statement of cash flows. The comparative balance sheet of ASCO Company at June 30 of the current year and the preceding year is as follows:

Assets	Current Year	Preceding Year
Cash	$ 40,750	$ 55,250
Trade receivables (net)	85,400	95,000
Merchandise inventory	255,300	249,200
Prepaid expenses	3,825	2,700
Plant assets	321,500	289,500
Accumulated depreciation—plant assets	(172,100)	(197,500)
	$534,675	$494,150
Liabilities and Stockholders' Equity		
Accounts payable (merchandise creditors)	$ 53,525	$ 49,150
Mortgage note payable	—	75,000
Common stock, $20 par	250,000	200,000
Premium on common stock	40,000	25,000
Retained earnings	191,150	145,000
	$534,675	$494,150

Additional data obtained from the income statement and from an examination of the accounts in the ledger are as follows:

(a) Net income, $91,150.
(b) Depreciation reported on the income statement, $28,600.
(c) An addition to the building was constructed at a cost of $86,000, and fully depreciated equipment costing $54,000 was discarded, with no salvage realized.
(d) The mortgage note payable was not due until 1992, but the terms permitted earlier payment without penalty.
(e) 2,500 shares of common stock were issued at 26 for cash.
(f) Cash dividends declared, $45,000.

Instructions: Prepare a statement of cash flows.

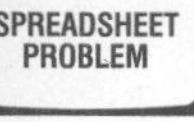
SPREADSHEET PROBLEM

14–37. Statement of cash flows. The comparative balance sheet of A. R. Katz Corporation at December 31 of the current year and the preceding year is as follows.

Assets	Current Year	Preceding Year
Cash	$ 89,900	$ 82,400
Trade receivables (net)	117,200	132,700
Inventories	260,070	238,070
Prepaid expenses	4,500	3,900
Land	100,000	100,000
Buildings	622,500	422,500
Accumulated depreciation—buildings	(210,000)	(192,000)
Machinery and equipment	275,000	275,000
Accumulated depreciation—machinery and equipment	(130,600)	(108,400)
Patents	40,500	50,000
	$1,169,070	$1,004,170

Assets	Current Year	Preceding Year
Liabilities and Stockholders' Equity		
Accounts payable (merchandise creditors)	$ 36,280	$ 51,780
Dividends payable	25,000	20,000
Salaries payable	10,550	19,400
Mortgage note payable, due 1995	150,000	—
Bonds payable	—	100,000
Common stock, $15 par	550,000	475,000
Premium on common stock	75,000	50,000
Retained earnings	322,240	287,990
	$1,169,070	$1,004,170

An examination of the income statement and the accounting records revealed the following additional information applicable to the current year:

(a) Net income, $84,250.
(b) Depreciation expense reported on the income statement: buildings, $18,000; machinery and equipment, $22,200.
(c) Patent amortization reported on the income statement, $9,500.
(d) A building was constructed for $200,000 cash.
(e) A mortgage note for $150,000 was issued for cash.
(f) 5,000 shares of common stock were issued at 20 in exchange for the bonds payable.
(g) Cash dividends declared, $50,000.

Instructions: Prepare a statement of cash flows.

14–38. Statement of cash flows. The comparative balance sheet of C. R. Lucas Inc. at December 31 of the current year and the preceding year is as follows:

Assets	Current Year	Preceding Year
Cash	$ 97,600	$ 84,500
Trade receivables (net)	140,500	125,250
Income tax refund receivable	7,500	—
Inventories	214,150	225,650
Prepaid expenses	8,100	9,250
Investments	70,000	200,000
Land	110,000	150,000
Buildings	650,000	375,000
Accumulated depreciation—buildings	(173,100)	(161,500)
Equipment	507,000	392,000
Accumulated depreciation—equipment	(181,620)	(171,420)
	$1,450,130	$1,228,730
Liabilities and Stockholders' Equity		
Accounts payable (merchandise creditors)	$ 71,400	$ 90,600
Income tax payable	—	9,000
Bonds payable	300,000	—
Discount on bonds payable	(24,375)	—
Common stock, $5 par	525,000	500,000
Premium on common stock	70,000	60,000
Appropriation for plant expansion	200,000	175,000
Retained earnings	308,105	394,130
	$1,450,130	$1,228,730

The noncurrent asset, the noncurrent liability, and the stockholders' equity accounts for the current year are as follows:

ACCOUNT INVESTMENTS — ACCOUNT NO.

Date		Item	Debit	Credit	Balance Debit	Balance Credit
19--						
Jan.	1	Balance			200,000	
May	5	Realized $155,000 cash from sale		130,000	70,000	

ACCOUNT LAND — ACCOUNT NO.

Date		Item	Debit	Credit	Balance Debit	Balance Credit
19--						
Jan.	1	Balance			150,000	
Aug.	15	Realized $50,000 from sale		40,000	110,000	

ACCOUNT BUILDINGS — ACCOUNT NO.

Date		Item	Debit	Credit	Balance Debit	Balance Credit
19--						
Jan.	1	Balance			375,000	
June	30	Acquired for cash	275,000		650,000	

ACCOUNT ACCUMULATED DEPRECIATION—BUILDINGS — ACCOUNT NO.

Date		Item	Debit	Credit	Balance Debit	Balance Credit
19--						
Jan.	1	Balance				161,500
Dec.	31	Depreciation for year		11,600		173,100

ACCOUNT EQUIPMENT — ACCOUNT NO.

Date		Item	Debit	Credit	Balance Debit	Balance Credit
19--						
Jan.	1	Balance			392,000	
Apr.	4	Discarded, no salvage		40,000		
July	11	Purchased for cash	80,000			
Oct.	10	Purchased for cash	75,000		507,000	

ACCOUNT ACCUMULATED DEPRECIATION—EQUIPMENT — ACCOUNT NO.

Date		Item	Debit	Credit	Balance Debit	Balance Credit
19--						
Jan.	1	Balance				171,420
Apr.	4	Equipment discarded	40,000			
Dec.	31	Depreciation for year		50,200		181,620

ACCOUNT BONDS PAYABLE — ACCOUNT NO.

Date		Item	Debit	Credit	Balance Debit	Balance Credit
19--						
June	30	Issued 20-year bonds		300,000		300,000

ACCOUNT DISCOUNT ON BONDS PAYABLE — ACCOUNT NO.

Date		Item	Debit	Credit	Balance Debit	Balance Credit
19--						
June	30	Bonds issued	25,000		25,000	
Dec.	31	Amortization		625	24,375	

ACCOUNT COMMON STOCK, $5 PAR — ACCOUNT NO.

Date		Item	Debit	Credit	Balance Debit	Balance Credit
19--						
Jan.	1	Balance				500,000
July	1	Stock dividend		25,000		525,000

ACCOUNT PREMIUM ON COMMON STOCK — ACCOUNT NO.

Date		Item	Debit	Credit	Balance Debit	Balance Credit
19--						
Jan.	1	Balance				60,000
July	1	Stock dividend		10,000		70,000

ACCOUNT APPROPRIATION FOR PLANT EXPANSION — ACCOUNT NO.

Date		Item	Debit	Credit	Balance Debit	Balance Credit
19--						
Jan.	1	Balance				175,000
Dec.	31	Appropriation		25,000		200,000

ACCOUNT RETAINED EARNINGS — ACCOUNT NO.

Date		Item	Debit	Credit	Balance Debit	Balance Credit
19--						
Jan.	1	Balance				394,130
July	1	Stock dividend	35,000			
Dec.	31	Net loss	1,025			
	31	Cash dividends	25,000			
	31	Appropriated	25,000			308,105

Instructions: Prepare a statement of cash flows.

14–39. Statement of cash flows. An income statement and a comparative balance sheet for Lee Company are as follows:

Lee Company
Income Statement
For Current Year Ended December 31

Sales	$962,500
Cost of merchandise sold	617,500
Gross profit	$345,000
Operating expenses (including depreciation of $32,200)	220,600
Income from operations	$124,400

Other income:		
Gain on sale of land	$15,000	
Gain on sale of investments	7,500	
Interest income	1,600	24,100
		$148,500
Interest expense		24,000
Income before income tax		$124,500
Income tax		43,000
Net income		$ 81,500

Lee Company
Comparative Balance Sheet
December 31, Current and Preceding Year

Assets	Current Year	Preceding Year
Cash	$ 39,900	$ 46,600
Trade receivables (net)	109,750	94,250
Inventories	169,200	152,100
Prepaid expenses	4,150	4,900
Investments	27,600	75,000
Land	70,000	60,000
Buildings	330,000	180,000
Accumulated depreciation—buildings	(73,000)	(65,000)
Equipment	395,000	350,000
Accumulated depreciation—equipment	(143,800)	(119,600)
Total assets	$928,800	$778,250
Liabilities and Stockholders' Equity		
Accounts payable (merchandise creditors)	$ 64,750	$ 50,400
Income tax payable	5,000	7,800
Dividends payable	12,500	10,000
Mortgage note payable	150,000	—
Bonds payable	100,000	200,000
Common stock, $25 par	350,000	300,000
Premium on common stock	38,000	33,000
Retained earnings	208,550	177,050
Total liabilities and stockholders' equity	$928,800	$778,250

The following additional information on funds flow during the year was obtained from an examination of the ledger:

(a) Investments (long-term) were purchased for $27,600.
(b) Investments (long-term) were sold for $82,500.
(c) Equipment was purchased for $45,000. There were no disposals.
(d) A building valued at $150,000 and land valued at $50,000 were acquired by a cash payment of $200,000.
(e) Land which cost $40,000 was sold for $55,000 cash.
(f) A mortgage note payable for $150,000 was issued for cash.
(g) Bonds payable of $100,000 were retired by the payment of their face amount.
(h) 2,000 shares of common stock were issued for cash at 27 1/2.
(i) Cash dividends of $50,000 were declared.

Instructions: Prepare a statement of cash flows.

14–40. Real World Focus. The current asset and current liability sections of the May 31, 1987 and 1986 balance sheets of The Pillsbury Company are as follows (dollars in millions):

	1987	1986
Current assets:		
Cash and equivalents	$ 80.7	$ 96.5
Receivables	522.7	492.7
Inventories	572.2	490.2
Prepaid and other assets	98.0	79.7
Total current assets	$1,273.6	$1,159.1
Current liabilities:		
Notes payable	$ 51.9	$ 22.1
Current portion of long-term debt	44.9	52.1
Accounts and drafts payable	620.7	513.6
Advances on sales	113.7	91.4
Employee compensation payable	121.7	118.6
Income taxes payable	—	49.8
Other liabilities	289.7	287.9
Total current liabilities	$1,242.6	$1,135.5

Selected data from Pillsbury Company's 1987 income statement (dollars in millions) were as follows:

Net income	$181.9
Depreciation	197.6
Amortization	23.9
Deferred income taxes (expense)	54.0

Instructions: Prepare the cash flows from operating activities section of the statement of cash flows for The Pillsbury Company.

ALTERNATE PROBLEMS

14–35A. Statement of cash flows. The comparative balance sheet of C. D. Collins Co. for June 30 of the current year and the preceding year is as follows:

	June 30	
	Current Year	Preceding Year
Cash	$ 64,200	$ 49,900
Trade receivables (net)	91,500	80,000
Inventories	105,900	90,500
Investments	—	75,000
Land	85,000	—
Equipment	355,000	275,000
Accumulated depreciation	(149,000)	(119,000)
	$552,600	$451,400
Accounts payable (merchandise creditors)	$ 62,450	$ 55,000
Dividends payable	12,000	10,000
Common stock, $20 par	300,000	250,000
Premium on common stock	22,000	12,000
Retained earnings	156,150	124,400
	$552,600	$451,400

The following additional information was taken from the records of Collins:

(a) Equipment and land were acquired for cash.
(b) There were no disposals of equipment during the year.
(c) The investments were sold for $80,000 cash.
(d) The common stock was issued for cash.

(e) There was a $76,750 credit to Retained Earnings for net income.
(f) There was a $45,000 debit to Retained Earnings for cash dividends declared.

Instructions: Prepare a statement of cash flows.

14–36A. Statement of cash flows. The comparative balance sheet of AIA Corporation at December 31 of the current year and the preceding year is as follows:

Assets	Current Year	Preceding Year
Cash	$ 62,600	$ 51,250
Trade receivables (net)	55,800	58,500
Merchandise inventory	97,500	77,300
Prepaid expenses	5,300	4,650
Plant assets	375,000	337,500
Accumulated depreciation—plant assets	(110,000)	(125,000)
	$486,200	$404,200

Liabilities and Stockholders' Equity	Current Year	Preceding Year
Accounts payable (merchandise creditors)	$ 55,600	$ 40,100
Mortgage note payable	—	50,000
Common stock, $25 par	250,000	200,000
Premium on common stock	55,000	25,000
Retained earnings	125,600	89,100
	$486,200	$404,200

Additional data obtained from the income statement and from an examination of the accounts in the ledger are as follows:

(a) Net income, $72,500.
(b) Depreciation reported on the income statement, $27,500.
(c) An addition to the building was constructed at a cost of $80,000, and fully depreciated equipment costing $42,500 was discarded, with no salvage realized.
(d) The mortgage note payable was not due until 1993, but the terms permitted earlier payment without penalty.
(e) 2,000 shares of common stock were issued at 40 for cash.
(f) Cash dividends declared and paid, $36,000.

Instructions: Prepare a statement of cash flows.

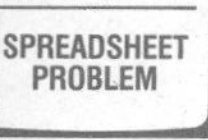

14–37A. Statement of cash flows. The comparative balance sheet of Dina Corporation at December 31 of the current year and the preceding year is as follows:

Assets	Current Year	Preceding Year
Cash	$ 53,400	$ 46,200
Trade receivables (net)	82,100	67,450
Inventories	110,500	119,750
Prepaid expenses	4,000	2,900
Land	60,000	60,000
Buildings	345,000	265,000
Accumulated depreciation—buildings	(140,600)	(130,400)
Machinery and equipment	275,000	275,000
Accumulated depreciation—machinery and equipment	(92,000)	(65,000)
Patents	30,000	35,000
	$727,400	$675,900

Assets	Current Year	Preceding Year
Liabilities and Stockholders' Equity		
Accounts payable (merchandise creditors)	$ 52,750	$ 80,000
Dividends payable	10,000	7,500
Salaries payable	4,500	4,950
Mortgage note payable, due 1992	50,000	—
Bonds payable	—	100,000
Common stock, $20 par	380,000	300,000
Premium on common stock	80,000	60,000
Retained earnings	150,150	123,450
	$727,400	$675,900

An examination of the income statement and the accounting records revealed the following additional information applicable to the current year:

(a) Net income, $66,700.
(b) Depreciation expense reported on the income statement: buildings, $10,200; machinery and equipment, $27,000.
(c) A building was constructed for $80,000 cash.
(d) Patent amortization reported on the income statement, $5,000.
(e) A mortgage note for $50,000 was issued for cash.
(f) 4,000 shares of common stock were issued at 25 in exchange for the bonds payable.
(g) Cash dividends declared, $40,000.

Instructions: Prepare a statement of cash flows.

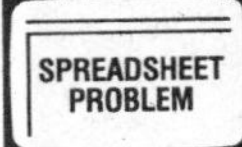

14–38A. Statement of cash flows. The comparative balance sheet of ACF Inc. at December, of the current year and the preceding year is as follows:

Assets	Current Year	Preceding Year
Cash	$ 56,125	$ 60,525
Trade receivables (net)	110,500	99,400
Inventories	218,750	192,700
Prepaid expenses	6,400	6,750
Investments	—	75,000
Land	47,500	47,500
Buildings	305,000	210,000
Accumulated depreciation—buildings	(76,400)	(69,000)
Equipment	470,500	395,500
Accumulated depreciation—equipment	(143,500)	(129,000)
	$994,875	$889,375
Liabilities and Stockholders' Equity		
Accounts payable (merchandise creditors)	$ 64,500	$ 80,500
Income tax payable	5,900	4,800
Bonds payable	100,000	—
Discount on bonds payable	(4,875)	—
Common stock, $20 par	550,000	500,000
Premium on common stock	67,000	55,000
Appropriation for plant expansion	75,000	50,000
Retained earnings	137,350	199,075
	$994,875	$889,375

The noncurrent asset, the noncurrent liability, and the stockholders' equity accounts for the current year are as follows:

ACCOUNT INVESTMENTS — ACCOUNT NO.

Date		Item	Debit	Credit	Balance Debit	Balance Credit
19--						
Jan.	1	Balance			75,000	
Aug.	3	Realized $67,500 cash from sale		75,000	—	—

ACCOUNT LAND — ACCOUNT NO.

Date		Item	Debit	Credit	Balance Debit	Balance Credit
19--						
Jan.	1	Balance			47,500	

ACCOUNT BUILDINGS — ACCOUNT NO.

Date		Item	Debit	Credit	Balance Debit	Balance Credit
19--						
Jan.	1	Balance			210,000	
July	1	Acquired for cash	95,000		305,000	

ACCOUNT ACCUMULATED DEPRECIATION — BUILDINGS — ACCOUNT NO.

Date		Item	Debit	Credit	Balance Debit	Balance Credit
19--						
Jan.	1	Balance				69,000
Dec.	31	Depreciation for year		7,400		76,400

ACCOUNT EQUIPMENT — ACCOUNT NO.

Date		Item	Debit	Credit	Balance Debit	Balance Credit
19--						
Jan.	1	Balance			395,500	
Mar.	28	Discarded, no salvage		35,000		
Sept.	12	Purchased for cash	65,000			
Nov.	21	Purchased for cash	45,000		470,500	

ACCOUNT ACCUMULATED DEPRECIATION — EQUIPMENT — ACCOUNT NO.

Date		Item	Debit	Credit	Balance Debit	Balance Credit
19--						
Jan.	1	Balance				129,000
Mar.	28	Equipment discarded	35,000			
Dec.	31	Depreciation for year		49,500		143,500

ACCOUNT BONDS PAYABLE — ACCOUNT NO.

Date		Item	Debit	Credit	Balance Debit	Balance Credit
19--						
July	1	Issued 20-year bonds		100,000		100,000

ACCOUNT DISCOUNT ON BONDS PAYABLE — ACCOUNT NO.

Date		Item	Debit	Credit	Balance Debit	Balance Credit
19--						
July	1	Bonds issued	5,000		5,000	
Dec.	31	Amortization		125	4,875	

ACCOUNT COMMON STOCK, $20 PAR — ACCOUNT NO.

Date		Item	Debit	Credit	Balance Debit	Balance Credit
19--						
Jan.	1	Balance				500,000
July	22	Stock dividend		50,000		550,000

ACCOUNT PREMIUM ON COMMON STOCK — ACCOUNT NO.

Date		Item	Debit	Credit	Balance Debit	Balance Credit
19--						
Jan.	1	Balance				55,000
July	22	Stock dividend		12,000		67,000

ACCOUNT APPROPRIATION FOR PLANT EXPANSION — ACCOUNT NO.

Date		Item	Debit	Credit	Balance Debit	Balance Credit
19--						
Jan.	1	Balance				50,000
Dec.	31	Appropriation		25,000		75,000

ACCOUNT RETAINED EARNINGS — ACCOUNT NO.

Date		Item	Debit	Credit	Balance Debit	Balance Credit
19--						
Jan.	1	Balance				199,075
July	22	Stock dividend	62,000			
Dec.	31	Net income		100,275		
	31	Cash dividends	75,000			
	31	Appropriated	25,000			137,350

Instructions: Prepare a statement of cash flows.

Mini-Case 14

a.j.jenkinsinc.

Ann Jenkins is the president and majority shareholder of A. J. Jenkins Inc., a small retail store chain. Recently, Jenkins submitted a loan application for A. J. Jenkins Inc. to Paxton State Bank. It called for a $150,000, 13%, 10-year loan to help finance the construction of a building and the purchase of store equipment costing a total of $200,000 to enable A. J. Jenkins Inc. to open another store in Paxton. Land for this purpose was acquired last year. The bank's loan officer requested a statement of cash flows in addition to the most recent income statement, balance sheet, and retained earnings statement that Jenkins had submitted with the loan application.

As a close family friend, Jenkins asked you to prepare a statement of cash flows. From the records provided, you prepared the following statement:

A. J. Jenkins Inc.
Statement of Cash Flows
For Year Ended December 31, 19--

Cash flows from operating activities:			
Net income, per income statement		$ 82,500	
Add: Depreciation	$25,500		
Decrease in trade receivables	9,000	34,500	
		$117,000	
Deduct: Increase in inventory	$ 7,500		
Increase in prepaid expenses	500		
Decrease in accounts payable	2,000		
Gain on sale of investments	5,000	15,000	
Net cash flow from operating activities			$102,000
Cash flows from financing activities:			
Cash paid for dividends		$ 50,000	
Net cash flow used for financing activities			(50,000)
Cash flows from investing activities:			
Cash received from investments sold		$ 35,000	
Less: Cash paid for purchase of store equipment		30,000	
Net cash flow from investing activities			5,000
Increase in cash			57,000
Cash at the beginning of the year			30,000
Cash at the end of the year			$ 87,000

Schedule of Noncash Financing and Investing Activities

Issuance of common stock at par for land	$40,000

After reviewing the statement, Jenkins telephoned you and commented, "Are you sure this statement is right?" Jenkins then raised the following questions:

(a) "How can depreciation be a cash flow?"
(b) "The issuance of common stock for the land is listed in a separate schedule. This transaction has nothing to do with cash! Shouldn't this transaction be eliminated from the statement?"
(c) "How can the gain on sale of investments be a deduction from net income in determining the cash flow from operating activities?"
(d) "Why does the bank need this statement anyway? They can compute the increase in cash from the balance sheets for the last two years."

After jotting down Jenkins' questions, you assured her that this statement was "right". However, to alleviate Jenkins' concern, you arranged a meeting for the following day.

Instructions:

(1) How would you respond to each of Jenkins' questions?
(2) Do you think that the statement of cash flows enhances the chances of A. J. Jenkins Inc. receiving the loan? Discuss.

Answers to Self-Examination Questions

1. D A full set of financial statements for a corporation includes a balance sheet (answer A), an income statement (answer B), a statement of cash flows (answer C), and a statement of retained earnings.

2. D Cash flows from operating activities relate to transactions that enter into the determination of net income (answer D). Receipts of cash from the sale of capital stock (answer A) and the sale of bonds (answer B) and payments of cash for dividends (answer C) are cash flows from financing activities.

3. D Cash flows from financing activities include receipts from the issuance of equity (answer A) and debt (answer B) securities and payments for dividends (answer C), repurchase of equity securities, and redemption of debt securities.

4. A Cash flows from investing activities include receipts from the sale of noncurrent assets, such as equipment (answer A), and payments for the acquisition of noncurrent assets. Receipts of cash from the sale of capital stock (answer B) and payments of cash for dividends (answer C) and for the repurchase of equity securities (answer D) are cash flows from financing activities.

5. D The cash flows from operating activities section of the statement of cash flows would report net cash flow from operating activities of $65,500, determined as follows:

Net income		$55,000	
Add:			
Depreciation	$22,000		
Decrease in inventories	5,000		
Decrease in prepaid expenses	500	27,500	
		$82,500	
Deduct:			
Increase in trade receivables	$10,000		
Decrease in accounts payable	7,000	17,000	
Net cash flow from operating activities			$65,500

Part Five

Managerial Accounting Concepts and Systems

15
The Nature of Managerial Accounting; Cost Concepts

CHAPTER OBJECTIVES

Describe the basic functions of the management process and the role of accounting in this process.

Describe the basic characteristics of managerial accounting reports.

Describe the organization of the managerial accounting function within a business enterprise.

Distinguish between costs and expenses.

Describe and illustrate the three manufacturing costs: direct materials, direct labor, and factory overhead.

Distinguish between product costs and period costs.

Describe and illustrate the statement of cost of goods manufactured.

Describe the basic cost classifications useful for planning and control:
Variable costs and fixed costs
Direct costs and indirect costs
Controllable costs and noncontrollable costs
Differential costs
Opportunity costs
Sunk costs

The **management** of an organization consists of those individuals charged with the responsibility for directing an enterprise toward achieving its goals. The primary goal of most enterprises is to earn a profit by rendering services or selling products. The primary goal of nonprofit organizations, such as governmental units, churches, and the Red Cross, is the rendering of humanitarian services to the needy at the lowest possible cost. Regardless of the goals, managers of all enterprises and organizations rely heavily on both historical and estimated accounting data in attempting to achieve their goals.

As discussed in Chapter 1 and illustrated in the diagram on page 13, managerial accounting overlaps financial accounting to the extent that management uses the financial statements or reports in directing current operations and in planning future operations. However, managerial accounting extends beyond financial accounting by providing additional information for management decision making, based upon the principle of usefulness. Thus, the managerial accountant is frequently concerned with identifying alternative courses of action and providing the necessary information for managers' use in deciding among the alternatives.

The primary focus of the remainder of this text is on the accounting data needed by the management of profit-oriented entities. Although the concepts and principles are presented in the context of a manufacturing enterprise, many of them apply to service and merchandising enterprises as well as to nonprofit organizations.[1]

This chapter begins with a discussion of the management process. This discussion is helpful in understanding the role of managerial accounting. The chapter concludes with a description and illustration of various cost concepts used by managerial accountants. Financial statements for a manufacturing enterprise are also illustrated.

THE MANAGEMENT PROCESS

The **management process** involves the four basic functions of (1) planning, (2) organizing and directing, (3) controlling, and (4) decision making. Although decision making has the central role in the management process, all four functions interact. As shown in the following diagram, these functions are the driving force for an enterprise's operations.

Diagram of Management Process

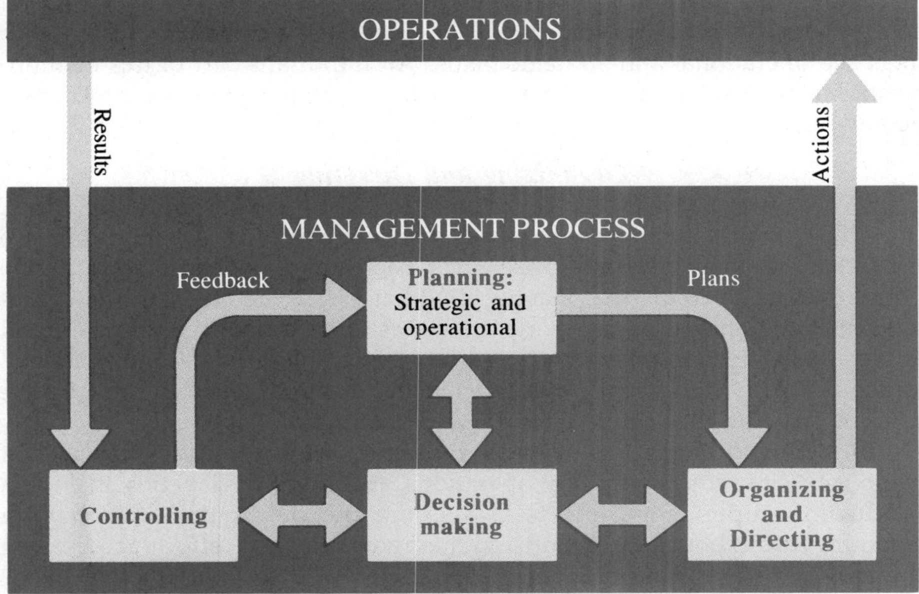

[1]Some specific applications of these concepts to service enterprises are presented in Appendix H.

Planning

Planning is the process by which management develops a course of action to attain enterprise goals. Planning involves such activities as setting selling prices, arranging for the financing of a plant expansion, and the development of new products. Planning can be categorized as either strategic planning or operational planning.

Strategic planning is the development of a long-range course of action to achieve goals. A strategic plan often encompasses periods ranging from five to ten years. Such a plan establishes enterprise policy and priorities for such activities as research and development, marketing, financing, and plant expansion. A strategic plan serves as the basis for the commitment of enterprise resources.

A strategic plan, which is normally approved by the highest levels of management, should integrate all aspects of the enterprise operations necessary for the achievement of long-range goals. Because the strategic plan is influenced by the changing environment within which the enterprise operates, the strategic plan should be periodically reviewed and revised. For example, rising interest rates might postpone a proposed plant expansion, or falling oil prices might postpone an enterprise's plan to expand operations into energy-saving products.

Operational planning, sometimes referred to as **tactical planning,** is the development of short-term plans to achieve goals identified in the strategic plan. Thus, operational plans complement the strategic plan and are typically established for time periods ranging from a week or a month to several years. Examples of operational planning are the setting of the current month's production levels by a manufacturer and determining the need for part-time employees during the holiday shopping period by a merchandising enterprise.

Effective communication between all levels of management within an enterprise is essential, so that day-to-day operations can be coordinated to meet the operational and strategic plans. An important part of this communication is the various accounting reports that management uses in planning operations.

Organizing and Directing

Organizing is the process by which management assigns responsibility to individuals for achieving enterprise goals. Each enterprise has its own unique organizational structure that management has established to implement strategic and operational plans. Some managers favor a highly centralized and autocratic organizational structure, while other managers favor decentralized structures with significant lower-management autonomy. No one organizational structure has proven best in all situations.

Directing is the process by which managers, given their assigned level of responsibilities, run day-to-day operations. Examples of directing include a production supervisor's efforts at keeping the production line moving smoothly throughout a work shift and the credit manager's efforts at assessing the creditworthiness of potential customers.

Controlling

Controlling is the process by which managers attempt to achieve the goals identified in the strategic and operational plans. This process normally involves monitoring the operating results of implemented plans and comparing the expected results with the actual results. This **feedback** allows management to isolate significant variations for further investigation and possible remedial action. It may also lead to a revision of future plans. This philosophy of controlling is sometimes referred to as **management by exception.** For example, if actual materials costs incurred in manufacturing a product exceed expected costs, an investigation may be conducted to determine the cause of the difference so that corrective action may be taken.

Decision Making

Decision making is the process by which managers determine to follow one course of action as opposed to an alternative. Decision making is inherent in each of the three management functions described in the preceding paragraphs. For example, in developing a strategic plan, managers must decide between competing courses of action to achieve long-range goals and objectives. Likewise, in organizing and directing operations, managers must decide on an organizational structure and on specific actions to take in day-to-day operations. In controlling operations, managers must decide whether variances are worth investigating.

ROLE OF MANAGERIAL ACCOUNTING

An essential ingredient for a management process to be successful is relevant information. **Managerial accounting** is the area of accounting that provides this information to management for use in planning, organizing, directing, and controlling of an enterprise. In this role, managerial accounting contributes to the efficient allocation of resources within the business enterprise.

Managerial accounting aids managers in planning by providing reports which estimate the effects of alternative actions on an enterprise's ability to achieve desired goals. For example, an enterprise might establish a 25% market share as a long-term strategic goal. To achieve this goal, the enterprise might consider increasing its advertising expenditures and/or decreasing its unit selling prices. Managerial accounting could report the estimated effects of the increased advertising, based on past experience, industry advertising statistics, market surveys, and other data, as well as the estimated effects of the decreased selling prices.

Managerial accounting aids managers in their organizing and directing functions by providing reports which allow them to adjust daily operations for changing conditions. For example, scrap reports could be provided to production supervisors for use in monitoring waste and efficiency of production on a daily basis. Likewise, daily or weekly sales reports could be used by a store manager in deciding which items are selling well and should be reordered and which items are not selling well and should not be reordered.

Managerial accounting aids managers in controlling operations by providing performance reports of variances between expected and actual operating results. Such reports serve as the basis for taking necessary corrective action to control operations. For example, a production supervisor might receive weekly or daily performance reports comparing actual materials costs with estimated costs. Significant variances could be isolated and corrective action could be taken. An excess of actual materials costs over estimated costs might be caused by the use of poor quality materials, in which case a change in suppliers might be warranted. Another example would be a partner in a law firm receiving weekly progress reports on the amount of staff time spent on each case. An excessive amount of staff time spent on any particular case would warrant an investigation and an explanation from the staff.

Managerial accounting aids managers in decision making by providing the basic information which the manager uses in selecting among alternative courses of action. For example, an accounting report indicating the contribution of the automotive service department to total store profits would aid the store manager in deciding whether to discontinue that department. Likewise, a similar accounting report would aid an ophthalmologist in deciding whether to sell eyeglass frames as a service to patients.

Managerial accounting thus provides information for all four basic functions of the management process. Without this information, it would be difficult for management to manage effectively and efficiently. The use of accounting information by managers is similar to the use of dashboard information by the driver of an automobile. The driver (manager) uses data on speed, oil pressure, and fuel (accounting information) to drive (manage) the automobile (enterprise) properly to an intended destination (goal).

CHARACTERISTICS OF MANAGERIAL ACCOUNTING REPORTS

As indicated, accounting reports provide much of the information useful for management in planning, organizing and directing, controlling, and decision making. The principle of "usefulness to management" is the primary criterion for the preparation of managerial accounting reports. To be useful, these reports should possess the characteristics of (1) relevance, (2) timeliness, (3) accuracy, (4) clarity, and (5) conciseness. Each of these characteristics is described in the following paragraphs.

Relevance

Relevance means that the economic information reported must be pertinent to the specific action being considered by management. In applying this concept, the accountant must be familiar with the operations of the firm and the needs of management in order to select what is important from the masses of data that are available. Especially in this modern age of the information explosion, this selection process can be difficult. To accomplish this task, the accountant must determine the needs of management for the decision at hand, examine the available data, and select only the relevant data for reporting to management. To illustrate, assume that management is considering the replacement of fully depreciated equipment, which cost $100,000, with new equipment costing $150,000. It is the $150,000 that is relevant for an analysis of financing the replacement. The original cost, $100,000, is irrelevant.

In applying the concept of relevance, it is important to recognize that some accounting information may have little or no relevance for one use but may have a high degree of relevance for another use. For example, in the previous illustration, the $100,000 was irrelevant for purposes of evaluating the financing of the replacement equipment. For financial reporting purposes, however, the $100,000 was relevant for determining the amount of the periodic depreciation from the use of the asset.

Timeliness

Timeliness refers to the need for accounting reports to contain the most up-to-date information. In many cases, outdated data can lead to unwise decisions. For example, if prior years' costs are relied upon in setting the selling price of a product, the resulting selling price may not be sufficient to cover the current year's costs and to provide a satisfactory profit.

In some cases, the timeliness concept may require the accountant to prepare reports on a prearranged schedule, such as daily, weekly, or monthly. For example, daily reports of cash receipts and disbursements assist management in effectively managing the use of cash on a day-to-day basis. On the other hand, weekly reports of the cost of products manufactured may be satisfactory to assist management in the control of costs. In other cases, reports are prepared on an irregular basis or only when needed. For example, if management is evaluating a proposed advertising promotion for the month of May, a report of current costs and other current relevant data for this specific proposal would be needed in sufficient time for management to make and implement the decision.

Accuracy

Accuracy refers to the need for the report to be correct within the constraints of the use of the report and the inherent inaccuracies in the measurement process. If the report is not accurate, management's decision may not be prudent. For example, if an inaccurate report on a customer's past payment practices is presented to management, an unwise decision in granting credit may be made.

As previously indicated, the concept of accuracy must be applied within the constraint of the use to be made of the report. In other words, there are occasions when accuracy should be sacrificed for less precise data that are more useful to management. For example, in planning production, estimates (forecasts) of future sales may be more useful than more accurate data from past sales. In addition, it should be noted that there are inherent inaccuracies in accounting data that are based on estimates and approximations. For example, in determining the unit cost of a product manufactured, an estimate of depreciation expense on factory equipment used in the manufacturing process must be made. Without this estimate, the cost of the product would be of limited usefulness in establishing the product selling price.

Clarity

Clarity refers to the need for reports to be clear and understandable in both format and content. Reports that are clear and understandable will enable management to focus on significant factors in planning and controlling operations. For example, for management's use in controlling the costs of manufacturing a product, a report that compares actual costs with expected costs and clearly indicates the differences enables management to give its attention to significant differences and to take any necessary corrective action.

Conciseness

Conciseness refers to the requirement that the report should be brief and to the point. Although the report must be complete and include all relevant information, the inclusion of unnecessary information wastes management's time and makes it more difficult for management to focus on the significant factors related to a decision. For example, reports prepared for the top level of management should usually be broad in scope and present summaries of data rather than small details.

Costs vs. Benefits of Managerial Accounting Reports

The characteristics of managerial accounting reports provide general guidelines for the preparation of reports to meet the various needs of management. In applying these guidelines, consideration must be given to the specific needs of each manager, and the reports should be tailored to meet these needs. In preparing reports, costs are incurred, and a primary consideration is that the value of the management reports must at least equal the cost of producing them. The relationship between the general guidelines and the cost-benefit consideration is illustrated as follows:

Managerial Accounting Reports

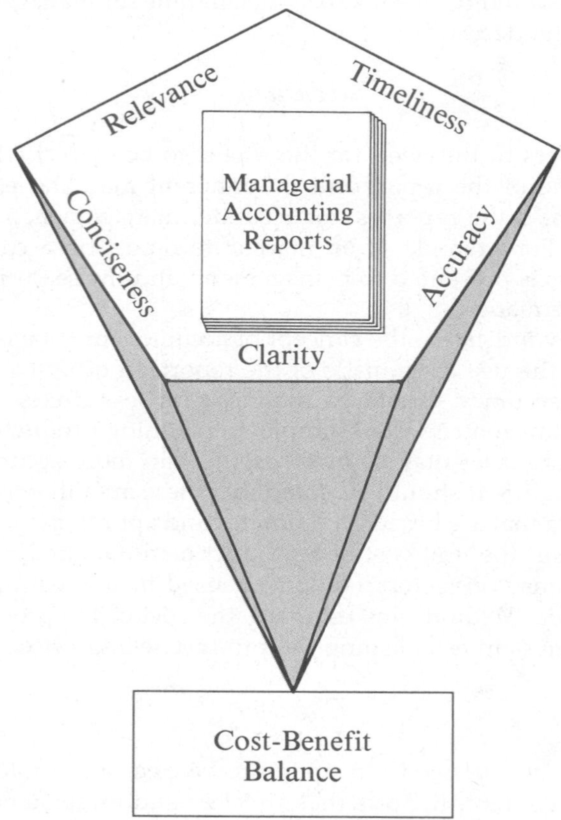

Costs and benefits must be considered, no matter how informational a report may be. A report should not be prepared if its cost exceeds the benefits derived by management.

ORGANIZATION OF THE MANAGERIAL ACCOUNTING FUNCTION

Managers organize business enterprises into departments or similar units with responsibilities for specific functions or activities. This operating structure of an enterprise can be diagrammed in an **organization chart.** An organization chart for Baker Inc., a small manufacturing enterprise, is as follows:

Organization Chart For Baker Inc.

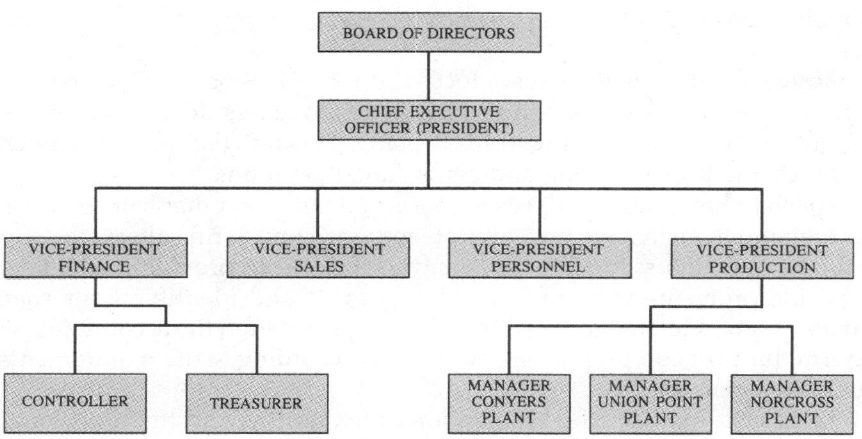

The Controller

In most business organizations, the chief accountant is called the **controller**. The controller, who commonly reports to the vice-president of finance, provides advice and assistance to management but assumes no direct responsibility for the operations of the business. The controller's function might be compared to that of an airplane's navigator. The navigator, with special skills and training, assists the pilot, but the pilot is responsible for flying the airplane. Likewise, the controller, with special accounting training and skills, advises management, but management is responsible for planning and controlling operations.

The controller usually has a staff consisting of several managerial accountants. Each accountant is responsible for a specialized accounting function, such as systems and procedures, general accounting, budgets and budget analyses, special reports and analyses and taxes. The following organization chart is typical for an accounting department that reports to the controller:

Organization Chart— Controller's Department

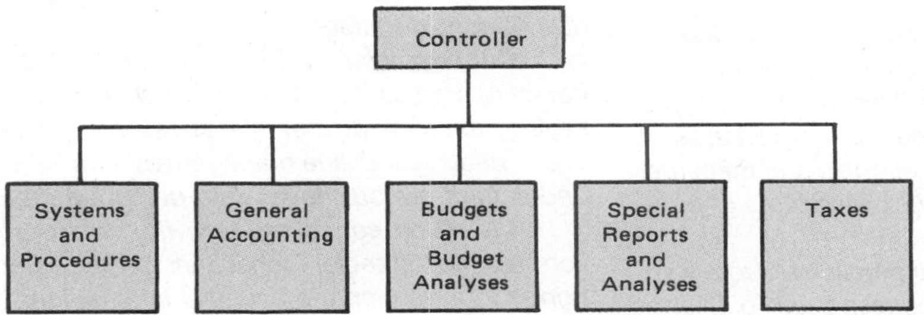

Systems and procedures is concerned with the design and implementation of procedures for the accumulation and reporting of accounting data to all interested users. In performing this function, the accountant must evaluate the usefulness of various types of data processing equipment for the firm. The systems accountant must also devise appropriate "checks and balances" to safeguard business assets and provide for an information flow that will be efficient and helpful to management.

General accounting is primarily concerned with the recording of transactions and periodic preparation of the basic financial statements. Of particular importance to this area is the gathering of data in conformity with the generally accepted accounting principles for preparing the basic financial statements.

Budgets and budget analyses focuses on the plan for financial operations for future periods, and through records and summaries, focuses on the comparison of actual operations with these plans. This function provides much of the information for planning and controlling operations.

Special reports and analyses is concerned with data that will be useful to management in analyzing current problems and considering alternate courses for future operations. Much of the analysis focuses on providing data related to specific problems that confront management and identifying alternative courses of action related to proposed new projects. Often the accountants who perform this function prepare special reports according to the requirements of regulatory agencies.

Taxes encompasses the preparation of tax returns and the consideration of the tax consequences of proposed business transactions or alternate courses of action. Accountants in this area must be familiar with the tax statutes affecting their business and must also keep up-to-date on administrative regulations and court decisions on tax cases.

The Magic of 3M

3M was listed along with 61 other corporate high achievers in the best seller, *In Search of Excellence,* by Thomas J. Peters and Robert H. Waterman, Jr. In *A Passion for Excellence,* by Peters and Nancy Austin, 3M was again listed as a model for product innovation and entrepreneurship.

Some of the reasons for 3M's success, based on interviews with 3M executives, are as follows:

"Financial expertise, long recognized as one of 3M's greatest assets, is a major contributor to the corporation's success. 3M uses its financial control system to encourage rather than curtail innovation and creativity. Numbers are used to set goals and measure performance rather than to deny expenditures or punish unmet expectations."

"... we (controllers) get intimately involved with day-to-day activities ... with forecasting and planning activities of business units. As an example, in new product development we try to lay out for the managers the cost implications of bringing on a new product and what it means in relation to their total business and whether or not they can still reach their financial targets. We work with them, developing the analysis to help them prioritize what products they want to go after. ... Our controllers view their roles as not to always challenge management, but as being a cooperative effort to develop a better business."

"3M's (division) controllers have been able to support 3M's strategic objectives while keeping management focused on operational objectives... we do a fair, if not a good, job of balancing strategic and operational considerations."

"Our organization is not a negatively focused accounting organization. We aren't always coming in and saying 'you can't do that.' We are supportive and positive in dealing with line management. We have tried to understand the business while doing our jobs."

"I (division controller) view the controller's function as the financial consultant... the person who brings to a division the financial information."

"I (vice president of finance) tell our people, 'Your job is to help the operating people achieve what they're trying to achieve. Then if you have to say no, you'll be respected for it.' The first principle is working with the operating people."

Source: Kathy Williams, "The Magic of 3M: Management Accounting Excellence," *Management Accounting* (February, 1986), pp. 20–27.

Profession of Managerial Accounting

Managerial accounting is gaining recognition as a profession for its importance to society and to the effective management of business enterprises. To provide some of this recognition, the **Institute of Certified Management Accounting,** which is an affiliate of the National Association of Accountants, grants the **Certificate in Management Accounting (CMA)** as evidence of professional competence in managerial accounting.

Individual holders of the CMA certificate are required to have a baccalaureate degree or equivalent, two years of experience in managerial accounting, pass a 2½-day examination, participate in a program of continuing education, and adhere to a professional code of ethics.

COST CONCEPTS

As described in the preceding paragraphs, the role of managerial accounting is to provide economic information to management. This information is often related to the "costs" associated with operations. Although it can take many forms, the information provided by managerial accountants should be communicated in common cost terminology that avoids confusion and misunderstanding.[2] For example, the terms "cost" and "expense" are sometimes used interchangeably. However, the terms have different meanings.

All disbursements of cash (or the commitment to pay cash in the future) for the purpose of generating revenues are **costs**. For example, when store supplies are purchased for cash or credit (on account), the disbursement represents the cost of the supplies. In contrast, although the payment of dividends to stockholders is a disbursement, it is not a cost, since the payment of dividends does not generate revenues.

All costs initially represent assets to the enterprise. As the assets are used in generating revenues, the cost of the assets must be recognized as **expenses** in order to match revenues and expenses properly in the process of determining the net income of the period. Thus, depreciation expense is recognized as plant assets are used in generating revenues, and prepaid insurance premiums are written off as an expense over the periods benefiting from the insurance policies.

To simplify the recording process, costs that will benefit only the current period are often initially recorded as expenses rather than as assets. This procedure avoids the need to record the use of the assets as expenses, as would be the case if the costs were initially recorded as assets. For example, the payment of $1,500 for the current month's rent would be recorded by most enterprises as an expense (Rent Expense) rather than as an asset (Prepaid Rent).

The distinction between costs and expenses is summarized in the following diagram:

[2]The terminology in this chapter is consistent with the recommendations in *Statement on Management Accounting No. 2,* "Management Accounting Terminology" (Montvale, New Jersey: National Association of Accountants, 1983).

Costs and Expenses Distinguished

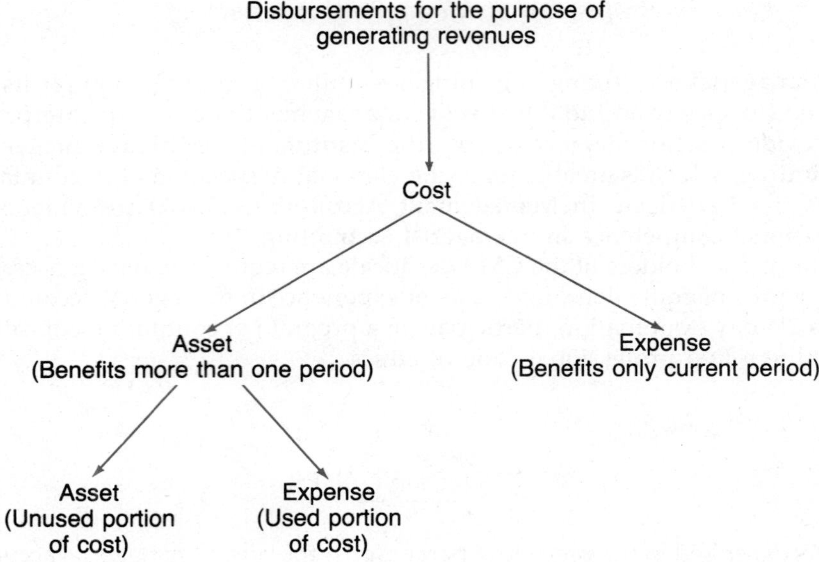

The distinction between the terms cost and expense is especially important for the preparation of financial statements for service, merchandising, and manufacturing enterprises. However, this distinction has more importance for manufacturing enterprises. Costs incurred in manufacturing products are assets, and these costs do not become expenses until the manufactured products are sold, thereby generating revenue. Likewise, products for which manufacturing has been partially or fully completed but which have not been sold should continue to be recognized as assets.

MANUFACTURING COSTS

The cost of manufacturing a product includes not only the cost of tangible materials entering into the manufacturing process, but also the costs incurred in changing the materials into a finished product ready for sale. The cost of a manufactured product generally consists of direct materials cost, direct labor cost, and factory overhead cost.

Direct Materials Cost

The cost of materials entering directly into the manufactured product is classified as **direct materials cost,** sometimes referred to as **raw materials cost.** For example, the direct materials for Seawind Company, a manufacturer of fishing boats, would include fiberglass and paint.

As a practical matter, in order for a cost to be classified as a direct materials cost, the cost must not only be an integral part of the end product, but it must be a significant dollar portion of the total cost of the product. For Seawind Company, the costs of fiberglass and paint are a significant portion of the total cost of each boat.

Other examples of direct materials costs include the cost of paper and ink for a printer, lumber for a furniture manufacturer, silicon wafers for a producer of microcomputer chips, and steel for an automobile manufacturer.

The finished product of one manufacturer may become the direct materials for another manufacturer. For example, the finished products of a lumber mill become the direct materials for a construction contractor.

Direct Labor Cost

The cost of wages paid to employees directly involved in changing direct materials into finished product is classified as **direct labor cost.** For example, the direct labor cost of Seawind Company includes the wages of the employees who paint the boat hulls in the manufacturing process. Other examples of direct labor costs include the wages of carpenters for a construction contractor, mechanics' wages in an automotive repair shop, machine operators' wages in a tool manufacturing plant, and assemblers' wages in a microcomputer manufacturing plant.

As a practical matter, for the cost of employee wages to be classified as direct labor cost, the employee must not only be directly involved in the creation of the finished product, but the wages must be a significant portion of the total product cost. For Seawind Company, the painters' wages are a significant portion of the total cost of each boat.

Factory Overhead Cost

Costs other than direct materials cost and direct labor cost incurred in the manufacturing process are classified as **factory overhead cost,** sometimes referred to as **manufacturing overhead** or **factory burden.** For example, factory overhead cost includes the cost of heating and lighting the factory, repair and maintenance of factory equipment, and property taxes, insurance, and depreciation on factory plant and equipment. Factory overhead cost also includes materials and labor costs which do not enter directly into the finished product. For example, the cost of oil used to lubricate machinery is a materials cost which does not enter directly into finished products. Other examples of such costs include the wages of janitorial, supervisory, and quality control personnel.

As a practical matter, if the costs of direct materials or direct labor are not a significant portion of the total product cost, these costs are classified as factory overhead. In Seawind Company, for example, glue enters directly into the finished product (boats), but its cost is insignificant and it is therefore classified as factory overhead. For many industries, the increased use of automated machinery and robotics has decreased labor costs to a level where they are a small portion of total product costs. In this situation, direct labor costs of manufactured products are often included as part of factory overhead cost[3].

Prime Costs and Conversion Costs

As previously discussed, the total cost of a manufactured product consists of three elements: direct materials, direct labor, and factory overhead costs. These costs are often grouped in various classifications for analysis and

[3]Trends in the development and use of managerial accounting in the rapidly changing business environment are further discussed in Appendix I.

reporting purposes. As will be illustrated in later chapters, two common classifications of manufacturing costs often reported to management for planning and decision making purposes are prime costs and conversion costs.

Prime costs are the combination of direct materials and direct labor costs. As the name implies, prime costs are generally the largest component of the total cost of a manufactured product. **Conversion costs** are the combination of direct labor and factory overhead costs. Conversion costs are the costs of converting the materials into a finished, manufactured product.

The diagram below summarizes the classification of manufacturing costs into prime costs and conversion costs.

Prime Costs and Conversion Costs

PRIME COSTS

Direct Materials Cost:

(1) Enters directly into the product, and

(2) Is significant amount of total product cost.

Example: Memory chips for a microcomputer manufacturer.

Direct Labor Cost:

(1) Enters directly into manufacturing the product, and

(2) Is significant amount of total product cost.

Example: Hourly wages of assemblers of microcomputers.

CONVERSION COSTS

Factory Overhead Cost:

Is cost other than direct materials cost and direct labor cost incurred in the manufacturing of products.

Example: Depreciation on testing equipment for a microcomputer manufacturer.

NONMANUFACTURING COSTS

Nonmanufacturing costs are generally classified into two categories: selling and administrative. **Selling costs** are costs that are incurred in marketing the product and delivering the sold product to customers. Examples of selling costs include salaries of marketing personnel, advertising expenditures, sales commissions, salespersons' salaries, and depreciation on store equipment. **Administrative costs** are costs that are incurred in the administration of the business and that are not related to the manufacturing or selling functions. Examples of administrative costs include office salaries, office supplies, and depreciation on office buildings and equipment.

By classifying nonmanufacturing costs into selling and administrative, the managerial accountant enables management to establish accountability and control over the cost of two major functional activities: selling activities and administrative activities. Different levels of accountability for these activities may be shown in managerial reports. For example, selling costs may be reported by product, salespersons, departments, divisions, or geographic territories. Likewise, administrative costs may be reported by functional area, such as personnel, computer services, accounting, finance, or office support.

The accounting for nonmanufacturing costs is similar for manufacturing, merchandising, and service enterprises. Most selling and administrative costs are initially recognized as expenses because they benefit only the period in which they are incurred.

The concepts and principles discussed throughout this text for planning and controlling manufacturing costs are also applicable to selling and administrative costs. Where applicable, these concepts and principles will be illustrated for both manufacturing costs and selling and administrative costs.

PRODUCT COSTS AND PERIOD COSTS

In the preceding section, costs were classified as manufacturing or nonmanufacturing. These costs may also be classified as either product costs or period costs.

Product costs are composed of the three elements of manufacturing cost: direct materials, direct labor, and factory overhead.[4] These costs are treated as assets until the product is sold. In other words, during the period beginning when product costs are initially incurred until the products are sold, product costs are accounted for as assets and are reported as a part of inventory on the balance sheet. In this sense, product costs are sometimes referred to as **inventoriable costs.** Thus, direct materials, direct labor, and factory overhead costs incurred in one period will not appear on the income statement as expenses until the products with which they are associated are sold.

Period costs are those costs that are used up in generating revenue during the current period and that are not involved in the manufacturing process. Selling and administrative costs are period costs. They are recognized as expenses on the current period's income statement. Many period costs are time-oriented, in the sense that the costs are incurred or used as time passes.

---

[4]For merchandising enterprises, product costs include the costs associated with a product purchased in finished form and ready for sale.

The following diagram relates the manufacturing and nonmanufacturing cost concepts to the product cost and period cost concepts for a furniture manufacturer.

Examples of Product Costs and Period Costs

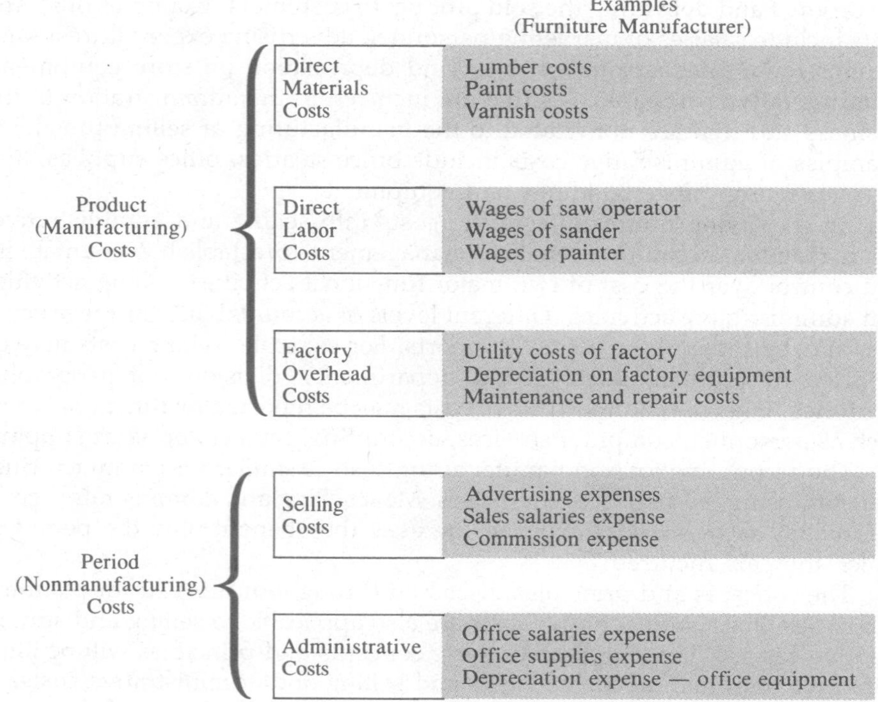

FINANCIAL STATEMENTS FOR MANUFACTURING ENTERPRISES

The financial statements for manufacturing enterprises are more complex than those for service and merchandising enterprises. Since a manufacturing enterprise manufactures the products that it sells, the manufacturing costs described in the preceding paragraphs must be properly accounted for and reported in the financial statements. These manufacturing costs primarily affect the preparation of the balance sheet and income statement, which are described in the following paragraphs. The retained earnings and cash flow statements for merchandising and manufacturing enterprises are similar and therefore are not discussed.

Balance Sheet for a Manufacturing Enterprise

A manufacturing enterprise reports three types of inventory on its balance sheet: direct materials inventory, work in process inventory, and finished goods inventory. The **direct materials inventory** for a manufacturing enterprise consists of the cost of the direct materials which have not yet entered into the manufacturing process.[5] The **work in process inventory** for

[5]Direct materials inventory, sometimes simply called materials inventory, includes only direct materials to be used in the manufacturing process. Indirect materials are classified as factory supplies.

a manufacturing enterprise consists of the direct materials costs, the direct labor costs, and the factory overhead costs which have entered into the manufacturing process, but are associated with products that have not been finished. The **finished goods inventory** of a manufacturing enterprise consists of the finished products on hand that have not been sold. For example, The Proctor & Gamble Company reported the following inventories on its 1987 balance sheet.

Inventories (in millions of dollars):	
Materials	$ 807
Work in process	270
Finished products	1,087

The flow of manufacturing costs into the manufacturing process and the related inventories of a manufacturing enterprise is illustrated in the following diagram:

Flow of Manufacturing Costs to Balance Sheet

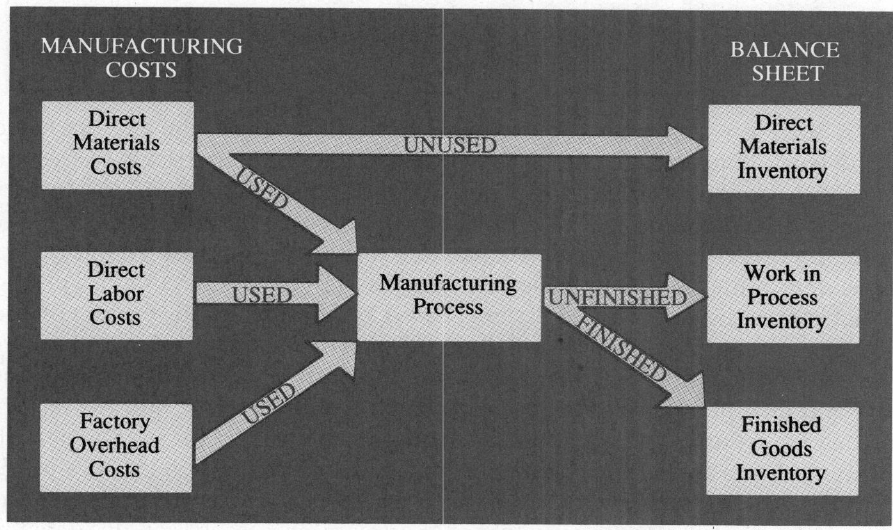

Income Statement for a Manufacturing Enterprise

The major difference in the income statements for merchandising and manufacturing enterprises is in the reporting of cost of merchandise sold for a merchandising enterprise and cost of goods sold for a manufacturing enterprise. For a merchandising enterprise, merchandise is purchased in a finished state for resale to customers. The merchandise that is sold is called the **cost of merchandise sold.**

For a manufacturing enterprise, the product to be sold is manufactured by processing direct materials, using direct labor and factory overhead. The cost of the product sold is called the **cost of goods sold.** The costs of manufacturing the product, which are comparable to the purchases reported by a merchandising enterprise, can be reported in a **statement of cost of goods manufactured.** To illustrate the difference between the income statements for a merchandising enterprise and a manufacturing enterprise, the income statements for Loose Inc., a merchandiser, and Burleson Manufacturing Company are shown below and on the following page. The Burleson Manufacturing Company income statement is supported by a statement of cost of goods manufactured.

Merchandising Enterprise—Income Statement

Loose Inc.
Income Statement
For the Year Ended December 31, 1989

Sales		$1,100,000
Cost of merchandise sold:		
Merchandise inventory, Jan. 1, 1989	$ 90,000	
Purchases	900,000	
Merchandise available for sale	$990,000	
Less merchandise inventory, Dec. 31, 1989	120,000	
Cost of merchandise sold		870,000
Gross profit		$ 230,000
Operating expenses:		
Selling expenses	$ 85,000	
Administrative expenses	75,000	
Total operating expenses		160,000
Net income		$ 70,000

In Burleson's statement of cost of goods manufactured, the amount listed for the work in process inventory at the beginning of the period is composed of the estimated cost of the direct materials, the direct labor, and the factory overhead applicable to the inventory of partially processed products at the end of the preceding period. The cost of the direct materials placed in production is determined by adding the beginning inventory of direct materials and the net cost of the direct materials purchased and deducting the ending inventory. The amount of direct labor is then listed. The factory overhead costs are listed individually in the statement or in a separate schedule. The sum of the costs of direct materials placed in production, the direct labor, and the factory overhead represents the total manufacturing costs incurred during the period. Addition of this amount to the beginning inventory of work in process yields the total cost of the work that has been in process during the period. The estimated cost of the ending inventory of work in process is then deducted to yield the cost of goods manufactured.

ADDITIONAL COST CONCEPTS FOR MANAGERIAL PLANNING

The cost concepts and classifications described to this point are used primarily in the preparation of financial statements. For purposes of planning, organizing and directing, decision making, and controlling operations, managers require a variety of managerial reports in which cost data are classified in various ways. In the remainder of this chapter, the following cost concepts that are frequently reported to management for use in directing current operations and planning future operations are briefly described:

Variable costs and fixed costs	Differential costs
Direct costs and indirect costs	Discretionary costs
Controllable costs and noncontrollable costs	Opportunity costs
	Sunk costs

Manufacturing Enterprise—Income Statement

Burleson Manufacturing Company
Income Statement
For Year Ended December 31, 1989

Sales		$915,800
Cost of goods sold:		
Finished goods inventory, January 1, 1989	$ 78,500	
Cost of goods manufactured	550,875	
Cost of finished goods available for sale	$629,375	
Less finished goods inventory, December 31, 1989	91,000	
Cost of goods sold		538,375
Gross profit		$377,425
Operating expenses:		
Selling expenses	$165,000	
Administrative expenses	84,425	
Total operating expenses		249,425
Net income		$128,000

Statement of Cost of Goods Manufactured

Burleson Manufacturing Company
Statement of Cost of Goods Manufactured
For Year Ended December 31, 1989

Work in process inventory, January 1, 1989			$ 55,000
Direct materials:			
Inventory, January 1, 1989	$ 62,000		
Purchases	220,800		
Cost of materials available for use	$282,800		
Less inventory, December 31, 1989	58,725		
Cost of materials placed in production		$224,075	
Direct labor		218,750	
Factory overhead:			
Indirect labor	$ 49,300		
Depreciation of factory equipment	22,300		
Heat, light, and power	21,800		
Property taxes	9,750		
Depreciation of buildings	6,000		
Insurance expense	4,750		
Factory supplies expense	2,900		
Miscellaneous factory costs	2,050		
Total factory overhead		118,850	
Total manufacturing costs			561,675
Total work in process during period			$616,675
Less work in process inventory, December 31, 1989			65,800
Cost of goods manufactured			$550,875

The use of these cost concepts by managers will be described and illustrated in more detail in later chapters.

Variable Costs and Fixed Costs

For management's use, costs are often classified by cost behavior; that is, costs are classified as to how they respond to changes in the volume of business activity. As the volume of business activity rises or falls, some costs tend to change proportionally to the rise or fall, while other costs do not change significantly as the volume of business activity changes. For directing current operations and planning future operations, a knowledge of the response pattern of costs to changing or anticipated changes in activity levels is useful.

Variable Costs. A **variable cost** varies in total dollar amount as the level of activity changes. The level of activity is normally expressed in units of production, although other activity bases may be used. Direct materials cost is a variable cost because the total direct materials cost varies directly with the number of units produced. For example, assume that Micro-Systems Inc. produces a standard microcomputer containing a 256K memory board. The cost of each memory board is a variable cost because it varies with the number of computers produced. If each memory board costs $50, the total direct materials cost of the memory boards for the production of 1,000 computers is $50,000 ($50 × 1,000); for 2,000 computers, the total cost is $100,000. Other common variable manufacturing costs include direct labor cost and factory overhead items, such as electricity, lubricants, and supplies.

The variable cost concept is also applicable to nonmanufacturing costs. For example, a 5% sales commission is a cost that varies with total sales. Likewise, the administrative cost of billing customers is a cost that varies directly with the number of billings.

Fixed Costs. A **fixed cost** remains constant in total dollar amount as the level of activity changes. As with variable costs, the level of activity is normally expressed in units of production, although other activity bases may be used. Straight-line depreciation on manufacturing equipment is a fixed cost because the total annual depreciation does not vary with the number of units produced. For example, straight-line depreciation of $15,000 per year on Micro-Systems Inc.'s assembly and testing equipment would not vary with the number of computers produced. The total straight-line depreciation would be $15,000, regardless of whether 1,000, 2,000, or 6,000 microcomputers are produced. Other common fixed manufacturing costs include costs of renting factory equipment or buildings, property taxes on factory plant and equipment, property insurance, and salaries of factory supervisory personnel. Although these examples are factory overhead costs, some factory overhead costs, such as electricity, are variable costs.

The fixed cost concept is also applicable to nonmanufacturing costs. For example, straight-line depreciation on store equipment and a sales manager's salary do not vary with the volume of sales. Likewise, officers' salaries is a fixed cost.

Mixed Costs. Some costs have both variable and fixed characteristics. These costs are often called **mixed costs** or **semivariable** or **semifixed** costs. These mixed costs can often be separated into their variable and fixed components. For example, the rental charge for a copier might be $100 per month plus $.01 per copy. The $100 per month portion of the rental charge is a fixed cost, and the $.01 per copy portion is a variable cost.

Direct and Indirect Costs

A **direct cost** is a cost that can be traced directly to a unit within the enterprise. Costs which are not direct are said to be **indirect costs**. Critical to separating costs into direct and indirect classifications is relating costs to some unit within the enterprise. The unit may be a product line, a department, a plant, a sales territory, or some other unit.

Direct costs for a manufactured product, such as spark plugs produced by an automobile parts manufacturer, would include direct materials and direct labor because these costs can be directly traced to the spark plugs. Indirect costs for the spark plugs product line would include factory overhead costs, such as depreciation on the factory building, because these costs cannot be directly traced to the product line. For a nonmanufacturing enterprise, such as a department store, the salaries paid to the salespersons in the shoe department would be a direct cost to that department. The store's officers' salaries would be an indirect cost to the shoe department.

Controllable Costs and Noncontrollable Costs

All costs are controllable by someone within a business enterprise, but not all costs are controllable at the same level of management. For example, plant supervisors, as members of operating management, are responsible for controlling the use of direct materials in their departments. They have no control, however, of the amount of insurance coverage or premium costs related to the buildings housing their departments. For a specific level of management, **controllable costs** are costs that it controls directly, and **noncontrollable costs** are costs that another level of management controls. This distinction, as applied to specific levels of management, is useful in fixing the responsibility for the incurrence of costs and then for reporting the cost data to those responsible for cost control.

In some cases, there is a time dimension to the classification of costs as controllable or noncontrollable. Some costs cannot be controlled in the short run but can be controlled in the long run. For example, a plant manager cannot, in the short run, control the wages of factory employees who have union contracts. In the long run, however, the wages become controllable because the contracts expire and are subject to renegotiation.

Differential Costs

Differential cost, sometimes referred to as **incremental cost,** is the increase or decrease in cost that is expected from a particular course of action as compared with an alternative course of action. For example, the management of a microcomputer manufacturer must decide on whether to purchase carrying cases for the computers from an outside supplier or to produce the carrying cases. If the cost of purchasing the carrying cases is $20 per case and the cost of producing the carrying cases is $18 per case, the cost difference between the two alternatives ($2) is referred to as the differential cost. As another example, if an increase in advertising expenditures from $100,000 to $150,000 is being considered, the differential cost of the proposal would be $50,000.

Discretionary Costs

A **discretionary cost** is a cost that is not essential to short-term operations. For example, costs incurred in continuing education courses for management are classified as discretionary. Other examples of discretionary costs include advertising expenses, management consulting fees, sponsorship of employee social events (such as a company picnic), sponsorship of local athletic teams (such as a Little League team), charitable contributions to community activities, and a subsidized employee cafeteria.

Management reviews discretionary costs periodically, usually yearly, to determine whether the cost should continue to be incurred. Discretionary costs are usually the first to be reduced or eliminated during periods of worsening economic conditions, since their discontinuance does not affect short-term operations or profitability. Although discretionary costs do not have an immediate effect on short-term operations or profitability, their discontinuance can have a long-term impact on the enterprise. For example, research and development costs are often viewed as discretionary, but their discontinuance could be disastrous in the long run, especially in high-tech industries such as the computer industry. Likewise, the discontinuance of management continuing education could jeopardize the quality of managerial decision making in the long run.

Sunk Costs

Sunk costs are costs which have been incurred and cannot be reversed by subsequent decisions. Sunk costs are irrelevant for future decision making and are therefore excluded from managerial accounting reports prepared to assist management in making such decisions. To illustrate, assume that a major airline is currently operating a fleet of Boeing 727 passenger jets, which originally cost $300 million and on which depreciation of $250 million has been taken. In considering whether to spend $500 million to upgrade its fleet of aircraft to the newer, more fuel-efficient and technologically advanced 767 passenger jets, the original $300 million cost is irrelevant. The $300 million has been spent, and regardless of whether the original decision was wise or unwise, the $300 million expenditure cannot be reversed. For this reason, the original cost of $300 million is referred to as a sunk cost. Likewise, the $50 million book value of the 727 jets (the original cost of $300 million less accumulated depreciation of $250 million) is also irrelevant. The cost savings resulting from the use of the more fuel-efficient 767, when compared to the proposed expenditure of $500 million, are the relevant costs that would be considered by management in making the decision.

Opportunity Costs

An **opportunity cost** is the amount of income that is forgone by selecting one alternative over another. To illustrate, assume that the treasurer of

Faulkner Inc. invested $100,000 in a money market account yielding 5% interest. If United States Treasury bills are currently yielding 6%, the opportunity cost of not investing in the Treasury bills is $6,000 ($100,000 × 6%). Hence, the treasurer might consider switching investments to maximize the return to Faulkner Inc. and to minimize the opportunity cost.

Opportunity cost differs fundamentally from the other classifications of costs that have been discussed previously because an opportunity cost does not represent a transaction involving a disbursement. Opportunity costs should be considered, however, in all decisions that management makes involving the commitment of resources. For example, in deciding whether to expand manufacturing capacity for the current product line, management should consider the opportunity cost of investing the resources in other product lines.

SUMMARY OF COST CONCEPTS

Many of the costs described in this chapter can be classified in more than one way, depending upon decision-making situations. For example, direct materials cost may be classified as a variable cost or a product cost. Each specific decision-making situation must be analyzed carefully by the managerial accountant in order to classify and report costs properly for managerial use. Such decision-making situations are discussed in the following chapters.

Chapter Review

KEY POINTS

1. The Management Process.
The management of an organization consists of those individuals charged with the responsibility of directing the enterprise toward achieving its goals. The management process involves the four basic functions of (1) planning, (2) organizing and directing, (3) controlling, and (4) decision making.

Planning is the process by which management develops a course of action to attain enterprise goals. Long-range goals involve strategic planning, while short-term goals involve operational planning. Organizing is the process by which management assigns responsibility to individuals for achieving enterprise goals, while directing is the process by which managers run day-to-day operations. Controlling is the process by which managers attempt to achieve the goals identified in the strategic and operational plans. Decision making, which involves choosing among alternative courses of action, has a central role in planning, organizing and directing, and controlling operations.

2. Role of Managerial Accounting.
Managerial accounting is the area of accounting that provides relevant information to management. Managerial accounting aids managers in planning

(by providing reports which estimate the effects of alternative actions on an enterprise's ability to achieve desired goals), in organizing and directing (by providing information which is used to adjust daily operations for changing conditions), in controlling operations (by providing performance reports of variances between expected and actual operating results), and in decision making (by providing the basic information which the manager uses in selecting among alternative courses of action). Without accounting information, it would be difficult for management to manage effectively and efficiently.

3. Characteristics of Managerial Accounting Reports.
The principle of usefulness to management is the primary criterion for preparation of managerial accounting reports. In preparing useful managerial accounting reports, five characteristics should be considered. Relevance means that the economic information reported must be pertinent to the specific action being considered by management. Timeliness refers to the need for accounting reports to contain the most up-to-date information. Accuracy refers to the need for the report to be correct within the constraints of the use of the report and the inherent inaccuracies in the measurement process. Clarity refers to the need for the report to be clear and understandable in both format and content. Conciseness refers to the requirement that the report should be brief and to the point. A report should not be prepared if the cost of preparing it exceeds the benefits derived by management from its use.

4. Organization of the Managerial Accounting Function.
Managers organize business enterprises into departments or similar units with responsibilities for specific functions or activities. This operating structure of an enterprise can be diagrammed in an organization chart.

The chief accountant in a corporation is called the controller. The controller provides advice and assistance to management but assumes no direct responsibility for the operations of the business. The functions most commonly provided by the controller's staff include systems and procedures, general accounting, budgets and budget analyses, special reports and analyses, and taxes.

The Institute of Certified Management Accounting grants the Certificate in Management Accounting (CMA) as evidence of professional competence in managerial accounting. Holders of the CMA certificate are required to pass a two and one-half-day examination, participate in a program of continuing education, and adhere to a professional code of ethics.

5. Costs Concepts.
All disbursements of cash (or the commitment to pay cash in the future) for the purpose of generating revenues are costs that initially represent assets to the enterprise. As the assets are used in generating revenues, the cost of the assets must be recognized as expenses in order to match revenues and expenses properly in the process of determining the net income for the period. To simplify the recording process, costs that will benefit only the current period are often initially recorded as expenses rather than as assets. This distinction between the terms cost and expense is especially important for the preparation of financial statements. This distinction has more importance for manufacturing enterprises. Costs incurred in manufacturing products are

assets, and these costs do not become expenses until the manufactured products are sold.

6. Manufacturing Costs.

The cost of a manufactured product consists of direct materials cost, direct labor cost, and factory overhead cost. The cost of materials entering directly into the product is classified as direct materials cost. For a cost to be classified as a direct materials cost, the cost must not only be an integral part of the end product, but it must also be a significant dollar amount of the total cost of the product.

The cost of wages paid to employees directly involved in changing direct materials into finished products is classified as direct labor cost. For the cost of employee wages to be classified as direct labor cost, the employee must not only be directly involved in the creation of the product, but the wages must be a significant portion of the total product cost.

Costs other than direct materials cost and direct labor cost incurred in the manufacturing process are classified as factory overhead cost. If the costs of direct materials or direct labor are not a significant portion of the total product cost, these costs may be classified as factory overhead.

Two common classifications of manufacturing costs are prime costs and conversion costs. Prime costs are the combination of direct materials cost and direct labor cost. Conversion costs are the combination of direct labor cost and factory overhead cost.

7. Nonmanufacturing Costs.

Nonmanufacturing costs are generally classified into two categories: selling and administrative. These classifications enable management to establish accountability and control over the costs of each of these two major functional areas. Different levels of accountability and control may be shown in managerial reports.

8. Product Costs and Period Costs.

Product costs are composed of the three elements of manufacturing costs: direct materials, direct labor, and factory overhead. These costs are treated as assets until the product with which they are associated is sold. Product costs are sometimes referred to as inventoriable costs. Period costs are those costs that are used up in generating revenue during the current period. These costs are recognized as expenses on the current period's income statement. Many period costs are time-oriented, in the sense that the costs are incurred or used as time passes.

9. Financial Statements for Manufacturing Enterprises.

The financial statements for manufacturing enterprises are more complex than those for service and merchandising enterprises. A manufacturing enterprise reports three types of inventory on its balance sheet: direct materials, work in process, and finished goods. The direct materials inventory consists of the cost of direct materials which have not yet entered into the manufacturing process. The work in process inventory consists of direct materials costs, direct labor costs, and factory overhead costs which have entered into the manufacturing process, but are associated with products that have not been finished. The finished goods inventory consists of the finished products on hand that have not been sold.

The major difference in income statements for merchandising and manufacturing enterprises is that a merchandising enterprise reports cost of merchandise sold and a manufacturing enterprise reports cost of goods sold. For a manufacturing enterprise, the product to be sold is manufactured by processing direct materials, using direct labor and factory overhead. The cost of the product sold is called the cost of goods sold. The costs of manufacturing the product can be reported in a statement of cost of goods manufactured.

10. Additional Cost Concepts for Managerial Planning.
A variable cost varies in total dollar amount as the level of activity changes. The level of activity is normally expressed in units of production. The variable cost concept is also applicable to nonmanufacturing costs. An example of a variable cost is direct materials cost. A fixed cost remains constant in total dollar amount as the level of activity changes. The level of activity is normally expressed in units of production. The fixed cost concept is also applicable to nonmanufacturing costs. An example of a fixed cost is straight-line depreciation on factory equipment. Costs that have both variable and fixed characteristics are called mixed costs or semivariable or semifixed costs.

A direct cost is a cost that can be traced directly to a unit within the enterprise. Costs that are not direct are said to be indirect costs.

A controllable cost is one that can be controlled by a specific level of management. Over time all costs are controllable at some level of management. Therefore, when classifying a cost as controllable or noncontrollable, the time period and level of management are critical reference points.

A differential cost, sometimes referred to as an incremental cost, is the difference in cost from one course of action compared to alternative courses of action. Differential costs are an important consideration for managers in deciding among alternative courses of action.

A discretionary cost is a cost that is not essential to short-term operations. Management reviews discretionary costs periodically, usually yearly, to determine whether the costs should continue to be incurred. Although discretionary costs do not have an immediate effect on short-term operations or profitability, their discontinuance can have a long-term impact on the enterprise.

Sunk costs are costs which have been incurred and cannot be reversed by a subsequent decision. Sunk costs are irrelevant for future decision making and are therefore excluded from managerial accounting reports.

An opportunity cost is the amount of income that is forgone by selecting one alternative over another. Opportunity cost differs fundamentally from the other classifications of costs that have been discussed previously because an opportunity cost does not represent a transaction involving a disbursement. Opportunity costs should be considered in all decisions that management makes involving the commitment of resources.

KEY TERMS

costs 575
expenses 575
direct materials cost 576
direct labor cost 577
factory overhead cost 577
prime costs 578
conversion costs 578
product costs 579
period costs 579
direct materials inventory 580
work in process inventory 580
finished goods inventory 581
statement of cost of goods manufactured 581
cost of merchandise sold 581
cost of goods sold 581
variable cost 584
fixed cost 584
mixed (semivariable or semifixed) cost 585
direct cost 585
indirect cost 585
controllable cost 585
noncontrollable cost 585
differential cost 585
discretionary cost 586
sunk cost 586
opportunity cost 587

SELF-EXAMINATION QUESTIONS

(Answers at End of Chapter)

1. Which of the following is *not* one of the four basic functions of the management process?
   A. Planning
   B. Controlling
   C. Decision making
   D. Operations

2. Which of the following designations serves as evidence of professional competence in managerial accounting?
   A. Certified Public Accountant
   B. Certified Management Accountant
   C. Certified Internal Auditor
   D. Certified Financial Planner

3. Which of the following costs would be included as part of the factory overhead costs of a microcomputer manufacturer?
   A. The cost of memory chips
   B. Depreciation on testing equipment
   C. Wages of computer assemblers
   D. The cost of disk drives

4. Which of the following are considered conversion costs?
   A. Direct labor cost and factory overhead cost
   B. Factory overhead cost
   C. Direct materials cost and direct labor cost
   D. Direct materials cost and factory overhead cost

5. Which of the following costs would normally be considered a variable cost?
   A. Direct materials cost
   B. Direct labor cost
   C. Electricity to operate factory equipment
   D. All of the above

ILLUSTRATIVE PROBLEM

The following pre-closing trial balance of Mahaney Inc. was prepared as of December 31, 1990, the end of the current fiscal year:

Account	Debit	Credit
Cash	50,000	
Accounts Receivable	160,000	
Allowance for Doubtful Accounts		20,000
Finished Goods Inventory	180,000	
Work in Process Inventory	75,000	
Direct Materials Inventory	40,000	
Prepaid Insurance	12,000	
Factory Supplies	7,000	
Land	100,000	
Factory Buildings	400,000	
Accumulated Depreciation—Factory Buildings		220,000
Factory Equipment	250,000	
Accumulated Depreciation—Factory Equipment		125,000
Accounts Payable		30,000
Wages Payable		14,000
Income Tax Payable		10,000
Common Stock		100,000
Retained Earnings		711,000
Dividends	20,000	
Sales		1,500,000
Direct Materials Purchases	750,000	
Direct Labor	300,000	
Indirect Factory Labor	150,000	
Depreciation—Factory Equipment	25,000	
Factory Heat, Light, and Power	20,000	
Depreciation—Factory Building	20,000	
Factory Property Taxes	18,000	
Insurance Expense—Factory	12,000	
Factory Supplies Expense	6,000	
Miscellaneous Factory Costs	4,000	
Selling Expenses	60,000	
Administrative Expenses	50,000	
Income Tax	21,000	
	2,730,000	2,730,000

Inventories at December 31, 1990, were as follows:

Finished goods	$200,000
Work in process	70,000
Direct materials	42,000

Instructions:

1. Prepare a statement of cost of goods manufactured.
2. Prepare an income statement.
3. Prepare a retained earnings statement.
4. Prepare a balance sheet.

SOLUTION

(1)

MAHANEY INC.
Statement of Cost of Goods Manufactured
For Year Ended December 31, 1990

Work in process inventory, January 1, 1990....			$ 75,000
Direct materials:			
Inventory, January 1, 1990..................		$ 40,000	
Purchases		750,000	
Cost of materials available for use..........		$790,000	
Less inventory, December 31, 1990.........		42,000	
Cost of materials placed in production.....		$748,000	
Direct labor		300,000	
Factory overhead:			
Indirect labor..............................	$150,000		
Depreciation—factory equipment...........	25,000		
Factory heat, light and power	20,000		
Depreciation—factory buildings	20,000		
Factory property taxes	18,000		
Insurance expense—factory...............	12,000		
Factory supplies expense..................	6,000		
Miscellaneous factory costs	4,000		
Total factory overhead..................		255,000	
Total manufacturing costs....................			1,303,000
Total work in process during period			$1,378,000
Less work in process inventory, December 31, 1990......................			70,000
Cost of goods manufactured			$1,308,000

(2)

MAHANEY INC.
Income Statement
For Year Ended December 31, 1990

Sales..		$1,500,000
Cost of goods sold:		
Finished goods inventory, January 1, 1990	$ 180,000	
Cost of goods manufactured.......................	1,308,000	
Cost of finished goods available for sale	$1,488,000	
Less finished goods inventory, December 31, 1990....	200,000	
Cost of goods sold		1,288,000
Gross profit		$ 212,000
Operating expenses:		
Selling expenses	$ 60,000	
Administrative expenses........................	50,000	
Total operating expenses......................		110,000
Income before income tax		$ 102,000
Income tax....................................		21,000
Net income		$ 81,000

(3)

MAHANEY INC.
Retained Earnings Statement
For Year Ended December 31, 1990

Retained earnings, January 1, 1990		$711,000
Net income for year	$81,000	
Less dividends	20,000	
Increase in retained earnings		61,000
Retained earnings, December 31, 1990		$772,000

(4)

MAHANEY INC.
Balance Sheet
December 31, 1990

Assets			
Current assets:			
Cash		$ 50,000	
Accounts receivable	$160,000		
Less allowance for doubtful accounts	20,000	140,000	
Inventories:			
Finished goods	$200,000		
Work in process	70,000		
Direct materials	42,000	312,000	
Prepaid insurance		12,000	
Factory supplies		7,000	
Total current assets			$521,000
Plant assets:			
Land		$100,000	
Buildings	$400,000		
Less accumulated depreciation	220,000	180,000	
Factory equipment	$250,000		
Less accumulated depreciation	125,000	125,000	
Total plant assets			405,000
Total assets			$926,000
Liabilities			
Current liabilities:			
Accounts payable		$ 30,000	
Wages payable		14,000	
Income tax payable		10,000	
Total current liabilities			$54,000
Stockholders' Equity			
Common stock		$100,000	
Retained earnings		772,000	
Total stockholders' equity			872,000
Total liabilities and stockholders' equity			$926,000

Discussion Questions

15–1. What term refers to the individuals who are responsible for directing an enterprise?

15–2. What are the four basic functions of the management process?

15–3. What is the term for a plan that encompasses a period ranging from five to ten years and that serves as a basis for commitment of enterprise resources?

15–4. What is the process by which management assigns responsibility to individuals for achieving enterprise goals?

15–5. Describe what is meant by "management by exception."

15–6. What is the dominant principle that guides the managerial accountant in preparing management reports?

15–7. Zarnoch Company is contemplating the expansion of its operations through the purchase of the assets of Keefe Lumber Company. Included among the assets of Keefe Lumber Company is lumber purchased for $150,000 and having a current replacement cost of $205,000. Which cost ($150,000 or $205,000) is relevant for the decision to be made by Zarnoch Company? Briefly explain the reason for your answer.

15–8. A bank loan officer is evaluating a request for a loan that is to be secured by a mortgage on the borrower's property. The property cost $300,000 twenty years ago and has a current market value of $450,000. Which figure, $300,000 or $450,000, is relevant for the loan officer's use in evaluating the request for the loan? Discuss.

15–9. What is meant by cost-benefit balance as it relates to the preparation of management reports?

15–10. What is the role of the controller in a business organization?

15–11. (a) What do the initials CMA signify? (b) Briefly describe the requirements for the CMA designation.

15–12. What term describes all disbursements of cash (or the commitment to pay cash in the future) for the purpose of generating revenues?

15–13. What three costs make up the cost of manufacturing a product?

15–14. What manufacturing cost term is used to describe the cost of wages paid to employees directly involved in converting direct materials to a finished product?

15–15. If the cost of wages paid to employees is not a significant portion of the total product cost, the wages cost would normally be classified as what type of manufacturing cost?

15–16. Indicate whether each of the following costs of an automobile manufacturer would be classified as (a) direct materials cost, (b) direct labor cost, or (c) factory overhead cost:
(1) tires
(2) transmission
(3) factory machinery lubricants
(4) depreciation on factory machinery
(5) wages of assembly-line worker
(6) windshield
(7) engine
(8) wages of assembly-line supervisor

15–17. Distinguish between prime costs and conversion costs.

15–18. What is the difference between a product cost and a period cost?

15–19. Name the three inventory accounts for a manufacturing business and describe what each balance represents at the end of an accounting period.

15–20. What are the three categories of manufacturing costs included in the cost of finished goods and the cost of work in process?

15–21. What statement is used to summarize the manufacturing costs incurred during a period?

15–22. For a manufacturing enterprise, what is the description of the amount that is comparable to a merchandising concern's net cost of merchandise purchased?

15–23. Classify each of the following costs as either (a) a variable cost or (b) a fixed cost:
(1) straight-line depreciation on factory equipment
(2) direct materials cost
(3) $1,000 per month rent on factory building
(4) property taxes on factory plant and equipment
(5) electricity usage
(6) direct labor cost
(7) property insurance
(8) 15% sales commission

15–24. For a company that produces microcomputers, would memory chips be considered a direct or an indirect cost of each microcomputer produced?

15–25. For a production line supervisor, would depreciation on the factory plant be considered a controllable or a noncontrollable cost?

15–26. In deciding between the purchase of truck A or truck B, what would be the differential cost?

15–27. How might the discontinuance or reduction of discretionary costs affect long-term operations? Use research and development costs as the basis for an example.

15–28. (a) What is meant by *sunk costs?* (b) A company is contemplating replacing an old piece of machinery which cost $320,000 and has $280,000 accumulated depreciation to date. A new machine costs $400,000. What is the sunk cost in this situation?

15–29. In considering the purchase of a new automobile, would the book value (the original cost less accumulated depreciation) of the automobile traded in be considered a sunk cost?

15–30. (a) What is meant by *opportunity cost?* (b) Lieu Company is currently earning 10% on $200,000 invested in marketable securities. It proposes to use the $200,000 to acquire plant facilities to manufacture a new product line that is expected to add $30,000 annually to net income. What is the opportunity cost involved in the decision to manufacture the new product?

15–31. Real World Focus. The following paragraphs were taken from an article in *The Wall Street Journal* on April 13, 1987, describing actions taken by General Motors Corporation:

> *General Motors Corp. has lowered its market-share goal in the U.S. through 1990, but "is now in a strong position to provide maximum profitability," Roger B. Smith, GM chairman, told securities analysts.*
>
> *Mr. Smith said GM's goal is to get about 40% of the U.S. car market. That is higher than the 37.9% GM got in the first quarter, but below the 42% goal that GM officials were setting a few months ago and below the 45% share that GM has averaged over the past decade. The new goal reflects GM's "changing focus towards profitability," Leon J. Krain, the company's treasurer, said in a telephone interview Friday.*

Do the actions taken by General Motors Corporation impact on strategic or operational planning? Explain.

Exercises

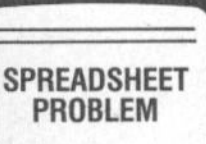

15-32. Statement of cost of goods manufactured. The following accounts were selected from the pre-closing trial balance of Jarvis Co. at July 31, 1990, the end of the current fiscal year:

Direct Labor	$192,000
Direct Materials Inventory	51,600
Direct Materials Purchases	230,100
Factory Overhead	76,800
Finished Goods Inventory	76,500
General Expense	54,750
Interest Expense	8,500
Sales	717,600
Selling Expense	76,500
Work in Process Inventory	55,500

Inventories at July 31 were as follows:

Finished Goods	$81,000
Work in Process	59,550
Direct Materials	54,000

Prepare a statement of cost of goods manufactured.

15-33. Cost of goods sold. On the basis of the data presented in Exercise 15-32, prepare the cost of goods sold section of the income statement.

15-34. Terminology. Choose the appropriate term for completing each of the following sentences.

(a) The wages of an assembly worker are considered an inventoriable or (fixed, product) cost.
(b) Direct materials costs combined with direct labor costs are called (prime, conversion) costs.
(c) Because the total wages of the assembly workers change as the level of production changes, the wages of assembly workers are considered a (fixed, variable) cost.
(d) Since the amount of overtime work by assembly workers can be determined by the production supervisor through proper scheduling, overtime pay is considered a (controllable, noncontrollable) cost for the production supervisor.
(e) Straight-line depreciation on factory equipment does not vary with changes in level of production and therefore is considered a (fixed, variable) cost.
(f) Factory overhead costs combined with direct labor costs are called (prime, conversion) costs.
(g) Sales salaries paid during the current period are shown on the income statement as an expense and are (product, period) costs.
(h) A cost that has been incurred and cannot be reversed by subsequent decisions is an example of a (fixed, sunk) cost.
(i) The (opportunity, prime) cost of not investing in U.S. Treasury securities, which are yielding 10%, is the interest forgone on the possible investment.

15-35. Classification as product or period costs. For a manufacturing enterprise, classify each of the following costs as either a product (inventoriable) cost or period cost:

(a) Sales commissions
(b) Controller's salary
(c) Direct materials used during production
(d) Depreciation on factory equipment

(e) Depreciation on office equipment
(f) Property taxes on factory building and equipment
(g) Advertising expenses
(h) Factory supervisors' salaries
(i) Repairs and maintenance costs for factory equipment
(j) Wages of assembly workers
(k) Oil used to lubricate factory equipment.
(l) Travel costs of salespersons
(m) Utility costs for office building
(n) Factory janitorial supplies
(o) Salary of production quality control supervisor

15-36. Classification of costs. The following is a list of various costs that could be incurred in producing this textbook. With respect to the manufacture and sale of this text, classify each cost as either variable or fixed, and as either indirect or direct.

(a) paper on which the text is written
(b) wages of vice-president of marketing
(c) sales commissions paid to textbook representatives for each text sold
(d) straight-line depreciation on the printing presses used to manufacture the text
(e) electricity used to run the presses during the printing of the text
(f) hourly wages of printing press operators during production
(g) property taxes on the factory building and equipment
(h) ink used to print the text
(i) salary of staff used to develop artwork for the text
(j) royalty paid to the authors for each text sold

15-37 Analysis of differential costs. Grainger Company has been purchasing carrying cases for its portable typewriters at a price of $15 per typewriter. If Grainger Company manufactures the carrying cases, the manufacturing costs are expected to be $16. (a) What is the differential cost of manufacturing the carrying cases, compared to the alternative of purchasing the cases? (b) Should Grainger Company purchase or manufacture the cases? Explain.

Problems

15-38. Classification as product or period costs. The following is a list of costs incurred by several business enterprises.

(a) Production supervisor's salary
(b) Steel for an automobile manufacturer
(c) Oil lubricants for factory plant and equipment
(d) Advertising costs
(e) Memory chips for a microcomputer manufacturer
(f) Wages of assembly worker on the production line
(g) Salary of the vice-president of marketing
(h) Wages of a machine operator on the production line
(i) Property taxes on factory building
(j) Factory operating supplies
(k) Salary of the president of the company
(l) Depreciation on factory equipment
(m) Wages of production quality control personnel
(n) Maintenance and repair costs for factory equipment
(o) Sales commissions
(p) Bonuses paid to president and other officers
(q) Health insurance premiums paid for factory workers

(r) Lumber used by furniture manufacturer
(s) Paper used by textbook publisher in printing texts
(t) Paper used by computer department in processing various managerial reports
(u) Insurance premiums paid on salespersons' automobiles
(v) Coffee for executive lounge
(w) Janitorial supplies used in cleaning the production line
(x) Protective glasses for factory machine operators
(y) Blank diskettes for the producer and distributor of microcomputer software
(z) Sales catalogs distributed free of charge to potential customers

Instructions: Classify each of the preceding costs as product costs or period costs. For those costs classified as product costs, indicate whether the product cost is a direct materials cost, a direct labor cost, or a factory overhead cost. For those costs classified as period costs, indicate whether the period cost is a selling expense or an administrative expense. Use the following tabular headings for preparing your answer. Place an X in the appropriate columns.

	Product Cost			Period Cost	
Cost	Direct Materials Cost	Direct Labor Cost	Factory Overhead Cost	Selling Expense	Administrative Expense

15-39. Statement of cost of goods manufactured; cost of goods sold. The following accounts related to manufacturing operations of Henry Inc. were selected from the pre-closing trial balance at June 30, 1990, the end of the current fiscal year:

Depreciation of Factory Buildings	$ 10,000
Depreciation of Factory Equipment	14,500
Direct Labor	110,000
Direct Materials Inventory	30,000
Direct Materials Purchases	145,600
Factory Supplies Expense	3,200
Finished Goods Inventory	45,000
Heat, Light, and Power	14,300
Indirect Labor	23,500
Insurance Expense	5,000
Miscellaneous Factory Costs	2,400
Property Taxes	6,100
Work in Process Inventory	28,400

Inventories at June 30 were as follows:

Finished Goods	52,000
Work in Process	33,200
Direct Materials	32,500

Instructions: (1) Prepare a statement of cost of goods manufactured.
(2) Prepare the cost of goods sold section of the income statement.

15-40. Determination of missing income statement data. Data for Childers Inc. and Marlowe Co., manufacturing companies, are as follows:

	Childers Inc.	Marlowe Co.
Work in process inventory, Jan. 1, 1990	$ 100,000	$ 80,000
Cost of direct materials placed in production	(a)	200,000
Direct labor	300,000	105,000
Total factory overhead	200,000	(f)
Total manufacturing costs	900,000	400,000
Work in process inventory, Dec. 31, 1990	(b)	(g)

	Childers Inc.	Marlowe Co.
Cost of goods manufactured	$ 780,000	$390,000
Finished goods inventory, Jan. 1, 1990	50,000	80,000
Finished goods inventory, Dec. 31, 1990	60,000	(h)
Cost of goods sold	(c)	370,000
Sales	1,200,000	(i)
Gross profit	(d)	380,000
Total operating expenses	140,000	(j)
Net income	(e)	180,000

Instructions: Determine the missing items, identifying each by the letters (a) through (j).

15-41. Financial statements for a manufacturing enterprise. The pre-closing trial balance of Ayers Inc. as of August 31, 1990, the end of the current fiscal year, is shown below. Inventories at August 31, 1990, were as follows:

Finished Goods	$90,000
Work in Process	60,000
Direct Materials	55,000

Cash	20,000	
Accounts Receivable	80,000	
Allowance for Doubtful Accounts		2,000
Finished Goods Inventory	85,000	
Work in Process Inventory	70,000	
Direct Materials Inventory	60,000	
Prepaid Insurance	9,000	
Factory Supplies	8,000	
Land	75,000	
Factory Buildings	300,000	
Accumulated Depreciation—Factory Buildings		150,000
Factory Equipment	450,000	
Accumulated Depreciation—Factory Equipment		210,000
Accounts Payable		60,000
Wages Payable		8,000
Income Tax Payable		5,000
Common Stock		100,000
Retained Earnings		578,000
Dividends	40,000	
Sales		800,000
Direct Materials Purchases	200,000	
Direct Labor	175,000	
Indirect Labor	50,000	
Depreciation—Factory Equipment	32,000	
Factory Heat, Light, and Power	22,000	
Factory Property Taxes	14,000	
Depreciation—Factory Buildings	18,000	
Insurance Expense—Factory	6,000	
Factory Supplies Expense	5,500	
Miscellaneous Factory Costs	3,500	
Selling Expenses	100,000	
Administrative Expenses	60,000	
Income Tax	30,000	
	1,913,000	1,913,000

Instructions: (1) Prepare a statement of cost of goods manufactured.
(2) Prepare an income statement.
(3) Prepare a retained earnings statement.
(4) Prepare a balance sheet.

15-42. Cost identification and classification. The management of Ferguson Inc., a boat retailer and distributor, is considering expanding operations by adding a repair and maintenance department. Originally, Ferguson Inc. built its building to accommodate future expansion. For the past several years, it has rented a 2,500-foot section of the building to Ron's Motorcycle Shop for $2,000 per month. This section of the building will be converted for use by the maintenance and repair department.

New equipment costing $10,000 will be purchased. It will be depreciated using the straight-line method. Existing equipment that has no resale value or other use and has a book value of $3,000 will be converted for use by the repair and maintenance department. A supervisory mechanic will be hired for $1,500 per month, and an assistant mechanic will be hired for $6 per hour. An inventory of $20,000 of spare parts will be ordered. Ferguson Inc.'s business insurance premiums are expected to increase by $200 per month, once the repairs and maintenance department opens for business.

To obtain as much visibility as possible, a one-time special advertising promotion is planned at a cost of $2,500.

Instructions: (1) Classify the costs of the proposed repairs and maintenance operations into the following categories:

variable costs
fixed costs
differential costs of expansion
sunk costs of expansion

(2) What is the opportunity cost for Ferguson Inc. of expanding operations?

ALTERNATE PROBLEMS

15-38A. Classification as product or period costs. The following is a list of costs incurred by several business enterprises.

(a) Disk drives for a microcomputer manufacturer
(b) Wages of a painter for an automotive repair shop
(c) Salary of the vice-president of finance
(d) Wages of a machine operator on the production line
(e) Life insurance premiums paid for company president
(f) Coal used to heat furnaces of steel manufacturer
(g) Ink used by textbook publisher in printing texts
(h) Pens, paper, and other supplies used by accounting department in preparing various managerial reports
(i) Employer's portion of factory workers' FICA taxes
(j) Electricity used to operate factory machinery
(k) Janitorial supplies used in cleaning the office building
(l) Fees paid lawn service for office grounds
(m) Wages of computer programmer for producer and distributor of microcomputer software
(n) Depreciation on copying machine used by the marketing department
(o) Production supervisor's salary
(p) Tires for an automobile manufacturer
(q) Oil lubricants for factory plant and equipment
(r) Cost of a 30-second television commercial
(s) Depreciation on robot used to assemble a product
(t) Wages of production quality control personnel
(u) Maintenance and repair costs for factory equipment
(v) Depreciation on tools used in production
(w) Bonuses paid to salespersons
(x) Insurance on factory building
(y) Salary of the secretary of the president of the company
(z) Cost of company picnic

Instructions: Classify each of the preceding costs as product costs or period costs. For those costs classified as product costs, indicate whether the product cost is a direct materials cost, a direct labor cost, or a factory overhead cost. For those costs classified as period costs, indicate whether the period cost is a selling expense or an administrative expense. Use the following tabular headings for preparing your answer. Place an X in the appropriate columns.

	Product Cost			Period Cost	
Cost	Direct Materials Cost	Direct Labor Cost	Factory Overhead Cost	Selling Expense	Administrative Expense

15-39A. Statement of cost of goods manufactured; cost of goods sold. The following accounts related to manufacturing operations of Miles Inc. were selected from the pre-closing trial balance at March 31, 1990, the end of the current fiscal year:

Depreciation of Factory Buildings	$ 56,000
Depreciation of Factory Equipment	81,200
Direct Labor	590,000
Direct Materials Inventory	170,000
Direct Materials Purchases	800,000
Factory Supplies Expense	17,200
Finished Goods Inventory	250,000
Heat, Light, and Power	80,500
Indirect Labor	132,000
Insurance Expense	25,400
Miscellaneous Factory Costs	13,500
Property Taxes	35,000
Work in Process Inventory	160,000

Inventories at March 31 were as follows:

Finished Goods	$285,000
Work in Process	180,800
Direct Materials	200,000

Instructions: (1) Prepare a statement of cost of goods manufactured.
(2) Prepare the cost of goods sold section of the income statement.

15-40A. Determination of missing income statement data. Data for Bormann Inc. and Fender Co., manufacturing companies, are as follows:

	Bormann Inc.	Fender Co.
Work in process inventory, Jan. 1, 1990	$ 30,000	$ 40,000
Cost of direct materials placed in production	100,000	(f)
Direct labor	150,000	80,000
Total factory overhead	80,000	120,000
Total manufacturing costs	(a)	440,000
Work in process inventory, Dec. 31, 1990	20,000	(g)
Cost of goods manufactured	(b)	390,000
Finished goods inventory, Jan. 1, 1990	(c)	100,000
Finished goods inventory, Dec. 31, 1990	70,000	80,000
Cost of goods sold	320,000	(h)
Sales	(d)	610,000
Gross profit	280,000	(i)
Total operating expenses	150,000	(j)
Net income	(e)	80,000

Instructions: Determine the missing items, identifying each by the letters (a) through (j).

15-41A. Financial statements for a manufacturing enterprise. The following pre-closing trial balance of Whitehead Inc. was prepared as of March 31, 1990, the end of the current fiscal year:

Account	Debit	Credit
Cash	40,000	
Accounts Receivable	120,000	
Allowance for Doubtful Accounts		10,000
Finished Goods Inventory	170,000	
Work in Process Inventory	50,000	
Direct Materials Inventory	40,000	
Prepaid Insurance	12,000	
Factory Supplies	7,000	
Land	90,000	
Factory Buildings	350,000	
Accumulated Depreciation—Factory Buildings		220,000
Factory Equipment	175,000	
Accumulated Depreciation—Factory Equipment		80,000
Accounts Payable		45,000
Wages Payable		15,000
Income Tax Payable		10,000
Common Stock		200,000
Retained Earnings		439,000
Dividends	30,000	
Sales		1,200,000
Direct Materials Purchases	500,000	
Direct Labor	250,000	
Indirect Factory Labor	110,000	
Factory Heat, Light, and Power	18,000	
Depreciation—Factory Equipment	20,000	
Factory Property Taxes	15,000	
Depreciation—Factory Buildings	14,000	
Insurance Expense—Factory	10,000	
Factory Supplies Expense	8,000	
Miscellaneous Factory Costs	5,000	
Selling Expenses	100,000	
Administrative Expenses	60,000	
Income Tax	25,000	
	2,219,000	2,219,000

Inventories at March 31, 1990, were as follows:

Finished Goods	$160,000
Work in Process	40,000
Direct Materials	45,000

Instructions: (1) Prepare a statement of cost of goods manufactured.
(2) Prepare an income statement.
(3) Prepare a retained earnings statement.
(4) Prepare a balance sheet.

Mini-Case 15

Rutkosky's Pizza Inc. began operations on June 20, 1986, in the garage of Helen Rutkosky. The business specializes in fast delivery of home-made pizzas on weekends. At the request of customers, Rutkosky is considering moving to a vacant office building and devoting full time to the business. Rutkosky is currently employed at Eats' Grocery as an assistant store manager, where she makes $15,000 a year.

Rutkosky has estimated the following costs of opening the new business:

Purchase of new oven	$5,000
Purchase of additional delivery truck	$12,000
Purchase of furnishings	$8,000
Monthly rent	$1,000
Wages of employees	$5.50 per hour
Insurance	$500 per year
Local advertising	$600 per month
Additional business licenses	$300 per year

Rutkosky plans to move the existing equipment from her garage to the new business. The existing equipment has an original cost of $15,000 and accumulated depreciation of $3,000. Straight-line depreciation is used to depreciate all plant and equipment.

Instructions:

(1) Classify each of the preceding costs of opening the new busi ness, using the following categories:
variable costs
fixed costs
differential costs
discretionary costs
opportunity costs
sunk costs
Note: Some costs may be classified into more than one category.

(2) Assuming that Rutkosky opens the new business, list (a) costs which are controllable on a day-to-day basis, and (b) costs which are noncontrollable on a day-to-day basis.

(3) List three direct costs and three indirect costs of making pizzas.

Answers to Self-Examination Questions

1. D The four basic functions of the management process are planning (answer A), organizing and directing, controlling (answer B), and decision making (answer C). Operations (answer D) is not one of the four basic functions, but is the activity which managers attempt to manage.
2. B The Certified Management Accountant designation (answer B) serves as evidence of professional competence in managerial accounting. A Certified Public Accountant (answer A) has professional competence in financial accounting. A Certified Internal Auditor (answer C) has professional competence in internal auditing. A Certified Financial Planner (answer D) has professional competence in financial planning.
3. B Depreciation on testing equipment (answer B) is included as part of the factory overhead costs of the microcomputer manufacturer. The cost of memory chips (answer A) and the cost of disk drives (answer D) are both considered a part of direct materials cost. The wages of microcomputer assemblers (answer C) are part of direct labor cost.
4. A Conversion cost is the combination of direct labor cost and factory overhead cost (answer A). Factory overhead cost (answer B) is a separate cost of manufacturing a product. Direct materials cost and direct labor cost (answer C) are prime costs. The combination of direct materials cost and factory overhead cost (answer D) is not considered a separate cost classification.
5. D Direct materials cost (answer A), direct labor cost (answer B), and electricity to operate factory equipment (answer C) all vary with changes in the level of activity and are therefore variable costs.

16
Accounting Systems For Manufacturing Enterprises: Job Order Cost Systems

CHAPTER OBJECTIVES

Describe the usefulness of product costs.

Describe the basic types of accounting systems used by manufacturing enterprises.

Describe the basic characteristics of cost accounting systems.

Describe and illustrate the flow of data through a cost accounting system of a manufacturing enterprise.

Describe alternative cost accounting systems for manufacturing operations.

Describe and illustrate a job order cost accounting system.

A variety of cost concepts and classifications were described and illustrated in Chapter 15. For manufacturing enterprises, the importance of distinguishing between product costs and period costs was emphasized. Period costs are used up in generating revenues of the current period and are shown on the current period's income statement as expenses. Product costs are composed of the three elements of manufacturing costs: direct materials, direct labor, and factory overhead. Until the units to which they relate are sold, product costs are treated as part of inventory.

To account for product costs properly, a manufacturing enterprise must use an accounting system that will accumulate and assign all product costs to the related units of production. This chapter briefly describes the basic types of accounting systems used by manufacturing enterprises. The chapter then focuses on a discussion and illustration of one of these systems, the job order cost system.

USEFULNESS OF PRODUCT COSTS

In studying product costs, it is important to keep in mind that the primary function of the managerial accountant is to provide useful information to managers for planning, organizing and directing, decision making, and controlling operations. Much of this information is developed in the process of accounting for product costs.

A primary use of product costs by managers is for preparation of the financial statements of the enterprise. To present materials, work in process, and finished goods inventories properly on the balance sheet, product costs must be accounted for and assigned to the individual units in inventory. Because the cost of materials, direct labor, and factory overhead may vary throughout the period, product costs are usually assigned to inventory on the basis of an average per unit cost for the period. For example, if 1,000,000 pounds of materials were purchased throughout the period at a total cost of $2,500,000, the materials product cost per pound would be $2.50.

The assignment of product costs to direct materials, work in process, and finished goods inventories allows for the proper determination of net income for the period. The statement of cost of goods manufactured (illustrated in Chapter 15) serves as a basis for determining the cost of goods sold. An improper assignment of product costs to inventory would lead to a misstatement of the cost of goods sold and net income.

Product costs are also needed by management for a wide variety of purposes. For example, the per unit cost of finished goods inventory is vital information for the setting of long-term product prices. Product cost information is also necessary in deciding whether to continue making a product internally for use in further processing or to purchase the product from an outside supplier. A variety of other managerial decisions which require the use of product cost information will be illustrated throughout the remainder of this text. Without accurate product cost information, managers could not effectively or efficiently manage operations.

TYPES OF ACCOUNTING SYSTEMS

Two basic accounting systems may be used by manufacturers: general accounting systems and cost accounting systems. Although accounting for manufacturing operations is usually more complex than for merchandising operations, a **general accounting system** may be used if a single product or several similar products are manufactured. A general accounting system is essentially an extension of the periodic system of inventory accounting used in merchandising enterprises to the three manufacturing inventories: direct materials, work in process, and finished goods. Because such simple manufacturing situations are rare, the basic principles of a general accounting system for manufacturing operations are not discussed further in this chapter.

Through the use of perpetual inventory systems, a **cost accounting system** achieves greater accuracy in the determination of product costs than is possible with a general accounting system that uses periodic inventory procedures. Cost accounting procedures also permit far more effective control by supplying data on the costs incurred by each manufacturing department or process and the unit cost of manufacturing each type of product. Such procedures provide not only data useful to management in minimizing costs, but also other valuable information about production methods to use and quantities to produce.

Types of Cost Accounting Systems

There are two main types of cost systems for manufacturing operations—job order cost and process cost. Each of the two systems is widely used, and a manufacturer may use a job order cost system for some of its products and a process cost system for others.

A **job order cost system** provides for a separate record of the cost of each particular quantity of product that passes through the factory. It is best suited to industries that manufacture goods to fill special orders from customers and to industries that produce different lines of products for stock. It is also appropriate when standard products are manufactured in batches rather than on a continuous basis. In a job order cost system, a summary such as the following would show the cost incurred in completing a job:

Job 565
1,000 Units of Product X200

Direct materials used	$2,380
Direct labor used	4,400
Factory overhead applied	3,080
Total cost	$9,860
Unit cost ($9,860 ÷ 1,000)	$ 9.86

Under a **process cost system,** the costs are accumulated for each of the departments or processes within the factory. A process system is best used by manufacturers of like units of product that are not distinguishable from each other during a continuous production process.

Perpetual Inventory Procedures

In a cost accounting system, perpetual inventory controlling accounts and subsidiary ledgers are maintained for materials, work in process, and finished goods.[1] Each of these accounts is debited for all additions and is credited for all deductions. The balance of each account thus represents the inventory on hand.

All expenditures incidental to manufacturing move through the work in process account, the finished goods account, and eventually into the cost of goods sold account. The flow of costs through the perpetual inventory accounts and into the cost of goods sold account is illustrated as follows:

Flow of Costs Through Perpetual Inventory Accounts

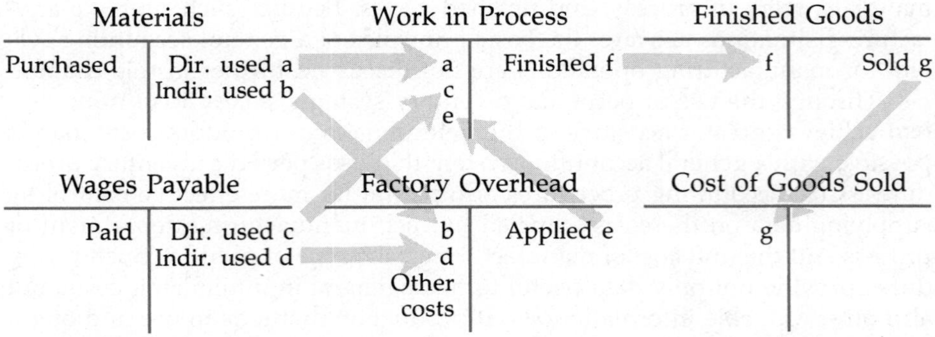

[1]In this chapter and in subsequent chapters, the titles of the three manufacturing inventories will be shortened to "Materials," "Work in Process," and "Finished Goods."

Materials and labor used in production are classified as direct and indirect. The materials and the labor used directly in the process of manufacturing are debited to Work in Process (a and c in the diagram). The materials and the labor used that do not enter directly into the finished product are debited to Factory Overhead (b and d in the diagram). Examples of indirect materials are oils and greases, abrasives and polishes, cleaning supplies, gloves, and brushes. Examples of indirect labor are salaries of supervisors, inspectors, material handlers, security guards, and janitors. The applied factory overhead cost is computed by using a predetermined factory overhead rate, as explained later in this chapter, and is debited to Work in Process (e in the diagram). The costs of the goods finished are transferred from Work in Process to Finished Goods (f in the diagram). When the goods are sold, their costs are transferred from Finished Goods to Cost of Goods Sold (g in the diagram).

The number of accounts presented in the flowchart was limited in order to simplify the illustration. In practice, manufacturing operations may require many processing departments, each requiring separate work in process and factory overhead accounts.

JOB ORDER COST SYSTEMS

The basic concepts of job order cost systems are illustrated in this chapter, while process cost systems are discussed in Chapter 17. In the following paragraphs, the discussion focuses attention on the source documents that serve as the basis for the entries in the job order cost system and on the managerial uses of cost accounting in planning and controlling operations.

Materials

Procedures used in the procurement and issuance of materials differ considerably among manufacturers and even among departments of a particular manufacturer. The discussion that follows is confined to the basic principles, however, and will disregard relatively minor variations and details.

Some time in advance of the date that production of a certain commodity is to begin, the department responsible for scheduling informs the purchasing department, by means of **purchase requisitions,** of the materials that will be needed. The purchasing department then issues the necessary **purchase orders** to suppliers. After the goods have been received and inspected, the receiving department personnel prepare a **receiving report,** showing the quantity received and its condition. Quantities, unit costs, and total costs of the goods billed, as reported on the supplier's invoice, are then compared with the purchase order and the receiving report to make sure that the amounts billed agree with the materials ordered and received. After such verifications, the invoice is recorded as a debit to Materials and a credit to Accounts Payable.

The account Materials in the general ledger is a controlling account. A separate account for each type of material is maintained in a subsidiary ledger called the **materials ledger.** Details as to quantity and cost of materials received are recorded in the materials ledger on the basis of the purchase invoices, or receiving reports. A typical form of materials ledger account is illustrated as follows:

Materials Ledger Account

MATERIAL NO. 23									ORDER POINT 1,000
RECEIVED			ISSUED				BALANCE		
REC. REPORT NO.	QUANTITY	AMOUNT	MAT. REQ. NO.	QUANTITY	AMOUNT	DATE	QUANTITY	AMOUNT	UNIT PRICE
						JAN. 1	1,200	600.00	.50
			672	500	250.00	4	700	350.00	.50
196	3,000	1,620.00				8	700	350.00	.50
							3,000	1,620.00	.54
			704	800	404.00	18	2,900	1,566.00	.54

The accounts in the materials ledger may also be used as an aid in maintaining proper inventory quantities of stock items. Frequent comparisons of quantity balances with predetermined order points enable management to avoid costly idle time caused by lack of materials. The subsidiary ledger form may also include columns for recording quantities ordered and dates of the purchase orders.

Materials are transferred from the storeroom to the factory in response to **materials requisitions,** which may be issued by the manufacturing department concerned or by a central scheduling department. Storeroom personnel record the issuances on the materials requisition by inserting the physical quantity data. Transfer of responsibility for the materials is evidenced by the signature or initials of the storeroom and factory personnel concerned. The requisition is then routed to the materials ledger clerk, who inserts unit prices and amounts. A typical materials requisition is illustrated as follows:

Materials Requisition

MATERIALS REQUISITICN

Job No. 62 Requisition No. 704

Authorized by R. A. Sanders Date January 18, 19--

Description	Quantity Authorized	Quantity Issued	Unit Price	Amount
Material No. 23	800	700 100	$.50 .54	$350 54
Total issued				$404

Issued by M. K. Received by J. B.

The completed requisition serves as the basis for posting quantities and dollar data to the materials ledger accounts. In the illustration, the first-in, first-out costing method was used. A summary of the materials requisitions completed during the month serves as the basis for transferring the cost of the materials from the controlling account in the general ledger to the controlling accounts for work in process and factory overhead. The flow of materials into production is illustrated by the following entry:

Work in Process	13,000	
Factory Overhead..	840	
Materials..		13,840

The perpetual inventory system for materials has three important advantages: (1) it provides for prompt and accurate charging of materials to jobs and factory overhead, (2) it permits the work of inventory-taking to be spread out rather than concentrated at the end of a fiscal period, and (3) it aids in the disclosure of inventory shortages or other irregularities. As physical quantities of the various materials are determined, the actual inventories are compared with the balances of the respective subsidiary ledger accounts. The causes of significant differences between the two should be determined and the responsibility for the differences assigned to specific individuals. Remedial action can then be taken.

Factory Labor

Unlike materials, factory labor is not tangible, nor is it acquired and stored in advance of its use. Hence, there is no perpetual inventory account for labor. The two main objectives in accounting for labor are (1) determination of the correct amount to be paid each employee for each payroll period, and (2) appropriate allocation of labor costs to factory overhead and individual job orders.

The amount of time spent by an employee in the factory is usually recorded on **clock cards,** which are also called **in-and-out cards.** The amount of time spent by each employee and the labor cost incurred for each individual job, or for factory overhead, are recorded on **time tickets.** A typical time ticket form is illustrated on page 612.

The times reported on an employee's time tickets are compared with the related clock cards as an internal check on the accuracy of payroll disbursements. A summary of the time tickets at the end of each month serves as the basis for recording the direct and indirect labor costs incurred. The flow of labor costs into production is illustrated by the following entry:

Work in Process	10,000	
Factory Overhead..	2,200	
Wages Payable..		12,200

Time Ticket

Time Ticket				
Employee Name Gail Berry			No. 4521	
Employee No. 240			Date January 18, 19--	
Description of work Finishing			Job No. 62	
Time Started	Time Stopped	Hours Worked	Hourly Rate	Cost
10:00	12:00	2	$6.50	$13.00
1:00	2:00	1	6.50	6.50
Total cost				$19.50
Approved by T. D.				

Factory Overhead

Factory overhead includes all manufacturing costs, except direct materials and direct labor. Examples of factory overhead costs, in addition to indirect materials and indirect labor, are depreciation, electricity, fuel, insurance, and property taxes. It is customary to have a factory overhead controlling account in the general ledger. Details of the various types of cost are accumulated in a subsidiary ledger.

Debits to Factory Overhead come from various sources. For example, the cost of indirect materials is obtained from the summary of the materials requisitions, the cost of indirect labor is obtained from the summary of the time tickets, costs of electricity and water are obtained from invoices, and the cost of depreciation and expired insurance may be recorded as adjustments at the end of the accounting period.

Although factory overhead cannot be specifically identified with particular jobs, it is as much a part of manufacturing costs as direct materials and direct labor. As the use of machines and automation has increased, factory overhead has represented an ever larger part of total costs. Many items of factory overhead cost are incurred for the entire factory and cannot be directly related to the finished product. The problem is further complicated because some items of factory overhead cost are relatively fixed in amount while others tend to vary according to changes in productivity.

To wait until the end of an accounting period to allocate factory overhead to the various jobs would be quite acceptable from the standpoint of accuracy but highly unsatisfactory in terms of timeliness. If the cost system is to be of maximum usefulness, it is imperative that cost data be available as each job is completed, even though there is a sacrifice in accuracy. It is only through timely reporting that management can make whatever adjustments seem necessary in pricing and manufacturing methods to achieve the best possible combination of revenue and cost on future jobs. Therefore, in order that job costs may be available currently, it is customary to apply factory overhead to production by using a **predetermined factory overhead rate.**

Predetermined Factory Overhead Rate. The factory overhead rate is determined by relating the estimated amount of factory overhead for the forthcoming year to some common activity base, one that will equitably apply the factory overhead costs to the goods manufactured. The common bases include direct labor costs, direct labor hours, and machine hours. For example, if it is estimated that the total factory overhead costs for the year will be $100,000 and that the total direct labor cost will be $125,000, an overhead rate of 80% ($100,000÷$125,000) will be applied to the direct labor cost incurred during the year.

As factory overhead costs are incurred, they are debited to the factory overhead account. The factory overhead costs applied to production are periodically credited to the factory overhead account and debited to the work in process account. The application of factory overhead costs to production (80% of direct labor cost of $10,000) is illustrated by the following entry:

Work in Process	8,000	
Factory Overhead....................................		8,000

Inevitably, factory overhead costs applied and actual factory overhead costs incurred during a particular period will differ. If the amount applied exceeds the actual costs, the factory overhead account will have a credit balance and the overhead is said to be **overapplied** or **overabsorbed.** If the amount applied is less than the actual costs, the account will have a debit balance and the overhead is said to be **underapplied** or **underabsorbed.** Both cases are illustrated in the following account:

ACCOUNT FACTORY OVERHEAD ACCOUNT NO.

Date		Item	Debit	Credit	Balance Debit	Balance Credit
May	1	Balance				200
	31	Costs incurred	8,320			
	31	Cost applied		8,000	120	

Underapplied Balance

Overapplied Balance

Disposition of Factory Overhead Balance. The balance in the factory overhead account is carried forward from month to month until the end of the year. The amount of the balance is reported on interim balance sheets as a deferred item.

The nature of the balance in the factory overhead account (underapplied or overapplied), as well as the amount, may change during the year. If there is a decided trend in either direction and the amount is substantial, the reason should be determined. If the variation is caused by alterations in manufacturing methods or by substantial changes in production goals, it may be advisable to revise the factory overhead rate. The accumulation of a large underapplied balance is more serious than a trend in the opposite direction and may indicate inefficiencies in production methods, excessive expenditures, or a combination of factors.

Despite any corrective actions that may be taken to avoid an underapplication or overapplication of factory overhead, the account will usually have a balance at the end of the fiscal year. Since the balance represents the underapplied or overapplied factory overhead applicable to the operations of the year just ended, it is not proper to report it in the year-end balance sheet as a deferred item.

There are two main alternatives for disposing of the balance of factory overhead at the end of the year: (1) by allocation of the balance among work in process, finished goods, and cost of goods sold accounts on the basis of the total amounts of applied factory overhead included in those accounts at the end of the year, or (2) by transfer of the balance to the cost of goods sold account. Theoretically, only the first alternative is sound because it represents a correction of the estimated overhead rate and brings the accounts into agreement with the costs actually incurred. On the other hand, much time and expense may be required to make the allocation and to revise the unit costs of the work in process and finished goods inventories. Furthermore, in most manufacturing enterprises, a very large part of the total manufacturing costs for the year passes through the work in process and the finished goods accounts into the cost of goods sold account before the end of the year. Therefore, unless the total amount of the underapplied or overapplied balance is great, it is satisfactory to transfer it to Cost of Goods Sold.

The Implications of Automation for Allocating Factory Overhead—A Case Study

For some departments at Amerock Corporation, the allocation of overhead on the basis of direct labor became less accurate and less useful as manufacturing processes became more automated. The solution was to change from direct labor hours to machine hours for these departments.

Amerock Corporation, a manufacturer of cabinet and decorative hardware, found that the only disadvantages to using machine hours as a basis for allocating factory overhead were the time it would take to develop the system and the need for additional reporting by the machine operators. The potential benefits clearly outweighed any disadvantages. In the accounting area, a major advantage would be the ability to allocate overhead when one worker tended several machines. Better cost estimating would also be possible because overhead allocation would be more accurate. Forecasting and the calculation of actual costs would be easier. In the manufacturing area, machine utilization information would be more useful in understanding and controlling production and reporting.

Amerock Corporation's change in its overhead allocation basis has made it possible for accounting to capture costs accurately and for manufacturing to measure performance efficiently. The results have been so successful that Amerock plans to convert most of its departments to a machine hour basis as more of its plants become automated.

Source: Gregory Hakala, "Measuring Costs with Machine Hours," *Management Accounting* (October, 1985), pp. 57–61.

Work in Process

Costs incurred for the various jobs are debited to Work in Process. The job costs described in the preceding sections may be summarized as follows:

Direct materials, $13,000—Work in Process debited and Materials credited; data obtained from summary of materials requisitions.

Direct labor, $10,000—Work in Process debited and Wages Payable credited; data obtained from summary of time tickets.

Factory overhead, $8,000—Work in process debited and Factory Overhead credited; data obtained by applying overhead rate to direct labor cost (80% of $10,000).

The work in process account to which these costs were charged is illustrated as follows:

ACCOUNT WORK IN PROCESS ACCOUNT NO.

Date		Item	Debit	Credit	Balance Debit	Balance Credit
May	1	Balance			3,000	
	31	Direct materials	13,000		16,000	
	31	Direct labor	10,000		26,000	
	31	Factory overhead	8,000		34,000	
	31	Jobs completed		31,920	2,080	

The work in process account is a controlling account that contains summary information only. The details concerning the costs incurred on each job order are accumulated in a subsidiary ledger known as the **cost ledger.** Each cost ledger account, called a **job cost sheet,** has spaces for recording all direct materials and direct labor chargeable to the job and for applying factory overhead at the predetermined rate. Postings to the job cost sheets are made from materials requisitions and time tickets or from summaries of these documents.

The four cost sheets in the subsidiary ledger for the work in process account illustrated are summarized as follows:

COST LEDGER

Job 71 (Summary)	
Balance	3,000
Direct materials	2,000
Direct labor	2,400
Factory overhead	1,920
	9,320

Job 73 (Summary)	
Direct materials	6,000
Direct labor	4,000
Factory overhead	3,200
	13,200

Job 72 (Summary)	
Direct materials	4,000
Direct labor	3,000
Factory overhead	2,400
	9,400

Job 74 (Summary)	
Direct materials	1,000
Direct labor	600
Factory overhead	480
	2,080

The relationship between the work in process controlling account on page 615 and the subsidiary cost ledger may be observed in the following tabulation:

Work in Process (Controlling)			Cost Ledger (Subsidiary)	
Beginning balance	$ 3,000	⟷	Beginning balance	
			Job 71	$ 3,000
Direct materials	$13,000	⟷	Direct materials	
			Job 71	$ 2,000
			Job 72	4,000
			Job 73	6,000
			Job 74	1,000
				$13,000
Direct labor	$10,000	⟷	Direct labor	
			Job 71	$ 2,400
			Job 72	3,000
			Job 73	4,000
			Job 74	600
				$10,000
Factory overhead	$ 8,000	⟷	Factory overhead	
			Job 71	$ 1,920
			Job 72	2,400
			Job 73	3,200
			Job 74	480
				$ 8,000
Jobs completed	$31,920	⟷	Jobs completed	
			Job 71	$ 9,320
			Job 72	9,400
			Job 73	13,200
				$31,920
Ending balance	$ 2,080	⟷	Ending balance	
			Job 74	$ 2,080

The data in the cost ledger were presented in summary form for illustrative purposes. A job cost sheet for Job 72, providing for the current accumulation of cost elements entering into the job order and for a summary when the job is completed, is as follows:

Job Cost Sheet

Job No. 72				Date May 7, 19--			
Item 5,000 Type C Containers				Date wanted May 23, 19--			
For Stock				Date completed May 21, 19--			
Direct Materials		Direct Labor				Summary	
Mat. Req. No.	Amount	Time Summary No.	Amount	Time Summary No.	Amount	Item	Amount
834	800.00	2202	83.60	2248	122.50	Direct materials	4,000.00
838	1,000.00	2204	208.40	2250	187.30	Direct labor	3,000.00
841	1,400.00	2205	167.00	2253	155.40	Factory overhead (80% of direct labor cost)	2,400.00
864	800.00	2210	229.00		3,000.00	Total cost	9,400.00
	4,000.00	2211	198.30			No. of units finished	5,000
		2213	107.20			Cost per unit	1.88
		2216	110.00				
		2222	277.60				
		2224	217.40				
		2225	106.30				
		2231	153.20				
		2234	245.20				
		2237	170.00				
		2242	261.60				

When Job 72 was completed, the direct materials costs and the direct labor costs were totaled and entered in the Summary column. Factory overhead was added at the predetermined rate of 80% of the direct labor cost, and the total cost of the job was determined. The total cost of the job, $9,400, divided by the number of units produced, 5,000, yielded a unit cost of $1.88 for the Type C Containers produced.

Upon the completion of Job 72, the job cost sheet was removed from the cost ledger and filed for future reference. At the end of the accounting period, the sum of the total costs on all cost sheets completed during the period is determined and the following entry is made:

Finished Goods..	31,920	
Work in Process		31,920

The remaining balance in the work in process account represents the total cost charged to the uncompleted job cost sheets.

Finished Goods and Cost of Goods Sold

The finished goods account is a controlling account. The related subsidiary ledger, which has an account for each kind of commodity produced, is called the **finished goods ledger** or **stock ledger.** Each account in the subsidiary finished goods ledger provides columns for recording the quantity and the cost of goods manufactured, the quantity and the cost of goods shipped, and the quantity, the total cost, and the unit cost of goods on hand. An account in the finished goods ledger is illustrated as follows:

Finished Goods Ledger Account

ITEM: TYPE C CONTAINER

MANUFACTURED			SHIPPED			BALANCE			
JOB ORDER NO.	QUANTITY	AMOUNT	SHIP ORDER NO.	QUANTITY	AMOUNT	DATE	QUANTITY	AMOUNT	UNIT COST
						May 1	2,000	3,920.00	1.96
			643	2,000	3,920.00	8	—	—	—
72	5,000	9,400.00				21	5,000	9,400.00	1.88
			646	2,000	3,760.00	23	3,000	5,640.00	1.88

Just as there are various methods of costing materials entering into production, there are various methods of determining the cost of the finished goods sold. In the illustration, the first-in, first-out method is used. The quantities shipped are posted to the finished goods ledger from a copy of the shipping order or other memorandum. The finished goods ledger clerk then records on the copy of the shipping order the unit cost and the total amount of the commodity sold. A summary of the cost data on these shipping orders becomes the basis for the following entry:

Cost of Goods Sold	30,168	
Finished Goods		30,168

If goods are returned by a buyer and are put back in stock, it is necessary to debit Finished Goods and credit Cost of Goods Sold for the cost.

Sales

For each sale of finished goods, it is necessary to maintain a record of both the cost price and the selling price of the goods sold. As previously stated, the cost data may be recorded on the shipping orders. As each sale occurs, the cost of the goods billed is recorded by debiting Cost of Goods Sold and crediting Finished Goods. The selling price of the goods sold is recorded by debiting Accounts Receivable (or Cash) and crediting Sales.

ILLUSTRATION OF JOB ORDER COST ACCOUNTING

To illustrate further a job order cost accounting system, assume that Spencer Co. has the following general ledger trial balance on January 1, the first day of the fiscal year:

Spencer Co.
Trial Balance
January 1, 19--

Account	Debit	Credit
Cash	85,000	
Accounts Receivable	73,000	
Finished Goods	40,000	
Work in Process	20,000	
Materials	30,000	
Prepaid Expenses	2,000	
Plant Assets	850,000	
Accumulated Depreciation—Plant Assets		473,000
Accounts Payable		70,000
Wages Payable		15,000
Common Stock		500,000
Retained Earnings		42,000
	1,100,000	1,100,000

Although in practice the transactions for Spencer Co. would be recorded daily, the January transactions and adjustments are summarized as follows, along with the related journal entries:

(a) Materials purchased and prepaid expenses incurred.

Summary of invoices and receiving reports:

Material A	$29,000
Material B	17,000
Material C	16,000
Material D	4,000
Total	$66,000

Entry:		
Materials	66,000	
Prepaid Expenses	1,000	
Accounts Payable		67,000

(b) Materials requisitioned for use.

Summary of requisitions:

By Use

Job 1001	$12,000	
Job 1002	26,000	
Job 1003	22,000	$60,000
Factory Overhead		3,000
Total		$63,000

By Types

Material A	$27,000
Material B	18,000
Material C	15,000
Material D	3,000
Total	$63,000

Entry:		
Work in Process	60,000	
Factory Overhead	3,000	
Materials		63,000

(c) Factory labor used.

Summary of time tickets:

Job 1001	$60,000	
Job 1002	30,000	
Job 1003	10,000	$100,000
Factory Overhead		20,000
Total		$120,000

Entry: Work in Process	100,000	
Factory Overhead	20,000	
Wages Payable		120,000

(d) Other costs incurred.

Entry: Factory Overhead	56,000	
Selling Expenses	25,000	
General Expenses	10,000	
Accounts Payable		91,000

(e) Expiration of prepaid expenses.

Entry: Factory Overhead	1,000	
Selling Expenses	100	
General Expenses	100	
Prepaid Expenses		1,200

(f) Depreciation.

Entry: Factory Overhead	7,000	
Selling Expenses	200	
General Expenses	100	
Accumulated Depreciation—Plant Assets		7,300

(g) Application of factory overhead costs to jobs. The predetermined rate was 90% of direct labor cost.

Summary of factory overhead applied:

Job 1001 (90% of $60,000)	$54,000
Job 1002 (90% of $30,000)	27,000
Job 1003 (90% of $10,000)	9,000
Total	$90,000

Entry: Work in Process	90,000	
Factory Overhead		90,000

(h) Jobs completed.

Summary of completed job cost sheets:

Job 1001	$146,000
Job 1002	83,000
Total	$229,000

Entry: Finished Goods	229,000	
Work in Process		229,000

(i) Sales and cost of goods sold.

Summary of sales invoices and shipping orders:

	Sales Price	Cost Price
Product X	$ 19,600	$ 15,000
Product Y	165,100	125,000
Product Z	105,300	80,000
Total	$290,000	$220,000

		Debit	Credit
Entry:	Accounts Receivable	290,000	
	Sales		290,000
Entry:	Cost of Goods Sold	220,000	
	Finished Goods		220,000

(j) Cash received.

		Debit	Credit
Entry:	Cash	300,000	
	Accounts Receivable		300,000

(k) Cash disbursed.

		Debit	Credit
Entry:	Accounts Payable	190,000	
	Wages Payable	125,000	
	Cash		315,000

The flow of costs through the manufacturing accounts, together with summary details of the subsidiary ledgers, is illustrated below. Entries in the accounts are identified by letters to facilitate comparisons with the foregoing summary journal entries.

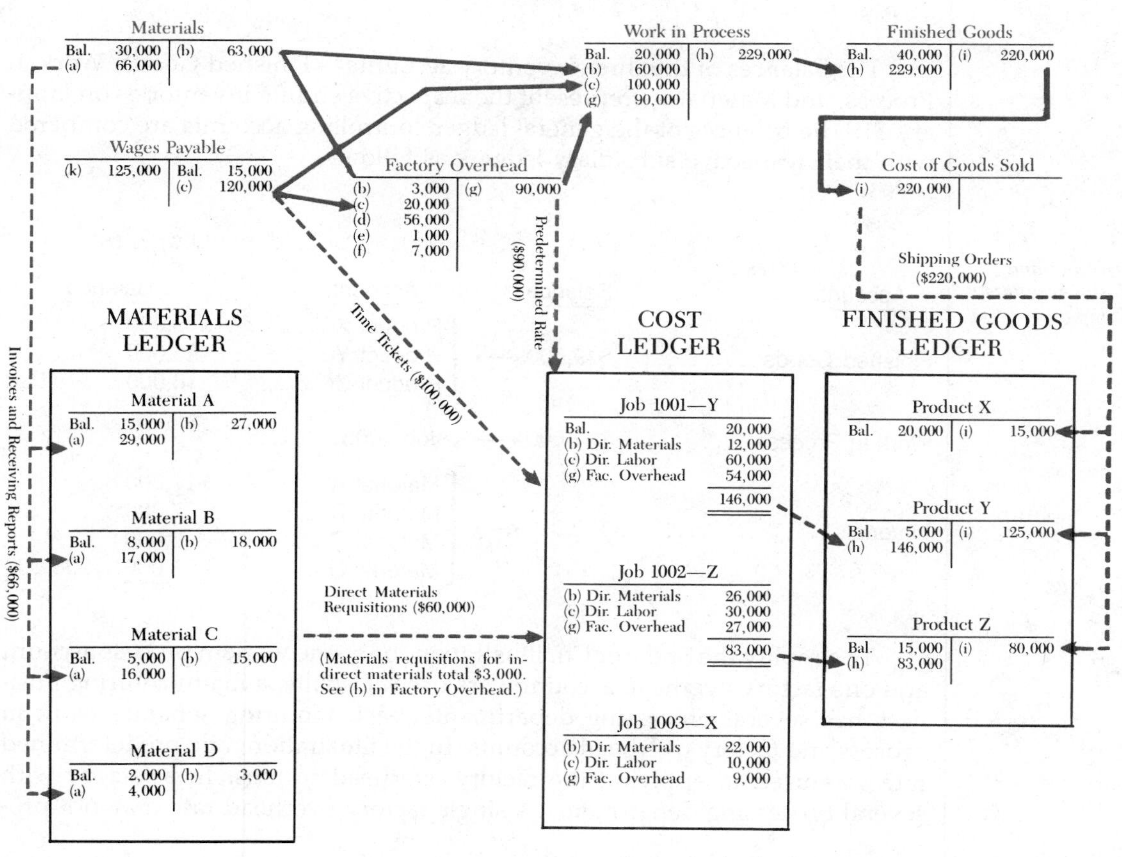

Flow of Costs Through Job Order Cost Accounts

The trial balance taken from the general ledger of Spencer Co. on January 31 is as follows:

Spencer Co.
Trial Balance
January 31, 19--

Account	Debit	Credit
Cash	70,000	
Accounts Receivable	63,000	
Finished Goods	49,000	
Work in Process	41,000	
Materials	33,000	
Prepaid Expenses	1,800	
Plant Assets	850,000	
Accumulated Depreciation—Plant Assets		480,300
Accounts Payable		38,000
Wages Payable		10,000
Common Stock		500,000
Retained Earnings		42,000
Sales		290,000
Cost of Goods Sold	220,000	
Factory Overhead		3,000
Selling Expenses	25,300	
General Expenses	10,200	
	1,363,300	1,363,300

The balances of the three inventory accounts—Finished Goods, Work in Process, and Materials—represent the respective ending inventories on January 31. The balances of the general ledger controlling accounts are compared with their respective subsidiary ledgers as follows:

Controlling and Subsidiary Accounts Compared

Controlling Accounts: Account	Balance		Subsidiary Ledgers: Account	Balance	
Finished Goods	$49,000	⟷	Product X	$ 5,000	
			Product Y	26,000	
			Product Z	18,000	$49,000
Work in Process	$41,000	⟷	Job 1003		$41,000
Materials	$33,000	⟷	Material A	$17,000	
			Material B	7,000	
			Material C	6,000	
			Material D	3,000	$33,000

To simplify the Spencer Co. illustration, only one work in process account and one factory overhead account were used. Usually, a manufacturing business has several processing departments, each requiring separate work in process and factory overhead accounts. In the illustration, one predetermined rate was used in applying the factory overhead to jobs. In a factory with several processing departments, a single factory overhead rate may not provide accurate product costs and effective cost control. A single rate for the entire factory cannot take into consideration such factors as differences among departments in the nature of their operations and in amounts of factory overhead incurred. In such cases, each factory department should have a separate factory overhead rate. For example, in a factory with twenty distinct operating departments, one department might have an overhead rate of 110% of direct labor cost, another a rate of $4 per direct labor hour, and another a rate of $3.50 per machine hour.

The following financial statements are based on the data for Spencer Co. It should be noted that the overapplied factory overhead on January 31 is reported on the balance sheet as a deferred item. It should also be noted that a separate statement of cost of goods manufactured, as illustrated in Chapter 15, is not shown. Under a perpetual inventory cost accounting system, the balances of the cost of goods sold, materials, work in process, and finished goods accounts are kept up to date. Hence, the finished goods ledger will indicate the costs of manufacturing the various products during the period. Likewise, the cost ledger will indicate the costs assigned to jobs still in process. The balance of the cost of goods sold account will indicate the cost of products sold during the period. The statement of cost of goods manufactured is normally prepared only for enterprises using periodic inventory procedures under a general accounting system.

Spencer Co.
Income Statement
For Month Ended January 31, 19--

Sales		$290,000
Cost of goods sold		220,000
Gross profit		$ 70,000
Operating expenses:		
Selling expenses	$25,300	
General expenses	10,200	
Total operating expenses		35,500
Income from operations		$ 34,500

Spencer Co.
Retained Earnings Statement
For Month Ended January 31, 19--

Retained earnings, January 1, 19--	$42,000
Income for the month	34,500
Retained earnings, January 31, 19--	$76,500

Spencer Co. Balance Sheet January 31, 19--			
Assets			
Current assets:			
Cash		$ 70,000	
Accounts receivable		63,000	
Inventories:			
Finished goods	$49,000		
Work in process	41,000		
Materials	33,000	123,000	
Prepaid expenses		1,800	
Total current assets			$257,800
Plant assets		$850,000	
Less accumulated depreciation		480,300	369,700
Total assets			$627,500
Liabilities			
Current liabilities:			
Accounts payable	$38,000		
Wages payable	10,000		
Total current liabilities		$ 48,000	
Deferred credits:			
Factory overhead		3,000	
Total liabilities			$ 51,000
Stockholders' Equity			
Common stock		$500,000	
Retained earnings		76,500	
Total stockholders' equity			576,500
Total liabilities and stockholders' equity			$627,500

Chapter Review

KEY POINTS

1. Usefulness of Product Costs.
Product costs are useful to managers for the preparation of financial statements. Product costs are also needed by management for a wide variety of decisions, such as setting long-term product prices. Without accurate product cost information, managers could not effectively or efficiently manage operations.

2. Types of Accounting Systems.
Two basic accounting systems may be used by manufacturers: general accounting systems and cost accounting systems. A general accounting system

uses periodic inventory procedures for materials, work in process, and finished goods inventories. For more complex manufacturing operations, a cost accounting system using perpetual inventory procedures is usually employed. A cost accounting system also uses controlling accounts and subsidiary ledgers for materials, work in process, and finished goods. The two main types of cost accounting systems for manufacturing operations are the job order cost and process cost systems.

3. Job Order Cost Systems.
A job order cost system provides for a separate record of the cost of each particular quantity of product that passes through the factory. The details concerning the costs incurred on each job order are accumulated in a subsidiary ledger known as the cost ledger. Each cost ledger account, called a job cost sheet, has spaces for recording all direct materials and direct labor chargeable to the job and for applying factory overhead at the predetermined rate. Work in Process is the controlling account for the cost ledger. As a job is finished, it is transferred to the finished goods ledger, for which Finished Goods is the controlling account.

KEY TERMS

general accounting system 607
cost accounting system 607
job order cost system 608
process cost system 608
purchase requisitions 609
purchase orders 609
receiving report 609
materials ledger 609
materials requisitions 610
time tickets 611
predetermined factory overhead rate 613
overapplied overhead 613
underapplied overhead 613
cost ledger 615
job cost sheet 615
finished goods ledger 617

SELF-EXAMINATION QUESTIONS

(Answers at End of Chapter)

1. The account maintained by a manufacturing business for inventory of goods in the process of manufacture is:
   A. Finished Goods
   B. Materials
   C. Work in Process
   D. None of the above

2. For a manufacturing business, finished goods inventory includes:
   A. direct materials costs
   B. direct labor costs
   C. factory overhead costs
   D. all of the above

3. An example of a factory overhead cost is:
   A. wages of factory assembly-line workers
   B. salaries for factory plant supervisors
   C. bearings for electric motors being manufactured
   D. all of the above

4. For which of the following would the job order cost system be appropriate?
   A. Antique furniture repair shop
   B. Rubber manufacturer
   C. Coal manufacturer
   D. All of the above

5. If the factory overhead account has a credit balance, factory overhead is said to be:
   A. underapplied C. underabsorbed
   B. overapplied D. none of the above

ILLUSTRATIVE PROBLEM

Shelton Signs Inc. specializes in the production of neon signs and uses a job order cost system. The following data summarize the operations related to product for November, the first month of operations:

(a) Materials purchased on account, $21,750.
(b) Materials requisitioned and factory labor used:

	Materials	Factory Labor
Job No. 1	$2,750	$1,700
Job No. 2	3,800	2,000
Job No. 3	2,990	1,450
Job No. 4	5,950	3,800
Job No. 5	3,250	1,900
Job No. 6	900	600
For general factory use	595	500

(c) Factory overhead costs incurred on account, $4,300.
(d) Depreciation of machinery, $1,450.
(e) The factory overhead rate is 60% of direct labor cost.
(f) Jobs completed: Nos. 1, 2, 4, and 5.
(g) Jobs Nos. 1, 2, and 4 were shipped and customers were billed for $7,900, $10,500, and $18,100, respectively.

Instructions:

1. Prepare entries to record the foregoing summarized operations.
2. Determine the account balances for Work in Process and Finished Goods.
3. Prepare a schedule of unfinished jobs to support the balance in the work in process account.
4. Prepare a schedule of completed jobs on hand to support the balance in the finished goods account.

SOLUTION

(1)

	Debit	Credit
(a) Materials	21,750	
Accounts Payable		21,750
(b) Work in Process	31,090	
Factory Overhead	1,095	
Materials		20,235
Wages Payable		11,950
(c) Factory Overhead	4,300	
Accounts Payable		4,300

	Debit	Credit
(d) Factory Overhead	1,450	
Accumulated Depreciation—Machinery		1,450
(e) Work in Process	6,870	
Factory Overhead (60% of $11,450)		6,870
(f) Finished Goods	30,790	
Work in Process		30,790

Computation of the cost of jobs finished:

Job	Direct Materials	Direct Labor	Overhead	Total
Job No. 1	$2,750	$1,700	$1,020	$ 5,470
Job No. 2	3,800	2,000	1,200	7,000
Job No. 4	5,950	3,800	2,280	12,030
Job No. 5	3,250	1,900	1,140	6,290
				$30,790

	Debit	Credit
(g) Accounts Receivable	36,500	
Sales		36,500
Cost of Goods Sold	24,500	
Finished Goods		24,500

Computation of the cost of jobs sold:

Job No. 1	$ 5,470
Job No. 2	7,000
Job No. 4	12,030
	$24,500

(2) Work in Process: $7,170 ($31,090 + $6,870 − $30,790)
Finished Goods: $6,290 ($30,790 − $24,500)

(3) Schedule of Unfinished Jobs

	Direct Materials	Direct Labor	Factory Overhead	Total
Job No. 3	$2,990	$1,450	$870	$5,310
Job No. 6	900	600	360	1,860
Balance of Work in Process, November 30				$7,170

(4) Schedule of Completed Jobs

Job No. 5: Direct materials	$3,250
Direct labor	1,900
Factory overhead	1,140
Balance of Finished Goods, November 30	$6,290

Discussion Questions

16–1. What are two important uses of product cost information by managers?

16–2. What are the two basic accounting systems commonly used by manufacturers?

16–3. (a) Name the two principal types of cost accounting systems. (b) Which system provides for a separate record of each particular quantity of product that passes through the factory? (c) Which system accumulates the costs for each department or process within the factory?

16–4. Distinguish between the purchase requisition and the purchase order used in the procurement of materials.

16–5. Briefly discuss how the purchase order, purchase invoice, and receiving report can be used to assist in controlling cash disbursements for materials acquired.

16–6. What document is the source for (a) debiting the accounts in the materials ledger, and (b) crediting the accounts in the materials ledger?

16–7. Briefly discuss how the accounts in the materials ledger can be used as an aid in maintaining appropriate inventory quantities of stock items.

16–8. How does use of the materials requisition help control the issuance of materials from the storeroom?

16–9. Discuss the major advantages of a perpetual inventory system over a periodic system for materials.

16–10. (a) Differentiate between the clock card and the time ticket. (b) Why should the total time reported on an employee's time tickets for a payroll period be compared with the time reported on the employee's clock cards for the same period?

16–11. Which of the following items are properly classified as part of factory overhead?

(a) factory supplies used
(b) interest expense
(c) amortization of factory patents
(d) property taxes on factory buildings
(e) sales commissions
(f) direct materials

16–12. Discuss how the predetermined factory overhead rate can be used in job order cost accounting to assist management in pricing jobs.

16–13. (a) How is a predetermined factory overhead rate calculated? (b) Name three common bases used in calculating the rate.

16–14. (a) What is (1) overapplied factory overhead and (2) underapplied factory overhead? (b) If the factory overhead account has a debit balance, was factory overhead underapplied or overapplied? (c) If the factory overhead account has a credit balance at the end of the first month of the fiscal year, where will the amount of this balance be reported on the interim balance sheet?

16–15. At the end of a fiscal year, there was a relatively minor balance in the factory overhead account. What is the simplest satisfactory procedure for the disposition of the balance in the account?

16–16. What name is given to the individual accounts in the cost ledger?

16–17. What document serves as the basis for posting to (a) the direct materials section of the job cost sheet, and (b) the direct labor section of the job cost sheet?

16–18. Describe the source of the data for debiting Work in Process for (a) direct materials, (b) direct labor, and (c) factory overhead.

16–19. What account is the controlling account for (a) the materials ledger, (b) the cost ledger, and (c) the finished goods ledger or stock ledger?

16–20. Real World Focus. Hewlett-Packard Company manufactures printed circuit boards in which a high volume of standardized units are fabricated, machined, assembled, and tested. Is the job order cost system appropriate in this situation?

Exercises

16–21. Cost of materials issuances by fifo and lifo methods. The balance of Material G on April 1 and the receipts and issuances during April are as follows:

Balance:	April 1	240 units at $40.00
Received:	April 6	600 units at $42.00
	14	480 units at $42.60
	26	360 units at $43.20
Issued:	April 7	360 units for Job 410
	17	300 units for Job 415
	28	420 units for Job 430

Determine the cost of each of the three issuances under a perpetual system, using (a) the first-in, first-out method and (b) the last-in, first-out method.

16–22. Entry for issuance of materials. The issuances of materials for the current month are as follows:

Requisition No.	Material	Job No.	Amount
841	F-10	1020	$5,140
842	H-60	1060	1,690
843	W-3	1035	3,860
844	A-16	General factory use	750
845	J-48	1018	4,320

Present the journal entry to record the issuances of materials.

16–23. Entry for factory labor costs. A summary of the time tickets for the current month follows:

Job No.	Amount	Job No.	Amount
673	$1,250	677	$ 800
674	8,100	Indirect labor	1,180
675	2,670	678	6,250
676	4,500	679	5,200

Present the journal entry to record the factory labor costs.

16–24. Factory overhead rates, entries, and account balance. Logan Company, which maintains departmental accounts for work in process and factory overhead, applies factory overhead to jobs on the basis of machine hours in Department 30 and on the basis of direct labor costs in Department 40. Estimated factory overhead costs, direct labor costs, and machine hours for January are as follows:

	Department 30	Department 40
Estimated factory overhead cost for year	$65,000	$243,600
Estimated direct labor costs for year		$580,000
Estimated machine hours for year	20,000	
Actual factory overhead costs for January	$ 6,050	$ 20,100
Actual direct labor costs for January		$ 48,500
Actual machine hours for January	1,800	

(a) Determine the factory overhead rate for Department 30. (b) Determine the factory overhead rate for Department 40. (c) Prepare the journal entries to apply factory overhead to production for January. (d) Determine the balances of the departmental factory overhead accounts as of January 31 and indicate whether the amounts represent overapplied or underapplied factory overhead.

16–25. Entry for jobs completed; cost of unfinished jobs. The following account appears in the ledger after only part of the postings have been completed for November:

Work in Process

Balance, November 1	17,150	
Direct Materials	43,100	
Direct Labor	67,500	
Factory Overhead	37,000	

Jobs finished during November are summarized as follows:

Job 1320............	$25,400	Job 1327............	$40,800
Job 1326............	45,600	Job 1330............	26,100

(a) Prepare the journal entry to record the jobs completed and (b) determine the cost of the unfinished jobs at November 30.

16–26. Entries for factory costs and jobs completed. Hill Enterprises Inc. began manufacturing operations on February 1. Jobs 201 and 202 were completed during the month, and all costs applicable to them were recorded on the related cost sheets. Jobs 203 and 204 are still in process at the end of the month, and all applicable costs except factory overhead have been recorded on the related cost sheets. In addition to the materials and labor charged directly to the jobs, $10,500 of indirect materials and $25,200 of indirect labor were used during the month. The cost sheets for the four jobs entering production during the month are as follows, in summary form:

Job 201		Job 202	
Direct materials............	15,750	Direct materials	28,200
Direct labor	12,600	Direct labor................	20,160
Factory overhead..........	7,560	Factory overhead...........	12,096
Total	35,910	Total......................	60,456

Job 203		Job 204	
Direct materials............	21,400	Direct materials	5,500
Direct labor	17,640	Direct labor................	7,800
Factory overhead..........		Factory overhead...........	

Prepare an entry to record each of the following operations for the month (one entry for each operation):

(a) Direct and indirect materials used.
(b) Direct and indirect labor used.
(c) Factory overhead applied (a single overhead rate is used, based on direct labor cost).
(d) Completion of Jobs 201 and 202.

Problems

16–27. Entries and schedules for unfinished and completed jobs. Logan Printing Company uses a job order cost system. The following data summarize the operations related to production for June, the first month of operations:

(a) Materials purchases on account, $110,160.
(b) Materials requisitioned and factory labor used:

	Materials	Factory Labor
Job 601	$15,840	$9,500
Job 602	10,380	7,040
Job 603	13,900	5,100
Job 604	20,950	13,380
Job 605	11,440	6,680
Job 606	7,100	2,900
For general factory use	2,300	1,760

(c) Factory overhead costs incurred on account, $21,200.
(d) Depreciation of machinery and equipment, $7,760.
(e) The factory overhead rate is 75% of direct labor cost.
(f) Jobs completed: 601, 602, 603, and 605.
(g) Jobs 601, 602, and 605 were shipped and customers were billed for $49,250, $31,100, and $31,280 respectively.

Instructions: (1) Prepare entries to record the foregoing summarized operations.
(2) Open T accounts for Work in Process and Finished Goods and post the appropriate entries, using the identifying letters as dates. Insert memorandum account balances as of the end of the month.
(3) Prepare a schedule of unfinished jobs to support the balance in the work in process account.
(4) Prepare a schedule of completed jobs on hand to support the balance in the finished goods account.

If the working papers correlating with the textbook are not used, omit Problem 16–28.

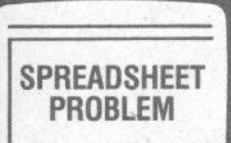

16–28. Job order cost sheet. Stein Furniture Company repairs, refinishes, and reupholsters furniture. A job order cost system was installed recently to facilitate (1) the determination of price quotations to prospective customers, (2) the determination of actual costs incurred on each job, and (3) cost reductions.

In response to a prospective customer's request for a price quotation on a job, the estimated cost data are inserted on an unnumbered job cost sheet. If the offer is accepted, a number is assigned to the job and the costs incurred are recorded in the usual manner on the job cost sheet. After the job is completed, reasons for the variances between the estimated and actual costs are noted on the sheet. The data are then available to management in evaluating the efficiency of operations and in preparing quotations on future jobs.

On June 10, an estimate of $665 for reupholstering a couch was given to Nancy Westbrook. The estimate was based on the following data:

Estimated direct materials:	
10 meters at $8.50 per meter	$ 85
Estimated direct labor:	
20 hours at $13 per hour	260
Estimated factory overhead (50% of direct labor cost)	130
Total estimated costs	$475
Markup (40% of production costs)	190
Total estimate	$665

On June 14, the couch was picked up from the residence of Nancy Westbrook, 2408 Bobolink Way, Tampa, with a commitment to return it on June 28.

The job was completed on June 24. The related materials requisitions and time tickets are summarized as follows:

Materials Requisition No.	Description	Amount
3480	10 meters at $8.50	$ 85
3492	2 meters at $8.50	17

Time Ticket No.	Description	Amount
H143	15 hours at $13	$195
H151	7 hours at $13	91

Instructions: (1) Complete that portion of the job order cost sheet that would be prepared when the estimate is given to the customer.

(2) Assign number R6-18 to the job, record the costs incurred, and complete the job order cost sheet. In commenting upon the variances between actual costs and estimated costs, assume that 2 meters of materials were spoiled, the factory overhead rate has been proved to be satisfactory, and an inexperienced employee performed the work.

16–29. Preparation of financial statements. The trial balance of F. R. Conrad Inc., at the beginning of the current fiscal year, is as follows:

F. R. Conrad Inc.
Trial Balance
May 1, 19--

Cash	46,300	
Accounts Receivable	70,260	
Finished Goods	66,500	
Work in Process	24,360	
Materials	32,200	
Prepaid Expenses	8,600	
Plant Assets	582,400	
Accumulated Depreciation—Plant Assets		330,500
Accounts Payable		23,700
Wages Payable		—
Common Stock		100,000
Retained Earnings		376,420
Sales		—
Cost of Goods Sold	—	
Factory Overhead	—	
Selling Expenses	—	
General Expenses	—	
	830,620	830,620

Transactions completed during May and adjustments required on May 31 are summarized as follows:

(a) Materials purchased on account		$27,480
(b) Materials requisitioned for factory use:		
Direct	$25,800	
Indirect	320	26,120
(c) Factory labor costs incurred:		
Direct	$12,960	
Indirect	1,840	14,800
(d) Other costs and expenses incurred on account:		
Factory overhead	$ 6,750	
Selling expenses	6,570	
General expenses	4,800	18,120

(e) Cash disbursed:		
Accounts payable	$49,200	
Wages payable	13,300	62,500
(f) Depreciation charged:		
Factory equipment	$ 4,320	
Office equipment	360	4,680
(g) Prepaid expenses expired:		
Chargeable to factory	$ 640	
Chargeable to selling expenses	150	
Chargeable to general expenses	140	930
(h) Applied factory overhead at a predetermined rate: 110% of direct labor cost.		
(i) Total cost of jobs completed		51,600
(j) Sales, all on account:		
Selling price		67,200
Cost		43,600
(k) Cash received on account		68,400

Instructions: (1) Open T accounts and record the initial balances indicated in the May 1 trial balance, identifying each as "Bal."

(2) Record the transactions directly in the accounts, using the identifying letters in place of dates.

(3) Prepare an income statement for the month ended May 31, 19--.

(4) Prepare a retained earnings statement for the month ended May 31, 19--.

(5) Prepare a balance sheet as of May 31, 19--.

16–30. Entries, trial balance, and financial statements. The trial balance of the general ledger of R. Staub Co. as of March 31, the end of the first month of the current fiscal year, is as follows:

R. Staub Co.
Trial Balance
March 31, 19--

Cash	92,000	
Accounts Receivable	185,300	
Finished Goods	187,600	
Work in Process	62,000	
Materials	72,900	
Plant Assets	810,000	
Accumulated Depreciation—Plant Assets		360,000
Accounts Payable		125,000
Wages Payable		15,000
Capital Stock		100,000
Retained Earnings		738,700
Sales		280,000
Cost of Goods Sold	168,000	
Factory Overhead	900	
Selling and General Expenses	40,000	
	1,618,700	1,618,700

As of the same date, balances in the accounts of selected subsidiary ledgers are as follows:

Finished goods ledger:
Commodity X, 2,000 units, $40,000; Commodity Y, 6,000 units, $90,000; Commodity Z, 3,200 units, $57,600.

Cost ledger:
Job 700, $62,000.

Materials ledger:
Material R15, $38,600; Material Z10, $31,600; Material W01, $2,700.

The transactions completed during April are summarized as follows:

(a) Materials were purchased on account as follows:

Material R15	$55,000
Material Z10	38,500
Material W01	1,500

(b) Materials were requisitioned from stores as follows:

Job 700, Material R15, $21,040; Material Z10, $16,800	$37,840
Job 701, Material R15, $27,000; Material Z10, $23,120	50,120
Job 702, Material R15, $13,800; Material Z10, $6,130	19,930
For general factory use, Material W01	1,600

(c) Time tickets for the month were chargeable as follows:

Job 700	$19,600	Job 702	$16,400
Job 701	16,800	Indirect labor	5,000

(d) Factory payroll checks for $59,400 were issued.
(e) Various factory overhead charges of $11,200 were incurred on account.
(f) Selling and general expenses of $38,200 were incurred on account.
(g) Payments on account were $140,000.
(h) Depreciation of $10,300 on factory plant and equipment was recorded.
(i) Factory overhead was applied to jobs at 60% of direct labor cost.
(j) Jobs completed during the month were as follows: Job 700 produced 6,400 units of Commodity X; Job 701 produced 5,000 units of Commodity Y.
(k) Total sales on account were $383,200. The goods sold were as follows (use first-in, first-out method): 4,600 units of Commodity X; 7,500 units of Commodity Y; 2,000 units of Commodity Z.
(l) Cash of $250,000 was received on accounts receivable.

Instructions: (1) Open T accounts for the general ledger, the finished goods ledger, the cost ledger, and the materials ledger. Record directly in these accounts the balances as of March 31, identifying them as "Bal." Record the quantities as well as the dollar amounts in the finished goods ledger.
(2) Prepare entries to record the April transactions. After recording each transaction, post to the T accounts, using the identifying letters as dates. When posting to the finished goods ledger, record quantities as well as dollar amounts.
(3) Prepare a trial balance.
(4) Prepare schedules of the account balances in the finished goods ledger, the cost ledger, and the materials ledger.
(5) Prepare an income statement for the two months ended April 30.

16–31. Determination of amounts missing from selected accounts in job cost system. Following are selected accounts for Watson Products. For the purposes of this problem, some of the debits and credits have been omitted.

Accounts Receivable

Oct. 1	Balance	47,600	Oct. 31	Collections	102,000
31	Sales	(A)			

Materials

Oct. 1	Balance	11,500	Oct. 31	Requisitions	(B)
31	Purchases	16,900			

Work in Process

Oct. 1	Balance	21,000	Oct. 31	Goods finished	(E)
31	Direct materials	(C)			
31	Direct labor	22,400			
31	Factory overhead	(D)			

Finished Goods

Oct. 1	Balance	38,900	Oct. 31	Cost of goods sold	(G)
31	Goods finished	(F)			

Factory Overhead

Oct. 1	Balance	120	Oct. 31	Applied (80% of direct labor cost)	(H)
1–31	Costs incurred	17,500			

Cost of Goods Sold

Oct. 31		(I)			

Sales

			Oct. 31		(J)

Selected balances at October 31:

Accounts receivable	$52,000
Finished goods	24,000
Work in process	17,800
Materials	9,500

Materials requisitions for October included $500 of materials issued for general factory use. All sales are made on account, terms n/30.

Instructions: (1) Determine the amounts represented by the letters (A) through (J), presenting your computations.

(2) Determine the amount of factory overhead overapplied or underapplied as of October 31.

ALTERNATE PROBLEMS

16–27A. Entries and schedules for unfinished and completed jobs. Owens Printing Company uses a job order cost system. The following data summarize the operations related to production for November, the first month of operations:

(a) Materials purchased on account, $57,420.

(b) Materials requisitioned and factory labor used:

	Materials	Factory Labor
Job 101	$11,600	$9,150
Job 102	3,400	1,960
Job 103	8,520	4,690
Job 104	4,280	1,900
Job 105	6,830	2,800
Job 106	6,180	4,610
For general factory use	1,310	3,000

(c) Factory overhead costs incurred on account, $11,300.

(d) Depreciation of machinery and equipment, $5,400.

(e) The factory overhead rate is 70% of direct labor cost.

(f) Jobs completed: 101, 102, 104, and 105.

(g) Jobs 101, 102, and 104 were shipped and customers were billed for $36,200, $8,400, and $10,350 respectively.

Instructions: (1) Prepare entries to record the foregoing summarized operations.

(2) Open T accounts for Work in Process and Finished Goods and post the appropriate entries, using the identifying letters as dates. Insert memorandum account balances as of the end of the month.

(3) Prepare a schedule of unfinished jobs to support the balance in the work in process account.

(4) Prepare a schedule of completed jobs on hand to support the balance in the finished goods account.

If the working papers correlating with the textbook are not used, omit Problem 16–28A.

16–28A. Job order cost sheet. Katz Furniture Company repairs, refinishes, and reupholsters furniture. A job order cost system was installed recently to facilitate (1) the determination of price quotations to prospective customers, (2) the determination of actual costs incurred on each job, and (3) cost reductions.

In response to a prospective customer's request for a price quotation on a job, the estimated cost data are inserted on an unnumbered job cost sheet. If the offer is accepted, a number is assigned to the job and the costs incurred are recorded in the usual manner on the job cost sheet. After the job is completed, reasons for the variances between the estimated and actual costs are noted on the sheet. The data are then available to management in evaluating the efficiency of operations and in preparing quotations on future jobs.

On February 6, an estimate of $360 for reupholstering a chair and couch was given to John Bergman. The estimate was based on the following data:

Estimated direct materials:	
12 meters at $10 per meter	$120
Estimated direct labor:	
8 hours at $15 per hour	120
Estimated factory overhead (40% of direct labor cost)	48
Total estimated costs	$288
Markup (25% of production costs)	72
Total estimate	$360

On February 10, the chair and couch were picked up from the residence of John Bergman, 1454 Spartan Lane, Des Moines, with a commitment to return it on February 21. The job was completed on February 19.

The related materials requisitions and time tickets are summarized as follows:

Materials Requisition No.	Description	Amount
U642	12 meters at $10	$120
U651	3 meters at $10	30

Time Ticket No.	Description	Amount
1519	6 hours at $15	$ 90
1520	3 hours at $15	45

Instructions: (1) Complete that portion of the job order cost sheet that would be prepared when the estimate is given to the customer.

(2) Assign number 89-10-1 to the job, record the costs incurred, and complete the job order cost sheet. In commenting upon the variances between actual costs and

estimated costs, assume that 3 meters of materials were spoiled, the factory overhead rate has been proved to be satisfactory, and an inexperienced employee performed the work.

16–30A. Entries, trial balance, and financial statements. The trial balance of the general ledger of Thurman Corporation as of January 31, the end of the first month of the current fiscal year, is shown as follows:

Thurman Corporation
Trial Balance
January 31, 19--

Account	Debit	Credit
Cash	54,840	
Accounts Receivable	111,180	
Finished Goods	106,800	
Work in Process	36,840	
Materials	44,340	
Plant Assets	474,600	
Accumulated Depreciation—Plant Assets		211,740
Accounts Payable		79,780
Wages Payable		9,000
Capital Stock		200,000
Retained Earnings		311,700
Sales		160,980
Cost of Goods Sold	120,000	
Factory Overhead	1,200	
Selling and General Expenses	23,400	
	973,200	973,200

As of the same date, balances in the accounts of selected subsidiary ledgers are as follows:

Finished goods ledger:
Commodity E, 3,500 units, $42,000; Commodity F, 1,800 units, $27,000; Commodity G, 1,400 units, $37,800.
Cost ledger:
Job 580, $36,840.
Materials ledger:
Material M, $17,700; Material N, $22,140; Material O, $4,500.

The transactions completed during February are summarized as follows:

(a) Materials were purchased on account as follows:

Material M	$33,000
Material N	23,100
Material O	900

(b) Materials were requisitioned from stores as follows:

Job 580, Material M, $16,200; Material N, $14,178	$30,378
Job 581, Material M, $8,280; Material N, $3,324	11,604
Job 582, Material M, $12,720; Material N, $10,118	22,838
For general factory use, Material O	960

(c) Time tickets for the month were chargeable as follows:

Job 580	$11,760	Job 582	$9,840
Job 581	10,080	Indirect labor	3,600

(d) Factory payroll checks for $38,640 were issued.
(e) Various factory overhead charges of $13,425 were incurred on account.
(f) Depreciation of $5,400 on factory plant and equipment was recorded.
(g) Factory overhead was applied to jobs at 70% of direct labor cost.
(h) Jobs completed during the month were as follows: Job 580 produced 5,700 units of Commodity F; Job 582 produced 1,460 units of Commodity G.
(i) Selling and general expenses of $22,920 were incurred on account.
(j) Payments on account were $85,800.
(k) Total sales on account were $167,800. The goods sold were as follows (use first-in, first-out method): 1,500 units of Commodity E; 3,200 units of Commodity F; 1,600 units of Commodity G.
(l) Cash of $150,600 was received on accounts receivable.

Instructions: (1) Open T accounts for the general ledger, the finished goods ledger, the cost ledger, and the materials ledger. Record directly in these accounts the balances as of January 31, identifying them as "Bal." Record the quantities as well as the dollar amounts in the finished goods ledger.
(2) Prepare entries to record the February transactions. After recording each transaction, post to the T accounts, using the identifying letters as dates. When posting to the finished goods ledger, record quantities as well as dollar amounts.
(3) Prepare a trial balance.
(4) Prepare schedules of the account balances in the finished goods ledger, the cost ledger, and the materials ledger.
(5) Prepare an income statement for the two months ended February 28.

16–31A. Determination of amounts missing from selected accounts in job cost system. Following are selected accounts for Nowell Products. For the purposes of this problem, some of the debits and credits have been omitted.

Accounts Receivable

Mar.	1	Balance	81,600	Mar. 31	Collections	120,500
	31	Sales	(A)			

Materials

Mar.	1	Balance	21,000	Mar. 31	Requisitions	(B)
	31	Purchases	41,500			

Work in Process

Mar.	1	Balance	24,000	Mar. 31	Goods finished	(E)
	31	Direct materials	(C)			
	31	Direct labor	48,200			
	31	Factory overhead	(D)			

Finished Goods

Mar.	1	Balance	12,800	Mar. 31	Cost of goods sold	(G)
	31	Goods finished	(F)			

Factory Overhead

Mar.	1	Balance	300	Mar. 31	Applied (60% of direct labor cost)	(H)
	1–31	Costs incurred	28,800			

Cost of Goods Sold

Mar. 31	(I)		

Sales

		Mar. 31	(J)

Selected balances at March 31:

Accounts receivable	$78,750
Finished goods	22,000
Work in process	27,300
Materials	15,000

Materials requisitions for March included $1,300 of materials issued for general factory use. All sales are made on account, terms n/30.

Instructions: (1) Determine the amounts represented by the letters (A) through (J), presenting your computations.

(2) Determine the amount of factory overhead overapplied or underapplied as of March 31.

Mini-Case 16

As an assistant cost accountant for Atkinson Industries, you have been assigned to review the activity base for the predetermined factory overhead rate. The president, J. C. Atkinson, has expressed concern that the over- or underapplied overhead has fluctuated excessively over the years.

An analysis of the company's operations and use of the current overhead base (direct materials usage) have narrowed the possible alternative overhead bases to direct labor cost and machine hours. For the past five years, the following data have been gathered:

	1990	1989	1988	1987	1986
Actual overhead	$ 840,000	$ 820,000	$ 900,000	$ 735,000	$ 705,000
Applied overhead	812,000	847,500	921,000	750,000	656,000
(Over) underapplied overhead	$ 28,000	$ (27,500)	$ (21,000)	$ (15,000)	$ 49,000
Direct labor cost	$3,350,000	$3,300,000	$3,625,000	$2,925,000	$2,800,000
Machine hours	663,000	645,000	726,000	597,000	569,000

Instructions:

(1) Calculate a predetermined factory overhead rate for each alternative base, assuming that the rates would have been determined by relating the amount of factory overhead for the past five years to the base.
(2) For each of the past five years, determine the over- or underapplied overhead, based on the two predetermined overhead rates developed in (1).
(3) Which predetermined overhead rate would you recommend? Discuss the basis for your recommendation.

Answers to Self-Examination Questions

1. C Three inventory accounts are maintained by manufacturing businesses for (1) goods in the process of manufacture (Work in Process—answer C), (2) goods in the state in which they are to be sold (Finished Goods—answer A), and (3) goods in the state in which they were acquired (Materials—answer B).

2. D The finished goods inventory is composed of three categories of manufacturing costs: direct materials (answer A), direct labor (answer B), and factory overhead (answer C).

3. B Factory overhead includes all manufacturing costs, except direct materials and direct labor. Salaries of plant supervisors (answer B) is an example of a factory overhead item. Wages of factory assembly-line workers (answer A) is a direct labor item, and bearings for electric motors (answer C) are direct materials.

4. A Job order cost systems are best suited to businesses manufacturing for special orders from customers, such as would be the case for a repair shop for antique furniture (answer A). A process cost system is best suited for manufacturers of homogeneous units of product, such as rubber (answer B) and coal (answer C).

5. B If the amount of factory overhead applied during a particular period exceeds the actual overhead costs, the factory overhead account will have a credit balance and is said to be overapplied (answer B) or overabsorbed. If the amount applied is less than the actual costs, the account will have a debit balance and is said to be underapplied (answer A) or underabsorbed (answer C).

17
Process Cost Systems

CHAPTER OBJECTIVES

Distinguish process cost accounting systems from job order cost accounting systems.

Describe and illustrate the basic concepts for a process cost accounting system.

Describe and illustrate the preparation and the use of a cost of production report.

Describe and illustrate the accounting for joint products.

Describe and illustrate the accounting for by-products.

Describe and illustrate the use of the average cost method of inventory costing for process cost accounting systems.

In many industries, job orders as described in Chapter 16 are not suitable for scheduling production and accumulating the manufacturing costs. Companies manufacturing cement, flour, or paint, for example, do so on a continuous basis. The principal product is a homogeneous mass rather than a collection of distinct units. No useful purpose would be served by maintaining job orders for particular amounts of a product as the material passes through the several stages of production.

PROCESS COST AND JOB ORDER COST SYSTEMS DISTINGUISHED

Many of the methods, procedures, and managerial applications presented in the preceding chapter in the discussion of job order cost systems apply equally to process cost systems. For example, perpetual inventory accounts with subsidiary ledgers for materials, work in process, and finished goods are requisites of both systems. In job order cost accounting, however, the costs of direct materials, direct labor, and factory overhead are charged directly to job orders. In process cost accounting, the costs are charged to processing departments, and the cost of a finished unit is determined by dividing the total cost incurred in each process among the number of units produced. Since all goods produced in a department are identical units, it is not necessary to classify production into job orders.

In factories with departmentalized operations, costs are accumulated in factory overhead and work in process accounts maintained for each department. If there is only one processing department in a factory, the cost accounting procedures are simple. The manufacturing cost elements are charged to the single work in process account, and the unit cost of the finished product is determined by dividing the total cost by the number of units produced.

When the manufacturing procedure requires a sequence of different processes, the output of Process 1 becomes the direct materials of Process 2, the output of Process 2 becomes the direct materials of Process 3, and so on until the finished product emerges. Additional direct materials requisitioned from stores may also be introduced during subsequent processes.

A work in process account for Haworth Manufacturing Company, which is departmentalized, is illustrated as follows. In this illustration, the total cost of $96,000 is divided by the output, 10,000 units, to obtain a unit cost of $9.60.

Work in Process—Assembly Department

Direct materials	32,000	To Sanding Dept., 10,000 units	96,000
Direct labor	40,000	Cost per unit:	
Factory overhead	24,000	$96,000 ÷ 10,000 = $9.60	
	96,000		96,000

A New Way To Build Cars

One of the major industries that uses process cost accounting is the automobile manufacturing industry. Typically, cars are built as they move along an assembly line that provides little flexibility for the installation of the many options common to today's vehicles. Therefore, automakers are turning to modern technology in modifying the traditional assembly line. For example, in two new assembly plants in Kansas City, Kansas, and Doraville, Georgia, General Motors Corporation is using hundreds of motorized, unmanned carriers to move cars through the assembly process. The effect of using these carriers, called automated guided vehicles, in the production of cars is described in the following excerpts from an article in the *New York Times*:

When Henry Ford perfected the assembly line, he was making only one type of car, the Model T, which came in just one color, black. Since then, options have proliferated and today there can be as much as a 30 percent difference in the content of a stripped-down model and one fully loaded.

Because current lines move at a constant speed, regardless of the model mix, plant managers have had to hire enough workers to build the most complex car in the assigned amount of time. This means that some people are idle when base models come down the line. And because stopping the line to fix something would idle thousands, most workers only tag an incorrectly fitting part and hope it will be repaired at the end of the line.

With the carriers, the notion of a "line" begins to fade, although the vehicles generally follow a prescribed path, receiving their instructions from wires buried in the plant floor. If a particular car has a heavy load of options, though, the vehicle may be directed to move out of the main [path] to have those parts installed, while less heavily equipped models continue along the route. G.M. engineers call this "decoupling the line." With this flexibility, plant managers will be able to balance the work force more closely with the workload. . . .

The carriers also fit into the modular assembly concept that G.M. officials have called one of the keys to cutting manufacturing costs in its Saturn program. Instead of installing thousands of parts, one by one, on a car, a whole module, such as an instrument panel, will be built off the line, tested and only installed if it passes the tests. Since a carrier can be programmed to stop and go as needed, it could roll to the completed instrument panels and then stop to ease the installation. . . .

"We couldn't have done this a few years ago," said David D. Campbell, the director of operations for G.M.'s Chevrolet-Pontiac-Canada group. "We need computers that can keep track of hundreds of carriers and decide on a minute-by-minute basis what station to assign them to, based on variations in the model mix."

Source: John Holusha, "A New Way to Build Cars," *The New York Times,* March 13, 1986.

SERVICE DEPARTMENTS AND PROCESS COSTS

In a factory with several processes, there may be one or more **service departments** that do not process the materials directly. Examples of service departments are the factory office, the power plant, and the maintenance and repair shop. These departments perform services for the benefit of other production departments. The costs that they incur, therefore, are part of the total manufacturing costs and must be charged to the processing departments.

The services performed by a service department give rise to internal transactions with the processing departments benefited. These internal transactions are recorded periodically in order to charge the factory overhead accounts of the processing departments with their share of the costs incurred by the service departments. The period usually chosen is a month, although a different period of time may be used. To illustrate, assume that the Power Department of Haworth Manufacturing Company produced 600 000 kilowatt-hours (kwh) during the month at a total cost of $30,000, or 5¢ per kilowatt-hour ($30,000 ÷ 600 000). The factory overhead accounts for the departments that used the power are accordingly charged for power at the 5¢ rate. Assuming that during the month the Assembly Department used 100 000 kwh, the Sanding Department used 300 000 kwh, and the Polishing Department used 200 000 kwh, the accounts affected by the interdepartmental transfer of cost would appear as follows:

Service Department Costs Charged to Processing Departments

Power Department

Fuel	12,000	To Factory Overhead—Assembly Dept.	5,000
Wages	8,500	To Factory Overhead—Sanding Dept.	15,000
Depreciation	3,000	To Factory Overhead—Polishing Dept.	10,000
Maintenance	2,500		
Insurance	2,000		
Taxes	1,500		
Miscellaneous	500		
	30,000		30,000

Factory Overhead—Assembly Dept.

Power	5,000	

Factory Overhead—Sanding Dept.

Power	15,000	

Factory Overhead—Polishing Dept.

Power	10,000	

Some service departments render services to other service departments. For example, the power department may supply electric current to light the factory office and to operate data processing equipment. At the same time, the factory office provides general supervision for the power department, maintains its payroll records, buys its fuel, and so on. In such cases, the costs of the department rendering the greatest service to other service departments may be distributed first, despite the fact that it receives benefits from other service departments.

PROCESSING COSTS

The accumulated costs transferred from preceding departments and the costs of direct materials and direct labor incurred in each processing department are debited to the related work in process account. Each work in process account is also debited for the factory overhead applied. The costs incurred are summarized periodically, usually at the end of the month. The costs related to the output of each department during the month are then transferred to the next processing department or to Finished Goods, as the case may be. This flow of costs through a work in process account is illustrated as follows:

Work in Process—Sanding Department

10,000 units at $9.60			To Polishing Dept., 10,000 units	160,000
from Assembly Dept.		96,000	Cost per unit:	
Direct labor	36,800		$160,000 ÷ 10,000 = $16	
Factory overhead	27,200	64,000		
		160,000		160,000

The three debits in the preceding account may be grouped into two separate categories: (1) direct materials or partially processed materials received from another department, which in this case is composed of 10,000 units received from the Assembly Department, with a total cost of $96,000, and (2) direct labor and factory overhead applied in the Sanding Department, which in this case totaled $64,000. This second group of costs, as described in Chapter 15, is called the **conversion cost.**

Again referring to the illustration, all of the 10,000 units were completely processed in the Sanding Department and were passed on to the Polishing Department. The $16 unit cost of the product transferred to the Polishing Department is made up of Assembly Department cost of $9.60 ($96,000 ÷ 10,000 units) and conversion cost of $6.40 ($64,000 ÷ 10,000 units) incurred in the Sanding Department.

INVENTORIES OF PARTIALLY PROCESSED MATERIALS

In the preceding illustration, all materials entering a process were completely processed at the end of the accounting period. In such a case, the determination of unit costs is quite simple. The total of the costs transferred from other departments, the direct materials, the direct labor, and the factory overhead charged to a department is divided by the number of units completed and passed on to the next department or to finished goods. Often, however, some partially processed materials remain in various stages of production in a department at the end of a period. In this case, the costs in work in process must be allocated between the units that have been completed and transferred to the next process or to finished goods and those that are only partially completed and remain within the department.

Flow of Manufacturing Costs

To allocate direct materials and transferred costs between the output completed and transferred to the next process and inventory of goods within the department, it is necessary to determine the manner in which materials are placed in production and flow through the production processes. For some products, materials may be added to production in about the same proportion as conversion costs are incurred. In still other situations, materials may enter the process at relatively few points, which may or may not be evenly spaced throughout the process. For most manufacturing processes, however, the materials are on hand when production begins, and they move through the production processes in a first-in, first-out flow; that is, the first units entering the production process are the first to be completed. Therefore, the following discussion and illustrations will assume a normal production process, whereby all materials are placed into the process in a fifo (first-in, first-out) order. The manufacturing costs associated with such a process will also be allocated by the fifo cost method. Later in the chapter, an alternate method—the average cost method—will be discussed.

Equivalent Units of Production

To allocate processing costs between the output completed and transferred to the next process and the inventory of goods within the process, it is necessary to determine the number of *equivalent units* of production during the period. The **equivalent units of production** are the number of units that could have been manufactured from start to finish during the period. To illustrate, assume that there is no inventory of goods in process in a certain processing department at the beginning of the period, that 1,000 units of materials enter the process during the period, and that at the end of the period all of the units are 75% completed. The equivalent production in the processing department for the period would be 750 units (75% of 1,000).

Usually there is an inventory of partially processed units in the department at the beginning of a period. These units are normally completed during the period and transferred to the next department along with units started and completed in the current period. Other units started in the period are only partially processed and thus make up the ending inventory. To illustrate the computation of equivalent units under such circumstances, the following data are assumed for the Polishing Department of Haworth Manufacturing Company:

Inventory within Polishing Department on March 1.......	600 units, 1/3 completed
Completed in Polishing Department and transferred to finished goods during March	9,800 units, completed
Inventory within Polishing Department on March 31......	800 units, 2/5 completed

The equivalent units of production are determined as follows:

Determination of Equivalent Units of Production

To process units in inventory on March 1.........	600 units × 2/3	400
To process units started and completed in March.....	9,800 units − 600 units	9,200
To process units in inventory on March 31........	800 units × 2/5.........	320
Equivalent units of production in March..........		9,920

The 9,920 equivalent units of production represent the number of units that would have been produced if there had been no inventories within the process either at the beginning or at the end of the period.

Continuing with the illustration, the next step is to allocate the costs incurred in the Polishing Department between the units completed during March and those remaining in process at the end of the month. If all materials were introduced at the beginning of the process, the full materials cost per unit must be assigned to the uncompleted units. The conversion costs would then be allocated to the finished and the uncompleted units on the basis of equivalent units of production, as shown in the following account:

ACCOUNT WORK IN PROCESS—POLISHING DEPARTMENT ACCOUNT NO.

Date		Item	Debit	Credit	Balance Debit	Balance Credit
Mar.	1	Bal., 600 units, ⅓ completed			10,200	
	31	Sanding Dept., 10,000 units at $16	160,000		170,200	
	31	Direct labor	26,640		196,840	
	31	Factory overhead	18,000		214,840	
	31	Goods finished, 9,800 units		200,600		
	31	Bal., 800 units, ⅖ completed			14,240	

The conversion costs incurred in the Polishing Department during March total $44,640 ($26,640 + $18,000). The equivalent units of production for March, determined above, is 9,920. The conversion cost per equivalent unit is therefore $4.50 ($44,640 ÷ 9,920). Of the $214,840 debited to the Polishing Department, $200,600 was transferred to Finished Goods and $14,240 remained in the account as work in process inventory. The computation of the allocations to finished goods and to inventory is as follows:

Allocation of Departmental Charges to Finished Goods and Inventory

Goods Finished During March

600 units:	Inventory on March 1, 1/3 completed	$ 10,200	
	Conversion cost in March:		
	600 × 2/3, or 400 units at $4.50	1,800	
	Total..		$ 12,000
	(Unit cost: $12,000 ÷ 600 = $20)		
9,200 units:	Materials cost in March, at $16 per unit	$147,200	
	Conversion cost in March:		
	9,200 at $4.50 per unit	41,400	
	Total..		188,600
	(Unit cost: $188,600 ÷ 9,200 = $20.50)		
9,800 units:	Goods finished during March		$200,600

Polishing Department Inventory on March 31

800 units:	Materials cost in March, at $16 per unit	$ 12,800	
	Conversion cost in March:		
	800 × 2/5, or 320 at $4.50	1,440	
800 units:	Polishing Department inventory on March 31...		$ 14,240

COST OF PRODUCTION REPORT

A report prepared periodically for each processing department summarizes (1) the units for which the department is accountable and the disposition of these units, and (2) the costs charged to the department and the allocation of these costs. This report, termed the **cost of production report,** may be used as the source of the computation of unit production costs and the allocation of the processing costs in the general ledger to the finished and the uncompleted units. More importantly, the report is used to control costs. Each department head is held responsible for the units entering production and the costs incurred in the department. Any differences in unit product costs from one month to another are studied carefully and the causes of significant differences are determined.

The cost of production report based on the data presented in the preceding section for the Polishing Department of Haworth Manufacturing Company is shown below.

Haworth Manufacturing Company
Cost of Production Report—Polishing Department
For the Month Ended March 31, 19--

Quantities:		
Charged to production:		
In process, March 1		600
Received from Sanding Department		10,000
Total units to be accounted for		10,600
Units accounted for:		
Transferred to finished goods		9,800
In process, March 31		800
Total units accounted for		10,600
Costs:		
Charged to production:		
In process, March 1		$ 10,200
March costs:		
Direct materials from Sanding Department ($16 per unit)		160,000
Conversion costs:		
Direct labor	$ 26,640	
Factory overhead	18,000	
Total conversion costs ($4.50 per unit)		44,640
Total costs to be accounted for		$214,840
Costs allocated as follows:		
Transferred to finished goods:		
600 units at $20	$ 12,000	
9,200 units at $20.50	188,600	
Total cost of finished goods		$200,600
In process, March 31:		
Direct materials (800 units at $16)	$ 12,800	
Conversion costs (800 units × 2/5 × $4.50)	1,440	
Total cost of inventory in process, March 31		14,240
Total costs accounted for		$214,840
Computations:		
Equivalent units of production:		
To process units in inventory on March 1:		
600 units × 2/3		400
To process units started and completed in March:		
9,800 units − 600 units		9,200
To process units in inventory on March 31:		
800 units × 2/5		320
Equivalent units of production		9,920
Unit conversion cost:		
$44,640 ÷ 9,920		$ 4.50

JOINT PRODUCTS AND BY-PRODUCTS

In some manufacturing processes, more than one product is produced. In processing cattle, for example, the meat packer produces dressed beef, hides, and other products. In processing logs, the lumber mill produces several grades of lumber in addition to scraps and sawdust. When the output of a manufacturing process consists of two or more different products, the products may be joint products, or one or more of the products may be a by-product.

When two or more goods of significant value are produced from a single principal direct material, the products are termed **joint products.** Similarly, the costs incurred in the manufacture of joint products are called **joint costs.** Common examples of joint products are gasoline, naphtha, kerosene, paraffin, benzine, and other related goods, all of which come from the processing of crude oil.

If one of the products resulting from a process has little value in relation to the main product or joint products, it is known as a **by-product.** The emergence of a by-product is only incidental to the manufacture of the main product or joint products. By-products may be leftover materials, such as sawdust and scraps of wood in a lumber mill, or they may be separated from the material at the beginning of production, as in the case of cottonseed from raw cotton.

Accounting for Joint Products

In management decisions concerning the production and sale of joint products, only the relationship of the total revenue to be derived from the entire group to their total production cost is relevant. Nothing is to be gained from an allocation of joint costs to each product because one product cannot be produced without the others. A decision to produce a single joint product is in effect a decision to produce all of the joint products.

Since joint products come from the processing of a common parent material, the assignment of cost to each separate product cannot be based on actual expenditures. It is impossible to determine the amount of cost incurred in the manufacture of each separate product. However, for purposes of inventory valuation, it is necessary to allocate joint costs among the joint products.

One method of allocation commonly used is the **market (sales) value method.** Its main feature is the assignment of costs to the different products according to their relative sales values. To illustrate, assume that 10,000 units of Product X and 50,000 units of Product Y were produced at a total cost of $63,000. The sales values of the two products and the allocation of the joint costs are as follows:

Allocation of Joint Costs

Joint Costs	Joint Product	Units Produced	Sales Value per Unit	Total Sales Value
$63,000	X	10,000	$3.00	$30,000
	Y	50,000	1.20	60,000
Total sales value				$90,000

Allocation of joint costs:

X: $\frac{\$30,000}{\$90,000} \times \$63,000$ $21,000

Y: $\frac{\$60,000}{\$90,000} \times \$63,000$ 42,000

Unit cost:

X: $21,000 ÷ 10,000 units $2.10

Y: $42,000 ÷ 50,000 units .... .84

Accounting for By-Products

The amount of manufacturing cost usually assigned to a by-product is the sales value of the by-product reduced by any additional costs necessary to complete and sell it. The amount of cost thus determined is removed from the proper work in process account and transferred to a finished goods inventory account. To illustrate, assume that for a certain period the costs accumulated in Department 4 total $24,400, and during the same period of time, 1,000 units of by-product B emerge from the processing in Department 4. If the estimated value of the by-product is $200, after estimated completion and selling costs have been deducted, Finished Goods—Product B would be debited for $200 and Work in Process—Department 4 would be credited for the same amount, as illustrated in the following accounts:

Work in Process—Department 4	
24,400	200

Finished Goods—Product B	
200	

ILLUSTRATION OF PROCESS COST ACCOUNTING

To illustrate further the basic procedures of the process costing system, assume that Conway Company manufactures Product A. The manufacturing activity begins in Department 1, where all materials enter production. The materials remain in Department 1 for a relatively short time, and there is usually no inventory of work in process in that department at the end of the accounting period. From Department 1, the materials are transferred to Department 2. In Department 2, there are usually inventories at the end of the accounting period. Separate factory overhead accounts are maintained for Departments 1 and 2. Factory overhead is applied at 80% and 50% of direct labor cost for Departments 1 and 2 respectively. There are two service departments, Maintenance and Power. All inventories are costed by the first-in, first-out method.

The trial balance of the general ledger on January 1, the first day of the fiscal year, is as follows:

Conway Company
Trial Balance
January 1, 19--

Cash	39,400	
Accounts Receivable	45,000	
Finished Goods—Product A (1,000 units at $36.50)	36,500	
Work in Process—Department 2 (800 units, 1/2 completed)	24,600	
Materials	32,000	
Prepaid Expenses	6,150	
Plant Assets	510,000	
Accumulated Depreciation—Plant Assets		295,000
Accounts Payable		51,180
Wages Payable		3,400
Common Stock		250,000
Retained Earnings		94,070
	693,650	693,650

To reduce the illustrative entries to a manageable number and to avoid repetition, the transactions and the adjustments for January are stated as summaries. In practice, the transactions would be recorded from day to day in various journals. The descriptions of the transactions, followed in each case by the entry, are as follows:

(a) Materials purchased and prepaid expenses incurred.

Entry:	Materials	80,500	
	Prepaid Expenses	3,300	
	Accounts Payable		83,800

(b) Materials requisitioned for use.

Entry:	Maintenance Department	1,200	
	Power Department	6,000	
	Factory Overhead—Department 1	3,720	
	Factory Overhead—Department 2	2,700	
	Work in Process—Department 1	58,500	
	Materials		72,120

(c) Factory labor used.

Entry:	Maintenance Department	3,600	
	Power Department	4,500	
	Factory Overhead—Department 1	2,850	
	Factory Overhead—Department 2	2,100	
	Work in Process—Department 1	24,900	
	Work in Process—Department 2	37,800	
	Wages Payable		75,750

(d) Other costs incurred.

Entry:	Maintenance Department	600	
	Power Department	900	
	Factory Overhead—Department 1	1,800	
	Factory Overhead—Department 2	1,200	
	Selling Expenses	15,000	
	General Expenses	13,500	
	Accounts Payable		33,000

(e) Expiration of prepaid expenses.

Entry:		
Maintenance Department	300	
Power Department	750	
Factory Overhead—Department 1	1,350	
Factory Overhead—Department 2	1,050	
Selling Expenses	900	
General Expenses	600	
Prepaid Expenses		4,950

(f) Depreciation.

Entry:		
Maintenance Department	300	
Power Department	1,050	
Factory Overhead—Department 1	1,800	
Factory Overhead—Department 2	2,700	
Selling Expenses	600	
General Expenses	300	
Accumulated Depreciation—Plant Assets		6,750

(g) Distribution of Maintenance Department costs.

The portion of services rendered was 5%, 45%, and 50% for the Power Department, Department 1, and Department 2, respectively.

Entry:		
Power Department	300	
Factory Overhead—Department 1	2,700	
Factory Overhead—Department 2	3,000	
Maintenance Department		6,000

(h) Distribution of Power Department costs.

Power was provided at 5¢ per kwh for 108 000 and 162 000 kwh for Departments 1 and 2, respectively.

Entry:		
Factory Overhead—Department 1	5,400	
Factory Overhead—Department 2	8,100	
Power Department		13,500

(i) Application of factory overhead costs to work in process.

The predetermined rates were 80% and 50% of direct labor cost for Departments 1 and 2 respectively. See transaction (c) for the monthly direct labor costs.

Entry:		
Work in Process—Department 1	19,920	
Work in Process—Department 2	18,900	
Factory Overhead—Department 1		19,920
Factory Overhead—Department 2		18,900

(j) Transfer of production costs from Department 1 to Department 2.

4,100 units were fully processed, and there is no work in process in Department 1 at the beginning or at the end of the month.

Total costs charged to Department 1:	
Direct materials	$ 58,500
Direct labor	24,900
Factory overhead	19,920
Total costs	$103,320

Unit cost of product transferred to Department 2:		
$103,320 ÷ 4,100		$ 25.20

Entry: Work in Process—Department 2	103,320	
Work in Process—Department 1		103,320

(k) *Transfer of production costs from Department 2 to Finished Goods.* 4,000 units were completed, and the remaining 900 units were 2/3 completed at the end of the month.

Equivalent units of production:	
To process units in inventory on January 1:	
800 × 1/2	400
To process units started and completed in January:	
4,000 − 800	3,200
To process units in inventory on January 31:	
900 × 2/3	600
Equivalent units of production in January	4,200

Conversion costs:	
Direct labor [transaction (c)]	$ 37,800
Factory overhead [transaction (i)]	18,900
Total conversion costs	$ 56,700

Unit conversion cost:	
$56,700 ÷ 4,200	$ 13.50

Allocation of costs of Department 2:		
Units started in December, completed in January:		
Inventory on January 1, 800 units 1/2 completed	$ 24,600	
Conversion costs in January, 400 at $13.50	5,400	
Total ($30,000 ÷ 800 = $37.50 unit cost)		$ 30,000
Units started and completed in January:		
From Department 1, 3,200 units at $25.20	$ 80,640	
Conversion costs, 3,200 at $13.50	43,200	
Total ($123,840 ÷ 3,200 = $38.70 unit cost)		123,840
Total transferred to Product A		$153,840
Units started in January, 2/3 completed:		
From Department 1, 900 units at $25.20	$ 22,680	
Conversion costs, 600 at $13.50	8,100	
Total work in process—Department 2		30,780
Total costs charged to Department 2		$184,620

Entry: Finished Goods—Product A	153,840	
Work in Process—Department 2		153,840

(l) Cost of goods sold.

Product A, 3,800 units:		
1,000 units at $36.50		$ 36,500
800 units at $37.50		30,000
2,000 units at $38.70		77,400
Total cost of goods sold		$143,900

Entry: Cost of Goods Sold	143,900	
Finished Goods—Product A		143,900

(m) Sales.

Entry: Accounts Receivable	210,500	
Sales		210,500

(n) Cash received.

Entry: Cash	200,000	
Accounts Receivable		200,000

(o) Cash disbursed.

Entry: Accounts Payable	120,000	
Wages Payable	72,500	
Cash		192,500

A chart of the flow of costs from the service and processing department accounts into the finished goods account and then to the cost of goods sold account is as follows. Entries in the accounts are identified by letters to aid the comparison with the summary journal entries.

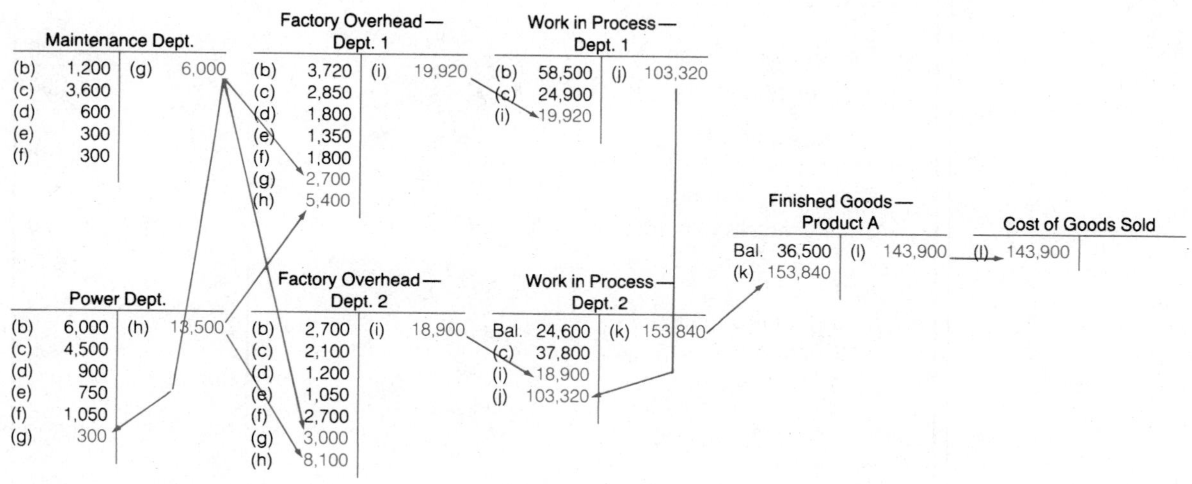

The cost of production reports for Departments 1 and 2 are as follows:

Conway Company
Cost of Production Report—Department 1
For Month Ended January 31, 19--

Quantities:	
Units charged to production and to be accounted for	4,100
Units accounted for and transferred to Department 2	4,100
Costs:	
Costs charged to production in January:	
Direct materials	$ 58,500
Direct labor	24,900
Factory overhead	19,920
Total costs to be accounted for	$103,320
Total costs accounted for and transferred to Department 2 (4,100 units × $25.20)	$103,320

Conway Company
Cost of Production Report—Department 2
For Month Ended January 31, 19--

Quantities:		
Charged to production:		
In process, January 1		800
Received from Department 1		4,100
Total units to be accounted for		4,900
Units accounted for:		
Transferred to finished goods		4,000
In process, January 31		900
Total units accounted for		4,900
Costs:		
Charged to production:		
In process, January 1		$ 24,600
January costs:		
Direct materials from Department 1 ($25.20 per unit)		103,320
Conversion costs:		
Direct labor	$ 37,800	
Factory overhead	18,900	
Total conversion costs ($13.50 per unit)		56,700
Total costs to be accounted for		$184,620

Costs allocated as follows:		
Transferred to finished goods:		
800 units at $37.50	$ 30,000	
3,200 units at $38.70	123,840	
Total cost of finished goods		$153,840
In process, January 31:		
Direct materials (900 units at $25.20)	$ 22,680	
Conversion costs (900 units × 2/3 × $13.50)	8,100	
Total cost of inventory in process, January 31		30,780
Total costs accounted for		$184,620
Computations:		
Equivalent units of production:		
To process units in inventory on January 1:		
800 units × 1/2		400
To process units started and completed in January:		
4,000 units − 800 units		3,200
To process units in inventory on January 31:		
900 units × 2/3		600
Equivalent units of production		4,200
Unit conversion cost:		
$56,700 ÷ 4,200		$13.50

Financial Statements

The financial statements for process cost systems are similar to those for job order cost systems. To illustrate, the trial balance and the condensed financial statements for Conway Company are presented as follows. Note that the net underapplied factory overhead of $1,650 ($1,950 − $300) on January 31 is reported on the balance sheet as a deferred item.

Conway Company
Trial Balance
January 31, 19--

Cash	46,900	
Accounts Receivable	55,500	
Finished Goods—Product A (1,200 units at $38.70)	46,440	
Work in Process—Department 2 (900 units, 2/3 completed)	30,780	
Materials	40,380	
Prepaid Expenses	4,500	
Plant Assets	510,000	
Accumulated Depreciation—Plant Assets		301,750
Accounts Payable		47,980
Wages Payable		6,650
Common Stock		250,000
Retained Earnings		94,070
Sales		210,500
Cost of Goods Sold	143,900	
Factory Overhead—Department 1		300
Factory Overhead—Department 2	1,950	
Selling Expenses	16,500	
General Expenses	14,400	
	911,250	911,250

Conway Company
Income Statement
For Month Ended January 31, 19--

Sales		$210,500
Cost of goods sold		143,900
Gross profit		$ 66,600
Operating expenses:		
Selling expenses	$16,500	
General expenses	14,400	
Total operating expenses		30,900
Income from operations		$ 35,700

Conway Company
Retained Earnings Statement
For Month Ended January 31, 19--

Retained earnings, January 1, 19--	$ 94,070
Income for the month	35,700
Retained earnings, January 31, 19--	$129,770

Conway Company
Balance Sheet
January 31, 19--

Assets

Current assets:			
Cash		$ 46,900	
Accounts receivable		55,500	
Inventories:			
Finished goods	$46,440		
Work in process	30,780		
Materials	40,380	117,600	
Prepaid expenses		4,500	
Total current assets			$224,500
Plant assets		$510,000	
Less accumulated depreciation		301,750	208,250
Deferred debits:			
Factory overhead underapplied			1,650
Total assets			$434,400

Liabilities		
Current liabilities:		
Accounts payable	$ 47,980	
Wages payable	6,650	
Total liabilities		$ 54,630
Stockholders' Equity		
Common stock	$250,000	
Retained earnings	129,770	
Total stockholders' equity		379,770
Total liabilities and stockholders' equity		$434,400

INVENTORY COSTING METHODS

In the preceding discussion and illustrations, the **first-in, first-out (fifo) cost method** was used to determine unit product costs. Another method, known as the average cost method, is sometimes used in practice. Under the **average cost method,** all costs incurred in manufacturing the goods completed during a period are averaged, and this average is used in determining the unit product cost of the goods completed during the period and the work in process at the end of the period. Although the average cost method is not as accurate and not as useful to management in controlling costs as the fifo method, it is simpler to use and is therefore encountered in practice.

First-In, First-Out (Fifo) Cost Method

In most manufacturing processes, the products flow through the processes in a first-in, first-out manner; that is, the first units entering the process are the first completed. In such processes, the work in process at the beginning of the period is completed before work is completed on additional materials entered into the process. The fifo cost method is consistent with the flow of products in such manufacturing processes and is widely used.

When the fifo cost method is used, the beginning work in process inventory costs are kept separate from the costs incurred during the current period. As a result, the fifo cost method generally provides two unit cost figures for products completed during a period: (1) units completed from the beginning work in process, and (2) units started and completed during the current period. These two unit cost figures are useful to management in controlling manufacturing costs because current costs are used to determine the cost of products started and completed during the current period. Management can therefore focus on these current costs in evaluating and controlling current operations.

Using two separate costs adds some complexity to the calculation of unit costs. It also complicates the determination of product costs when the products completed by one process are used in subsequent processes. Primarily for these reasons, some enterprises prefer to use the average cost method.

Average Cost Method

The average cost method is *based on the assumption that the work in process at the beginning of the current period was started and completed during the current period*. Using this method, one unit cost figure for all products completed during the current period is determined. Although not as accurate as the fifo cost method, the average cost method avoids the problem of having two unit cost figures for products completed during a period. When the average cost method is used, it is more difficult for management to evaluate and control current operations, since past costs and current costs are averaged.

To illustrate the use of the average cost method, assume the following data for the Cutting Department of Perrin Company for July of the current year. In addition, assume that all materials used in the Cutting Department are added at the beginning of the process.

Inventory in process, July 1, 500 units:	
Materials cost, 500 units	$24,550
Conversion costs, 500 units, 60% completed	3,600
Materials cost for July, 1,000 units	50,000
Conversion costs for July, 1,000 units	9,660
Goods finished in July (includes units in process on July 1), 1,100 units	—
Inventory in process, July 31, 400 units, 50% completed	—

To apply the average cost method in the determination of the unit cost for the 1,100 units finished in July and the 400 units that are 50% completed on July 31, the average materials cost and the average conversion cost are determined as follows:

Materials cost for 500 units in process at July 1	$24,550
Materials cost for 1,000 units for July	50,000
Total materials cost (1,500 units)	$74,550
Average materials cost per unit ($74,550 ÷ 1,500)	$ 49.70
Conversion costs for units in process at July 1	$ 3,600
Conversion costs for July	9,660
Total conversion costs	$13,260
Equivalent units of production:	
To process units in inventory on July 1	500
To process units started and completed in July (1,100 units − 500 units)	600
To process units in inventory on July 31 (400 units × 50%)	200
Equivalent units of production in July	1,300
Average conversion cost per unit ($13,260 ÷ 1,300)	$ 10.20

It should be noted that in determining the average unit materials cost, the cost of materials in work in process on July 1 (the beginning inventory) is added to the materials cost for July before dividing by the total units of materials in the cutting process during July. A similar procedure is followed for computing the average unit conversion cost. The conversion costs in work in process on July 1 (the beginning inventory) are added to the conversion costs for July before dividing by the equivalent units of production for July. As mentioned earlier, in computing these equivalent units, the units in the beginning inventory are treated as if they were all started and completed during the current period. In other words, the beginning inventory of

500 units is treated as 500 units fully completed during the current period, not 500 units 40% completed (200 units) during the current period.

The average unit costs for Perrin Company are used to determine the cost of goods finished during July and the cost of the work in process on July 31 (the ending inventory), as follows:

Goods finished during July:		
1,100 units:	1,100 units at $49.70 for materials costs	$54,670
	1,100 units at $10.20 for conversion costs...........	11,220
	Total (1,100 units at $59.90)	$65,890
Work in process, July 31:		
400 units:	400 units at $49.70 for materials costs................	$19,880
	400 units × 50% × $10.20 for conversion costs	2,040
	Total..	$21,920

In many manufacturing processes, there is no significant difference between the unit cost figures determined under the average cost and the fifo cost methods. This similarity in unit costs is especially true where the beginning and ending work in process inventories are uniform and materials costs do not fluctuate widely from period to period. Therefore, the simplification of the calculations by using the average cost method and the lack of significant variation in unit costs under the two methods have been the principal reasons for the use of the average cost method. Computers, however, have removed the complexity from the calculations of unit product costs.

Chapter Review

KEY POINTS

1. Process Cost and Job Order Cost Systems Distinguished.
No useful purpose would be served for companies manufacturing a homogeneous product, such as cement, flour, or paint, to maintain job orders for each particular amount of product. In these cases, a process cost system is normally utilized. In process cost accounting, costs are charged to processing departments, and the cost of the finished unit is determined by dividing the total cost incurred in each process among the number of units produced.

2. Service Departments and Process Costs.
In a factory with several processes, there may be one or more service departments that do not process the materials directly. Examples include the factory office, the power plant, and the maintenance and repair shop. Periodically, the costs incurred by service departments are allocated to the factory overhead accounts of the processing departments.

3. Processing Costs.
The accumulated costs transferred from preceding departments and the costs of direct materials and direct labor incurred in each processing department are

debited to the related work in process account. Each work in process account is also debited for the factory overhead applied. The direct labor and the factory overhead applied are referred to as the conversion costs.

4. Inventories of Partially Processed Materials.
Frequently, partially processed materials remain in various stages of production in a department at the end of a period. In this case, the manufacturing costs must be allocated between the units that have been completed and those that are only partially completed and remain within the department. In allocating costs between completed products and work remaining in process, either the first-in, first-out method or the average cost method may be used. To allocate processing costs between the output completed and the inventory of goods within the department, it is necessary to determine the number of equivalent units of production during the period. The equivalent units of production are the number of units that could have been manufactured from start to finish during the period.

5. Cost of Production Report.
A report prepared periodically for each processing department summarizes (1) the units for which the department is accountable and the disposition of these units and (2) the costs charged to the department and the allocation of these costs. This report, termed the cost of production report, may be used as the source of the computation of unit production costs and the allocation of the processing costs to the finished and the uncompleted units. More importantly, the report is used to control costs.

6. Joint Products and By-Products.
In some manufacturing processes, more than one product is produced. When the output of a manufacturing process consists of two or more different products, the products are either joint products or by-products. When two or more goods of significant value are produced from a single principal direct material, the products are termed joint products. Similarly, the costs incurred in the manufacture of joint products are called joint costs. If one of the products resulting from a process has little value in relation to the main product or joint products, it is known as a by-product.

Since joint products come from the processing of a common parent material, the assignment of cost to each separate product cannot be based on actual expenditures. The allocation of joint costs among the joint products is usually performed using the market (sales) value method. The amount of manufacturing cost usually assigned to a by-product is the sales value of the by-product reduced by any additional costs necessary to complete and sell it.

7. Inventory Costing Methods.
The first-in, first-out (fifo) cost method of accounting for manufacturing costs is consistent with the flow of product costs through most manufacturing processes. The average cost method, although not as useful for cost control as the fifo method, is also used in practice. The simplification of the computations of unit product costs under the average cost method is the major reason for use of the method. Under the average cost method, one unit cost figure (rather than two, as under the fifo method) for all products completed during a period is computed.

KEY TERMS

service departments 643
conversion cost 644
equivalent units of production 645
cost of production report 646
joint products 648
joint costs 648
by-product 648
market (sales) value method 648
first-in, first-out method 657
average cost method, 657

SELF-EXAMINATION QUESTIONS

(Answers at End of Chapter)

1. For which of the following businesses would the process cost system be most appropriate?
   A. Custom furniture manufacturer
   B. Commercial building contractor
   C. Crude oil refinery
   D. None of the above

2. The group of manufacturing costs referred to as *conversion costs* includes:
   A. direct materials and direct labor
   B. direct materials and factory overhead
   C. direct labor and factory overhead
   D. none of the above

3. Information relating to production in Department A for May is as follows:

May	1	Balance, 1,000 units, 3/4 completed	$22,150
	31	Direct materials, 5,000 units	75,000
	31	Direct labor	32,500
	31	Factory overhead	16,250

   If 500 units were 1/4 completed at May 31, 5,500 units were completed during May, and inventories are costed by the first-in, first-out method, what was the number of equivalent units of production for May?
   A. 4,500
   B. 4,875
   C. 5,500
   D. None of the above

4. Based on the data presented in Question 3, what is the unit conversion cost?
   A. $10
   B. $15
   C. $25
   D. None of the above

5. If one of the products resulting from a process has little value in relation to the principal products, it is known as a:
   A. joint product
   B. by-product
   C. direct material
   D. none of the above

ILLUSTRATIVE PROBLEM

Tate Company manufactures Product A by a series of four processes, all materials being introduced in Department 1. From Department 1 the materials pass through Departments 2, 3, and 4, emerging as finished Product A. All inventories are costed by the first-in, first-out method.

The balances in the accounts Work in Process—Department 4 and Finished Goods were as follows on May 1:

Work in Process—Department 4 (1,000 units, 1/4 completed)	$17,800
Finished Goods (1,800 units at $23.50 a unit)	42,300

The following costs were charged to Work in Process—Department 4 during May:

Direct materials transferred from Department 3: 4,700 units at $16 a unit	$75,200
Direct labor	25,500
Factory overhead	15,300

During May, 5,000 units of A were completed and 4,800 units were sold. Inventories on May 31 were as follows:

Work in Process—Department 4: 700 units, 1/2 completed
Finished Goods: 2,000 units

Instructions:

Determine the following, presenting the computations in good order:

(a) Equivalent units of production for Department 4 during May.
(b) Unit conversion cost for Department 4 for May.
(c) Total and unit cost of Product A started in a prior period and finished in May.
(d) Total and unit cost of Product A started and finished in May.
(e) Total cost of goods transferred to finished goods.
(f) Work in process inventory for Department 4, May 31.
(g) Cost of goods sold (indicate number of units and unit costs.)
(h) Finished goods inventory, May 31.

SOLUTION

(a) Equivalent units of production:

To process units in inventory on May 1:	
1,000 units × 3/4	750
To process units started and completed	
in May: 5,000 units − 1,000 units	4,000
To process units in inventory on May 31:	
700 units × 1/2	350
Equivalent units of production in May	5,100

(b) Unit conversion cost: $\frac{\$25,500 + \$15,300}{5,100} = \$8$

(c) Cost of Product A started in a prior period and finished in May:

1,000 units:	Inventory on May 1, 1/4 completed	$ 17,800
	Conversion cost in May, 750 × $8	6,000
	Total	$ 23,800

Unit cost: $23,800 ÷ 1,000 = $23.80

(d) Cost of Product A started and finished in May:

4,000 units:	Materials from Department 3, 4,000 × $16	$ 64,000
	Conversion cost in May, 4,000 × $8	32,000
	Total	$ 96,000
	Unit cost: $96,000 ÷ 4,000 = $24	

(e) Total cost of goods transferred to finished goods:

Cost of Product A started in a prior period and finished in May (1,000 units at $23.80)	$ 23,800
Cost of Product A started and finished in May (4,000 units at $24)	96,000
Total	$119,800

(f) Work in process inventory, May 31:

700 units:	Materials cost, 700 × $16	$ 11,200
	Conversion costs in May, 350 × $8	2,800
	Work in process inventory, May 31	$ 14,000

(g) Cost of goods sold:

1,800 units at $23.50	$ 42,300
1,000 units at $23.80	23,800
2,000 units at $24.00	48,000
4,800 units	$114,100

(h) Finished goods inventory, May 31:

2,000 units at $24	$ 48,000

Discussion Questions

17–1. Which type of cost system, process or job order, would be best suited for each of the following: (a) paint manufacturer, (b) oil refinery, (c) furniture upholsterer, (d) building contractor, (e) refrigerator manufacturer? Give reasons for your answers.

17–2. Are perpetual inventory accounts for materials, work in process, and finished goods generally used for (a) job order cost systems and (b) process cost systems?

17–3. In job order cost accounting, the three elements of manufacturing cost are charged directly to job orders. Why is it not necessary to charge manufacturing costs in process cost accounting to job orders?

17–4. (a) How does a service department differ from a processing department? (b) Give two examples of a service department.

17–5. Cowen Company maintains a cafeteria for its employees at a cost of $2,250 per month. On what basis would the company most likely allocate the cost of the cafeteria among the production departments?

17–6. What two groups of manufacturing costs are referred to as conversion costs?

17–7. In the manufacture of 1,000 units of a product, direct materials cost incurred was $20,000, direct labor cost incurred was $8,000, and factory overhead applied was

$4,000. (a) What is the total conversion cost? (b) What is the conversion cost per unit? (c) What is the total manufacturing cost? (d) What is the manufacturing cost per unit?

17–8. What is meant by the term "equivalent units"?

17–9. If Department A had no work in process at the beginning of the period, 5,000 units were completed during the period, and 1,000 units were 25% completed at the end of the period, what was the number of equivalent units of production for the period?

17–10. The following information concerns production in the Mixing Department for January. All direct materials are placed in process at the beginning of production. Determine the number of units in work in process inventory at the end of the month.

WORK IN PROCESS — MIXING DEPARTMENT

Date		Item	Debit	Credit	Balance	
					Debit	Credit
Jan.	1	Bal., 6,000 units, ¾ completed			9,500	
	31	Direct materials, 15,000 units	7,500			
	31	Direct labor	14,450			
	31	Factory overhead	7,225			
	31	Goods finished, 13,500 units		28,550		
	31	Bal., ____ units, ½ completed			10,125	

17–11. For Question No. 17–10, determine the equivalent units of production for January, assuming that the first-in, first-out method is used to cost inventories.

17–12. What data are summarized in the two principal sections of the cost of production report?

17–13. What is the most important purpose of the cost of production report?

17–14. Distinguish between a joint product and a by-product.

17–15. The Refining Department produces two products. How should the costs be allocated (a) if the products are joint products and (b) if one of the products is a by-product?

17–16. Factory employees in the Assembly Department of Farr Co. are paid widely varying wage rates. In such circumstances, would direct labor hours or direct labor cost be the more equitable base for applying factory overhead to the production of the department? Explain.

17–17. In a factory with several processing departments, a separate factory overhead rate may be determined for each department. Why is a single factory overhead rate often inadequate in such circumstances?

17–18. What are the two common inventory costing methods used in process cost accounting?

17–19. What are the principal advantages of the use of the first-in, first-out method for costing inventories for process cost systems?

17–20. What are the principal advantages of the use of the average method for costing inventories for process cost systems?

17–21. Real World Focus. As production processes become more and more automated in what many see as the "age of robotics," materials may enter into and leave a production process without human intervention. For example, in the manufacture of automobiles, General Motors uses state-of-the-art paint systems, which are operated from an automated video control room. The control room supervisor monitors the preparation of the bare metal body of the automobile as it is submerged in a primer. Next, the body passes through nine pairs of robot painters teamed with other robot devices that open and close doors and paint inside surfaces. (a) In this type of production environment, would direct labor hours be an appropriate base for allocation of predetermined factory overhead? (b) Can you suggest other possible factory overhead bases?

Exercises

17–22. Flowchart of accounts related to service and processing departments. Yates Co. manufactures two products. The entire output of Department 1 is transferred to Department 2. Part of the fully processed goods from Department 2 are sold as Product P and the remainder of the goods are transferred to Department 3 for further processing into Product Q. The service department, Factory Office, provides services for each of the processing departments.

Prepare a chart of the flow of costs from the service and processing department accounts into the finished goods accounts and then into the cost of goods sold account. The relevant accounts are as follows:

Cost of Goods Sold	Finished Goods—Product P
Factory Office	Finished Goods—Product Q
Factory Overhead—Department 1	Work in Process—Department 1
Factory Overhead—Department 2	Work in Process—Department 2
Factory Overhead—Department 3	Work in Process—Department 3

17–23. Entry for allocation of service department costs. The Maintenance and Repair Department provides services to processing departments C, D, and E. During July of the current year, the total cost incurred by the Maintenance and Repair Department was $80,000. During July, it was estimated that 60% of the services were provided to Department C, 25% to Department D, and 15% to Department E.

Prepare an entry to record the allocation of the Maintenance and Repair Department cost for July to the processing departments.

17–24. Entries for flow of factory costs for process cost system. Lunn Company manufactures a single product by a continuous process, involving four production departments. The records indicate that $65,000 of direct materials were issued to and $90,000 of direct labor was incurred by Department 1 in the manufacture of the product; the factory overhead rate is 60% of direct labor cost; work in process in the department at the beginning of the period totaled $37,500; and work in process at the end of the period totaled $35,000.

Prepare entries to record (a) the flow of costs into Department 1 during the period for (1) direct materials, (2) direct labor, and (3) factory overhead; (b) the transfer of production costs to Department 2.

17–25. Factory overhead rate, entry for application of factory overhead, and factory overhead account balance. The chief cost accountant for R. D. Evans Co. estimates total factory overhead cost for the Blending Department for the year at $72,000 and total direct labor costs at $96,000. During March, the actual direct labor cost totaled $8,100, and factory overhead cost incurred totaled $6,250. (a) What is the predetermined factory overhead rate based on direct labor cost? (b) Prepare the entry to apply factory overhead to production for March. (c) What is the March 31 balance of the account Factory Overhead—Blending Department? (d) Does the balance in (c) represent overapplied or underapplied factory overhead?

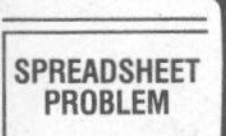

17–26. Equivalent units of production and related costs. The charges to Work in Process—Finishing Department for a period, together with information concerning production, are as follows. All direct materials are placed in process at the beginning of production, and the first-in, first-out method is used to cost inventories.

Work in Process—Finishing Department

2,000 units, 80% completed	49,100	To Dept. 2, 6,200 units	169,600
Direct materials, 4,200 at $15	63,000		
Direct labor	46,000		
Factory overhead	11,500		

Determine the following, presenting your computations: (a) equivalent units of production, (b) conversion cost per equivalent unit of production, (c) total and unit cost of product started in prior period and completed in the current period, and (d) total and unit cost of product started and completed in the current period.

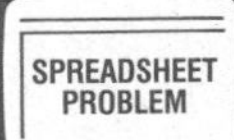

17–27. Cost of production report. Prepare a cost of production report for the Assembly Department of Cohen Company for May of the current fiscal year, using the following data and assuming that the first-in, first-out method is used to cost inventories:

Inventory, May 1, 5,000 units, 40% completed	$120,000
Materials from the Sanding Department, 15,000 units	337,500
Direct labor for May	51,875
Factory overhead for May	31,125
Goods finished during May (includes units in process, May 1) 16,500 units	—
Inventory, May 31, 3,500 units, 60% completed	—

17–28. Allocation of costs for by-product and joint products. The charges to Work in Process—Department 4, together with units of product completed during the period, are indicated in the following account:

Work in Process—Department 4

From Department 3	125,600	By-product A, 1,000 units
Direct labor	30,300	Joint product P, 4,000 units
Factory overhead	10,100	Joint product Q, 10,000 units

There is no inventory of goods in process at either the beginning or the end of the period. The value of A is $1 a unit; P sells at $25 a unit, and Q sells at $15 a unit.

Allocate the costs to the three products and determine the unit cost of each, presenting your computations.

17–29. Unit cost of product by average cost method. The debits to Work in Process—Melting Department for a period, together with information concerning production, are as follows:

Work in process, beginning of period:	
Materials costs, 2,000 units	$28,760
Conversion costs, 2,000 units, 80% completed	15,000
Materials added during period, 4,200 units	63,000
Conversion costs during period	46,000
Work in process, end of period, 200 units, 50% completed	—
Goods finished during period, 6,000 units	—

All direct materials are placed in process at the beginning of the process, and the average cost method is used to cost inventories. Determine the following, presenting your computations: (a) average materials cost per unit for period, (b) equivalent units of production for period, (c) average conversion cost per unit for period, (d) cost of goods finished during the period, and (e) cost of work in process at end of period.

17–30. Entries for process cost system. Sellers Company manufactures Product Z. Material A is placed in process in Department 1, where it is ground and partially refined. The output of Department 1 is transferred to Department 2, where Material B is added at the beginning of the process and the refining is completed. On June 1, Sellers Company had the following inventories:

Finished goods (6,150 units)	$107,625
Work in process—Department 1	—
Work in process—Department 2 (3,150 units, 2/3 completed)	51,345
Materials	61,470

Departmental accounts are maintained for factory overhead, and there is one service department, Factory Office. The first-in, first-out method is used to cost inventories. Manufacturing operations for June are summarized as follows:

(a) Materials purchased on account	$32,700
(b) Materials requisitioned for use:	
Material A	$51,705
Material B	9,840
Indirect materials—Department 1	2,160
Indirect materials—Department 2	540
(c) Labor used:	
Direct labor—Department 1	$73,050
Direct labor—Department 2	29,175
Indirect labor—Department 1	4,200
Indirect labor—Department 2	1,920
Factory Office	3,450
(d) Depreciation charged on plant assets:	
Department 1	$29,850
Department 2	14,400
Factory Office	1,650
(e) Miscellaneous costs incurred on account:	
Department 1	$ 5,535
Department 2	3,465
Factory Office	1,800
(f) Expiration of prepaid expenses:	
Department 1	$ 3,420
Department 2	735
Factory Office	1,125
(g) Distribution of Factory Office costs:	
Department 1	60% of total Factory Office costs
Department 2	40% of total Factory Office costs
(h) Application of factory overhead costs:	
Department 1	70% of direct labor cost
Department 2	80% of direct labor cost

(i) Production costs transferred from Department 1 to Department 2:
12,300 units were fully processed, and there was no inventory of work in process in Department 1 at June 30.

(j) Production costs transferred from Department 2 to finished goods:
11,250 units, including the inventory at June 1, were fully processed. There were 4,200 units 3/5 completed at June 30.

(k) Cost of goods sold during June:
12,000 units (Use the first-in, first-out method in crediting the finished goods account.)

Instructions: (1) Prepare entries to record the foregoing operations. Identify each entry by letter.
(2) Compute the June 30 work in process inventory for Department 2.

17–31. Cost of production report. The data related to production during June of the current year for Department 2 of Sellers Company are presented in Problem 17–30.

Instructions: Prepare a cost of production report for Department 2 for June.

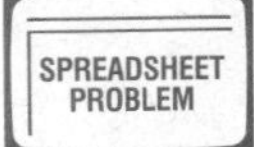

17–32. Financial statements for process cost system. The trial balance of Sarnoff Inc. at January 31, the end of the first month of the current fiscal year, is as follows:

Sarnoff Inc.
Trial Balance
January 31, 19--

Cash	80,600	
Marketable Securities	60,000	
Accounts Receivable	245,000	
Allowance for Doubtful Accounts		9,900
Finished Goods — Product A1	91,600	
Finished Goods — Product A2	155,000	
Work in Process — Department 1	17,750	
Work in Process — Department 2	33,150	
Work in Process — Department 3	29,400	
Materials	60,500	
Prepaid Insurance	14,750	
Office Supplies	5,250	
Land	105,000	
Buildings	660,000	
Accumulated Depreciation — Buildings		319,200
Machinery and Equipment	342,000	
Accumulated Depreciation — Machinery and Equipment		216,600
Office Equipment	59,400	
Accumulated Depreciation — Office Equipment		25,560
Patents	66,000	
Accounts Payable		122,150
Wages Payable		19,750
Income Tax Payable		6,500
Mortgage Note Payable (due 1995)		120,000
Common Stock ($15 par)		600,000
Retained Earnings		518,220
Sales		755,500
Cost of Goods Sold	502,300	
Factory Overhead — Department 1	400	
Factory Overhead — Department 2	370	
Factory Overhead — Department 3		290
Selling Expenses	99,750	
General Expenses	68,800	
Interest Expense	1,000	
Interest Income		350
Income Tax	16,000	
	2,714,020	2,714,020

Instructions: (1) Prepare an income statement.
(2) Prepare a retained earnings statement.
(3) Prepare a balance sheet.

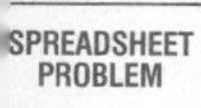

17–33. Equivalent units and related costs; cost of production report. Drysdale Company manufactures Product C by a series of four processes, all materials being introduced in Department 1. From Department 1, the materials pass through Departments 2, 3, and 4, emerging as finished Product C. All inventories are costed by the first-in, first-out method.

The balances in the accounts Work in Process—Department 4 and Finished Goods were as follows on July 1:

Work in Process—Department 4 (6,000 units, 3/4 completed) .	$ 66,300
Finished Goods (8,000 units at $13 a unit)	104,000

The following costs were charged to Work in Process—Department 4 during July:

Direct materials transferred from Department 3: 26,000 units at $5.20 a unit	$135,200
Direct labor	144,000
Factory overhead	72,000

During July, 25,000 units of C were completed and 26,800 units were sold. Inventories on July 31 were as follows:

Work in Process—Department 4: 7,000 units, 1/2 completed
Finished Goods: 6,200 units

Instructions: (1) Determine the following, presenting computations in good order:
- (a) Equivalent units of production for Department 4 during July.
- (b) Unit conversion cost for Department 4 for July.
- (c) Total and unit cost of Product C started in a prior period and finished in July.
- (d) Total and unit cost of Product C started and finished in July.
- (e) Total cost of goods transferred to finished goods.
- (f) Work in process inventory for Department 4, July 31.
- (g) Cost of goods sold (indicate number of units and unit costs).
- (h) Finished goods inventory, July 31.

(2) Prepare a cost of production report for Department 4 for July.

17–34. Entries for process cost system, including joint products. I. C. Han Products manufactures joint products A and B. Materials are placed in production in Department 1, and after processing, are transferred to Department 2, where more materials are added. The finished products emerge from Department 2. There are two service departments: Factory Office, and Maintenance and Repair.

There were no inventories of work in process at the beginning or at the end of January. Finished goods inventories at January 1 were as follows:

Product A, 2,500 units	$75,000
Product B, 900 units	45,000

Transactions related to manufacturing operations for January are summarized as follows:

- (a) Materials purchased on account, $91,750.
- (b) Materials requisitioned for use: Department 1, $47,000 ($42,540 entered directly into the products); Department 2, $31,385 ($27,320 entered directly into the products); Maintenance and Repair, $1,990.
- (c) Labor costs incurred: Department 1, $36,100 ($31,500 entered directly into the products); Department 2, $38,800 ($33,600 entered directly into the products); Factory Office, $5,850; Maintenance and Repair, $13,650.
- (d) Miscellaneous costs and expenses incurred on account: Department 1, $5,570; Department 2, $4,150; Factory Office, $1,400; and Maintenance and Repair, $2,170.

(e) Depreciation charged on plant assets: Department 1, $6,900; Department 2, $5,360; Factory Office, $900; and Maintenance and Repair, $980.
(f) Expiration of various prepaid expenses: Department 1, $450; Department 2, $330; Factory Office, $350; and Maintenance and Repair, $490.
(g) Factory office costs allocated on the basis of hours worked: Department 1, 2,200 hours; Department 2, 1,760 hours; Maintenance and Repair, 440 hours.
(h) Maintenance and repair costs allocated on the basis of services rendered: Department 1, 60%; Department 2, 40%.
(i) Factory overhead applied to production at the predetermined rates: 120% and 90% of direct labor cost for Departments 1 and 2 respectively.
(j) Output of Department 1: 8,100 units.
(k) Output of Department 2: 4,000 units of Product A and 1,600 units of Product B. Unit selling price is $45 for Product A and $75 for Product B.
(l) Sales on account: 4,500 units of Product A at $45 and 1,700 units of Product B at $75. Credits to the finished goods accounts are to be made according to the first-in, first-out method.

Instructions: Present entries to record the transactions, identifying each by letter. Include as an explanation for entry (k) the computations for the allocation of the production costs for Department 2 to the joint products, and as an explanation for entry (l) the number of units and the unit costs for each product sold.

17–35. Work in process account data for two months and determination of difference in unit product cost between months. A process cost system is used to record the costs of manufacturing Product C, which requires a series of three processes. The inventory of Work in Process—Department 3 on July 1 and debits to the account during July were as follows:

Balance, 1,200 units, 2/3 completed.	$11,640
From Department 2, 5,250 units.	9,450
Direct labor	50,676
Factory overhead.	12,669

During July, the 1,200 units in process on July 1 were completed, and of the 5,250 units entering the department, all were completed except 2,000 units, which were 3/4 completed.

Charges to Work in Process—Department 3 for August were as follows:

From Department 2, 6,100 units.	$10,675
Direct labor	63,500
Factory overhead.	15,875

During August, the units in process at the beginning of the month were completed, and of the 6,100 units entering the department, all were completed except 500 units, which were 1/2 completed. All inventories are costed by the first-in, first-out method.

Instructions: (1) Set up an account for Work in Process—Department 3. Enter the balance as of July 1 and record the debits and credits in the account for July. Present computations for the determination of (a) equivalent units of production, (b) unit conversion cost, (c) cost of goods finished, differentiating between units started in the prior period and units started and finished in July, and (d) work in process inventory.
(2) Record the transactions for August in the account. Present the computations listed in (1).
(3) Determine the difference in unit cost between the product started and completed in July and the product started and completed in August. Determine also the amount of the difference attributable collectively to operations in Departments 1 and 2 and the amount attributable to operations in Department 3.

17–36. Unit cost of finished product by average cost method; cost of production report. Tupper Company manufactures Product F by a series of four processes, all materials being introduced in Department 1. From Department 1, the materials pass through Departments 2, 3, and 4, emerging as finished Product F. All inventories are costed by the average method.

The balance in the account Work in Process—Department 4 was as follows on March 1:

Materials cost (4,000 units)	$ 18,640
Conversion costs (4,000 units, 3/4 completed)	14,000

The following costs were charged to Work in Process—Department 4 during March:

Direct materials transferred from Department 3: 24,000 units at $4.80 per unit	$115,200
Direct labor	138,460
Factory overhead	42,420

During March, 21,600 units of Product F were completed and the work in process inventory on March 31 was 6,400 units, 1/4 completed.

Instructions: (1) Determine the following for Department 4, presenting computations in good order:

(a) Average materials cost per unit.
(b) Equivalent units of production in March.
(c) Average conversion cost per unit for March.
(d) Cost of goods finished during March.
(e) Cost of work in process at March 31.

(2) Prepare a cost of production report for Department 4 for March.

ALTERNATE PROBLEMS

17–30A. Entries for process cost system. Ryan Company manufacturers Product W. Material E is placed in process in Department 1, where it is ground and partially refined. The output of Department 1 is transferred to Department 2, where Material F is added at the beginning of the process and the refining is completed. On April 1, Ryan Company had the following inventories:

Finished goods (7,000 units)	$169,400
Work in process—Department 1	—
Work in process—Department 2 (1,400 units, 3/4 completed)	28,140
Materials	37,650

Departmental accounts are maintained for factory overhead, and there is one service department, Factory Office. All inventories are costed by the first-in, first-out method. Manufacturing operations for April are summarized as follows:

(a) Materials purchased on account	$68,500
(b) Materials requisitioned for use:	
Material E	$37,114
Material F	30,800
Indirect materials—Department 1	2,460
Indirect materials—Department 2	1,770
(c) Labor used:	
Direct labor—Department 1	$77,000
Direct labor—Department 2	54,950

Indirect labor—Department 1	$ 2,900
Indirect labor—Department 2	2,750
Factory Office	2,618

(d) Miscellaneous costs incurred on account:

Department 1	$ 9,950
Department 2	7,250
Factory Office	2,996

(e) Expiration of prepaid expenses:

Department 1	$ 1,490
Department 2	975
Factory Office	420

(f) Depreciation charged on plant assets:

Department 1	$20,500
Department 2	17,500
Factory Office	1,330

(g) Distribution of Factory Office costs:

Department 1	75% of total Factory Office costs
Department 2	25% of total Factory Office costs

(h) Application of factory overhead costs:

Department 1	55% of direct labor cost
Department 2	60% of direct labor cost

(i) Production costs transferred from Department 1 to Department 2:
12,320 units were fully processed, and there was no inventory of work in process in Department 1 at April 30.

(j) Production costs transferred from Department 2 to finished goods:
11,200 units, including the inventory at April 1, were fully processed. 2,520 units were 1/3 completed at April 30.

(k) Cost of goods sold during April:
13,300 units (Use the first-in, first-out method in crediting the finished goods account.)

Instructions: (1) Prepare entries to record the foregoing operations. Identify each entry by letter.
(2) Compute the April 30 work in process inventory for Department 2.

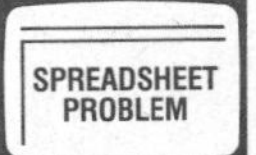

17–33A. Equivalent units and related costs; cost of production report. Bowers Company manufactures Product Z by a series of three processes, all materials being introduced in Department 1. From Department 1, the materials pass through Departments 2 and 3, emerging as finished Product Z. All inventories are costed by the first-in, first-out method.

The balances in the accounts Work in Process—Department 3 and Finished Goods were as follows on March 1:

Work in Process—Department 3 (7,000 units, 1/2 completed)	$212,100
Finished Goods (12,000 units at $36.20 a unit)	434,400

The following costs were charged to Work in Process—Department 3 during March:

Direct materials transferred from Department 2: 37,000 units at $24 a unit	$888,000
Direct labor	232,600
Factory overhead	140,000

During March, 35,000 units of Z were completed and 37,200 units were sold. Inventories on March 31 were as follows:

Work in Process—Department 3: 9,000 units, 1/3 completed
Finished Goods: 9,800 units

Instructions: (1) Determine the following, presenting computations in good order:
(a) Equivalent units of production for Department 3 during March.
(b) Unit conversion cost for Department 3 for March.
(c) Total and unit cost of Product Z started in a prior period and finished in March.
(d) Total and unit cost of Product Z started and finished in March.
(e) Total cost of goods transferred to finished goods.
(f) Work in process inventory for Department 3, March 31.
(g) Cost of goods sold (indicate number of units and unit costs).
(h) Finished goods inventory, March 31.
(2) Prepare a cost of production report for Department 3 for March.

17–35A. Work in process account data for two months and determination of difference in unit product cost between months. A process cost system is used to record the costs of manufacturing Product F10, which requires a series of four processes. The inventory of Work in Process—Department 4 on June 1 and debits to the account during June were as follows:

Balance, 800 units, 1/4 completed	$13,040
From Department 3, 4,600 units	51,520
Direct labor	77,000
Factory overhead	19,250

During June, the 800 units in process on June 1 were completed, and of the 4,600 units entering the department, all were completed except 1,100 units, which were 1/4 completed.

Charges to Work in Process—Department 4 for July were as follows:

From Department 3, 4,125 units	$47,850
Direct labor	83,448
Factory overhead	20,862

During July, the units in process at the beginning of the month were completed, and of the 4,125 units entering the department, all were completed except 750 units, which were 1/2 completed. All inventories are costed by the first-in, first-out method.

Instructions: (1) Set up an account for Work in Process—Department 4. Enter the balance as of June 1 and record the debits and the credits in the account for June. Present computations for the determination of (a) equivalent units of production, (b) unit conversion cost, (c) cost of goods finished, differentiating between units started in the prior period and units started and finished in June, and (d) work in process inventory.
(2) Record the transactions for July in the account. Present the computations listed in (1).
(3) Determine the difference in unit cost between the product started and completed in June and the product started and completed in July. Determine also the amount of the difference attributable collectively to operations in Departments 1 through 3 and the amount attributable to operations in Department 4.

Mini-Case 17

H and S Inc. manufactures product 3D by a series of four processes. All materials are placed in production in the Die Casting Department and, after processing, are transferred to the Tooling, Assembly, and Polishing Departments, emerging as a finished product 3D.

On June 1, the balance in the account Work in Process—Polishing was $201,960, determined as follows:

Direct materials: 12,000 units	$122,040
Direct labor: 12,000 units, 3/4 completed	64,530
Factory overhead: 12,000 units, 3/4 completed	15,390
Total	$201,960

The following costs were charged to Work in Process—Polishing during June:

Direct materials transferred from Assembly Dept., 136,000 units	$1,428,000
Direct labor	988,920
Factory overhead	217,080

During June, 138,000 units of 3D were completed and transferred to Finished Goods. On June 30, the inventory in the Polishing Department consisted of 10,000 units, one-half completed. All inventories are costed by the first-in, first-out method.

As a new cost accountant for H and S Inc., you have just received a phone call from Ann Pearlstein, the superintendent of the Polishing Department. She was extremely upset with the cost of production report, which she says does not balance. In addition, she commented:

> "I give up! These reports are a waste of time. My department has always been the best department in the plant, so why should I bother with these reports? Just what purpose do they serve?"

The report to which Pearlstein referred is as follows:

H and S Inc.
Cost of Production Report — Polishing Department
For Month Ended June 30, 19--

Quantities:		
Charged to production:		
In process, June 1		9,000
Received from Assembly Department		136,000
Total units to be accounted for		145,000
Units accounted for:		
Transferred to finished goods		138,000
In process, June 30		5,000
Total units accounted for		143,000
Costs:		
Charged to production:		
In process, June 1		$ 201,960
June costs:		
Direct materials from Assembly Department ($9.42 per unit)		1,428,000
Conversion costs:		
Direct labor	$988,920	
Factory overhead	217,080	
Total conversion costs ($8.04 per unit)		1,206,000
Total costs to be accounted for		$2,835,960
Costs allocated as follows:		
Transferred to finished goods:		
138,000 units at $17.46 ($9.42+$8.04)		$2,409,480
In process, June 30:		
Materials (5,000 units×$9.42)	$ 47,100	
Conversion costs (5,000 units×$8.04)	40,200	
Total cost of inventory in process		87,300
Total costs accounted for		$2,496,780
Computations:		
Equivalent units of production:		
To process units in inventory on June 1: 12,000 units×3/4		9,000
To process units started and completed in June		136,000
To process units in inventory on June 30: 10,000 units×1/2		5,000
Equivalent units of production		150,000
Unit conversion cost:		
$1,206,000÷150,000		$8.04

Instructions:

(1) Based upon the data for June, prepare a revised cost of production report for the Polishing Department.
(2) Assume that for May, the unit direct materials cost was $10.17 and the unit conversion cost was $8.88. Determine the change in the direct materials unit cost and unit conversion cost for June.
(3) Based on (2), what are some possible explanations for the changing unit costs?
(4) Describe how you would explain to Pearlstein that cost of production reports are useful.

Answers to Self-Examination Questions

1. C The process cost system is most appropriate for a business where manufacturing is conducted by continuous operations and involves a series of uniform production processes, such as the processing of crude oil (answer C). The job order cost system is most appropriate for a business where the product is made to customers' specifications, such as custom furniture manufacturing (answer A) and commercial building construction (answer B).

2. C The manufacturing costs that are necessary to convert direct materials into finished products are referred to as conversion costs. The conversion costs include direct labor and factory overhead (answer C).

3. B The number of units that could have been produced from start to finish during a period is termed equivalent units. The 4,875 equivalent units (answer B) is determined as follows:

To process units in inventory on May 1:	
1,000 units × 1/4	250
To process units started and completed	
in May: 5,500 units − 1,000 units	4,500
To process units in inventory on May 31:	
500 units × 1/4	125
Equivalent units of production in May	4,875

4. A The conversion costs (direct labor and factory overhead) totaling $48,750 are divided by the number of equivalent units (4,875) to determine the unit conversion cost of $10 (answer A).

5. B The product resulting from a process that has little value in relation to the principal product or joint products is known as a by-product (answer B). When two or more commodities of significant value are produced from a single direct material, the products are termed joint products (answer A). The raw material that enters directly into the finished product is termed direct material (answer C).

Part Six

Planning and Control

18
Cost Behavior and Cost Estimation

CHAPTER OBJECTIVES

Distinguish between cost behavior and cost estimation.

Describe and illustrate variable costs.

Describe the behavior of total and unit variable costs.

Describe and illustrate fixed costs.

Describe the behavior of total and unit fixed costs.

Describe and illustrate mixed costs.

Describe and illustrate the use of the high-low method to estimate total costs.

Describe and illustrate the use of the scattergraph method to estimate total costs.

Describe and illustrate the use of the least squares method to estimate total costs.

Describe the judgmental and engineering methods of estimating total costs.

Explain how the learning effect may influence cost estimation.

Describe cost trends in the United States.

A variety of managerial cost and expense terms, classifications, and concepts were introduced in Chapter 15. This chapter continues the discussion of cost concepts by focusing on cost behavior and cost estimation.

Cost behavior refers to the manner in which a cost changes in relation to its activity base. For example, direct materials costs vary proportionately with changes in the number of units produced. If the total units produced doubles, direct materials costs will also double. **Cost estimation** refers to the methods used to estimate costs for use in managerial decision making. For example, the managerial accountant must develop reliable product cost estimates for use by managers in setting selling prices.

A thorough understanding of cost behavior and cost estimation methods is essential for planning and controlling operations. For example, classifying costs by their behavior as production varies allows management to establish standards for evaluating (controlling) the efficiency of current operations and for predicting (planning) the costs of future levels of operations. Cost estimation methods may be used to analyze past cost behavior so that future production costs can be estimated.

COST BEHAVIOR

The behavior of costs can be classified in a variety of ways. The three most common cost classifications are variable costs, fixed costs, and mixed costs. Each of these classifications was briefly described in Chapter 15. This chapter expands upon this discussion to include additional issues which must be considered if the managerial accountant is to classify cost behavior properly into these three types.

Variable Costs

Variable costs are costs that vary in total in direct proportion to changes in an activity base. As mentioned in Chapter 15, direct materials and direct labor costs are generally treated as variable costs because, as production volume changes, the totals of these costs change proportionately. To illustrate, assume that Wilson Inc. produces stereophonic sound systems under the brand name of JimBo. The parts for the stereo systems are purchased from outside suppliers for $10 per unit and are assembled in Wilson's Augusta plant. The direct materials costs for Model JW-12 for differing levels of production are summarized in the following table:

Number of Units of Model JW-12 Produced	*Direct Materials Cost per Unit*	*Total Direct Materials Cost*
5,000 units	$10	$ 50,000
10,000 units	10	100,000
15,000 units	10	150,000
20,000 units	10	200,000
25,000 units	10	250,000
30,000 units	10	300,000

As the table illustrates, the total direct materials cost varies in direct proportion to the number of units of Model JW-12 produced. The direct materials cost for 25,000 units ($250,000) is 5 times the direct materials cost for 5,000 units ($50,000). However, the unit direct materials cost of $10 remains constant over all levels of production. A constant per unit cost is a characteristic of variable costs.

The following graphs illustrate how the variable costs for direct materials for Model JW-12 behave in total and on a per unit basis as production changes:

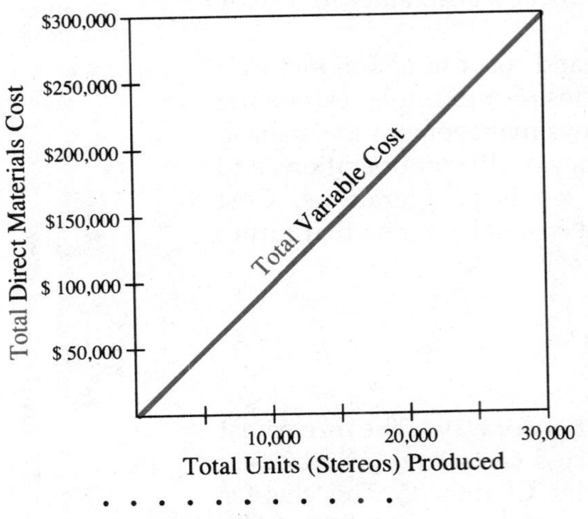

Total Variable Cost Graph

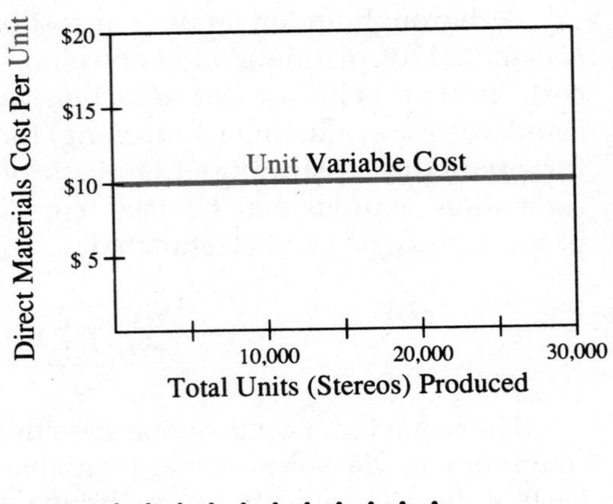

Unit Variable Cost Graph

Activity Base for Variable Costs. The preceding illustration of a variable cost used units produced as the activity base. The relevant activity base for a cost depends upon which base is most closely associated with the cost and the decision-making needs of management in using the cost in planning and controlling operations. To illustrate, food costs for a hospital are closely associated with the number of patients in the hospital. Thus, the number of patients would be the most appropriate activity base for making decisions related to food costs. On the other hand, because patients' diagnoses differ, the number of x-rays taken rather than the number of patients is a better activity base for decisions related to the cost of x-ray film.

To provide relevant information to management for decision making, managerial accountants must be thoroughly familiar with the operations of the entity, so that the most appropriate activity bases for various cost classifications are selected. Units sold and units produced are commonly used activity bases, but they may not always be the most appropriate. For example, miles driven rather than the number of orders delivered would be the most appropriate activity base for gasoline costs of a moving company.

Step-Wise Variable Costs. True variable costs remain constant on a per unit basis and change in total on a proportionate basis with changes in an activity base. For example, in the previous illustration of Wilson Inc., each additional Model JW-12 unit produced required $10 of direct materials. The materials cost per unit remained constant at $10, and the total materials cost increased by $10 with each additional unit produced. Hence, as the number of units of Model JW-12 produced doubled from 5,000 units to 10,000 units, the total direct materials cost doubled from $50,000 to $100,000. Likewise, as the number of units of Model JW-12 tripled, the total direct materials cost tripled.

In practice, some costs may be classified as variable costs, even though they may not change in exact proportion to changes in the activity base. For example, direct labor costs are generally treated as a variable cost. However, direct labor may be acquired in units that increase or decrease with a batch of products produced. In such cases, the direct labor cost is a step-wise variable cost. To illustrate, assume that Horn Inc. manufactures machine tools using semi-automated lathes. During an 8-hour work shift, a machine operator normally produces 50 tools. Thus, for each increase in production of 50 tools, an additional machine operator is required. If scheduled production for a machine operator is less than 50 tools, the operator is still paid for an 8-hour shift. Assuming that machine operators earn $12.50 per hour, the direct labor costs for increasing levels of production are summarized in the following table and graph:

Number of Units Produced	*Total Direct Labor Cost*
0– 50	$100
51–100	200
101–150	300
151–200	400
201–250	500
251–300	600

Total Step-Wise Variable Cost

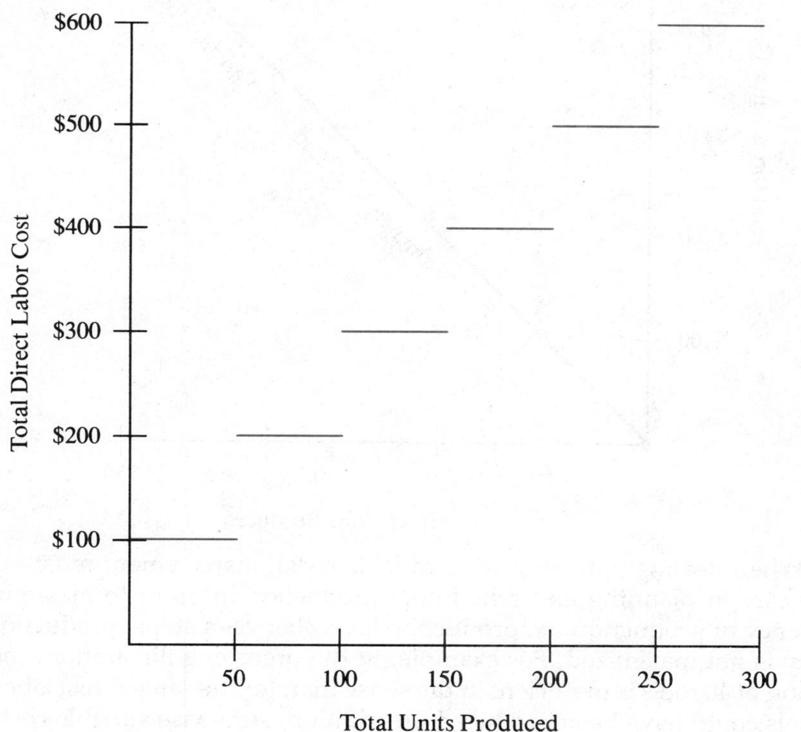

Step-wise variable costs derive their name from their step-wise nature, as indicated in the preceding graph. In practice, when the length of the steps is relatively small, step-wise variable costs are often treated as simple variable costs. For example, in the preceding illustration, the direct labor cost could be treated as a variable cost with a constant per unit cost of $2, as illustrated in the following table:

Number of Units Produced	Total Direct Labor Cost	Direct Labor Cost per Unit
50	$100	$2
100	200	2
150	300	2
200	400	2
250	500	2
300	600	2

These direct labor costs are shown in the following graph, where the step-wise variable cost data are indicated by dotted lines and the estimated variable cost data are indicated by a solid line.

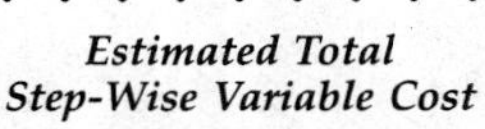

Estimated Total Step-Wise Variable Cost

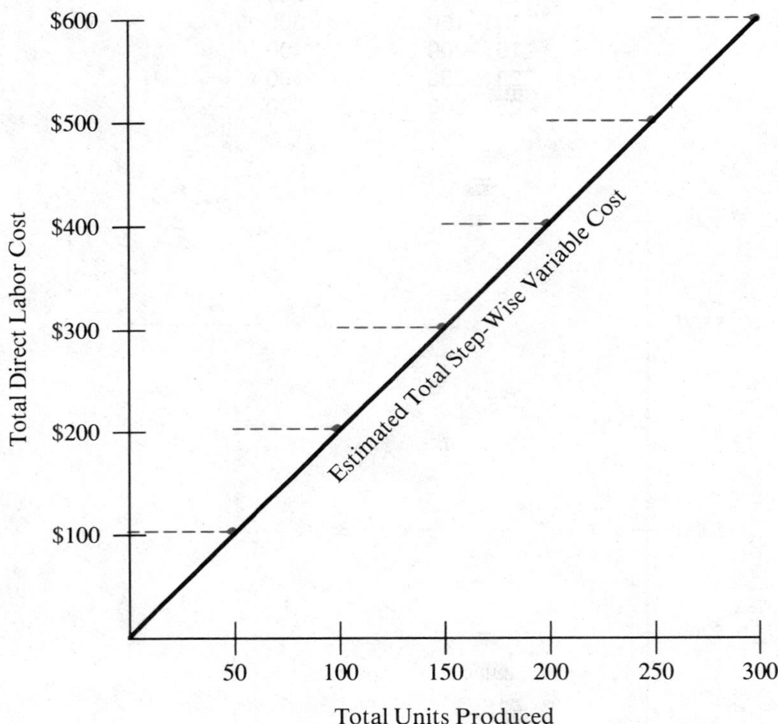

When dealing with step-wise variable costs, management must exercise extra care in planning and scheduling production in order to maximize the efficiency of production. At production levels between steps, production efficiency is not maximized. For example, in the preceding illustration, the production of 40 tools is inefficient in the sense that, for the same direct labor cost, 50 tools could have been produced. In addition, step-wise variable costs may be difficult to reduce when production decreases, thus creating further inefficiencies. For example, if workers are laid off every time a significant decrease in production occurs, employee morale may suffer, additional training costs may be necessary in hiring replacement workers when production resumes, and the company may have difficulty hiring workers who view the likelihood of layoffs as high.

Relevant Range for Variable Costs. Because variable costs are assumed to change in a constant proportion with changes in the activity base, the graph of a variable cost when plotted against the activity base appears as a straight line, as illustrated on page 680. In this sense, variable costs are said to be **linear** in nature.

Over a wide range of production, some costs vary in differing proportions to changes in an activity base, rather than vary in a constant proportion. This phenomenon of changing proportions of costs to changes in an activity base is referred to by economists as the principle of **economies of scale.** This principle recognizes that, when production facilities are limited, some variable costs increase but at a decreasing rate as production increases from a relatively low level. This behavior occurs because, as operations expand, workers learn to be more efficient and division of labor is possible. Therefore, the rate of increase in direct labor costs is not constant. At some point, however, variable costs may begin to increase at an increasing rate, rather than at a constant rate, because of inefficiencies created by such factors as employee fatigue and poor morale.

Graphically, the effect of differing proportions of costs to changes in an activity base is a curvilinear line rather than a straight line. The following graph illustrates the principle of economies of scale for the direct labor costs of John Manufacturing Inc.:

Economies of Scale

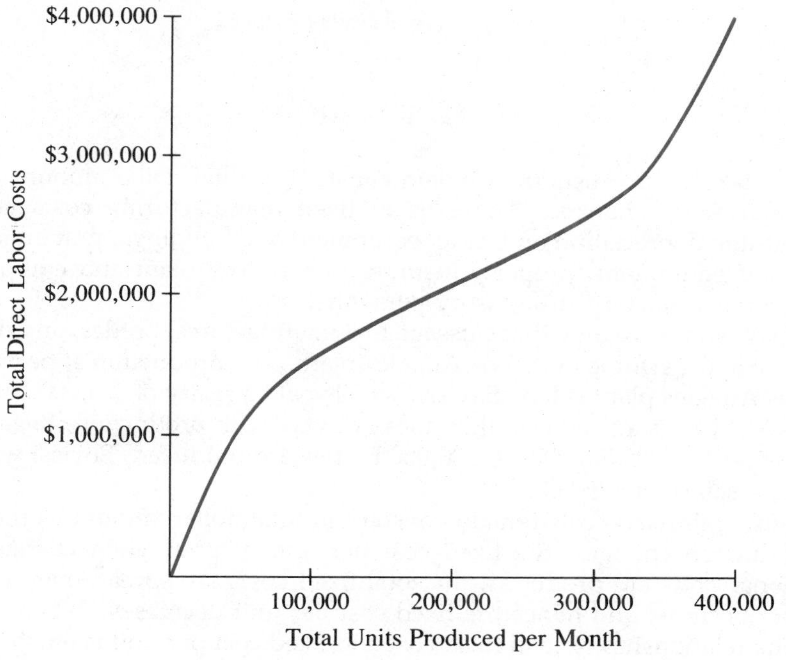

Managerial accountants recognize the curvilinear nature of total costs for wide ranges of production. However, most operating decisions by management focus on a narrow range of relevant activity within which the enterprise is planning to operate. This range of activity is referred to as the **relevant range.** Generally, within the relevant range, variable costs vary so closely to a constant rate that they may be represented by a straight line without a significant loss of accuracy. For example, the direct labor costs of John Manufacturing Inc. are considered to be linear in nature for the relevant range of production, 100,000 units to 300,000 units, as shown in the following graph:

Relevant Range for Variable Costs

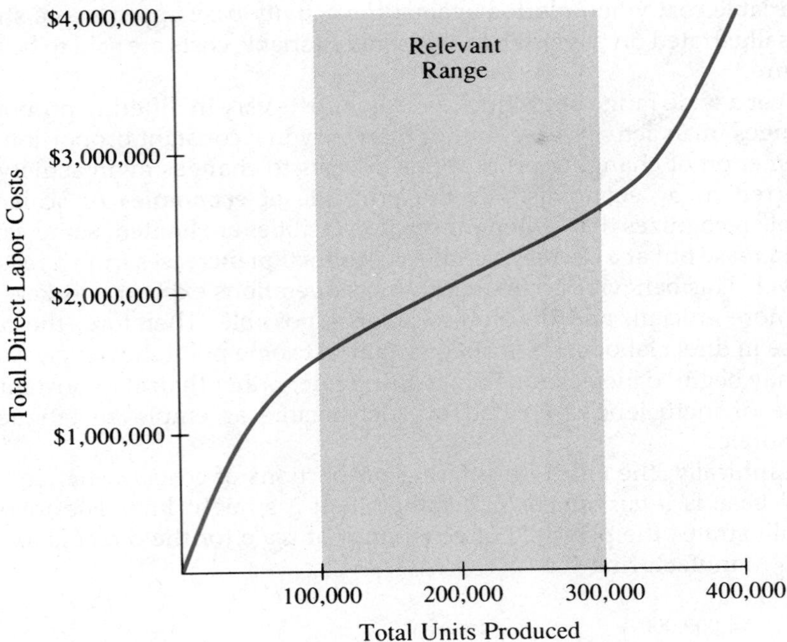

Fixed Costs

Fixed costs are costs that remain constant in total dollar amount as the level of activity changes. Examples of fixed manufacturing costs include straight-line depreciation on factory equipment and buildings, rent on factory plant and equipment, property insurance on factory plant and equipment, and salaries of factory supervisory personnel.

To illustrate, assume that Gossage Inc. manufactures, bottles, and distributes La Fleur Perfume at its Los Angeles plant. The production supervisor at the Los Angeles plant is Jane Sovissi, who is paid a salary of $75,000 per year. Sovissi's salary is a fixed cost that does not vary with production. Regardless of whether 50,000, 100,000, or 300,000 bottles are produced, Sovissi will still receive a salary of $75,000.

Although fixed costs remain constant in total dollar amount as the level of production changes, the fixed cost per unit of production changes. As additional units are produced, the total fixed costs are spread over a larger number of units, and hence the fixed cost per unit decreases.

The relationship of total fixed cost and fixed cost per unit is illustrated in the following table and graphs for the $75,000 salary of Jane Sovissi:

Number of Bottles of Perfume Produced	Total Salary for Jane Sovissi	Salary per Bottle Produced
50,000 bottles	$75,000	$1.500
100,000	75,000	.750
150,000	75,000	.500
200,000	75,000	.375
250,000	75,000	.300
300,000	75,000	.250

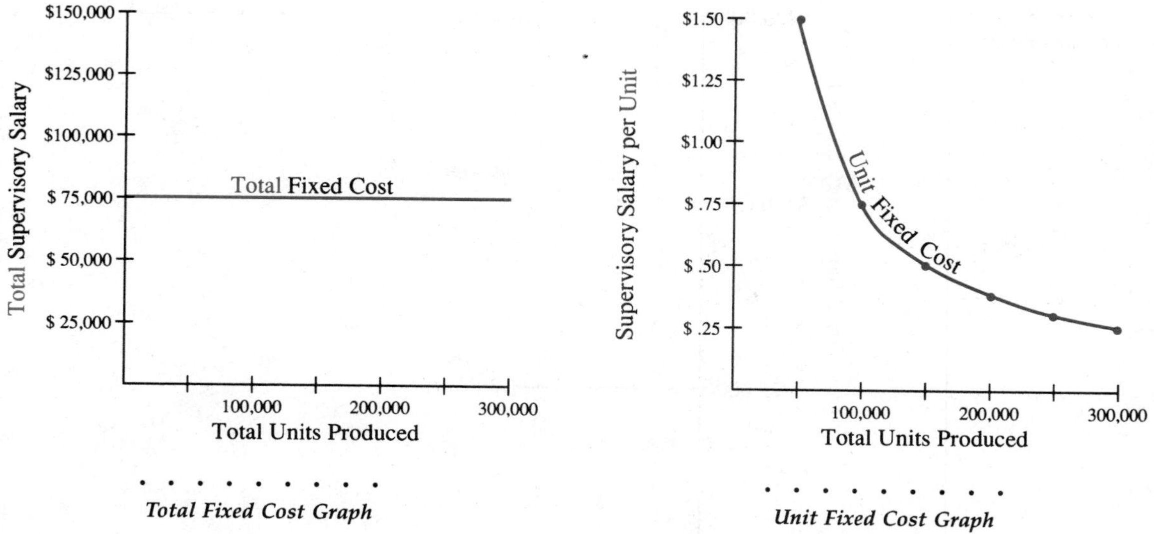

Total Fixed Cost Graph

Unit Fixed Cost Graph

Activity Base for Fixed Costs. Like variable costs, fixed costs are defined relative to an activity base. In most situations, the activity base for fixed costs will be expressed as either units produced, units sold, or sales dollars. In the preceding illustration, the activity base was expressed in terms of units of production—bottles of perfume produced.

Step-Wise Fixed Costs. As discussed earlier, many costs behave in a step-wise fashion over a wide range of production. **Step-wise fixed costs** differ from step-wise variable costs in the width of the range of production over which total costs change: the steps are longer for step-wise fixed costs than for step-wise variable costs. For example, a step-wise variable cost might vary with every 50 units produced, while a step-wise fixed cost might vary with every 300,000 units produced.

To illustrate, assume that Gossage Inc. can only produce 300,000 bottles of La Fleur Perfume during an 8-hour shift. To produce between 300,000 to 600,000 bottles of perfume, an additional shift has to be added and another production supervisor hired at a salary of $75,000. Likewise, to produce between 600,000 to 900,000 bottles of perfume, yet another production supervisor must be hired. Graphically, the step-wise nature of the production supervisory salary costs is illustrated at the top of page 686.

Another example of step-wise fixed costs is straight-line depreciation on machinery. As demand for a product increases and new machines are purchased to produce additional units, total straight-line depreciation costs will vary in a step-wise fashion.

Step-wise fixed costs tend to be long-term in nature and therefore are not easily changed. For this reason, managers should be careful in incurring step-wise fixed costs. Since fixed costs cannot be easily changed, managers often focus on maximizing the usage of existing resources. Later chapters will discuss commonly used methods by which managers evaluate decisions that involve the incurrence of fixed costs.

Relevant Range for Fixed Costs. As discussed in the preceding paragraphs, there exists a relevant range of activity for which management normally focuses its attention for operating purposes. The usefulness of this relevant range for classifying step-wise variable costs was discussed previously. The relevant range is also useful in classifying step-wise fixed costs for

Step-Wise Fixed Costs

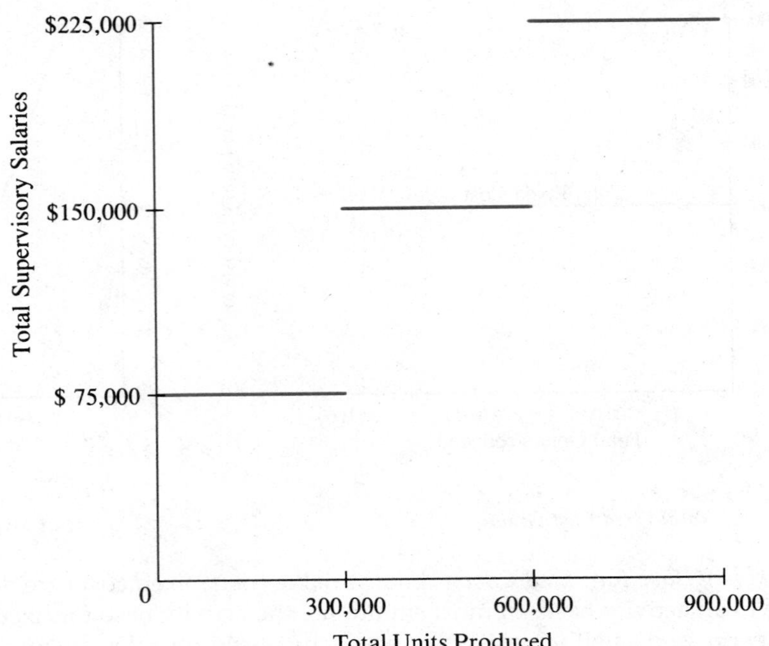

management decision-making purposes. To illustrate, if the relevant range of production for Gossage Inc. is between 300,000 and 600,000 bottles of perfume, the salary cost of production supervisors is a fixed cost of $150,000, as shown in the following graph:

Relevant Range for Fixed Costs

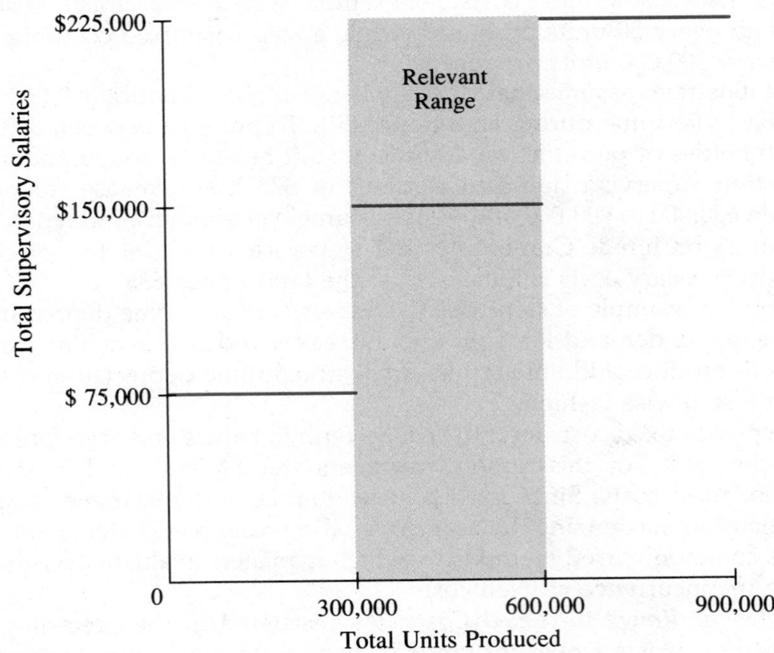

Mixed Costs

A **mixed cost** has characteristics of both a variable and a fixed cost. For example, over one range of the activity base, the mixed cost may remain constant in total amount, and it will therefore be a fixed cost. Over another range of activity, the mixed cost may change in proportion to changes in the activity base, and it will therefore be a variable cost. Mixed costs are sometimes referred to as **semivariable** or **semifixed** costs.

To illustrate, assume that Simpson Inc. manufactures sails, using rented machinery. The rental charges are $20,000 per year plus $1 for each machine hour used. If the machinery is used 20,000 hours, the total rental charge is $40,000 [$20,000 + (20,000 × $1)]. If the machinery is used 30,000 hours, the total rental charge is $50,000 [$20,000 + (30,000 × $1)], and so on. This mixed cost behavior is illustrated graphically below.

Mixed Costs – $20,000 + $1 per Hour

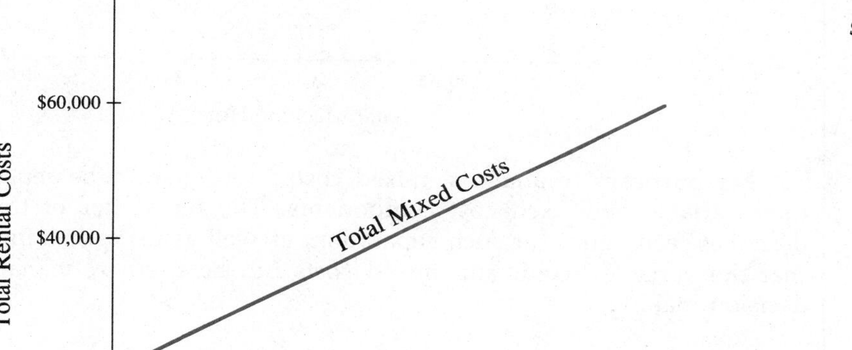

In this illustration, which is the most common type of mixed cost behavior, a rental cost of $20,000 will be incurred, even if the machinery is not used at all. The $20,000 is constant over all levels of production and represents the fixed cost component of the mixed cost. The rental charge of $1 per hour, which represents the variable cost component of the mixed cost, causes the total mixed cost to increase as machine hours are used.

The behavior of mixed costs can vary widely. For example, if the rental charges in the preceding illustration had been $15,000 per year plus $1 for each machine hour used over 10,000 hours, the mixed cost graph would appear as shown at the top of page 688.

In this graph, the fixed cost component is $15,000 and the rental charge of $1 per hour is the variable cost component of the mixed cost. The variable cost component causes the total mixed cost to increase after 10,000 machine hours have been used.

Mixed Costs — $15,000 + $1 per Hour Over 10,000 Hours

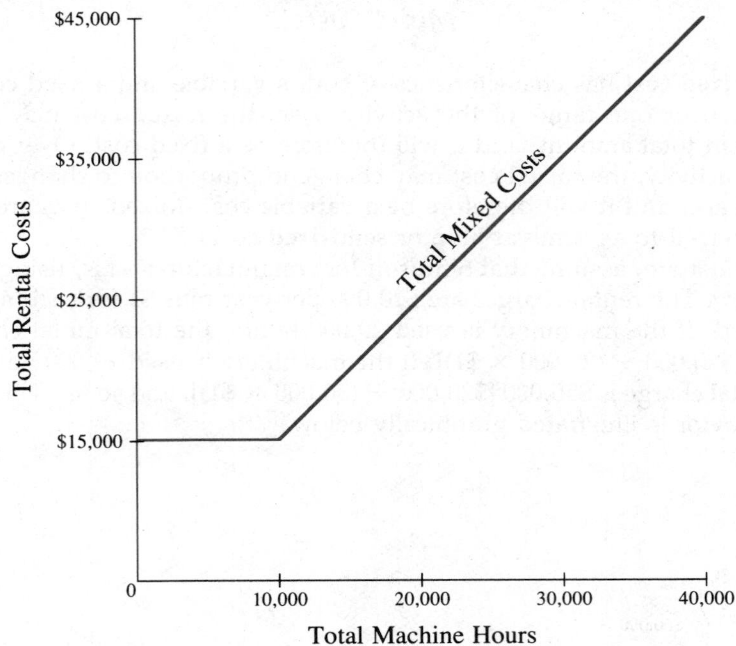

For purposes of analysis, mixed costs can generally be separated into their variable and fixed cost components. The remainder of this chapter describes techniques for such separation, as well as for estimating costs, so that the variable, fixed, and mixed costs can be used by management in decision making.

Summary of Cost Behavior Concepts

As indicated in the preceding paragraphs, costs can be classified as variable costs, fixed costs, or mixed costs. Step-wise variable costs and step-wise fixed costs are normally treated as either simple variable costs or fixed costs. Likewise, for purposes of analysis, mixed costs are generally separated into their variable and fixed cost components. The following table summarizes the cost behavior characteristics of variable costs and fixed costs:

	Effect of Changing Activity Level	
Cost	*Total Amount*	*Per Unit Amount*
Variable	Increases and decreases proportionately with activity level.	Remains constant regardless of activity level.
Fixed	Remains constant regardless of activity level.	Increases and decreases inversely with activity level.

COST ESTIMATION

Although the costs from past operations are known, it is the estimation of future costs that is important for many analyses useful in decison making. In addition, the separation of estimated total costs into fixed and variable cost components is necessary for many decisions. These decisions may involve cost control, product pricing, and production planning, which will be discussed in later chapters. The following paragraphs describe methods of cost estimation, including the high-low method, the scattergraph method, and the least squares method.

High-Low Method

The **high-low method** is used to estimate costs at a desired production level, as well as the variable and fixed components, for either a particular mixed cost or for total costs in general. In this chapter, the examples will use the highest and lowest total costs revealed by past cost patterns. The activity base associated with past cost patterns is usually units of production, although other activity bases, such as machine hours, direct labor hours, or direct labor cost, could be used.

To estimate the variable cost per unit and the fixed cost, the following steps are used:

1. a. The difference between the *total costs* at the highest and lowest levels of production is determined.
   b. The difference between the *total units* produced at the highest and lowest levels of production is determined.
2. Since only the total variable cost will change as the number of units of production changes, the difference in total costs as determined in (1a) is divided by the diference in units produced as determined in (1b) to determine the variable cost per unit.
3. The total variable cost (variable cost per unit × total units produced) at either the highest or the lowest level of production is determined, and the amount is subtracted from the total cost at that level to determine the fixed cost per period.

To illustrate, assume that Sutton Company, which produces sports jerseys, has incurred total costs for the following levels of production during the past 5 months:

	Units Produced	*Total Costs*
June	175,000 units	$185,000
July	75,000	80,000
August	200,000	210,000
September	325,000	320,000
October	300,000	270,000

The units produced and the total costs at the highest and lowest levels of production and the differences are as follows:

	Units Produced	*Total Costs*
Highest level	325,000 units	$320,000
Lowest level	75,000	80,000
Differences	250,000 units	$240,000

Since the total fixed cost does not change with changes in volume of production, the $240,000 difference in the total cost represents the change in the total variable cost. Hence, dividing the difference in total costs by the change in production provides an estimate of the variable cost per unit. In this illustration, the variable cost per unit is $.96, as shown in the following computation:

$$\text{Variable Cost per Unit} = \frac{\text{Difference in Total Costs}}{\text{Difference in Production}}$$

$$\text{Variable Cost per Unit} = \frac{\$240{,}000}{250{,}000\text{ units}} = \$.96\text{ per unit}$$

The fixed costs will be the same at both the highest and the lowest levels of production. Thus, the fixed cost of $8,000 per month can be estimated by subtracting the estimated total variable cost from the total cost at either the highest or the lowest levels of production, using the total cost equation as follows:

$$\text{Total Cost} = (\text{Variable Cost per Unit} \times \text{Units of Production}) + \text{Fixed Cost}$$

Highest level:

$$\$320{,}000 = (\$.96 \times 325{,}000) + \text{Fixed Cost}$$
$$\$320{,}000 = \$312{,}000 + \text{Fixed Cost}$$
$$\$\ \ 8{,}000 = \text{Fixed Cost}$$

Lowest level:

$$\$\ 80{,}000 = (\$.96 \times 75{,}000) + \text{Fixed Cost}$$
$$\$\ 80{,}000 = \$72{,}000 + \text{Fixed Cost}$$
$$\$\ \ 8{,}000 = \text{Fixed Cost}$$

The variable and fixed cost components of the total cost have now been identified and can be incorporated into the total cost equation:

$$\text{Total Cost} = (\text{Variable Cost per Unit} \times \text{Units of Production}) + \text{Fixed Cost}$$
$$\text{Total Cost} = (\$.96 \times \text{Units of Production}) + \$8{,}000$$

The cost data and the related total cost for Sutton Company are plotted on the graph illustrated on page 691. The graph is constructed in the following manner:

1. Levels of units of production are spread along the horizontal axis. For Sutton Company, it is assumed that a maximum of 400,000 units could be produced per month.
2. The total costs are spread along the vertical axis. For Sutton Company, it is assumed that the total costs could not exceed $400,000 per month.
3. The total cost at the highest and lowest levels of production is then plotted on the graph. For example, the total cost of September's 325,000 units of

production would be indicated on the graph by a point representing $320,000. The total cost of July's 75,000 units would be indicated by a point representing $80,000.

4. After the total costs for the highest and lowest levels of production have been plotted on the graph, a straight line (the total cost line) is drawn through the highest and lowest total cost points. The point at which the total cost line intersects the vertical axis represents the estimated fixed cost per month, approximately $8,000. The variable cost per unit, $.96, is represented by the slope of the total cost line. The relevant range on the graph represents the range from which the cost data were gathered.

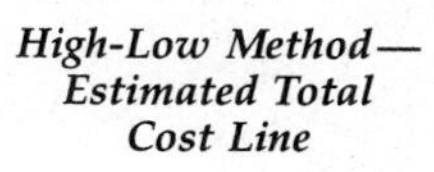

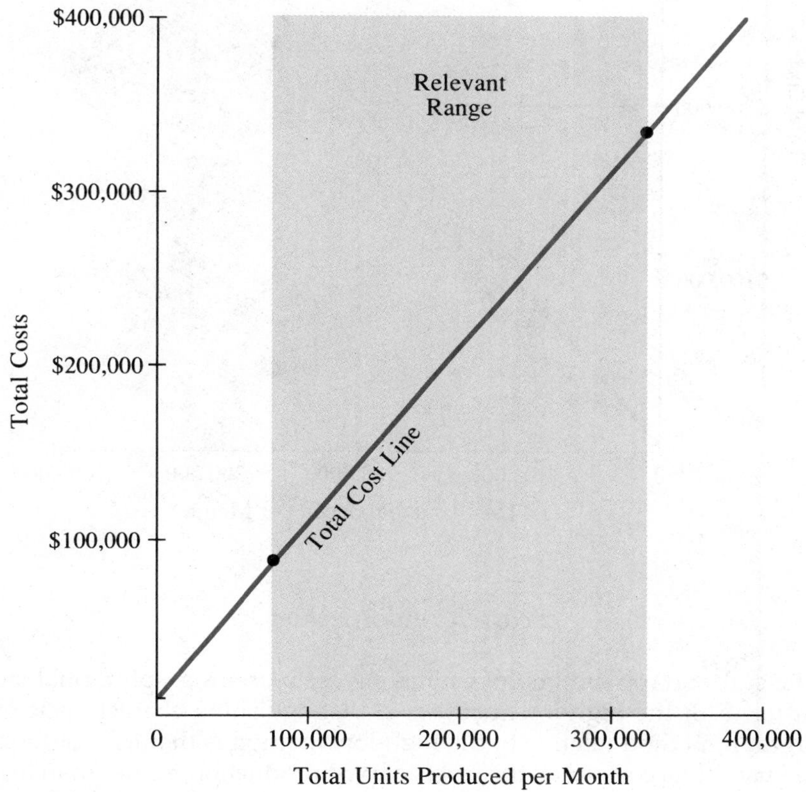

For any level of production within the relevant range, total costs can be estimated using either the graph or the total cost equation. For example, for 200,000 units of production in one month, the estimated total cost would be determined as follows, using the total cost equation:

Total Cost = ($.96 × 200,000 units) + $8,000
Total Cost = $200,000

Alternatively, the total cost can be estimated directly from the graph by locating the total units of production on the horizontal axis, proceeding vertically upward until the total cost line is intersected, and then proceeding horizontally to the left until the vertical axis is intersected. In this way, the estimated total cost of producing 200,000 units is determined to be $200,000, as shown in the following graph:

High-Low Method—Estimated Total Cost for 200,000 Units of Production

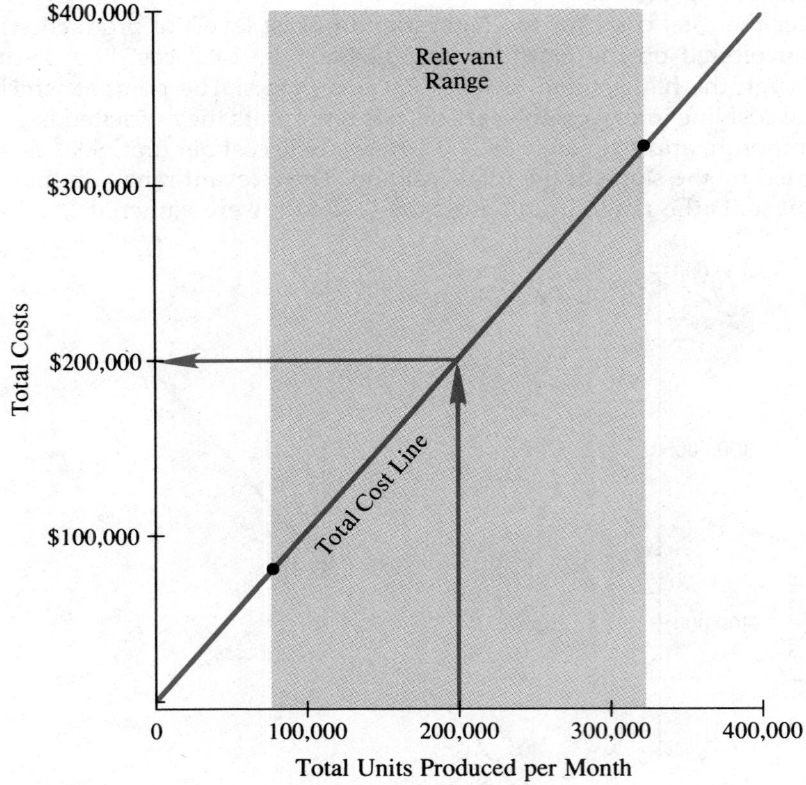

Scattergraph Method

The **scattergraph method** of estimating costs uses a graph format similar to that used for the high-low method. A distinguishing characteristic of the scattergraph method relative to the high-low method is that the scattergraph method uses total costs at all the levels of past production, rather than just the highest and lowest levels. Because the scattergraph method uses all the data available, it tends to be more accurate than the high-low method.

The following cost and production data for Sutton Company, which were used in illustrating the high-low method, are used to illustrate the scattergraph method:

	Units Produced	*Total Costs*
June	170,000	$185,000
July	75,000	80,000
August	200,000	210,000
September	325,000	320,000
October	300,000	270,000

The following scattergraph was constructed with these data:

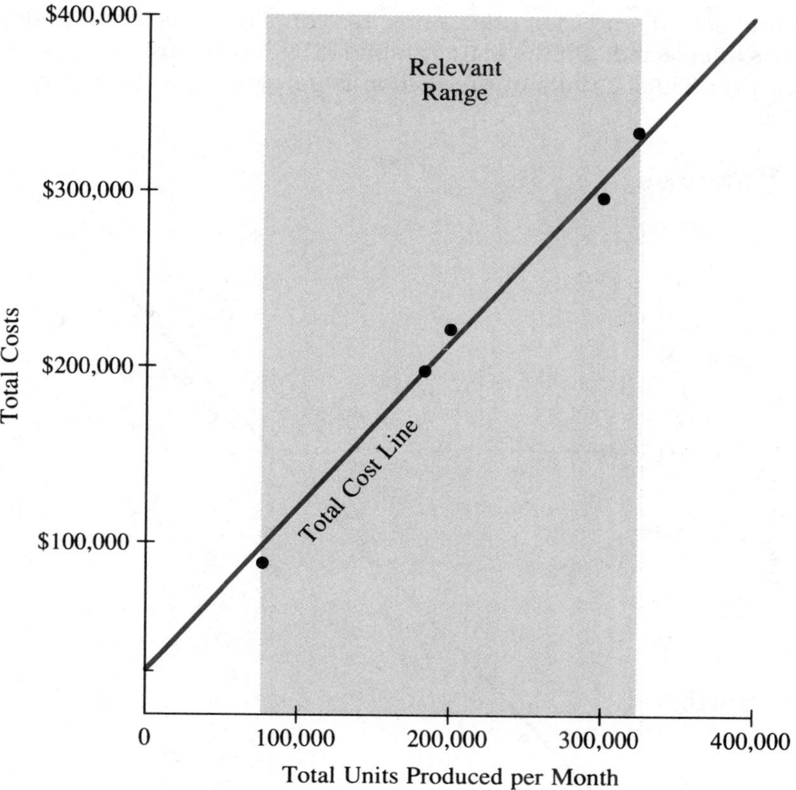

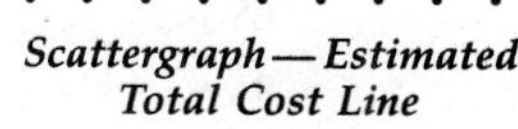

Scattergraph—Estimated Total Cost Line

The scattergraph is constructed in the following manner:

1. Levels of units of production are spread along the horizontal axis. For Sutton Company, it is assumed that a maximum of 400,000 units could be produced per month.
2. The total costs are spread along the vertical axis. For Sutton Company, it is assumed that the total costs could not exceed $400,000 per month.
3. The total cost at each past level of production is then plotted on the graph. For example, the total cost of June's 175,000 units of production would be indicated on the graph by a point representing $185,000. The total cost of July's 75,000 units would be indicated by a point representing $80,000.
4. After the total costs for the past levels of production have been plotted on the graph, a straight line representing the total costs is drawn on the graph. *This line is drawn so that the differences between each point and the line are at a minimum in the judgment of the preparer of the graph.*

The scattergraph is similar to the high-low graph, except for the total cost line. In the high-low method, the total cost line connects the highest and lowest cost points.

From the following scattergraph for Sutton Company, the estimated total costs for various levels of production and the fixed and variable cost components can be determined. The estimated total cost for any level of production within the relevant range can be determined by locating the units of production on the horizontal axis, proceeding vertically upward until the total cost line is intersected, and then proceeding horizontally to the left until the vertical axis is intersected. On the scattergraph for Sutton Company, the estimated total cost for 250,000 units of production is determined to be approximately $240,000.

Scattergraph Method—Estimated Total Cost for 250,000 Units of Production

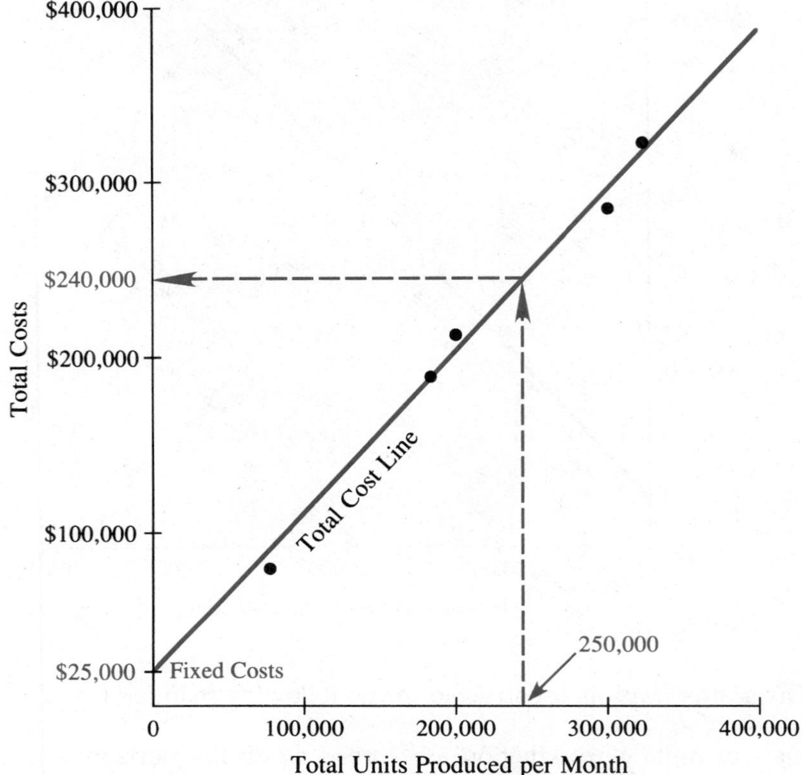

The point at which the total cost line intersects the vertical axis of the scattergraph indicates the estimated fixed cost of production. For Sutton Company, the fixed cost component is approximately $25,000 per month.

The total variable cost for any level of production within the relevant range is the difference between the estimated total cost and the estimated fixed cost. For Sutton Company, the estimated total variable cost for 250,000 units of production is $215,000 ($240,000 − $25,000). The estimated variable cost per unit is $.86 ($215,000 ÷ 250,000 units).

For 200,000 units of production, the estimated total cost would be determined as follows, using the total cost equation:

Total Cost = (Variable Cost per Unit × Units of Production) + Fixed Cost
Total Cost = ($.86 × Units of Production) + $25,000
Total Cost = ($.86 × 200,000 units) + $25,000
Total Cost = $197,000

Least Squares Method

While the scattergraph method requires the judgmental drawing of a total cost line through the plotted total cost points, the **least squares method** uses statistics to determine the total cost line. Thus, the resulting estimated total cost line is based on more objective statistical criteria.

The least squares method fits a straight line through the plotted total cost points according to the following total cost equation:

Total Cost = (Variable Cost per Unit × Units of Production) + Fixed Cost

The variable cost per unit component of this equation is estimated statistically, using the following computational formula:

$$\text{Variable Cost per Unit} = \frac{n(\Sigma P_iC_i) - (\Sigma P_i)(\Sigma C_i)}{n(\Sigma P_i^2) - (\Sigma P_i)^2}$$

The symbols in the preceding formula are explained as follows:

- n is the number of total cost observations
- Σ is the sum of the numbers
- P_i is an observed level of production, in units, at period *i*
- C_i is an observation of total cost, in dollars, at period *i*
- P_i^2 is the square of the value P_i; likewise, $(\Sigma P_i)^2$ is the square of the value (ΣP_i)

The formula can be easily solved through the use of a computational table with columns for P_i, C_i, P_i^2, and P_iC_i. To illustrate, the following computational table for the estimation of the variable cost per unit for Sutton Company is prepared, based on the cost and production data that were used in the preceding illustrations. To simplify the computations, the thousands have been deleted from both the cost and production data.

Units Produced *(P_i)*	*Total Costs* *(C_i)*	P_i^2	P_iC_i
175	$ 185	30,625	$ 32,375
75	80	5,625	6,000
200	210	40,000	42,000
325	320	105,625	104,000
300	270	90,000	81,000
1,075	$1,065	271,875	$265,375
↑ ΣP_i	↑ ΣC_i	↑ ΣP_i^2	↑ ΣP_iC_i

Using the values from the table, the computational formula yields the following results:

$$\text{Variable Cost per Unit} = \frac{n(\Sigma P_iC_i) - (\Sigma P_i)(\Sigma C_i)}{n(\Sigma P_i^2) - (\Sigma P_i)^2}$$

$$\text{Variable Cost per Unit} = \frac{5(\$265{,}375) - (1{,}075)(\$1{,}065)}{5(271{,}875) - (1{,}075)^2}$$

$$\text{Variable Cost per Unit} = \frac{\$1{,}326{,}875 - \$1{,}144{,}875}{1{,}359{,}375 - 1{,}155{,}625}$$

$$\text{Variable Cost per Unit} = \frac{\$182{,}000}{203{,}750} = \$.89 \text{ per unit}$$

The fixed cost component of total cost is estimated statistically, using the following computational formula:

$$\text{Fixed Cost} = \overline{C} - (\text{Variable Cost per Unit} \times \overline{P})$$

The symbols are explained as follows:

$\overline{C}$ is the average of the monthly total costs
$\overline{P}$ is the average of the monthly units of production

For Sutton Company, the average total cost is $213,000 ($1,065,000 ÷ 5), and the average units of production is 215,000 units (1,075,000 units ÷ 5). When these values are substituted into the formula, the fixed cost per month is computed as follows:

Fixed Cost = $213,000 − ($.89 × 215,000 units)
Fixed Cost = $213,000 − $191,350
Fixed Cost = $21,650

The estimated fixed cost of $21,650 per month and the variable cost of $.89 per unit are represented in the total cost equation as follows:

Total Cost = Variable Cost + Fixed Cost
Total Cost = ($.89 × Total Units of Production) + $21,650

The estimated total cost can be shown graphically by fitting the estimated total cost line to the plotted data, as illustrated at the top of page 697 in the graph of the Sutton Company data. This line, which is sometimes referred to as a **regression line,** is fitted so that the sum of the squares of deviations from each plotted point to the line is smaller (hence, the name *least squares*) than it would be for any other line. Regression lines are discussed in detail in more advanced texts.

For 200,000 units of production in one month, the estimated total cost could be determined by using the graph at the top of page 697 or the total cost equation, as follows:

Total Cost = ($.89 × 200,000 units) + $21,650
Total Cost = $199,650

Comparison of Cost Estimation Methods

Each of the three methods described provided different estimates of fixed and variable costs, summarized as follows:

	Variable Cost per Unit	*Fixed Cost per Month*
High-low method	$.96	$ 8,000
Scattergraph method	.86	25,000
Least squares method	.89	21,650

The cost estimation method that should be used in any given situation depends on such considerations as the cost of gathering data for the estimates and the importance of the accuracy of the estimates. Although the high-low

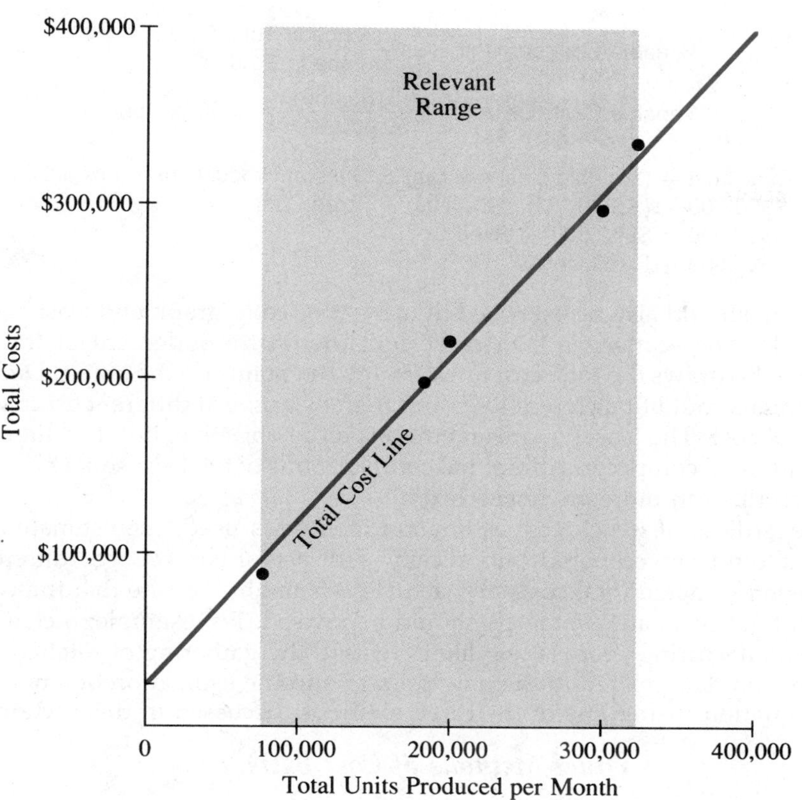

Least-Squares Method—Estimated Total Cost Line

method is the easiest and the least costly to apply, it is also normally the least accurate. The least squares method is generally more accurate, but it is more complex and more costly to use.

In this illustration, the high-low method differs significantly in its estimates of variable and fixed costs, $.96 and $8,000, compared to the variable and fixed cost estimates of the scattergraph and least squares method, $.86 and $25,000, and $.89 and $21,650, respectively. These differences result because the high-low method uses only two cost and production observations to estimate costs for all levels of production. If these two observations are not representative of the normal cost and production patterns for all levels of production, then inaccurate variable and fixed cost estimates may be obtained. To illustrate, if the July production and total cost data for Sutton Company are eliminated because they are seasonal and not typical of normal operations, then the high-low method yields representative estimates which are comparable to the estimates provided by the scattergraph and least squares methods, as shown in the following computations. In these computations, the fixed cost is estimated at the highest level of production.

	Total Units Produced	*Total Costs*
Highest level	325,000 units	$320,000
Lowest level (excluding July data)	175,000	185,000
Differences	150,000 units	$135,000

$$\text{Variable Cost per Unit} = \frac{\text{Difference in Total Cost}}{\text{Difference in Production}}$$

$$\text{Variable Cost per Unit} = \frac{\$135{,}000}{150{,}000 \text{ units}} = \$.90 \text{ per unit}$$

$$\begin{aligned} \text{Total Cost} &= (\text{Variable Cost per Unit} \times \text{Units of Production}) + \text{Fixed Cost} \\ \$320{,}000 &= (\$.90 \times 325{,}000 \text{ units}) + \text{Fixed Cost} \\ \$320{,}000 &= \$292{,}500 + \text{Fixed Cost} \\ \$27{,}500 &= \text{Fixed Cost} \end{aligned}$$

Care should also be exercised in using the scattergraph and least squares methods. The scattergraph method depends on the judgment of the individual who draws the total cost line through the points on the graph. Different individuals could fit different lines and thereby arrive at different estimates of the total cost. The least squares method is more objective, but it is difficult to use without a computer. Additional complications of the least squares method are described in more advanced texts.

Regardless of which cost estimation method is used, the estimated total costs should be compared periodically with actual costs. Large differences between estimated total costs and actual costs might indicate that the way in which total costs are estimated should be revised. For example, a change in the manufacturing process will likely require the gathering of total cost and production data related to the new process and the estimation of a new total cost equation, using one of the three methods discussed in this section.

Other Methods of Cost Estimation

The preceding paragraphs have described three common methods of cost estimation. Two other methods used in practice include the judgmental method and the engineering method. Each of these methods is briefly discussed in the following paragraphs.

Judgmental Method. The use of the **judgmental method** is viewed by some accountants as an alternative method of cost estimation. Under this method, managers use their experience and past observations of cost-volume relationships to estimate fixed and variable costs. The advantage of this method is its simplicity and its reliance on the seasoned experience of the manager. In some cases, managers use either the high-low, scattergraph, or least-squares method as an initial starting point and then refine the estimates, using experienced judgment. The use of the judgmental method has the further advantage of allowing the manager to incorporate anticipated cost trends into the estimates, rather than relying solely on past cost data. The disadvantage of the judgmental method is its heavy reliance on the judgment of the manager or the accountant who is estimating the costs. If this individual does not exercise good judgment, a significant potential for errors exists. Such errors could have a major effect on related managerial decisions.[1]

Engineering Method. In situations where little or no past cost data are available for use in estimating costs, the **engineering method** may be used to estimate costs. Under this method, industrial engineers provide estimates based on studies of such factors as production methods, materials and labor requirements, equipment needs, and utility demands. The following excerpt

[1] A recent study sponsored by the National Association of Accountants concluded that managerial judgment is a widely used method of estimating costs. Maryanne M. Mowen, *Accounting for Costs as Fixed and Variable* (National Association of Accountants: Montvale, New Jersey, 1986), p. 19.

taken from a National Association of Accountants Research Report summarizes the use of the engineering method:

The industrial engineering approach to determination of how costs should vary with volume proceeds by systematic study of materials, labor, services, and facilities needed at varying volumes.... These studies generally make use of... results obtained by direct study of the production methods and facilities. Where no past experience is available, as with a new product, plant, or method, this approach can be applied to estimate the changes in cost that will accompany changes in volume.[2]

THE LEARNING EFFECT IN ESTIMATING COSTS

Total costs are affected by how efficiently and effectively employees perform their tasks. In a manufacturing environment, costs will be affected by how rapidly new employees learn their jobs and by how rapidly experienced employees learn new job assignments. For example, after production for a new product begins or as a new manufacturing process is implemented, workers usually increase their efficiency as more units are produced and they become more experienced. This **learning effect** is known as the **learning curve phenomenon.** When learning occurs, it can have a significant impact on costs and should be considered in estimating costs.

To illustrate, assume that Barker Company manufactures yachts and has added a new yacht to its product line. Past experience indicates that every time a new line of yachts is added, the total time to manufacture each yacht declines by 10% as each of the next 5 yachts is produced. Thus, the second yacht requires 90% of the total time to manufacture the first yacht, the third yacht requires 90% of the time of the second yacht, and so on. However, past experience also indicates that after the sixth yacht is produced, further reductions in time are insignificant.

For Barker Company, it is estimated that the first yacht will require 500 direct labor hours at $20 per hour, and that 10 yachts are scheduled for initial production. The following table illustrates the learning effect on the total direct labor cost per yacht:

Yacht	Total Direct Labor Hours per Yacht	Direct Labor Cost per Hour	Total Direct Labor Cost per Yacht
1	500	$20	$10,000
2	450	20	9,000
3	405	20	8,100
4	365	20	7,300
5	329	20	6,580
6	296	20	5,920
7	296	20	5,920
8	296	20	5,920
9	296	20	5,920
10	296	20	5,920

In this table, the total direct labor hours per yacht declined by 10% each time an additional yacht was produced, from a high of 500 hours to a low of 296 hours. The total direct labor cost per yacht declined from a high of $10,000 to a low of $5,920. After the sixth yacht was produced, the employees had

[2]National Association of Accountants, *The Analysis of Cost-Volume-Profit Relationships: Research Report No. 16* (New York, 1960).

learned enough from their experience in building the first 6 yachts that no additional reductions in time could be achieved.

The learning effect for Barker Company in terms of total direct labor hours per yacht is shown in the following graph:

Graph of Learning Effect

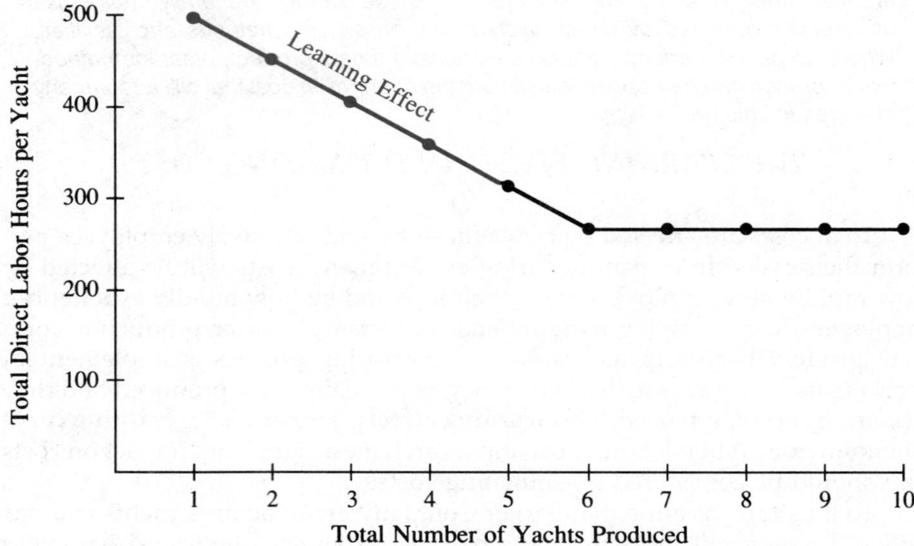

The learning effect does not occur for all production processes, nor does it affect all production processes in the same way. In the preceding illustration of Barker Company, for example, instead of a 10% learning effect each time an additional yacht was produced, the learning effect could have been 10% for the first 3 yachts and 5% for the following 3 yachts. Generally, the more labor that is used in the production process, the greater the opportunity for the learning effect to occur. As production processes become more automated, less opportunity for learning exists.

The learning effect is important to managers, since it directly affects cost estimation. Estimated costs affect the development of reports and analyses used by management in decision making.

COST TRENDS

There are several important cost trends in the United States which may be relevant in the preparation of reports for use by managers in decision making. One such trend is the increased automation of manufacturing processes through the use of robotics and advanced technology. As a result of this automation, the percentage of product cost that is attributable to direct labor cost has steadily declined over the years. In contrast, an increasing percentage of the product cost is fixed cost and factory overhead cost. The increasing fixed cost is due in large measure to increased depreciation charges, rental charges, property taxes, and insurance costs. Since fixed costs are often more difficult to reduce than variable costs, incurring an increasing percentage of fixed costs may limit the ability of an enterprise's managers to react quickly to changing environmental and market conditions.

As the percentage of direct labor costs has decreased significantly for many businesses in recent years, some managerial accountants have started to classify direct labor cost for such businesses as part of factory overhead cost, rather than as a separate product cost. This treatment is especially valid when the only direct labor cost entering into a manufacturing process is the wages of machine operators who operate or monitor several machines at one time. In this situation, it is difficult to trace the direct labor cost to any particular product or process.

The Explosive Growth of Overhead Costs

In order for American industry to remain competitive in world markets, it is critical for managers to control overhead costs and the forces behind them. Yet control of overhead costs is more difficult to achieve as overhead costs become a more significant part of product cost. This growth in overhead costs is described in the following excerpts from an article in the *Harvard Business Review:*

While the world's attention is focused on the fight to increase productivity and develop new technologies, manufacturing managers—especially those in the electronics and mechanical equipment (machinery) industries—are quietly waging a different battle: the battle to conquer [increasing] overhead costs. Indeed, our research shows that overhead costs rank behind only quality and getting new products out on schedule as a primary concern of manufacturing executives.

. . . Overhead costs as a percentage of value added in American industry and as a percentage of overall manufacturing costs have been rising steadily for more than 100 years as the ratio of direct labor costs to value added has declined [as indicated in the graph on page 167]. Moreover, in today's environment, production managers have more direct leverage on improving productivity through cutting overhead than they do through pruning direct labor.

As America's factories step up the pace of automation, they find that they are being hit twice: first, overhead costs grow in percentage terms as direct labor costs fall (everything has to add up to 100%); and second, overhead costs grow in real terms because of the increased support costs associated with maintaining and running automated equipment. . . .

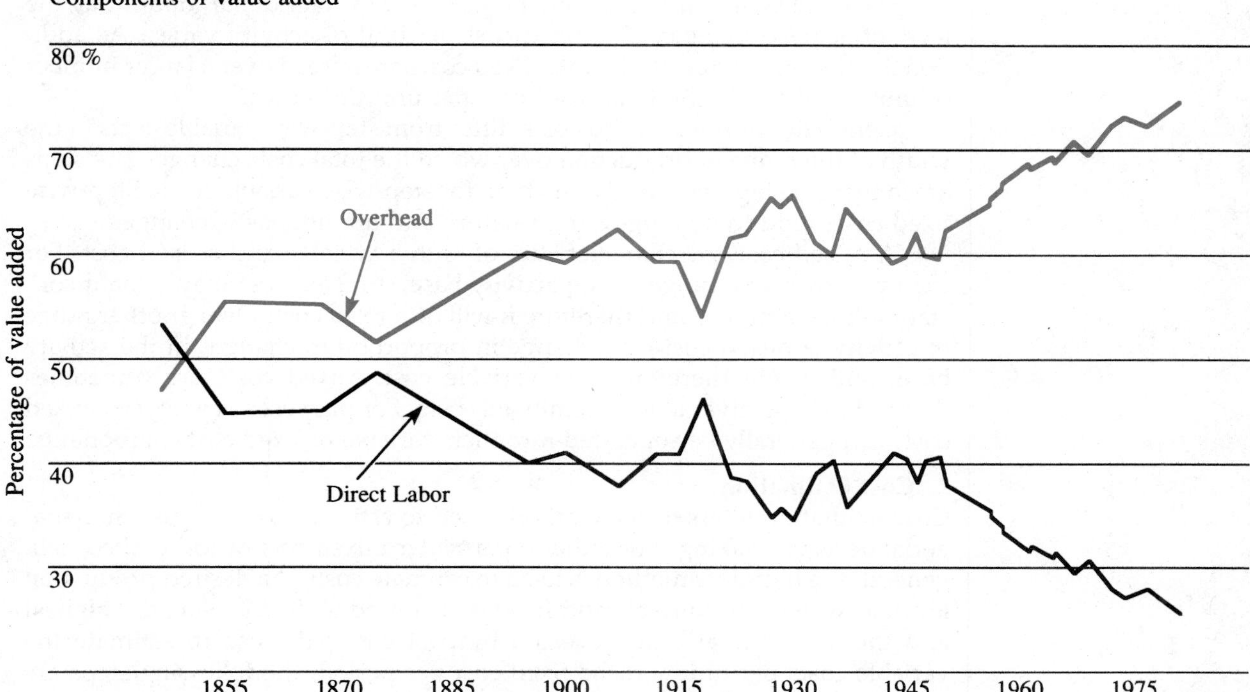

Source: Jeffrey G. Miller and Thomas E. Vollmann, "The Hidden Factory," *Harvard Business Review* (September–October, 1985),pp. 142–150.

Chapter Review

KEY POINTS

1. Cost Behavior.
Cost behavior refers to the manner in which a cost changes as its activity base changes. The three most common cost classifications are variable costs, fixed costs, and mixed costs.

Variable costs are costs that vary in total in direct proportion to changes in an activity base. Variable costs remain constant on a per unit basis with changes in the activity base. The relevant activity base for a variable cost depends upon which base is most closely associated with the cost and the decision-making needs of management. In practice, some costs may be classified as variable costs, even though they may not change in exact proportion to changes in the activity base. Step-wise variable costs change on a step-wise basis with changes in an activity base.

Because variable costs are assumed to change in constant proportion to changes in the activity base, the graph of a variable cost when plotted against the activity base appears as a straight line. In this sense, variable costs are said to be linear in nature. Over a wide range of production, costs often vary in different proportions to changes in an activity base, rather than in a constant proportion. This phenomenon is known as the principle of economies of scale. The narrow range of activity within which an enterprise is planning to operate is referred to as the relevant range. Within the relevant range, variable costs vary so closely to a constant rate that they may be represented by a straight line.

Fixed costs are costs that remain constant in total dollar amount as the level of activity changes. The fixed cost per unit of activity varies. As additional units are produced, the total fixed costs are spread over a larger number of units, and hence the total fixed cost per unit decreases.

Generally, step-wise fixed costs differ from step-wise variable costs in the width of the range of production over which the total costs change. The steps are longer for step-wise fixed costs than for step-wise variable costs. Step-wise fixed costs tend to be long-term in nature and are not easily changed.

A mixed cost has characteristics of both a variable and a fixed cost. For example, over one range of the activity base, a mixed cost may remain constant in total amount, and therefore it will be a fixed cost. Over another range of activity, a mixed cost may change in proportion to changes in the activity base, and it will therefore be a variable cost. Mixed costs are sometimes referred to as semivariable or semifixed costs. For purposes of analysis, mixed costs can generally be separated into their variable or fixed cost components.

2. Cost Estimation.
Cost estimation refers to the methods used to estimate costs for use in managerial decision making. For either a particular mixed cost or for total costs in general, the high-low method is used to estimate costs at a desired production level, as well as the variable and fixed cost components, by using the highest and the lowest total costs revealed by past cost patterns. To estimate the variable costs per unit and the fixed cost per period, the following steps are used:

1. a. The difference between the total costs at the highest and lowest levels of production is determined.
   b. The difference between the total units produced at the highest and lowest levels of production is determined.
2. The difference in total costs as determined in (1a) is divided by the difference in units produced as determined in (1b) to determine the variable cost per unit.
3. The total variable cost (variable cost per unit × total units produced) at either the highest or the lowest level of production is determined, and the amount is subtracted from the total cost at that level to determine the fixed cost per period.

The estimated total cost line for the high-low method can be plotted on a graph by connecting the highest and the lowest total cost points by a straight line. The point at which the total cost line intersects the vertical axis represents the estimated fixed cost per period. The variable cost per unit is represented by the slope of the total cost line.

The scattergraph method of estimating costs uses a graph format similar to that used for the high-low method. A distinguishing characteristic of the scattergraph method relative to the high-low method is that the scattergraph method uses total costs at all the levels of past production, rather than just the highest and lowest levels.

The scattergraph is constructed using similar procedures as for the high-low graph, except that the total cost line is drawn so that the differences between each plotted point and the line are at a minimum in the judgment of the preparer of the graph.

The least squares method of estimating costs uses statistics to determine the total cost line. The least squares method fits a straight line through the plotted total cost points according to the following total cost equation:

$$\text{Total Cost} = (\text{Variable Cost per Unit} \times \text{Units of Production}) + \text{Fixed Cost}$$

The variable cost per unit component of the equation is estimated statistically, using the following computational formula:

$$\text{Variable Cost per Unit} = \frac{n(\Sigma P_i C_i) - (\Sigma P_i)(\Sigma C_i)}{n(\Sigma P_i^2) - (\Sigma P_i)^2}$$

The fixed cost component of total cost is estimated statistically, using the following computational formula:

$$\text{Fixed Cost} = \overline{C} - (\text{Variable Cost per Unit} \times \overline{P})$$

The high-low method, scattergraph method, and least squares method provide different estimates of fixed and variable costs. The cost estimation method that should be used in any given situation depends upon such considerations as the cost of gathering data for the estimates and the importance of the accuracy of the estimates. Although the high-low method is the easiest and the least costly to apply, it is also normally the least accurate. The least squares method is generally more accurate, but it is more complex and more costly to use.

Two other methods of cost estimation used in practice include the judgmental method and the engineering method. Under the judgmental method, managers use their experience and past observations to estimate fixed and variable costs. Under the engineering method, industrial engineers estimate fixed and variable costs by studying such factors as production methods, materials and labor requirements, equipment needs, and utility demands.

3. The Learning Effect in Estimating Costs.
Total costs are affected by how efficiently and effectively employees perform their tasks. After production for a new product begins or as a manufacturing process is implemented, workers usually increase their efficiency as more units are produced and they become more experienced. This learning effect is known as the learning curve phenomenon.

4. Cost Trends.
There are several important cost trends in the United States which may be relevant to managers for decision making. One such trend is the increased automation of manufacturing processes through the use of robotics and advanced technology. As a result of this automation, the percentage of product cost that is attributable to direct labor cost has declined. In contrast, an increasing percentage of product cost is fixed cost and factory overhead cost. Since fixed costs are often more difficult to reduce, an increasing percentage of fixed costs may limit the ability of an enterprise's managers to react quickly to changing environmental and market conditions.

KEY TERMS

cost behavior 678
cost estimation 678
variable costs 679
step-wise variable costs 680
economies of scale 683
relevant range 683
fixed costs 684
step-wise fixed costs 685
mixed costs 687
semivariable costs 687
high-low method 689
scattergraph method 692
least squares method 694
judgmental method 698
engineering method 698
learning effect 699
learning curve 699

SELF-EXAMINATION QUESTIONS

(Answers at End of Chapter)

1. Which of the following statements describes variable costs?
   A. Costs that vary on a per unit basis as the activity base changes
   B. Costs that vary in total in direct proportion to changes in the activity base
   C. Costs that remain constant in total dollar amount as the level of activity changes
   D. Costs that vary on a per unit basis, but remain constant in total as the level of activity changes

2. Which of the following is an example of a mixed cost?
   A. Straight-line depreciation on factory equipment
   B. Direct materials cost

C. Utility costs of $5,000 per month plus $.50 per kilowatt-hour
D. Supervisory salaries of $10,000 per month

3. The point at which the total cost line intersects the vertical axis of the scattergraph indicates:
   A. total variable cost
   B. total fixed cost
   C. variable cost per unit
   D. none of the above

4. Which of the following methods of cost estimation always uses statistical formulas to determine the total cost and the variable and fixed cost components?
   A. High-low method
   B. Judgmental method
   C. Least squares method
   D. Scattergraph method

5. Which of the following methods is normally considered the least accurate method of estimating total costs and fixed and variable cost components?
   A. High-low method
   B. Scattergraph method
   C. Least squares method
   D. Engineering method

ILLUSTRATIVE PROBLEM

Hinderman Manufacturing Inc., which began operations in January, 1990, is in the process of estimating variable costs per unit and fixed costs based upon the past year's results. The following production and cost data have been gathered from the accounting and production records for the past 10 months:

	Units Produced	Total Costs
March	80,000	$170,000
April	90,000	190,000
May	100,000	200,000
June	110,000	220,000
July	120,000	224,000
August	115,000	218,000
September	110,000	210,000
October	100,000	205,000
November	110,000	215,000
December	120,000	220,000

January and February cost and production data have been excluded, since operations during these months were in a start-up stage and were not typical.

Instructions:

1. Estimate (a) the variable cost per unit and (b) the fixed cost per month, using the high-low method of cost estimation. Use the cost data for December's production of 120,000 units, rather than the July cost data, since the December costs are more recent.
2. Prepare a least squares computational table for the estimation of variable cost per unit, using the following form. Do not include thousands in the table.

Units Produced (P_i)	Total Costs (C_i)	P_i^2	P_iC_i

3. Determine the estimated variable cost per unit, using the table in (2) and the appropriate least squares formula. Round to the nearest cent.

4. Determine the estimated fixed cost per month, using (2) and (3) and the appropriate least squares formula.
5. Estimate the total cost of 100,000 units of production per month, using (a) the high-low method and (b) the least squares method.

SOLUTION

(1) (a)

	Units Produced	Total Costs
Highest level	120,000	$220,000
Lowest level	80,000	170,000
Difference	40,000	$ 50,000

$$\text{Variable Cost per Unit} = \frac{\text{Difference in Total Costs}}{\text{Difference in Production}}$$

$$\text{Variable Cost per Unit} = \frac{\$220{,}000 - \$170{,}000}{120{,}000 \text{ units} - 80{,}000 \text{ units}}$$

$$\text{Variable Cost per Unit} = \frac{\$50{,}000}{40{,}000} = \$1.25 \text{ per unit}$$

(b) The fixed cost per month can be determined by subtracting the estimated total variable cost from the total cost at either the highest or lowest level of production, as follows:

Total Cost = (Variable Cost per Unit × Units of Production) + Fixed Cost

Highest Level:

$220,000 = ($1.25 × 120,000 units) + Fixed Cost
$220,000 = $150,000 + Fixed Cost
$ 70,000 = Fixed Cost

Lowest Level:

$170,000 = ($1.25 × 80,000 units) + Fixed Cost
$170,000 = $100,000 + Fixed Cost
$ 70,000 = Fixed Cost

(2)

Units Produced (P_i)	Total Costs (C_i)	P_i^2	P_iC_i
80	$ 170	6,400	$ 13,600
90	190	8,100	17,100
100	200	10,000	20,000
110	220	12,100	24,200
120	224	14,400	26,880
115	218	13,225	25,070
110	210	12,100	23,100
100	205	10,000	20,500
110	215	12,100	23,650
120	220	14,400	26,400
1,055	$2,072	112,825	$220,500

(3) $\text{Variable Cost per Unit} = \dfrac{n(\Sigma P_i C_i) - (\Sigma P_i)(\Sigma C_i)}{n(\Sigma P_i^2) - (\Sigma P_i)^2}$

$\text{Variable Cost per Unit} = \dfrac{10(\$220{,}500) - (1{,}055)(\$2{,}072)}{10(112{,}825) - (1{,}055)^2}$

$\text{Variable Cost per Unit} = \dfrac{\$2{,}205{,}000 - \$2{,}185{,}960}{1{,}128{,}250 - 1{,}113{,}025}$

$\text{Variable Cost per Unit} = \dfrac{\$19{,}040}{15{,}225} = \$1.25 \text{ per unit}$

(4) Fixed Cost = $\overline{C}$ − (Variable Cost per Unit × $\overline{P}$)
$\overline{C}$ = ($2,072,000 ÷ 10) = $207,200
$\overline{P}$ = (1,055,000 units ÷ 10) = 105,500 units
Fixed Cost = $207,200 − ($1.25 × 105,500 units)
Fixed Cost = $207,200 − $131,875
Fixed Cost = $75,325

(5) (a) Total Cost = (Variable Cost per Unit × Units of Production) + Fixed Cost
Total Cost = ($1.25 × 100,000 units) + $70,000
Total Cost = $125,000 + $70,000
Total Cost = $195,000

(b) Total Cost = (Variable Cost per Unit × Units of Production) + Fixed Cost
Total Cost = ($1.25 × 100,000 units) + $75,325
Total Cost = $125,000 + $75,325
Total Cost = $200,325

Discussion Questions

18–1. Distinguish between cost behavior and cost estimation.

18–2. What are the three most common classifications used for classifying cost behavior?

18–3. Describe how total variable costs and unit variable costs behave with changes in the activity base.

18–4. Which of the following costs would be classified as variable costs for units produced?
(a) Direct materials cost
(b) Straight-line depreciation
(c) Factory supervisor's salary
(d) Electricity costs of $.25 per kilowatt-hour
(e) Insurance premiums on factory plant and equipment of $3,000 per month
(f) Direct labor costs
(g) Oil used in operating factory machinery
(h) Janitorial supplies of $750 per month

18–5. Which of the following graphs illustrates how total variable costs behave with changes in total units produced?

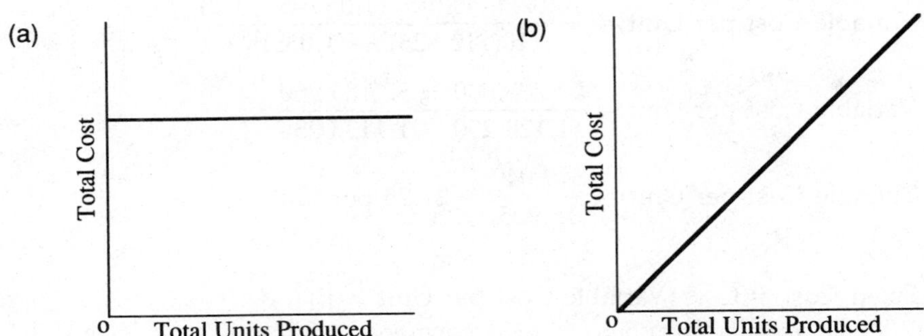

18–6. Which of the following graphs illustrates how unit variable costs behave with changes in total units produced?

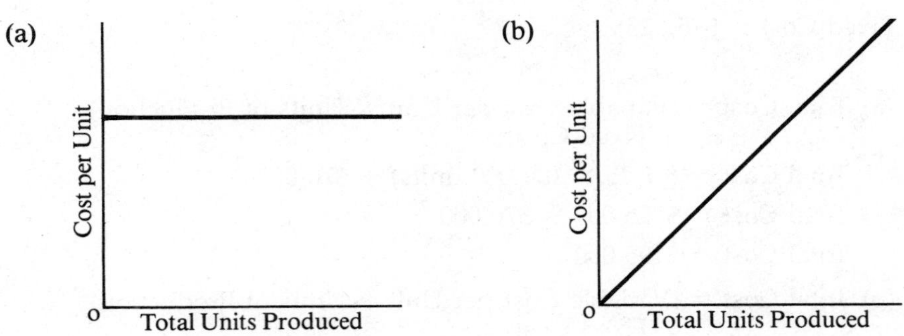

18–7. For Weber Tree Farm Inc., match each cost in the following table with the activity base most appropriate to it. An activity base may be used more than once.

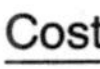

Cost	Activity Base
(1) Fertilizer	(a) Number of trees planted in the fields
(2) Dirt and packaging materials for shipping mature trees	(b) Number of trees shipped
(3) The cost of water used to water the trees	(c) Number of fields
(4) Sales commissions	(d) Dollar amount of trees sold
(5) Field managers' salaries	(e) Dollar amount of trees planted in the fields

18–8. Which of the following graphs best illustrates the nature of a step-wise cost?

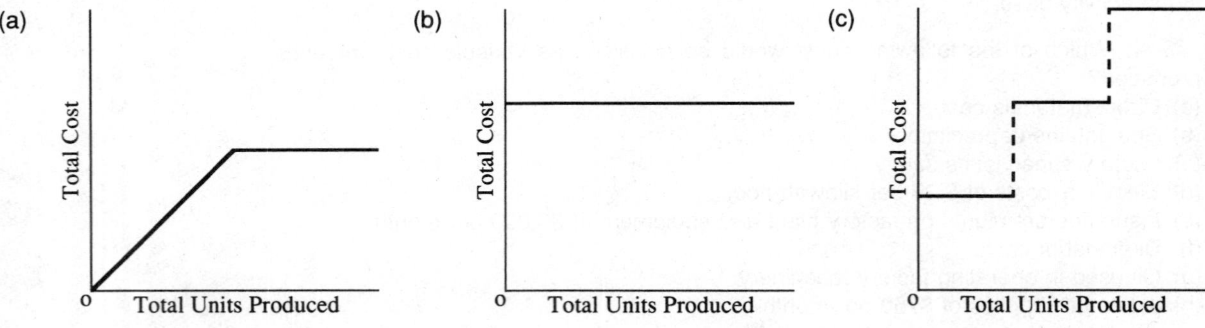

18–9. Why must management exercise added care in planning and scheduling production in order to maximize the efficiency of operations for step-wise costs?

18–10. Does the total cost graph of a variable cost appear as a straight line or as a curvilinear line when plotted against its activity base?

18–11. What term refers to the economic phenomenon of changing proportions of costs to changes in an activity base?

18–12. What term refers to the narrow range of activity within which the enterprise is planning to operate?

18–13. Describe the behavior of (a) total fixed costs and (b) unit fixed costs as the activity base increases.

18–14. Which of the following costs are fixed costs of production?

(a) Property insurance premiums of $4,000 per month on plant and equipment
(b) Straight-line depreciation on plant and equipment
(c) Direct labor costs
(d) Salary of factory supervisor, $40,000 per year
(e) Rent of $25,000 per month on factory building
(f) Electricity used in running machinery, $.02 per kilowatt-hour
(g) Direct materials
(h) Oil and other lubricants used on factory machinery

18–15. Which of the following graphs best illustrates fixed costs per unit as the activity base changes?

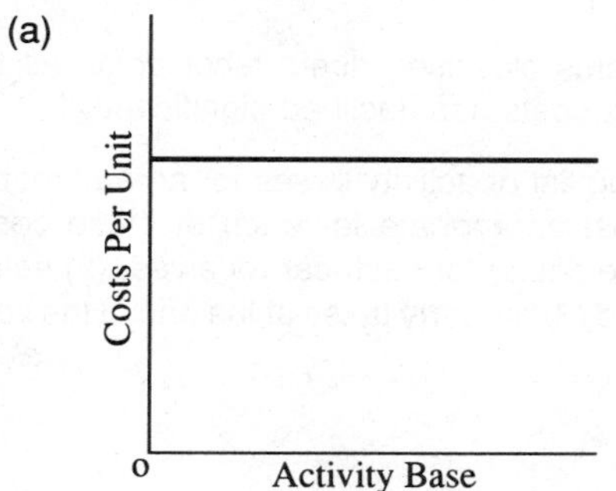

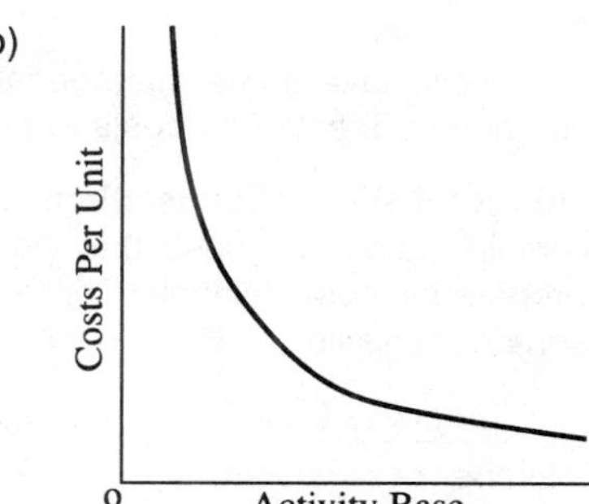

18–16. How do step-wise fixed costs differ from step-wise variable costs?

18–17. What type of cost has both fixed and variable cost characteristics?

18–18. Miller Inc. rents factory machinery for $14,000 per year and $.25 per machine hour. Which of the following graphs best illustrates the behavior of the rental costs?

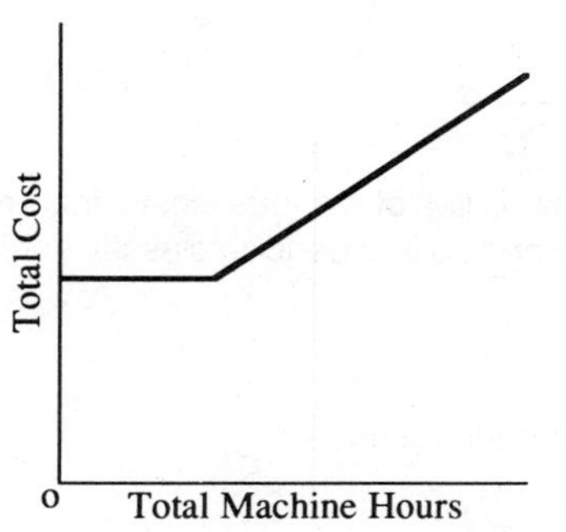

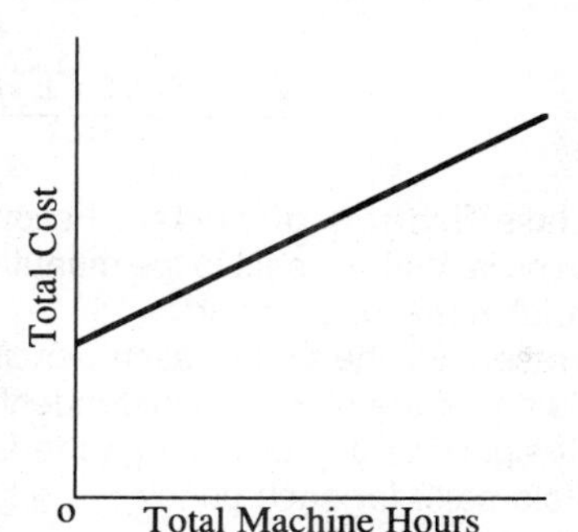

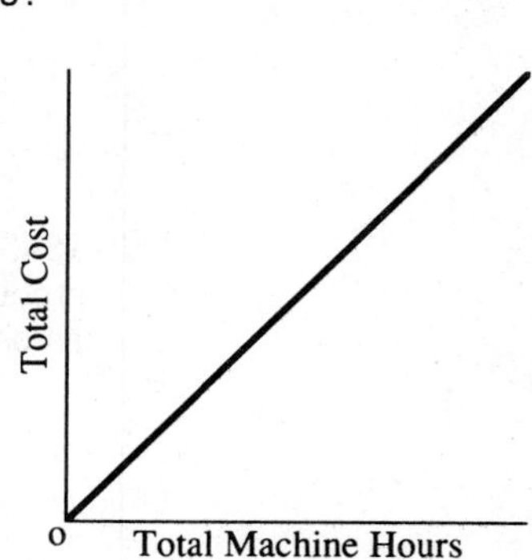

18–19. Name five methods of cost estimation that may be useful to the managerial accountant.

18–20. In applying the high-low method of cost estimation, how is the total fixed cost estimated?

18–21. If the variable cost per unit is $2.50 and the total fixed cost is $300,000, what is the estimated total cost for the production of 50,000 units?

18–22. Describe how the total cost line is drawn on a scattergraph.

18–23. How is the scattergraph method used to determine the estimated total cost for any level of production?

18–24. Assuming that the least squares method of cost estimation is used to estimate a variable cost per unit of $1.30, the average of the observed total costs is $82,000, and the average of the observed levels of production is 40,000 units, what is the least squares estimate of the total fixed cost?

18–25. What might be indicated by large differences between estimated total costs and actual costs?

18–26. As production for a new product begins or as a new manufacturing process is implemented, workers usually increase their efficiency as they produce more units and acquire more experience. What is this phenomenon called?

18–27. Why is the learning effect important to managers?

18–28. What is an implication of the increasing percentage of fixed costs to total product costs?

18–29. How have some managerial accountants classified direct labor costs as the percentage of direct labor costs to total product costs has declined significantly?

18–30. Real World Focus. From the following list of activity bases for an automobile dealership, select the base that would be most appropriate for each of these costs: (1) preparation costs (cleaning, oil, and gasoline costs) for each car received, (2) salespersons' commission of 5% for each car sold, and (3) property taxes at the end of the year.

Activity Base

(a) Number of cars sold
(b) Number of cars received
(c) Number of cars ordered
(d) Number of cars on hand
(e) Dollar amount of cars sold
(f) Dollar amount of cars received
(g) Dollar amount of cars ordered
(h) Dollar amount of cars on hand

Exercises

18–31. Classification of costs. Following is a list of various costs incurred in producing pencils. With respect to the manufacture and sale of pencils, classify each cost as either variable, fixed, or mixed.

1. Erasers for the end of each pencil.
2. Salary of the plant superintendent.
3. Straight-line depreciation on the factory equipment.
4. Gold paint for each pencil.
5. Number 2 lead.

6. Property taxes on factory building and equipment.
7. Hourly wages of machine operators.
8. Pension cost of $.20 per employee hour on the job.
9. Lubricants used to oil machinery.
10. Rent on warehouse of $3,000 per month plus $2 per square foot of storage used.
11. Metal to hold the eraser on the end of the pencil.
12. Electricity costs of $.025 per kilowatt-hour.
13. Janitorial costs of $2,000 per month.
14. Wood costs per pencil.
15. Property insurance premiums of $1,500 per month plus $.003 for each dollar of insurance over $2,000,000.

18–32. Identification of cost graphs. The following cost graphs illustrate various types of cost behavior:

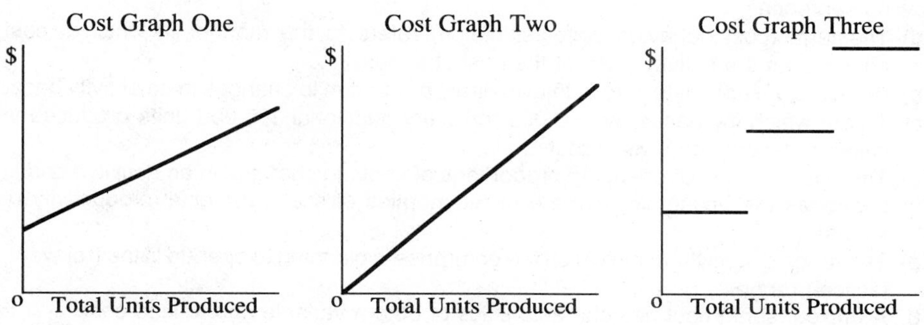

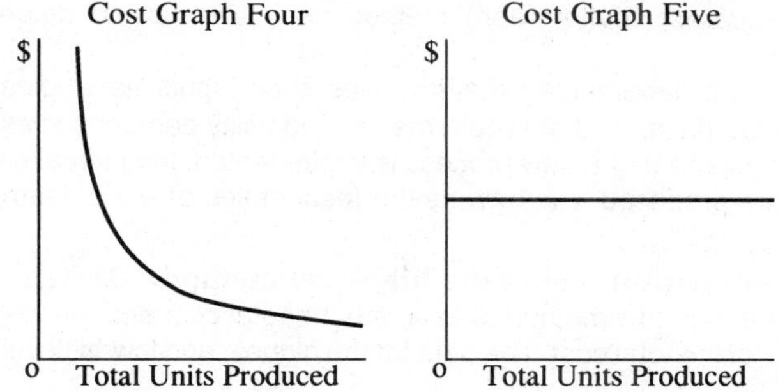

For each of the following costs, identify the cost graph that best illustrates its cost behavior as the number of units produced increases.

(a) Total direct materials cost.
(b) Per unit cost of straight-line depreciation on factory equipment.
(c) Utility costs of $2,000 per month plus $.0002 per kilowatt-hour.
(d) Salary of quality control supervisor, $2,500 per month. One quality control supervisor is needed for each 10,000 units produced.
(e) Per unit cost of direct labor.

18–33. Relevant range and computation of fixed and variable costs. Reynolds Inc. manufactures tool sets within a relevant range of 100,000 to 300,000 sets a year. Within this range, the following partially completed manufacturing cost schedule has been prepared:

	Tool Sets Produced		
	100,000	200,000	300,000
Total costs:			
Total variable costs	$ 700,000	(d)	(j)
Total fixed costs	450,000	(e)	(k)
Total costs	$1,150,000	(f)	(l)
Cost per unit:			
Variable cost per unit	(a)	(g)	(m)
Fixed cost per unit	(b)	(h)	(n)
Total cost per unit	(c)	(i)	(o)

Complete the cost schedule, identifying each cost by the appropriate letter (a) through (o).

18–34. Terminology. Choose the appropriate term for completing each of the following sentences.

(a) The term (cost behavior, cost estimation) refers to the manner in which a cost changes as the activity base of the cost changes.
(b) (Variable, Fixed) costs vary in total in direct proportion to changes in an activity base.
(c) A cost which increases by $50,000 for every additional 100,000 units produced is called a (mixed, step-wise) cost.
(d) The phenomenon of changing proportions of costs to changes in an activity base is known as the economic principle of (economies of scale, marginal productivity of inputs).
(e) The range of activity within which the enterprise is planning to operate is the (relevant, tactical) range.
(f) A (mixed, sunk) cost has characteristics of both a variable and a fixed cost.
(g) The (high-low, scattergraph) method uses total costs at all levels of past production in estimating costs.
(h) The (least squares, scattergraph) method uses statistics to determine the total cost line.
(i) The (engineering, judgmental) method uses such inputs as studies of production processes, material and labor requirements, and utility demands in estimating costs.
(j) When new equipment or a new process is implemented, the increase in efficiency as more units are produced is known as the (economies of scale, learning effect.)

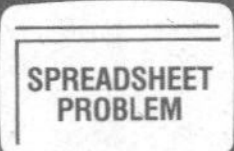

18–35. Cost estimation, using the high-low method. McKean Company has decided to use the high-low method to estimate the total cost and the fixed and variable cost components of the total cost. The data for the highest and lowest levels of production are as follows:

	Units Produced	Total Costs
Highest level	80,000	$370,000
Lowest level	40,000	220,000

(a) Determine the variable cost per unit and the fixed cost for McKean Company.
(b) Based on (a), estimate the total cost for 60,000 units of production.

18–36. Cost estimation, using the scattergraph method. Using data for an 8-month period, a cost accountant for Kadrmas Company has prepared the following scattergraph as a basis for cost estimation:

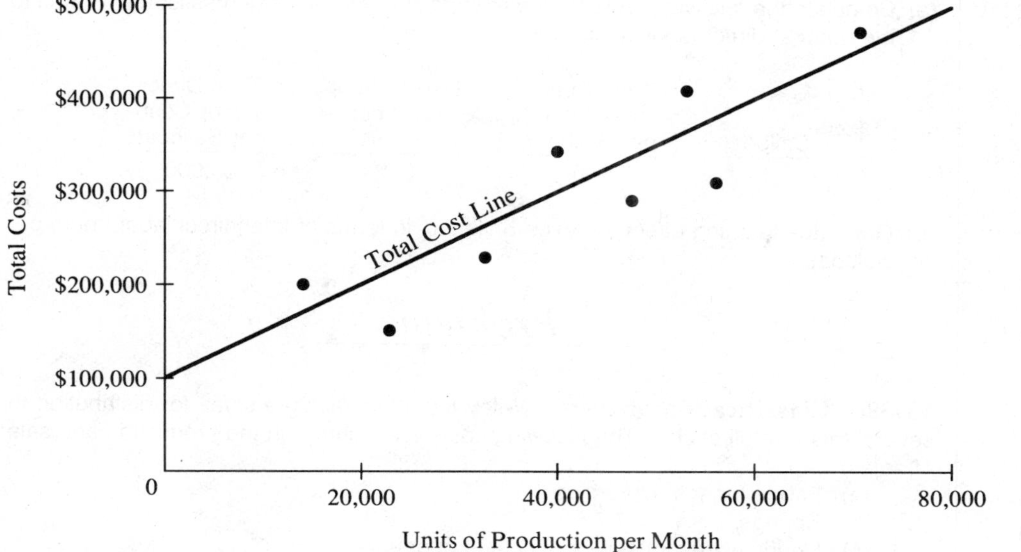

(a) Determine the estimated fixed cost per month for Kadrmas Company.
(b) Determine the estimated total cost for 40,000 units of production.
(c) Compute the estimated variable cost per unit, based on the total cost of producing 40,000 units.

SPREADSHEET PROBLEM

18–37. Cost estimation, using the least squares method. Using data for the first six months of the year, the assistant controller for Zavor Company prepared the following table for use in estimating costs:

Units Produced (P_i)	Total Costs (C_i)	P_i^2	P_iC_i
50	$ 200	2,500	$ 10,000
100	302	10,000	30,200
80	258	6,400	20,640
60	220	3,600	13,200
90	280	8,100	25,200
70	240	4,900	16,800
450	$1,500	35,500	$116,040

The thousands have been deleted from the table. Thus, 50 units in the table represents 50,000 units of production, and $100 represents $100,000.

(a) Determine the estimated variable cost per unit, using the table and the appropriate least squares formula. Round to the nearest cent.
(b) Determine the estimated fixed cost per month, using the preceding data and the appropriate least squares formula.
(c) Based on (a) and (b), estimate the total cost for 65,000 units of production.

18–38. Learning effect. Miles Sails Inc. manufactures sailboats and has added a new model of sailboat to its product line. Past experience indicates that every time a new model of sailboat is added, the total time to manufacture each sailboat declines by 8% as each of the next six sailboats is produced. After the seventh sailboat, no further reduction in time is possible. It is estimated that the first sailboat will require 500 direct labor hours at a cost of $12 per hour.

(a) Complete the following table for the manufacture of the first ten sailboats. Round to the nearest direct labor hour.

Sailboat	Total Direct Labor Hours per Sailboat	Direct Labor Cost per Hour	Total Direct Labor Cost per Sailboat
1	500	$12	$6,000

(b) Graph the learning effect for Miles Sails Inc. in terms of total direct labor hours per sailboat.

Problems

18–39. Classification of costs. Wiley Inc. manufactures sofas for distribution to several major retail chains. The following costs are incurred in the production and sale of sofas:

(a) Fabric for sofa coverings.
(b) Springs.
(c) Hourly wages of sewing machine operators.
(d) Foam rubber for cushion fillings.
(e) Insurance premiums on property, plant, and equipment, $5,000 per year plus $.002 per insured value over $8,000,000.
(f) Straight-line depreciation on factory equipment.
(g) Wood for framing the sofas.
(h) Salary of designers.
(i) Salary of production vice-president.
(j) Rent on experimental equipment, $50 for every sofa produced.
(k) Consulting fee of $15,000 paid to efficiency specialists.
(l) Janitorial supplies, $40 for each sofa produced.
(m) Salesperson's salary, $12,000 plus 5% of the selling price of each sofa sold.
(n) Employer's FICA taxes on controller's salary of $65,000.
(o) Sewing supplies.
(p) Cartons used to ship sofas.
(q) Rental costs of warehouse, $14,000 per month.
(r) Legal fees paid to attorneys in defense of the company in a patent infringement suit, $10,000 plus $30 per hour.
(s) Property taxes on property, plant, and equipment.
(t) Electricity costs of $.00035 per kilowatt-hour.

Instructions: Classify the preceding costs as either variable, fixed, or mixed. Use the following tabular headings and place an X in the appropriate column:

Cost	Variable Cost	Fixed Cost	Mixed Cost

18–40. Identification of cost graphs. The following costs were incurred by Johnson Manufacturing Co. in the production of utility trailers:

(a) Aluminum for sides of trailers.
(b) Hourly wages of assemblers, $15 per hour plus time and one half for all hours in excess of 40 per week.
(c) Property taxes paid to city, $1,000, unless 200 trailers are produced, in which case no tax is paid.
(d) Per unit cost of straight-line depreciation.
(e) Electricity costs of $1,000 per month plus $.0004 per kilowatt-hour.
(f) Safety chain, where the cost per foot of chain is $.06 per foot for the first 1,000 feet purchased, and $.05 per foot after the purchase of 1,000 feet.
(g) Rental of welding equipment, $500 for the first 100 trailers produced plus $3 for each trailer after 100.

(h) Water costs according to the following schedule:

First 1,000 gallons	$.20 per gallon
1,001–3,000 gallons....................	$.18 per gallon
3,001–8,000 gallons....................	$.15 per gallon
over 8,000 gallons	$.12 per gallon

(i) Salary of superintendent of production, $60,000.
(j) Rental costs for metal stamping equipment, per machine:

1–100 trailers	$600 per month
101–200 trailers	$500 per month
201–300 trailers	$400 per month

(k) Health insurance costs, $200 per employee plus $.003 per hour worked for first 2,000 hours and $.005 per hour worked for all hours over 2,000.
(l) Maintenance contract for factory overhead: $1,000 for first 100 trailers produced, $1,200 for second 100 trailers produced, and $1,400 for third 100 trailers produced.

Instructions: For each of the costs, identify the cost graph, from the following group of various graphs, that best describes the cost behavior as the number of units produced increases. For each graph, the vertical axis represents dollars of cost and the horizontal axis represents units of production.

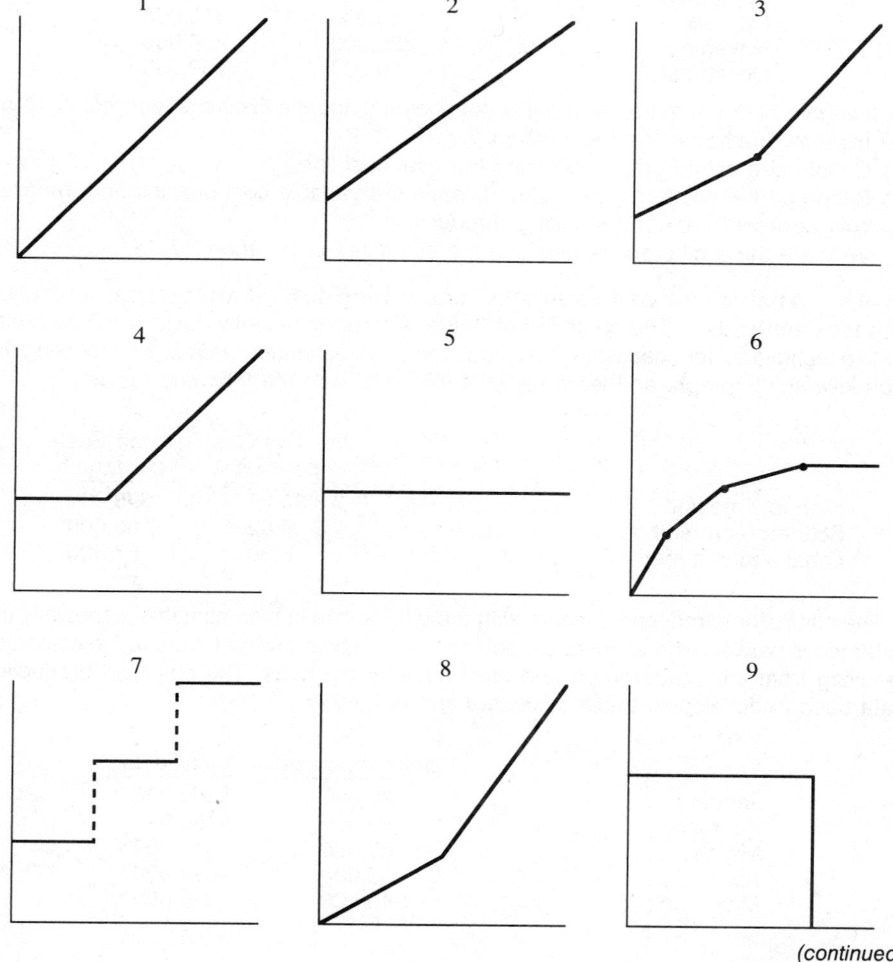

(continued)

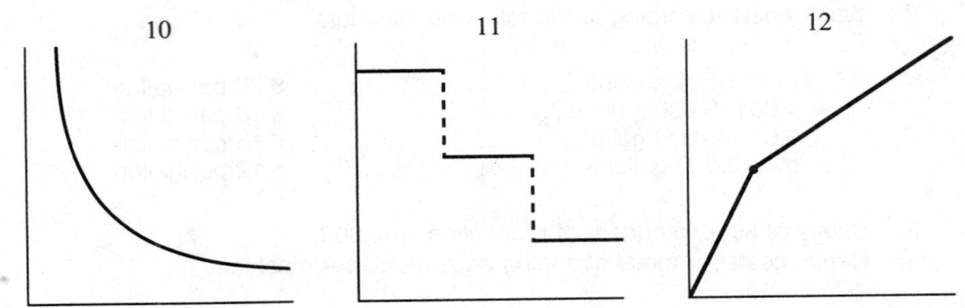

18–41. Cost estimation, using high-low and scattergraph methods. The controller for Shaut Company is preparing some preliminary cost projections for the 1990 budget and has accumulated the following cost and production data for 1989:

	Units Produced	Total Costs
January	20,000	$250,000
February	50,000	500,000
March	40,000	400,000
April	30,000	300,000
May	60,000	550,000
June	65,000	600,000
July	70,000	620,000
August	85,000	750,000
September	80,000	700,000
October	45,000	410,000
November	25,000	280,000
December	10,000	150,000

Instructions: (1) Estimate the variable cost per unit and the fixed cost per month, using the high-low method of cost estimation.
(2) Construct a scattergraph, including the total cost line.
(3) Based on the scattergraph in (2), estimate the variable cost per unit and the fixed cost per month at 40,000 units of production.
(4) Why are there differences between the estimates in (1) and (3)?

18–42. Analysis of cost estimates, using high-low, scattergraph, and least squares methods. The controller of Sauter Company recently decided to use quantitative techniques for cost estimation purposes. Cost estimates were prepared using the high-low, scattergraph, and least squares methods, with the following results:

	Variable Cost per Unit	Fixed Costs per Month
High-low method	$8.25	$35,000
Scattergraph method	8.02	60,000
Least squares method	8.00	57,300

The controller expressed concern with the differences in the estimates, especially the differences between the estimates resulting from the high-low method and the estimates resulting from the scattergraph and least squares methods. The cost and production data used in developing these estimates are as follows:

	Units Produced	Total Costs
January	20,000	$200,000
February	50,000	460,000
March	60,000	540,000
April	65,000	600,000
May	40,000	380,000

	Units Produced	Total Costs
June	65,000	$580,000
July	94,000	780,000
August	100,000	860,000
September	80,000	700,000
October	75,000	665,000

Instructions: (1) Based on each of the preceding cost estimates for the high-low, scattergraph, and least squares methods, (a) compute the estimated total cost for 75,000 units of production, and (b) compute the differences between each of the total cost estimates in (a) and the actual cost of $665,000.

(2) Assuming that the January production and cost data are not typical of normal operations, recompute the variable cost per unit and the fixed cost per month, using the high-low method.

(3) Based on (2), recompute the estimated total cost for 75,000 units of production, using the high-low method.

(4) Based on the total cost estimate computed in (3), what is the difference between this estimate and the actual cost of $665,000?

(5) Regardless of which cost estimation method is used, why should the estimated total cost be compared periodically with the actual cost?

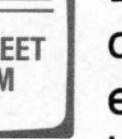

18–43. Cost estimation, using least squares method. Mitchell Company began operations in January, 1989, and has decided to use the least squares method for estimating variable costs per unit and fixed costs. The following production and cost data have been gathered from the accounting and production records for the past 10 months:

	Units Produced	Total Costs
March	300,000	$ 665,000
April	400,000	810,000
May	650,000	1,170,000
June	690,000	1,250,000
July	720,000	1,270,000
August	780,000	1,400,000
September	510,000	980,000
October	320,000	700,000
November	270,000	600,000
December	90,000	350,000

January and February cost and production data have been excluded, since operations during these months were in a start-up stage and were not typical.

Instructions: (1) Prepare a computational table for the estimation of the variable cost per unit, using the following form. Do not include thousands in the table.

Units Produced (P_i)	Total Costs (C_i)	P_i^2	P_iC_i

(2) Determine the estimated variable cost per unit, using the table in (1) and the appropriate least squares formula. Round to the nearest cent.

(3) Determine the estimated fixed cost per month, using (1) and (2) and the appropriate least squares formula.

(4) Estimate the total cost of 600,000 units of production, using the results of (2) and (3).

ALTERNATE PROBLEMS

18–39A. Classification of costs. Gardner Inc. manufactures blue jeans for distribution to several major retail chains. The following costs are incurred in the production and sale of blue jeans:

(a) Blue denim fabric.
(b) Insurance premiums on property, plant, and equipment, $10,000 per year plus $.003 per insured value over $5,000,000.
(c) Hourly wages of sewing machine operators.
(d) Property taxes on property, plant, and equipment.
(e) Thread.
(f) Brass buttons.
(g) Legal fees paid to attorneys in defense of the company in a patent infringement suit, $20,000 plus $50 per hour.
(h) Salary of designers.
(i) Salary of production vice-president.
(j) Rent on experimental equipment, $15,000 per year.
(k) Consulting fee of $80,000 paid to industry specialist for marketing advice.
(l) Janitorial supplies, $1,000 per month.
(m) Salesperson's salary, $12,000 plus 5% of the total sales.
(n) Electricity costs of $.00040 per kilowatt-hour.
(o) Sewing supplies.
(p) Shipping boxes used to ship orders.
(q) Rental costs of warehouse, $2,000 per month plus $.50 per square foot of storage used.
(r) Leather for patches identifying each jean style.
(s) Blue dye.
(t) Straight-line depreciation on sewing machines.

Instructions: Classify the preceding costs as either variable, fixed, or mixed. Use the following tabular headings and place an X in the appropriate column:

Cost	Variable Cost	Fixed Cost	Mixed Cost

18–40A. Identification of cost graphs. The following costs were incurred by Brown Manufacturing Co. in the production of ironing boards:

(a) Wood for top of board.
(b) Hourly wages of assemblers, $15 per hour plus time and one half for all hours in excess of 40 per week.
(c) Property taxes paid to city, $5,000, unless 10,000 ironing boards are produced, in which case no tax is paid.
(d) Per unit cost of straight-line depreciation.
(e) Electricity costs of $500 per month plus $.0006 per kilowatt-hour.
(f) Rental of experimental shipping equipment, $1,000 for first 5,000 shipments and $.04 for each shipment after 5,000.
(g) Special heat-resistant cloth for covering top of board, where the cost per yard is $1.50 per yard for the first 5,000 yards, and $1 per yard thereafter.
(h) Water costs according to the following schedule:

First 5,000 gallons	$.30 per gallon
5,001–10,000 gallons	$.25 per gallon
10,001–15,000 gallons	$.20 per gallon
over 15,000 gallons	$.15 per gallon

(i) Maintenance contract for factory equipment; $600 for first 2,000 hours of use, $900 for next 500 hours of use, and $1,200 for remaining hours of use.
(j) Rental of cutting machine according to the following schedule:

1–500 hours of use	$700
501–1,000 hours of use	$500
1,001–2,000 hours of use	$300

(k) Health insurance costs, $300 per employee plus $.002 per hour worked for first 2,000 hours and $.004 per hour worked for all hours over 2,000.

(l) Salary of superintendent of production, $80,000.

Instructions: For each of the costs, identify the cost graph, from the following group of various graphs, that best describes the cost behavior as the number of units produced increases. For each graph, the vertical axis represents dollars of cost, and the horizontal axis represents units of production.

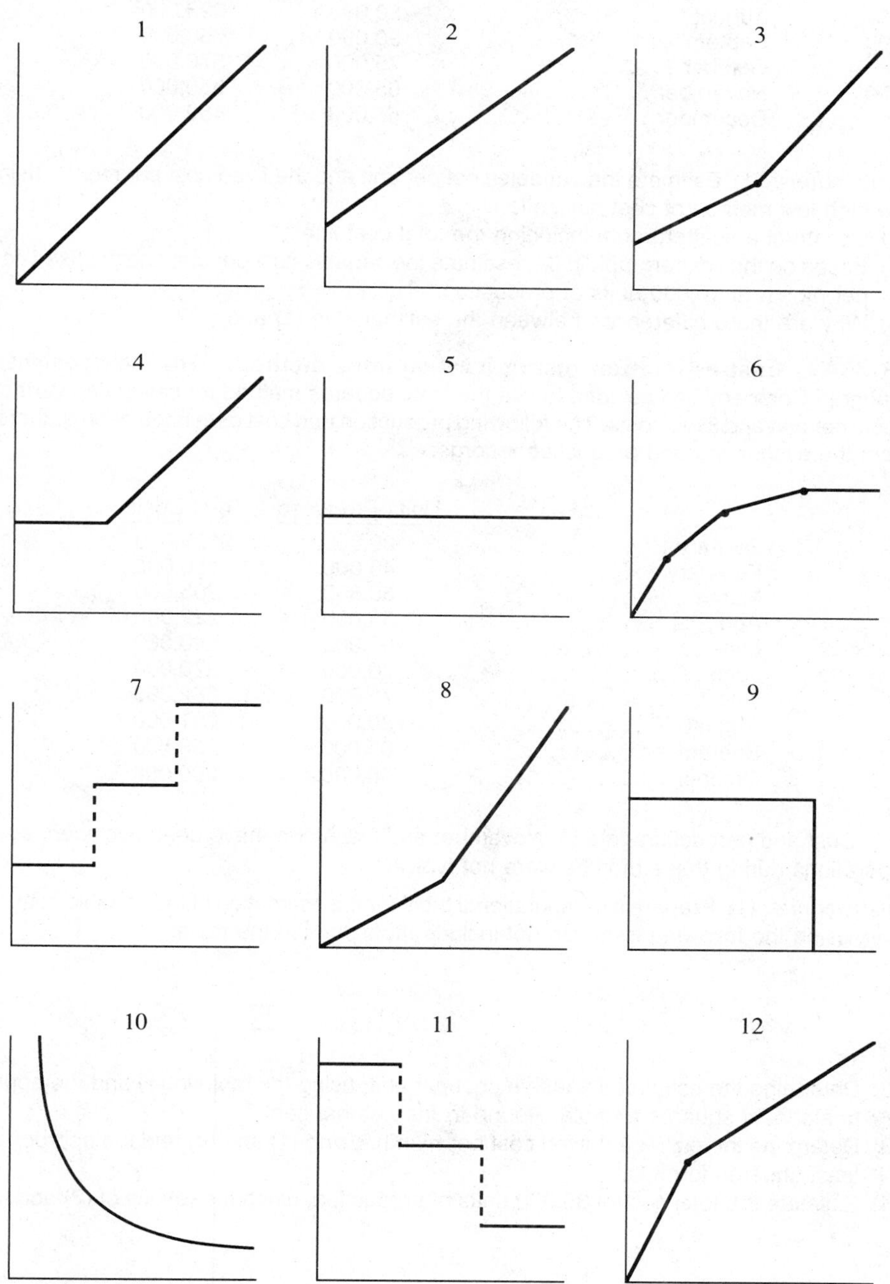

18–41A. Cost estimation, using high-low and scattergraph methods. The controller for Valdes Company is preparing some preliminary cost projections for the 1990 budget and has accumulated the following cost and production data for 1989:

	Units Produced	Total Costs
January	30,000	$380,000
February................	20,000	330,000
March	10,000	210,000
April....................	35,000	360,000
May.....................	42,000	450,000
June	60,000	490,000
July	70,000	595,000
August	80,000	695,000
September..............	90,000	650,000
October	75,000	570,000
November	65,000	550,000
December	50,000	450,000

Instructions: (1) Estimate the variable cost per unit and the fixed cost per month, using the high-low method of cost estimation.

(2) Construct a scattergraph, including the total cost line.

(3) Based on the scattergraph in (2), estimate the variable cost per unit and the fixed cost per month at 40,000 units of production.

(4) Why are there differences between the estimates in (1) and (3)?

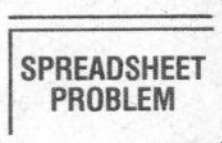

18–43A. Cost estimation, using least squares method. The management of Lindgren Company has decided to use the least squares method for estimating variable costs per unit and fixed costs. The following production and cost data have been gathered from the accounting and production records:

	Units Produced	Total Costs
January	20,000	$125,000
February................	40,000	180,000
March	50,000	205,000
April....................	55,000	222,000
May.....................	60,000	240,000
June	70,000	270,000
July	75,000	282,000
August	80,000	291,000
September..............	65,000	258,000
October	45,000	200,000

Cost and production data for November and December have been excluded, since operations during these months were not typical.

Instructions: (1) Prepare a computational table for the estimation of the variable cost per unit, using the following form. Do not include thousands in the table.

Units Produced (P_i)	Total Costs (C_i)	P_i^2	P_iC_i

(2) Determine the estimated variable cost per unit, using the table in (1) and the appropriate least squares formula. Round to the nearest cent.

(3) Determine the estimated fixed cost per month, using (1) and (2) and the appropriate least squares formula.

(4) Estimate the total cost of 35,000 units of production, using the results of (2) and (3).

Mini-Case 18

Beckel Company has recently become concerned with the accuracy of its cost estimates because of large monthly differences between actual and estimated total costs. In the past, the senior managerial accountant has used the high-low method to develop estimates of variable costs per unit and fixed costs. These cost estimates are as follows:

Variable cost per unit.	$1.50
Fixed cost	$52,500

As a new junior accountant, the controller has asked you to determine whether the least squares method of cost estimation would provide more accurate estimates. The following twelve-month cost and production data have been gathered as a basis for developing the least squares cost estimates:

	Units Produced	Total Costs
January	40,000	$127,000
February.	45,000	131,000
March	50,000	136,000
April.	55,000	143,000
May.	60,000	150,000
June	70,000	155,000
July	80,000	170,000
August	85,000	180,000
September.	75,000	157,000
October	65,000	144,000
November	46,000	133,000
December	25,000	90,000

Instructions:

(1) Prepare a least squares computational table for the estimation of variable cost per unit, using the following form. Do not include thousands in the table.

Units Produced (P_i)	Total Costs (C_i)	P_i^2	P_iC_i

(2) Determine the estimated variable cost per unit, using the table in (1) and the appropriate least squares formula. Round to the nearest cent.

(3) Determine the estimated fixed cost per month, using (1) and (2) and the appropriate least squares formula.

(4) Prepare a table comparing the monthly differences between actual and estimated total costs for the high-low and least squares methods. Use the following headings:

Month	Units Produced	Total Actual Costs	Total Estimated Costs: High-Low Method	Total Estimated Costs: Least Squares Method	Monthly Differences: High-Low Method	Monthly Differences: Least Squares Method

(5) Which method is more accurate in estimating total costs? Explain.
(6) Which cost estimation method would you recommend to the controller?

Answers to Self-Examination Questions

1. B Variable costs vary in total in direct proportion to changes in the activity base (answer B). Costs that vary on a per unit basis as the activity base changes (answer A) or remain constant in total dollar amount as the level of activity changes (answer C), or both (answer D), are fixed costs.

2. C Mixed costs have characteristics of both variable and fixed costs. Utility costs of $5,000 per month (the fixed component) plus $.50 per kilowatt-hour (the variable component) (answer C) are a mixed cost. Straight-line depreciation on factory equipment (answer A) and supervisory salaries of $10,000 per month (answer D) are fixed costs. Direct materials cost (answer B) is a variable cost.

3. B The point at which the total cost line intersects the vertical axis of the scattergraph indicates the estimated total fixed cost of production (answer B). The total variable cost (answer A) for any level of production is the difference between the estimated total cost indicated on the scattergraph and the estimated total fixed cost. The estimated variable cost per unit (answer C) can be computed by dividing the total variable cost by the total units of production for a given level of production.

4. C The least squares method (answer C) uses statistical formulas to estimate the total cost and the variable and fixed cost components. The high-low method (answer A) uses only data for the highest and lowest levels of production in estimating costs. The scattergraph method (answer D) uses a graph to estimate costs. The judgmental method (answer B) uses experience and past observations of cost-volume relationships to estimate costs. It may also use the high-low, scattergraph, or least squares method as a starting point.

5. A The high-low method (answer A) is normally considered the least accurate method of estimating costs because it uses data for only the highest and lowest levels of production. On the other hand, the scattergraph method (answer B) and the least squares method (answer C) both utilize data for all the observed levels of production. The engineering method (answer D) will provide estimates that are as accurate as the engineering studies upon which the estimates are based.

19
Cost-Volume-Profit Analysis

CHAPTER OBJECTIVES

Describe the use of analyses of cost-volume-profit relationships in planning operations.

Describe and illustrate the mathematical approach to cost-volume-profit analysis.

Describe and illustrate the graphic approach to cost-volume-profit analysis.

Describe the use of computers in cost-volume-profit analysis.

Describe and illustrate the impact of sales mix considerations in cost-volume-profit analysis.

Describe and illustrate special cost-volume-profit relationships.

Describe the limitations of cost-volume-profit analysis.

Cost-volume-profit analysis is a commonly used tool that provides management with useful information for decision making. For example, cost-volume-profit analysis may be used in setting selling prices, selecting the mix of products to sell, choosing among alternative marketing strategies, and analyzing the effects of cost increases or decreases on the profitability of the business enterprise. In this chapter, the study of the relationship of costs to volume and profit is based on the cost behavior and cost estimation discussion of Chapter 18. Cost-volume-profit analysis is then applied in the calculation of the break-even point, desired profit, sales mix, margin of safety, and contribution margin ratio.

COST-VOLUME-PROFIT RELATIONSHIPS

Cost-volume-profit analysis is the systematic examination of the interrelationships between selling prices, volume of sales and production, costs, expenses, and profits. This analysis is a complex matter, since these relationships are often affected by forces entirely or partially beyond management's control. For example, the determination of the selling price of a product is often affected by not only the costs of production, but also by uncontrollable factors in the marketplace. On the other hand, the cost of producing the product is affected by such controllable factors as the efficiency of operations and the volume of production.

Accountants can play an important role in cost-volume-profit analysis by providing management with information on the relative profitability of its various products, the probable effects of changes in selling price, and other variables. Such information can help management improve the relationship between these variables. For example, an analysis of sales and cost data can be helpful in determining the level of sales volume necessary for the business to earn a satisfactory profit.

In cost-volume-profit analysis, all costs[1] must be classified into two categories: (1) variable and (2) fixed. As described in Chapter 18, **variable costs** are costs that change, in total, as the volume of activity changes. **Fixed costs** remain constant, in total, as the volume of activity changes. **Mixed costs,** sometimes referred to as **semivariable** or **semifixed costs,** are costs that have both variable and fixed characteristics. Using the cost estimation methods described in Chapter 5, a mixed cost can generally be separated into its variable and fixed components.

MATHEMATICAL APPROACH TO COST-VOLUME-PROFIT ANALYSIS

After the costs and expenses have been classified into fixed and variable components, the effect on profit of these costs and expenses, along with revenues and volume, can be expressed in the form of cost-volume-profit analysis. Although accountants have proposed various approaches for cost-volume-profit analysis, the mathematical approach is one of two common approaches described and illustrated in this chapter.

The mathematical approach to cost-volume-profit analysis generally uses equations (1) to indicate the revenues necessary to achieve the break-even point in operations or (2) to indicate the revenues necessary to achieve a desired or target profit. These two equations and their use by management in profit planning are described and illustrated in the paragraphs that follow.

Break-Even Point

The level of operations of an enterprise at which revenues and expired costs are exactly equal is called the **break-even point.** At this level of operations, an enterprise will neither realize an operating income nor incur an operating loss. Break-even analysis can be applied to past periods, but it is most useful when applied to future periods as a guide to business planning, particularly if either an expansion or a curtailment of operations is expected. In such cases, it is concerned with future prospects and future operations and hence relies upon estimates. The reliability of the analysis is greatly influenced by the accuracy of the estimates.

[1] In this chapter, the term "costs" is often used as a convenience to represent both "costs" and "expenses."

The break-even point can be computed by means of a mathematical formula which indicates the relationship between revenue, costs, and capacity. The data required are (1) total estimated fixed costs for a future period, such as a year, and (2) the total estimated variable costs for the same period, stated as a percent of net sales. To illustrate, assume that fixed costs are estimated at $90,000 and that variable costs are expected to be 60% of sales. The break-even point is $225,000 of sales, computed as follows:

Break-Even Sales (in $) = Fixed Costs (in $) + Variable Costs (as % of Break-Even Sales)
S = $90,000 + 60%S
40%S = $90,000
S = $225,000

The validity of the preceding computation is shown in the following income statement:

Sales		$225,000
Expenses:		
Variable costs ($225,000 × 60%)	$135,000	
Fixed costs	90,000	225,000
Operating profit		-0-

The break-even point can be expressed either in terms of total sales dollars, as in the preceding illustration, or in terms of units of sales. For example, in the preceding illustration, if the unit selling price is $25, the break-even point can be expressed as either $225,000 of sales or 9,000 units ($225,000 ÷ $25).

The break-even point can be affected by changes in the fixed costs, unit variable costs, and unit selling price. The effect of each of these factors on the break-even point is briefly described in the following paragraphs.

Effect of Changes in Fixed Costs. Although fixed costs do not change in total with changes in volume of activity, they may change because of other factors, such as changes in property tax rates and salary increases given to factory supervisors. Increases in fixed costs will raise the break-even point. Similarly, decreases in fixed costs will lower the break-even point.

To illustrate, assume that Bishop Co. is evaluating a proposal to budget an additional $100,000 for advertising. Fixed costs (before the additional expenditure of $100,000 is considered) are estimated at $600,000, and variable costs are estimated at 75% of sales. The break-even point (before the additional expenditure is considered) is $2,400,000, computed as follows:

Break-Even Sales (in $) = Fixed Costs (in $) + Variable Costs (as % of Break-Even Sales)
S = $600,000 + 75%S
25%S = $600,000
S = $2,400,000

If advertising expense is increased by $100,000, the break-even point is raised to $2,800,000, computed as follows:

Break-Even Sales (in $) = Fixed Costs (in $) + Variable Costs (as % of Break-Even Sales)
S = $700,000 + 75%S
25%S = $700,000
S = $2,800,000

The increased fixed cost of $100,000 increases the break-even point by $400,000 of sales, since 75 cents of each sales dollar must cover variable costs.

Hence, $4 of additional sales are needed for each $1 increase in fixed costs if the operating profit for Bishop Co. is to remain unchanged.

Effect of Changes in Variable Costs. Although unit variable costs do not change with changes in volume of activity, they may change because of other factors, such as changes in the price of direct materials and salary increases given to factory workers providing direct labor. Increases in unit variable costs will raise the break-even point. Similarly, decreases in unit variable costs will lower the break-even point.

To illustrate, assume that Park Co. is evaluating a proposal to pay an additional 2% sales commission to its sales representatives as an incentive to increase sales. Fixed costs are estimated at $84,000, and variable costs are estimated at 58% of sales (before the additional 2% commission is considered). The break-even point (before the additional commission is considered) is $200,000, computed as follows:

Break-Even Sales (in $) = Fixed Costs (in $) + Variable Costs (as % of Break-Even Sales)
S = $84,000 + 58%S
42%S = $84,000
S = $200,000

If the sales commission proposal is adopted, the break-even point is raised to $210,000, computed as follows:

Break-Even Sales (in $) = Fixed Costs (in $) + Variable Costs (as % of Break-Even Sales)
S = $84,000 + 60%S
40%S = $84,000
S = $210,000

The additional 2% sales commission (a variable cost) increases the break-even point by $10,000 of sales. If the proposal is adopted, 2% less of each sales dollar is available to cover the fixed costs of $84,000.

Effect of Changing Unit Selling Price. Increases in the unit selling price will lower the break-even point, while decreases in the unit selling price will raise the break-even point. To illustrate the effect of changing the unit selling price, assume that Graham Co. is evaluating a proposal to increase the unit selling price of its product from its current price of $50 to $60 and has accumulated the following relevant data:

	Current	*Proposed*
Unit selling price	$50	$60
Unit variable cost	$30	$30
Variable costs (as % of break-even sales):		
$30 unit variable cost ÷ $50 unit selling price	60%	
$30 unit variable cost ÷ $60 unit selling price		50%
Total fixed costs	$600,000	$600,000

The break-even point based on the current selling price is $1,500,000, computed as follows:

Break-Even Sales (in $) = Fixed Costs (in $) + Variable Costs (as % of Break-Even Sales)
S = $600,000 + 60%S
40%S = $600,000
S = $1,500,000

If the selling price is increased by $10 per unit, the break-even point is decreased to $1,200,000, computed as follows:

Break-Even Sales (in \$) = Fixed Costs (in \$) + Variable Costs (as % of Break-Even Sales)

$$S = \$600,000 + 50\%S$$
$$50\%S = \$600,000$$
$$S = \$1,200,000$$

The increase in selling price of \$10 per unit decreases the break-even point by \$300,000 (from \$1,500,000 to \$1,200,000). In terms of units of sales, the decrease is from 30,000 units (\$1,500,000 ÷ \$50) to 20,000 units (\$1,200,000 ÷ \$60).

Desired Profit

At the break-even point, sales and costs are exactly equal. However, business enterprises do not use the break-even point as their goal for future operations. Rather, they seek to achieve the largest possible volume of sales above the break-even point. By modifying the break-even equation, the sales volume required to earn a desired amount of profit may be estimated. For this purpose, a factor for desired profit is added to the standard break-even formula. To illustrate, assume that fixed costs are estimated at \$200,000, variable costs are estimated at 60% of sales, and the desired profit is \$100,000. The sales volume is \$750,000, computed as follows:

Sales (in \$) = Fixed Costs (in \$) + Variable Costs (as % of Sales) + Desired Profit

$$S = \$200,000 + 60\%S + \$100,000$$
$$40\%S = \$300,000$$
$$S = \$750,000$$

The validity of the preceding computation is shown in the following income statement:

Sales		\$750,000
Expenses:		
Variable costs (\$750,000 × 60%)	\$450,000	
Fixed costs	200,000	650,000
Operating profit		\$100,000

GRAPHIC APPROACH TO COST-VOLUME-PROFIT ANALYSIS

Cost-volume-profit analysis can be presented graphically as well as in equation form. Many managers prefer the graphic format because the operating profit or loss for any given level of capacity can be readily determined, without the necessity of solving an equation. The following paragraphs describe two graphic approaches which managers find useful.

Cost-Volume-Profit (Break-Even) Chart

A **cost-volume-profit chart,** sometimes called a **break-even chart,** is used to assist management in understanding the relationships between costs, sales, and operating profit or loss. To illustrate the cost-volume-profit chart, assume that fixed costs are estimated at \$90,000, and variable costs are estimated as 60% of sales. The maximum sales at 100% of capacity is \$400,000. The following cost-volume-profit chart is based on the foregoing data:

Cost-Volume-Profit Chart

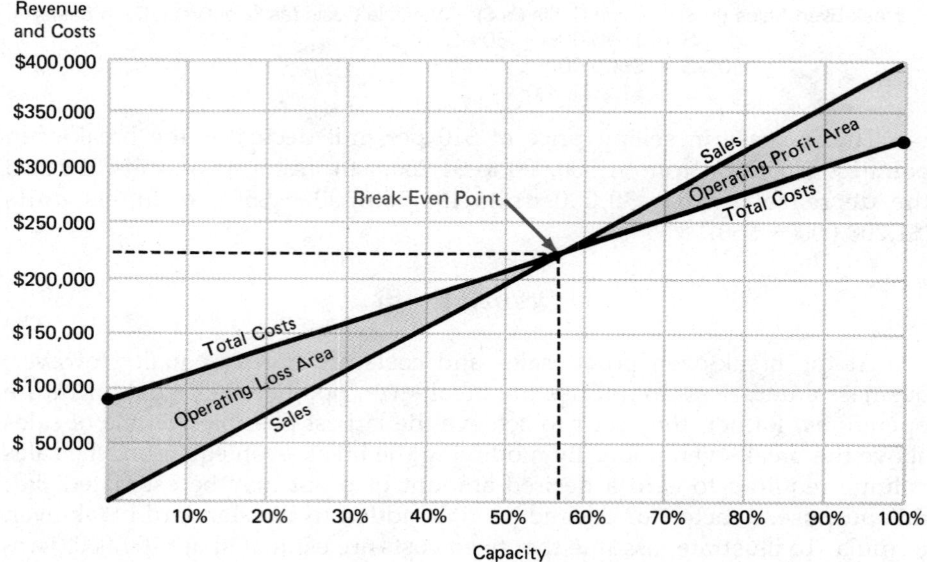

The cost-volume-profit chart is constructed in the following manner:

1. Percentages of capacity of the enterprise are spread along the horizontal axis, and dollar amounts representing operating data are spread along the vertical axis. The outside limits of the chart represent 100% of capacity and the maximum sales potential at that level of capacity.
2. A diagonal line representing sales is drawn from the lower left corner to the upper right corner.
3. A point representing fixed costs is plotted on the vertical axis at the left, and a point representing total costs at maximum capacity is plotted at the right edge of the chart. A diagonal line representing total costs at various percentages of capacity is then drawn connecting these two points.
4. Horizontal and vertical lines are drawn at the point of intersection of the sales and cost lines, which is the break-even point, and the areas representing operating profit and operating loss are identified.

In the illustration, the total costs at maximum capacity are $330,000 (fixed costs of $90,000 plus variable costs of $240,000, which is 60% of $400,000). The dotted line drawn from the point of intersection to the vertical axis identifies the break-even sales amount of $225,000. The dotted line drawn from the point of intersection to the horizontal axis identifies the break-even point in terms of capacity of approximately 56%. Operating profits will be earned when sales levels are to the right of the break-even point (operating profit area), and operating losses will be incurred when sales levels are to the left of the break-even point (operating loss area).

Changes in the unit selling price, total fixed costs, and unit variable costs can also be analyzed using a cost-volume-profit chart. To illustrate, using the preceding example, assume that a proposal to reduce fixed costs by $42,000 is to be evaluated. In this situation, the total fixed costs would be $48,000 ($90,000 – $42,000), and the total costs at maximum capacity would amount to $288,000 ($48,000 of fixed costs plus variable costs of $240,000). The preceding cost-volume-profit chart is revised by plotting the points representing the total fixed cost and the total cost and drawing a line between the two points, indicating the proposed total cost line. The following revised chart indicates that the break-even point would decrease to $120,000 of sales (30% of capacity).

Revised Cost-Volume-Profit Chart

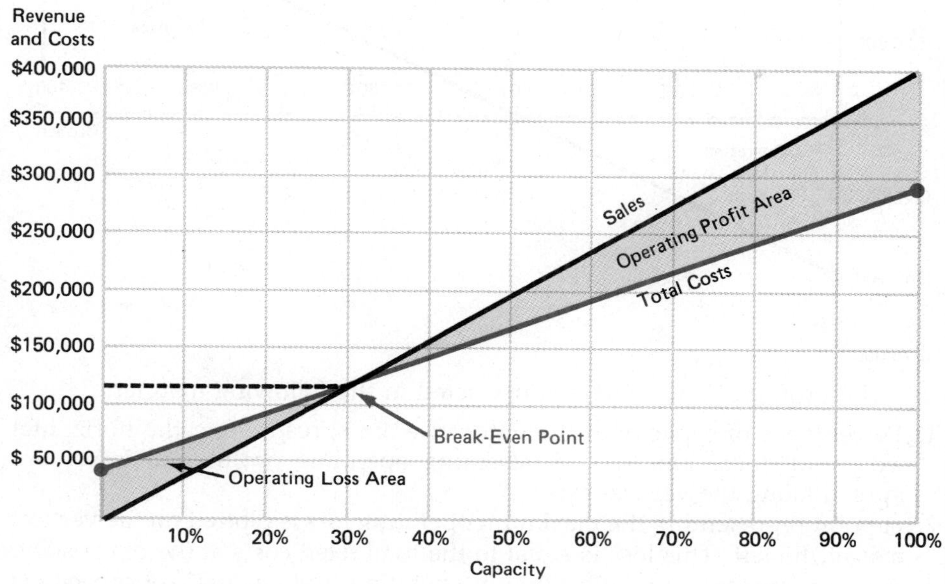

Profit-Volume Chart

Rather than focusing on sales revenues and costs, as was the case for the cost-volume-profit chart, another graphic approach to cost-volume-profit analysis, called the **profit-volume chart,** focuses on profitability. On the profit-volume chart, only the difference between total sales revenues and total costs is plotted, which enables management to determine the operating profit (or loss) for various levels of operations.

To illustrate the profit-volume chart, assume that fixed costs are estimated at $50,000, variable costs are estimated at 75% of sales, and the maximum capacity is $500,000 of sales. The maximum operating loss is equal to the fixed costs of $50,000, and the maximum operating profit at 100% of capacity is $75,000, computed as follows:

Sales		$500,000
Expenses:		
Variable costs ($500,000 × 75%)	$375,000	
Fixed costs	50,000	425,000
Operating profit		$ 75,000

The following profit-volume chart is based on the foregoing data:

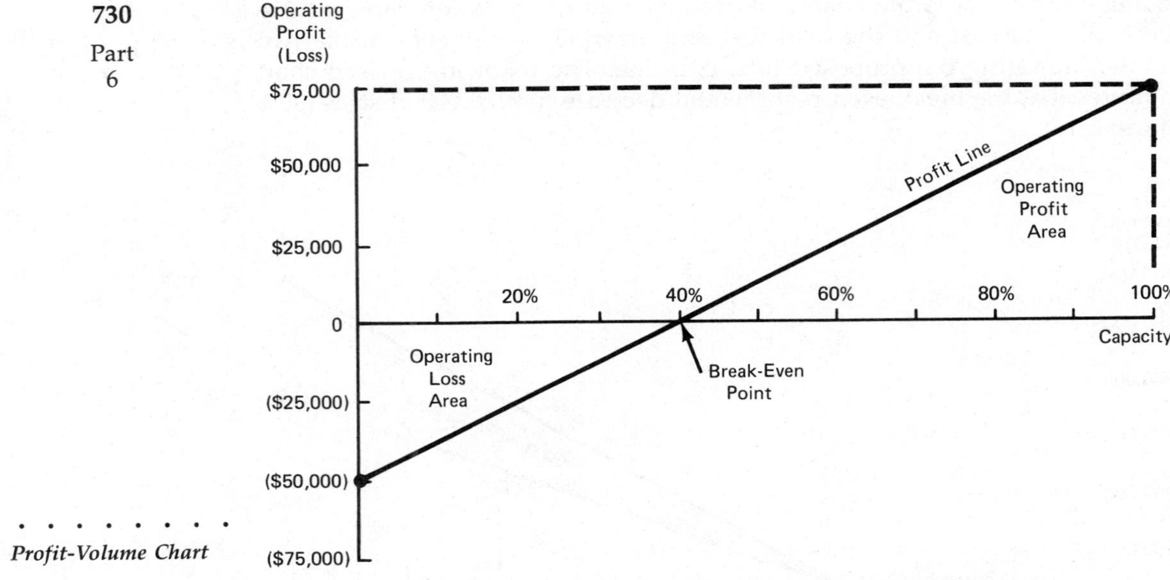

Profit-Volume Chart

The profit-volume chart is constructed in the following manner:

1. Percentages of capacity of the enterprise are spread along the horizontal axis, and dollar amounts representing operating profits and losses are spread along the vertical axis.
2. A point representing the maximum operating loss is plotted on the vertical axis at the left. This loss is equal to the total fixed costs at 0% of capacity.
3. A point representing the maximum operating profit at 100% of capacity is plotted on the right.
4. A diagonal profit line is drawn connecting the maximum operating loss point with the maximum operating profit point.
5. The profit line intersects the horizontal axis at the break-even point expressed as a percentage of capacity, and the areas representing operating profit and operating loss are identified.

In the illustration, the break-even point is 40% of productive capacity, which can be converted to $200,000 of total sales (maximum capacity of $500,000 × 40%). Operating profit will be earned when sales levels are to the right of the break-even point (operating profit area), and operating losses will be incurred when sales levels are to the left of the break-even point (operating loss area). For example, at 60% of productive capacity, an operating profit of $25,000 will be earned, as indicated in the profit-volume chart at the top of page 731.

The effect of changes in the unit selling price, total fixed costs, and unit variable costs on profit can be analyzed using a profit-volume chart. To illustrate, using the preceding example, assume that the effect on profit of an increase of $25,000 in fixed costs is to be evaluated. In this case, the total fixed costs would be $75,000 ($50,000 + $25,000), and the maximum operating loss at 0% of capacity would be $75,000. The maximum operating profit at 100% of capacity would be $50,000, computed as follows:

Sales		$500,000
Expenses:		
Variable costs ($500,000 × 75%)	$375,000	
Fixed costs	75,000	450,000
Operating profit		$ 50,000

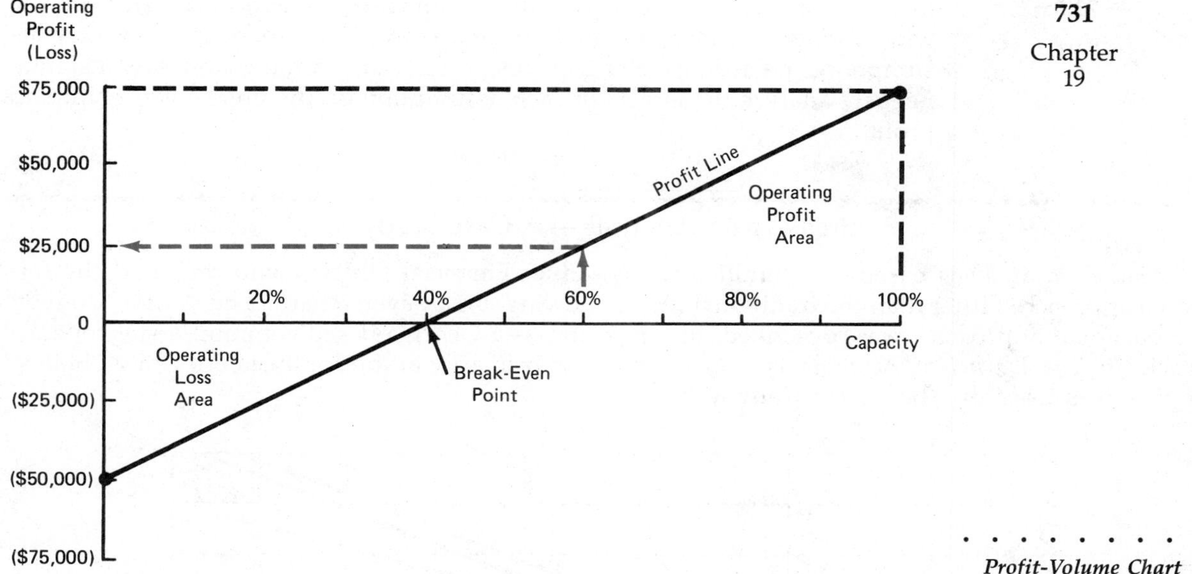

Profit-Volume Chart

A revised profit-volume chart is constructed by plotting the maximum operating loss and maximum operating profit points and drawing a line between the two points, indicating the revised profit line. The original and the revised profit-volume charts are as follows:

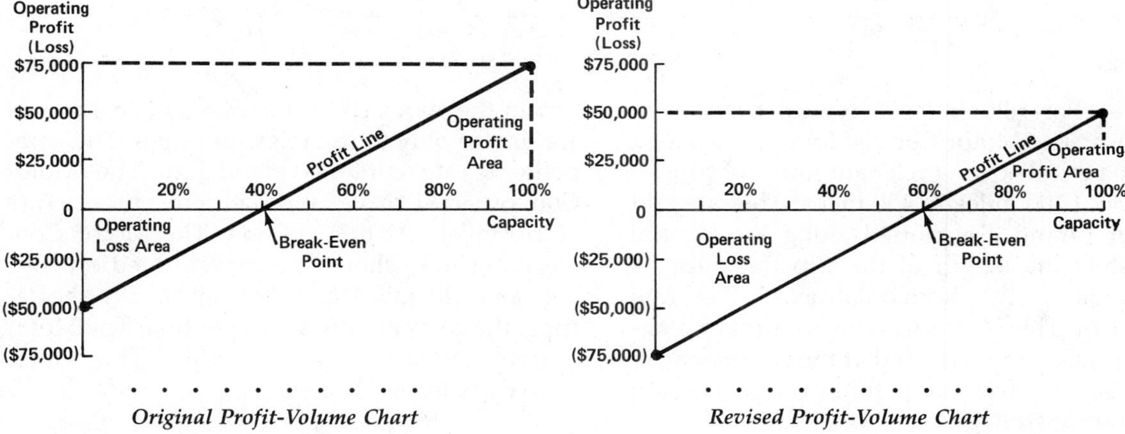

Original Profit-Volume Chart

Revised Profit-Volume Chart

The revised profit-volume chart indicates that the break-even point is 60% of capacity, which can be converted to total sales of $300,000 (maximum capacity of $500,000 × 60%). Note that the operating loss area of the chart has increased, while the operating profit area has decreased under the proposed change in fixed costs.

USE OF COMPUTERS IN COST-VOLUME-PROFIT ANALYSIS

In the preceding paragraphs, the use of the mathematical approach to cost-volume-profit analysis and the use of the cost-volume-profit chart and the profit-volume chart for analyzing the effect of changes in selling price, costs, and volume on profits have been demonstrated. Both the mathematical and graphic approaches are becoming increasingly popular and easy to use when managers have access to a computer terminal or a microcomputer. With the wide variety of computer software that is available, managers can vary assumptions regarding selling prices, costs, and volume and can instantaneously analyze the effects of each assumption on the break-even point and profit.

Break-Even Analysis—A Case Study

A break-even analysis based on a multidimensional approach, rather than the traditional two-dimensional approach, was described in an article in *The Journal of Accountancy*. Such an approach is used by The Motor Convoy Inc.'s Chief Financial Officer, who prepared the following break-even chart. The Motor Convoy Inc. is a Georgia-based common carrier operating primarily in the southeastern United States.

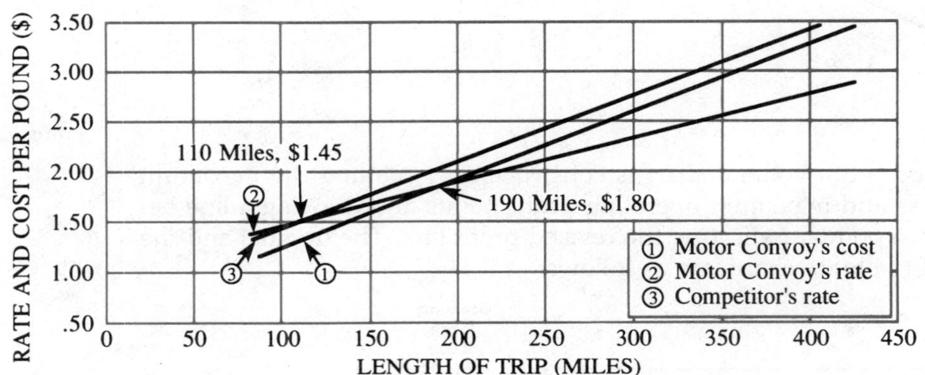

The chart illustrates a typical break-even analysis at The Motor Convoy for a normal load of 2,000 pounds over a relevant range of trips—from about 100 miles to 450 miles. The rate and cost per pound are plotted along the vertical axis, while the length of the trip (in miles) is plotted along the horizontal axis. The rate charged by The Motor Convoy's primary competitor is also graphed, so that the company can assess the effect of competition on developing its operating strategy.

In the above chart, the rate and cost curves are drawn only in the relevant range. The competitor's rate curve is parallel to The Motor Convoy's cost curve, and both rate curves cross at 110 miles. At this volume, The Motor Convoy's business should be concentrated on trips between 110 miles and 190 miles. On shorter trips, the competition is cheaper than The Motor Convoy, while on longer trips, The Motor Convoy is losing money.

Source: "Multidimensional Break-Even Analysis," *The Journal of Accountancy* (January, 1987), pp. 132–133.

SALES MIX CONSIDERATIONS

In many businesses, more than one product is sold at varying selling prices. In addition, the products often have different unit variable costs, and each product makes a different contribution to profits. Thus, the total business profit, as well as the break-even point, depends upon the proportions in which the products are sold.

Sales mix is the relative distribution of sales among the various products sold by an enterprise. For example, assume that the sales for Cascade Company during the past year, a typical year for the company, are as follows:

Product	Units Sold	Sales Mix
A	8,000	80%
B	2,000	20
	10,000	100%

The sales mix for products A and B can be expressed as a relative percentage, as shown above, or as the ratio of 80:20.

Sales Mix and the Break-Even Point

The break-even point for an enterprise selling two or more products must be calculated on the basis of a specified sales mix. If the sales mix is assumed to be constant, the break-even point and the sales necessary to achieve desired levels of operating profit can be computed using the standard calculations.

To illustrate the computation of the break-even point for Cascade Company, assume that fixed costs are $200,000. In addition, assume that the unit selling prices, unit variable costs, and sales mix for products A and B are as follows:

Product	Selling Price per Unit	Variable Cost per Unit	Sales Mix
A	$ 90	$70	80%
B	140	95	20

To compute the break-even point when several products are sold, it is useful to think of the individual products as components of one overall enterprise product. For Cascade Company, assume that this overall enterprise product is arbitrarily labeled E. The unit selling price of E can be thought of as equal to the total of the unit selling prices of the individual products A and B, multiplied by their respective sales mix percentages. Likewise, the unit variable cost of E can be thought of as equal to the total of the unit variable costs of products A and B, multiplied by the sales mix percentages. These computations are as follows:

Unit selling price of E: ($90 × .8) + ($140 × .2) = $100
Unit variable cost of E: ($70 × .8) + ($95 × .2) = $75

The variable costs for enterprise product E are therefore expected to be 75% of sales ($75 ÷ 100). The break-even point can be determined in the normal manner, using the equation, as follows:

Break-Even Sales (in $) = Fixed Costs (in $) + Variable Costs (as % of Break-Even Sales)
S = $200,000 + 75%S
25%S = $200,000
S = $800,000

The break-even point of $800,000 of sales of enterprise product E is equivalent to 8,000 total sales units ($800,000 ÷ $100). Since the sales mix for products A and B is 80% and 20% respectively, the break-even quantity of A is 6,400 (8,000 × 80%) and B is 1,600 (8,000 × 20%) units.

The validity of the preceding analysis can be verified by preparing the following income statement:

Cascade Company
Income Statement
For Year Ended December 31, 19--

	Product A	*Product B*	*Total*
Sales:			
6,400 units × $90	$576,000		$576,000
1,600 units × $140		$224,000	224,000
Total sales	$576,000	$224,000	$800,000
Variable costs:			
6,400 units × $70	$448,000		$448,000
1,600 units × $95		$152,000	152,000
Total variable costs	$448,000	$152,000	$600,000
Fixed costs			200,000
Total costs			$800,000
Operating profit			-0-

The effects of changes in the sales mix on the break-even point can be determined by repeating the preceding analysis, assuming a different sales mix.

Sales Mix and Desired Profit

The sales volume needed to earn an amount of profit when an enterprise sells two or more products can be computed using an approach similar to that described in the previous section. For example, the total sales necessary for Cascade Company to earn an operating profit of $40,000, with the original sales mix of 80% and 20% (where fixed costs were $200,000 and variable costs were 75% of sales), can be computed by use of the concept of an overall enterprise product E and solving the following equation:

Sales (in $) = Fixed Costs (in $) + Variable Costs (as a % of Sales) + Desired Profit
S = $200,000 + 75%S + $40,000
25%S = $240,000
S = $960,000

Sales of $960,000 of enterprise product E is equivalent to 9,600 total sales units ($960,000 ÷ $100). Since the sales mix for products A and B is 80% and 20% respectively, the quantity of A to be sold is 7,680 (9,600 × 80%) and B is 1,920 (9,600 × 20%) units. The validity of this approach can be verified by preparing the following income statement:

Cascade Company
Income Statement
For Year Ended December 31, 19--

	Product A	Product B	Total
Sales:			
7,680 units × $90	$691,200		$691,200
1,920 units × $140		$268,800	268,800
Total sales	$691,200	$268,800	$960,000
Variable costs:			
7,680 units × $70	$537,600		$537,600
1,920 units × $95		$182,400	182,400
Total variable costs	$537,600	$182,400	$720,000
Fixed costs			200,000
Total costs			$920,000
Operating profit			$ 40,000

SPECIAL COST-VOLUME-PROFIT RELATIONSHIPS

Additional relationships can be developed from the information presented in both the mathematical and graphic approaches to cost-volume-profit analysis. Two of these relationships that are especially useful to management in decision making are discussed in the following paragraphs.

Margin of Safety

The difference between the current sales revenue and the sales at the break-even point is called the **margin of safety.** It represents the possible decrease in sales revenue that may occur before an operating loss results, and it may be stated either in terms of dollars or as a percentage of sales. For example, if the volume of sales is $250,000 and sales at the break-even point amount to $200,000, the margin of safety is $50,000 or 20%, as shown by the following computation:

$$\text{Margin of Safety} = \frac{\text{Sales} - \text{Sales at Break-Even Point}}{\text{Sales}}$$

$$\text{Margin of Safety} = \frac{\$250,000 - \$200,000}{\$250,000} = 20\%$$

The margin of safety is useful in evaluating past operations and as a guide to business planning. For example, if the margin of safety is low, management should carefully study forecasts of future sales because even a small decline in sales revenue will result in an operating loss.

Contribution Margin Ratio

Another relationship between cost, volume, and profits that is especially useful in business planning because it gives an insight into the profit potential of a firm is the **contribution margin ratio,** sometimes called the **profit-volume ratio.** This ratio indicates the percentage of each sales dollar available to cover the fixed expenses and to provide operating income. For example, if the volume of sales is $250,000 and variable expenses amount to $175,000, the contribution margin ratio is 30%, as shown by the following computation:

$$\text{Contribution Margin Ratio} = \frac{\text{Sales} - \text{Variable Expenses}}{\text{Sales}}$$

$$\text{Contribution Margin Ratio} = \frac{\$250{,}000 - \$175{,}000}{\$250{,}000} = 30\%$$

The contribution margin ratio permits the quick determination of the effect on operating income of an increase or a decrease in sales volume. To illustrate, assume that the management of a firm with a contribution margin ratio of 30% is studying the effect on operating income of adding $25,000 in sales orders. Multiplying the ratio (30%) by the change in sales volume ($25,000) indicates an increase in operating income of $7,500 if the additional orders are obtained. In using the analysis in such a case, factors other than sales volume, such as the amount of fixed expenses, the percentage of variable expenses to sales, and the unit sales price, are assumed to remain constant. If these factors are not constant, the effect of any change must be considered in applying the analysis.

The contribution margin ratio is also useful in setting business policy. For example, if the contribution margin ratio of a firm is large and production is at a level below 100% capacity, a comparatively large increase in operating income can be expected from an increase in sales volume. On the other hand, a comparatively large decrease in operating income can be expected from a decline in sales volume. A firm in such a position might decide to devote more effort to additional sales promotion because of the large change in operating income that will result from changes in sales volume. On the other hand, a firm with a small contribution margin ratio will probably want to give more attention to reducing costs and expenses before concentrating large efforts on additional sales promotion.

LIMITATIONS OF COST-VOLUME-PROFIT ANALYSIS

The reliability of cost-volume-profit analysis depends upon the validity of several assumptions. One major assumption is that there is no change in inventory quantities during the year; that is, the quantity of units in the beginning inventory equals the quantity of units in the ending inventory. When changes in inventory quantities occur, the computations for cost-volume-profit analysis become more complex.

For cost-volume-profit analysis, a relevant range of activity is assumed, within which all costs can be classified as either fixed or variable. Within the relevant range, which is usually a range of activity within which the company is likely to operate, the unit variable costs and the total fixed costs will not change. For example, within the relevant range of activity, factory supervisory salaries are fixed. For cost-volume-profit analysis, it is assumed that a significant change in activity that would cause these salaries to change, such as adding a night shift that would double production, will not occur.

These assumptions simplify cost-volume-profit relationships, and since substantial variations in the assumptions are often uncommon in practice, cost-volume-profit analysis can be used quite effectively in decision making. Under conditions of substantial variations from the assumptions, the analysis of the cost-volume-profit relationships must be used cautiously.

Chapter Review

KEY POINTS

1. Cost-Volume-Profit Relationships.
Cost-volume-profit analysis is the systematic examination of the interrelationships between selling prices, volume of sales and production, costs, expenses, and profits. Accountants can play an important role in cost-volume-profit analysis by providing management with information on the relative profitability of its various products, the probable effects of changes in selling price, and other variables.

In cost-volume-profit analysis, costs are subdivided into two categories: (1) variable and (2) fixed. Variable costs are costs that change, in total, as the volume of activity changes. Fixed costs remain constant, in total, as the volume of activity changes. Mixed costs are costs that have both variable and fixed characteristics. For purposes of analysis, mixed costs can generally be separated into variable and fixed components.

2. Mathematical Approach to Cost-Volume-Profit Analysis.
The mathematical approach to cost-volume-profit analysis uses equations (1) to indicate the revenues necessary to achieve the break-even point in operations or (2) to indicate the revenues necessary to achieve a desired or target profit. The level of operations of an enterprise at which revenues and expired costs are exactly equal is called the break-even point. The break-even point can be determined using the following equation:

Break-Even Sales (in $) = Fixed Costs (in $) + Variable Costs (as % of Break-Even Sales)

The break-even point is raised by increases in fixed costs, increases in variable costs, or decreases in the unit selling price. The break-even point is lowered by decreases in fixed costs, decreases in variable costs, or increases in the unit selling price. By modifying the break-even equation and adding a factor for desired profit, the sales volume required to earn a desired amount of profit may be estimated.

3. Graphic Approach to Cost-Volume-Profit Analysis.
Many managers prefer to use a graphic format for cost-volume-profit analysis because the operating profit or loss for any given level of capacity can be readily determined, without the necessity of solving an equation. A cost-volume-profit chart is used to assist management in understanding the relationships between costs, sales, and operating profit or loss. Changes in the unit selling price, total fixed costs, and unit variable costs can also be analyzed using a cost-volume-profit chart. Another graphic approach to cost-volume-profit analysis, called the profit-volume chart, focuses on profitability rather

than on sales revenues and costs. The effect of changes in unit selling price, total fixed costs, and unit variable costs on profit can also be analyzed using a profit-volume chart.

4. Use of Computers in Cost-Volume-Profit Analysis.
Both the mathematical and graphic approaches to cost-volume-profit analysis are becoming increasingly popular and easy to use when managers have access to a computer terminal or a microcomputer. With the wide variety of computer software that is available, managers can vary assumptions regarding selling prices, costs, and volume and can instantaneously analyze the effects of each assumption on the break-even point and profit.

5. Sales Mix Considerations.
The break-even point for an enterprise selling two or more products must be calculated on the basis of a specified sales mix. If the sales mix is assumed to be constant, the break-even point can be computed using the standard approaches.

6. Special Cost-Volume-Profit Relationships.
The difference between the current sales revenue and the sales at the break-even point is called the margin of safety. The margin of safety is useful in evaluating past operations and as a guide to business planning. Another relationship between costs, volume, and profits that is especially useful in business planning because it gives an insight into the profit potential of a firm is the contribution margin ratio. This ratio indicates the percentage of each sales dollar available to cover the fixed costs and expenses and to provide operating income. The contribution margin ratio permits the quick determination of the effect on operating income of an increase or a decrease in sales volume.

7. Limitations of Cost-Volume-Profit Analysis.
The reliability of cost-volume-profit analysis depends upon the validity of several assumptions. One major assumption is that there is no change in inventory quantities during the year. Another assumption is that the analysis is conducted within a relevant range of activity within which all costs can be classified as fixed or variable. These assumptions simplify cost-volume-profit relationships, and since substantial variations in the assumptions are often uncommon in practice, cost-volume-profit analysis can be used quite effectively in decision making.

KEY TERMS

cost-volume-profit analysis 723
variable costs 724
fixed costs 724
mixed costs 724
break-even point 724
cost-volume-profit chart 727
profit-volume chart 729
sales mix 732
margin of safety 735
contribution margin ratio 736

SELF-EXAMINATION QUESTIONS

(Answers at End of Chapter)

1. For cost-volume-profit analysis, costs must be classified as either fixed or variable. Variable costs:
   A. change in total as the volume of activity changes
   B. do not change in total as the volume of activity changes

C. change on a per unit basis as the volume of activity changes
D. none of the above

2. If variable costs are 40% of sales and fixed costs are $240,000, what is the break-even point?
   A. $200,000 C. $400,000
   B. $240,000 D. None of the above

3. Based on the data presented in Question 2, how much sales would be required to realize operating profit of $30,000?
   A. $400,000 C. $600,000
   B. $450,000 D. None of the above

4. If sales were $500,000, variable costs are $200,000, and fixed costs are $240,000, what is the margin of safety?
   A. 20% C. 60%
   B. 40% D. None of the above

5. Based on the data presented in Question 4, what is the contribution margin ratio?
   A. 40% C. 88%
   B. 48% D. None of the above.

ILLUSTRATIVE PROBLEM

Nissat Company expects to maintain the same inventories at the end of the year as at the beginning of the year. The estimated fixed costs and expenses for the year are $360,000 and the estimated variable costs and expenses per unit are $9. It is expected that 75,000 units will be sold at a selling price of $15 per unit. Capacity output is 80,000 units.

Instructions:

1. Determine the break-even point (a) in dollars of sales, (b) in units, and (c) in terms of capacity.
2. Construct a cost-volume-profit chart, indicating the break-even point in dollars of sales.
3. Construct a profit-volume chart, indicating the break-even point as a percentage of capacity.
4. What is the expected margin of safety?
5. What is the contribution margin ratio?

SOLUTION

(1) (a) Break-even point in dollars of sales:

$$S = \$360,000 + 60\%S$$
$$S - 60\%S = \$360,000$$
$$S = \$900,000$$

(b) Break-even point in units:

$$\$900,000 \div \$15 = 60,000 \text{ units}$$

(c) Break-even point in terms of capacity:

$$60,000 \div 80,000 = 75\%$$

(2)

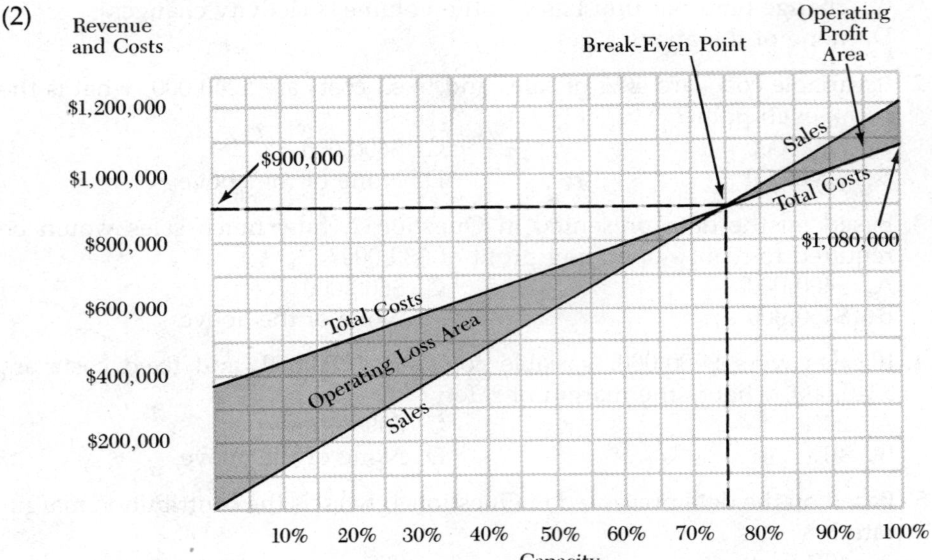

(3)

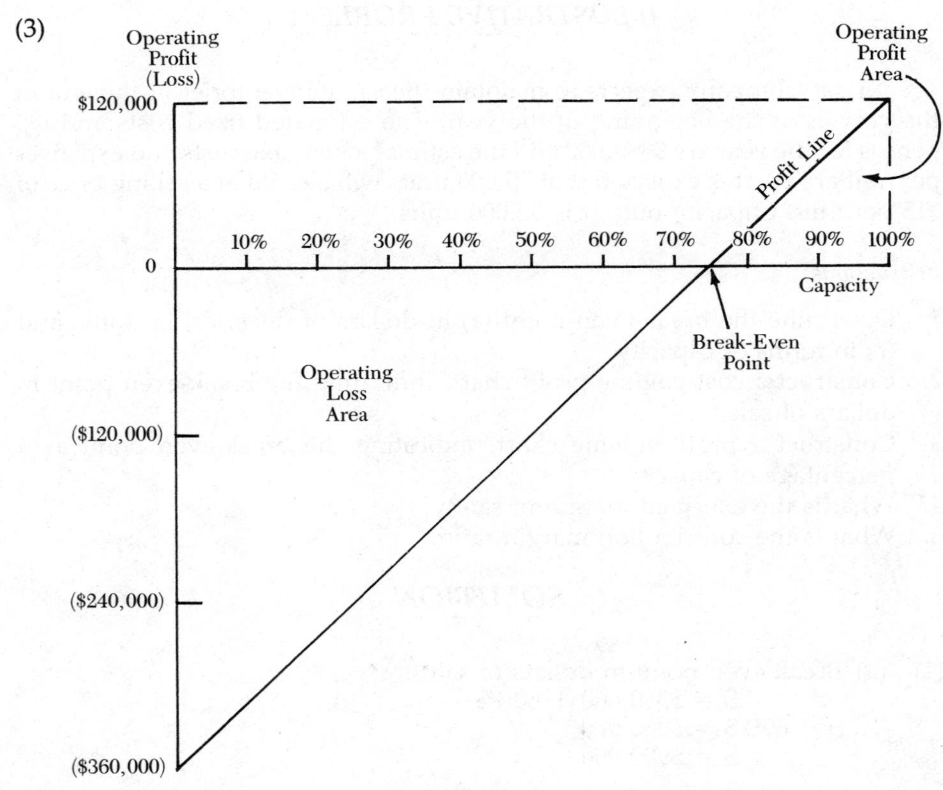

(4) Margin of safety:

Expected sales (75,000 units @ $15)	$1,125,000
Break-even point	900,000
Margin of safety	$ 225,000 or 20%

$$(5)\ \text{Contribution margin ratio} = \frac{\text{Sales} - \text{Variable Expenses}}{\text{Sales}}$$

$$= \frac{\$1,125,000 - (75,000 \times \$9)}{\$1,125,000}$$

$$= \frac{\$450,000}{\$1,125,000}$$

$$= 40\%$$

Discussion Questions

19–1. How do changes in volume of activity affect (a) total variable costs and (b) total fixed costs?

19–2. If total fixed costs are $84,000, what is the unit fixed cost if production is (a) 20,000 units and (b) 35,000 units?

19–3. (a) What is the break-even point? (b) What equation can be used to determine the break-even point?

19–4. If sales are $800,000, variable costs are $520,000, and fixed costs are $175,000, what is the break-even point?

19–5. If fixed costs are $320,000 and variable costs are 60% of sales, what is the break-even point?

19–6. If the unit cost of direct materials is decreased, what effect will this change have on the break-even point?

19–7. If the property tax rates are increased, what effect will this change in fixed costs have on the break-even point?

19–8. If fixed costs are $250,000 and variable costs are 65% of sales, what sales are required to realize an operating profit of $100,000?

19–9. What is the advantage of presenting cost-volume-profit analysis in the chart form over the equation form?

19–10. Name the following chart and identify the items represented by the letters *a* through *f*.

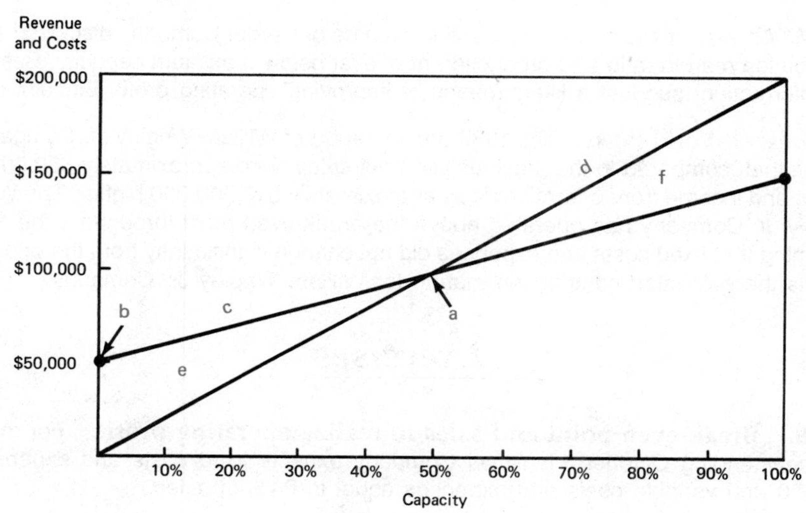

19–11. Name the following chart and identify the items represented by the letters *a* through *f*.

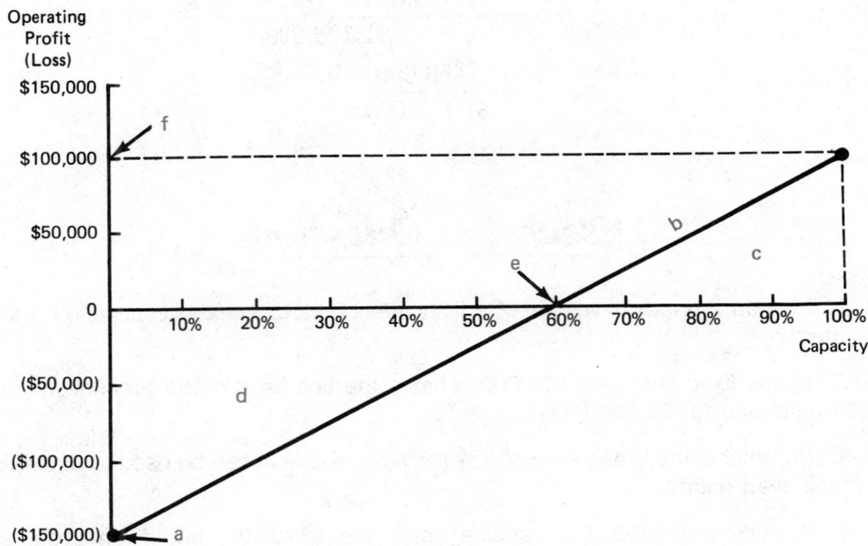

19–12. Both Harris Company and Lammers Company had the same sales, total costs, and operating profit for the current fiscal year, yet Harris Company had a lower break-even point than Lammers Company. Explain the reason for this difference in break-even points.

19–13. (a) What is meant by *sales mix?* (b) For conventional break-even analysis, is the sales mix assumed to be constant?

19–14. (a) What is meant by the term *margin of safety?* (b) If sales are $600,000, net income is $50,400, and sales at the break-even point are $480,000, what is the margin of safety?

19–15. What ratio indicates the percentage of each sales dollar that is available to cover fixed costs and to provide a profit?

19–16. (a) If sales are $180,000 and variable costs are $126,000, what is the contribution margin ratio? (b) What is the contribution margin ratio if variable costs are 65% of sales?

19–17. An examination of the accounting records of Cardel Company disclosed a high contribution margin ratio and production at a level below maximum capacity. Based on this information, suggest a likely means of improving operating profit. Explain.

19–18. Real World Focus. The 1987 annual report of William Wrigley Jr. Company indicates that, compared to the previous year, net sales were approximately $80,000,000 higher, and income from operations was approximately $16,000,000 higher. The William Wrigley Jr. Company has operated above the break-even point throughout the 1980s. Assuming that fixed costs and expenses did not change significantly from the prior year, what is the estimated contribution margin for William Wrigley Jr. Company?

Exercises

19–19. Break-even point and sales to realize operating profit. For the current year ending October 31, Duval Company expects fixed costs and expenses of $72,000 and variable costs and expenses equal to 64% of sales.

(a) Compute the anticipated break-even point.
(b) Compute the sales required to realize operating profit of $43,200.

SPREADSHEET PROBLEM

19–20. Break-even point. For the past year, DeLong Company had fixed costs of $342,000 and variable costs equal to 55% of sales. All revenues and costs are expected to remain constant for the coming year, except that property taxes are expected to increase by $27,000 during the year.

(a) Compute the break-even point for the past year.
(b) Compute the anticipated break-even point for the coming year.

19–21. Break-even point. For the current year ending May 31, Lynch Company expects fixed costs of $420,000 and variable costs equal to 65% of sales. For the coming year, a new wage contract will increase variable costs to 70% of sales.

(a) Compute the break-even point for the current year.
(b) Compute the anticipated break-even point for the coming year, assuming that all revenues and costs are to remain constant, with the exception of the costs represented by the new wage contract.

19–22. Break-even point. Currently the unit selling price of a product is $40, the unit variable cost is $27, and the total fixed costs are $52,000. A proposal is being evaluated to increase the unit selling price to $45.

(a) Compute the current break-even point.
(b) Compute the anticipated break-even point, assuming that the unit selling price is increased and all costs remain constant.

19–23. Profit-volume chart. For the coming year, Inwood Inc. anticipates fixed costs of $200,000, variable costs equal to 60% of sales, and maximum capacity of $1,000,000 of sales.

(a) What is the maximum possible operating loss?
(b) Compute the maximum possible operating profit.
(c) Construct a profit-volume chart.
(d) Determine the break-even point as a percentage of capacity by using the profit-volume chart constructed in (c).

19–24. Margin of safety. (a) If Tucker Company, with a break-even point at $420,000 of sales, has actual sales of $700,000, what is the margin of safety expressed (1) in dollars and (2) as a percentage of sales? (b) If the margin of safety for Faust Company was 25%, fixed costs were $240,000, and variable costs were 60% of sales, what was the amount of actual sales?

19–25. Contribution margin ratio. (a) If Woodall Company budgets sales of $750,000, fixed costs and expenses of $120,000, and variable costs and expenses of $480,000, what is the anticipated contribution margin ratio? (b) If the contribution margin ratio for Austin Company is 28%, sales were $850,000, and fixed costs and expenses were $88,000, what was the operating profit?

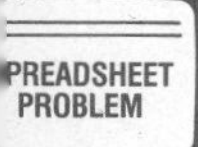

19–26. Computation of break-even point, variable and fixed costs, and operating profit. For the past year, Gonzales Company had sales of $1,200,000, a margin of safety of 15%, and a contribution margin ratio of 40%. Compute:

(a) The break-even point.
(b) The variable costs and expenses.
(c) The fixed costs and expenses.
(d) The operating profit.

19–27. Computation of break-even point, sales, and operating profit. For 1989, a company had sales of $1,800,000, fixed costs of $300,000, and a contribution margin ratio of 25%. During 1990, the variable costs were 75% of sales, the fixed costs did not change from the previous year, and the margin of safety was 20%.

(a) What was the operating profit for 1989?
(b) What was the break-even point for 1990?
(c) What was the amount of sales for 1990?
(d) What was the operating profit for 1990?

19–28. Real World Focus. The following income statement data were taken from the 1987 financial statements of Pillsbury Company:

	(In millions)
Net Sales	$6,127.8
Costs and expenses:	
Cost of sales	$4,292.2
Selling, general, and administrative expenses	1,387.5
Interest expense	95.6
	$5,775.3
Income before income tax	$ 352.5

Assume that the costs and expenses have been classified into the following fixed and variable components:

	Fixed	Variable
Cost of sales	20%	80%
Selling, general, and administrative expenses	40%	60%
Interest expense	100%	0%

Based on the above data, determine (a) the break-even point for Pillsbury Company and (b) the margin of safety expressed in sales dollars and as a percentage of 1987 sales. Round computations to one decimal place.

Problems

19–29. Break-even point and cost-volume-profit chart. For the coming year, Peak Company anticipates fixed costs of $300,000 and variable costs equal to 70% of sales.

Instructions: (1) Compute the anticipated break-even point.
(2) Compute the sales required to realize an operating profit of $90,000.
(3) Construct a cost-volume-profit chart, assuming sales of $2,000,000 at full capacity.
(4) Determine the probable operating profit if sales total $1,600,000.

19–30. Break-even point and cost-volume-profit chart. Hooper Company operated at 80% of capacity last year, when sales were $800,000. Fixed costs were $240,000, and variable costs were 60% of sales. Hooper Company is considering a proposal to spend an additional $40,000 on billboard advertising during the current year in an attempt to increase sales and utilize additional capacity.

Instructions: (1) Construct a cost-volume-profit chart indicating the break-even point for last year.
(2) Using the cost-volume-profit chart prepared in (1), determine (a) the operating profit for last year and (b) the maximum operating profit that could have been realized during the year.
(3) Construct a cost-volume-profit chart indicating the break-even point for the current year, assuming that a noncancelable contract is signed for the additional billboard advertising. No changes are expected in unit selling price or other costs.
(4) Using the cost-volume-profit chart prepared in (3), determine (a) the operating profit if sales total $800,000 and (b) the maximum operating profit that could be realized during the year.

19–31. Break-even point and profit-volume chart. Last year, Randall Company had sales of $300,000, fixed costs of $50,000, and variable costs of $225,000. Randall Company is considering a proposal to spend $12,500 to hire a public relations firm, hoping that the company's image can be improved and sales increased. Maximum operating capacity is $500,000 of sales.

Instructions: (1) Construct a profit-volume chart for last year.
(2) Using the profit-volume chart prepared in (1), determine for last year (a) the break-even point, (b) the operating profit, and (c) the maximum operating profit that could have been realized.
(3) Construct a profit-volume chart for the current year, assuming that the additional $12,500 expenditure is made and there is no change in unit selling price or other costs.
(4) Using the profit-volume chart prepared in (3), determine (a) the break-even point, (b) the operating profit if sales total $300,000, and (c) the maximum operating profit that could be realized.

19–32. Sales mix and break-even point. Data related to the expected sales of products A and B for Gowdy Company for the current year, which is typical of recent years, are as follows:

Product	Selling Price per Unit	Variable Cost per Unit	Sales Mix
A	$160	$ 88	75%
B	200	144	25

The estimated fixed costs for the current year are $544,000.

Instructions: (1) Determine the estimated sales revenues necessary to reach the break-even point for the current year.
(2) Based on the break-even point in (1), determine the unit sales of both A and B for the current year.
(3) Determine the estimated sales revenues necessary for Gowdy Company to realize an operating profit of $136,000 for the current year.
(4) Based on the sales revenues determined in (3), determine the unit sales of both A and B for the current year.

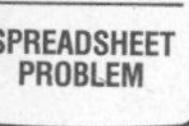

19–33. Break-even point and cost-volume-profit chart, margin of safety, and contribution margin ratio. Joyce Company expects to maintain the same inventories at the end of 1990 as at the beginning of the year. The total of all production costs for the year is therefore assumed to be equal to the cost of goods sold. With this in mind, the various department heads were asked to submit estimates of the expenses for their departments during 1990. A summary report of these estimates is as follows:

	Estimated Fixed Expense	Estimated Variable Expense (per unit sold)
Production costs:		
Direct materials	—	$ 5.40
Direct labor	—	12.60
Factory overhead	$150,000	2.00
Selling expenses:		
Sales salaries and commissions	50,000	.60
Advertising	25,400	—
Travel	5,600	—
Miscellaneous selling expense	1,200	.15
General expenses:		
Office and officers' salaries	30,000	—
Supplies	5,100	.20
Miscellaneous general expense	2,700	.05
	$270,000	$21.00

It is expected that 40,000 units will be sold at a selling price of $30 a unit. Capacity output is 50,000 units.

Instructions: (1) Determine the break-even point (a) in dollars of sales, (b) in units, and (c) in terms of capacity.
(2) Prepare an estimated income statement for 1990.
(3) Construct a cost-volume-profit chart, indicating the break-even point in dollars of sales.
(4) What is the expected margin of safety?
(5) What is the expected contribution margin ratio?

19–34. Break-even point under present and proposed conditions. Fain Company operated at full capacity during 1990. Its income statement for 1990 is as follows:

Sales		$4,000,000
Cost of goods sold		2,400,000
Gross profit		$1,600,000
Operating expenses:		
Selling expenses	$850,000	
General expenses	250,000	
Total operating expenses		1,100,000
Operating profit		$ 500,000

The division of costs and expenses between fixed and variable is as follows:

	Fixed	Variable
Cost of goods sold	15%	85%
Selling expenses	10%	90%
General expenses	22%	78%

Management is considering a plant expansion program that will permit an increase of $800,000 in yearly sales. The expansion will increase fixed costs and expenses by $150,000, but will not affect the relationship between sales and variable costs and expenses.

Instructions: (1) Determine for present capacity (a) the total fixed costs and expenses and (b) the total variable costs and expenses.
(2) Determine the percentage of total variable costs and expenses to sales.
(3) Compute the break-even point under present conditions.
(4) Compute the break-even point under the proposed program.
(5) Determine the amount of sales that would be necessary under the proposed program to realize the $500,000 of operating profit that was earned in 1990.
(6) Determine the maximum operating profit possible with the expanded plant.
(7) If the proposal is accepted and sales remain at the 1990 level, what will the operating profit or loss be for 1991?
(8) Based on the data given, would you recommend accepting the proposal? Explain.

ALTERNATE PROBLEMS

19–29A. Break-even point and cost-volume-profit chart. For the coming year, Reece Company anticipates fixed costs of $140,000 and variable costs equal to 60% of sales.

Instructions: (1) Compute the anticipated break-even point.
(2) Compute the sales required to realize an operating profit of $40,000.
(3) Construct a cost-volume-profit chart, assuming sales of $500,000 at full capacity.
(4) Determine the probable operating profit if sales total $400,000.

19–30A. Break-even point and cost-volume-profit chart. Chadwick Company operated at 70% of capacity last year, when sales totaled $700,000. Fixed costs were $125,000, and variable costs were 75% of sales. Chadwick Company is considering a proposal to spend an additional $25,000 on billboard advertising during the current year in an attempt to increase sales and utilize additional capacity.

Instructions: (1) Construct a cost-volume-profit chart indicating the break-even point for last year.

(2) Using the cost-volume-profit chart prepared in (1), determine (a) the operating profit for last year and (b) the maximum operating profit that could have been realized during the year.

(3) Construct a cost-volume-profit chart indicating the break-even point for the current year, assuming that a noncancelable contract is signed for the additional billboard advertising. No changes are expected in unit selling price or other costs.

(4) Using the cost-volume-profit chart prepared in (3), determine (a) the operating profit if sales total $700,000 and (b) the maximum operating profit that could be realized during the year.

19–31A. Break-even point and profit-volume chart. Last year, Coggins Company had sales of $400,000, fixed costs of $50,000, and variable costs of $320,000. Coggins Company is considering a proposal to spend $10,000 to hire a public relations firm, hoping that the company's image can be improved and sales increased. Maximum operating capacity is $500,000 of sales.

Instructions: (1) Construct a profit-volume chart for last year.

(2) Using the profit-volume chart prepared in (1), determine for last year (a) the break-even point, (b) the operating profit, and (c) the maximum operating profit that could have been realized.

(3) Construct a profit-volume chart for the current year, assuming that the additional $10,000 expenditure is made and there is no change in unit selling price or other costs.

(4) Using the profit-volume chart prepared in (3), determine (a) the break-even point, (b) the operating profit if sales total $400,000, and (c) the maximum operating profit that could be realized.

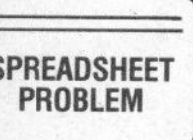

19–33A. Break-even point and cost-volume-profit chart, margin of safety, and contribution margin ratio. Spencer Company expects to maintain the same inventories at the end of 1990 as at the beginning of the year. The total of all production costs for the year is therefore assumed to be equal to the cost of goods sold. With this in mind, the various department heads were asked to submit estimates of the expenses for their departments during 1990. A summary report of these estimates is as follows:

	Estimated Fixed Expense	Estimated Variable Expense (per unit sold)
Production costs:		
Direct materials	—	$ 3.25
Direct labor	—	8.70
Factory overhead	$120,000	1.80
Selling expenses:		
Sales salaries and commissions	60,000	.80
Advertising	35,200	—
Travel	21,800	—
Miscellaneous selling expense	7,000	.20
General expenses:		
Office and officers' salaries	40,000	—
Supplies	11,600	.15
Miscellaneous general expense	4,400	.10
	$300,000	$15.00

It is expected that 50,000 units will be sold at a selling price of $25 a unit. Capacity output is 60,000 units.

Instructions: (1) Determine the break-even point (a) in dollars of sales, (b) in units, and (c) in terms of capacity.

(2) Prepare an estimated income statement for 1990.

(3) Construct a cost-volume-profit chart, indicating the break-even point in dollars of sales.

(4) What is the expected margin of safety?

(5) What is the expected contribution margin ratio?

Mini-Case 19

Owens Company manufactures product M, which sold for $45 per unit in 1989. For the past several years, sales and operating profit have been declining. On sales of $495,000 in 1989, the company operated near the break-even point and used only 55% of its productive capacity. Bill Owens, your father-in-law, is considering several proposals to reverse the trend of declining sales and operating profit, and to more fully use production facilities. One proposal under consideration is to reduce the unit selling price to $40.

Your father-in-law has asked you to aid him in assessing the proposal to reduce the sales price by $5. For this purpose, he provided the following summary of the estimated fixed and variable costs and expenses for 1990, which are unchanged from 1989:

Variable costs and expenses:	
Production costs	$18.60 per unit
Selling expenses	6.20 per unit
General expenses	4.00 per unit
Fixed costs and expenses:	
Production costs	$120,000
Selling expenses	30,000
General expenses	26,400

Instructions:

(1) Determine the break-even point for 1990 in dollars, assuming (a) no change in sales price and (b) the proposed sales price.

(2) How much additional sales are necessary for Owens Company to break even in 1990 under the proposal?

(3) Determine the operating profit for 1990, assuming (a) no change in sales price and volume from 1989 and (b) the new sales price and no change in volume from 1989.

(4) Determine the maximum operating profit for 1990, assuming the proposed sales price.

(5) Briefly list factors that you would discuss with your father-in-law in evaluating the proposal.

Answers to Self-Examination Questions

1. A Variable costs change in total as the volume of activity changes (answer A) or, expressed in another way, the unit variable cost remains constant with changes in volume.

2. C The break-even point of $400,000 (answer C) is that level of operations at which revenue and expired costs are exactly equal and is determined as follows:

$$\text{Break-Even Sales (in \$)} = \text{Fixed Costs (in \$)} + \text{Variable Costs (as \% of Sales)}$$
$$S = \$240{,}000 + 40\%S$$
$$60\%S = \$240{,}000$$
$$S = \$400{,}000$$

3. B $450,000 of sales (answer B) would be required to realize operating profit of $30,000, computed as follows:

$$\text{Sales (in \$)} = \text{Fixed Costs (in \$)} + \text{Variable Costs (as \% of Sales)} + \text{Desired Profit}$$
$$S = \$240{,}000 + 40\%S + \$30{,}000$$
$$60\%S = \$270{,}000$$
$$S = \$450{,}000$$

4. A The margin of safety of 20% (answer A) represents the possible decrease in sales revenue that may occur before an operating loss results and is determined as follows:

$$\text{Margin of Safety} = \frac{\text{Sales} - \text{Sales at Break-Even Point}}{\text{Sales}}$$
$$= \frac{\$500{,}000 - \$400{,}000}{\$500{,}000}$$
$$= 20\%$$

The margin of safety can also be expressed in terms of dollars and would amount to $100,000, determined as follows:

Sales	$500,000
Less sales at break-even point	400,000
Margin of safety	$100,000

5. D The contribution margin ratio indicates the percentage of each sales dollar available to cover the fixed expenses and provide operating income and is determined as follows:

$$\text{Contribution Margin Ratio} = \frac{\text{Sales} - \text{Variable Expenses}}{\text{Sales}}$$
$$\text{Contribution Margin Ratio} = \frac{\$500{,}000 - \$200{,}000}{\$500{,}000}$$
$$= 60\%$$

20
Profit Reporting for Management Analysis

CHAPTER OBJECTIVES

Describe and illustrate absorption costing concepts.

Describe and illustrate variable costing concepts.

Describe management's use of variable costing and absorption costing for:
Cost control
Product pricing
Production planning
Sales analysis
Contribution margin analysis

The basic accounting systems used by manufacturers to provide accounting information useful to management in planning, organizing and directing, controlling, and decision making were described and illustrated in preceding chapters. In planning operations, the use of cost-volume-profit analysis, which was based on the discussion of cost behavior and cost estimation, was also discussed. In this chapter, two alternate concepts useful to management in planning and controlling operations—absorption costing and variable costing—are described and illustrated.

ABSORPTION COSTING AND VARIABLE COSTING

One of the most important items affecting an enterprise's net income is the cost of goods sold. In many cases, the cost of goods sold is larger than all of the other operating expenses combined. In determining the cost of goods sold, either the absorption costing or variable costing concept can be used.

The cost of manufactured products consists of direct materials, direct labor, and factory overhead. All such costs become a part of the finished goods inventory and remain there as an asset until the goods are sold. This conventional treatment of manufacturing costs is sometimes called **absorption costing** because all costs are "absorbed" into finished goods. Although the concept is necessary in determining taxable income and historical costs for the basic financial statements, another costing concept may be more useful to management in making decisions.

In **variable costing,** which is also termed **direct costing,** the cost of goods manufactured is composed only of variable costs—those manufacturing costs that increase or decrease as the volume of production rises or falls. These costs are the direct materials, direct labor, and only those factory overhead costs which vary with the rate of production. The remaining factory overhead costs, which are the fixed or nonvariable items, are related to the productive capacity of the manufacturing plant and are not affected by changes in the quantity of product manufactured. Accordingly, the fixed factory overhead does not become a part of the cost of goods manufactured, but is considered an expense of the period.

The distinction between absorption costing and variable costing is illustrated in the following diagram. Note that the difference between the two costing concepts is in the treatment of the fixed manufacturing costs, which consist of the fixed factory overhead costs.

Absorption Costing Compared with Variable Costing

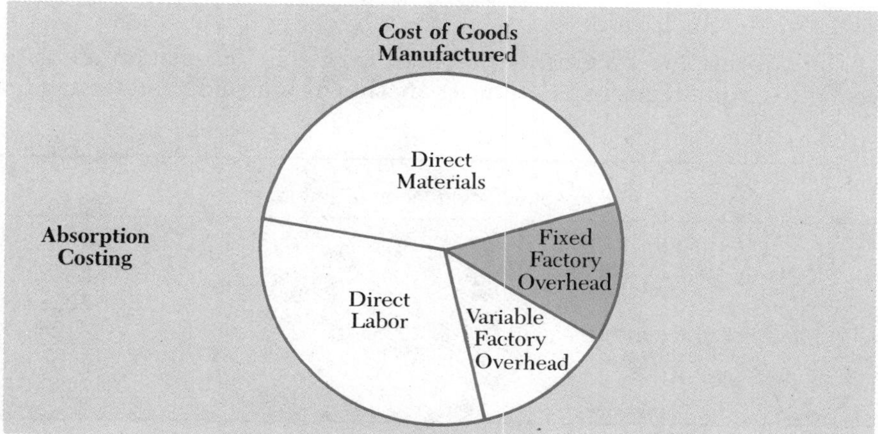

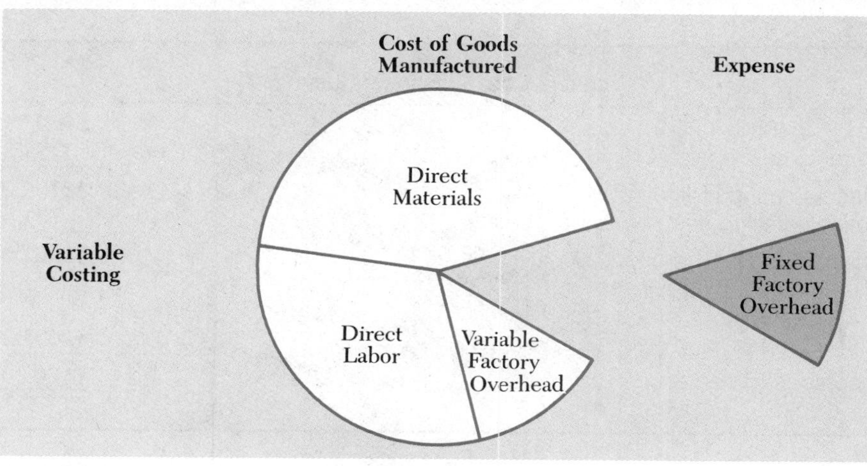

Variable Costing and the Income Statement

The arrangement of data in the variable costing income statement differs considerably from the format of the conventional income statement. Variable costs and expenses are presented separately from fixed costs and expenses, with significant summarizing amounts inserted at intermediate points. As a basis for illustrating the differences between the two forms, assume that 15,000 units were manufactured and sold at a unit price of $50 and the costs and expenses were as follows:

	Total Cost or Expense	Number of Units	Unit Cost
Manufacturing costs:			
Variable	$375,000	15,000	$25
Fixed	150,000	15,000	10
Total	$525,000		$35
Selling and general expenses:			
Variable ($5 per unit sold)	$ 75,000		
Fixed	50,000		
Total	$125,000		

The two income statements prepared from this information are as follows. The computations in parentheses are shown as an aid to understanding.

Absorption Costing Income Statement

Absorption Costing Income Statement

Sales (15,000 × $50)	$750,000
Cost of goods sold (15,000 × $35)	525,000
Gross profit	$225,000
Selling and general expenses ($75,000 + $50,000)	125,000
Income from operations	$100,000

Variable Costing Income Statement

Variable Costing Income Statement

Sales (15,000 × $50)		$750,000
Variable cost of goods sold (15,000 × $25)		375,000
Manufacturing margin		$375,000
Variable selling and general expenses		75,000
Contribution margin		$300,000
Fixed costs and expenses:		
Fixed manufacturing costs	$150,000	
Fixed selling and general expenses	50,000	200,000
Income from operations		$100,000

The absorption costing income statement does not distinguish between variable and fixed costs and expenses. All manufacturing costs are included in the cost of goods sold. The deduction of the cost of goods sold from sales yields the intermediate amount, gross profit. Deduction of selling and general expenses then yields income from operations.

In contrast, the variable costing income statement includes only the variable manufacturing costs in the cost of goods sold. Deduction of the cost of goods sold from sales yields an intermediate amount, termed **manufacturing margin.** Deduction of the variable selling and general expenses yields the **contribution margin,** or **marginal income.** The fixed costs and expenses are then deducted from the contribution margin to yield income from operations.

Units Manufactured Equal Units Sold. In the preceding illustration, 15,000 units were manufactured and sold. Both the absorption and the variable costing income statements reported the same income from operations of $100,000. Assuming no other changes, this equality of income will always be the case when the number of units manufactured and the number of units sold are equal. Only when the number of units manufactured and the number of units sold are not equal, which creates a change in the quantity of finished goods in inventory, will the income from operations differ under the two concepts.

Units Manufactured Exceed Units Sold. For any period in which the number of units manufactured exceeds the number of units sold, the operating income reported under the absorption costing concept will be larger than the operating income reported under the variable costing concept. To illustrate, assume that in the preceding example only 12,000 units of the 15,000 units manufactured were sold. The two income statements that result are as follows. Computations are inserted parenthetically as an aid to understanding.

Absorption Costing Income Statement

Absorption Costing Income Statement

Sales (12,000 × $50)		$600,000
Cost of goods sold:		
Cost of goods manufactured (15,000 × $35)	$525,000	
Less ending inventory (3,000 × $35)	105,000	
Cost of goods sold		420,000
Gross profit		$180,000
Selling and general expenses ($60,000 + $50,000)		110,000
Income from operations		$ 70,000

Variable Costing Income Statement

Variable Costing Income Statement

Sales (12,000 × $50)		$600,000
Variable cost of goods sold:		
Variable cost of goods manufactured (15,000 × $25)	$375,000	
Less ending inventory (3,000 × $25)	75,000	
Variable cost of goods sold		300,000
Manufacturing margin		$300,000
Variable selling and general expenses		60,000
Contribution margin		$240,000
Fixed costs and expenses:		
Fixed manufacturing costs	$150,000	
Fixed selling and general expenses	50,000	200,000
Income from operations		$ 40,000

The $30,000 difference in the amount of income from operations ($70,000 − $40,000) is due to the different treatment of the fixed manufacturing costs. The entire amount of the $150,000 of fixed manufacturing costs is included as an expense of the period in the variable costing statement. The ending inventory in the absorption costing statement includes $30,000 (3,000 × $10) of fixed manufacturing costs. This $30,000, by being included in inventory on hand, is thus excluded from the current cost of goods sold and instead is deferred to another period.

Units Manufactured Less Than Units Sold. For any period in which the number of units manufactured is less than the number of units sold, the operating income reported under the absorption costing concept will be less than the operating income reported under the variable costing concept. To illustrate, assume that 5,000 units of inventory were on hand at the beginning of a period, 10,000 units were manufactured during the period, and 15,000 units were sold (10,000 units manufactured during the period plus the 5,000 units on hand at the beginning of the period) at $50 per unit. The manufacturing costs and selling and general expenses are as follows:

	Total Cost or Expense	*Number of Units*	*Unit Cost*
Beginning inventory:			
Manufacturing costs:			
Variable	$125,000	5,000	$25
Fixed	50,000	5,000	10
Total	$175,000		$35

	Total Cost or Expense	*Number of Units*	*Unit Cost*
Current period:			
Manufacturing costs:			
Variable	$250,000	10,000	$25
Fixed	150,000	10,000	15
Total	$400,000		$40
Selling and general expenses:			
Variable ($5 per unit sold)	$ 75,000		
Fixed	50,000		
Total	$125,000		

The two income statements prepared from this information are as follows. Computations are inserted parenthetically as an aid to understanding.

Absorption Costing Income Statement

Absorption Costing Income Statement

Sales (15,000 × $50)		$750,000
Cost of goods sold:		
Beginning inventory (5,000 × $35)	$175,000	
Cost of goods manufactured (10,000 × $40)	400,000	
Cost of goods sold		575,000
Gross profit		$175,000
Selling and general expenses ($75,000 + $50,000)		125,000
Income from operations		$ 50,000

Variable Costing Income Statement

Variable Costing Income Statement		
Sales (15,000 × $50)		$750,000
Variable cost of goods sold:		
Beginning inventory (5,000 × $25)	$125,000	
Variable cost of goods manufactured (10,000 × $25)	250,000	
Variable cost of goods sold		375,000
Manufacturing margin		$375,000
Variable selling and general expenses		75,000
Contribution margin		$300,000
Fixed costs and expenses:		
Fixed manufacturing costs	$150,000	
Fixed selling and general expenses	50,000	200,000
Income from operations		$100,000

The $50,000 difference ($100,000 − $50,000) in the amount of income from operations is attributable to the different treatment of the fixed manufacturing costs. The beginning inventory in the absorption costing income statement includes $50,000 (5,000 units × $10) of fixed manufacturing costs incurred in the preceding period. By being included in the beginning inventory, this $50,000 is included in the cost of goods sold for the current period. Under variable costing, however, this $50,000 was included as an expense in an income statement of a prior period. Therefore, none of it is included as an expense in the current period variable costing income statement.

Comparison of Income Reported Under the Two Concepts

The examples presented in the preceding sections illustrated the effects of the absorption costing and variable costing concepts on income from operations when the level of inventory changes during a period. These effects may be summarized as follows:

Units manufactured:	
Equal units sold	Absorption costing income equals variable costing income.
Exceed units sold	Absorption costing income is greater than variable costing income.
Less than units sold	Absorption costing income is less than variable costing income

Income Analysis Under Absorption Costing

As was illustrated in the preceding examples, changes in the quantity of the finished goods inventory, caused by differences in the levels of sales and production, directly affect the amount of income from operations reported under absorption costing. Management should therefore be aware of the possible effects of changing inventory levels on operating income reported under absorption costing in analyzing and evaluating operations. To illustrate, assume that the following two proposed production levels are being evaluated by the management of Brownstein Manufacturing Company:

Proposal 1: 20,000 Units To Be Manufactured

	Total Cost or Expense	Number of Units	Unit Cost
Manufacturing costs:			
Variable	$ 700,000	20,000	$35
Fixed	400,000	20,000	20
Total	$1,100,000		$55
Selling and general expenses:			
Variable ($5 per unit sold)	$ 100,000		
Fixed	100,000		
Total	$ 200,000		

Proposal 2: 25,000 Units To Be Manufactured

	Total Cost or Expense	Number of Units	Unit Cost
Manufacturing costs:			
Variable	$ 875,000	25,000	$35
Fixed	400,000	25,000	16
Total	$1,275,000		$51
Selling and general expenses:			
Variable ($5 per unit sold)	$ 100,000		
Fixed	100,000		
Total	$ 200,000		

Brownstein Manufacturing Company has no beginning inventory, and sales are estimated to be 20,000 units at $75 per unit, regardless of production levels. If the company manufactures 20,000 units, which is an amount equal to the estimated sales, income from operations under absorption costing would be $200,000. However, the reported income from operations could be increased by $80,000 by manufacturing 25,000 units and adding 5,000 units to the finished goods inventory. The absorption costing income statements illustrating this effect are as follows:

Absorption Costing Income Statements

Absorption Costing Income Statements

	20,000 Units Manufactured	25,000 Units Manufactured
Sales (20,000 units × $75)	$1,500,000	$1,500,000
Cost of goods sold:		
Cost of goods manufactured:		
(20,000 units × $55)	$1,100,000	
(25,000 units × $51)		$1,275,000
Less ending inventory:		
(5,000 units × $51)		255,000
Cost of goods sold	$1,100,000	$1,020,000
Gross profit	$ 400,000	$ 480,000
Selling and general expenses ($100,000 + $100,000)	200,000	200,000
Income from operations	$ 200,000	$ 280,000

The $80,000 increase in operating income would be caused by the allocation of the fixed manufacturing costs of $400,000 over a greater number of units of production. Specifically, an increase in production from 20,000 units to 25,000 units meant that the fixed manufacturing costs per unit decreased from $20 ($400,000 ÷ 20,000 units) to $16 ($400,000 ÷ 25,000 units). Thus, the cost of goods sold when 25,000 units are manufactured would be $4 per unit less, or $80,000 less in total (20,000 units sold times $4). Since the cost of goods sold is less, operating income is $80,000 more when 25,000 units are manufactured rather than 20,000 units.

Under the variable costing concept, income from operations would have been $200,000, regardless of the amount by which units manufactured exceeded sales, because no fixed manufacturing costs are allocated to the units manufactured. To illustrate, the following variable costing income statements are presented for Brownstein for the production of 20,000 units, 25,000 units, and 30,000 units. In each case, the income from operations is $200,000.

Variable Costing Income Statements

Variable Costing Income Statements

	20,000 Units Manufactured	25,000 Units Manufactured	30,000 Units Manufactured
Sales (20,000 units × $75)	$1,500,000	$1,500,000	$1,500,000
Variable cost of goods sold:			
Variable cost of goods manufactured:			
(20,000 units × $35)	$ 700,000		
(25,000 units × $35)		$ 875,000	
(30,000 units × $35)			$1,050,000
Less ending inventory:			
(0 units × $35)	0		
(5,000 units × $35)		175,000	
(10,000 units × $35)			350,000
Variable cost of goods sold	$ 700,000	$ 700,000	$ 700,000
Manufacturing margin	$ 800,000	$ 800,000	$ 800,000
Variable selling and general expenses	100,000	100,000	100,000
Contribution margin	$ 700,000	$ 700,000	$ 700,000
Fixed costs and expenses:			
Fixed manufacturing costs	$ 400,000	$ 400,000	$ 400,000
Fixed selling and general expenses	100,000	100,000	100,000
Total fixed costs and expenses	$ 500,000	$ 500,000	$ 500,000
Income from operations	$ 200,000	$ 200,000	$ 200,000

As illustrated, if absorption costing is used, management should be careful in analyzing income from operations when large changes in inventory levels occur. Otherwise, increases or decreases in income from operations due to changes in inventory levels could be misinterpreted to be the result of operating efficiencies or inefficiencies.

MANAGEMENT'S USE OF VARIABLE COSTING AND ABSORPTION COSTING

Both variable costing and absorption costing serve useful purposes for management. However, there are limitations to the use of both concepts in certain circumstances. Therefore, managerial accountants must carefully analyze each situation in evaluating whether variable costing reports or absorption costing reports would be more useful. In many situations, the preparation of reports under both concepts will provide useful insights. Such reports and their advantages and disadvantages are discussed in the following paragraphs.

Cost Control

As discussed in Chapter 15, all costs are controllable by someone within a business enterprise, but they are not all controllable at the same level of management. For example, plant supervisors, as members of operating management, are responsible for controlling the use of direct materials in their departments. They have no control, however, of the amount of insurance coverage or premium costs related to the buildings housing their departments. For a specific level of management, **controllable costs** are costs that it controls directly, and **noncontrollable costs** are costs that another level of management controls. This distinction, as applied to specific levels of management, is useful in fixing the responsibility for incurrence of costs and then for reporting the cost data to those responsible for cost control.

Variable manufacturing costs are controlled at the operating level because the amount of such costs varies with changes in the volume of production. By including only variable manufacturing costs in the cost of the product, variable costing provides a product cost figure that can be controlled by operating management. The fixed factory overhead costs are ordinarily the responsibility of a higher level of management. When the fixed factory overhead costs are reported as a separate item in the variable costing income statement, they are easier to identify and control than when they are spread among units of product as they are under absorption costing.

As is the case with the fixed and variable manufacturing costs, the control of the variable and fixed operating expenses is usually the responsibility of different levels of management. Under variable costing, the variable selling and general expenses are reported in a separate category from the fixed selling and general expenses. Because they are reported in this manner, both types of operating expenses are easier to identify and control than is the case under absorption costing, where they are not reported separately.

Product Pricing

Many factors enter into the determination of the selling price of a product. The cost of making the product is clearly significant. Microeconomic theory deduces, from a set of restrictive assumptions, that income is maximized by expanding output to the volume where the revenue realized by the sale of the final unit (marginal revenue) equals the cost of that unit (marginal cost). Although the degree of exactness assumed in economic theory is rarely attainable, the concepts of marginal revenue and marginal cost are useful in setting selling prices.

In the short run, an enterprise is committed to the existing capacity of its manufacturing facilities. The pricing decision should be based upon making the best use of such capacity. The fixed costs and expenses cannot be avoided, but the variable costs and expenses can be eliminated if the company does not manufacture the product. The selling price of a product, therefore, should at least be equal to the variable costs and expenses of making and selling it. Any price above this minimum selling price contributes an amount toward covering fixed costs and expenses and providing operating income. Variable costing procedures yield data that emphasize these relationships.

In the long run, plant capacity can be increased or decreased. If an enterprise is to continue in business, the selling prices of its products must cover all costs and expenses and provide a reasonable operating income. Hence, in establishing pricing policies for the long run, information provided by absorption costing procedures is needed.

The results of a recent research study sponsored by the National Association of Accountants indicated that the companies studied used absorption costing in making routine pricing decisions. However, these companies regularly used variable costing as a basis for setting prices in many short-run situations.[1]

There are no simple solutions to most pricing problems. Consideration must be given to many factors of varying importance. Accounting can contribute by preparing analyses of various pricing plans for both the short run and the long run.

Variable Costing in Pricing Decisions — Two Case Studies

A firm may find it profitable to sell its existing products in new markets. For example, consumer products may be targeted for industrial usage, or the firm may decide to expand into national or international markets. Variable costing can aid management in pricing decisions related to such products, as the following case studies illustrate.

Case One

This company is a division of a Fortune 500 firm. The division identified good opportunities in Third World countries for selling its products through distributors. Since there is usually an independent agent acting as an intermediary in arranging sales between the company and the distributors in the United States, dealing with distributors eliminates the commission paid to these agents. In addition, freight costs are lower, since the distributors provide the transportation. The company passes on these cost savings and quotes prices based on variable costs rather than full costs. In this way, the company is able to meet stiff foreign competition.

Case Two

This company is engaged primarily in the manufacture and sale of wire and cable made from nonferrous metals. The company has 25 major product lines. In the initial stages of introducing a product to a new market, price is not a major factor — quality, reliability, and timeliness of delivery are far more important. Hence, in this initial introductory stage, a full cost approach is used to establish the product price. However, once a product has passed the introductory stage and has achieved a good market share, it normally runs into stiff price competition from within the market. It is at this point that variable costing enters into the pricing decision to determine the price floor. If management decides to remain in the market, a price will be set, based upon variable cost, to fight off short-run price wars from competitors.

Source: Thomas M. Bruegelmann, Gaile A. Haessly, Michael Schiff, and Claire P. Wolfangel, *The Use of Variable Costing in Pricing Decisions,* National Association of Accountants (Montvale, New Jersey, 1986), pp. 45–46.

---

[1]Thomas M. Bruegelmann, Gaile A. Haessly, Michael Schiff, and Claire P. Wolfangel, *The Use of Variable Costing in Pricing Decisions,* National Association of Accountants (Montvale, New Jersey, 1986), p. vii.

Production Planning

Production planning also has both short-run and long-run implications. In the short run, production is limited to existing capacity, and operating decisions must be made quickly before opportunities are lost. For example, a company manufacturing products with a seasonal demand may have an opportunity to obtain an off-season order that will not interfere with its production schedule nor reduce the sales of its other products. The relevant factors for such a short-run decision are the revenues and the variable costs and expenses. If the revenues from the special order will provide a contribution margin, the order should be accepted because it will increase the company's operating income. For long-run planning, management must also consider the fixed costs and expenses.

Sales Analysis

The primary objective of the marketing and sales functions is to offer the company's products for sale at prices that will result in an adequate amount of income relative to the total assets employed. To evaluate these functions properly, management needs information concerning the profitability of various types of products and sales mixes, sales territories, and salespersons. Variable costing can make a significant contribution to management decision making in such areas.

Sales Mix Analysis. **Sales mix,** sometimes referred to as product mix, is generally defined as the relative distribution of sales among the various products sold. Some products are more profitable than others, and management should concentrate its sales efforts on those that will provide the maximum total operating income.

Sales mix studies are based on assumptions, such as the ability to sell one product in place of another and the ability to convert production facilities to accommodate the manufacture of one product instead of another. Proposed changes in the sales mix often affect only small segments of a company's total operations. In such cases, changes in sales mix may be possible within the limits of existing capacity, and the presentation of cost and revenue data in the variable costing form is useful in achieving the most profitable sales mix.

Two very important factors that should be determined for each product are (1) the production facilities needed for its manufacture and (2) the amount of contribution margin to be gained from its manufacture. If two or more products require equal use of limited production facilities, then management should concentrate its sales and production efforts on the product or products with the highest contribution margin per unit. The following report, which focuses on product contribution margins, is an example of the type of data needed for an evaluation of sales mix. The enterprise, which manufactures two products and is operating at full capacity, is considering whether to change the emphasis of its advertising and other promotional efforts.

Contribution Margin Statement—Unit of Product

Contribution Margin by Unit of Product
April 15, 19--

	Product A	Product B
Sales price	$6.00	$8.50
Variable cost of goods sold	3.50	5.50
Manufacturing margin	$2.50	$3.00
Variable selling and general expenses	1.00	1.00
Contribution margin	$1.50	$2.00

The statement indicates that Product B yields a greater amount of contribution margin per unit than Product A. Therefore, Product B provides the larger contribution to the recovery of fixed costs and expenses and realization of operating income. If the amount of production facilities used for each product is assumed to be equal, it would be desirable to increase the sales of Product B.

If two or more products require unequal use of production resources, management should concentrate its sales and production efforts on that product or products with the highest contribution margin per unit of resource. For example, assume that in the above illustration, to manufacture Product B requires twice the machine hours required for Product A. Specifically, Product B requires 2 machine hours per unit, while Product A requires only 1 machine hour per unit. Under this assumption, the contribution margin per unit of resource (machine hours) is \$1.50 (\$1.50 contribution margin ÷ 1 machine hour) for Product A and \$1 (\$2 contribution margin ÷ 2 machine hours) for Product B. Under such circumstances, a change in sales mix designed to increase sales of Product A would be desirable.

To illustrate, if 2,000 additional units of Product A (requiring 2,000 machine hours) could be sold in place of 1,000 units of Product B (also requiring 2,000 machine hours), the total company contribution margin would increase by \$1,000, as follows:

Additional contribution margin from sale of additional 2,000 units of Product A (\$1.50 × 2,000 units)	\$3,000
Less contribution margin from forgoing production and sale of 1,000 units of Product B (\$2 × 1,000 units)	2,000
Increase in total contribution margin	\$1,000

Sales Territory Analysis. An income statement presenting the contribution margin by sales territories is often useful to management in appraising past performance and in directing future sales efforts. The following income statement is prepared in such a format, in abbreviated form:

Contribution Margin Statement—Sales Territories

Contribution Margin Statement by Sales Territory
For Month Ended July 31, 19--

	Territory A	Territory B	Total
Sales	\$315,000	\$502,500	\$817,500
Less variable costs and expenses	189,000	251,250	440,250
Contribution margin	\$126,000	\$251,250	\$377,250
Less fixed costs and expenses			242,750
Income from operations			\$134,500

In addition to the contribution margin, the **contribution margin ratio** (contribution margin divided by sales) for each territory is useful in evaluating sales territories and directing operations toward more profitable activities. For Territory A, the contribution margin ratio is 40% (\$126,000 ÷ \$315,000), and for Territory B the ratio is 50% (\$251,250 ÷ \$502,500). Consequently, more profitability could be achieved by efforts to increase the sales of Territory B relative to Territory A.

Salespersons' Analysis. A report to management for use in evaluating the sales performance of each salesperson could include total sales, gross profit, gross profit percentage, total selling expenses, and contribution to company profit. Such a report is illustrated as follows:

Salespersons' Analysis

Salespersons' Analysis
For Six Months Ended June 30, 19--

Salesperson	Total Sales	Gross Profit	Gross Profit Percentage	Total Selling Expenses	Contribution to Company Profit
A	$300,000	$120,000	40%	$24,000	$ 96,000
B	250,000	75,000	30	22,500	52,500
C	500,000	125,000	25	35,000	90,000
D	180,000	72,000	40	18,000	54,000
E	460,000	197,800	43	27,600	170,200
F	320,000	112,000	35	22,400	89,600

The preceding report illustrates that the total sales figure is not the only consideration in evaluating a salesperson. For example, although salesperson C has the highest total sales, C's sales are not contributing as much to overall company profits as are the sales of A and E, primarily because C's sales have the lowest gross profit percentage. Of the six salespersons, E is generating the highest dollar contribution to company profit and is selling the most profitable mix of products, as measured by a gross profit percentage of 43%.

Other factors should also be considered in evaluating the performance of salespersons. For example, sales growth rates, years of experience, and actual performance compared to budgeted performance may be more important than total sales.

Contribution Margin Analysis

Another use of the contribution margin concept to assist management in planning and controlling operations focuses on differences between planned and actual contribution margins. However, mere knowledge of the differences is insufficient. Management needs information about the causes of the differences. The systematic examination of the differences between planned and actual contribution margin is termed **contribution margin analysis**.

Since contribution margin is the excess of sales over variable costs and expenses, a difference between the planned and actual contribution margin can be caused by (1) an increase or decrease in the amount of sales or (2) an increase or decrease in the amount of variable costs and expenses. An increase or decrease in either element may in turn be due to (1) an increase or decrease in the number of units sold or (2) an increase or decrease in the unit sales price or unit cost. The effect of these two factors on either sales or variable costs and expenses may be stated as follows:

1. **Quantity factor**—the effect of a difference in the number of units sold, assuming no change in unit sales price or unit cost. The quantity factor is computed as the difference between the actual quantity sold and the planned quantity sold, multiplied by the planned unit sales price or unit cost.

2. **Unit price or unit cost factor**—the effect of a difference in unit sales price or unit cost on the number of units sold. The unit price or unit cost factor is computed as the difference between the actual unit price or unit cost and the planned unit price or unit cost, multiplied by the actual quantity sold.

The following data for Noble Inc. are used as a basis for illustrating contribution margin analysis. For the sake of simplicity, a single commodity is assumed. The amount of detail entering into the analysis would be greater if several different commodities were sold, but the basic principles would not be affected.

	For Year Ended December 31, 1990		
	Actual	*Planned*	*Difference (Increase or Decrease*)*
Sales	$937,500	$800,000	$137,500
Less:			
Variable cost of goods sold	$425,000	$350,000	$ 75,000
Variable selling and administrative expenses	162,500	125,000	37,500
Total	$587,500	$475,000	$112,500
Contribution margin	$350,000	$325,000	$ 25,000
Number of units sold	125,000	100,000	
Per unit:			
Sales price	$7.50	$8.00	
Variable cost of goods sold	$3.40	$3.50	
Variable selling and administrative expenses	$1.30	$1.25	

The analysis of these data in the report on page 764 shows that the favorable increase of $25,000 in the contribution margin was due in large part to an increase in the number of units sold. This increase was partially offset by a decrease in the unit sales price and an increase in the unit cost for variable selling and administrative expenses. The decrease in the unit cost for the variable cost of goods sold was an additional favorable result of 1990 operations.

The data presented in the contribution margin analysis report are useful to management in evaluating past performance and in planning future operations. For example, the impact of the $.50 reduction in the unit sales price on the number of units sold and on the total sales for the year is information that management can use in determining whether further price reductions might be desirable. The contribution margin analysis report also highlights the impact of changes in unit variable costs and expenses, but not necessarily the reasons for these changes. For example, the $.05 increase in the unit variable selling and administrative expenses might be a result of increased advertising expenditures. If so, the increase in the number of units sold in 1990 could be attributed to both the $.50 price reduction and the increased advertising.

Noble Inc.
Contribution Margin Analysis
For Year Ended December 31, 1990

Increase in amount of sales attributed to:			
Quantity factor:			
Increase in number of units sold in 1990	25,000		
Planned sales price in 1990	× $8.00	$200,000	
Price factor:			
Decrease in unit sales price in 1990	$.50		
Number of units sold in 1990	×125,000	62,500	
Net increase in amount of sales			$137,500
Increase in amount of variable cost of goods sold attributed to:			
Quantity factor:			
Increase in number of units sold in 1990	25,000		
Planned unit cost in 1990	× $3.50	$ 87,500	
Unit cost factor:			
Decrease in unit cost in 1990	$.10		
Number of units sold in 1990	×125,000	12,500	
Net increase in amount of variable cost of goods sold			75,000
Increase in amount of variable selling and administrative expenses attributed to:			
Quantity factor:			
Increase in number of units sold in 1990	25,000		
Planned unit cost in 1990	× $1.25	$ 31,250	
Unit cost factor:			
Increase in unit cost in 1990	$.05		
Number of units sold in 1990	×125,000	6,250	
Net increase in the amount of variable selling and administrative expenses			37,500
Increase in contribution margin			$ 25,000

Contribution Margin Analysis Report

Chapter Review

KEY POINTS

1. Absorption Costing and Variable Costing.
The costs of manufacturing are direct materials, direct labor, and factory overhead. Under absorption costing, all such costs become part of the cost of goods manufactured. Under variable costing, the cost of goods manufactured

is composed of only variable costs—those manufacturing costs that increase or decrease as the volume of production rises or falls. These costs are the direct materials, direct labor, and only those factory overhead costs which vary with the rate of production. The fixed factory overhead costs do not become a part of the cost of goods manufactured, but are considered an expense of the period. In the variable costing income statement, the deduction of the cost of goods sold from sales yields an intermediate amount, termed manufacturing margin. Deduction of the variable selling and general expenses yields the contribution margin. Fixed costs and expenses are then deducted from the contribution margin to yield income from operations.

A comparison of income reported under the absorption costing and variable costing concepts when the level of inventory changes during the period is summarized in the following table:

Units manufactured:	
Equal units sold................	Absorption costing income equals variable costing income.
Exceed units sold..............	Absorption costing income is greater than variable costing income.
Less than units sold............	Absorption costing income is less than variable costing income.

The possible effects of any changes in inventory levels on operating income should be considered when management analyzes and evaluates operations.

2. Management's Use of Variable Costing and Absorption Costing. Variable costing is especially useful at the operating level of management because the amount of variable manufacturing costs varies with changes in the volume of production and thus is controllable at this level. The fixed factory overhead costs are ordinarily controllable by a higher level of management.

In the short run, variable costing may be useful in establishing the selling price of a product. This price should be at least equal to the variable costs and expenses of making and selling the product. In the long run, however, absorption costing procedures are useful in establishing selling prices, in that all costs and expenses and a reasonable amount of operating income must be earned.

Variable costing can make a significant contribution to management decision making in analyzing and evaluating sales. Management should concentrate its sales efforts on those products that will provide the maximum total operating income. Sales mix studies emphasize the contribution margin of each product in evaluating sales territories and directing operations towards more profitable activities. In addition, a salespersons' analysis report may be useful to management in evaluating the sales performance of each salesperson. Such a report emphasizes the contribution of each salesperson to the overall company profit.

Contribution margin analysis is the systematic examination of differences between planned and actual contribution margin. Since contribution margin is the excess of sales over variable costs and expenses, a difference between the planned and actual contribution margins can be caused by (1) an increase or decrease in the amount of sales or (2) an increase or decrease in the amount of variable costs and expenses. An increase or decrease in either element may in turn be due to (1) an increase or decrease in the number of units sold or (2) an increase or decrease in the unit sales price or unit cost. The effect of these two factors on either sales or variable costs and expenses may be stated as follows:

> Quantity factor—the effect of a difference in the number of units sold, assuming no change in unit sales price or unit cost. The quantity factor is computed as the difference between the actual quantity sold and the planned quantity sold, multiplied by the planned unit sales price or unit cost.
>
> Unit price or unit cost factor—the effect of a difference in unit sales price or unit cost on the number of units sold. The unit price or unit cost factor is computed as the difference between the actual unit price or unit cost and the planned unit price or unit cost, multiplied by the actual quantity sold.

KEY TERMS

absorption costing 750
variable costing 751
manufacturing margin 753
contribution margin 753
controllable costs 758
noncontrollable costs 758
sales mix 760
contribution margin ratio 761
contribution margin analysis 762

SELF-EXAMINATION QUESTIONS

(Answers at End of Chapter)

1. The concept that considers the cost of products manufactured to be composed only of those manufacturing costs that vary with the rate of production is known as:
   A. absorption costing
   B. variable costing
   C. replacement cost
   D. none of the above

2. In an income statement prepared under the variable costing concept, the deduction of the variable cost of goods sold from sales yields an intermediate amount referred to as:
   A. gross profit
   B. contribution margin
   C. manufacturing margin
   D. none of the above

3. Sales were $750,000, variable cost of goods sold was $400,000, variable selling and general expenses were $90,000, and fixed costs and expenses were $200,000. The contribution margin was:
   A. $60,000 C. $350,000
   B. $260,000 D. none of the above

4. During a year in which the number of units manufactured exceeded the number of units sold, the operating income reported under the absorption costing concept would be:
   A. larger than the operating income reported under the variable costing concept
   B. smaller than the operating income reported under the variable costing concept
   C. the same as the operating income reported under the variable costing concept
   D. none of the above

5. If actual sales totaled $800,000 for the current year (80,000 units at $10 each), and planned sales were $765,000 (85,000 units at $9 each), the difference between actual and planned sales due to the quantity factor is:
   A. a $50,000 increase C. a $45,000 decrease
   B. a $35,000 decrease D. none of the above

ILLUSTRATIVE PROBLEM

During the current period, McLaughlin Company sold 60,000 units of product at a selling price of $30 per unit. At the beginning of the period, there were 10,000 units in inventory and McLaughlin Company manufactured 50,000 units during the period. The manufacturing costs and selling and general expenses were as follows:

	Total Cost or Expense	Number of Units	Unit Cost
Beginning inventory:			
Direct materials	$ 67,000	10,000	$ 6.70
Direct labor	155,000	10,000	15.50
Variable factory overhead	18,000	10,000	1.80
Fixed factory overhead	20,000	10,000	2.00
Total	$ 260,000		$26.00
Current period costs:			
Direct materials	$ 350,000	50,000	$ 7.00
Direct labor	810,000	50,000	16.20
Variable factory overhead	90,000	50,000	1.80
Fixed factory overhead	100,000	50,000	2.00
Total	$1,350,000		$27.00

Selling and general expenses:	
Variable	$ 65,000
Fixed	45,000
Total	$ 110,000

Instructions:

1. Prepare an income statement based on the absorption costing concept.
2. Prepare an income statement based on the variable costing concept.
3. Explain the reason for the difference in the amount of operating income reported in *1* and *2*.

SOLUTION

(1) Absorption Costing Income Statement

Sales (60,000 × $30)		$1,800,000
Cost of goods sold:		
Beginning inventory (10,000 × $26)	$ 260,000	
Cost of goods manufactured (50,000 × $27)	1,350,000	
Cost of goods sold		1,610,000
Gross profit		$ 190,000
Selling and general expenses ($65,000 + $45,000)		110,000
Income from operations		$ 80,000

(2) Variable Costing Income Statement

Sales (60,000 × $30)		$1,800,000
Variable cost of goods sold:		
Beginning inventory (10,000 × $24)	$ 240,000	
Variable cost of goods manufactured (50,000 × $25)	1,250,000	
Variable cost of goods sold		1,490,000
Manufacturing margin		$ 310,000
Variable selling and general expenses		65,000
Contribution margin		$ 245,000
Fixed costs and expenses:		
Fixed manufacturing costs	$ 100,000	
Fixed selling and general expenses	45,000	145,000
Income from operations		$ 100,000

(3) The difference of $20,000 ($100,000 − $80,000) in the amount of income from operations is attributable to the different treatment of the fixed manufacturing costs. The beginning inventory in the absorption costing income statement includes $20,000 (10,000 units × $2) of fixed manufacturing costs incurred in the preceding period. This $20,000 was included as an expense in a variable costing income statement of a prior period, however. Therefore, none of it is included as an expense in the current period variable costing income statement.

Discussion Questions

20–1. What types of costs are customarily included in the cost of manufactured products under (a) the *absorption costing* concept and (b) the *variable costing* concept?

20–2. Which type of manufacturing cost (direct materials, direct labor, variable factory overhead, fixed factory overhead) is included in the cost of goods manufactured under the absorption costing concept but is excluded from the cost of goods manufactured under the variable costing concept?

20–3. At the end of the first year of operations, 500 units remained in the finished goods inventory. The unit manufacturing costs during the year were as follows:

Direct materials	$ 3.00
Direct labor	24.00
Fixed factory overhead	1.50
Variable factory overhead	.50

What would be the cost of the finished goods inventory reported on the balance sheet under (a) the absorption costing concept and (b) the variable costing concept?

20–4. Which of the following costs would be included in the cost of a manufactured product according to the variable costing concept: (a) electricity purchased to operate factory equipment, (b) property taxes on factory building, (c) direct labor, (d) salary of factory supervisor, (e) direct materials, (f) depreciation on factory building, and (g) rent on factory building?

20–5. In the following equations, based on the variable costing income statement, identify the items designated by **X**:
(a) Net sales − **X** = manufacturing margin
(b) Manufacturing margin − **X** = contribution margin
(c) Contribution margin − **X** = income from operations

20–6. In the variable costing income statement, how are the fixed manufacturing costs reported and how are the fixed selling and general expenses reported?

20–7. If the quantity of the ending inventory is larger than that of the beginning inventory, will the amount of income from operations determined by absorption costing be more than or less than the amount determined by variable costing? Explain.

20–8. Since all costs of operating a business are controllable, what is the significance of the term *noncontrollable cost?*

20–9. Discuss how financial data prepared on the basis of variable costing can assist management in the development of short-run pricing policies.

20–10. What term is used to refer to the relative distribution of sales among the various products manufactured?

20–11. A company, operating at full capacity, manufactures two products, with Product E requiring three times the production facilities as Product F. The contribution margin is $50 per unit for Product E and $15 per unit for Product F. How much would the total contribution margin be increased or decreased for the coming year if the sales of Product E could be increased by 1,000 units by changing the emphasis of promotional efforts?

20–12. Explain why rewarding sales personnel on the basis of total sales might not be in the best interests of an enterprise whose goal is to maximize profits.

20–13. What term is used to describe the systematic examination of differences between planned and actual contribution margin?

20–14. In 1989, Jarad Inc. sold 100,000 units at $5 per unit. In 1990, Jarad Inc. sold 90,000 units at $6 per unit. If Jarad Inc. had planned for 1990 based upon preceding years' operating results, what is the sales quantity factor for 1990?

20–15. Based upon the data in Question 20–14, what is the sales price factor for 1990 for Jarad Inc.

20–16. Based upon the data in Questions 20–14 and 20–15, what was the difference between actual and planned sales for Jarad Inc. in 1990?

20–17. Real World Focus. Dutch Pantry Inc. operates 53 full-service family restaurants in 12 eastern states. To assure consistent quality, many of the items served in the restaurants are prepared in a central food processing plant. Classify each of the following costs and expenses of the food processing plant as either variable or fixed.
(a) Cooking oil
(b) Office salaries
(c) Electricity
(d) Experimental costs and expenses
(e) Depreciation on equipment (straight-line method)
(f) Garbage collection expense
(g) Water
(h) Cleaning supplies
(i) Property taxes
(j) Salad dressing
(k) Spices

Exercises

20–18. Income statements under absorption costing and variable costing. Casey Company began operations on July 1 and operated at 100% of capacity during the first month. The following data summarize the results for July:

Sales (12,000 units)		$600,000
Production costs (15,000 units):		
Direct materials	$150,000	
Direct labor	180,000	
Variable factory overhead	45,000	
Fixed factory overhead	30,000	405,000
Selling and general expenses:		
Variable selling and general expenses	$ 60,000	
Fixed selling and general expenses	18,000	78,000

(a) Prepare an income statement in accordance with the absorption costing concept. (b) Prepare an income statement in accordance with the variable costing concept. (c) What is the reason for the difference in the amount of operating income reported in (a) and (b)?

20–19. Cost of goods manufactured, using variable costing and absorption costing. On October 31, the end of the first year of operations, Kanter Company manufactured 40,000 units and sold 35,000 units. The following income statement was prepared, based on the variable costing concept:

Kanter Company
Income Statement
For Year Ended October 31, 19--

Sales		$700,000
Variable cost of goods sold:		
Variable cost of goods manufactured	$480,000	
Less ending inventory	60,000	
Variable cost of goods sold		420,000
Manufacturing margin		$280,000
Variable selling and general expenses		70,000
Contribution margin		$210,000
Fixed costs and expenses:		
Fixed manufacturing costs	$ 60,000	
Fixed selling and general expenses	50,000	110,000
Income from operations		$100,000

Determine the unit cost of goods manufactured, based on (a) the variable costing concept and (b) the absorption costing concept.

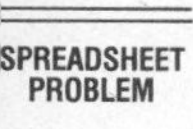

20–20. Variable costing income statement. On June 30, the end of the first month of operations, Lloyd Company prepared the following income statement, based on the absorption costing concept:

Lloyd Company
Income Statement
For Month Ended June 30, 19--

Sales (4,400 units)		$66,000
Cost of goods sold:		
Cost of goods manufactured	$45,000	
Less ending inventory (600 units)	5,400	
Cost of goods sold		39,600
Gross profit		$26,400
Selling and general expenses		15,800
Income from operations		$10,600

If the fixed manufacturing costs were $15,000 and the variable selling and general expenses were $7,700, prepare an income statement in accordance with the variable costing concept.

20–21. Absorption costing income statement. On April 30, the end of the first month of operations, Moyer Company prepared the following income statement, based on the variable costing concept:

Moyer Company
Income Statement
For Month Ended April 30, 19--

Sales (18,000 units)		$360,000
Variable cost of goods sold:		
Variable cost of goods manufactured	$200,000	
Less ending inventory (2,000 units)	20,000	
Variable cost of goods sold		180,000
Manufacturing margin		$180,000
Variable selling and general expenses		36,000
Contribution margin		$144,000
Fixed costs and expenses:		
Fixed manufacturing costs	$ 50,000	
Fixed selling and general expenses	29,000	79,000
Income from operations		$ 65,000

Prepare an income statement in accordance with the absorption costing concept.

20–22. Estimated income statements, using absorption and variable costing. Prior to the first month of operations ending January 31, Lester Company estimated the following operating results:

Sales (1,000 × $50)	$50,000
Manufacturing costs (1,000 units):	
Direct materials	15,000
Direct labor	10,000
Variable factory overhead	7,000
Fixed factory overhead	4,800
Fixed selling and general expenses	6,500
Variable selling and general expenses	2,000

The company is evaluating a proposal to manufacture 1,200 units instead of 1,000 units.

(a) Assuming no change in sales, unit variable manufacturing costs, and fixed factory overhead and total selling and general expenses, prepare an estimated income statement, comparing operating results if 1,000 and 1,200 units are manufactured, in the (1) absorption costing format and (2) variable costing format. (b) What is the reason for the difference in income from operations reported for the two levels of production by the absorption costing income statement?

20–23. Change in sales mix and contribution margin. Van Cleave Company manufactures Products A and B and is operating at full capacity. To manufacture Product A requires four times the number of machine hours as required for Product B. Market research indicates that 2,000 additional units of Product B could be sold. The contribution margin by unit of product is as follows:

	Product A	Product B
Sales price	$120	$50
Variable cost of goods sold	70	36
Manufacturing margin	$ 50	$14
Variable selling and general expenses	32	9
Contribution margin	$ 18	$ 5

Prepare a tabulation indicating the increase or decrease in total contribution margin if 2,000 additional units of Product B are produced and sold.

20–24. Contribution margin analysis—sales. The following data for Wenstrup Inc. are available:

	For Year Ended June 30, 1990		
	Actual	Planned	Difference (Increase or Decrease*)
Sales	$544,000	$600,000	$56,000*
Less:			
Variable cost of goods sold	$289,000	$280,000	$ 9,000
Variable selling and administrative expenses	149,600	180,000	30,400*
Total	$438,600	$460,000	$21,400*
Contribution margin	$105,400	$140,000	$34,600*
Number of units sold	34,000	40,000	
Per unit:			
Sales price	$16.00	$15.00	
Variable cost of goods sold	$ 8.50	$ 7.00	
Variable selling and administrative expenses	$ 4.40	$ 4.50	

Prepare a contribution analysis of the sales quantity and price factors.

20–25. Contribution margin analysis—variable costs and expenses. Based upon the data in Exercise 20–24, prepare a contribution analysis of the variable costs and expenses for Wenstrup Inc. for the year ended June 30, 1990.

20–26. Real World Focus. The following data were adapted from the income statement of General Electric Company for the year ended December 31, 1987:

	In Millions
Sales of products and services to customers	$39,315
Operating costs:	
Cost of goods sold	29,657
Selling, general, and administrative expense	5,979
Operating costs	$35,636
Income from operations	$ 3,679

Assume that the variable amount of each category of operating costs is as follows:

Cost of goods sold	$19,500
Selling, general, and administrative expense	3,600

Based on the above data, prepare a variable costing income statement for General Electric Company for the year ended December 31, 1987.

Problems

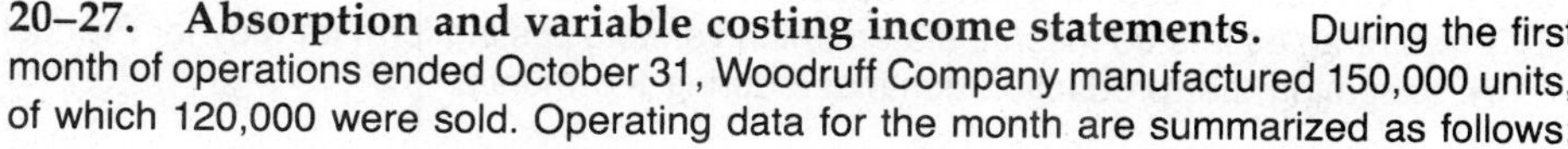

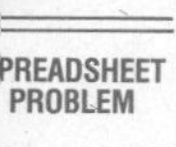

20–27. Absorption and variable costing income statements. During the first month of operations ended October 31, Woodruff Company manufactured 150,000 units, of which 120,000 were sold. Operating data for the month are summarized as follows:

Sales		$840,000
Manufacturing costs:		
Direct materials	$150,000	
Direct labor	330,000	
Variable factory overhead	120,000	
Fixed factory overhead	60,000	660,000
Selling and general expenses:		
Variable	$ 72,000	
Fixed	48,000	120,000

Instructions: (1) Prepare an income statement based on the absorption costing concept.

(2) Prepare an income statement based on the variable costing concept.

(3) Explain the reason for the difference in the amount of operating income reported in (1) and (2).

20–28. Income statements under absorption costing and variable costing. The demand for Product H, one of numerous products manufactured by Sommer Inc., has dropped sharply because of recent competition from a similar product. The company's chemists are currently completing tests of various new formulas, and it is anticipated that the manufacture of a superior product can be started on June 1, one month hence. No changes will be needed in the present production facilities to manufacture the new product because only the mixture of the various materials will be changed.

The controller has been asked by the president of the company for advice on whether to continue production during May or to suspend the manufacture of Product H until June 1. The controller has assembled the following pertinent data:

Sommer Inc.
Estimated Income Statement—Product H
For Month Ending April 30, 19--

Sales (20,000 units)	$800,000
Cost of goods sold	760,500
Gross profit	$ 39,500
Selling and general expenses	84,000
Loss from operations	$ 44,500

The estimated production costs and selling and general expenses, based on a production of 20,000 units, are as follows:

Direct materials	$14.50 per unit
Direct labor	18.00 per unit
Variable factory overhead	2.50 per unit
Variable selling and general expenses	3.00 per unit
Fixed factory overhead	$60,500 for April
Fixed selling and general expenses	24,000 for April

Sales for May are expected to drop about 30% below those of the preceding month. No significant changes are anticipated in the production costs or operating expenses. No extra costs will be incurred in discontinuing operations in the portion of the plant associated with Product H. The inventory of Product H at the beginning and end of May is expected to be inconsequential.

Instructions: (1) Prepare an estimated income statement in absorption costing form for May for Product H, assuming that production continues during the month.

(2) Prepare an estimated income statement in variable costing form for May for Product H, assuming that production continues during the month.

(3) State the estimated operating loss arising from the activities associated with Product H for May if production is temporarily suspended.
(4) Prepare a brief statement of the advice the controller should give.

20–29. Salespersons' report and analysis. Lin Company employs seven salespersons to sell and distribute its product throughout the state. Data extracted from reports received from the salespersons during the current year ended December 31 are as follows:

Salesperson	Total Sales	Cost of Goods Sold	Total Selling Expenses
Barr	$900,000	$585,000	$217,500
Farmer	675,000	418,500	175,500
Griffith	560,000	341,600	118,400
Murray	600,000	372,000	141,000
Owens	375,000	225,000	78,000
Thom	480,000	278,400	112,500
York	525,000	315,000	114,000

Instructions: (1) Prepare a report for the year, indicating total sales, gross profit, gross profit percentage, total selling expenses, and contribution to company profit by salesperson.
(2) Which salesperson contributed the highest dollar amount to company profit during the year?
(3) Briefly list factors other than contribution to company profit that should be considered in evaluating the performance of salespersons.

20–30. Variable costing income statement and effect on income of change in operations. T. E. Collins Company manufactures three styles of folding chairs, A, B, and C. The income statement has consistently indicated a net loss for Style B, and management is considering three proposals: (1) continue Style B, (2) discontinue Style B and reduce total output accordingly, or (3) discontinue Style B and conduct an advertising campaign to expand the sales of Style A so that the entire plant capacity can continue to be used.

If Proposal 2 is selected and Style B is discontinued and production curtailed, the annual fixed production costs and fixed operating expenses could be reduced by $22,500 and $12,000 respectively. If Proposal 3 is selected, it is anticipated that an additional annual expenditure of $40,000 for advertising Style A would yield an increase of 40% in its sales volume, and that the increased production of Style A would utilize the plant facilities released by the discontinuance of Style B.

The sales, costs, and expenses have been relatively stable over the past few years, and they are expected to remain so for the foreseeable future. The income statement for the past year ended August 31 is:

	Style			
	A	B	C	Total
Sales	$650,000	$190,000	$600,000	$1,440,000
Cost of goods sold:				
Variable costs	$370,000	$132,300	$330,000	$ 832,300
Fixed costs	125,000	40,700	120,000	285,700
Total cost of goods sold	$495,000	$173,000	$450,000	$1,118,000
Gross profit	$155,000	$ 17,000	$150,000	$ 322,000
Less operating expenses:				
Variable expenses	$ 64,800	$ 18,900	$ 60,000	$ 143,700
Fixed expenses	36,000	16,000	35,000	87,000
Total operating expenses	$100,800	$ 34,900	$ 95,000	$ 230,700
Income from operations	$ 54,200	$ (17,900)	$ 55,000	$ 91,300

Instructions: (1) Prepare an income statement for the past year in the variable costing format. Use the following headings:

Style			
A	B	C	Total

Data for each style should be reported through contribution margin. The fixed costs and expenses should be deducted from the total contribution margin, as reported in the "Total" column, to determine income from operations.

(2) Based on the income statement prepared in (1) and the other data presented above, determine the amount by which total annual operating income would be reduced below its present level if Proposal 2 is accepted.

(3) Prepare an income statement in the variable costing format, indicating the projected annual operating income if Proposal 3 is accepted. Use the following headings:

Style		
A	C	Total

Data for each style should be reported through contribution margin. The fixed costs and expenses should be deducted from the total contribution margin as reported in the "Total" column. For purposes of this problem, the additional expenditure of $40,000 for advertising can be added to the fixed operating expenses.

(4) By how much would total annual income increase above its present level if Proposal 3 is accepted? Explain.

20–31. Contribution margin analysis. Power Inc. manufactures only one product. For the year ended December 31, 1990, the contribution margin decreased by $86,000 from the planned level of $150,000. The president of Power Inc. has expressed serious concern about the size of this decrease and has requested a follow-up report.

The following data have been gathered from the accounting records:

	For the Year Ended December 31, 1990		
	Actual	Planned	Difference (Increase or Decrease*)
Sales	$920,000	$900,000	$ 20,000
Less:			
Variable cost of goods sold	$476,000	$450,000	$ 26,000
Variable selling and administrative expenses	380,000	300,000	80,000
Total	$856,000	$750,000	$106,000
Contribution margin	$ 64,000	$150,000	$ 86,000*
Number of units sold	80,000	75,000	
Per unit:			
Sales price	$11.50	$12.00	
Variable cost of goods sold	$ 5.95	$ 6.00	
Variable selling and administrative expenses	$ 4.75	$ 4.00	

Instructions: (1) Prepare a contribution margin analysis report for the year ended December 31, 1990.

(2) At a meeting of the board of directors on March 2, 1991, the president, after reviewing the contribution analysis report, made the following comment:

"It looks as if the price decrease of $.50 had the effect of increasing sales. However, we lost control over the variable costs of goods sold and variable selling and administrative expenses. Let's look into these expenses and get them under control! Also, let's consider decreasing the sales price to $11 to increase sales further."

Do you agree with the president's comment? Explain.

ALTERNATE PROBLEMS

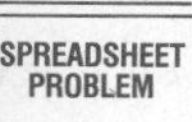

20–27A. Absorption and variable costing income statements. During the first month of operations ended April 30, Hyatt Company manufactured 80,000 units, of which 60,000 were sold. Operating data for the month are summarized as follows:

Sales		$480,000
Manufacturing costs:		
Direct materials	$ 96,000	
Direct labor	192,000	
Variable factory overhead	60,000	
Fixed factory overhead	120,000	468,000
Selling and general expenses:		
Variable	$ 66,000	
Fixed	35,000	101,000

Instructions: (1) Prepare an income statement based on the absorption costing concept.
(2) Prepare an income statement based on the variable costing concept.
(3) Explain the reason for the difference in the amount of operating income reported in (1) and (2).

20–28A. Income statements under absorption costing and variable costing. The demand for Product X, one of numerous products manufactured by Engel Inc., has dropped sharply because of recent competition from a similar product. The company's chemists are currently completing tests of various new formulas, and it is anticipated that the manufacture of a superior product can be started on August 1, one month hence. No changes will be needed in the present production facilities to manufacture the new product because only the mixture of the various materials will be changed.

The controller has been asked by the president of the company for advice on whether to continue production during July or to suspend the manufacture of Product X until August 1. The controller has assembled the following pertinent data:

Engel Inc.
Estimated Income Statement—Product X
For Month Ending June 30, 19--

Sales (10,000 units)	$200,000
Cost of goods sold	157,000
Gross profit	$ 43,000
Selling and general expenses	50,000
Loss from operations	$ 7,000

The estimated production costs and selling and general expenses, based on a production of 10,000 units, are as follows:

Direct materials	$4.50 per unit
Direct labor	6.00 per unit
Variable factory overhead	1.20 per unit
Variable selling and general expenses	2.00 per unit
Fixed factory overhead	$40,000 for June
Fixed selling and general expenses	30,000 for June

Sales for July are expected to drop about 50% below those of the preceding month. No significant changes are anticipated in the production costs or operating expenses. No extra costs will be incurred in discontinuing operations in the portion of the plant associated with Product X. The inventory of Product X at the beginning and end of July is expected to be inconsequential.

Instructions: (1) Prepare an estimated income statement in absorption costing form for July for Product X, assuming that production continues during the month.

(2) Prepare an estimated income statement in variable costing form for July for Product X, assuming that production continues during the month.

(3) State the estimated operating loss arising from the activities associated with Product X for July if production is temporarily suspended.

(4) Prepare a brief statement of the advice the controller should give.

20–31A. Contribution margin analysis. Ohngren Inc. manufactures only one product. For the year ended December 31, 1990, the contribution margin decreased by $68,000 from the planned level of $180,000. The president of Ohngren Inc. has expressed serious concern about the size of this decrease and has requested a follow-up report.

The following data have been gathered from the accounting records:

	For the Year Ended December 31, 1990		
	Actual	Planned	Difference (Increase or Decrease*)
Sales	$805,000	$750,000	$ 55,000
Less:			
Variable cost of goods sold	$553,000	$480,000	$ 73,000
Variable selling and administrative expenses	140,000	90,000	50,000
Total	$693,000	$570,000	$123,000
Contribution margin	$112,000	$180,000	$ 68,000*
Number of units sold	700,000	600,000	
Per unit:			
Sales price	$1.15	$1.25	
Variable cost of goods sold	$ .79	$ .80	
Variable selling and administrative expenses	$ .20	$ .15	

Instructions: (1) Prepare a contribution margin analysis report for the year ended December 31, 1990.

(2) At a meeting of the board of directors on February 23, 1991, the president, after reviewing the contribution analysis report, made the following comment:

> "It looks as if the price decrease of $.10 had the effect of increasing sales. However, we lost control over the variable costs of goods sold and variable selling and administrative expenses. Let's look into these expenses and get them under control! Also, let's consider decreasing the sales price to $1 to increase sales further."

Do you agree with the president's comment? Explain.

Mini-Case 20

Reynolds Company is a family-owned business in which you own 15% of the common stock and your brothers and sisters own the remaining shares. The employment contract of Reynolds' new president, Grace McKean, stipulates a base salary of $60,000 per year plus 8% of income from operations in excess of $2,000,000. Reynolds uses the absorption costing method of reporting income from operations, which has averaged approximately $2,000,000 for the past several years.

Sales for 1990, McKean's first year as president of Reynolds Company, are estimated at 50,000 units at a selling price of $180 per unit. To maximize the use of Reynolds' productive capacity, McKean has decided to manufacture 60,000 units, rather than the 50,000 units of estimated sales. The beginning inventory at January 1, 1990, is insignificant in amount, and the manufacturing costs and selling and general expenses for the production of 50,000 and 60,000 units are as follows:

50,000 Units To Be Manufactured

	Total Cost or Expense	Number of Units	Unit Cost
Manufacturing costs:			
Variable	$4,000,000	50,000	$ 80
Fixed	1,500,000	50,000	30
Total	$5,500,000		$110
Selling and general expenses:			
Variable	$1,000,000		
Fixed	500,000		
Total	$1,500,000		

60,000 Units To Be Manufactured

	Total Cost or Expense	Number of Units	Unit Cost
Manufacturing costs:			
Variable	$4,800,000	60,000	$ 80
Fixed	1,500,000	60,000	25
Total	$6,300,000		$105
Selling and general expenses:			
Variable	$1,000,000		
Fixed	500,000		
Total	$1,500,000		

Instructions:

(1) Prepare absorption costing income statements for the year ending December 31, 1990, based upon sales of 50,000 units and the manufacture of (a) 50,000 units and (b) 60,000 units.

(2) Explain the difference in the income from operations reported in (1).

(3) Compute McKean's total salary for 1990, based on sales of 50,000 units and the manufacture of (a) 50,000 units and (b) 60,000 units.
(4) In addition to maximizing the use of Reynolds Company's productive capacity, why might McKean wish to manufacture 60,000 units rather than 50,000 units?
(5) Can you suggest an alternative way in which McKean's salary could be determined, using a base salary of $60,000 and 8% of income from operations in excess of $2,000,000, so that the salary could not be increased by simply manufacturing more units?

Answers to Self-Examination Questions

1. B Under the variable costing concept (answer B), the cost of products manufactured is composed of only those manufacturing costs that increase or decrease as the volume of production rises or falls. These costs include direct materials, direct labor, and variable factory overhead. Under the absorption costing concept (answer A), all manufacturing costs become a part of the cost of the products manufactured. The absorption costing concept is required in the determination of historical cost and taxable income. The variable costing concept is often useful to management in making decisions.
2. C In the variable costing income statement, the deduction of the variable cost of goods sold from sales yields the manufacturing margin (answer C). Deduction of the variable selling and general expenses from manufacturing margin yields the contribution margin (answer B).
3. B The contribution margin of $260,000 (answer B) is determined by deducting all of the variable costs and expenses ($400,000 + $90,000) from sales ($750,000).
4. A In a period in which the number of units manufactured exceeds the number of units sold, the operating income reported under the absorption costing concept is larger than the operating income reported under the variable costing concept (answer A) because a portion of the fixed manufacturing costs are deferred when the absorption costing concept is used. This deferment has the effect of excluding a portion of the fixed manufacturing costs from the current cost of goods sold.
5. C A difference between planned and actual sales can be attributed to (1) a difference in the number of units sold—quantity factor and (2) a difference in the unit price—price factor. The $45,000 decrease (answer C) attributed to the quantity factor is determined as follows:

Decrease in number of units sold	5,000
Planned unit sales price	× $9
Quantity factor—decrease	$45,000

The unit price factor can be determined as follows:

Increase in unit sales price	$1
Actual number of units sold	×80,000
Price factor—increase	$80,000

The increase of $80,000 attributed to the price factor less the decrease of $45,000 attributed to the quantity factor accounts for the $35,000 increase in total sales.

21
Budgeting

CHAPTER OBJECTIVES

Describe the nature and objectives of budgeting and the budget process.

Describe and illustrate the master budget and the preparation of the following components of a master budget for a small manufacturing enterprise:

Sales budget
Production budget
Direct materials purchases budget
Direct labor cost budget
Factory overhead cost budget
Cost of goods sold budget
Operating expenses budget
Budgeted income statement
Capital expenditures budget
Cash budget
Budgeted balance sheet

Describe and illustrate budget performance reports.

Describe and illustrate flexible budgets.

Describe automated budgeting systems.

Describe the impact of budgeting on human behavior.

Effective planning and control are requisites of successful operations. Various uses of accounting data by management in performing these functions have been described and illustrated in earlier chapters. For example, the role of accounting in planning production and controlling costs has been discussed and illustrated. This chapter and Chapter 22 are devoted to budgeting and standard costs, two additional accounting devices that aid management in planning and controlling the operations of the business.

NATURE AND OBJECTIVES OF BUDGETING

A **budget** is a formal written statement of management's plans for the future, expressed in financial terms. A budget charts the course of future action. Thus, it serves management's primary functions in the same manner that the architect's blueprints aid the builder and the navigator's flight plan aids the pilot.

A budget, like a blueprint and flight plan, should contain sound, attainable objectives. If the budget is to contain such objectives, planning must be based on careful study, investigation, and research. Management's reliance on data thus obtained lessens the role of guesswork and intuition in managing a business enterprise.

In a recent survey, the corporate boards of directors of 600 of the 1,000 largest U.S. corporations emphasized the importance of planning to the success of a business. The results of this survey, which asked the boards to identify the most important issues facing them now, and five years from now, are shown in the following bar graph:[1]

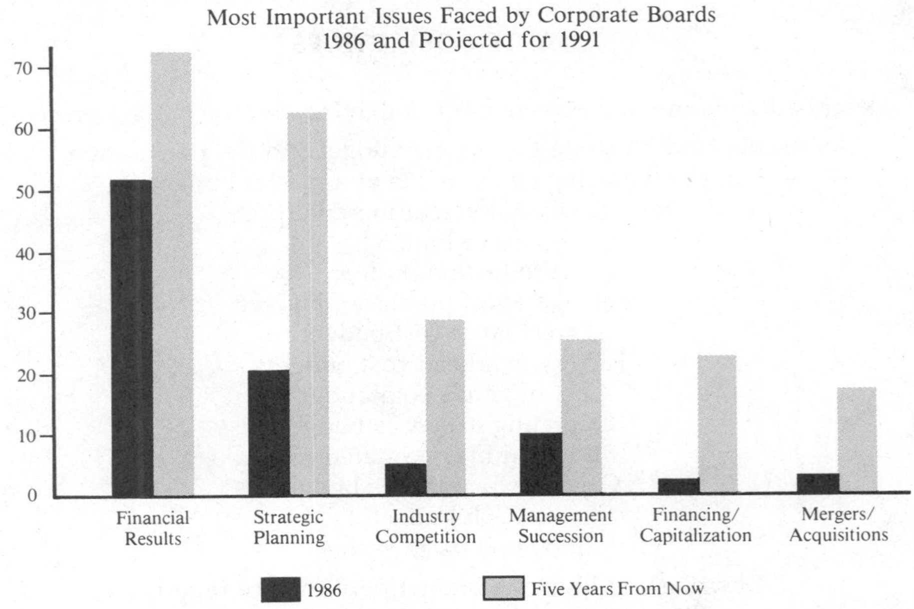

The essentials of budgeting are (1) the establishment of specific goals for future operations and (2) the periodic comparison of actual results with these goals. The establishment of specific goals for future operations encompasses the planning function of management. The periodic comparison of actual results with these goals encompasses the control function of management.

Although budgets are commonly associated with profit-making enterprises, they play an important role in operating most instrumentalities of government, ranging from rural school districts and small villages to gigantic agencies of the federal government. They are also an important part of the operations of churches, hospitals, and other nonprofit institutions. Individuals and family units often use budgeting techniques as an aid to careful

[1]Deloitte Haskins & Sells, "Major Issues Facing Boards of Directors," *DH+S Review,* October 25, 1987, p. 3.

management of resources. In this chapter, the principles of budgeting are discussed in the context of profit-making enterprises.

BUDGET PERIOD

Budgets of operating activities usually include the fiscal year of an enterprise. A year is short enough to make possible fairly dependable estimates of future operations, and yet long enough to make it possible to view the future in a reasonably broad context. However, to achieve effective control, the annual budgets must be subdivided into shorter time periods, such as quarters of the year, months, or weeks. It is also necessary to review the budgets from time to time and make any changes that become necessary as a result of unforeseen changes in general business conditions, in the particular industry, or in the individual enterprise.

A frequent variant of fiscal-year budgeting, sometimes called **continuous budgeting,** provides for maintenance of a twelve-month projection into the future. At the end of each time interval used, the twelve-month budget is revised by removing the data for the period just ended and adding the newly estimated budget data for the same period next year.

BUDGETING PROCEDURES

The details of budgeting systems are affected by the type and degree of complexity of a particular company, the amount of its revenues, the relative importance of its various divisions, and many other factors. Budget procedures used by a large manufacturer of automobiles would obviously differ in many ways from a system designed for a small manufacturer of paper products. The differences between a system designed for factory operations of any type and a financial enterprise such as a bank would be even more marked.

The development of budgets for a following fiscal year usually begins several months prior to the end of the current year. The responsibility for their development is ordinarily assigned to a committee made up of the budget director and such high-level executives as the controller, treasurer, production manager, and sales manager. The process is started by requesting estimates of sales, production, and other operating data from the various administrative units concerned. It is important that all levels of management and all departments participate in the preparation and submission of budget estimates. The involvement of all supervisory personnel fosters cooperation both within and among departments and also heightens awareness of each department's importance in the overall processes of the company. All levels of management are thus encouraged to set goals and to control operations in a manner that strengthens the possibilities of achieving the goals.

The process of developing budget estimates differs among enterprises. One method is to require all levels of management to start from zero and estimate sales, production, and other operating data as though operations were being started for the first time. Although this concept, called **zero-base budgeting,** has received wide attention in regard to budgeting for governmental units, it is equally useful to commercial enterprises. Another method of developing estimates is for each level of management to modify last year's budgeted amounts in light of last year's operating results and expected changes for the coming year.

The various estimates received by the budget committee are revised, reviewed, coordinated, cross-referenced, and finally put together to form the

master budget. The estimates submitted should not be substantially revised by the committee without first giving the originators an opportunity to defend their proposals. After agreement has been reached and the master budget has been adopted by the budget committee, copies of the pertinent sections are distributed to the proper personnel in the chain of accountability. Periodic reports comparing actual results with the budget should likewise be distributed to all supervisory personnel.

As a framework for describing and illustrating budgeting, a small manufacturing enterprise will be assumed. The major parts of its master budget are as follows:

Components of Master Budget

Budgeted income statement
- Sales budget
- Cost of goods sold budget
  - Production budget
  - Direct materials purchases budget
  - Direct labor cost budget
  - Factory overhead cost budget
- Operating expenses budget

Budgeted balance sheet
- Capital expenditures budget
- Cash budget

Sales Budget

The first budget to be prepared is usually the sales budget. An estimate of the dollar volume of sales revenue serves as the foundation upon which the other budgets are based. Sales volume will have a significant effect on all of the factors entering into the determination of operating income.

The sales budget ordinarily indicates (1) the quantity of forecasted sales for each product and (2) the expected unit selling price of each product. These data are often classified by areas and/or sales representatives.

In forecasting the quantity of each product expected to be sold, the starting point is generally past sales volumes. These amounts are revised for various factors expected to affect future sales, such as a backlog of unfilled sales orders, planned advertising and promotion, expected industry and general economic conditions, productive capacity, projected pricing policy, and market research study findings. Statistical analysis can be used in this process to evaluate the effect of these factors on past sales volume. Such analysis can provide a mathematical association between past sales and the several variables expected to affect future sales.

Once the forecast of sales volume is completed, the anticipated sales revenue is then determined by multiplying the volume of forecasted sales by the expected unit sales price, as shown in the sales budget at the top of page 785.

Frequent comparisons of actual sales with the budgeted volume, by product, area, and/or sales representative, will show differences between the two. Management is then able to investigate the probable cause of the significant differences and attempt corrective action.

Production Budget

The number of units of each commodity expected to be manufactured to meet budgeted sales and inventory requirements is set forth in the production

Sales Budget

Bowers Company
Sales Budget
For Year Ending December 31, 19--

Product and Area	Unit Sales Volume	Unit Selling Price	Total Sales
Product X:			
Area A.	208,000	$ 9.90	$2,059,200
Area B.	162,000	9.90	1,603,800
Area C	158,000	9.90	1,564,200
Total.	528,000		$5,227,200
Product Y:			
Area A.	111,600	$16.50	$1,841,400
Area B.	78,800	16.50	1,300,200
Area C	89,600	16.50	1,478,400
Total.	280,000		$4,620,000
Total revenue from sales.			$9,847,200

budget. The budgeted volume of production is based on the sum of (1) the expected sales volume and (2) the desired year-end inventory, less (3) the inventory expected to be available at the beginning of the year. A production budget is illustrated as follows:

Production Budget

Bowers Company
Production Budget
For Year Ending December 31, 19--

	Units	
	Product X	Product Y
Sales	528,000	280,000
Plus desired ending inventory, December 31, 19--	80,000	60,000
Total.	608,000	340,000
Less estimated beginning inventory, January 1, 19--	88,000	48,000
Total production	520,000	292,000

The production needs must be carefully coordinated with the sales budget to assure that production and sales are kept in balance during the period. Ideally, manufacturing operations should be maintained at capacity, and inventories should be neither excessive nor insufficient to fill sales orders.

Direct Materials Purchases Budget

The production needs shown by the production budget, combined with data on direct materials needed, provide the data for the direct materials purchases budget. The quantities of direct materials purchases necessary to meet production needs is based on the sum of (1) the materials expected to be needed to meet production requirements and (2) the desired year-end inventory, less (3) the inventory expected to be available at the beginning of the year. The quantities of direct materials required are then multiplied by the expected unit purchase price to determine the total cost of direct materials purchases.

In the following direct materials purchases budget, materials A and C are required for Product X, and materials A, B, and C are required for Product Y.

Direct Materials Purchases Budget

Bowers Company
Direct Materials Purchases Budget
For Year Ending December 31, 19--

	Direct Materials		
	A	B	C
Units required for production:			
Product X	390,000	—	520,000
Product Y	146,000	292,000	294,200
Plus desired ending inventory, Dec. 31, 19--	80,000	40,000	120,000
Total	616,000	332,000	934,200
Less estimated beginning inventory, Jan. 1, 19--	103,000	44,000	114,200
Total units to be purchased	513,000	288,000	820,000
Unit price	$ .60	$ 1.70	$ 1.00
Total direct materials purchases	$307,800	$489,600	$820,000

The timing of the direct materials purchases requires close coordination between the purchasing and production departments so that inventory levels can be maintained within reasonable limits.

Direct Labor Cost Budget

The needs indicated by the production budget provide the starting point for the preparation of the direct labor cost budget. The direct labor hours necessary to meet production needs are multiplied by the estimated hourly rate to yield the total direct labor cost. The manufacturing operations for both Products X and Y are performed in Departments 1 and 2. A direct labor cost budget is illustrated as follows:

Direct Labor Cost Budget

Bowers Company
Direct Labor Cost Budget
For Year Ending December 31, 19--

	Department 1	Department 2
Hours required for production:		
Product X	75,000	104,000
Product Y	46,800	116,800
Total	121,800	220,800
Hourly rate	$10	$8
Total direct labor cost	$1,218,000	$1,766,400

The direct labor requirements must be carefully coordinated with available labor time to assure that sufficient labor will be available to meet production needs. Efficient manufacturing operations minimize idle time and labor shortages.

Factory Overhead Cost Budget

The factory overhead costs estimated to be necessary to meet production needs are presented in the factory overhead cost budget. For use as part of the master budget, the factory overhead cost budget usually presents the total estimated cost for each item of factory overhead. A factory overhead cost budget is illustrated as follows:

Factory Overhead Cost Budget

Bowers Company
Factory Overhead Cost Budget
For Year Ending December 31, 19--

Indirect factory wages	$ 732,800
Supervisory salaries	360,000
Power and light	306,000
Depreciation of plant and equipment	288,000
Indirect materials	182,800
Maintenance	140,280
Insurance and property taxes	79,200
Total factory overhead cost	$2,089,080

Supplemental schedules are often prepared to present the factory overhead cost for each individual department. Such schedules enable department supervisors to direct attention to those costs for which each is solely responsible. They also aid the production manager in evaluating performance in each department.

Cost of Goods Sold Budget

The budget for the cost of goods sold is prepared by combining data on estimated inventories with the relevant estimates of quantities and costs in the budgets for (1) direct materials purchases, (2) direct labor costs, and (3) factory overhead costs. A cost of goods sold budget is illustrated as follows:

Cost of Goods Sold Budget

Bowers Company
Cost of Goods Sold Budget
For Year Ending December 31, 19--

Finished goods inventory, January 1, 19--			$1,095,600
Work in process inventory, January 1, 19--		$ 214,400	
Direct materials:			
Direct materials inventory, January 1, 19--	$ 250,800		
Direct materials purchases	1,617,400		
Cost of direct materials available for use	$1,868,200		
Less direct materials inventory, December 31, 19--	236,000		
Cost of direct materials placed in production	$1,632,200		
Direct labor	2,984,400		
Factory overhead	2,089,080		
Total manufacturing costs		6,705,680	
Total work in process during period		$6,920,080	
Less work in process inventory, December 31, 19--		220,000	
Cost of goods manufactured			6,700,080
Cost of finished goods available for sale			$7,795,680
Less finished goods inventory, December 31, 19--			1,195,000
Cost of goods sold			$6,600,680

Operating Expenses Budget

Based on past experiences, which are adjusted for future expectations, the estimated selling and general expenses are set forth in the operating expenses budget. For use as part of the master budget, the operating expenses budget ordinarily presents the expenses by nature or type of expenditure, such as sales salaries, rent, insurance, and advertising. An operating expenses budget is illustrated as follows:

Operating Expenses Budget

Bowers Company
Operating Expenses Budget
For Year Ending December 31, 19--

Selling expenses:		
Sales salaries expense	$595,000	
Advertising expense	360,000	
Travel expense	115,000	
Telephone expense—selling	95,000	
Miscellaneous selling expense	25,000	
Total selling expenses		$1,190,000
General expenses:		
Officers salaries expense	$360,000	
Office salaries expense	105,000	
Heating and lighting expense	75,000	
Taxes expense	60,000	
Depreciation expense—office equipment	27,000	
Telephone expense—general	18,000	
Insurance expense	17,500	
Office supplies expense	7,500	
Miscellaneous general expense	25,000	
Total general expenses		695,000
Total operating expenses		$1,885,000

Detailed supplemental schedules based on departmental responsibility are often prepared for major items in the operating expenses budget. The advertising expense schedule, for example, should include such details as the advertising media to be used (newspaper, direct mail, television), quantities (column inches, number of pieces, minutes), cost per unit, frequency of use, and sectional totals. A realistic budget is prepared through careful attention to details, and effective control is achieved through assignment of responsibility to departmental supervisors.

Budgeted Income Statement

A budgeted income statement can usually be prepared from the estimated data presented in the budgets for sales, cost of goods sold, and operating expenses, with the addition of data on other income, other expense, and income tax. A budgeted income statement is illustrated as follows:

Bowers Company
Budgeted Income Statement
For Year Ending December 31, 19--

Revenue from sales		$9,847,200
Cost of goods sold		6,600,680
Gross profit		$3,246,520
Operating expenses:		
Selling expenses	$1,190,000	
General expenses	695,000	
Total operating expenses		1,885,000
Income from operations		$1,361,520
Other income:		
Interest income	$ 98,000	
Other expense:		
Interest expense	90,000	8,000
Income before income tax		$1,369,520
Income tax		610,000
Net income		$ 759,520

Budgeted Income Statement

The budgeted income statement brings together in condensed form the projection of all profit-making phases of operations and enables management to weigh the effects of the individual budgets on the profit plan for the year. If the budgeted net income in relationship to sales or to stockholders' equity is disappointingly low, additional review of all factors involved should be undertaken in an attempt to improve the plans.

Capital Expenditures Budget

The capital expenditures budget summarizes future plans for acquisition of plant facilities and equipment.[2] Substantial expenditures may be needed to replace machinery and other plant assets as they wear out, become obsolete, or for other reasons fall below minimum standards of efficiency. In addition, an expansion of plant facilities may be planned to keep pace with increasing demand for a company's product or to provide for additions to the product line.

The useful life of many plant assets extends over relatively long periods of time, and the amount of the expenditures for such assets usually changes

[2]The methods of evaluating alternate capital expenditure proposals are discussed in Chapter 26.

a great deal from year to year. The customary practice, therefore, is to project the plans for a number of years into the future in preparing the capital expenditures budget. A five-year capital expenditures budget is illustrated as follows:

Capital Expenditures Budget

Bowers Company
Capital Expenditures Budget
For Five Years Ending December 31, 1992

Item	1988	1989	1990	1991	1992
Machinery— Department 1	$400,000			$280,000	$360,000
Machinery— Department 2	180,000	$260,000	$560,000	200,000	
Office equipment		90,000			60,000
Total	$580,000	$350,000	$560,000	$480,000	$420,000

The various proposals recognized in the capital expenditures budget must be considered in preparing certain operating budgets. For example, the expected amount of depreciation on new equipment to be acquired in the current year must be taken into consideration when the budgets for factory overhead and operating expenses are prepared. The manner in which the proposed expenditures are to be financed will also affect the cash budget.

Cash Budget

The cash budget presents the expected inflow and outflow of cash for a day, week, month, or longer period. Receipts are classified by source and disbursements by purpose. The expected cash balance at the end of the period is then compared with the amount established as the minimum balance and the difference is the anticipated excess or deficiency for the period.

The minimum cash balance represents a safety buffer for mistakes in cash planning and for emergencies. However, the amount stated as the minimum balance need not remain fixed. It should perhaps be larger during periods of "peak" business activity than during the "slow" season. In addition, for effective cash management, much of the minimum cash balance can often be deposited in interest-bearing accounts.

The interrelationship of the cash budget with other budgets may be seen from the following illustration. Data from the sales budget, the various budgets for manufacturing costs and operating expenses, and the capital expenditures budget affect the cash budget. Consideration must also be given to dividend policies, plans for equity or long-term debt financing, and other projected plans that will affect cash.

Cash Budget

Bowers Company
Cash Budget
For Three Months Ending March 31, 19--

	January	February	March
Estimated cash receipts from:			
Cash sales	$168,000	$185,000	$115,000
Collections of accounts receivable	699,000	712,800	572,000
Other sources (issuance of securities, interest, etc.)	—	—	27,000
Total cash receipts	$867,000	$897,800	$714,000
Estimated cash disbursements for:			
Manufacturing costs	$541,200	$557,000	$536,000
Operating expenses	150,200	151,200	140,800
Capital expenditures	—	144,000	80,000
Other purposes (notes, income tax, etc.)	47,000	20,000	160,000
Total cash disbursements	$738,400	$872,200	$916,800
Cash increase (decrease)	$128,600	$ 25,600	$(202,800)
Cash balance at beginning of month	280,000	408,600	434,200
Cash balance at end of month	$408,600	$434,200	$231,400
Minimum cash balance	300,000	300,000	300,000
Excess (deficiency)	$108,600	$134,200	$ (68,600)

In some cases, it is useful to present supplemental schedules to indicate the details of some of the amounts in the cash budget. For example, the following schedule illustrates the determination of the estimated cash receipts arising from collections of accounts receivable. For the illustration, it is assumed that the accounts receivable balance was $295,800 on January 1, and sales for each of the three months ending March 31 are $840,000, $925,000, and $575,000, respectively. Bowers Company expects to sell 20% of its merchandise for cash. Of the sales on account, 60% are expected to be collected in the month of the sale and the remainder in the following month.

Schedule of Collections of Accounts Receivable

Bowers Company
Schedule of Collections of Accounts Receivable
For Three Months Ending March 31, 19--

	January	February	March
January 1 balance	$295,800		
January sales on account (80% × $840,000):			
Collected in January (60% × $672,000)	403,200		
Collected in February (40% × $672,000)		$268,800	
February sales on account (80% × $925,000):			
Collected in February (60% × $740,000)		444,000	
Collected in March (40% × $740,000)			$296,000
March sales on account (80% × $575,000):			
Collected in March (60% × $460,000)			276,000
Totals	$699,000	$712,800	$572,000

The importance of accurate cash budgeting can scarcely be overemphasized. An unanticipated lack of cash can result in loss of discounts, unfavorable borrowing terms on loans, and damage to the credit rating. On the other hand, an excess amount of idle cash also shows poor management. When the budget shows periods of excess cash, such funds can be used to reduce loans or purchase investments in readily marketable income-producing securities. Reference to the Bowers Company cash budget shows excess cash during January and February and a deficiency during March.

Getting the Most Out of Your Cash

Most businesses could reduce their interest expenses if they would improve their management of cash. The goal of cash management is to use the company's money to maximize earnings while paying all liabilities and maintaining adequate liquidity. Accelerating collections, delaying disbursements, and getting the needed information about the cash status are the foundation of effective cash management.

One of the most efficient cash management tools is the wire transfer, which is the safest and fastest way to move a large sum of money quickly. It is used by having your customers who monthly pay you large amounts wire the money directly to your bank.

Another efficient cash management tool is the lockbox, which is a system that has your customers mail their remittance checks directly to a post office box in the name of your company. You authorize your bank to collect the customers' payments, and each item is deposited directly to the bank, according to your instructions. A lockbox greatly accelerates the transformation of your receivables into cash, and it eliminates delays from mail and processing.

If your company is borrowing from a bank and not using its cash as effectively as it can, your company is losing interest every day. If the money is not needed on a day-by-day basis, you should invest the excess money in overnight, one- or two-week or 30-day instruments. If you are required to keep a compensating balance, monitor the account so that you do not keep more than the required amount.

Every morning, through phone calls or through a third party, you can receive information on your previous night's bank balances, credits, and disbursements in order to determine what you have available for investments that day. You can arrange for your bank to transfer the money out of your account and into investments every day.

Source: Allen E. Fishman, "Getting the Most Out of Your Cash," *St. Louis Post-Dispatch* (May 5, 1986), p. 14A.

Budgeted Balance Sheet

The budgeted balance sheet may reveal weaknesses in financial position, such as an abnormally large amount of current liabilities in relation to current assets, or excessive long-term debt in relation to stockholders' equity. If such conditions are indicated, the relevant factors should be given further study, so that the proper corrective action may be taken.

The budgeted balance sheet presents estimated details of financial condition at the end of a budget period, assuming that all budgeted operating and financing plans are fulfilled. A budgeted balance sheet is illustrated as follows:

Bowers Company
Budgeted Balance Sheet
December 31, 19--

Assets				
Current assets:				
Cash			$ 360,000	
Accounts receivable			214,000	
Marketable securities			650,000	
Inventories:				
Finished goods		$1,195,000		
Work in process		220,000		
Materials		236,000	1,651,000	
Prepaid expenses			37,500	
Total current assets				$2,912,500
	Cost	Accumulated Depreciation	Book Value	
Plant assets:				
Land	$ 275,000	—	$ 275,000	
Buildings	3,100,000	$1,950,000	1,150,000	
Machinery	950,000	380,000	570,000	
Office equipment	180,000	75,000	105,000	
Total plant assets	$4,505,000	$2,405,000		2,100,000
Total assets				$5,012,500
Liabilities				
Current liabilities:				
Accounts payable		$ 580,000		
Accrued liabilities		175,000		
Total current liabilities			$ 755,000	
Long-term liabilities:				
Mortgage note payable			900,000	
Total liabilities				$1,655,000
Stockholders' Equity				
Common stock			$2,000,000	
Retained earnings			1,357,500	
Total stockholders' equity				3,357,500
Total liabilities and stockholders' equity				$5,012,500

BUDGET PERFORMANCE REPORTS

A **budget performance report** comparing actual results with the budgeted figures should be prepared periodically for each budget. This "feedback" enables management to investigate significant differences to determine their cause and to seek means of preventing their recurrence. If corrective action cannot be taken because of changed conditions that have occurred since the budget was prepared, future budget figures should be revised accordingly. A budget performance report is illustrated as follows:

Budget Performance Report

Bowers Company
Budget Performance Report—Factory Overhead Cost, Department 1
For Month Ended June 30, 19--

	Budget	Actual	Over	Under
Indirect factory wages	$30,200	$30,400	$200	
Supervisory salaries	15,000	15,000		
Power and light	12,800	12,750		$ 50
Depreciation of plant and equipment	12,000	12,000		
Indirect materials	7,600	8,250	650	
Maintenance	5,800	5,700		100
Insurance and property taxes	3,300	3,300		
	$86,700	$87,400	$850	$150

The amounts reported in the "Budget" column were obtained from supplemental schedules accompanying the master budget. The amounts in the "Actual" column are the costs actually incurred. The last two columns show the amounts by which actual costs exceeded or were below budgeted figures. As shown in the illustration, there were differences between the actual and budgeted amounts for some of the items of overhead cost. The cause of the significant difference in indirect materials cost should be investigated, and an attempt to find means of corrective action should be made. For example, if the difference in indirect materials cost were found to be caused by a marketwide increase in the price of materials used, a corrective action may not be possible. On the other hand, if the difference resulted from the inefficient use of materials in the production process, it may be possible to eliminate the inefficiency and effect a savings in future indirect materials costs.

FLEXIBLE BUDGETS

In the discussion of budget systems, it has been assumed that the amount of sales and the level of manufacturing activity achieved during a period approximated the goals established in the budgets. When substantial changes in expectations occur during a budget period, the budgets should be revised to give effect to such changes. Otherwise, they will be of questionable value as incentives and instruments for controlling costs and expenses.

The effect of changes in volume of activity can be "built in" to the system by what are termed **flexible budgets.** Particularly useful in estimating and controlling factory overhead costs and operating expenses, a flexible budget is in reality a series of budgets for varying rates of activity. To illustrate, assume that because of extreme variations in demand and other uncontrollable factors, the output of a particular manufacturing enterprise fluctuates widely from month to month. In such circumstances, the total factory overhead costs incurred during periods of high activity are certain to be greater than during periods of low activity. It is equally certain, however, that fluctuations in total factory overhead costs will not be exactly proportionate to the volume of production. For example, if $100,000 of factory overhead costs are usually incurred during a month in which production totals 10,000 units, the factory overhead for a month in which only 5,000 units are produced would unquestionably be more than $50,000.

As discussed in previous chapters, items of factory cost and operating expense that tend to remain constant in amount regardless of changes in volume of activity may be said to be **fixed.** Real estate taxes, property insurance, and depreciation expense on buildings are examples of fixed costs. The amounts incurred are substantially independent of the level of operations. Costs and expenses which tend to fluctuate in amount according to changes in volume of activity are called **variable.** Supplies and indirect materials used and sales commissions are examples of variable costs and expenses. The degree of variability is not the same for all variable items; few, if any, vary in exact proportion to sales or production. The terms **mixed cost, semivariable cost,** or **semifixed cost** are sometimes applied to items that have both fixed and variable characteristics to a significant degree. An example is electric power, for which there is often an initial flat fee and a rate for additional usage. For example, the charge for electricity used might be $700 for the first 10 000 kwh consumed during a month and $.05 per kwh used above 10 000.

Although there are many approaches to the preparation of a flexible budget, the first step is to identify the fixed and variable components of the various factory overhead and operating expenses being budgeted. The costs and expenses can then be presented in variable and fixed categories. For example, in the following flexible budget for factory overhead cost for one department and one product, "electric power" is broken down into its fixed and variable cost components for three different levels of production.

Flexible Budget for Factory Overhead Cost

Collins Manufacturing Company
Monthly Factory Overhead Cost Budget

Units of product	8,000	9,000	10,000
Variable cost:			
Indirect factory wages	$ 32,000	$ 36,000	$ 40,000
Electric power	24,000	27,000	30,000
Indirect materials	12,000	13,500	15,000
Total variable cost	$ 68,000	$ 76,500	$ 85,000
Fixed cost:			
Supervisory salaries	$ 40,000	$ 40,000	$ 40,000
Depreciation of plant and equipment	25,000	25,000	25,000
Property taxes	15,000	15,000	15,000
Insurance	12,000	12,000	12,000
Electric power	10,000	10,000	10,000
Total fixed cost	$102,000	$102,000	$102,000
Total factory overhead cost	$170,000	$178,500	$187,000

The fixed portion of electric power is $10,000 for all levels of production. The variable portion is $30,000 for 10,000 units of product, $27,000 ($30,000 × 9,000/10,000) for 9,000 units of product, and $24,000 ($30,000 × 8,000/10,000) for 8,000 units of product.

In practice, the number of production levels and the interval between levels in a flexible budget will vary with the range of production volume. For example, instead of budgeting for 8,000, 9,000, and 10,000 units of product, it might be necessary to provide for levels, at intervals of 500, from 6,000 to 12,000 units. Alternative bases, such as hours of departmental operation or direct labor hours, may also be used in measuring the volume of activity.

In preparing budget performance reports, the actual results would be compared with the flexible budget figures for the level of operations achieved.

For example, if Collins Manufacturing Company manufactured 10,000 units during a month, the budget figures reported in the budget performance report would be those appearing in the "10,000 units" column of Collins' flexible budget.

AUTOMATED BUDGETING SYSTEMS

Many firms use computers in the budgeting process. Computers can not only speed up the budgeting process, but they can also reduce the cost of budget preparation when large quantities of data need to be processed. Computers are especially useful in preparing flexible budgets and in continuous budgeting. Budget performance reports can also be prepared on a timely basis by the use of the computer.

By using computerized simulation models, which are mathematical statements of the relationships among various operating activities, management can determine the impact of various operating alternatives on the master budget. For example, if management wishes to evaluate the impact of a proposed change in direct labor wage rates, the computer can quickly provide a revised master budget that reflects the new rates. If management wishes to evaluate a proposal to add a new product line, the computer can quickly update current budgeted data and indicate the effect of the proposal on the master budget.

BUDGETING AND HUMAN BEHAVIOR

The budgeting process sets the overall goals of the business as well as the specific goals for individual units. Significant human behavior problems can develop if these goals are viewed as unrealistic or unachievable by management personnel. In such a case, management may become discouraged as well as uncommitted to the achievement of the goals. As a result, the budget becomes worthless as a tool for planning and controlling operations. On the other hand, goals set within a range that management considers attainable are likely to inspire management's efforts to achieve the goals. Therefore, it is important that all levels of management be involved in establishing the goals which they will be expected to achieve. In such an environment, the budget is a planning tool that will favorably affect human behavior and increase the possibility of achieving the goals.

Human behavior problems can also arise when the budgeted and actual results are compared and reported. These problems can be minimized if budget performance reports are used exclusively to evaluate operating performance and to initiate corrective action when performance can be improved. However, if budget performance reports are also used to evaluate management performance, management may concentrate more on defending its performance than on using the budgeting system to plan and control operations.

There is little doubt that budgets and budget performance reports can have a significant influence on management behavior. Behavioral factors have received increased attention by management accountants and behavioral scientists in recent years, and many behavioral issues are the subject of ongoing research.

Chapter Review

KEY POINTS

1. Nature and Objectives of Budgeting.
The essentials of budgeting are (1) the establishment of specific goals for future operations and (2) the periodic comparison of actual results with these goals. The establishment of specific goals for future operations encompasses the planning function of management. The periodic comparison of actual results with these goals encompasses the control function of management.

2. Budget Period.
Although budgets may be prepared for quarters of the year, months, or weeks, budgets of operating activities usually include the fiscal year of an enterprise. A variant of fiscal-year budgeting, continuous budgeting, provides for maintenance of a twelve-month projection into the future.

3. Budgeting Procedures.
All levels of management should be encouraged to participate in the budgeting process. Usually a budget committee has final responsibility for preparation of the master budget.

The sales budget is usually the first component of the master budget that is prepared. The production budget sets forth the number of units of each commodity expected to be manufactured to meet budgeted sales and inventory requirements. The direct materials budget is based on the needs shown by the production budget. The production budget also serves as a starting point for the preparation of the direct labor cost budget and factory overhead cost budget. The cost of goods sold budget is prepared by combining data on estimated inventories with the relevant estimates of quantities and costs in the budgets for (1) direct materials purchases, (2) direct labor costs, and (3) factory overhead costs. After the operating expenses budget is prepared, the budgeted income statement can be prepared.

The capital expenditures budget summarizes future plans for the acquisition of plant facilities and equipment, while the cash budget represents the expected inflow and outflow of cash for a day, week, month, or a longer period. The budgeted balance sheet presents estimated details of financial condition at the end of a budget period, assuming that all the budgeted operating and financing plans are fulfilled.

4. Budget Performance Reports.
A budget performance report provides feedback to management by reporting actual results compared with budgeted figures. Significant differences can then be investigated and corrective action taken.

5. Flexible Budgets.
Through the use of flexible budgets, the effect of changes in volume of activity can be built into the budgetary system. The preparation of flexible budgets requires the separation of costs and expenses into fixed and variable components. The use of flexible budgets facilitates the preparation of budget performance reports based on the actual level of operations achieved.

6. Automated Budgeting Systems.
Computers can be useful in speeding up the budgetary process and in preparing timely budget performance reports. In addition, through the use of simulation models, management can determine the impact of operating alternatives on the various budgets.

7. Budgeting and Human Behavior.
Significant human behavior problems can develop if managers view a budget as unrealistic or unachievable. Human behavior problems can also arise when budgeted and actual results are compared. These problems can be minimized if managers are involved in establishing budgets initially and budgets are revised for changes and expectations that occur during a budget period.

KEY TERMS

budget 782
continuous budgeting 783
zero-base budgeting 784
master budget 784
budget performance report 793
flexible budgets 794
fixed costs and expenses 795
variable cost and expenses 795
mixed costs 795

SELF-EXAMINATION QUESTIONS

(Answers at End of Chapter)

1. Budgeting of operating activities to provide at all times for maintenance of a twelve-month projection into the future is called:
   A. fixed budgeting
   B. variable budgeting
   C. continuous budgeting
   D. none of the above
2. The budget that summarizes future plans for acquisition of plant facilities and equipment is the:
   A. cash budget
   B. sales budget
   C. capital expenditures budget
   D. none of the above
3. A report comparing actual results with the budget figures is called a:
   A. budget report
   B. budget performance report
   C. flexible budget report
   D. none of the above
4. Costs that tend to remain constant in amount, regardless of variations in volume of activity, are called:
   A. fixed costs
   B. variable costs
   C. semifixed costs
   D. semivariable costs

5. The system that "builds in" the effect of fluctuations in volume of activity into the various budgets is termed:
   A. budget performance reporting
   B. continuous budgeting
   C. flexible budgeting
   D. none of the above

ILLUSTRATIVE PROBLEM

Hamilton Company prepared the following factory overhead cost budget for the Finishing Department for June of the current year:

Hamilton Company
Factory Overhead Cost Budget—Finishing Department
For Month Ending June 30, 19--

Direct labor hours budgeted		9,000
Variable cost:		
Indirect factory wages	$9,450	
Indirect materials	6,750	
Power and light	5,400	
Total variable cost		$21,600
Fixed cost:		
Supervisory salaries	$8,000	
Indirect factory wages	3,300	
Depreciation of plant and equipment	3,100	
Insurance	1,500	
Power and light	1,200	
Property taxes	900	
Total fixed cost		18,000
Total factory overhead cost		$39,600

Instructions:

1. Prepare a flexible budget for the month of July, indicating capacities of 8,000, 9,000, 10,000, and 11,000 direct labor hours.
2. Prepare a budget performance report for July. The Finishing Department was operated for 8,000 direct labor hours and the following factory overhead costs were incurred:

Indirect factory wages	$11,500
Supervisory salaries	8,000
Power and light	6,350
Indirect materials	6,050
Depreciation of plant and equipment	3,100
Insurance	1,500
Property taxes	900
Total factory overhead costs incurred	$37,400

SOLUTION

(1)

Hamilton Company
Factory Overhead Cost Budget—Finishing Department
For Month Ending July 31, 19--

Direct labor hours	8,000	9,000	10,000	11,000
Budgeted factory overhead:				
Variable cost:				
Indirect factory wages	$ 8,400	$ 9,450	$10,500	$11,550
Indirect materials	6,000	6,750	7,500	8,250
Power and light	4,800	5,400	6,000	6,600
Total variable cost	$19,200	$21,600	$24,000	$26,400
Fixed cost:				
Supervisory salaries	$ 8,000	$ 8,000	$ 8,000	$ 8,000
Indirect factory wages	3,300	3,300	3,300	3,300
Depreciation of plant and equipment	3,100	3,100	3,100	3,100
Insurance	1,500	1,500	1,500	1,500
Power and light	1,200	1,200	1,200	1,200
Property taxes	900	900	900	900
Total fixed cost	$18,000	$18,000	$18,000	$18,000
Total factory overhead cost	$37,200	$39,600	$42,000	$44,400

(2)

Hamilton Company
Budget Performance Report—Finishing Department
For Month Ended July 31, 19--

	Budget	Actual	Over	Under
Variable cost:				
Indirect factory wages	$ 8,400	$ 8,200		$ 200
Indirect materials	6,000	6,050	$ 50	
Power and light	4,800	5,150	350	
Total variable cost	$19,200	$19,400		
Fixed cost:				
Supervisory salaries	$ 8,000	$ 8,000		
Indirect factory wages	3,300	3,300		
Depreciation of plant and equipment	3,100	3,100		
Insurance	1,500	1,500		
Power and light	1,200	1,200		
Property taxes	900	900		
Total fixed cost	$18,000	$18,000		
Total factory overhead cost	$37,200	$37,400	$400	$ 200

Discussion Questions

21–1. What is a budget?

21–2. (a) Name the two basic functions of management in which accounting is involved. (b) How does a budget aid management in the discharge of these basic functions?

21–3. What is meant by *continuous budgeting?*

21–4. Why should all levels of management and all departments participate in the preparation and submission of budget estimates?

21–5. Which budgetary concept requires all levels of management to start from zero and estimate sales, production, and other operating data as though the operations were being initiated for the first time?

21–6. Why should the production requirements as set forth in the production budget be carefully coordinated with the sales budget?

21–7. Why should the timing of direct materials purchases be closely coordinated with the production budget?

21–8. What is a capital expenditures budget?

21–9. (a) Discuss the purpose of the cash budget. (b) If the cash budget for the first quarter of the fiscal year indicates excess cash at the end of each of the first two months, how might the excess cash be used?

21–10. What is a budget performance report?

21–11. What is a flexible budget?

21–12. Distinguish between (a) fixed costs and (b) variable costs.

21–13. Which of the following costs incurred by a manufacturing enterprise tend to be fixed and which tend to be variable: (a) cost of direct materials entering into finished product, (b) salary of factory superintendent, (c) indirect materials, (d) rent on factory building, (e) depreciation on factory building, (f) property taxes on factory building, (g) direct labor entering into finished product?

21–14. What is a mixed cost?

21–15. Drake Corporation uses flexible budgets. For each of the following variable operating expenses, indicate whether there has been a saving or an excess of expenses, assuming that actual sales were $500,000.

Expense Item	Actual Amount	Budget Allowance Based on Sales
Factory supplies expense.......	$15,800	3%
Uncollectible accounts expense .	9,500	2%

21–16. Briefly discuss the type of human behavior problem that might arise if goals used in developing budgets are unrealistic or unachievable.

21–17. Real World Focus. During a ten-year period from 1977 to 1987, the ratio of cost of sales to net sales for PepsiCo Inc. declined from 48.2% to 38.8%. During this same period, the net sales of PepsiCo increased by approximately 400%. As the sales increase, why would management normally expect the ratio of cost of sales to net sales to decline?

Exercises

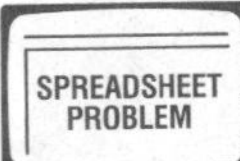

21–18. Sales and production budgets. Husley Company manufactures two models of humidifiers, M3 and P4. Based on the following production and sales data for June of the current year, prepare (a) a sales budget and (b) a production budget.

	M3	P4
Estimated inventory (units), June 1	45,000	27,600
Desired inventory (units), June 30	54,000	24,000
Expected sales volume (units):		
Region A	81,500	40,800
Region B	66,200	24,800
Unit sales price	$14.50	$20

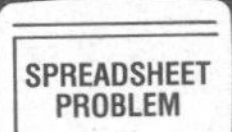

21–19. Schedule of cash collections of accounts receivable. Mattox Company was organized on August 1 of the current year. Projected sales for each of the first three months of operations are as follows:

August	$160,000
September	200,000
October	280,000

The company expects to sell 25% of its merchandise for cash. Of sales on account, 60% are expected to be collected in the month of the sale, 30% in the month following the sale, and the remainder in the following month. Prepare a schedule indicating cash collections of accounts receivable for August, September, and October.

21–20. Schedule of cash disbursements. Sirmons Company was organized on February 28 of the current year. Projected operating expenses for each of the first three months of operations are as follows:

March	$ 98,000
April	122,000
May	136,000

Depreciation, insurance, and property taxes represent $18,000 of the estimated monthly operating expenses. Insurance was paid on February 28, and property taxes will be paid in December. Three fourths of the remainder of the operating expenses are expected to be paid in the month in which they are incurred, with the balance to be paid in the following month. Prepare a schedule indicating cash disbursements for operating expenses for March, April, and May.

21–21. Flexible budget for operating expenses. Daniel Company uses flexible budgets that are based on the following data:

Sales commissions	6% of sales
Advertising expense	$10,000 for $200,000 of sales
	$15,000 for $300,000 of sales
	$20,000 for $400,000 of sales
Miscellaneous selling expense	$1,000 plus 1/2% of sales
Office salaries expense	$15,000
Office supplies expense	2% of sales
Miscellaneous general expense	$500 plus 1/4% of sales

Prepare a flexible operating expenses budget for November of the current year for sales volumes of $200,000, $300,000, and $400,000.

21–22. Budget performance report. The operating expenses incurred during November of the current year by Daniel Company were as follows:

Sales commissions	$23,800
Advertising expense	22,600
Miscellaneous selling expense	3,050
Office salaries expense	15,000
Office supplies expense	7,810
Miscellaneous general expense	1,620

Assuming that the total sales for November were $400,000, prepare a budget performance report for operating expenses on the basis of the data presented above and in Exercise 21–21.

21–23. Flexible factory overhead cost budget. Spang Company prepared the following factory overhead cost budget for Department L for March of the current year, during which it expected to manufacture 20,000 units:

Variable cost:		
Indirect factory	$16,000	
Power and light	12,500	
Indirect materials	4,000	
Total variable cost		$32,500
Fixed cost:		
Supervisory salaries	$15,000	
Depreciation of plant and equipment	4,000	
Insurance and property taxes	2,000	
Total fixed cost		21,000
Total factory overhead cost		$53,500

Assuming that the estimated costs in March are applicable to April operations, prepare a flexible factory overhead cost budget for Department L for April for 18,000, 20,000, and 22,000 units of product.

21–24. Budget performance report. During April, Spang Company manufactured 22,000 units, and the factory overhead costs incurred in Department L were: indirect factory wages, $17,300; power and light, $14,000; indirect materials, $4,500; supervisory salaries, $15,000; depreciation of plant and equipment, $4,000; and insurance and property taxes, $2,000.

Prepare a budget performance report for Department L for April. To be useful for cost control, the budgeted amounts should be based on the data for 22,000 units, as revealed in Exercise 21–23.

Problems

21–25. Sales, production, direct materials, and direct labor budgets. The budget director of Greaves Company requests estimates of sales, production, and other operating data from the various administrative units every month. Selected information concerning sales and production for August of the current year are summarized as follows:

(a) Estimated sales for August by sales territory:
Northeast:
Product A: 24,000 units at $45 per unit
Product B: 20,000 units at $60 per unit
Southeast:
Product A: 15,000 units at $45 per unit
Product B: 27,000 units at $60 per unit
Southwest:
Product A: 32,000 units at $45 per unit
Product B: 43,000 units at $60 per unit

(b) Estimated inventories at August 1:
Direct materials:
Material W: 21,000 lbs. Material Y: 21,500 lbs.
Material X: 15,600 lbs. Material Z: 27,600 lbs.
Finished products:
Product A: 10,000 units Product B: 15,000 units

(c) Desired inventories at August 31:
Direct materials:
Material W: 18,000 lbs. Material Y: 28,000 lbs.
Material X: 22,000 lbs. Material Z: 20,000 lbs.
Finished products:
Product A: 12,000 units Product B: 25,000 units

(d) Direct materials used in production:
In manufacture of Product A:
Material X: 1.2 lbs. per unit of product
Material Y: .8 lbs. per unit of product
Material Z: 1.0 lb. per unit of product
In manufacture of Product B:
Material W: 1.5 lbs. per unit of product
Material Y: .9 lbs. per unit of product
Material Z: 1.4 lbs. per unit of product

(e) Anticipated purchase price for direct materials:
Material W: $1.40 per lb. Material Y: $2.00 per lb.
Material X: $ .50 per lb. Material Z: $1.75 per lb.

(f) Direct labor requirements:
Product A:
Department 20: 1.0 hour at $14 per hour
Department 30: .6 hours at $20 per hour
Product B:
Department 10: 1.4 hours at $15 per hour
Department 20: .5 hours at $14 per hour

Instructions: (1) Prepare a sales budget for August.
(2) Prepare a production budget for August.
(3) Prepare a direct materials purchases budget for August.
(4) Prepare a direct labor cost budget for August.

21–26. Budgeted income statement and supporting budgets. The budget director of Martin Inc., with the assistance of the controller, treasurer, production manager, and sales manager, has gathered the following data for use in developing the budgeted income statement for July:

(a) Estimated sales for July:

Product J: 50,000 units at $120 per unit
Product K: 30,000 units at $90 per unit

(b) Estimated inventories at July 1:

Direct materials:
Material A: 5,000 lbs.
Material B: 40,000 lbs.
Material C: 8,000 lbs.

Finished products:
Product J: 10,000 units at $92 per unit
Product K: 7,000 units at $75 per unit

(c) Desired inventories at July 31:

Direct materials:
Material A: 8,000 lbs.
Material B: 35,000 lbs.
Material C: 10,000 lbs.

Finished products:
Product J: 15,000 units at $92 per unit
Product K: 9,000 units at $75 per unit

(d) Direct materials used in production:

In manufacture of Product J:
Material A: .75 lbs. per unit of product
Material B: 1.5 lbs. per unit of product

In manufacture of Product K:
Material B: 1.0 lb. per unit of product
Material C: 1.2 lbs. per unit of product

(e) Anticipated cost of purchases and beginning and ending inventory of direct materials:

Material A: $14.00 per lb.
Material B: $ .80 per lb.
Material C: $20.00 per lb.

(f) Direct labor requirements:

Product J:
Department 100: 3.0 hours at $15 per hour
Department 200: 1.0 hour at $20 per hour

Product K:
Department 200: .5 hours at $20 per hour
Department 300: 2.0 hours at $18 per hour

(g) Estimated factory overhead costs for July:

Indirect factory wages	$250,000
Depreciation of plant and equipment	220,000
Supervisory salaries	125,000
Power and light	115,700
Indirect materials	81,000
Maintenance	33,400
Insurance and property taxes	25,900

(h) Estimated operating expenses for July:

Sales salaries expense	$462,000
Officers salaries expense	300,000
Advertising expense	286,000
Office salaries expense	125,000
Depreciation expense—office equipment	84,500
Telephone expense—selling	47,900
Telephone expense—general	22,000
Travel expense—selling	14,500
Travel expense—general	8,300
Office supplies expense	4,000
Miscellaneous selling expense	11,200
Miscellaneous general expense	7,500

(i) Estimated other income and expense for July:

Interest income	$180,000
Interest expense	145,000

(j) Estimated tax rate: 30%.

Instructions: (1) Prepare a sales budget for July.
(2) Prepare a production budget for July.
(3) Prepare a direct materials purchases budget for July.
(4) Prepare a direct labor cost budget for July.
(5) Prepare a factory overhead cost budget for July.
(6) Prepare a cost of goods sold budget for July. Work in process at the beginning of July is estimated to be $140,000, and work in process at the end of July is estimated to be $150,000.
(7) Prepare an operating expenses budget for July. Classify the expenses as either selling or general expenses.
(8) Prepare a budgeted income statement for July.

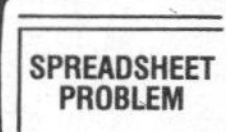

21–27. Cash budget. The treasurer of Flores Company instructs you to prepare a monthly cash budget for the next three months. You are presented with the following budget information:

	April	May	June
Sales	$600,000	$550,000	$700,000
Manufacturing costs	390,000	360,000	450,000
Operating expenses	125,000	115,000	145,000
Capital expenditures	—	160,000	—

The company expects to sell about 25% of its merchandise for cash. Of sales on account, 60% are expected to be collected in full in the month following the sale and the remainder the following month. Depreciation, insurance, and property taxes represent $30,000 of the estimated monthly manufacturing costs and $5,000 of the probable monthly operating expenses. Insurance and property taxes are paid in December. Of the remainder of the manufacturing costs and operating expenses, 70% are expected to be paid in the month in which they are incurred and the balance in the following month.

Current assets as of April 1 are composed of cash of $70,200, marketable securities of $60,000, and accounts receivable of $570,000 ($442,000 from March sales and $128,000 from February sales). Current liabilities as of April 1 are composed of a $100,000, 12%, 120-day note payable due June 20, $105,000 of accounts payable incurred in March for manufacturing costs, and accrued liabilities of $30,200 incurred in March for operating expenses.

It is expected that $4,000 in dividends will be received in May. An estimated income tax payment of $31,200 will be made in June. Flores Company's regular semiannual dividend of $20,000 is expected to be declared in May and paid in June. Management desires to maintain a minimum cash balance of $60,000.

Instructions: (1) Prepare a monthly cash budget for April, May, and June.
(2) On the basis of the cash budget prepared in (1), what recommendation should be made to the treasurer?

21–28. Forecast sales volume and sales budget. Ingram Company prepared the following sales budget for the current year:

Ingram Company
Sales Budget
For Year Ending December 31, 1989

Product and Area	Unit Sales Volume	Unit Selling Price	Total Sales
Product R:			
East	20,000	$15.00	$ 300,000
Central	30,000	15.00	450,000
West	50,000	15.00	750,000
Total	100,000		$1,500,000
Product S:			
East	15,000	$10.00	$ 150,000
Central	12,000	10.00	120,000
West	8,000	10.00	80,000
Total	35,000		$ 350,000
Total revenue from sales			$1,850,000

At the end of September, 1989, the following unit sales data were reported for the first nine months of the year:

	Unit Sales	
	Product R	Product S
East	14,100	11,475
Central	23,400	9,270
West	36,000	5,700

For the year ending December 31, 1990, unit sales are expected to follow the patterns established during the first nine months of the year ending December 31, 1989. The unit selling price for Product R is not expected to change, and the unit selling price for Product S is expected to be increased to $10.50, effective January 1, 1990.

Instructions: (1) Compute the increase or decrease of actual *unit* sales for the nine months ended September 30, 1989, over expectations for this nine-month period. Since sales have historically occurred evenly throughout the year, budgeted sales for the first nine months of a year would be 75% of the year's budgeted sales. Comparison of this amount with actual sales will indicate the percentage increase or decrease of actual sales for the nine months over budgeted sales for the nine months. (Round percent changes to the nearest whole percent.) Place your answers in a columnar table with the following format:

	Unit Budgeted Sales		Actual Sales	Increase (Decrease)	
	Year	**Nine Months**	**for Nine Months**	**Amount**	**Percent**
Product R					
East					
Central					
West					
Product S					
East					
Central					
West					

(2) Assuming that the trend of sales indicated in (1) is to continue in 1990, compute the unit sales volume to be used for preparing the sales budget for the year ending December 31, 1990. Place your answers in a columnar table with the following format:

	1989 Budgeted Units	Percentage Increase (Decrease)	1990 Budgeted Units
Product R			
East			
Central			
West			
Product S			
East			
Central			
West			

(3) Prepare a sales budget for the year ending December 31, 1990.

21–29. Flexible factory overhead cost budget and budget performance report. Sims Inc. prepared the following factory overhead cost budget for July of the current year for 12,000 units of product:

Sims Inc.
Factory Overhead Cost Budget
For Month Ending July 31, 19--

Variable cost:		
Indirect factory wages	$36,000	
Indirect materials	21,000	
Power and light	13,200	
Total variable cost		$ 70,200
Fixed cost:		
Supervisory salaries	$16,200	
Indirect factory wages	13,800	
Depreciation of plant and equipment	10,000	
Insurance	7,100	
Power and light	6,300	
Property taxes	2,000	
Total fixed cost		55,400
Total factory overhead cost		$125,600

The following factory overhead costs were incurred in producing 11,000 units in July:

Indirect factory wages	$ 47,500
Supervisory salaries	16,200
Power and light	18,000
Indirect materials	19,100
Depreciation of plant and equipment	10,000
Insurance	7,100
Property taxes	2,000
Total factory overhead cost incurred	$119,900

Instructions: (1) Prepare a flexible factory overhead cost budget for July, indicating capacities of 9,000, 10,000, 11,000, and 12,000 units of product.
(2) Prepare a budget performance report for July.

21–30. Budgeted income statement and balance sheet. As a preliminary to requesting budget estimates of sales, costs, and expenses for the fiscal year beginning January 1, 1990, the following tentative trial balance as of December 31 of the preceding year is prepared by the accounting department of Calmer Company:

Cash	85,000	
Accounts Receivable	90,000	
Finished Goods	150,000	
Work in Process	78,800	
Materials	52,200	
Prepaid Expenses	10,200	
Plant and Equipment	800,000	
Accumulated Depreciation—Plant and Equipment		320,000
Accounts Payable		100,000
Notes Payable		60,000
Common Stock, $20 par		150,000
Retained Earnings		636,200
	1,266,200	1,266,200

Factory output and sales for 1990 are expected to total 60,000 units of product, which are to be sold at $20 per unit. The quantities and costs of the inventories (lifo method) at December 31, 1990, are expected to remain unchanged from the balances at the beginning of the year.

Budget estimates of manufacturing costs and operating expenses for the year are summarized as follows:

	Estimated Costs and Expenses	
	Fixed (Total for Year)	Variable (Per Unit Sold)
Cost of goods manufactured and sold:		
Direct materials	—	$2.50
Direct labor	—	6.00
Factory overhead:		
Depreciation of plant and equipment	$25,000	—
Other factory overhead	18,000	1.95
Selling expenses:		
Sales salaries and commissions	30,000	.60
Advertising	15,000	—
Miscellaneous selling expense	1,000	.05
General expenses:		
Office and officers salaries	40,000	.30
Supplies	2,000	.10
Miscellaneous general expense	1,000	.04

Balances of accounts receivable, prepaid expenses, and accounts payable at the end of the year are expected to differ from the beginning balances by only inconsequential amounts.

For purposes of this problem, assume that federal income tax of $160,500 on 1990 taxable income will be paid during 1990. Regular quarterly cash dividends of $.30 a share are expected to be declared and paid in March, June, September, and December. It is anticipated that plant and equipment will be purchased for $200,000 cash in November.

Instructions: (1) Prepare a budgeted income statement for 1990.
(2) Prepare a budgeted balance sheet as of December 31, 1990.

ALTERNATE PROBLEMS

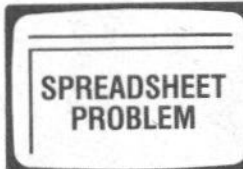

21–27A. Cash budget. The treasurer of Inman Company instructs you to prepare a monthly cash budget for the next three months. You are presented with the following budget information:

	October	November	December
Sales	$240,000	$360,000	$410,000
Manufacturing costs	140,000	220,000	250,000
Operating expenses	38,000	54,000	62,000
Capital expenditures	—	90,000	—

The company expects to sell about 30% of its merchandise for cash. Of sales on account, 80% are expected to be collected in full in the month following the sale and the remainder the following month. Depreciation, insurance, and property taxes represent $20,000 of the estimated monthly manufacturing costs and $8,000 of the probable monthly operating expenses. Insurance and property taxes are paid in March and August respectively. Of the remainder of the manufacturing costs and operating expenses, 65% are expected to be paid in the month in which they are incurred and the balance in the following month.

Current assets as of October 1 are composed of cash of $28,500, marketable securities of $40,000, and accounts receivable of $176,400 ($140,000 from September sales and $36,400 from August sales). Current liabilities as of October 1 are composed of a $50,000, 10%, 90-day note payable due November 5, $42,500 of accounts payable incurred in September for manufacturing costs, and accrued liabilities of $10,200 incurred in September for operating expenses.

It is expected that $2,000 in dividends will be received in October. An estimated income tax payment of $15,000 will be made in November. Inman Company's regular quarterly dividend of $10,000 is expected to be declared in November and paid in December. Management desires to maintain a minimum cash balance of $25,000.

Instructions: (1) Prepare a monthly cash budget for October, November, and December.
(2) On the basis of the cash budget prepared in (1), what recommendation should be made to the treasurer?

21–28A. Forecast sales volume and sales budget. Johnson Company prepared the following sales budget for the current year:

Johnson Company
Sales Budget
For Year Ending December 31, 1989

Product and Area	Unit Sales Volume	Unit Selling Price	Total Sales
Product R:			
East	20,000	$18.00	$ 360,000
Central	30,000	18.00	540,000
West	40,000	18.00	720,000
Total	90,000		$1,620,000
Product S:			
East	50,000	$20.00	$1,000,000
Central	60,000	20.00	1,200,000
West	75,000	20.00	1,500,000
Total	185,000		$3,700,000
Total revenue from sales			$5,320,000

At the end of September, 1989, the following unit sales data were reported for the first nine months of the year:

	Unit Sales	
	Product R	Product S
East	14,400	39,750
Central	22,950	44,100
West	28,500	60,750

For the year ending December 31, 1990, unit sales are expected to follow the patterns established during the first nine months of the year ending December 31, 1989. The unit selling price for Product R is expected to be increased to $19, effective January 1, 1990, and the unit selling price for Product S is not expected to change.

Instructions: (1) Compute the increase or decrease of actual *unit* sales for the nine months ended September 30, 1989, over expectations for this nine-month period. Since sales have historically occurred evenly throughout the year, budgeted sales for the first nine months of a year would be 75% of the year's budgeted sales. Comparison of this amount with actual sales will indicate the percentage increase or decrease of actual sales for the nine months over budgeted sales for the nine months. Place your answers in a columnar table with the following format:

	Unit Budgeted Sales		Actual Sales	Increase (Decrease)	
	Year	**Nine Months**	**for Nine Months**	**Amount**	**Percent**
Product R					
East					
Central					
West					
Product S					
East					
Central					
West					

(2) Assuming that the trend of sales indicated in (1) is to continue in 1990, compute the unit sales volume to be used for preparing the sales budget for the year ending December 31, 1990. Place your answers in a columnar table with the following format:

	1989 Budgeted Units	Percentage Increase (Decrease)	1990 Budgeted Units
Product R			
East			
Central			
West			
Product S			
East			
Central			
West			

(3) Prepare a sales budget for the year ending December 31, 1990.

21–29A. Flexible factory overhead cost budget and budget performance report. Southern Company prepared the following factory overhead cost budget for June of the current year for 20,000 units of product:

Southern Company
Factory Overhead Cost Budget
For Month Ending June 30, 19--

Variable cost:		
Indirect factory wages	$30,000	
Indirect materials	18,500	
Power and light	9,500	
Total variable cost		$ 58,000
Fixed cost:		
Supervisory salaries	$25,000	
Indirect factory wages	7,500	
Depreciation of plant and equipment	6,000	
Insurance	4,500	
Power and light	4,000	
Property taxes	3,000	
Total fixed cost		50,000
Total factory overhead cost		$108,000

The following factory overhead costs were incurred in producing 19,000 units in June:

Indirect factory wages	$ 36,800
Supervisory salaries	25,000
Indirect materials	17,100
Power and light	12,600
Depreciation of plant and equipment	6,000
Insurance	4,500
Property taxes	3,000
Total factory overhead cost incurred	$105,000

Instructions: (1) Prepare a flexible factory overhead cost budget for June, indicating capacities of 18,000, 19,000, 20,000, and 21,000 units of product.

(2) Prepare a budget performance report for June.

Mini-Case 21

BARNES MANUFACTURING COMPANY

Your father is president and chief operating officer of Barnes Manufacturing Company and has hired you as a summer intern to assist the controller. The controller has asked you to visit with the production supervisor of the Polishing Department and evaluate the supervisor's concern with the budgeting process. After this evaluation, you are to meet with the controller to discuss suggestions for improving the budgeting process.

This morning, you met with the supervisor, who expressed dissatisfaction with the budgets and budget performance reports prepared for the factory overhead costs for the Polishing Department. Specifically, July's budget performance report was mentioned as an example. The supervisor indicated that this report is not useful in evaluating the efficiency of the department, because most of the overages for the individual factory overhead items are not caused by inefficiencies, but by variations in the volume of activity between actual and budget. Although you were not provided with a copy of the budget for July, the supervisor indicated that it is standard practice for the plant manager to prepare a budget based on the production of 20,000 units. Actual production varies widely, however, with approximately 22,000 to 24,000 units being produced each month for the past several months. You are provided with the following budget performance report for July of the current year, when actual production was 24,000 units. All of the overages relate to variable costs, and the other costs are fixed.

Barnes Manufacturing Company
Budget Performance Report—Factory Overhead Cost, Polishing Department
For Month Ended July 31, 19--

	Budget	Actual	Over	Under
Indirect factory wages	$18,000	$21,800	$3,800	
Electric power	15,000	17,500	2,500	
Supervisory salaries	12,000	12,000		
Depreciation of plant assets	8,100	8,100		
Indirect materials	7,500	9,100	1,600	
Insurance and property taxes	5,000	5,000		
	$65,600	$73,500	$7,900	$0

In your discussion, you learned that the department supervisor has little faith in the budgeting process. The supervisor views the budgets as worthless and the budget performance reports as a waste of time, because they require an explanation of the budget overages, which, for the most part, are not departmentally controlled.

Instructions:

Prepare a list of suggestions for improving the budgeting process. Include any reports that you might find useful when you meet with the controller to discuss your suggestions.

Answers to Self-Examination Questions

1. C Continuous budgeting (answer C) is a type of budgeting that continually provides for maintenance of a twelve-month projection into the future.
2. C The capital expenditures budget (answer C) summarizes the plans for the acquisition of plant facilities and equipment for a number of years into the future. The cash budget (answer A) presents the expected inflow and outflow of cash for a budget period, and the sales budget (answer B) presents the expected sales for the budget period.
3. B A budget performance report (answer B) compares actual results with budgeted figures.
4. A Costs that tend to remain constant in amount, regardless of variations in volume of activity, are called fixed costs (answer A). Costs that tend to fluctuate in amount in accordance with variations in volume are called variable costs (answer B). Costs that have both fixed and variable characteristics are called semifixed costs (answer C) or semivariable costs (answer D).
5. C Flexible budgeting (answer C) provides a series of budgets for varying rates of activity and thereby builds into the budgeting system the effect of fluctuations in volume of activity. Budget performance reporting (answer A) is a system of reports that compares actual results with budgeted figures. Continuous budgeting (answer B) is a variant of fiscal-year budgeting that provides for continuous twelve-month projections into the future. This is achieved by periodically deleting from the current budget the data for the elapsed period and adding newly estimated budget data for the same period next year.

22
Standard Cost Systems

CHAPTER OBJECTIVES

Describe the nature and objectives of standards.

Describe the use of standard cost systems in planning and controlling operations.

Describe the use of variance analysis in controlling operations.

Compute and illustrate the use of the following variances in controlling costs:
- Direct materials quantity variance
- Direct materials price variance
- Direct labor time variance
- Direct labor rate variance
- Factory overhead volume variance
- Factory overhead controllable variance

Describe and illustrate the use of standards in the accounts.

Describe and illustrate the reporting of variances on the income statement.

Describe the conditions requiring the revision of standards.

Describe the use of standards for nonmanufacturing expenses.

The preceding chapter focused on the use of budgets as an aid to management in planning and controlling the operations of a business. This chapter will focus on standard cost systems and variance analysis, which can also be used by management in planning and controlling operations.

THE NATURE AND OBJECTIVES OF STANDARDS

Standards are used to measure and evaluate performance in many areas of life. For example, colleges and universities set standards for graduation, such as a C average. They may establish a B+ average for graduation with honors. Golfers use par as a standard in evaluating their play on the golf course. In each of these cases, the predetermined standard is used to measure and evaluate an individual's performance. In a like manner, business enterprises may use carefully predetermined standards to evaluate and control operations.

Service, merchandising, and manufacturing enterprises can all use standards. For example, an automobile repair garage may use a *standard* amount of time, as expressed in service manuals, as the basis for computing the labor charges for automobile repairs and measuring the performance of the mechanic. The driver of a truck delivering merchandise may be expected to make a *standard* number of deliveries each day. The widest use of standards is by manufacturing enterprises, which establish standard costs for the three categories of manufacturing costs: direct materials, direct labor, and factory overhead.

Accounting systems that use standards for each element of manufacturing cost entering into the finished product are sometimes called **standard cost systems.** Such systems enable management to determine how much a product should cost (**standard**), how much it does cost (actual), and the causes of any difference (**variance**) between the two. Standard costs thus serve as a device for measuring efficiency. If the actual costs are compared with the standard costs, unfavorable conditions can be determined and corrective actions taken. Thus, management has a device for controlling costs and motivating employees to become more cost conscious.

Setting Standards

The starting point in setting standards is often a review of past operations. In this review, management and the management accountant rely on their knowledge and judgment of past processes and costs to estimate the costs to produce a unit of product. However, standards should not be merely an extension of past costs. Inefficiencies may be reflected in past costs, and these inefficiencies should be considered in determining what the costs should be (standards). In addition, changes in technology, machinery, production methods, and economic conditions must be considered.

The setting of standards is both an art and a science. Although the standard-setting process varies among enterprises, it often requires the joint efforts of accountants, engineers, personnel administrators, and other management personnel. The management accountant plays an important role by expressing the results of judgments and studies in terms of dollars and subsequently reporting how actual results compare with these standards. Engineers contribute to the standard-setting process by studying the requirements of the product and the production process. For example, direct materials requirements can be determined by studying such factors as the materials specifications for the product and the normal spoilage in production. Time and motion studies may be used to determine the length of time required for each of the various manufacturing operations. Engineering studies may also be used to determine standards for some of the elements of factory overhead, such as the amount of power needed to operate machinery.

The Development of Standard Costs

An example of a company that uses standard costs is Dutch Pantry Inc., which operates 53 family restaurants in 12 eastern states. To assure consistent quality in the items served in these restaurants, much of the food preparation is done in a central commissary. Because the commissary produces more than 150 different items, it uses a standard cost system based on the production of a batch of product. This system allows the costs for the many products to flow through the various operations involved in food preparation.

The food processing activity of the central commissary consists of the following operations:

Spice room	Trim
Butcher shop	Weigh
Pan/stuffing	Pop-out
Bake/roast	Sure flow
Meat/broth	Bulk pack
Cooking kettles	Salad dressing
Frying	Case packing
Slicing	Warehouse

As production passes through each of these operations, the various elements of cost are incurred. How standard costs are developed for Dutch Pantry's raw materials, ingredients, packaging, and direct labor is described in the following excerpts from an article in *Management Accounting:*

. . . The standard costs of raw materials, ingredients and packaging are calculated by the use of a Recipe Sheet. . . , which is actually a bill of materials for a batch of the product. For costing purposes, the recipes are input to a computer program called the Recipe Master List. All costs are calculated on a hundred weight (CWT) basis. . . .

The standard costs of the component items are updated monthly on the Inventory Master Listing. At the same time, the updated costs are input to the Recipe Master List. This permits a timely revision of the costs of the finished products for changes in the standards of any components.

Direct labor dollars are [incurred in] production [as] the product passes through [the various operations.] A labor grid is prepared for each product. This grid lists the various [operations] for the product and the number of workers required to staff each [operation]. The various worker classifications and hourly rates are used to calculate a weighted-average cost per hour for direct labor.

Next, a standard poundage of product processed per hour is developed for each [operation]. A weighted average of the actual production runs from the prior year is used for this calculation. The direct labor cost per CWT is recorded on the product rate master (report) by [operation]. . . .

[Finally, the] budgeted direct labor dollars for the warehouse are divided by the forecasted quantity of production (cases). The result is the warehousing cost per case. . . .

Source: Dennis M. Boll, "How Dutch Pantry Accounts for Standard Costs," *Management Accounting* (December, 1982), pp. 32–35.

Types of Standards

Implicit in the use of standards is the concept of an acceptable level of production efficiency. One of the major objectives in selecting this performance level is to motivate workers to expend the efforts necessary to achieve the most efficient operations.

Standards that are too high, that is, standards that are unrealistic, may have a negative impact on performance because workers may become frustrated with their inability to meet the standards and, therefore, may not be motivated to do their best. Such standards represent levels of performance that can be achieved only under perfect operating conditions, such as no idle time, no machine breakdown, and no materials spoilage. Such standards, often called **theoretical standards** or **ideal standards,** are not widely used.

Standards that are too low might not motivate employees to perform at their best because the standard level of performance can be reached too easily. As a result, productivity may be lower than that which could be achieved.

Most companies use **currently attainable standards** (sometimes called **normal standards**), which represent levels of operation that can be attained with reasonable effort. Such currently attainable standards allow for reasonable production problems and errors, such as normal materials spoilage and machinery downtime for maintenance. When reasonable standards are used, employees often become cost conscious and expend their best efforts to achieve the best possible results at the lowest possible cost. Also, if employees are given bonuses for exceeding normal standards, the standards may be even more effective in motivating employees to perform at their best.

VARIANCES FROM STANDARDS

One of the primary purposes of a standard cost system is to facilitate control over costs by comparing actual costs with standard costs. Control is achieved by the action of management in investigating significant deviations of performance from standards and taking corrective action. Differences between the standard costs of a department or product and the actual costs incurred are termed **variances.** If the actual cost incurred is less than the standard cost, the variance is favorable. If the actual cost exceeds the standard cost, the variance is unfavorable. When actual costs are compared with standard costs, only the "exceptions" or variances are reported to the person responsible for cost control. This reporting by the "principle of exceptions" enables the one responsible for cost control to concentrate on the cause and correction of the variances.

When manufacturing operations are automated, standard cost data can be integrated with the computer that directs operations. Variances can then be detected and reported automatically by the computer system, and adjustments can be made to operations in progress.

The total variance for a certain period is usually made up of several variances, some of which may be favorable and some unfavorable. There may be variances from standards in direct materials costs, in direct labor costs, and in factory overhead costs. Illustrations and analyses of these variances for Ballard Company, a manufacturing enterprise, are presented in the following paragraphs. For illustrative purposes, it is assumed that only one type of direct material is used, that there is a single processing department, and that Product X is the only commodity manufactured by the enterprise. The standard costs for direct materials, direct labor, and factory overhead for a unit of Product X are as follows:

Direct materials:	
2 pounds at $1 per pound	$ 2.00
Direct labor:	
.4 hour at $16 per hour	6.40
Factory overhead:	
.4 hour at $8.40 per hour	3.36
Total per unit	$11.76

Direct Materials Cost Variance

Two major factors enter into the determination of standards for direct materials cost: (1) the quantity (usage) standard and (2) the price standard. If the actual quantity of direct materials used in producing a commodity differs from the standard quantity, there is a **quantity variance.** If the actual unit price of the materials differs from the standard price, there is a **price variance.** To illustrate, assume that the standard direct materials cost of producing 10,000 units of Product X and the direct materials cost actually incurred during June were as follows:

Actual:	20,600 pounds at $1.04	$21,424
Standard:	20,000 pounds at $1.00	20,000

The unfavorable variance of $1,424 resulted in part from an excess usage of 600 pounds of direct materials and in part from an excess cost of $.04 per pound. The analysis of the direct materials cost variance is as follows:

Direct Materials Cost Variance

Quantity variance:		
Actual quantity	20,600 pounds	
Standard quantity	20,000 pounds	
Variance—unfavorable	600 pounds × standard price, $1	$ 600
Price variance:		
Actual price	$1.04 per pound	
Standard price	1.00 per pound	
Variance—unfavorable	$ .04 per pound × actual quantity, 20,600	824
Total direct materials cost variance—unfavorable		$1,424

Direct Materials Quantity Variance. The direct materials quantity variance is the difference between the actual quantity used and the standard quantity, multiplied by the standard price per unit. If the standard quantity exceeds the actual quantity used, the variance is favorable. If the actual quantity of materials used exceeds the standard quantity, the variance is unfavorable, as shown for Ballard Company in the following illustration:

Direct Materials Quantity Variance

Direct Materials Quantity Variance = Actual Quantity Used − Standard Quantity × Standard Price per Unit

Quantity variance = (20,600 pounds − 20,000 pounds) × $1.00 per pound
Quantity variance = 600 pounds × $1.00 per pound
Quantity variance = $600 unfavorable

Direct Materials Price Variance. The direct materials price variance is the difference between the actual price per unit and the standard price per unit, multiplied by the actual quantity used. If the standard price per unit exceeds the actual price per unit, the variance is favorable. If the actual price per unit exceeds the standard price per unit, the variance is unfavorable, as shown for Ballard Company in the following illustration:

Direct Materials Price Variance

Direct Materials Price Variance = (Actual Price per Unit − Standard Price) × Actual Quantity Used

Price variance = ($1.04 per pound − $1.00 per pound) × 20,600 pounds
Price variance = $.04 per pound × 20,600 pounds
Price variance = $824 unfavorable

Reporting Direct Materials Cost Variance. The physical quantity and the dollar amount of the quantity variance should be reported to the factory superintendent and other personnel responsible for production. If excessive amounts of direct materials were used because of the malfunction of equipment or some other failure within the production department, those responsible should correct the situation. However, an unfavorable direct materials quantity variance is not necessarily the result of inefficiency within the production department. If the excess usage of 600 pounds of materials in the example above had been caused by inferior materials, the purchasing department should be held responsible.

The unit price and the total amount of the materials price variance should be reported to the purchasing department, which may or may not be able to control this variance. If materials of the same quality could have been purchased from another supplier at the standard price, the variance was controllable. On the other hand, if the variance resulted from a marketwide price increase, the variance was not subject to control.

Direct Labor Cost Variance

As in the case of direct materials, two major factors enter into the determination of standards for direct labor cost: (1) the time (usage or efficiency) standard, and (2) the rate (price or wage) standard. If the actual direct labor hours spent producing a product differ from the standard hours, there is a **time variance.** If the wage rate paid differs from the standard rate, there is a **rate variance.** The standard cost and the actual cost of direct labor in the production of 10,000 units of Product X during June are assumed to be as follows:

Actual:	3,950 hours at $16.40	$64,780
Standard:	4,000 hours at 16.00	64,000

The unfavorable direct labor variance of $780 is made up of a favorable time variance and an unfavorable rate variance, determined as follows:

Direct Labor Cost Variance

Time variance:		
Actual time...............	3,950 hours	
Standard time	4,000 hours	
Variance—favorable....	−50 hours × standard rate, $16.........	$ 800
Rate variance:		
Actual rate...............	$16.40 per hour	
Standard rate	16.00 per hour	
Variance—unfavorable..	$ .40 per hour × actual time, 3,950 hours.	1,580
Total direct labor cost variance—unfavorable	....	$ 780

Direct Labor Time Variance. The direct labor time variance is the difference between the actual hours worked and the standard hours, multiplied by the standard rate per hour. If the actual hours worked exceed the standard hours, the variance is unfavorable. If the actual hours worked are less than the standard hours, the variance is favorable, as shown for Ballard Company in the following illustration:

Direct Labor Time Variance

Direct Labor Time Variance	=	Actual Hours Worked − Standard Hours	×	Standard Rate per Hour
Time variance	=	(3,950 hours − 4,000 hours)	×	$16 per hour
Time variance	=	−50 hours	×	$16 per hour
Time variance	=	$800 favorable		

In the illustration, when the standard hours (4,000) are subtracted from the actual hours worked (3,950), the difference is "−50 hours." The minus sign indicates that the variance of 50 hours, or $800 (50 hours × $16), is favorable.

Direct Labor Rate Variance. The direct labor rate variance is the difference between the actual rate per hour and the standard rate per hour, multiplied by the actual hours worked. If the standard rate per hour exceeds the actual rate per hour, the variance is favorable. If the actual rate per hour exceeds the standard rate per hour, the variance is unfavorable, as shown for Ballard Company in the following illustration:

Direct Labor Rate Variance

Direct Labor Rate Variance	=	Actual Rate per Hour − Standard Rate	×	Actual Hours Worked
Rate variance	=	($16.40 per hour − $16.00 per hour)	×	3,950 hours
Rate variance	=	$.40 per hour	×	3,950 hours
Rate variance	=	$1,580 unfavorable		

Reporting Direct Labor Cost Variance. The control of direct labor cost is often in the hands of production supervisors. To aid them, periodic reports analyzing the cause of any direct labor variance may be prepared. A comparison of standard direct labor hours and actual direct labor hours will provide the basis for an investigation into the efficiency of direct labor (time variance). A comparison of the rates paid for direct labor with the standard rates highlights the efficiency of the supervisors or the personnel department in selecting the proper grade of direct labor for production (rate variance).

Factory Overhead Cost Variance

Some of the difficulties encountered in allocating factory overhead costs among products manufactured have been considered in Chapter 16. These difficulties stem from the great variety of costs that are included in factory overhead and their nature as indirect costs. For the same reasons, the procedures used in determining standards and variances for factory overhead cost are more complex than those used for direct materials cost and direct labor cost.

A flexible budget, described in Chapter 21, is used to establish the standard factory overhead rate and to aid in determining subsequent variations from standard. The standard rate is determined by dividing the standard factory overhead costs by the standard amount of productive activity, generally expressed in direct labor hours, direct labor cost, or machine hours. A flexible budget showing the standard factory overhead rate for a month is as follows:

Factory Overhead Cost Budget Indicating Standard Factory Overhead Rate

Ballard Company
Factory Overhead Cost Budget
For Month Ending June 30, 19--

Percent of productive capacity	80%	90%	100%	110%
Direct labor hours	4,000	4,500	5,000	5,500
Budgeted factory overhead:				
Variable cost:				
Indirect factory wages	$12,800	$14,400	$16,000	$17,600
Power and light	5,600	6,300	7,000	7,700
Indirect materials	3,200	3,600	4,000	4,400
Maintenance	2,400	2,700	3,000	3,300
Total variable cost	$24,000	$27,000	$30,000	$33,000
Fixed cost:				
Supervisory salaries	$ 5,500	$ 5,500	$ 5,500	$ 5,500
Depreciation of plant and equipment	4,500	4,500	4,500	4,500
Insurance and property taxes	2,000	2,000	2,000	2,000
Total fixed cost	$12,000	$12,000	$12,000	$12,000
Total factory overhead cost	$36,000	$39,000	$42,000	$45,000
Factory overhead rate per direct labor hour ($42,000 ÷ 5,000)			$8.40	

The standard factory overhead cost rate is determined on the basis of the projected factory overhead costs at 100% of productive capacity, where this level of capacity represents the general expectation of business activity under normal operating conditions. In the illustration, the standard factory overhead rate is $8.40 per direct labor hour. This rate can be subdivided into $6 per hour for variable factory overhead ($30,000 ÷ 5,000 hours) and $2.40 per hour for fixed factory overhead ($12,000 ÷ 5,000 hours).

Variances from standard for factory overhead cost result (1) from operating at a level above or below 100% of capacity and (2) from incurring a total amount of factory overhead cost greater or less than the amount budgeted for the level of operations achieved. The first factor results in the **volume variance,** which is a measure of the penalty of operating at less than 100% of productive capacity or the benefit from operating at a level above 100% of productive capacity. The second factor results in the **controllable variance,** which is the difference between the actual amount of factory overhead incurred and the amount of factory overhead budgeted for the level of production achieved during the period. To illustrate, assume that the actual cost and standard cost of factory overhead for Ballard Company's production of 10,000 units of Product X during June were as follows:

Actual:	Variable factory overhead	$24,600	
	Fixed factory overhead	12,000	$36,600
Standard:	4,000 hours at $8.40		33,600

The unfavorable factory overhead cost variance of $3,000 is made up of a volume variance and a controllable variance, determined as follows:

Volume variance:		
Productive capacity of 100%	5,000 hours	
Standard for amount produced	4,000 hours	
Productive capacity not used	1,000 hours	
Standard fixed factory overhead cost rate	×$2.40	
Variance—unfavorable		$2,400
Controllable variance:		
Actual factory overhead cost incurred	$36,600	
Budgeted factory overhead for standard product produced	36,000	
Variance—unfavorable		600
Total factory overhead cost variance—unfavorable		$3,000

Factory Overhead Cost Variance

Factory Overhead Volume Variance. The factory overhead volume variance is the difference between the productive capacity at 100% and the standard productive capacity, multiplied by the standard fixed factory overhead rate. If the standard capacity for the amount produced exceeds the productive capacity at 100%, the variance is favorable. If the productive capacity at 100% exceeds the standard capacity for the amount produced, the variance is unfavorable, as shown for Ballard Company in the following illustration:

Factory Overhead Volume Variance

Factory Overhead Volume Variance	=	Productive Capacity at 100% − Standard Capacity for Amount Produced	×	Standard Fixed Factory Overhead Rate
Volume variance	=	(5,000 hours − 4,000 hours)	×	$2.40 per hour
Volume variance	=	1,000 hours	×	$2.40 per hour
Volume variance	=	$2,400 unfavorable		

In the illustration, the unfavorable volume variance of $2,400 can be viewed as the cost of the available but unused productive capacity (1,000 hours). It should also be noted that the variable portion of the factory overhead cost rate was ignored in determining the volume variance. Variable factory overhead costs vary with the level of production. Thus, a curtailment of production should be accompanied by a comparable reduction of such costs. On the other hand, fixed factory overhead costs are not affected by changes in the volume of production. The fixed factory overhead costs represent the costs of providing the capacity for production, and the volume variance measures the amount of the fixed factory overhead cost due to the variance between capacity used and 100% of capacity.

The idle time that resulted in a volume variance may be due to such factors as failure to maintain an even flow of work, machine breakdowns or repairs causing work stoppages, and failure to obtain enough sales orders to keep the factory operating at full capacity. Management should determine the causes of the idle time and should take corrective action. A volume variance caused by failure of supervisors to maintain an even flow of work, for example, can be remedied. Volume variances caused by lack of sales orders may be corrected through increased advertising or other sales effort, or it may be advisable to develop other means of using the excess plant capacity.

Factory Overhead Controllable Variance. The factory overhead controllable variance is the difference between the actual factory overhead and the budgeted factory overhead for the standard amount produced. If the budgeted factory overhead for the standard amount produced exceeds the actual factory overhead, the variance is favorable. If the actual factory overhead exceeds the budgeted factory overhead for the standard amount produced, the variance is unfavorable. For Ballard Company, the standard direct labor hours for the amount produced during June was 4,000 (80% of productive capacity). Therefore, the factory overhead budgeted at this level of production, according to the budget on page 822, was $36,000. When this budgeted factory overhead is compared with the actual factory overhead, as shown in the following illustration for Ballard Company, an unfavorable variance results.

Factory Overhead Controllable Variance

Factory Overhead Controllable Variance	=	Actual Factory Overhead	−	Budgeted Factory Overhead for Standard Amount Produced
Controllable variance	=	$36,600	−	$36,000
Controllable variance	=	$600 unfavorable		

The amount and the direction of the controllable variance show the degree of efficiency in keeping the factory overhead costs within the limits established by the budget. Most of the controllable variance is related to the cost of the variable factory overhead items because generally there is little or no variation in the costs incurred for the fixed factory overhead items. Therefore, responsibility for the control of this variance generally rests with department supervisors.

Reporting Factory Overhead Cost Variance. The best means of presenting standard factory overhead cost variance data is through a factory overhead cost variance report. Such a report, illustrated as follows, can present both the controllable variance and the volume variance in a format that pinpoints the causes of the variances and aids in placing the responsibility for control.

Factory Overhead Cost Variance Report

Ballard Company
Factory Overhead Cost Variance Report
For Month Ended June 30, 19--

	Budget	Actual	Variances Favorable	Variances Unfavorable
Productive capacity for the month				5,000 hours
Actual production for the month				4,000 hours
Variable cost:				
Indirect factory wages	$12,800	$13,020		$ 220
Power and light	5,600	5,550	$50	
Indirect materials	3,200	3,630		430
Maintenance	2,400	2,400		
Total variable cost	$24,000	$24,600		
Fixed cost:				
Supervisory salaries	$ 5,500	$ 5,500		
Depreciation of plant and equipment	4,500	4,500		
Insurance and property taxes	2,000	2,000		
Total fixed cost	$12,000	$12,000		
Total factory overhead cost	$36,000	$36,600		
Total controllable variances			$50	$ 650
Net controllable variance—unfavorable				$ 600
Volume variance—unfavorable:				
Idle hours at the standard rate for fixed factory overhead—1,000 × $2.40				2,400
Total factory overhead cost variance—unfavorable				$3,000

The variance in many of the individual cost items in factory overhead can be subdivided into quantity and price variances, as were the variances in direct materials and direct labor. For example, the indirect factory wages variance may include both time and rate variances, and the indirect materials variance may be made up of both a quantity variance and a price variance.

The foregoing brief introduction to analysis of factory overhead cost variance suggests the many difficulties that may be encountered in actual practice. The rapid increase of automation in factory operations has been accompanied by increased attention to factory overhead costs. The use of predetermined standards and the analysis of variances from such standards provides management with the best possible means of establishing responsibility and controlling factory overhead costs.

STANDARDS IN THE ACCOUNTS

Although standard costs can be used solely as a statistical device apart from the ledger, it is generally considered preferable to incorporate them in the accounts. One approach, when this plan is used, is to identify the variances in the accounts at the time the manufacturing costs are recorded in the accounts. To illustrate, assume that Marin Corporation purchased, on account, 10,000 pounds of direct materials at $1 per pound, when the standard price was $.95 per pound. The entry to record the purchase and the unfavorable direct materials price variance is as follows:

Materials	9,500	
Direct Materials Price Variance	500	
Accounts Payable		10,000

The materials account is debited for the 10,000 pounds at the standard price of $.95 per pound. The unfavorable direct materials price variance is $500 [($1.00 actual price per pound − $.95 standard price per pound) × 10,000 pounds purchased] and is recorded by a debit to Direct Materials Price Variance. Accounts Payable is credited for the actual amount owed, $10,000 (10,000 pounds at $1 per pound). If the variance had been favorable, Direct Materials Price Variance would have been credited for the amount of the variance.

The accounts affected by the purchase of direct materials would appear as follows:

ACCOUNT MATERIALS — ACCOUNT NO.

Date	Item	Debit	Credit	Balance Debit	Balance Credit
	Purchased	9,500		9,500	

ACCOUNT DIRECT MATERIALS PRICE VARIANCE — ACCOUNT NO.

Date	Item	Debit	Credit	Balance Debit	Balance Credit
	Purchased	500		500	

ACCOUNT ACCOUNTS PAYABLE — ACCOUNT NO.

Date	Item	Debit	Credit	Balance Debit	Balance Credit
	Actual cost		10,000		10,000

Variances in other manufacturing costs are recorded in a manner similar to the direct materials price variance. For example, if Marin Corporation used 4,900 pounds of direct materials to produce a product with a standard of 5,000 pounds, the entry to record the variance and the materials used would be as follows:

Work in Process	4,750	
Materials		4,655
Direct Materials Quantity Variance		95

The work in process account is debited for the standard price of the standard amount of direct materials required, \$4,750 (5,000 pounds × \$.95). Materials is credited for the actual amount of materials used at the standard price, \$4,655 (4,900 pounds × \$.95). The favorable direct materials quantity variance of \$95 [(5,000 standard pounds − 4,900 actual pounds) × \$.95 standard price per pound] is credited to Direct Materials Quantity Variance. If the variance had been unfavorable, Direct Materials Quantity Variance would have been debited for the amount of the variance.

The accounts affected by the use of direct materials would appear as follows:

ACCOUNT MATERIALS — ACCOUNT NO.

Date		Item	Debit	Credit	Balance Debit	Balance Credit
		Purchased	9,500		9,500	
		Used		4,655	4,845	

ACCOUNT DIRECT MATERIALS QUANTITY VARIANCE — ACCOUNT NO.

Date		Item	Debit	Credit	Balance Debit	Balance Credit
		Used		95		95

ACCOUNT WORK IN PROCESS — ACCOUNT NO.

Date		Item	Debit	Credit	Balance Debit	Balance Credit
		Direct materials (actual)	4,750		4,750	

For Marin Corporation, the entries for direct labor, factory overhead, and other variances are recorded in a manner similar to the entries for direct materials. The work in process account is debited for the standard costs of direct labor and factory overhead as well as direct materials. Likewise, the work in process account is credited for the standard cost of the product completed and transferred to the finished goods account.

In a given period, it is possible to have both favorable and unfavorable variances. For example, if a favorable variance has been recorded, such as the direct materials quantity variance for Marin Corporation, and unfavorable direct materials quantity variances occur later in the period, the unfavorable variances would be recorded as debits in the direct materials quantity variance account. Analyses of this account may provide management with insights for controlling direct materials usage.

Another means of incorporating standards in the accounts is to debit the work in process account for the actual cost of direct materials, direct labor, and factory overhead entering into production. The same account is credited for the standard cost of the product completed and transferred to the finished goods account. The balance remaining in the work in process account is then made up of the ending inventory of work in process and the variances of actual cost from standard cost. In the following illustrative accounts for Ballard Company, there is assumed to be no ending inventory of work in process:

Standard Costs in Accounts

ACCOUNT WORK IN PROCESS — ACCOUNT NO.

Date		Item	Debit	Credit	Balance Debit	Balance Credit
June	30	Direct materials (actual)	21,424		21,424	
	30	Direct labor (actual)	64,780		86,204	
	30	Factory overhead (actual)	36,600		122,804	
	30	Units finished (standard)		117,600		
	30	Balance (variances)			5,204	

ACCOUNT FINISHED GOODS — ACCOUNT NO.

Date		Item	Debit	Credit	Balance Debit	Balance Credit
June	1	Inventory (standard)			88,800	
	30	Units finished (standard)	117,600		206,400	
	30	Units sold (standard)		113,500	92,900	

The balance in the work in process account is the sum of the variances between the standard and actual costs. In the illustration, the debit balance of $5,204 indicates a net unfavorable variance. If the balance had been a credit, it would have indicated a net favorable variance.

REPORTING VARIANCES ON THE INCOME STATEMENT

Variances from standard costs are usually not reported to stockholders and others outside of management. If standards are recorded in the accounts, however, it is customary to disclose the variances on income statements prepared for management. An interim monthly income statement prepared for Ballard Company's internal use is illustrated at the top of page 828.

At the end of the fiscal year, the variances from standard are usually transferred to the cost of goods sold account. However, if the variances are significant or if many of the products manufactured are still on hand, the variances should be allocated to the work in process, finished goods, and cost of goods sold accounts. The result of such an allocation is to convert these account balances from standard cost to actual cost.

REVISION OF STANDARDS

Standard costs should be continuously reviewed, and when they no longer represent the conditions that were present when the standards were set, they should be changed. Standards should not be revised merely because they differ from actual costs, but because they no longer reflect the conditions that they were intended to measure. For example, the direct labor cost stan-

Variances From Standards in Income Statement

Ballard Company
Income Statement
For Month Ended June 30, 19--

	Favorable	Unfavorable	
Sales			$185,400
Cost of goods sold—at standard			113,500
Gross profit—at standard			$ 71,900
Less variances from standard cost:			
Direct materials quantity		$ 600	
Direct materials price		824	
Direct labor time	$800		
Direct labor rate		1,580	
Factory overhead volume		2,400	
Factory overhead controllable		600	5,204
Gross profit			$ 66,696
Operating expenses:			
Selling expenses		$22,500	
General expenses		19,225	41,725
Income before income tax			$ 24,971

dard would not be revised simply because workers were unable to meet properly determined standards. On the other hand, standards should be revised when prices, product designs, labor rates, manufacturing methods, or other circumstances change to such an extent that the current standards no longer represent a useful measure of performance.

STANDARDS FOR NONMANUFACTURING EXPENSES

The use of standards for nonmanufacturing expenses is not as common as the use of standards for manufacturing costs. This difference in the use of standards is due in part to the fact that nonmanufacturing expenses are, in many cases, not nearly as large as the manufacturing costs. Another major reason is that while many manufacturing operations are repetitive and thus subject to the determination of a per unit cost of output, many nonmanufacturing expenses do not lend themselves to such measurement. In many cases, for example, the costs associated with an assembly line can be measured and related to a uniform product unit. On the other hand, the expenses associated with the work of the office manager are not easily related to any unit of output.

When nonmanufacturing activities are repetitive and generate a somewhat homogeneous product, the concept of standards can be applied. In these cases, the process of estimating and using standards can be similar to that described for a manufactured product. For example, standards can be applied to the work of office personnel who process sales orders, and a standard unit expense for processing a sales order could be determined. The variance between the actual cost of processing a sales order with the standard expense can then be evaluated by management and corrective action taken.

In practice, standards are not widely used for nonmanufacturing expenses. Instead, these expenses are generally controlled by the use of budgets and budget performance reports, as discussed in Chapter 21. However, the use of standards appears to be gaining in acceptance as more attention is being given to the nonmanufacturing expenses by the managerial accountant.

Chapter Review

KEY POINTS

1. The Nature and Objectives of Standards.
Accounting systems that use standards for each element of manufacturing cost entering into the finished product are called standard cost systems. Such systems enable management to determine how much a product should cost (standard), how much it does cost (actual), and the causes of any difference (variance) between the two. Standard costs thus serve as a device for measuring efficiency.

The setting of standards is both an art and a science. Although the standard-setting process varies among enterprises, it often requires the joint efforts of accountants, engineers, personnel administrators, and other management personnel. Standards that represent levels of performance that can be achieved only under perfect operating conditions, such as no idle time, no machine breakdowns, and no materials spoilage, are called theoretical standards or ideal standards. Standards that represent levels of operation that can be attained with reasonable effort are called currently attainable standards or normal standards.

2. Variances from Standards.
One of the primary purposes of a standard cost system is to facilitate control over costs by comparing actual costs with standard costs and thus determining variances. The two major variances for direct materials cost are the (1) direct materials quantity variance and (2) direct materials price variance. The two major variances for direct labor costs are the (1) direct labor time variance and (2) direct labor rate variance. The two major variances for factory overhead costs are the (1) factory overhead volume variance and (2) factory overhead controllable variance.

3. Standards in the Accounts.
It is generally preferable to incorporate standards in the accounts. One approach is to identify the variances in the accounts at the time the manufacturing costs are recorded in the accounts. Under this approach, the work in process account is debited for the standard costs of direct materials, direct labor, and factory overhead. Likewise, the work in process account is credited for the standard cost of the product completed and transferred to the finished goods account.

Another approach to incorporating standards in the accounts is to debit the work in process account for the actual costs of direct materials, direct labor, and factory overhead entering into production. The same account is then credited for the standard costs of the product completed and transferred to the finished goods account. Thus, the variances of actual costs from standard costs are isolated along with the ending inventory in the work in process account. At the end of the fiscal year, the variances are usually transferred to the cost of goods sold account.

4. Reporting Variances on the Income Statement.
Variances from standard costs are usually not reported to stockholders and others outside management. If standards are recorded in the accounts, however, it is customary to disclose the variances on interim income statements prepared for management. At the end of the year, the variances from standard are usually transferred to the cost of goods sold account. However, if the variances are significant or if many of the products manufactured are still on hand, the variances should be allocated to the work in process, finished goods, and cost of goods sold accounts.

5. Revision of Standards.
Established standards should be continually reviewed. If the standards no longer represent present conditions, they should be revised.

6. Standards for Nonmanufacturing Expenses.
The use of standards for nonmanufacturing expenses is not as common as the use of standards for manufacturing costs. When nonmanufacturing activities are repetitive and generate a somewhat homogeneous product, the concept of standards can be applied. In these cases, the process of estimating and using standards is similar to that described for a manufactured product.

KEY TERMS

standard cost systems 816
standard costs 816
variances 816
theoretical standards 817
currently attainable standards 818
direct materials quantity variance 819
direct materials price variance 819
direct labor time variance 820
direct labor rate variance 820
factory overhead volume variance 822
factory overhead controllable variance 822

SELF-EXAMINATION QUESTIONS

(Answers at End of Chapter)

1. The actual and standard direct materials costs for producing a specified quantity of product are as follows:

Actual:	51,000 pounds at $5.05	$257,550
Standard:	50,000 pounds at $5.00	250,000

The direct materials price variance is:

A. $2,500 unfavorable
B. $2,550 unfavorable
C. $7,550 unfavorable
D. none of the above

2. The actual and standard direct labor costs for producing a specified quantity of product are as follows:

Actual:	990 hours at $10.90..........	$10,791
Standard:	1,000 hours at $11.00..........	11,000

The direct labor cost time variance is:

A. $99 favorable
B. $99 unfavorable
C. $110 favorable
D. $110 unfavorable

3. The actual and standard factory overhead costs for producing a specified quantity of product are as follows:

Actual:	Variable factory overhead	$72,500	
	Fixed factory overhead	40,000	$112,500
Standard:	19,000 hours at $6		
	($4 variable and $2 fixed)		114,000

If 1,000 hours of productive capacity were unused, the factory overhead volume variance would be:

A. $1,500 favorable
B. $2,000 unfavorable
C. $4,000 unfavorable
D. none of the above

4. Based on the data in Question 3, the factory overhead controllable variance would be:

A. $3,500 favorable
B. $3,500 unfavorable
C. $1,500 favorable
D. none of the above

5. Variances from standard costs are reported on interim income statements as:

A. selling expenses
B. general expenses
C. other expenses
D. none of the above

ILLUSTRATIVE PROBLEM

Wolfram Inc. manufactures Product S for distribution nationally. The standard costs and actual costs for direct materials, direct labor, and factory overhead incurred for the manufacture of 1,000 units of Product S were as follows:

	Standard Costs	Actual Costs
Direct materials............	1,000 pounds at $75	980 pounds at $75.50
Direct labor................	12,500 hours at $9	12,600 hours at $8.95
Factory overhead	Rates per direct labor hour, based on 100% of capacity of 15,000 labor hours:	
	Variable cost, $3.50	$44,150 variable cost
	Fixed cost, $1.00	$15,000 fixed cost

Instructions:

1. Determine the quantity variance, price variance, and total direct materials cost variance for Product S.
2. Determine the time variance, rate variance, and total direct labor cost variance for Product S.
3. Determine the volume variance, controllable variance, and total factory overhead cost variance for Product S.

SOLUTION

(1) Direct Materials Cost Variance

Quantity Variance:		
Actual quantity	980 pounds	
Standard quantity	1,000 pounds	
Variance—favorable	20 pounds × standard price, $75	$1,500
Price Variance:		
Actual price	$75.50 per pound	
Standard price	75.00 per pound	
Variance—unfavorable	$ .50 per pound × actual quantity, 980	490
Total Direct Materials Cost Variance—favorable		$1,010

(2) Direct Labor Cost Variance

Time Variance:		
Actual time	12,600 hours	
Standard time	12,500 hours	
Variance—unfavorable	100 hours × standard rate, $9	$ 900
Rate Variance:		
Actual rate	$8.95	
Standard rate	9.00	
Variance—favorable	$ .05 per hour × actual time, 12,600	$ 630
Total Direct Labor Cost Variance—unfavorable		$ 270

(3) Factory Overhead Cost Variance

Volume Variance:		
Productive capacity of 100%	15,000 hours	
Standard for amount produced	12,500 hours	
Productive capacity not used	2,500 hours	
Standard fixed factory overhead cost rate	× $1	
Variance—unfavorable		$2,500
Controllable Variance:		
Actual factory overhead cost incurred	$59,150	
Budgeted factory overhead for 12,500 hrs.	58,750	
Variance—unfavorable		400
Total Factory Overhead Cost Variance—unfavorable		$2,900

Discussion Questions

22–1. What are the basic objectives in the use of standard costs?

22–2. (a) Describe theoretical (ideal) standards and discuss the possible impact of theoretical standards on worker performance. (b) Describe currently attainable (normal) standards and discuss the possible impact of currently attainable standards on worker performance.

22–3. How can standards be used by management to achieve control over costs?

22–4. As the term is used in reference to standard costs, what is a *variance*?

22–5. What is meant by reporting by the "principle of exceptions" as the term is used in reference to cost control?

22–6. (a) What are the two variances between actual cost and standard cost for direct materials? (b) Discuss some possible causes of these variances.

22–7. The materials cost variance report for Jachino Inc. indicates a large favorable materials price variance and a significant unfavorable materials quantity variance. What might have caused these offsetting variances?

22–8. (a) What are the two variances between actual cost and standard cost for direct labor? (b) Who generally has control over the direct labor cost?

22–9. A new assistant controller recently was heard to remark: "All the assembly workers in this plant are covered by union contracts, so there should be no labor variances." Was the controller's remark correct? Discuss.

22–10. (a) Describe the two variances between actual costs and standard costs for factory overhead. (b) What is a factory overhead cost variance report?

22–11. If variances are recorded in the accounts at the time the manufacturing costs are incurred, what does a credit balance in Direct Materials Price Variance represent?

22–12. If variances are recorded in the accounts at the time the manufacturing costs are incurred, what does a debit balance in Direct Materials Quantity Variance represent?

22–13. If standards are recorded in the accounts and Work in Process is debited for the actual manufacturing costs and credited for the standard cost of products produced, what does the balance in Work in Process represent?

22–14. Are variances from standard costs usually reported in financial statements issued to stockholders and others outside the firm?

22–15. Assuming that the variances from standards are not significant at the end of the period, to what account are they transferred?

22–16. How often should standards be revised?

22–17. Are standards for nonmanufacturing expenses as widely used as standards for manufacturing costs?

22–18. Real World Focus. Concrete Pipe & Products Co. Inc. manufactures concrete pipe in its operations in Richmond, Virginia. The primary materials used in producing concrete are cement, sand, and gravel. The costs for a batch of concrete weighing 13,250 pounds are as follows:

	Pounds per batch	Price per pound
Cement	2,350	$.03000
Sand	6,700	.00205
Gravel	4,200	.00270
	13,250	

Assuming 5% waste, compute the standard cost per pound for concrete. Use the following tabular headings for organizing the computations:

	Pounds per batch	Price per pound	Batch cost	5% waste	Total batch cost	Cost per pound
Cement...	2,350	$.03000				
Sand	6,700	.00205				
Gravel....	4,200	.00270				
	13,250					

Exercises

22–19. Direct materials variances. The following data relate to the direct materials cost for the production of 30,000 units of product:

Actual:	78,000 pounds at $1.82	$141,960
Standard:	75,000 pounds at 1.80	135,000

Determine the quantity variance, price variance, and total direct materials cost variance.

22–20. Standard direct materials cost per unit from variance data. The following data relating to direct materials cost for July of the current year are taken from the records of J. Ledbetter Company:

Quantity of direct materials used	16,000 pounds
Unit cost of direct materials	$2.50 per pound
Units of finished product manufactured	20,625 units
Standard direct materials per unit of finished product.......	.8 pounds
Direct materials quantity variance—favorable	$1,200
Direct materials price variance—unfavorable..............	$1,600

Determine the standard direct materials cost per unit of finished product, assuming that there was no inventory of work in process at either the beginning or the end of the month. Present your computations.

22–21. Direct labor variances. The following data relate to direct labor cost for the production of 15,000 units of product:

Actual:	42,500 hours at $15.80.........................	$671,500
Standard:	42,000 hours at $16.00.........................	672,000

Determine the time variance, rate variance, and total direct labor cost variance.

22–22. Factory overhead cost variances. The following data relate to factory overhead cost for the production of 40,000 units of product:

Actual:	Variable factory overhead.....................	$152,000
	Fixed factory overhead........................	120,000
Standard:	60,000 hours at $4...........................	240,000

If productive capacity of 100% was 80,000 hours and the factory overhead costs budgeted at the level of 60,000 standard hours was $270,000, determine the volume variance, controllable variance, and total factory overhead cost variance. The fixed factory overhead rate was $1.50 per hour.

22–23. Flexible budget. Blackmon Company prepared the following factory overhead cost budget for Department M for November of the current year, when the company expected to operate at 9,900 direct labor hours:

Variable cost:		
Indirect factory wages	$21,600	
Power and light	12,600	
Indirect materials	7,380	
Total variable cost		$41,580
Fixed cost:		
Supervisory salaries	$15,000	
Depreciation of plant and equipment	10,700	
Insurance and property taxes	4,000	
Total fixed cost		29,700
Total factory overhead cost		$71,280

Blackmon Company has decided to install a standard cost system and has determined that productive capacity is 11,000 direct labor hours. Prepare a flexible budget indicating production levels of 8,800, 9,900, and 11,000 direct labor hours and showing the standard factory overhead rate.

22–24. Entries for recording standards in accounts. Smith Manufacturing Company incorporates standards in the accounts and identifies variances at the time the manufacturing costs are incurred. Prepare entries to record the following transactions:

(a) Purchased 1,000 units of direct material W at $15.50 per unit. The standard price is $15 per unit.

(b) Used 400 units of direct material W in the process of manufacturing 140 units of finished product. Three units of material W are required, at standard, to produce a finished unit.

Problems

SPREADSHEET PROBLEM

22–25. Direct materials, direct labor, and factory overhead cost variance analysis. Standard costs and actual costs for direct materials, direct labor, and factory overhead incurred for the manufacture of 5,000 units of product were as follows:

	Standard Costs	Actual Costs
Direct materials	7,000 pounds at $12	7,200 pounds at $11.50
Direct labor	2,000 hours at $15	1,850 hours at $15.50
Factory overhead	Rates per direct labor, based on 100% of capacity of 2,500 labor hours:	
	Variable cost, $13.20	$28,000 variable cost
	Fixed cost, $8.00	$20,000 fixed cost

Instructions: Determine (a) the quantity variance, price variance, and total direct materials cost variance; (b) the time variance, rate variance, and total direct labor cost variance; and (c) the volume variance, controllable variance, and total factory overhead cost variance.

22–26. Standard factory overhead variance report. Hiram Company prepared the following factory overhead cost budget for Department F for April of the current year.

The company expected to operate the department at 100% of capacity of 15,000 direct labor hours.

Variable cost:		
Indirect factory wages	$25,000	
Power and light	14,600	
Indirect materials	6,400	
Total variable cost		$46,000
Fixed cost:		
Supervisory salaries	$18,000	
Depreciation of plant and equipment	10,000	
Insurance and property taxes	3,500	
Total fixed cost		31,500
Total factory overhead cost		$77,500

During April, the department operated at 12,750 direct labor hours, and the factory overhead costs incurred were: indirect factory wages, $22,100; power and light, $12,000; indirect materials, $6,000; supervisory salaries, $18,000; depreciation of plant and equipment, $10,000; and insurance and property taxes, $3,500.

Instructions: Prepare a standard factory overhead variance report for April. To be useful for cost control, the budgeted amounts should be based on 12,750 direct labor hours.

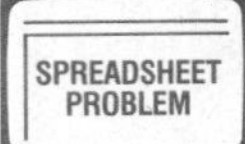

22–27. Flexible factory overhead cost budget and variance report. Yates Company prepared the following factory overhead cost budget for the Painting Department for October of the current year:

Yates Company
Factory Overhead Cost Budget—Painting Department
For Month Ending October 31, 19--

Direct labor hours:		
Productive capacity of 100%		20,000
Hours budgeted		16,000
Variable cost:		
Indirect factory wages	$24,000	
Indirect materials	9,600	
Power and light	4,800	
Total variable cost		$38,400
Fixed cost:		
Supervisory salaries	$18,000	
Indirect factory wages	12,400	
Depreciation of plant and equipment	7,500	
Insurance	6,200	
Power and light	4,100	
Property taxes	3,800	
Total fixed cost		52,000
Total factory overhead cost		$90,400

During October, the Painting Department was operated for 16,000 direct labor hours, and the following factory overhead costs were incurred:

Indirect factory wages	$38,000
Supervisory salaries	18,000
Indirect materials	9,400
Power and light	9,100
Depreciation of plant and equipment	7,500
Insurance	6,200
Property taxes	3,800
Total factory overhead cost incurred	$92,000

Instructions: (1) Prepare a flexible budget for October, indicating capacities of 14,000, 16,000, 18,000, and 20,000 direct labor hours and the determination of a standard factory overhead rate per direct labor hour.
(2) Prepare a standard factory overhead cost variance report for October.

22–28. Entries and standard cost variance analysis. Walters Inc. maintains perpetual inventory accounts for materials, work in process, and finished goods and uses a standard cost system based on the following data:

	Standard Cost per Unit
Direct materials: 4 kilograms at $1.25 per kg	$ 5
Direct labor: 3 hours at $15 per hour	45
Factory overhead: $1.00 per direct labor hour	3
Total	$53

There was no inventory of work in process at the beginning or end of January, the first month of the current fiscal year. The transactions relating to production completed during January are summarized as follows:

(a) Materials purchased on account, $75,600.
(b) Direct materials used, $36,400. The amount represented 28 000 kilograms at $1.30 per kilogram.
(c) Direct labor paid, $315,700. This amount represented 20,500 hours at $15.40 per hour. There were no accruals at either the beginning or the end of the period.
(d) Factory overhead incurred during the month was composed of depreciation on plant and equipment, $8,500; indirect labor, $7,400; insurance, $4,750; and miscellaneous factory costs, $4,150. The indirect labor and miscellaneous factory costs were paid during the period, and the insurance represents an expiration of prepaid insurance. Of the total factory overhead of $24,800, fixed costs amounted to $12,000 and variable costs were $12,800.
(e) Goods finished during the period, 6,900 units.

Instructions: (1) Prepare entries to record the transactions, assuming that the work in process account is debited for actual production costs and credited with standard costs for goods finished.
(2) Prepare a T account for Work in Process and post to the account, using the identifying letters as dates.
(3) Prepare schedules of variances for direct materials cost, direct labor cost, and factory overhead cost. Productive capacity for the plant is 30,000 direct labor hours.
(4) Total the amount of the standard cost variances and compare this total with the balance of the work in process account.

22–29. Income statement indicating standard cost variances. The following data were taken from the records of Watkins Company for May of the current year:

Cost of goods sold (at standard)	$390,000
Direct materials quantity variance—unfavorable	2,560
Direct materials price variance—favorable	1,320
Direct labor time variance—unfavorable	3,270
Direct labor rate variance—favorable	900
Factory overhead volume variance—unfavorable	10,000
Factory overhead controllable variance—favorable	1,600
General expenses	25,000
Sales	500,000
Selling expenses	42,000

Instructions: Prepare an income statement for presentation to management.

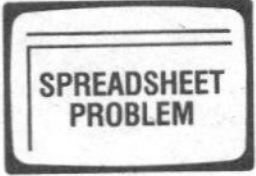

22–25A. Direct materials, direct labor, and factory overhead cost variance analysis. Standard costs and actual costs for direct materials, direct labor, and factory overhead incurred for the manufacture of 2,000 units of product were as follows:

	Standard Costs	Actual Costs
Direct materials	3,000 pounds at $8	3,100 pounds at $8.20
Direct labor	6,200 hours at $12	6,000 hours at $13.25
Factory overhead	Rates per direct labor hour, based on 100% of capacity of 8,000 labor hours:	
	Variable cost, $1.20	$8,200 variable cost
	Fixed cost, $3.50	$28,000 fixed cost

Instructions: Determine (a) the quantity variance, price variance, and total direct materials cost variance; (b) the time variance, rate variance, and total direct labor cost variance; and (c) the volume variance, controllable variance, and total factory overhead cost variance.

22–27A. Flexible factory overhead cost budget and variance report. Wooten Inc. prepared the following factory overhead cost budget for the Polishing Department for March of the current year:

Wooten Inc.
Factory Overhead Cost Budget—Polishing Department
For Month Ending March 31, 19--

Direct labor hours:		
Productive capacity of 100%		25,000
Hours budgeted		28,750
Variable cost:		
Indirect factory wages	$16,100	
Indirect materials	9,430	
Power and light	7,360	
Total variable cost		$32,890
Fixed cost:		
Supervisory salaries	$13,500	
Indirect factory wages	7,780	
Depreciation of plant and equipment	5,220	
Insurance	3,160	
Power and light	2,800	
Property taxes	1,940	
Total fixed cost		34,400
Total factory overhead cost		$67,290

During March, the Polishing Department was operated for 28,750 direct labor hours, and the following factory overhead costs were incurred:

Indirect factory wages	$25,780
Supervisory salaries	13,500
Power and light	10,000
Indirect materials	9,700
Depreciation of plant and equipment	5,220
Insurance	3,160
Property taxes	1,940
Total factory overhead cost incurred	$69,300

Instructions: (1) Prepare a flexible budget for March, indicating capacities of 17,500, 21,250, 25,000, and 28,750 direct labor hours and the determination of a standard factory overhead rate per direct labor hour.
(2) Prepare a standard factory overhead cost variance report for March.

22–28A. Entries and standard cost variance analysis. Duckworth Inc. maintains perpetual inventory accounts for materials, work in process, and finished goods and uses a standard cost system based on the following data:

	Standard Cost per Unit
Direct materials: 4 kilograms at $2.50 per kg	$10
Direct labor: 2 hours at $16.50 per hour	33
Factory overhead: $2.50 per direct labor hour	5
Total	$48

There was no inventory of work in process at the beginning or end of August, the first month of the current fiscal year. The transactions relating to production completed during August are summarized as follows:

(a) Materials purchased on account, $120,600.
(b) Direct materials used, $49,920. This represented 20 800 kilograms at $2.40 per kilogram.
(c) Direct labor paid, $169,320. This represented 10,200 hours at $16.60 per hour. There were no accruals at either the beginning or the end of the period.
(d) Factory overhead incurred during the month was composed of depreciation on plant and equipment, $13,700; indirect labor, $9,480; insurance, $2,400; and miscellaneous factory costs, $5,320. The indirect labor and miscellaneous factory costs were paid during the period, and the insurance represents an expiration of prepaid insurance. Of the total factory overhead of $30,900, fixed costs amounted to $18,000, and variable costs were $12,900.
(e) Goods finished during the period, 5,000 units.

Instructions: (1) Prepare entries to record the transactions, assuming that the work in process account is debited for actual production costs and credited with standard costs for goods finished.
(2) Prepare a T account for Work in Process and post to the account, using the identifying letters as dates.
(3) Prepare schedules of variances for direct materials cost, direct labor cost, and factory overhead cost. Productive capacity for the plant is 15,000 direct labor hours.
(4) Total the amount of the standard cost variances and compare this total with the balance of the work in process account.

Mini-Case 22

Pany Company operates a plant in Columbus, Iowa, where you have been assigned as the new cost analyst. To familiarize yourself with your new responsibilities, you have gathered the following cost variance data for May. During May, 34,000 units of product were manufactured.

Factory Overhead Cost Variance Report

Productive capacity for the month (100%) .... 20,000 hours
Standard for amount produced during month .... 17,000 hours

	Budget	Actual	Variances Favorable	Variances Unfavorable
Variable cost:				
Indirect factory wages	$27,200	$28,000		$ 800
Power and light	17,850	18,000		150
Indirect materials	10,200	10,000	$200	
Maintenance	4,250	4,000	250	
Total variable cost	$59,500	$60,000		
Fixed cost:				
Supervisory salaries	$20,000	$20,000		
Depreciation of plant and equipment	15,000	15,000		
Insurance and property taxes	3,000	3,000		
Total fixed cost	$38,000	$38,000		
Total factory overhead cost	$97,500	$98,000		
Total controllable variances			$450	$ 950
Net controllable variance—unfavorable				$ 500
Volume variance—unfavorable:				
Idle hours at the standard rate for fixed factory overhead − 3,000 × $1.90				5,700
Total factory overhead cost variance—unfavorable				$6,200

Direct Materials Cost Variance

Quantity variance:		
Actual quantity	41,000 pounds	
Standard quantity	40,800 pounds	
Variance—unfavorable	200 pounds × standard price, $2.25	$ 450
Price variance:		
Actual price	$2.40 per pound	
Standard price	2.25 per pound	
Variance—unfavorable	$ .15 per pound × actual quantity, 41,000	6,150
Total direct materials cost variance—unfavorable		$6,600

Direct Labor Cost Variance

Time variance:		
Actual time	17,500 hours	
Standard time	17,000 hours	
Variance—unfavorable	500 hours × standard rate, $12	$6,000
Rate variance:		
Actual rate	$11.50 per hour	
Standard rate	12.00 per hour	
Variance—favorable	$ .50 per hour × actual hours, 17,500	8,750
Total direct labor cost—favorable		$2,750

After your review of the May cost variance data, you arranged a meeting with the factory superintendent to discuss manufacturing operations. During this meeting, the factory superintendent made the following comment:

"Why do you have to compute a factory overhead volume variance? I don't have any control over the level of operations. I can only control costs for the level of production at which I am told to operate. Why not just eliminate the volume variance from the factory overhead cost variance report?"

You next discussed the direct materials variance analyses with the purchasing department manager, who made the following comment:

"The materials price variance is computed incorrectly. The computations should be actual price minus standard price times the standard quantity of materials for the amount produced. By multiplying the difference in the actual and standard price by the actual quantity of materials used, my department is being penalized for the inefficiencies of the production department."

During June, the standard costs were not changed, productive capacity was 20,000 hours, and the following data were taken from the records for the production of 36,000 units of product:

Quantity of direct materials used	43,500 pounds
Cost of direct materials	$2.42 per pound
Quantity of direct labor used	18,600 hours
Cost of direct labor	$11.60 per hour
Factory overhead costs:	
Indirect factory wages	$29,800
Supervisory salaries	20,000
Power and light	19,400
Depreciation of plant and equipment	15,000
Indirect materials	10,700
Maintenance	4,450
Insurance and property taxes	3,000

Instructions:

(1) Prepare a factory overhead cost variance report for June.
(2) Determine (a) the quantity variance, price variance, and total direct materials cost variance, and (b) the time variance, rate variance, and total direct labor cost variance for June.
(3) Based upon the cost variances for May and June, what areas of operations would you investigate and why?
(4) How would you respond to the comments of the factory superintendent?
(5) How would you respond to the comments of the manager of the purchasing department?

Answers to Self-Examination Questions

1. B The unfavorable direct materials price variance of $2,550 (answer B) is determined as follows:

Actual price	$5.05 per pound
Standard price	5.00 per pound
Price variance—unfavorable	$ .05 per pound

$.05 × 51,000 actual quantity = $2,550

2. C The favorable direct labor cost time variance of $110 (answer C) is determined as follows:

Actual time	990 hours
Standard time	1,000 hours
Time variance—favorable	10 hours
10 hours × $11 standard	$110

3. B The unfavorable factory overhead volume variance of $2,000 (answer B) is determined as follows:

Productive capacity not used	1,000 hours
Standard fixed factory overhead cost rate	× $2
Factory overhead volume variance—unfavorable	$2,000

4. A The favorable factory overhead controllable variance of $3,500 (answer A) is determined as follows:

Actual factory overhead cost incurred	$112,500
Budgeted factory overhead for standard product produced [(19,000 hours at $4 variable) + (20,000 hours at $2 fixed)]	116,000
Factory overhead controllable variance—favorable	$ 3,500

5. D Since variances from standard costs represent the differences between the standard cost of manufacturing a product and the actual costs incurred, the variances relate to the product. Therefore, they should be reported on interim income statements as an adjustment to gross profit—at standard.

Part Seven

Accounting for Decentralized Operations

23
Responsibility Accounting for Cost and Profit Centers

CHAPTER OBJECTIVES

Describe the nature of centralized and decentralized operations.

Describe the advantages and disadvantages of decentralized operations.

Describe the three types of decentralized operations.

Describe and illustrate responsibility accounting for cost centers.

Describe and illustrate responsibility accounting for profit centers.

In a small business, virtually all plans and decisions can be made by one individual. As a business grows or its operations become more diverse, it becomes difficult, if not impossible, for one individual to perform these functions. For example, the responsibility for planning and controlling operations is clear in a one-person real estate agency. If the agency expands by opening an office in a distant city, some of the authority and responsibility for planning and decision making in a given area of operations might be delegated to others. In other words, if centralized operations become unwieldy as a business grows, the need to delegate responsibility for portions of operations arises. This separation of a business into more manageable units is termed **decentralization.** In a decentralized business, an important function of the managerial accountant is to assist individual managers in evaluating and controlling their areas of responsibility.

A term frequently applied to the process of measuring and reporting operating data by areas of responsibility is **responsibility accounting.** Some of the concepts useful in responsibility accounting were presented in preceding chapters. For example, in discussing budgetary control of operations, the use of the master budget, budgets for various departments, and budget performance reports in controlling operations by areas of responsibility were discussed. In this chapter, the concept of responsibility accounting as it relates to two types of decentralized operations is described and illustrated. A third type of decentralization is discussed in Chapter 24.

CENTRALIZED AND DECENTRALIZED OPERATIONS

A completely centralized business organization is one in which all major planning and operating decisions are made by the top echelon of management. For example, a one-person, owner-manager-operated business is centralized because all plans and decisions are made by one person. In a small owner-manager-operated business, centralization may be desirable, since the owner-manager's close supervision ensures that the business will be operated in conformity with the manager's wishes and desires.

In a decentralized business organization, responsibility for planning and controlling operations is delegated among managers. These managers have the authority to make decisions without first seeking the approval of higher management. The level of decentralization varies significantly, and there is no one best level of decentralization for all businesses. In some companies, for example, plant managers have authority over all plant operations, including plant asset acquisitions and retirements. In other companies, a plant manager may only have authority for scheduling production and for controlling the costs of direct materials, direct labor, and factory overhead. The proper level of decentralization for a company depends on the advantages and disadvantages of decentralization as they apply to a company's specific, unique circumstances.

Advantages of Decentralization

As a business grows, it becomes more difficult for top management to maintain close daily contact with all operations. Hence, a top management that delegates authority in such circumstances has a better chance of sound decisions being made, and the managers closest to the operations may anticipate and react to operating information more quickly. In addition, as a company diversifies into a wide range of products and services, it becomes more difficult for top management to maintain operating expertise in all product lines and services. In such cases, decentralization allows managers to concentrate on acquiring expertise in their areas of responsibility. For example, in a company that maintains diversified operations in oil refining, banking, and the manufacture of office equipment, individual managers could become "expert" in the area of their responsibility.

The delegation of responsibility for day-to-day operations from top management to middle management frees top management to concentrate more on strategic planning. **Strategic planning** is the process of establishing long-term goals for an enterprise and developing plans to achieve these goals. For example, a goal to expand an enterprise's product line into new markets and a plan to finance this expansion through the issuance of long-term debt rather than additional common stock are examples of strategic planning decisions. As the business environment becomes more complex and as companies grow, strategic planning assumes an increasingly important role in the long-run success of a company.

Decentralized decision making provides excellent training for managers, which may be a factor in enabling a company to retain quality managers. Since the art of management can best be acquired through experience, the delegation of responsibility enables managers to acquire and develop managerial expertise early in their careers. Also, the operating personnel may be more creative in suggesting operating improvements, since personnel in a decentralized company tend to identify closely with the operations for which they are responsible.

The delegation of responsibility also serves as a positive reinforcement for managers, in that they may view such delegation as an indication of top management's confidence in their abilities. Thus, manager morale tends to increase because managers feel that they have more control over factors affecting their careers and their performance evaluation.

Disadvantages of Decentralization

The primary disadvantage of decentralized operations is that decisions made by one manager may affect other managers in such a way that the profitability of the entire company may suffer. For example, two managers competing in a common product market may engage in price cutting to win customers. However, the overall company profits are less than the profits that could have been if the price cutting had not occurred.

Other potential disadvantages of decentralized operations may be the duplication of various assets and costs in the operating divisions. For example, each manager of a product line might have a separate sales force and administrative office staff, but centralization of these personnel could save money. Likewise, the costs of gathering and processing operating information in a decentralized operation might be greater than if such information were gathered and processed centrally.

Thinking Small

One company that experienced positive results from decentralizing was NCR (formerly National Cash Register Co.), a Dayton-based multinational electronics and computer manufacturing corporation. In 1979, NCR was a troubled company. Management began to examine NCR's problems and to reevaluate the company's structure, which appeared to be inhibiting NCR'S ability to innovate and adapt. Additional background and the results of NCR's changes were reported in *Inc.*, as follows:

As part of this reevaluation process, NCR commissioned the McKinsey & Co. consulting group to study the attributes of a number of highly successful companies. The researchers looked at such corporations as Sperry, IBM, and Hewlett-Packard, to determine what they had done that might be applied to NCR.

Using this study as background, NCR developed a plan for restructuring itself. Analyzing the path of a product from idea to implementation, it discovered some obvious impediments. The development, production, and marketing of a new product involved three separate divisions. This cumbersome system created opportunities for false starts and misinterpreting . . . the market . . . It took a long time to get a product through this entire process, and sometimes products got lost in translation. . . .

So NCR proceeded to break up its product-management organization and move the parts to units that would develop, manufacture, and market products. In consulting jargon, this is called shifting from a "functional" to a "divisional" organization, and it has been done many times before in other industries. . . .

These changes transformed NCR Corp. from a highly centralized operation into a series of standalone [or decentralized] units. Today there is no requirement that one unit buy components from another NCR unit if it can find better or cheaper products outside the company. Moreover, based upon the nature of their products, the different divisions make their own decisions about how they want to structure themselves with regard to such activities as marketing.

Source: Eugene Linden, "Let a Thousand Flowers Bloom," *Inc.*, April, 1984, pp. 64–76.

TYPES OF DECENTRALIZED OPERATIONS

Decentralized operations can be classified by the scope of responsibility assigned and the decision making authority given to individual managers. The three common types of decentralized operations are referred to as cost centers, profit centers, and investment centers. Each of these types of decentralized operations is briefly described in the following paragraphs. Responsibility accounting for cost centers and profit centers is then discussed and illustrated in the remainder of this chapter, while responsibility accounting for investment centers is discussed in Chapter 24.

Cost Centers

In a **cost center,** the department or division manager has responsibility for the control of costs incurred and the authority to make decisions that affect these costs. For example, the marketing manager has responsibility for the costs of the Marketing Department, and the supervisor of the Power Department has responsibility for the costs incurred in providing power. The department manager does not make decisions concerning sales of the cost center's output, nor does the department manager have control over the plant assets available to the cost center.

Cost centers are the most widely used type of decentralization, because the organization and operation of most businesses allow for an easy identification of areas where managers can be assigned responsibility for and authority over costs. Cost centers may vary in size from a small department with a few employees to an entire manufacturing plant. In addition, cost centers may exist within other cost centers. For example, a manager of a manufacturing plant organized as a cost center may treat individual departments within the plant as separate cost centers, with the department managers reporting directly to the plant manager.

Profit Centers

In a **profit center,** the manager has the responsibility and the authority to make decisions that affect both costs and revenues (and thus profits) for the department or division. For example, a retail department store might decentralize its operations by product line. The manager of each product line would have responsibility for the cost of merchandise and decisions regarding revenues, such as the determination of sales prices. The manager of a profit center does not make decisions concerning the plant assets available to the center. For example, the manager of the Sporting Goods Department does not make the decision to expand the available floor space for that department.

Profit centers are widely used in businesses in which individual departments or divisions sell products or services to those outside the company. A partial organization chart for a department store decentralized by retail departments as profit centers is as follows:

Partial Organization Chart for Department Store with Profit Centers

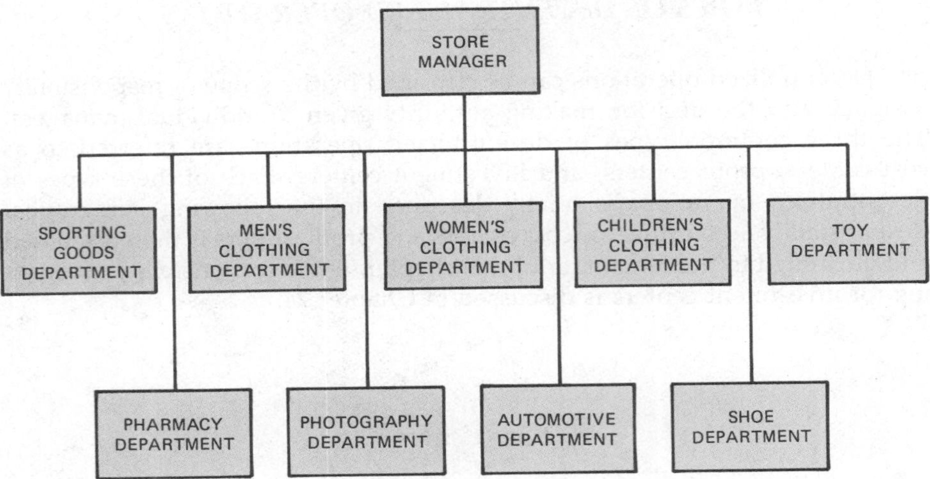

Occasionally, profit centers are established when the center's product or service is consumed entirely within the company. For example, a Repairs and Maintenance Department of a manufacturing plant could be treated as a profit center if its manager were allowed to bill other departments, such as the various production departments, for services rendered. Likewise, the Data Processing Department of a company might bill each of the company's administrative and operating units for computing services.

In a sense, a profit center may be viewed as a business within a business. While the primary concern of a cost center manager is the control of costs, the profit center is concerned with both revenues and costs.

Profit centers are often viewed as an excellent training assignment for new managers. For example, Lester B. Korn, Chairman and Chief Executive Officer of Korn/Ferry International, recently offered the following strategy for young executives enroute to top management positions:

> *Get Profit-Center Responsibility—Obtain a position where you can prove yourself as both a specialist with particular expertise and a generalist who can exercise leadership, authority, and inspire enthusiasm among colleagues and subordinates.*

Investment Centers

In an **investment center,** the manager has the responsibility and the authority to make decisions that affect not only costs and revenues, but also the plant assets available to the center. For example, a plant manager sets selling prices of products and establishes controls over costs. In addition, the plant manager could, within general constraints established by top management, expand production facilities through equipment acquisitions and retirements.

The manager of an investment center has more authority and responsibility than the manager of either a cost center or a profit center. The manager of an investment center occupies a position similar to that of a chief operating officer or president of a separate company. As such, an investment center manager is evaluated in much the same way as a manager of a separate company is evaluated.

Investment centers are widely used in highly diversified companies. A partial organizational chart for a diversified company with divisions organized as investment centers is as follows:

Partial Organization Chart for Diversified Company with Investment Centers

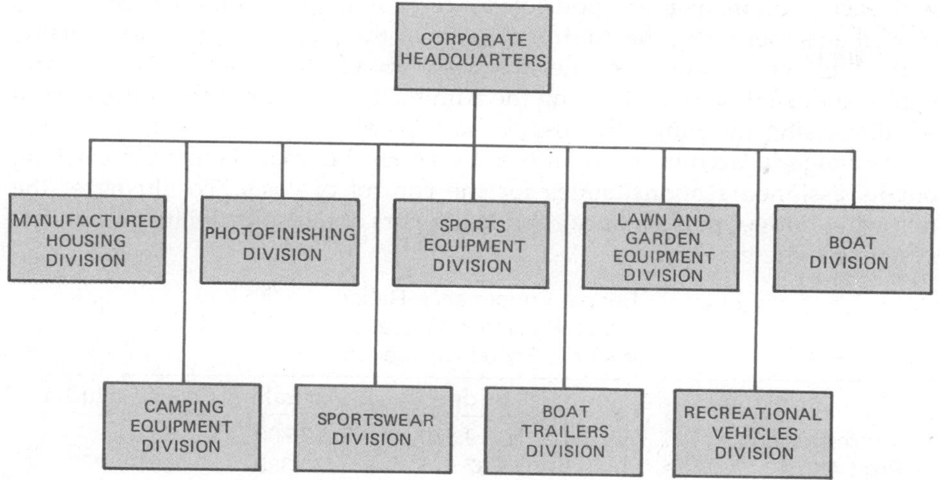

RESPONSIBILITY ACCOUNTING FOR COST CENTERS

Since managers of cost centers have responsibility for and authority to make decisions regarding costs, responsibility accounting for cost centers focuses on costs. The primary accounting tools appropriate for controlling and reporting costs are budgets and standard costs. Since budgets and standard costs were described and illustrated in Chapters 21 and 22, they will not be discussed in detail in this chapter. Instead, responsibility accounting for a cost center which uses budgeting to assist in the control of costs will be illustrated. The basic concepts of responsibility accounting, as illustrated, are equally applicable to cost centers that use standard cost systems to aid in cost control.

For purposes of illustration, assume that the responsibility for the manufacturing operations of an enterprise is as represented in the following organization chart:

Organization Chart Depicting Management Responsibility for Production

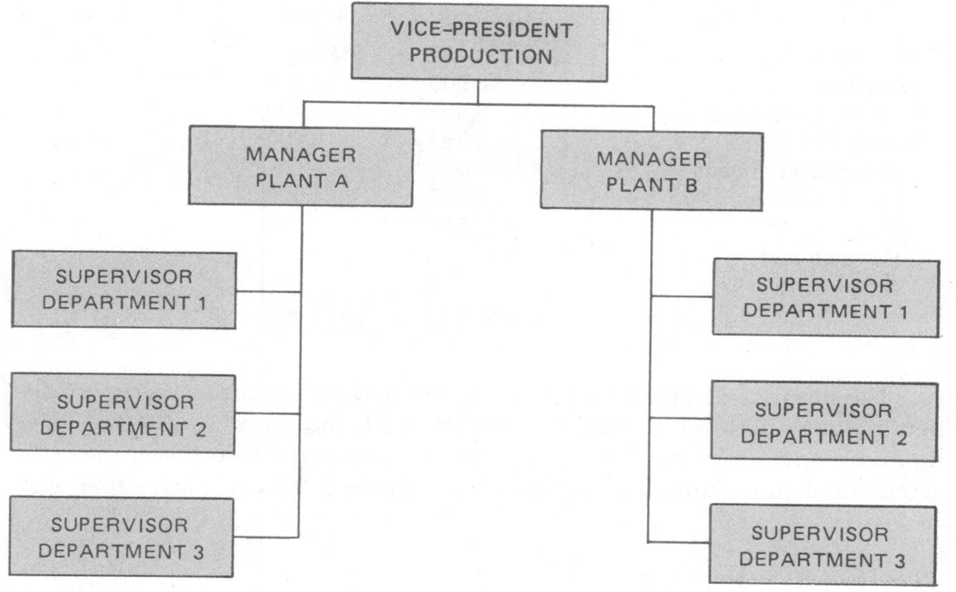

Within the organizational structure illustrated, there are three levels of cost centers. At the operating level, each department is a cost center, with the department supervisors responsible for controlling costs within their departments. At the next level of the organization, each plant is a cost center, with each plant manager responsible for controlling plant administrative costs as well as supervising the control of costs in the plant departments. Finally, at the top level, the office of the vice-president of production is a cost center with responsibility for controlling the administrative costs of the office as well as supervising the control of costs in each plant.

Managerial accounting reports aid each level of management in carrying out its assigned responsibilities for the control of costs. To illustrate, the following budget performance reports are part of a responsibility accounting system for the enterprise:

Responsibility Accounting

Budget Performance Report—
Vice-President, Operations
For Month Ended October 31, 19--

	Budget	Actual	Over	Under
Administration	$ 19,500	$ 19,700	$ 200	
Plant A	467,475	470,330	2,855	
Plant B	395,225	394,300		$925
	$882,200	$884,330	$3,055	$925

Budget Performance Report—Manager, Plant A
For Month Ended October 31, 19--

	Budget	Actual	Over	Under
Administration	$ 17,500	$ 17,350		$150
Department 1	109,725	111,280	$1,555	
Department 2	190,500	192,600	2,100	
Department 3	149,750	149,100		650
	$467,475	$470,330	$3,655	$800

Budget Performance Report—Supervisor,
Department 1-Plant A
For Month Ended October 31, 19--

	Budget	Actual	Over	Under
Factory wages	$ 58,100	$ 58,000		$100
Materials	32,500	34,225	$1,725	
Supervisory salaries	6,400	6,400		
Power and light	5,750	5,690		60
Depreciation of plant and equipment	4,000	4,000		
Maintenance	2,000	1,990		10
Insurance and property taxes	975	975		
	$109,725	$111,280	$1,725	$170

The amount of detail presented in the budget performance report depends upon the level of management to which the report is directed. The reports prepared for the department supervisors present details of the budgeted and actual manufacturing costs for their departments. Each supervisor can then concentrate on the individual items that resulted in significant variations. In the illustration, the budget performance report for Department 1-Plant A indicates a significant variation between the budget and actual amounts for materials. It is clear that supplemental reports providing detailed data on the causes of the variation would aid the supervisor in taking corrective action. One such report, a scrap report, is illustrated as follows. This report indicates the cause of a significant part of the variation.

Scrap Report

Materials Scrap Report—Department 1-Plant A
For Month Ended October 31, 19--

Material No.	Units Spoiled	Unit Cost	Dollar Loss	Remarks
A392	50	$3.10	$ 155.00	Machine malfunction
C417	76	.80	60.80	Inexperienced employee
G118	5	1.10	5.50	
J510	120	8.25	990.00	Substandard materials
K277	2	1.50	3.00	
P719	7	2.10	14.70	
V112	22	4.25	93.50	Machine malfunction
			$1,322.50	

The scrap report is one example of the type of supplemental report that can be provided to department supervisors. Other examples would include reports on factory wages and the cost of idle time.

The budget performance reports for the plant managers contain summarized data on the budgeted and actual costs for the departments under their jurisdiction. These reports enable them to identify the department supervisors responsible for significant variances. The report for the vice-president in charge of operations summarizes the data by plant. The persons responsible for plant operations can thus be held accountable for significant variations from predetermined objectives.

RESPONSIBILITY ACCOUNTING FOR PROFIT CENTERS

Since managers of profit centers have responsibility for and authority to make decisions regarding expenses and revenues, responsibility accounting reports for profit centers are normally in the form of income statements. These income statements for individual profit centers report expenses and revenues by departments through either gross profit or operating income. Alternatively, profit center income statements may include a breakdown of revenues and expenses by responsibility for their incurrence, and may identify contributions made by each department to overall company profit.

Since profit centers are widely used by merchandising enterprises, such as department stores, a merchandising enterprise is used as the basis for the following discussion and illustration of responsibility accounting for profit centers. Although the degree to which profit centers are used by a merchandising enterprise varies, profit centers are typically established for each major retail department. The enterprise in the illustrations, Garrison Company, has established Departments A and B as profit centers.

Gross Profit by Departments

To compute gross profit by departments, it is necessary to determine by departments each element entering into gross profit. An income statement showing gross profit by departments for Garrison Company appears below. For illustrative purposes, the operating expenses are shown in condensed form. Usually they would be listed in detail.

For a merchandising enterprise, the gross profit is one of the most significant figures in the income statement. Since the sales and the cost of goods sold are both controlled by departmental management, the reporting of gross profit by departments is useful in cost analysis and control. In addition, such reports aid management in directing its efforts toward obtaining a mix of sales that will maximize profits. For example, after studying the reports, management may decide to change sales or purchases policies to achieve a higher gross profit for each department. Caution must be exercised in the use of such reports to insure that proposed changes affecting gross profit do not have an adverse effect on net income. A change that increases gross profit could result in an even greater increase in operating expenses and thereby decrease net income.

Operating Income by Departments

Departmental reporting may be extended to operating income. In such cases, each department must be assigned not only the related revenues and

Income Statement Departmentalized Through Gross Profit

Garrison
Income
For Year Ended

	Department A		
Revenue from sales:			
Sales		$630,000	
Less sales returns and allowances		15,300	
Net sales			$614,700
Cost of goods sold:			
Inventories, January 1, 19--		$ 80,150	
Purchases	$334,550		
Less purchases discounts	6,200	328,350	
Goods available for sale		$408,500	
Less inventories, December 31, 19--		85,150	
Cost of goods sold			323,350
Gross profit			$291,350
Operating expenses:			
Selling expenses			
General expenses			
Total operating expenses			
Income from operations			
Other expense:			
Interest expense			
Income before income tax			
Income tax			
Net income			

the cost of goods sold (as in the preceding illustration), but also that part of operating expenses incurred for its benefit. Some of these expenses may be easily identified with the department benefited. For example, if each salesperson is restricted to a certain sales department, the sales salaries may be assigned to the proper departmental salary accounts each time the payroll is prepared. On the other hand, the salaries of company officers, executives, and office personnel are not identifiable with specific sales departments and must therefore be allocated if an equitable and reasonable basis for allocation exists.

When operating expenses are allocated, they should be apportioned to the respective departments as nearly as possible in accordance with the cost of services rendered to them. Determining the amount of an expense chargeable to each department is not always a simple matter. In the first place, it requires the exercise of judgment; and accountants of equal ability may well differ in their opinions as to the proper basis for the apportionment of operating expenses. Second, the cost of collecting data for use in making an apportionment must be kept within reasonable bounds. Consequently, information that is readily available and is substantially reliable may be used instead of more accurate information that would be more costly to collect.

To illustrate the apportionment of operating expenses, assume that Garrison Company extends its departmental reporting through income from operations. The company's operating expenses for the year and the methods used in apportioning them are presented in the paragraphs that follow.

Sales Salaries Expense is apportioned to the two departments according to the distributions shown in the payroll records. Of the $84,900 total in the

Company
Statement
December 31, 19--

Department B			Total		
	$270,000			$900,000	
	7,100			22,400	
		$262,900			$877,600
	$ 61,750			$141,900	
$200,350			$534,900		
2,400	197,950		8,600	526,300	
	$259,700			$668,200	
	78,950			164,100	
		180,750			504,100
		$ 82,150			$373,500
				$113,000	
				110,200	
					223,200
					$150,300
					2,500
					$147,800
					37,800
					$110,000

account, $54,000 is chargeable to Department A and $30,900 is chargeable to Department B.

Advertising Expense, covering billboard advertising and newspaper advertising, is apportioned according to the amount of advertising incurred for each department. The billboard advertising totaling $5,000 emphasizes the name and the location of the company. This expense is allocated on the basis of sales, the assumption being that this basis represents a fair allocation of billboard advertising to each department. Analysis of the newspaper space costing $14,000 indicates that 65% of the space was devoted to Department A and 35% to Department B. The computations of the apportionment of the total advertising expense are as follows:

	Total		*Department A*		*Department B*	
Sales—dollars	$900,000		$630,000		$270,000	
Sales—percent	100%		70%		30%	
Billboard advertising		$ 5,000		$ 3,500		$ 1,500
Newspaper space—percent	100%		65%		35%	
Newspaper advertising		14,000		9,100		4,900
Advertising expense		$19,000		$12,600		$6,400

Depreciation Expense—Store Equipment is apportioned according to the average cost of the equipment in each of the two departments. The computations for the apportionment of the depreciation expense are as follows:

	Total	*Department A*	*Department B*
Cost of store equipment:			
January 1	$28,300	$16,400	$11,900
December 31	31,700	19,600	12,100
Total	$60,000	$36,000	$24,000
Average	$30,000	$18,000	$12,000
Percent	100%	60%	40%
Depreciation expense	$ 4,400	$ 2,640	$ 1,760

Officers' Salaries Expense and **Office Salaries Expense** are apportioned on the basis of the relative amount of time devoted to each department by the officers and by the office personnel. Obviously, this can be only an approximation. The number of sales transactions may have some bearing on the matter, as may billing and collection procedures and other factors such as promotional campaigns that might vary from period to period. Of the total officers' salaries of $52,000 and office salaries of $17,600, it is estimated that 60%, or $31,200 and $10,560 respectively, is chargeable to Department A and that 40%, or $20,800 and $7,040 respectively, is chargeable to Department B.

Rent Expense and **Heating and Lighting Expense** are usually apportioned on the basis of floor space devoted to each department. In apportioning rent expense for a multistory building, differences in the value of the various floors and locations may be taken into account. For example, the space near the main entrance of a department store is more valuable than the same amount of floor space located far from the elevator on the sixth floor. For

Garrison Company, rent expense is apportioned on the basis of floor space used because there is no significant difference in the value of the floor areas used by each department. In allocating heating and lighting expense, it is assumed that the number of lights, their wattage, and the extent of use are uniform throughout the sales departments. If there are major variations and the total lighting expense is material, further analysis and separate apportionment may be advisable. The rent expense and the heating and lighting expense are apportioned as follows:

	Total	*Department A*	*Department B*
Floor space, square feet	160,000	104,000	56,000
Percent	100%	65%	35%
Rent expense	$15,400	$10,010	$ 5,390
Heating and lighting expense	$ 5,100	$ 3,315	$ 1,785

Property Tax Expense and **Insurance Expense** are related primarily to the cost of the inventories and the store equipment. Although the cost of these assets may differ from their assessed value for tax purposes and their value for insurance purposes, the cost is most readily available and is considered to be satisfactory as a basis for apportioning these expenses. The computations of the apportionment of the personal property tax expense and the insurance expense are as follows:

	Total	*Department A*	*Department B*
Inventories:			
January 1	$141,900	$ 80,150	$ 61,750
December 31	164,100	85,150	78,950
Total	$306,000	$165,300	$140,700
Average	$153,000	$ 82,650	$ 70,350
Average cost of store equipment (computed previously)	30,000	18,000	12,000
Total	$183,000	$100,650	$ 82,350
Percent	100%	55%	45%
Property tax expense	$ 6,800	$ 3,740	$ 3,060
Insurance expense	$ 3,900	$ 2,145	$ 1,755

Uncollectible Accounts Expense, Miscellaneous Selling Expense, and **Miscellaneous General Expense** are apportioned on the basis of sales. Although the uncollectible accounts expense may be apportioned on the basis of an analysis of accounts receivable written off, it is assumed that the expense is closely related to sales. The miscellaneous selling and general expenses are apportioned on the basis of sales, which are assumed to be a reasonable measure of the benefit to each department. The computation of the apportionment is as follows:

	Total	Department A	Department B
Sales	$900,000	$630,000	$270,000
Percent	100%	70%	30%
Uncollectible accounts expense	$ 4,600	$ 3,220	$ 1,380
Miscellaneous selling expense	$ 4,700	$ 3,290	$ 1,410
Miscellaneous general expense	$ 4,800	$ 3,360	$ 1,440

An income statement presenting income from operations by departments for Garrison Company appears below. The amounts for sales and the cost of goods sold are presented in condensed form. Details could be reported if desired, in the manner illustrated on pages 852 and 853.

Income Statement Departmentalized Through Income From Operations

Garrison
Income
For Year Ended

	Department A		
Net sales			$614,700
Cost of goods sold			323,350
Gross profit			$291,350
Operating expenses:			
Selling expenses:			
Sales salaries expense	$ 54,000		
Advertising expense	12,600		
Depreciation expense—store equipment	2,640		
Miscellaneous selling expense	3,290		
Total selling expenses		$ 72,530	
General expenses:			
Officers' salaries expense	$ 31,200		
Office salaries expense	10,560		
Rent expense	10,010		
Property tax expense	3,740		
Heating and lighting expense	3,315		
Uncollectible accounts expense	3,220		
Insurance expense	2,145		
Miscellaneous general expense	3,360		
Total general expenses		67,550	
Total operating expenses			140,080
Income (loss) from operations			$151,270
Other expense:			
Interest expense			
Income before income tax			
Income tax			
Net income			

In a recent research study, 85% of the companies surveyed indicated that they allocate some operating expenses to profit centers (departments), as discussed in the preceding section.[1] Caution should be used, however, in relying on income statements departmentalized through income from operations, since the use of arbitrary bases in allocating operating expenses is likely to yield incorrect amounts of departmental operating income. In addition, the reporting of operating income by departments may be misleading, since the departments are not independent operating units. The departments are segments of a business enterprise, and no single department of a business can earn an income independently. For these reasons, income statements of segmented businesses may follow a somewhat different format than the one illustrated below. The alternative format emphasizes the contribution of each department to overall company net income and to covering the overall opera-

Company
Statement
December 31, 19--

Department B			Total		
		$262,900			$877,600
		180,750			504,100
		$ 82,150			$373,500
$ 30,900			$ 84,900		
6,400			19,000		
1,760			4,400		
1,410			4,700		
	$ 40,470			$113,000	
$ 20,800			$ 52,000		
7,040			17,600		
5,390			15,400		
3,060			6,800		
1,785			5,100		
1,380			4,600		
1,755			3,900		
1,440			4,800		
	42,650			110,200	
		83,120			223,200
		$ (970)			$150,300
					2,500
					$147,800
					37,800
					$110,000

[1]James M. Fremgen and Shu S. Liao, *The Allocation of Corporate Indirect Costs* (New York: National Association of Accountants, 1981), pp. 33–34.

ting expenses incurred on behalf of the business. Income statements prepared in this alternative format are said to follow the **departmental margin** or **contribution margin** approach to responsibility accounting.

Prior to the preparation of an income statement in the departmental margin format, it is necessary to differentiate between operating expenses that are direct and those that are indirect. The two categories may be described in general terms as follows:

1. **Direct expense**—Operating expenses directly traceable to or incurred for the sole benefit of a specific department and usually subject to the control of the department manager.
2. **Indirect expense**—Operating expenses incurred for the entire enterprise as a unit and hence not subject to the control of individual department managers.

The details of departmental sales and the cost of goods sold are presented on the income statement in the usual manner. The direct expenses of each department are then deducted from the related departmental gross profit, yielding balances which are identified as the departmental margin. The remaining expenses, including the indirect operating expenses, are not departmentalized. They are reported separately below the total departmental margin.

An income statement in the departmental margin format for Garrison Company is presented on the following page. The basic revenue, cost, and expense data for the period are identical with those reported in the earlier illustration. The expenses identified as "direct" are sales salaries, property tax, uncollectible accounts, insurance, depreciation, and the newspaper advertising portion of advertising. The billboard portion of advertising, which is for the benefit of the business as a whole, as well as officers' and office salaries, and the remaining operating expenses, are identified as "indirect." Although a $970 net loss from operations is reported for Department B on page 857, a departmental margin of $38,395 is reported for the same department on the statement on page 859.

With departmental margin income statements, the manager of each department can be held responsible for operating expenses traceable to the department. A reduction in the direct expenses of a department will have a favorable effect on that department's contribution to the net income of the enterprise.

The departmental margin income statement may also be useful to management in making plans for future operations. For example, this type of analysis can be used when the discontinuance of a certain operation or department is being considered. If a specific department yields a departmental margin, it generally should be retained, even though the allocation of the indirect operating expenses would result in a net loss for that department. This observation is based upon the assumption that the department in question represents a relatively small segment of the enterprise. Its termination, therefore, would not cause any significant reduction in the amount of indirect expenses.

To illustrate the application of the departmental margin approach to long-range planning, assume that a business occupies a rented three-story building. If the enterprise is divided into twenty departments, each occupying

Garrison Company
Income Statement
For Year Ended December 31, 19--

	Department A		Department B		Total	
Net sales	......	$614,700	......	$262,900	......	$877,600
Cost of goods sold	......	323,350	......	180,750	......	504,100
Gross profit	......	$291,350	......	$ 82,150	......	$373,500
Direct departmental expenses:						
Sales salaries expense	$54,000	....	$30,900	....	$84,900	....
Advertising expense	9,100	....	4,900	....	14,000	....
Property tax expense	3,740	....	3,060	....	6,800	....
Uncollectible accounts expense	3,220	....	1,380	....	4,600	....
Depreciation expense—store equipment	2,640	....	1,760	....	4,400	....
Insurance expense	2,145	....	1,755	....	3,900	....
Total direct departmental expenses	......	74,845	......	43,755	......	118,600
Departmental margin	......	$216,505	......	$ 38,395	......	$254,900
Indirect expenses:						
Officers' salaries expense	......	....	......	....	$52,000	....
Office salaries expense	......	....	......	....	17,600	....
Rent expense	......	....	......	....	15,400	....
Heating and lighting expense	......	....	......	....	5,100	....
Advertising expense	......	....	......	....	5,000	....
Miscellaneous selling expense	......	....	......	....	4,700	....
Miscellaneous general expense	......	....	......	....	4,800	....
Total indirect expenses	......	....	......	....	......	104,600
Income from operations	......	....	......	....	......	$150,300
Other expense:						
Interest expense	......	....	......	....	......	
Income before income tax	......	....	......	....	......	
Income tax	......	....	......	....	......	
Net income	......	....	......	....	......	

Income Statement Departmentalized Through Departmental Margin

about the same amount of space, termination of the least profitable department would probably not cause any reduction in rent or other occupancy expenses. The space vacated would probably be absorbed by the remaining nineteen departments. On the other hand, if the enterprise were divided into three departments, each occupying approximately equal areas, the discontinuance of one could result in vacating an entire floor and significantly reducing occupancy expenses. When the departmental margin analysis is applied to problems of this type, consideration should be given to proposals for the use of the vacated space.

To further illustrate the departmental margin approach, assume that an enterprise with six departments has earned $70,000 before income tax during the past year, which is fairly typical of recent operations. Assume also that recent income statements, in which all operating expenses are allocated, indicate that Department F has been incurring losses, the net loss having amounted to $5,000 for the past year. Departmental margin analysis shows that, in spite of the losses, Department F should not be discontinued unless there is enough assurance that a proportionate increase in the gross profit of other departments or a decrease in indirect expenses can be effected. The following analysis, which is considerably condensed, shows a possible reduction of $10,000 in net income (the amount of the departmental margin for Department F) if Department F is discontinued.

Departmental Analysis—Discontinuance of Unprofitable Department

Proposal to Discontinue Department F
January 25, 19--

	Current Operations			Discontinuance of Department F
	Department F	Departments A–E	Total	
Sales	$100,000	$900,000	$1,000,000	$900,000
Cost of goods sold	70,000	540,000	610,000	540,000
Gross profit	$ 30,000	$360,000	$ 390,000	$360,000
Direct departmental expenses	20,000	210,000	230,000	210,000
Departmental margin	$ 10,000	$150,000	$ 160,000	$150,000
Indirect expenses			90,000	90,000
Income before income tax			$ 70,000	$ 60,000

In addition to departmental margin analysis, there are other factors that may need to be considered. For example, there may be problems regarding the displacement of sales personnel. Or customers attracted by the least profitable department may make large purchases in other departments, so that discontinuance of that department may adversely affect the sales of other departments.

The foregoing discussion of departmental income statements has suggested various ways in which income data may be made useful to management in making important policy decisions. Note that the format selected for the presentation of income data to management must be that which will be most useful for evaluating, controlling, and planning departmental operations.

Chapter Review

KEY POINTS

1. Centralized and Decentralized Operations.
Responsibility accounting is the process of measuring and reporting operating data to management by areas of responsibility. In a centralized business organization, all major planning and operating decisions are made by the top echelon of management. In a decentralized business organization, the responsibility for planning and controlling operations is delegated among managers who have authority to make decisions without first seeking the approval of higher management. In a decentralized organization, an important function of the managerial accountant is to assist managers in the process of measuring and reporting data by their areas of responsibility.

2. Types of Decentralized Operations.
Decentralized operations can be classified by the scope of the responsibility assigned and the decision-making authority given to individual managers. In a cost center, the manager has the responsibility for the control of costs incurred and the authority to make decisions that affect those costs. In a profit center, the manager has the responsibility and the authority to make decisions that affect both costs and revenue (and thus profits) for the department or division. In an investment center, the manager has the responsibility and the authority to make decisions that affect not only costs and revenues, but also the plant assets available to the center.

3. Responsibility Accounting for Cost Centers.
Since managers of cost centers have responsibility for and authority to make decisions regarding costs, responsibility accounting for cost centers focuses on costs. The primary accounting tools for planning and controlling costs for a cost center are budgets and standard costs.

4. Responsibility Accounting for Profit Centers.
Since managers of profit centers have responsibility for and authority to make decisions regarding expenses and revenues, responsibility accounting reports for profit centers are normally in the form of income statements. One such statement determines gross profit by departments. Departmental reporting may be extended to operating income, in which case the operating expenses incurred by the company must be allocated to the departments. These expenses are usually allocated on the basis of the departmental benefit received from the expenditure. Some accountants, who consider the allocation of operating expenses to be arbitrary, advocate the preparation of departmental income statements based upon departmental margin or contribution margin. Departmental margin is determined by deducting the direct expenses of each department from departmental gross profit. The remaining expenses are not allocated to a department, but are reported in the income statement separately below the total departmental margin.

KEY TERMS

decentralization 844	investment center 848
responsibility accounting 844	departmental margin 856
strategic planning 845	contribution margin 856
cost center 847	direct expense 858
profit center 847	indirect expense 858

SELF-EXAMINATION QUESTIONS

(Answers at End of Chapter)

1. When the manager has the responsibility and authority to make decisions that affect costs and revenues, but no responsibility for or authority over assets invested in the department, the department is referred to as:
   A. a cost center
   B. a profit center
   C. an investment center
   D. none of the above
2. Which of the following would be the most appropriate basis for allocating rent expense for use in arriving at operating income by departments?
   A. Departmental sales
   B. Physical space occupied
   C. Cost of inventory
   D. Time devoted to departments
3. The term used to describe the excess of departmental gross profit over direct departmental expenses is:
   A. income from operations
   B. net income
   C. departmental margin
   D. none of the above
4. On an income statement departmentalized through departmental margin, sales commissions expense would be reported as:
   A. a direct expense
   B. an indirect expense
   C. an other expense
   D. none of the above
5. On an income statement departmentalized through departmental margin, office salaries would be reported as:
   A. a direct expense
   B. an indirect expense
   C. an other expense
   D. none of the above

ILLUSTRATIVE PROBLEM

Perry Home Appliances operates two sales departments—Department F for freezers, and Department R for ranges and ovens. The following data were obtained from the ledger on April 30, the end of the current fiscal year:

Sales—Department F	350,000
Sales—Department R	650,000
Sales Returns and Allowances—Department F	6,400
Sales Returns and Allowances—Department R	10,200

Cost of Goods Sold — Department F	280,200
Cost of Goods Sold — Department R	526,800
Sales Salaries	43,400
Advertising Expense	10,800
Depreciation Expense — Store Equipment	8,800
Store Supplies Expense	1,250
Miscellaneous Selling Expense	800
Office Salaries	10,000
Rent Expense	9,800
Heating and Lighting Expense	4,000
Property Tax Expense	3,000
Insurance Expense	1,800
Uncollectible Accounts Expense	1,100
Miscellaneous General Expense	900
Interest Income	1,000
Income Tax	15,700

The bases to be used in apportioning expenses, together with other essential information, are as follows:

Sales salaries — payroll records: Department F, $17,300; Department R, $26,100

Advertising expense — usage: Department F, $4,000; Department R, $6,800.

Depreciation expense — average cost of equipment. Equipment balances at beginning of year: Department F, $17,000; Department R, $26,000. Equipment balances at end of year: Department F, $18,200; Department R, $26,800.

Store supplies expense — requisitions: Department F, $550; Department R, $700.

Office salaries — Department F, 30%; Department R, 70%.

Rent expense and heating and lighting expense — floor space: Department F, 1,200 sq. ft.; Department R, 2,800 sq. ft.

Property tax expense and insurance expense — average cost of equipment plus average cost of inventories. Inventory balances at the beginning of the year: Department F, $17,200; Department R, $36,000. Inventory balances at the end of the year: Department F, $17,600; Department R, $41,200.

Uncollectible accounts expense, miscellaneous selling expense, and miscellaneous general expense — volume of gross sales.

Instructions:

Prepare an income statement departmentalized through income from operations.

SOLUTION

PERRY HOME
Income
For Year Ended

	Department F		
Revenue from sales:			
Sales	....	$350,000	....
Less sales returns and allowances	....	6,400	....
Net sales	....	......	$343,600
Cost of goods sold	....	......	280,200
Gross profit	....	......	$ 63,400
Operating expenses:			
Selling expenses:			
Sales salaries	$17,300	......	....
Advertising expense	4,000	......	....
Depreciation expense—store equipment	3,520	......	....
Store supplies expense	550	......	....
Miscellaneous selling expense	280	......	....
Total selling expenses	....	$ 25,650	....
General expenses:			
Office salaries	$ 3,000	......	....
Rent expense	2,940	......	....
Heating and lighting expense	1,200	......	....
Property tax expense	1,050	......	....
Insurance expense	630	......	....
Uncollectible accounts expense	385	......	....
Miscellaneous general expense	315	......	....
Total general expenses	....	9,520	....
Total operating expenses	....	......	35,170
Income from operations	....	......	$ 28,230
Other income:			
Interest income	....	......	....
Income before income tax	....	......	....
Income tax	....	......	....
Net income	....	......	....

APPLIANCES
Statement
April 30, 19--

Department R			Total		
....	$650,000	....	......	$1,000,000	......
....	10,200	....	......	16,600	......
....	......	$639,800	......	....	$983,400
....	......	526,800	......	....	807,000
....	......	$113,000	......	....	$176,400
$26,100	......	....	$43,400	....	......
6,800	......	....	10,800	....	......
5,280	......	....	8,800	....	......
700	......	....	1,250	....	......
520	......	....	800	....	......
....	$ 39,400	....	......	$ 65,050	......
$ 7,000	......	....	$10,000	....	......
6,860	......	....	9,800	....	......
2,800	......	....	4,000	....	......
1,950	......	....	3,000	....	......
1,170	......	....	1,800	....	......
715	......	....	1,100	....	......
585	......	....	900	....	......
....	21,080	....	......	30,600	......
....	......	60,480	......	....	95,650
....	......	$ 52,520	......	....	$ 80,750
....	......	....	......	....	1,000
....	......	....	......	....	$ 81,750
....	......	....	......	....	15,700
....	......	....	......	....	$ 66,050

Discussion Questions

23–1. What is responsibility accounting?

23–2. What is a decentralized business organization?

23–3. Name three common types of responsibility centers for decentralized operations.

23–4. Differentiate between a cost center and a profit center.

23–5. Differentiate between a profit center and an investment center.

23–6. In what major respect would budget performance reports prepared for the use of plant managers of a manufacturing enterprise with cost centers differ from those prepared for the use of the various department supervisors who report to the plant managers?

23–7. The newly appointed manager of the Appliance Department in a department store is studying the income statements presenting gross profit by departments in an attempt to adjust operations to achieve the highest possible gross profit for the department. (a) Suggest ways in which an income statement departmentalized through gross profit can be used in achieving this goal. (b) Suggest reasons why caution must be exercised in using such statements.

23–8. Describe the underlying principle of apportionment of operating expenses to departments for income statements departmentalized through income from operations.

23–9. For each of the following types of expenses, select the allocation basis listed that is most appropriate for use in arriving at operating income by departments.

Expense:	Basis of allocation:
(a) Property tax expense	(1) Cost of inventory and equipment
(b) Sales salaries	(2) Departmental sales
(c) Rent expense	(3) Time devoted to departments
(d) Advertising expense	(4) Physical space occupied

23–10. Describe an appropriate basis for apportioning Officers' Salaries Expense among departments for purposes of the income statement departmentalized through income from operations.

23–11. Differentiate between a direct and an indirect operating expense.

23–12. Indicate whether each of the following operating expenses incurred by a department store is a direct or an indirect expense:

(a) Uncollectible accounts expense
(b) General manager's salary
(c) Depreciation of store equipment
(d) Insurance expense on building
(e) Sales commissions
(f) Heating and lighting expense

23–13. What term is applied to the dollar amount representing the excess of departmental gross profit over direct departmental expenses?

23–14. Recent income statements departmentalized through income from operations report operating losses for Department J, a relatively minor segment of the business. Management studies indicate that discontinuance of Department J would not affect sales of other departments or the volume of indirect expenses. Under what circumstances would the discontinuance of Department J result in a decrease of net income of the enterprise?

23–15. A portion of an income statement in condensed form, departmentalized through departmental margin for the year just ended, is as follows:

	Department 9
Net sales	$135,750
Cost of goods sold	109,500
Gross profit	$ 26,250
Direct expenses	30,000
Departmental margin	$ (3,750)

It is believed that the discontinuance of Department 9 would not affect the sales of the other departments nor reduce the indirect expenses of the enterprise. Based on this information, what would have been the effect on the income from operations of the enterprise if Department 9 had been discontinued prior to the year just ended?

23–16. Real World Focus. Many business enterprises maintain a computer information system. In such systems, there are three types of costs: systems development costs, operating costs, and software maintenance costs. Systems development costs include feasibility analysis, design, testing, and training costs. Operating costs are the expenses incurred in the day-to-day operation of the data processing facility. They include the use of hardware, software, and telecommunications resources. Software maintenance costs include the costs of assuring that all valid transactions are processed properly, and that new procedures are designed, tested, and used.

For purposes of allocating information system costs to user departments, which allocation base — labor time or machine processing time — would be most appropriate for each type of information system cost?

Exercises

23–17. Budget performance report. The budget for Department P of Plant 11 for the current month ended April 30 is as follows:

Direct materials	$140,000
Direct labor	157,500
Power and light	51,000
Supervisory salaries	36,000
Indirect materials	7,000
Indirect factory wages	10,500
Depreciation of plant and equipment	21,300
Maintenance	19,300
Insurance and property taxes	12,000

During April, the costs incurred in Department P of Plant 11 were: direct materials, $145,130; direct labor, $158,200; power and light, $50,400; supervisory salaries, $36,000; indirect materials, $7,020; indirect factory wages, $10,550; depreciation of plant and equipment, $21,300; maintenance, $19,180; insurance and property taxes, $12,000. (a) Prepare a budget performance report for the supervisor of Department P, Plant 11, for the month of April. (b) For what significant variations might the supervisor be expected to request supplemental reports?

23–18. Idle time report. The chief accountant of Allen Company prepares weekly reports of idleness of direct labor employees. These reports for the plant manager classify the idle time by departments. Idle time data for the week ended June 11 of the current year are as follows:

Department	Standard Hours	Actual Hours
A	5,200	4,940
B	3,700	3,700
C	4,100	4,018
D	2,000	1,880

The hourly direct labor rates are $22, $19, $24, and $16 respectively for Departments A through D. The idleness was caused by a machine breakdown in Department A, a materials shortage in Department C, and a lack of sales orders in Department D. Prepare an idle time report, classified by departments, for the week ended June 11. Use the following columnar headings for the report:

	Production			Idle Time		
Dept.	Standard Hours	Actual Hours	Percentage of Standard	Hours	Cost of Idle Time	Remarks

23–19. Apportionment of rent expense to departments. Hobbs Company occupies a two-story building. The departments and the floor space occupied by each department are as follows:

Receiving and Storage	basement	1,800 sq. ft.
Department 1	basement	4,200
Department 2	first floor	3,500
Department 3	first floor	6,500
Department 4	second floor	1,000
Department 5	second floor	1,600
Department 6	second floor	1,400

The building is leased at an annual rental of $100,000, allocated to the floors as follows: basement, 30%; first floor, 50%; second floor, 20%. Determine the amount of rent to be apportioned to each department.

23–20. Apportionment of depreciation and property tax expense to departments. In income statements prepared for Beeman Company, depreciation expense on equipment is apportioned on the basis of the average cost of the equipment, and property tax expense is apportioned on the basis of the combined total of the average cost of the equipment and the average cost of the inventories. Depreciation expense on equipment amounted to $150,000, and property tax expense amounted to $30,000 for the year. Determine the apportionment of the depreciation expense and the property tax expense, based on the following data:

	Average Cost	
Departments	Equipment	Inventories
Service:		
A	$ 360,000	
B	240,000	
Sales:		
X	720,000	$360,000
Y	480,000	120,000
Z	600,000	120,000
Total	$2,400,000	$600,000

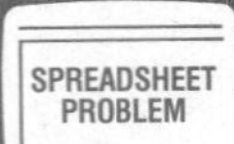

23–21. Departmental income statement. The following data were summarized from the accounting records for Crow Company for the current year ended October 31:

Cost of goods sold:	
Department E	$166,800
Department F	237,000
Direct expenses:	
Department E	88,000
Department F	119,200
Income tax	38,400
Indirect expenses	76,400
Interest Income	16,000

Net sales:	
Department E	328,400
Department F	466,200

Prepare an income statement departmentalized through departmental margin.

23–22. Decision on discontinuance of department. A portion of an income statement in condensed form, departmentalized through loss from operations for the year just ended, is as follows:

	Department C
Net sales	$271,200
Cost of goods sold	218,700
Gross profit	$ 52,500
Operating expenses	64,000
Loss from operations	$(11,500)

The operating expenses of Dept. C include $20,000 for indirect expenses. It is believed that the discontinuance of Department C would not affect the sales of the other departments nor reduce the indirect expenses of the enterprise. Based on this information, determine the increase or decrease in income from operations of the enterprise if Department C had been discontinued prior to the year just ended.

Problems

If the working papers correlating with the textbook are not used, omit Problem 23–23.

23–23. Budget performance reports. The organization chart for the manufacturing operations of Hubble Inc. is presented in the working papers, along with the completed budget performance reports for the Machine Shop and Assembly Departments of Plant 2. Partially completed budget performance reports for the Painting Department of Plant 2 and the vice-president in charge of operations are also presented.

Instructions: (1) Complete the budget performance report for the supervisor of the Painting Department of Plant 2.

(2) Prepare a budget performance report for the use of the manager of Plant 2, detailing the relevant data from the three departments in the plant. Assume that the budgeted and actual administration expenses for the plant were $22,600 and $23,850, respectively.

(3) Complete the budget performance report for the vice-president in charge of operations.

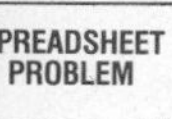

23–24. Departmental income statement through income from operations. Waller Appliances operates two sales departments—Department S for small appliances, such as radios and televisions, and Department L for large appliances, such as refrigerators and washing machines. The following data were obtained from the ledger on October 31, the end of the current fiscal year:

Sales—Department S	280,000
Sales—Department L	520,000
Sales Returns and Allowances—Department S	2,800
Sales Returns and Allowances—Department L	4,200
Cost of Goods Sold—Department S	171,360
Cost of Goods Sold—Department L	344,640
Sales Salaries Expense	33,900
Advertising Expense	12,090
Depreciation Expense—Store Equipment	6,200

Store Supplies Expense	1,620
Miscellaneous Selling Expense	2,600
Office Salaries Expense	30,000
Rent Expense	12,000
Heating and Lighting Expense	10,200
Property Tax Expense	3,800
Insurance Expense	1,800
Uncollectible Accounts Expense	1,500
Miscellaneous General Expense	1,700
Interest Expense	1,800
Income Tax	46,500

Inventories at the beginning of the year: Department S, $15,600; Department L, $49,400. Inventories at the end of the year: Department S, $12,240; Department L, $42,760.

The bases to be used in apportioning expenses, together with other essential information, are as follows:

Sales salaries expense—payroll records: Department S, $11,800; Department L, $22,100.
Advertising expense—usage: Department S, $4,250; Department L, $7,840.
Depreciation expense—average cost of equipment. Equipment balances at beginning of year: Department S, $19,360; Department L, $29,320. Equipment balances at end of year: Department S, $22,240; Department L, $33,080.
Store supplies expense—requisitions: Department S, $580; Department L, $1,040.
Office salaries expense—Department S, 32%; Department L, 68%.
Rent expense and heating and lighting expense—floor space: Department S, 4,200 sq. ft.; Department L, 10,800 sq. ft.
Property tax expense and insurance expense—average cost of equipment plus average cost of inventories.
Uncollectible accounts expense, miscellaneous selling expense, and miscellaneous general expense—volume of gross sales.

Instructions: Prepare an income statement departmentalized through income from operations.

23–25. Decision on discontinuance of department. Wood-Cutler Company is considering discontinuance of one of its ten departments. If operations in Department 4 are discontinued, it is estimated that the indirect operating expenses and the level of operations in the other departments will not be affected.

Data from the income statement for the past year ended December 31, which is considered to be a typical year, are as follows:

	Department 4		Other Departments	
Sales		$61,500		$995,500
Cost of goods sold		40,000		603,100
Gross profit		$21,500		$392,400
Operating expenses:				
Direct expenses	$18,400		$208,000	
Indirect expenses	9,500	27,900	114,000	322,000
Income (loss) before income tax		$(6,400)		$ 70,400

Instructions: (1) Prepare an estimated income statement for the current year ending December 31, assuming the discontinuance of Department 4.
(2) On the basis of the data presented, would it be advisable to retain Department 4?

23–26. Departmental income statement through departmental margin. Coastland Fashions has 16 departments. Those with the least sales volume are Department G and Department K, which were established about eighteen months ago on a trial basis. The board of directors believes that it is now time to consider the retention or the termination of these two departments. The following adjusted trial balance as of August 31, the end of the first month of the current fiscal year, is severely condensed. August is considered to be a typical month. The income tax accrual has no bearing on the decision and is excluded from consideration.

Coastland Fashions
Trial Balance
August 31, 19--

Current Assets	228,700	
Plant Assets	792,900	
Accumulated Depreciation—Plant Assets		218,600
Current Liabilities		150,100
Common Stock		250,000
Retained Earnings		403,505
Cash Dividends	50,000	
Sales—Department G		37,500
Sales—Department K		26,900
Sales—Other Departments		998,900
Cost of Goods Sold—Department G	26,125	
Cost of Goods Sold—Department K	20,480	
Cost of Goods Sold—Other Departments	619,160	
Direct Expenses—Department G	8,125	
Direct Expenses—Department K	7,490	
Direct Expenses—Other Departments	227,665	
Indirect Expenses	94,860	
Interest Expense	10,000	
	2,085,505	2,085,505

Instructions: (1) Prepare an income statement for August, departmentalized through departmental margin.

(2) State your recommendations concerning the retention of Departments G and K, giving reasons.

23–27. Departmental income statement through departmental margin. Wilson Corporation consists of two departments, J and M. The bases to be used in apportioning expenses between the two departments, together with other essential data, are as follows:

Sales salaries and commissions expense—basic salary plus 5% of sales. Basic salaries for Department J, $40,800; Department M, $18,200.

Advertising expense for brochures—usage within each department advertising specific products: Department J, $9,400; Department M, $4,350.

Depreciation expense—average cost of store equipment: Department J, $63,800, Department M, $46,200.

Insurance expense—average cost of store equipment plus average cost of inventories. Average cost of inventories was $49,950 for Department J and $15,050 for Department M.

Uncollectible accounts expense—.4% of sales. Departmental managers are responsible for the granting of credit on the sales made by their respective departments.

The following data are obtained from the ledger on May 31, the end of the current fiscal year:

Sales—Department J	550,000
Sales—Department M	220,000

Cost of Goods Sold — Department J	357,500	
Cost of Goods Sold — Department M	145,200	
Sales Salaries and Commissions Expense	97,500	
Advertising Expense	13,750	
Depreciation Expense — Store Equipment	9,500	
Miscellaneous Selling Expense	1,520	
Administrative Salaries Expense	32,800	
Rent Expense	18,000	
Utilities Expense	11,200	
Insurance Expense	4,800	
Uncollectible Accounts Expense	3,080	
Miscellaneous General Expense	720	
Interest Income		5,000
Income Tax	24,200	

Instructions: (1) Prepare an income statement departmentalized through departmental margin.
(2) Determine the rate of gross profit for each department.
(3) Determine the rate of departmental margin to sales for each department.

ALTERNATE PROBLEMS

If the working papers correlating with the textbook are not used, omit Problem 23–23A.

23–23A. Budget performance reports. The organization chart for the manufacturing operations of Hubble Inc. is presented in the working papers, along with the completed budget performance reports for the Machine Shop and Assembly Departments of Plant 2. Partially completed budget performance reports for the Painting Department of Plant 2 and the vice-president in charge of operations are also presented.

Instructions: (1) Complete the budget performance report for the supervisor of the Painting Department of Plant 2.
(2) Prepare a budget performance report for the use of the manager of Plant 2, detailing the relevant data from the three departments in the plant. Assume that the budgeted and actual administration expenses for the plant were $15,800 and $14,300, respectively.
(3) Complete the budget performance report for the vice-president in charge of operations.

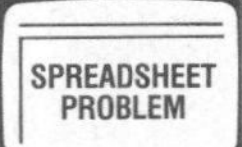

23–24A. Departmental income statement through income from operations. Sparkman Co. operates two sales departments — Department S for sporting goods and Department T for camping equipment. The following data were obtained from the ledger on June 30, the end of the current fiscal year.

Sales — Department S	280,000
Sales — Department T	120,000
Sales Returns and Allowances — Department S	2,500
Sales Returns and Allowances — Department T	1,700
Cost of Goods Sold — Department S	134,030
Cost of Goods Sold — Department T	68,770
Sales Salaries Expense	70,000
Advertising Expense	11,000
Depreciation Expense — Store Equipment	5,500
Store Supplies Expense	3,600
Miscellaneous Selling Expense	3,000
Office Salaries Expense	30,000
Rent Expense	10,000
Heating and Lighting Expense	6,000

Property Tax Expense	3,200
Insurance Expense	2,800
Uncollectible Accounts Expense	2,200
Miscellaneous General Expense	1,050
Interest Expense	1,100
Income Tax	6,500

Inventories at the beginning of the year: Department S, $26,730; Department T, $14,770. Inventories at the end of the year: Department S, $24,300; Department T, $16,400.

The bases to be used in apportioning expenses, together with other essential information, are as follows:

Sales salaries expense—payroll records: Department S, $45,000; Department T, $25,000.
Advertising expense—usage: Department S, $7,200; Department T, $3,800.
Depreciation expense—average cost of equipment. Balances of equipment at beginning of year: Department S, $48,490; Department T, $26,110. Balances at end of year: Department S, $54,080; Department T, $29,120.
Store supplies expense—requisitions: Department S, $2,420; Department T, $1,180.
Office salaries expense—Department S, 80%; Department T, 20%.
Rent expense and heating and lighting expense—floor space: Department S, 14,400 sq. ft.; Department T, 5,600 sq. ft.
Property tax expense and insurance expense—average cost of equipment plus average cost of inventories.
Uncollectible accounts expense, miscellaneous selling expense, and miscellaneous general expense—volume of gross sales.

Instructions: Prepare an income statement departmentalized through income from operations.

23–25A. Decision on discontinuance of department. R. E. Ziegler Company is considering discontinuance of one of its twelve departments. If operations in Department L are discontinued, it is estimated that the indirect operating expenses and the level of operations in the other departments will not be affected.

Data from the income statement for the past year ended December 31, which is considered to be a typical year, are as follows:

	Department L		Other Departments	
Sales		$66,000		$855,000
Cost of goods sold		35,250		510,750
Gross profit		$30,750		$344,250
Operating expenses:				
Direct expenses	$24,750		$192,500	
Indirect expenses	13,500	38,250	99,000	291,500
Income (loss) before income tax		$ (7,500)		$ 52,750

Instructions: (1) Prepare an estimated income statement for the current year ending December 31, assuming the discontinuance of Department L.
(2) On the basis of the data presented, would it be advisable to retain Department L?

23–26A. Departmental income statement through departmental margin. Weaver's Department Store has 18 departments. Those with the least sales volume are Department 16 and Department 17, which were established about a year ago on a trial basis. The board of directors feels that it is now time to consider the retention or the termination of these two departments. The following adjusted trial balance as of May 31, the end of the first month of the current fiscal year, is severely condensed. May is considered to be a typical month. The income tax accrual has no bearing on the decision and is excluded from consideration.

Weaver's Department Store
Trial Balance
May 31, 19--

Current Assets	383,200	
Plant Assets	692,700	
Accumulated Depreciation—Plant Assets		282,370
Current Liabilities		190,920
Common Stock		200,000
Retained Earnings		291,860
Cash Dividends	20,000	
Sales—Department 16		40,000
Sales—Department 17		25,000
Sales—Other Departments		881,750
Cost of Goods Sold—Department 16	31,500	
Cost of Goods Sold—Department 17	15,200	
Cost of Goods Sold—Other Departments	531,750	
Direct Expenses—Department 16	12,750	
Direct Expenses—Department 17	5,800	
Direct Expenses—Other Departments	125,000	
Indirect Expenses	85,000	
Interest Expense	9,000	
	1,911,900	1,911,900

Instructions: (1) Prepare an income statement for May, departmentalized through departmental margin.

(2) State your recommendations concerning the retention of Departments 16 and 17, giving reasons.

Mini-Case 23

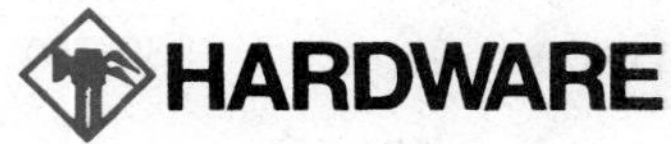

Assume that you recently started to work in your family-owned hardware store as an assistant store manager. Your father, the store manager and major stockholder, is considering the elimination of the Garden Supply Department, which has been incurring net losses for several years. Condensed revenue and expense data for the most recent year ended December 31, are presented on the following page. These data are typical of recent years. Bases used in allocating operating expenses among departments are listed at the top of page 876.

Petry Hardware
Income Statement
For Year Ended December 31, 19--

	Garden Supply Department			Other Departments			Total		
Net sales			$68,000			$796,800			$864,800
Cost of goods sold			49,600			500,000			549,600
Gross profit			$18,400			$296,800			$315,200
Operating expenses:									
Selling expenses:									
Sales commissions expense	$5,440			$63,744			$69,184		
Advertising expense	2,040			24,000			26,040		
Depreciation expense—store equipment	1,600			18,800			20,400		
Miscellaneous selling expense	1,020			11,952			12,972		
Total selling expenses		$10,100			$118,496			$128,596	
General expenses:									
Administrative salaries expense	$6,920			$62,280			$69,200		
Rent expense	2,272			18,176			20,448		
Utilities expense	2,044			16,360			18,404		
Insurance and property tax expense	1,400			13,360			14,760		
Miscellaneous general expense	612			7,172			7,784		
Total general expenses		13,248			117,348			130,596	
Total operating expenses			23,348			235,844			259,192
Income (loss) from operations			$ (4,948)			$ 60,956			$ 56,008
Other expense:									
Interest expense									1,700
Income before income tax									$ 54,308
Income tax									8,500
Net income									$ 45,808

Expense	Basis
Sales commissions expense	Actual: 8% of net sales
Advertising expense	Actual: all advertising consists of brochures distributed by the various departments advertising specific products
Depreciation expense	Average cost of store equipment used
Miscellaneous selling expense	Amount of net sales
Administrative salaries expense	Each of the 10 departments apportioned an equal share
Rent expense	Floor space occupied
Utilities expense	Floor space occupied
Insurance and property tax expense	Average cost of equipment used average cost of inventory
Miscellaneous general expense	Amount of net sales

Since the Garden Supply Department is under your supervision, your father has asked your opinion as to whether the Garden Supply Department should be eliminated.

Instructions:

Prepare a brief statement of your recommendation to your father, supported by such schedule(s) as you think will be helpful to him in reaching a decision.

Answers to Self-Examination Questions

1. B The manager of a profit center (answer B) has responsibility for and authority over costs and revenues. If the manager has responsibility and authority for only costs, the department is referred to as a cost center (answer A). If the responsibility and authority extend to the investment in assets as well as costs and revenues, it is referred to as an investment center (answer C).

2. B Operating expenses should be apportioned to the various departments as nearly as possible in accordance with the cost of services rendered to them. For rent expense, generally the most appropriate basis is the floor space devoted to each department (answer B).

3. C When the departmental margin approach to income reporting is employed, the direct departmental expenses for each department are deducted from the gross profit for each department to yield departmental margin for each department (answer C). The indirect expenses are deducted from the total departmental margin to yield income from operations (answer A). The final total income is identified as net income (answer B).

4. A Operating expenses traceable to or incurred for the sole benefit of a specific department, such as sales commissions expense, are termed direct expenses (answer A) and should be so reported on the income statement departmentalized through departmental margin.

5. B Operating expenses incurred for the entire enterprise as a unit and hence not subject to the control of individual department managers, such as office salaries, are termed indirect expenses (answer B) and should be so reported on the income statement departmentalized through departmental margin.

24
Responsibility Accounting for Investment Centers; Transfer Pricing

CHAPTER OBJECTIVES

Describe and illustrate responsibility accounting for investment centers, including three common measures of management performance:
Operating income
Rate of return on investment
Residual income

Describe the nature of transfer pricing for decentralized operations.

Describe and illustrate three common approaches to establishing transfer prices:
Market price approach
Negotiated price approach
Cost price approach

Describe and illustrate the effect of transfer prices on the evaluation of decentralized performance.

Describe and illustrate the potential impact of transfer prices on overall enterprise income.

Businesses that are separated into two or more manageable units in which divisional managers have authority and responsibility for operations are said to be decentralized. Three types of decentralized operations — cost centers, profit centers, and investment centers — were described in Chapter 23. The role of the managerial accountant in providing useful reports to assist individual managers in evaluating and controlling cost centers and profit centers was also described.

This chapter completes the discussion of decentralized business operations by focusing on responsibility accounting and reporting for investment centers. In addition, the pricing of products or services that are transferred between decentralized segments of a company is discussed.

RESPONSIBILITY ACCOUNTING FOR INVESTMENT CENTERS

Since investment center managers have responsibility for revenues and expenses, operating income is an essential part of investment center reporting. In addition, because the investment center manager also has responsibility for the assets invested in the center, two additional measures of performance are often used. These additional measures are the rate of return on investment and residual income. Each of these measures of investment center performance will be described and illustrated for Marsh Company, a diversified company with three operating divisions, as shown in the following organization chart:

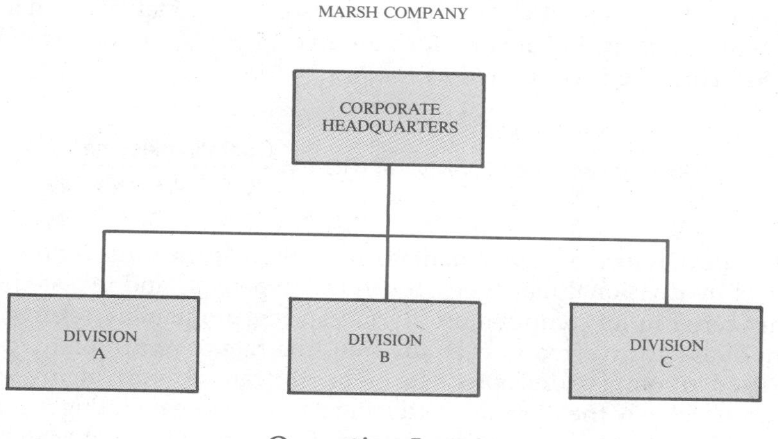

Partial Organization Chart for a Decentralized Company with Investment Centers

Operating Income

Because investment centers are evaluated as if they were separate companies, traditional financial statements are normally prepared for each center. For purposes of assessing profitability, operating income is the focal point of analysis. Since the determination of operating income for decentralized operations was described and illustrated in Chapter 23, only condensed divisional income statements will be used for illustrative purposes. The condensed divisional income statements for Marsh Company are as follows:

Marsh Company
Divisional Income Statements
For Year Ended December 31, 19--

	Division A	Division B	Division C
Sales	$560,000	$672,000	$750,000
Cost of goods sold	336,000	470,400	562,500
Gross profit	$224,000	$201,600	$187,500
Operating expenses	154,000	117,600	112,500
Operating income	**$ 70,000**	**$ 84,000**	**$ 75,000**

Based on the amount of divisional operating income, Division B is the most profitable of Marsh Company's divisions, with income from operations of $84,000. Divisions A and C are less profitable, with Division C reporting $5,000 more operating income than Division A.

Although operating income is a useful measure of investment center profitability, it does not reflect the amount of investment in assets committed to each center. For example, if the amount of assets invested in Division B is twice that of the other divisions, then Division B is the least profitable of the divisions in terms of the rate of return on investment. Since investment center managers also control the amount of assets invested in their centers, they should be held accountable for the use of invested assets.

Rate of Return on Investment

One of the most widely used measures of divisional performance for investment centers is the **rate of return on investment (ROI),** or **rate of return on assets.** This rate is computed as follows:

$$\text{Rate of Return on Investment (ROI)} = \frac{\text{Operating Income}}{\text{Invested Assets}}$$

The rate of return on investment is useful because the three factors subject to control by divisional managers (revenues, expenses, and invested assets) are considered in its computation. By measuring profitability relative to the amount of assets invested in each division, the rate of return on investment can be used to compare divisions. The higher the rate of return on investment, the more effectively the division is utilizing its assets in generating income. To illustrate, the rate of return on investment for each division of Marsh Company, based on the book value of invested assets, is as follows:

	Operating Income	*Invested Assets*	*Rate of Return on Investment*
Division A	$70,000	$350,000	20%
Division B	84,000	700,000	12
Division C	75,000	500,000	15

Although Division B generated the largest operating income, its rate of return on investment (12%) is the lowest. Hence, relative to the assets invested, Division B is the least profitable division. In comparison, the rates of return on investment of Divisions A and C are 20% and 15% respectively. These differences in the rates of return on investment may be analyzed by restating the expression for the rate of return on investment in expanded form, as follows:

$$\text{Rate of Return on Investment (ROI)} = \frac{\text{Operating Income}}{\text{Sales}} \times \frac{\text{Sales}}{\text{Invested Assets}}$$

In the expanded form, the rate of return on investment is the product of two factors: (1) the ratio of operating income to sales, often termed the **profit margin,** and (2) the ratio of sales to invested assets, often termed the **in-**

vestment turnover. As shown in the following computation, the use of this expanded expression yields the same rate of return for Division A, 20%, as the previous expression for the rate of return on investment:

$$\text{Rate of Return on Investment (ROI)} = \frac{\text{Operating Income}}{\text{Sales}} \times \frac{\text{Sales}}{\text{Invested Assets}}$$

$$\text{ROI} = \frac{\$70{,}000}{\$560{,}000} \times \frac{\$560{,}000}{\$350{,}000}$$

$$\text{ROI} = 12.5\% \times 1.6$$

$$\text{ROI} = 20\%$$

The expanded expression for the rate of return on investment is useful in management's evaluation and control of decentralized operations because the profit margin and the investment turnover focus on the underlying operating relationships of each division. The profit margin component focuses on profitability by indicating the rate of profit earned on each sales dollar. When efforts are aimed at increasing a division's profit margin by changing the division's sales mix, for example, the division's rate of return on investment may increase.

The investment turnover component focuses on efficiency in the use of assets and indicates the rate at which sales are being generated for each dollar of invested assets. The more sales per dollar invested, the greater the efficiency in the use of the assets. When efforts are aimed at increasing a division's investment turnover through special sales promotions, for example, the division's rate of return on investment may increase.

The rate of return on investment, using the expanded expression for each division of Marsh Company, is summarized as follows:

$$\text{Rate of Return on Investment (ROI)} = \text{Profit Margin} \times \text{Investment Turnover}$$

$$\text{ROI} = \frac{\text{Operating Income}}{\text{Sales}} \times \frac{\text{Sales}}{\text{Invested Assets}}$$

Division A:

$$\text{ROI} = \frac{\$70{,}000}{\$560{,}000} \times \frac{\$560{,}000}{\$350{,}000}$$

$$\text{ROI} = 12.5\% \times 1.6$$

$$\text{ROI} = 20\%$$

Division B:

$$\text{ROI} = \frac{\$84{,}000}{\$672{,}000} \times \frac{\$672{,}000}{\$700{,}000}$$

$$\text{ROI} = 12.5\% \times .96$$

$$\text{ROI} = 12\%$$

Division C:

$$\text{ROI} = \frac{\$75{,}000}{\$750{,}000} \times \frac{\$750{,}000}{\$500{,}000}$$

$$\text{ROI} = 10\% \times 1.5$$

$$\text{ROI} = 15\%$$

Although Divisions A and B have the same profit margins, Division A's investment turnover is larger than that of Division B (1.6 to .96). Thus, by more efficiently utilizing its invested assets, Division A's rate of return on investment is higher than Division B's. Division C's profit margin of 10% and investment turnover of 1.5 are lower than the corresponding factors for Division A. The product of these factors results in a return on investment of 15% for Division C, as compared to 20% for Division A.

To determine possible ways of increasing the rate of return on investment, the profit margin and investment turnover for a division should be analyzed. For example, if Division A is in a highly competitive industry where the profit margin cannot be easily increased, the division manager should concentrate on increasing the investment turnover. To illustrate, assume that sales of Division A could be increased by $56,000 through changes in advertising expenditures. The cost of goods sold is expected to be 60% of sales, and operating expenses will increase to $169,400. If the advertising changes are undertaken, Division A's operating income would increase from $70,000 to $77,000, as shown in the following condensed income statement:

Sales ($560,000 + $56,000)	$616,000
Cost of goods sold ($616,000 × 60%)	369,600
Gross profit	$246,400
Operating expenses	169,400
Operating income	$ 77,000

The rate of return on investment for Division A, using the expanded expression, is recomputed as follows:

$$\text{Rate of Return on Investment (ROI)} = \frac{\text{Operating Income}}{\text{Sales}} \times \frac{\text{Sales}}{\text{Invested Assets}}$$

$$\text{ROI} = \frac{\$77{,}000}{\$616{,}000} \times \frac{\$616{,}000}{\$350{,}000}$$

$$\text{ROI} = 12.5\% \times 1.76$$

$$\text{ROI} = 22\%$$

Although Division A's profit margin remains the same (12.5%), the division's investment turnover has increased from 1.6 to 1.76, an increase of 10% (.16 ÷ 1.6). The 10% increase in investment turnover has the effect of also increasing the rate of return on investment by 10% (from 20% to 22%).

The major advantage of the use of the rate of return on investment instead of operating income as a divisional performance measure is that the amount of divisional investment is directly considered. Thus, divisional performances can be compared, even though the sizes of the divisions may vary significantly.

In addition to its use as a performance measure, the rate of return on investment can assist management in other ways. For example, in considering a decision to expand the operations of Marsh Company, management should consider giving priority to Division A because it earns the highest rate of return on investment. If the current rates of return on investment can be maintained in the future, an investment in Division A will return 20 cents (20%) on each dollar invested, while investments in Divisions B and C will return only 12 cents and 15 cents respectively.

A major disadvantage of the rate of return on investment as a performance measure is that it may lead divisional managers to reject new investment proposals, even though the rate of return on these investments exceeds the minimum considered acceptable by the company. For example, a division might have an overall rate of return on investment of 25%, and the company might have an overall rate of return on investment of 15%. If the division accepts a new investment that would earn a 20% rate of return on investment, the overall rate of return for the division would decrease, but the overall rate of return for the company as a whole would increase. Thus, the division manager might reject the proposal, even though its acceptance would be in the best interests of the company.

Residual Income

In the previous illustration for Marsh Company, two measures of evaluating divisional performance were discussed and illustrated. The advantages and disadvantages of both measures were also discussed. An additional measure, residual income, is useful in overcoming some of the disadvantages associated with the operating income and rate of return on investment measures.

Residual income is the excess of divisional operating income over a minimum amount of desired operating income. The minimum amount of desired divisional operating income is set by top management by establishing a minimum rate of return for the invested assets and then multiplying this rate by the amount of divisional assets. To illustrate, assume that the top management of Marsh Company has established 10% as the minimum rate of return on divisional assets. The residual incomes for Divisions A, B, and C are computed as follows:

Residual Income by Division

	Division A	Division B	Division C
Divisional operating income	$70,000	$84,000	$75,000
Minimum amount of divisional operating income:			
$350,000 × 10%	35,000		
$700,000 × 10%		70,000	
$500,000 × 10%			50,000
Residual income	$35,000	$14,000	$25,000

The major advantage of residual income as a performance measure is that it gives consideration not only to a minimum rate of return on investment, but also to the total magnitude of the operating income earned by each division. For example, Division A has more residual income than the other divisions of Marsh Company, even though it has the least operating income. Also, Division C earns $11,000 more residual income than Division B, even though Division B generates more operating income than Division C. The reason for this difference is that Division B has $200,000 more assets than Division C. Hence, Division B's operating income is reduced by $20,000 ($200,000 × 10%) more than Division C's operating income in determining residual income.

The preceding paragraphs have described and illustrated three measures—operating income, rate of return on investment, and residual income—which management can use in evaluating and controlling investment center performance. In practice, most companies use some combination of all these measures.

Measuring a Foreign Subsidiary's Performance

Managers of foreign subsidiaries face a major problem: achieving accurately measured levels of performance. Because a foreign subsidiary is not isolated from its environment, it is influenced significantly by local sociological, economic, political-legal, and educational factors. Between countries, these factors are likely to be quite different, which destroys the comparability of subsidiary operating results. For example, there may be differences in social structures and religious customs that interact with inflation, foreign exchange rates, and taxes. A country's attitudes toward foreigners may cause the country's government to issue laws and regulations that affect a foreign subsidiary's operations in that country. Special training programs may be required for a foreign subsidiary operating in an educationally underdeveloped country.

The following table illustrates the variability of traditional measures between the foreign subsidiaries of four U.S.-based corporations. Because of the factors mentioned above, the managers of multinational corporations must be especially careful in using such measures to evaluate their foreign subsidiary operations. For example, the relatively high 100% profit margin and the relatively low 4% rate of return on investment for Company Four's Venezuelan subsidiary would be totally misleading if the local environmental factors were not considered.

The name of the company (assumed)	Industry	Foreign Countries
Company One	Measuring, Analyzing, and Control Instruments	Canada, the U.K., Belgium, Australia, and South Africa
Company Two	Oil and Gas	Canada, Mexico, Brazil, the Philippines, and Thailand
Company Three	Electric and Electronic	Germany, Canada, South Africa, Brazil, and Australia
Company Four	Fabricated Metal	Italy, Spain, France, Mexico, and Venezuela

Actual Financial Information (in millions of dollars)

Foreign Country	(1) Total Assets	(2) Gross Revenues	(3) Income After Taxes	(4) Profit Margin (3) ÷ (2)	(5) Investment Turnover (2) ÷ (1)	(6) Actual ROI (3) ÷ (1)
			Company One			
Canada	9	6.50	1.60	24.6%	0.72	17.8%
The U.K.	6	4.20	1.20	28.6%	0.70	20 %
Belgium	15	13.60	.40	2.9%	0.90	2.7%
Australia	12	11.80	2.00	22.0%	0.98	21.7%
South Africa	9	7.60	1.40	18.4%	0.84	15.6%
			Company Two			
Canada	60	110	10	9.1%	1.83	16.7%
Mexico	80	130	16	12.3%	1.63	20 %
Brazil	30	30	6	20 %	1.00	20 %
Phillippines	20	50	8	16 %	2.50	40 %
Thailand	15	30	12	40 %	2.00	80 %

Foreign Country	(1) Total Assets	(2) Gross Revenues	(3) Income After Taxes	(4) Profit Margin (3) ÷ (2)	(5) Investment Turnover (2) ÷ (1)	(6) Actual ROI (3) ÷ (1)
			Company Three			
Germany	5.4	1.96	1.22	62.2%	0.36	22.6%
Canada	6.0	1.80	.94	52.2%	0.30	15.7%
South Africa	2.4	1.44	.80	55.6%	0.60	33.3%
Brazil	1.0	.52	.30	57.7%	0.52	30 %
Australia	6.0	2.52	1.32	52.4%	0.42	22 %
			Company Four			
Italy	29.6	29.8	14.4	48.3%	1.01	48.6%
Spain	18.6	13.4	10.2	76.1%	0.72	54.8%
France	5.2	4.8	1.60	33.3%	0.92	30.8%
Mexico	7	4.4	2.0	45.5%	0.63	28.6%
Venezuela	15	0.60	.60	100 %	.04	4 %

Actual Financial Information (in millions of dollars)

Source: Wagdy M. Abdallah, "Change the Environment or Change the System," *Management Accounting* (October, 1986), pp. 33–36.

TRANSFER PRICING

The use of responsibility accounting and reporting in measuring performance in decentralized companies can be important in motivating managers to achieve common profit goals. However, when decentralized units transfer products or render services to each other, the **transfer price**—the price to charge for the products or services—becomes an issue. Since transfer prices affect the revenues and expenses of both the receiving unit and the unit providing the product or service, transfer prices affect the performance measures used for evaluating divisional performance.

The objective of transfer pricing is to encourage each divisional manager to transfer goods and services between divisions if overall company income can be increased by doing so. As will be illustrated, however, transfer prices may be misused to the detriment of overall company income.

The following paragraphs describe and illustrate various approaches to establishing transfer prices, the effect of transfer prices on the evaluation of decentralized performance, and their potential impact on overall company income. Three commonly used approaches are (1) the market price approach, (2) the negotiated price approach, and (3) the cost price approach.

Although transfer prices may apply when decentralized units are organized as cost or profit centers, a diversified company (Wilson Company) with two operating divisions (M and N) organized as investment centers will be used for the illustrations in the remainder of this chapter. Condensed income statements for Wilson Company's divisions, with no intracompany transfers and a breakdown of expenses into variable and fixed components, are as follows:

Wilson Company
Divisional Income Statements
For Year Ended December 31, 19--

	Division M	Division N	Total
Sales:			
50,000 units × $20 per unit	$1,000,000		$1,000,000
20,000 units × $40 per unit		$800,000	800,000
			$1,800,000
Expenses:			
Variable:			
50,000 units × $10 per unit	$ 500,000		$ 500,000
20,000 units × $30* per unit		$600,000	600,000
Fixed	300,000	100,000	400,000
Total expenses	$ 800,000	$700,000	$1,500,000
Operating income	$ 200,000	$100,000	$ 300,000

*$20 of the $30 per unit represents materials costs, and the remaining $10 per unit represents other expenses incurred within Division N.

Market Price Approach

Under the **market price approach,** the transfer price is the price at which the product or service transferred could be sold to outside buyers. If an outside market exists for the product or service transferred, then the current market price at which the purchasing division could buy the product or service outside the company would seem to be a reasonable transfer price for intracompany transfers. However, the appropriateness of the market price approach depends on whether the division supplying the product or service is operating at full capacity and can sell all it produces.

To illustrate, assume that materials used by Wilson Company in producing Division N's product are currently purchased from an outside supplier at $20 per unit. The same materials are produced by Division M. If Division M is operating at full capacity of 50,000 units and can sell all it produces to either Division N or to outside buyers, then the use of a transfer price of $20 per unit (the market price) has no effect on the income of Division M or total company income. Division M will earn revenues of $20 per unit on all its production and sales, regardless of who buys its product, and Division N will pay $20 per unit for materials, regardless of whether it purchases the materials from Division M or from an outside supplier. In this situation, the use of the market price as the transfer price is appropriate. The condensed divisional income statements for Wilson Company under such circumstances would be as shown above.

If unused capacity exists in the supplying division, the use of the market price approach may not lead to the maximization of total company income. To illustrate, assume that Division M has unused capacity of 20,000 units and it can continue to sell only 50,000 units to outside buyers. In this situation, the transfer price should be set to motivate the manager of Division N to purchase from Division M if the variable cost per unit of product of Division M is less than the market price. If the variable costs are less than $20 per unit but the transfer price is set equal to the market price of $20, then the manager of Division N is indifferent as to whether materials are purchased from Division

M or from outside suppliers, since the cost per unit to Division N would be the same, $20. However, Division N's purchase of 20,000 units of materials from outside suppliers at a cost of $20 per unit would not maximize overall company income, since this market price per unit is greater than the unit variable expenses of Division M, $10. Hence, the intracompany transfer could save the company the difference between the market price per unit and Division M's unit variable expenses. This savings of $10 per unit would add $200,000 (20,000 units × $10) to overall company income.

Negotiated Price Approach

In the previous illustration, the manager of Division N should be encouraged to purchase from Division M by establishing a transfer price at an amount less than the market price of $20 per unit. Division N's materials cost per unit would thus decrease, and its operating income would increase. In such situations, the negotiated price approach can be used to establish an appropriate transfer price.

The **negotiated price approach** allows the managers of decentralized units to agree (negotiate) among themselves as to the proper transfer price. If agreement cannot be reached among the division managers, the company's top management may have to intervene to set the transfer price. To illustrate, assume that Wilson Company's division managers agree to a transfer price of $15 for Division M's product. By purchasing from Division M, Division N would then report $5 per unit less materials cost. At the same time, Division M would increase its sales to a total of 70,000 units (50,000 units to outside buyers and 20,000 units to Division N). The effect of increasing Division M's sales by $300,000 (20,000 units × $15 per unit) is to increase its income by $100,000 ($300,000 sales − $200,000 variable expenses). The effect of reducing Division N's materials cost by $100,000 (20,000 units × $5 per unit) is to increase its income by $100,000. Therefore, Wilson Company's income is increased by $200,000 ($100,000 reported by Division M and $100,000 reported by Division N), as shown in the following condensed income statements:

Wilson Company
Divisional Income Statements
For Year Ended December 31, 19--

	Division M	Division N	Total
Sales:			
50,000 units × $20 per unit	$1,000,000		$1,000,000
20,000 units × $15 per unit	300,000		300,000
20,000 units × $40 per unit		$800,000	800,000
	$1,300,000	$800,000	$2,100,000
Expenses:			
Variable:			
70,000 units × $10 per unit	$ 700,000		$ 700,000
20,000 units × $25* per unit		$500,000	500,000
Fixed	300,000	100,000	400,000
Total expenses	$1,000,000	$600,000	$1,600,000
Operating income	**$ 300,000**	**$200,000**	**$ 500,000**

*$10 per unit of the $25 is incurred solely within Division N, and $15 per unit represents the transfer price per unit from Division M.

In the Wilson Company illustration, any transfer price less than the market price of $20 but greater than Division M's unit variable expenses of $10 would increase each division's income and would increase overall company income by $200,000. By establishing a range of $20 to $10 for the negotiated transfer price, each division manager will have an incentive to negotiate the intracompany transfer of the materials. For example, a transfer price of $18 would increase Division M's income by $160,000 (from $200,000 to $360,000) and Division N's income by $40,000 (from $100,000 to $140,000). Overall company income would still be increased by $200,000 (from $300,000 to $500,000), as shown in the following condensed income statements:

Wilson Company
Divisional Income Statements
For Year Ended December 31, 19--

	Division M	Division N	Total
Sales:			
50,000 units × $20 per unit	$1,000,000		$1,000,000
20,000 units × $18 per unit	360,000		360,000
20,000 units × $40 per unit		$800,000	800,000
	$1,360,000	$800,000	$2,160,000
Expenses:			
Variable:			
70,000 units × $10 per unit	$ 700,000		$ 700,000
20,000 units × $28* per unit		$560,000	560,000
Fixed	300,000	100,000	400,000
Total expenses	$1,000,000	$660,000	$1,660,000
Operating income	**$ 360,000**	**$140,000**	**$ 500,000**

*$10 per unit of the $28 is incurred solely within Division N, and $18 per unit represents the transfer price per unit from Division M.

Cost Price Approach

Under the **cost price approach,** cost is used as the basis for setting transfer prices. With this approach, a variety of cost concepts may be used. For example, cost may refer to either total product cost per unit or variable product cost per unit. If total product cost per unit is used, direct materials, direct labor, and factory overhead are included in the transfer price. If variable product cost per unit is used, the fixed factory overhead component of total product cost is excluded from the transfer price.

Either actual costs or standard (budgeted) costs may be used in applying the cost price approach. If actual costs are used, inefficiencies of the producing division are transferred to the purchasing division, and thus there is little incentive for the producing division to control costs carefully. For this reason, most companies use standard costs in the cost price approach, so that differences between actual and standard costs are isolated in the producing divisions for cost control purposes.

When division managers have responsibility for only costs incurred in their divisions, the cost price approach to transfer pricing is frequently used. However, many accountants argue that the cost price approach is inappropriate for decentralized operations organized as profit or investment centers. In profit and investment centers, division managers have responsibility for both revenues and expenses. The use of cost as a transfer price, however, ignores the supplying division manager's responsibility over revenues. When a supplying division's sales are all intracompany transfers, for example, the use of the cost price approach would prevent the supplying division from reporting any operating income. A cost-based transfer price would therefore not motivate the division manager to make intracompany transfers, even though they are in the best interests of the company.

Transfer Pricing for an Automobile Dealership—A Case Analysis

The importance of developing appropriate transfer prices can be demonstrated by the following case, which was reported in *Management Accounting*. The case is based on an actual company, an automobile dealership that is one of the largest volume import dealers in the state of Pennsylvania.

... With sales expected to exceed 1,000 new units in [the] calendar year, ... the dealership serves as a leader in the field. Dollar sales of new units will top $9 million by calendar year-end. In addition to the sales department, the dealership also has separate parts and service departments. [The sales department] is a major customer of both [the] service and parts [departments]....

[The transfer prices for floormats, rustproofing, paint protection, AM-FM stereo cassettes, and air conditioning transferred from the parts and service departments to the sales department were determined as follows:]

Item	Cost*	Markup	Transfer Price
Deluxe floormats ..	$ 27.49	27%	$ 35.00
Rustproofing	25.54	135	60.00
Paint protection....	25.54	135	60.00
AM-FM stereo cassette	225.60	13	255.00
A/C	484.70	34	650.00

*Includes installation costs.

All of the above prices were set by the dealer-owner in conjunction with his service manager and parts manager with the implied intention of giving these departments a share of the sales department's profit. These prices are not retail prices, nor are they legitimate wholesale prices; they are simply arbitrary transfer prices.

[The above transfer prices illustrate] the haphazard method by which [the sales department] is charged for goods from the two supporting departments. Notice that floormats are charged to sales at approximately a 27% mark-up on cost, rustproofing and paint protection at 135% mark-up, and air conditioning at 34% mark-up. The lowest mark-up occurs on radios, a mere 13% increase....

Because of perceived excess charges, the frustrated sales manager looked outside the company for the products and services he needed. After minimal investigation he found a subcontractor willing to supply comparable performance radios and air conditioners at considerable savings. He was able to and did buy radios for $227.00 installed and air conditioners for $525.00 installed. This practice continued for approximately two years. During this period the sales manager was noticeably ecstatic over his increased bonuses, while the parts and service managers were long-faced and moody due to declining profits. In this period 618 air conditioners and 267 AM-FM stereo cassettes were sold by the sales department. Of these, 112 air conditioners and three stereo cassettes were purchased internally. Although the sales department saved $63,250.00 (506 units @ $125.00 savings) on air conditioners, and [$7,392.00 (264 units @ $28.00 savings)] on cassette radios, the company as a whole lost money. By buying 506 air conditioners from a third party the company lost $20,391.80 [506 units × ($525.00 price paid − $484.70 cost to internally install)]. By purchasing 264 AM-FM stereo cassettes from an outsider the company gave up $369.60 [264 units × ($227.00 price paid − $225.60 cost to internally install)]. Total company losses totalled $20,761.40.

After two years the dealer-owner realized the extent of his lost profits and immediately called all three managers together in conference to discuss the problem.... After several days of negotiation, ... the parties settled on what they believed were fair and reasonable transfer prices for the products involved as well as all other products sold internally to the sales department....

Source: Joseph A. Scarpo, Jr., "Auto Dealers Lag in Transfer Pricing," *Management Accounting* (July, 1984), pp. 54–56.

Chapter Review

KEY POINTS

1. Responsibility Accounting for Investment Centers.
Since investment center managers have responsibility for expenses and revenues of the center and plant assets assigned to the center, they are evaluated as if they were managers of separate companies. Three common measures of performance for investment centers are (1) operating income, (2) rate of return on investment, and (3) residual income.

Because investment centers are evaluated as if they were separate companies, traditional financial statements are normally prepared for each center. For purposes of assessing profitability, operating income is the focal point of the analysis.

The rate of return on investment is one of the most widely used measures of divisional performance for investment centers and is computed as follows:

$$\text{Rate of Return on Investment (ROI)} = \frac{\text{Operating Income}}{\text{Invested Assets}}$$

The rate of return on investment may be expressed in expanded form as follows:

$$\text{Rate of Return on Investment (ROI)} = \frac{\text{Operating Income}}{\text{Sales}} \times \frac{\text{Sales}}{\text{Invested Assets}}$$

In the expanded form, the rate of return on investment is the product of two factors: (1) the ratio of operating income to sales, often termed the profit margin, and (2) the ratio of sales to invested assets, often termed the investment turnover.

Residual income is the excess of divisional operating income over a minimum amount of desired operating income. The minimum amount of desired divisional operating income is set by top management by establishing a minimum rate of return for the invested assets and then multiplying this rate by the amount of divisional assets.

2. Transfer Pricing.
The transfer price is the price charged by a unit for products or services provided to another unit in a decentralized company. The objective of transfer pricing is to encourage each divisional manager to transfer goods and services between divisions if overall company income can be increased by doing so. Three commonly used approaches to establishing transfer prices are (1) the market price approach, (2) the negotiated price approach, and (3) the cost price approach.

Under the market price approach to transfer pricing, the transfer price is set at the price at which the product or services transferred between units could be sold to outsider buyers.

Under the negotiated price approach to transfer pricing, the transfer price is the price agreed to (negotiated) among the managers of the decentralized units.

Under the cost price approach, cost is used as the basis for setting transfer prices. The cost may be either total product cost per unit or variable product cost per unit, and most companies use the standard cost rather than the actual cost.

KEY TERMS

rate of return on investment (ROI) 880
profit margin 880
investment turnover 881
residual income 883
transfer price 885
market price approach 886
negotiated price approach 887
cost price approach 888

Self-Examination Questions

(Answers at End of Chapter)

1. Managers of what type of decentralized units have authority and responsibility over revenues, expenses, and invested assets?
   A. Profit center
   B. Cost center
   C. Investment center
   D. None of the above

2. Division A of Kern Co. has sales of $350,000, cost of goods sold of $200,000, operating expenses of $30,000, and invested assets of $600,000. What is the rate of return on investment for Division A?
   A. 20%
   B. 25%
   C. 40%
   D. None of the above

3. Which of the following expressions is frequently referred to as the turnover factor in determining the rate of return on investment?
   A. Operating Income ÷ Sales
   B. Operating Income ÷ Invested Assets
   C. Sales ÷ Invested Assets
   D. None of the above

4. Division L of Liddy Co. has a rate of return on investment of 24% and an investment turnover of 1.6. What is the profit margin?
   A. 6%
   B. 15%
   C. 24%
   D. None of the above

5. Which approach to transfer pricing uses the price at which the product or service transferred could be sold to outside buyers as the transfer price?
   A. Cost price approach
   B. Negotiated price approach
   C. Market price approach
   D. None of the above

ILLUSTRATIVE PROBLEM

Reese Company has two divisions, A and B. Invested assets and condensed income statement data for each division for the past year ended December 31 are as follows:

	Division A	Division B
Sales	$3,125,000	$5,100,000
Cost of goods sold	2,500,000	4,000,000
Operating expenses	150,000	590,000
Invested assets	2,500,000	3,000,000

Instructions:

1. Prepare condensed income statements for the past year for each division.
2. Using the expanded expression, determine the profit margin, investment turnover, and rate of return on investment for each division.
3. If management desires a minimum rate of return of 12%, determine the residual income for each division.

SOLUTION

(1)

Reese Company
Divisional Income Statements
For Year Ended December 31, 19--

	Division A	Division B
Sales	$3,125,000	$5,100,000
Cost of goods sold	2,500,000	4,000,000
Gross profit	$ 625,000	$1,100,000
Operating expenses	150,000	590,000
Operating income	$ 475,000	$ 510,000

(2)

Rate of Return on Investment (ROI) = Profit Margin × Investment Turnover

$$\text{ROI} = \frac{\text{Operating Income}}{\text{Sales}} \times \frac{\text{Sales}}{\text{Invested Assets}}$$

$$\text{Division A: ROI} = \frac{\$475{,}000}{\$3{,}125{,}000} \times \frac{\$3{,}125{,}000}{\$2{,}500{,}000}$$

$$\text{ROI} = 15.2\% \times 1.25$$

$$\text{ROI} = 19\%$$

$$\text{Division B: ROI} = \frac{\$510{,}000}{\$5{,}100{,}000} \times \frac{\$5{,}100{,}000}{\$3{,}000{,}000}$$

$$\text{ROI} = 10\% \times 1.7$$

$$\text{ROI} = 17\%$$

(3) Division A: $175,000 ($475,000 − $300,000)
Division B: $150,000 ($510,000 − $360,000)

Discussion Questions

24–1. What are three ways in which decentralized operations may be organized?

24–2. Name three performance measures useful in evaluating investment centers.

24–3. What is the major shortcoming of using operating income as a performance measure for investment centers?

24–4. Why should the factors under the control of the investment center manager (revenues, expenses, and invested assets) be considered in the computation of the rate of return on investment?

24–5. Halbert Co. has $300,000 invested in Division R, which earned $81,000 of operating income. What is the rate of return on investment for Division R?

24–6. If Halbert Co. in Question 24–5 had sales of $540,000, what is (a) the profit margin and (b) the investment turnover for Division R?

24–7. What are two ways of expressing the rate of return on investment?

24–8. In evaluating investment centers, what does multiplying the profit margin by the investment turnover equal?

24–9. In a decentralized company in which the divisions are organized as investment centers, how could a division be considered the least profitable, even though it earned the largest amount of operating income?

24–10. Which component of the rate of return on investment (profit margin factor or investment turnover factor) focuses on efficiency in the use of assets and indicates the rate at which sales are generated for each dollar of invested assets?

24–11. Division C of Austin Co. has a rate of return on investment of 20%. (a) If Division C increases its investment turnover by 15%, what would be the new rate of return on investment? (b) If Division C also increases its profit margin from 10% to 12%, what would be the new rate of return on investment?

24–12. How does the use of the rate of return on investment facilitate comparability of divisions of decentralized companies?

24–13. The rates of return on investment for Horn Co.'s three divisions, X, Y, and Z, are 22%, 18%, and 12%, respectively. In expanding operations, which of Horn Co.'s divisions should be given priority? Explain.

24–14. What term is used to describe the excess of divisional operating income over a minimum amount of desired operating income?

24–15. Division M of Jones Co. reported operating income of $260,000, based on invested assets of $800,000. If the minimum rate of return on divisional investments is 15%, what is the residual income for Division M?

24–16. What term is used to describe the amount charged for products transferred or services rendered to other decentralized units in a company?

24–17. What is the objective of transfer pricing?

24–18. Name three commonly used approaches to establishing transfer prices.

24–19. What transfer price approach uses the price at which the product or service transferred could be sold to outside buyers as the transfer price?

24–20. When is the negotiated price approach preferred over the market price approach in setting transfer prices?

24–21. If division managers cannot agree among themselves on a transfer price when using the negotiated price approach, how is the transfer price established?

24–22. When using the negotiated price approach to transfer pricing, within what range should the transfer price be established?

24–23. Real World Focus. Tandy Corporation's annual report for the year ended June 30, 1987 reports a profit margin of 7.0% and an investment turnover rate of 1.76. (a) What was the rate of return on investment for the year ended June 30, 1987? (b) If the investment turnover rate does not change for the year ended June 30, 1988, what must the profit margin be to earn a rate of return on investment of 15%? (Round to the nearest tenth of one percent.)

Exercises

24–24. Determination of missing items on income statements. One item is omitted from each of the following condensed divisional income statements of Bormann Company:

	Division G	Division H	Division I
Sales	$450,000	$640,000	(e)
Cost of goods sold	270,000	(c)	320,000
Gross profit	(a)	$330,000	$260,000
Operating expenses	30,000	(d)	100,000
Operating income	(b)	$130,000	(f)

(a) Determine the amount of the missing items, identifying them by letter. (b) Based on operating income, which division is the most profitable?

24–25. Rate of return on investment. The operating income and the amount of invested assets in each division of Enders Company are as follows:

	Operating Income	Invested Assets
Division A	$221,000	$850,000
Division B	158,400	480,000
Division C	136,800	720,000

(a) Compute the rate of return on investment for each division. (b) Which division is the most profitable per dollar invested?

24–26. Residual income. Based on the data in Exercise 24–25, assume that management has established a minimum rate of return for invested assets of 15%. (a) Determine the residual income for each division. (b) Based on residual income, which of the divisions is the most profitable?

24–27. Determination of missing items for computations of rate of return on investment. One item is omitted from each of the following computations of the rate of return on investment:

Rate of Return on Investment	=	Profit Margin	×	Investment Turnover
26%		20%		(a)
(b)		12%		1.5
36%		(c)		2.4
24%		15%		(d)
(e)		15%		.8

Determine the missing items, identifying each by the appropriate letter.

24–28. Profit margin, investment turnover, and rate of return on investment. The condensed income statement for Division E of Farmer Company is as follows:

Sales	$600,000
Cost of goods sold	360,000
Gross profit	$240,000
Operating expenses	144,000
Operating income	$ 96,000

The manager of Division E is considering ways to increase the rate of return on investment. (a) Using the expanded expression, determine the profit margin, investment turnover, and rate of return on investment of Division E, assuming that $400,000 of assets have been invested in Division E. (b) If expenses could be reduced by $12,000 without decreasing sales, what would be the impact on the profit margin, investment turnover, and rate of return on investment for Division E?

SPREADSHEET PROBLEM

24–29. Determination of missing items for computations of rate of return on investment and residual income. One or more items is missing from the following tabulation of rate of return on investment and residual income:

Invested Assets	Operating Income	Rate of Return on Investment	Minimum Rate of Return	Minimum Amount of Operating Income	Residual Income
$750,000	$150,000	(a)	16%	(b)	(c)
$420,000	(d)	15%	(e)	$42,000	$21,000
$600,000	(f)	(g)	(h)	$72,000	$36,000
$900,000	$216,000	(i)	20%	(j)	(k)

Determine the missing items, identifying each item by the appropriate letter.

24–30. Decision on transfer pricing. Materials used by Burr Company in producing Division C's product are currently purchased from outside suppliers at a cost of $40 per unit. However, the same materials are available from Division W. Division W has unused capacity and can produce the materials needed by Division C at a variable cost of $30 per unit. (a) If a transfer price of $35 per unit is established and 50,000 units of material are transferred, with no reduction in Division W's current sales, how much would Burr Company's total operating income increase? (b) How much would operating income of Division C increase? (c) How much would the operating income of Division W increase?

24–31. Decision on transfer pricing. Based on the Burr Company data in Exercise 24–30, assume that a transfer price of $32 has been established and 50,000 units of materials are transferred, with no reduction in Division W's current sales. (a) How much would Burr Company's total operating income increase? (b) How much would Division C's operating income increase? (c) How much would Division W's operating income increase? (d) If the negotiated price approach is used, what would be the range of acceptable transfer prices?

Problems

SPREADSHEET PROBLEM

24–32. Divisional income statements and rate of return on investment analysis. Mitchell Company is a diversified company with three operating divisions organized as investment centers. Condensed data taken from the records of the three divisions for the year ended August 31 are as follows:

	Division A	Division B	Division C
Sales	$1,000,000	$1,500,000	$1,800,000
Cost of goods sold	600,000	975,000	1,350,000
Operating expenses	280,000	345,000	252,000
Invested assets	800,000	1,000,000	1,200,000

The management of Mitchell Company is evaluating each division as a basis for planning a future expansion of operations.

Instructions: (1) Prepare condensed divisional income statements for Divisions A, B, and C.
(2) Using the expanded expression, compute the profit margin, investment turnover, and rate of return on investment for each division.
(3) If available funds permit the expansion of operations of only one division, which of the divisions would you recommend for expansion, based on (1) and (2)?

24–33. Effect of proposals on divisional performance. A condensed income statement for Division H of Searcy Company for the year ended October 31 is as follows:

Sales	$2,400,000
Cost of goods sold	1,440,000
Gross profit	$ 960,000
Operating expenses	660,000
Operating income	$ 300,000

The president of Searcy Company is concerned with Division H's rate of return on invested assets of $2,000,000, and has indicated that the division's rate of return on investment must be increased to at least 18% by the end of the next year if operations are to continue. The division manager is considering the following three proposals:

Proposal 1: Transfer equipment with a book value of $400,000 to other divisions at no gain or loss and lease similar equipment. The annual lease payments would exceed the amount of depreciation expense on the old equipment by $16,800. This increase in expense would be included as part of the cost of goods sold. Sales would remain unchanged.

Proposal 2: Reduce invested assets by discontinuing a product line. This action would eliminate sales of $150,000, cost of goods sold of $120,000, and operating expenses of $45,000. Assets of $200,000 would be transferred to other divisions at no gain or loss.

Proposal 3: Purchase new and more efficient machinery and thereby reduce the cost of goods sold by $134,400. Sales would remain unchanged, and the old machinery, which has no remaining book value, would be scrapped at no gain or loss. The new machinery would increase invested assets by $400,000 for the year.

Instructions: (1) Using the expanded expression, determine the profit margin, investment turnover, and rate of return on investment for Division H for the past year.
(2) Prepare condensed estimated income statements for Division H for each proposal.
(3) Using the expanded expression, determine the profit margin, investment turnover, and rate of return on investment for Division H under each proposal.
(4) Which of the three proposals would meet the required 18% rate of return on investment?
(5) If Division H were in an industry where the investment turnover could not be increased, how much would the profit margin have to increase to meet the president's required 18% rate of return on investment?

24–34. Determination of missing items from computations. Data for Divisions A, B, C, D, and E of Young Company are as follows:

	Sales	Operating Income	Invested Assets	Rate of Return on Investment	Profit Margin	Investment Turnover
Division A....	$750,000	$120,000	$500,000	(a)	(b)	(c)
Division B....	(d)	(e)	$600,000	12%	(f)	1.25
Division C....	$420,000	(g)	(h)	(i)	15%	1.2
Division D....	$375,000	(j)	(k)	(l)	16%	1.25
Division E....	(m)	$ 88,000	(n)	22%	11%	(o)

Instructions: (1) Determine the missing items, identifying each by letters (a) through (o).
(2) Determine the residual income for each division, assuming that the minimum rate of return established by management is 10%.
(3) Which division is the most profitable?

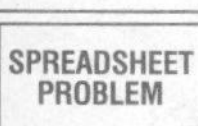

24–35. Divisional performance analysis and evaluation. The vice-president of operations of Carney Company is evaluating the performance of two divisions organized as investment centers. Division F generates the largest amount of operating income but has the lowest rate of return on investment. Division E has the highest rate of return on investment but generates the smallest operating income. Invested assets and condensed income statement data for the past year for each division are as follows:

	Division E	Division F
Sales.	$5,000,000	$6,750,000
Cost of goods sold.	3,000,000	4,320,000
Operating expenses.	1,200,000	1,620,000
Invested assets.	4,000,000	4,500,000

Instructions: (1) Prepare condensed divisional income statements for each division for the year ended October 31.
(2) Using the expanded expression, determine the profit margin, investment turnover, and rate of return on investment for each division.
(3) If management desires a minimum rate of return of 12%, determine the residual income for each division.
(4) Discuss the evaluation of Divisions E and F, using the performance measures determined in (1), (2), and (3).

24–36. Divisional performance analysis and evaluation. The vice-president of operations of Swann Inc. recently resigned, and the president is considering which one of two division managers to promote to the vacated position. Both division managers have been with the company approximately ten years. Operating data for each division for the past three years are as follows:

	1990	1989	1988
Division M:			
Sales.	$ 1,520,000	$ 1,360,000	$ 1,200,000
Cost of goods sold	900,000	800,000	720,000
Gross profit	$ 620,000	$ 560,000	$ 480,000
Operating expenses.	460,400	410,400	345,600
Operating income	$ 159,600	$ 149,600	$ 134,400
Invested assets.	$ 950,000	$ 800,000	$ 600,000
Total industry sales.	$15,200,000	$10,880,000	$ 8,000,000
Division N:			
Sales.	$ 900,000	$ 770,000	$ 500,000
Cost of goods sold	540,000	460,000	300,000
Gross profit	$ 360,000	$ 310,000	$ 200,000
Operating expenses.	216,000	194,500	128,000
Operating income	$ 144,000	$ 115,500	$ 72,000
Invested assets.	$ 600,000	$ 550,000	$ 400,000
Total industry sales.	$11,250,000	$11,000,000	$10,000,000

Instructions: (1) For each division for each of the three years, use the expanded expression to determine the profit margin, investment turnover, and rate of return on investment.
(2) Assuming that 15% has been established as a minimum rate of return, determine the residual income for each division for each of the three years.
(3) Determine each division's market share (division sales divided by total industry sales) for each of the three years.
(4) Based on (1), (2), and (3), which division manager would you recommend for promotion to vice-president of operations?
(5) What other factors should be considered in the promotion decision?

24–37. Real World Focus. The following data (in millions) for the four primary business segments of Rockwell International Corporation were taken from Rockwell International's 1986 financial statements:

	Sales	Operating Income	Assets
Aerospace	$5,545	$571.1	$1,431
Electornics	4,221	400.5	3,549
Automotive	1,588	153.6	995
General Industries	942	87.9	567

Instructions: (1) For each of the four segments, use the expanded expression to determine the profit margin, investment turnover, and rate of return on investment. Round the profit margin to one decimal place, round the investment turnover to two decimal places, and determine the rate of return on investment by multiplying the profit margin by the investment turnover.
(2) Rank the segments from the highest to the lowest in terms of rate of return on investment.

24–38. Transfer pricing. Pane Company is diversified, with two operating divisions, X and Y. Condensed divisional income statements, which involve no intracompany transfers and which include a breakdown of expenses into variable and fixed components, are as follows:

Pane Company
Divisional Income Statements
For Year Ended December 31, 19--

	Division X	Division Y	Total
Sales:			
75,000 units × $120 per unit	$9,000,000		$ 9,000,000
25,000 units × $160 per unit		$4,000,000	4,000,000
			$13,000,000
Expenses:			
Variable:			
75,000 units × $60 per unit	$4,500,000		$ 4,500,000
25,000 units × $100* per unit		$2,500,000	2,500,000
Fixed	3,000,000	1,000,000	4,000,000
Total expenses	$7,500,000	$3,500,000	$11,000,000
Operating income	$1,500,000	$ 500,000	$ 2,000,000

*$80 of the $100 per unit represents materials costs, and the remaining $20 per unit represents other expenses incurred within Division Y.

Division X is operating at three fourths of capacity of 100,000 units. Materials used in producing Division Y's product are currently purchased from outside suppliers at a price of $80 per unit. The materials used by Division Y are produced by Division X.

Except for the possible transfer of materials between divisions, no changes are expected in sales and expenses.

Instructions: (1) Would the market price of $80 per unit be an appropriate transfer price for Pane Company? Explain.

(2) If Division Y purchases 25,000 units from Division X and a transfer price of $70 per unit is negotiated between the managers of Divisions X and Y, how much would the operating income of each division and total company operating income increase?

(3) Prepare condensed divisional income statements for Pane Company, based on the data in (2).

(4) If a transfer price of $65 per unit is negotiated, how much would the operating income of each division and total company income increase?

(5) (a) What is the range of possible negotiated transfer prices that would be acceptable for Pane Company?

(b) Assuming that the division managers of X and Y cannot agree on a transfer price, what price would you suggest as the transfer price?

ALTERNATE PROBLEMS

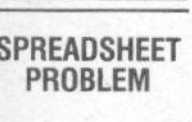

24–32A. Divisional income statements and rate of return on investment analysis. Zavor Company is a diversified company with three operating divisions organized as investment centers. Condensed data taken from the records of the three divisions for the year ended August 31 are as follows:

	Division X	Division Y	Division Z
Sales	$960,000	$1,875,000	$1,350,000
Cost of goods sold	624,000	1,200,000	810,000
Operating expenses	192,000	525,000	324,000
Invested assets	800,000	750,000	900,000

The management of Zavor Company is evaluating each division as a basis for planning a future expansion of operations.

Instructions: (1) Prepare condensed divisional income statements for Divisions X, Y, and Z.

(2) Using the expanded expression, compute the profit margin, investment turnover, and rate of return on investment for each division.

(3) If available funds permit the expansion of operations of only one division, which of the divisions would you recommend for expansion, based on (1) and (2)?

24–34A. Determination of missing items from computations. Data for Divisions M, N, O, P, and Q of Reid Company are as follows:

	Sales	Operating Income	Invested Assets	Rate of Return on Investment	Profit Margin	Investment Turnover
Division M	$ 500,000	$ 60,000	$400,000	(a)	(b)	(c)
Division N	$1,080,000	(d)	$600,000	18%	(e)	(f)
Division O	(g)	$174,000	(h)	(i)	24%	1.25
Division P	$ 840,000	(j)	(k)	24%	20%	(l)
Division Q	(m)	$ 75,600	$360,000	(n)	(o)	1.5

Instructions: (1) Determine the missing items, identifying each by letters (a) through (o).

(2) Determine the residual income for each division, assuming that the minimum rate of return established by management is 12%.

(3) Which division is the most profitable?

24–35A. Divisional performance analysis and evaluation. The vice-president of operations of Eaton Company is evaluating the performance of two divisions organized as investment centers. Division Y has the highest rate of return on investment, but generates the smallest amount of operating income. Division X generates the largest operating income, but has the lowest rate of return on investment. Invested assets and condensed income statement data for the past year for each division are as follows:

	Division X	Division Y
Sales.	$3,375,000	$3,840,000
Cost of goods sold.	2,025,000	2,496,000
Operating expenses.	756,000	768,000
Invested assets.	2,700,000	2,400,000

Instructions: (1) Prepare condensed divisional income statements for each division for the year ended October 31.

(2) Using the expanded expression, determine the profit margin, investment turnover, and rate of return on investment for each division.

(3) If management desires a minimum rate of return of 16%, determine the residual income for each division.

(4) Discuss the evaluation of Divisions X and Y, using the performance measures determined in (1), (2), and (3).

24–38A. Transfer pricing. Cowen Company is diversified, with two operating divisions, F and G. Condensed divisional income statements, which involve no intracompany transfers and which include a breakdown of expenses into variable and fixed components, are as follows:

Cowen Company
Divisional Income Statements
For Year Ended December 31, 19--

	Division F	Division G	Total
Sales:			
240,000 units × $20 per unit . .	$4,800,000		$4,800,000
80,000 units × $25 per unit . . .		$2,000,000	2,000,000
			$6,800,000
Expenses:			
Variable:			
240,000 units × $12 per unit	$2,880,000		$2,880,000
80,000 units × $16* per unit		$1,280,000	1,280,000
Fixed	920,000	520,000	1,440,000
Total expenses	$3,800,000	$1,800,000	$5,600,000
Operating income	$1,000,000	$ 200,000	$1,200,000

*$14 of the $16 per unit represents materials costs, and the remaining $2 per unit represents other expenses incurred within Division G.

Division F is operating at two thirds of its capacity of 360,000 units. Materials used in producing Division G's product are currently purchased from outside suppliers at a price of $14 per unit. The materials used by Division G are produced by Division F. Except for the possible transfer of materials between divisions, no changes are expected in sales and expenses.

Instructions: (1) Would the market price of $14 per unit be an appropriate transfer price for Cowen Company? Explain.

(2) If Division G purchases 80,000 units from Division F and a transfer price of $13 per unit is negotiated between the managers of Divisions F and G, how much would the operating income of each division and total company operating income increase?

(3) Prepare condensed divisional income statements for Cowen Company, based on the data in (2).

(4) If a transfer price of $13.50 per unit had been negotiated, how much would the operating income of each division and total company income have increased?

(5) (a) What is the range of possible negotiated transfer prices that would be acceptable for Cowen Company?

(b) If the division managers of F and G cannot agree on a transfer price, what price would you suggest as the transfer price?

Mini-Case 24

NEWMAN COMPANY

Your father is the president of Newman Company, a privately held, diversified company with five separate divisions organized as investment centers. A condensed income statement for the Sporting Goods Division for the past year is as follows:

Newman Company—Sporting Goods Division
Income Statement
For Year Ended December 31, 19--

Sales	$22,500,000
Cost of goods sold	13,500,000
Gross profit	$ 9,000,000
Operating expenses	5,400,000
Operating income	$ 3,600,000

The manager of the Sporting Goods Division was recently presented with the opportunity to add an additional product line, which would require invested assets of $5,000,000. A projected income statement for the new product line is as follows:

New Product Line
Projected Income Statement
For Year Ended December 31, 19--

Sales	$ 6,000,000
Cost of goods sold	3,600,000
Gross profit	$ 2,400,000
Operating expenses	1,500,000
Operating income	$ 900,000

The Sporting Goods Division currently has $15,000,000 in invested assets, and Newman Company's overall rate of return on investment, including all divisions, is 15%. Each division manager is evaluated on the basis of divisional rate of return on investment, and a bonus equal to $4,000 for each percentage point by which the division's rate of return on investment exceeds the company average is awarded each year.

Your father is concerned that the manager of the Sporting Goods Division rejected the addition of the new product line, when all estimates indicated that the product line would be profitable and would increase overall company income. You have been asked to analyze the possible reasons why the Sporting Goods Division manager rejected the new product line.

Instructions:

(1) Determine the rate of return on investment for the Sporting Goods Division for the past year.
(2) Determine the Sporting Goods Division manager's bonus for the past year.
(3) Determine the estimated rate of return on investment for the new product line.
(4) Why might the manager of the Sporting Goods Division decide to reject the new product line?
(5) Can you suggest an alternative performance measure for motivating division managers to accept new investment opportunities that would increase the overall company income and rate of return on investment?

Answers to Self-Examination Questions

1. C Managers of investment centers (answer C) have authority and responsibility for revenues, expenses, and assets. Managers of profit centers (answer A) have authority and responsibility for revenues and expenses. Managers of cost centers (answer B) have authority and responsibility for costs.

2. A The rate of return on investment for Division A is 20% (answer A), computed as follows:

$$\text{Rate of Return on Investment (ROI)} = \frac{\text{Operating Income}}{\text{Invested Assets}}$$

$$\text{ROI} = \frac{\$350{,}000 - \$200{,}000 - \$30{,}000}{\$600{,}000}$$

$$\text{ROI} = \frac{\$120{,}000}{\$600{,}000}$$

$$\text{ROI} = 20\%$$

3. C Investment turnover is the ratio of sales to invested assets (answer C). The ratio of operating income to sales is the profit margin (answer A). The ratio of operating income to invested assets is the rate of return on investment (answer B).

4. B The profit margin for Division L of Liddy Co. is 15% (answer B), computed as follows:

$$\text{Rate of Return on Investment (ROI)} = \text{Profit Margin} \times \text{Investment Turnover}$$
$$24\% = \text{Profit Margin} \times 1.6$$
$$15\% = \text{Profit Margin}$$

5. C The market price approach (answer C) to transfer pricing uses the price at which the product or service transferred could be sold to outside buyers as the transfer price. The cost price approach (answer A) uses cost as the basis for setting transfer prices. The negotiated price approach (answer B) allows managers of decentralized units to agree (negotiate) among themselves as to the proper transfer price.

Part Eight

Analyses For Decision Making

25
Differential Analysis and Product Pricing

CHAPTER OBJECTIVES

Describe the nature of differential analysis.

Illustrate the use of differential analysis in decisions involving:
- Leasing or selling
- Discontinuing an unprofitable segment
- Making or buying
- Replacing equipment
- Processing or selling
- Accepting business at a special price

Describe and illustrate the setting of normal product prices, using the:
- Total cost concept
- Product cost concept
- Variable cost concept

Describe and illustrate the economic theory of product pricing.

Describe the use of alternative price strategies during a product's life cycle.

A primary objective of accounting is to provide management with analyses and reports that will be useful in resolving current problems and planning for the future. The types of analyses and reports depend on the nature of the decisions to be made. However, all decisions require careful consideration of the consequences of alternative courses of action. This chapter discusses differential analysis, which provides management with data on the differences in total revenues and costs associated with alternative actions.

This chapter also describes and illustrates practical approaches frequently used by managers in setting normal product prices. The relationship of economic theory to the more practical approaches to product pricing is briefly discussed. Finally, the alternative price strategies used by management during a product's life cycle are discussed.

DIFFERENTIAL ANALYSIS

Planning for future operations is chiefly decision making. For some decisions, revenue and cost information drawn from the general ledger and other basic accounting records is very useful. For example, historical cost data in the absorption costing format are helpful in planning production for the long run. Historical cost data in the variable costing format are useful in planning production for the short run. However, the revenue and cost data needed to evaluate courses of future operations or to choose among competing alternatives are often not available in the basic accounting records.

The relevant revenue and cost data in the analysis of future possibilities are the differences between the alternatives under consideration. The amounts of such differences are called **differentials** and the area of accounting concerned with the effect of alternative courses of action on revenues and costs is called **differential analysis.**

Differential revenue is the amount of increase or decrease in revenue expected from a particular course of action as compared with an alternative. To illustrate, assume that certain equipment is being used to manufacture a product that provides revenue of $150,000. If the equipment could be used to make another product that would provide revenue of $175,000, the differential revenue from the alternative would be $25,000.

Differential cost is the amount of increase or decrease in cost that is expected from a particular course of action as compared with an alternative. For example, if an increase in advertising expenditures from $100,000 to $150,000 is being considered, the differential cost of the action would be $50,000.

The main advantage of differential analysis is its selection of relevant revenues and costs related to alternative courses of action. Differential analysis reports emphasize the significant factors bearing on the decision, help to clarify the issues, and save the time of the reader.

Differential analysis can aid management in making decisions on a variety of alternatives, including (1) whether equipment should be leased or sold, (2) whether to discontinue an unprofitable segment, (3) whether to manufacture or purchase a needed part, (4) whether to replace usable plant assets, (5) whether to process further or sell an intermediate product, and (6) whether to accept additional business at a special price. The following discussion relates to the use of differential analysis in analyzing these alternatives.

Lease or Sell

Management often has a choice between leasing or selling a piece of equipment that is no longer needed in the business. In deciding which option is best, management can use differential analysis. To illustrate, assume that Company A is considering the disposal of equipment that originally cost $200,000 and has been depreciated a total of $120,000 to date. Company A can sell the equipment through a broker for $100,000 less a 6% commission. Alternatively, Company B has tentatively offered to lease the equipment for a number of years for a total of $160,000, after which Company A would sell it for a small amount as scrap. During the period of the lease, Company A would incur repair, insurance, and property tax expenses estimated at $35,000. Company A's analysis of whether to lease or sell the equipment is as follows:

Differential Analysis Report—Lease or Sell

Proposal To Lease or Sell Equipment
June 22, 19--

Differential revenue from alternatives:		
Revenue from lease	$160,000	
Revenue from sale	100,000	
Differential revenue from lease		$60,000
Differential cost of alternatives:		
Repair, insurance, and property tax expenses	$ 35,000	
Commission expense on sale	6,000	
Differential cost of lease		29,000
Net advantage of lease alternative		$31,000

It should be noted that it was not necessary to consider the $80,000 book value ($200,000 − $120,000) of the equipment. The $80,000 is a **sunk cost**; that is, it is a cost that will not be affected by later decisions. In the illustration, the expenditure to acquire the equipment had already been made, and the choice is now between leasing or selling the equipment. The relevant factors to be considered are the differential revenues and differential costs associated with the lease or sell decision. The undepreciated cost of the equipment is irrelevant. The validity of the foregoing report can be shown by the following conventional analysis:

Lease alternative:			
Revenue from lease		$160,000	
Depreciation expense	$80,000		
Repair, insurance, and property tax expenses	35,000	115,000	
Net gain			$45,000
Sell alternative:			
Sale price		$100,000	
Book value of equipment	$80,000		
Commission expense	6,000	86,000	
Net gain			14,000
Net advantage of lease alternative			$31,000

The alternatives presented in the illustration were relatively uncomplicated. Regardless of the number and complexity of the additional factors that may be involved, the approach to differential analysis remains basically the same. Two factors that often need to be considered are (1) the differential revenue from investing the funds generated by the alternatives and (2) the income tax differential. In the example, there would undoubtedly be a differential advantage to the immediate investment of the $94,000 net proceeds ($100,000 − $6,000) from the sale over the investment of the net proceeds from the lease arrangement, which would become available over a period of years. The income tax differential would be that related to the differences in timing of the income from the alternatives and the differences in the amount of investment income.

Discontinuance of an Unprofitable Segment

When a department, branch, territory, or other segment of an enterprise has been operating at a loss, management should consider eliminating the unprofitable segment. It might be natural to assume (sometimes mistakenly) that the total operating income of the enterprise would be increased if the operating loss could be eliminated. Discontinuance of the unprofitable segment will usually eliminate all of the related variable costs and expenses. However, if the segment represents a relatively small part of the enterprise, the fixed costs and expenses (depreciation, insurance, property taxes, etc.) will not be reduced by its discontinuance. It is entirely possible in this situation for the total operating income of a company to be reduced rather than increased by eliminating an unprofitable segment. As a basis for illustrating this type of situation, the following income statement is presented for the year just ended, which was a normal year. For purposes of the illustration, it is assumed that discontinuance of Product A, on which losses are incurred annually, will have no effect on total fixed costs and expenses.

Condensed Income Statement
For Year Ended August 31, 19--

	Product			
	A	B	C	Total
Sales	$100,000	$400,000	$500,000	$1,000,000
Cost of goods sold:				
Variable costs	$ 60,000	$200,000	$220,000	$ 480,000
Fixed costs	20,000	80,000	120,000	220,000
Total cost of goods sold	$ 80,000	$280,000	$340,000	$ 700,000
Gross profit	$ 20,000	$120,000	$160,000	$ 300,000
Operating expenses:				
Variable expenses	$ 25,000	$ 60,000	$ 95,000	$ 180,000
Fixed expenses	6,000	20,000	25,000	51,000
Total operating expenses	$ 31,000	$ 80,000	$120,000	$ 231,000
Income (loss) from operations	$ (11,000)	$ 40,000	$ 40,000	$ 69,000

Data on the estimated differential revenue and differential cost related to discontinuing Product A, on which an operating loss of $11,000 was incurred during the past year, may be assembled in a report such as the following. This report emphasizes the significant factors bearing on the decision.

Differential Analysis Report—Discontinuance of Unprofitable Segment

Proposal To Discontinue Product A
September 29, 19--

Differential revenue from annual sales of product:		
Revenue from sales		$100,000
Differential cost of annual sales of product:		
Variable cost of goods sold	$60,000	
Variable operating expenses	25,000	85,000
Annual differential income from sales of Product A		$ 15,000

Instead of an increase in annual operating income to $80,000 (Product B, $40,000; Product C, $40,000) that might seem to be indicated by the income statement, the discontinuance of Product A would reduce operating income to an estimated $54,000 ($69,000 − $15,000). The validity of this conclusion can be shown by the following conventional analysis:

Proposal To Discontinue Product A
September 29, 19--

	Current Operations			Discontinuance
	Product A	Products B and C	Total	of Product A
Sales	$100,000	$900,000	$1,000,000	$900,000
Cost of goods sold:				
Variable costs	$ 60,000	$420,000	$ 480,000	$420,000
Fixed costs	20,000	200,000	220,000	220,000
Total cost of goods sold	$ 80,000	$620,000	$ 700,000	$640,000
Gross profit	$ 20,000	$280,000	$ 300,000	$260,000
Operating expenses:				
Variable expenses	$ 25,000	$155,000	$ 180,000	$155,000
Fixed expenses	6,000	45,000	51,000	51,000
Total operating expenses	$ 31,000	$200,000	$ 231,000	$206,000
Income (loss) from operations	$ (11,000)	$ 80,000	$ 69,000	$ 54,000

For purposes of the illustration, it was assumed that the discontinuance of Product A would not cause any significant reduction in the volume of fixed costs and expenses. If plant capacity made available by discontinuance of a losing operation can be used in some other manner or if plant capacity can be reduced, with a resulting reduction in fixed costs and expenses, additional analysis would be needed.

In decisions involving the elimination of an unprofitable segment, management must also consider such other factors as its effect on employees and customers. If a segment of the business is discontinued, some employees may have to be laid off and others may have to be relocated and retrained. Also important is the possible decline in sales of the more profitable products to customers who were attracted to the firm by the discontinued product.

Make or Buy

The assembly of many parts is often a substantial element in manufacturing operations. Many of the large factory complexes of automobile manufacturers are specifically called assembly plants. Some of the parts of the finished automobile, such as the motor, are produced by the automobile manufacturer, while other parts, such as tires, are often purchased from other manufacturers. Even in manufacturing the motors, such items as spark plugs and nuts and bolts may be acquired from suppliers in their finished state. When parts or components are purchased, management has usually evaluated the question of "make or buy" and has concluded that a savings in cost results from buying the part rather than manufacturing it. However, "make or buy" options are likely to arise anew when a manufacturer has excess productive capacity in the form of unused equipment, space, and labor.

As a basis for illustrating such alternatives, assume that a manufacturer has been purchasing a component, Part X, for $5 a unit. The factory is currently operating at 80% of capacity, and no significant increase in production is anticipated in the near future. The cost of manufacturing Part X, determined by absorption costing methods, is estimated at $1 for direct materials,

$2 for direct labor, and $3 for factory overhead (at the predetermined rate of 150% of direct labor cost), or a total of $6. The decision based on a simple comparison of a "make" price of $6 with a "buy" price of $5 is obvious. However, to the extent that unused capacity could be used in manufacturing the part, there would be no increase in the total amount of fixed factory overhead costs. Hence, only the variable factory overhead costs need to be considered. Variable factory overhead costs such as power and maintenance are determined to amount to approximately 65% of the direct labor cost of $2, or $1.30. The cost factors to be considered are summarized in the following report:

Differential Analysis Report—Make or Buy

Proposal To Manufacture Part X
February 15, 19--

Purchase price of part		$5.00
Differential cost to manufacture part:		
Direct materials	$1.00	
Direct labor	2.00	
Variable factory overhead	1.30	4.30
Cost reduction from manufacturing Part X		$ .70

Other possible effects of a change in policy should also be considered, such as the possibility that a future increase in volume of production would require the use of the currently idle capacity of 20%. The possible effect of the alternatives on employees and on future business relations with the supplier of the part, who may be providing other essential components, are additional factors that might need study.

Equipment Replacement

The usefulness of plant assets may be impaired long before they are considered to be "worn out." Equipment may no longer be ideally adequate for the purpose for which it is used, but on the other hand it may not have reached the point of complete inadequacy. Similarly, the point in time when equipment becomes obsolete may be difficult to determine. Decisions to replace usable plant assets should be based on studies of relevant costs rather than on whims or subjective opinions. The costs to be considered are the alternative future costs of retention as opposed to replacement. The book values of the plant assets being replaced are sunk costs and are irrevelant.

To illustrate some of the factors involved in replacement decisions, assume that an enterprise is considering the disposal of several identical machines having a total book value of $100,000 and an estimated remaining life of five years. The old machines can be sold for $25,000. They can be replaced by a single high-speed machine at a cost of $250,000, with an estimated useful life of five years and no residual value. Analysis of the specifications of the new machine and of accompanying changes in manufacturing methods indicate an estimated annual reduction in variable manufacturing costs from $225,000 to $150,000. No other changes in the manufacturing costs or the operating expenses are expected. The basic data to be considered are summarized in the following report:

Differential Analysis Report—Equipment Replacement

Proposal To Replace Equipment November 28, 19--		
Annual variable costs—present equipment	$225,000	
Annual variable costs—new equipment	150,000	
Annual differential decrease in cost	$ 75,000	
Number of years applicable	× 5	
Total differential decrease in cost	$375,000	
Proceeds from sale of present equipment	25,000	$400,000
Cost of new equipment		250,000
Net differential decrease in cost, 5-year total		$150,000
Annual differential decrease in cost—new equipment		$ 30,000

Complicating features could be added to the foregoing illustration, such as a disparity between the remaining useful life of the old equipment and the estimated life of the new equipment, or possible improvement in the product due to the new machine, with a resulting increase in selling price or volume of sales. Another factor that should be considered is the importance of alternative uses for the cash outlay needed to obtain the new equipment. The amount of income that would result from the best available alternative to the proposed use of cash or its equivalent is sometimes called **opportunity cost.** If, for example, it is assumed that the cash outlay of $250,000 for the new equipment, less the $25,000 proceeds from the sale of the present equipment, could be used to yield a 10% return, the opportunity cost of the proposal would amount to 10% of $225,000, or $22,500.

The term "opportunity cost" introduces a new concept of "cost." In reality, it is not a cost in any usual sense of the word. Instead, it represents the forgoing of possible income associated with a lost opportunity. Although opportunity cost computations do not appear as a part of historical accounting data, they are unquestionably useful in analyses involving choices between alternative courses of action.

Process or Sell

When a product is manufactured, it progresses through various stages of production. Often, a product can be sold at an intermediate stage of production, or it can be processed further and then sold. In deciding whether to sell a product at an intermediate stage or to process it further, the differential revenues that would be provided and the differential costs that would be incurred from further processing must be considered. Since the costs of producing the intermediate product do not change, regardless of whether the intermediate product is sold or processed further, these costs are not differential costs and are not considered.

To illustrate, assume that an enterprise produces Product Y in batches of 4,000 gallons by processing standard quantities of 4,000 gallons of direct materials, which cost $1.20 per gallon. Product Y can be sold without further processing for $2 per gallon. It is possible for the enterprise to process Product Y further to yield Product Z, which can be sold for $5 per gallon. Product Z will require additional processing costs of $5,760 per batch, and 20% of the gallons of Product Y will evaporate during production. The differential revenues and costs to be considered in deciding whether to process Product Y to produce Product Z are summarized in the following report:

Proposal To Process Product Y Further October 1, 19--		
Differential revenue from further processing per batch:		
Revenue from sale of Product Z [(4,000 gallons − 800 gallons evaporation) × $5]	$16,000	
Revenue from sale of Product Y (4,000 gallons × $2)	8,000	
Differential revenue		$8,000
Differential cost per batch:		
Additional cost of producing Product Z		5,760
Net advantage of further processing Product Y per batch		$2,240

Differential Analysis Report—Process or Sell

The net advantage of further processing Product Y into Product Z is $2,240 per batch. Note that the initial cost of producing the intermediate Product Y, $4,800 (4,000 gallons × $1.20), is not considered in deciding whether to process Product Y further. This initial cost will be incurred regardless of whether Product Z is produced.

Acceptance of Business at a Special Price

In determining whether to accept additional business at a special price, management must consider the differential revenue that would be provided and the differential cost that would be incurred. If the company is operating at full capacity, the additional production will increase both fixed and variable production costs. But if the normal production of the company is below full capacity, additional business may be undertaken without increasing fixed production costs. In the latter case, the variable costs will be the differential cost of the additional production. Variable costs are the only costs to be considered in making a decision to accept or reject the order. If the operating expenses are likely to increase, these differentials must also be considered.

To illustrate, assume that the usual monthly production of an enterprise is 10,000 units of a certain commodity. At this level of operation, which is well below capacity, the manufacturing cost is $20 per unit, composed of variable costs of $12.50 and fixed costs of $7.50. The normal selling price of the product in the domestic market is $30. The manufacturer receives an offer from an exporter for 5,000 units of the product at $18 each. Production costs can be spread over a three-month period without interfering with normal production or incurring overtime costs. Pricing policies in the domestic market will not be affected. Comparison of a sales price of $18 with the present unit cost of $20 would indicate that this offer should be rejected. However, if attention is limited to the differential cost, which in this case is composed of the variable costs and expenses, the conclusion is quite different. The essentials of the analysis are presented in the following brief report:

Proposal To Sell to Exporter March 10, 19--	
Differential revenue from acceptance of offer:	
Revenue from sale of 5,000 additional units at $18	$90,000
Differential cost of acceptance of offer:	
Variable costs and expenses of 5,000 additional units at $12.50	62,500
Gain from acceptance of offer	$27,500

Differential Analysis Report—Sale at Special Price

Proposals to sell an increased output in the domestic market at a reduction from the normal price may require additional considerations of a difficult nature. It would clearly be unwise to increase sales volume in one territory by means of a price reduction if sales volume would thereby be jeopardized in other areas. Manufacturers must also exercise care to avoid violations of the Robinson-Patman Act, which prohibits price discrimination within the United States unless the difference in price can be justified by a difference in the cost of serving different customers.

SETTING NORMAL PRODUCT PRICES

Differential analysis, as illustrated, is useful to management in setting product selling prices for special short-run decisions, such as whether to accept business at a price lower than the normal price. In such situations, the short-run price is set high enough to cover all variable costs and expenses plus provide an excess to cover some of the fixed costs and perhaps provide for profit. Such a pricing plan will improve profits in the short run. In the long run, however, the normal selling price must be set high enough to cover all costs and expenses (both fixed and variable) and provide a reasonable amount for profit. Otherwise, the long-run survival of the firm may be jeopardized.

The normal selling price can be viewed as the target selling price which must be achieved in the long run, but which may be deviated from in the short run because of such factors as competition and general market conditions. A practical approach to setting the normal price is the cost-plus approach. Using this approach, managers determine product prices by adding to a "cost" amount a plus, called a **markup,** so that all costs plus a profit are covered in the price.

Three cost concepts commonly used in applying the cost-plus approach are (1) total cost, (2) product cost, and (3) variable cost. Each of these cost concepts is described and illustrated in the following paragraphs.

Total Cost Concept

Using the **total cost concept** of determining the product price, all costs of manufacturing a product plus the selling and general expenses are included in the cost amount to which the markup is added. Since all costs and expenses are included in the cost amount, the dollar amount of the markup equals the desired profit.

The first step in applying the total cost concept is to determine the total cost of manufacturing the product. Under the absorption costing system of accounting for manufacturing operations, the costs of direct materials, direct labor, and factory overhead should be available from the accounting records. The next step is to add the estimated selling and general expenses to the total cost of manufacturing the product. The cost amount per unit is then computed by dividing the total costs and expenses by the total units expected to be produced and sold.

After the cost amount per unit has been determined, the dollar amount of the markup is determined. For this purpose, the markup is expressed as a percentage of cost. This percentage is then multiplied by the cost amount per unit. The dollar amount of the markup is then added to the cost amount per unit to arrive at the selling price.

The markup percentage for the total cost concept is determined by applying the following formula:

$$\text{Markup Percentage} = \frac{\text{Desired Profit}}{\text{Total Costs and Expenses}}$$

The numerator of the markup percentage formula includes only the desired profit, since all costs and expenses will be covered by the cost amount to which the markup will be added. The denominator of the formula includes the total costs and expenses, which are covered by the cost amount.

To illustrate the use of the total cost concept, assume that the costs and expenses for Product N of Moyer Co. are as follows:

Variable costs and expenses:	
Direct materials	$ 3.00 per unit
Direct labor	10.00
Factory overhead	1.50
Selling and general expenses	1.50
Total	$16.00 per unit
Fixed costs and expenses:	
Factory overhead	$50,000
Selling and general expenses	20,000

Moyer Co. desires a profit equal to a 20% rate of return on assets, $800,000 of assets are devoted to producing Product N, and 100,000 units are expected to be produced and sold. The cost amount for Product N is $1,670,000, or $16.70 per unit, computed as follows:

Variable costs and expenses ($16.00 × 100,000 units)		$1,600,000
Fixed costs and expenses:		
Factory overhead	$50,000	
Selling and general expenses	20,000	70,000
Total costs and expenses		$1,670,000
Cost amount per unit ($1,670,000 ÷ 100,000 units)		$16.70

The desired profit is $160,000 (20% × $800,000), and the markup percentage for Product N is 9.6%, computed as follows:

$$\text{Markup Percentage} = \frac{\text{Desired Profit}}{\text{Total Costs and Expenses}}$$

$$\text{Markup Percentage} = \frac{\$160{,}000}{\$1{,}670{,}000}$$

$$\text{Markup Percentage} = 9.6\%$$

Based on the cost amount per unit and the markup percentage for Product N, Moyer Co. would price Product N at $18.30 per unit, as shown in the following computation:

Cost amount per unit	$16.70
Markup ($16.70 × 9.6%)	1.60
Selling price	$18.30

The ability of the selling price of $18.30 to generate the desired profit of $160,000 is shown in the following condensed income statement for Moyer Co.:

Moyer Co.
Income Statement
For Year Ended December 31, 19--

Sales (100,000 units × $18.30)		$1,830,000
Expenses:		
Variable (100,000 units × $16.00)	$1,600,000	
Fixed ($50,000 + $20,000)	70,000	1,670,000
Income from operations		$ 160,000

The total cost concept of applying the cost-plus approach to product pricing is frequently used by contractors who sell products to government agencies. In many cases, government contractors are required by law to be reimbursed for their products on a total-cost-plus-profit basis.

Product Cost Concept

Using the **product cost concept** of determining the product price, only the costs of manufacturing the product, termed the product cost, are included in the cost amount to which the markup is added. Selling expenses, general expenses, and profit are covered in the markup. The markup percentage is determined by applying the following formula:

$$\text{Markup Percentage} = \frac{\text{Desired Profit} + \text{Total Selling and General Expenses}}{\text{Total Manufacturing Costs}}$$

The numerator of the markup percentage formula includes the desired profit plus the total selling and general expenses. Selling and general expenses must be covered by the markup, since they are not covered by the cost amount to which the markup will be added. The denominator of the formula includes the costs of direct materials, direct labor, and factory overhead, which are covered by the cost amount.

To illustrate the use of the product cost concept, assume the same data that were used in the preceding illustration. The cost amount for Moyer Co.'s Product N is $1,500,000, or $15 per unit, computed as follows:

Direct materials ($3 × 100,000 units)		$ 300,000
Direct labor ($10 × 100,000 units)		1,000,000
Factory overhead:		
Variable ($1.50 × 100,000 units)	$150,000	
Fixed	50,000	200,000
Total manufacturing costs		$1,500,000
Cost amount per unit ($1,500,000 ÷ 100,000 units)		$15

The desired profit is $160,000 (20% × $800,000), and the total selling and general expenses are $170,000 [(100,000 units × $1.50 per unit) + $20,000]. The markup percentage for Product N is 22%, computed as follows:

$$\text{Markup Percentage} = \frac{\text{Desired Profit + Total Selling and General Expenses}}{\text{Total Manufacturing Costs}}$$

$$\text{Markup Percentage} = \frac{\$160{,}000 + \$170{,}000}{\$1{,}500{,}000}$$

$$\text{Markup Percentage} = \frac{\$330{,}000}{\$1{,}500{,}000}$$

$$\text{Markup Percentage} = 22\%$$

Based on the cost amount per unit and the markup percentage for Product N, Moyer Co. would price Product N at $18.30 per unit, as shown in the following computation:

Cost amount per unit	$15.00
Markup ($15 × 22%)	3.30
Selling price	$18.30

Variable Cost Concept

Using the **variable cost concept** of determining the product price, only variable costs and expenses are included in the cost amount to which the markup is added. All variable manufacturing costs, as well as variable selling and general expenses, are included in the cost amount. Fixed manufacturing costs, fixed selling and general expenses, and profit are covered in the markup.

The markup percentage for the variable cost concept is determined by applying the following formula:

$$\text{Markup Percentage} = \frac{\text{Desired Profit + Total Fixed Manufacturing Costs + Total Fixed Selling and General Expenses}}{\text{Total Variable Costs and Expenses}}$$

The numerator of the markup percentage formula includes the desired profit plus the total fixed manufacturing costs and the total fixed selling and general expenses. Fixed manufacturing costs and fixed selling and general expenses must be covered by the markup, since they are not covered by the cost amount to which the markup will be added. The denominator of the formula includes the total variable costs and expenses, which are covered by the cost amount.

To illustrate the use of the variable cost concept, assume the same data that were used in the two preceding illustrations. The cost amount for Product N is $1,600,000, or $16.00 per unit, computed as follows:

Variable costs and expenses:	
Direct materials ($3 × 100,000 units)	$ 300,000
Direct labor ($10 × 100,000 units)	1,000,000
Factory overhead ($1.50 × 100,000 units)	150,000
Selling and general expenses ($1.50 × 100,000 units)	150,000
Total variable costs and expenses	$1,600,000
Cost amount per unit ($1,600,000 ÷ 100,000 units)	$16.00

The desired profit is $160,000 (20% × $800,000), the total fixed manufacturing costs are $50,000, and the total fixed selling and general expenses are $20,000. The markup percentage for Product N is 14.4%, computed as follows:

$$\text{Markup Percentage} = \frac{\text{Desired Profit + Total Fixed Manufacturing Costs + Total Fixed Selling and General Expenses}}{\text{Total Variable Costs and Expenses}}$$

$$\text{Markup Percentage} = \frac{\$160,000 + \$50,000 + \$20,000}{\$1,600,000}$$

$$\text{Markup Percentage} = \frac{\$230,000}{\$1,600,000}$$

$$\text{Markup Percentage} = 14.4\%$$

Based on the cost amount per unit and the markup percentage for Product N, Moyer Co. would price Product N at $18.30 per unit, as shown in the following computation:

Cost amount per unit	$16.00
Markup ($16.00 × 14.4%)	2.30
Selling price	$18.30

The variable cost concept emphasizes the distinction between variable and fixed costs and expenses in product pricing. This distinction is similar to the distinction between absorption and variable costing described in Chapter 20.

Choosing a Cost-Plus Approach Cost Concept

The three cost concepts commonly used in applying the cost-plus approach to product pricing are summarized as follows:

Cost Concept	*Covered in Cost Amount*	*Covered in Markup*
Total cost	Total costs and expenses	Desired profit
Product cost	Total manufacturing costs	Desired profit + Total selling and general expenses
Variable cost	Total variable costs and expenses	Desired profit + Total fixed manufacturing costs + Total fixed selling and general expenses

As demonstrated in the Moyer Co. illustration, all three cost concepts will yield the same selling price ($18.30) when the concepts are properly applied. Which of the three cost concepts should be used by management depends on such factors as the cost of gathering the data and the decision needs of management. For example, the data for the product cost concept can be easily gathered by a company using an absorption cost accounting system.

To reduce the costs of gathering data, standard costs rather than actual costs may be used with any of the three cost concepts. However, caution should be exercised by management when using standard costs in applying the cost-plus approach. As discussed in Chapter 22, the standards should be based on normal (attainable) operating levels and not theoretical (ideal) levels of performance. In product pricing, the use of standards based on ideal or maximum capacity operating levels might lead to the establishment of product prices which are too low, since the costs of such factors as normal spoilage or normal periods of idle time would not be covered in the price. As a result, the desired profit would be reduced by these costs and expenses.

ECONOMIC THEORY OF PRODUCT PRICING

In addition to costs, as discussed in the preceding paragraphs, other factors may influence the pricing decision. In considering these factors, which include the general economic conditions of the marketplace, a knowledge of the economic theory underlying product pricing is useful to the managerial accountant. Although the study of **price theory** is generally considered a separate discipline in the area of microeconomics, the following paragraphs present an overview of the economic models for explaining pricing behavior.

Maximization of Profits

In microeconomic theory, management's primary objective is assumed to be the maximization of profits. Profits will be maximized at the point at which the difference between total revenues and total costs and expenses is the greatest amount. Consequently, microeconomic theory focuses on the behavior of total revenues as price and sales volume vary and the behavior of total costs and expenses as production varies.

Revenues

Generally, it is not possible to sell an unlimited number of units of product at the same price. At some point, price reductions will be necessary in order to sell more units. Total revenue may increase as the price is reduced, but there comes a point when further price decreases will reduce total revenue. To illustrate, the following revenue schedule shows the effect on revenue when each $1 reduction in the unit selling price increases by 1 unit the number of units sold:

REVENUE SCHEDULE

Price	*Units Sold*	*Total Revenue*	*Marginal Revenue*
$11	1	$11	$11
10	2	20	9
9	3	27	7
8	4	32	5
7	5	35	3
6	6	36	1
5	7	35	−1

In the revenue schedule illustrated, a price reduction from $11 to $10 increases total revenue by $9 (from $11 to $20). This increase (or decrease) in total revenue realized from the sale of an additional unit of product is called the **marginal revenue.** With each successive price reduction from $11 to $6, the total revenue increase is less. Finally, a price reduction from $6 to $5 decreases total revenue by $1.

Costs

As production and sales increase, the total cost increases. The amount by which total cost increases, however, varies as more and more production and sales are squeezed from limited facilities. Economists assume that as the total number of units produced and sold increases from a relatively low level, the total cost increases but in decreasing amounts. This assumption is based on efficiencies created by **economies of scale.** Economies of scale generally imply that, for a given amount of facilities, it is more efficient to produce and sell large quantities than small quantities. At some point, however, the total cost will begin to increase by increasing amounts because of inefficiencies created by such factors as employees getting in each other's way and machine breakdowns caused by heavy use. The increase in total cost from producing and selling an additional unit of product is known as **marginal cost.** To illustrate, the following cost schedule shows the effect on cost when one additional unit is produced and sold:

COST SCHEDULE

Units Produced and Sold	*Total Cost*	*Marginal Cost*
1	$ 9	$9
2	17	8
3	24	7
4	30	6
5	37	7
6	45	8
7	54	9

In the cost schedule, the cost of producing 1 unit is $9, and for each additional unit the total cost per unit increases by $8, $7, $6, $7, $8, and $9 respectively. The marginal cost of producing and selling the second unit is $8, which is the difference between the total cost of producing and selling 2 units ($17) and the total cost of 1 unit ($9). As production and sales increase from 1 unit to 4 units, the marginal cost decreases from $9 to $6. After the production and sale of 4 units, however, the marginal cost increases from $6 for the fourth unit to $7 for producing and selling the fifth unit.

Product Price Determination

A price-cost combination that maximizes the total profit of an enterprise can be determined by plotting the marginal revenues and marginal costs on a **price graph.** To illustrate, the marginal revenues and marginal costs for the preceding illustration are plotted on the following graph:

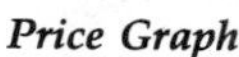

Price Graph

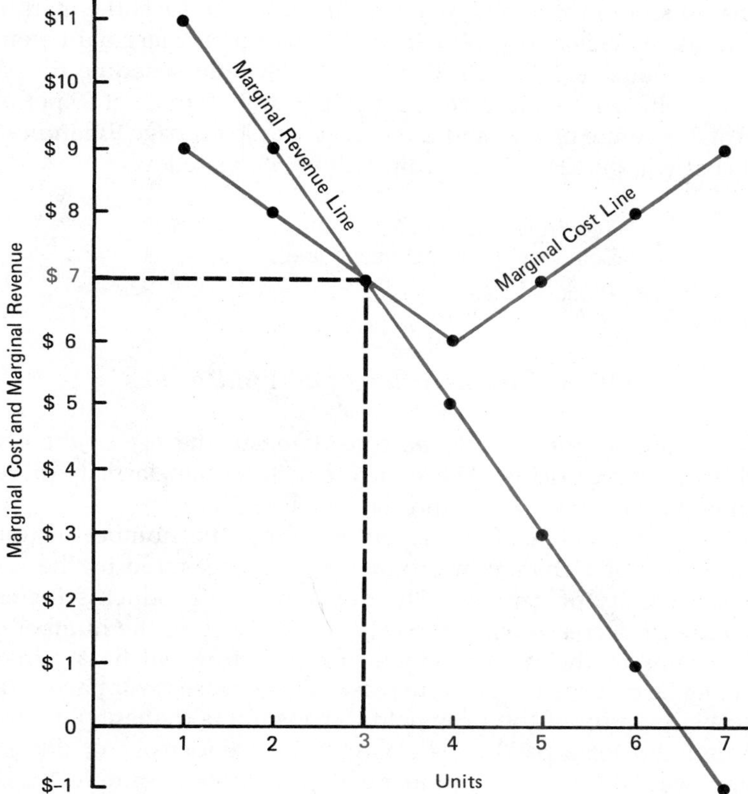

A price graph is constructed in the following manner:

1. The horizontal axis is drawn to represent units of production and sales.
2. The vertical axis is drawn to represent dollars for marginal revenues and marginal costs.
3. The marginal revenue for each unit of sales is plotted on the graph by first locating the number of units of sales along the horizontal axis and then proceeding upward until the proper amount of marginal revenue is indicated on the vertical axis.
4. The marginal revenue line is drawn on the price graph by connecting the marginal revenue points.
5. The marginal cost for each unit of production is plotted on the graph by first locating the number of units of production along the horizontal axis and then proceeding upward until the proper amount of marginal cost is indicated on the vertical axis.
6. The marginal cost line is drawn on the price graph by connecting the marginal cost points.

The point at which the marginal revenue line intersects the marginal cost line on the price graph indicates a level of sales and production at which profits are maximized. In other words, there is no other level of production and sales that will provide a larger amount of profit. For example, at higher levels of production and sales, the change in total cost is greater than the change in total revenue. Therefore, less profit would be achieved by manufacturing and selling more units.

In the illustration, the marginal revenue line intersects the marginal cost line at 3 units of sales and production. At this point, marginal revenue and marginal cost equal $7. To sell 3 units, the revenue schedule on page 917 indicates that the price should be set at $9 per unit. A price of $9 per unit will provide total revenue of $27, and the cost schedule on page 918 indicates that the total cost will be $24. Thus, profit will be $3, as follows:

Total revenue (3 units × $9)	$27
Total cost (from cost schedule).....	24
Profit	$ 3

Other Considerations and Limitations

Several other factors should be considered in the use of the economic approach to product pricing. These factors include the elasticity of demand, competitive market conditions, and data availability.

Elasticity of demand. The degree by which the number of units sold changes because of a change in product price is measured by the economic concept of **elasticity of demand.** The demand for a product is **inelastic** if a price increase or decrease will have little or no effect on the number of units sold. For example, the demand for a medical drug, such as penicillin or insulin, is inelastic because price increases or decreases will have little or no effect on the quantity of the drug sold to consumers (patients).

The demand for a product is **elastic** if a price increase or decrease will have a significant effect on the number of units sold. For example, the demand for most automobiles is elastic. As a consequence, automobile manufacturers will periodically offer special rebates or other price reductions to consumers in order to stimulate sales.[1]

Economists employ various techniques to estimate the elasticity of demand. A description of these techniques is normally covered in economic texts and is not described in this chapter.

Competitive market conditions. One limitation of the economic concepts described in the preceding paragraphs is that the concepts directly apply only to conditions of monopoly and monopolistic competition. In a **monopoly market,** no competing products exist. For example, many cable television companies offer their services in a monopoly market. In a **monopolistic competitive market,** there exist many sellers of similar products, with no one seller having a large enough share of the market to influence the total sales of the other products. For example, many retail businesses operate within monopolistic competitive markets.

The concepts described in the preceding paragraphs are not directly applicable to purely competitive and oligopoly markets. In a **purely competitive market,** the price for the product is established solely by the market conditions, and the quantity that a firm sells has no impact on the total market

[1]Managers must be careful in classifying the demand for products as either elastic or inelastic. For example, although the demand for most automobiles is elastic, the demand for specialty automoblies, such as Porsches and Ferraris, is inelastic.

for the product. Thus, a firm can sell all it produces at the market price. Agriculture is an example of a purely competitive market.

In an **oligopoly market,** there exist a few large sellers competing against each other with similar products. Hence, the amount sold by each seller has a direct effect on the sales of the other companies. An example is the auto industry. In this market, price increases by a company will bring no response by competitors and will result in a decrease in total units sold because competitors will not change their prices. In contrast, a price decrease will bring retaliatory price decreases by competitors.

Data availability. The economic approach to product pricing is not often used because the data required to estimate demand elasticity and marginal revenue are often unavailable. For example, it is difficult to estimate the amount that consumers will purchase over a range of prices without actually offering the product for sale at those prices. Since total cost data can be estimated reliably from accounting records, the cost-plus approach to product pricing is frequently used.

The Art of Pricing Air Fares

One industry in which pricing plays a very significant role is the airline industry, which operates in an oligopoly market. Fare wars and constantly changing fares are commonplace among the major airlines. The fine tuning involved in pricing fares is described in the following excerpt from an article in *The Wall Street Journal*.

The latest round of fare wars... has put a spotlight on how carriers use state-of-the-art computer software, complex forecasting techniques and a little intuition to divine how many seats at what prices they will offer on any given flight....

Too many wrong projections can lead to huge losses of revenue, or even worse. The inability of People Express to manage its inventory of seats properly, for example, was one of the major causes of its demise.

"It's a sophisticated guessing game," said [the] vice president of pricing and product planning at American Airlines.... "You don't want to sell a seat to a guy for $69 when he's willing to pay $400."

With the industry now adopting very low discount but nonrefundable fares, the complex task of managing seat inventory may become easier because airlines will be better able to predict how many people will show up for a flight.

Some airlines have already seen a drop in their no-shows, which means they can overbook less and spare more customers from being bumped. The nonrefundable fares could also enable carriers to sell more discount seats weeks before a flight, rather than putting them on sale at the last minute in an effort to fill up the plane.

American's inventory operation illustrates just how complicated the process can be. At the airline's corporate headquarters [in Dallas], 90 yield managers are linked by terminals to five International Business Machines mainframe computers in Tulsa, Okla. The managers monitor and adjust the fare mixes on 1,600 daily flights as well as 528,000 future flights involving nearly 50 million passengers. Their work is hectic: A fare's average life span is two weeks, and industrywide about 200,000 fares change daily.

American and the other airlines base their forecasts largely on historical profiles of each flight. Business travelers, for example, book heavily on many Friday afternoon flights, but often not until the day of departure. The airlines reserve blocks of seats for those frequent fliers. Few, if any, discounts are made available....

For the bargain hunter, finding a discount will increasingly depend on the season, day and time of travel, destination and length of stay....

The following table indicates the difference between the number of seats sold at each fare for a Wednesday and Friday flight of American Airlines:

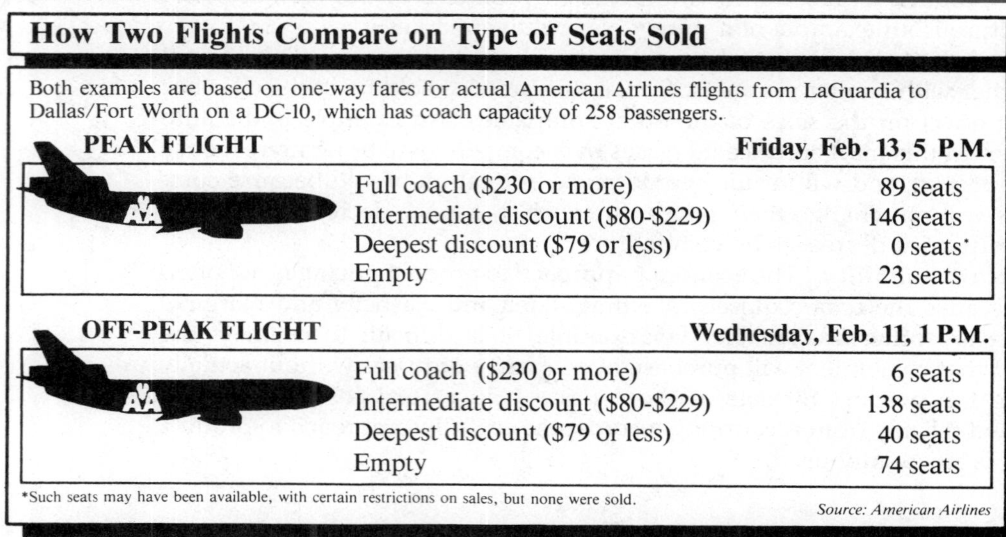

How Two Flights Compare on Type of Seats Sold

Both examples are based on one-way fares for actual American Airlines flights from LaGuardia to Dallas/Fort Worth on a DC-10, which has coach capacity of 258 passengers.

PEAK FLIGHT	**Friday, Feb. 13, 5 P.M.**
Full coach ($230 or more)	89 seats
Intermediate discount ($80-$229)	146 seats
Deepest discount ($79 or less)	0 seats*
Empty	23 seats

OFF-PEAK FLIGHT	**Wednesday, Feb. 11, 1 P.M.**
Full coach ($230 or more)	6 seats
Intermediate discount ($80-$229)	138 seats
Deepest discount ($79 or less)	40 seats
Empty	74 seats

*Such seats may have been available, with certain restrictions on sales, but none were sold.

Source: American Airlines

Source: Eric Schmitt, "The Art of Pricing Air Fares," *The Wall Street Journal,* March 4, 1987.

PRICING STRATEGIES

Within the constraints of market conditions, managers must decide upon a pricing strategy for a company's various products. The pricing strategy chosen for a product depends upon the factors previously discussed. In addition, the stage in the product's life cycle at which the product is offered for sale has an important effect. The **product life cycle** concept is based on the idea that a product normally passes through various stages from the time that it is introduced until the time that it disappears from the market.

The normal life cycle for a product is divided into five stages: the introductory stage, the rapid growth stage, the turbulent stage, the maturity stage, and the terminating stage. Graphically, the relationship of these stages to total dollar sales during a product's life cycle can be illustrated as follows:

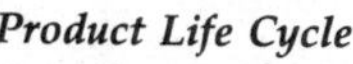

Product Life Cycle

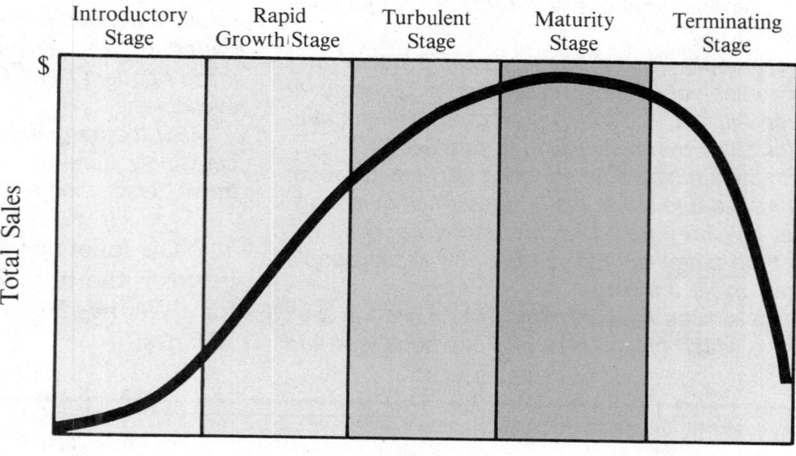

In the introductory stage, the product is new to the market and no direct competition exists. During this stage, management normally spends large amounts on promotional activities in order to develop a market for the product. Since no competition exists, prices are normally set to provide coverage of all costs and to provide high profit margins. Total sales begin low and expand rapidly as more consumers discover the product.

In the rapid growth stage, the product has caught on with consumers and competitors begin to enter the market. Total sales expand rapidly, since the industry cannot meet consumer demand for the product. Prices normally remain high during this stage, but begin to decrease as competition increases. Management normally continues to set prices high enough to cover all costs and provide for a reasonable profit.

In the turbulent stage, competition increases dramatically as more and more competitors enter the market. Although sales continue to be strong, increasing price competition causes total sales to increase at a decreasing rate. Management normally continues to set prices high enough to cover all costs, but profit margins are reduced to meet competition. For short periods of time, management may offer the product for sale at special prices that cover only variable costs. During this stage, one or two companies may achieve dominant positions in the market as less efficient competitors are driven out of the market.

In the maturity stage, competition stabilizes and few, if any, new competitors enter the market. Management normally sets prices at a relatively low level to cover all costs and to allow for a low profit margin. The consumer demand for the product levels off and may decline. Total sales reach a maximum and begin to decline.

In the terminating stage, the strategy of management is to reduce the chance of any losses and to get as much profit out of the remaining product demand as possible. Near the end of this stage, prices are often set to cover only product variable costs in order to reduce the chance that the company will be left with excess inventories after consumer demand has disappeared.

One example of the product life cycle concept is the market for the IBM personal computer during the early and mid-1980's. During this period, the price of a standard IBM personal computer decreased from approximately $3,500 in 1980, when it was first introduced, to less than $1,000 in 1987. IBM attempted to prolong the computer's relatively brief life cycle by introducing new enhancements, such as hard disk drives, additional memory, and color monitors.

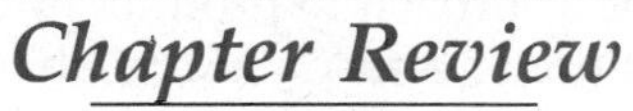

Chapter Review

KEY POINTS

1. Differential Analysis.

The area of accounting concerned with the effect of alternative courses of action on revenues and costs is called differential analysis. Differential revenue is the amount of increase or decrease in revenue expected from a particular course of action as compared with an alternative. Differential cost is the amount of increase or decrease in cost that is expected from a particular course of action as compared with an alternative.

Differential analysis can aid management in making decisions on a variety of alternatives, including (1) whether equipment should be leased or sold, (2) whether to discontinue an unprofitable segment, (3) whether to manufacture or purchase a needed part, (4) whether to replace plant assets, (5) whether to process further or sell an intermediate product, and (6) whether to accept additional business at a special price.

2. Setting Normal Product Prices.
The normal selling price can be viewed as the target selling price, which must be achieved in the long run but may be deviated from in the short run because of such factors as competition and general market conditions. A practical approach to setting the normal price is the cost-plus approach. Using this approach, managers determine product prices by adding to a "cost" amount a markup, so that all costs plus a profit are covered in the price.

The three cost concepts commonly used in applying the cost-plus approach to product pricing are summarized as follows:

Cost Concept	Covered in Cost Amount	Covered in Markup
Total cost	Total costs and expenses	Desired profit
Product cost	Total manufacturing costs	Desired profit + Total selling and general expenses
Variable cost	Total variable costs and expenses	Desired profit + Total fixed manufacturing costs + Total fixed selling and general expenses

The markup percentage for each cost concept is determined by dividing the amount covered in the markup by the amount covered in the cost.

3. Economic Theory of Product Pricing.
The theory underlying product pricing is a separate economic discipline known as price theory. In this theory, management's primary objective is assumed to be the maximization of profits. The increase (decrease) in total revenue realized from the sale of an additional unit of product is called marginal revenue. The increase in total cost from producing and selling an additional unit of product is called marginal cost. A cost schedule prepared under the assumption of economies of scale is used for determining marginal costs. The point on the price graph where the marginal revenue line and the marginal cost line intersect indicates the level of sales and production at which profits are maximized.

In using the economic approach to product pricing, elasticity of demand, competitive market conditions, and data availability should be considered.

4. Pricing Strategies.
The stage in its life cycle at which a product is offered for sale has an important effect on management's choice of a pricing strategy. During the introductory stage, product prices are set to cover all costs and to provide for high profit margins. During the rapid growth stage, product prices remain high, but begin to decrease as new competitors enter the market. During the turbulent stage, profit margins are reduced as prices fall and special prices covering only variable costs may be established for short periods. During the maturity stage,

prices remain at low levels as total sales reach a maximum and begin to fall. During the terminating stage, prices may be lowered to cover only variable costs in order to reduce losses and excess inventories.

KEY TERMS

differential analysis 905
differential revenue 905
differential cost 905
sunk cost 906
opportunity cost 910
markup 912
total cost concept 912
product cost concept 914
variable cost concept 915
price theory 917
marginal revenue 917
economies of scale 918
marginal cost 918
price graph 918
elasticity of demand 920
inelastic demand 920
elastic demand 920
monopoly market 920
monopolistic competitive market 920
purely competitive market 920
oligopoly market 921
product life cycle 922

SELF-EXAMINATION QUESTIONS

(Answers at End of Chapter)

1. The amount of increase or decrease in cost that is expected from a particular course of action as compared with an alternative is referred to as:
   A. differential cost
   B. replacement cost
   C. sunk cost
   D. none of the above
2. Victor Company is considering the disposal of equipment that was originally purchased for $200,000 and has accumulated depreciation to date of $150,000. The same equipment would cost $310,000 to replace. What is the sunk cost?
   A. $50,000
   B. $150,000
   C. $200,000
   D. None of the above
3. The amount of income that would result from the best available alternative to a proposed use of cash or its equivalent is referred to as:
   A. actual cost
   B. historical cost
   C. opportunity cost
   D. none of the above
4. For which cost concept used in applying the cost-plus approach to product pricing are fixed manufacturing costs, fixed selling and general expenses, and desired profit allowed for in the determination of markup?
   A. Total cost
   B. Product cost
   C. Variable cost
   D. None of the above
5. According to microeconomic theory, profits of a business enterprise will be maximized at the point where:
   A. marginal revenue equals marginal cost
   B. the change in total revenue is greater than the change in total cost
   C. the change in total cost is greater than the change in total revenue
   D. none of the above

ILLUSTRATIVE PROBLEM

Berry Company recently began production of a new product, M, which required the investment of $2,000,000 in assets. The costs and expenses of producing and selling 100,000 units of Product M are estimated as follows:

Variable costs and expenses:	
Direct materials	$ 2.40 per unit
Direct labor	6.50
Factory overhead	.90
Selling and general expenses	.20
Total	$10.00 per unit
Fixed costs and expenses:	
Factory overhead	$ 60,000
Selling and general expenses	140,000

Berry Company is currently considering the establishment of a selling price for Product M. The president of Berry Company has decided to use the cost-plus approach to product pricing and has indicated that Product M must earn an 18% rate of return on invested assets.

Instructions:

1. Determine the amount of desired profit from the production and sale of Product M.
2. Assuming that the total cost concept is used, determine (a) the cost amount per unit, (b) the markup percentage, and (c) the selling price of Product M.
3. Assuming that the product cost concept is used, determine (a) the cost amount per unit, (b) the markup percentage, and (c) the selling price of Product M.
4. Assuming that the variable cost concept is used, determine (a) the cost amount per unit, (b) the markup percentage, and (c) the selling price of Product M.

SOLUTION

(1) $360,000 ($2,000,000 × 18%)

(2) (a) Total costs and expenses:

Variable ($10 × 100,000 units)	$1,000,000
Fixed ($60,000 + $140,000)	200,000
Total	$1,200,000

Cost amount per unit: $1,200,000 ÷ 100,000 units = $12

(b) $$\text{Markup Percentage} = \frac{\text{Desired Profit}}{\text{Total Costs and Expenses}}$$

$$\text{Markup Percentage} = \frac{\$360{,}000}{\$1{,}200{,}000}$$

Markup Percentage = 30%

(c)

Cost amount per unit	$12.00
Markup ($12 × 30%)	3.60
Selling price	$15.60

(3) (a) Total manufacturing costs:

Variable ($9.80 × 100,000 units)	$ 980,000
Fixed factory overhead	60,000
Total	$1,040,000

Cost amount per unit: $1,040,000 ÷ 100,000 units = $10.40

(b) $$\text{Markup Percentage} = \frac{\text{Desired Profit} + \text{Total Selling and General Expenses}}{\text{Total Manufacturing Costs}}$$

$$\text{Markup Percentage} = \frac{\$360{,}000 + \$140{,}000 + (\$.20 \times 100{,}000 \text{ units})}{\$1{,}040{,}000}$$

$$\text{Markup Percentage} = \frac{\$360{,}000 + \$140{,}000 + \$20{,}000}{\$1{,}040{,}000}$$

$$\text{Markup Percentage} = \frac{\$520{,}000}{\$1{,}040{,}000}$$

Markup Percentage = 50%

(c)

Cost amount per unit	$10.40
Markup ($10.40 × 50%)	5.20
Selling price	$15.60

(4) (a) Total variable costs and expenses: $10 × 100,000 units = $1,000,000
Cost amount per unit: $1,000,000 ÷ 100,000 units = $10

(b) $$\text{Markup Percentage} = \frac{\text{Desired Profit} + \text{Total Fixed Manufacturing Costs} + \text{Total Fixed Selling and General Expenses}}{\text{Total Variable Costs and Expenses}}$$

$$\text{Markup Percentage} = \frac{\$360{,}000 + \$60{,}000 + \$140{,}000}{\$1{,}000{,}000}$$

$$\text{Markup Percentage} = \frac{\$560{,}000}{\$1{,}000{,}000}$$

Markup Percentage = 56%

(c)

Cost amount per unit	$10.00
Markup ($10 × 56%)	5.60
Selling price	$15.60

Discussion Questions

25–1. What term is applied to the type of analysis that emphasizes the difference between the revenues and costs for proposed alternative courses of action?

25–2. Explain the meaning of (a) *differential revenue* and (b) *differential cost.*

25–3. Phillips Lumber Company incurs a cost of $80 per thousand board feet in processing a certain "rough-cut" lumber which it sells for $120 per thousand board feet. An alternative is to produce a "finished-cut" at a total processing cost of $96 per thousand board feet, which can be sold for $160 per thousand board feet. What is the amount of (a) the differential revenue and (b) the differential cost associated with the alternative?

25–4. (a) What is meant by *sunk costs?* (b) A company is contemplating replacing an old piece of machinery which cost $320,000 and has $280,000 accumulated depreciation to date. A new machine costs $400,000. What is the sunk cost in this situation?

25–5. The condensed income statement for Irving Company for the current year is as follows:

	Product			
	A	B	C	Total
Sales	$200,000	$170,000	$ 80,000	$450,000
Less variable costs and expenses	120,000	100,000	60,000	280,000
Contribution margin	$ 80,000	$ 70,000	$ 20,000	$170,000
Less fixed costs and expenses	40,000	31,000	30,000	101,000
Income (loss) from operations	$ 40,000	$ 39,000	$(10,000)	$ 69,000

Management decided to discontinue the manufacture and sale of Product C. Assuming that the discontinuance will have no effect on the total fixed costs and expenses or on the sales of Products A and B, has management made the correct decision? Explain.

25–6. (a) What is meant by *opportunity cost?* (b) Lieu Company is currently earning 10% on $200,000 invested in marketable securities. It proposes to use the $200,000 to acquire plant facilities to manufacture a new product that is expected to add $30,000 annually to net income. What is the opportunity cost involved in the decision to manufacture the new product?

25–7. In the long run, the normal selling price must be set high enough to cover what factors?

25–8. What are three cost concepts commonly used in applying the cost-plus approach to product pricing?

25–9. In using the product cost concept of applying the cost-plus approach to product pricing, what factors are included in the markup?

25–10. The variable cost concept used in applying the cost-plus approach to product pricing includes what costs in the cost amount to which the markup is added?

25–11. In determining the markup percentage for the variable cost concept of applying the cost-plus approach, what is included in the denominator?

25–12. Why might the use of ideal standards in applying the cost-plus approach to product pricing lead to setting product prices which are too low?

25–13. Although the cost-plus approach to product pricing may be used by management as a general guideline, what are some examples of other factors that managers should also consider in setting product prices?

25–14. In microeconomic theory, what is assumed to be management's primary objective for a business enterprise?

25–15. Why is it generally not possible to sell an unlimited number of units of product at the same price?

25–16. As the terms are used in microeconomic theory, what is meant by (a) marginal revenue and (b) marginal cost?

25–17. If the total revenue for selling 4 units of Product F is $40 and the total revenue for selling 5 units is $45, what is the marginal revenue associated with selling the fifth unit?

25–18. What does the concept of economies of scale generally imply?

25–19. For a given amount of facilities, why will the total costs and expenses begin to increase by increasing amounts at some point?

25–20. What point on the price graph indicates a maximum level of profit?

25–21. (a) If an increase in a price of a product has little or no effect on the number of units sold, is the demand for the product said to be elastic or inelastic? (b) Is the demand for bath soap by college students elastic or inelastic?

25–22. What is the economic term used to describe the market for a product in which there are many sellers of similar products, with no one seller having a large enough share of the market to influence the total sales of the other products?

25–23. Why is the more theoretical economic approach to product pricing not used as often as the cost-plus approach?

25–24. For the following graph of total sales for a product, identify each stage of the product's life cycle.

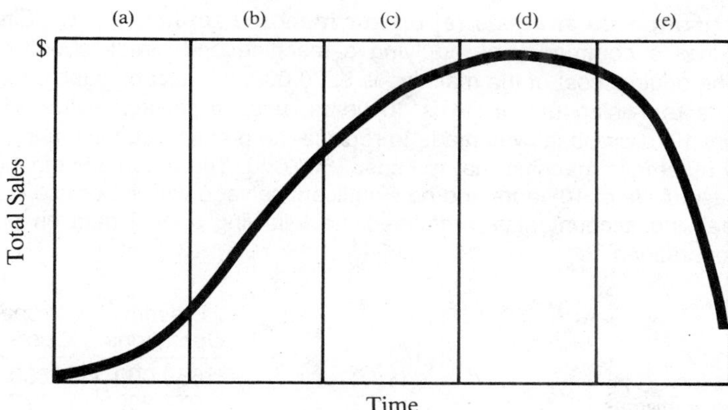

25–25. Real World Focus. In the personal computer hardware market, at what stage in the product life cycle is the 5 1/4-inch disk drives and the 3 1/2-inch drive?

25–26. Real World Focus. In July, 1986 *The Wall Street Journal* reported that the brakes that General Motors produces at its Delco Moraine division for its automobile assembly plants cost up to 15% more to make than they would cost to buy from an outside supplier. The same article reported that Ford Motor Co. and Chrysler Corp. buy almost all their brakes from outside suppliers as far away as Brazil, and these companies save money in the process. The decision of General Motors to produce its brakes internally is an example of what type of decision illustrated in this chapter?

Exercises

25–27. Differential analysis report for discontinuance of product. A condensed income statement by product line for Chow Co. indicated the following for Product H for the past year:

Sales	$120,000
Cost of goods sold	70,000
Gross profit	$ 50,000
Operating expenses	60,000
Loss from operations	$ (10,000)

It is estimated that 20% of the cost of goods sold represents fixed factory overhead costs and that 40% of operating expenses is fixed. Since Product H is only one of many products, the fixed costs and expenses will not be materially affected if the product is discontinued. (a) Prepare a differential analysis report, dated January 3 of the current year, for the proposed discontinuance of Product H. (b) Should Product H be retained? Explain.

25–28. Make or buy decision. Hernandez Company has been purchasing carrying cases for its portable typewriters at a delivered cost of $20 per unit. The company, which is currently operating below full capacity, charges factory overhead to production at the rate of 40% of direct labor cost. The direct materials and direct labor costs per unit to produce comparable carrying cases are expected to be $7 and $10 respectively. If Hernandez Company manufactures the carrying cases, fixed factory overhead costs will not increase and variable factory overhead costs associated with the cases are expected to be 15% of direct labor costs. (a) Prepare a differential analysis report, dated May 10 of the current year, for the make or buy decision. (b) On the basis of the data presented, would it be advisable to make or to continue buying the carrying cases? Explain.

SPREADSHEET PROBLEM

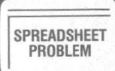

25–29. Differential analysis report for machine replacement. Elmore Company produces a commodity by applying a machine and direct labor to the direct material. The original cost of the machine is $270,000, the accumulated depreciation is $160,000, its remaining useful life is 10 years, and its salvage value is negligible. On February 10, a proposal was made to replace the present manufacturing procedure with a fully automatic machine that will cost $500,000. The automatic machine has an estimated useful life of 10 years and no significant salvage value. For use in evaluating the proposal, the accountant accumulated the following annual data on present and proposed operations:

	Present Operations	Proposed Operations
Sales	$650,000	$650,000
Direct materials	277,200	277,200
Direct labor	118,800	—
Power and maintenance	20,400	47,200
Taxes, insurance, etc.	13,200	19,200
Selling and general expenses	52,800	52,800

(a) Prepare a differential analysis report for the proposal to replace the machine. Include in the analysis both the net differential decrease in costs and expenses anticipated over the 10 years and the annual differential decrease in costs and expenses anticipated. (b) Based only on the data presented, should the proposal be accepted? (c) What are some of the other factors that should be considered before a final decision is made?

25–30. Decision on acceptance of additional business. Bailey Company has a plant capacity of 60,000 units, and current production is 40,000 units. Monthly fixed costs and expenses are $130,000, and variable costs and expenses are $14.20 per unit. The present selling price is $25 per unit. On November 23, the company received an offer from EMI Company for 10,000 units of the product at $16 each. The EMI Company will market the units in a foreign country under its own brand name. The additional business is not expected to affect the regular selling price or quantity of sales of Bailey Company. (a) Prepare a differential analysis report for the proposed sale to EMI Company. (b) Briefly explain the reason why the acceptance of this additional business will increase operating income. (c) What is the minimum price per unit that would produce a contribution margin?

25–31. Use of absorption costing or variable costing in bidding on contract. Adams Company expects to operate at 90% of productive capacity during

November. The total manufacturing costs for November for the production of 18,000 grinders are budgeted as follows:

Direct materials	$ 23,400
Direct labor	45,000
Variable factory overhead	10,800
Fixed factory overhead	27,000
Total manufacturing costs	$106,200

The company has an opportunity to submit a bid for 2,000 grinders to be delivered by November 30 to a government agency. If the contract is obtained, it is anticipated that the additional activity will not interfere with normal production during November or increase the selling or general expenses. (a) What is the unit cost below which Adams Company should not go in bidding on the government contract? (b) Is a unit cost figure based on absorption costing or one based on variable costing more useful in arriving at a bid on this contract? Explain.

25–32. Total cost concept of product pricing. Hargrave Company uses the total cost of applying the cost-plus approach to product pricing. The costs and expenses of producing and selling 10,000 units of Product M are as follows:

Variable costs and expenses:	
Direct materials	$ 5.60 per unit
Direct labor	2.80
Factory overhead	.60
Selling and general expenses	1.50
Total	$10.50 per unit
Fixed costs and expenses:	
Factory overhead	$30,000
Selling and general expenses	15,000

Hargrave Company desires a profit equal to an 18% rate of return on invested assets of $100,000. (a) Determine the amount of desired profit from the production and sale of Product M. (b) Determine the total costs and expenses and the cost amount per unit for the production and sale of 10,000 units of Product M. (c) Determine the markup percentage for Product M. (d) Determine the selling price of Product M.

25–33. Product cost concept of product pricing. Based on the data presented in Exercise 25–32, assume that Hargrave Company uses the product cost concept of applying the cost-plus approach to product pricing. (a) Determine the total manufacturing costs and the cost amount per unit for the production and sale of 10,000 units of Product M. (b) Determine the markup percentage for Product M. (c) Determine the selling price of Product M.

25–34. Variable cost concept of product pricing. Based on the data presented in Exercise 25–32, assume that Hargrave Company uses the variable cost concept of applying the cost-plus approach to product pricing. (a) Determine the cost amount per unit for the production and sale of 10,000 units of Product M. (b) Determine the markup percentage for Product M. (c) Determine the selling price of Product M.

25–35. Price graph and analysis. For the following revenue schedule and cost schedule for Product E (a) construct a price graph, (b) determine the level of sales and production at which the marginal cost and marginal revenue lines intersect, (c) determine the unit sales price at the level of sales determined in, (b) and (d) determine the maximum profit for Product E at the level of sales determined in (b).

Revenue Schedule

Price	Units Sold	Total Revenue	Marginal Revenue
$10	1	$10	$10
9	2	18	8
8	3	24	6
7	4	28	4
6	5	30	2
5	6	30	0
4	7	28	−2

Cost Schedule

Units Produced and Sold	Total Cost	Marginal Cost
1	$ 7	$ 7
2	13	6
3	18	5
4	22	4
5	25	3
6	29	4
7	34	5

Problems

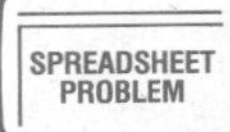

25–36. Differential analysis report involving opportunity costs. On August 1, Waters Company is considering leasing a building and purchasing the necessary equipment to operate a public warehouse. The project would be financed by selling $800,000 of 9% U.S. Treasury bonds that mature in 20 years. The bonds were purchased at face value and are currently selling at face value. The following data have been assembled:

Cost of equipment	$800,000
Life of equipment	20 years
Estimated residual value of equipment	$200,000
Yearly costs to operate the warehouse, in addition to depreciation of equipment	$ 50,000
Yearly expected revenues—first 8 years	$180,000
Yearly expected revenues—next 12 years	$150,000

Instructions: (1) Prepare a differential analysis report presenting the differential revenue and the differential cost associated with the proposed operation of the warehouse for the 20 years as compared with present conditions.

(2) Based on the results disclosed by the differential analysis, should the proposal be accepted?

(3) If the proposal is accepted, what is the total estimated income from operation of the warehouse for the 20 years?

25–37. Differential analysis report for machine replacement proposal. Lee Company is considering the replacement of a machine that has been used in its factory for three years. Relevant data associated with the operations of the old machine and the new machine, neither of which has any residual value, are as follows:

Old Machine

Cost of machine, 9-year life	$300,000
Annual depreciation	33,333

Annual manufacturing costs, exclusive of depreciation	$ 510,000
Related annual operating expenses	320,000
Associated annual revenue	1,120,000
Current estimated selling price	180,000

New Machine

Cost of machine, 6-year life	$630,000
Annual depreciation	105,000
Estimated annual manufacturing costs, exclusive of depreciation	380,000

Annual operating expenses and revenue are not expected to be affected by purchase of the new machine.

Instructions: (1) Prepare a differential analysis report as of October 4 of the current year, comparing operations utilizing the new machine with operations using the present equipment. The analysis should indicate the total differential decrease or increase in costs that would result over the 6-year period if the new machine is acquired.
(2) List other factors that should be considered before a final decision is reached.

25–38. Differential analysis report for sales promotion proposal. Gorksi Company is planning a one-month campaign for June to promote sales of one of its two products. A total of $35,000 has been budgeted for advertising, contests, redeemable coupons, and other promotional activities. The following data have been assembled for their possible usefulness in deciding which of the products to select for the campaign:

	Product D		Product E	
Unit selling price		$50		$60
Unit production costs:				
Direct materials	$14		$18	
Direct labor	10		14	
Variable factory overhead	8		8	
Fixed factory overhead	6		6	
Total unit production costs		$38		$46
Unit variable operating expenses		5		5
Unit fixed operating expenses		3		3
Total unit costs and expenses		$46		$54
Operating income per unit		$ 4		$ 6

No increase in facilities would be necessary to produce and sell the increased output. It is anticipated that 10,000 additional units of Product D or 8,000 additional units of Product E could be sold without changing the unit selling price of either product.

Instructions: (1) Prepare a differential analysis report as of May 5 of the current year, presenting the additional revenue and additional costs and expenses anticipated from the promotion of Product D and Product E.
(2) The sales manager had tentatively decided to promote Product E, estimating that operating income would be increased by $13,000 ($6 operating income per unit for 8,000 units, less promotion expenses of $35,000). It was also believed that the selection of Product D would increase operating income by only $5,000 ($4 operating income per unit for 10,000 units, less promotion expenses of $35,000). State briefly your reasons for supporting or opposing the tentative decision.

25–39. Differential analysis report for further processing. The management of Beeman Company is considering whether to process further Product X into Product Y. Product Y can be sold for $50 per pound, and Product X can be sold without further processing for $10 per pound. Product X is produced in batches of 300 pounds by processing 400 pounds of raw material, which costs $7 per pound. Product Y will require additional processing costs of $2.50 per pound of Product X, and 3 pounds of Product X will produce 1 pound of Product Y.

Instructions: (1) Prepare a differential analysis report as of April 10, presenting the differential revenue and differential cost per batch associated with the further processing of Product X to produce Product Y.
(2) Briefly report your recommendations.

25–40. Differential analysis report for further processing. Childers Refining Inc. refines Product V in batches of 100,000 gallons, which it sells for $4.80 per gallon. The associated unit costs and expenses are currently as follows:

Direct materials	$2.70
Direct labor	.72
Variable factory overhead	.28
Fixed factory overhead	.18
Sales commissions	.48
Fixed selling and general expenses	.12

The company is presently considering a proposal to put Product V through several additional processes to yield Products V and W. Although the company had determined such further processing to be unwise, new processing methods have now been developed. Existing facilities can be used for the additional processing, but since the factory is operating at full 8-hour-day capacity, the processing would have to be performed at night. Additional costs of processing would be $6,500 per batch, and there would be an evaporation loss of 10%, with 65% of the processed material evolving as Product V and 25% as Product W. The selling price of Product W is $7.20 per gallon. Sales commissions are a uniform percentage based on the sales price.

Instructions: (1) Prepare a differential analysis report as of January 20, presenting the differential revenue and the differential cost per batch associated with the processing to produce Products V and W, compared with processing to produce Product V only.
(2) Briefly report your recommendations.

25–41. Product pricing using the cost-plus approach concepts. Wilson Company recently began production of a new product, J, which required the investment of $500,000 in assets. The costs and expenses of producing and selling 50,000 units of Product J are estimated as follows:

Variable costs and expenses:	
Direct materials	$ 6.20
Direct labor	7.40
Factory overhead	1.40
Selling and general expenses	1.00
Total	$16.00
Fixed costs and expenses:	
Factory overhead	$150,000
Selling and general expenses	50,000

Wilson Company is currently considering the establishment of a selling price for Product J. The president of Wilson Company has decided to use the cost-plus approach to product pricing and has indicated that Product J must earn a 16% rate of return on invested assets.

Instructions: (1) Determine the amount of desired profit from the production and sale of Product J.
(2) Assuming that the total cost concept is used, determine (a) the cost amount per unit, (b) the markup percentage, and (c) the selling price of Product J.
(3) Assuming that the product cost concept is used, determine (a) the cost amount per unit, (b) the markup percentage, and (c) the selling price of Product J.
(4) Assuming that the variable cost concept is used, determine (a) the cost amount per unit, (b) the markup percentage, and (c) the selling price of Product J.

(5) Comment on any additional considerations that could influence the establishment of the selling price for Product J.

ALTERNATE PROBLEMS

SPREADSHEET PROBLEM

25–36A. Differential analysis report involving opportunity costs. On July 1, Stuart Company is considering leasing a building and purchasing the necessary equipment to operate a public warehouse. The project would be financed by selling $750,000 of 8% U.S. Treasury bonds that mature in 10 years. The bonds were purchased at face value and are currently selling at face value. The following data have been assembled:

Cost of equipment	$750,000
Life of equipment	10 years
Estimated residual value of equipment	$ 50,000
Yearly costs to operate the warehouse, in addition to depreciation of equipment	$ 74,000
Yearly expected revenues—first 6 years	$220,000
Yearly expected revenues—next 4 years	$200,000

Instructions: (1) Prepare a differential analysis report presenting the differential revenue and the differential cost associated with the proposed operation of the warehouse for the 10 years as compared with present conditions.

(2) Based on the results disclosed by the differential analysis, should the proposal be accepted?

(3) If the proposal is accepted, what is the total estimated income from operation of the warehouse for the 10 years?

25–37A. Differential analysis report for machine replacement proposal. Greeley Company is considering the replacement of a machine that has been used in its factory for four years. Relevant data associated with the operations of the old machine and the new machine, neither of which has any residual value, are as follows:

Old Machine	
Cost of machine, 9-year life	$585,000
Annual depreciation	65,000
Annual manufacturing costs, exclusive of depreciation	375,000
Related annual operating expenses	138,500
Associated annual revenue	920,000
Current estimated selling price	210,000

New Machine	
Cost of machine, 5-year life	$750,000
Annual depreciation	150,000
Estimated annual manufacturing costs, exclusive of depreciation	220,000

Annual operating expenses and revenue are not expected to be affected by purchase of the new machine.

Instructions: (1) Prepare a differential analysis report as of April 2 of the current year, comparing operations utilizing the new machine with operations using the present equipment. The analysis should indicate the total differential decrease or increase in costs that would result over the 5-year period if the new machine is acquired.

(2) List other factors that should be considered before a final decision is reached.

25–41A. Product pricing using the cost-plus approach concepts. Alman Company recently began production of a new product, W, which required the investment of $800,000 in assets. The costs and expenses of producing and selling 25,000 units of Product W are as follows:

Variable costs and expenses:	
Direct materials	$ 6.00
Direct labor	2.75
Factory overhead	1.25
Selling and general expenses	2.00
Total	$12.00
Fixed costs and expenses:	
Factory overhead	$70,000
Selling and general expenses	30,000

Alman Company is currently considering the establishment of a selling price for Product W. The president of Alman Company has decided to use the cost-plus approach to product pricing and has indicated that Product W must earn a 10% rate of return on invested assets.

Instructions: (1) Determine the amount of desired profit from the production and sale of Product W.

(2) Assuming that the total cost concept is used, determine (a) the cost amount per unit, (b) the markup percentage, and (c) the selling price of Product W.

(3) Assuming that the product cost concept is used, determine (a) the cost amount per unit, (b) the markup percentage, and (c) the selling price of Product W. Round to the nearest cent.

(4) Assuming that the variable cost concept is used, determine (a) the cost amount per unit, (b) the markup percentage, and (c) the selling price of Product W.

(5) Comment on any additional considerations that could influence the establishment of the selling price for Product W.

Mini-Case 25

SCHOOLCRAFT MOTORS

Your father operates a family-owned automotive dealership. Recently, the city government has requested bids on the purchase of 10 sedans for use by the city police department. Although the city prefers to purchase from local dealerships, state law requires the acceptance of the lowest bid. The past several contracts for automotive purchases have been granted to dealerships from surrounding communities.

The following data were taken from the dealership records for the normal sale of the automobile for which current bids have been requested:

Retail list price of sedan	$13,600
Cost allocated to normal sale:	
Dealer cost from manufacturer	10,800
Fixed overhead	500
Shipping charges from manufacturer	420
Preparation charges	100
Sales commission based on selling price	6%

Your father has asked you to help him in arriving at a "winning" bid price for this contract. In the past, your father has always bid $300 above the total cost (including fixed overhead). No sales commissions will be paid if the bid is accepted, and your father has indicated that the bid price must contribute at least $300 per car to the profits of the dealership.

Instructions:

(1) Do you think that your father has used good bidding procedures for prior contracts? Explain.
(2) What should be the bid price, based upon your father's profit objectives?
(3) Explain why the bid price determined in (2) would not be an acceptable price for normal customers.

Answers to Self-Examination Questions

1. A Differential cost (answer A) is the amount of increase or decrease in cost that is expected from a particular course of action compared with an alternative. Replacement cost (answer B) is the cost of replacing an asset at current market prices, and sunk cost (answer C) is a past cost that will not be affected by subsequent decisions.

2. A A sunk cost is not affected by later decisions. For Victor Company, the sunk cost is the $50,000 (answer A) book value of the equipment, which is equal to the original cost of $200,000 (answer C) less the accumulated depreciation of $150,000 (answer B).

3. C The amount of income that could have been earned from the best available alternative to a proposed use of cash is called opportunity cost (answer C). Actual cost (answer A) or historical cost (answer B) is the cash or equivalent outlay for goods or services actually acquired.

4. C Under the variable cost concept of product pricing (answer C), fixed manufacturing costs, fixed general and selling expenses, and desired profit are allowed for in the determination of the markup. Only desired profit is allowed for in the markup under the total cost concept (answer A). Under the product cost concept (answer B), total selling and general expenses, and desired profit are allowed for in the determination of markup.

5. A Microeconomic theory indicates that profits of a business enterprise will be maximized at the point where marginal revenue equals marginal cost (answer A). At lower levels of production and sales, the change in total revenue is greater than the change in total cost (answer B); hence, more profit can be achieved by manufacturing and selling more units. At higher levels of production and sales, the change in total cost is greater than the change in total revenue (answer C); hence, less profit will be achieved by manufacturing and selling more units.

26
Capital Investment Analysis

CHAPTER OBJECTIVES

Describe the nature and importance of long-term investment decisions involving property, plant, and equipment.

Describe and illustrate the use of the present value concept in capital investment decisions.

Describe the nature of capital investment analysis and illustrate the evaluation of capital investment proposals by the following methods:
Average rate of return
Cash payback
Discounted cash flow
Discounted internal rate of return

Describe and illustrate factors that complicate capital investment analysis, including:
Income tax
Unequal proposal lives
Lease versus capital investment
Uncertainty
Changes in price levels

Describe and illustrate the capital rationing process.

Describe the basic concepts for planning and controlling capital investment expenditures.

With the accelerated growth of American industry, increasing attention has been given to long-term investment decisions involving property, plant, and equipment. The process by which management plans, evaluates, and controls such investments is called **capital investment analysis,** or **capital budgeting.** This chapter describes analyses useful for making capital investment decisions, which may involve thousands, millions, or even billions of dollars. The similarities and differences between the most commonly used methods of evaluating capital investment proposals, as well as the uses of each method, are emphasized. Finally, considerations complicating capital investment analyses, the process of allocating available investment funds among competing proposals (capital rationing), and planning and controlling capital expenditures are briefly discussed.

NATURE OF CAPITAL INVESTMENT ANALYSIS

Capital investment expenditures normally involve a long-term commitment of funds and thus affect operations for many years. These expenditures must earn a reasonable rate of return, so that the enterprise can meet its obligations to creditors and provide dividends to stockholders. Because capital investment decisions are some of the most important decisions that management makes, the systems and procedures for evaluating, planning, and controlling capital investments must be carefully developed and implemented.

A capital investment program should include a plan for encouraging employees at all levels of an enterprise to submit proposals for capital investments. The plan should provide for communicating to the employees the long-range goals of the enterprise, so that useful proposals are submitted. In addition, the plan may provide for rewarding employees whose proposals are implemented. All reasonable proposals should be given serious consideration, and the effects of the economic implications expected from these proposals should be identified.

METHODS OF EVALUATING CAPITAL INVESTMENT PROPOSALS

The methods of evaluating capital investment proposals can be grouped into two general categories that can be referred to as (1) methods that ignore present value and (2) present value methods. The characteristic that distinguishes one category from the other is the way in which the concept of the time value of money is treated. Both the time value of money and the concept of present value are discussed in more detail later in this chapter. Because cash on hand can be invested to earn more cash, while cash to be received in the future cannot, money has a time value. However, the methods that ignore present value do not give consideration to the fact that cash on hand is more valuable than cash to be received in the future. The two methods in this category are (1) the average rate of return method and (2) the cash payback method.

By converting dollars to be received in the future into current dollars, using the concept of present value, the present value methods take into consideration the fact that money has a time value. The two common present value methods used in evaluating capital investment proposals are (1) the discounted cash flow method and (2) the discounted internal rate of return method.

Each of the four methods of analyzing capital investment proposals has both advantages and limitations. Often management will use some combination of the four methods in evaluating the various economic aspects of capital investment proposals.

Methods That Ignore Present Value

The average rate of return and the cash payback methods of evaluating capital investment proposals are simple to use and are especially useful in screening proposals. Management often establishes a minimum standard, and proposals not meeting this minimum standard are dropped from further consideration. When several alternative proposals meet the minimum standard, management will often rank the proposals from the most desirable to the least desirable.

The methods that ignore present value are also useful in evaluating capital investment proposals that have relatively short useful lives. In such situations, the timing of the cash flows is less important, and management generally focuses its attention on the amount of income to be earned from the investment and the total net cash flows to be received from the investment.

Average Rate of Return Method. The expected **average rate of return,** sometimes referred to as the **accounting rate of return,** is a measure of the expected profitability of an investment in plant assets. The amount of income expected to be earned from the investment is stated as an annual average over the number of years the asset is to be used. The amount of the investment may be considered to be the original cost of the plant asset, or recognition may be given to the effect of depreciation on the amount of the investment. According to the latter view, the investment gradually declines from the original cost to the estimated residual value at the end of its useful life. If straight-line depreciation and no residual value are assumed, the average investment would be equal to one half of the original expenditure.

To illustrate, assume that management is considering the purchase of a certain machine at a cost of $500,000. The machine is expected to have a useful life of 4 years, with no residual value, and its use during the 4 years is expected to yield total income of $200,000. The estimated average annual income is therefore $50,000 ($200,000 ÷ 4), and the average investment is $250,000 [($500,000 + $0 residual value) ÷ 2]. Accordingly, the expected average rate of return on the average investment is 20%, computed as follows:

$$\text{Average Rate of Return} = \frac{\text{Estimated Average Annual Income}}{\text{Average Investment}}$$

$$\text{Average Rate of Return} = \frac{\$200{,}000 \div 4}{(\$500{,}000 + \$0) \div 2}$$

$$\text{Average Rate of Return} = 20\%$$

The expected average rate of return of 20% should be compared with the rate established by management as the minimum reward for the risks involved in the investment. The attractiveness of the proposed purchase of additional equipment is indicated by the difference between the expected rate and the minimum desired rate.

When several alternative capital investment proposals are being considered, the proposals can be ranked by their average rates of return. The higher the average rate of return, the more desirable the proposal. For example, assume that management is considering the following alternative capital investment proposals and has computed the indicated average rates of return:

	Proposal A	Proposal B
Estimated average annual income.........	$ 30,000	$ 36,000
Average investment	$120,000	$180,000
Average rate of return:		
$30,000 ÷ $120,000..................	25%	
$36,000 ÷ $180,000..................		20%

If only the average rate of return is considered, Proposal A, based on its average rate of return of 25%, would be preferred over Proposal B.

The primary advantages of the average rate of return method are its ease of computation and the fact that it emphasizes the amount of income earned over the entire life of the proposal. Its main disadvantages are its lack of consideration of the expected cash flows from the proposal and the timing of these cash flows. These cash flows are important because cash coming from an investment can be reinvested in other income-producing activities. Therefore, the more funds and the sooner the funds become available, the more income that can be generated from their reinvestment.

Cash Payback Method. The expected period of time that will pass between the date of a capital investment and the complete recovery in cash (or equivalent) of the amount invested is called the **cash payback period**. To simplify the analysis, the revenues and the out-of-pocket operating expenses expected to be associated with the operation of the plant assets are assumed to be entirely in the form of cash. The excess of the cash flowing in from revenue over the cash flowing out for expenses is termed **net cash flow.** The time required for the net cash flow to equal the initial outlay for the plant asset is the payback period.

For purposes of illustration, assume that the proposed investment in a plant asset with an 8-year life is $200,000 and that the annual net cash flow is expected to be $40,000. The estimated cash payback period for the investment is 5 years, computed as follows:

$$\frac{\$200,000}{\$40,000} = \text{5-year cash payback period}$$

In the preceding illustration, the annual net cash flows were equal ($40,000 per year). If these annual net cash flows are not equal, the cash payback period is determined by summing the annual net cash flows until the cumulative sum equals the amount of the proposed investment. To illustrate, assume that for a proposed investment of $400,000, the annual net cash flows and cumulative net cash flows over the proposal's 6-year life are as follows:

Year	Net Cash Flow	Cumulative Net Cash Flow
1	$ 60,000	$ 60,000
2	80,000	140,000
3	105,000	245,000
4	155,000	400,000
5	140,000	540,000
6	90,000	630,000

The cumulative net cash flow at the end of the fourth year equals the amount of the investment, $400,000. Therefore, the payback period is 4 years.

The cash payback method is widely used in evaluating proposals for expansion and for investment in new projects. A relatively short payback period is desirable, because the sooner the cash is recovered the sooner it becomes available for reinvestment in other projects. In addition, there is likely to be less possibility of loss from changes in economic conditions, obsolescence, and other unavoidable risks when the commitment is short-term. The cash payback concept is also of interest to bankers and other creditors who may be dependent upon net cash flow for the repayment of claims associated with the initial capital investment. The sooner the cash is recovered, the sooner the debt or other liabilities can be paid. Thus, the cash payback method would be especially useful to managers whose primary concern is liquidity.

One of the primary disadvantages of the cash payback method as a basis for decisions is its failure to take into consideration the expected profitability of a proposal. A project with a very short payback period, coupled with relatively poor profitability, would be less desirable than one with a longer payback period but with satisfactory profitability. Another disadvantage of the cash payback method is that the cash flows occurring after the payback period are ignored. A 5-year project with a 3-year payback period and two additional years of substantial cash flows is more desirable than a 5-year project with a 3-year payback period that has lower cash flows in the last two years.

Present Value Methods

An investment in plant and equipment may be viewed as the acquisition of a series of future net cash flows composed of two elements: (1) recovery of the initial investment and (2) income. The period of time over which these net cash flows will be received may be an important factor in determining the value of an investment.

The concept of the time value of money is that any specified amount of cash to be received at some date in the future is not the equivalent of the same amount of cash held at an earlier date. A sum of cash to be received in the future is not as valuable as the same sum on hand today, because cash on hand today can be invested to earn income. For example, $10,000 on hand today would be more valuable than $10,000 to be received a year from today. In other words, if cash can be invested to earn 10% per year, the $10,000 on hand today will accumulate to $11,000 ($10,000 plus $1,000 earnings) by one year from today. The $10,000 on hand today can be referred to as the **present value** amount that is equivalent to $11,000 to be received a year from today.

Discounted Cash Flow Method. The **discounted cash flow method,** sometimes referred to as the **net present value method,** uses present value concepts to compute the present value of the cash flows expected from a proposal. To illustrate, if the rate of earnings is 12% and the cash to be received in one year is $1,000, the present value amount is $892.86 ($1,000 ÷ 1.12). If the cash is to be received one year later (two years in all), with the earnings compounded at the end of the first year, the present value amount would be $797.20 ($892.86 ÷ 1.12).

Instead of determining the present value of future cash flows by a series of divisions in the manner just illustrated, it is customary to find the present value of $1 from a table of present values and to multiply it by the amount of the future cash flow. Reference to the following partial table indicates that the present value of $1 to be received two years hence, with earnings at the rate of 12% a year, is .797. Multiplication of .797 by $1,000 yields $797, which is the same amount that was determined in the preceding paragraph by two successive divisions. The small difference is due to rounding the present value factors in the table to three decimal places.[1]

Present Value of $1 at Compound Interest

Year	6%	10%	12%	15%	20%
1	.943	.909	.893	.870	.833
2	.890	.826	.797	.756	.694
3	.840	.751	.712	.658	.579
4	.792	.683	.636	.572	.482
5	.747	.621	.567	.497	.402
6	.705	.564	.507	.432	.335
7	.665	.513	.452	.376	.279
8	.627	.467	.404	.327	.233
9	.592	.424	.361	.284	.194
10	.558	.386	.322	.247	.162

The particular rate of return selected in discounted cash flow analysis is affected by the nature of the business enterprise and its relative profitability, the purpose of the capital investment, the cost of securing funds for the investment, the minimum desired rate of return, and other related factors. If the present value of the net cash flow expected from a proposed investment, at the selected rate, equals or exceeds the amount of the investment, the proposal is desirable. For purposes of illustration, assume a proposal for the acquisition of $200,000 of equipment with an expected useful life of 5 years and a minimum desired rate of return of 10%. The anticipated net cash flow for each of the 5 years and the analysis of the proposal are as follows. The calculation shows that the proposal is expected to recover the investment and provide more than the minimum rate of return.

Discounted Cash Flow Analysis

Year	Present Value of $1 at 10%	Net Cash Flow	Present Value of Net Cash Flow
1	.909	$ 70,000	$ 63,630
2	.826	60,000	49,560
3	.751	50,000	37,550
4	.683	40,000	27,320
5	.621	40,000	24,840
Total		$260,000	$202,900
Amount to be invested			200,000
Excess of present value over amount to be invested			$ 2,900

When several alternative investment proposals of the same amount are being considered, the one with the largest excess of present value over the amount to be invested is the most desirable. If the alternative proposals involve different amounts of investment, it is useful to prepare a relative ranking of the proposals by using a **present value index.** The present value index for the previous illustration is computed by dividing the total present value of the net cash flow by the amount to be invested, as follows:

[1]More complete tables of both present values and future values are in Appendix G.

$$\text{Present Value Index} = \frac{\text{Total Present Value of Net Cash Flow}}{\text{Amount To Be Invested}}$$

$$\text{Present Value Index} = \frac{\$202{,}900}{\$200{,}000}$$

$$\text{Present Value Index} = 1.01$$

To illustrate the ranking of the proposals by use of the present value index, assume that the total present values of the net cash flow and the amounts to be invested for three alternative proposals are as follows:

	Proposal A	*Proposal B*	*Proposal C*
Total present value of net cash flow . . .	$107,000	$86,400	$93,600
Amount to be invested	100,000	80,000	90,000
Excess of present value over amount to be invested	$ 7,000	$ 6,400	$ 3,600

The present value index for each proposal is as follows:

	Present Value Index
Proposal A.	1.07 ($107,000 ÷ $100,000)
Proposal B.	1.08 ($ 86,400 ÷ $ 80,000)
Proposal C.	1.04 ($ 93,600 ÷ $ 90,000)

The present value indexes indicate that although Proposal A has the largest excess of present value over the amount to be invested, it is not as attractive as Proposal B in terms of the amount of present value per dollar invested. It should be noted, however, that Proposal B requires an investment of only $80,000, while Proposal A requires an investment of $100,000. The possible use of the $20,000 if B is selected should be considered before a final decision is made.

The primary advantage of the discounted cash flow method is that it gives consideration to the time value of money. A disadvantage of the method is that the computations are more complex than those for the methods that ignore present value. In addition, this method assumes that the cash received from the proposal during its useful life will be reinvested at the rate of return used to compute the present value of the proposal. Because of changing economic conditions, this assumption may not always be reasonable.

Discounted Internal Rate of Return Method. The **discounted internal rate of return method,** sometimes called the **internal rate of return** or **time-adjusted rate of return method,** uses present value concepts to compute the rate of return from the net cash flows expected from capital investment proposals. Thus, it is similar to the discounted cash flow method, in that it focuses on the present value of the net cash flows. However, the discounted internal rate of return method starts with the net cash flows and, in a sense, works backwards to determine the discounted rate of return expected from the proposal. The discounted cash flow method requires management to specify a minimum rate of return, which is then used to determine the excess (deficiency) of the present value of the net cash flow over the investment.

To illustrate the use of the discounted internal rate of return method, assume that management is evaluating a proposal to acquire equipment costing $33,530, which is expected to provide annual net cash flows of $10,000 per year for 5 years. If a rate of return of 12% is assumed, the present value of the net cash flows can be computed using the present value of $1 table on page 943, as follows:

Year	Present Value of $1 at 12%	Net Cash Flow	Present Value of Net Cash Flow
1	.893	$10,000	$ 8,930
2	.797	10,000	7,970
3	.712	10,000	7,120
4	.636	10,000	6,360
5	.567	10,000	5,670
Total		$50,000	$36,050

Since the present value of the net cash flow based on a 12% rate of return, $36,050, is greater than the $33,530 to be invested, 12% is obviously not the discounted internal rate of return. The following analysis indicates that 15% is the rate of return that equates the $33,530 cost of the investment with the present value of the net cash flows.

Year	Present Value of $1 at 15%	Net Cash Flow	Present Value of Net Cash Flow
1	.870	$10,000	$ 8,700
2	.756	10,000	7,560
3	.658	10,000	6,580
4	.572	10,000	5,720
5	.497	10,000	4,970
Total		$50,000	$33,530

In the illustration, the discounted internal rate of return was determined by trial and error. A rate of 12% was assumed before the discounted internal rate of return of 15% was identified. Such procedures are tedious and time consuming. When equal annual net cash flows are expected from a proposal, as in the illustration, the computations can be simplified by using a table of the present value of an annuity.[2]

A series of equal cash flows at fixed intervals is termed an **annuity**. The **present value of an annuity** is the sum of the present values of each cash flow. From another point of view, the present value of an annuity is the amount of cash that would be needed today to yield a series of equal cash flows at fixed intervals in the future. For example, reference to the following table of the present value of an annuity of $1 shows that the present value of cash flows at the end of each of five years, with a discounted internal rate of return of 15% per year, is 3.353. Multiplication of $10,000 by 3.353 yields the same amount ($33,530) that was determined in the preceding illustration by five successive multiplications.

---

[2]In the illustration, equal annual net cash flows are assumed, so that attention can be focused on the basic concepts. If the annual net cash flows are not equal, the procedures are more complex, but the basic concepts are not affected. In such cases, computers can be used to perform the computations.

Present Value of an Annuity of $1 at Compound Interest

Year	6%	10%	12%	15%	20%
1	.943	.909	.893	.870	.833
2	1.833	1.736	1.690	1.626	1.528
3	2.673	2.487	2.402	2.283	2.106
4	3.465	3.170	3.037	2.855	2.589
5	4.212	3.791	3.605	3.353	2.991
6	4.917	4.355	4.111	3.785	3.326
7	5.582	4.868	4.564	4.160	3.605
8	6.210	5.335	4.968	4.487	3.837
9	6.802	5.759	5.328	4.772	4.031
10	7.360	6.145	5.650	5.019	4.192

The procedures for using the present value of an annuity of $1 table to determine the discounted internal rate of return are as follows:

1. A present value factor for an annuity of $1 is determined by dividing the amount to be invested by the annual net cash flow, as expressed in the following formula:

$$\text{Present Value Factor for an Annuity of \$1} = \frac{\text{Amount To Be Invested}}{\text{Annual Net Cash Flow}}$$

2. The present value factor determined in (1) is located in the present value of an annuity of $1 table by first locating the number of years of expected useful life of the investment in the Year column and then proceeding horizontally across the table until the present value factor determined in (1) is found.
3. The discounted internal rate of return is then identified by the heading of the column in which the present value factor in (2) is located.

To illustrate the use of the present value of an annuity of $1 table, assume that management is considering a proposal to acquire equipment costing $97,360, which is expected to provide equal annual net cash flows of $20,000 for 7 years. The present value factor for an annuity of $1 is 4.868, computed as follows:

$$\text{Present Value Factor for an Annuity of \$1} = \frac{\text{Amount To Be Invested}}{\text{Annual Net Cash Flow}}$$

$$\text{Present Value Factor for an Annuity of \$1} = \frac{\$97{,}360}{\$20{,}000}$$

$$\text{Present Value Factor for an Annuity of \$1} = 4.868$$

For a period of 7 years, the following table for the present value of an annuity of $1 indicates that the factor 4.868 is associated with a percentage of 10%. Thus, 10% is the discounted internal rate of return for this proposal.

Present Value of an Annuity of $1 at Compound Interest

Year	6%	10%	12%
1	.943	.909	.893
2	1.833	1.736	1.690
3	2.673	2.487	2.402
4	3.465	3.170	3.037
5	4.212	3.791	3.605
6	4.917	4.355	4.111
7	5.582	4.868	4.564
8	6.210	5.335	4.968
9	6.802	5.759	5.328
10	7.360	6.145	5.650

If the minimum acceptable rate of return for similar proposals is 10% or less, then the proposed equipment acquisition should be considered desirable. When several proposals are under consideration, management often ranks the proposals by their discounted internal rates of return, and the proposal with the highest rate is considered the most attractive.

The primary advantage of the discounted internal rate of return method is that the present values of the net cash flows over the entire useful life of the proposal are considered. An additional advantage of the method is that by determining a rate of return for each proposal, all proposals are automatically placed on a common basis for comparison, without the need to compute a present value index as was the case for the discounted cash flow method. The primary disadvantage of the discounted internal rate of return method is that the computations are somewhat more complex than for some of the other methods. In addition, like the discounted cash flow method, this method assumes that the cash received from a proposal during its useful life will be reinvested at the discounted internal rate of return. Because of changing economic conditions, this assumption may not always be reasonable.

The Discounted Internal Rate of Return Method—An Application Using the Microcomputer

The complexity of using the present value methods of evaluating capital investment proposals can be significantly reduced by using a microcomputer. The following computer program, which was written in the BASIC programming language, computes the discounted internal rate of return for an investment proposal with a series of equal net cash flows.

```
10   INPUT "periods";N: INPUT "investment";I: INPUT "annual net cash flow";C
20   INPUT "guess";G
30   X=(X+G)/100+1:S=I
40   FOR J=1 TO N:S=S+C/X^J:NEXT:X=(X-1)*100
50   IF ABS(Y-X)<=.001 THEN END
60   LPRINT X:Y=X:RESTORE:IF S>0 THEN 30
70   X=X-G:G=G/3:GOTO 30
```

To run this program, the user must have access to the BASIC programming system. The manual accompanying this system will describe the procedures for calling up the system and entering, saving, loading, and running a program. In using the above program, the program steps must be keyboarded exactly as shown. When the program is run, the user will be required to input (1) the number of periods for which the proposed capital investment will yield annual cash inflows, (2) the cost of the investment expressed as a negative initial cash flow, (3) the annual net cash flows, and (4) an initial guess as to the approximate discounted internal rate of return. The initial guess does not necessarily have to be close to the true value, since the computer will estimate the true value regardless of the accuracy of the initial guess. The initial guess only adds efficiency to the estimation process. An example of the use of this computer program for the illustration presented on page 946 is as follows:

```
periods? 7
investment? -97360
annual net cash flow? 20000
guess? 15
  15
  4.999995
  9.999991
  14.99999
  11.66666
  10.55554
  10.18517
  10.06172
  10.02057
  10.00685
  10.00227
  10.00456
  10.00303
```

Note: This program was written for the BASIC programming language using the IBM personal computer.

The program will stop computing the estimated discounted internal rate of return when successive estimates are reasonably close to one another and additional precision is not warranted. In the above example, the approximate discounted internal rate of return is 10%. Note that the difference between the above estimate and the illustration in the text is due to rounding within the computer program.

FACTORS THAT COMPLICATE CAPITAL INVESTMENT ANALYSIS

In the preceding paragraphs, the basic concepts for four widely used methods of evaluating capital investment proposals were discussed. In practice, additional factors may have an impact on a capital investment decision. Some of the most important of these factors, which are described in the following paragraphs, are the federal income tax, the unequal lives of alternate proposals, the leasing alternative, uncertainty, and changes in price levels.

Income Tax

In many cases, the impact of the federal income tax on capital investment decisions can be significant. One provision of the Internal Revenue Code (IRC) which should be considered in capital investment analysis is the allowable deduction for depreciation expense.

For determining **depreciation,** or the *cost recovery deduction,* which is the expensing of the cost of plant assets over their useful lives, the IRC specifies the use of the **Accelerated Cost Recovery System (ACRS). Modified ACRS (MACRS),** under the Tax Reform Act of 1986, provides for eight classes of useful lives for plant assets acquired after 1986. The two most common classes for assets other than real estate are the 5-year class and the 7-year class.[3] The 5-year class includes automobiles and light-duty trucks, and the 7-year class includes most machinery and equipment. Depreciation for these two classes approximates the use of the 200-percent declining-balance method.

The Internal Revenue Service has prescribed methods that result in annual percentages to be used in determining depreciation for each class. In using these rates, salvage value is ignored, and all plant assets are assumed to be placed in service in the middle of the year and taken out of service in the middle of the year. For the 5-year-class assets, for example, depreciation is spread over six years; for the 7-year-class assets, depreciation is spread over eight years, as shown in the following schedule of MACRS depreciation rates:

[3]Real estate is classified into 27½-year classes and 31½-year classes and is depreciated by the straight-line method.

Year	5-Year-Class Depreciation Rates	7-Year-Class Depreciation Rates
1	20.0%	14.3%
2	32.0	24.5
3	19.2	17.5
4	11.5	12.5
5	11.5	8.9
6	5.8	8.9
7		8.9
8		4.5
	100.0%	100.0%

MACRS Depreciation Rate Schedule

MACRS simplifies depreciation accounting by eliminating the need to estimate useful life and salvage value and to decide on a depreciation method. Although a short-run tax saving can usually be realized by using the regular MACRS cost recovery allowance, a taxpayer may elect to use a straight-line deduction based on the property classes prescribed under MACRS. The accelerated write-off of depreciable assets provided by MACRS does not, however, effect a long-run net saving in income tax. The tax reduction of the early years of use is offset by higher taxes as the annual cost recovery allowance diminishes.

To illustrate the potential impact of MACRS depreciation on capital investment decisions, assume that Sierra Company is using the discounted cash flow method in evaluating a proposal.[4] The cost of the investment acquired in year 1 is $300,000, with an expected useful life of 5 years, no residual value, and a minimum desired rate of return of 12%. If Sierra Company elects the straight-line method of depreciation, the IRC requires one half of a full year's depreciation to be taken in the first year and one half of a full year's depreciation to be taken in the sixth year. Thus, Sierra Company would deduct the following depreciation amounts during the 5-year life of the asset:

	Depreciation Expense
First year	$30,000 [($300,000 ÷ 5) × 1/2]
Second year	$60,000 ($300,000 ÷ 5)
Third year	$60,000 ($300,000 ÷ 5)
Fourth year	$60,000 ($300,000 ÷ 5)
Fifth year	$60,000 ($300,000 ÷ 5)
Sixth year	$30,000 [($300,000 ÷ 5) × 1/2]

During the six years in which depreciation expense is deducted, the investment is expected to yield annual operating income, before depreciation and income taxes, of $120,000, $100,000, $90,000, $70,000, $60,000, and $30,000, respectively. To simplify the illustration, all revenues and operating expenses except depreciation represent current period cash flows. If the income tax rate is 34%, the annual net aftertax cash flows from acquisition of the asset are as follows:

[4] The same general impact of depreciation on capital investment decisions would occur, regardless of which of the four capital investment evaluation methods was used. To simplify the discussion in this chapter, only the discounted cash flow method is illustrated.

	Year 1	2	3	4	5	6
Net cash flow before income taxes	$120,000	$100,000	$90,000	$70,000	$60,000	$30,000
Income tax expense*	30,600	13,600	10,200	3,400	0	0
Net cash flow	$ 89,400	$ 86,400	$79,800	$66,600	$60,000	$30,000
*Income tax expense:						
Operating income before depreciation and income taxes	$120,000	$100,000	$90,000	$70,000	$60,000	$30,000
Depreciation expense	30,000	60,000	60,000	60,000	60,000	30,000
Income before income taxes	$ 90,000	$ 40,000	$30,000	$10,000	0	0
Income tax rate	34%	34%	34%	34%	0	0
Income tax expense	$ 30,600	$ 13,600	$10,200	$ 3,400	0	0

Based on the preceding data and using the discounted cash flow method, a $2,899 deficiency of the present value over the amount to be invested is computed as follows:

Year	*Present Value of 1 at 12%*	*Net Cash Flow*	*Present Value of Net Cash Flow*
1	.893	$ 89,400	$ 79,834
2	.797	86,400	68,861
3	.712	79,800	56,818
4	.636	66,600	42,358
5	.567	60,000	34,020
6	.507	30,000	15,210
Total		$412,200	$297,101
Amount to be invested			300,000
Deficiency of present value over amount to be invested			$ 2,899

Because the discounted cash flow method indicates that there is a deficiency of the present value over the amount to be invested, the decision would be to reject the proposal. However, if the accelerated depreciation provided by the IRC is used, the present value of the acquisition changes significantly and might lead to a different decision. To illustrate, assume that Sierra Company is permitted to deduct depreciation over a 5-year period, beginning with the year the asset is acquired. Using the MACRS percentages shown on page 949, the depreciation for Sierra Company will be as follows:

	Depreciation Expense
First year	$60,000 ($300,000 × 20.0%)
Second year	$96,000 ($300,000 × 32.0%)
Third year	$57,600 ($300,000 × 19.2%)
Fourth year	$34,500 ($300,000 × 11.5%)
Fifth year	$34,500 ($300,000 × 11.5%)
Sixth year	$17,400 ($300,000 × 5.8%)

The annual aftertax net cash flows from the acquisition of the plant asset, including the effect of MACRS depreciation, are as follows:

	Year					
	1	2	3	4	5	6
Net cash flow before income taxes	$120,000	$100,000	$90,000	$70,000	$60,000	$30,000
Income tax expense*..................	20,400	1,360	11,016	12,070	8,670	4,284
Net cash flow	$ 99,600	$ 98,640	$78,984	$57,930	$51,330	$25,716
*Income tax expense:						
Operating income before depreciation and income taxes..................	$120,000	$100,000	$90,000	$70,000	$60,000	$30,000
Depreciation expense	60,000	96,000	57,600	34,500	34,500	17,400
Income before income taxes	$ 60,000	$ 4,000	$32,400	$35,500	$25,500	$12,600
Income tax rate......................	34%	34%	34%	34%	34%	34%
Income tax expense	$ 20,400	$ 1,360	$11,016	$12,070	$ 8,670	$ 4,284

Based on the preceding data and using the discounted cash flow method, a $2,781 excess of the present value over the amount to be invested is computed as follows:

Year	Present Value of 1 at 12%	Net Cash Flow	Present Value of Net Cash Flow
1	.893	$ 99,600	$ 88,943
2	.797	98,640	78,616
3	.712	78,984	56,237
4	.636	57,930	36,843
5	.567	51,330	29,104
6	.507	25,716	13,038
Total		$412,200	$302,781
Amount to be invested			300,000
Excess of present value over amount to be invested................			$ 2,781

The specific dollar effects of tax considerations on the evaluation of capital investment proposals will depend on the deductions and credits allowed by the Internal Revenue Code at the time the capital investment decision is to be made. In this illustration, the discounted cash flow analysis indicates an excess of the present value over the amount to be invested, and the decision would be to invest in the asset.

Unequal Proposal Lives

In the preceding sections, the discussion of the methods of analyzing capital investment proposals was based on the assumption that alternate proposals had the same useful lives. In practice, however, alternate proposals may have unequal lives. In such cases, the proposals must be made comparable. One widely used method is to adjust the lives of projects with the longest lives to a time period that is equal to the life of the project with the shortest life. In this manner, the useful lives of all proposals are made equal. To illustrate, assume that the discounted cash flow method is being used to compare the following two proposals, each of which has an initial investment of $100,000:

Year	Net Cash Flows Proposal X	Proposal Y
1	$30,000	$30,000
2	30,000	30,000
3	25,000	30,000
4	20,000	30,000
5	15,000	30,000
6	15,000	—
7	10,000	—
8	10,000	—

If the desired rate of return is 10%, the proposals have an excess of present value over the amount to be invested, as follows:

Proposal X

Year	Present Value of 1 at 10%	Net Cash Flow	Present Value of Net Cash Flow
1	.909	$ 30,000	$ 27,270
2	.826	30,000	24,780
3	.751	25,000	18,775
4	.683	20,000	13,660
5	.621	15,000	9,315
6	.564	15,000	8,460
7	.513	10,000	5,130
8	.467	10,000	4,670
Total.		$155,000	$112,060
Amount to be invested			100,000
Excess of present value over amount to be invested.			$ 12,060

Proposal Y

Year	Present Value of 1 at 10%	Net Cash Flow	Present Value of Net Cash Flow
1	.909	$ 30,000	$ 27,270
2	.826	30,000	24,780
3	.751	30,000	22,530
4	.683	30,000	20,490
5	.621	30,000	18,630
Total.		$150,000	$113,700
Amount to be invested			100,000
Excess of present value over amount to be invested.			$ 13,700

The two proposals cannot be compared by focusing on the amount of the excess of the present value over the amount to be invested, because Proposal Y has a life of 5 years while Proposal X has a life of 8 years. Proposal X can be adjusted to a 5-year life by assuming that it is to be terminated at the end of 5 years and the asset sold. This assumption requires that the residual value be estimated at the end of 5 years and that this value be considered a cash flow at that date. Both proposals will then cover 5 years, and the results of the discounted cash flow analysis can be used to compare the relative attractiveness of the two proposals. For example, assume that Proposal X has an estimated residual value at the end of year 5 of $40,000. For Proposal X, the excess of the present value over the amount to be invested is $18,640 for a 5-year life, as follows:

Proposal X

Year	*Present Value of 1 at 10%*	*Net Cash Flow*	*Present Value of Net Cash Flow*
1	.909	$ 30,000	$ 27,270
2	.826	30,000	24,780
3	.751	25,000	18,775
4	.683	20,000	13,660
5	.621	15,000	9,315
5 (Residual value)	.621	40,000	24,840
Total		$160,000	$118,640
Amount to be invested			100,000
Excess of present value over amount to be invested			$ 18,640

Since the present value over the amount to be invested for Proposal X exceeds that for Proposal Y by $4,940 ($18,640 − $13,700), Proposal X may be viewed as the more attractive of the two proposals.

Lease Versus Capital Investment

Leasing of plant assets has become common in many industries in recent years. Leasing allows an enterprise to acquire the use of plant assets without the necessity of using large amounts of cash to purchase them. In addition, if management believes that a plant asset has a high degree of risk of becoming obsolete before the end of its useful life, then leasing rather than purchasing the asset may be more attractive. By leasing the asset, management reduces the risk of suffering a loss due to obsolescence. Finally, the Internal Revenue Code provisions which allow the lessor (the owner of the asset) to pass tax deductions on to the lessee (the party leasing the asset) have increased the popularity of leasing in recent years. For example, a company that leases for its use a $200,000 plant asset with a life of 8 years for $50,000 per year is permitted to deduct the annual lease payments of $50,000.

In many cases, before a final decision is made, management should consider the possibility of leasing assets instead of purchasing them. Ordinarily, leasing assets is more costly than purchasing because the lessor must include in the rental price not only the costs associated with owning the assets but also a profit. Nevertheless, using the methods of evaluating capital investment proposals, management should consider whether or not the profitability and cash flows from the lease alternative with its risks compares favorably to the profitability and cash flows from the purchase alternative with its risks.

Uncertainty

All capital investment analyses rely on factors that are uncertain; that is, the accuracy of the estimates involved, including estimates of expected revenues, expenses, and cash flows, are uncertain. Although the estimates are subject to varying degrees of risk or uncertainty, the long-term nature of capital investments suggests that many of the estimates are likely to involve considerable uncertainty. Errors in one or more of the estimates could lead to unwise decisions.

Because of the importance of capital investment decisions, management should be aware of the potential impact of uncertainty on their decisions. Some techniques that can be used to assist management in evaluating the effects of uncertainties on capital investment proposals are presented in Chapter 27.

Changes in Price Levels

The past three decades, which have been characterized by increasing price levels, are described as periods of **inflation.** In recent years, the rates of inflation have fluctuated widely, making the estimation of future revenues, expenses, and cash flows more difficult. Therefore, management should consider the expected future price levels and their likely effect on the estimates used in capital investment analyses. Fluctuations in the price levels assumed could significantly affect the analyses.

CAPITAL RATIONING

Capital rationing refers to the process by which management allocates available investment funds among competing capital investment proposals. Generally, management will use various combinations of the evaluation methods described in this chapter in developing an effective approach to capital rationing.

In capital rationing, an initial screening of alternative proposals is usually performed by establishing minimum standards for the cash payback and the average rate of return methods. The proposals that survive this initial screening are subjected to the more rigorous discounted cash flow and discounted internal rate of return methods of analysis. The proposals that survive this final screening are evaluated in terms of nonfinancial factors, such as employee morale. For example, the acquisition of new, more efficient equipment which eliminates several jobs could lower employee morale to a level that could decrease overall plant productivity.

The final step in the capital rationing process is a ranking of the proposals and a comparison of proposals with the funds available to determine which proposals will be funded. The unfunded proposals are reconsidered if funds subsequently become available. The flowchart on page 955 portrays the capital rationing decision process.

CAPITAL EXPENDITURES BUDGET

Once capital investment expenditures for a period have been approved, a **capital expenditures budget** should be prepared and procedures should be established for controlling the expenditures. After the assets are placed in service, the actual results of operations should be compared to the initial projected results to determine whether the capital expenditures are meeting management's expectations.

The capital expenditures budget facilitates the planning of operations and the financing of capital expenditures. A capital expenditures budget, which is

Capital Rationing Decision Process

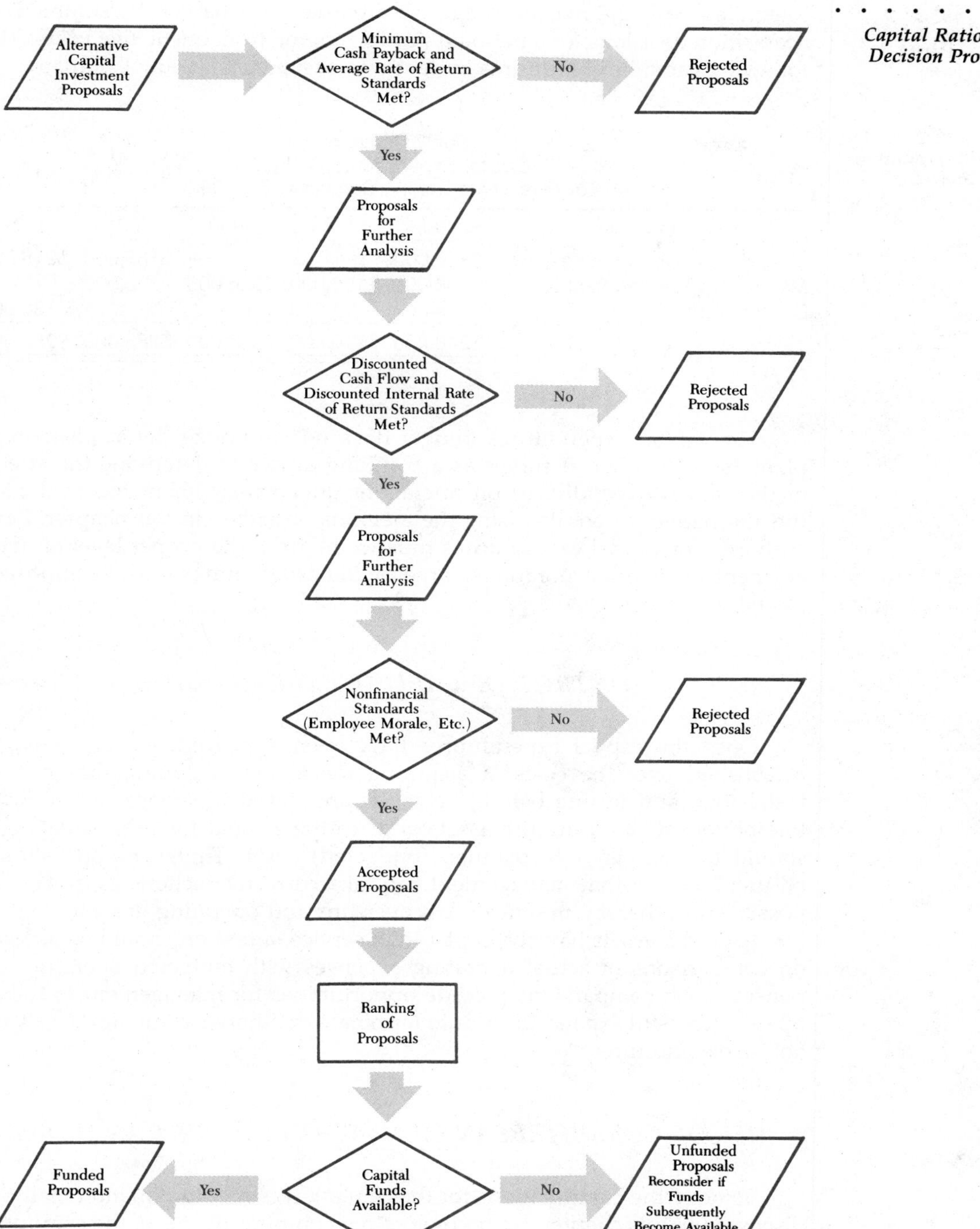

Alternative Capital Investment Proposals
Minimum Cash Payback and Average Rate of Return Standards Met?
No
Rejected Proposals
Yes
Proposals for Further Analysis
Discounted Cash Flow and Discounted Internal Rate of Return Standards Met?
No
Rejected Proposals
Yes
Proposals for Further Analysis
Nonfinancial Standards (Employee Morale, Etc.) Met?
No
Rejected Proposals
Yes
Accepted Proposals
Ranking of Proposals
Capital Funds Available?
Yes
Funded Proposals
No
Unfunded Proposals
Reconsider if Funds Subsequently Become Available

integrated with the master budget as discussed in Chapter 21, summarizes acquisition decisions for a period typically ranging from one to five years. The following capital expenditures budget was prepared for Sealy Company:

Capital Expenditures Budget

Sealy Company
Capital Expenditures Budget
For Five Years Ending December 31, 1992

Item	1988	1989	1990	1991	1992
Machinery—Department A . . .	$240,000	—	—	$168,000	$216,000
Machinery—Department B . . .	108,000	$156,000	$336,000	120,000	—
Delivery equipment	—	54,000	—	—	36,000
Total	$348,000	$210,000	$336,000	$288,000	$252,000

The capital expenditures budget does not authorize the acquisition of plant assets. Rather, it serves as a planning device to determine the effects of the capital expenditures on operations after management has evaluated the alternative proposals, using the methods described in this chapter. Final authority for capital expenditures must come from the proper level of management. In some corporations, large capital expenditures must be approved by the board of directors.

CONTROL OF CAPITAL EXPENDITURES

Once the capital expenditures have been approved, control must be established over the costs of acquiring the assets, including the costs of installation and testing before the assets are placed in service. Throughout this period of acquiring the assets and readying them for use, actual costs should be compared to planned (budgeted) costs. Timely reports should be prepared, so that management can take corrective actions as quickly as possible and thereby minimize cost overruns and operating delays.

After the assets have been placed in service, attention should be focused on comparisons of actual operating expenses with budgeted operating expenses. Such comparisons provide opportunities for management to follow up on successful expenditures or to terminate or otherwise attempt to salvage failing expenditures.

USE OF COMPUTERS IN CAPITAL INVESTMENT ANALYSIS

Some of the computations for the capital investment evaluation methods discussed in this chapter can become rather complex. By use of the computer, the calculations can be performed easily and quickly. The most important use of the computer, however, is in developing various models which indicate the effect of changes in key factors on the results of capital investment proposals. For example, the effect of various potential changes in future price levels on a proposal could be simulated and the results presented to management for its use in decision making.

Chapter Review

KEY POINTS

1. Nature of Capital Investment Analysis.
The process by which management plans, evaluates, and controls investments involving property, plant, and equipment is called capital investment analysis. A capital investment program should include a plan for encouraging employees at all levels of an enterprise to submit proposals for capital investments. All reasonable proposals should be given serious consideration, and the effects of the economic implications expected from these proposals should be identified.

2. Methods of Evaluating Capital Investment Proposals.
The methods of evaluating capital investment proposals can be grouped into two general categories: (1) methods that ignore present value and (2) present value methods. The methods that ignore present value include (1) the average rate of return method and (2) the cash payback method. Methods that use present values in evaluating capital investment proposals are (1) the discounted cash flow method and (2) the discounted internal rate of return method.

The expected average rate of return is a measure of the expected profitability of an investment in plant assets. When several alternative capital investment proposals are being considered, the proposals can be ranked by their average rates of return. The higher the average rate of return, the more desirable the proposal. The primary advantage of the average rate of return method is its simplicity, and its primary disadvantage is its lack of consideration of expected cash flows from a proposal and the timing of those cash flows.

The cash payback method measures the cash payback period, which is the expected period of time that will pass between the date of a capital investment and the complete recovery in cash (or equivalent) of the amount invested. The cash payback method is especially useful to managers whose primary concern is liquidity. The primary disadvantage of the cash payback method is its failure to take into consideration the expected profitability of a proposal. Another disadvantage of the cash payback method is that the cash flows occurring after the payback period are ignored.

The discounted cash flow method uses present value concepts to compute the present value of the cash flows expected from a proposal. When several alternative investment proposals of the same amount are being considered, the one with the largest excess of present value over the amount to be invested is the most desirable. If the alternative proposals involve different amounts of investment, it is useful to prepare a ranking of the proposals by using a present value index. The primary advantage of the discounted cash flow method is that it gives consideration to the time value of money. A disadvantage of the method is that the computations are more complex than those for the methods that ignore present value. In addition, it assumes that the cash received from the proposal during its useful life will be reinvested at the rate of return used to compute the present value of the proposal.

The discounted internal rate of return method uses present value concepts to compute the rate of return from the net cash flows expected from capital investment proposals. When several proposals are under consideration, management often ranks proposals by their discounted internal rates of return, and the proposal with the highest rate is considered the most attractive. The primary advantage of the discounted internal rate of return method is that the present values of the net cash flows over the entire useful life of the proposal are considered. The primary disadvantage of the discounted internal rate of return method is that the computations are somewhat more complex than for some of the other methods. In addition, like the discounted cash flow method, this method assumes that the cash received from a proposal during its useful life will be reinvested at the discounted internal rate of return.

3. Factors that Complicate Capital Investment Analysis.
Factors that may complicate capital investment analysis include the impact of the federal income tax, unequal lives of alternative proposals, the leasing alternative, uncertainty, and changes in price levels.

4. Capital Rationing.
Capital rationing refers to the process by which management allocates available investment funds among competing capital investment proposals. In capital rationing, an initial screening of alternative proposals is usually performed by establishing minimum standards for the cash payback and the average rate of return methods. The final step in the capital rationing process is a ranking of the proposals and a comparison of proposals with the funds available to determine which proposals will be funded.

5. Capital Expenditures Budget.
Once capital investment expenditures for a period have been approved, a capital expenditures budget should be prepared and procedures should be established for controlling the expenditures.

6. Control of Capital Expenditures.
Throughout the period of acquiring plant assets and readying them for use, actual costs should be compared to planned costs, and timely reports should be prepared, so that management can minimize cost overruns and operating delays.

7. Use of Computers in Capital Investment Analysis.
Some of the computations for the capital investment evaluation methods can become complex. By the use of the computer, the calculations can be performed easily and quickly. In addition, the computer can be used in developing various models which indicate the effect of changes in key factors on the results of capital investment proposals.

KEY TERMS

capital investment analysis 938
average rate of return 940
cash payback period 941
present value 942
discounted cash flow method 942
present value index 943
discounted internal rate of return method 944
annuity 945
present value of an annuity 945
Modified Accelerated Cost Recovery System (MACRS) 948
inflation 954
capital rationing 954
capital expenditures budget 954

SELF EXAMINATION QUESTIONS

(Answers at End of Chapter)

1. Methods of evaluating capital investment proposals that ignore present value include:
   A. average rate of return
   B. cash payback
   C. both A and B
   D. neither A nor B

2. Management is considering a $100,000 investment in a project with a 5-year life and no residual value. If the total income from the project is expected to be $60,000 and recognition is given to the effect of straight-line depreciation on the investment, the average rate of return is:
   A. 12%
   B. 24%
   C. 60%
   D. none of the above

3. As used in the analysis of proposed capital investments, the expected period of time that will elapse between the date of a capital investment and the complete recovery of the amount of cash invested is called:
   A. the average rate of return period
   B. the cash payback period
   C. the discounted cash flow period
   D. none of the above

4. Which method of analyzing capital investment proposals determines the total present value of the cash flows expected from the investment and compares this value with the amount to be invested?
   A. Average rate of return
   B. Cash payback
   C. Discounted cash flow
   D. Discounted internal rate of return

5. The process by which management allocates available investment funds among competing capital investment proposals is referred to as:
   A. capital rationing
   B. capital expenditure budgeting
   C. leasing
   D. none of the above

ILLUSTRATIVE PROBLEM

The capital investment committee of Bormann Company is currently considering two projects. The estimated operating income and net cash flows expected from each project are as follows:

	Project A		Project B	
Year	Operating Income	Net Cash Flow	Operating Income	Net Cash Flow
1	$ 9,000	$19,000	$ 5,000	$15,000
2	7,000	17,000	6,000	16,000
3	6,000	16,000	8,000	18,000
4	5,000	15,000	7,000	17,000
5	3,000	13,000	4,000	14,000
	$30,000	$80,000	$30,000	$80,000

Each project requires an investment of $50,000. Straight-line depreciation will be used, and no residual value is expected. The committee has selected a rate of 15% for purposes of the discounted cash flow analysis.

Instructions:

1. Compute the following:
   a. The average rate of return for each project, giving effect to depreciation on the investment.
   b. The excess or deficiency of present value over the amount to be invested, as determined by the discounted cash flow method for each project. Use the present value of $1 table appearing in this chapter.
2. Prepare a brief report for the capital investment committee, advising it on the relative merits of the two projects.

SOLUTION

(1) (a) Average annual rate of return for both projects:

$$\frac{\$30{,}000 \div 5}{(\$50{,}000 + \$0) \div 2} = 24\%$$

(b) Discounted cash flow analysis:

Year	Present Value of 1 at 15%	Net Cash Flow Project A	Net Cash Flow Project B	Present Value of Net Cash Flow Project A	Present Value of Net Cash Flow Project B
1	.870	$19,000	$15,000	$16,530	$13,050
2	.756	17,000	16,000	12,852	12,096
3	.658	16,000	18,000	10,528	11,844
4	.572	15,000	17,000	8,580	9,724
5	.497	13,000	14,000	6,461	6,958
Total		$80,000	$80,000	$54,951	$53,672
Amount to be invested				50,000	50,000
Excess of present value over amount to be invested				$ 4,951	$ 3,672

(2) (a) Both projects offer the same average annual rate of return.
(b) Although both projects exceed the selected rate established for discounted cash flows, Project A offers a larger excess of present value over the amount to be invested. Thus, if only one of the two projects can be accepted, Project A would be the more attractive.

Discussion Questions

26–1. Which two methods of capital investment analysis ignore present value?

26–2. Which two methods of capital investment analysis can be described as present value methods?

26–3. What is the "time value of money" concept?

26–4. (a) How is the average rate of return computed for capital investment analysis, assuming that consideration is given to the effect of straight-line depreciation on the amount of the investment? (b) If the amount of an 8-year investment is $100,000, the straight-line method of depreciation is used, there is no residual value, and the total income expected from the investment is $140,000, what is the average rate of return?

26–5. What are the principal objections to the use of the average rate of return method in evaluating capital investment proposals?

26–6. (a) As used in analyses of proposed capital investments, what is the cash payback period? (b) Discuss the principal limitations of the cash payback method for evaluating capital investment proposals.

26–7. What is the present value of $6,720 to be received one year from today, assuming an earnings rate of 12%?

26–8. Which method of evaluating capital investment proposals reduces their expected future net cash flows to present values and compares the total present values to the amount of the investment?

26–9. A discounted cash flow analysis used to evaluate a proposed equipment acquisition indicated an $18,000 excess of present value over the amount to be invested. What is the meaning of the $18,000 as it relates to the desirability of the proposal?

26–10. How is the present value index for a proposal determined?

26–11. What are the major disadvantages of the use of the discounted cash flow method of analyzing capital investment proposals?

26–12. What is an annuity?

26–13. What are the major disadvantages of the use of the discounted internal rate of return method of analyzing capital investment proposals?

26–14. What provision of the Internal Revenue Code is especially important for consideration in analyzing capital investment proposals?

26–15. What method can be used to place two capital investment proposals with unequal useful lives on a comparable basis?

26–16. What are the major advantages of leasing a plant asset rather than purchasing it?

26–17. What is capital rationing?

26–18. Which budget summarizes the acquisition decisions for a period?

26–19. Real World Focus. Boston Metal Products, a small manufacturer in Medford, Mass., was considering the purchase of a robot. The company controller was asked to calculate whether the $200,000 investment made financial sense. Using traditional accounting techniques, the controller concluded that the investment did not meet the financial criteria that had been established. However, the company went ahead and made the investment. What qualitative techniques could Boston Metal Products have used to justify the capital investment in a robot?

Exercises

26–20. Average rate of return. The following data are accumulated by Frantz Company in evaluating two competing capital investment proposals:

	Proposal E	Proposal F
Amount of investment	$450,000	$180,000
Useful life	6 years	8 years
Estimated residual value	-0-	-0-
Estimated total income	$243,000	$108,000

Determine the expected average rate of return for each proposal, giving effect to straight-line depreciation on each investment.

26–21. Cash payback period. Burke Company is evaluating two capital investment proposals, each requiring an investment of $150,000 and each with an 8-year life and expected total net cash flows of $240,000. Proposal 1 is expected to provide equal annual net cash flows of $30,000, and Proposal 2 is expected to have the following unequal annual net cash flows:

Year 1	$60,000
Year 2	50,000
Year 3	40,000
Year 4	20,000
Year 5	20,000
Year 6	20,000
Year 7	20,000
Year 8	10,000

Determine the cash payback period for both proposals.

26–22. Discounted cash flow method. The following data are accumulated by Auerbach Company in evaluating the purchase of $120,000 of equipment having a 4-year useful life:

	Net Income	Net Cash Flow
Year 1	$25,000	$55,000
Year 2	10,000	40,000
Year 3	6,000	36,000
Year 4	4,000	34,000

(a) Assuming that the desired rate of return is 12%, determine the excess (deficiency) of present value over the amount to be invested for the proposal. Use the table of the present value of $1 appearing in this chapter. (b) Would management be likely to look with favor on the proposal? Explain.

26–23. Present value index. Grayson Company has computed the excess of present value over the amount to be invested for capital expenditure proposals P and Q, using the discounted cash flow method. Relevant data related to the computation are as follows:

	Proposal P	Proposal Q
Total present value of net cash flow	$318,000	$441,000
Amount to be invested	300,000	420,000
Excess of present value over amount to be invested	$ 18,000	$ 21,000

Determine the present value index for each proposal.

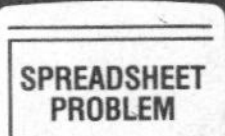

26–24. Average rate of return, cash payback period, discounted cash flow method. Linston Company is considering the acquisition of machinery at a cost of $400,000. The machinery has an estimated life of 5 years and no residual value. It is expected to provide yearly income of $40,000 and yearly net cash flows of $120,000. The company's minimum desired rate of return for discounted cash flow analysis is 10%. Compute the following:

(a) The average rate of return, giving effect to straight-line depreciation on the investment.
(b) The cash payback period.

(c) The excess (deficiency) of present value over the amount to be invested, as determined by the discounted cash flow method. Use the table of the present value of $1 appearing in this chapter.

26–25. Discounted internal rate of return method. The discounted internal rate of return method is used by Ramsey Company in analyzing a capital expenditure proposal that involves an investment of $342,600 and annual net cash flows of $120,000 for each of the 4 years of useful life. (a) Determine a "present value factor for an annuity of $1" which can be used in determining the discounted internal rate of return. (b) Using the factor determined in (a) and the present value of an annuity of $1 table appearing in this chapter, determine the discounted internal rate of return for the proposal.

26–26. Discounted cash flow method and discounted internal rate of return method. Emerson Inc. is evaluating a proposed expenditure of $121,480 on a 4-year project whose estimated net cash flows are $40,000 for each of the four years.

(a) Compute the excess (deficiency) of present value over the amount to be invested, using the discounted cash flow method and an assumed rate of return of 15%. (b) Based on the analysis prepared in (a), is the rate of return (1) more than 15%, (2) 15%, or (3) less than 15%? Explain. (c) Determine the discounted internal rate of return by computing a "present value factor for an annuity of $1" and using the table of the present value of an annuity of $1 presented in the text.

Problems

26–27. Average rate of return method, discounted cash flow method, and analysis. The capital investments budget committee is considering two projects. The estimated operating income and net cash flows from each project are as follows:

	Project G		Project H	
Year	Operating Income	Net Cash Flow	Operating Income	Net Cash Flow
1	$15,000	$ 39,000	$ 7,000	$ 31,000
2	10,000	34,000	9,000	33,000
3	8,000	32,000	10,000	34,000
4	6,000	30,000	10,000	34,000
5	6,000	30,000	9,000	33,000
Total	$45,000	$165,000	$45,000	$165,000

Each project requires an investment of $120,000. Straight-line depreciation will be used, and no residual value is expected. The committee has selected a rate of 10% for purposes of the discounted cash flow analysis.

Instructions: (1) Compute the following:

(a) The average rate of return for each project, giving effect to depreciation on the investment.

(b) The excess (deficiency) of present value over the amount to be invested, as determined by the discounted cash flow method for each project. Use the present value of $1 table appearing in this chapter.

(2) Prepare a brief report for the capital investment committee, advising it on the relative merits of the two projects.

26–28. Cash payback period, discounted cash flow method, and analysis. Enders Company is considering two projects. The estimated net cash flows from each project are as follows:

Year	Project L	Project M
1	$ 50,000	$200,000
2	250,000	100,000
3	100,000	100,000
4	50,000	80,000
5	50,000	20,000
Total	$500,000	$500,000

Each project requires an investment of $300,000, with no residual value expected. A rate of 20% has been selected for the discounted cash flow analysis.

Instructions: (1) Compute the following for each project:

(a) Cash payback period.

(b) The excess (deficiency) of present value over the amount to be invested, as determined by the discounted cash flow method. Use the present value of $1 table appearing in this chapter.

(2) Prepare a brief report advising management on the relative merits of each of the two projects.

26–29. Discounted cash flow method, present value index, and analysis. Farmer Company wishes to evaluate three capital investment proposals by using the discounted cash flow method. Relevant data related to the proposals are summarized as follows:

	Proposal A	Proposal B	Proposal C
Amount to be invested	$100,000	$100,000	$150,000
Annual net cash flows:			
Year 1	60,000	45,000	75,000
Year 2	45,000	40,000	70,000
Year 3	30,000	30,000	60,000

Instructions: (1) Assuming that the desired rate of return is 15%, prepare a discounted cash flow analysis for each proposal. Use the present value of $1 table appearing in this chapter.

(2) Determine a present value index for each proposal.

(3) Which proposal offers the largest amount of present value per dollar of investment? Explain.

26–30. Discounted cash flow method, discounted internal rate of return method, and analysis. Management is considering two capital investment proposals. The estimated net cash flows from each proposal are as follows:

Year	Proposal A	Proposal B
1	$50,000	$160,000
2	50,000	160,000
3	50,000	160,000
4	50,000	160,000

Proposal A requires an investment of $129,450, while Proposal B requires an investment of $456,800. No residual value is expected from either proposal.

Instructions: (1) Compute the following for each proposal:

(a) The excess (deficiency) of present value over the amount to be invested, as determined by the discounted cash flow method. Use a rate of 12% and the present value of $1 table appearing in this chapter.

(b) A present value index.

(2) Determine the discounted internal rate of return for each proposal by (a) computing a "present value factor for an annuity of $1" and (b) using the present value of an annuity of $1 table appearing in this chapter.
(3) What advantage does the discounted internal rate of return method have over the discounted cash flow method in comparing proposals?

26–31. Effect of income tax on capital investment decision. Using the discounted cash flow method, the accountant for Collins Company prepared the following analysis of a project expected to be undertaken during Year 1:

Year	Present Value of 1 at 12%	Net Cash Flow	Present Value of Net Cash Flow
1	.893	$152,000	$135,736
2	.797	136,000	108,392
3	.712	136,000	96,832
4	.636	112,000	71,232
5	.567	100,000	56,700
6	.507	50,000	25,350
Total		$686,000	$494,242
Amount to be invested			500,000
Deficiency of present value over amount to be invested			$ 5,758

A review of the analysis and related items disclosed the following:
(a) The straight-line method was used for computing depreciation, with one half of a year's depreciation taken in the first year and the sixth year.
(b) Operating income (and net cash flow) before depreciation and taxes is expected to be $220,000, $160,000, $160,000, $120,000, $100,000, and $50,000 for the first through sixth years, respectively.
(c) The income tax rate is 40%.

Instructions: (1) Assuming the use of the straight-line depreciation method with a 5-year life and no residual value, compute the following:
(a) Amount of depreciation expense for each of the six years covered by the project.
(b) Income tax expense for each of the six years covered by the project.
(c) Net cash flow for each of the six years covered by the project. (Note: The net cash flows calculated should agree with those included in the analysis presented in the first paragraph of this problem.)
(2) Compute the following:
(a) Depreciation expense for each of the six years covered by the project, assuming that the 5-year-class MACRS depreciation rates appearing in this chapter are used.
(b) Income tax expense for each of the six years, based on the use of MACRS depreciation.
(c) Net cash flow for each of the six years covered by the project, based on the income tax expense computed in (b).
(d) The excess (deficiency) of present value over the amount to be invested, based on the net cash flows determined in (c) and as determined by the discounted cash flow method. Use the present value of 1 table appearing in this chapter and round computations to the nearest dollar.
(3) Should the project be accepted? Explain.

26–32. Evaluation of alternative capital investment decisions. The investment committee of Beaver Company is evaluating two projects. The projects have different useful lives, but each requires an investment of $160,000. The estimated net cash flows from each project are as follows:

Year	Net Cash Flows	
	Project A	Project B
1	$45,000	$60,000
2	45,000	60,000
3	45,000	60,000
4	45,000	60,000
5	45,000	
6	45,000	

The committee has selected a rate of 15% for purposes of discounted cash flow analysis. It also estimates that the residual value at the end of each project's useful life is $0, but at the end of the fourth year, Project A's residual value would be $90,000.

Instructions: (1) For each project, compute the excess (deficiency) of present value over the amount to be invested, as determined by the discounted cash flow method. Use the present value of 1 table appearing in this chapter. (Ignore the unequal lives of the projects.)

(2) For each project, compute the excess (deficiency) of present value over the amount to be invested, as determined by the discounted cash flow method, assuming that Project A is adjusted to a four-year life for purposes of analysis. Use the present value of 1 table appearing in this chapter.

(3) In reporting to the investment committee, what advice would you give on the relative merits of the two projects?

ALTERNATE PROBLEMS

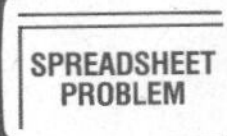

26–27A. Average rate of return method, discounted cash flow method, and analysis. The capital investments budget committee is considering two projects. The estimated operating income and net cash flows from each project are shown as follows:

Year	Project J		Project K	
	Operating Income	Net Cash Flow	Operating Income	Net Cash Flow
1	$ 25,000	$ 75,000	$ 40,000	$ 90,000
2	25,000	75,000	30,000	80,000
3	25,000	75,000	20,000	70,000
4	15,000	65,000	6,000	56,000
5	10,000	60,000	4,000	54,000
Total	$100,000	$350,000	$100,000	$350,000

Each project requires an investment of $250,000. Straight-line depreciation will be used, and no residual value is expected. The committee has selected a rate of 12% for purposes of the discounted cash flow analysis.

Instructions: (1) Compute the following:

(a) The average rate of return for each project, giving effect to depreciation on the investment.

(b) The excess (deficiency) of present value over the amount to be invested, as determined by the discounted cash flow method for each project. Use the present value of $1 table appearing in this chapter.

(2) Prepare a brief report for the capital investment committee, advising it on the relative merits of the two projects.

26–28A. Cash payback period, discounted cash flow method, and analysis. Cuthbert Company is considering two projects. The estimated net cash flows from each project are as follows:

Year	Project D	Project E
1	$200,000	$ 50,000
2	200,000	150,000
3	100,000	300,000
4	100,000	100,000
5	100,000	100,000
Total	$700,000	$700,000

Each project requires an investment of $500,000, with no residual value expected. A rate of 12% has been selected for the discounted cash flow analysis.

Instructions: (1) Compute the following for each project:
(a) Cash payback period.
(b) The excess (deficiency) of present value over the amount to be invested, as determined by the discounted cash flow method. Use the present value of 1 table appearing in this chapter.
(2) Prepare a brief report advising management on the relative merits of each of the two projects.

26–29A. Discounted cash flow method, present value index, and analysis. J. Wilson Company wishes to evaluate three capital investment projects by using the discounted cash flow method. Relevant data related to the projects are summarized as follows:

	Project P	Project Q	Project R
Amount to be invested	$480,000	$240,000	$240,000
Annual net cash flows:			
Year 1	300,000	180,000	60,000
Year 2	240,000	120,000	120,000
Year 3	180,000	60,000	180,000

Instructions: (1) Assuming that the desired rate of return is 20%, prepare a discounted cash flow analysis for each project. Use the present value of $1 table appearing in this chapter.
(2) Determine a present value index for each project.
(3) Which project offers the largest amount of present value per dollar of investment? Explain.

26–30A. Discounted cash flow method, discounted internal rate of return method, and analysis. Management is considering two capital investment projects. The estimated net cash flows from each project are as follows:

Year	Project S	Project T
1	$120,000	$30,000
2	120,000	30,000
3	120,000	30,000
4	120,000	30,000

Project S requires an investment of $364,440, while Project T requires an investment of $85,650. No residual value is expected from either project.

Instructions: (1) Compute the following for each project:
(a) The excess (deficiency) of present value over the amount to be invested, as determined by the discounted cash flow method. Use a rate of 10% and the present value of $1 table appearing in this chapter.
(b) A present value index.

(continued)

(2) Determine the discounted internal rate of return for each project by (a) computing a "present value factor for an annuity of $1" and (b) using the present value of an annuity of $1 table appearing in this chapter.
(3) What advantage does the discounted internal rate of return method have over the discounted cash flow method in comparing projects?

Mini-Case 26

Your father is considering an investment of $400,000 in either Project X or Project Y. In discussing the two projects with an advisor, it was decided that, for the risk involved, a return of 12% on the cash investment would be required. For this purpose, your father estimated the following economic factors for the projects:

	Project X	Project Y
Useful life	4 years	4 years
Residual value	-0-	-0-
Net income:		
Year 1	$ 20,000	$ 55,000
2	30,000	40,000
3	35,000	15,000
4	43,000	10,000
Net cash flows:		
Year 1	$120,000	$155,000
2	130,000	140,000
3	135,000	115,000
4	143,000	110,000

Although the average rate of return exceeded 12% on both projects, your father has tentatively decided to invest in Project X because the rate was higher for Project X. Although he doesn't fully understand the importance of cash flow, he has heard others talk about its importance in evaluating investments. In this respect, he noted that the total net cash flow from Project X is $528,000, which exceeds that from Project Y by $8,000.

Instructions:

(1) Determine the average rate of return for both projects.
(2) How would you explain the importance of net cash flows in the analysis of investment projects? Include a specific example to demonstrate the importance of net cash flows and their timing to these two projects.

Answers to Self-Examination Questions

1. C Methods of evaluating capital investment proposals that ignore the time value of money are categorized as methods that ignore present value. This category includes the average rate of return method (answer A) and the cash payback method (answer B).

2. B The average rate of return is 24% (answer B), determined by dividing the expected average annual earnings by the average investment, as indicated below:

$$\frac{\$60,000 \div 5}{(\$100,000 + \$0) \div 2} = 24\%$$

3. B Of the three methods of analyzing proposals for capital investments, the cash payback method (answer B) refers to the expected period of time required to recover the amount of cash to be invested. The average rate of return method (answer A) is a measure of the anticipated profitability of a proposal. The discounted cash flow method (answer C) reduces the expected future net cash flows originating from a proposal to their present values.

4. C The discounted cash flow method (answer C) uses the concept of present value to determine the total present value of the cash flows expected from a proposal and compares this value with the amount to be invested. The average rate of return method (answer A) and the cash payback method (answer B) ignore present value. The discounted internal rate of return method (answer D) uses the present value concept to determine the discounted internal rate of return expected from the proposal.

5. A Capital rationing (answer A) is the process by which management allocates available investment funds among competing capital investment proposals. Capital expenditure budgeting (answer B) is the process of summarizing the decisions that have been made for the acquisition of plant assets and preparing a capital expenditures budget to reflect these decisions. Leasing (answer C) is an alternative that management should consider before making a final decision on the acquisition of assets.

27
Quantitative Techniques for Controlling Inventory and Making Decisions Under Uncertainty

CHAPTER OBJECTIVES

Describe and illustrate the use of the economic order quantity for inventory control.

Describe and illustrate the use of the inventory order point and safety stock for inventory control.

Describe and illustrate the use of linear programming for inventory control.

Describe the use of the expected value concept for decision making under uncertainty.

Illustrate the use of payoff tables and decision trees in applying the concept of expected value in managerial decision making.

Describe the value of information concept and illustrate its use in managerial decision making.

Describe and illustrate the use of expected value concepts in variance analysis.

Describe and illustrate the use of the maximin and maximax concepts in managerial decision making under uncertainty.

Previous chapters have discussed many ways in which accounting data can be used by management in planning and controlling business operations, including such analyses as cost-volume-profit analysis, differential analysis, and capital investment analysis. These analyses can be performed using rather simple mathematical relationships, since they usually involve a limited number of objectives and variables. This chapter focuses on the use of quantitative techniques that rely on more sophisticated mathematical relationships and statistical methods. Such techniques enable management to consider a larger number of objectives and variables in planning and controlling operations.

The discussions and illustrations in this chapter relate to the use of quantitative techniques in controlling inventory and making decisions under uncertainty. These techniques often lead to a clarification of management decision alternatives and their expected effects on the business enterprise. For example, the most economical plan for purchasing materials for a single plant may be easily determined, based on the lowest overall cost per unit of materials. However, the most economical plan for purchasing materials for several plants may not be as easily determined, because transportation costs to the various plant locations may be different, and the amount of purchases from any one supplier may be limited. In this latter case, a quantitative technique known as linear programming may be useful in determining the most economical plan for purchasing materials.

The primary disadvantages of quantitative techniques are their complexity and their reliance on mathematical relationships and statistical methods which may be understood by only the most highly trained experts. When computers are used, however, it is less important to understand these complexities, so that quantitative techniques can be used by all levels of management.

Decision Support Systems for Managerial Use

A decision support system [DSS] is a computerized aid to ease or enhance the decision-making process. It is geared toward facilitating unstructured or semi-structured decisions. . . .

Unstructured decision situations are those that contain many unknowns, in the areas of both decision criteria and the variables upon which the decisions are based. For example, if we are dealing with a problem in which the interest rates and the unemployment rate a year from today will have some effect, but we are unsure of the exact relationship between those factors and the outcome, we are in an unstructured decision situation. We don't know what the interest rates or unemployment rate will be one year hence, nor do we know the exact relationship between those factors and our outcome.

Semistructured decision situations occur when either the decision criteria or the decision variables are unknown, but not both. For example, in a semistructured decision situation we know how to quantify the relationship between interest rates, the unemployment rate, and our outcome, but we don't know what the rates will be.

Decision support systems also may be employed to make structured decisions when the number of variables is so great it becomes too difficult to organize and execute calculations manually. For example, if [a business enterprise is negotiating a mortgage to finance the acquisition of a plant asset and] different banks are offering different [mortgage] packages with different [interest] rates [and different loan provisions, such as compensating balance requirements, working capital requirements, payment options, and initiation fees,] we would have an ideal application for a decision support system. The [enterprise] would have to define the necessary criteria (for example, maximum [quarterly] payments. . .) and supply the variables offered by each of the banks.

. . . This is a fully structured decision as both the decision criteria and the decision variables are known. The automation of the tedious calculation process and the ability to change the decision criteria or decision variables quickly qualify it as a decision support system.

A DSS does not replace the decision maker by making the actual decision. As the name suggests, the DSS serves to support the decision-making process.

Source: Susan Davis-Stemp, Joshua E. Minkin, John Thomopoulos, Morris W. Stemp, and Robert Howell, *Decision Support Systems* (Montvale, New Jersey: National Association of Accountants, 1986).

For a business enterprise that needs large quantities of inventory to meet sales orders or production requirements, inventory is one of its most important assets. The lack of sufficient inventory can result in lost sales, idle production facilities, production bottlenecks, and additional purchasing costs due to placing special orders or rush orders. On the other hand, excess inventory can result in large storage costs and large spoilage losses, which reduce the profitability of the enterprise. Thus, it is important for a business enterprise to know the ideal quantity to be purchased in a single order and the minimum and maximum quantities to be on hand at any time. Such factors as economies of large-scale buying, storage costs, work interruption due to shortages, and seasonal and cyclical changes in production schedules need to be considered. Three quantitative techniques that are especially useful in inventory control are (1) the economic order quantity formula, (2) the inventory order point formula, and (3) linear programming.[1]

Economic Order Quantity

The optimum quantity of inventory to be ordered at one time is termed the **economic order quantity (EOQ).** Important factors to be considered in determining the optimum quantity are the costs involved in processing an order for the materials and the costs involved in storing the materials.

The annual cost of processing orders for a specified material (cost of placing orders, verifying invoices, processing payments, etc.) increases as the number of orders placed increases. On the other hand, the annual cost of storing the materials (taxes, insurance, occupancy of storage space, etc.) decreases as the number of orders placed increases. The economic order quantity is therefore that quantity that will minimize the combined annual costs of ordering and storing materials.

The combined annual cost incurred in ordering and storing materials can be computed under various assumptions as to the number of orders to be placed during a year. To illustrate, assume the following data for an inventoriable material which is used at the same rate during the year:

Units required during the year..........	1,200
Ordering cost, per order placed	$10.00
Annual storage cost, per unit..........	.60

If a single order were placed for the entire year's needs, the cost of ordering the 1,200 units would be $10. The average number of units held in inventory during the year would therefore be 600 (1,200 units ÷ 2) and would result in an annual storage cost of $360 (600 units × $.60). The combined order and storage costs for placing only one order during the year would thus be $370 ($10 + $360). If, instead of a single order, two orders were placed during the year, the order cost would be $20 (2 × $10), 600 units would need to be purchased on each order, the average inventory would be 300 units, and the annual storage cost would be $180 (300 units × $.60). Accordingly, the combined order and storage costs for placing two orders during the year would be $200 ($20 + $180). Successive computations will disclose the EOQ

[1]The development and use of "just-in-time" inventory control procedures are discussed in Appendix I, "Trends in Managerial Accounting."

when the combined cost reaches its lowest point and starts upward. The following table shows an optimum of 200 units of materials per order, with 6 orders per year, at a combined cost of $120:

Tabulation of Economic Order Quantity

Number of Orders	Number of Units per Order	Average Units in Inventory	Order and Storage Costs		
			Order Cost	Storage Cost	Combined Cost
1	1,200	600	$10	$360	$370
2	600	300	20	180	200
3	400	200	30	120	150
4	300	150	40	90	130
5	240	120	50	72	122
6	200	100	60	60	120
7	171	86	70	52	122

The economic order quantity may also be determined by a formula based on differential calculus. The formula and its application to the illustration is as follows:

Economic Order Quantity Formula

$$\text{EOQ} = \sqrt{\frac{2 \times \text{Annual Units Required} \times \text{Cost per Order Placed}}{\text{Annual Storage Cost per Unit}}}$$

$$\text{EOQ} = \sqrt{\frac{2 \times 1{,}200 \times \$10}{\$.60}}$$

$$\text{EOQ} = \sqrt{40{,}000}$$

$$\text{EOQ} = 200 \text{ units}$$

Inventory Order Point

The **inventory order point,** usually expressed in units, is the level to which inventory is allowed to fall before an order for additional inventory is placed. The inventory order point depends on the (1) daily usage of inventory that is expected to be consumed in production or sold, (2) number of production days that it takes to receive an order for inventory, termed the **lead time,** and (3) **safety stock,** which is the amount of inventory that is available for use when unforeseen circumstances arise, such as delays in receiving ordered inventory as a result of a national truckers' strike. Once the order point is reached, the most economical quantity should be ordered.

The inventory order point is computed by using the following formula:

Inventory Order Point = (Daily Usage × Days of Lead Time) + Safety Stock

To illustrate, assume that Beacon Company, a printing company, estimates daily usage of 3,000 pounds of paper and a lead time of 30 days to receive an order of paper. Beacon Company desires a safety stock of 10,000 pounds. The inventory order point for the paper is 100,000 pounds, computed as follows:

Inventory Order Point = (Daily Usage × Lead Time) + Safety Stock
Inventory Order Point = (3,000 lbs. × 30 days) + 10,000 lbs.
Inventory Order Point = 90,000 lbs. + 10,000 lbs.
Inventory Order Point = 100,000 lbs.

In this illustration, a safety stock of 10,000 pounds of paper was assumed. This level of safety stock should be established by management after considering many factors, such as the uncertainty in the estimates of daily inventory usage and lead time. If management were 100% certain that estimates of the daily usage and lead time were correct, no safety stock would be required. As the uncertainty in these estimates increases, the amount of safety stock normally increases. In addition, the level of safety stock carried by an enterprise will also depend on the costs of carrying inventory and the costs of being out of inventory when materials are needed for production or sales. If the costs of carrying inventory are low and the costs of being out of inventory are high, then relatively large amounts of safety stock would normally be carried by a business enterprise.

Inventory Cardiogram

Henry C. Ekstein, the former chief financial officer of Remington Aluminum, developed an inventory cardiogram for use in controlling inventory. The cardiogram is a graph of inventory levels over time, which portrays the normal inventory usage cycle for a company. For example, the cardiogram indicates when and how many times inventory was overstocked and back ordered, the inventory reorder point, and the safety stock levels. In the following cardiogram, both desired and actual inventory usage are plotted. The reorder point is 275 units, the safety stock is 225 units, and the inventory was back ordered twice during the 12-week period. The economic order quantity is 400 units, indicated by the length of the vertical lines. The vertical lines also indicate the receipt of additional inventory.

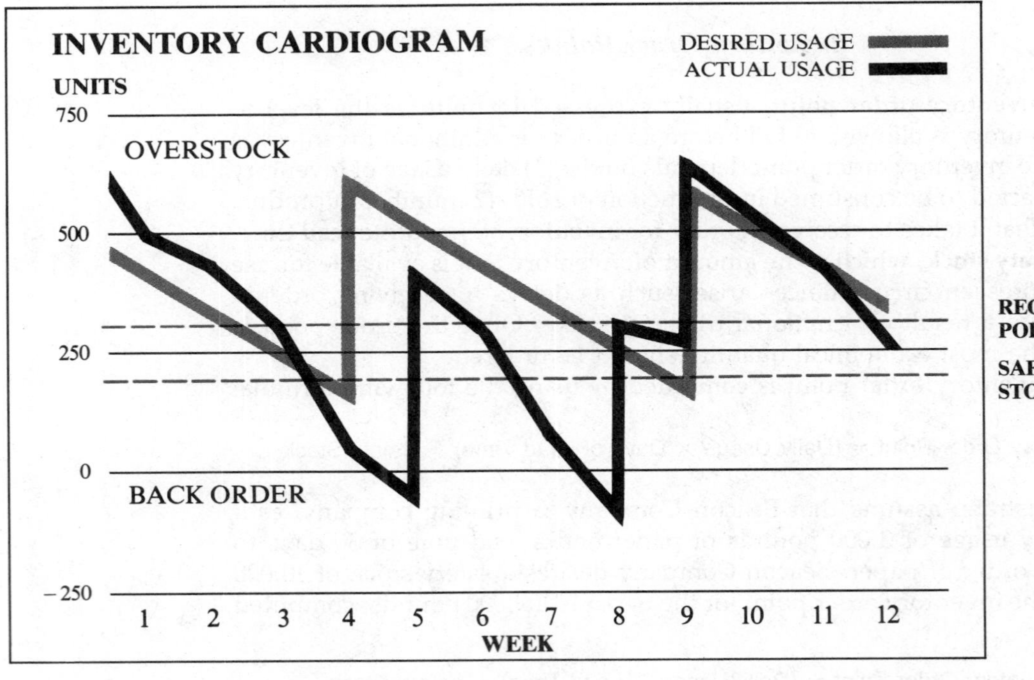

Ekstein believes that the cardiogram is most effective in managing a limited number of inventory items that were previously uncontrolled. "Once you show someone the inventory cardiogram, " Ekstein claims, "all of a sudden it makes sense to them — how inventories behave, what the problem is, how many times it occurred over the past year, and what to do about it."

Source: Paul Susca, "Checking the Vital Signs," *CFO* (February, 1986), p. 13.

Quantitative techniques using statistics and probability theory may be useful to managers in establishing order point and safety stock levels. Such techniques are described in advanced texts.

Linear Programming for Inventory Control

Linear programming is a quantitative method that can provide data for solving a variety of business problems in which management's objective is to minimize costs or maximize profits, subject to several limiting factors. Although a thorough discussion of linear programming is appropriate for more advanced courses, the following simplified illustration demonstrates the way in which linear programming can be applied to determine the most economical purchasing plan. In this situation, management's objective is to minimize the total cost of purchasing materials for several branch locations, subject to the availability of materials from suppliers.

Assume that a manufacturing company purchases Part P for use at both its West Branch and East Branch. Part P is available in limited quantities from two suppliers. The total unit cost price varies considerably for parts acquired from the two suppliers mainly because of differences in transportation charges. The relevant data for the decision regarding the most economical purchase arrangement are summarized in the following diagram:

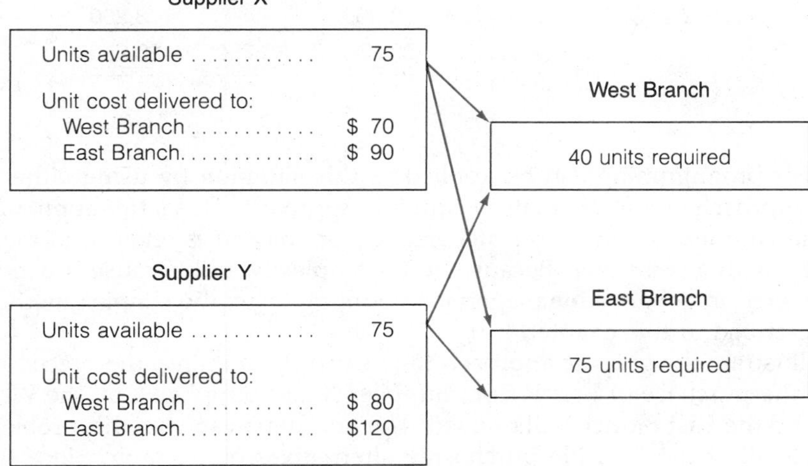

It might appear that the most economical course of action would be to purchase (1) the 40 units required by West Branch from Supplier X at $70 a unit, (2) 35 units for East Branch from Supplier X at $90 a unit, and (3) the remaining 40 units required by East Branch from Supplier Y at $120 a unit.

If this course of action were followed, the total cost of the parts needed by the two branches would amount to $10,750, as indicated by the following computation:

	Cost of Purchases		
	By West Branch	*By East Branch*	*Total*
From Supplier X:			
40 units at $70	$2,800		$ 2,800
35 units at $90		$3,150	3,150
From Supplier Y:			
40 units at $120		4,800	4,800
Total	$2,800	$7,950	$10,750

Although many different purchasing programs are possible, the most economical course of action would be to purchase (1) the 75 units required by East Branch from Supplier X at $90 a unit and (2) the 40 units required by West Branch from Supplier Y at $80 a unit. If this plan were used, no units would be purchased at the lowest available unit cost, and the total cost of the parts would be $9,950, calculated as follows:

	Cost of Purchases		
	By West Branch	*By East Branch*	*Total*
From Supplier X:			
75 units at $90		$6,750	$6,750
From Supplier Y:			
40 units at $80	$3,200		3,200
Total	$3,200	$6,750	$9,950

Linear programming can be applied to this situation by using either a graphic approach or a mathematical equation approach. This latter approach, called the **simplex method,** uses algebraic equations and is often used more practically with a computer. Because of its complexity and because it is normally covered in advanced managerial accounting texts, the simplex method is not described in this chapter.

To illustrate the graphic approach to linear programming, the preceding facts for the purchase of Part P from Supplier X and Supplier Y by the West Branch and the East Branch will be used. The first step in solving this problem is to place all of the possible purchasing alternatives on a graph. Since the amount purchased from Supplier X will determine the amount purchased from Supplier Y, and vice versa, only a graph showing all possible purchase plans for Supplier X (or Supplier Y) is necessary. The following graph for Supplier X is based on the foregoing data.

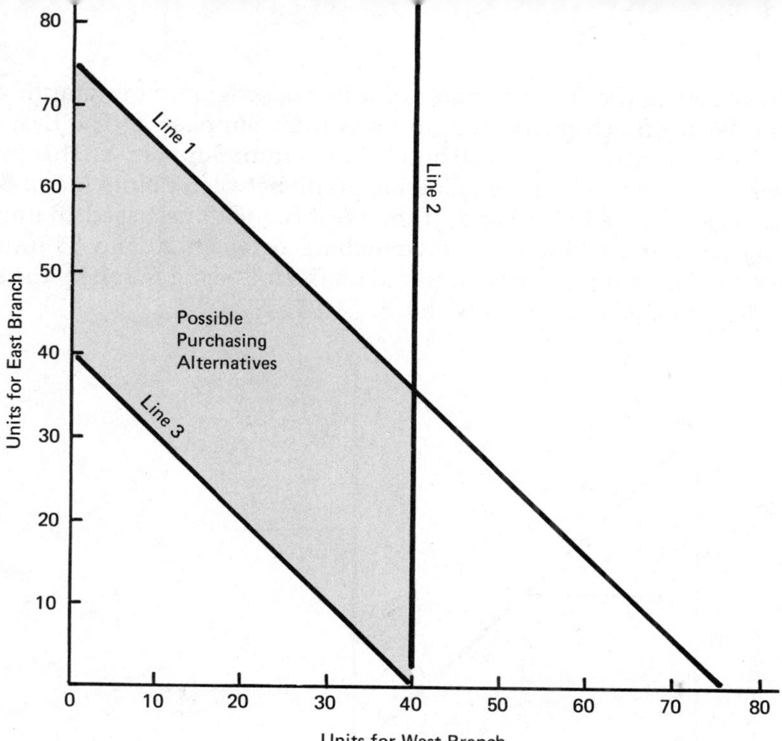

Linear Programming Graph—Units Purchased From Supplier X

Line 1: Maximum number of units that can be purchased from Supplier X.

Line 2: Maximum number of units that will be purchased by West Branch.

Line 3: Minimum number of units that must be purchased from Supplier X.

The linear programming graph is constructed in the following manner:

1. Units for the West Branch are plotted on the horizontal axis, and units for the East Branch are plotted on the vertical axis.
2. A point representing the maximum number of units that could be purchased from Supplier X by the West Branch (75 units) is located on the horizontal axis. A point representing the maximum number of units that could be purchased from Supplier X by the East Branch (75 units) is located on the vertical axis.
3. A diagonal line (labeled Line 1) is drawn connecting the points representing the 75 units on the vertical axis with 75 units on the horizontal axis. This line represents the constraint on the maximum number of units (75) that can be purchased from Supplier X by either branch or both branches.
4. The constraint on the number of units that the West Branch would purchase from Supplier X (40) is indicated by a line (labeled Line 2) which is drawn vertically upward from the point of 40 units on the horizontal axis to intersect Line 1.
5. A line (labeled Line 3) is drawn connecting 40 units on the vertical axis with 40 units on the horizontal axis. This line represents the constraint on minimum purchases from Supplier X (115 units required by the branches less 75 units available from each supplier).
6. The area bounded by the vertical axis and Lines 1, 2, and 3 is shaded. This area represents the set of all possible alternatives for purchases from Supplier X.

To illustrate the interpretation of a linear programming graph, assume that the West Branch purchased no units from Supplier X. The East Branch could then purchase between 40 and 75 units from Supplier X. This purchase alternative is indicated on the following graph between points A and B on the vertical axis. On the other hand, if the West Branch purchased 20 units from Supplier X, the East Branch could purchase between 20 and 55 units from Supplier X. This alternative is indicated on the following graph by the colored dotted line connecting points E and F.

Linear Programming Graph—Alternative Purchase Plans

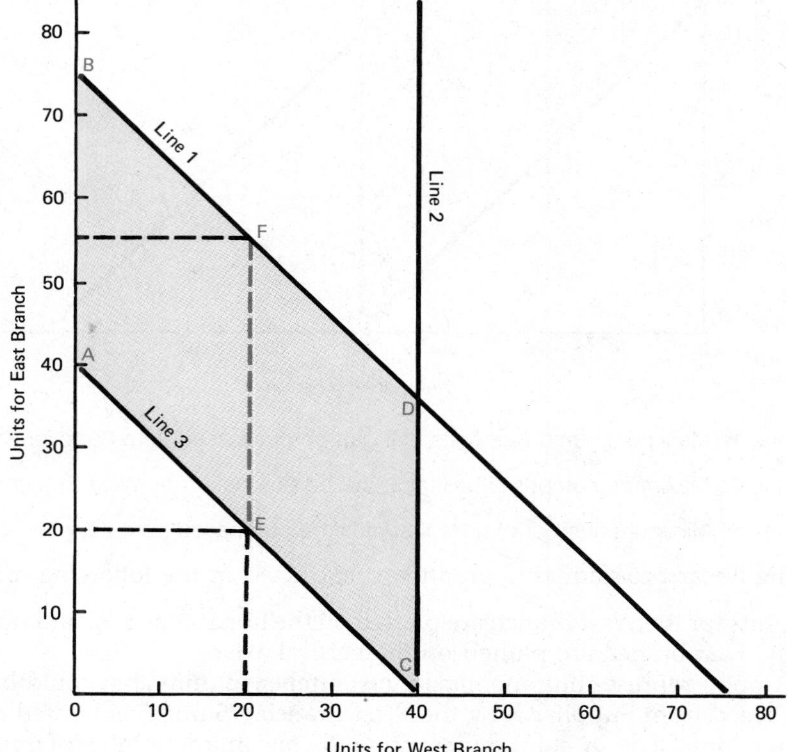

Although any point in the shaded area of the graph is a possible purchasing plan, managers are interested in selecting the most economical plan. According to the mathematical properties of linear programming, an economical purchase plan is located at one of the four points representing the corners of the shaded area of the graph. These corners are labeled A through D on the graph.

Each of the four corners represents the following purchases from Supplier X by the West Branch and the East Branch:

	Purchases by West Branch	Purchases by East Branch
Corner A:		
From Supplier X	0 units	40 units
Corner B:		
From Supplier X	0	75
Corner C:		
From Supplier X	40	0
Corner D:		
From Supplier X	40	35

Since the amount purchased from Supplier X affects the amount purchased from Supplier Y, the four corners identified above can be rewritten in terms of four separate purchase plans. In other words, if only 40 units are purchased from Supplier X and are shipped to the East Branch (Corner A), then the West Branch must obtain its purchases of 40 units from Supplier Y, and the East Branch must obtain an additional 35 units from Supplier Y to fulfill its total needs of 75 units. The four purchase plans represented by the four corners are as follows:

	Purchases by West Branch	*Purchases by East Branch*
Plan 1 (Corner A):		
From Supplier X	0 units	40 units
From Supplier Y	40	35
Plan 2 (Corner B):		
From Supplier X	0	75
From Supplier Y	40	0
Plan 3 (Corner C):		
From Supplier X	40	0
From Supplier Y	0	75
Plan 4 (Corner D):		
From Supplier X	40	35
From Supplier Y	0	40

By computing the total cost of the purchases for the West Branch and the East Branch for each of the purchase plans, the most economical purchase plan can be determined. As described earlier on page 976 and as shown in the following computation, Plan 2 is the most economical of the four purchase plans.

	Cost of Purchases		
	By West Branch	*By East Branch*	*Total*
Plan 1:			
From Supplier X:			
40 units at $90.		$3,600	$ 3,600
From Supplier Y:			
40 units at $80.	$3,200		3,200
35 units at $120.		4,200	4,200
Total	$3,200	$7,800	$11,000
Plan 2:			
From Supplier X:			
75 units at $90.		$6,750	$ 6,750
From Supplier Y:			
40 units at $80.	$3,200		3,200
Total	$3,200	$6,750	$ 9,950

	Cost of Purchases		
	By West Branch	By East Branch	Total
Plan 3:			
From Supplier X:			
40 units at $70	$2,800		$ 2,800
From Supplier Y:			
75 units at $120		$9,000	9,000
Total	$2,800	$9,000	$11,800
Plan 4:			
From Supplier X:			
40 units at $70	$2,800		$ 2,800
35 units at $90		$3,150	3,150
From Supplier Y:			
40 units at $120		4,800	4,800
Total	$2,800	$7,950	$10,750

The preceding illustration of the graphic approach to linear programming required the construction of a graph and the consideration of four alternative purchase plans. Although an economical purchasing plan decision could have been determined by trial and error, such an approach can be time-consuming and costly. The trial and error approach could potentially require consideration of a much larger number of possible purchase plans before the most economical plan is found.

DECISION MAKING UNDER UNCERTAINTY

Quantitative techniques are especially useful to management in making decisions under uncertainty, which is characteristic of the environment in which managers must make decisions. The managerial accountant can aid management in making decisions under uncertainty by providing data useful in assessing the chances that future events will occur and the impact of those events. One technique useful for this purpose is the expected value concept. Two alternative concepts that managers may also find useful in special situations are the maximin and maximax concepts. These three concepts are discussed and illustrated in the remainder of this chapter.

MANAGERIAL USE OF THE EXPECTED VALUE CONCEPT

The concept of **expected value** involves identifying the possible outcomes from a decision and estimating the likelihood that each outcome will occur. By using the expected value concept, managers can better evaluate the uncertainty of the occurrence of predicted outcomes from decisions.

The likelihood that an outcome will occur from a decision is usually expressed in terms of a probability or chance of occurrence. For example, the probability or chance that, on the flip of a coin, a head will appear is .50 or 50%. Likewise, the probability or chance that the introduction of a new product will be successful might be expressed as .60 or 60%.

The expected value of a decision is the sum of the values that result when the dollar value of each outcome is multiplied by the probability or chance of its occurrence. Thus, expected value can be thought of as an average value.

That is, each possible outcome is weighted by its chance of occurrence to obtain an average expected outcome. For example, assume that you are playing a game in which a coin is flipped. If a head appears, you win $10,000; if a tail appears, you lose $6,000. The expected value of this game is $2,000, computed as follows:

Expected Value = .50($10,000) + .50(−$6,000)
Expected Value = $5,000 − $3,000
Expected Value = $2,000

If you played the preceding game a large number of times, 50% of the time you would win $10,000, 50% of the time you would lose $6,000, and on the average you would win $2,000 per game. For example, if you played the game twice and won once and lost once, you would have won $10,000 and lost $6,000. Hence, you would have net winnings of $4,000 ($10,000 − $6,000). Since you played the game twice, your average winnings would be $2,000 per game ($4,000 ÷ 2). Consequently, the expected value of playing the game is $2,000.

To illustrate the expected value concept within a managerial context, assume that the management of Faxon Company is faced with deciding on a location for a new hotel. The search for the best site has been narrowed to two choices within a large metropolitan area. One site is in the center of the city. The accessibility to the city's business and entertainment district makes this site attractive for conventions. The other location is twenty miles from the center of the city at the intersection of two interstate highways. The site is attractive because of its proximity to the city's international airport. After the hotel is constructed, the management of Faxon Company plans to operate the hotel for one year and then sell the hotel for a profit. Over the past five years, Faxon has successfully constructed and sold four hotels in this fashion.

The estimated profit or loss at each site depends on whether the occupancy rate the first year is high or low. Based on marketing studies, the following profit and loss data have been estimated:

City Site	*Profit or Loss*	*Chance of Occurrence*
High occupancy	$1,500,000	70%
Low occupancy	(500,000)	30
Interstate site	*Profit or Loss*	*Chance of Occurrence*
High occupancy	$1,000,000	60%
Low occupancy	100,000	40

The expected value of each site is computed by weighting each outcome by its chance of occurrence, as follows:

City Site

Expected value = .7($1,500,000) + .3(−$500,000)
Expected value = $1,050,000 − $150,000
Expected value = $900,000

Interstate Site

Expected value = .6($1,000,000) + .4($100,000)
Expected value = $600,000 + $40,000
Expected value = $640,000

Based on the expected values, the city site is more attractive than the interstate site because the city site has a higher expected value. Thus, on the average, the city site is expected to yield a higher profit than the interstate site.

The expected values for the city site and the interstate site of $900,000 and $640,000, respectively, will not actually occur. These values are weighted averages of the estimated profit or loss for each site. For the city site, the estimated outcome will be either a profit of $1,500,000 or a loss of $500,000. Likewise, for the interstate site, the estimated outcome will be either a profit of $1,000,000 or a profit of $100,000.

In the face of uncertainty, expected value is one of the most important pieces of information available to the manager for making a decision. Because expected value is an average concept, however, the range of possible outcomes (the variability of the outcomes) may also be valuable information for management's assessment of the uncertainty surrounding a decision. Although the city site in the preceding illustration has a higher expected value than the interstate site, the city site also has a wider range of possible outcomes (a profit of $1,500,000 or a loss of $500,000) than does the interstate site (a profit of $1,000,000 or $100,000). Consequently, the management of Faxon Company might select the interstate site in order to minimize the variability of the possible outcomes from the site decision. As with many other decisions, management must exercise judgment after weighing all available data and analyses.

The use of the expected value concept by management can be facilitated through the use of payoff tables and decision trees. In addition, the expected value concept may be used by managers in assessing the value of collecting additional information before a decision is made. The remainder of this section describes and illustrates the use of payoff tables and decision trees and discusses the value of obtaining additional information.

Payoff Tables

A **payoff table** presents a summary of the possible outcomes of one or more decisions. A payoff table is especially useful in managerial decision making when a wide variety of possible outcomes exists. One such situation might involve a decision facing a store manager who must decide on the amount of merchandise to purchase for various levels of possible consumer demand. To illustrate, assume that the new manager of Grocery Wholesalers Inc. must decide how many pounds of a perishable product to purchase on Monday for sale during the week. The product is purchased in 100-pound units, and by the end of the week, any unsold product is spoiled and lost. In the past, the former manager had noted that the maximum weekly sales had been 900 pounds. Therefore, to be assured that all demand could be met, 1,000 pounds were purchased.

The variable cost of the product is $1.50 per pound, and the selling price is $1.80 per pound. Thus, for each pound sold, Grocery Wholesalers Inc. earns a contribution margin of $.30 ($1.80 selling price − $1.50 variable cost per pound) to cover fixed costs and earn a profit. For each pound unsold at the end of the week, the $1.50 variable cost per pound is lost.

Based on sales records, it was determined that sales during the past ten weeks were as follows:

Number of Weeks	Actual Demand (Sales)
2	700 lbs.
5	800
3	900

The new manager must determine whether to purchase 700, 800, or 900 pounds. If the past ten weeks of sales data are used as an indication of future customer demand, the new manager should not purchase 1,000 pounds, since the recent sales data indicate that the maximum demand (sales) has not exceeded 900 pounds.

The outcomes (payoffs) in terms of contribution margin for each of the possible purchase amounts and possible levels of customer demand are summarized in the following payoff table:

Payoff Table of Possible Outcomes

Possible Demand	Contribution Margin of Purchases		
	700 lbs.	800 lbs.	900 lbs.
700 lbs.	$210	$ 60	$ (90)
800	210	240	90
900	210	240	270

The entries in the payoff table indicate that if 700 pounds are demanded and 700 pounds are purchased, for example, then 700 pounds will be sold and a total contribution margin of $210 (700 lbs. × $.30 per lb.) will result. If 700 pounds are demanded and 800 pounds are purchased, then 700 pounds will be sold and 100 pounds will spoil. In this case, the 700 pounds sold will generate a contribution margin of $210 (700 lbs. × $.30 per lb.), the 100 pounds that spoil will generate a loss of $150 (100 lbs. × $1.50 per lb.), and the net contribution margin will be $60 ($210 − $150). If 700 pounds are demanded and 900 pounds are purchased, then 700 pounds will be sold and 200 pounds will spoil. In this case, the 700 pounds sold will generate a contribution margin of $210 (700 lbs. × $.30 per lb.), the 200 pounds that spoil will generate a loss of $300 (200 lbs. × $1.50 per lb.), and the net contribution margin will be a loss of $90 ($210 − $300). If 800 pounds are demanded and 700 pounds are purchased, then 700 pounds will be sold and a total contribution margin of $210 (700 lbs. × $.30 per lb.) will result. The remaining entries in the payoff table are determined in a similar manner.

Based on the past ten weeks of sales data, the chances that the various levels of customer demand will occur can be estimated as follows:

Possible Demand	Number of Weeks	Chance of Occurrence
700 lbs.	2	20% (2/10)
800	5	50% (5/10)
900	3	30% (3/10)
	10	

A payoff table of expected values can now be constructed. Each entry in the payoff table of possible outcomes is multiplied by its chance of occurrence, as indicated above, to determine its expected value. The resulting amounts are entered in the following payoff table:

Payoff Table of Expected Value of Possible Outcomes

Possible Demand	Expected Value of Contribution Margin of Purchases 700 lbs.	800 lbs.	900 lbs.
700 lbs.	$ 42	$ 12	$ (18)
800	105	120	45
900	63	72	81
Totals	$210	$204	$ 108

The expected value of the outcome that 700 pounds are demanded and 700 pounds are purchased is computed by multiplying the contribution margin of $210 by the 20% chance that 700 pounds will be demanded. The resulting expected value is $42 ($210 × 20%). Likewise, the expected value of the outcome that 700 pounds are demanded and 800 pounds are purchased is computed by multiplying the contribution margin of $60 by the 20% chance that 700 pounds will be demanded. The resulting expected value is $12 ($60 × 20%). The expected value of the outcome that 700 pounds are demanded and 900 pounds are purchased is a loss of $18 (−$90 × 20%). Similarly, the expected value of the outcome that 800 pounds are demanded and 700 pounds are purchased is computed by multiplying the contribution margin of $210 by the 50% chance that 800 pounds will be demanded. The resulting expected value is $105 ($210 × 50%). The remaining entries in the payoff table are determined in a similar manner.

The total expected value of each possible purchase is determined by summing the individual expected values at each level of possible demand. In the above table, this total expected value is represented by the totals of each column. For example, the total expected value of a purchase of 700 pounds is equal to the sum of expected values of a purchase of 700 pounds and possible demand of 700 pounds ($42), a purchase of 700 pounds and possible demand of 800 pounds ($105), and a purchase of 700 pounds and possible demand of 900 pounds ($63). The resulting total expected value of purchasing 700 pounds is $210 (the total of the first column). Likewise, the total expected value of a purchase of 800 pounds is $204, and the total expected value of purchasing 900 pounds is $108.

Based solely on the above payoff table of expected values, the new manager should select that purchase with the highest total expected value. Thus, the best purchase decision, on the average, will be the purchase of 700 pounds, since its expected value of $210 is higher than any other purchase alternative. Even though this decision will result in lost sales in some weeks, on the average it will result in the largest possible profits.

Decision Trees

Decision trees are graphical representations of decisions, possible outcomes, and chances that outcomes will occur. Decision trees are especially useful to managers who are choosing among alternatives when possible outcomes are dependent on several decisions. For example, if management decides to produce a new product, it must consider whether to offer the product in all consumer markets or only in specific markets, whether to offer special introductory rebates, whether to offer special warranties, and whether and how much to advertise. In this case, the expected profit from producing the new product depends on many decisions, each of which has an effect on the profitability of the new product.

To illustrate the use of decision trees, assume that Lampe Company is considering disposing of unimproved land. If the unimproved land is to be sold as is, its sales price would be $80,000. If the land is improved, however, there is a 40% chance that it can be rezoned for commercial development and sold for $120,000 more than the cost incurred in making improvements. There is a 60% chance that the improved land would be rezoned for residential use, in which case the land could be sold to a real estate developer for $70,000 more than the cost of improvements.

The decision tree for the preceding example can be diagrammed as follows:

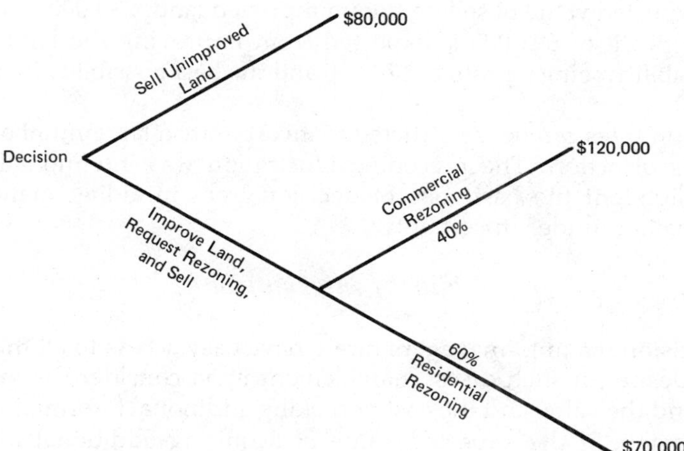

Decision Tree—Profit From Sale of Unimproved or Improved Land

The expected values can be computed directly from the decision tree by tracing back through each branch of the decision tree and multiplying each of the possible outcomes by the chance of its occurrence. For example, the expected value of the land being rezoned for commercial use and sold for $120,000 is $48,000 ($120,000 × .4). The expected value of the residential rezoning is computed in a similar manner and is $42,000 ($70,000 × .6). Since there is no uncertainty concerning the selling of the unimproved land for $80,000, the expected value of selling the unimproved land is $80,000. These expected values are summarized in the following decision tree:

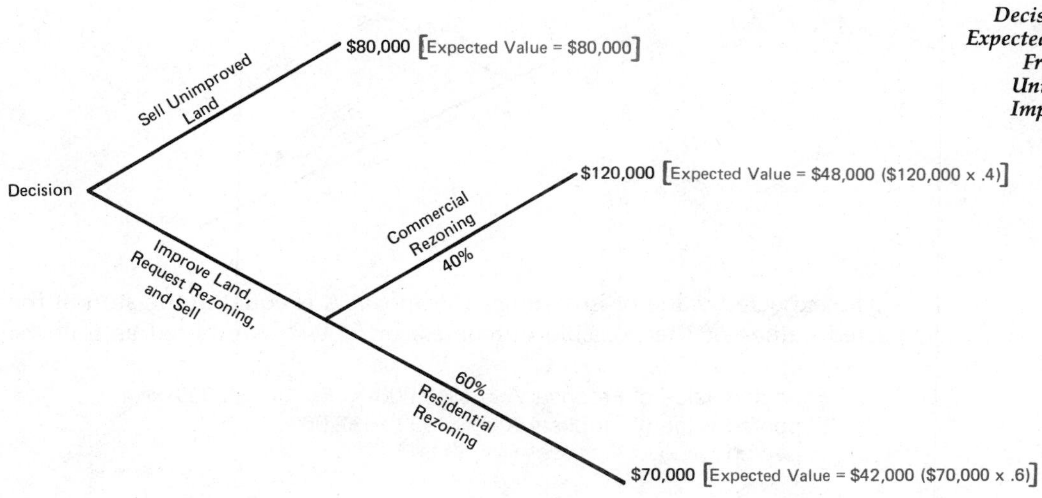

Decision Tree with Expected Values—Profit From Sale of Unimproved or Improved Land

The total expected value of improving the land is equal to the sum of the expected values of the possible outcomes from the land improvement, or $90,000, computed as follows:

Commercial rezoning	$48,000
Residential rezoning	42,000
Total expected value of improving the land	$90,000

The preceding analysis indicates that the land should be improved and sold, since the expected value of this course of action, $90,000, is higher than the expected value of selling the unimproved land, $80,000. Thus, on the average, a profit of $90,000 is expected from improving the land, with the worst possibility being a profit of $70,000 and the best possibility being a profit of $120,000.

Decision trees can be constructed to incorporate a large number of possible courses of action. The preceding illustration was intentionally brief in order to highlight the basic use of decision trees in aiding management's decision making under uncertainty.

Value of Information

In decision making, managers rarely have easy access to all the information they desire. In such cases, management must consider the information available and the value and the cost of seeking additional information relevant to the decision. If the expected value of acquiring additional information exceeds its expected cost, then the additional information should be acquired.

To illustrate, assume that an investment in Proposal A is expected to have a 60% chance of earning net income of $10,000 and a 40% chance of suffering a net loss of $5,000. This situation is diagrammed in the following decision tree:

Decision Tree—Proposal A

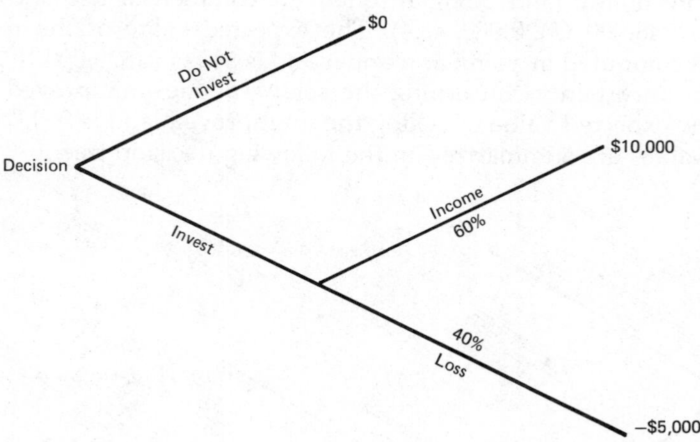

The expected value of investing in Proposal A is equal to the sum of the expected values of the possible outcomes, or $4,000, computed as follows:

Expected value of Proposal A = ($10,000 × .6) + (–$5,000 × .4)
Expected value of Proposal A = $6,000 – $2,000
Expected value of Proposal A = $4,000

Since the expected value of Proposal A is positive, the manager would normally invest in the proposal, even though there is a 40% chance of a loss of $5,000. Assume, however, that the manager could acquire additional information that would indicate with certainty whether Proposal A would earn the $10,000 income or suffer the loss of $5,000. How much would the manager be willing to pay for this additional (perfect) information?

The maximum amount (cost) that would be paid to obtain perfect information concerning a decision is termed the **value of perfect information.** It is the difference between (1) the expected value of a decision based on the perfect information and (2) the expected value of a decision based on existing information. To illustrate, the maximum amount that would be paid to obtain perfect information concerning Proposal A is determined by first computing the expected value of the proposal as if it is known beforehand whether the proposal would be successful or not. If the manager knows that the proposal will be successful, then a decision to invest would be made and income of $10,000 would be earned. If the manager knows that the proposal will be unsuccessful, then a decision not to invest would be made and no income or loss would result. For Proposal A, 60% of the time the perfect information will indicate that the proposal would be successful and therefore income of $10,000 would be earned. Also, 40% of the time the information will indicate that the proposal would be unsuccessful and therefore management would not invest. The expected value of perfect information is equal to the sum of the expected values of the possible outcomes, or $6,000, computed as follows:

Expected value of Proposal A,
based on perfect information = ($10,000 × .6) + ($0 × .4)
Expected value of Proposal A,
based on perfect information = $6,000

The value of perfect information concerning Proposal A is then determined by subtracting $4,000, the expected value of Proposal A, based on existing information, from the $6,000 computed above. Thus, as shown in the following computation, the manager would be willing to pay $2,000 to obtain perfect information concerning Proposal A.

Expected value of Proposal A, based on perfect information	$6,000
Less expected value of Proposal A, based on existing information .	4,000
Value of perfect information concerning Proposal A	$2,000

VARIANCE ANALYSIS USING EXPECTED VALUE

When variances from standard costs occur, management must decide whether to investigate the causes and attempt corrective actions. To assist management in making this decision, the managerial accountant can use the expected value concept to focus on the expected costs relevant to the decision.

In prior illustrations, the use of the expected value concept focused on choosing among alternatives, so that the alternative with the highest expected value in terms of profit was chosen. Since management's primary focus in variance analysis is to minimize costs, however, the decision whether to investigate a variance is one of choosing that alternative with the lowest expected cost. In other words, in deciding whether to investigate a variance, management should compare the expected costs if an investigation is made with the expected costs if no investigation is made. It will then choose the alternative (investigate or not investigate) that provides the lowest expected costs.

To illustrate, assume that an unfavorable direct materials quantity variance of $1,000 has been reported for July and is expected to continue for one month if not corrected. Past experience indicates that 60% of the time the variance is caused by poor quality materials and can be eliminated (is controllable) by switching suppliers. On the other hand, 40% of the time the variance is caused by machine wear and tear and cannot be eliminated (is uncontrollable) without a major overhaul of the machinery. Due to sales commitments, production cannot be delayed for a machinery overhaul until the end of August, when regular maintenance is scheduled.

If the variance is not investigated, it will continue for August and the expected cost is the amount of the variance, $1,000. If the variance is investigated, using personnel who are available to conduct the investigation at no additional cost, the investigation may indicate that the variance is caused by poor quality materials and therefore is controllable. Management will then change suppliers and there will be no variance in August. If the investigation indicates that the variance is caused by machine wear and tear (and therefore is uncontrollable), the variance will continue for August at a cost of $1,000. However, the variance will be caused by machine wear and tear only 40% of the time, and thus the expected cost is $400 ($1,000 × 40%). These possible outcomes are diagrammed in the following decision tree:

Decision Tree — Variance Investigation with Expected Costs

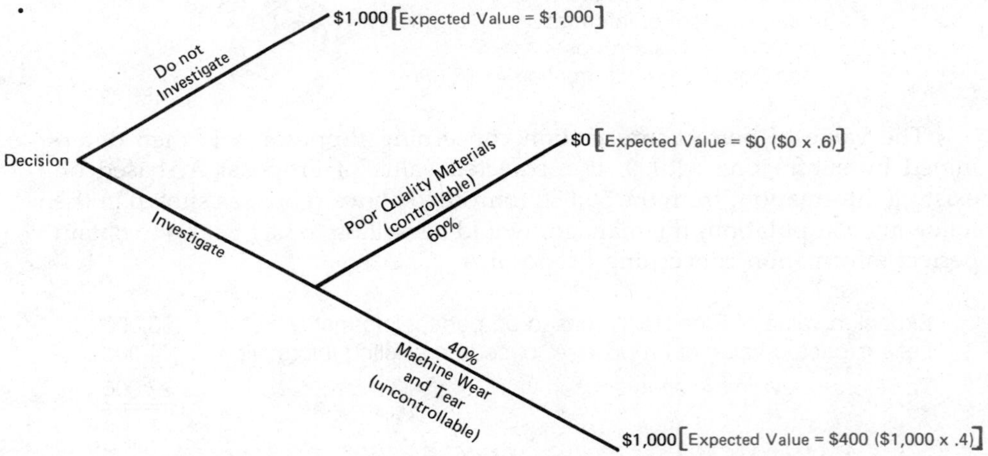

The total expected cost if the variance is investigated is the sum of the expected costs of the two possible outcomes, as shown in the following computation:

Expected cost if variance is caused by poor quality materials (controllable)...	$ 0
Plus expected cost if variance is caused by machine wear and tear (uncontrollable)	400
Total expected cost if variance is investigated	$400

As indicated previously, management should select the alternative with the lowest expected cost. Since the total expected cost if the variance is investigated ($400) is less than the expected cost if no investigation is undertaken ($1,000), management should investigate the variance.

In this illustration, the cost of conducting the investigation was assumed to be zero. In practice, however, the cost may not be zero, and the important question therefore becomes: how much should management be willing to spend to investigate the variance? The answer for the direct materials variance illustration is $600, which is the difference between the total expected costs if (1) no investigation is undertaken and (2) an investigation is undertaken, as shown in the following computation:

Expected cost—no investigation	$1,000
Less expected cost—investigation	400
Value of conducting an investigation	$ 600

In the above illustration, $600 is the maximum amount that management would spend to conduct an investigation of the direct materials variance. In other words, the value of conducting an investigation and obtaining perfect information concerning the cause of the variance is $600. Thus, if it is estimated that the cost to conduct an investigation would be $700, no investigation should be undertaken. If, on the other hand, the estimated cost to conduct an investigation is $500, the investigation should be undertaken. In the latter case, the expected cost savings would be $100, as shown in the following computation:

Value of conducting an investigation	$600
Less cost of conducting the investigation	500
Expected cost savings from investigation	$100

MAXIMIN AND MAXIMAX CONCEPTS OF DECISION MAKING UNDER UNCERTAINTY

Alternative concepts to expected value are useful to management when it is extremely difficult to estimate the chances of occurrence of the various outcomes or when the potential loss or gain for a proposal is so great that management would ignore the expected value in making the decision. For example, management might be considering the possibility of introducing a revolutionary new product, which has a chance of earning extraordinarily large profits but which requires a total commitment of company resources. If the product is successful, the company will earn record profits; but if the product fails, the company may go bankrupt. In such a situation, the expected value concept may not be useful because management may not be willing to risk bankruptcy. The remainder of this chapter describes and illustrates two alternative concepts to expected value: (1) the maximin concept and (2) the maximax concept. These concepts depend on different philosophies of risk and thus lead to different decisions.

Maximin Concept

The use of the **maximin concept** leads management to decide in favor of the alternative with the maximum (largest) minimum profit. The maximin concept is applied as follows:

1. The minimum (smallest) profit for each decision alternative is listed.
2. The decision alternative with the maximum (largest) profit from the list in (1) is chosen.

To illustrate, assume that the management of Hayes Company is considering building a condominium development in one of three locations. Because of limited funds, only one of the locations can be selected. The success of each location depends on demand. The estimated profit and loss from two levels of demand (low and high) for the condominium units for each location are as follows:

	Low Demand	*High Demand*
Location 1	$(500,000)	$4,000,000
Location 2	100,000	1,200,000
Location 3	150,000	800,000

In applying the maximin concept, the maximum minimum profit (or loss) from each alternative is selected. In this illustration, the minimum profit (loss) for each location appears in the low demand column. For Hayes Company, the maximin concept indicates that Location 3 should be chosen, since under conditions of low demand, Location 3 will earn more than either Locations 1 or 2. In this way, management is assured that in the worst possible case (that of low demand), a maximum profit of $150,000 will be earned. By using the maximin concept, management has avoided the possibility of losing $500,000 from the selection of Location 1 and earning only $100,000 profit from the selection of Location 2. At the same time, however, management has also forgone the possibility of earning a maximum profit of $4,000,000 from the selection of Location 1 under the most favorable (high demand) condition.

The maximin concept is used by managers when the primary concern is minimizing the risk of any loss. In such situations, managers are said to be risk averse.

Maximax Concept

The use of the **maximax concept** leads management to decide in favor of the alternative with the maximum (largest) profit. The maximax concept is applied as follows:

1. The maximum (largest) profit for each decision alternative is listed.
2. The decision alternative with the maximum (largest) profit from the list in (1) is chosen.

To illustrate, assume the same facts as in the preceding illustration for Hayes Company. In applying the maximax concept, only the maximum (largest) profit for each location is considered. In this illustration, the maximum profit for each location appears in the high demand column of the table above. For Hayes Company, the maximax concept indicates that Location 1 should be selected, since under conditions of high demand, Location 1 will earn more than either Locations 2 or 3. In this way, management is assured that in the best possible case (that of high demand), the maximum profit of $4,000,000 will be earned. At the same time, however, management has also taken the risk of losing $500,000 from the selection of Location 1 under the worst (low demand) condition.

The maximax concept is used by managers when the primary concern is earning the largest possible profit, regardless of the risks. In such situations, managers are said to be risk takers.

Chapter Review

KEY POINTS

1. Inventory Control.
For a business enterprise that needs large quantities of inventory, one of the most important assets is inventory. The lack of sufficient inventory can result in lost sales, idle production facilities, production bottlenecks, and additional purchasing costs due to placing special orders or rush orders. On the other hand, excess inventory can result in large storage costs and large spoilage losses, which reduce the profitability of the enterprise.

The optimum quantity of inventory to be ordered at one time is the economic order quantity (EOQ). Important factors to be considered in determining the EOQ are the costs involved in processing an order for materials and the costs involved in storing materials. The EOQ can be determined in either tabular form or through the following formula:

$$\text{EOQ} = \sqrt{\frac{2 \times \text{Annual Units Required} \times \text{Cost per Order Placed}}{\text{Storage Cost per Unit}}}$$

The inventory order point is the level to which inventory is allowed to fall before an order for additional inventory is placed. The inventory order point depends on the (1) daily usage of inventory that is expected to be consumed in production or sold, (2) number of production days (lead time) that it takes to receive an order for inventory, and (3) the amount of inventory (safety stock) that is available for use when unforeseen circumstances arise. The inventory order point is computed using the following formula:

$$\text{Inventory Order Point} = (\text{Daily Usage} \times \text{Days of Lead Time}) + \text{Safety Stock}$$

Linear programming is a quantitative method that can provide data for solving a variety of problems in which management's objective is to minimize costs or maximize profits, subject to several limiting factors. Linear programming can be used to determine the most economical merchandise purchasing plan.

2. Decision Making Under Uncertainty.
Quantitative techniques are especially useful to management in making decisions under uncertainty. The managerial accountant can aid management in making such decisions by providing data useful in assessing the chances that future events will occur and the impact of those events.

3. Managerial Use of the Expected Value Concept.
The concept of expected value involves identifying the possible outcomes from a decision and estimating the likelihood that each outcome will occur. The likelihood that an outcome will occur is usually expressed in terms of a probability or chance of occurrence. The expected value of the decision is the sum of the values that result when the dollar value of each outcome is

multiplied by the probability of its occurrence. That is, each possible outcome is weighted by its chance of occurrence to obtain an average expected outcome.

The use of the expected value concept by management may be facilitated through the use of payoff tables and decision trees. A payoff table presents a summary of possible outcomes of one or more decisions. A payoff table is especially useful when a wide variety of possible outcomes exist. Decision trees are graphical representations of decisions, possible outcomes, and chances that outcomes will occur. Decision trees are especially useful when possible outcomes are dependent on several decisions.

In decision making, managers must consider the information available and the value and the cost of seeking additional information relevant to the decision. If the expected value of acquiring additional information exceeds its expected cost, then the additional information should be acquired. The maximum amount that would be paid to obtain perfect information concerning a decision is termed the value of perfect information. It is the difference between (1) the expected value of a decision based on perfect information and (2) the expected value of a decision based on existing information.

The expected value concept may be useful to managers in deciding whether to investigate the causes of variances from standard costs and to attempt corrective actions. Management should compare the expected cost if an investigation is made with the expected cost if no investigation is made, and then choose the alternative that provides the lowest expected cost.

4. Maximin and Maximax Concepts of Decision Making Under Uncertainty. Alternative concepts to expected value are useful when it is extremely difficult to estimate the chances of occurrence of the various outcomes or when the potential loss or gain for a proposal is so great that management would ignore the expected value in making the decision.

The maximin concept leads management to decide in favor of the alternative with the maximum (largest) minimum profit. The maximin concept is used when the primary concern is minimizing the risk of any loss. In such situations, managers are risk averse.

The use of the maximax concept leads management to decide in favor of the alternative with the maximum (largest) profit. The maximax concept is used when the primary concern is earning the largest possible profit, regardless of the risks. In such situations, managers are risk takers.

KEY TERMS

economic order quantity (EOQ) 972
inventory order point 973
lead time 973
safety stock 973
linear programming 975
simplex method 976
expected value 980
payoff table 982
decision trees 984
value of perfect information 987
maximin concept 989
maximax concept 990

SELF-EXAMINATION QUESTIONS

(Answers at End of Chapter)

1. In determing the economic order quantity, which, if any, of the following factors are important to consider?
   A. Storage cost per unit
   B. Annual units required
   C. Cost per order placed
   D. All of the above

2. Proposal R has a 60% chance of earning a profit of $80,000 and a 40% chance of incurring a loss of $60,000. What is the expected value of Proposal R?
   A. $24,000
   B. $48,000
   C. $72,000
   D. None of the above

3. Management's use of expected value can be facilitated through the use of payoff tables and:
   A. the maximax concept
   B. decision trees
   C. the maximin concept
   D. none of the above

4. The expected value of Proposal A, based on existing information, is $5,000, and the expected value of Proposal A, based on perfect information, is $8,000. What is the value of the perfect information concerning Proposal A?
   A. $3,000
   B. $5,000
   C. $8,000
   D. None of the above

5. The management of Freeman Co. is considering an investment in one of four real estate projects. The success of each project depends on whether demand is high or low. Based on the following data, which project would management select, using the maximin concept?

	Low Demand	High Demand
Project W	$120,000	$600,000
Project X	(40,000)	800,000
Project Y	110,000	500,000
Project Z	(60,000)	900,000

   A. Project W
   B. Project X
   C. Project Y
   D. Project Z

ILLUSTRATIVE PROBLEM

Shiver News Distributors recently purchased a newsstand on the corner of 5th Avenue South and 2nd Street in downtown Clinton. The new manager of the newsstand must decide how many copies of the local newspaper to stock on a daily basis. The former manager had noted that the maximum daily sales, in the past, had been 175 papers, and to be assured that all demand could be met, 200 papers were purchased daily. The cost of the newspaper is $.20 per paper, and the paper is sold for $.30. Any papers remaining at the end of the day are worthless and are thrown away. The paper is published five days a week.

The records for the past month indicate the following sales:

Number of Days	Actual Demand (Sales)
2	100 papers
8	125
6	150
4	175

Instructions:

1. Prepare a payoff table of possible outcomes in terms of contribution margin, using the format shown in this chapter.
2. Based on the sales data for the past 20 days, estimate the chances of each level of possible demand for the newspaper.

3. Prepare a payoff table of expected values of possible outcomes in terms of contribution margin, using the format shown in this chapter.
4. Based on (3), how many newspapers should be purchased? Explain.

SOLUTION

(1)

Possible Demand	Contribution Margin of Purchases: 100 papers	125 papers	150 papers	175 papers
100 papers	$10.00	$ 5.00	$ 0.00	$ (5.00)
125	10.00	12.50	7.50	2.50
150	10.00	12.50	15.00	10.00
175	10.00	12.50	15.00	17.50

(2)

Possible Demand	Number of Days	Chance of Occurrence
100 papers	2	10% (2/20)
125	8	40% (8/20)
150	6	30% (6/20)
175	4	20% (4/20)

(3)

Possible Demand	Expected Value of Contribution Margin of Purchases: 100 papers	125 papers	150 papers	175 papers
100 papers	$ 1.00	$ .50	$ 0.00	$ (.50)
125	4.00	5.00	3.00	1.00
150	3.00	3.75	4.50	3.00
175	2.00	2.50	3.00	3.50
Totals	$10.00	$11.75	$10.50	$7.00

(4) 125 newspapers should be purchased, because the daily total expected value of this purchase is the highest. On the average, 125 papers is the best purchase.

Discussion Questions

27–1. What is the primary advantage of quantitative techniques?

27–2. What are the primary disadvantages of quantitative techniques?

27–3. For a business enterprise that needs large quantities of inventories to meet sales orders or production requirements, what can result from insufficient inventory?

27–4. What term is used to describe the optimum quantity of inventory to be ordered at one time?

27–5. Assuming that Product S is used at the same rate throughout the year, 10,000 units are required during the year, the cost per order placed is $5, and the storage cost per unit is $2.50, what is the economic order quantity for Product S?

27–6. The inventory order point depends on what factors?

27–7. Assuming that Parish Co. estimates daily usage of 1,200 pounds of Material X, the lead time to receive an order of Material X is 10 days, and a safety stock of 3,600 pounds is desired, what is the inventory order point?

27–8. If everything else remains the same, as the cost of carrying inventory decreases, would the level of safety stock normally carried by a company increase or decrease?

27–9. What quantitative technique is often useful in determining the most economical plan for purchasing materials for several locations?

27–10. How can the managerial accountant aid management in making decisions under uncertainty?

27–11. What concept involves identifying possible outcomes from a decision and estimating the likelihood that each outcome will occur?

27–12. How is the expected value of a decision calculated?

27–13. Assume that you are playing a game in which a coin is flipped. If a head appears, you win $1,000, and if a tail appears, you lose $700. What is the expected value of playing this game?

27–14. Rawlings Co. is considering an investment in a real estate project with the following outcomes and chances of occurrence. What is the expected value of the project?

Profit	Chance of Occurrence
$2,000,000	40%
1,000,000	60%

27–15. What term is used to describe a table frequently used by managers to summarize the possible outcomes of one or more decisions?

27–16. The following data have been taken from the sales records of Sims Co.:

Number of Weeks	Actual Demand (Sales)
5	5,000 units
2	8,000
6	7,000
4	4,000
3	6,000

Estimate the chance that each sales level will reoccur.

27–17. Based on the following payoff table of expected values, what should be the amount of monthly purchases?

Possible Demand	Expected Value of Contribution Margin of Purchases	
	20,000 units	30,000 units
20,000 units.........	$ 40,000	$ 30,000
30,000 units.........	60,000	90,000
Totals	$100,000	$120,000

27–18. What term is used to describe graphical representations of decisions, possible outcomes, and chances that outcomes will occur?

27–19. When are decision trees especially useful to managers in choosing among alternatives?

27–20. When should management acquire additional information before making a decision?

27–21. What term is used to describe the maximum amount that would be paid to obtain perfect information?

27–22. How is the value of perfect information computed?

27–23. Wolfe Co. is evaluating Proposal B as an investment. The expected value of Proposal B based on existing information is $30,000, and the expected value of Proposal B based on perfect information is $42,000. Wolfe Co. can obtain perfect information concerning Proposal B at a cost of $10,000. Should Wolfe Co. pay the $10,000 for the perfect information? Explain.

27–24. Using the expected value concept, how should management decide when to incur the costs necessary to investigate a variance?

27–25. What two alternative concepts to expected value can be used by management in making decisions under uncertainty?

27–26. When might the alternative concepts of maximax and maximin be more useful to management in decision making than the concept of expected value?

27–27. The president of Lundy Co. recently made the following statement concerning a proposed investment: "I don't care if the expected value is $3,000,000. I am not going to take the risk of losing $2,000,000 on Proposal X. I'm selecting Proposal W, with its expected value of $1,200,000, because its maximum possible loss is estimated to be $100,000." What decision-making concept was the president of Lundy Co. using?

27–28. Describe how the maximax concept of decision making is applied.

27–29. Would the use of the maximin and maximax concepts normally lead management to make the same decisions? Explain.

27–30. Real World Focus. On August 1, 1986, Grandview Resources Inc. reported in a news release the planned opening of a gold mine east of Stockton, California. The company expected to produce 60,000 to 80,000 ounces of gold annually from this mine. The chance of producing 60,000 ounces is equally as likely as producing 80,000 ounces annually. (a) What is the expected annual production of gold from the mine? (b) Assuming that gold will average $350 per ounce, what is the expected annual revenue from the gold mine?

Exercises

27–31. Economic order quantity and inventory order point. Jewell Company estimates that 4,080 units of Material W will be required during the coming year. The materials will be used at the rate of 15 units per day throughout the 272-day period of budgeted production for the year. Past experience indicates that the annual storage cost is $.15 per unit, the cost to place an order is $34, the lead time to receive an order is 30 days, and the desired amount of safety stock is 225 units. Determine (a) the economic order quantity, (b) the inventory order point, and (c) the number of units to be purchased when the inventory order point is reached.

27–32. Linear programming graph. Ralls Company purchases Part F for use at both its Austell and Tucker branches. Part F is available in limited quantities from two suppliers. The relevant data for determining an economical purchase plan are as follows:

Units required:	
Austell Branch	50 units
Tucker Branch	100 units

Supplier G:

Total units available	100 units
Unit cost delivered to:	
Austell Branch	$80 per unit
Tucker Branch	$120 per unit

Supplier H:

Total units available	100 units
Unit cost delivered to:	
Austell branch	$90 per unit
Tucker Branch	$150 per unit

The following linear programming graph for units purchased from Supplier G has been constructed, based on the above data:

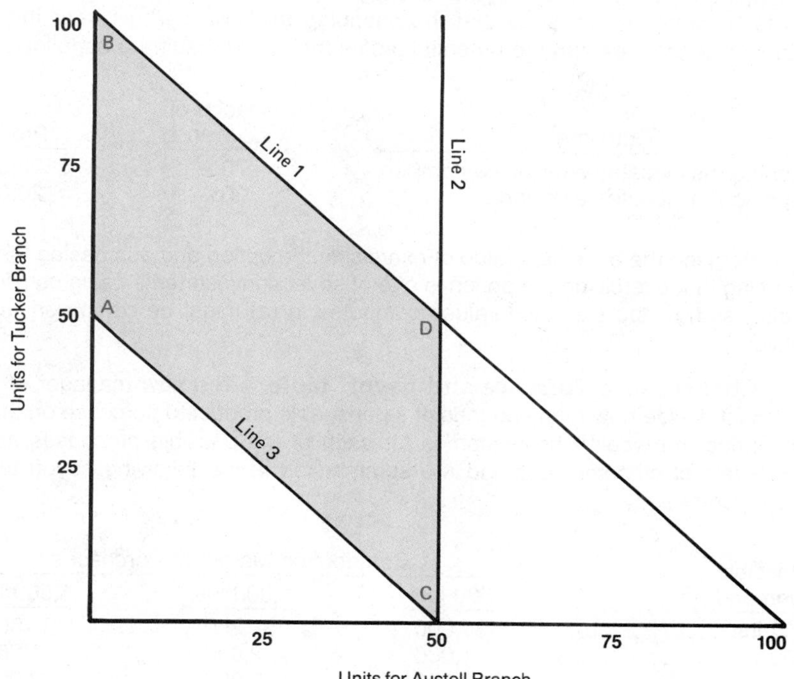

(a) For each of the four corners identified on the above graph by letters A through D, determine the purchases from Supplier G for the Austell and Tucker Branches. Use the same format as shown in this chapter.

(b) For each of the four corners in (a), indicate the units purchased from both Suppliers G and H for the Austell and Tucker Branches. Use the same format as shown in this chapter and identify Plan 1 with Corner A, Plan 2 with Corner B, Plan 3 with Corner C, and Plan 4 with Corner D.

(c) Determine the most economical purchase plan by computing the total cost of each purchase plan determined in (b).

27–33. Expected value of playing game. While on vacation in Atlantic City, you are offered the opportunity to play one game of chance in which a die is thrown. The die is numbered one through six, and each number has an equal chance of appearing on any throw of the die. The winnings and losses established for each number on a throw of the die are as follows:

Number	Winnings (Losses)
1	$1,500
2	900
3	600
4	450
5	(300)
6	(3,000)

(a) Determine the expected value of playing the game. (b) If the cost of playing the game is $20, would you play? Explain.

27–34. Expected value of exercising option to purchase land. Based on a rumor that a new shopping mall will locate near its office complex, Ritter Company is considering exercising an option to purchase thirty acres of land surrounding its offices. If the shopping mall is constructed, the land should increase substantially in value and be sold for a profit. The chance that the shopping mall will be built near the Ritter Company office complex and the potential profits that could result are as follows:

Outcome	Chance of Occurrence	Profit
Shopping mall locates near office complex	70%	$600,000
Shopping mall locates elsewhere	30%	20,000

(a) Determine the expected value of exercising the option and purchasing the land. (b) Assuming that exercising the option is one of several investments being considered, briefly discuss how the expected values computed in (a) might be compared with the alternatives.

27–35. Chances of occurrence and payoff table. The new manager of Gatlin Grocery must decide how many pounds of a perishable product to purchase on Monday for sale during the week. The outcomes for each of the possible purchases and the possible levels of customer demand are summarized in the following payoff table of possible outcomes:

Possible Demand	Contribution Margin of Purchases		
	500 lbs.	1,000 lbs.	1,500 lbs.
500 lbs.	$1,000	$ 250	$ (500)
1,000	1,000	2,000	1,250
1,500	1,000	2,000	3,000

The sales records for the past twenty weeks indicate the following levels of sales:

Number of Weeks	Actual Demand (Sales)
10	500 lbs.
6	1,000
4	1,500

(a) Based on the sales data for the past twenty weeks, determine the chances that the various levels of customer demand (500 lbs., 1,000 lbs., 1,500 lbs.) will occur. (b) Construct a payoff table of expected values of possible outcomes, using the format shown in this chapter. (c) What amount should Gatlin Grocery purchase?

27–36. Decision tree and analysis. Chapman Company is considering whether to offer a new product for sale in the Midwest or in the Northeast. Because of the uncertainty associated with introducing a new product, the decision will be made on the basis of expected annual income. The possible outcomes and chances of occurrence are summarized as follows:

Customer Demand	Midwestern Region Annual Income	Midwestern Region Chance of Occurrence	Northeastern Region Annual Income	Northeastern Region Chance of Occurrence
High	$20,000,000	40%	$35,000,000	35%
Moderate	10,000,000	35	15,000,000	20
Low............	4,000,000	25	2,000,000	45

(a) To aid management in deciding in which region to offer the new product, prepare a decision tree with expected values. (b) Which region should be selected for the introduction of the new product, based on the expected value concept?

27–37. Value of perfect information. The management of Ramsay Company has the opportunity to invest in Proposal A, which is expected to have a 60% chance of earning income of $100,000 and a 40% chance of suffering a loss of $140,000. (a) What is the expected value of Proposal A, based on existing information? (b) What is the expected value of Proposal A, based on perfect information? (c) What is the value of perfect information concerning Proposal A? (d) If the management of Ramsay Company could purchase perfect information concerning Proposal A for $40,000, should the perfect information be purchased?

27–38. Expected cost of investigating a variance; analysis. The controller of Lien Company must decide whether to investigate an unfavorable direct labor quantity variance of $5,000 for July. The variance is expected to continue for August if no investigation is undertaken. Based on past experience, there is a 75% chance that the variance is controllable and can be eliminated for August if an investigation is conducted. There is a 25% chance that the variance is uncontrollable and cannot be eliminated for August. (a) Determine the expected cost if the variance is investigated, assuming that no additional cost will be incurred in conducting the investigation. (b) How much should management be willing to spend to investigate the variance?

27–39. Decision trees. Prepare a decision tree of expected values (costs) for (a) Exercise 27–37 and (b) Exercise 27–38.

27–40. Maximin and maximax concepts analysis. Siefer Company is considering an investment in one of three projects. The success of each project depends on whether customer demand is low or high. The possible profit or loss for each project is summarized as follows:

	Low Demand	High Demand
Project X...............................	$300,000	$500,000
Project Y...............................	(100,000)	400,000
Project Z...............................	(200,000)	750,000

(a) Using the maximin concept, which project should management choose? (b) Using the maximax concept, which project should management choose? (c) Explain why the answers to (a) and (b) are not the same.

Problems

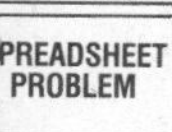

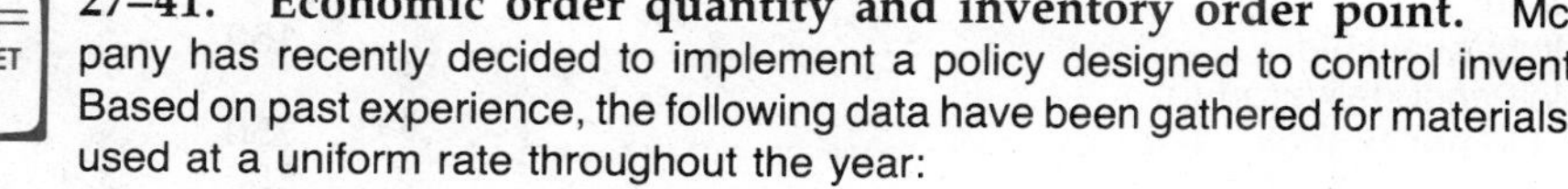

27–41. Economic order quantity and inventory order point. McCay Company has recently decided to implement a policy designed to control inventory better. Based on past experience, the following data have been gathered for materials, which are used at a uniform rate throughout the year:

Units required during the year 2,760
Units of safety stock.......... 180
Days of scheduled production 230
Days of lead time to receive an order 25
Ordering cost, per order placed.......... $34.50
Annual storage cost, per unit .... $ .40

Instructions: (1) Complete the following table for "number of orders" of 1 through 6.

Number of Orders	Number of Units per Order	Average Units in Inventory	Order and Storage Costs		
			Order Cost	Storage Cost	Combined Cost
1	2,760	1,380	$34.50	$552.00	$586.50

(2) Determine the economic order quantity, based on the table completed in (1).
(3) Determine the economic order quantity, using the economic order quantity formula.
(4) Determine the inventory order point.

27–42. Economic order quantity under present and proposed conditions. Based on the data presented in Problem 27–41, assume that McCay Company is considering the purchase of new automated storage equipment to facilitate access to materials and to increase storage capacity. In addition, the manager of the purchasing department has requested authorization to purchase five microcomputers to expedite the processing of purchase orders.

Instructions: (1) Assuming that the new storage equipment will increase the storage cost from $.40 to $1.60 per unit, determine the economic order quantity for McCay Company, using the economic order quantity formula.
(2) Assuming that the new storage equipment is not purchased and the acquisition of the microcomputer equipment will decrease the cost per order placed fron $34.50 to $5.52, determine the economic order quantity, using the economic order quantity formula.
(3) Assuming that both the new storage equipment and the microcomputer equipment are purchased, determine the economic order quantity, using the economic order quantity formula. As indicated in (1) and (2), the purchase of the storage equipment is expected to increase the storage cost per unit from $.40 to $1.60, and the microcomputer equipment is expected to decrease the cost per order placed from $34.50 to $5.52.
(4) Based on the answers to Problem 27–41 and (1), (2), and (3) above, what generalizations can be made concerning how changes in the cost per order placed and the storage cost per unit affect the economic order quantity?

27–43. The most economical purchasing plan, using linear programming graph. Collins Company purchases Part Q for use at both its Comer and Lilburn branches. Part Q is available in limited quantities from two suppliers. The relevant data are as follows:

Units required:
Comer Branch.......... 100
Lilburn Branch.......... 150

Supplier E:
Units available.......... 150
Unit cost delivered to:
Comer Branch.......... $40
Lilburn Branch.......... $70

Supplier F:
Units available.......... 150
Unit cost delivered to:
Comer Branch.......... $50
Lilburn Branch.......... $90

The manager of the purchasing department has prepared the following purchase plan for the Comer and Lilburn branches:

(1) Purchase all units for Comer Branch from Supplier E.
(2) Purchase remaining available units of Supplier E for the Lilburn Branch.
(3) Purchase any additional units required by the Lilburn Branch from Supplier F.

Instructions: (1) Construct a linear programming graph for units to be purchased from Supplier E. Plot the units for the Comer Branch along the horizontal axis.
(2) Identify the four corners at which an economical purchase plan might be identified on the linear programming graph. Label the corners A through D, as shown in the illustration in this chapter.
(3) For each corner in (2), indicate purchases from Suppliers E and F for the Comer and Lilburn branches. Identify Plan 1 with Corner A, Plan 2 with Corner B, Plan 3 with Corner C, and Plan 4 with Corner D.
(4) Determine the most economical purchase plan by computing the total cost of purchases for each plan identified in (3).
(5) Was the purchasing department manager's plan the most economical? Explain.

27–44. Expected value and analysis. Interamerica Films Inc. is considering purchasing the rights to one of two autobiographies for the purposes of producing and marketing a motion picture. Each autobiography has the potential for development and sale as one of the following: (1) a cable TV movie, (2) a network (noncable) TV movie, (3) a weekly TV series, or (4) a commercial theater movie. The estimated profit for development and sale of each autobiography and the estimated chances of occurrence are as follows:

Autobiography S

	Estimated Profit	Chance of Occurrence
Cable TV movie	$15,000,000	25%
Network TV movie	8,000,000	15
Weekly TV series	20,000,000	30
Theater movie	10,000,000	30

Autobiography T

	Estimated Profit	Chance of Occurrence
Cable TV movie	$16,000,000	30%
Network TV movie	18,000,000	35
Weekly TV series	5,000,000	25
Theater movie	40,000,000	10

Instructions: (1) Determine the expected value of each autobiography.
(2) Based on the results of (1), which autobiography rights should be purchased?

27–45. Payoff table, chances of occurrence, and analysis. Shugart News Distributors recently purchased a newsstand on the corner of Chase Street and Prince Avenue in downtown Hampton. The new manager of the newsstand must decide how many copies of a magazine to stock on a weekly basis. The magazine is published locally and features local civic and social events and has a large classified advertising section. The former manager had noted that the maximum weekly sales, in the past, had been 400 magazines, and to be assured that all demand could be met, 450 magazines were purchased. The cost of the magazine is $60 for quantities of 50 ($1.20 per magazine), and the magazine is sold for $2. Any magazines remaining at the end of the week are worthless and are thrown away.

The records for the past ten weeks indicate the following sales:

Number of Weeks	Actual Demand (Sales)
3	200
2	250
4	300
1	400

Instructions: (1) Prepare a payoff table of possible outcomes in terms of contribution margin, using the format shown in this chapter.

(2) Based on the sales data for the past ten weeks, estimate the chances of each level of possible demand for the magazine.

(3) Prepare a payoff table of expected values of possible outcomes in terms of contribution margin, using the format shown in this chapter.

(4) Based on (3), how many magazines should be purchased? Explain.

27–46. Decision tree and analysis. Gem Mines Inc. is preparing to bid on the purchase of mining rights to one of two plats of federally owned land: Plat #600 and Plat #900. Both plats of land are known to contain deposits of coal; however, the quality of deposits will not be known until actual mining begins.

Preliminary estimates indicate that, for Plat #600, there is a 45% chance that the deposit is of high quality and will yield total profits of $20,000,000. There is a 30% chance that the deposit is of moderate quality and will yield total profits of $10,000,000. Finally, there is a 25% chance that the deposit is of low quality and will yield total profits of $2,000,000.

Preliminary estimates indicate that, for Plat #900, there is a 25% chance that the deposit is of high quality and will yield total profits of $40,000,000. There is a 20% chance that the deposit is of moderate quality and will yield total profits of $15,000,000. Finally, there is a 55% chance that the deposit is of low quality and will yield total profits of $1,000,000.

Instructions: (1) Prepare a decision tree with expected values to aid management in deciding on which plat rights to bid.

(2) On which plat rights should the management of Gem Mines Inc. bid?

27–47. Expected cost of conducting an investigation of a variance and analysis. The controller of Crowley Company must decide whether to investigate an unfavorable direct labor rate variance of $8,000 reported for May. The variance is expected to continue for June if not corrected. Past experience indicates that 75% of the time the variance is caused by use of more experienced, higher paid employees in jobs budgeted for less experienced, lower paid employees. In this case, the variance can be eliminated by the rescheduling of job assignments. On the other hand, 25% of the time the variance is caused by overtime created by production commitments in excess of normal operations. If production demands continue, additional employees will be hired. However, because of training commitments, any new employees would not be available for assignment to normal operations until the end of June.

Instructions: (1) Assuming that no additional costs would be incurred in conducting an investigation, what is the expected cost of investigation of the direct labor rate variance?

(2) What is the value of conducting an investigation of the direct labor rate variance?

(3) If the estimated cost to investigate the variance is $5,000, should the controller authorize an investigation? Explain.

(4) If the estimated cost to investigate the variance is $7,000, should the controller authorize an investigation? Explain.

27–48. Maximin and maximax concepts and analysis. The management of Dawson Realty Corporation is considering an investment in one of three real estate projects. The first project involves the construction of a medical office complex which will be sold to a group of practicing physicians.

The second project involves the construction of a professional office building in which space will be sold to nonmedical professional businesses, such as law firms and insurance agencies. The third project is the construction of a small shopping mall in which space will be sold to small businesses. The success of each project depends on whether demand for the constructed space is high, moderate, or low. The estimated profit or loss for each project is as follows:

	Demand for Space		
Project	High	Moderate	Low
Medical office complex	$2,000,000	$1,500,000	$1,200,000
Professional office complex ...	3,300,000	2,500,000	1,100,000
Shopping mall...............	4,000,000	2,000,000	(400,000)

Instructions: (1) If the management of Dawson Realty Corporation uses the maximin concept, which of the three projects would be chosen?

(2) If the management of Dawson Realty Corporation uses the maximax concept, which of the three projects would be chosen?

(3) Assuming that the Moderate column is the most likely estimate of profit for each of the projects, what alternative decision concept can be used by Dawson Realty Corporation?

27–49. Expected value; maximin concept; maximax concept; and analysis. Kincaid Company is considering building a condominium development in one of three locations: a city location, a country club location, and a lakefront location. The success of each location depends on buyer demand. Based on marketing studies, the following profits and losses have been estimated for each location, along with the chances of occurrence:

	High Buyer Demand		Low Buyer Demand	
	Profit (Loss)	Chance of Occurrence	Profit (Loss)	Chance of Occurrence
City	$30,000,000	60%	$(12,000,000)	40%
Country club ..	60,000,000	70	(40,000,000)	30
Lakefront	50,000,000	75	(20,000,000)	25

Instructions: (1) Determine the expected value of each location.

(2) Which location should be chosen, using the expected value concept?

(3) Which location should be chosen, using the maximin concept?

(4) Which location should be chosen, using the maximax concept?

(5) Which location should be chosen if management's primary objective is to choose that location with the smallest range of possible outcomes?

(6) Which location would be chosen if management uses the concept of selecting that location with the highest chance of profit?

ALTERNATE PROBLEMS

27–41A. Economic order quantity and inventory order point. Colson Company has recently decided to implement a policy designed to control inventory better. Based on past experience, the following data have been gathered for materials, which are used at a uniform rate throughout the year:

Units required during the year	3,960
Units of safety stock..	270
Days of scheduled production	220
Days of lead time to receive an order	20
Ordering cost, per order placed......................................	$33.00
Annual storage cost, per unit	$ .15

Instructions: (1) Complete the following table for "number of orders" of 1 through 6.

Number of Orders	Number of Units per Order	Average Units in Inventory	Order and Storage Costs: Order Cost	Storage Cost	Combined Cost
1	3,960	1,980	$33.00	$297.00	$330.00

(2) Determine the economic order quantity, based on the table completed in (1).
(3) Determine the economic order quantity, using the economic order quantity formula.
(4) Determine the inventory order point.

27–43A. The most economical purchasing plan, using linear programming graph. Parks Company purchases Part R for use at both its Clinton and Moline branches. Part R is available in limited quantities from two suppliers. The relevant data are as follows:

Units required:	
Clinton Branch	120
Moline Branch	200
Supplier J:	
Units available	200
Unit cost delivered to:	
Clinton Branch	$ 50
Moline Branch	$100
Supplier K:	
Units available	200
Unit cost delivered to:	
Clinton Branch	$ 60
Moline Branch	$140

The new manager of the purchasing department of Parks Company has prepared the following purchase plan for the Clinton and Moline Branches:

	Purchases by Clinton Branch	Purchases by Moline Branch
From Supplier J	120 units	80 units
From Supplier K	0	120

Instructions: (1) Construct a linear programming graph for units to be purchased from Supplier J. Plot the units for the Clinton Branch along the horizontal axis.
(2) Identify the four corners at which an economical purchase plan might be identified on the linear programming graph. Label the corners A through D, as shown in the illustration in this chapter.
(3) For each corner in (2), indicate purchases from Suppliers J and K for the Clinton and Moline branches. Identify Plan 1 with Corner A, Plan 2 with Corner B, Plan 3 with Corner C, and Plan 4 with Corner D.
(4) Determine the most economical purchase plan by computing the total cost of purchases for each plan identified in (3).
(5) Was the purchasing department manager's plan the most economical? Explain.

27–44A. Expected value and analysis. Fielder Science Corporation is considering purchasing the rights to one of two laser patents for purposes of research and development. Patent 1002 has potential developmental applications in the areas of medicine, computer science, pharmacology, and military weaponry. Patent 1010 has potential developmental applications in the areas of mining, automobile manufacturing, telecommunications, and energy. Whichever patent rights are purchased, it is likely that only one of the potential applications will yield research and development results promising enough to market commercially. The estimated profit for each patent application and the estimated chances of occurrence are as follows:

Patent 1002

Application	Estimated Profit	Chance of Occurrence
Medicine	$15,000,000	20%
Computer science	4,000,000	30
Pharmacology	6,000,000	35
Military weaponry	12,000,000	15

Patent 1010

Application	Estimated Profit	Chance of Occurrence
Mining	$2,000,000	10%
Automobile manufacturing	8,000,000	30
Telecommunications	10,000,000	40
Energy	30,000,000	20

Instructions: (1) Determine the expected value of each patent.
(2) Based on the results of (1), which patent rights should be purchased?

27–45A. Payoff table, chances of occurrence, and analysis. Martel News Distributors recently purchased a newsstand on the corner of 2nd Avenue South and 5th Avenue in downtown Morrison. The new manager of the newsstand must decide how many copies of the local newspaper to stock on a daily basis. The former manager had noted that the maximum daily sales, in the past, had been 200 papers, and to be assured that all demand could be met, 220 papers were purchased daily. The cost of the newspaper is $.20 per paper, and the paper is sold for $.40. Any papers remaining at the end of the day are worthless and are thrown away. The paper is published five days a week.

The records for the past month indicate the following sales:

Number of Days	Actual Demand (Sales)
2	100
4	150
8	175
6	200

Instructions: (1) Prepare a payoff table of possible outcomes in terms of contribution margin, using the format shown in this chapter.
(2) Based on the sales data for the past 20 days, estimate the chances of each level of possible demand for the newspaper.
(3) Prepare a payoff table of expected values of possible outcomes in terms of contribution margin, using the format shown in this chapter.
(4) Based on (3), how many newspapers should be purchased? Explain.

27–46A. Decision tree and analysis. Jewel Mines Inc. is preparing to bid on the purchase of mining rights to one of two plats of federally owned land: Plat #100 and Plat #300. Both plats of land are known to contain deposits of uranium; however, the quality of the deposits will not be known until actual mining begins.

Preliminary estimates indicate that, for Plat #100, there is a 60% chance that the deposit is of high quality and will yield total profits of $50,000,000. There is a 25% chance that the deposit is of moderate quality and will yield total profits of $20,000,000. Finally, there is a 15% chance that the deposit is of low quality and will yield total profits of $5,000,000.

Preliminary estimates indicate that, for Plat #300, there is a 30% chance that the deposit is of high quality and will yield total profits of $80,000,000. There is a 30% chance that the deposit is of moderate quality and will yield total profits of $40,000,000. Finally, there is a 40% chance that the deposit is of low quality and will yield total profits of $1,000,000.

Instructions: (1) Prepare a decision tree with expected values to aid management in deciding on which plat rights to bid.

(2) On which plat rights should the management of Jewel Mines Inc. bid?

27–47A. Expected cost of conducting an investigation of a variance and analysis. The controller of Hodges Company must decide whether to investigate an unfavorable direct labor time variance of $4,000 reported for August. The variance is expected to continue for September if not corrected. Past experience indicates that 80% of the time the variance is caused by lack of proper supervision and can be eliminated by reminding the supervisors of their responsibilities. On the other hand, 20% of the time the variance is caused by inexperienced personnel who lack proper training. Due to sales and production commitments, the appropriate training cannot be scheduled until the end of September.

Instructions: (1) Assuming that no additional costs would be incurred in conducting an investigation, what is the expected cost of investigating the direct labor time variance?

(2) What is the value of conducting an investigation of the direct labor time variance?

(3) If the estimated cost to investigate the variance is $5,000, should the controller authorize an investigation? Explain.

(4) If the estimated cost to investigate the variance is $2,500, should the controller authorize an investigation? Explain.

27–48A. Maximin and maximax concepts and analysis. The management of Investors Systems Inc. is considering a speculative investment in one of three oil and gas ventures. The success or failure of each venture depends on the quantity of oil and gas discovered. The estimated profit or loss for each venture is as follows:

	Amount of Oil and Gas Discovered		
	Small Quantities	Moderate Quantities	Large Quantities
Venture X.	$(100,000)	$8,000,000	$20,000,000
Venture Y.	400,000	7,500,000	15,000,000
Venture Z.	300,000	10,000,000	18,500,000

Instructions: (1) If the management of Investors Systems Inc. uses the maximin concept, which of the three ventures would be chosen?

(2) If the management of Investors Systems Inc. uses the maximax concept, which of the three ventures would be chosen?

(3) Assuming that the Moderate Quantities column is the most likely estimate of profit from the oil and gas that will be discovered, what alternative decision concept can be used by Investors Systems Inc.?

Mini-Case 27

International Oil Inc.

International Oil Inc. must decide between two sites at which to drill for oil. At a desert site, there is a 70% chance that oil will be discovered, resulting in an estimated profit of $30,000,000. There is a 30% chance that no oil will be discovered at the desert site, resulting in an estimated loss of $5,000,000. At a mountain site, there is a 65% chance that oil will be discovered, resulting in an estimated profit of $40,000,000. There is a 35% chance that no oil will be discovered at the mountain site, resulting in an estimated loss of $20,000,000.

As a special assistant to the president, Susan Satterfield, you have been asked to analyze which site should be selected for drilling. In the past, Satterfield has selected that site with the largest possible profit.

Instructions:

(1) What decision concept has Satterfield used in the past?
(2) Using the concept identified in (1), which site should be selected?
(3) Prepare a decision tree with expected values to aid in the site selection decision.
(4) Based on the expected value concept, which site should be selected?
(5) Assuming that a new technology, using infrared photographs from satellites, can provide perfect information concerning the location of oil deposits, how much should International Oil Inc. be willing to pay for perfect information concerning (a) the desert site and (b) the mountain site?
(6) Assuming that the perfect information described in (5) costs $3,000,000 per site, should each site be analyzed at a cost of $3,000,000 per analysis to obtain perfect information?
(7) Assuming that Satterfield agrees to use the expected value concept in the selection of a drilling site, prepare a final recommendation using the results of (3) through (6).

Answers to Self-Examination Questions

1. D Storage cost per unit (answer A), annual units required (answer B), and cost per order (answer C) are all important in the determination of economic order quantity.

2. A The expected value of Proposal R is $24,000 (answer A), computed as follows:

Expected Value = .60($80,000) + .40(−$60,000)
Expected Value = $48,000 − $24,000
Expected Value = $24,000

3. B Management's use of expected value can be facilitated through the use of payoff tables and decision trees (answer B). The maximax concept (answer A) and the maximin concept (answer C) do not use expected values.

4. A The value of perfect information concerning Proposal A is $3,000 (answer A), which is the difference between (1) the expected value of Proposal A based on perfect information, $8,000 (answer C), and (2) the expected value of a decision based on existing information, $5,000 (answer B).

5. A The maximin concept leads management to decide in favor of that alternative with the maximum minimum profit. For Freeman Co., the minimum profit (loss) for each alternative appears in the low demand column. This column indicates that Project W (answer A) has the highest minimum profit ($120,000) of the four alternatives.

Part Nine

Financial Analysis for Management Use

28
Financial Statement Analysis and Annual Reports

CHAPTER OBJECTIVES

Describe the usefulness of financial statement analysis to management.

Describe the types of financial statement analysis.

Describe basic financial statement analytical procedures.

Illustrate the application of financial statement analysis in assessing solvency and profitability.

Identify and illustrate the content of corporate annual reports.

Describe the content of interim financial reports.

One of the primary objectives of accounting is to provide useful data to management for directing operations. In providing data to assist management, the accountant relies on a variety of concepts and techniques. Many of these concepts and techniques, such as budgeting, standard costs, differential analysis, break-even analysis, and variable costing, were discussed in preceding chapters. In this chapter, management's use of analyses of the data reported in the basic financial statements will be presented. In addition, the annual reports and the interim reports that are issued by corporations are discussed. These reports often contain some financial analyses as well as much of the basic information used by outsiders in evaluating management's performance.

USEFULNESS OF FINANCIAL STATEMENT ANALYSIS

The financial condition and the results of operations, as reported in the basic financial statements, are of interest to many groups external to the reporting enterprise. Since the basic statements will be evaluated by outsiders, such as creditors and owners, management is concerned with the basic financial statements and how they are viewed by these external parties. Management is also interested in the basic financial statements for other reasons. For example, the basic financial statements are used to assess the effectiveness of management in planning and controlling operations. In addition, management recognizes that the evaluation of past operations, as revealed by the analysis of the basic statements, represents a good starting point in planning future operations. Management uses financial statement analysis, therefore, as an important means of assessing past performance and in forecasting and planning future performance.

TYPES OF FINANCIAL STATEMENT ANALYSIS

Most of the items in the basic statements are of limited significance when considered individually. Their usefulness can be enhanced through studying relationships and comparisons of items (1) within a single year's financial statements, (2) in a succession of financial statements, and (3) with other enterprises. The selection and the preparation of analytical aids are a part of the work of the accountant.

Certain aspects of financial condition or of operations are of greater importance to management than are other aspects. However, management is especially interested in the ability of a business to pay its debts as they come due and to earn a reasonable amount of income. These two aspects of the status of an enterprise are called factors of **solvency** and **profitability.** An enterprise that cannot meet its obligations to creditors on a timely basis is likely to experience difficulty in obtaining credit, and this may lead to a decline in profitability. Similarly, an enterprise whose earnings are less than those of its competitors is likely to be at a disadvantage in obtaining credit or new capital from stockholders. In addition to this interrelationship between solvency and profitability, it is important to recognize that analysis of historical data is useful in assessing the past performance of an enterprise and in forecasting its future performance.

The basic analytical procedures and the various types of financial analysis useful in evaluating the solvency and profitability of an enterprise are discussed in the following paragraphs.

BASIC ANALYTICAL PROCEDURES

The analytical measures obtained from financial statements are usually expressed as ratios or percentages. For example, the relationship of $150,000 to $100,000 ($150,000/$100,000 or $150,000:$100,000) may be expressed as 1.5, 1.5:1, or 150%. This ease of computation and simplicity of form for expressing financial relationships are major reasons for the widespread use of ratios and percentages in financial analysis.

Analytical procedures may be used to compare the amount of specific items on a current statement with the corresponding amounts on earlier statements. For example, in comparing cash of $150,000 on the current balance sheet with cash of $100,000 on the balance sheet of a year earlier, the current amount may be expressed as 1.5 or 150% of the earlier amount. The relationship may also be expressed in terms of change, that is, the increase of $50,000 may be stated as a 50% increase.

Analytical procedures are also widely used to show the relationships of individual items to each other and of individual items to totals on a single statement. To illustrate, assume that included in the total of $1,000,000 of assets on a balance sheet are cash of $50,000 and inventories of $250,000. In relative terms, the cash balance is 5% of total assets and the inventories represent 25% of total assets. Individual items in the current asset group could also be related to total current assets. Assuming that the total of current assets in the example is $500,000, cash represents 10% of the total and inventories represent 50% of the total.

Increases or decreases in items may be expressed in percentage terms only when the base figure is positive. If the base figure is zero or a negative value, the amount of change cannot be expressed as a percentage. For example, if comparative balance sheets indicate no liability for notes payable on the first, or base, date and a liability of $10,000 on the later date, the increase of $10,000 cannot be stated as a percent of zero. Similarly, if a net loss of $10,000 in a particular year is followed by a net income of $5,000 in the next year, the increase of $15,000 cannot be stated as a percent of the loss of the base year.

In the following discussion and illustrations of analytical procedures, the basic significance of the various measures will be emphasized. The measures developed are not ends in themselves; they are only guides to the evaluation of financial and operating data. Many other factors, such as trends in the industry, changes in price levels, and general economic conditions and prospects, may also need consideration in order to arrive at sound conclusions.

Horizontal Analysis

The percentage analysis of increases and decreases in corresponding items in comparative financial statements is called **horizontal analysis.** The amount of each item on the most recent statement is compared with the corresponding item on one or more earlier statements. The increase or decrease in the amount of the item is then listed, together with the percent of increase or decrease. When the comparison is made between two statements, the earlier statement is used as the base. If the analysis includes three or more statements, there are two alternatives in the selection of the base: the earliest date or period may be used as the basis for comparing all later dates or periods, or each statement may be compared with the immediately preceding statement. The two alternatives are illustrated as follows:

BASE: EARLIEST YEAR

				Increase (Decrease*)			
				1989–90		1989–91	
Item	1989	1990	1991	Amount	Percent	Amount	Percent
A	$100,000	$150,000	$200,000	$ 50,000	50%	$100,000	100%
B	100,000	200,000	150,000	100,000	100%	50,000	50%

BASE: PRECEDING YEAR

				Increase (Decrease*)			
				1989–90		1990–91	
Item	1989	1990	1991	Amount	Percent	Amount	Percent
A	$100,000	$150,000	$200,000	$ 50,000	50%	$ 50,000	33%
B	100,000	200,000	150,000	100,000	100%	50,000*	25%*

Comparison of the amounts in the last two columns of the first analysis with the amounts in the corresponding columns of the second analysis reveals the effect of the base year on the direction of change and the amount and percent of change.

A condensed comparative balance sheet for two years, with horizontal analysis, is illustrated as follows:

Comparative Balance Sheet—Horizontal Analysis

Chung Company
Comparative Balance Sheet
December 31, 1990 and 1989

	1990	1989	Increase (Decrease*) Amount	Percent
Assets				
Current assets	$ 550,000	$ 533,000	$ 17,000	3.2%
Long-term investments	95,000	177,500	82,500*	46.5%*
Plant assets (net)	444,500	470,000	25,500*	5.4%*
Intangible assets	50,000	50,000	—	
Total assets	$1,139,500	$1,230,500	$ 91,000*	7.4%*
Liabilities				
Current liabilities	$ 210,000	$ 243,000	$ 33,000*	13.6%*
Long-term liabilities	100,000	200,000	100,000*	50.0%*
Total liabilities	$ 310,000	$ 443,000	$133,000*	30.0%*
Stockholders' Equity				
Preferred 6% stock, $100 par	$ 150,000	$ 150,000	—	—
Common stock, $10 par	500,000	500,000	—	—
Retained earnings	179,500	137,500	$ 42,000	30.5%
Total stockholders' equity	$ 829,500	$ 787,500	$ 42,000	5.3%
Total liabilities and stockholders' equity	$1,139,500	$1,230,500	$ 91,000*	7.4%*

The significance of the various increases and decreases in the items shown cannot be fully determined without additional information. Although total assets at the end of 1990 were $91,000 (7.4%) less than at the beginning of the year, liabilities were reduced by $133,000 (30%) and stockholders' equity increased $42,000 (5.3%). It would appear that the reduction of $100,000 in long-term liabilities was accomplished, for the most part, through the sale of long-term investments.

The foregoing balance sheet may be expanded to include the details of the various categories of assets and liabilities, or the details may be presented in separate schedules. Opinions differ as to which method presents the clearer picture. A supporting schedule with horizontal analysis is illustrated by the following comparative schedule of current assets:

Comparative Schedule of Current Assets—Horizontal Analysis

Chung Company
Comparative Schedule of Current Assets
December 31, 1990 and 1989

	1990	1989	Increase (Decrease*) Amount	Percent
Cash	$ 90,500	$ 64,700	$25,800	39.9%
Marketable securities	75,000	60,000	15,000	25.0%
Accounts receivable (net)	115,000	120,000	5,000*	4.2%*
Inventories	264,000	283,000	19,000*	6.7%*
Prepaid expenses	5,500	5,300	200	3.8%
Total current assets	$550,000	$533,000	$17,000	3.2%

The reduction in accounts receivable may have come about through changes in credit terms or improved collection policies. Similarly, a reduction in inventories during a period of increased sales probably indicates an improvement in the management of inventories.

The changes in the current assets would appear to be favorable, particularly in view of the 24.8% increase in net sales, shown in the following comparative income statement with horizontal analysis:

Comparative Income Statement—Horizontal Analysis

Chung Company
Comparative Income Statement
For Years Ended December 31, 1990 and 1989

	1990	1989	Increase (Decrease*) Amount	Percent
Sales	$1,530,500	$1,234,000	$296,500	24.0%
Sales returns and allowances	32,500	34,000	1,500*	4.4%*
Net sales	$1,498,000	$1,200,000	$298,000	24.8%
Cost of goods sold	1,043,000	820,000	223,000	27.2%
Gross profit	$ 455,000	$ 380,000	$ 75,000	19.7%
Selling expenses	$ 191,000	$ 147,000	$ 44,000	29.9%
General expenses	104,000	97,400	6,600	6.8%
Total operating expenses	$ 295,000	$ 244,400	$ 50,600	20.7%
Operating income	$ 160,000	$ 135,600	$ 24,400	18.0%
Other income	8,600	11,000	2,400*	21.8%*
	$ 168,600	$ 146,600	$ 22,000	15.0%
Other expense	13,100	18,000	4,900*	27.2%*
Income before income tax	$ 155,500	$ 128,600	$ 26,900	20.9%
Income tax	64,500	52,100	12,400	23.8%
Net income	$ 91,000	$ 76,500	$ 14,500	19.0%

An increase in net sales, considered alone, is not necessarily favorable. The increase in Chung Company's net sales was accompanied by a somewhat greater percentage increase in the cost of goods (merchandise) sold, which indicates a narrowing of the gross profit margin. Selling expenses increased markedly and general expenses increased slightly, making an overall increase in operating expenses of 20.7%, as contrasted with a 19.7% increase in gross profit.

Although the increase in operating income and in the final net income figure is favorable, it would be incorrect for management to conclude that its operations were at maximum efficiency. A study of the expenses and additional analysis and comparisons of individual expense accounts should be made.

The income statement illustrated is in condensed form. Such a condensed statement usually provides enough information for all interested groups except management. If desired, the statement may be expanded or supplemental schedules may be prepared to present details of the cost of goods sold, selling expenses, general expenses, other income, and other expense.

A comparative retained earnings statement with horizontal analysis is illustrated as follows:

Comparative Retained Earnings Statement—Horizontal Analysis

Chung Company
Comparative Retained Earnings Statement
For Years Ended December 31, 1990 and 1989

	1990	1989	Increase (Decrease*) Amount	Percent
Retained earnings, January 1	$137,500	$100,000	$37,500	37.5%
Net income for year	91,000	76,500	14,500	19.0%
Total	$228,500	$176,500	$52,000	29.5%
Dividends:				
On preferred stock	$ 9,000	$ 9,000	—	—
On common stock	40,000	30,000	$10,000	33.3%
Total	$ 49,000	$ 39,000	$10,000	25.6%
Retained earnings, December 31	$179,500	$137,500	$42,000	30.5%

Examination of the statement reveals an increase of 30.5% in retained earnings for the year. The increase was attributable to the retention of $42,000 of the net income for the year ($91,000 net income − $49,000 dividends paid).

Vertical Analysis

Percentage analysis may also be used to show the relationship of the component parts to the total in a single statement. This type of analysis is called **vertical analysis.** As in horizontal analysis, the statements may be prepared in either detailed or condensed form. In the latter case, additional details of the changes in the various categories may be presented in supporting schedules. If such schedules are prepared, the percentage analysis may be based on either the total of the schedule or the balance sheet total. Although vertical analysis is confined within each individual statement, the significance of both the amounts and the percentages is increased by preparing comparative statements.

In vertical analysis of the balance sheet, each asset item is stated as a percent of total assets, and each liability and stockholders' equity item is stated as a percent of total liabilities and stockholders' equity. A condensed comparative balance sheet with vertical analysis is illustrated as follows:

Comparative Balance Sheet— Vertical Analysis

Chung Company
Comparative Balance Sheet
December 31, 1990 and 1989

	1990		1989	
	Amount	Percent	Amount	Percent
Assets				
Current assets	$ 550,000	48.3%	$ 533,000	43.3%
Long-term investments	95,000	8.3	177,500	14.4
Plant assets (net)	444,500	39.0	470,000	38.2
Intangible assets	50,000	4.4	50,000	4.1
Total assets	$1,139,500	100.0%	$1,230,500	100.0%
Liabilities				
Current liabilities	$ 210,000	18.4%	$ 243,000	19.7%
Long-term liabilities	100,000	8.8	200,000	16.3
Total liabilities	$ 310,000	27.2%	$ 443,000	36.0%
Stockholders' Equity				
Preferred 6% stock, $100 par	$ 150,000	13.2%	$ 150,000	12.2%
Common stock, $10 par	500,000	43.9	500,000	40.6
Retained earnings	179,500	15.7	137,500	11.2
Total stockholders' equity	$ 829,500	72.8%	$ 787,500	64.0%
Total liabilities and stockholders' equity	$1,139,500	100.0%	$1,230,500	100.0%

The major relative changes in Chung Company's assets were in the current asset and long-term investment groups. In the lower half of the balance sheet, the greatest relative change was in long-term liabilities and retained earnings. Stockholders' equity increased from 64% of total liabilities and stockholders' equity at the end of 1989 to 72.8% at the end of 1990, with a corresponding decrease in the claims of creditors.

In vertical analysis of the income statement, each item is stated as a percent of net sales. A condensed comparative income statement with vertical analysis is illustrated as follows:

Chung Company
Comparative Income Statement
For Years Ended December 31, 1990 and 1989

	1990		1989	
	Amount	Percent	Amount	Percent
Sales	$1,530,500	102.2%	$1,234,000	102.8%
Sales returns and allowances	32,500	2.2	34,000	2.8
Net sales	$1,498,000	100.0%	$1,200,000	100.0%
Cost of goods sold	1,043,000	69.6	820,000	68.3
Gross profit	$ 455,000	30.4%	$ 380,000	31.7%
Selling expenses	$ 191,000	12.8%	$ 147,000	12.3%
General expenses	104,000	6.9	97,400	8.1
Total operating expenses	$ 295,000	19.7%	$ 244,400	20.4%
Operating income	$ 160,000	10.7%	$ 135,600	11.3%
Other income	8,600	.6	11,000	.9
	$ 168,600	11.3%	$ 146,600	12.2%
Other expense	13,100	.9	18,000	1.5
Income before income tax	$ 155,500	10.4%	$ 128,600	10.7%
Income tax	64,500	4.3	52,100	4.3
Net income	$ 91,000	6.1%	$ 76,500	6.4%

Comparative Income Statement— Vertical Analysis

Care must be used in judging the significance of differences between percentages for the two years. For example, the decline of the gross profit rate from 31.7% in 1989 to 30.4% in 1990 is only 1.3 percentage points. In terms of dollars of potential gross profit, however, it represents a decline of approximately $19,500 (1.3% × $1,498,000).

Common-Size Statements

Horizontal and vertical analyses with both dollar and percentage figures are helpful in disclosing relationships and trends in financial condition and operations of individual enterprises. Vertical analysis with both dollar and percentage figures is also useful in comparing one company with another or with industry averages. Such comparisons may be made easier by the use of **common-size statements,** in which all items are expressed only in relative terms.

Common-size statements may be prepared in order to compare percentages of a current period with past periods, to compare individual businesses, or to compare one business with industry percentages published by trade associations and financial information services. A comparative common-size income statement for two enterprises is illustrated as follows:

Common-Size Income Statement

Chung Company and Ross Corporation
Condensed Common-Size Income Statement
For Year Ended December 31, 1990

	Chung Company	Ross Corporation
Sales	102.2%	102.3%
Sales returns and allowances	2.2	2.3
Net sales	100.0%	100.0%
Cost of goods sold	69.6	70.0
Gross profit	30.4%	30.0%
Selling expenses	12.8%	11.5%
General expenses	6.9	4.1
Total operating expenses	19.7%	15.6%
Operating income	10.7%	14.4%
Other income	.6	.6
	11.3%	15.0%
Other expense	.9	.5
Income before income tax	10.4%	14.5%
Income tax	4.3	5.5
Net income	6.1%	9.0%

Examination of the statement reveals that although Chung Company has a slightly higher rate of gross profit than Ross Corporation, the advantage is more than offset by its higher percentage of both selling and general expenses. As a consequence, the operating income of Chung Company is 10.7% of net sales as compared with 14.4% for Ross Corporation, an unfavorable difference of 3.7 percentage points.

Other Analytical Measures

In addition to the percentage analyses previously discussed, there are a number of other relationships that may be expressed in ratios and percentages. The items used in the measures are taken from the financial statements of the current period and hence are a further development of vertical analysis. Comparison of the items with corresponding measures of earlier periods is an extension of horizontal analysis.

Some of the more important ratios useful in the evaluation of solvency and profitability are discussed in the sections that follow. The examples are based on the illustrative statements presented earlier. In a few instances, data from a company's statements of the preceding year and from other sources are also used.

SOLVENCY ANALYSIS

Solvency is the ability of a business to meet its financial obligations as they come due. Solvency analysis, therefore, focuses mainly on balance sheet relationships that indicate the ability to liquidate current and noncurrent liabilities. Major analyses used in assessing solvency include (1) current position analysis, (2) accounts receivable analysis, (3) inventory analysis, (4) the ratio of plant assets to long-term liabilities, (5) the ratio of stockholders' equity to liabilities, and (6) the number of times interest charges are earned.

Current Position Analysis

To be useful, ratios relating to a firm's solvency must show the firm's ability to liquidate its liabilities. The use of ratios showing the ability to liquidate current liabilities is called **current position analysis** and is of particular interest to short-term creditors.

Working Capital. The excess of the current assets of an enterprise over its current liabilities at a certain moment of time is called **working capital.** The absolute amount of working capital and the flow of working capital during a period of time may be used in evaluating a company's ability to meet currently maturing obligations. Although useful for making intraperiod comparisons for a company, these absolute amounts are difficult to use in comparing companies of different sizes or in comparing such amounts with industry figures. For example, working capital of $250,000 may be very adequate for a small building contractor specializing in residential construction, but it may be completely inadequate for a large building contractor specializing in industrial and commerical construction.

Current Ratio. Another means of expressing the relationship between current assets and current liabilities is through the **current ratio,** sometimes referred to as the **working capital ratio** or **bankers' ratio.** The ratio is computed by dividing the total of current assets by the total of current liabilities. The determination of working capital and the current ratio for Chung Company is illustrated as follows:

	1990	*1989*
Current assets	$550,000	$533,000
Current liabilities	210,000	243,000
Working capital	$340,000	$290,000
Current ratio	2.6:1	2.2:1

The current ratio is a more dependable indication of solvency than is working capital. To illustrate, assume that as of December 31, 1990, the working capital of a competing corporation is much greater than $340,000, but its current ratio is only 1.3:1. Considering these factors alone, Chung Company, with its current ratio of 2.6:1, is in a more favorable position to obtain short-term credit than the corporation with the greater amount of working capital.

Acid-Test Ratio. The amount of working capital and the current ratio are two solvency measures that indicate a company's ability to meet currently maturing obligations. However, these two measures do not take into account the composition of the current assets. To illustrate the significance of this additional factor, the following current position data for Chung Company and Randall Corporation as of December 31, 1990, are as follows:

	Chung Company	Randall Corporation
Current assets:		
Cash	$ 90,500	$ 45,500
Marketable securities	75,000	25,000
Accounts receivable (net)	115,000	90,000
Inventories	264,000	380,000
Prepaid expenses	5,500	9,500
Total current assets	$550,000	$550,000
Current liabilities	210,000	210,000
Working capital	$340,000	$340,000
Current ratio	2.6:1	2.6:1

Both companies have working capital of $340,000 and a current ratio of 2.6:1. But the ability of each company to meet its currently maturing debts is vastly different. Randall Corporation has more of its current assets in inventories, which must be sold and the receivables collected before the current liabilities can be paid in full. A considerable amount of time may be required to convert these inventories into cash. Declines in market prices and a reduction in demand could also impair the ability to pay current liabilities. Conversely, Chung Company has enough cash and current assets (marketable securities and accounts receivable) which can generally be converted to cash rather quickly to meet its current liabilities.

A ratio that measures the "instant" debt-paying ability of a company is called the **acid-test ratio** or **quick ratio.** It is the ratio of the total **quick assets,** which are the cash, the marketable securities, and the receivables, to the total current liabilities. The acid-test ratio data for Chung Company are as follows:

	1990	1989
Quick assets:		
Cash	$ 90,500	$ 64,700
Marketable securities	75,000	60,000
Accounts receivable (net)	115,000	120,000
Total	$280,500	$244,700
Current liabilities	$210,000	$243,000
Acid-test ratio	1.3:1	1.0:1

A thorough analysis of a firm's current position would include the determination of the amount of working capital, the current ratio, and the acid-test ratio. The current and acid-test ratios are most useful when viewed together and when compared with similar ratios for previous periods and with those of other firms in the industry.

Accounts Receivable Analysis

The size and composition of accounts receivable change continually during business operations. The amount is increased by sales on account and reduced by collections. Firms that grant long credit terms tend to have relatively greater amounts tied up in accounts receivable than those granting short credit terms. Increases or decreases in the volume of sales also affect the amount of outstanding accounts receivable.

Accounts receivable yield no revenue, hence it is desirable to keep the amount invested in them at a minimum. The cash made available by prompt collection of receivables improves solvency and may be used for purchases of merchandise in larger quantities at a lower price, for payment of dividends to stockholders, or for other purposes. Prompt collection also lessens the risk of loss from uncollectible accounts.

Accounts Receivable Turnover. The relationship between credit sales and accounts receivable may be stated as the **accounts receivable turnover.** It is computed by dividing net sales on account by the average net accounts receivable. It is preferable to base the average on monthly balances, which gives effect to seasonal changes. When such data are not available, it is necessary to use the average of the balances at the beginning and the end of the year. If there are trade notes receivable as well as accounts, the two should be combined. The accounts receivable turnover data for Chung Company are as follows. All sales were made on account.

	1990	*1989*
Net sales on account	$1,498,000	$1,200,000
Accounts receivable (net):		
Beginning of year	$ 120,000	$ 140,000
End of year	115,000	120,000
Total	$ 235,000	$ 260,000
Average	$ 117,500	$ 130,000
Accounts receivable turnover	12.7	9.2

The increase in the accounts receivable turnover for 1990 indicates that there has been an acceleration in the collection of receivables, due perhaps to improvement in either the granting of credit or the collection practices used, or both.

Number of Days' Sales in Receivables. Another means of expressing the relationship between credit sales and accounts receivable is the **number of days' sales in receivables.** This measure is determined by dividing the net accounts receivable at the end of the year by the average daily sales on account (net sales on account divided by 365), illustrated as follows for Chung Company:

	1990	*1989*
Accounts receivable (net), end of year	$ 115,000	$ 120,000
Net sales on account	$1,498,000	$1,200,000
Average daily sales on account	$ 4,104	$ 3,288
Number of days' sales in receivables	28.0	36.5

The number of days' sales in receivables gives a rough measure of the length of time the accounts receivable have been outstanding. A comparison of this measure with the credit terms, with figures for comparable firms in the same industry, and with figures of Chung Company for prior years will help reveal the efficiency in collecting receivables and the trends in the management of credit.

Inventory Analysis

Although an enterprise must maintain sufficient inventory quantities to meet the demands of its operations, it is desirable to keep the amount invested in inventory to a minimum. Inventories in excess of the needs of business reduce solvency by tying up funds. Excess inventories may also cause increases in the amount of insurance, property taxes, storage, and other related expenses, further reducing funds that could be used to better advantage. There is also added risk of loss through price declines and deterioration or obsolescence of the inventory.

Inventory Turnover. The relationship between the volume of goods (merchandise) sold and inventory may be stated as the **inventory turnover.** It is computed by dividing the cost of goods sold by the average inventory. If monthly data are not available, it is necessary to use the average of the inventories at the beginning and the end of the year. The inventory turnover data for Chung Company are as follows:

	1990	*1989*
Cost of goods sold	$1,043,000	$820,000
Inventories:		
Beginning of year	$ 283,000	$311,000
End of year	264,000	283,000
Total	$ 547,000	$594,000
Average	$ 273,500	$297,000
Inventory turnover	3.8	2.8

The improvement in the turnover resulted from an increase in the cost of goods sold, combined with a decrease in average inventory. The variation in types of inventories is too great to permit any broad generalizations as to what is a satisfactory turnover. For example, a firm selling food should have a much higher turnover than one selling furniture or jewelry, and the perishable foods department of a supermarket should have a higher turnover than the soaps and cleansers department. However, for each business or each department within a business, there is a reasonable turnover rate. A turnover below this rate means that the company or the department is incurring extra expenses such as those for administration and storage, is increasing its risk of loss because of obsolescence and adverse price changes, is incurring interest charges in excess of those considered necessary, and is failing to free funds for other uses.

Number of Days' Sales in Inventory. Another means of expressing the relationship between the cost of goods sold and inventory is the **number of days' sales in inventory.** This measure is determined by dividing the inventories at the end of the year by the average daily cost of goods sold (cost of goods sold divided by 365), illustrated as follows for Chung Company:

	1990	*1989*
Inventories, end of year	$ 264,000	$283,000
Cost of goods sold	$1,043,000	$820,000
Average daily cost of goods sold	$ 2,858	$ 2,247
Number of days' sales in inventory	92.4	125.9

The number of days' sales in inventory gives a rough measure of the length of time it takes to acquire, sell, and then replace the average inventory. Although there was a substantial improvement in the second year, comparison of the measure with those of earlier years and of comparable firms is an essential element in judging the effectiveness of Chung Company's inventory control.

As with many attempts to analyze financial data, it is possible to determine more than one measure to express the relationship between the cost of goods sold and inventory. Both the inventory turnover and number of days' sales in inventory are useful for evaluating the efficiency in the management of inventory. Whether both measures are used or whether one measure is preferred over the other is a matter for the individual analyst to decide.

Ratio of Plant Assets to Long-Term Liabilities

Long-term notes and bonds are often secured by mortgages on plant assets. *The* **ratio of total plant assets to long-term liabilities** *provides a solvency measure that shows the margin of safety of the noteholders or bondholders. It also gives an indication of the potential ability of the enterprise to borrow additional funds on a long-term basis.* The ratio of plant assets to long-term liabilities of Chung Company is as follows:

	1990	*1989*
Plant assets (net)	$444,500	$470,000
Long-term liabilities	$100,000	$200,000
Ratio of plant assets to long-term liabilities	4.4:1	2.4:1

The marked increase in the ratio at the end of 1990 was mainly due to the liquidation of one half of Chung Company's long-term liabilities. If the company should need to borrow additional funds on a long-term basis, it is in a stronger position to do so.

Ratio of Stockholders' Equity to Liabilities

Claims against the total assets of an enterprise are divided into two basic groups, those of the creditors and those of the owners. *The relationship between the total claims of the creditors and owners provides a solvency measure that indicates the margin of safety for the creditors and the ability of the enterprise to withstand adverse business conditions.* If the claims of the creditors are large in proportion to the equity of the stockholders, there are likely to be substantial charges for interest payments. If earnings decline to the point where the company is unable to meet its interest payments, control of the business may pass to the creditors.

The relationship between stockholder and creditor equity is shown in the vertical analysis of the balance sheet. For example, the balance sheet of Chung Company presented on page 1016 indicates that on December 31, 1990, stockholders' equity represented 72.8% and liabilities represented 27.2% of the sum of the liabilities and stockholders' equity (100.0%). Instead of expressing each item as a percent of the total, the relationship may be expressed as a ratio of one to the other, as follows:

	1990	1989
Total stockholders' equity	$829,500	$787,500
Total liabilities	$310,000	$443,000
Ratio of stockholders' equity to liabilities	2.7:1	1.8:1

The balance sheet of Chung Company shows that the major factor affecting the change in the ratio was the $100,000 reduction in long-term liabilities during 1990. The ratio at both dates shows a large margin of safety for the creditors.

Number of Times Interest Charges Earned

Some corporations, such as railroads and public utilities, have a high ratio of debt to stockholders' equity. In analyzing such corporations, it is customary to express *the solvency measure that shows the relative risk of the debtholders in terms of the* **number of times the interest charges are earned** during the year. The higher the ratio, the greater the assurance of continued interest payments in case of decreased earnings. *The measure also provides an indication of general financial strength,* which is of concern to stockholders and employees, as well as to creditors.

In the following data, the amount available to meet interest charges is not affected by taxes on income because interest is deductible in determining taxable income.

	1990	1989
Income before income tax	$ 900,000	$ 800,000
Add interest charges	300,000	250,000
Amount available to meet interest charges	$1,200,000	$1,050,000
Number of times interest charges earned	4	4.2

Analyses like the above can be applied to dividends on preferred stock. In such cases, net income would be divided by the amount of preferred dividends to yield the number of times preferred dividends were earned. This measure gives an indication of the relative assurance of continued dividend payments to preferred stockholders.

PROFITABILITY ANALYSIS

Profitability is the ability of an entity to earn income. It can be assessed by computing various relevant measures, including (1) the ratio of net sales to assets, (2) the rate earned on total assets, (3) the rate earned on stockholders' equity, (4) the rate earned on common stockholders' equity, (5) earnings per share on common stock, (6) the price-earnings ratio, and (7) dividend yield.

Ratio of Net Sales to Assets

The **ratio of net sales to assets** *is a profitability measure that shows how effectively a firm utilizes its assets.* Assume that two competing enterprises have equal amounts of assets, but the amount of the sales of one is double the amount of the sales of the other. Obviously, the former is making better use of its assets. In computing the ratio, any long-term investments should be excluded from total assets because they are wholly unrelated to sales of goods or services. Assets used in determining the ratio may be the total at the end of the year, the average of the beginning and end of the year totals, or the average of the monthly totals. The basic data and the ratio of net sales to assets for Chung Company are as follows:

	1990	1989
Net sales	$1,498,000	$1,200,000
Total assets (excluding long-term investments):		
Beginning of year	$1,053,000	$1,010,000
End of year	1,044,500	1,053,000
Total	$2,097,500	$2,063,000
Average	$1,048,750	$1,031,500
Ratio of net sales to assets	1.4:1	1.2:1

The ratio improved to a minor degree in 1990, largely due to the increased sales volume. A comparison of the ratio with those of other enterprises in the same industry would be helpful in assessing Chung Company's effectiveness in the utilization of assets.

Rate Earned on Total Assets

The **rate earned on total assets** *is a measure of the profitability of the assets, without regard to the equity of creditors and stockholders in the assets.* The rate is therefore not affected by differences in methods of financing an enterprise.

The rate earned on total assets is derived by adding interest expense to net income and dividing this sum by the average total assets held throughout the year. By adding interest expense to net income, the profitability of the assets is determined without considering the means of financing the acquisition of the assets. The rate earned by Chung Company on total assets is determined as follows:

	1990	1989
Net income	$ 91,000	$ 76,500
Plus interest expense	13,100	18,000
Total	$ 104,100	$ 94,500
Total assets:		
Beginning of year	$1,230,500	$1,187,500
End of year	1,139,500	1,230,500
Total	$2,370,000	$2,418,000
Average	$1,185,000	$1,209,000
Rate earned on total assets	8.8%	7.8%

The rate earned on total assets of Chung Company for 1990 indicates an improvement over that for 1989. A comparison with other companies and with industry averages would also be useful in evaluating the effectiveness of management performance.

It is sometimes preferable to determine the rate of operating income (income before nonoperating income, nonoperating expense, extraordinary items, and income tax) to total assets. If nonoperating income is not considered, the investments yielding such income should be excluded from the assets. The use of income before income tax eliminates the effect of changes in the tax structure on the rate of earnings. When considering published data on rates earned on assets, the reader should note the exact nature of the measure.

Rate Earned on Stockholders' Equity

Another relative measure of profitability is obtained by dividing net income by the total stockholders' equity. In contrast to the rate earned on total assets, **the rate earned on stockholders' equity** *emphasizes the income yield in relationship to the amount invested by the stockholders.*

The amount of the total stockholders' equity throughout the year varies for several reasons—the issuance of additional stock, the retirement of a class of stock, the payment of dividends, and the gradual accrual of net income. If monthly figures are not available, the average of the stockholders' equity at the beginning and the end of the year is used, as in the following illustration:

	1990	*1989*
Net income	$ 91,000	$ 76,500
Stockholders' equity:		
Beginning of year	$ 787,500	$ 750,000
End of year	829,500	787,500
Total	$1,617,000	$1,537,500
Average	$ 808,500	$ 768,750
Rate earned on stockholders' equity	11.3%	10.0%

The rate earned by a thriving enterprise on the equity of its stockholders is usually higher than the rate earned on total assets. The reason for the difference is that the amount earned on assets acquired through the use of funds provided by creditors is more than the interest charges paid to creditors. This tendency of the rate on stockholders' equity to vary disproportionately from the rate on total assets is sometimes called **leverage.** The Chung Company rate on stockholders' equity for 1990, 11.3%, compares favorably with the rate of 8.8% earned on total assets, as reported on the preceding page. The leverage factor of 2.5% (11.3% − 8.8%) for 1990 also compares favorably with the 2.2% (10.0% − 7.8%) differential for the preceding year. These leverage factors for Chung Company are illustrated graphically in the following charts:

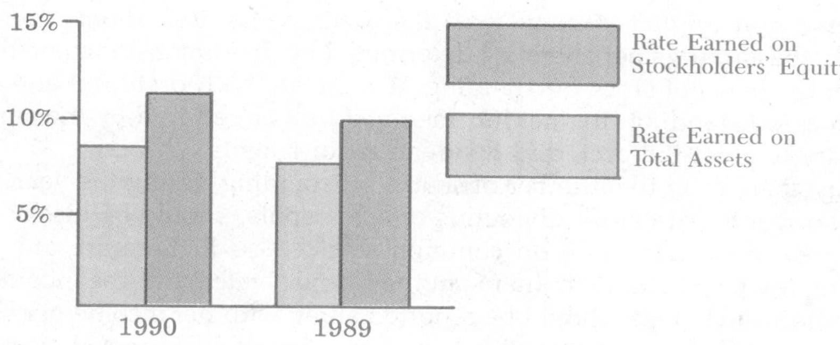

Chart of Rate Earned on Stockholders' Equity and Total Assets

Rate Earned on Common Stockholders' Equity

When a corporation has both preferred and common stock outstanding, the holders of the common stock have the residual claim on earnings. The **rate earned on common stockholders' equity** is the net income less preferred dividend requirements for the period, stated as a percent of the average equity of the common stockholders.

Chung Company has $150,000 of 6% nonparticipating preferred stock outstanding at both balance sheet dates, hence annual preferred dividends amount to $9,000. The common stockholders' equity is the total stockholders' equity, including retained earnings, reduced by the par of the preferred stock ($150,000). The basic data and the rate earned on common stockholders' equity are as follows:

	1990	*1989*
Net income	$ 91,000	$ 76,500
Preferred dividends	9,000	9,000
Remainder—identified with common stock	$ 82,000	$ 67,500
Common stockholders' equity:		
Beginning of year	$ 637,500	$ 600,000
End of year	679,500	637,500
Total	$1,317,000	$1,237,500
Average	$ 658,500	$ 618,750
Rate earned on common stockholders' equity	12.5%	10.9%

The rate earned on common stockholders' equity differs from the rates earned by Chung Company on total assets and total stockholders' equity. This situation will occur if there are borrowed funds and also preferred stock outstanding, which rank ahead of the common shares in their claim on earnings. Thus the concept of leverage, as discussed in the preceding section, can be applied to the use of funds from the sale of preferred stock as well as from borrowing. Funds from both sources can be used in an attempt to increase the return on common stockholders' equity.

Earnings per Share on Common Stock

One of the profitability measures most commonly quoted by the financial press and included in the income statement in corporate annual reports is

earnings per share on common stock. If a company has issued only one class of stock, the earnings per share are determined by dividing net income by the number of shares of stock outstanding. If there are both preferred and common stock outstanding, the net income must first be reduced by the amount necessary to meet the preferred dividend requirements.

Any changes in the number of shares outstanding during the year, such as would result from stock dividends or stock splits, should be disclosed in quoting earnings per share on common stock. Also if there are any nonrecurring (extraordinary, etc.) items in the income statement, the income per share before such items should be reported along with net income per share. In addition, if there are convertible bonds or convertible preferred stock outstanding, the amount reported as net income per share should be stated without considering the conversion privilege, followed by net income per share assuming conversion had occurred.

The data on the earnings per share of common stock for Chung Company are as follows:

	1990	*1989*
Net income	$91,000	$76,500
Preferred dividends	9,000	9,000
Remainder—identified with common stock	$82,000	$67,500
Shares of common stock outstanding	50,000	50,000
Earnings per share on common stock	$1.64	$1.35

Since earnings form the primary basis for dividends, earnings per share and dividends per share on common stock are commonly used by investors in weighing the merits of alternative investment opportunities. Earnings per share data can be presented in conjunction with dividends per share data to indicate the relationship between earnings and dividends and the extent to which the corporation is retaining its earnings for use in the business. The following chart shows this relationship for Chung Company:

Chart of Earnings and Dividends per Share of Common Stock

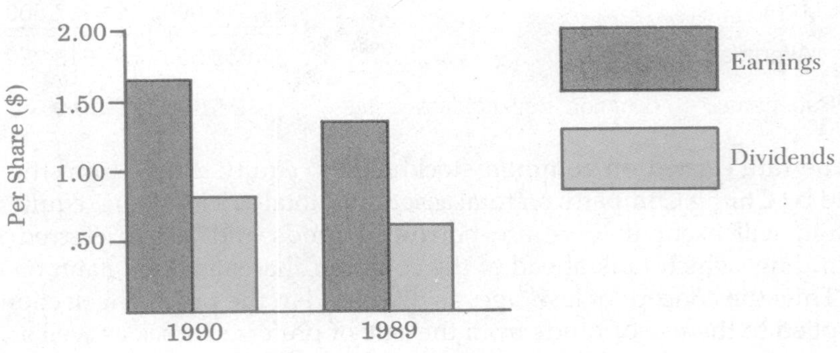

Price-Earnings Ratio

A profitability measure commonly quoted by the financial press is the **price-earnings (P/E) ratio** on common stock. *The price-earnings ratio is used as an indicator of a firm's future earnings prospects.* It is computed by dividing the market price per share of common stock at a specific date by the annual earnings per share. Assuming market prices per common share of 20 1/2 at the end of 1990 and 13 1/2 at the end of 1989, the price-earnings ratio on common stock of Chung Company is as follows:

	1990	1989
Market price per share of common stock	$20.50	$13.50
Earnings per share on common stock	$ 1.64	$ 1.35
Price-earnings ratio on common stock	12.5	10.0

The price-earnings ratio indicates that a share of common stock of Chung Company was selling for 12.5 and 10 times the amount of earnings per share at the end of 1990 and 1989 respectively.

Dividend Yield

The **dividend yield** on common stock is a profitability measure that shows the rate of return to common stockholders in terms of cash dividend distributions. It is of special interest to investors whose main investment objective is to receive a current return on the investment rather than an increase in the market price of the investment. The dividend yield is computed by dividing the annual dividends paid per share of common stock by the market price per share at a specific date. Assuming dividends of $.80 and $.60 per common share and market prices per common share of 20 1/2 and 13 1/2 at the end of 1990 and 1989 respectively, the dividend yield on common stock of Chung Company is as follows:

	1990	1989
Dividends per share on common stock	$ .80	$ .60
Market price per share of common stock	$20.50	$13.50
Dividend yield on common stock	3.9%	4.4%

SUMMARY OF ANALYTICAL MEASURES

The following presentation is a summary of the method of computation and use of the analytical measures discussed in this chapter:

	Method of Computation	Use
Solvency measures		
Working capital	Current assets − current liabilities	To indicate the ability to meet currently maturing obligations
Current ratio	$\frac{\text{Current assets}}{\text{Current liabilities}}$	
Acid-test ratio	$\frac{\text{Quick assets}}{\text{Current liabilities}}$	To indicate instant debt-paying ability
Accounts receivable turnover	$\frac{\text{Net sales on account}}{\text{Average accounts receivable}}$	To assess the efficiency in collecting receivables and in the management of credit
Number of days' sales in receivables	$\frac{\text{Accounts receivable, end of year}}{\text{Average daily sales on account}}$	

	Method of Computation	Use
Inventory turnover	Cost of goods sold / Average inventory	To assess the efficiency in the management of inventory
Number of days' sales in inventory	Inventory, end of year / Average daily cost of goods sold	
Ratio of plant assets to long-term liabilities	Plant assets (net) / Long-term liabilities	To indicate the margin of safety to long-term creditors
Ratio of stockholders' equity to liabilities	Total stockholders' equity / Total liabilities	To indicate the margin of safety to creditors
Number of times interest charges earned	Income before income tax + interest expense / Interest expense	To assess the risk to debtholders in terms of number of times interest charges were earned
Profitability measures		
Ratio of net sales to assets	Net sales / Average total assets (excluding long-term investments)	To assess the effectiveness in the use of assets
Rate earned on total assets	Net income + interest expense / Average total assets	To assess the profitability of the assets
Rate earned on stockholders' equity	Net income / Average stockholders' equity	To assess the profitability of the investment by stockholders
Rate earned on common stockholders' equity	Net income − preferred dividends / Average common stockholders' equity	To assess the profitability of the investment by common stockholders
Earnings per share on common stock	Net income − preferred dividends / Shares of common stock outstanding	
Dividends per share of common stock	Dividends / Shares of common stock outstanding	To indicate the extent to which earnings are being distributed to common stockholders
Price-earnings ratio	Market price per share of common stock / Earnings per share on common stock	To indicate future earnings prospects, based on the relationship between market value of common stock and earnings
Dividend yield	Dividends per common share / Market price per common share	To indicate the rate of return to common stockholders in terms of dividends

The analytical measures that have been discussed and illustrated are representative of many that can be developed for a medium-size merchandising enterprise. Some of them might well be omitted in analyzing a specific firm, or additional measures could be developed. The type of business activity, the capital structure, and the size of the enterprise usually affect the measures used.

Percentage analyses, ratios, turnovers, and other measures of financial position and operating results are useful analytical devices. They are helpful in appraising the present performance of an enterprise and in forecasting its future. They are not, however, a substitute for sound judgment, nor do they provide definitive guides to action. In selecting and interpreting analytical indexes, proper consideration should be given to any conditions peculiar to the enterprise or to the industry of which the enterprise is a part. The possible influence of the general economic and business environment should also be weighed.

To determine trends, the interrelationship of the measures used in appraising a certain enterprise should be carefully studied, as should comparable indexes of earlier fiscal periods. Data from competing enterprises may also be compared in order to determine the relative efficiency of the firm being analyzed. In making such comparisons, however, it is essential to consider the potential effects of any significant differences in the accounting methods used by the enterprises.

Perceptions of Financial Ratios

A survey of the views of financial executives on important issues relating to financial ratios indicated that financial ratios are an important tool in analyzing the financial results of a company and in managing a company. In addition, 93 of the 100 respondents to the survey indicated that their firms use financial ratios as part of their corporate objectives. The ratios most significant to the respondents are those that measure the ability of the firm to earn a profit.

Source: Charles H. Gibson, "How Industry Perceives Financial Ratios," *Management Accounting* (April, 1982), pp. 13–19.

Financial ratios are often more useful when they are compared with similar ratios of other companies or groups of companies. For this purpose, average ratios for many industries are compiled by various financial services and trade associations. In this process, however, it should be remembered that averages are just that—averages—and care should be taken in their use. The danger in interpreting averages was graphically illustrated by Eldon Grimm, a Wall Street analyst who said: "A statistician is an individual who has his head in the refrigerator, his feet in the oven and on the average feels comfortable."

Source: "Twenty-Five Years Ago in *Forbes*," *Forbes* (August 16, 1982), p. 107.

CORPORATE ANNUAL REPORTS

Corporations ordinarily issue to their stockholders and other interested parties annual reports summarizing activities of the past year and any significant plans for the future. Although there are many differences in the form and sequence of the major sections of annual reports, one section is always devoted to the financial statements, including the accompanying notes. In addition, annual reports usually include (a) selected data referred to as financial highlights, (b) a letter from the president of the corporation, which is sometimes also signed by the chairperson of the board of directors, (c) the independent auditors' report, (d) the management report, and (e) a five- or ten-year historical summary of financial data. A description of financial reporting for segments of a business and supplemental data on the effects of price-level changes may also be included, either separately or as footnotes to the financial statements. As a way to strengthen the relationship with stockholders, many corporations also include pictures of their products and officers or other materials. The following subsections describe the portions of annual reports commonly related to financial matters, with the exception of the principal financial statements, examples of which appear in Appendix J.

Financial Highlights

This section, sometimes called *Results in Brief,* typically summarizes the major financial results for the last year or two. It is usually presented on the first one or two pages of the annual report. Although there are many variations in format and content of this section, such items as sales, income before income taxes, net income, net income per common share, cash dividends, cash dividends per common share, and the amount of capital expenditures are typically presented. In addition to the selected income statement data, information about the financial position at year end, such as the amount of working capital, total assets, long-term debt, and stockholders' equity, is often provided. Other year-end data often reported are the number of common and preferred shares outstanding, number of common and preferred stockholders, and number of employees. An example of a financial highlights section from a corporation's annual report is as follows:

Financial Highlights Section

FINANCIAL HIGHLIGHTS

(Dollars in thousands except per share amounts)

For the Year	Current Year	Preceding Year
Sales	$1,336,750	$ 876,400
Income before income tax	149,550	90,770
Net income	105,120	66,190
Per common share	4.03	2.62
Dividends declared on common stock	34,990	33,150
Per common share	1.48	1.40
Capital expenditures and investments	265,120	157,050
At Year-End		
Working capital	$ 415,410	$ 423,780
Total assets	1,712,170	1,457,240
Long-term debt	440,680	457,350
Stockholders' equity	840,350	692,950

President's Letter

A letter by the president to the stockholders, discussing such items as reasons for an increase or decrease in net income, changes in existing plant or purchase or construction of new plants, significant new financing commitments, attention given to social responsibility issues, and future prospects, is also found in most annual reports. A condensed version of a president's letter adapted from a corporation's annual report is as follows:

To the Stockholders:

FISCAL YEAR REVIEWED

The record net income in this fiscal year resulted from very strong product demand experienced for about two thirds of the fiscal year, more complete utilization of plants, and a continued improvement in sales mix. Income was strong both domestically and internationally during this period.

PLANT EXPANSION CONTINUES

Capital expenditures during the year were $14.5 million. Expansions were in progress or completed at all locations. Portions of the Company's major new expansion at one of its West Coast plants came on stream in March of this year and will provide much needed capacity in existing and new product areas. Capital expenditures will be somewhat less during next year.

ENVIRONMENTAL CONCERN

The Company recognizes its responsibility to provide a safe and healthy environment at each of its plants. The Company expects to spend approximately $1 million in the forthcoming year to help continue its position as a constructive corporate citizen.

OUTLOOK

During the past 10 years the Company's net income and sales have more than tripled. Net income increased from $3.1 million to $10.7 million, and sales from $45 million to $181 million.

The Company's employees are proud of this record and are determined to carry the momentum into the future. The current economic slowdown makes results for the new fiscal year difficult to predict. However, we are confident and enthusiastic about the Company's prospects for continued growth over the longer term.

Respectfully submitted,

Frances B. Davis

Frances B. Davis
President

March 24, 1990

During recent years, corporate enterprises have become increasingly active in accepting environmental and other social responsibilities. In addition to the brief discussion that may be contained in the president's letter, a more detailed analysis of the company's social concerns may be included elsewhere in the annual report. Knowledgeable investors recognize that the failure of a business enterprise to meet acceptable social norms can have long-run unfavorable implications. In the near future, an important function of accounting may be to assist management in developing a statement covering the social responsibilities of corporate enterprises and what management is doing about them.

Independent Auditors' Report

Before issuing annual statements, all publicly held corporations, as well as many other corporations, engage independent public accountants, usually CPAs, to conduct an *examination* of the financial statements. Such an examination is for the purpose of adding credibility to the statements that have been prepared by management. Upon completion of the examination, which for large corporations may engage many accountants for several weeks or longer, an **independent auditors' report** is prepared. This report accompanies the financial statements. A typical report includes three paragraphs: (1) an introductory paragraph identifying the financial statements being audited, (2) a "scope" paragraph describing the nature of the audit, and (3) an "opinion" paragraph presenting the auditor's opinion as to the fairness of the statements. The recommended report is as follows:[1]

Independent Auditors' Report Section

Independent Auditor's Report

We have audited the accompanying balance sheets of X Company as of December 31, 19X2 and 19X1, and the related statements of income, retained earnings, and cash flows for the years then ended. These financial statements are the responsibility of the Company's management. Our responsibility is to express an opinion on these financial statements based on our audits.

We conducted our audits in accordance with generally accepted auditing standards. Those standards require that we plan and perform the audit to obtain reasonable assurance about whether the financial statements are free of material misstatement. An audit includes examining, on a test basis, evidence supporting the amounts and disclosures in the financial statements. An audit also includes assessing the accounting principles used and significant estimates made by management, as well as evaluating the overall financial statement presentation. We believe that our audits provide a reasonable basis for our opinion.

In our opinion, the financial statements referred to above present fairly, in all material respects, the financial position of X Company as of [at] December 31, 19X2 and 19X1, and the results of its operations and its cash flows for the years then ended in conformity with generally accepted accounting principles.

[*Signature*]

[*Date*]

In most instances, the auditors can render a report such as the one illustrated, which may be said to be "unqualified." However, it is possible that accounting methods used by a client do not conform with generally accepted accounting principles. In such cases, a "qualified" opinion must be rendered and the exception briefly described. If the effect of the departure from accepted principles is sufficiently material, an "adverse" or negative opinion must be issued and the exception described. In rare circumstances, the auditors may be unable to perform sufficient auditing procedures to enable them to reach a conclusion as to the fairness of the financial statements. In such circumstances, the auditors must issue a "disclaimer" and briefly describe the reasons for their failure to be able to reach a decision as to the fairness of the statements.

Professional accountants cannot disregard their responsibility in attesting to the fairness of financial statements without seriously jeopardizing their reputations. This responsibility is described as follows:

> *The report shall either contain an expression of opinion regarding the financial statements, taken as a whole, or an assertion to the effect that an opinion cannot be expressed. When an overall opinion cannot be expressed, the reasons therefor should be stated. In all cases where an auditor's name is associated with financial statements, the report should contain a clear-cut indication of the*

[1]*Statements on Auditing Standards No. 58,* "Reports on Audited Financial Statements," (New York: American Institute of Certified Public Accountants, 1988), par. 8.

character of the auditor's examination, if any, and the degree of responsibility he is taking.[2]

Management Report

Responsibility for the accounting system and the resultant financial statements rests mainly with the principal officers of a corporation. In the **management report,** the chief financial officer or other representative of management (1) states that the financial statements are management's responsibility and that they have been prepared according to generally accepted accounting principles, (2) presents management's assessment of the company's internal accounting control system, and (3) comments on any other pertinent matters related to the accounting system, the financial statements, and the examination by the independent auditor.

Although the concept of a management report is relatively new, an increasing number of corporations are including such a report in the annual report. An example of such a report for Alcoa is as follows:

Management Report Section

Management's Report to Alcoa Shareholders

The accompanying financial statements of Alcoa and consolidated subsidiaries were prepared by management, which is responsible for their integrity and objectivity. The statements were prepared in accordance with generally accepted accounting principles and include amounts that are based on management's best judgments and estimates. The other financial information included in this annual report is consistent with that in the financial statements.

The company maintains a system of internal controls, including accounting controls, and a strong program of internal auditing. The system of controls provides for appropriate division of responsibility and the application of policies and procedures that are consistent with high standards of accounting and administration. The company believes that its system of internal controls provides reasonable assurance that assets are safeguarded against losses from unauthorized use or disposition and that financial records are reliable for use in preparing financial statements.

The Audit Committee of the Board of Directors, composed solely of directors who are not officers or employees, meets regularly with management, with the company's internal auditors, and with its independent certified public accountants, to discuss their evaluation of internal accounting controls and the quality of financial reporting. The independent auditors and the internal auditors have free access to the Audit Committee, without management's presence.

Management also recognizes its responsibility for conducting the company's affairs according to the highest standards of personal and corporate conduct. This responsibility is characterized and reflected in key policy statements issued from time to time regarding, among other things, conduct of its business activities within the laws of the host countries in which the company operates and potentially conflicting outside business interests of its employees. The company maintains a systematic program to assess compliance with these policies.

Charles W. Parry
Chairman of the Board
and Chief Executive Officer

James W. Wirth
Senior Vice President--Finance

---

[2] *Ibid.,* par. 509.04.

Historical Summary

This section, for which there are many variations in title, reports selected financial and operating data of past periods, usually for five or ten years. It is usually presented in close proximity to the financial statements for the current year, and the types of data reported are varied. An example of a portion of such a report is as follows:

Historical Summary Section

Five-Year Consolidated Financial and Statistical Summary
for Years Ended December 31
(Dollar amounts in millions except for per share data)

For the Year	1990	1989	1986
Net sales	$1,759.7	$1,550.1	$ 997.4
Gross profit	453.5	402.8	270.8
Percent to net sales	25.8%	26.0%	27.2%
Interest expense	33.9	21.3	15.0
Income before income tax	172.7	163.4	87.5
Income tax	62.8	57.8	30.2
Net income	109.9	105.6	57.3
Percent to net sales	6.2%	6.8%	5.7%
Per common share:			
Net income	5.19	4.84	2.54
Dividends	1.80	1.65	1.40
Return on stockholders' equity	19.4%	20.2%	13.6%
Common share market price:			
High	31	41 ½	40 ⅝
Low	18	22 ⅜	22 ¼
Depreciation and amortization	43.3	41.0	23.6
Capital expenditures	98.5	72.1	55.5
At Year End			
Working capital	$ 443.9	$ 434.8	$ 254.6
Plant assets—gross	704.7	620.3	453.7
Plant assets—net	420.0	362.7	263.4
Stockholders' equity	594.3	536.9	447.6
Stockholders' equity per common share	33.07	29.69	23.02
Number of holders of common shares	39,503	39,275	43,852
Number of employees	50,225	50,134	42,826

Segment of a Business

Many companies diversify their operations; that is, they are involved in more than one type of business activity. These companies may also operate in foreign markets. The individual segments of such diversified companies ordinarily experience differing rates of profitability, degrees of risk, and opportunities for growth. To help financial statement users in assessing past performance and future potential of diversified companies, financial statements should disclose such information as the enterprise's operations in different industries, its foreign markets, and its major customers. The required information for each significant reporting segment includes the following: revenue, income from operations, and identifiable assets associated with the segment.[3] An example of financial reporting for segments of a business is illustrated by the following note adapted from the 1987 financial statements of The Procter & Gamble Company:

Millions of Dollars	Segments					
	Laundry and Cleaning	Personal Care	Food and Beverage	Other	Corporate	Total
Net Sales						
1985	$4,884	$5,107	$2,815	$1,237	$(491)	$13,552
1986	5,348	6,451	2,923	1,161	(444)	15,439
1987	**5,748**	**7,512**	**2,976**	**1,186**	**(458)**	**17,000**
Earnings Before Income Taxes						
1985	691	332	(110)	104	(13)	1,004
1986	667	625	(64)	74	(127)	1,175
1987	**510**	**498**	**(282)**	**148**	**(257)**	**617**
Assets						
1985	2,038	3,776	1,717	1,244	908	9,683
1986	2,369	6,446	1,761	1,279	1,200	13,055
1987	**2,690**	**6,679**	**1,690**	**1,273**	**1,383**	**13,715**

Supplemental Data on the Effects of Price-Level Changes

Financial statements are expressed in terms of money. Because money changes in value as prices change, changing price levels will affect financial reporting. The means of disclosing the effects of these changing prices on financial reporting have been the subject of much experimentation by the accounting profession. Currently there are two widely discussed possibilities for supplementing conventional statements and thus resolving financial reporting problems created by changing price levels: (1) supplemental financial data based on current costs, and (2) supplemental financial data based on constant dollars. The discussion in the following sections is confined to the basic concepts and problems of these recommendations.

Current Cost Data. **Current cost** is the amount of cash that would have to be paid currently to acquire assets of the same age and in the same condition as existing assets. When current costs are used as the basis for financial reporting, assets, liabilities, and owner's equity are stated at current values, and expenses are stated at the current cost of doing business. The use of current costs permits the identification of gains and losses that result from holding assets during periods of changes in price levels. To illustrate, assume that a firm acquired land at the beginning of the fiscal year for $50,000 and that at the end of the year its current cost (value) is $60,000. The land could be reported at its current cost of $60,000, and the $10,000 increase in value could be reported as an unrealized gain from holding the land.

[3]*Statement of Financial Accounting Standards, No. 14,* "Financial Reporting for Segments of a Business Enterprise" (Stamford: Financial Accounting Standards Board, 1976). Nonpublic corporations are exempted from this requirement by *Statement of Financial Accounting Standards, No. 21,* "Suspension of the Reporting of Earnings per Share and Segment Information by Nonpublic Enterprises" (Stamford: Financial Accounting Standards Board, 1978).

The major disadvantage in the use of current costs is the absence of established standards and procedures for determining such costs. However, many accountants believe that adequate standards and procedures will evolve through experimentation with actual applications.

Constant Dollar Data. **Constant dollar** data, also known as general price-level data, are historical costs that have been converted to constant dollars through the use of a price-level index. In this manner, financial statement elements are reported in dollars, each of which has the same (that is, constant) general purchasing power.

A **price-level index** is the ratio of the total cost of a group of commodities prevailing at a particular time to the total cost of the same group of commodities at an earlier base time. The total cost of the commodities at the base time is assigned a value of 100 and the price-level indexes for all later times are expressed as a ratio to 100. For example, assume that the cost of a selected group of commodities amounted to \$12,000 at a particular time and \$13,200 today. The price index for the earlier, or base, time becomes 100 and the current price index is 110 [(13,200 ÷ 12,000) × 100].

A general price-level index may be used to determine the effect of changes in price levels on certain financial statement items. To illustrate, assume a price index of 120 at the time of purchase of a plot of land for \$10,000 and a current price index of 150. The **constant dollar equivalent** of the original cost of \$10,000 may be computed as follows:

$$\frac{\text{Current Price Index}}{\text{Price Index at Date of Purchase}} \times \text{Original Cost} = \text{Constant Dollar Equivalent}$$

$$\frac{150}{120} \times \$10{,}000 = \$12{,}500$$

Current Annual Reporting Requirements for Price-Level Changes. In 1979, the Financial Accounting Standards Board undertook an experimental program for reporting the effects of changing prices by requiring approximately 1,300 large, publicly held enterprises to disclose certain current cost information and constant dollar information annually as supplemental data. In 1984, after reviewing the experiences with these 1979 disclosure requirements, the FASB concluded that current cost information was more useful than constant dollar information as a supplement to the basic financial statements. In addition, the FASB concluded that requiring two different methods of reporting the effects of changing prices may detract from the usefulness of the information. As a result, the requirement to report constant dollar information was dropped for those companies that report current cost information. Finally, in 1986, the FASB concluded that the supplemental data had been used very little and therefore made the supplemental disclosure of current cost/constant dollar information voluntary.[4] However, the FASB continues to encourage companies to experiment with different methods of providing the information.

The following footnote from the 1986 annual report of The Pillsbury Company illustrates the reporting of the effects of changing prices:

---

[4]*Statement of Financial Accounting Standards, No. 89,* "Financial Reporting and Changing Prices" (Stamford: Financial Accounting Standards Board, 1986).

> **Information on effects of changing prices and inflation**
>
> Financial statements, prepared using historical costs as required by generally accepted accounting principles, may not reflect the full impact of current costs and general inflation.
>
> The following supplementary disclosures attempt to remeasure certain historical financial information to recognize the effects of changes in current costs using specific price indices. The current cost information is then expressed in average Fiscal 1986 dollars to reflect the effects of general inflation based on the U.S. Consumer Price Index. . . .

Other Information

The preceding paragraphs described the most commonly presented sections of annual reports related to financial matters. Some annual reports may include other financial information, such as forecasts which indicate financial plans and expectations for the year ahead.

INTERIM FINANCIAL REPORTS

Corporate enterprises customarily issue interim financial reports to their stockholders. Corporations that are listed on a stock exchange or file reports with the Securities and Exchange Commission or other regulatory agencies are required to submit interim reports, usually on a quarterly basis. Such reports often have a significant influence on the valuation of a corporation's equity securities on stock exchanges.

Interim reports of an enterprise should disclose such information as gross revenue, costs and expenses, provision for income taxes, extraordinary or infrequently occurring items, net income, earnings per share, contingent items, and cash flows.[5] The particular accounting principles used on an annual basis, such as depreciation methods and inventory cost flow assumptions, are usually followed in preparing interim statements. However, if changes in accounting principles occur before the end of a fiscal year, there are detailed guidelines for their disclosure.[6]

Much of the value of interim financial reports to the investing public is based on their timeliness. Lengthy delays between the end of a quarter and the issuance of reports would usually greatly reduce their value. This is one of the reasons that interim reports are usually not audited by independent CPAs. In some cases, the interim reports are subjected to a "limited review" by the CPA and a report on this limited review is issued.

---

[5]*Opinions of the Accounting Principles Board, No. 28,* "Interim Financial Reporting" (New York: American Institute of Certified Public Accountants, 1973).

[6]*Statement of Financial Accounting Standards, No. 3,* "Reporting Accounting Changes in Interim Financial Statements" (Stamford: Financial Accounting Standards Board, 1974).

Chapter Review

KEY POINTS

1. Usefulness of Financial Statement Analysis.
The financial condition and the results of operations, as reported in the basic financial statements, are of interest to many groups external to the reporting enterprise. Because the basic financial statements are used to assess the effectiveness of management in planning and controlling operations and because financial statements can be used to plan future operations, financial statement analysis is also important to management.

2. Types of Financial Statement Analysis.
Users of financial statements often gain a clearer picture of the economic condition of an entity by studying relationships and comparisons of items (1) within a single year's statements, (2) in a succession of statements, (3) with other enterprises, and (4) with industry averages. Users are especially interested in solvency and profitability. Analysis of historical data in financial statements is useful in assessing the past performance of an enterprise and in forecasting its future performance.

3. Basic Analytical Procedures.
The analytical measures obtained from financial statements are usually expressed as ratios or percentages. The basic measures developed through the use of analytical procedures are not ends in themselves. They are only guides to the evaluation of financial and operating data. Many other factors, such as trends in the industry, changes in price levels, and general economic conditions and prospects, may also need consideration in order to arrive at sound conclusions.

The percentage analysis of increases and decreases in corresponding items in comparative financial statements is called horizontal analysis. Percentage analysis may also be used to show the relationship of the component parts to the total in a single statement. This type of analysis is called vertical analysis. Although vertical analysis is confined within each individual statement, the significance of both the amounts and the percentages is increased by preparing comparative statements. Vertical analysis with both dollar and percentage figures is also useful in comparing one company with another or with industry averages. Such comparisons may be made easier by the use of common-size statements, in which all items are expressed only in relative terms.

4. Solvency Analysis.
Solvency is the ability of a business to meet its financial obligations as they come due. Solvency analysis, therefore, focuses mainly on balance sheet relationships that indicate the ability to liquidate liabilities. Major analyses used in assessing solvency include (1) current position analysis, (2) accounts receivable analysis, (3) inventory analysis, (4) the ratio of plant assets to long-term liabilities, (5) the ratio of stockholders' equity to liabilities, and (6) the number of times interest charges are earned.

Current position analysis includes the assessment of working capital, the current ratio, and the acid-test ratio. Accounts receivable analysis includes the assessment of accounts receivable turnover and number of days' sales in receivables. Inventory analysis includes the assessment of inventory turnover and number of days' sales in inventory. The ratio of plant assets to long-term liabilities shows the margin of safety for the creditors. The ratio of stockholders' equity to liabilities indicates the margin of safety for the creditors and the ability of the enterprise to withstand adverse business conditions. The number of times interest charges are earned indicates the relative risk of the debtholders' continuing to receive interest payments.

5. Profitability Analysis.
Profitability is the ability of an entity to earn income. It can be assessed by computing various relevant measures, including (1) the ratio of net sales to assets, (2) the rate earned on total assets, (3) the rate earned on stockholders' equity, (4) the rate earned on common stockholders' equity, (5) the earnings per share on common stock, (6) the price-earnings ratio, and (7) the dividend yield.

6. Summary of Analytical Measures.
The type of business activity, the capital structure, and the size of the enterprise usually affect the measures used in financial statement analysis. These analytical measures, however, are not a substitute for sound judgment, nor do they provide definitive guides to action. In selecting and interpreting analytical indexes, proper consideration should be given to any conditions peculiar to the enterprise or to the industry of which the enterprise is a part.

7. Corporate Annual Reports.
Corporations ordinarily issue to their stockholders and other interested parties annual reports summarizing activities of the past year and any significant plans for the future. These reports normally include the financial highlights section, the president's letter, the independent auditors' report, the management report, and a historical summary of operations. Reporting of segments and supplementary data on the effects of price-level changes may also be included.

8. Interim Financial Reports.
Corporations customarily issue interim financial reports to their stockholders. Interim reports disclose such information as gross revenue, expenses, net income, and cash flows, following the accounting principles that are used on an annual basis.

KEY TERMS

solvency 1011
profitability 1011
horizontal analysis 1012
vertical analysis 1015
common-size statements 1017
working capital 1019
current ratio 1019
acid-test ratio 1020
quick assets 1020
accounts receivable turnover 1021
number of days' sales in receivables 1021
inventory turnover 1022
number of days' sales in inventory 1022
rate earned on total assets 1025
rate earned on stockholders' equity 1026
leverage 1026
rate earned on common stockholders' equity 1027
earnings per share on common stock 1028
price-earnings (P/E) ratio 1028
current cost 1037
constant dollar 1038
price-level index 1038

SELF-EXAMINATION QUESTIONS

(Answers at End of Chapter)

1. What type of analysis is indicated by the following?

	Amount	Percent
Current assets	$100,000	20%
Plant assets	400,000	80
Total assets	$500,000	100%

A. Vertical analysis
B. Horizontal analysis
C. Current position analysis
D. None of the above

2. Which of the following measures is useful as an indication of the ability of a firm to liquidate current liabilities?
A. Working capital
B. Current ratio
C. Acid-test ratio
D. All of the above

3. The ratio determined by dividing total current assets by total current liabilities is:
A. current ratio
B. working capital ratio
C. bankers' ratio
D. all of the above

4. The ratio of the quick assets to current liabilities, which indicates the "instant" debt-paying ability of a firm, is:
A. current ratio
B. working capital ratio
C. acid-test ratio
D. none of the above

5. A measure useful in evaluating the efficiency in the management of inventories is:
A. inventory turnover
B. number of days' sales in inventory
C. both A and B
D. none of the above

ILLUSTRATIVE PROBLEM

Fleming Inc.'s comparative financial statements for the years ended December 31, 1990 and 1989, are as follows. The market price of Fleming Inc.'s common stock was $30 on December 31, 1989, and $25 on December 31, 1990.

Fleming Inc.
Comparative Income Statement
For Years Ended December 31, 1990 and 1989

	1990	1989
Sales (all on account)	$5,125,000	$3,257,600
Sales returns and allowances	125,000	57,600
Net sales	$5,000,000	$3,200,000
Cost of goods sold	3,400,000	2,080,000
Gross profit	$1,600,000	$1,120,000
Selling expenses	$ 785,000	$ 499,000
General expenses	325,000	224,000
Total operating expenses	$1,110,000	$ 723,000

Operating income	$ 490,000	$ 397,000
Other income	25,000	19,200
	$ 515,000	$ 416,200
Other expense (interest)	105,000	64,000
Income before income tax	$ 410,000	$ 352,200
Income tax	165,000	141,000
Net income	$ 245,000	$ 211,200

Fleming Inc.
Comparative Retained Earnings Statement
For Years Ended December 31, 1990 and 1989

	1990	1989
Retained earnings, January 1	$ 723,000	$ 581,800
Add net income for year	245,000	211,200
Total	$ 968,000	$ 793,000
Deduct dividends:		
On preferred stock	$ 40,000	$ 40,000
On common stock	45,000	30,000
Total	$ 85,000	$ 70,000
Retained earnings, December 31	$ 883,000	$ 723,000

Fleming Inc.
Comparative Balance Sheet
December 31, 1990 and 1989

Assets	1990	1989
Current assets:		
Cash	$ 175,000	$ 125,000
Marketable securities	150,000	50,000
Accounts receivable (net)	425,000	325,000
Inventories	720,000	480,000
Prepaid expenses	30,000	20,000
Total current assets	$1,500,000	$1,000,000
Long-term investments	250,000	225,000
Plant assets (net)	2,093,000	1,948,000
Total assets	$3,843,000	$3,173,000
Liabilities		
Current liabilities	$ 750,000	$ 650,000
Long-term liabilities:		
Mortgage note payable, 10%, due 1995	$ 410,000	—
Bonds payable, 8%, due 1997	800,000	$ 800,000
Total long-term liabilities	$1,210,000	$ 800,000
Total liabilities	$1,960,000	$1,450,000
Stockholders' Equity		
Preferred 8% stock, $100 par	$ 500,000	$ 500,000
Common stock, $10 par	500,000	500,000
Retained earnings	883,000	723,000
Total stockholders' equity	$1,883,000	$1,723,000
Total liabilities and stockholders' equity	$3,843,000	$3,173,000

Instructions:

Determine the following measures for 1990:

(1) Working capital.
(2) Current ratio.
(3) Acid-test ratio.
(4) Accounts receivable turnover.
(5) Number of days' sales in receivables.
(6) Inventory turnover.
(7) Number of days' sales in inventory.
(8) Ratio of plant assets to long-term liabilities.
(9) Ratio of stockholders' equity to liabilities.
(10) Number of times interest charges earned.
(11) Number of times preferred dividends earned.
(12) Ratio of net sales to assets.
(13) Rate earned on total assets.
(14) Rate earned on stockholders' equity.
(15) Rate earned on common stockholders' equity.
(16) Earnings per share on common stock.
(17) Price-earnings ratio.
(18) Dividend yield.

SOLUTION

(1) Working capital: $750,000
$1,500,000 − $750,000

(2) Current ratio: 2.0:1
$1,500,000 ÷ $750,000

(3) Acid-test ratio: 1.0:1
$750,000 ÷ $750,000

(4) Accounts receivable turnover: 13.3

$$\$5{,}000{,}000 \div \frac{\$425{,}000 + \$325{,}000}{2}$$

(5) Number of days' sales in receivables: 31 days
$5,000,000 ÷ 365 = $13,699
$ 425,000 ÷ $13,699

(6) Inventory turnover: 5.7

$$\$3{,}400{,}000 \div \frac{\$720{,}000 + \$480{,}000}{2}$$

(7) Number of days' sales in inventory: 77.3 days
$3,400,000 ÷ 365 = $9,315
$ 720,000 ÷ $9,315

(8) Ratio of plant assets to long-term liabilities: 1.7:1
$2,093,000 ÷ $1,210,000

(9) Ratio of stockholders' equity to liabilities: 1.0:1
$1,883,000 ÷ $1,960,000

(10) Number of times interest charges earned: 4.9
($410,000 + $105,000) ÷ $105,000

(11) Number of times preferred dividends earned: 6.1
$245,000 ÷ $40,000

(12) Ratio of net sales to assets: 1.5:1

$$\$5{,}000{,}000 \div \frac{\$3{,}593{,}000 + \$2{,}948{,}000}{2}$$

(13) Rate earned on total assets: 10.0%

$$(\$245{,}000 + \$105{,}000) \div \frac{\$3{,}843{,}000 + \$3{,}173{,}000}{2}$$

(14) Rate earned on stockholders' equity: 13.6%

$$\$245{,}000 \div \frac{\$1{,}883{,}000 + \$1{,}723{,}000}{2}$$

(15) Rate earned on common stockholders' equity: 15.7%

$$(\$245{,}000 - \$40{,}000) \div \frac{\$1{,}383{,}000 + \$1{,}223{,}000}{2}$$

(16) Earnings per share on common stock: $4.10
($245,000 − $40,000) ÷ 50,000

(17) Price-earnings ratio: 6.1
$25 ÷ $4.10

(18) Dividend yield: 3.6%

$$\frac{(\$45{,}000 \div 50{,}000 \text{ shares})}{\$25}$$

Discussion Questions

28–1. In the analysis of the financial status of an enterprise, what is meant by *solvency* and *profitability*?

28–2. Using the following data taken from a comparative balance sheet, illustrate (a) horizontal analysis and (b) vertical analysis.

	Current Year	Preceding Year
Accounts payable	$ 600,000	$ 400,000
Total current liabilities	1,250,000	1,000,000

28–3. What is the advantage of using comparative statements for financial analysis rather than statements for a single date or period?

28–4. The current year's amount of net income (after income tax) is 20% larger than that of the preceding year. Does this indicate an improved operating performance? Discuss.

28–5. What are common-size financial statements?

28–6. (a) Name the major ratios useful in assessing solvency and profitability.
(b) Why is it important not to rely on only one ratio or measure in assessing the solvency or profitability of an enterprise?

28–7. Identify the measure of current position analysis described by each of the following: (a) the excess of current assets over current liabilities, (b) the ratio of current assets to current liabilities, (c) the ratio of quick assets to current liabilities.

28–8. Selected condensed data taken from the balance sheet of Young Corporation at June 30, the end of the current fiscal year, are as follows:

Cash, marketable securities, and receivables	$300,000
Other current assets	450,000
Total current assets	$750,000
Current liabilities	$250,000

At June 30, what are (a) the working capital, (b) the current ratio, and (c) the acid-test ratio?

28–9. For Stapp Company, the working capital at the end of the current year is $75,000 greater than the working capital at the end of the preceding year, reported as follows. Does this mean that the current position has improved? Explain.

	Current Year	Preceding Year
Current assets:		
Cash, marketable securities, and receivables	$360,000	$300,000
Inventories	540,000	325,000
Total current assets	$900,000	$625,000
Current liabilities	450,000	250,000
Working capital	$450,000	$375,000

28–10. A company that grants terms of n/30 on all sales has an accounts receivable turnover for the year, based on monthly averages, of 6. Is this a satisfactory turnover? Discuss.

28–11. What does an increase in the number of days' sales in receivables ordinarily indicate about the credit and collection policy of the firm?

28–12. (a) Why is it advantageous to have a high inventory turnover? (b) Is it possible for the inventory turnover to be too high? Discuss. (c) Is it possible to have a high inventory turnover and a high number of days' sales in inventory? Discuss.

28–13. What does the following data taken from a comparative balance sheet indicate about the company's current ability to borrow additional funds on a long-term basis as compared to the preceding year?

	Current Year	Preceding Year
Plant assets (net)	$1,800,000	$1,700,000
Long-term liabilities	600,000	850,000

28–14. What does an increase in the ratio of stockholders' equity to liabilities indicate about the margin of safety for the firm's creditors and the ability of the firm to withstand adverse business conditions?

28–15. In determining the number of times interest charges are earned, why are interest charges added to income before income tax?

28–16. In computing the ratio of net sales to assets, why are long-term investments excluded in determining the amount of the total assets?

28–17. In determining the rate earned on total assets, why is interest expense added to net income before dividing by total assets?

28–18. (a) Why is the rate earned on stockholders' equity by a thriving enterprise ordinarily higher than the rate earned on total assets?
(b) Should the rate earned on common stockholders' equity normally be higher or lower than the rate earned on total stockholders' equity? Explain.

28–19. The net income (after income tax) of Olson Company was $20 per common share in the latest year and $30 per common share for the preceding year. At the beginning of the latest year, the number of shares outstanding was doubled by a stock split. There were no other changes in the amount of stock outstanding. What were the earnings per share in the preceding year, adjusted to place them on a comparable basis with the latest year?

28–20. The price-earnings ratio for the common stock of Daytona Company was 12 at December 31, the end of the current fiscal year. What does the ratio indicate about the selling price of the common stock in relation to current earnings?

28–21. Why would the dividend yield differ significantly from the rate earned on common stockholders' equity?

28–22. Favorable business conditions may bring about certain seemingly unfavorable ratios, and unfavorable business operations may result in apparently favorable ratios. For example, Almond Company increased its sales and net income substantially for the current year, yet the current ratio at the end of the year is lower than at the beginning of the year. Discuss some possible causes of the apparent weakening of the current position while sales and net income have increased substantially.

28–23. (a) What are the major components of an annual report? (b) Indicate the purpose of the financial highlights section and the president's letter.

28–24. (a) The typical independent auditors' report expressing an unqualified opinion consists of three paragraphs. What is reported in each paragraph? (b) Under what conditions does an auditor give a qualified opinion?

28–25. Conventional financial statements do not give recognition to the instability of the purchasing power of the dollar. How can the effect of the fluctuating dollar on business operations be presented to the users of the financial statements?

28–26. What is the current cost of an asset?

28–27. If land was purchased for $80,000 when the general price-level index was 220, and the general price-level index has risen to 242, what is the constant dollar equivalent of the original cost of the land?

28–28. Real World Focus. Tandy Corporation's 1987 annual report indicates that the rate earned on total assets was 13.2% for the year ended June 30, 1987. For the same period, the rate earned on stockholders' equity was 18%. What is the explanation for the difference in the two rates?

Exercises

28–29. Vertical analysis of income statement. Revenue and expense data for P. A. Good Company are as follows:

	1990	1989
Sales	$900,000	$800,000
Cost of goods sold	531,000	464,000
Selling expenses	135,000	144,000
General expenses	63,000	64,000
Income tax	63,000	48,000

(a) Prepare an income statement in comparative form, stating each item for both 1990 and 1989 as a percent of sales.
(b) Comment on the significant changes disclosed by the comparative income statement.

28–30. Horizontal analysis of balance sheet. Balance sheet data for Dennis Company on December 31, the end of the fiscal year, are as follows:

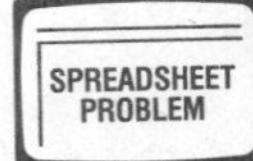

	1990	1989
Current assets	$451,000	$410,000
Plant assets	449,000	413,800
Intangible assets	50,000	56,200
Current liabilities	100,000	90,000
Long-term liabilities	250,000	275,000
Common stock	400,000	350,000
Retained earnings	200,000	165,000

Prepare a comparative balance sheet with horizontal analysis, indicating the increase (decrease) for 1990 when compared with 1989.

28–31. Current position analysis. The following data were abstracted from the balance sheet of Concepcion Company:

	Current Year	Preceding Year
Cash	$ 95,500	$112,500
Marketable securities	45,000	50,000
Accounts and notes receivable (net)	189,500	187,500
Inventories	279,500	189,000
Prepaid expenses	20,500	11,000
Accounts and notes payable (short-term)	275,000	222,500
Accrued liabilities	25,000	27,500

(a) Determine for each year (1) the working capital, (2) the current ratio, and (3) the acid-test ratio. (Present figures used in your computations.)
(b) What conclusions can be drawn from these data as to the company's ability to meet its currently maturing debts?

28–32. Accounts receivable analysis. The following data are taken from the financial statements for Shula Company:

	Current Year	Preceding Year
Accounts receivable, end of year	$ 662,100	$ 601,350
Monthly average accounts receivable (net)	627,000	550,100
Net sales on account	5,016,000	3,850,700

Terms of all sales are 1/10, n/60.

(a) Determine for each year (1) the accounts receivable turnover and (2) the number of days' sales in receivables.
(b) What conclusions can be drawn from these data concerning the composition of the accounts receivable?

28–33. Inventory analysis. The following data were abstracted from the income statement of McHale Corporation:

	Current Year	Preceding Year
Sales	$4,275,500	$4,160,000
Beginning inventories	648,000	558,000
Purchases	2,664,000	2,790,000
Ending inventories	672,000	648,000

(a) Determine for each year (1) the inventory turnover and (2) the number of days' sales in inventory.
(b) What conclusions can be drawn from these data concerning the composition of the inventories?

SPREADSHEET PROBLEM

28–34. Six measures of solvency or profitability. The following data were taken from the financial statements of John Britz and Co. for the current fiscal year:

Plant assets (net)			$1,250,000
Liabilities:			
Current liabilities			$ 400,000
Mortgage note payable, 10%, issued 1982, due 1992			500,000
Total liabilities			$ 900,000
Stockholders' equity:			
Preferred 8% stock, $100 par, cumulative, nonparticipating (no change during year)			$ 200,000
Common stock, $10 par (no change during year)			1,000,000
Retained earnings:			
Balance, beginning of year	$687,500		
Net income	193,500	$881,000	
Preferred dividends	$ 16,000		
Common dividends	65,000	81,000	
Balance, end of year			800,000
Total stockholders' equity			$2,000,000
Net sales			$3,975,000
Interest expense			50,000

Assuming that long-term investments totaled $150,000 throughout the year and that total assets were $2,700,000 at the beginning of the year, determine the following, presenting figures used in your computations: (a) ratio of plant assets to long-term liabilities, (b) ratio of stockholders' equity to liabilities, (c) ratio of net sales to assets, (d) rate earned on total assets, (e) rate earned on stockholders' equity, (f) rate earned on common stockholders' equity.

28–35. Five measures of solvency or profitability. The balance sheet for Culp Corporation at the end of the current fiscal year indicated the following:

Bonds payable, 12% (issued in 1975, due in 1995)	$2,000,000
Preferred 8% stock, $100 par	1,000,000
Common stock, $50 par	2,500,000

Income before income tax was $720,000, and income taxes were $320,000 for the current year. Cash dividends paid on common stock during the current year totaled $300,000. The common stock was selling for $64 per share at the end of the year. Determine each of the following: (a) number of times bond interest charges were earned, (b) number of times preferred dividends were earned, (c) earnings per share on common stock, (d) price-earnings ratio, and (e) dividend yield.

28–36. Earnings per share. The net income reported on the income statement of Burger and Co. was $2,900,000. There were 500,000 shares of $10 par common stock and 100,000 shares of $8 preferred stock outstanding throughout the current year. The income statement included two extraordinary items: a $900,000 gain from condemnation of land and a $300,000 loss arising from flood damage, both after applicable income tax. Determine the per share figures for common stock for (a) income before extraordinary items and (b) net income.

28–37. Effect of price-level change on investment in land. Several years ago, Manley Company purchased land as a future building site for $60,000. The price-level index at that time was 120. On October 11 of the current year, when the price-level index was 132, the land was sold for $71,500.

(a) Determine the amount of the gain that would be realized according to conventional accounting.
(b) Indicate the amount of the gain that may be (1) attributed to the change in purchasing power and (2) considered a true gain in terms of current dollars.

28–38. Real World Focus. The following comparative income statement (in thousands of dollars) for the years ending December 31, 1986 and 1985, was adapted from the 1986 annual report of William Wrigley Jr. Company:

	1986	1985
Revenues:		
Net sales	$698,982	$620,267
Investment income	6,980	6,787
Total revenues	$705,962	$627,054
Cost and expenses:		
Cost of sales	$318,280	$295,430
Selling, distribution, and general administrative	283,480	250,375
Interest	544	788
Total costs and expenses	$602,304	$546,593
Earnings before income taxes	$103,658	$ 80,461
Income taxes	49,840	36,963
Net earnings	$ 53,818	$ 43,498

(a) Prepare a comparative income statement for 1986 and 1985 in vertical form, stating each item as a percent of revenues. (b) Based upon (a), which 1986 income statement item(s) might warrant additional investigation?

Problems

28–39. Horizontal analysis for income statement. For 1990, Talman Company reported its most significant increase in net income in years. At the end of the year, Ann Talman, the president, is presented with the following condensed comparative income statement:

Talman Company
Comparative Income Statement
For Years Ended December 31, 1990 and 1989

	1990	1989
Sales	$909,000	$804,500
Sales returns and allowances	9,000	4,500
Net sales	$900,000	$800,000
Cost of goods sold	548,000	480,000
Gross profit	$352,000	$320,000
Selling expenses	$117,000	$144,000
General expenses	81,000	65,000
Total operating expenses	$198,000	$209,000
Operating income	$154,000	$111,000
Other income	2,000	1,000
Income before income tax	$156,000	$112,000
Income tax	58,000	42,000
Net income	$ 98,000	$ 70,000

Instructions: (1) Prepare a comparative income statement with horizontal analysis for the two-year period, using 1989 as the base year.
(2) To the extent the data permit, comment on the significant relationships revealed by the horizontal analysis prepared in (1).

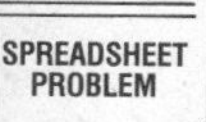

28–40. Vertical analysis for income statement. For 1990, Knight Company initiated an extensive sales promotion campaign that included the expenditure of an additional $75,000 for advertising. At the end of the year, John Knight, the president, is presented with the following condensed comparative income statement:

Knight Company
Comparative Income Statement
For Years Ended December 31, 1990 and 1989

	1990	1989
Sales	$841,500	$687,480
Sales returns and allowances	16,500	7,480
Net sales	$825,000	$680,000
Cost of goods sold	519,750	435,200
Gross profit	$305,250	$244,800
Selling expenses	$198,000	$102,000
General expenses	36,300	40,800
Total operating expenses	$234,300	$142,800
Operating income	$ 70,950	$102,000
Other expense	2,475	2,720
Income before income tax	$ 68,475	$ 99,280
Income tax	14,850	24,480
Net income	$ 53,625	$ 74,800

Instructions: (1) Prepare a comparative income statement for the two-year period, presenting an analysis of each item in relationship to net sales for each of the years.
(2) To the extent the data permit, comment on the significant relationships revealed by the vertical analysis prepared in (1).

28–41. Common-size income statement. Revenue and expense data for the current calendar year for Regal Publishing Company and for the publishing industry are as follows. The Regal Publishing Company data are expressed in dollars; the publishing industry averages are expressed in percentages.

	Regal Publishing Company	Publishing Industry Average
Sales	$8,080,000	100.6%
Sales returns and allowances	80,000	.6
Cost of goods sold	5,760,000	69.0
Selling expenses	656,000	9.0
General expenses	496,000	8.2
Other income	40,000	.6
Other expense	96,000	1.4
Income tax	384,000	5.0

Instructions: (1) Prepare a common-size income statement comparing the results of operations for Regal Publishing Company with the industry average.
(2) As far as the data permit, comment on significant relationships revealed by the comparisons.

28–42. Effect of transactions on current position analysis. Data pertaining to the current position of Mullins Company are as follows:

Cash	$ 90,000
Marketable securities	40,000
Accounts and notes receivable (net)	120,000
Inventories	225,000
Prepaid expenses	25,000
Accounts payable	140,000
Notes payable (short-term)	75,000
Accrued liabilities	35,000

Instructions: (1) Compute (a) the working capital, (b) the current ratio, and (c) the acid-test ratio.

(2) List the following captions on a sheet of paper:

Transaction	Working Capital	Current Ratio	Acid-Test Ratio

Compute the working capital, the current ratio, and the acid-test ratio after each of the following transactions, and record the results in the appropriate columns. Consider each transaction separately and assume that only that transaction affects the data given above.

(a) Declared a cash dividend, $50,000.
(b) Issued additional shares of stock for cash, $100,000.
(c) Purchased goods on account, $50,000.
(d) Paid accounts payable, $60,000.
(e) Borrowed cash from bank on a long-term note, $50,000.
(f) Paid cash for office supplies, $20,000.
(g) Received cash on account, $75,000.
(h) Paid notes payable, $75,000.
(i) Declared a common stock dividend on common stock, $100,000.
(j) Sold marketable securities, $40,000.

28–43. Effect of errors on current position analysis. Prior to approving an application for a short-term loan, Tolono National Bank required that Morgan Company provide evidence of working capital of at least $300,000, a current ratio of at least 1.5:1, and an acid-test ratio of at least 1.0:1. The chief accountant of Morgan Company compiled the following data pertaining to the current position:

Morgan Company
Schedule of Current Assets and Current Liabilities
December 31, 1989

Current assets:	
Cash	$ 54,750
Marketable securities	72,500
Accounts receivable	341,500
Notes receivable	125,000
Interest receivable	6,250
Inventories	188,250
Supplies	11,750
Total current assets	$800,000
Current liabilities:	
Accounts payable	$300,000
Notes payable	100,000
Total current liabilities	$400,000

Instructions: (1) Compute (a) the working capital, (b) the current ratio, and (c) the acid-test ratio.

(2) At the request of the bank, a firm of independent auditors was retained to examine data submitted with the loan application. This examination disclosed several errors. Prepare correcting entries for each of the following errors:

(a) A canceled check indicates that a bill for $28,750 for repairs on factory equipment had not been recorded in the accounts.
(b) Accounts receivable of $41,500 are uncollectible and should be immediately written off. In addition, it was estimated that of the remaining receivables, 5% would eventually become uncollectible. An allowance should be made for these future uncollectible accounts.
(c) Six months' interest had been accrued on the $125,000, 10%, six-month note receivable dated October 1, 1989.
(d) Supplies on hand at December 31, 1989, total $4,750.
(e) The marketable securities portfolio includes $50,000 of Dixon Company stock that is held as a long-term investment.
(f) The notes payable account consists of a 12%, 90-day note dated November 1, 1989. No interest had been accrued on the note.
(g) Accrued wages as of December 31, 1989, totaled $30,000.
(h) Rental Income had been credited upon receipt of $72,000, which was the full amount of a year's rent for warehouse space leased to C. A. Cox Inc., effective July 1, 1989.

(3) Giving effect to each of the preceding errors separately and assuming that only that error affects the current position of Morgan Company, compute (a) the working capital, (b) the current ratio, and (c) the acid-test ratio. Use the following column headings for recording your answers:

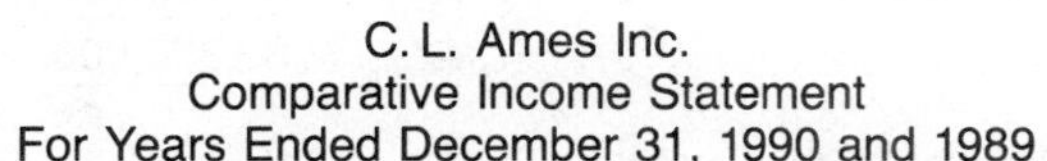

Error	Working Capital	Current Ratio	Acid-Test Ratio

(4) Prepare a revised schedule of working capital as of December 31, 1989, and recompute the current ratio and the acid-test ratio, giving effect to the corrections of all of the preceding errors.
(5) Discuss the action you would recommend that the bank take regarding the pending loan application.

28–44. Eighteen measures of solvency and profitability. The comparative financial statements of C. L. Ames Inc. are as follows. The market price of C. L. Ames Inc.'s common stock was $60.50 on December 31, 1989, and $51 on December 31, 1990.

C. L. Ames Inc.
Comparative Income Statement
For Years Ended December 31, 1990 and 1989

	1990	1989
Sales (all on account)	$9,396,750	$8,024,000
Sales returns and allowances	46,750	24,000
Net sales	$9,350,000	$8,000,000
Cost of goods sold	5,984,000	4,800,000
Gross profit	$3,366,000	$3,200,000
Selling expenses	$1,496,000	$1,232,000
General expenses	673,200	658,000
Total operating expenses	$2,169,200	$1,890,000
Operating income	$1,196,800	$1,310,000
Other income	149,600	136,000
	$1,346,400	$1,446,000
Other expense (interest)	240,000	210,000
Income before income tax	$1,106,400	$1,236,000
Income tax	506,400	596,000
Net income	$ 600,000	$ 640,000

C. L. Ames Inc.
Comparative Retained Earnings Statement
For Years Ended December 31, 1990 and 1989

	1990	1989
Retained earnings, January 1	$2,770,000	$2,420,000
Add net income for year	600,000	640,000
Total	$3,370,000	$3,060,000
Deduct dividends:		
On preferred stock	$ 90,000	$ 90,000
On common stock	210,000	200,000
Total	$ 300,000	$ 290,000
Retained earnings, December 31	$3,070,000	$2,770,000

C. L. Ames Inc.
Comparative Balance Sheet
December 31, 1990 and 1989

Assets	1990	1989
Current assets:		
Cash	$ 412,500	$ 363,000
Marketable securities	137,500	132,000
Accounts receivable (net)	550,000	495,000
Inventories	792,000	726,000
Prepaid expenses	88,000	44,000
Total current assets	$1,980,000	$1,760,000
Long-term investments	275,000	220,000
Plant assets (net)	5,665,000	5,280,000
Total assets	$7,920,000	$7,260,000
Liabilities		
Current liabilities	$1,100,000	$ 990,000
Long-term liabilities:		
Mortgage note payable, 12%, due 1997	$ 250,000	—
Bonds payable, 14%, due 2007	1,500,000	$1,500,000
Total long-term liabilities	$1,750,000	$1,500,000
Total liabilities	$2,850,000	$2,490,000
Stockholders' Equity		
Preferred 9% stock, $100 par	$1,000,000	$1,000,000
Common stock, $10 par	1,000,000	1,000,000
Retained earnings	3,070,000	2,770,000
Total stockholders' equity	$5,070,000	$4,770,000
Total liabilities and stockholders' equity	$7,920,000	$7,260,000

Instructions: Determine the following measures for 1990, presenting the figures used in your computations:

(1) Working capital.
(2) Current ratio.
(3) Acid-test ratio.
(4) Accounts receivable turnover.
(5) Number of days' sales in receivables.
(6) Inventory turnover.
(7) Number of days' sales in inventory.
(8) Ratio of plant assets to long-term liabilities.
(9) Ratio of stockholders' equity to liabilities.

(10) Number of times interest charges earned.
(11) Number of times preferred dividends earned.
(12) Ratio of net sales to assets.
(13) Rate earned on total assets.
(14) Rate earned on stockholders' equity.
(15) Rate earned on common stockholders' equity.
(16) Earnings per share on common stock.
(17) Price-earnings ratio.
(18) Dividend yield.

28–45. Report on detailed financial analysis. Ralph Lamor is considering making a substantial investment in C. L. Ames Inc. The company's comparative financial statements for 1990 and 1989 are given in Problem 28–44. To assist in the evaluation of the company, Lamor secured the following additional data taken from the balance sheet at December 31, 1988:

Accounts receivable (net)	$ 440,000
Inventories	674,000
Long-term investments	100,000
Total assets	6,700,000
Total stockholders' equity (preferred and common stock outstanding same as in 1989)	4,200,000

Instructions: Prepare a report for Lamor, based on an analysis of the financial data presented. In preparing your report, include all ratios and other data that will be useful in arriving at a decision regarding the investment.

ALTERNATE PROBLEMS

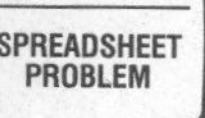

28–40A. Vertical analysis for income statement. For 1990, Paret Company initiated an extensive sales promotion campaign that included the expenditure of an additional $50,000 for advertising. At the end of the year, Ray Paret, the president, is presented with the following condensed comparative income statement:

Paret Company
Comparative Income Statement
For Years Ended December 31, 1990 and 1989

	1990	1989
Sales	$609,000	$361,800
Sales returns and allowances	9,000	1,800
Net sales	$600,000	$360,000
Cost of goods sold	372,000	216,000
Gross profit	$228,000	$144,000
Selling expenses	$108,000	$ 57,600
General expenses	24,000	16,200
Total operating expenses	$132,000	$ 73,800
Operating income	$ 96,000	$ 70,200
Other income	1,800	1,440
Income before income tax	$ 97,800	$ 71,640
Income tax	24,000	18,000
Net income	$ 73,800	$ 53,640

Instructions: (1) Prepare a comparative income statement for the two-year period, presenting an analysis of each item in relationship to net sales for each of the years.
(2) To the extent the data permit, comment on the significant relationships revealed by the vertical analysis prepared in (1).

28–42A. Effect of transactions on current position analysis. Data pertaining to the current position of D. Ellis Inc. are as follows:

Cash	$132,500
Marketable securities	50,000
Accounts and notes receivable (net)	297,500
Inventories	482,500
Prepaid expenses	37,500
Accounts payable	302,500
Notes payable (short-term)	75,000
Accrued liabilities	22,500

Instructions: (1) Compute (a) the working capital, (b) the current ratio, and (c) the acid-test ratio.
(2) List the following captions on a sheet of paper:

Transaction	Working Capital	Current Ratio	Acid-Test Ratio

Compute the working capital, the current ratio, and the acid-test ratio after each of the following transactions, and record the results in the appropriate columns. Consider each transaction separately and assume that only that transaction affects the data given above.

(a) Paid accounts payable, $100,000.
(b) Sold marketable securities, $50,000.
(c) Purchased goods on account, $80,000.
(d) Paid notes payable, $75,000.
(e) Declared a cash dividend, $50,000.
(f) Declared a common stock dividend on common stock, $72,500.
(g) Borrowed cash from bank on a long-term note, $200,000.
(h) Received cash on account, $150,000.
(i) Issued additional shares of stock for cash, $150,000.
(j) Paid cash for office supplies, $30,000.

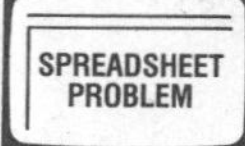

28–44A. Eighteen measures of solvency and profitability. The comparative financial statements of A. B. Peters Company are as follows. The market price of A. B. Peters Company's common stock was $64 on December 31, 1989, and $82 on December 31, 1990.

A. B. Peters Company
Comparative Income Statement
For Years Ended December 31, 1990 and 1989

	1990	1989
Sales (all on account)	$6,860,000	$4,880,000
Sales returns and allowances	110,000	80,000
Net sales	$6,750,000	$4,800,000
Cost of goods sold	4,590,000	3,120,000
Gross profit	$2,160,000	$1,680,000
Selling expenses	$ 877,500	$ 741,000
General expenses	438,750	336,000
Total operating expenses	$1,316,250	$1,077,000
Operating income	$ 843,750	$ 603,000
Other income	33,750	30,000
	$ 877,500	$ 633,000
Other expense (interest)	193,800	120,000
Income before income tax	$ 683,700	$ 513,000
Income tax	316,200	226,500
Net income	$ 367,500	$ 286,500

A. B. Peters Company
Comparative Retained Earnings Statement
For Years Ended December 31, 1990 and 1989

	1990	1989
Retained earnings, January 1	$1,084,500	$ 903,000
Add net income for year	367,500	286,500
Total	$1,452,000	$1,189,500
Deduct dividends:		
On preferred stock	$ 60,000	$ 60,000
On common stock	67,500	45,000
Total	$ 127,500	$ 105,000
Retained earnings, December 31	$1,324,500	$1,084,500

A. B. Peters Company
Comparative Balance Sheet
December 31, 1990 and 1989

Assets	1990	1989
Current assets:		
Cash	$ 337,500	$ 262,500
Marketable securities	150,000	—
Accounts receivable (net)	637,500	487,500
Inventories	1,080,000	720,000
Prepaid expenses	45,000	30,000
Total current assets	$2,250,000	$1,500,000
Long-term investments	375,000	337,500
Plant assets (net)	3,139,500	2,922,000
Total assets	$5,764,500	$4,759,500
Liabilities		
Current liabilities	$1,125,000	$ 975,000
Long-term liabilities:		
Mortgage note payable, 12%, due 1999	$ 615,000	—
Bonds payable, 10%, due 1997	1,200,000	$1,200,000
Total long-term liabilities	$1,815,000	$1,200,000
Total liabilities	$2,940,000	$2,175,000
Stockholders' Equity		
Preferred $8 stock, $100 par	$ 750,000	$ 750,000
Common stock, $25 par	750,000	750,000
Retained earnings	1,324,500	1,084,500
Total stockholders' equity	$2,824,500	$2,584,500
Total liabilities and stockholders' equity	$5,764,500	$4,759,500

Instructions: Determine the following measures for 1990, presenting the figures used in your computations:

(1) Working capital.
(2) Current ratio.
(3) Acid-test ratio.
(4) Accounts receivable turnover.
(5) Number of days' sales in receivables.
(6) Inventory turnover.
(7) Number of days' sales in inventory.

(continued)

(8) Ratio of plant assets to long-term liabilities.
(9) Ratio of stockholders' equity to liabilities.
(10) Number of times interest charges earned.
(11) Number of times preferred dividends earned.
(12) Ratio of net sales to assets.
(13) Rate earned on total assets.
(14) Rate earned on stockholders' equity.
(15) Rate earned on common stockholders' equity.
(16) Earnings per share on common stock.
(17) Price-earnings ratio.
(18) Dividend yield.

Mini-Case 28

You and your sister are both presidents of companies in the same industry, CDP Inc. and RST Inc., respectively. Both companies were originally operated as a single-family business; but, shortly after your father's death in 1975, the business was divided into two companies. Your sister took over CDP Inc., located in Indianapolis, while you took over RST Inc., located in Cincinnati.

During a recent family reunion, your sister referred to the much larger rate of return to her stockholders than was the case in your company and suggested that you consider rearranging the method of financing your corporation. The difference is highlighted by the following chart, which compares the rates earned on the stockholders' equity and the assets of the two companies:

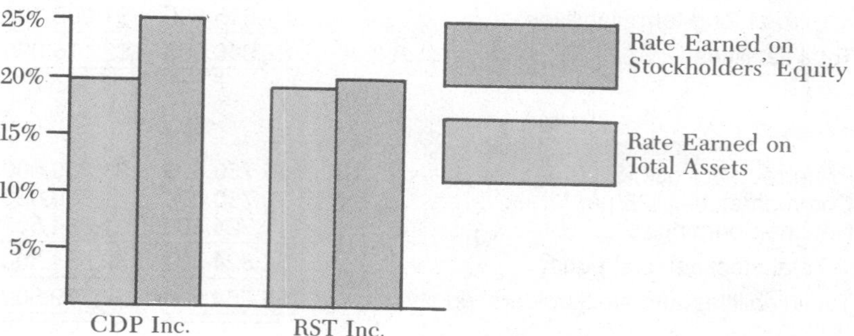

Since 1975, the growth in your sister's company has been financed largely through borrowing and yours largely through the issuance of additional common stock. Both companies have about the same volume of sales, gross profit, operating income, and total assets.

The income statements for the year ended December 31, 1990, and the balance sheets at December 31, 1990, for both companies are as follows:

Income Statements

	CDP Inc.	RST Inc.
Sales	$2,029,500	$1,952,500
Sales returns and allowances	29,500	22,500
Net sales	$2,000,000	$1,930,000
Cost of goods sold	1,225,000	1,179,000
Gross profit	$ 775,000	$ 751,000
Selling expenses	$ 335,000	$ 305,750
General expenses	195,000	175,250
Total operating expenses	$ 530,000	$ 481,000
Operating income	$ 245,000	$ 270,000
Interest expense	31,000	10,500
Income before income tax	$ 214,000	$ 259,500
Income tax	86,000	103,500
Net income	$ 128,000	$ 156,000

Balance Sheets

Assets	CDP Inc.	RST Inc.
Current assets	$ 62,500	$ 65,000
Plant assets (net)	775,000	810,000
Intangible assets	12,500	25,000
Total assets	$ 850,000	$ 900,000
Liabilities		
Current liabilities	$ 25,000	$ 40,000
Long-term liabilities	310,000	100,000
Total liabilities	$ 335,000	$ 140,000
Stockholders' Equity		
Common stock ($10 par)	$ 100,000	$ 400,000
Retained earnings	415,000	360,000
Total stockholders' equity	$ 515,000	$ 760,000
Total liabilities and stockholders' equity	$ 850,000	$ 900,000

In addition to the 1990 financial statements, the following data were taken from the balance sheet at December 31, 1989:

	CDP Inc.	RST Inc.
Total assets	$ 800,000	$ 860,000
Total stockholders' equity	495,000	740,000

Instructions:

(1) Determine for 1990 the following ratios and other measures for both companies.
  (a) Ratio of plant assets to long-term liabilities.
  (b) Ratio of stockholders' equity to liabilities.
  (c) Ratio of net sales to assets.
  (d) Rate earned on total assets.
  (e) Rate earned on stockholders' equity.

(2) For both CDP Inc. and RST Inc., the rate earned on stockholders' equity is greater than the rate earned on total assets. Explain.

(3) Why is the rate of return on stockholders' equity for CDP Inc. approximately 20% greater than for RST Inc.?

(4) Comment on your sister's suggestion for rearranging the financing of RST Inc.

Answers to Self-Examination Questions

1. A Percentage analysis indicating the relationship of the component parts to the total in a financial statement, such as the relationship of current assets to total assets (20% to 100%) in the question, is called vertical analysis (answer A). Percentage analysis of increases and decreases in corresponding items in comparative financial statements is called horizontal analysis (answer B). An example of horizontal analysis would be the presentation of the amount of current assets in the preceding balance sheet along with the amount of current assets at the end of the current year, with the increase or decrease in current assets between the periods expressed as a percentage. Current position analysis (answer C), relates to analysis of various current asset and current liability items.

2. D Various solvency measures, categorized as current position analysis, indicate a firm's ability to meet currently maturing obligations. Each measure contributes in the analysis of a firm's current position and is most useful when viewed with other measures and when compared with similar measures for other periods and for other firms. Working capital (answer A) is the excess of current assets over current liabilities; the current ratio (answer B) is the ratio of current assets to current liabilities; and the acid-test ratio (answer C) is the ratio of the sum of cash, receivables, and marketable securities to current liabilities.

3. D The ratio of current assets to current liabilities is usually referred to as the current ratio (answer A) and is sometimes referred to as the working capital ratio (answer B) or bankers' ratio (answer C).

4. C The ratio of the sum of cash, receivables, and marketable securities (sometimes called quick assets) to current liabilities is called the acid-test ratio (answer C) or quick ratio. The current ratio (answer A) and working capital ratio (answer B) are two terms that describe the ratio of current assets to current liabilities.

5. C As with many attempts at analyzing financial data, it is possible to determine more than one measure that is useful for evaluating the efficiency in the management of inventories. Both the inventory turnover (answer A), which is determined by dividing the cost of goods sold by the average inventory, and the number of days' sales in inventory (answer B), which is determined by dividing the inventories at the end of the year by the average daily cost of goods sold, express the relationship between the cost of goods sold and inventory.

Appendixes

Appendix A
Glossary

A

Absorption costing. The concept that considers the cost of manufactured products to be composed of direct materials, direct labor, and factory overhead.

Accelerated depreciation method. A depreciation method that provides for a high depreciation charge in the first year of use of an asset and gradually declining periodic charges thereafter.

Account. The form used to record additions and deductions for each individual asset, liability, owner's equity, revenue, and expense.

Account form of balance sheet. A balance sheet with assets on the left-hand side and liabilities and owner's equity on the right-hand side.

Accounting. The process of identifying, measuring, and communicating economic information to permit informed judgments and decisions by users of the information.

Accounting equation. The expression of the relationship between assets, liabilities, and owner's equity; most commonly stated as Assets=Liabilities+Owner's Equity.

Accounting system. The system that provides the information for use in conducting the affairs of the business and reporting to owners, creditors, and other interested parties.

Account payable. A liability created by a purchase made on credit.

Account receivable. A claim against a customer for sales made on credit.

Accounts payable ledger. The subsidiary ledger containing the individual accounts with suppliers (creditors).

Accounts receivable ledger. The subsidiary ledger containing the individual accounts with customers (debtors).

Accounts receivable turnover. The relationship between credit sales and accounts receivable, computed by dividing net sales on account by the average net accounts receivable.

Accrual. An expense or a revenue that gradually increases with the passage of time.

Accrual basis. Revenues are recognized in the period earned and expenses are recognized in the period incurred in the process of generating revenues.

Accrued asset (accrued revenue) or accrued liability (accrued expense). An asset (revenue) or a liability (expense) that gradually increases with the passage of time and that is recorded at the end of the accounting period by an adjusting entry.

Accumulated depreciation account. The contra asset account used to accumulate the depreciation recognized to date on plant assets.

Acid-test ratio. The ratio of the sum of cash, receivables, and marketable securities to current liabilities.

Adjusting entry. An entry required at the end of an accounting period to record an internal transaction and to bring the ledger up to date.

Aging the receivables. The process of analyzing the accounts receivable and classifying them according to various age groupings, with the due date being the base point for determining age.

Allowance method. The method of accounting for uncollectible receivables, by which advance provision for the uncollectibles is made.

Amortization. The periodic expense attributed to the decline in usefulness of an intangible asset or the allocation of bond premium or discount over the life of a bond issue.

Annuity. A series of equal cash flows at fixed intervals.

Appropriation. A designated use of revenues for which a potential liability is recognized by nonprofit organizations.

Appropriation of retained earnings. The amount of a corporation's retained earnings that has been restricted and therefore is not available for distribution to shareholders as dividends.

Articles of partnership. The formal written contract creating a partnership.

Asset. Property owned by a business enterprise.

Average cost method. The method of costing inventory in a merchandising enterprise that is based on the assumption that costs should be charged against revenue in accordance with the weighted average unit costs of the commodities sold. A method of determining manufactured product costs in which all costs incurred in manufacturing the goods completed during a period are averaged, and this average is used in determining the unit product cost of the goods completed during the period and the work in process at the end of the period.

Average rate of return. A method of evaluating capital investment proposals that focuses on the expected profitability of the investment.

B

Balance sheet. A financial statement listing the assets, liabilities, and owner's equity of a business entity as of a specific date.

Bank reconciliation. The method of analysis that details the items that are responsible for the difference between the cash balance reported in the bank statement and the balance of the cash account in the ledger.

Bond. A form of interest-bearing note employed by corporations to borrow on a long-term basis.

Bond indenture. The contract between a corporation issuing bonds and the bondholders.

Book value of an asset. The cost of an asset less the balance of any related contra asset account.

Boot. The balance owed the supplier when an old asset is traded for a new asset.

Break-even point. The point in the operations of an enterprise at which revenues and expired costs are equal.

Budget. A formal written statement of management's plans for the future, expressed in financial terms.

Budget performance report. A report comparing actual results with budget figures.

Business entity concept. The concept that assumes that accounting applies to individual economic units and that each unit is separate and distinct from the persons who supply its assets.

Business transaction. The occurrence of an event or of a condition that must be recorded in the accounting records.

By-product. A product resulting from a manufacturing process and having little value in relation to the principal product or joint products.

C

Capital expenditure. A cost that adds to the utility of an asset for more than one accounting period.

Capital expenditures budget. The budget summarizing future plans for acquisition of plant facilities and equipment.

Capital investment analysis. The process by which management plans, evaluates, and controls long-term capital investments involving property, plant, and equipment.

Capital lease. A lease which includes one or more of four provisions that result in treating the leased asset as a purchased asset in the accounts.

Capital stock. Shares of ownership of a corporation.

Capital rationing. The process by which management allocates available investment funds among competing capital investment proposals.

Carrying amount. The amount at which a temporary or a long-term investment or a long-term liability is reported on the balance sheet; also called basis or book value.

Cash basis. Revenue is recognized in the period cash is received, and expenses are recognized in period cash is paid.

Cash discount. The deduction allowable if an invoice is paid by a specified date.

Cash dividend. A cash distribution of earnings by a corporation to its shareholders.

Cash flows from financing activities. The section of the statement of cash flows in which is reported the transactions involving cash receipts from the issuance of equity and debt securities; and cash payments for dividends, repurchase of equity securities, and redemption of debt securities.

Cash flows from investing activities. The section of the statement of cash flows in which is reported the activities involving cash receipts from the sale of investments, plant assets, and other noncurrent assets; and cash payments for the acquisition of investments, plant assets, and other noncurrent assets.

Cash flows from operating activities. The section of the statement of cash flows in which is reported the cash transactions that entered into the determination of net income.

Cash payback period. The expected period of time that will elapse between the date of a capital investment and the complete recovery in cash (or equivalent) of the amount invested.

Cash payments journal. The journal in which all cash payments are recorded.

Cash receipts journal. The journal in which all cash receipts are recorded.

Chart of accounts. A listing of all the accounts used by a business enterprise.

Closing entry. An entry necessary to eliminate the balance of a temporary account in preparation for the following accounting period.

Combined line-program budget. A budget in which the items of expenditure are presented by the object of the expenditure and the program associated with the expenditure.

Common-size statement. A financial statement in which all items are expressed only in relative terms.

Common stock. The basic ownership class of corporate capital stock.

Completed-contract method. The method that recognizes revenue from long-term construction contracts when the project is completed.

Composite-rate depreciation method. A method of depreciation based on the use of a single rate that applies to entire groups of assets.

Consistency. The concept that assumes that the same generally accepted accounting principles have been applied in the preparation of successive financial statements.

Consolidated statement. A financial statement resulting from combining parent and subsidiary company statements.

Consolidation. The creation of a new corporation by the transfer of assets and liabilities from two or more existing corporations.

Constant dollar. Historical costs that have been converted into dollars of constant value through the use of a price-level index.

Contingent liability. A potential obligation that will materialize only if certain events occur in the future.

Continuous budgeting. A method of budgeting that provides for maintenance of a twelve-month projection into the future.

Contra account. An account that is offset against another account.

Contract rate of interest. The interest rate specified on a bond.

Contribution margin. Sales less variable cost of goods sold and variable selling and general expenses.

Contribution margin analysis. The systematic examination of the differences between planned and actual contribution margins.

Contribution margin ratio. The percentage of each sales dollar that is available to cover the fixed expenses and provide an operating income. Sometimes called the profit-volume ratio.

Controllable cost. For a specific level of management, a cost that can be directly controlled.

Controller. The chief managerial accountant of an organization.

Controlling. The process by which managers attempt to achieve the goals identified in an enterprise's strategic and operational plans.

Controlling account. The account in the general ledger that summarizes the balances of a subsidiary ledger.

Conversion costs. The combination of direct labor and factory overhead costs.

Corporation. A separate legal entity that is organized in accordance with state or federal statutes and in which ownership is divided into shares of stock.

Cost accounting system. An accounting system which uses the perpetual system of inventory accounting for the three manufacturing inventories: direct materials, work in process, and finished goods.

Cost behavior. The manner in which a cost changes in relation to its activity base.

Cost center. A decentralized unit in which the responsibility for control of costs incurred and the authority to make decisions that affect these costs is the responsibility of the unit's manager.

Cost driver. An activity measure used to allocate overhead cost.

Cost estimation. The method or methods used to estimate costs for use in managerial decision making.

Cost ledger. A subsidiary ledger employed in a job order cost system and which contains an account for each job order.

Cost method. A method of accounting for an investment in stock, by which the investor recognizes as income its share of cash dividends of the investee.

Cost of goods sold. The cost of a product (direct materials, direct labor, and factory overhead costs) that has been sold during a period by a manufacturing enterprise.

Cost of merchandise sold. The cost of the merchandise purchased and sold.

Cost of production report. A report prepared periodically by a processing department, summarizing (1) the units for which the department is accountable and the disposition of these units and (2) the costs charged to the department and the allocation of these costs.

Cost price approach. An approach to transfer pricing that uses cost as the basis for setting the transfer price.

Cost principle. The principle that assumes that the monetary record for properties and services purchased by a business should be maintained in terms of cost.

Costs. The disbursement of cash (or the commitment to pay cash in the future) for the purpose of generating revenues.

Cost-volume-profit analysis. The systematic examination of the interrelationships between selling prices, volume of sales and production, costs, expenses, and profits.

Cost-volume-profit chart. A chart used to assist management in understanding the relationships between costs, expenses, sales, and operating profit or loss. Sometimes referred to as a break-even chart.

Credit. (1) The right side of an account; (2) the amount entered on the right side of an account; (3) to enter an amount on the right side of an account.

Credit memorandum. The form issued by a seller to inform a debtor that a credit has been posted to the debtor's account receivable.

Cumulative preferred stock. Preferred stock that is entitled to current and past dividends before dividends may be paid on common stock.

Current asset. Cash or another asset that may reasonably be expected to be realized in cash or sold or consumed, usually within a year or less, through the normal operations of a business.

Current cost. The amount of cash that would have to be paid currently to acquire assets of the same age and in the same condition as existing assets.

Current liability. A liability that will be due within a short time (usually one year or less) and that is to be paid out of current assets.

Current ratio. The ratio of current assets to current liabilities.

Currently attainable standards. Standards which represent levels of operation that can be attained with reasonable effort.

D

Data base. The entire amount of data needed by an enterprise.

Debit. (1) The left side of an account; (2) the amount entered on the left side of an account; (3) to enter an amount on the left side of an account.

Debit memorandum. The form issued by a buyer to inform a creditor that a debit has been posted to the creditor's account payable.

Debt security. A bond or a note payable.

Decentralization. The separation of a business into more manageable units.

Decision making. The process by which managers determine to follow one course of action as opposed to an alternative.

Decision tree. A graphical representation of decisions, possible outcomes, and chances that outcomes will occur.

Declining-balance depreciation method. A method of depreciation that provides declining periodic depreciation charges to expense over the estimated life of an asset.

Deferral. A postponement of the recognition of an expense already paid or a revenue already received.

Deficit. A debit balance in the retained earnings account.

Departmental margin. Departmental gross profit less direct departmental expenses.

Depletion. The cost of metal ores and other minerals removed from the earth.

Depreciation. The decrease in usefulness of all plant assets except land.

Differential analysis. The area of accounting concerned with the effect of alternative courses of action on revenues and costs.

Differential cost. The amount of increase or decrease in cost that is expected from a particular course of action as compared with an alternative. Sometimes referred to as incremental cost.

Differential revenue. The amount of increase or decrease in revenue expected from a particular course of action as compared with an alternative.

Direct cost. A cost that can be traced directly to a unit within an enterprise or organization.

Direct expense. An expense directly traceable to or incurred for the sole benefit of a specific department and ordinarily subject to the control of the department manager.

Directing. The process by which managers, given their assigned level of responsibilities, run day-to-day operations.

Direct labor cost. The cost of wages paid to employees directly involved in changing direct materials into finished products.

Direct labor rate variance. The cost associated with the difference between the actual rate paid for direct labor used in producing a commodity and the standard rate for the commodity.

Direct labor time variance. The cost associated with the difference between the actual direct labor hours spent producing a commodity and the standard hours for the commodity.

Direct materials cost. The cost of materials entering directly into the manufactured product. Sometimes referred to as raw materials costs.

Direct materials inventory. The cost of direct materials which have not yet entered into the manufacturing process.

Direct materials price variance. The cost associated with the difference between the actual price of direct materials used in producing a commodity and the standard price for the commodity.

Direct materials quantity variance. The cost associated with the difference between the actual quantity of direct materials used in producing a commodity and the standard quantity for the commodity.

Direct method. A method of reporting the cash flows from operating activities as the difference between the operating cash receipts and the operating cash payments.

Direct write-off method. A method of accounting for uncollectible receivables, whereby an expense is recognized only when specific accounts are judged to be uncollectible.

Discontinued operations. The operations of a business segment that has been disposed of.

Discount. (a) The interest deducted from the maturity value of a note; (b) excess of par value of stock over its sales price; (c) excess of the face amount of bonds over their issue price.

Discount rate. The rate used in computing the interest to be deducted from the maturity value of a note.

Discounted cash flow method. A method of analysis of proposed capital investments that focuses on the present value of the cash flows expected from the investment.

Discounted internal rate of return method. A method of analysis of proposed capital investments that focuses on using present value concepts to compute the rate of return from the net cash flows expected from the investment.

Dishonored note receivable. A note which the maker fails to pay on the due date.

Discretionary cost. A cost that is not essential to short-term operations.

Dividend. A distribution of earnings of a corporation to its owners (stockholders).

Double-entry accounting. A system for recording transactions based on recording increases and decreases in accounts so that debits always equal credits.

E

Earnings per share (EPS) on common stock. The profitability ratio of net income available to common shareholders to the number of common shares outstanding.

Economic order quantity (EOQ). The optimum quantity of specified inventoriable materials to be ordered at one time.

Economies of scale. An economic concept that recognizes that over a wide range of production, costs vary in differing proportions to changes in an activity base. When production facilities are limited, costs tend to increase but at a decreasing rate as production increases from a relatively low level.

Effective rate of interest. The market rate of interest at the time bonds are issued.

Elastic demand. An economic concept in which a price increase or decrease for a product will have a significant effect on the number of units of the product sold.

Elasticity of demand. The degree to which the number of units sold changes because of a change in product price.

Electronic funds transfer (EFT). A payment system that uses computerized electronic impulses rather than paper (money, checks, etc.) to effect a cash transaction.

Employee's earnings record. A detailed record of each employee's earnings.

Encumbrance. A commitment by a nonprofit organization to incur expenditures in the future.

Engineering method. A cost estimation method in which engineers estimate total cost, as well as variable and fixed components, based on studies of such factors as production methods, materials and labor requirements, equipment needs, and utility demands.

Equity. The right or claim to the properties of a business enterprise.

Equity method. A method of accounting for investments in common stock, by which the investment account is adjusted for the investor's share of periodic net income and property dividends of the investee.

Equity per share. The ratio of stockholders' equity to the related number of shares of stock outstanding.

Equity security. Preferred or common stock.

Equivalent units of production. The number of units that could have been manufactured from start to finish during a period.

Exchange rate. The rate at which one unit of currency can be converted into another currency.

Expected value. A concept useful for managers in decision making which involves identifying the possible outcomes from a decision and estimating the likelihood that each outcome will occur.

Expense. The amount of assets consumed or services used in the process of earning revenue.

Extraordinary item. An event or transaction that is unusual and infrequent.

F

Factory overhead controllable variance. The difference between the actual amount of factory overhead cost incurred and the amount of factory overhead budgeted for the level of operations achieved.

Factory overhead cost. Costs other than direct materials cost and direct labor cost incurred in the manufacturing process. Sometimes referred to as manufacturing overhead or factory burden.

Factory overhead volume variance. The cost or benefit associated with operating at a level above or below 100% of productive capacity.

FICA tax. Federal Insurance Contributions Act tax used to finance federal programs for old-age and disability benefits and health insurance for the aged.

Financial accounting. The branch of accounting that is concerned with the recording of transactions using generally accepted accounting principles (GAAP) for a business enterprise or other economic unit and with a periodic preparation of various statements from such records.

Financial Accounting Standards Board (FASB). The current authoritative body for the development of accounting principles for all entities except state and municipal governments.

Finished goods inventory. The cost of finished products on hand that have not been sold.

Finished goods ledger. The subsidiary ledger that contains the individual accounts for each kind of commodity produced.

First-in, first-out method. A method of inventory costing based on the assumption that the costs of merchandise sold should be charged against revenue in the order in which the costs were incurred. Also, a method of determining costs of goods manufactured in which the beginning work in process inventory costs are kept separate from the costs incurred during the period and these costs are assigned to the goods manufactured in the order incurred.

Fiscal year. The annual accounting period adopted by an enterprise.

Fixed cost. A cost that remains constant in total dollar amount as the level of activity changes.

Flexible budgets. A series of budgets for varying rates of activity.

FOB destination. Terms of agreement between buyer and seller, whereby ownership passes when merchandise is received by the buyer, and the seller absorbs the transportation costs.

FOB shipping point. Terms of agreement between buyer and seller, whereby ownership passes when merchandise is delivered to the shipper, and the buyer absorbs the transportation costs.

Fund. A term with multiple meanings, including (1) segregations of cash for a special purpose, (2) in accounting for nonprofit organizations, an accounting entity with accounts maintained for recording assets, liabilities, fund equity, revenues, and expenditures for a particular purpose.

Funded. An appropriation of retained earnings accompanied by a segregation of cash or marketable securities.

Fund equity. The excess of assets over liabilities in a nonprofit organization.

Future value. The amount that will accumulate at some future date as a result of an investment or a series of investments.

G

General accounting system. An accounting system which extends the periodic system of inventory accounting used by merchandising enterprises to the three manufacturing inventories: direct materials, work in process, and finished goods.

General expense. Expense incurred in the general operation of a business.

General journal. The two-column form used to record journal entries that do not "fit" in any special journals.

General ledger. The principal ledger, when used in conjunction with subsidiary ledgers, that contains all of the balance sheet and income statement accounts.

Generally accepted accounting principles (GAAP). Generally accepted guidelines for the preparation of financial statements.

Going concern concept. The concept that assumes that a business entity has a reasonable expectation of continuing in business at a profit for an indefinite period of time.

Goodwill. An intangible asset that attaches to a business as a result of such favorable factors as location, product superiority, reputation, and managerial skill.

Governmental Accounting Standards Board (GASB). The current authoritative body for the development of accounting principles for state and municipal governments.

Gross pay. The total earnings of an employee for a payroll period.

Gross profit. The excess of net revenue from sales over the cost of merchandise sold.

Gross profit analysis. The procedure used to develop information concerning the effect of changes in quantities and unit prices on sales and cost of goods sold.

Gross profit method. A means of estimating inventory on hand without the need for a physical count.

H

High-low method. A method used to estimate total cost, as well as variable and fixed components, by using the highest and lowest total costs revealed by past cost patterns.

Horizontal analysis. The percentage analysis of increases and decreases in corresponding items in comparative financial statements.

I

Income from operations. The excess of gross profit over total operating expenses.

Income statement. A summary of the revenues and expenses of a business entity for a specific period of time.

Income summary account. The account used in the closing process for summarizing the revenue and expense accounts.

Indirect cost. A cost that for a specific unit within an enterprise or organization cannot be traced directly to that unit.

Indirect expense. An expense that is incurred for an entire business enterprise as a unit and that is not subject to the control of individual department managers.

Indirect method. A method of reporting the cash flows from operating activities as the net income from operations adjusted for all deferrals of past cash receipts and payments and all accruals of expected future cash receipts and payments.

Inelastic demand. An economic concept in which a price increase or decrease for a product will have little or no effect on the number of units of the product sold.

Inflation. A period when prices in general are rising and the purchasing power of money is declining.

Installment method. The method of recognizing revenue, whereby each receipt of cash from installment sales is considered to be composed of partial payment of cost of merchandise sold and gross profit.

Intangible asset. A long-lived asset that is useful in the operations of an enterprise, is not held for sale, and is without physical qualities.

Internal controls. The policies and procedures established by an enterprise to provide reasonable assurance that the enterprise's goals will be achieved.

Inventory order point. The level to which inventory is allowed to fall before an order for additional inventory is placed.

Inventory turnover. The relationship between the volume of goods sold and inventory, computed by dividing the cost of goods sold by the average inventory.

Investment center. A decentralized unit in which the manager has the responsibility and authority to make decisions that affect not only cost and revenues, but also the plant assets available to the center.

Investment turnover. A component of the rate of return on investment, computed as the ratio of sales to invested assets.

Invoice. The bill provided by the seller (who refers to it as a sales invoice) to a buyer (who refers to it as a purchase invoice) for items purchased.

J

Job cost sheet. An account in the cost ledger in which the costs charged to a particular job order are recorded.

Job order cost system. A type of cost accounting system that provides for a separate record of the cost of each particular quantity of product that passes through the factory.

Joint costs. The costs common to the manufacture of two or more products (joint products).

Joint products. Two or more commodities of significant value produced from a single principal direct material.

Journal. The initial record in which the effects of a transaction on accounts are recorded.

Judgmental method. A cost estimation method in which managers estimate total cost, as well as variable and fixed components, using experience and past observations of cost-volume-relationships.

Just-in-time inventory system. A system whose goal is to reduce inventories to the lowest possible point. Sometimes referred to as a kanban system.

Just-in-time manufacturing system. A system of manufacturing in which a primary emphasis is on the reduction of work in process inventories by combining processing functions and organizing mini-production lines.

L

Last-in, first-out (lifo) method. A method of inventory costing based on the assumption that the most recent merchandise costs incurred should be charged against revenue.

Lead time. The time, usually expressed in days, that it takes to receive an order for inventory.

Learning effect (learning curve). The effect on costs determined by how rapidly new employees learn their jobs or by how rapidly experienced employees learn new job assignments.

Least squares method. A cost estimation method that uses statistics to estimate total cost and the fixed and variable cost components.

Ledger. The group of accounts used by an enterprise.

Leverage. The tendency of the rate earned on stockholders' equity to vary from the rate earned on total assets because the amount earned on assets acquired through the use of funds provided by creditors varies from the interest paid to these creditors.

Liability. A debt of a business enterprise.

Linear programming. A quantitative method that can be used in providing data for solving a variety of business problems in which management's objective is to minimize cost or maximize profits, subject to several limiting factors.

Line budget. A budget in which the items of expenditure are presented by the object of the expenditure. Sometimes referred to as a functional budget.

Liquidating dividend. A distribution out of paid-in capital when a corporation permanently reduces its operations or winds up its affairs completely.

Liquidation. The winding-up process when a partnership goes out of business.

Long-term investment. An investment that is not intended to be a ready source of cash in the normal operations of a business and that is listed in the "investments" section of the balance sheet.

Long-term liability. A liability that is not due for a comparatively long time (usually more than one year).

Lower of cost or market. A method of costing inventory or valuing temporary investments that carries those assets at the lower of their cost or current market prices.

M

Management. Individuals who are charged with the responsibility of directing the operations of enterprises.

Management by exception. The philosophy of managing which involves monitoring the operating results of implemented plans and comparing the expected results with the actual results. This feedback allows management to isolate significant variations for further investigation and possible remedial action.

Management process. The four basic functions of (1) planning, (2) organizing and directing, (3) controlling, and (4) decision making used in managing an organization.

Managerial accounting. The area of accounting that provides relevant information to management for use in planning, organizing and directing, controlling, and decision making.

Manufacturing margin. Sales less variable cost of goods sold.

Marginal cost. The increase in total cost of producing and selling an additional unit of product.

Marginal revenue. The increase in total revenue realized from the sale of an additional unit of product.

Margin of safety. The difference between current sales revenue and the sales at the break-even point.

Market price approach. An approach to transfer pricing that uses the price at which the product or service transferred could be sold to outside buyers as the transfer price.

Marketable security. An investment in a security that can be readily sold when cash is needed.

Markup. An amount which is added to a "cost" amount to determine product price.

Market (sales) value method. A method of allocating joint costs among products according to their relative sales values.

Master budget. The comprehensive budget plan encompassing all the individual budgets related to sales, cost of goods sold, operating expenses, capital expenditures, and cash.

Matching. The principle of accounting that all revenues should be matched with the expenses incurred in earning those revenues during a period of time.

Materiality. The concept that recognizes the practicality of ignoring small or insignificant deviations from generally accepted accounting principles.

Materials. Goods in the state in which they were acquired for use in manufacturing operations.

Materials ledger. The subsidiary ledger containing the individual accounts for each type of material.

Materials requirements planning (MRP). A system which uses computers to project materials requirements by developing purchasing schedules and manufacturing schedules based on projected demand. Sometimes termed materials resource planning.

Materials requisition. The form used by the appropriate manufacturing department to authorize the issuance of materials from the storeroom.

Maturity value. The amount due at the maturity or due date of a note.

Maximax concept. A concept useful for managerial decision making, which leads management to decide in favor of that alternative with the maximum (largest) profit.

Maximin concept. A concept useful for managerial decision making, which leads management to decide in favor of that alternative with the maximum (largest) minimum profit.

Merchandise inventory. Merchandise on hand and available for sale.

Merger. The fusion of two corporations by the acquisition of the properties of one corporation by another, with the dissolution of one of the corporations.

Minority interest. The portion of a subsidiary corporation's capital stock that is not owned by the parent corporation.

Mixed cost. A cost with both variable and fixed characteristics, sometimes referred to as semivariable or semifixed cost.

Modified Accelerated Cost Recovery System (MACRS). The system described in the Internal Revenue Code for determining depreciation (cost recovery) of plant asset acquisitions.

Monopolistic competitive market. A market in which there exists many sellers of similar products with no one seller having a large enough share of the market to influence the total sales of the other products.

Monopoly market. A market in which no directly competing products exist.

Multiple-step income statement. An income statement with numerous sections and subsections with several intermediate balances before net income.

N

Natural business year. A year that ends when a business's activities have reached the lowest point in its annual operating cycle.

Negotiated price approach. An approach to transfer pricing that allows the managers of decentralized units to agree (negotiate) among themselves as to the proper transfer price.

Net income. The final figure in the income statement when revenues exceed expenses.

Net loss. The final figure in the income statement when expenses exceed revenues.

Net pay. Gross pay less payroll deductions; the amount the employer is obligated to pay the employee.

Net realizable value. The amount at which merchandise that can be sold only at prices below cost should be valued, determined as the estimated selling price less any direct cost of disposition.

Net worth. The owner's equity in a business.

Noncontrollable cost. For a specific level of management, a cost that cannot be directly controlled.

Note receivable. A written promise to pay, representing an amount to be received by a business.

Number of days' sales in inventory. The relationship between the volume of sales and inventory, computed by dividing the inventory at the end of the year by the average daily cost of goods sold.

Number of days' sales in receivables. The relationship between credit sales and accounts receivable, computed by dividing the net accounts receivable at the end of the year by the average daily sales on account.

O

Oligopoly market. A market in which there exists a few large sellers competing against each other with similar products, and the amount sold by each seller has a direct effect on the sales of the other companies.

Operational planning. The development of short-term plans to achieve goals identified in an enterprise's strategic plan. Sometimes referred to as tactical planning.

Operating lease. A lease which does not meet the criteria for a capital lease, and thus which is accounted for as an operating expense, so that neither future lease obligations nor future rights to use the leased asset are recognized in the accounts.

Opportunity cost. The amount of income that is foregone by selecting one alternative over another.

Organizing. The process by which management assigns responsibility to individuals for achieving enterprise goals.

Other expense. An expense that cannot be associated definitely with operations.

Other income. Revenue from sources other than the principal activity of a business.

Overapplied overhead. The amount of overhead applied in excess of the actual overhead costs incurred for production during a period.

Owner's equity. The rights of the owners in a business enterprise.

P

Paid-in capital. The capital acquired from stockholders.

Par. The arbitrary monetary figure printed on a stock certificate.

Parent company. The company owning all or a majority of the voting stock of another corporation.

Participating preferred stock. Preferred stock that could receive dividends in excess of the specified amount granted by its preferential rights.

Partnership. An unincorporated business owned by two or more individuals.

Payoff table. A table that summarizes the possible outcomes of one or more decisions for management's use in decision making.

Payroll. The total amount paid to employees for a certain period.

Payroll register. A multi-column form used to assemble and summarize payroll data at the end of each payroll period.

Percentage-of-completion method. The method of recognizing revenue from long-term contracts over the entire life of the contract.

Period costs. Those costs that are used up in generating revenue during the current period and that are not involved in the manufacturing process. These costs are recognized as expenses on the current period's income statement.

Periodic inventory system. A system of inventory accounting in which only the revenue from sales is recorded each time a sale is made; the cost of merchandise on hand at the end of a period is determined by a detailed listing (physical inventory) of the merchandise on hand.

Perpetual inventory system. A system of inventory accounting that employs records that continually disclose the amount of the inventory on hand.

Petty cash fund. A special cash fund used to pay relatively small amounts.

Physical inventory. The detailed listing of merchandise on hand.

Planning. The process by which management develops a course of action to attain enterprise goals.

Plant asset. A tangible asset of a relatively fixed or permanent nature owned by a business enterprise.

Point of sale method. The method of recognizing revenue, whereby the revenue is determined to be realized at the time that title passes to the buyer.

Pooling of interests method. A method of accounting for an affiliation of two corporations resulting from an exchange of voting stock of one corporation for substantially all of the voting stock of the other corporation.

Post-closing trial balance. A trial balance prepared after all of the temporary accounts have been closed.

Posting. The process of transferring debits and credits from a journal to the accounts.

Predetermined factory overhead rate. The rate used to apply factory overhead costs to the goods manufactured.

Preemptive right. The right of each shareholder to maintain the same fractional interest in the corporation by purchasing a proportionate number of shares of any additional issuances of stock.

Preferred stock. A class of stock with preferential rights over common stock.

Premium. (a) The excess of the sales price of stock over its par amount; (b) excess of the issue price of bonds over the face amount.

Prepaid expense. A purchased commodity or service that has not been consumed at the end of an accounting period.

Present value. The estimated present worth of an amount of cash to be received (or paid) in the future.

Present value index. An index computed by dividing the total present value of the net cash flow to be received from a proposed capital investment by the amount to be invested.

Present value of an annuity. The sum of the present values of a series of equal cash flows to be received at fixed intervals.

Price-earnings (P/E) ratio. The ratio of the market price per share of common stock, at a specific date, to the annual earnings per share.

Price graph. A graph used to determine the price-cost combination that maximizes the total profit of an enterprise by plotting the marginal revenues and marginal costs.

Price-level index. The ratio of the total cost of a group of commodities prevailing at a particular time to the total cost of the same group of commodities at an earlier base time.

Price theory. A separate discipline in the area of microeconomics which studies the setting of product prices.

Prime costs. The combination of direct materials and direct labor costs.

Prior period adjustment. Correction of a material error related to a prior period or periods, excluded from the determination of net income.

Proceeds. The net amount available from discounting a note.

Process cost system. A type of cost accounting system that accumulates costs for each of the various departments or processes within a factory.

Product cost concept. A concept used in applying the cost-plus approach to product pricing in which only the costs of manufacturing the product, termed the product cost, are included in the cost amount to which the markup is added.

Product costs. The three components of manufacturing cost: direct materials, direct labor, and factory overhead costs.

Product life cycle. A concept that assumes that a product passes through various stages from the time that it is introduced until the time that it disappears from the market.

Profit center. A decentralized unit in which the manager has the responsibility and the authority to make decisions that affect both cost and revenues (and thus profits).

Profit margin. A component of the rate of return on investment, computed as the ratio of operating income to sales.

Profit-volume chart. A chart used to assist management in understanding the relationship between profit and volume.

Profitability. The ability of a firm to earn income.

Program budget. A budget in which the items of expenditure are presented by the program associated with the expenditure.

Promissory note. A written promise to pay a sum in money on demand or at a definite time.

Purchase method. The accounting method employed when a parent company acquires a controlling share of the voting stock of a subsidiary other than by the exchange of voting common stock.

Purchase orders. The form issued by the purchasing department to suppliers, requesting the delivery of materials.

Purchase requisitions. The form used to inform the purchasing department that materials are needed by an enterprise.

Purchases discounts. An available discount taken by the purchaser for early payment of an invoice; a contra account to Purchases.

Purchases journal. The journal in which all items purchased on account are recorded.

Purchases returns and allowances. Reduction in purchases, resulting from merchandise returned to the vendor or from the vendor's reduction in the original purchase price; a contra account to Purchases.

Purely competitive market. A market in which the price for a product is established solely by the market conditions, and the quantity that a firm sells has no impact on the total market for the product. Thus, a firm can sell all it produces at the market price.

Q

Quality circle. A group of employees who meet periodically to identify and discuss problems and, when appropriate, to implement solutions to those problems.

Quality control chart. A chart, often developed using statistical methods, which shows desired operating conditions and limits within which production may vary.

Quick assets. The sum of cash, receivables and marketable securities.

R

Rate earned on common stockholders' equity. A measure of profitability computed by dividing net income, reduced by preferred dividend requirements, by common stockholders' equity.

Rate earned on stockholders' equity. A measure of profitability computed by dividing net income by total stockholders' equity.

Rate earned on total assets. A measure of the profitability of assets, without regard to the equity of creditors and stockholders in the assets.

Rate of return on investment (ROI). A measure of managerial efficiency in the use of investments in assets, computed by dividing operating income by invested assets.

Realization principle. Sales are recorded when title to the merchandise passes to the buyer.

Receiving report. The form used by the receiving department to indicate that materials have been received and inspected.

Relevant range. The range of activity within which the enterprise is planning to operate.

Report form of balance sheet. The form of balance sheet with the liability and owner's equity sections presented below the asset section.

Residual income. The excess of divisional operating income over a "minimum" amount of desired operating income.

Residual value. The estimated recoverable cost of a depreciable asset as of the time of its removal from service.

Responsibility accounting. The process of measuring and reporting operating data by areas of responsibility.

Retail inventory method. A method of inventory costing based on the relationship of the cost and retail price of merchandise.

Retained earnings. Net income retained in a corporation.

Retained earnings statement. A statement for a corporate enterprise, summarizing the changes in retained earnings during a specific period of time.

Revenues. The gross increases in owner's equity as a result of business and professional activities entered into for the purpose of earning income.

Revenue expenditure. An expenditure that benefits only the current period.

Reversing entry. An entry that reverses a specific adjusting entry to facilitate the recording of routine transactions in the subsequent period.

S

Safety stock. The amount of inventory that serves as a reserve for unforeseen circumstances, and therefore is not normally used in regular operations.

Sales discounts. An available discount granted by the seller for early payment of an invoice; a contra account to Sales.

Sales journal. The journal in which all sales of merchandise on account are recorded.

Sales mix. The relative distribution of sales among the various products available for sale.

Sales returns and allowances. Reductions in sales, resulting from merchandise returned by customers or from the seller's reduction in the original sales price; a contra account to Sales.

Scattergraph method. A cost estimation method that uses a graph to estimate total cost and the fixed and variable cost components.

Selling expense. An expense incurred directly and entirely in connection with the sale of merchandise.

Semivariable cost. A cost with both variable and fixed characteristics, sometimes referred to as a mixed or semifixed cost.

Service departments. Factory departments that do not process materials directly, but render services for the benefit of production departments.

Simplex method. A mathematical equation approach to linear programming, which is often used more practically with a computer.

Single-step income statement. An income statement with the total of all expenses deducted from the total of all revenues.

Sinking fund. Assets set aside in a special fund to be used for a specific purpose.

Slide. The erroneous movement of all digits in a number, one or more spaces to the right or the left, such as writing $542 as $5,420.

Sole proprietorship. A business owned by one individual.

Solvency. The ability of a firm to pay its debts as they come due.

Special journal. A journal designed to record a single type of transaction.

Standard costs. Detailed estimates of what a product should cost.

Standard cost system. An accounting system that uses standards for each element of manufacturing costs entering into the finished product.

Stated value. An amount assigned by the board of directors to each share of no-par stock.

Statement of cash flows. A summary of the major cash receipts and cash payments for a period.

Statement of cost of goods manufactured. A separate statement for a manufacturer that reports the cost of goods manufactured during a period.

Statement of revenues, expenditures, and changes in fund balance. The statement for a nonprofit enterprise that provides a comparison of budgeted and actual revenues and expenditures along with the effect of operations on the unreserved fund balance.

Step-wise fixed cost. A cost which varies in a step-wise fashion with changes in an activity base. Because of the long width of the range of production (steps) over which the total cost changes, the cost is classified as a fixed cost for managerial decision making.

Step-wise variable cost. A cost which varies in a step-wise fashion with changes in an activity base. Because of the short width of the range of production (steps) over which the total cost changes, the cost is classified as a variable cost for managerial decision making.

Stock dividend. Distribution of a company's own stock to its shareholders.

Stockholders. The owners of a corporation.

Stockholders' equity. The equity of the shareholders in a corporation.

Stock options. Rights given by a corporation to its employees to purchase shares of the corporation's stock at a stated price.

Stock outstanding. The stock in the hands of the stockholders.

Stock split. A reduction in the par or stated value of a share of common stock and the issuance of a proportionate number of additional shares.

Straight-line depreciation method. A method of depreciation that provides for equal periodic charges to expense over the estimated life of an asset.

Strategic planning. The development of a long-range course of action to achieve enterprise goals.

Subsidiary company. The corporation that is controlled by a parent company.

Subsidiary ledger. A ledger containing individual accounts with a common characteristic.

Sum-of-the-years-digits depreciation method. A method of depreciation that provides for declining periodic depreciation charges to expense over the estimated life of an asset.

Sunk cost. Costs which have been incurred and cannot be reversed by subsequent decisions.

T

T account. A form of account resembling the letter T.

Taxable income. The base on which the amount of income tax is determined.

Temporary investment. An investment in securities that can be readily sold when cash is needed.

Theoretical standards. Standards that represent levels of performance that can be achieved only under perfect operating conditions, such as no idle time, no machine breakdowns, and no materials spoilage.

Time tickets. The form on which the amount of time spent by each employee and the labor cost incurred for each individual job, or for factory overhead, are recorded.

Total cost concept. A concept used in applying the cost-plus approach to product pricing in which all costs of manufacturing a product plus the selling and general expenses are included in the cost amount to which the markup is added.

Transfer price. The price charged one decentralized unit by another for the goods or services provided.

Transposition. The erroneous arrangement of digits in a number, such as writing $542 as $524.

Treasury stock. A corporation's own outstanding stock that has been reacquired.

Trial balance. A summary listing of the balances and the titles of the accounts.

U

Underapplied overhead. The amount of actual overhead in excess of the overhead applied to production during a period.

Unearned revenue. Revenue received in advance of its being earned.

Units-of-production depreciation method. A method of depreciation that provides for depreciation expense based on the expected productive capacity of an asset.

V

Value of perfect information. The maximum amount (cost) that will be paid to obtain perfect information concerning a decision.

Variable cost. A cost that varies in total dollar amount as the level of activity changes.

Variable cost concept. A concept used in applying the cost-plus approach to product pricing in which only variable costs and expenses are included in the cost amount to which the markup is added.

Variable costing. The concept that considers the cost of products manufactured to be composed only of those manufacturing costs that increase or decrease as the volume of production rises or falls (direct materials, direct labor, and variable factory overhead).

Variance. The difference between what a product should cost (standard) and how much it does cost (actual).

Vertical analysis. The percentage analysis of component parts in relation to the total of the parts in a single financial statement.

Voucher. A document that serves as evidence of authority to pay cash.

Voucher system. Records, methods, and procedures employed in verifying and recording liabilities and paying and recording cash payments.

W-Z

Working capital. The excess of total current assets over total current liabilities at some point in time.

Work in process. Goods in the process of manufacture.

Work sheet. A working paper used to assist in the preparation of financial statements.

Zero-base budgeting. A concept of budgeting that requires all levels of management to start from zero and estimate budget data as if there had been no previous activities in their unit.

Appendix B

Alternative Method of Recording Merchandise Inventories

The recording of merchandise inventory at the end of the accounting period is described and illustrated in Chapter 4. The alternative method presented in this appendix classifies the entries for the beginning and the ending merchandise inventories as *adjusting* entries instead of *closing* entries. The difference in viewpoint has a minor effect on the work sheet, the sequence of entries in the journal, and the income summary account. It does not alter the financial statements in any way. The data for Midtown Electric Corporation presented in Chapter 4 is used for the illustrations in this appendix.

MERCHANDISE INVENTORY ADJUSTMENTS

At the end of the period it is necessary to remove from Merchandise Inventory the amount representing the inventory at the beginning of the period and to replace it with the amount representing the inventory at the end of the period. This can be accomplished by two adjusting entries. The first entry transfers the beginning inventory to Income Summary. Since this beginning inventory is part of the cost of merchandise sold, it is debited to Income Summary. It is also a subtraction from the asset account, Merchandise Inventory, and hence is credited to that account. The first adjusting entry for Midtown Electric Corporation is as follows:

Dec. 31	Income Summary	59,700	
	Merchandise Inventory		59,700

The second adjusting entry debits the cost of the merchandise inventory at the end of the period to the asset account, Merchandise Inventory. The credit portion of the entry effects a deduction of the unsold merchandise from the total cost of the merchandise available for sale during the period. The second adjusting entry for Midtown Electric Corporation is as follows:

Dec. 31	Merchandise Inventory	62,150	
	Income Summary		62,150

The effect of the two inventory adjustments is indicated by the following T accounts for Merchandise Inventory and Income Summary:

Merchandise Inventory

Dec. 31, 1988	59,700	Dec. 31, 1988	59,700
Dec. 31, 1989	62,150		

Income Summary

Dec. 31, 1989	59,700	Dec. 31, 1989	62,150

In the accounts, the inventory of $59,700 at the end of the preceding year (December 31, 1988), which is the beginning of the current year, has been transferred to Income Summary as a part of the cost of merchandise available for sale. It is replaced by a debit of $62,150, the merchandise inventory at the end of the current year (December 31, 1989). The credit of the same amount to Income Summary is a deduction from the cost of merchandise available for sale.

WORK SHEET

All adjustments are recorded in the Adjustments columns of the work sheet in the same manner as was illustrated on pages 132 and 133, except that by this method entries are required in the Adjustments columns for merchandise inventory. The balances are then extended to the Income Statement and Balance Sheet columns, and the work sheet is completed. An exception to the usual practice of extending only the account balances should be noted. Both the debit and credit amounts for Income Summary are extended to the Income Statement columns. Since both the amount of the debit adjustment (beginning inventory of $59,700) and the amount of the credit adjustment (ending inventory of $62,150) may be reported on the income statement, there is no need to determine the difference between the two amounts. A work sheet for Midtown Electric Corporation employing this alternative procedure is illustrated on page B-3. Note that the Income Statement and Balance Sheet columns, including column totals and the amount of net income, are the same as those on the work sheet on pages 132 and 133.

ADJUSTING ENTRIES

The adjusting entries made from the alternative work sheet are illustrated as follows. They are exactly the same as those illustrated on page 141, except for the inclusion of adjustments for inventory.

Adjusting Entries

JOURNAL PAGE 28

DATE		DESCRIPTION	POST. REF.	DEBIT	CREDIT
		Adjusting Entries			
1989 Dec.	31	Income Summary	313	59 700 00	
		Merchandise Inventory	114		59 700 00
	31	Merchandise Inventory	114	62 150 00	
		Income Summary	313		62 150 00
	31	Office Supplies Expense	717	610 00	
		Office Supplies	116		610 00
	31	Insurance Expense	716	1 910 00	
		Prepaid Insurance	117		1 910 00
	31	Depreciation Expense — Store Equip.	613	3 100 00	
		Accumulated Depr. — Store Equip.	122		3 100 00
	31	Depreciation Expense — Office Equip.	715	2 490 00	
		Accumulated Depr. — Office Equip.	124		2 490 00
	31	Sales Salaries Expense	611	780 00	
		Office Salaries Expense	711	360 00	
		Salaries Payable	213		1 140 00

Midtown Electric Corporation
Work Sheet
For Year Ended December 31, 1989

ACCOUNT TITLE	TRIAL BALANCE		ADJUSTMENTS		INCOME STATEMENT		BALANCE SHEET	
	DEBIT	CREDIT	DEBIT	CREDIT	DEBIT	CREDIT	DEBIT	CREDIT
Cash	62,950						62,950	
Notes Receivable	40,000						40,000	
Accounts Receivable	60,880						60,880	
Merchandise Inventory	59,700		(b) 62,150	(a) 59,700			62,150	
Office Supplies	1,090			(c) 610			480	
Prepaid Insurance	4,560			(d) 1,910			2,650	
Store Equipment	27,100						27,100	
Accumulated Depreciation—Store Equipment		12,600		(e) 3,100				15,700
Office Equipment	15,570						15,570	
Accumulated Depreciation—Office Equipment		7,230		(f) 2,490				9,720
Accounts Payable		22,420						22,420
Salaries Payable				(g) 1,140				1,140
Mortgage Note Payable		25,000						25,000
Capital Stock		100,000						100,000
Retained Earnings		41,200						41,200
Dividends	18,000						18,000	
Income Summary			(a) 59,700	(b) 62,150	59,700	62,150		
Sales		720,185				720,185		
Sales Returns and Allowances	6,140				6,140			
Sales Discounts	5,790				5,790			
Purchases	521,980				521,980			
Purchases Returns and Allowances		9,100				9,100		
Purchases Discounts		2,525				2,525		
Transportation In	17,400				17,400			
Sales Salaries Expense	59,250		(g) 780		60,030			
Advertising Expense	10,860				10,860			
Depreciation Expense—Store Equipment			(e) 3,100		3,100			
Miscellaneous Selling Expense	630				630			
Office Salaries Expense	20,660		(g) 360		21,020			
Rent Expense	8,100				8,100			
Depreciation Expense—Office Equipment			(f) 2,490		2,490			
Insurance Expense			(d) 1,910		1,910			
Office Supplies Expense			(c) 610		610			
Miscellaneous General Expense	760				760			
Interest Income		3,600				3,600		
Interest Expense	2,440				2,440			
	943,860	943,860	131,100	131,100	722,960			
Net income					74,600			74,600
					797,560	797,560	289,780	289,780

CLOSING ENTRIES

All accounts with balances in the Income Statement Credit column of the work sheet, with the exception of the amount for Income Summary, which represents the ending merchandise inventory balance, are closed in one compound journal entry by debiting each account and crediting Income Summary. All accounts with balances in the Income Statement Debit column, with the exception of the amount for Income Summary, which represents the beginning merchandise inventory balance, are closed in one entry by debiting Income Summary and crediting each account. The Income Summary and the dividends accounts are then closed to the retained earnings account. All of the closing entries for the alternative procedure for Midtown Electric Corporation are as follows:

Income Summary Account

JOURNAL PAGE 29

DATE		DESCRIPTION	POST. REF.	DEBIT	CREDIT
		Closing Entries			
1989 Dec.	31	Sales	411	720185 00	
		Purchases Returns and Allowances	512	9100 00	
		Purchases Discounts	518	2525 00	
		Interest Income	812	3600 00	
		Income Summary	313		735410 00
	31	Income Summary	313	663260 00	
		Sales Returns and Allowances	412		6140 00
		Sales Discounts	413		5790 00
		Purchases	511		521980 00
		Transportation In	514		17400 00
		Sales Salaries Expense	611		60030 00
		Advertising Expense	612		10860 00
		Depreciation Exp.—Store Equip.	613		3100 00
		Miscellaneous Selling Expense	619		630 00
		Office Salaries Expense	711		21020 00
		Rent Expense	712		8100 00
		Depreciation Exp.—Office Equip.	715		2490 00
		Insurance Expense	716		1910 00
		Office Supplies Expense	717		610 00
		Miscellaneous General Expense	719		760 00
		Interest Expense	911		2440 00
	31	Income Summary	313	74600 00	
		Retained Earnings	311		74600 00
	31	Retained Earnings	311	18000 00	
		Dividends	312		18000 00

The income summary account, as it will appear after the merchandise inventory adjustments and the closing entries have been posted, is as follows. Each item in the account is identified as an aid to understanding. Such notations are not an essential part of the posting procedure.

ACCOUNT Income Summary ACCOUNT NO. 313

DATE		ITEM	POST. REF.	DEBIT	CREDIT	BALANCE DEBIT	BALANCE CREDIT
1989 Dec.	31	Mer. inv.,					
		Jan. 1	28	59 700 00		59 700 00	
	31	Mer. inv.,					
		Dec. 31	28		62 150 00		2 450 00
	31	Revenue, etc.	29		735 410 00		737 860 00
	31	Expense, etc.	29	663 260 00			74 600 00
	31	Net income	29	74 600 00		—	—

Appendix C
Special Journals and Subsidiary Ledgers

A manual accounting system is used in the text because such a system enables the student to focus most easily on the basic principles of accounting. In practice, when the manual system is used, it is often modified somewhat in order to process accounting data more effectively. One such modification is discussed in this appendix.

In the text, all transactions were initially recorded in a two-column journal, then posted individually to the appropriate accounts in the ledger. Applying such detailed procedures to a large number of transactions that are often repeated is impractical. For example, if many credit sales are made, each of these transactions would require an entry debiting Accounts Receivable and crediting Sales. In addition, the accounts receivable account in the ledger would include receivables from a large number of customers. In such cases, special journals can be used to record like kinds of transactions, and subsidiary ledgers can be used for accounts with a common characteristic.

Special Journals

One of the simplest methods of processing data more efficiently in a manual accounting system is to expand the two-column journal to a **multicolumn** journal. Each amount column included in a multicolumn journal is restricted to the recording of transactions affecting a certain account. For example, a special column could be used only for recording debits to the cash account and another special column could be used only for recording credits to the cash account. The addition of the two special columns would eliminate the writing of "Cash" in the journal for every receipt and payment of cash. Furthermore, there would be no need to post each individual debit and credit to the cash account. Instead, the "Cash Dr." and "Cash Cr." columns could be totaled periodically and only the totals posted, yielding additional economies. In a similar manner, special columns could be added for recording credits to Sales, debits and credits to Accounts Receivable and Accounts Payable, and for other entries that are repeated. Although there is no exact number of columns that may be effectively used in a multicolumn journal, there is a maximum number beyond which the journal would become unmanageable. Also, the possibilities of errors in recording become greater as the number of columns and the width of the page increase.

An all-purpose multicolumn journal is usually satisfactory for a small business enterprise that needs the services of only one bookkeeper. If the number of transactions is enough to require two or more bookkeepers, the use of a single journal is usually not efficient. The next logical development in expanding the system is to replace an all-purpose journal with a number of **special journals,** each designed to record a single kind of transaction. Special journals would be needed only for the kinds of transactions that occur frequently. Since most enterprises have many transactions in which cash is received and many in which cash is paid out, it is common practice to use a special journal for recording cash receipts and another special journal for recording cash payments. An enterprise that sells services or merchandise to customers on account might use a special journal designed for recording only such transactions. On the other hand, a business that does not give credit would have no need for such a journal.

The transactions that occur most often in a medium-size merchandising firm and the special journals in which they are recorded are as follows:

Purchase of merchandise or other items *on account* → recorded in → Purchases journal

Payments of cash for *any* purpose → recorded in → Cash payments journal

Sale of merchandise *on account* → recorded in → Sales journal

Receipt of cash from *any* source → recorded in → Cash receipts journal

Sometimes the business documents evidencing purchases and sales transactions are used as special journals. When there are a large number of such transactions on a credit basis, the use of this procedure may result in a substantial savings in bookkeeping expenses and a reduction of bookkeeping errors.

The two-column form illustrated in earlier chapters can be used for miscellaneous entries, such as adjusting and closing entries, that do not "fit" in any of the special journals. The two-column form is commonly called the **general journal** or simply the **journal.**

Subsidiary Ledgers

As the number of purchases and sales on account increase, the need for maintaining a separate account for each creditor and debtor is clear. If such accounts are numerous, their inclusion in the same ledger with all other accounts would cause the ledger to become unmanageable. The chance of posting errors would also be increased and the preparation of the trial balance and the financial statements would be delayed.

When there are a large number of individual accounts with a common characteristic, it is common to place them in a separate ledger called a **subsidiary ledger.** The principal ledger, which contains all of the balance sheet and income statement accounts, is then called the **general ledger.** Each subsidiary ledger is represented by a summarizing account in the general ledger called a **controlling account.** The sum of the balances of the accounts in a subsidiary ledger must agree with the balance of the related controlling account. Thus, a subsidiary ledger may be said to be *controlled* by its controlling account.

The individual accounts with creditors are arranged in alphabetical order in a subsidiary ledger called the **accounts payable ledger** or **creditors ledger.** The related controlling account in the general ledger is Accounts Payable.

A subsidiary ledger for credit customers is needed for most business enterprises. This ledger containing the individual accounts is called the **accounts receivable ledger** or **customers ledger.** The controlling account in the general ledger that summarizes the debits and credits to the individual customers accounts is Accounts Receivable.

Purchases Journal

Property most frequently purchased on account by a merchandising concern is of the following types: (1) merchandise for resale to customers, (2) supplies for use in conducting the business, and (3) equipment and other plant assets. Because of the variety of items acquired on credit terms, the **purchases journal** should be designed to allow for the recording of everything purchased on account. The form of purchases journal used by Kannon Corporation is illustrated at the top of pages C-3 and C-4.

For each transaction recorded in the purchases journal, the credit is entered in the Accounts Payable Cr. column. The next three amount columns are used for accumulating debits to the particular accounts most frequently affected. Invoice amounts for merchandise purchased for sale to customers are recorded in the Purchases Dr. column. The purpose of the Store Supplies Dr. and Office Supplies Dr. columns is

Purchases Journal

	PAGE 19				PURCHASES
	DATE		ACCOUNT CREDITED	POST. REF.	ACCOUNTS PAYABLE CR.
1	1989 Oct.	2	Video Co.	✓	5724 00
2		3	Marsh Inc.	✓	7406 00
3		9	Parker Supply Co.	✓	257 00
4		11	Marsh Inc.	✓	3208 00
5		16	Dunlap Corporation	✓	3593 00
6		17	Robinson Supply	✓	1500 00
7		20	Walton Co.	✓	15125 00
8		23	Parker Supply Co.	✓	132 00
9		27	Dunlap Corporation	✓	6375 00
10		31			43320 00
11					(211)

readily apparent. If supplies of these two categories were purchased only once in a while, the two columns could be omitted from the journal.

The final set of columns, under the main heading Sundry Accounts Dr., is used to record acquisitions, on account, of items not provided for in the special debit columns. The title of the account to be debited is entered in the Account column and the amount is entered in the Amount column. A separate posting reference column is provided for this section of the purchases journal.

Posting the Purchases Journal. The special journals used in recording most of the transactions affecting creditors accounts are designed to allow the posting of individual transactions to the accounts payable ledger and a single monthly total to Accounts Payable. The basic techniques of posting credits from a purchases journal to an accounts payable ledger and the controlling account are shown in the flowchart below.

Flow of Credits From Purchases Journal to Ledgers

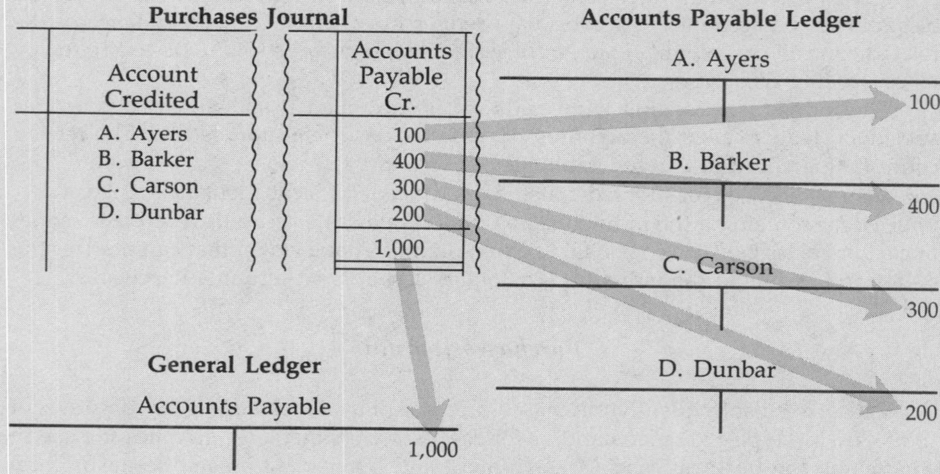

The individual credits of $100, $400, $300, and $200 to Ayers, Barker, Carson, and Dunbar respectively are posted to their accounts in the accounts payable ledger. The sum of the credits to the four individual accounts in the subsidiary ledger is posted as a single $1,000 credit to Accounts Payable, the controlling account in the general ledger.

JOURNAL PAGE 19

PURCHASES DR.	STORE SUPPLIES DR.	OFFICE SUPPLIES DR.	SUNDRY ACCOUNTS DR. ACCOUNT	POST. REF.	AMOUNT	
5724 00						1
7406 00						2
	131 00	126 00				3
3208 00						4
3593 00						5
1500 00						6
			Store Equipment	121	15125 00	7
	75 00	57 00				8
6375 00						9
27806 00	206 00	183 00			15125 00	10
(511)	(115)	(116)			(✓)	11

The source of the entries posted to the subsidiary and general ledgers is indicated in the posting reference column of each account by inserting the letter "P" and the page number of the purchases journal. An account in the accounts payable ledger of Kannon Corporation is presented as an example.

An Account in the Accounts Payable Ledger

NAME Robinson Supply
ADDRESS 3800 Mission Street, San Francisco, CA 94110-1732

DATE		ITEM	POST. REF.	DEBIT	CREDIT	BALANCE
1989 Oct.	17		P19		1500 00	1500 00

Since the balances in the creditors accounts are usually credit balances, a three-column account form is used instead of the four-column account form illustrated earlier. When a creditor's account is overpaid and a debit balance occurs, that fact should be indicated by an asterisk or parentheses in the Balance column. When an account's balance is zero, a line may be drawn in the Balance column.

The creditors accounts in the subsidiary ledger are not numbered, because the order changes each time a new account is inserted alphabetically or an old account is removed. Thus, instead of a number, a check mark (✓) is inserted in the posting reference column of the purchases journal after a credit is posted.

The amounts in the Sundry Accounts Dr. column of the purchases journal are posted to the appropriate accounts in the general ledger and the posting reference ("P" and page number) are inserted in the accounts. As each amount is posted, the related general ledger account number is inserted in the posting reference column of the Sundry Accounts section.

At the end of each month, the purchases journal is totaled and ruled in the manner illustrated on pages C-3 and C-4. Before posting the totals to the general ledger, the sum of the totals of the four debit columns should be compared with the total of the credit column to prove their equality.

The totals of the four special columns are posted to the appropriate general ledger accounts in the usual manner, with the related account numbers inserted below the columnar totals. Because each amount in the Sundry Accounts Dr. was posted individually, a check mark is placed below the $15,125 total to show that no further action is needed.

Two of the general ledger accounts to which postings were made are presented as examples. The debit posting to Store Equipment was from the Sundry Accounts Dr. column; the credit posting to Accounts Payable was from the total of the Accounts Payable Cr. column.

General Ledger Accounts After Posting From Purchases Journal

ACCOUNT Store Equipment — ACCOUNT NO. 121

DATE		ITEM	POST. REF.	DEBIT	CREDIT	BALANCE DEBIT	BALANCE CREDIT
1989 Oct.	1	Balance	✓			11,975 00	
	20		P19	15,125 00		27,100 00	

ACCOUNT Accounts Payable — ACCOUNT NO. 211

DATE		ITEM	POST. REF.	DEBIT	CREDIT	BALANCE DEBIT	BALANCE CREDIT
1989 Oct.	1	Balance	✓				21,975 00
	31		P19		43,320 00		65,295 00

The flow of data from the purchases journal of Kannon Corporation to its two related ledgers is presented graphically in the diagram below. Two procedures revealed by the flow diagram should be given special attention:

1. Postings are made from the purchases journal to both (a) accounts in the subsidiary ledger and (b) accounts in the general ledger.
2. The sum of the postings to individual accounts payable in the subsidiary ledger equals the columnar total posted to Accounts Payable (controlling account) in the general ledger.

Flow of Data From Purchases Journal to Ledgers

Purchases Journal

Account Credited	P. R.	Accts. Payable Cr.	Purchases Dr.	Store Sup. Dr.	Office Sup. Dr.	Sundry Accounts Debit: Account	P. R.	Amount
Video Co.	✓	5,724	5,724					
Marsh Inc.	✓	7,406	7,406					
Parker Supply Co.	✓	257		131	126			
Walton Co.	✓	15,125				Store Equip.	121	15,125
Parker Supply Co.	✓	132		75	57			
Dunlap Corporation	✓	6,375	6,375					
		43,320	27,806	206	183			15,125

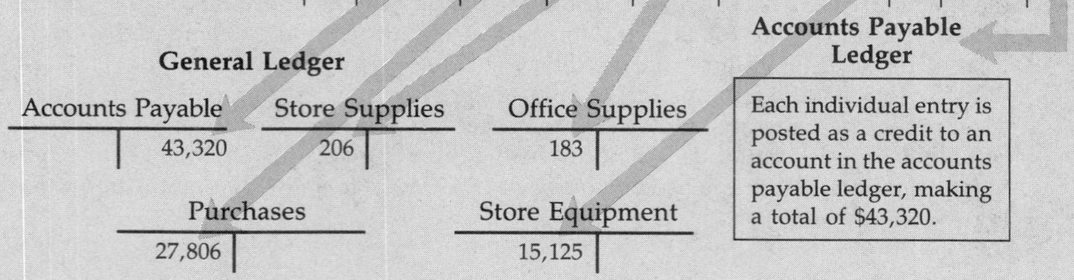

General Ledger

Accounts Payable	
	43,320

Store Supplies	
206	

Office Supplies	
183	

Purchases	
27,806	

Store Equipment	
15,125	

Accounts Payable Ledger

Each individual entry is posted as a credit to an account in the accounts payable ledger, making a total of $43,320.

Purchases Returns and Allowances. When merchandise purchased is returned or a price adjustment is granted, an entry is made in the general journal according to the principles described in Chapter 2. To illustrate, assume that during October, Kannon Corporation issued a debit memorandum for a return of merchandise. The entry may be recorded in a two-column general journal, as follows:

General Journal Entry for Returns and Allowances

JOURNAL — PAGE 18

	DATE		DESCRIPTION	POST. REF.	DEBIT	CREDIT	
17	Oct.	20	Accounts Payable—Dunlap Corp.	211 / ✓	97 50		17
18			Purchases Returns and Allowances	512		97 50	18
19			Debit Memo No. 20.				19

The debit portion of the entry is posted to the accounts payable account in the general ledger (No. 211) and also to the creditor's account in the subsidiary ledger (✓). The need for posting the debits to two different accounts is indicated, at the time these entries are journalized, by drawing a *diagonal line* in the posting reference column. The account number and check mark are inserted, in the usual manner, at the time the entry is posted.

After the entry has been recorded, the memorandum is attached to the related unpaid invoice. If the invoice had been paid before the return or allowance was granted, the settlement might be a cash refund.

If goods other than merchandise are returned or a price adjustment is granted, the account to which the goods were first debited should be credited. For example, if a purchase of office equipment is returned, the credit would be to Office Equipment rather than Purchases Returns and Allowances.

Cash Payments Journal

The standards for determining the special columns to be provided in the **cash payments journal** are the same as for the purchases journal, namely, the kind of transactions to be recorded and the frequency of their occurrence. It is necessary to have a Cash Cr. column. Payments to creditors on account happen often enough to require columns for Accounts Payable Dr. and Purchases Discounts Cr. The cash payments journal illustrated at the top of page C-7 has these three columns and an additional column for Sundry Accounts Dr.

All payments by Kannon Corporation are made by check. As each transaction is recorded in the cash payments journal, the related check number is entered in the column at the right of the Date column. The check numbers provide a convenient cross-reference, and their use also is helpful in controlling cash payments.

The Sundry Accounts Dr. column is used to record debits to any account for which there is no special column. On October 2, for example, Kannon Corporation paid $1,275 for a cash purchase of merchandise. The transaction was recorded by writing "Purchases" in the space provided and $1,275 in the Sundry Accounts Dr. and the Cash Cr. columns. The posting reference (511) was inserted later, at the time the debit was posted.

Debits to creditors accounts for invoices paid are recorded in the Accounts Payable Dr. column and credits for the amounts paid are recorded in the Cash Cr. column. If a discount is taken, the debit to the account payable will, of course, differ from the amount of the payment. Cash discounts taken on merchandise purchased for resale are recorded in the Purchases Discounts Cr. column.

At frequent intervals during the month, the amounts entered in the Accounts Payable Dr. column are posted to the creditors accounts in the accounts payable

Cash Payments Journal After Posting

CASH PAYMENTS JOURNAL — PAGE 16

	DATE		CK. NO.	ACCOUNT DEBITED	POST. REF.	SUNDRY ACCOUNTS DR.	ACCOUNTS PAYABLE DR.	PURCHASES DISCOUNTS CR.	CASH CR.	
1	1989 Oct.	2	312	Purchases	511	1275 00			1275 00	1
2		4	313	Store Equipment	121	350 00			350 00	2
3		12	314	Marsh Inc.	✓		7406 00	74 06	7331 94	3
4		12	315	Sales Salaries Exp.	611	2560 00			2560 00	4
5		12	316	Office Salaries Exp.	711	880 00			880 00	5
6		14	317	Misc. Gen. Exp.	719	56 40			56 40	6
7		16	318	Prepaid Insurance	117	984 00			984 00	7
8		20	319	Marsh Inc.	✓		3208 00	32 08	3175 92	8
9		20	320	Heath Co.	✓		4850 00		4850 00	9
10		21	321	Sales Ret. & Allow.	412	462 00			462 00	10
11		23	322	Robinson Supply	✓		1500 00	30 00	1470 00	11
12		23	323	Video Co.	✓		7600 00		7600 00	12
13		23	324	Rent Expense	712	789 20			789 20	13
14		24	325	Walton Co.	✓		9525 00		9525 00	14
15		26	326	Sales Salaries Exp.	611	2560 00			2560 00	15
16		26	327	Office Salaries Exp.	711	880 00			880 00	16
17		26	328	Advertising Expense	612	786 00			786 00	17
18		27	329	Misc. Selling Exp.	619	41 50			41 50	18
19		28	330	Office Equipment	123	900 00			900 00	19
20		31				12524 10	34089 00	136 14	46476 96	20
21						(✓)	(211)	(513)	(111)	21

ledger. After each posting, "CP" and the page number of the journal are inserted in the posting reference column of the account. Check marks are placed in the posting reference column of the cash payments journal to indicate that the amounts have been posted. The items in the Sundry Accounts Dr. column are also posted to the appropriate accounts in the general ledger at frequent intervals. The posting is indicated by writing the account numbers in the posting reference column of the cash payments journal. At the end of the month, each of the amount columns in the cash payments journal is footed, the sum of the two debit totals is compared with the sum of the two credit totals to determine their equality, and the journal is ruled.

A check mark is placed below the total of the Sundry Accounts Dr. column to indicate that it is not posted. As each of the totals of the other three columns is posted to a general ledger account, the proper account numbers are inserted below the column totals.

Accounts Payable Control and Subsidiary Ledger

During October, the following postings were made to Accounts Payable in the general ledger of Kannon Corporation:

Credits to Accounts Payable

Oct. 31 Total purchases on account (purchases journal) $43,320.00

Debits to Accounts Payable

Oct. 20 A return of merchandise (general journal) 97.50
31 Total cash payments on account
(cash payments journal) $34,089.00

The accounts payable controlling account and the subsidiary accounts payable ledger of Kannon Corporation as of October 31 are presented on pages C-8 and C-9.

GENERAL LEDGER

ACCOUNT Accounts Payable ACCOUNT NO. 211

DATE		ITEM	POST. REF.	DEBIT	CREDIT	BALANCE DEBIT	BALANCE CREDIT
1989 Oct.	1	Balance	✓				21 975 00
	20		J18	97 50			21 877 50
	31		P19		43 320 00		65 197 50
	31		CP16	34 089 00			31 108 50

Accounts Payable Account in the General Ledger at the End of the Month

ACCOUNTS PAYABLE LEDGER

NAME Dunlap Corporation

ADDRESS 521 Scottsdale Blvd., Phoenix, AZ 85004-1100

DATE		ITEM	POST. REF.	DEBIT	CREDIT	BALANCE
1989 Oct.	16		P19		3 593 00	3 593 00
	20		J18	97 50		3 495 50
	27		P19		6 375 00	9 870 50

Accounts Payable Ledger at the End of the Month

NAME Heath Co.

ADDRESS 9950 Ridge Ave., Los Angeles, CA 90048-3694

DATE		ITEM	POST. REF.	DEBIT	CREDIT	BALANCE
1989 Sept.	21		P18		4 850 00	4 850 00
Oct.	20		CP16	4 850 00		——

NAME Marsh Inc.

ADDRESS 650 Wilson, Portland, OR 97209-1406

DATE		ITEM	POST. REF.	DEBIT	CREDIT	BALANCE
1989 Oct.	3		P19		7 406 00	7 406 00
	11		P19		3 208 00	10 614 00
	12		CP16	7 406 00		3 208 00
	20		CP16	3 208 00		——

NAME Parker Supply Co.

ADDRESS 142 West 8th, Los Angeles, CA 90014-1225

DATE		ITEM	POST. REF.	DEBIT	CREDIT	BALANCE
1989 Oct.	9		P19		257 00	257 00
	23		P19		132 00	389 00

Accounts Payable Ledger at the End of the Month — Concluded

NAME Robinson Supply

ADDRESS 3800 Mission Street, San Francisco, CA 94110-1732

DATE		ITEM	POST. REF.	DEBIT	CREDIT	BALANCE
1989 Oct.	17		P19		1,500 00	1,500 00
	23		CP16	1,500 00		—

NAME Video Co.

ADDRESS 1200 Capital Ave., Sacramento, CA 95814-1048

DATE		ITEM	POST. REF.	DEBIT	CREDIT	BALANCE
1989 Sept.	25		P18		7,600 00	7,600 00
Oct.	2		P19		5,724 00	13,324 00
	23		CP16	7,600 00		5,724 00

NAME Walton Co.

ADDRESS 9554 W. Colorado Blvd., Pasadena, CA 91107-1318

DATE		ITEM	POST. REF.	DEBIT	CREDIT	BALANCE
1989 Sept.	28		P18		9,525 00	9,525 00
Oct.	20		P19		15,125 00	24,650 00
	24		CP16	9,525 00		15,125 00

After all posting has been completed for the month, the sum of the balances in the accounts payable ledger should be compared with the balance of the accounts payable account in the general ledger. If the controlling account and the subsidiary ledger do not agree, the error or errors must be located and corrected. The balances of the individual creditors accounts may be summarized on a calculator tape, or a schedule such as the following may be prepared. The total of the schedule, $31,108.50, agrees with the balance of the accounts payable account shown on page C-8.

Schedule of Accounts Payable

Kannon Corporation
Schedule of Accounts Payable
October 31, 1989

Dunlap Corporation	$ 9,870.50
Parker Supply Co.	389.00
Video Co.	5,724.00
Walton Co.	15,125.00
Total accounts payable	$31,108.50

Sales Journal

The **sales journal** is used only for recording *sales of merchandise on account;* sales of merchandise for cash are recorded in the cash receipts journal. Sales of non-merchandise assets are recorded in the cash receipts journal or the general journal, depending upon whether the sale was made for cash or on account. The sales journal of Kannon Corporation for October is as follows:

Sales Journal After Posting

SALES JOURNAL — PAGE 35

	DATE		INVOICE NO.	ACCOUNT DEBITED	POST. REF.	ACCTS. REC. DR. SALES CR.	
1	1989 Oct.	2	615	Barnes Inc.	✓	9350 00	1
2		3	616	Standard Supply Co.	✓	1604 00	2
3		5	617	David T. Mattox	✓	15305 00	3
4		9	618	Barnes Inc.	✓	1396 00	4
5		10	619	Adler Company	✓	6750 00	5
6		17	620	Hamilton Inc.	✓	7865 00	6
7		23	621	Cooper & Co.	✓	1502 00	7
8		26	622	Tracy & Lee Inc.	✓	3260 00	8
9		27	623	Standard Supply Co.	✓	1908 00	9
10		31				48940 00	10
11						(113) (411)	11

Details of the first sale recorded by Kannon Corporation in October are taken from Invoice No. 615. The customer is Barnes Inc., and the invoice total is $9,350. Since the amount of the debit to Accounts Receivable is the same as the credit to Sales, a single amount column in the sales journal is sufficient. However, if sales are subject to a sales tax, a special column may be added to the sales journal for recording the credit to Sales Tax Payable.

Posting the Sales Journal. The principles used in posting the sales journal compare to those used in posting the purchases journal. The source of the entry being posted is shown in the posting reference column of an account by the letter "S" and the proper page number. A customer's account with a posting from the sales journal is as follows:

An Account in the Accounts Receivable Ledger

NAME Adler Company

ADDRESS 7608 Melton Ave., Los Angeles, CA 90025-3942

DATE		ITEM	POST. REF.	DEBIT	CREDIT	BALANCE
1989 Oct.	10		S35	6750 00		6750 00

As each debit to a customer's account is posted, a check mark (✓) is inserted in the posting reference column of the sales journal. At the end of each month, the amount column of the sales journal is added, the journal is ruled, and the total is posted as a debit to Accounts Receivable and a credit to Sales. The respective account numbers are then inserted below the total to indicate that the posting is completed.

Sales Returns and Allowances. When merchandise sold is returned or a price adjustment is granted, an entry is made in the general journal according to the principles described in Chapter 2. During October, Kannon Corporation issued a credit memorandum and prepared the entry shown in the two-column general journal at the top of page C-11.

Note the *diagonal line* and *double posting* in the entry to record the credit memorandum. The diagonal line is placed in the posting reference column *at the time the entry is recorded in the general journal.*

If a cash refund is made because of merchandise returned or for an allowance, Sales Returns and Allowances is debited and Cash is credited. The entry would be recorded in the cash payments journal.

General Journal Entry For Sales Returns and Allowances

	JOURNAL				PAGE 18	
	DATE		**DESCRIPTION**	**POST. REF.**	**DEBIT**	**CREDIT**	
1	1989 Oct.	13	Sales Returns and Allowances	412	225 00		1
2			Accounts Receivable—				2
3			Adler Company	113 ✓		225 00	3
4			Credit Memo No. 32				4

Cash Receipts Journal

All transactions that increase the amount of cash are recorded in a **cash receipts journal.** In a typical merchandising business, the most frequent sources of cash receipts are likely to be cash sales and collections from customers on account.

The cash receipts journal has a special column entitled Cash Dr. The frequency of the various kinds of transactions in which cash is received determines the titles of the other columns. The cash receipts journal of Kannon Corporation for October is as follows:

CASH RECEIPTS JOURNAL — PAGE 14

	DATE		ACCOUNT CREDITED	POST. REF.	SUNDRY ACCOUNTS CR.	SALES CR.	ACCOUNTS REC. CR.	SALES DISCOUNTS DR.	CASH DR.	
1	1989 Oct.	2	Notes Receivable	112	2400 00				2544 00	1
2			Interest Income	812	144 00					2
3		5	Barnes Inc.	✓			5800 00	116 00	5684 00	3
4		6	Fogarty & Jacobs	✓			2625 00	52 50	2572 50	4
5		7	Sales	✓		3700 00			3700 00	5
6		10	David T. Mattox	✓			600 00	12 00	588 00	6
7		13	Standard Supply Co.	✓			1604 00	32 08	1571 92	7
8		14	Sales	✓		1632 00			1632 00	8
9		17	Adler Company	✓			6525 00	130 50	6394 50	9
10		19	Hamilton Inc.	✓			4850 00		4850 00	10
11		21	Sales	✓		1920 30			1920 30	11
12		23	Purchases Returns							12
13			and Allowances	512	86 20				86 20	13
14		24	Wallace Corporation	✓			2200 00		2200 00	14
15		27	Hamilton Inc.	✓			7865 00	157 30	7707 70	15
16		28	Sales	✓		2086 00			2086 00	16
17		31	Sales	✓		2423 40			2423 40	17
18		31			2630 20	11761 70	32069 00	500 38	45960 52	18
19					(✓)	(411)	(113)	(413)	(111)	19

Cash Receipts Journal After Posting

The Sundry Accounts Cr. column is used for recording credits to any account for which there is no special column. For example, as of October 2, in the illustration, the receipt of $2,544 in payment of an interest-bearing note was recorded by a credit to Notes Receivable of $2,400 and a credit to Interest Income of $144. Both amounts were entered in the Sundry Accounts Cr. column. The posting references for the credits were inserted at the time the amounts were posted.

The Sales Cr. column is used for recording sales of merchandise for cash. Each individual sale is recorded on a cash register, and the totals thus accumulated are recorded in the cash receipts journal daily, weekly, or at other regular intervals. This is illustrated by the entry of October 7 recording weekly sales and cash receipts of $3,700. Since the total of the Sales Cr. column will be posted at the end of the month, a check mark is inserted in the posting reference column to show that the $3,700 item needs no further attention.

Credits to customers accounts for payments of invoices are recorded in the Accounts Receivable Cr. column. The amount of the cash discount granted, if any, is recorded in the Sales Discounts Dr. column, and the amount of cash actually received is recorded in the Cash Dr. column. The entry on October 5 illustrates the use of these columns. Cash in the amount of $5,684 was received from Barnes Inc. in payment of its account of $5,800, the cash discount being 2% of $5,800, or $116.

Each amount in the Sundry Accounts Cr. column of the cash receipts journal is posted to the proper account in the general ledger at frequent intervals during the month. The posting is indicated by inserting the account number in the posting reference column. At regular intervals the amounts in the Accounts Receivable Cr. column are posted to the customers accounts in the subsidiary ledger, and "CR" and the proper page number are inserted in the posting reference columns of the accounts. Check marks are placed in the posting reference column of the journal to show that the amounts have been posted. None of the individual amounts in the remaining three columns of the cash receipts journal are posted.

At the end of the month, all of the amount columns are footed, the equality of the debits and credits is proved, and the journal is ruled. Because each amount in the Sundry Accounts Cr. column has been posted individually to a general ledger account, a check mark is inserted below the column total to indicate that no further action is needed. The totals of the other four columns are posted to the proper accounts in the general ledger and their account numbers are inserted below the totals to show that the posting has been completed.

The flow of data from the cash receipts journal to the ledgers of Kannon Corporation is illustrated in the following diagram:

Flow of Data From Cash Receipts Journal to Ledgers

Cash Receipts Journal

Account Credited	P. R.	Sundry Accounts Cr.	Sales Cr.	Accounts Receivable Cr.	Sales Discounts Dr.	Cash Dr.
Notes Receivable	112	2,400.00				2,544.00
Interest Income	811	144.00				
Barnes Inc.	✓			5,800.00	116.00	5,684.00
Fogarty & Jacobs	✓			2,625.00	52.50	2,572.50
Sales	✓		3,700.00			3,700.00
David T. Mattox	✓			600.00	12.00	588.00
Sales	✓		2,423.40			2,423.40
		2,630.20	11,761.70	32,069.00	500.38	45,960.52

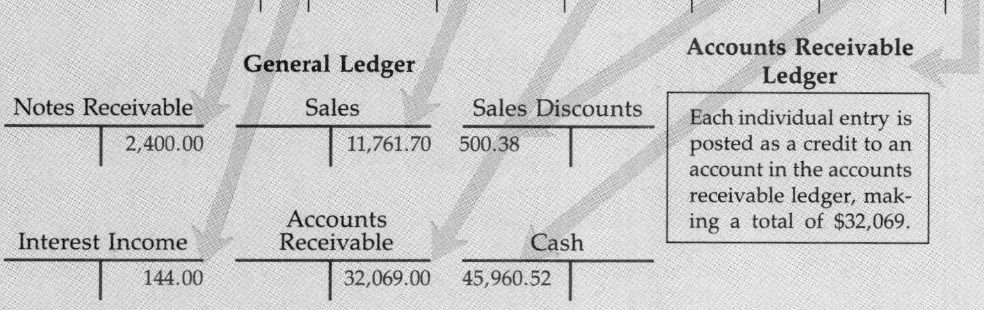

General Ledger

Notes Receivable	
2,400.00	

Sales	
	11,761.70

Sales Discounts	
500.38	

Interest Income	
	144.00

Accounts Receivable	
	32,069.00

Cash	
45,960.52	

Accounts Receivable Ledger

Each individual entry is posted as a credit to an account in the accounts receivable ledger, making a total of $32,069.

Accounts Receivable Control and Subsidiary Ledger

During October, the following postings were made to Accounts Receivable in the general ledger of Kannon Corporation:

Debits

Oct. 31	Total sales on account (sales journal)	$48,940.00

Credits

Oct. 13	A sales return (general journal)	225.00
Oct. 31	Total cash received on account (cash receipts journal)	32,069.00

The accounts receivable controlling account of Kannon Corporation as of October 31 is as follows:

Accounts Receivable Account in the General Ledger at the End of the Month

GENERAL LEDGER

ACCOUNT Accounts Receivable — ACCOUNT NO. 113

DATE		ITEM	POST. REF.	DEBIT	CREDIT	BALANCE DEBIT	BALANCE CREDIT
1989 Oct.	1	Balance	✓			17 260 00	
	13		J18		225 00	17 035 00	
	31		S35	48 940 00		65 975 00	
	31		CR14		32 069 00	33 906 00	

The posting procedures and determination of the balances of the accounts in the accounts receivable ledger and the preparation of the schedule of accounts receivable are comparable to those for accounts payable and are therefore not illustrated.

Problems

C–1. Determination of proper special journals to use. For the past few years, your aunt has operated a small jewelry store, Kal Jewelers. Its current annual revenues are approximately $450,000. Because the company's bookkeeper has been taking more and more time each month to record all transactions in a two-column journal and to prepare the financial statements, your aunt is considering improving the company's accounting system by adding special journals and subsidiary ledgers. Your aunt has asked you to help her with this project. She has compiled the following information:

(1)

Type of Transaction	Estimated Frequency per Month
Purchases of merchandise on account	200
Sales on account	175
Cash receipts from customers on account	150
Daily cash register summaries of cash sales	25
Purchases of merchandise for cash	20
Purchases of office supplies on account	5
Purchases of store supplies on account	5
Cash payments for utilities expenses	4
Cash purchases of office supplies	4
Cash purchases of store supplies	4

(2) For merchandise purchases of high dollar-value items, Kal Jewelers issues notes payable at current interest rates to vendors. These notes are issued because many of the high-value items may not sell immediately and the issuance of the notes reduces the need to maintain large balances of cash or assets that can be readily converted to cash. Notes are issued for approximately 10% of the purchases on account.
(3) All purchases discounts are taken when available.
(4) A sales discount of 1/10, n/30 is offered to all credit customers.
(5) A local sales tax of 6% is collected on all intrastate sales of merchandise.
(6) Monthly financial statements are prepared.

Instructions: (1) Based upon the preceding description of Kal Jewelers, indicate which special journals you would recommend as part of Kal Jewelers' accounting system.
(2) Assume that your aunt has decided to use a sales journal and a purchases journal. Design the format for each journal, giving special consideration to the needs of Kal Jewelers.
(3) Which subsidiary ledgers would you recommend for Kal Jewelers?

C–2. Purchases and purchases returns, accounts payable account, and accounts payable ledger. Purchases on account and related returns and allowances completed by Video Sales during May of the current year are as follows:

May 2. Purchased merchandise on account from Yu Co., $6,150.50
4. Purchased merchandise on account from O'Grady Corp. $9,250.
5. Received a credit memorandum from Yu Co. for merchandise returned, $200.
9. Purchased office supplies on account from Tyler Supply, $175.30.
13. Purchased merchandise on account from Yu Co., $4,370.50.
14. Purchased office equipment on account from Diamond Equipment Co., $5,500.
17. Purchased merchandise on account from James Co., $3,100.
May 19. Received a credit memorandum from Tyler Supply for office supplies returned, $22.50.
20. Purchased merchandise on account from Craig Co., $1,130.30.
24. Purchased store supplies on account from Tyler Supply, $325.
27. Received a credit memorandum from O'Grady Corp. as an allowance for damaged merchandise, $500.
29. Purchased merchandise on account from James Co., $475.15
31. Purchased office supplies on account from Tyler Supply, $210.50.

Instructions: (1) Open the following accounts in the general ledger and enter the balances as of May 1:

114	Store Supplies	$ 460.00
115	Office Supplies	327.40
122	Office Equipment	32,500.00
211	Accounts Payable	12,212.30
511	Purchases	89,917.40
512	Purchases Returns and Allowances	2,170.10

(2) Open the following accounts in the accounts payable ledger and enter the balances in the balance columns as of May 1: Craig Co., $2,177.70; Diamond Equipment Co.; James Co., $4,550.25; O'Grady Corp., $5,484.35; Tyler Supply; Yu Co.
(3) Record the transactions for May, posting to the creditors accounts in the accounts payable ledger immediately after each entry. Use a purchases journal, similar to the one illustrated on pages C-3 and C-4, and a two-column general journal.
(4) Post the general journal and the purchases journal to the accounts in the general ledger.
(5) (a) What is the sum of the balances in the subsidiary ledger at May 31?
(b) What is the balance of the controlling account at May 31?

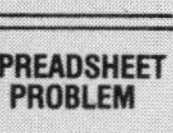

C–3. Purchases and cash payments journals; accounts payable and general ledgers. Ladd Co. was established on March 15 of the current year. Transactions related to purchases, returns and allowances, and cash payments during the remainder of March are as follows:

Mar. 16. Issued Check No. 1 in payment of rent for March, $1,000.
16. Purchased store equipment on account from Harper Equipment Corp., $9,900.
17. Purchased merchandise on account from Carter Clothing, $3,250.
18. Issued Check No. 2 in payment of store supplies, $140, and office supplies, $75.
19. Purchased merchandise on account from Hernandez Clothing Co., $5,920.
20. Purchased merchandise on account from Adams Co., $4,600.
22. Received a credit memorandum from Hernandez Clothing Co. for returned merchandise, $220.
Post the journals to the accounts payable ledger.
24. Issued Check No. 3 to Harper Equipment Corp. in payment of invoice of $9,900.
25. Received a credit memorandum from Adams Co. for defective merchandise, $300.
26. Issued Check No. 4 to Carter Clothing in payment of invoice of $3,250, less 2% discount.
28. Issued Check No. 5 to a cash customer for merchandise returned, $65.
28. Issued Check No. 6 to Hernandez Clothing Co. in payment of the balance owed, less 2% discount.
28. Purchased merchandise on account from Adams Co., $5,250.
Post the journals to the accounts payable ledger.
30. Purchased the following from Harper Equipment Corp. on account: store supplies, $110; office supplies, $42; office equipment, $3,450.
30. Issued Check No. 7 to Adams Co. in payment of invoice of $4,600, less the credit of $300 and 1% discount.
30. Purchased merchandise on account from Carter Clothing, $1,200.
31. Issued Check No. 8 in payment of store supplies, $170.
31. Issued Check No. 9 in payment of sales salaries, $2,200.
31. Received a credit memorandum from Harper Equipment Corp. for defect in office equipment, $50.
Post the journals to the accounts payable ledger.

Instructions: (1) Open the following accounts in the general ledger, using the account numbers indicated:

111	Cash	412	Sales Returns and Allowances
116	Store Supplies	511	Purchases
117	Office Supplies	512	Purchases Returns and Allowances
121	Store Equipment	513	Purchases Discounts
122	Office Equipment	611	Sales Salaries Expense
211	Accounts Payable	712	Rent Expense

(2) Open the following accounts in the accounts payable ledger: Adams Co.; Carter Clothing; Harper Equipment Corp.; Hernandez Clothing Co.
(3) Record the transactions for March, using a purchases journal similar to the one illustrated on pages C-3 and C-4, a cash payments journal similar to the one illustrated on page C-8, and a two-column general journal. Post to the accounts payable ledger at the points indicated in the narrative of transactions.
(4) Post the appropriate individual entries to the general ledger (Sundry Accounts columns of the purchases journal and the cash payments journal; both columns of the general journal).
(5) Total each of the columns of the purchases journal and the cash payments journal, and post the appropriate totals to the general ledger. (Because the problem does not include transactions related to cash receipts, the cash account in the ledger will have a credit balance.)
(6) Prepare a schedule of accounts payable.

C–4. Sales journal; accounts receivable and general ledgers. RGM Company was established on May 15 of the current year. Its sales of merchandise on account and related returns and allowances during the remainder of the month are as follows. Terms of all sales were 1/10, n/30, FOB destination.

May 20. Sold merchandise on account to Bows Co., Invoice No. 1, $1,200.
22. Sold merchandise on account to Stark Inc., Invoice No. 2, $2,750.
24. Sold merchandise on account to Morris Co., Invoice No. 3, $3,175.
25. Issued Credit Memorandum No. 1 for $100 to Bows Co. for merchandise returned.
27. Sold merchandise on account to C. D. Walters Co., Invoice No. 4, $2,500.
28. Sold merchandise on account to Unisac Inc., Invoice No. 5, $1,500.
28. Issued Credit Memorandum No. 2 for $150 to Stark Inc. for merchandise returned.
30. Sold merchandise on account to Stark Inc., Invoice No. 6, $2,925.
30. Issued Credit Memorandum No. 3 for $75 to C. D. Walters Co. for damages to merchandise caused by faulty packing.
31. Sold merchandise on account to Morris Co., Invoice No. 7, $995.

Instructions: (1) Open the following accounts in the general ledger, using the account numbers indicated: Accounts Receivable, 113; Sales, 411; Sales Returns and Allowances, 412.

(2) Open the following accounts in the accounts receivable ledger: Bows Co.; Morris Co.; Stark Inc.; Unisac Inc.; C. D. Walters Co.

(3) Record the transactions for May, posting to the customers accounts in the accounts receivable ledger and inserting the balance immediately after recording each entry. Use a sales journal, similar to the one illustrated on page C-12, and a two-column general journal.

(4) Post the general journal and the sales journal to the three accounts opened in the general ledger, inserting the account balances only after the last postings.

(5) (a) What is the sum of the balances of the accounts in the subsidiary ledger at May 31?

(b) What is the balance of the controlling account at May 31?

If the working papers correlating with the textbook are not used, omit Problem C–5.

C–5. Sales and cash receipts journals; accounts receivable and general ledgers. Three journals, the accounts receivable ledger, and portions of the general ledger of White Company are presented in the working papers. Sales invoices and credit memorandums were entered in the journals by an assistant. Terms of sales on account are 1/10, n/30, FOB shipping point. Transactions in which cash and notes receivable were received during July are as follows:

July 2. Received $5,940 from C. D. Martin Co. in payment of June 22 invoice, less discount.
3. Received $20,200 in payment of $20,000 note receivable and interest of $200.
Post transactions of July 2 and 6 to accounts receivable ledger.
8. Received $6,435 from Janet Rowe Co. in payment of June 28 invoice, less discount.
10. Received $2,200 from R. C. Fellows Inc. in payment of June 10 invoice, no discount.
15. Cash sales for first half of July totaled $14,915.
Post transactions of July 8, 10, 12, and 15 to accounts receivable ledger.
19. Received $1,250 refund for return of defective equipment purchased for cash in June.
20. Received $2,871 from C. D. Martin Co. in payment of balance due on July 10 invoice, less discount.
22. Received $5,742 from R. C. Fellows Inc. in payment of July 12 invoice, less discount.
Post transactions of July 17, 20, 22, and 23 to accounts receivable ledger.
28. Received $50 for sale of office supplies at cost.
31. Received $1,750 cash and a $2,500 note receivable from Ignacio and Co. in settlement of the balance due on the invoice of July 2, no discount. (Record receipt of note in the general journal.)

July 31. Cash sales for the second half of July totaled $16,100.
Post transactions of July 27, 28, 30, and 31 to accounts receivable ledger.

Instructions: (1) Record the cash receipts in the cash receipts journal and the note in the general journal. Before recording a receipt of cash on account, determine the balance of the customer's account. Post the entries from the three journals, in date sequence, to the accounts receivable ledger in accordance with the instructions in the narrative of transactions. Insert the new balance after each posting to an account.
(2) Post the appropriate individual entries from the cash receipts journal and the general journal to the general ledger.
(3) Total each of the columns of the sales journal and the cash receipts journal and post the appropriate totals to the general ledger. Insert the balance of each account after the last posting.
(4) Prepare a schedule of the accounts receivable as of July 31 and compare the total with the balance of the controlling account.

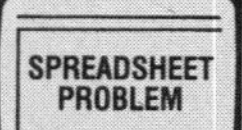

C–6. Sales and cash receipts journals; accounts receivable and general ledgers. Transactions related to sales and cash receipts completed by W. A. Duke Company during the period June 15–30 of the current year are as follows. The terms of all sales on account are 1/10, n/30, FOB shipping point.

June 15. Issued Invoice No. 717 to Towers Co., $6,100.
16. Received cash from F. G. Black Co. for the balance owed on its account, less discount.
17. Issued Invoice No. 718 to Halloway Co., $7,700.
18. Issued Invoice No. 719 to Ross and Son, $2,600.
Post all journals to the accounts receivable ledger.
21. Received cash from Halloway Co. for the balance owed on June 15, no discount.
22. Issued Credit Memorandum No. 55 to Towers Co., $200.
24. Issued Invoice No. 720 to Halloway Co., $7,000.
24. Received $1,050 in payment of a $1,000 note receivable and interest of $50.
Post all journals to the accounts receivable ledger.
25. Received cash from Towers Co. for the balance due on invoice of June 15, less discount.
27. Received cash from Halloway Co. for invoice of June 17, less discount.
29. Issued Invoice No. 721 to F. G. Black Co., $8,500.
30. Recorded cash sales for the second half of the month, $11,750.
30. Issued Credit Memorandum No. 56 to F. G. Black Co., $150.
Post all journals to the accounts receivable ledger.

Instructions: (1) Open the following accounts in the general ledger, inserting the balances indicated, as of June 1:

111	Cash	$13,705
112	Notes Receivable	7,500
113	Accounts Receivable	15,975
411	Sales	—
412	Sales Returns and Allowances	—
413	Sales Discounts	—
811	Interest Income	—

(2) Open the following accounts in the accounts receivable ledger, inserting the balances indicated, as of June 15: F. G. Black Co., $8,900; Halloway Co., $9,825; Ross and Son; Towers Co.
(3) In a sales journal similar to the one illustrated on page C-12 and a cash receipts journal similar to the one illustrated on page C-14, insert "June 15 Total(s) Forwarded" on the first line of the Account Debited or Account Credited column, "✔" in the Post. Ref. column, and the following dollar figures in the respective amount columns:

Sales journal: 25,350
Cash receipts journal: 3,467; 13,470; 22,600; 366; 39,171.

(4) Using the two special journals and a two-column general journal, record the transactions for the remainder of June. Post to the accounts receivable ledger, and insert the balances at the points indicated in the narrative of transactions. *Determine the balance in the customer's account before recording a cash receipt.*

(5) Total each of the columns of the special journals and post the individual entries and totals to the general ledger. Insert account balances after the last posting.

(6) Determine that the subsidiary ledger agrees with the controlling account in the general ledger.

C–7. **All journals and general ledger; trial balance.** The transactions completed by C. E. Dunn Co. during July, the first month of the current fiscal year, were as follows:

July 1. Issued Check No. 920 for July rent, $2,000.
2. Purchased equipment on account from Mann Co., $7,500.
2. Purchased merchandise on account from Evans Corp., $4,250.
3. Issued Invoice No. 832 to Black Co., $1,975.
7. Received check for $2,475 from Owens Corp. in payment of $2,500 invoice, less discount.
7. Issued Check No. 921 for miscellaneous selling expense, $190.
7. Received credit memorandum from Evans Corp. for returned merchandise, $250.
8. Issued Invoice No. 833 to Kane Co., $5,000.
9. Issued Check No. 922 for $9,310 to Frank Inc. in payment of $9,500 invoice, less 2% discount.
9. Received check for $7,425 from Baker Manufacturing Co. in payment of $7,500 invoice, less discount.
10. Issued Check No. 923 to Davis Enterprises in payment of $3,100 invoice, no discount.
12. Issued Invoice No. 834 to Owens Corp., $3,500.
12. Issued Check No. 924 for $930 to Ross Corp. in payment of account, no discount.
12. Received check for $775 from Black Co. on account, no discount.
14. Issued credit memorandum to Owens Corp. for damaged merchandise, $500.
15. Issued Check No. 925 for $3,920 to Evans Corp. in payment of $4,000 balance, less 2% discount.
15. Issued Check No. 926 for $2,250 for cash purchase of merchandise.
15. Cash sales for July 1–15, $23,750.
18. Purchased merchandise on account from Davis Enterprises, $6,420.
19. Received check for return of merchandise that had been purchased for cash, $90.
19. Issued Check No. 927 for miscellaneous general expense, $145.
21. Purchased the following on account from Cass Supply Inc.: store supplies, $225; office supplies, $195.
22. Issued Check No. 928 in payment of advertising expense, $945.
23. Issued Invoice No. 835 to Baker Manufacturing Co., $1,950.
24. Purchased the following on account from Frank Inc.: merchandise, $4,170; store supplies, $130.
25. Issued Invoice No. 836 to Jackson Co., $3,290.
25. Received check for $2,970 from Owens Corp. in payment of $3,000 balance, less discount.
29. Issued Check No. 929 for $7,500 to Mann Co. in payment of invoice of July 2, no discount
30. Issued Check No. 930 in payment of dividends, $3,000.
31. Issued Check No. 931 for monthly salaries as follows: sales salaries, $11,100; office salaries, $4,500.
31. Cash sales for July 16–31, $26,150.
31. Issued Check No. 932 in payment of transportation charges for merchandise purchased during the month, $465.

Instructions: (1) Open the following accounts in the general ledger, entering the balances indicated as of July 1:

111	Cash	$ 9,850
113	Accounts Receivable	12,975
114	Merchandise Inventory	35,500
115	Store Supplies	545
116	Office Supplies	360
117	Prepaid Insurance	2,100
121	Equipment	47,250
122	Accumulated Depreciation	22,250
211	Accounts Payable	13,530
311	Capital Stock	50,000
312	Retained Earnings	22,800
313	Dividends	—
411	Sales	—
412	Sales Returns and Allowances	—
413	Sales Discounts	—
511	Purchases	—
512	Purchases Returns and Allowances	—
513	Purchases Discounts	—
514	Transportation In	—
611	Sales Salaries Expense	—
612	Advertising Expense	—
619	Miscellaneous Selling Expense	—
621	Office Salaries Expense	—
622	Rent Expense	—
629	Miscellaneous General Expense	—

(2) Record the transactions for July, using a purchases journal (as on pages C-3 and C-4), a sales journal (as on page C-12), a cash payments journal (as on page C-8), a cash receipts journal (as on page C-14), and a two-column general journal. The terms of all sales on account are FOB shipping point, 1/10, n/30. Assume that an assistant makes daily postings to the individual accounts in the accounts payable ledger and the accounts receivable ledger.

(3) Post the appropriate individual entries to the general ledger.

(4) Total each of the columns of the special journals and post the appropriate totals to the general ledger; insert the account balances.

(5) Prepare a trial balance.

(6) Balances of the accounts in the subsidiary ledgers as of July 31 are as follows:

Accounts receivable: 2,200; 1,975; 5,000; 1,950; 3,290.
Accounts payable: 6,420; 420; 4,300.

Verify the agreement of the subsidiary ledgers with their respective controlling accounts.

Appendix D
Income Taxes

The federal government and more than three-fourths of the states levy an income tax. In addition, some of the states permit municipalities or other political subdivisions to levy income taxes. In operating a business or determining one's personal income tax, it is only good management to plan to keep these taxes to a minimum. This idea was expressed by Judge Learned Hand in *Newman* [35 AFTR 857], as follows:

> *Over and over again courts have said that there is nothing sinister in so arranging one's affairs as to keep taxes as low as possible. Everybody does so, rich or poor; and all do right, for nobody owes any public duty to pay more than the law demands; taxes are enforced exactions, not voluntary contributions. To demand more in the name of morals is mere cant.*

An understanding of any but the simplest aspects of income taxes is almost impossible without some knowledge of accounting concepts. Conversely, an understanding of the basic concepts of income taxes enable an individual or business to minimize taxes. In many cases, this understanding of the basic concepts leads one to seek the advice and assistance of professional accountants who specialize in determining the tax or developing plans to minimize the tax.

The explanations and illustrations of the federal system presented in this appendix are illustrative of the nature of income taxes. They are brief and relatively free of the many complexities encountered in actual practice. In addition, it should be noted that the federal tax laws are often changed, and that major tax bills have been enacted on the average of every 18 months since the original tax law was passed in 1913. The tax law upon which this discussion is based was changed significantly by the Tax Reform Act of 1986 (as amended by the Revenue Act of 1987), and the provisions of this act will not be fully implemented until 1991. Therefore, the current tax law and the current tax rates should be examined before tax-related decisions are made.

FEDERAL INCOME TAX SYSTEM

The present system of federal income tax began with the Revenue Act of 1913, which was enacted soon after the ratification of the Sixteenth Amendent to the Constitution. All current income tax statutes, as well as other federal tax laws, are now codified in the Internal Revenue Code (IRC).

The Treasury Department is charged with responsibility in federal tax matters. The division of the Department concerned specifically with enforcement and collection of the income tax is the Internal Revenue Service (IRS), headed by the Commissioner of Internal Revenue. Interpretations of the law and directives formulated according to express provisions of the IRC are issued in various forms. The most important and comprehensive are the "Regulations," which extend to more than two thousands pages.

The data required for the determination of income tax liability are supplied by the taxpayer on official forms and supporting schedules that are referred to collectively as a tax return. Failure to receive the forms from the IRS or failure to maintain adequate records does not relieve taxpayers of their legal obligations to file annual tax returns. Willful failure to comply with the income tax laws may result in the imposition of severe civil and criminal penalties.

Taxpayers alleged by the IRS to be deficient in reporting or paying their tax may, if they disagree with the determination, present their case in informal conferences at district and regional levels. Unresolved disputes may be taken to the federal courts for settlement. The taxpayer may seek relief in the Tax Court or may pay the disputed amount and sue to recover it.

The income tax is not imposed upon business units as such, but upon taxable entities. The principal taxable entities are individuals, corporations, estates, and trusts.

Business enterprises organized as sole proprietorships are not taxable entities. The revenues and expenses of such business enterprises are reported in the individual tax returns of the owners. Partnerships are not taxable entities but are required to report on an informational return the details of their revenues, expenses, and allocations to partners. The partners then report on their individual tax returns the amount of net income and other special items allocated to them on the partnership return.

Corporations engaged in business for profit are generally treated as distinct taxable entities. However, it is possible for two or more corporations with common ownership to join in filing a consolidated return. Subchapter S of the IRC also permits a nonpublic corporation that conforms to specified requirements to elect to be treated in a manner similar to a partnership. The effect of the election is to tax the shareholders on their distributive shares of the net income instead of taxing the corporation.

ACCOUNTING METHODS

Although neither the IRC nor the Regulations provide uniform systems of accounting for use by all taxpayers, detailed procedures are prescribed in certain cases. In addition, the IRS has the authority to prescribe accounting methods where those used by a taxpayer fail to yield a fair determination of taxable income. In general, taxpayers have the option of using either the cash basis or the accrual basis.

Cash Basis

Because of its greater simplicity, the cash basis of determining taxable income is usually used by individuals whose sources of income are limited to salary, dividends, and interest. Professional and other service enterprises (e.g., physicians, attorneys, insurance agencies) also ordinarily use the cash basis in determining taxable income. One of the advantages is that the fees charged to clients or customers are not considered to be earned until payment is received. Similarly, it is not necessary to accrue expenses incurred but not paid within the tax year. It is not permissible, however, to treat the entire cost of long-lived assets as an expense of the period in which the cash payment is made.[1] Deductions for depreciation on equipment and buildings used for business purposes may be claimed in the same manner as under the accrual basis, regardless of when payment is made.

Recognition of revenue according to the cash basis is not always contingent upon the actual receipt of cash. In some cases, revenue is said to be constructively received at the time it becomes available to the taxpayer, regardless of when it is actually converted to cash. For example, a check for services rendered which is received before the end of a taxable year is income of that year, even though the check is not deposited or cashed until the following year. Other examples of constructive receipt are bond interest coupons due within the taxable year and interest credited to a savings account as of the last day of the taxable year.

Accrual Basis

For businesses in which production or trading in merchandise is an important factor, purchases and sales must be accounted for on the accrual basis. Thus, revenues from sales must be reported in the year in which the goods are sold, regardless of when the cash is received. Similarly, the cost of goods purchased must be reported in the year in which the liabilities are incurred, regardless of when payment is made. The usual adjustments must also be made for the beginning and ending inventories in order to determine the cost of goods sold and the gross profit. However, enterprises are not required to extend the accrual basis to every other phase of their operations. A mixture

[1]The current tax law allows small businesses to write off as an expense as much as $10,000 of annual equipment purchases.

of the cash and accrual methods of accounting is permissible, if it yields reasonable results and is used consistently from year to year.

INCOME TAX ON INDIVIDUALS

Methods of accounting in general, as well as many of the regulations affecting the determination of net business or professional income, are not affected by the legal nature or the organizational structure of the taxpayer. On the other hand, the tax base and the tax rate structure for individuals differ markedly from those which apply to corporations.

The individual's tax base, upon which the amount of income tax is determined, is called taxable income. Taxable income is gross income less certain deductions as specified by the IRC. It is determined as follows:

Determination of Taxable Income for Individuals

GROSS INCOME
minus
DEDUCTIONS FROM GROSS INCOME
equals
ADJUSTED GROSS INCOME
minus
ITEMIZED DEDUCTIONS AND EXEMPTIONS
equals
TAXABLE INCOME

The basic concepts underlying the determination of taxable income are discussed in the paragraphs that follow.

Gross Income

Items of gross income subject to tax are sometimes called taxable gross income. Some of the taxable and nontaxable items of gross income of indi-viduals are as follows:

Partial List of Taxable and Nontaxable Gross Income Items

TAXABLE ITEMS	NONTAXABLE ITEMS
Wages and other remuneration from employer.	All or portions of federal old-age pension benefits, depending on amounts of other income.
Tips and gratuities for services rendered.	Value of property received as a gift.
Cash dividends.	Value of property received by bequest, devise, or inheritance.
Rents and royalties.	Life insurance proceeds received because of death of insured.
Income from a business or profession.	Interest on most obligations of a state or political subdivision.
Gains from the sale of real estate, securities, and other property.	Scholarships for tuition and fees.
Distributive share of partnership income.	Compensation for injuries or for damages related to personal or family rights.
Income from an estate or trust.	Worker's compensation insurance for sickness or injury.
Prizes won in contests.	
Gambling winnings.	
Jury fees.	
Gains from illegal transactions.	
Unemployment compensation.	

Deductions from Gross Income

Business expenses and other expenses related to earning revenue are deductible in full or in part from gross income to yield adjusted gross income. For example, ordinary and necessary expenses incurred in the operations of a sole proprietorship are deductible from gross income. Also, expenses that are directly connected with earning rent or royalty income are allowable as deductions from gross income.

A self-employed individual may establish a qualified retirement fund (called a Keogh plan) and deduct the annual contribution from gross income in determining adjusted gross income. Also, certain employees may deduct contributions to plans provided by employers (called 401K plans), and low- and middle-income workers can deduct contributions to individual retirement accounts (called IRAs). The IRC and related regulations state many limitations on the amount of such deductions from gross income.

Adjusted Gross Income

The expenses described in the preceding section are deducted from an amount of related gross income. The resulting figure is the adjusted gross income. The amount of adjusted gross income is used in determining the amount of some of the deductions described in the following section. For example, the medical deduction is limited to the portion of total medical expenses which exceed 7 1/2% of adjusted gross income.

Itemized Deductions, the Standard Deduction, and Exemptions

After the amount of adjusted gross income of an individual is determined, two categories of deductions are subtracted to yield taxable income: (1) itemized deductions or the standard deduction and (2) exemptions. These two deductions from adjusted gross income are described in the following paragraphs.

Itemized Deductions. Certain specified expenditures and losses may be *itemized* and deducted from adjusted gross income. The deductions that are generally available to individuals who itemize deductions are described in the paragraphs that follow.

Charitable contributions. Contributions made by an individual to domestic organizations created exclusively for religious, charitable, scientific, literary, or educational purposes, or for the prevention of cruelty to children or animals are deductible, provided the organization is nonprofit and does not devote a substantial part of its activities to influencing legislation. Contributions to domestic governmental units and to organizations of war veterans are also deductible.

The limitation on the amount of qualified contributions that may be deducted ranges from 20% of adjusted gross income for contributions to private foundations to 50% of adjusted gross income for contributions to public charities, with 50% being the overall maximum. There are other intermediate limitations related to contributions of various types of property other than cash.

Interest expense. Interest expense on indebtedness for the taxpayer's principal and second residences is deductible, subject to certain limitations. Interest expense on indebtedness used for investment purposes is fully deductible up to an amount equal to investment income.

Taxes. Most of the taxes levied by the federal government are not deductible from adjusted gross income. Some of the taxes of a nonbusiness or personal nature levied by states or their political subdivisions are deductible from adjusted gross income. The common deductible state and local taxes are real estate, personal property, and income taxes.

Medical expenses. Amounts paid for prescription drugs and insulin and other medical expenses are generally deductible to the extent that they exceed 7 1/2% of adjusted gross income. Other medical expenses deductible in total or in part include medical care insurance, doctors' fees, hospital expenses, etc.

Standard Deduction. As an alternative to itemizing deductions, the taxpayer may take a standard deduction. The amount of the deduction depends upon whether the taxpayer is filing as a single taxpayer, as a head of household, or with a spouse (joint return). In 1988, for example, the standard deduction for a single taxpayer is $3,000. Beginning in 1989, the deduction is adjusted annually for inflation.

Exemptions. In general, each taxpayer is entitled to a personal exemption.[2] An additional exemption is allowed for each dependent. The amount of the personal exemption is $2,000 in 1989. Beginning in 1990, the exemption is adjusted annually for inflation.

Taxable Income and Determination of Income Tax

After the taxable income is determined, the taxpayer uses various tax rate schedules to determine the amount of the income tax. For example, the individual tax rates for a single taxpayer are as follows for 1988:

Taxable Income	Tax Rate[3]
$0– $17,850	15%
Over $17,850	28%

To illustrate the use of the tax rate schedules, assume that a single taxpayer has taxable income of $27,850. The tax is determined as follows:

Individual Tax Rates—Single Taxpayer

Tax on $17,850 at 15%	$2,678 (rounded)
Tax on 10,000 at 28%	2,800
Total on $27,850	$5,478

Credits Against the Tax

After the amount of the income tax has been determined, the tax may be reduced on a dollar-for-dollar basis by the amount of various credits. These credits are therefore quite different from deductions and exemptions, which are reductions of the income subject to tax. The most common credits are described in the paragraphs that follow.

Credit for the Elderly. Some elderly taxpayers receive nontaxable retirement income, while others receive taxable retirement income. The credit for the elderly is an attempt to overcome this perceived inequity. The formula for determining the credit is complex and the IRC should be consulted for the details.

Child and Disabled Dependent Care Expenses Credit. Taxpayers who maintain a household are allowed a tax credit for expenses, including household expenses, involved in the care of a dependent child under age 15 or a physically or mentally incapacitated dependent or spouse, provided the expenses were incurred to enable the taxpayer to be gainfully employed. The amount of the credit is on a sliding scale, depending on the amount of adjusted gross income and the number of dependents.

Earned Income Credit. This credit against the tax is available to low-income workers who maintain a household for at least one of their dependent children and who have earned income (wages and self-employment income). Unlike the other credits, which cannot exceed the amount of the tax before applying the credit, if the earned income credit reduces the tax liability below zero, the negative amount is paid to the taxpayer. For example, if a worker's tax liability before applying the credit is $150 and the earned income credit is $375, the taxpayer will receive a direct payment of $225. Direct payments of tax revenues to individuals who have no liability for federal

[2]Certain high-income taxpayers are not eligible for the personal exemption. For single taxpayers, the personal exemption is phased out by applying a surtax to taxable income that exceeds $89,560.

[3]For certain high-income taxpayers, a surtax is added to offset the benefit of the 15% tax rate.

income tax is a concept with significant socioeconomic implications. The concept is often called a "negative income tax."

Filing Returns; Payment of Tax

The income tax withheld from an employee's earnings by an employer represents current payments on account. An individual whose income is not subject to withholding, or only partially so, or an individual whose income is fairly large must estimate the income tax in advance. The estimated tax for the year, after deducting the estimated amount to be withheld and any credit for overpayment from prior years, must be paid currently, usually in quarterly installments.

Annual income tax returns must be filed at the appropriate Internal Revenue Service office within 3 1/2 months following the end of the taxpayer's taxable year. Any balance owed must accompany the return. If there has been an overpayment of the tax liability, the taxpayer may request that the overpayment be refunded or credited against the estimated tax for the following year.

INCOME TAX ON CORPORATIONS

The taxable income of a corporation is determined, in general, by deducting its ordinary business expenses from the total amount of its includable gross income. The corporate tax rates, in general, are as follows for 1988:

Corporate Income Tax Rates

Taxable Income	Tax Rate[4]
$0– $50,000	15%
$50,001–$75,000	25%
Over $75,000	34%

TAX PLANNING TO MINIMIZE INCOME TAXES

There are various legal means of minimizing or reducing federal income taxes, some of which are of broader applicability than others. Much depends upon the volume and the sources of a taxpayer's gross income, the nature of the expenses and other deductions, and the accounting methods used. Examples of means to minimize income taxes are presented in the following paragraphs.

Alternative Accounting Principles

There are many cases in which an enterprise may choose from among two or more optional accounting principles in determining the amount of its taxable income. The particular principle chosen may have an effect on the amount of income tax, not only in the year in which the choice is made but also in later years. To illustrate, the tax law generally permits an enterprise to choose its method of determining the cost of inventory. Two widely used methods are fifo (first-in, first-out) and lifo (last-in, first-out). The more traditional method is fifo, while the more widely used method is lifo. The method chosen may have a significant effect on income and the tax on income in periods of changing price levels.

Under fifo, the first goods purchased during a year are assumed to be the first goods sold. During a period of rising prices, the first goods purchased are the least costly. If the least costly goods are sold, they are charged against revenue, and the most costly goods are included in inventory. Under lifo, however, the last goods

[4] The benefits of the 15% and 25% tax rates would be phased out for companies whose income exceeds $100,000. For those companies, a 5% tax on income over $100,000 would be added until the tax is equal to a flat rate of 34%.

purchased during a year are assumed to be the first goods sold. During a period of rising prices, the last goods purchased are the most costly. If the most costly goods are sold, they are charged against revenue, and the least costly goods are included in inventory. Thus, in periods of rising prices, lifo results in higher cost of goods sold, lower income, and lower taxes than fifo.

To illustrate the effects of fifo and lifo on the cost of goods sold and gross profit (and consequently net income and income taxes) in a period of rising prices, assume the following activity for a year for a firm that sells one product:

Sales, 1,000 units at $200	$200,000
Beginning inventory, 500 units at $150	75,000
Purchases, 1,000 units at $160	160,000
Ending inventory, 500 units	—

The effect of using fifo and lifo on the year's gross profit is as follows:

	Fifo		*Lifo*	
Sales		$200,000		$200,000
Cost of goods sold:				
Beginning inventory	$ 75,000		$ 75,000	
Purchases	160,000		160,000	
Goods available for sale	$235,000		$235,000	
Ending inventory:				
500 units at $160	80,000			
500 units at $150			75,000	
Cost of goods sold		155,000		160,000
Gross profit		$ 45,000		$ 40,000

Under fifo, the 1,000 units sold include the 500 in beginning inventory at $150, or $75,000, plus 500 of those purchased at $160, or $80,000, for a total of $155,000. Under lifo, the 1,000 units sold would be the 1,000 purchased at $160, or $160,000. Thus, using lifo results in a $5,000 higher cost of goods sold (and lower gross profit). From another view, the $5,000 difference in gross profit can be viewed as the difference in the ending inventory amounts ($80,000 − $75,000).

The income tax effect of using fifo versus lifo during periods of declining prices would be the reverse of that illustrated. During periods of declining prices, gross profit (and net income and income taxes) under lifo would exceed that of fifo.

In times of inflation, which has been the long-term trend in the United States since World War II, the use of lifo not only results in a lower annual income tax, but it also permits the taxpayer to retain more funds, by lowering tax payments, to replace goods sold with higher-priced goods. Clearly, this advantage is one of the most important reasons for lifo's popularity.

Use of Corporate Debt

If a corporation is in need of relatively permanent funds, it generally considers borrowing money on a long-term basis or issuing stock. Since interest on debt is a deductible expense in determining taxable income and dividends paid on stock are not, this impact on income tax is one of the important factors to consider in evaluating the two methods of financing. To illustrate, assume that a corporation which expects a tax rate of 34% is considering issuing (1) $1,000,000 of 10% bonds or (2) $1,000,000 of 10% cumulative preferred stock. If the bonds are issued, the deduction of the yearly $100,000 of interest in determining taxable income results in an annual net borrowing cost of $66,000 ($100,000 less tax savings of 34% of $100,000). If the preferred stock is issued, the dividends are not deductible in determining taxable income and the net annual outlay for this method of financing is $100,000. Thus, issuing bonds instead of preferred stock reduced the annual financing expenditures by $34,000 ($100,000 − $66,000).

Nontaxable Investment Income

Interest on bonds issued by a state or political subdivision is exempt from the federal income tax. To illustrate, the following table compares the income after tax on a $100,000 investment in a 10% industrial bond and a $100,000 investment in an 8% municipal bond for a corporation with a tax rate of 34%.

	Taxable 10% Industrial Bond	*Nontaxable 8% Municipal Bond*
Income	$10,000	$8,000
Tax (34% of $10,000)	3,400	—
Income after tax	$ 6,600	$8,000

Although the interest rate on the municipal bond (8%) is less than the rate on the industrial bond (10%), the aftertax income is larger from the investment in the municipal bond.

GENERAL IMPACT OF INCOME TAXES

The foregoing description of the federal income tax system and discussion of tax minimization demonstrates the importance of income taxes to individuals and to business enterprises. Many accountants, in both private and public practice, devote their entire attention to tax planning for their employers or their clients. The statutes and the administrative regulations, which are often changed, must be studied continuously by anyone who engages in this phase of accounting.

Discussion Questions

D–1. (a) Does the failure to receive the tax forms from the IRS qualify as a legitimate means of tax avoidance? (b) Does the failure to maintain adequate records qualify as a legitimate means of tax avoidance?

D–2. (a) What are the principal taxable entities subject to the federal income tax? (b) How is the income of a sole proprietorship taxed?

D–3. Describe briefly the system employed in subjecting the income of partnerships to the federal income tax.

D–4. The adjusted gross income of a sole proprietorship for the year was $60,000, of which the owner withdrew $45,000. What amount of income from the business enterprise must be reported on the owner's income tax return?

D–5. Do corporations electing partnership treatment (Subchapter S) pay federal income tax? Discuss.

D–6. Which of the two methods of accounting, cash or accrual, is more commonly used by individual taxpayers?

D–7. Describe constructive receipt of gross income as it applies to (a) a salary check received from an employer, (b) interest credited to a savings account, and (c) bond interest coupons.

D–8. Arrange the following items in their proper sequence for the determination of taxable income of an individual.
(a) Adjusted gross income
(b) Gross income

(c) Itemized deductions and exemptions
(d) Taxable income
(e) Expenses related to business or specified revenue

D–9. Which inventory method (lifo or fifo) would result in the lower income tax during a period of rising prices? Explain.

Exercises

D–10. Determination of income using cash method and accrual method. Nancy Young, DDS, opened her dental office after graduation from dental school in early January of the current year. On December 31, the accounting records indicated the following for the current year to date:

	Total	Cash Received	Cash Paid
Fees earned	$92,000	$79,000	—
Lease of dental office and equipment	24,000	—	$22,000
Dental assistant salary	18,000	—	16,500
Dental supplies, utilities, etc.	9,000	—	7,400

(a) Determine the amount of net income Young would report from her dental practice for the current year under the (a) cash method and (b) accrual method.
(b) List the advantages of using the cash method rather than the accrual method in accounting for Young's dental practice.
(c) What is the principal advantage of using the accrual method rather than the cash method in accounting for Young's dental practice?

D–11. Determination of corporation income tax. During the current year, three corporations realized the following taxable income:

Corporation A	$ 10,000
Corporation B	60,000
Corporation C	100,000

Using the tax rates indicated in the chapter, determine the amount of income tax owed by each corporation.

D–12. Effects of using fifo and lifo for inventory costing. On January 10 of the current year, Linda Marie Fell opened the Old Fashioned Ice Cream Parlor. During the year, ice cream was purchased at three different prices, as follows:

	Price per Gallon
January 10–May 1	$1.50
May 2–August 20	1.55
August 21–December 31	1.65

Sales averaged 400 gallons of ice cream per month, and 150 gallons were on hand at December 31.

(a) Assuming the use of the fifo (first-in, first-out) inventory method, determine the cost of the inventory at December 31.
(b) Assuming the use of the lifo (last-in, first-out) inventory method, determine the cost of the inventory at December 31.
(c) Which inventory method, fifo or lifo, will result in the lower net income, and by how much will the income be lower?

D–13. Effects of using fifo and lifo for inventory costing. Acme Limousine Sales sold 25 limousines for $22,500 each during the first year of operations. Data related to purchases during the year are as follows:

	Quantity	Unit Cost
January 3.	5	$20,000
April 10.	4	20,100
June 30	7	20,250
August 22	10	20,300
November 5	5	20,500

Sales of limousines are the company's only source of income, and operating expenses for the current year are $19,750.

(a) Determine the net income for the current year, using the fifo (first-in, first-out) inventory method.

(b) Determine the net income for the current year, using the lifo (last-in, first-out) inventory method.

(c) Which method of inventory costing, fifo or lifo, would you recommend for tax purposes? Discuss.

D–14. Effects of corporation income tax on two financing plans. The board of directors of Highland Inc. is planning an expansion of plant facilities expected to cost $2,000,000. The board is undecided about the method of financing this expansion and is considering two plans:

Plan 1. Issue 20,000 shares of $100, 10% cumulative preferred stock at par.
Plan 2. Issue $2,000,000 of 20-year, 12% bonds at face amount.

The condensed balance sheet of the corporation at the end of the most recent fiscal year is as follows:

Highland Inc.
Balance Sheet
December 31, 19--

Assets		Liabilities and Stockholders' Equity	
Current assets	$1,400,000	Current liabilities.	$1,140,000
Plant assets	4,600,000	Common stock, $25 par.	2,500,000
		Premium on common stock. . .	1,000,000
		Retained earnings	1,360,000
Total assets.	$6,000,000	Total liabilities and stock-holders' equity	$6,000,000

Net income has remained relatively constant over the past several years. As a result of the expansion program, yearly income after tax but before bond interest and related income tax is expected to increase to $450,000.

(a) Prepare a tabulation indicating the net annual outlay (dividends and interest after tax) for financing under each plan. (Use the 34% income tax rate indicated in the chapter.)

(b) List factors other than the net cost of financing that the board should consider in evaluating the two plans.

Appendix E

The Direct Method of Reporting Cash Flows From Operating Activities

There are two alternative formats for reporting cash flows from operating activities on the statement of cash flows: (1) the indirect method and (2) the direct method. The amount reported as the net cash flow from operating activities will not be affected by the format used. The indirect method is more widely used in practice and was discussed and illustrated in Chapter 14. The basic concepts of reporting cash flows from operating activities by the direct method are briefly discussed in this appendix.

In reporting cash flows from operating activities by the direct method, the major classes of operating cash receipts (cash received from customers, for example) and operating cash payments (cash payments to suppliers for merchandise, for example) are presented on the statement of cash flows. The difference between the total cash receipts by major classes and the total cash payments by major classes is the net cash flow from operating activities.[1]

ASSEMBLING DATA FOR CASH FLOWS FROM OPERATING ACTIVITIES

To collect data for reporting cash flows from operating activities by the direct method, all of the operating cash receipts and operating cash payments for a period could be analyzed and classified for reporting on the statement of cash flows. However, this procedure would be expensive and time consuming. A more efficient procedure is to examine the revenues and expenses reported on the income statement and to determine the cash flows related to these revenues and expenses. In performing this analysis, supplementary data can be obtained from other records as needed. To illustrate this approach to assembling data for reporting cash flows from operating activities, the following income statement for Johnson Company for the year ended December 31, 1989, will be used:

Johnson Company
Income Statement
For Year Ended December 31, 1989

Sales		$990,000
Cost of merchandise sold		580,000
Gross profit		$410,000
Operating expenses:		
Depreciation expense	$ 38,000	
Other operating expenses	256,500	
Total operating expenses		294,500
Income before income tax		$115,500
Income tax		27,500
Net income		$ 88,000

[1]A reconciliation of net income and net cash flow from operating activities, as illustrated in the footnote on page E-4, may be included as a supplement to the cash flow statement when the direct method of reporting cash flows from operating activities is used.

Additional data showing the change in relevant account balances from the beginning to the end of 1989 are as follows:

Accounts	December 31 1989	December 31 1988	Increase Decrease*
Trade receivables (net)	$ 72,500	$ 65,000	$ 7,500
Inventories	155,000	165,000	10,000*
Prepaid expenses	6,500	5,000	1,500
Accounts payable (merchandise creditors)	60,000	46,000	14,000
Accrued operating expenses	13,000	8,500	4,500
Income tax payable	5,500	7,500	2,000*

The determination of the cash receipts and cash payments by major classes are discussed and illustrated in the following paragraphs.

Cash Received from Customers

The $990,000 of sales reported on the income statement for Johnson Company is determined by the accrual method. To determine the cash received from sales made to customers, the $990,000 must be converted to the cash basis. The procedure to convert the sales reported on the income statement to the cash received from customers can be summarized as follows:

Sales (reported on the income statement)	......	+ decrease in trade receivables **or** − increase in trade receivables	=	Cash Received from Customers

For Johnson Company, the cash received from customers is $982,500, determined as follows:

Sales	$990,000
Less increase in trade receivables	7,500
Cash received from customers	$982,500

The additions to **trade receivables** for sales on account during the year were $7,500 more than the deductions for amounts collected from customers on account. The amount reported on the income statement as sales therefore included $7,500 that did not yield cash inflow during the year. In other words, the increase in trade receivables of $7,500 during 1989 indicates that sales exceeded cash received from customers by $7,500. Accordingly, $7,500 must be deducted from sales to determine the cash received from customers.

The $982,500 of cash received from customers would be reported in the cash flows from operating activities section of the cash flow statement. For Johnson Company, this section is presented on page E-4.

Cash Payments for Merchandise

The $580,000 of cost of merchandise sold reported on the income statement for Johnson Company is determined by the accrual method. The conversion of the cost of merchandise sold to the cash payments made during 1989 for merchandise can be summarized as follows:

Cost of Merchandise Sold (reported on the income statement)	......	+ increase in inventories or − decrease in inventories AND + decrease in accounts payable or − increase in accounts payable	=	Cash Payments for Merchandise

In the illustration for Johnson Company, the cash payments for merchandise is $556,000, determined as follows:

Cost of merchandise sold		$580,000
Deduct: Decrease in inventories	$10,000	
Increase in accounts payable	14,000	24,000
Cash payments for merchandise		$556,000

The $10,000 decrease in **inventories** indicates that the merchandise sold exceeded the cost of the merchandise purchased by $10,000. The amount reported on the income statement as a deduction from sales revenue therefore included $10,000 that did not require cash outflow during the year. Accordingly, $10,000 must be deducted from cost of merchandise sold in determining the cash payments for merchandise.

The effect of the increase in **accounts payable,** which is the amount owed creditors for merchandise, was to include in merchandise purchases the sum of $14,000 for which there had been no cash outlay during the year. In other words, the increase in accounts payable indicates that cash payments for merchandise was $14,000 less than purchases made during 1989. Hence, $14,000 must be deducted from the cost of merchandise sold in determining the cash payments for merchandise.

Cash Payments for Operating Expenses

• • •

Since the $38,000 of depreciation expense reported on the income statement did not require an outlay of cash, it is not reported on the statement of cash flows. The conversion of the $256,500 reported for the other operating expenses to cash payments for operating expenses can be summarized as follows:

Operating Expenses other than Depreciation (reported on the income statement)	....	+ increase in prepaid expenses or − decrease in prepaid expenses AND + decrease in accrued expenses or − increase in accrued expenses	=	Cash Payments for Operating Expenses

For Johnson Company, the cash payments for operating expenses is $253,500, determined as follows:

Operating expenses other than depreciation	$256,500
Add increase in prepaid expenses	1,500
	$258,000
Deduct increase in accrued operating expenses	4,500
Cash payments for operating expenses	$253,500

The outlay of cash for **prepaid expenses** exceeded by $1,500 the amount deducted as an expense during the year. Hence, $1,500 must be added to the amount of operating expenses (other than depreciation) reported on the income statement in determining the cash payments for operating expenses.

The increase in **accrued operating expenses** indicates that the amount reported as an expense during the year exceeded the cash payments by $4,500. Hence, $4,500 must be deducted from the amount of operating expenses on the income statement in determining the cash payments for operating expenses.

Cash Payments for Income Taxes

The procedure to convert the amount of income tax reported on the income statement to the cash basis can be summarized as follows:

Income Tax (reported on income statement)	....	+ decrease in income tax payable **or** − increase in income tax payable	=	Cash Payments for Income Tax

For Johnson Company, the cash payments for income tax is $29,500, determined as follows:

Income tax.	$27,500
Add decrease in income tax payable	2,000
Cash payments for income tax.	$29,500

The outlay of cash for **income taxes** exceeded by $2,000 the amount of income tax deducted as an expense during the period. Accordingly, $2,000 must be added to the amount of income tax reported on the income statement to determine the cash payments for income tax.

REPORTING CASH FLOWS FROM OPERATING ACTIVITIES

The main classes of operating cash receipts and operating cash payments for Johnson Company, as determined in the preceding paragraphs, may be reported in the statement of cash flows as follows:

Cash flows from operating activities:			
Cash received from customers		$982,500	
Deduct: Cash payments for merchandise	$556,000		
Cash payments for operating expenses	253,500		
Cash payments for income tax	29,500	839,000	
Net cash flow from operating activities			$143,500[2]

[2]Regardless of whether the direct method or the indirect method is used, the same amount of net cash flow from operating activities will be reported in the cash flow statement. For example, as described and illustrated in Chapter 14, the indirect method would report net cash flow from operating activities of $143,500, which would be presented as follows:

Net income, per income statement		$88,000	
Add: Depreciation	$38,000		
Decrease in inventories	10,000		
Increase in accounts payable	14,000		
Increase in accrued operating expenses	4,500	66,500	
		$154,500	
Deduct: Increase in trade receivables	$ 7,500		
Increase in prepaid expenses	1,500		
Decrease in income tax payable	2,000	11,000	
Net cash flow from operating activities			$143,500

Exercises

E–1. Cash flows from operating activities section. The income statement of BCD Company for the current year ended June 30 is as follows:

Sales		$735,000
Cost of merchandise sold		440,000
Gross profit		$295,000
Operating expenses:		
Depreciation expense	$ 22,500	
Other operating expenses	177,500	
Total operating expenses		200,000
Income before income tax		$ 95,000
Income tax		20,000
Net income		$ 75,000

Changes in the balance of selected accounts from the beginning to the end of the current year are as follows:

	Increase (Decrease)
Trade receivables (net)	$(15,000)
Inventories	8,000
Prepaid expenses	(750)
Accounts payable (merchandise creditors)	(12,500)
Accrued operating expenses	5,000
Income tax payable	(1,500)

Prepare the cash flows from operating activities section of the statement of cash flows, using the direct method of presentation.

E–2. Cash flows from operating activities section. The income statement for AB&T Co. for the current year ended March 31 and the balances of selected accounts at the end and beginning of the year are as follows:

Sales		$975,000
Cost of merchandise sold		610,000
Gross profit		$365,000
Operating expenses:		
Depreciation expense	$ 55,000	
Other operating expenses	210,000	
Total operating expenses		265,000
Income before income tax		$100,000
Income tax		24,500
Net income		$ 75,500

	End of Year	Beginning of Year
Trade receivables (net)	$ 98,000	$ 89,000
Inventories	110,000	115,000
Prepaid expenses	4,500	3,000
Accounts payable (merchandise creditors)	67,500	75,000
Accrued operating expenses	9,000	6,000
Income tax payable	3,000	2,000

Prepare the cash flows from operating activities section of the statement of cash flows, using the direct method of presentation.

E–3. Cash flows from operating activities section. The income statement for the current year and balances of selected accounts at the beginning and end of the current year are as follows:

Sales		$870,000
Cost of merchandise sold		510,000
Gross profit		$360,000
Operating expenses:		
Depreciation expense	$ 32,250	
Other operating expenses	213,750	
Total operating expenses		246,000
Income before income tax		$114,000
Income tax		26,900
Net income		$ 87,100

	End of Year	Beginning of Year
Trade receivables	$ 87,500	$80,000
Inventories	110,000	95,000
Prepaid expenses	6,900	7,650
Accounts payable (merchandise creditors)	77,200	72,700
Accrued operating expenses	3,750	6,250
Income tax payable	1,100	1,100

Prepare the cash flows from operating activities section of the statement of cash flows, using the direct method of presentation.

E–4. Cash flows from operating activities section. The income statement for the current year and the balances of selected accounts at the beginning and end of the current year are as follows:

Sales		$1,300,000
Cost of merchandise sold		760,000
Gross profit		$ 540,000
Operating expenses:		
Depreciation expense	$ 43,500	
Other operating expenses	367,875	
Total operating expenses		411,375
Operating income		$ 128,625
Other expense:		
Interest expense		9,000
Income before income tax		$ 119,625
Income tax		27,500
Net income		$ 92,125

	End of Year	Beginning of Year
Accounts receivable (trade)	$ 80,500	$85,000
Inventories	110,000	97,000
Prepaid expenses	7,900	7,400
Accounts payable (merchandise creditors)	69,700	72,700
Accrued operating expenses	7,500	6,250
Interest payable	1,500	1,500
Income tax payable	2,500	4,000

Prepare the cash flows from operating activities section of a statement of cash flows, using the direct method of presentation.

Problems

E–5. Statement of cash flows. The comparative balance sheet of R. N. Corley Inc. for December 31 of the current year and the preceding year and the income statement for the current year are as follows:

	December 31	
	Current Year	Preceding Year
Cash	$ 72,000	$ 50,500
Trade receivables (net)	88,000	80,000
Inventories	105,900	91,400
Investments	—	50,000
Land	50,000	—
Equipment	375,000	275,000
Accumulated depreciation	(149,000)	(114,000)
	$541,900	$432,900
Accounts payable (merchandise creditors)	$ 59,000	$ 57,000
Accrued operating expenses	5,000	7,000
Dividends payable	15,000	10,000
Common stock, $40 par	320,000	250,000
Premium on common stock	17,000	12,000
Retained earnings	125,900	96,900
	$541,900	$432,900

Sales		$919,500
Cost of merchandise sold		550,000
Gross profit		$369,500
Operating expenses:		
Depreciation expense	$ 35,000	
Other operating expenses	260,000	
Total operating expenses		295,000
Operating income		$ 74,500
Other income:		
Gain on sale of investments		10,000
Income before income tax		$ 84,500
Income tax		20,000
Net income		$ 64,500

The following additional information was taken from Corley's records:

(a) The investments were sold for $60,000 cash at the beginning of the year.
(b) Equipment and land were acquired for cash.
(c) There were no disposals of equipment during the year.
(d) The common stock was issued for cash.
(e) There was a $35,500 debit to Retained Earnings for cash dividends declared.

Instructions: Prepare a statement of cash flows, using the direct method of presenting cash flows from operating activities.

E–6. Statement of Cash Flows. The comparative balance sheet of C. D. Collins Co. for December 31 of the current year and the preceding year is as follows:

	December 31	
	Current Year	Preceding Year
Cash	$ 64,200	$ 49,900
Trade receivables (net)	91,500	80,000
Inventories	105,900	90,500
Investments	—	75,000
Land	85,000	—
Equipment	355,000	275,000
Accumulated depreciation	(149,000)	(119,000)
	$552,600	$451,400
Accounts payable (merchandise creditors)	$ 62,450	$ 55,000
Accrued operating expenses	6,000	4,000
Dividends payable	12,000	10,000
Common stock, $20 par	300,000	250,000
Premium on common stock	22,000	12,000
Retained earnings	150,150	120,400
	$552,600	$451,400

E-8

Appendix E

The income statement for the current year ended December 31 is as follows:

Sales		$995,000
Cost of merchandise sold		590,750
Gross profit		$404,250
Operating expenses:		
Depreciation expense	$ 30,000	
Other operating expenses	280,000	
Total operating expense		310,000
Operating income		$ 94,250
Other income:		
Interest income		5,000
Income before income tax		$ 99,250
Income tax		22,500
Net income		$ 76,750

The following additional information was taken from the records of Collins:

(a) Equipment and land were acquired for cash.
(b) There were no disposals of equipment during the year.
(c) The investments were sold for $75,000 cash.
(d) The common stock was issued for cash.
(e) There was a $47,000 debit to Retained Earnings for cash dividends declared.

Instructions: Prepare a statement of cash flows, using the direct method of presenting cash flows from operating activities.

Appendix F
Work Sheet for Statement of Cash Flows

Some accountants prefer to use a work sheet to assist them in assembling data for the statement of cash flows. Although a work sheet is not essential, it is especially useful when a large number of transactions must be analyzed. Also, whether or not a work sheet is used, the concept of cash flows and the statement of cash flows are not affected.

The following sections describe and illustrate the use of the work sheet in preparing the statement of cash flows for T. R. Morgan Corporation, based on the data in Chapter 14.

WORK SHEET PROCEDURES FOR STATEMENT OF CASH FLOWS

The comparative balance sheet and additional data obtained from the accounts of T. R. Morgan Corporation are presented on page F-2. The work sheet prepared from these data is presented on page F-3. The procedures to prepare the work sheet for the statement of cash flows are outlined as follows:

1. List the title of each *noncash* account in the Description column. For each account, enter the debit or credit representing the change (increase or decrease) in the account balance for the year in the Change During Year column.
2. Add the debits and credits in the Change During Year column and determine the subtotals. Enter the change (increase or decrease) in cash during the year in the appropriate column to balance the totals of the debits and credits.
3. Provide space in the bottom portion of the work sheet for later use in identifying the various cash flows from (1) operating activities, (2) financing activities, and (3) investing activities.
4. Analyze the change during the year in each noncash account to determine the cash flows by type of activity related to the transactions recorded in each account. Record these activities in the bottom portion of the work sheet by means of entries in the Work Sheet Entries columns.
5. Complete the work sheet.

These procedures are explained in detail in the following paragraphs.

Noncash Accounts

Since the analysis of transactions recorded in the noncash accounts reveals the cash flows, the work sheet focuses on noncash accounts. For this purpose, the titles of the noncash accounts are entered in the Description column. To facilitate reference in the illustration, noncash current accounts are listed first, followed by the noncurrent accounts. The order of the listing is not important. Next, the debit or credit change for the year in each account balance is entered in the Change During Year column. For example, the beginning and ending balances of Trade Receivables were $65,000 and $74,000, respectively. Thus, the change for the year was an increase, or debit, of $9,000. The beginning and ending balances of Inventories were $180,000 and $172,000, respectively. Thus, the change for the year was a decrease, or credit, of $8,000. The changes in the other accounts are determined in a like manner.

T. R. Morgan Corporation
Comparative Balance Sheet
December 31, 1989 and 1988

	1989	1988	Increase Decrease*
Assets			
Cash	$ 49,000	$ 26,000	$ 23,000
Trade receivables (net)	74,000	65,000	9,000
Inventories	172,000	180,000	8,000*
Prepaid expenses	4,000	3,000	1,000
Investments (long-term)	—	45,000	45,000*
Land	90,000	40,000	50,000
Building	200,000	200,000	—
Accumulated depreciation—building	(36,000)	(30,000)	(6,000)
Equipment	290,000	142,000	148,000
Accumulated depreciation—equipment	(43,000)	(40,000)	(3,000)
Total assets	$800,000	$631,000	$169,000
Liabilities			
Accounts payable (merchandise creditors)	$ 50,000	$ 32,000	$ 18,000
Income tax payable	2,500	4,000	1,500*
Dividends payable	15,000	8,000	7,000
Bonds payable	120,000	245,000	125,000*
Total liabilities	$187,500	$289,000	$101,500*
Stockholders' Equity			
Preferred stock	$150,000	—	$150,000
Premium on preferred stock	10,000	—	10,000
Common stock	280,000	$230,000	50,000
Retained earnings	172,500	112,000	60,500
Total stockholders' equity	$612,500	$342,000	$270,500
Total liabilities and stockholders' equity	$800,000	$631,000	$169,000

Additional data:

(1) Net income, $90,500.
(2) Cash dividends declared, $30,000.
(3) Common stock issued at par for land, $50,000.
(4) Preferred stock issued for cash, $160,000.
(5) Bonds payable retired for cash, $125,000.
(6) Depreciation for year: equipment, $12,000; building, $6,000.
(7) Fully depreciated equipment discarded, $9,000.
(8) Equipment purchased for cash, $157,000.
(9) Book value of investments sold for $75,000 cash, $45,000.

Work Sheet for Statement of Cash Flows

T. R. Morgan Corporation
Work Sheet for Statement of Cash Flows
For Year Ended December 31, 1989

Description	Change During Year Debit	Change During Year Credit	Work Sheet Entries Debit		Work Sheet Entries Credit	
Trade receivables	9,000				(q)	9,000
Inventories		8,000	(p)	8,000		
Prepaid expenses	1,000				(o)	1,000
Accounts payable		18,000	(n)	18,000		
Income tax payable	1,500				(m)	1,500
Dividends payable		7,000	(l)	7,000		
Investments		45,000	(k)	45,000		
Land	50,000				(j)	50,000
Building	—	—				
Accumulated depreciation—building		6,000	(i)	6,000		
Equipment	148,000		(g)	9,000	(h)	157,000
Accumulated depreciation—equipment		3,000	(f)	12,000	(g)	9,000
Bonds payable	125,000				(e)	125,000
Preferred stock		150,000	(d)	150,000		
Premium on preferred stock		10,000	(d)	10,000		
Common stock		50,000	(c)	50,000		
Retained earnings		60,500	(a)	90,500	(b)	30,000
	334,500	357,500				
Increase in cash	23,000					
Totals	357,500	357,500				
Operating activities:						
Net income					(a)	90,500
Depreciation of equipment					(f)	12,000
Depreciation of building					(i)	6,000
Gain on sale of investments			(k)	30,000		
Decrease in income tax payable			(m)	1,500		
Increase in accounts payable					(n)	18,000
Increase in prepaid expenses			(o)	1,000		
Decrease in inventories					(p)	8,000
Increase in trade receivables			(q)	9,000		
Financing activities:						
Declaration of cash dividends			(b)	30,000		
Increase in dividends payable					(l)	7,000
Issuance of common stock for land					(c)	50,000
Issuance of preferred stock					(d)	160,000
Retirement of bonds payable			(e)	125,000		
Investing activities:						
Purchase of equipment			(h)	157,000		
Acquisition of land by issuance of common stock			(j)	50,000		
Sale of investments					(k)	75,000
Totals				809,000		809,000

Change in Cash

Since transactions that result in changes in cash also result in changes in the noncash accounts, the change in cash for the period will equal the change in the noncash accounts for the period. Thus, if a subtotal of the debits and credits for the noncash accounts (as indicated in the Change During Year column) is determined, the increase or decrease in cash for the period can be inserted in the appropriate column and the two columns will balance. In the illustration, the subtotal of the credit column ($357,500) exceeds the subtotal of the debit column ($334,500) by $23,000, which is identified as the increase in cash. By entering the $23,000 as a debit in the Change During Year column, the debit and credit columns are balanced. This $23,000 increase in cash will also be reported on the statement of cash flows.

If the subtotals in the Change During Year columns indicate that the debits exceed the credits, the balancing figure would be identified as a decrease in cash.

Cash Flow Activities

After the Change During Year columns are totaled and ruled, "Operating activities," "Financing activities," and "Investing activities" are written in the Description column. Several lines are skipped between each category, so that at a later time the various cash flows can be entered, by type of activity. When the work sheet is completed, this bottom portion will contain the data necessary to prepare the statement.

To determine the various cash flows by activity for the year, the changes in the noncash accounts are analyzed. As each account is analyzed, entries made in the work sheet relate specific types of cash flows to the noncash accounts. For purposes of discussion, the noncash accounts can be classified as (1) noncurrent accounts and (2) current accounts (except cash).

Analysis of Noncurrent Accounts

As was discussed in Chapter 14, transactions that increase or decrease noncurrent accounts often result in cash flows. Therefore, the changes in the noncurrent accounts are analyzed to determine the various cash flows for the year. As each account is analyzed, entries that relate specific types of cash flow activity to the noncurrent account are made in the work sheet. It should be noted that the work sheet entries are not entered into the accounts. They are, as is the entire work sheet, strictly an aid in assembling the data for later use in preparing the statement.

The sequence in which the noncurrent accounts are analyzed is unimportant. However, because it is more convenient and efficient, and the chance for errors is reduced, the analysis illustrated will begin with the retained earnings account and proceed upward in the listing in sequential order.

Retained Earnings. The work sheet indicates that there was an increase of $60,500 in retained earnings for the year. The additional data, taken from an examination of the account, indicate that the increase was the result of two factors: (1) net income of $90,500 and (2) declaration of cash dividends of $30,000. To identify the cash flows by activity, two entries are made on the work sheet. These entries also serve to account for, or explain, the increase of $60,500.

Net income. In closing the accounts at the end of the year, the retained earnings account was credited for $90,500, representing the net income. The $90,500 is also reported on the statement of cash flows as "cash flows from operating activities." An entry on the work sheet to debit retained earnings and to credit "Operating activities—net income" accomplishes the following: (1) the credit portion of the closing entry (to retained earnings) is accounted for, or in effect canceled, and (2) the cash flow is identified in the bottom portion of the work sheet. The entry on the work sheet is as follows:

(a) Retained Earnings	90,500	
Operating Activities—Net Income		90,500

The cash flows from operating activities is affected by expenses that did not decrease cash. It is also affected by differences between the time an expense is incurred and the time cash flows out, and differences between the time a revenue is recognized and the time cash flows in to the business. In addition, gains and losses from investing and financing transactions affect the determination of cash flows from operating activities. These effects are discussed later in this appendix.

Dividends. In closing the accounts at the end of the year, the retained earnings account was debited for $30,000, representing the cash dividends declared. The $30,000 is also reported on the statement as a financing activity. An entry on the work sheet to debit "Financing Activities— declaration of cash dividends" and to credit retained earnings accomplishes the following: (1) the debit portion of the closing entry (to retained earnings) is accounted for, or in effect canceled, and (2) the cash flow is identified in the bottom portion of the work sheet. The entry on the work sheet is as follows:

(b) Financing Activities—Declaration of Cash Dividends	30,000	
Retained Earnings		30,000

The cash used for the payment of dividends is affected by a difference between the time a dividend is declared and the time it is paid. This effect is discussed later in this appendix.

Common Stock. The next noncurrent item on the work sheet, common stock, increased by $50,000 during the year. The additional data, taken from an examination of the account, indicate that the stock was exchanged for land. Although this is a noncash transaction, it should be reported in a separate schedule on the statement of cash flows. To account fully for the change of $50,000 in the common stock account and to provide the data for the separate schedule, the following entry is made on the work sheet:

(c) Common Stock	50,000	
Financing Activities—Issuance of Common Stock for Land		50,000

It should be noted that the effect of the exchange will also be analyzed when the land account is examined.

Preferred Stock. The work sheet indicates that the preferred stock account increased by $150,000 and the premium on preferred stock account increased by $10,000. The additional data indicate that these increases resulted from the sale of preferred stock for $160,000. The work sheet entry to account for these increases and to identify the cash flow is as follows:

(d) Preferred Stock	150,000	
Premium on Preferred Stock	10,000	
Financing Activities—Issuance of Preferred Stock		160,000

Bonds Payable. The decrease of $125,000 in the bonds payable account during the year resulted from the retirement of the bonds for cash. The work sheet entry to record the effect of this transaction on cash is as follows:

(e) Financing Activities—Retirement of Bonds Payable	125,000	
Bonds Payable		125,000

Accumulated Depreciation—Equipment. The work sheet indicates that the accumulated depreciation—equipment account increased by $3,000 during the year. The additional data indicate that the increase resulted from (1) depreciation expense of

$12,000 (credit) for the year and (2) discarding $9,000 (debit) of fully depreciated equipment. Since depreciation expense does not affect cash but does decrease the amount of net income, it should be added to net income to determine the amount of cash flows from operating activities. This effect is indicated on the work sheet by the following entry:

(f)	Accumulated Depreciation — Equipment	12,000	
	Operating Activities — Net Income: Depreciation of Equipment		12,000

It should be noted that the notation in the Description column is placed so that the $12,000 can be added to "Operating activities — net income."

Since the discarding of the fully depreciated equipment did not affect cash, the following entry is made on the work sheet in order to fully account for the change of $3,000 in the accumulated depreciation — equipment account:

(g)	Equipment	9,000	
	Accumulated Depreciation — Equipment		9,000

It should be noted that this entry, like the transaction that was recorded in the accounts, does not affect cash. It serves only to complete the accounting for all transactions that resulted in the change in the account during the year and thus helps assure that no transactions affecting cash are overlooked in the analysis.

Equipment. The work sheet indicates that the equipment account increased by $148,000 during the year. The additional data, determined from an examination of the ledger account, indicates that the increase resulted from (1) discarding $9,000 of fully depreciated equipment and (2) purchasing $157,000 of equipment. The discarding of the equipment was included in, or accounted for, in (g) and needs no additional attention. The use of cash to purchase equipment is recognized by the following entry on the work sheet:

(h)	Investing Activities — Purchase of Equipment	157,000	
	Equipment		157,000

Accumulated Depreciation — Building. The $6,000 increase in the accumulated depreciation — building account during the year resulted from the entry to record depreciation expense. Since depreciation expense does not affect cash but does decrease the amount of net income, it should be added to net income to determine the amount of cash flows from operating activities. This effect is accomplished by the following entry on the work sheet:

(i)	Accumulated Depreciation — Building	6,000	
	Operating Activities — Net Income: Depreciation of Building		6,000

Building. There was no change in the balance of the building account during the year, and reference to the account confirms that no entries were made in it during the year. Hence, no entry is necessary on the work sheet.

Land. As indicated in the analysis of the common stock account, the $50,000 increase in land resulted from an acquisition by issuance of common stock. To account fully for the change of $50,000 in the land account and to provide the data for the separate schedule reporting this noncash transaction, the following entry is made on the work sheet:

(j)	Investing Activities — Acquisition of Land by Issuance of Common Stock	50,000	
	Land		50,000

Investments. The work sheet indicates that investments decreased by $45,000. The examination of the ledger account indicates that investments were sold for

$75,000. As was explained on page 611, the $30,000 gain on the sale is included in net income and must be deducted from net income in the operating activities section. The $75,000 of cash flows from investments sold would be reported as an investing activity. To indicate this cash flow on the work sheet, the following entry is made:

(k)	Operating Activities—Net Income:		
	Gain on Sale of Investments	30,000	
	Investments	45,000	
	Investing Activities—Sale of Investments		75,000

Analysis of Current Accounts (Except Cash)

• • •

The amount of cash used to pay dividends may differ from the amount of cash dividends declared. Timing differences between the incurrence of an expense and the related cash outflow and between the recognition of revenue and the receipt of cash must be considered in determining the amount of cash flows from operating activities. Therefore, the current accounts (other than cash) are analyzed to determine (1) cash flows for payment of dividends and (2) cash flows from operating activities.

Cash Flows for Payment of Dividends. The additional data indicate that $30,000 of dividends had been declared, which was identified as a financing activity in entry (b). The $7,000 credit in the Change During Year column of the work sheet for Dividends Payable reveals a timing difference between the declaration and the payment. In other words, the $7,000 increase in Dividends Payable for the year indicates that dividends paid were $7,000 less than dividends declared. The work sheet entry to adjust the dividends declared of $30,000 to reflect the dividends paid of $23,000 is as follows:

(l)	Dividends Payable	7,000	
	Financing Activities—Declaration of Cash Dividends: Increase in Dividends Payable		7,000

When the $7,000, which represents the increase in dividends payable, is deducted from the $30,000 of "financing activities—declaration of cash dividends," $23,000 is subsequently reported on the statement as a cash flow from financing activity.

Cash Flows From Operating Activities. The starting point in the analysis of the effect of operations on cash is net income for the period. The effect of this amount, $90,500, is indicated by entry (a). As indicated in the earlier analysis, depreciation expense of $18,000 must be added [(f) and (i)] to the $90,500 because depreciation expense did not decrease the amount of cash. Also as explained in entry (k), the gain on the sale of investments, $30,000, must be deducted. In addition, it is necessary to recognize the relationship of the accrual method of accounting to the movement of cash. Ordinarily, a portion of some of the other costs and expenses reported on the income statement, as well as a portion of the revenue earned, is not accompanied by cash outflow or inflow.

The effect of timing differences is indicated by the amount and the direction of change in the balances of the asset and liability accounts affected by operations. Decreases in such assets and increases in such liabilities during the period must be added to the amount reported as net income to determine the amount of cash flows from operating activities. Conversely, increases in such assets and decreases in such liabilities must be deducted from the amount reported as net income.

The noncash current accounts (except Dividends Payable) provide the following data that indicate the effect of timing differences on the amount of cash inflow and outflow from operating activities:

Accounts	Increase Decrease*
Trade receivables (net)	$ 9,000
Inventories	8,000*
Prepaid expenses	1,000
Accounts payable (merchandise creditors)	18,000
Income tax payable	1,500*

The sequence in which the noncash current accounts are analyzed is unimportant. However, to continue the sequence used in analyzing preceding accounts, the analysis illustrated will begin with the income tax payable account and proceed upward in the listing in sequential order.

Income tax payable decrease. The outlay of cash for income taxes exceeded by $1,500 the amount of income tax deducted as an expense during the period. Accordingly, $1,500 must be deducted from income to determine the amount of cash flows from operating activities. This procedure is indicated on the work sheet by the following entry:

(m) Operating Activities—Net Income:		
Decrease in Income Tax Payable	1,500	
Income Tax Payable		1,500

Accounts payable increase. The effect of the increase in the amount owed creditors for goods and services was to include in expired costs and expenses the sum of $18,000. Income was thereby reduced by $18,000 for which there had been no cash outlay during the year. Hence, $18,000 must be added to income to determine the amount of cash flows from operating activities. The work sheet entry is as follows:

(n) Accounts Payable	18,000	
Operating Activities—Net Income:		
Increase in Accounts Payable		18,000

Prepaid expenses increase. The outlay of cash for prepaid expenses exceeded by $1,000 the amount deducted as an expense during the year. Hence $1,000 must be deducted from income to determine the amount of cash flows from operating activities. The work sheet entry is as follows:

(o) Operating Activities—Net Income:		
Increase in Prepaid Expenses	1,000	
Prepaid Expenses		1,000

Inventories decrease. The $8,000 decrease in inventories indicates that the merchandise sold exceeded the cost of the merchandise purchased by $8,000. The amount reported on the income statement as a deduction from the revenue therefore included $8,000 that did not require cash outflow during the year. Accordingly, $8,000 must be added to income to determine the amount of cash flows from operations. The work sheet entry is as follows:

(p) Inventories	8,000	
Operating Activities—Net Income:		
Decrease in Inventories		8,000

Trade receivables (net) increase. The additions to trade receivables for sales on account during the year exceeded by $9,000 the deductions for amounts collected from customers on account. The amount reported on the income statement as sales therefore included $9,000 that did not yield cash inflow during the year. Accordingly, $9,000 must be deducted from income to determine the amount of cash flows from operating activities. The work sheet entry is as follows:

(q) Operating Activities—Net Income:		
Increase in Trade Receivables	9,000	
Trade Receivables		9,000

Completing the Work Sheet

After all of the noncash accounts have been analyzed, all of the operating, financing, and investing activities are identified in the bottom portion of the work sheet. To assure the equality of the work sheet entries, the last step is to total the Work Sheet Entries columns.

Preparation of the Statement of Cash Flows

The data for the three sections of the statement of cash flows are obtained from the bottom portion of the work sheet. Some modifications are made to the work sheet data for presentation on the statement. For example, in presenting the cash flows from operating activities, the total depreciation expense ($18,000) is reported instead of the two separate amounts ($12,000 and $6,000). The cash paid for dividends is reported as $23,000 instead of the amount of dividends declared ($30,000), less the increase in dividends payable ($7,000). The issuance of the common stock for land ($50,000) is reported in a separate schedule. The increase (or decrease) in cash that is reported on the statement is also identified on the work sheet. The statement prepared from the work sheet is illustrated below.

T. R. Morgan Corporation
Statement of Cash Flows
For Year Ended December 31, 1989

Cash flows from operating activities:			
Net income, per income statement		$ 90,500	
Add: Depreciation	$ 18,000		
Decrease in inventories	8,000		
Increase in accounts payable	18,000	44,000	
		$134,500	
Deduct: Increase in trade receivables	$ 9,000		
Increase in prepaid expenses	1,000		
Decrease in income tax payable	1,500		
Gain on sale of investments	30,000	41,500	
Net cash flow from operating activities			$93,000
Cash flows from financing activities:			
Cash received from sale of preferred stock		$160,000	
Less: Cash paid for dividends	$ 23,000		
Cash paid to retire bonds payable	125,000	148,000	
Net cash flow provided by financing activities			12,000
Cash flows from investing activities:			
Cash received from sale of investments		$ 75,000	
Less: Cash paid for purchase of equipment		157,000	
Net cash flow used for investing activities			(82,000)
Increase in cash			$23,000
Cash at the beginning of the year			26,000
Cash at the end of the year			$49,000

Schedule of Noncash Financing and Investing Activities	
Issuance of common stock for land	$50,000

Appendix G
Interest Tables

The following present value and future value tables contain factors carried to six decimal places for interest rates of 1% to 15% for 50 periods.

Future Amount of 1 at Compound Interest Due in n Periods: $a_{\overline{n}|i} = (1 + i)^n$ **Table 1**

n \ i	1%	2%	3%	4%	5%	6%	7%	8%	9%	10%	12%	15%
1	1.010000	1.020000	1.030000	1.040000	1.050000	1.060000	1.070000	1.080000	1.090000	1.100000	1.120000	1.150000
2	1.020100	1.040400	1.060900	1.081600	1.102500	1.123600	1.144900	1.166400	1.188100	1.210000	1.254400	1.322500
3	1.030301	1.061208	1.092727	1.124864	1.157625	1.191016	1.225043	1.259712	1.295029	1.331000	1.404928	1.520875
4	1.040604	1.082432	1.125509	1.169859	1.215506	1.262477	1.310796	1.360489	1.411582	1.464100	1.573519	1.749006
5	1.051010	1.104081	1.159274	1.216653	1.276282	1.338226	1.402552	1.469328	1.538624	1.610510	1.762342	2.011357
6	1.061520	1.126162	1.194052	1.265319	1.340096	1.418519	1.500730	1.586874	1.677100	1.771561	1.973823	2.313061
7	1.072135	1.148686	1.229874	1.315932	1.407100	1.503630	1.605781	1.713824	1.828039	1.948717	2.210681	2.660020
8	1.082857	1.171659	1.266770	1.368569	1.477455	1.593848	1.718186	1.850930	1.992563	2.143589	2.475963	3.059023
9	1.093685	1.195093	1.304773	1.423312	1.551328	1.689479	1.838459	1.999005	2.171893	2.357948	2.773079	3.517876
10	1.104622	1.218994	1.343916	1.480244	1.628895	1.790848	1.967151	2.158925	2.367364	2.593742	3.105848	4.045558
11	1.115668	1.243374	1.384234	1.539454	1.710339	1.898299	2.104852	2.331639	2.580426	2.853117	3.478550	4.652391
12	1.126825	1.268242	1.425761	1.601032	1.795856	2.012196	2.252192	2.518170	2.812665	3.138428	3.895976	5.350250
13	1.138093	1.293607	1.468534	1.665074	1.885649	2.132928	2.409845	2.719624	3.065805	3.452271	4.363493	6.152788
14	1.149474	1.319479	1.512590	1.731676	1.979932	2.260904	2.578534	2.937194	3.341727	3.797498	4.887112	7.075706
15	1.160969	1.345868	1.557967	1.800944	2.078928	2.396558	2.759032	3.172169	3.642482	4.177248	5.473566	8.137062
16	1.172579	1.372786	1.604706	1.872981	2.182875	2.540352	2.952164	3.425943	3.970306	4.594973	6.130394	9.357621
17	1.184304	1.400241	1.652848	1.947901	2.292018	2.692773	3.158815	3.700018	4.327633	5.054470	6.866041	10.761264
18	1.196147	1.428246	1.702433	2.025817	2.406619	2.854339	3.379932	3.996019	4.717120	5.559917	7.689966	12.375454
19	1.208109	1.456811	1.753506	2.106849	2.526950	3.025600	3.616528	4.315701	5.141661	6.115909	8.612762	14.231772
20	1.220190	1.485947	1.806111	2.191123	2.653298	3.207135	3.869684	4.660957	5.604411	6.727500	9.646293	16.366537
21	1.232392	1.515666	1.860295	2.278768	2.785963	3.399564	4.140562	5.033834	6.108808	7.400250	10.803848	18.821518
22	1.244716	1.545980	1.916103	2.369919	2.925261	3.603537	4.430402	5.436540	6.658600	8.140275	12.100310	21.644746
23	1.257163	1.576899	1.973587	2.464716	3.071524	3.819750	4.740530	5.871464	7.257874	8.954302	13.552347	24.891458
24	1.269735	1.608437	2.032794	2.563304	3.225100	4.048935	5.072367	6.341181	7.911083	9.849733	15.178629	28.625176
25	1.282432	1.640606	2.093778	2.665836	3.386355	4.291871	5.427433	6.848475	8.623081	10.834706	17.000064	32.918953
26	1.295256	1.673418	2.156591	2.772470	3.555673	4.549383	5.807353	7.396353	9.399158	11.918177	19.040072	37.856796
27	1.308209	1.706886	2.221289	2.883369	3.733456	4.822346	6.213868	7.988061	10.245082	13.109994	21.324881	43.535315
28	1.321291	1.741024	2.287928	2.998703	3.920129	5.111687	6.648838	8.627106	11.167140	14.420994	23.883866	50.065612
29	1.334504	1.775845	2.356566	3.118651	4.116136	5.418388	7.114257	9.317275	12.172182	15.863093	26.749930	57.575454
30	1.347849	1.811362	2.427262	3.243398	4.321942	5.743491	7.612255	10.062657	13.267678	17.449402	29.959922	66.211772
31	1.361327	1.847589	2.500080	3.373133	4.538039	6.088101	8.145113	10.867669	14.461770	19.194342	33.555113	76.143538
32	1.374941	1.884541	2.575083	3.508059	4.764941	6.453387	8.715271	11.737083	15.763329	21.113777	37.581726	87.565068
33	1.388690	1.922231	2.652335	3.648381	5.003189	6.840590	9.325340	12.676050	17.182028	23.225154	42.091533	100.699829
34	1.402577	1.960676	2.731905	3.794316	5.253348	7.251025	9.978114	13.690134	18.728411	25.547670	47.142517	115.804803
35	1.416603	1.999890	2.813862	3.946089	5.516015	7.686087	10.676581	14.785344	20.413968	28.102437	52.799620	133.175523
40	1.488864	2.208040	3.262038	4.801021	7.039989	10.285718	14.974458	21.724521	31.409420	45.259256	93.050970	267.863546
45	1.564811	2.437854	3.781596	5.841176	8.985008	13.764611	21.002452	31.920449	48.327286	72.890484	163.987604	538.769269
50	1.644632	2.691588	4.383906	7.106683	11.467400	18.420154	29.457025	46.901613	74.357520	117.390853	289.002190	1083.657442

Future Amount of Ordinary Annuity of 1 per Period: $A_{\overline{n}|i} = \frac{(1+i)^n - 1}{i}$ **Table 2**

n \ i	1%	2%	3%	4%	5%	6%	7%	8%	9%	10%	12%	15%
1	1.000000	1.000000	1.000000	1.000000	1.000000	1.000000	1.000000	1.000000	1.000000	1.000000	1.000000	1.000000
2	2.010000	2.020000	2.030000	2.040000	2.050000	2.060000	2.070000	2.080000	2.090000	2.100000	2.120000	2.150000
3	3.030100	3.060400	3.090900	3.121600	3.152500	3.183600	3.214900	3.246400	3.278100	3.310000	3.374400	3.472500
4	4.060401	4.121608	4.183627	4.246464	4.310125	4.374616	4.439943	4.506112	4.573129	4.641000	4.779328	4.993375
5	5.101005	5.204040	5.309136	5.416323	5.525631	5.637093	5.750740	5.866601	5.984711	6.105100	6.352847	6.742381
6	6.152015	6.308121	6.468410	6.632975	6.801913	6.975319	7.153291	7.335929	7.523335	7.715610	8.115189	8.753738
7	7.213535	7.434283	7.662462	7.898294	8.142008	8.393838	8.654021	8.922803	9.200435	9.487171	10.089012	11.066799
8	8.285671	8.582969	8.892336	9.214226	9.549109	9.897468	10.259803	10.636628	11.028474	11.435888	12.299693	13.726819
9	9.368527	9.754628	10.159106	10.582795	11.026564	11.491316	11.977989	12.487558	13.021036	13.579477	14.775656	16.785842
10	10.462213	10.949721	11.463879	12.006107	12.577893	13.180795	13.816448	14.486562	15.192930	15.937425	17.548735	20.303718
11	11.566835	12.168715	12.807796	13.486351	14.206787	14.971643	15.783599	16.645487	17.560293	18.531167	20.654583	24.349276
12	12.682503	13.412090	14.192030	15.025805	15.917127	16.869941	17.888451	18.977126	20.140720	21.384284	24.133133	29.001667
13	13.809328	14.680332	15.617790	16.626838	17.712983	18.882138	20.140643	21.495297	22.953385	24.522712	28.029109	34.351917
14	14.947421	15.973938	17.086324	18.291911	19.598632	21.015066	22.550488	24.214920	26.019189	27.974983	32.392602	40.504705
15	16.096896	17.293417	18.598914	20.023588	21.578564	23.275970	25.129022	27.152114	29.360916	31.772482	37.279715	47.580411
16	17.257864	18.639285	20.156881	21.824531	23.657492	25.672528	27.888054	30.324283	33.003399	35.949730	42.753280	55.717472
17	18.430443	20.012071	21.761588	23.697512	25.840366	28.212880	30.840217	33.750226	36.973705	40.544703	48.883674	65.075093
18	19.614748	21.412312	23.414435	25.645413	28.132385	30.905653	33.999033	37.450244	41.301338	45.599173	55.749715	75.836357
19	20.810895	22.840559	25.116868	27.671229	30.539004	33.759992	37.378965	41.446263	46.018458	51.159090	63.439681	88.211811
20	22.019004	24.297370	26.870374	29.778079	33.065954	36.785591	40.995492	45.761964	51.160120	57.274999	72.052442	102.443583
21	23.239194	25.783317	28.676486	31.969202	35.719252	39.992727	44.865177	50.422921	56.764530	64.002499	81.698736	118.810120
22	24.471586	27.298984	30.536780	34.247970	38.505214	43.392290	49.005739	55.456755	62.873338	71.402749	92.502584	137.631638
23	25.716302	28.844963	32.452884	36.617889	41.430475	46.995828	53.436141	60.893296	69.531939	79.543024	104.602894	159.276384
24	26.973465	30.421862	34.426470	39.082604	44.501999	50.815577	58.176671	66.764759	76.789813	88.497327	118.155241	184.167841
25	28.243200	32.030300	36.459264	41.645908	47.727099	54.864512	63.249038	73.105940	84.700896	98.347059	133.333870	212.793017
26	29.525632	33.670906	38.553042	44.311745	51.113454	59.156383	68.676470	79.954415	93.323977	109.181765	150.333934	245.711970
27	30.820888	35.344324	40.709634	47.084214	54.669126	63.705766	74.483823	87.350768	102.723135	121.099942	169.374007	283.568766
28	32.129097	37.051210	42.930923	49.967583	58.402583	68.528112	80.697691	95.338830	112.968217	134.209936	190.698887	327.104080
29	33.450388	38.792235	45.218850	52.966286	62.322712	73.629798	87.346529	103.965936	124.135356	148.630930	214.582754	377.169693
30	34.784892	40.568079	47.575416	56.084938	66.438848	79.058186	94.460786	113.283211	136.307539	164.494023	241.332684	434.745146
31	36.132740	42.379441	50.002678	59.328335	70.760790	84.801677	102.073041	123.345868	149.575217	181.943425	271.292606	500.956918
32	37.494068	44.227030	52.502759	62.701469	75.298829	90.889778	110.218154	134.213537	164.036987	201.137767	304.847719	577.100456
33	38.869009	46.111570	55.077841	66.209527	80.063771	97.343165	118.933425	145.950620	179.800315	222.251544	342.429446	644.665525
34	40.257699	48.033802	57.730177	69.857909	85.066959	104.183755	128.258765	158.626670	196.982344	245.476699	384.520979	765.365353
35	41.660276	49.994478	60.462082	73.652225	90.320307	111.434780	138.236878	172.316804	215.710755	271.024368	431.663496	881.170156
40	48.886373	60.401983	75.401260	95.025516	120.799774	154.761966	199.635112	259.056519	337.882445	442.592556	767.091420	1779.090308
45	56.481075	71.892710	92.719861	121.029392	159.700156	212.743514	285.749311	386.505617	525.858734	718.904837	1358.230032	3585.128460
50	64.463182	84.579401	112.796867	152.667084	209.347996	290.335905	406.528929	573.770156	815.083556	1163.908529	2400.018249	7217.716277

Table 3

Present Value of 1 at Compound Interest Due in n Periods: $p_{\overline{n}|i} = \frac{1}{(1 + i)^n}$

n \ i	1%	2%	3%	4%	5%	6%	7%	8%	9%	10%	12%	15%
1	0.990099	0.980392	0.970874	0.961538	0.952381	0.943396	0.934580	0.925926	0.917431	0.909091	0.892857	0.869565
2	0.980296	0.961169	0.942596	0.924556	0.907029	0.889996	0.873439	0.857339	0.841680	0.826446	0.797194	0.756144
3	0.970590	0.942322	0.915142	0.888996	0.863838	0.839619	0.816298	0.793832	0.772183	0.751315	0.711780	0.657516
4	0.960980	0.923845	0.888487	0.854804	0.822702	0.792094	0.762895	0.735030	0.708425	0.683013	0.635518	0.571753
5	0.951466	0.905731	0.862609	0.821927	0.783526	0.747258	0.712986	0.680583	0.649931	0.620921	0.567427	0.497177
6	0.942045	0.887971	0.837484	0.790315	0.746215	0.704961	0.666342	0.630170	0.596267	0.564474	0.506631	0.432328
7	0.932718	0.870560	0.813092	0.759918	0.710681	0.665057	0.622750	0.583490	0.547034	0.513158	0.452349	0.375937
8	0.923483	0.853490	0.789409	0.730690	0.676839	0.627412	0.582009	0.540269	0.501866	0.466507	0.403883	0.326902
9	0.914340	0.836755	0.766417	0.702587	0.644609	0.591898	0.543934	0.500249	0.460428	0.424098	0.360610	0.284262
10	0.905287	0.820348	0.744094	0.675564	0.613913	0.558395	0.508349	0.463193	0.422411	0.385543	0.321973	0.247185
11	0.896324	0.804263	0.722421	0.649581	0.584679	0.526788	0.475093	0.428883	0.387533	0.350494	0.287476	0.214943
12	0.887449	0.788493	0.701380	0.624597	0.556837	0.496969	0.444012	0.397114	0.355535	0.318631	0.256675	0.186907
13	0.878663	0.773033	0.680951	0.600574	0.530321	0.468839	0.414964	0.367698	0.326179	0.289664	0.229174	0.162528
14	0.869963	0.757875	0.661118	0.577475	0.505068	0.442301	0.387817	0.340461	0.299246	0.263331	0.204620	0.141329
15	0.861349	0.743015	0.641862	0.555265	0.481017	0.417265	0.362446	0.315242	0.274538	0.239392	0.182696	0.122894
16	0.852821	0.728446	0.623167	0.533908	0.458112	0.393646	0.338735	0.291890	0.251870	0.217629	0.163122	0.106865
17	0.844377	0.714163	0.605016	0.513373	0.436297	0.371364	0.316574	0.270269	0.231073	0.197845	0.145644	0.092926
18	0.836017	0.700159	0.587395	0.493628	0.415521	0.350344	0.295864	0.250249	0.211994	0.179859	0.130040	0.080805
19	0.827740	0.686431	0.570286	0.474642	0.395734	0.330513	0.276508	0.231712	0.194490	0.163508	0.116107	0.070265
20	0.819544	0.672971	0.553676	0.456387	0.376889	0.311805	0.258419	0.214548	0.178431	0.148644	0.103667	0.061100
21	0.811430	0.659776	0.537549	0.438834	0.358942	0.294155	0.241513	0.198656	0.163698	0.135131	0.092560	0.053131
22	0.803396	0.646839	0.521893	0.421955	0.341850	0.277505	0.225713	0.183941	0.150182	0.122846	0.082643	0.046201
23	0.795442	0.634156	0.506692	0.405726	0.325571	0.261797	0.210947	0.170315	0.137781	0.111678	0.073788	0.040174
24	0.787566	0.621721	0.491934	0.390121	0.310068	0.246979	0.197147	0.157699	0.126405	0.101526	0.065882	0.034934
25	0.779768	0.609531	0.477606	0.375117	0.295303	0.232999	0.184249	0.146018	0.115968	0.092296	0.058823	0.030378
26	0.772048	0.597579	0.463695	0.360689	0.281241	0.219810	0.172195	0.135202	0.106393	0.083905	0.052521	0.026415
27	0.764404	0.585862	0.450189	0.346817	0.267848	0.207368	0.160930	0.125187	0.097608	0.076278	0.046894	0.022970
28	0.756836	0.574375	0.437077	0.333477	0.255094	0.195630	0.150402	0.115914	0.089548	0.069343	0.041869	0.019974
29	0.749342	0.563112	0.424346	0.320651	0.242946	0.184557	0.140563	0.107328	0.082155	0.063039	0.037383	0.017369
30	0.741923	0.552071	0.411987	0.308319	0.231377	0.174110	0.131367	0.099377	0.075371	0.057309	0.033378	0.015103
31	0.734577	0.541246	0.399987	0.296460	0.220359	0.164255	0.122773	0.092016	0.069148	0.052099	0.029802	0.013133
32	0.727304	0.530633	0.388337	0.285058	0.209866	0.154957	0.114741	0.085200	0.063438	0.047362	0.026609	0.011420
33	0.720103	0.520229	0.377026	0.274094	0.199873	0.146186	0.107235	0.078889	0.058200	0.043057	0.023758	0.009931
34	0.712973	0.510028	0.366045	0.263552	0.190355	0.137912	0.100219	0.073045	0.053395	0.039143	0.021212	0.008635
35	0.705914	0.500028	0.355383	0.253415	0.181290	0.130105	0.093663	0.067635	0.048986	0.035584	0.018940	0.007509
40	0.671653	0.452890	0.306557	0.208289	0.142046	0.097222	0.066780	0.046031	0.031838	0.022095	0.010747	0.003733
45	0.639055	0.410197	0.264439	0.171198	0.111297	0.072650	0.047613	0.031328	0.020692	0.013719	0.006098	0.001856
50	0.608039	0.371528	0.228107	0.140713	0.087204	0.054288	0.033948	0.021321	0.013449	0.008519	0.003460	0.000923

Table 4

Present Value of Ordinary Annuity of 1 per Period: $P_{\overline{n}|i} = \dfrac{1 - \dfrac{1}{(1+i)^n}}{i}$

n \ i	1%	2%	3%	4%	5%	6%	7%	8%	9%	10%	12%	15%
1	0.990099	0.980392	0.970874	0.961538	0.952381	0.943396	0.934579	0.925926	0.917431	0.909091	0.892857	0.869565
2	1.970395	1.941561	1.913470	1.886095	1.859410	1.833393	1.808018	1.783265	1.759111	1.735537	1.690051	1.625709
3	2.940985	2.883883	2.828611	2.775091	2.723248	2.673012	2.624316	2.577097	2.531295	2.486852	2.401831	2.283225
4	3.901966	3.807729	3.717098	3.629895	3.545951	3.465106	3.387211	3.312127	3.239720	3.169865	3.037349	2.854978
5	4.853431	4.713460	4.579707	4.451822	4.329477	4.212364	4.100197	3.992710	3.889651	3.790787	3.604776	3.352155
6	5.795476	5.601431	5.417191	5.242137	5.075692	4.917324	4.766540	4.622880	4.485919	4.355261	4.111407	3.784483
7	6.728195	6.471991	6.230283	6.002055	5.786373	5.582381	5.389289	5.206370	5.032953	4.868419	4.563757	4.160420
8	7.651678	7.325481	7.019692	6.732745	6.463213	6.209794	5.971299	5.746639	5.534819	5.334926	4.967640	4.487322
9	8.566018	8.162237	7.786109	7.435332	7.107822	6.801692	6.515232	6.246888	5.995247	5.759024	5.328250	4.771584
10	9.471305	8.982585	8.530203	8.110896	7.721735	7.360087	7.023582	6.710081	6.417658	6.144567	5.650223	5.018769
11	10.367628	9.786848	9.252624	8.760477	8.306414	7.886875	7.498674	7.138964	6.805191	6.495061	5.937699	5.233712
12	11.255077	10.575341	9.954004	9.385074	8.863252	8.383844	7.942686	7.536078	7.160725	6.813692	6.194374	5.420619
13	12.133740	11.348374	10.634955	9.985648	9.393573	8.852683	8.357651	7.903776	7.486904	7.103356	6.423548	5.583147
14	13.003703	12.106249	11.296073	10.563123	9.898641	9.294984	8.745468	8.244237	7.786150	7.366687	6.628168	5.724476
15	13.865053	12.849264	11.937935	11.118387	10.379658	9.712249	9.107914	8.559479	8.060688	7.606080	6.810864	5.847370
16	14.717874	13.577709	12.561102	11.652296	10.837770	10.105895	9.446649	8.851369	8.312558	7.823709	6.973986	5.954235
17	15.562251	14.291872	13.166118	12.165669	11.274066	10.477260	9.763223	9.121638	8.543631	8.021553	7.119630	6.047161
18	16.398269	14.992031	13.753513	12.659297	11.689587	10.827603	10.059087	9.371887	8.755625	8.201412	7.249670	6.127966
19	17.226009	15.678462	14.323799	13.133939	12.085321	11.158116	10.335595	9.603599	8.950115	8.364920	7.365777	6.198231
20	18.045553	16.351433	14.877475	13.590326	12.462210	11.469921	10.594014	9.818147	9.128546	8.513564	7.469444	6.259331
21	18.856983	17.011209	15.415024	14.029160	12.821153	11.764077	10.835527	10.016803	9.292244	8.648694	7.562003	6.312462
22	19.660379	17.658048	15.936917	14.451115	13.163003	12.041582	11.061241	10.200744	9.442425	8.771540	7.644646	6.358663
23	20.455821	18.292204	16.443608	14.856842	13.488574	12.303379	11.272187	10.371059	9.580207	8.883218	7.718434	6.398837
24	21.243387	18.913926	16.935542	15.246963	13.798642	12.550358	11.469334	10.528758	9.706612	8.984744	7.784316	6.433771
25	22.023156	19.523456	17.413148	15.622080	14.093945	12.783356	11.653583	10.674776	9.822580	9.077040	7.843139	6.464149
26	22.795204	20.121036	17.876842	15.982769	14.375185	13.003166	11.825779	10.809978	9.928972	9.160945	7.895660	6.490564
27	23.559608	20.706898	18.327031	16.329586	14.643034	13.210534	11.986709	10.935165	10.026580	9.237223	7.942554	6.513534
28	24.316443	21.281272	18.764108	16.663063	14.898127	13.406164	12.137111	11.051078	10.116128	9.306567	7.984423	6.533508
29	25.065785	21.844385	19.188455	16.983715	15.141074	13.590721	12.277674	11.158406	10.198283	9.369606	8.021806	6.550877
30	25.807708	22.396456	19.600441	17.292033	15.372451	13.764831	12.409041	11.257783	10.273654	9.426914	8.055184	6.565980
31	26.542285	22.937702	20.000428	17.588494	15.592811	13.929086	12.531814	11.349799	10.342802	9.479013	8.084986	6.579113
32	27.269589	23.468335	20.388766	17.873552	15.802677	14.084043	12.646555	11.434999	10.406240	9.526376	8.111594	6.590533
33	27.989693	23.988564	20.765792	18.147646	16.002549	14.230230	12.753790	11.513888	10.464441	9.569432	8.135352	6.600463
34	28.702666	24.498592	21.131837	18.411198	16.192904	14.368141	12.854009	11.586934	10.517835	9.608575	8.156564	6.609099
35	29.408580	24.998619	21.487220	18.664613	16.374194	14.498246	12.947672	11.654568	10.566821	9.644159	8.175504	6.616607
40	32.834686	27.355479	23.114772	19.792774	17.159086	15.046297	13.331709	11.924613	10.757360	9.779051	8.243777	6.641778
45	36.094508	29.490160	24.518713	20.720040	17.774070	15.455832	13.605522	12.108402	10.881197	9.862808	8.282516	6.654293
50	39.196118	31.423606	25.729764	21.482185	18.255925	15.761861	13.800746	12.233485	10.961683	9.914814	8.304498	6.660515

Appendix H

Managerial Accounting for Service Enterprises and Activities

Accounting for the rendering of services is less complex than accounting for the production of products from raw materials. Specifically, for planning and controlling the operations of a service enterprise, management does not need detailed product cost information on a timely basis. Although most of the managerial concepts and techniques for manufacturing enterprises, as described and illustrated in this text, are also relevant for service enterprises, some techniques are less relevant. For example, although capital investment analysis may be used by service enterprises, by their very nature service enterprises are not capital intensive. Therefore, fewer capital investment decisions are made, and those that are made tend to have less of an impact on profitability and solvency than do the capital investment decisions of a manufacturing enterprise. Likewise, inventory analysis is generally not as important for service enterprises, since the only inventory for a service enterprise is usually supplies. Finally, since fixed costs are normally a small portion of the total costs, cost-volume-profit analysis and the computation of the break-even point is not as relevant for a service enterprise.

The managerial accounting concepts and procedures that are especially relevant for service enterprises include job order cost accounting systems, budgeting, responsibility accounting, standard costs, and pricing (setting professional fees). These concepts are described in the following paragraphs.

JOB ORDER COST ACCOUNTING

A cost accounting system is useful to management for planning and controlling the operations of a service enterprise. Since services are usually tailored to a particular client, a job order cost accounting system rather than a process cost system is generally appropriate for a service enterprise. The procedures described and illustrated in Chapter 16 are applicable to service enterprises. The major difference in a job order costing system for a service enterprise is that the planning and control of costs focus on direct labor and overhead. The cost of any materials or supplies used in rendering services for a client is usually small in amount and is normally included as part of the overhead.

The direct labor and overhead costs of rendering services to clients are accumulated in a work in process account, which is supported by a cost ledger. A job cost sheet is used to accumulate the costs for each client's job. When a job is completed and the client is billed, the costs are transferred to a cost of services account. This account is similar to the cost of merchandise sold account for a merchandising enterprise or the cost of goods sold account for a manufacturing enterprise. A finished goods account is not necessary, since the revenues associated with the services are recorded after the services have been rendered. The flow of costs through a service enterprise using a job order cost accounting system is illustrated as follows:

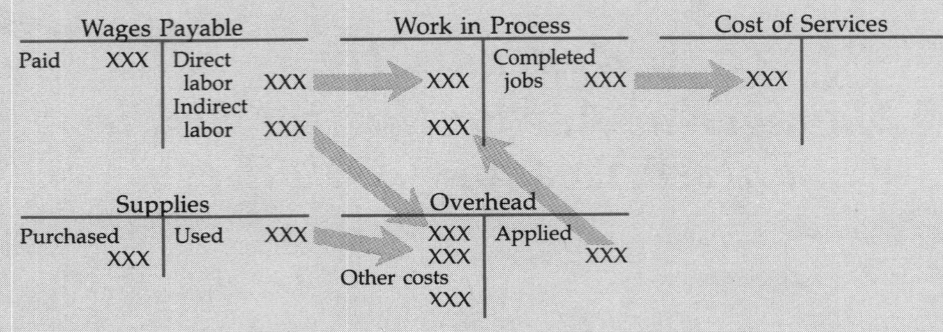

Flow of Costs Through a Service Enterprise

In practice, additional accounting considerations unique to service enterprises may need to be considered. For example, a service enterprise may bill clients on a weekly or monthly basis rather than waiting until a job is completed. In these situations, a portion of the costs related to each billing should be transferred from the work in process account to the cost of services account. This treatment is similar to the percentage-of-completion method used by construction contractors. A service enterprise may also have advance billings which would be accounted for as deferred revenue until the services have been completed.

Job Order Cost Accounting for an Advertising Agency

An article in the December, 1983 issue of *Management Accounting* discussed the importance of good financial planning and control for a service enterprise. The article described how an advertising agency, which develops advertising campaigns for clients, implemented a job order cost accounting system for planning and controlling its operations. Excerpts from the article follow:

...Formed in 1970 by the merging of two smaller agencies, the [New York-based advertising agency] grew [by the late 1970s] from $6 million in billings [revenues]...to $80 million in billings a year.... [Business expanded] so rapidly that management had its hands full just taking care of day-to-day business. This left little time to develop a formal accounting system.... The firm knew its total expenses (by adding employee salaries and overhead) and its total revenues, but had no idea which individual accounts [clients] were making or losing money.... Despite this lack of planning and control, [the company] remained profitable.... Then...the company suffered a major loss and senior management attempted to discover why the loss had occurred.

...[A] major reason for the loss was deemed to be the company's inadequate cost control system. Some accounts were highly profitable and others extremely unprofitable, but top management had no idea which were which....

...[The company] developed a [two-part] program [to address its problems]. First...a budgeting/cost control system designed to forecast revenue and expenses at least three to six months into the future by individual account [was established]. This system assured management that, well in advance of a given period, it would have a good idea of revenue and expenses, which would enable it to plan accordingly....

The second part of the program was to develop a control system which would monitor the actual amount of revenue or expense derived from each account on a monthly basis, and then analyze the variance between the actual amount and the original budget. Determining the actual revenue is relatively easy.... [Actual] direct costs are derived through a time sheet system which was developed to encompass all actual work performed by every employee in the company.... [The direct labor cost is computed by multiplying] the total number of hours worked by each employee on the account... [by] each person's cost to the agency [hourly wage rate].... Overhead is then calculated on a [direct labor cost] basis and a profit or loss [is computed for each account].

...Since devising the...system [the company] has become aware of which specific accounts are unprofitable and the reasons why. Since the budgeting and control system has been instituted, the agency has resigned several unprofitable accounts that otherwise would have gone unnoticed.... In brief, the new system has allowed [the company] to better plan and control its business.

Source: William B. Mills, "Drawing Up a Budgeting System for an Ad Agency," *Management Accounting* (December, 1983), pp. 46–51, 59.

To illustrate job order cost accounting for a service enterprise, assume that Grant and Lewis, CPAs, have organized as a professional corporation (designated by the initials *P.C.*) to practice public accounting. Selected transactions for November, followed by the entries to record them, are presented below.

(a) Labor incurred as reported by time reports for November:

Direct labor:	
Smith Co. (Job 101)	$ 12,000
Abel Inc. (Job 102)	50,000
Lybrand Co. (Job 103)	35,000
Martin Inc. (Job 104)	60,000
Young Inc. (Job 105)	23,000
	$180,000
Indirect labor	8,000
Total	$188,000

Work in Process	180,000	
Overhead	8,000	
Wages Payable		188,000

(b) Other costs incurred:

Overhead	33,800	
Advertising Expense	12,000	
Rent Expense	9,000	
Office Supplies Expense	4,000	
Accounts Payable		56,100
Supplies		2,700

(c) Application of overhead costs to jobs (the predetermined rate is 20% of direct labor cost):

Work in Process	36,000	
Overhead		36,000

(d) Cases completed and billed to clients:

Client	*Amount Billed*	*Cost*
Smith Co. (Job 101)	$ 35,000	$ 14,400
Able Inc. (Job 102)	120,000	60,000
Lybrand Co. (Job 103)	90,000	42,000
Total billings	$245,000	$116,400

Accounts Receivable	245,000	
Professional Fees		245,000
Cost of Services	116,400	
Work in Process		116,400

Assuming that there was no work in process on November 1, 1989, the balance of the work in process account on November 30, $99,600, should agree with the subsidiary cost ledger, as shown below. Note that, for a service enterprise, any materials or supplies cost is included in overhead cost, and hence, no direct materials account is needed.

Client	*Direct Labor Cost*	*Overhead Cost*	*Total Cost*
Martin Inc. (Job 104)	$60,000	$12,000	$72,000
Young Inc. (Job 105)	23,000	4,600	27,600
Total			$99,600

The financial statements of a service enterprise are similar to those for a merchandising and manufacturing enterprise and therefore are not illustrated. On the income statement, the balance of the cost of services account is deducted from the balance of the professional fees account to determine gross profit. Any underapplied or overapplied overhead cost is either transferred to the cost of services account or allocated between the cost of services account and the work in process account.

BUDGETING

The planning and control of service enterprises may be facilitated through management's use of budgeting. The budgeting process for a service enterprise is similar to that for a manufacturing enterprise, except that less emphasis is placed on materials budgets and more emphasis is placed on direct labor and overhead budgets.

For a service enterprise, a revenue (professional fees) budget is normally the first budget prepared. An estimate of the billable hours serves as the basis upon which the other budgets are prepared. To illustrate, the professional fees budget for Grant and Lewis, CPAs, is as follows:

Grant and Lewis, CPAs, P. C.
Professional Fees Budget
For the Year Ending December 31, 1989

	Billable Hours	Hourly Rate	Total Revenue
Audit Department:			
Staff	12,000	$30	$ 360,000
Supervisors	8,000	$40	320,000
Managers	6,000	$60	360,000
Partners	4,000	$80	320,000
Total	30,000		$1,360,000
Tax Department:			
Staff	22,000	$25	$ 550,000
Supervisors	15,000	$30	450,000
Managers	10,000	$50	500,000
Partners	8,000	$75	600,000
Total	55,000		$2,100,000
Consulting Group:			
Staff	4,000	$30	$ 120,000
Supervisors	3,000	$40	120,000
Managers	6,000	$60	360,000
Partners	2,000	$80	160,000
Total	15,000		$ 760,000
Total professional fees			$4,220,000

The direct labor cost budget is based upon the professional fees budget and indicates the number of professional staff hours required to meet the fee projections. To illustrate, the direct labor cost budget for Grant and Lewis, CPAs, is as follows:

Grant and Lewis, CPAs, P. C.
Direct Labor Cost Budget
For the Year Ending December 31, 1989

	Billable Hours Required			
	Staff	Supervisors	Managers	Partners
Audit Department	12,000	8,000	6,000	4,000
Tax Department	22,000	15,000	10,000	8,000
Consulting Group	4,000	3,000	6,000	2,000
Total	38,000	26,000	22,000	14,000
Average compensation per hour	× $15	× $20	× $35	× $60
Total direct labor cost	$570,000	$520,000	$770,000	$840,000

The remaining budgets for a service enterprise are similar to those for a merchandising or manufacturing enterprise. These budgets include the overhead cost budget, the operating expenses budget, the cash budget, and the capital expenditures budget. In combination, these supporting budgets form the master budget and are the basis for the preparation of the budgeted income statement and the budgeted balance sheet.

RESPONSIBILITY ACCOUNTING

The concept of responsibility accounting would be applied to a service enterprise in a manner similar to that for a manufacturing enterprise. Most service enterprises are organized as profit centers, with each different service offered established as a separate profit center. In these profit centers, the departmental manager has control over costs and revenues. Other departments within a service organization, such as a typing and reproduction department or a computer processing department, could be organized as cost centers. The departmental manager in such a cost center would be responsible for costs incurred in the department. Normally, service enterprises are not organized as investment centers, since service enterprises are not capital intensive. However, a branch office of a service enterprise might be organized as an investment center, in which case the branch manager would have responsibility for costs, revenues, and investment in the center.

The responsibility accounting reports for a service enterprise would be similar to those for a manufacturing enterprise. Cost center reports normally take the form of budget performance reports that compare budgeted costs with actual costs. Profit center reports emphasize profit measures, such as gross profit, departmental margin, or operating income. Budgeted profit measures could be compared with actual profit, using analyses such as gross profit analysis. Investment center performance reports emphasize the rate of return on investment or residual income as performance measures.

The profit center and cost center responsibility reports for Grant and Lewis, CPAs, P. C., are as follows:

Responsibility Report — Profit Center

Grant and Lewis, CPAs, P.C.
Tax Department
For Month Ended April 30, 1989

Professional fees		$500,000
Cost of services		420,000
Gross profit		$ 80,000
Operating expenses:		
Marketing expenses	$20,000	
General expenses	18,000	
Total operating expenses		38,000
Income from operations		$ 42,000

Responsibility Report — Cost Center

Grant and Lewis, CPAs, P.C.
Budget Performance Report — Typing and Reproduction Department
For Month Ended April 30, 1989

	Budget	Actual	Over	Under
Supervisory salaries	$ 45,000	$ 45,000		
Secretarial wages	30,000	31,500	$1,500	
Depreciation on equipment	15,000	15,000		
Supplies	11,000	14,100	3,100	
Power and light	8,000	7,500		$500
Rent	1,000	1,000		
	$110,000	$114,100	$4,600	$500

STANDARD COSTS

A full standard cost system associated with manufacturing enterprises would normally not be used by a service enterprise because it emphasizes standard costs for materials, direct labor, and factory overhead. Of these costs, a service enterprise would generally use only standard costs for direct labor to assist in planning and controlling operations. When direct labor standards are developed, the total direct labor cost variance, the direct labor time variance, and the direct labor rate variance can be determined as follows:

Total Direct Labor Cost Variance

$$\text{Total Direct Labor Cost Variance} = \text{Actual Direct Labor Cost} - \text{Standard Direct Labor Cost}$$

Direct Labor Time Variance

$$\text{Direct Labor Time Variance} = (\text{Actual Hours Worked} - \text{Standard Hours}) \times \text{Standard Rate per Hour}$$

Direct Labor Rate Variance

$$\text{Direct Labor Rate Variance} = (\text{Actual Rate per Hour} - \text{Standard Rate}) \times \text{Actual Hours Worked}$$

To illustrate, assume that the following data were gathered for the direct labor costs used in completing the audit of a client of Grant and Lewis, CPAs:

Actual:	1,500 hours at $28.00	$42,000
Standard:	1,400 hours at $28.50	39,900
Total variance		$ 2,100 unfavorable

The total unfavorable direct labor cost variance of $2,100 is made up of an unfavorable time variance and a favorable rate variance. The direct labor time variance is $2,850 unfavorable, computed as follows:

Direct Labor Time Variance = (Actual Hours Worked − Standard Hours) × Standard Rate per Hour

Time variance = (1,500 hours − 1,400 hours) × $28.50

Time variance = 100 hours × $28.50

Time variance = $2,850 unfavorable

The direct labor rate variance is $750 favorable, computed as follows:

Direct Labor Rate Variance = (Actual Rate per Hour − Standard Rate) × Actual Hours Worked

Rate variance = ($28.50 per hour − $28.50 per hour) × 1,500 hours

Rate variance = −$.50 per hour × 1,500 hours

Rate variance = −$750 favorable

To assist service enterprise managers in controlling direct labor costs, reports analyzing the cause of the variances may be prepared. For example, the direct labor time variance could have been caused by the use of inexperienced staff or staff with inadequate training. The direct labor rate variance could have been generated through the use of lower-paid staff for duties normally performed by higher-paid staff. For example, a tax manager rather than a tax partner might have reviewed a tax return.

Although overhead costs may be significant for a service enterprise, these costs are normally controlled through the use of budget performance reports, as illustrated in Chapter 22. Because service enterprises are not capital intensive, overhead volume variances are not applicable. Therefore, the only overhead variance generally analyzed for a service enterprise is the controllable (spending) variance, which is reported in a budget performance report.

PRICING

The total cost and variable cost concepts for determining product prices, described and illustrated in Chapter 25, are also relevant for setting professional billing rates for service enterprises. The product cost concept is generally not appropriate for service enterprises.

To illustrate the total cost concept of setting professional fees, assume the following costs and expenses for the rendering of 100,000 billable hours by Grant and Lewis, CPAs.

Variable costs and expenses:	
Direct labor	$27 per billable hour
Overhead	4
Marketing and general	4
Fixed costs and expenses:	
Overhead	$140,000
Marketing and general	360,000

Assume that Grant and Lewis, CPAs, desire a total income of $900,000 from the rendering of accounting services. The total cost for 100,000 billable hours during the year is $4,000,000 or $40 per billable hour, computed as follows:

Variable costs and expenses ($35 × 100,000 hours)		$3,500,000
Fixed costs and expenses:		
Overhead	$140,000	
Marketing and general	360,000	500,000
Total costs and expenses		$4,000,000

The markup percentage on each billable hour is 22.5%, computed as follows:

$$\text{Markup Percentage} = \frac{\text{Desired Income}}{\text{Total Costs and Expenses}}$$

$$\text{Markup Percentage} = \frac{\$900{,}000}{\$4{,}000{,}000}$$

$$\text{Markup Percentage} = 22.5\%$$

Based on the total cost per billable hour of $40 and the markup percentage of 22.5%, Grant and Lewis, CPAs, would charge an average billable rate per hour of $49, as shown in the following computation:

Total cost per billable hour	$40
Markup ($40 × 22.5%)	9
Rate per billable hour	$49

The variable cost concept of product pricing could also have been used by Grant and Lewis, CPAs. The markup percentage using the variable cost concept is 40%, computed as follows:

$$\text{Markup Percentage} = \frac{\text{Desired Income + Total Fixed Costs and Expenses}}{\text{Total Variable Costs and Expenses}}$$

$$\text{Markup Percentage} = \frac{\$900{,}000 + \$500{,}000}{\$3{,}500{,}000}$$

$$\text{Markup Percentage} = \frac{\$1{,}400{,}000}{\$3{,}500{,}000}$$

$$\text{Markup Percentage} = 40\%$$

Based on the variable cost per billable hour of $35 and the markup percentage of 40%, Grant and Lewis, CPAs, would charge an average billable rate per hour of $49, as shown in the following computation:

Variable cost per billable hour	$35
Markup ($35 × 40%)	14
Rate per billable hour	$49

As indicated in Chapter 25, the total cost and variable cost concepts of pricing only provide a general guide to setting prices. Other factors, such as competitive market pressures and general economic conditions, must also be considered. For example, because of uncertain economic conditions, Grant and Lewis, CPAs, might decide to round the estimated billable rate of $49 upward to $50 per hour. In addition, the billable rate of $49 is an average rate, and Grant and Lewis might establish different rates for each level of employee within the firm. For example, the services of new staff would normally be billed at a lower rate than the services of managers or partners.

Exercises

H-1. Job order cost accounting entries. Selected transactions for September for Marlowe and Sparkman, CPAs, are as follows:

(a) Labor incurred as reported by time reports for September:

Direct labor:	
Abel Inc. (Job 1)	$ 4,000
Nobel Co. (Job 2)	2,800
Anderson Co. (Job 3)	3,500
Nash Inc. (Job 4)	12,250
Thomas Inc. (Job 5)	1,250
	$23,800
Indirect labor	6,200
Total	$30,000

(b) The following other costs were incurred on account: overhead cost, $15,000; advertising expense, $3,000; rent expense, $5,000; and office supplies expense, $1,800.
(c) Overhead is applied to individual jobs at a rate of 60% of direct labor cost.
(d) Jobs completed and billed to clients:

Client	Amount Billed
Abel Inc. (Job 1)	$ 7,000
Nobel Co. (Job 2)	5,500
Anderson Co. (Job 3)	6,000
Total billings	$18,500

Instructions: (1) Prepare journal entries to record the preceding transactions.
(2) Prepare a summary of jobs in work in process as of September 30.

H-2. Professional fees budget. Mitchell and Momper, CPAs, offer three types of services to clients: auditing, tax, and computer installation. Based upon past experience and projected growth, the following billable hours have been estimated for the year ending December 31, 1989:

	Billable Hours
Audit Department:	
Staff	18,000
Partners	6,000
Tax Department:	
Staff	15,000
Partners	3,000
Computer Installation:	
Staff	12,000
Partners	2,000

The average billing rate for staff is $40 per hour, and the average billing rate for partners is $80 per hour.

Instructions: Prepare a professional fees budget for Mitchell and Momper, CPAs, for the year ending December 31, 1989, showing the estimated professional fees by type of service rendered.

H-3. Direct labor cost budget. Based upon the data in Exercise H-2 and assuming that the average compensation per hour for staff and partners is $25 and $50 respectively, prepare a direct labor cost budget for Mitchell and Momper, CPAs, for the year ending December 31, 1989.

H-4. Budget performance report. The Typing and Reproduction Department budget for March for Simpson and Ingram, CPAs, is as follows:

Simpson and Ingram, CPAs
Typing and Reproduction Department Budget
For Month Ended March 31, 1989

Supervisory salaries	$24,500
Secretarial wages	8,600
Depreciation on equipment	2,500
Supplies	1,000
Power and light	850
Rent	650
Total	$38,100

Simpson and Ingram, CPAs, treats the Typing and Reproduction Department as a cost center. The actual costs of the Typing and Reproduction Department for March were as follows: supervisory salaries, $24,500; secretarial wages, $9,000; depreciation on equipment, $2,500; supplies, $930; power and light, $1,200; and rent, $650.

Instructions: Prepare a budget performance report for the Typing and Reproduction Department for the month of March.

H-5. Direct labor cost variances. The following direct labor cost data for the Dysan Case have been gathered by Davis and Grainger, P. C., attorneys at law:

Actual:	2,200 hours at $19.50	$42,900
Standard:	2,000 hours at $20.00	40,000

Instructions: (1) Determine the total direct labor cost variance, the direct labor time variance, and the direct labor rate variance. Indicate whether each variance is favorable or unfavorable.
(2) Briefly describe possible causes of the time and rate variances determined in (1).

H-6. Total cost and variable cost concepts of pricing. Borman and Beeman, P. C., attorneys at law, have gathered the following cost data for the purpose of setting a billing rate for the rendering of professional services:

Variable costs and expenses:	
Direct labor	$20 per billable hour
Overhead	3
Marketing and general	2
Fixed costs and expenses:	
Overhead	$50,000
Marketing and general	10,000

Borman and Beeman desire a total income of $280,000, based upon the rendering of 20,000 hours of professional service.

Instructions: (1) Using the total cost concept of pricing, determine the markup percentage and estimated billing rate per hour.
(2) Using the variable cost concept of pricing, determine the markup percentage and estimated billing rate per hour.

Appendix I
Trends in Managerial Accounting

This text has described and illustrated traditional managerial accounting techniques useful to managers for planning and controlling operations. For example, Chapters 16 and 17 described and illustrated job order and process cost accounting systems, Chapter 18 described cost behavior and cost estimation, and Chapters 19 and 20 described cost-volume-profit analysis and profit reporting.

This appendix describes trends in the development and use of managerial accounting concepts. These trends reflect responses to a rapidly changing business environment.

CHANGES IN THE UNITED STATES ECONOMY

The stimulus for many of the trends in managerial accounting is changes in the economy of the United States. During the 1970s and throughout the 1980s, the competitive advantage in the manufacture and production of goods shifted from the United States to foreign producers. In 1970, the United States exported $42.5 billion of merchandise and imported $39.9 billion, for a net surplus of exports over imports of $2.6 billion. In 1985, the United States exported $214.4 billion of merchandise and imported $338.9 billion, for a net trade deficit (i.e., imports exceeded exports) of $124.5 billion.[1] This shift in exports and imports has been blamed on such factors as the high cost of American labor, trade barriers to foreign markets, unfavorable exchange rates, and the poor quality of American goods.

In response to competitive world markets, the U.S. economy has become more service oriented. In addition, many manufacturers have been forced to adopt new manufacturing techniques and processes. In turn, the managerial accounting methods which provide the basic information that management uses in planning and controlling operations have changed. Many of these changes are described in the remainder of this appendix.

MAJOR TRENDS IN MANUFACTURING

The major trends in manufacturing in the United States in recent years can be grouped into five general categories: (1) just-in-time manufacturing systems, (2) automation, (3) product quality, (4) inventory control, and (5) information technology. In the following paragraphs, each of these trends is briefly described, and its implications for managerial accounting are discussed.[2]

Just-In-Time Manufacturing Systems

Recently, manufacturers have begun to reorganize the traditional production line to achieve greater efficiency and to improve product quality. One such system that

[1]Council of Economic Advisers, *Economic Report of the President* (United States Printing Office: Washington, D.C., 1987), p. 358.

[2]These manufacturing trends and the implications for managerial accounting are described and illustrated in more detail in the articles, books, and monographs listed in the Selected Bibliography on pages I-10 and I-11.

has received much attention by industry is the **just-in-time manufacturing system,** sometimes referred to as the **flexible flow manufacturing system.**

In a traditional production process, a product moves through the process according to functional flows along a continuous production line. That is, the product moves from process to process as each function or step is completed. Each worker is assigned a specific job, which is performed repeatedly as unfinished products are received from the preceding department. In such a process, a product is often said to be "pushed through" production, since each manufacturing department "pushes" the unfinished product to the next stage (department) of manufacturing. For example, a furniture manufacturer might use seven production departments to perform the operating functions necessary to manufacture furniture, as shown in the diagram below.

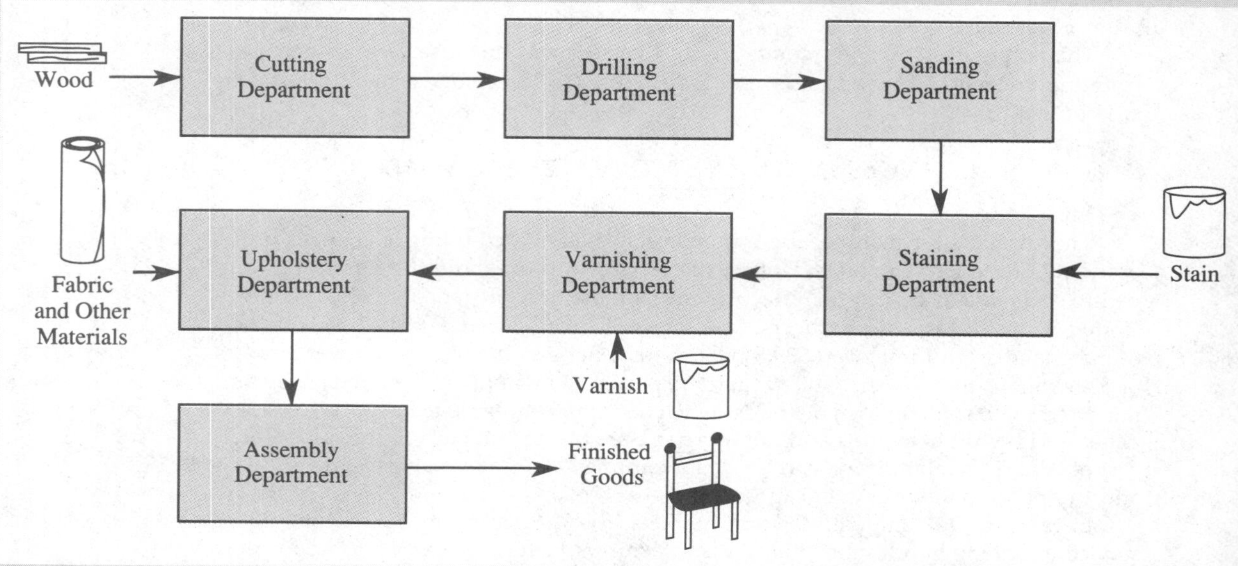

Traditional Production Line—Furniture Manufacturer

For the furniture maker in the illustration, manufacturing would begin in the Cutting Department, where the wood would be cut to design specifications. Next, the Drilling Department would perform the drilling function, after which the Sanding Department would sand the wood, the Staining Department would stain the furniture, and the Varnishing Department would apply varnish and other protective coatings. Then, the Upholstery Department would add fabric and other materials. Finally, the Assembly Department would assemble the furniture to complete the manufacturing process.

In the traditional production process, production supervisors attempt to enter enough materials into the manufacturing process to keep all the manufacturing departments operating. Some departments, however, may process materials more rapidly than others. In addition, if one department stops production because of machine breakdowns, for example, the preceding departments usually continue production in order to avoid idle time. This unevenness may result in a build-up of work in process between departments. Furthermore, if bottlenecks occur, the entire production line stops because the unfinished product is not passed on to the successive departments.

In a just-in-time manufacturing system, a primary emphasis is on the reduction of work in process inventories. Large amounts of work in process represent a large dollar investment in inventory that is not earning a return to the enterprise. Ideally, no work in process would exist among departments, but each department's processing finishes "just in time" for the next department's processing to begin. In a just-in-time system, the product is often said to be "pulled through" production, since a department finishing its processing "pulls" (demands) more materials from the preceding department.

One way in which just-in-time manufacturing systems attempt to reduce work in process is by combining processing functions into **work centers.** The seven departments illustrated above for the furniture manufacturer might be reorganized into three work centers, for example. As shown in the following diagram, Work Center One would perform the cutting, drilling, and sanding functions; Work Center Two would perform the staining and varnishing functions; and Work Center Three would perform the upholstery and assembly functions.

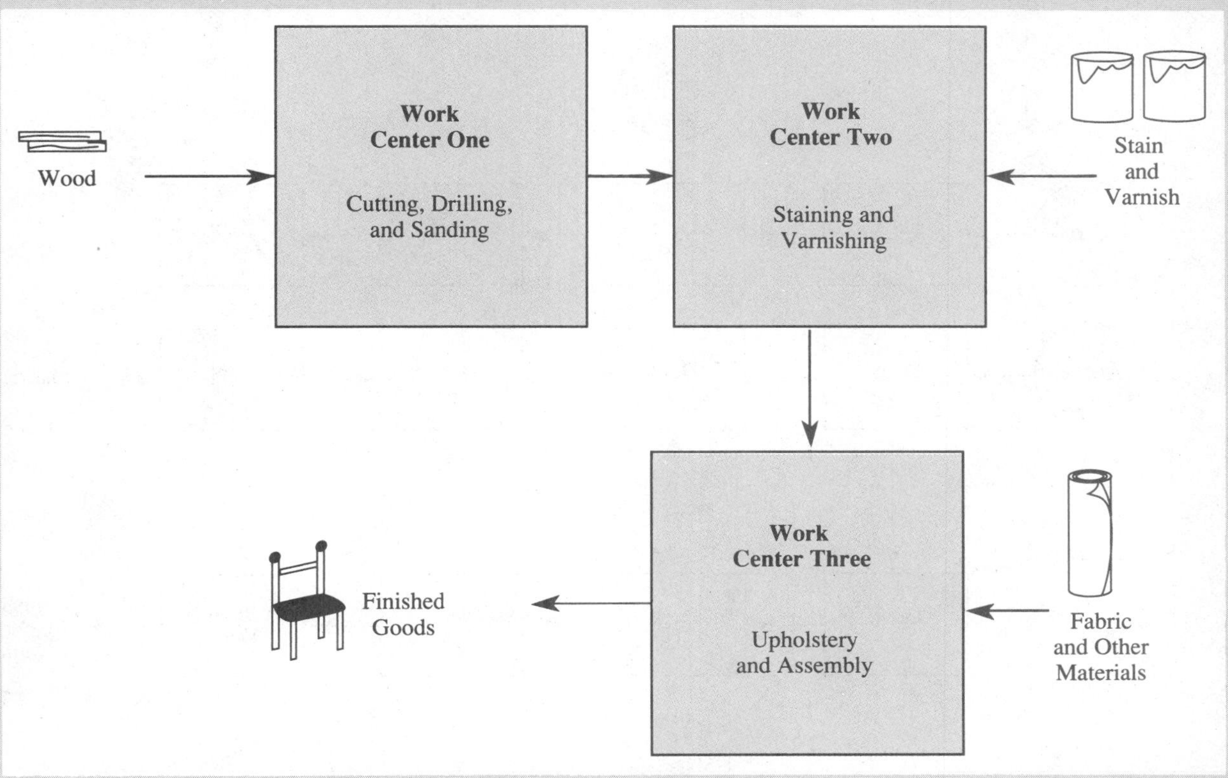

Just-In-Time Production Line—Furniture Manufacturer

In the traditional production line, as described previously, a worker typically performs only one function on a continous basis. However, in a work center in which several manufacturing functions take place, the workers are often cross-trained to perform more than one function. Research has indicated that workers who perform several manufacturing functions identify better with the end product. This identification creates pride in the products and improves quality and productivity.

The just-in-time reorganization of the manufacturing departments may also result in a reorganization of activities involving services to these departments. Specifically, the service activities may be assigned to individual work centers, rather than to the traditional centralized service departments. For example, each work center may be assigned the responsibility for the repair and maintenance of its machinery and equipment. The acceptance of this responsibility creates an environment in which workers gain a better understanding of the production process and machinery limitations. In turn, workers tend to take better care of the machinery, which decreases repairs and maintenance costs, reduces machine downtime, and improves product quality.

Another trend in just-in-time manufacturing systems is the splitting or "decoupling" of the traditional production process into one or more mini-production lines. For example, the mini-production lines of General Motors were described in Chapter 17 on page 642. Each mini-production line operates as if it were independent of the other production lines. Thus, the continuous nature of the traditional production line is eliminated, and there is less emphasis on pushing materials into production to keep all departments operating. Examples of a traditional production line and a decoupled, just-in-time manufacturing system are shown below and at the top of page I-5.

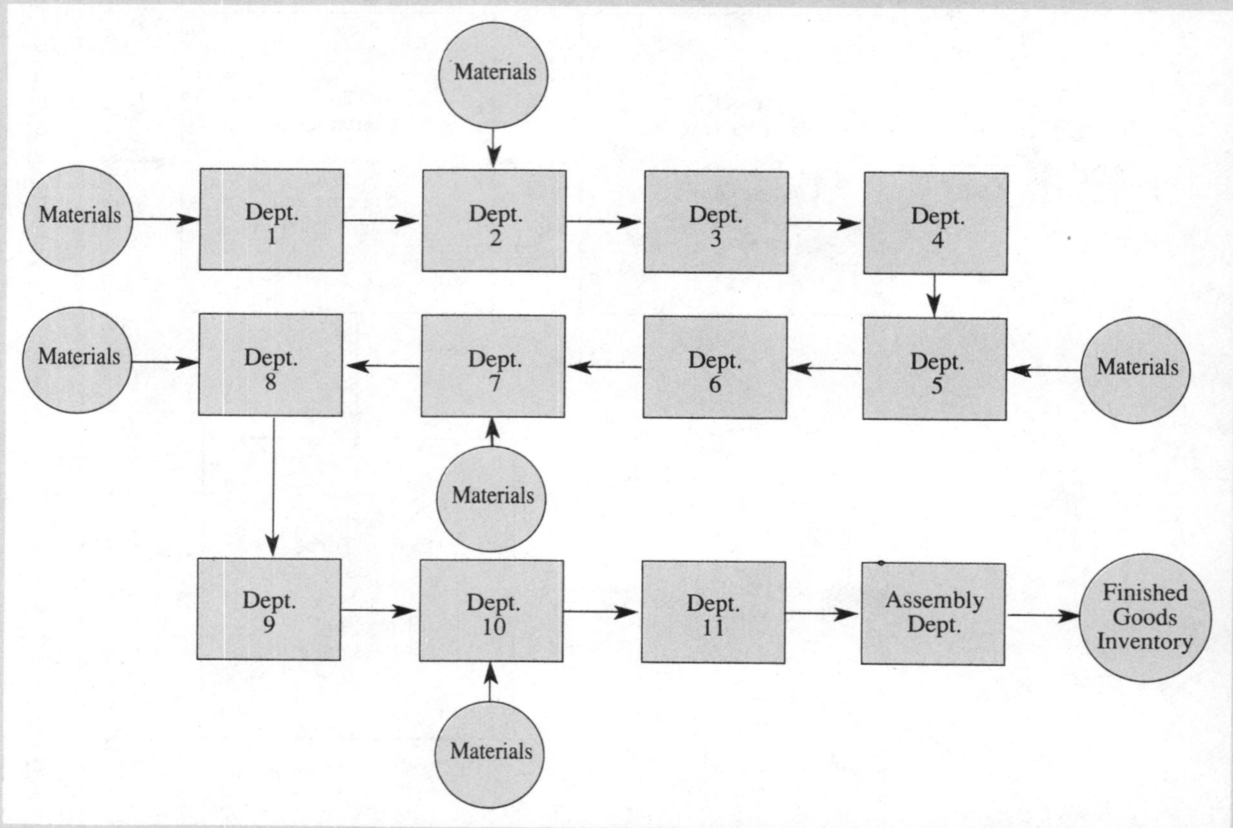

Traditional Production System — Continuous Production Line

In a just-in-time manufacturing system, handling costs are reduced because the product is not moved as frequently as in a traditional production line. The mini-production line is often set up so that the product is on a movable carrier that is centrally located in the work center. When the workers in each work center have completed their activities with the product, the entire carrier is then moved to the next work center.

Mini-production lines also provide additional flexibility in the manufacturing process. Since each line is viewed as separate from the other lines, a line having a slow period might contract for special jobs outside the company.

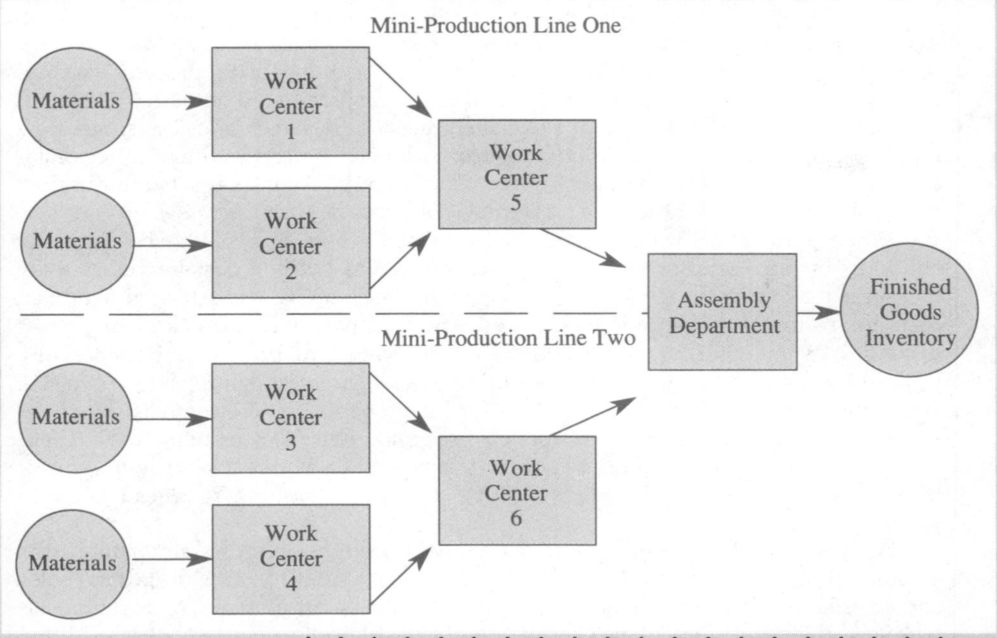

Just-In-Time Manufacturing System—Decoupled Production Line

The important implications of just-in-time manufacturing systems for managerial accountants are in the areas of cost allocation, cost accumulation, and cost control. When service functions, such as repairs and maintenance, are assigned to individual work centers, the costs of the services are accumulated in each work center, rather than allocated from a service department. As a result, the direct costs for each work center are determined more easily and are more accurate. In turn, cost control by work center and by mini-production line are facilitated.

The reduction of the amount of work in process inventory may make it unnecessary to account for work in process as a separate inventory item. Costs are accumulated in each work center as they enter the manufacturing process, and at the end of the period, these costs are transferred directly to finished goods inventory and to cost of goods sold, without flowing through the work in process account. Any work in process at the end of the period could be reported with the materials as "Materials and In Process Inventory."

Automation

One of the more visible trends in manufacturing is the increased use of automated machinery to perform routine, repetitive tasks with minimum human involvement in the manufacturing process. Automated machinery can take many forms, including computer-aided machinery and robots.

The use of automated machinery in the manufacturing process is often justified on the basis of labor and material savings. Other factors, however, such as improved quality control and reduced product development time, are often benefits of the use of automated machinery. For example, with the use of robotics, changes in products can be easily introduced into the manufacturing process by reprogramming robots. This ability to add or modify products quickly allows a company to react to changing market preferences and conditions.

The use of automated machinery increases overhead costs through increases in depreciation, maintenance, repairs, property taxes, and insurance. Automation also reduces the amount of direct labor required in the manufacturing process. Twenty-five years ago, for example, direct labor costs frequently accounted for 40% of production costs. With the use of automated machinery, direct labor costs may now represent no more than 5% of production costs. In such an environment, direct labor costs may be charged to overhead rather than accounted for as a separate product cost.[3] As a result, overhead as a percentage of product costs increases.

When a manufacturing process is automated, there is likely to be a greater emphasis on the control of overhead costs through analysis of cost trends. Activity measures may be developed to aid managers in determining the nature of overhead costs for control and allocation purposes. These activity measures, known as **cost drivers,** may include the number of orders received and processed for Receiving Department costs; the number of pounds, gallons, or liters shipped for Shipping Department costs; the number of repairs for Maintenance Department costs; and the number of engineering orders completed for Engineering Department costs. These cost drivers rather than traditional allocation bases, such as direct labor hours, direct labor costs, or units produced, would be used for allocating overhead costs to products.

An example of the results of a cost analysis brought about by automation was a company that found that 23% of its products accounted for 85% of its total sales and all of its profits. The remaining 77% of its products lost money. The cost analysis revealed that the direct-labor-based overhead allocation system was shifting costs from low-volume, special-order products to more profitable high-volume products. The allocation system was thereby disguising the true profitability of the products. The company immediately analyzed its product line and discontinued those products that were losing money.[4]

The increasing automation of manufacturing processes has also changed the way that managerial accountants use the traditional methods of capital investment analysis. In many situations, using the traditional quantitative methods, such as the average rate of return, discounted cash flow, and discounted internal rate of return methods, the purchase of automated equipment would not be recommended. However, companies often find that qualitative considerations achieved through automation, such as improved product quality and reliability, reduced development time for introducing new products, and manufacturing flexibility, often outweigh the quantitative considerations. To illustrate, Boston Metal Products purchased a robot, even though traditional capital investment analysis techniques did not justify the investment. The investment paid off quickly, and the robot improved the speed and the quality of welding. As a result, the company was able to speed up deliveries and to grow fourfold in three years with a higher quality product.[5]

Product Quality

During the 1950s and 1960s, price was a primary vehicle for competition among manufacturers. During that period, for example, Japanese products were primarily known for their low prices. During the last decade, however, foreign competitors, such as Japan, have implemented new manufacturing techniques and stringent quality control standards and have supplied world markets with higher quality products at lower prices than those of U.S. manufacturers. As a result, many U.S. manufacturers have been forced to move toward superior product quality as a major manufacturing goal in order to compete effectively.

To improve product quality, U.S. manufacturers have begun to use a Japanese method of organizing workers into **quality circles,** sometimes referred to as **quality**

[3]Ford S. Worthy, "Accounting Bores You? Wake Up," *Fortune* (October 12, 1987), p. 44.
[4]H. Thomas Johnson and Robert S. Kaplan, *Relevance Lost,* Harvard Business School Press (Boston: 1987).
[5]John Holusha, "Cost Accounting's Blind Spot," *The New York Times* (October 14, 1986).

control teams. A quality circle is a group of employees who meet periodically to identify and discuss problems and, when appropriate, to implement solutions to those problems. The use of such quality circles generates greater worker interest and commitment to the manufacturing process and to product quality. The team concept also generates a greater number of suggestions for improving manufacturing processes and cutting costs.

Quality control may be enhanced through the automation of manufacturing processes that allow robots or computer-controlled machinery to monitor the manufacturing process directly. When a weakness or defect in the manufactured product is detected, production is stopped and corrective action is taken.

Managerial accountants aid managers in their efforts to control product quality by analyzing defects and defective rates and by providing timely information on customer complaints, service calls, and warranty expenses. The monitoring of scrap provides managers with information on the quality of materials received from suppliers. In a quality control environment, less emphasis is placed on the price of materials and price variances, and more emphasis is placed on how the quality of the materials affects the final product.

The managerial accountant also aids managers in the control of the quality of production by preparing and interpreting quality control charts. **Quality control charts,** which may be developed by using statistical methods, show desired operating conditions and limits within which production may vary. Production observations outside these limits require investigation and possible corrective action.

In the following example of a quality control chart, the rate of defective units is represented by the vertical axis. The horizontal axis represents samples (1–14) taken from the production process over a period of time. The upper limit for the rate of defective units is 4%. The actual rates of defective units are plotted on the chart, based on the sample observations. For example, observation 3 indicates a rate of defective units of 2%.

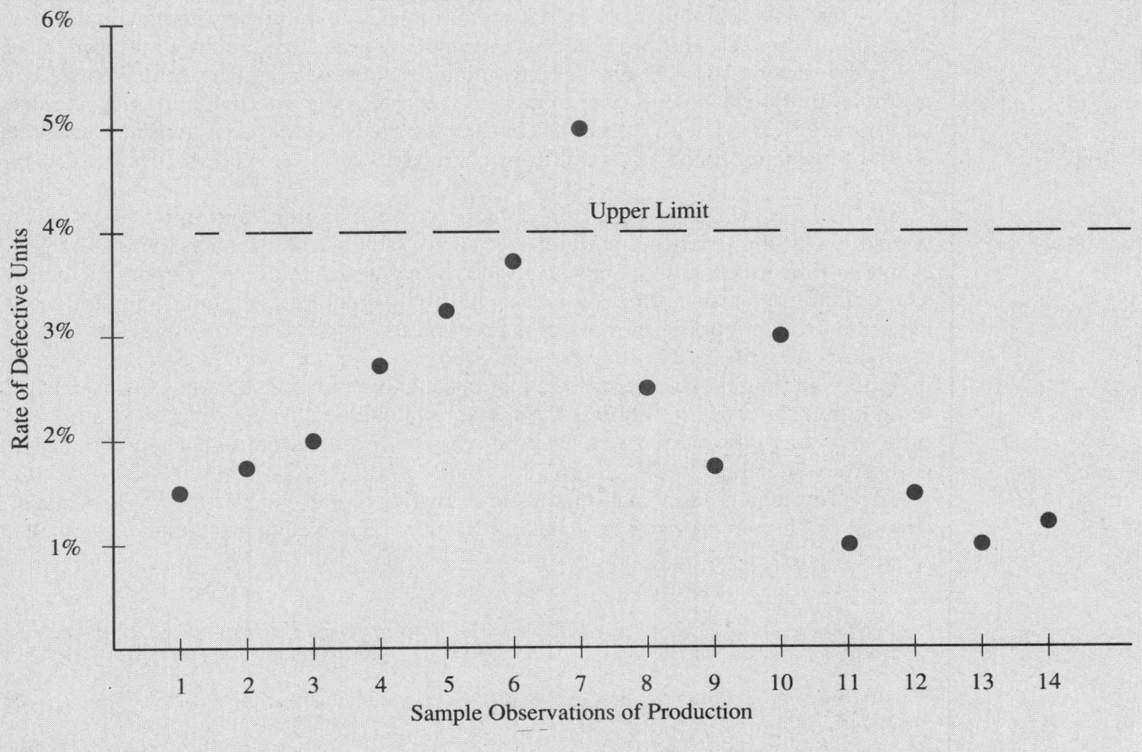

Quality Control Chart

Quality control charts aid managers in determining trends in the rate of defective units and whether the manufacturing process is in control or out of control. For example, in the preceding quality control chart, observations 1–6 indicate increasing rates of defective units, ending with observation 7. At this point, management took corrective action to bring the rate of defective units back into an acceptable range, as indicated by observations 8–14.

Inventory Control

Inventory control has been a major concern for managers for many years. The use of the economic order quantity, order point, and linear programming techniques for inventory control were described and illustrated in Chapter 27. Two additional techniques of inventory control — materials requirements planning and just-in-time inventory systems — are briefly described in the following paragraphs.

Materials Requirements Planning. **Materials requirements planning (MRP),** also known as **materials resource planning,** is a system developed in the 1970s. An MRP system uses computers to project materials requirements by developing purchasing schedules and manufacturing schedules based on projected demand. Included in the materials projections are allowances for such factors as machine breakdowns, which cause shortages or delays in receiving or processing materials. An MRP system is also reviewed and updated for such factors as changes in the product and in customer demand for the product.

The major disadvantages of MRP are that the models used to project materials requirements are often complex, require lengthy periods to develop, and must be used with computers. Therefore, an MRP system is costly. Although these disadvantages are significant, it has been estimated that between 2,000 and 5,000 companies in the United States are using an MRP system.[6] Most of these companies have annual sales exceeding $20 million. Black & Decker, for example, with sales of over $1 billion and nearly 20,000 products, has had remarkable success in using MRP.[7]

In the development of materials requirements planning systems, managerial accountants provide the product cost information necessary for the development of the computer models that are used to minimize materials and inventory costs. For example, the purchase cost of each item of material going into the final product must be estimated, along with handling and storage costs. Managerial accountants must also notify managers of any significant changes in costs, so that the system can be updated.[8]

Just-In-Time Inventory Systems. **Just-in-time inventory systems** were initially developed by the Japanese, who refer to such systems as **Kanban systems.** The goal of just-in-time inventory systems is to reduce inventories to the lowest possible point. The optimum of just-in-time systems would be to acquire just enough inventory to keep the production line moving on a continuous basis. No excess inventory would ever exist, and no interruptions in the production process would occur because of inventory shortages. The impact of a just-in-time inventory system on the profitability of an enterprise can be significant. For example, General Motors has used a just-in-time inventory approach since 1980 and has reduced its annual inventory-related costs from $8 billion to $2 billion.[9]

The implementation of a just-in-time inventory system usually requires major changes in an enterprise's purchasing system. These changes generally involve

---

[6]Sumer C. Aggarwal, "MRP, JIT, OPT, FMS?" *Harvard Business Review* (September-October 1985), p. 8.

[7]*Ibid.*, p. 9.

[8]Billy B. Bowers, "Product Costing in the MRP Environment," *Management Accounting* (December, 1982), pp. 24–27.

[9]David Whiteside and Jules Arbose, "Unsnarling Industrial Production: Why Top Management Is Starting to Care?" *International Management* (March, 1984), p. 20.

agreements with suppliers that will assure the receipt of high quality materials and a timely (just-in-time) delivery of the materials. Manufacturers may require suppliers to locate warehouses near production facilities in order to expedite delivery of materials. In some cases, a manufacturer's computer system is connected directly to a supplier's system, so that purchases may be made electronically when production reaches predetermined levels.

Just-in-time inventory systems are normally implemented with just-in-time manufacturing systems. In these cases, the managerial accountant provides input into the selection of suppliers and the design of innovative purchasing systems. Since materials may be shipped directly from suppliers to mini-production lines, where they will immediately enter production, methods are needed to assure the enterprise that proper quantities of materials have been received. Rather than delaying production by counting materials at the point of receipt, emphasis is likely to be placed on an analysis of the output of the manufacturing process and a reconciliation of the output quantities with the invoices received from the suppliers.

With just-in-time inventory and manufacturing systems, less emphasis is placed on traditional variance analysis, such as the computation of materials price variances, and more emphasis is placed on the timely delivery of materials. Long-term supplier-manufacturer relationships are negotiated with an emphasis on the quality of materials rather than the lowest possible price. As inventories are reduced, relevant product costs become more significant for managerial decision making in such areas as product pricing, cost control, and discontinuance of unprofitable products. The emphasis also changes in performance evaluations, where more nonfinancial measures are used, such as the time to produce a product from start to finish, or **throughput time,** the quantity of scrap generated, and numbers of service calls.

Information Technology

The use of advanced computer information technology in the manufacturing process allows managers to maintain real-time contact with the manufacturing process. With this information, managers can monitor and control operations on a minute-by-minute basis. This continuous monitoring of inputs and outputs of the manufacturing process increases production efficiency and product quality. For example, production supervisors can monitor the amount of scrap that is being generated at each stage of production and can take any corrective action that might be necessary on a timely basis. In contrast, in a traditional manufacturing system, managers often receive weekly or monthly scrap reports.

A primary concern of managerial accountants is providing managers with accurate and timely information on which to base decisions. Managerial accountants may need to become directly involved in the development and implementation of the advanced computer systems that are integrated with the manufacturing process. The challenge to managerial accountants is to develop innovative methods for providing information, so that managers are not overwhelmed by the amount of data, but are able to identify the essential information for decision-making purposes.

Designing the Factory Floor

Computer simulations can be used to design manufacturing operations to maximize efficiency and productivity. The following excerpts were taken from an article in *Business Week* that described how these simulations are used.

You pass by the factory manager's office, and what do you see? He and his top engineers are huddled around a computer screen where cute little symbols are threading their way through mazes. Are these well-paid professionals playing video games on company time?

Look again: The screen display is a recreation of the factory floor, replete with machine tools, robots, flexible manufacturing cells, and materials-handling vehicles. The goal of this game is to exploit those resources in the most efficient way and turn out the highest-quality lowest-cost product. Welcome to the era of manufacturing simulation.

While the exercise may have make-believe overtones, the payoff can be real. That's what the engineers at Northern Research & Engineering Corp., a consulting subsidiary of Ingersoll-Rand Co., learned when they designed a complicated line for making ball bearings. They figured they would need 77 machine tools performing 16 different processes. But when they fed the information into a computer and simulated the line in operation, they quickly realized the plan could be improved. They were able to [save] $750,000 for their client, Torrington Co. With computer simulation, says Northern Research senior engineer James M. Hanson, savings of several million dollars are "not unusual. . . ."

Source: William G. Wild Jr. and Otis Port, "This Video 'Game' Is Saving Manufacturers Millions," *Business Week* (August 17, 1987), pp. 82 and 84.

Selected Bibliography

Aggarwal, Sumer C. *"MRP, JIT, OPT, FMS?"* Harvard Business Review (September–October, 1985), pp. 8–10, 12, 16.

Bennett, Robert E., James A. Hendricks, David E. Keys, and Edward J. Rudnicki. *Cost Accounting for Factory Automation.* Montvale, N.J.: National Association of Accountants, 1987.

Bennett, Robert E., and James A. Hendricks. "Justifying the Acquisition of Automated Equipment." *Management Accounting* (July, 1987), pp. 39–46.

Bowers, Billy. "Product Costing in the MRP Environment." *Management Accounting* (December, 1982), pp. 24–27.

Bruns, William J., and Robert S. Kaplan. *Accounting & Management: Field Study Perspectives.* Boston: Harvard Business School Press, 1987.

Cook, James. "Kanban, American-Style." *Forbes* (October 8, 1984), pp. 66, 70.

Cooper, Robin, and Robert S. Kaplan. "How Cost Accounting Distorts Product Costs." *Management Accounting* (April, 1988), pp. 20–27.

Foster, George, and Charles T. Horngren. "JIT: Cost Accounting and Cost Management Issues." *Management Accounting* (June, 1987), pp. 19–25.

Galante, Steven P. "Small Manufacturers Shifting to 'Just-in-Time' Techniques." *The Wall Street Journal,* December 21, 1987, p. 25.

Holusha, John. "Cost Accounting's Blind Spot." *The New York Times,* October 14, 1986.

Holusha, John. "Designing for Assembly Lines." *The New York Times,* August 12, 1987.

Howell, Robert A., and Stephen R. Soucy. "Capital Investment in the New Manufacturing Environment." *Management Accounting* (November, 1987), pp. 26–32.

Howell, Robert A., and Stephen R. Soucy. "Cost Accounting in the New Manufacturing Environment." *Management Accounting* (August, 1987), pp. 42–48.

Howell, Robert A. and Stephen R. Soucy. "Management Reporting In the New Manufacturing Environment." *Management Accounting* (February, 1988), pp. 22–29.

Howell, Robert A., James D. Brown, Stephen R. Soucy, and Allen H. Seed, III. *Management Accounting in the New Manufacturing Environment.* Montvale, N.J.: National Association of Accountants, 1987.

Howell, Robert A., and Stephen R. Soucy. "Operating Controls in the New Manufacturing Environment." *Management Accounting* (October, 1987), pp. 23–31.

Howell, Robert A., and Stephen R. Soucy. The New Manufacturing Environment: Major Trends for Management Accounting." *Management Accounting* (July, 1987), pp. 21–27.

Jayson, Susan. "Cost Accounting for the 90s." *Management Accounting* (July, 1986), pp. 58–59.

Johnson, H. Thomas, and Robert S. Kaplan. "The Rise and Fall of Management Accounting." *Management Accounting* (January, 1987), pp. 22–30.

Johnson, H. Thomas, and Robert S. Kaplan. *Relevance Lost: The Rise and Fall of Management Accounting*. Boston: Harvard Business School Press, 1987.

Kaplan, Robert S. "Must CIM Be Justified by Faith Alone?" *Harvard Business Review* (March–April, 1986), pp. 87–95.

Lammert, Thomas B., and Robert Ehrsam. "The Human Element: The Real Challange in Modernizing Cost Systems." *Management Accounting* (July, 1987), pp. 32–37.

Mackey, James T. "11 Key Issues in Manufacturing Accounting." *Management Accounting* (January, 1987), pp. 32–37.

Marcom, John Jr. "Slimming Down: IBM Is Automating, Simplifying Products to Beat Asian Rivals." *The Wall Street Journal*, April 14, 1986, pp. 1, 10.

McIlhattan, Robert D. "How Cost Management Systems Can Support The JIT Philosophy." *Management Accounting* (September, 1987), pp. 20–26.

McNair, C. J., and William Mosconi. "Measuring Performance in an Advanced Manufacturing Environment." *Management Accounting* (July, 1987), pp. 28–31.

Neumann, Bruce R., and Pauline R. Jaouen. "Kanban, Zips and Cost Accounting: A Case Study." *Journal of Accountancy* (August, 1986), pp. 132–141.

Robinson, Michael A., and John E. Timmerman. "How Vendor Analysis Supports JIT Manufacturing." *Management Accounting* (December, 1987), pp. 20–24.

Sadhwani, A. T., and M. H. Sarhan. "The Impact of Just-In-Time Inventory Systems on Small Businesses." *Journal of Accountancy* (January, 1987), pp. 118–130.

Sadhwani, Arjan T. and M. H. Sarhan. "Electronic Systems Enhance JIT Operations." *Management Accounting* (December, 1987), pp. 25–30.

Sadhwani, Arjan T., M. H. Sarhan, and Dayal Kiringoda. "Just-In-Time: An Inventory System Whose Time Has Come." *Journal of Accountancy* (December, 1985), pp. 36–44.

Sauers, Dale G. "Analyzing Inventory Systems." *Management Accounting* (May, 1986), pp. 30–36.

Seglund, Ragnor, and Santiago Ibarreche. "Just-In-Time: The Accounting Implications." *Management Accounting* (August, 1984), pp. 43–45.

Whiteside, David, and Jules Arbose. "Unsnarling Industrial Production: Why Top Management Is Starting to Care?" *International Management* (March, 1984).

Wild, William G., Jr., and Otis Port. "This 'Video Game' is Saving Manufacturers Millions." *Business Week* (August 17, 1987), pp. 82, 84.

Worthy, Ford S. "Accounting Bores You? Wake Up." *Fortune* (October 12, 1987), pp. 43, 44, 48–50.

Appendix J

Specimen Financial Statements

This appendix contains selected statements and notes for real companies and financial statements based on the actual statements of a small, privately held manufacturing company. Because privately held companies are not required to release their financial statements to the public, the Carter Manufacturing Company statements were modified to protect the confidentiality of the company. We are grateful for the assistance of the public accounting firm of Deloitte Haskins & Sells and Mr. Mark Young in developing these statements.

Consolidated Statements of Earnings

Tonka Corporation and Subsidiaries

(In millions, except per share data)	Fiscal Year		
	1986	1985	1984
Net revenues	$ 293.4	$ 244.4	$ 139.0
Cost of goods sold	159.3	131.9	93.9
Gross profit	134.1	112.5	45.1
Advertising expense	45.7	40.2	13.8
Selling, general and administrative expenses	43.1	29.9	19.4
Other expense (income)	1.2	2.6	(1.9)
Interest expense — net	3.8	3.6	5.5
Earnings before income taxes	40.3	36.2	8.3
Income taxes	18.0	16.7	3.3
Net earnings	$ 22.3	$ 19.5	$ 5.0
Net earnings per share	$ 3.04	$ 2.99	$ .78
Average number of common shares	7.3	6.5	6.5

Consolidated Statements of Retained Earnings

Tonka Corporation and Subsidiaries

(In millions)	Fiscal Year		
	1986	1985	1984
Retained earnings at beginning of year	$ 46.4	$ 27.3	$ 22.7
Net earnings	22.3	19.5	5.0
Cash dividends	(.5)	(.4)	(.4)
Retained earnings at end of year	$ 68.2	$ 46.4	$ 27.3

Consolidated Balance Sheets
Tonka Corporation and Subsidiaries

(In millions)	January 3, 1987	December 28, 1985
Assets		
Current assets:		
Cash and short-term investments	$ 44.8	$ 22.9
Accounts receivable — net	58.4	44.1
Inventories	20.8	25.7
Prepaid expenses and other current assets	5.8	6.0
Deferred income taxes	4.8	4.5
Total current assets	134.6	103.2
Land, buildings and equipment:		
Land	2.0	2.0
Buildings	9.9	10.4
Equipment	44.6	40.6
Total land, buildings and equipment	56.5	53.0
Less accumulated depreciation	(34.1)	(33.1)
Net land, buildings and equipment	22.4	19.9
Other assets	1.6	.2
Total assets	$ 158.6	$ 123.3

Liabilities and Stockholders' Equity		
Current liabilities:		
Accounts payable	$ 17.6	$ 21.4
Accrued taxes	4.5	22.2
Accrued payroll	5.8	4.3
Accrued advertising	6.8	6.6
Accrued royalties	6.4	1.6
Current portion of long-term debt	7.9	.1
Other current liabilities	4.5	6.0
Total current liabilities	53.5	62.2
Long-term debt	8.2	8.1
Deferred income taxes and other	.6	1.7
Total liabilities	62.3	72.0
Stockholders' equity:		
Common stock, $.66 2/3 par, issued and outstanding 7.7 and 6.6 shares, respectively	5.1	4.3
Additional paid-in capital	25.3	3.0
Retained earnings	68.2	46.4
Cumulative translation adjustments	(2.3)	(2.4)
Total stockholders' equity	96.3	51.3
Total liabilities and stockholders' equity	$ 158.6	$ 123.3

Notes to Consolidated Financial Statements

Tonka Corporation and Subsidiaries
January 3, 1987, December 28, 1985 and December 29, 1984
(In millions, except share and per share data)

Note One — Summary of Significant Accounting Policies

Principles of Consolidation

The consolidated financial statements include the accounts of Tonka Corporation and subsidiaries (The "Company" or "Tonka"), all of which are wholly-owned. All material intercompany balances and transactions have been eliminated.

Short-term Investments

Short-term investments are carried at the lower of cost or market.

Land, Buildings, and Equipment

Land, buildings and equipment are stated on the basis of cost. Depreciation is computed by the straight-line method at rates expected to amortize the cost of buildings and equipment over their estimated useful lives.

Inventory Valuation

Inventories are valued at the lower of cost or market. Domestic inventories are valued using the last-in, first-out (LIFO) method, while other inventories are generally valued using the first-in, first-out (FIFO) method.

Research and Development

All expenditures for research and development are charged against operations in the year incurred. The charges for fiscal 1986, 1985 and 1984 were $8.3, $4.5 and $1.7, respectively.

Income Taxes

Deferred income taxes are provided for all significant timing differences between financial and taxable income. Investment tax credits are accounted for as a reduction of income tax expense in the year realized (flow-through method).

Reclassifications

The 1984 and 1985 financial statements have been reclassified to conform to 1986 presentations.

Earnings Per Share

Earnings per share are calculated based upon the weighted average number of shares outstanding during the year.

Note Two — Other Significant Transactions

In 1986, the Company decided to close out the GoBots product line. Proceeds from the GoBots inventory closeout were $7.9, which approximated the inventory value. All proceeds and inventory costs were included in cost of goods sold.

CONSOLIDATED STATEMENTS OF CASH FLOWS

Kelly Services, Inc. and Subsidiaries

(In thousands)	Fiscal Years		
	1987	1986	1985
Increase (decrease) in cash and cash equivalents			
Cash flows from operating activities:			
Net earnings	**$ 50,461**	$ 36,436	$ 32,615
Amounts that reconcile net earnings to net cash provided by operating activities—			
Depreciation	**6,363**	5,648	4,550
Changes in assets and liabilities:			
Increase in accounts receivable	**(8,685)**	(13,788)	(15,107)
Increase in prepaid expenses and other assets	**(2,767)**	(1,539)	(1,646)
Increase (decrease) in accounts payable	**(616)**	2,016	1,926
Increase in payroll and related taxes	**4,421**	5,820	2,697
Increase in insurance payable	**5,670**	5,344	3,201
Increase in income and other taxes payable	**1,556**	2,723	1,322
Net cash from operating activities	**56,403**	42,660	29,558
Cash flows used in investing activities:			
Capital expenditures	**(5,699)**	(7,417)	(8,396)
Increase in short-term investments	**(10,903)**	(4,631)	(3,937)
Cash used in investing activities	**(16,602)**	(12,048)	(12,333)
Cash flows from financing activities:			
Dividend payments	**(12,329)**	(10,131)	(8,697)
Purchase of treasury stock	**(3,350)**	(7,789)	(4,199)
Exercise of stock options	**582**	219	377
Net cash used in financing activities	**(15,097)**	(17,701)	(12,519)
Net increase in cash and cash equivalents	**24,704**	12,911	4,706
Cash and cash equivalents at beginning of year	**43,699**	30,788	26,082
Cash and cash equivalents at end of year	**$ 68,403**	$ 43,699	$ 30,788

See accompanying Notes to Consolidated Financial Statements.

Consolidated Balance Sheets

General Mills, Inc. and Subsidiaries

ASSETS	May 25, 1986	May 26, 1985
	Fiscal Year Ended (In Millions)	
CURRENT ASSETS:		
Cash	$ 56.4	$ 49.4
Short-term investments	133.9	17.4
Receivables, less allowance for doubtful accounts of $6.3 in 1986 and $4.0 in 1985	220.0	284.5
Inventories	350.9	377.7
Prepaid expenses	32.8	31.5
Net assets of discontinued operations and redeployments	10.4	517.5
TOTAL CURRENT ASSETS	804.4	1,278.0
LAND, BUILDINGS AND EQUIPMENT, AT COST:		
Land	100.9	93.3
Buildings	583.2	524.4
Equipment	894.7	788.1
Construction in progress	132.2	80.2
Total Land, Buildings and Equipment	1,711.0	1,486.0
Less accumulated depreciation	(626.1)	(530.0)
NET LAND, BUILDINGS AND EQUIPMENT	1,084.9	956.0
OTHER ASSETS:		
Net noncurrent assets of businesses to be spun off	—	206.5
Intangible assets, principally goodwill	53.4	50.8
Investments and miscellaneous assets	143.5	162.7
TOTAL OTHER ASSETS	196.9	420.0
TOTAL ASSETS	$2,086.2	$2,654.0

LIABILITIES AND STOCKHOLDERS' EQUITY	May 25, 1986	May 26, 1985
CURRENT LIABILITIES:		
Accounts payable	$ 382.4	$ 352.2
Current portion of long-term debt	10.5	59.4
Notes payable	4.7	379.8
Accrued taxes	97.5	1.4
Accrued payroll	100.6	91.8
Other current liabilities	167.1	164.0
TOTAL CURRENT LIABILITIES	762.8	1,048.6
LONG-TERM DEBT	458.3	449.5
DEFERRED INCOME TAXES	49.7	29.8
DEFERRED INCOME TAXES—TAX LEASES	78.1	60.8
OTHER LIABILITIES AND DEFERRED CREDITS	54.8	42.0
TOTAL LIABILITIES	1,403.7	1,630.7
STOCKHOLDERS' EQUITY:		
Common stock	215.9	213.7
Retained earnings	812.9	1,201.7
Less common stock in treasury, at cost	(314.1)	(333.9)
Cumulative foreign currency adjustment	(32.2)	(58.2)
TOTAL STOCKHOLDERS' EQUITY	682.5	1,023.3
TOTAL LIABILITIES AND STOCKHOLDERS' EQUITY	$2,086.2	$2,654.0

See accompanying notes to consolidated financial statements.

Consolidated Statements of Earnings

General Mills, Inc. and Subsidiaries

	Fiscal Year Ended		
	May 25, 1986	*May 26, 1985*	*May 27, 1984*
	(Amounts in Millions, Except Per Share Data)		
CONTINUING OPERATIONS:			
SALES	$4,586.6	$4,285.2	$4,118.4
COSTS AND EXPENSES:			
Cost of sales, exclusive of items below	2,563.9	2,474.8	2,432.8
Selling, general and administrative expenses	1,545.7	1,381.7	1,263.9
Depreciation and amortization expenses	113.1	110.4	99.0
Interest expense, net	38.8	46.6	19.1
TOTAL COSTS AND EXPENSES	4,261.5	4,013.5	3,814.8
EARNINGS FROM CONTINUING OPERATIONS—PRETAX	325.1	271.7	303.6
GAIN (LOSS) FROM REDEPLOYMENTS	(1.5)	(75.8)	53.0
EARNINGS FROM CONTINUING OPERATIONS AFTER REDEPLOYMENTS—PRETAX	323.6	195.9	356.6
INCOME TAXES	140.1	80.5	153.9
EARNINGS FROM CONTINUING OPERATIONS AFTER REDEPLOYMENTS	183.5	115.4	202.7
EARNINGS PER SHARE—CONTINUING OPERATIONS AFTER REDEPLOYMENTS	$ 4.11	$ 2.58	$ 4.32
DISCONTINUED OPERATIONS AFTER TAX	—	(188.3)	30.7
NET EARNINGS (LOSS)	$ 183.5	$ (72.9)	$ 233.4
NET EARNINGS (LOSS) PER SHARE	$ 4.11	$ (1.63)	$ 4.98
AVERAGE NUMBER OF COMMON SHARES	44.6	44.7	46.9

Consolidated Statements of Retained Earnings

	Fiscal Year Ended		
	May 25, 1986	*May 26, 1985*	*May 27, 1984*
	(Amounts in Millions, Except Per Share Data)		
RETAINED EARNINGS AT BEGINNING OF YEAR	$1,201.7	$1,375.0	$1,237.6
Net earnings (loss)	183.5	(72.9)	233.4
Deduct dividends of $2.26 per share in 1986, $2.24 per share in 1985 and $2.04 per share in 1984	(100.9)	(100.4)	(96.0)
Distribution of equity to stockholders from spin-off of Toy and Fashion operations	(471.4)	—	—
RETAINED EARNINGS AT END OF YEAR	$ 812.9	$1,201.7	$1,375.0

See accompanying notes to consolidated financial statements.

KMART CORPORATION

CONSOLIDATED STATEMENTS OF INCOME

(Millions, except per-share data)	Fiscal Year Ended January 28, 1987	January 29, 1986	January 30, 1985
Sales	**$23,812**	$22,035	$20,762
Licensee fees and rental income	**234**	223	206
Equity in income of affiliated retail companies	**83**	76	65
Interest income	**23**	23	39
	24,152	22,357	21,072
Cost of merchandise sold (including buying and occupancy costs)	**17,258**	15,987	15,095
Selling, general and administrative expenses	**4,936**	4,673	4,268
Advertising	**581**	554	543
Interest expense:			
Debt	**171**	205	147
Capital lease obligations	**178**	181	184
	23,124	21,600	20,237
Income from continuing retail operations before income taxes	**1,028**	757	835
Income taxes	**458**	285	332
Income from continuing retail operations	**570**	472	503
Discontinued operations (Note B)	**28**	(251)	(4)
Extraordinary item (Note I)	**(16)**	–	–
Net income for the year	**$ 582**	$ 221	$ 499
Earnings per common and common equivalent share:			
Continuing retail operations	**$ 2.84**	$ 2.42	$ 2.58
Discontinued operations	**.14**	(1.27)	(.02)
Extraordinary item	**(.08)**	–	–
Net income	**$ 2.90**	$ 1.15	$ 2.56
Weighted average shares outstanding	**201.5**	197.4	197.3

See accompanying Notes to Consolidated Financial Statements.

The consolidated statements of income for prior periods have been restated for discontinued operations.

Per share amounts and weighted average shares outstanding have been adjusted to reflect the three-for-two stock split declared March 24, 1987.

KMART CORPORATION

CONSOLIDATED BALANCE SHEETS

(Millions)	January 28, 1987	January 29, 1986
Assets		
Current Assets:		
Cash (includes temporary investments of $296 and $352, respectively)	$ 521	$ 627
Merchandise inventories	5,153	4,537
Accounts receivable and other current assets	390	363
Total current assets	6,064	5,527
Investments in Affiliated Retail Companies	317	293
Property and Equipment–net	3,594	3,644
Other Assets and Deferred Charges	603	527
	$10,578	$9,991
Liabilities and Shareholders' Equity		
Current Liabilities:		
Long-term debt due within one year	$ 4	$ 15
Notes payable	296	127
Accounts payable–trade	2,207	1,908
Accrued payrolls and other liabilities	639	624
Taxes other than income taxes	223	218
Income taxes	162	198
Total current liabilities	3,531	3,090
Capital Lease Obligations	1,600	1,713
Long-Term Debt	1,011	1,456
Other Long-Term Liabilities	315	345
Deferred Income Taxes	182	114
Shareholders' Equity	3,939	3,273
	$10,578	$9,991

See accompanying Notes to Consolidated Financial Statements.

KMART CORPORATION

CONSOLIDATED STATEMENTS OF SHAREHOLDERS' EQUITY

($ Millions)	Common Stock Shares	Common Stock Amount	Capital in Excess of Par Value	Retained Earnings	Treasury Shares	Foreign Currency Translation Adjustment	Total Shareholders' Equity
Balance at January 25, 1984	**188,866,208**	**$126**	**$293**	**$2,569**	**$**	**$ (48)**	**$2,940**
Net income for the year				499			499
Cash dividends declared, $.84 per share				(155)			(155)
Common stock sold under stock option and employees' savings plans and conversion of debentures	1,178,232	1	20				21
Purchase of 2,517,750 treasury shares, at cost					(51)		(51)
Foreign currency translation adjustment						(20)	(20)
Balance at January 30, 1985	**190,044,440**	**127**	**313**	**2,913**	**(51)**	**(68)**	**3,234**
Net income for the year				221			221
Cash dividends declared, $.92 per share				(176)			(176)
Common stock sold under stock option and employees' savings plans and conversion of debentures	1,478,041	1	30				31
Foreign currency translation adjustment						(37)	(37)
Balance at January 29, 1986	**191,522,481**	**128**	**343**	**2,958**	**(51)**	**(105)**	**3,273**
Net income for the year				582			582
Cash dividends declared, $1.00 per share				(193)			(193)
Three-for-two stock split		67	(67)				–
Common stock sold under stock option and employees' savings plans	2,792,834	2	63				65
Common stock issued for conversion of debentures	7,867,995	5	181				186
Reissue of 666,328 treasury shares for employees' savings plan			8		14		22
Foreign currency translation adjustment						4	4
Balance at January 28, 1987	**202,183,310**	**$202**	**$528**	**$3,347**	**$(37)**	**$(101)**	**$3,939**

Common stock, authorized 250,000,000 shares, $1.00 par value.

Ten million shares of no par value preferred stock with voting and cumulative dividend rights are authorized but unissued. Currently there are no plans for its issuance.

See accompanying Notes to Consolidated Financial Statements.

Cash dividends declared and common stock shares have been adjusted to reflect the three-for-two stock split declared March 24, 1987 [Note C].

Consolidated Statement of Income

(in millions except per share amounts)
PepsiCo, Inc. and Subsidiaries
Fifty-two weeks ended December 27, 1986, December 28, 1985 and December 29, 1984

	1986	1985	1984
Net Sales	$9,290.8	$7,653.4	$7,107.6
Costs and Expenses			
Cost of sales	3,731.8	3,148.3	2,974.4
Marketing, administrative and other expenses	4,738.4	3,760.4	3,407.4
Refranchising (credit) charge	–	(25.9)	156.0
Interest expense	263.2	195.4	205.1
Interest income	(122.9)	(96.4)	(86.1)
	8,610.5	6,981.8	6,656.8
Income From Continuing Operations Before Income Taxes	680.3	671.6	450.8
Provision for Income Taxes	222.5	251.5	175.8
Income From Continuing Operations	457.8	420.1	275.0
Discontinued Operations			
Income (loss) from discontinued operations (net of income tax provision of $6.7 in 1985 and none in 1984)	–	9.6	(47.5)
Gain (loss) on disposals (net of income tax provision of $28.8 in 1985 and benefit of $1.0 in 1984)	–	114.0	(15.0)
	–	123.6	(62.5)
Net Income	$ 457.8	$ 543.7	$ 212.5
Income (Loss) Per Share			
Continuing operations	$1.75	$1.50	$ .97
Discontinued operations	–	.44	(.22)
Net Income Per Share	$1.75	$1.94	$ .75
Average shares outstanding used to calculate income per share	262.2	280.7	287.5

See accompanying Notes to Consolidated Financial Statements.

Allocation of 1986 Net Sales

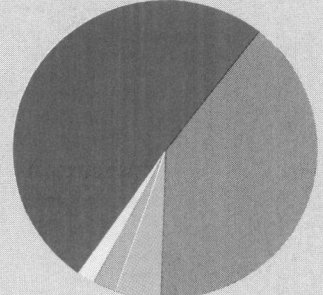

- Marketing, Administrative and Other Expenses 51.0%
- Cost of Sales 40.2%
- Net Interest Expense 1.5%
- Income Taxes 2.4%
- Net Income 4.9%

Business Segments

Net Sales

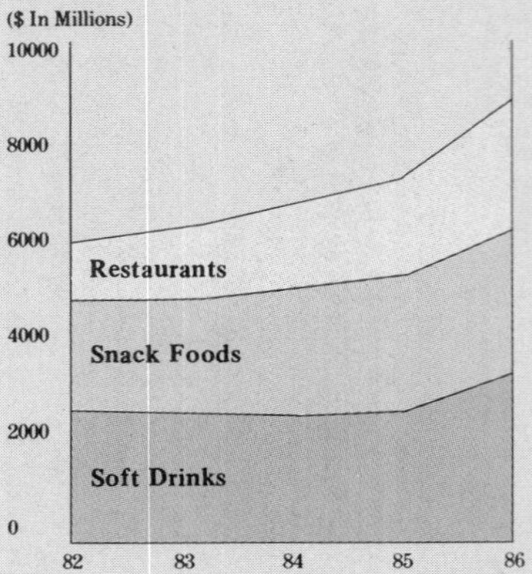

Capital Spending

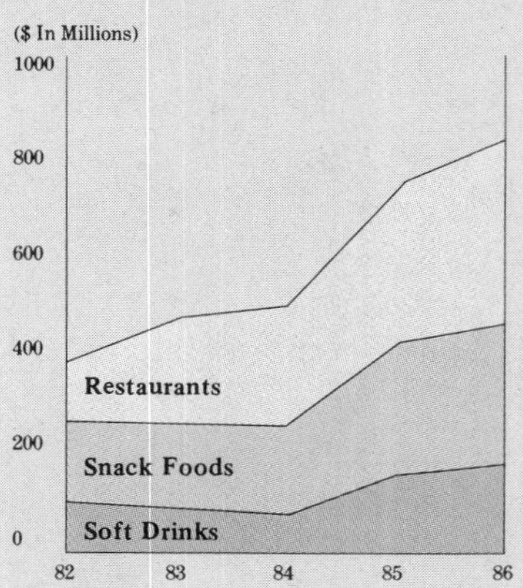

PepsiCo operates within three distinct business segments on a worldwide basis: soft drinks, snack foods and restaurants. Management's discussion and analysis of PepsiCo's business segments appears on pages 17, 23 and 30 under Management's Analysis.

The soft drinks segment primarily manufactures and markets Pepsi-Cola, Slice and their allied brands worldwide and Seven-Up internationally. For purposes of this Note, the operations of the soft drink concentrate manufacturing facility in Puerto Rico are allocated between domestic and foreign based upon the actual concentrate shipments to the respective markets. The snack foods segment primarily manufactures and markets salty snacks. The restaurants segment primarily includes the operations of Pizza Hut, Taco Bell and Kentucky Fried Chicken. The 1986 soft drinks and restaurants segment data included the results of the soft drink business of MEI Corporation, the international franchise soft drink business of The Seven-Up Company and Kentucky Fried Chicken operations from their respective dates of acquisition (see Note to the Consolidated Financial Statements on page 41).

In 1986 PepsiCo made three reclassifications to conform the reporting of segment net sales and operating profits to industry practices. Certain promotional discounts previously included in the soft drinks segment as marketing expense were reclassified as a reduction of net sales. State income taxes and net foreign currency translation gains previously included in the determination of segment operating profits were excluded and reclassified to "Provision for income taxes" and "Corporate expenses, net," respectively. The 1985 and 1984 amounts were reclassified on a comparable basis.

In December 1986 the Securities and Exchange Commission issued guidelines that clarified the reporting of certain unusual items. As a result, soft drinks segment operating profits were restated to include a $26 million credit recorded in 1985 and a $156 million charge recorded in 1984 related to the sale of several foreign company-owned bottling operations (see Note to the Consolidated Financial Statements on page 42).

Operating profits included research and development expenses of $82 million, $66 million and $49 million in 1986, 1985 and 1984, respectively.

Corporate expenses included unallocated corporate items, net interest expense and net foreign currency translation gains, which arose principally from the translation of foreign local currency borrowings. These foreign exchange translation gains were $33 million, $32 million and $53 million in 1986, 1985 and 1984, respectively.

Corporate identifiable assets principally consisted of short-term investments. Included in 1985 were the receivable from the sale of North American Van Lines and the investment in the Allegheny Pepsi-Cola Bottling Company, and in 1985 and 1984, the investment in Safe Harbor leases.

	1986	1985	1984
Net Sales:			
Soft drinks	**$3,588.4**	2,725.1	2,565.0
Snack foods	**3,018.4**	2,847.1	2,709.2
Restaurants	**2,684.0**	2,081.2	1,833.4
Total continuing operations	**$9,290.8**	7,653.4	7,107.6
Foreign portion	**$1,225.8**	951.9	963.9
Operating Profits:			
Soft drinks	**$ 348.6**	283.4	86.6
Snack foods	**342.8**	392.5	393.9
Restaurants	**210.1**	198.1	183.8
Corporate expenses, net	**(221.2)**	(202.4)	(213.5)
Income from continuing operations before income taxes	**$ 680.3**	671.6	450.8
Foreign portion	**$ 64.7**	70.0	(139.9)
Capital Spending:			
Soft drinks	**$ 193.9**	160.7	83.6
Snack foods	**298.6**	286.3	188.9
Restaurants	**384.6**	331.0	252.5
Corporate	**9.2**	7.9	30.8
Total continuing operations	**$ 886.3**	785.9	555.8
Foreign portion	**$ 81.4**	67.3	36.4
Identifiable Assets:			
Soft drinks	**$2,617.7**	1,318.6	1,038.9
Snack foods	**1,603.8**	1,487.1	1,254.5
Restaurants	**2,659.5**	1,326.7	1,020.7
Corporate	**1,147.6**	1,760.5	1,277.0
Total continuing operations	**$8,028.6**	5,892.9	4,591.1
Foreign portion	**$2,275.0**	1,054.3	687.5
Depreciation and Amortization Expense:			
Soft drinks	**$ 104.3**	69.2	71.1
Snack foods	**135.3**	107.7	93.6
Restaurants	**156.4**	109.2	75.7
Corporate	**4.7**	4.7	9.2
Total continuing operations	**$ 400.7**	290.8	249.6
Foreign portion	**$ 36.3**	25.3	36.8

This information constitutes a Note to the Consolidated Financial Statements.

Operating Profits

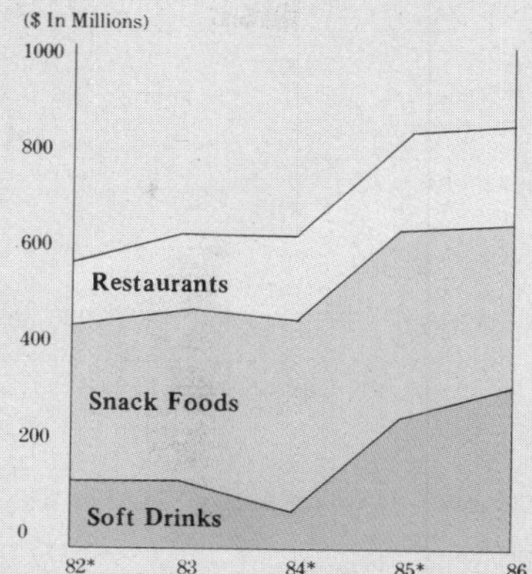

* Includes impact of unusual charges and credit related to foreign bottling operations. See pages 42 and 48.

Identifiable Assets

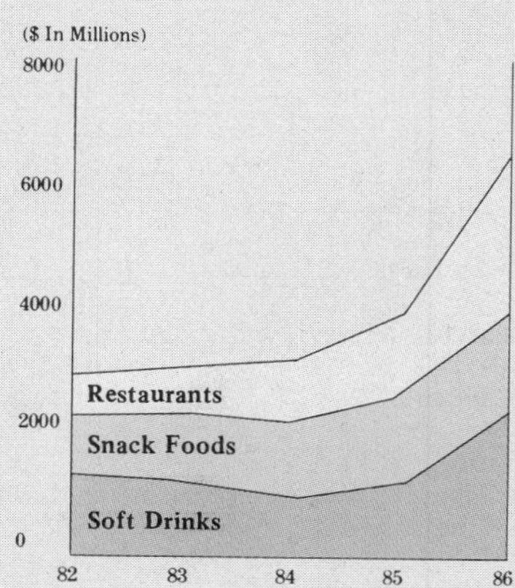

Consolidated Statement of Financial Condition

(in millions except per share amount)
PepsiCo, Inc. and Subsidiaries
December 27, 1986 and December 28, 1985

	1986	1985
Assets		
Current Assets		
Cash	$ 34.9	$ 26.0
Short-term investments	885.6	912.9
	920.5	938.9
Receivable from sale of North American Van Lines	–	375.5
Notes and accounts receivable, less allowance: 1986-$43.2, 1985-$30.4	820.2	653.3
Inventories	431.5	380.1
Prepaid expenses, taxes and other current assets	331.6	478.0
	2,503.8	2,825.8
Long-term Receivables, Investments and Other Assets	400.1	309.6
Property, Plant and Equipment	3,840.1	2,571.8
Goodwill	1,284.6	185.7
	$8,028.6	$5,892.9
Liabilities and Shareholders' Equity		
Current Liabilities		
Notes payable	$ 232.7	$ 344.1
Accounts payable	858.9	623.7
Income taxes payable	195.2	150.0
Other current liabilities	936.3	738.2
	2,223.1	1,856.0
Long-term Debt	2,492.9	1,035.6
Capital Lease Obligations	139.7	127.1
Other Liabilities and Deferred Credits	336.2	222.8
Deferred Income Taxes	777.6	813.7
Shareholders' Equity		
Capital stock, par value 1 2/3¢ per share: authorized 600.0 shares, issued 287.7 shares	4.8	4.8
Capital in excess of par value	287.0	282.5
Retained earnings	2,356.6	2,061.4
Cumulative translation adjustment	(40.0)	(40.9)
Cost of treasury stock: 1986-27.4 shares, 1985-24.6 shares	(549.3)	(470.1)
	2,059.1	1,837.7
	$8,028.6	$5,892.9

See accompanying Notes to Consolidated Financial Statements.

The Pillsbury Company and Subsidiaries
Consolidated Statement of Earnings

	Year ended May 31		
	1987	1986	1985
	(In millions except per share amounts)		
Net sales	$6,127.8	$5,847.9	$4,843.4
Costs and expenses:			
Cost of sales	4,292.2	4,102.6	3,465.5
Selling, general and administrative expenses	1,387.5	1,270.9	984.7
Interest expense, net	95.6	97.3	53.0
	5,775.3	5,470.8	4,503.2
Earnings before taxes on income	352.5	377.1	340.2
Taxes on income	170.6	169.0	148.4
Net earnings	$ 181.9	$ 208.1	$ 191.8
Average number of shares outstanding	86.7	87.3	86.8
Earnings per share	$ 2.10	$ 2.38	$ 2.21

Notes to Consolidated Financial Statements are an integral part of this statement.

UNITED CABLE TELEVISION CORPORATION and Subsidiaries

CONSOLIDATED BALANCE SHEETS

(In Thousands) As of May 31,	1986	1985
Assets		
Cash and cash equivalents	**$ 1,400**	$ 11,845
Trade accounts receivable, less allowance for doubtful receivables of $402,000 in 1986 and $401,000 in 1985	**3,758**	3,369
Notes and other receivables	**3,956**	6,264
Prepaid expenses and other assets	**8,739**	6,405
Investments in and advances to managed limited partnerships (Note 3)	**45,557**	16,602
Investments in and advances to affiliated companies (Note 1)	**982**	989
Investment in cable television systems (Notes 1, 2, 3, 4 and 12)		
Property, plant and equipment, at cost	**459,876**	383,411
Less—accumulated depreciation	**(164,927)**	(132,205)
	294,949	251,206
Cost in excess of net tangible assets of subsidiaries at acquisition, net of accumulated amortization of $3,863,000 in 1986 and $1,635,000 in 1985	**68,572**	33,783
Deferred cable television permit costs, net of accumulated amortization of $1,585,000 in 1986 and $1,279,000 in 1985	**7,013**	9,390
Total investment in cable television systems	**370,534**	294,379
Investments in broadcast television entities (Note 13)	**19,206**	7,639
Net assets of discontinued segment at estimated net realizable value (Notes 1 and 13)	**—**	10,991
	$454,132	$358,483

The accompanying notes to consolidated financial statements are an integral part of these balance sheets.

UNITED CABLE TELEVISION CORPORATION and Subsidiaries

CONSOLIDATED BALANCE SHEETS

(In Thousands) As of May 31,	1986	1985
Liabilities and stockholders' investment		
Accounts payable and accrued liabilities	**$ 31,140**	$ 17,402
Subscriber prepayments and deposits	**11,590**	9,879
Debt (Note 4)	**347,996**	276,842
Total liabilities	**390,726**	304,123
Minority interests	**462**	450
Deferred income taxes (Note 6)	**3,921**	3,702
Commitments (Note 11)		
Preferred stock, Series A, $1 par value, 10¼% cumulative, 100,000 shares authorized and outstanding in 1986 and 150,000 shares authorized and outstanding in 1985, issued at $100 per share, convertible into common stock, mandatory redemption requirements (Note 5)	**9,894**	14,828
Stockholders' investment (Notes 1, 2, 7, 8 and 9)		
Preferred stock, $1 par value, authorized 900,000 shares, none issued	**—**	—
Convertible preferred stock, Series B, $1 par value, none authorized or issued in 1986, 4,000 shares authorized and 3,650 shares outstanding in 1985	**—**	14,600
Common stock, $.10 par value, 40,000,000 shares authorized and 24,383,306 issued in 1986 and 20,000,000 shares authorized and 15,135,914 issued in 1985	**2,438**	1,513
Additional paid-in capital	**44,325**	18,232
Retained earnings (Note 4)	**2,459**	1,256
Treasury stock	**(93)**	(221)
Total stockholders' investment	**49,129**	35,380
	$454,132	$358,483

The accompanying notes to consolidated financial statements are an integral part of these balance sheets.

UNITED CABLE TELEVISION CORPORATION and Subsidiaries

CONSOLIDATED STATEMENTS OF OPERATIONS

(In Thousands Except Per Share Data) For The Years Ended May 31,	1986	1985	1984
Revenues	**$195,766**	$168,996	$140,741
Operating expenses	**68,223**	61,339	53,463
General and administrative expenses	**45,604**	39,154	33,782
Depreciation and amortization	**39,172**	32,465	27,008
	152,999	132,958	114,253
Operating income after depreciation	**42,767**	36,038	26,488
Other income (expense)			
Interest expense	**(33,477)**	(19,770)	(18,374)
Interest capitalized during construction (Note 1)	**1,224**	554	1,337
Acquisition cost write-off	**—**	(1,937)	—
Other, net	**(694)**	(538)	(476)
Income from continuing operations before income taxes	**9,820**	14,347	8,975
Income tax provision (benefit) (Note 6)			
Current	**18**	(10)	7
Deferred	**901**	1,890	807
	919	1,880	814
Income from continuing operations	**8,901**	12,467	8,161
Loss on disposal of discontinued segment, net of applicable income tax benefits of $575,000 in 1986 and $350,000 in 1984 (Note 13)	**(4,857)**	—	(4,226)
Net earnings before extraordinary item	**4,044**	12,467	3,935
Extraordinary loss, net of applicable income tax benefit of $224,000 (Note 4)	**—**	(1,925)	—
Net earnings	**$ 4,044**	$ 10,542	$ 3,935
Earnings (loss) per common and common equivalent share (Note 1)			
Primary and fully diluted			
Continuing operations	**$ .32**	$ .40	$ .27
Discontinued operations	**(.20)**	—	(.17)
Extraordinary item	**—**	(.07)	—
Net earnings	**$ .12**	$ .33	$ .10
Average number of common and common equivalent shares (Note 1)			
Primary	**24,511**	27,059	24,898
Fully diluted	**24,554**	27,108	24,916
Dividends per common share	**$ .07**	$ .06	$ .06

The accompanying notes to consolidated financial statements are an integral part of these statements.

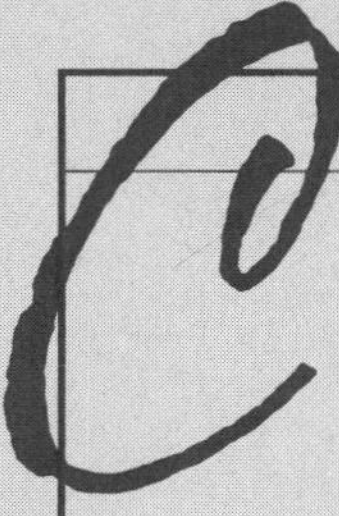

ONSOLIDATED STATEMENTS OF INCOME

Years ended February 28, 1987, 1986 and 1985
Thousands of dollars except per share amounts

	1987	1986	1985
Net sales	**$1,102,532**	$1,012,451	$919,371
Other income	**23,463**	23,200	26,287
Total Revenue	**1,125,995**	1,035,651	945,658
Costs and expenses:			
Material, labor and other production costs	**471,503**	416,322	377,755
Selling, distribution and marketing	**340,980**	308,745	274,095
Administrative and general	**145,012**	131,928	123,750
Depreciation and amortization	**29,059**	23,471	18,799
Interest	**24,875**	19,125	15,556
Divestiture loss	**12,371**	—	—
	1,023,800	899,591	809,955
Income Before Income Taxes	**102,195**	136,060	135,703
Income taxes	**38,834**	61,635	61,338
Net Income	**$ 63,361**	$ 74,425	$ 74,365
Net Income Per Share	**$1.97**	$2.32	$2.35

See notes to consolidated financial statements

ONSOLIDATED STATEMENTS OF FINANCIAL POSITION

February 28, 1987 and 1986
Thousands of dollars

ASSETS

	1987	1986
Current Assets		
Cash and equivalents	**$ 17,225**	$ 26,853
Trade accounts receivable, less allowances for sales returns of $67,033 ($57,382 in 1986) and for doubtful accounts of $3,992 ($3,378 in 1986)	**284,135**	240,471
Inventories:		
Raw material	**56,057**	59,343
Work in process	**69,668**	60,179
Finished products	**202,412**	181,237
	328,137	300,759
Less LIFO reserve	**75,392**	76,552
	252,745	224,207
Display material and factory supplies	**29,770**	26,826
Total inventories	**282,515**	251,033
Refundable and deferred income taxes	**26,593**	36,669
Prepaid expenses and other	**9,679**	6,228
Total current assets	**620,147**	561,254
Other Assets	**89,488**	47,085
Property, Plant and Equipment		
Land	**7,956**	7,523
Buildings	**183,481**	165,241
Equipment and fixtures	**269,644**	222,718
	461,081	395,482
Less accumulated depreciation and amortization	**148,097**	130,519
Property, plant and equipment—net	**312,984**	264,963
	$1,022,619	$873,302

LIABILITIES AND SHAREHOLDERS' EQUITY

	1987	1986
Current Liabilities		
Notes payable	**$ 25,092**	$ 15,921
Accounts payable	**69,175**	66,685
Payrolls and payroll taxes	**31,230**	28,675
Retirement plans	**10,966**	11,697
State and local taxes	**3,056**	2,763
Dividends payable	**5,343**	5,317
Income taxes	**—**	18,988
Sales returns	**29,964**	23,889
Current maturities of long-term debt	**10,894**	4,786
Total current liabilities	**185,720**	178,721
Long-Term Debt	**235,005**	147,592
Deferred Income Taxes	**77,451**	64,025
Shareholders' Equity		
Common shares—par value $1:		
Class A	**29,552**	29,203
Class B	**2,588**	2,982
Capital in excess of par value	**102,718**	94,744
Treasury stock	**(15,409)**	(1,689)
Cumulative translation adjustment	**(11,604)**	(16,801)
Retained earnings	**416,598**	374,525
Total shareholders' equity	**524,443**	482,964
	$1,022,619	$873,302

See notes to consolidated financial statements

MANAGEMENT ANALYSIS

Years ended February 28, 1987, 1986 and 1985

RESULTS OF OPERATIONS

Total revenue increased 8.7% in 1987 to $1.126 billion after increasing 9.5% in 1986. Although greeting card sales continued to increase, particularly everyday card sales, higher than expected returns of seasonal merchandise negatively affected net sales. Net greeting card dollar sales increased 7% in 1987 and 13% in 1986 while unit sales increased 2% in 1987 and 3% in 1986. Significant sales increases were also recorded by the Corporation's AmToy Division.

Sales by major product classification for the past three years, stated as a percent of net sales, were as follows:

	1987	1986	1985
Everyday greeting cards	38%	37%	37%
Holiday greeting cards	27	29	27
Gift wrapping and party goods	18	18	19
Consumer products (toys, candles and giftware)	8	7	8
Stationery and miscellaneous	9	9	9

Other income increased 1.1% in 1987, after being down 11.7% in 1986. Licensing income totaled $18.3 million in 1987, compared to $17.6 million in 1986 and $20.9 million in 1985. The decrease in 1986 was primarily due to the poor retail environment experienced by many of our licensees in that year.

Material, labor and other production costs were 41.9% of total revenue in 1987, up from 40.2% in 1986 after a slight increase from 39.9% in 1985. Higher costs associated with increased sales volume from non-greeting card subsidiaries and $7.5 million in unfavorable year end inventory adjustments were the significant factors responsible for the increased costs. Principally because of the inventory adjustments, material, labor and other production costs for the three months ended February 28, 1987 increased to 42.1% of total revenue from 36.3% in 1986.

Selling, distribution and marketing expenses were 30.3% of total revenue in 1987 as compared to 29.8% in 1986 and 29.0% in 1985. These increases are primarily the result of costs associated with competition for market share, revenues being less than original expectations, and in 1987, increased advertising costs.

As a percent of total revenue, administrative and general expenses did not change significantly from prior year levels, increasing slightly to 12.9% of revenue compared to 12.7% in 1986 and 13.1% in 1985.

Reflecting the Corporation's increased level of capital spending in recent years, depreciation expense increased $5.6 million in 1987 to 2.6% of total revenue (2.3% in 1986 and 2.0% in 1985).

Interest expense increased $5.8 million in 1987 and $3.6 million in 1986. Higher borrowing levels to fund capital expenditures, acquisitions, and (in 1987) treasury stock, along with increased inventory and accounts receivable levels, were the reasons for the increases.

During February, 1987 the assets and business of the Corporation's unprofitable German operations were sold. Although the pre-tax loss associated with the sale was $12.4 million, it was largely offset by income tax benefits of $11.9 million.

Because of the tax rate change resulting from the Tax Reform Act of 1986, the Corporation's investment in purchased tax benefits (made in 1983) was required under generally accepted accounting principles to be revalued and resulted in an unanticipated tax benefit of $8.2 million in 1987.

The tax benefits associated with the sale of the Corporation's German operations and the revaluation of the investments in tax benefits, both recorded in the fourth fiscal quarter of 1987, were the primary factors causing the effective tax rate to decrease to 38.0% in 1987, compared to 45.3% in 1986 and 45.2% in 1985.

During 1987, the Corporation adopted the installment sales method of tax accounting for certain domestic seasonal sales. Although this change had no impact on tax expense and reported earnings in 1987, it will have a significant overall favorable impact on cash flow in 1988.

CHANGES IN FINANCIAL POSITION

Cash provided from operations totaled $111.8 million in 1987 as compared to $116.7 million in 1986 and $114.2 million in 1985. Net cash from long-term financing (long-term debt and sale of stock under option plans) increased to $75.9 million in 1987 from $35.0 million in 1986 and $5.7 million in 1985. These funds were used to finance the Corporation's working capital requirements and other investments.

Accounts receivable as a percent of prior twelve months' net sales increased to 25.8% at the end of 1987 compared to 23.8% in 1986 and 18.9% in 1985. The difficult retail environment continued to cause slower collections from our accounts. Inventories, measured on the same basis, increased to 25.6% in 1987 from 24.8% in 1986 and 23.3% in 1985, principally due to higher inventories of non-greeting card products, display fixtures and factory supplies.

The Corporation invested $68.7 million in property, plant and equipment in 1987 ($61.8 million in 1986 and $43.6 million in 1985). To provide for future growth and productivity improvements, capital expenditures are expected to increase further in 1988. In addition, the Corporation acquired various businesses for $36.7 million as discussed in Note B to the Consolidated Financial Statements.

Dividend payments to shareholders increased to $21.3 million in 1987 from $19.9 million in 1986 and $17.1 million in 1985.

As a result of the Corporation's higher year-end 1987 borrowing levels, the ratio of total debt to total capitalization (equity plus short and long-term debt) increased to 34.1% from 25.8% in 1986 and 22.2% in 1985.

Shareholders' equity increased 8.6% to $524 million at February 28, 1987. Shareholders' equity per share was $16.32 at year-end 1987 ($15.01 in 1986 and $13.35 in 1985).

The Corporation finances its peak working capital requirements in the United States primarily through the issuance of commercial paper. Note C to the Consolidated Financial Statements more fully describes the Corporation's domestic and foreign credit facilities.

CASH FROM OPERATIONS
IN MILLIONS

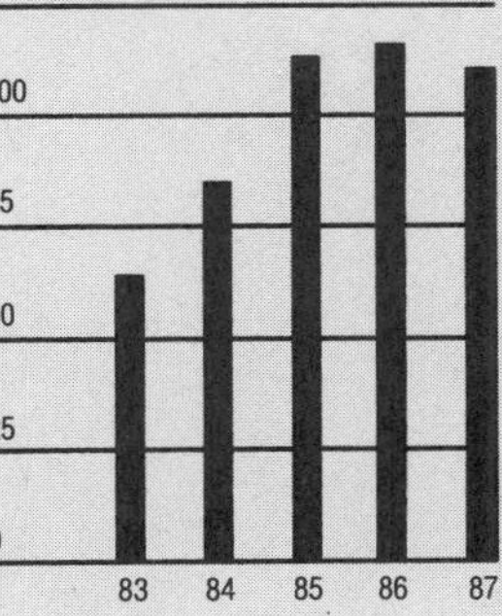

CAPITAL ADDITIONS
IN MILLIONS

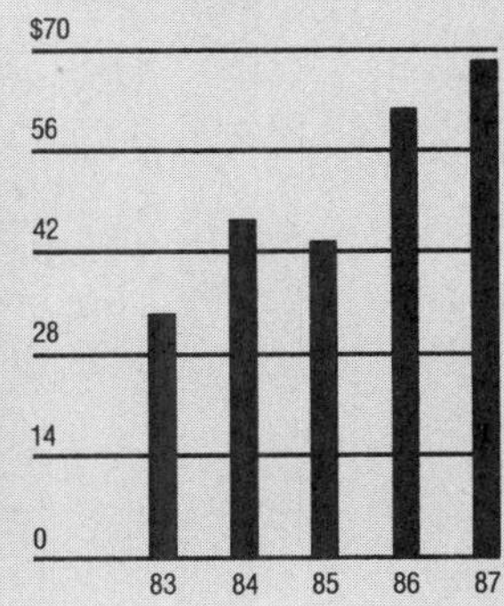

CAPITALIZATION
IN MILLIONS

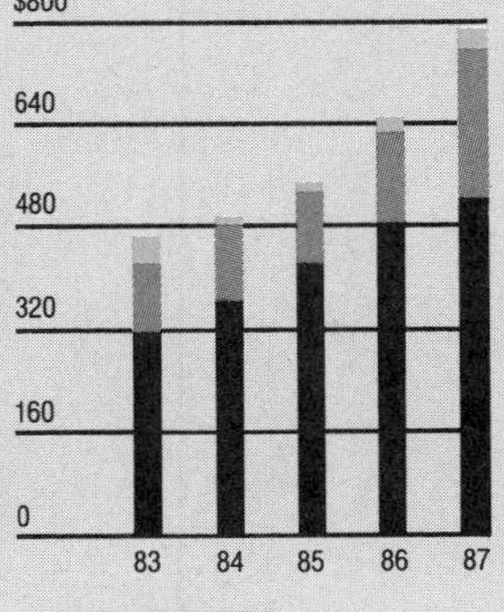

SHORT-TERM DEBT
LONG-TERM DEBT
SHAREHOLDERS' EQUITY

EFFECTS OF INFLATION

The effect of inflation on inventory is mitigated by the Corporation's use of the last-in, first-out method of inventory valuation for its principal domestic inventories. In addition, the Corporation attempts to offset any increase in costs through productivity improvements. For these reasons, as well as the moderate inflation rate experienced during fiscal year 1987, inflation had a negligible impact on the operating results of the Corporation.

AMERICAN GREETINGS

Consolidated Statements of Income

For the Years Ended January 31,	*1988*	*1987*	*1986*
Sales	$322,480,000	$316,366,000	$286,743,000
Cost of Sales	150,376,000	156,252,000	136,152,000
Gross Profit	172,104,000	160,114,000	150,591,000
Expenses:			
Store and Operating	122,596,000	117,563,000	108,451,000
Warehouse and Administrative	28,004,000	27,109,000	28,356,000
Total	150,600,000	144,672,000	136,807,000
Operating Profit	21,504,000	15,442,000	13,784,000
Provision for Loss on Sale and Disposition of Assets	—	—	4,100,000
Interest Expense	2,236,000	2,807,000	1,656,000
Income Before Income Taxes	19,268,000	12,635,000	8,028,000
Income Taxes	8,767,000	6,444,000	3,771,000
Net Income	$ 10,501,000	$ 6,191,000	$ 4,257,000
Net Income Per Share	$1.58	$.94	$.64

See notes to financial statements.

Consolidated Balance Sheets

	January 31,	*1988*	*1987*
Assets	Current Assets:		
	Cash	$ 571,000	$ 529,000
	Receivables	5,932,000	3,674,000
	Merchandise Inventories	133,608,000	111,698,000
	Prepaid Expenses and Other Current Assets	4,127,000	3,162,000
	Total Current Assets	144,238,000	119,063,000
	Property:		
	Land	589,000	589,000
	Buildings	6,443,000	6,441,000
	Furniture and Fixtures	40,016,000	37,203,000
	Leasehold Improvements	27,564,000	26,723,000
	Total	74,612,000	70,956,000
	Less Accumulated Depreciation and Amortization	34,906,000	33,617,000
	Property—Net	39,706,000	37,339,000
	Other Assets	680,000	1,638,000
	Total	$184,624,000	$158,040,000
Liabilities	Current Liabilities:		
	Accounts Payable	$ 48,129,000	$ 30,596,000
	Notes Payable to Banks	17,000,000	17,000,000
	Accrued Liabilities	10,168,000	9,288,000
	Income Taxes Payable	637,000	50,000
	Current Portion of Long-Term Debt	349,000	314,000
	Total Current Liabilities	76,283,000	57,248,000
	Deferred Income Taxes	3,887,000	3,420,000
	Long-Term Debt	11,736,000	12,085,000
Equity	Stockholders' Equity:		
	Preferred Stock, $.10 Par Value; Authorized 1,000,000 Shares; Outstanding, None		
	Common Stock, $.10 Par Value; Authorized 14,000,000 Shares; Outstanding 6,564,777 Shares in 1988 and 6,556,977 Shares in 1987	656,000	656,000
	Paid-In Capital	14,488,000	14,407,000
	Retained Earnings	77,574,000	70,224,000
	Total Stockholders' Equity	92,718,000	85,287,000
	Total	$184,624,000	$158,040,000

See notes to financial statements.

Consolidated Statements of Cash Flows

	For the Years Ended January 31,	*1988*	*1987*	*1986*
Cash Flows from Operating Activities	Net Income	$ 10,501,000	$ 6,191,000	$ 4,257,000
	Adjustments to Reconcile Net Income to Net Cash Provided by Operating Activities:			
	Depreciation and Amortization	5,954,000	5,844,000	5,444,000
	Loss on Disposal of Fixed Assets	980,000	920,000	4,800,000
	Deferred Taxes	467,000	2,723,000	(678,000)
	Other Assets	958,000	(1,121,000)	44,000
	Changes in Other Working Capital Components:			
	Accounts Receivable	(2,258,000)	(2,285,000)	1,074,000
	Inventories	(21,910,000)	320,000	(22,833,000)
	Prepaid Expenses and Other Current Assets	(965,000)	(212,000)	(1,631,000)
	Accounts Payable and Accrued Liabilities	18,650,000	(7,243,000)	10,885,000
	Income Taxes Payable	587,000	(950,000)	(681,000)
	Total Adjustments	2,463,000	(2,004,000)	(3,576,000)
	Net Cash Provided by Operating Activities	12,964,000	4,187,000	681,000
Cash Flows Used for Investing Activity	Capital Expenditures	(9,538,000)	(8,666,000)	(12,293,000)
Cash Flows from Financing Activities	Proceeds from Issuance of Long Term Debt	—	10,000,000	1,399,000
	(Reduction) Increase in Long Term Debt	(314,000)	(2,309,000)	749,000
	Payment of Dividends	(3,151,000)	(3,147,000)	(3,132,000)
	Proceeds from Exercise of Stock Options	81,000	149,000	249,000
	Change in Net Borrowings Under Lines of Credit Agreements	—	(1,000,000)	13,000,000
	Net Cash (Used for) Provided by Financing Activities	(3,384,000)	3,693,000	12,265,000
Net Increase (Decrease) in Cash		42,000	(786,000)	653,000
Cash at Beginning of Year		529,000	1,315,000	662,000
Cash at End of Year		$ 571,000	$ 529,000	$ 1,315,000

Supplemental Disclosures of Cash Flow Information

Cash Paid During the Year For	Interest	$2,442,000	$2,441,000	$1,570,000
	Income Taxes	$7,850,000	$4,970,000	$5,223,000

See notes to financial statements.

AUDITOR'S OPINION

Carter Manufacturing Company:

We have examined the balance sheets of Carter Manufacturing Company as of December 31, 1986 and 1985, and the related statements of income and retained earnings and of changes in financial position for the years then ended. Our examinations were made in accordance with generally accepted auditing standards and, accordingly, included such tests of the accounting records and such other auditing procedures as we considered necessary in the circumstances.

In our opinion, the accompanying financial statements present fairly the financial position of Carter Manufacturing Company as of December 31, 1986 and 1985, and the results of its operations and the changes in its financial position for the years then ended, in conformity with generally accepted accounting principles consistently applied.

February 22, 1987
Atlanta, Georgia

CARTER MANUFACTURING COMPANY

BALANCE SHEETS, DECEMBER 31, 1986 and 1985

ASSETS	NOTES	1986	1985
CURRENT ASSETS:			
Cash:			
Cash in bank		$ 38,526	$ 88,443
Petty cash		7,650	12,300
Savings certificates		375,000	235,344
Marketable securities	2, 5	332,238	361,842
Receivables:			
Customers—less allowance for doubtful accounts of $486,000 in 1986 and $45,000 in 1985	3	2,979,197	2,809,352
Interest		16,680	6,288
Other		22,893	10,125
Inventories	4	5,927,631	6,033,126
Prepaid insurance		38,604	45,234
Other prepayments		22,566	32,586
Total current assets		9,760,985	9,634,640
PLANT AND EQUIPMENT:			
Machinery and equipment		2,901,148	2,788,225
Delivery equipment		745,893	771,873
Furniture and fixtures		214,119	214,437
Leasehold improvements		97,758	94,011
Total		3,958,918	3,868,546
Less accumulated depreciation and amortization		2,172,171	2,085,417
Plant and equipment—net		1,786,747	1,783,129
TOTAL ASSETS		$11,547,732	$11,417,769

See notes to financial statements.

LIABILITIES AND SHAREHOLDERS' EQUITY	NOTES	1986	1985
CURRENT LIABILITIES:			
Trade accounts payable		$ 1,804,807	$ 1,700,652
Due under line of credit	5	120,000	180,000
Current portion of long-term debt	6	266,676	236,709
Accrued salaries, wages and commissions		369,009	194,910
Accrued and withheld payroll taxes		69,267	144,111
Income taxes payable		48,081	37,287
Contributions to employee benefit plans	8	277,521	100,647
Accrued rent		67,500	270,000
Total current liabilities		3,022,861	2,864,316
LONG-TERM DEBT	6, 7, 9	1,028,682	1,295,358
DEFERRED INCOME TAXES		56,091	44,877
SHAREHOLDERS' EQUITY:			
Capital stock—authorized and outstanding, 172,000 shares of $3 par value		516,000	516,000
Additional paid-in capital		36,927	36,927
Retained earnings		6,887,171	6,660,291
Shareholders' equity		7,440,098	7,213,218
TOTAL LIABILITIES AND SHAREHOLDERS' EQUITY		$11,547,732	$11,417,769

CARTER MANUFACTURING COMPANY

STATEMENTS OF INCOME AND RETAINED EARNINGS FOR THE YEARS ENDED DECEMBER 31, 1986 AND 1985

	NOTE	1986	1985
SALES (Less returns of $237,782 in 1986 and $345,762 in 1985)		$23,555,271	$23,401,635
COST OF GOODS SOLD		17,130,648	17,767,857
GROSS PROFIT		6,424,623	5,633,778
SELLING AND GENERAL EXPENSES		6,136,161	5,406,762
INCOME FROM OPERATIONS		288,462	227,016
OTHER INCOME (EXPENSES):			
Interest		167,978	84,732
Dividends		50,268	50,124
Sale of waste materials, etc.		183,526	91,365
Gain from sale of property and equipment		4,581	3,600
Unrealized loss on marketable securities	2	(28,824)	(80,388)
Interest expense		(233,385)	(112,641)
Cash discount lost		(63,924)	(108,987)
Total		80,220	(72,195)
INCOME BEFORE INCOME TAXES		368,682	154,821
INCOME TAX EXPENSE:			
Federal:			
Current		112,336	31,410
Deferred		9,303	18,036
Total federal		121,639	49,446
State:			
Current		18,252	11,955
Deferred		1,911	3,021
Total state		20,163	14,976
Total		141,802	64,422
NET INCOME		226,880	90,399
RETAINED EARNINGS, BEGINNING OF YEAR		6,660,291	6,569,892
RETAINED EARNINGS, END OF YEAR		$ 6,887,171	$ 6,660,291

See notes to financial statements.

STATEMENTS OF CHANGES IN FINANCIAL POSITION FOR THE YEARS ENDED DECEMBER 31, 1986 AND 1985

	1986	1985
SOURCES OF WORKING CAPITAL:		
Net income	$ 226,880	$ 90,399
Add charges not requiring an outlay of working capital:		
Depreciation and amortization	173,145	181,638
Deferred income taxes	11,214	21,057
Total from operations	411,239	293,094
Proceeds from sale of plant and equipment—net of gains included in operations	11,019	1,800
Increase in long-term debt		1,295,358
Total	422,258	1,590,252
USES OF WORKING CAPITAL:		
Purchase of plant and equipment	187,782	1,322,398
Reduction of long-term debt	266,676	
Total	454,458	1,322,398
INCREASE (DECREASE) IN WORKING CAPITAL	$ (32,200)	$ 267,854
COMPONENTS OF CHANGE IN WORKING CAPITAL:		
Cash and savings certificates and account	$ 85,089	$ 325,572
Marketable securities	(29,604)	(80,388)
Receivables	193,005	290,889
Inventories	(105,495)	(3,918)
Prepaid expenses	(16,650)	77,820
Trade accounts payable	(104,155)	(1,177)
Due under line of credit	60,000	(60,000)
Current portion of long-term debt	(29,967)	(236,709)
Accrued salaries, wages and commissions	(174,099)	(28,560)
Accrued and withheld payroll taxes	74,844	(102,966)
Income taxes payable—net	(10,794)	(35,937)
Contributions to employee benefits plans	(176,874)	123,228
Accrued rent	202,500	
INCREASE (DECREASE) IN WORKING CAPITAL	$ (32,200)	$ 267,854

See notes to financial statements.

CARTER MANUFACTURING COMPANY

NOTES TO FINANCIAL STATEMENTS FOR THE YEARS ENDED DECEMBER 31, 1986 AND 1985

1. SIGNIFICANT ACCOUNTING POLICIES

Nature of Business—The Company is principally engaged in the manufacture and sale of metal products.

Inventories

For the year ended December 31, 1984, the Company changed its method of accounting for inventories to a last-in, first-out (lifo) method. During a time of rapid price increases, the lifo method provides a better matching of revenue and expense than does the fifo method. The total effect of the change was included in the 1984 financial statements, and no restatement was made of amounts reported in prior years. The effect of this change was to reduce net income for 1984 by $298,944.

Plant and Equipment

Plant and equipment are stated at cost less accumulated depreciation and amortization. Depreciation on plant and equipment acquired after 1978 is computed using the straight-line method for financial reporting and accelerated methods for income tax purposes. Depreciation on previously acquired plant and equipment is computed using accelerated methods for financial reporting and income tax purposes, except that the straight-line method is used for tax purposes at such time as it results in a greater deduction than would result from continued use of an accelerated method. Rates are based upon the following estimated useful lives:

Classification	Useful Life
Machinery and equipment	7–10 Years
Delivery equipment	6–7 Years
Furniture and fixtures	8–10 Years
Leasehold improvements	5–6 Years

Revenue Recognition—Revenue from merchandise sales is recognized when the merchandise is shipped to the customer.

Deferred Income Taxes

Deferred income taxes are provided for timing differences between reported financial income before income taxes and taxable income. The timing differences arise from depreciation deductions for income tax purposes in excess of depreciation expense for financial reporting purposes.

2. MARKETABLE SECURITIES

The Company's marketable securities are stated at the lower of cost or market. At December 31, 1986 and 1985, the Company's investments had a cost of $582,876 and $583,656 respectively. To reduce the carrying amount of this investment to market, which was lower than cost at December 31, 1986 and 1985, valuation allowances of $250,638 and $221,814, respectively, were established. This resulted in a charge to earnings of $28,824 in 1986 and a charge to earnings of $80,388 in 1985.

3. RECEIVABLE DUE FROM A SINGLE CUSTOMER

At December 31, 1986, approximately $700,000 was due from a single distributor. Approximately $435,000 of the allowance for doubtful accounts at December 31, 1986, relates specifically to this receivable.

At December 31, 1985, approximately $350,000 was due from the distributor.

4. INVENTORIES

At December 31, 1986 and 1985, inventories (see Note 1) consisted of the following:

	1986	1985
Raw materials	$1,654,563	$1,491,876
Work in process	2,427,513	2,255,574
Finished goods	2,684,409	2,839,278
Total cost	6,766,485	6,586,728
Less lifo reserve	838,854	553,602
Total lifo	$5,927,631	$6,033,126

5. LINE OF CREDIT

The Company has an agreement with a bank for a line of credit, of which $180,000 was unused at December 31, 1986. Borrowings under the line are at an interest rate (12% at December 31, 1986) of 2% above the bank's prime lending rate. The Company's marketable securities are pledged as collateral for borrowing under the line.

6. LONG-TERM DEBT

At December 31, 1986 and 1985, the Company had three installment notes, payable to a bank as follows:

	1986	1985
Note dated February 2, 1986, due in $60,000 semiannual installments, with interest payable monthly at 12.625%	$ 120,000	$ 240,000
Note dated March 2, 1985, due in $10,000 semiannual installments, with interest payable monthly at 14.125%	20,000	40,000
Note dated December 12, 1985, due in 120 monthly payments of increasing amounts with interest at 14.00%	1,155,358	1,252,067
Total	1,295,358	1,532,067
Less amount due within one year	266,676	236,709
Total	$1,028,682	$1,295,358

NOTES TO FINANCIAL STATEMENTS

7. LONG-TERM LIABILITIES

The long-term liabilities have the following aggregate minimum maturities during the next five years:

1987	$ 266,676
1988	131,122
1989	135,103
1990	140,503
1991	146,299
After 1991	475,655
Total	$1,295,358

8. EMPLOYEE BENEFIT PLANS

The Company has a profit-sharing plan for its salaried employees and a defined benefit retirement plan for its hourly paid employees. Both plans are noncontributory, are funded annually, and have been amended to comply with the Employee Retirement Income Security Act of 1974.

The contributions to the profit-sharing plan are made at the discretion of the Board of Directors and were $138,261 for 1986 and $57,750 for 1985.

Annual contributions to the retirement plan were $139,260 for 1986 and $42,897 for 1985. The plan is being funded based upon actuarial computations of costs which include consideration of normal cost, interest on the unfunded prior service cost, and amortization of the prior service cost over a forty-year period.

At January 1, 1986 and 1985, net assets available for retirement plan benefits were $824,214 and $622,518 respectively; the actuarial present values of vested plan benefits were $984,666 and $885,435, respectively; and nonvested accumulated plan benefits were $87,522 and $90,788, respectively. The assumed rate of return used in determining the actuarial present values of accumulated plan benefits was 5%.

9. OPERATING LEASE

The Company leases land and buildings under a 5-year noncancelable operating lease which expires on December 31, 1989. Future minimum lease payments are as follows:

1987	$300,000
1988	330,000
1989	360,000
Total	$990,000

Index

Q

R

S

T

U

V

W-Z

INDEX OF REAL COMPANIES

Check Figures for Selected Problems

Agreement between the following "check" figures and those obtained in solving the problems is an indication that a significant portion of the solution is basically correct, aside from matters of form and procedure.

Problem 1–41	Trial balance totals, $92,500
1–42	Net income, $93,375
1–43	Trial balance totals, $65,840
1–44	Trial balance totals, $265,445
1–45	Trial balance totals, $248,065
1–46	Trial balance totals, $134,700
1–42A	Net income, $33,450
1–43A	Trial balance totals, $42,490
1–44A	Trial balance totals, $154,310
Problem 2–35	Trial balance totals, $200,590
2–36	Trial balance totals, $392,666
2–37	Trial balance totals, $33,338.10
2–38	Trial balance totals, $103,090
2–37A	Trial balance totals, $33,338.10
2–38A	Trial balance totals, $78,190
Problem 3–33	Insurance Expense, $1,365
3–33A	Insurance Expense, $808
Problem 4–35	Net income, $26,590
4–36	Net income, $52,490
4–37	Retained earnings, Nov. 30, $171,500
4–38	Retained earnings, Dec. 31, $212,950
4–39	Total assets, $495,300
4–40	Total assets, $500,600
4–41	Net income, $40,370
4–42	Retained earnings, Oct. 31, $112,840
4–35A	Net income, $47,750
4–36A	Net income, $70,000
4–37A	Retained earnings, Jan. 31, $346,000
4–38A	Retained earnings, April 30, $363,760
4–42A	Retained earnings, Nov. 30, $249,920
Comprehensive Problem	Total assets, May 31, $240,110
Problem 5–42	Adjusted balance, $22,627.55
5–43	Adjusted balance, $12,657.67
5–44	Adjusted balance, $9,798.02
5–42A	Adjusted balance, $15,225.75
5–43A	Adjusted balance, $12,730.98
5–44A	Adjusted balance, $15,905.79
Problem 6–38	Interest Income, March 11, balance, $1,260
6–39	Allowance for Doubtful Accounts, Dec. 31, $31,250
6–40	Allowance for Doubtful Accounts, end of 4th year, $11,900
6–41	Income from operations, third year, $39,200
6–42	Gain on repossession, $38
6–43	Total assets, $524,400
6–38A	Interest Income, March 16, balance, $646
6–39A	Allowance for Doubtful Accounts, Dec. 31, $15,000
6–41A	Income from operations, third year, $58,650
Problem 7–34	Inventory (2), $7,898
7–35	Inventory (4), $152,500
7–36	Total inventory, lower of C or M, $54,605
7–37	Inventory (1) $207,200; (2) $350,500
7–38	Net income, $86,250
7–39	Income from contracts, 1991, $275,000
7–34A	Inventory (2), $10,801
7–35A	Inventory (4), $2,910
7–36A	Total inventory, lower of C or M, $54,745
7–37A	Inventory, (1) $347,200; (2) $572,550
7–39A	Income from contracts, 1991, $465,000
Problem 8–48	Accumulated Depreciation, March 31, 1990, $262,350

	8–49	Accumulated Depreciation, Dec. 31, 1991, $1,525
	8–51	Net income, $103,000
	8–48A	Accumulated Depreciation, Sept. 30, 1990, $257,850
	8–49A	Accumulated Depreciation, June 30, 1991, $1,875
Problem	9–37	Total payroll taxes expense, $18,657.90
	9–37A	Total payroll taxes expense, $18,602.50
Problem	10–44	Total stockholders' equity, $381,450
	10–45	Total common dividends per share, $8.40
	10–47	Total stockholders' equity, $3,131,000
	10–45A	Total common dividends per share, $15.60
Problem	11–32	Deferred income tax payable, end of 4th year, $10,500
	11–34	Total retained earnings, $1,055,000
	11–35	Net income, $120,000
	11–36	Total stockholders' equity, $1,633,250
	11–37	Total stockholders' equity, $2,205,000
	11–38	Net income, $105,600
	11–32A	Deferred income tax payable, end of 4th year, $31,500
	11–34A	Total retained earnings, $940,000
	11–35A	Net income, $69,000
	11–36A	Total stockholders' equity, $2,993,980
Problem	12–37	Carrying amount of bonds, Dec. 31, 1990, $11,148,294
	12–38	Interest expense (4a), $620,545
	12–39	Discount on bonds, end of 1990, $288,960
	12–42	Net income, $81,986
	12–37A	Carrying value of bonds, Dec. 31, 1990, $7,573,194
	12–38A	Interest expense (4a), $1,165,696
	12–39A	Premium on bonds, end of 1990, $363,475
Problem	13–33	Total assets, $998,050
	13–34	Total assets, $2,053,110
	13–35	Total assets, $1,017,200
	13–36	Total assets, (1) $1,800,000; (2) $1,740,000; (3) $1,740,000
	13–37	Total assets, $1,828,575; net income, $317,800
	13–33A	Total assets, $1,479,700
	13–34A	Total assets, $3,132,490
	13–37A	Total assets, $1,570,000; net income, $250,000
Problem	14–35	Increase in cash, $21,500
	14–36	Decrease in cash, $14,500
	14–37	Increase in cash, $7,500
	14–38	Net cash flow used for operating activities, $11,900
	14–39	Net cash flow from operating activities, $70,900
	14–40	Net cash flow from operating activities, $411.6
	14–35A	Increase in cash, $14,300
	14–36A	Increase in cash, $11,350
	14–37A	Increase in cash, $7,200
	14–38A	Net cash flow from operating activities, $113,100
Problem	15–39	Cost of goods manufactured, $327,300
	15–41	Net income, $74,000
	15–39A	Cost of goods manufactured, $1,780,000
	15–41A	Net income, $50,000
Problem	16–27	Finished goods, $22,825
	16–29	Total assets, $509,986
	16–30	Trial balance totals, $2,017,680
	16–27A	Finished goods, $11,590
	16–30A	Trial balance totals, $1,150,585
Problem	17–30	Work in process, June 30, Department 2, $74,760
	17–31	Equivalent units of production, 11,670 units
	17–32	Total assets, $1,454,620
	17–33	Equivalent units of production, 24,000 units
	17–35	Work in process, Aug. 31, $4,000
	17–36	Equivalent units of production, 23,200 units
	17–30A	Work in process, April 30, Department 2, $45,024
	17–33A	Equivalent units of production, 34,500 units
	17–35A	Work in process, July 31, $17,250
Problem	18–43	Variable cost per unit, $1.50

18–43A	Variable cost per unit, $2.85
Problem 19–29	Break-even point, (1), $1,000,000
19–30	Maximum operating profit: (2), $160,000; (4), $120,000
19–31	Maximum operating profit: (2), $75,000; (4), $62,500
19–32	Break-even point, $1,360,000
19–33	Break-even point, $900,000
19–34	Present break-even point, $2,000,000
19–29A	Break-even point, (1), $350,000
19–30A	Maximum operating profit: (2), $125,000; (4), $100,000
19–31A	Maximum operating profit: (2), $50,000; (4), $40,000
19–33A	Break-even point, $750,000
Problem 20–27	Income from operations, (2), $180,000
20–28	Operating loss, $56,500
20–29	Contribution to company profit, Thom, $89,100
20–30	Total contribution margin, (1), $464,000; (3), $511,280
20–31	Decrease in contribution margin, $86,000
20–27A	Loss from operations, (2), $2,000
20–28A	Operating loss, $38,500
20–31A	Decrease in contribution margin, $68,000
Problem 21–25	Total production, Product A, 73,000 units
21–26	Net income, $425,900
21–27	Deficiency, June, $18,200
21–28	Total revenue from sales, $1,840,230
21–30	Net income, $215,100; cash, $116,100
21–27A	Deficiency, November, $22,500
21–28A	Total revenue from sales, $5,524,200
Problem 22–25	Total factory overhead cost variance — unfavorable, $5,600
22–26	Total factory overhead cost variance — unfavorable, $5,725
22–27	Total factory overhead cost variance — unfavorable, $12,000
22–28	Work in process account balance (debit), $11,200
22–25A	Total factory overhead cost variance — unfavorable, $7,060
22–27A	Total factory overhead cost variance — favorable, $3,150
22–28A	Work in process account balance (debit), $10,140
Problem 23–24	Net income, $111,290
23–27	Total departmental margin, $138,670
23–24A	Net income, $37,050
Problem 24–32	ROI, Division C, 16.5%
24–33	ROI, Proposal 3, 18.1%
24–34	Division A is most profitable
24–35	ROI, Division F, 18%
24–38	Total company income would increase by $500,000
24–32A	ROI, Division Z, 24%
24–33A	Division O is most profitable
24–35A	ROI, Division Y, 24%
24–38A	Total company income would increase by $160,000
Problem 25–36	Gain from operating warehouse, $200,000
25–37	Net cost reduction, $330,000
25–38	Gain from promotion campaign, Product D, $95,000
25–39	Net advantage, $1,250
25–40	Net advantage, $4,300
25–41	Selling price, $21.60
25–36A	Gain from operating warehouse, $80,000
25–37A	Net cost reduction, $235,000
25–41A	Selling price, $19.20
Problem 26–27	Excess of present value over amount to be invested, Project H, $4,686
26–28	Excess of present value over amount to be invested, Project M, $40,500
26–29	Present value index, Proposal C, 1.05
26–30	Discounted internal rate of return, Proposal B, 15%
26–31	(2), Excess of present value over amount to be invested, $5,381
26–32	(2), Excess of present value over amount to be invested, Project A, $20,000
26–27A	Excess of present value over amount to be invested Project K, $10,204
26–28A	Excess of present value over amount to be invested,

		Project D, $29,500
	26–29A	Present value index, Project Q, 1.12
	26–30A	Discounted internal rate of return, Project T, 15%
Problem	27–41	EOQ, 690 units
	27–42	EOQ, (3), 138 units
	27–43	Plan 2 is the most economical plan
	27–44	Expected value, T, $16,350,000
	27–45	250 magazines should be purchased
	27–46	Expected value, Plat #900, $13,550,000
	27–47	Value of conducting an investigation, $6,000
	27–48	(1), medical office complex
	27–49	(2), lakefront location
	27–41A	EOQ, 1,320 units
	27–43A	Plan 2 is the most economical plan
	27–44A	Expected value, Patent #1010, $12,600,000
	27–45A	175 newspapers should be purchased
	27–46A	Expected value, Plat #100, $35,750,000
	27–47A	Value of conducting an investigation, $3,200
	27–48A	(2), Venture X
Problem	28–43	Working capital, Dec. 31, 1989, $186,625
Problem	C–2	Accounts payable, $42,177.05
	C–3	Accounts payable, $10,002
	C–4	Accounts receivable, $14,720
	C–5	Accounts receivable, $10,360
	C–6	Accounts receivable, $17,950
	C–7	Trial balance totals, $172,415